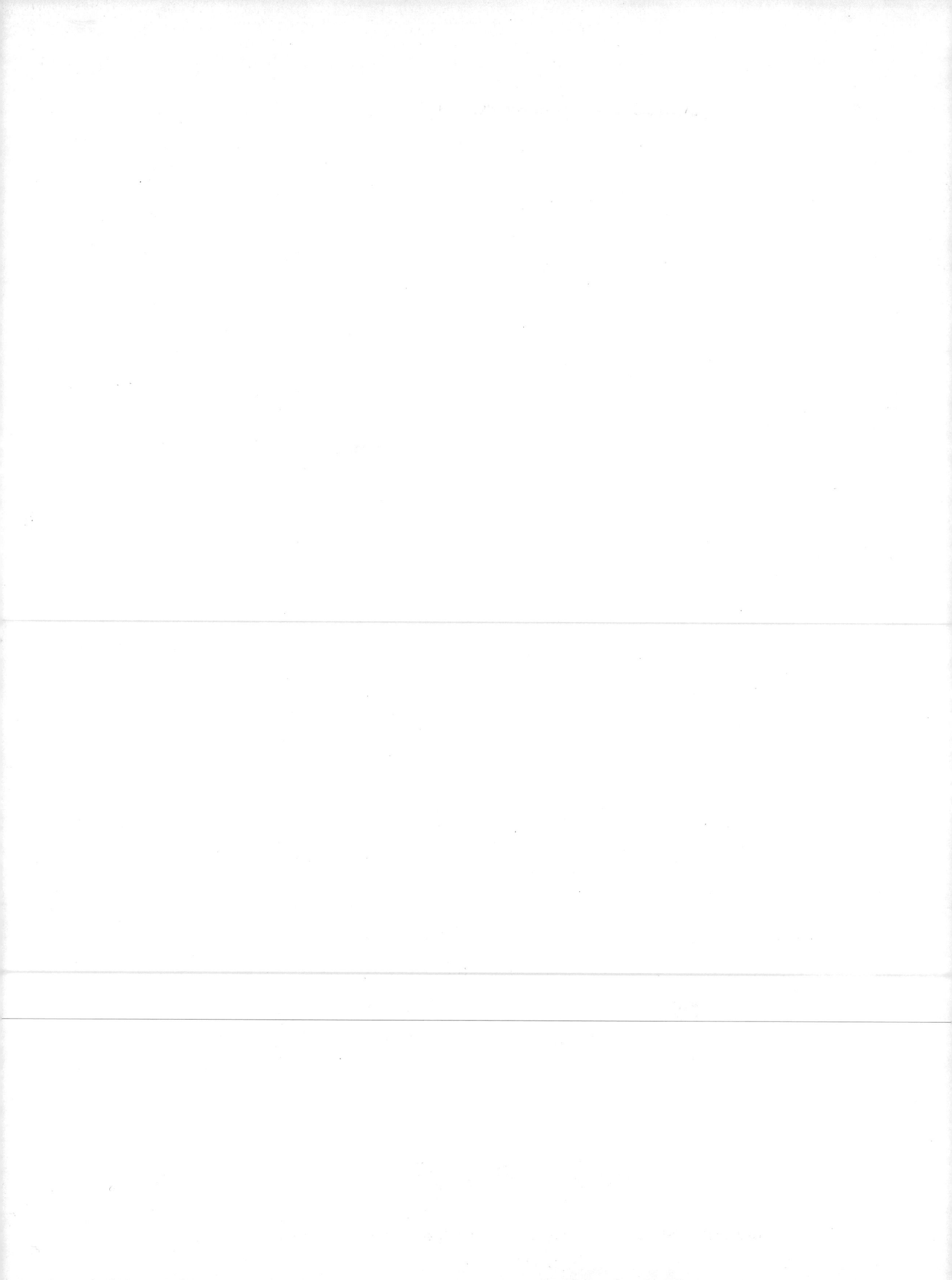

ANNOTATED TEACHER'S EDITION

HOLT

CALL TO FREEDOM

Beginnings to 1877

Sterling Stuckey ■ **Linda Kerrigan Salvucci**
Reading Consultant • Judith Irvin

HOLT, RINEHART AND WINSTON

A Harcourt Education Company

Austin • New York • Orlando • Atlanta • San Francisco • Boston • Dallas • Toronto • London

About the Authors

Sterling Stuckey is Professor of History and holds the Presidential Chair at the University of California, Riverside. Dr. Stuckey is the author of *Slave Culture: Nationalist Theory and the Foundations of Black America* and *Going Through the Storm: The Influence of African American Art in History.*

Linda Kerrigan Salvucci is Associate Professor of History at Trinity University, San Antonio, Texas. Dr. Salvucci is currently working on a book entitled *Ironies of Empire: The United States–Cuba Trade Under Spanish Rule.*

Cover photo: Hitchcock House Antiques, Inc., Woodbury, CT.

For acknowledgments, see page R70, which is an extension of the copyright page.

Printed in the United States of America

ISBN 0-03-065223-5

1 2 3 4 5 6 7 8 9 48 05 04 03 02 01

COVER: *An unknown artist created this pine statue of an American bald eagle, known as The Carved Eagle, about 1865.*

Content Reviewers

Dr. Richard Abbott
Eastern Michigan University
Reconstruction

Dr. Larry Conyers
University of Denver
Anthropology

Dr. R. Douglas Cope
Brown University
Colonial Latin America

Dr. Paul A. Gilje
University of Oklahoma
U.S., 1492–1865

Dr. Christopher Hendricks
Armstrong Atlantic State University
Early U.S.

Dr. Melvin Holli
University of Illinois at Chicago
U.S. urban and ethnic

Dr. Raymond Hyser
James Madison University
Gilded Age and Progressive Era

Dr. Elizabeth Jameson
University of New Mexico
American West and U.S. social

Dr. Beverly Jones
North Carolina Central University
Reconstruction

Dr. Yasuhide Kawashima
University of Texas at El Paso
*Colonial and revolutionary America,
American legal*

Dr. F. Daniel Larkin
State University of New York-Oneonta
19th-century U.S.

Dr. Helen Nader
University of Arizona
Renaissance, Spain

Dr. Edward Peters
University of Pennsylvania
Medieval European

Dr. Jack Rakove
Stanford University
*American Revolution, early
American political*

Dr. Leonard Richards
University of Massachusetts
Jacksonian America

Dr. Joel Silbey
Cornell University
19th-century U.S.

Dr. David Switzer
Plymouth State College
Civil War and Reconstruction

Dr. Jesús F. de la Teja
Southwest Texas State University
Spanish Borderlands

Dr. Patricia Tracy
Williams College
Colonial America

Dr. Clarence E. Walker
University of California at Davis
African American 1450–present

Dr. John R. Wunder
University of Nebraska
American West

Educational Reviewers

Anistacio Asuncion
Piedmont Middle School
San Jose, California

Michelle Bohanek
Orozco Academy
Chicago, Illinois

Jeri Goodspeed-Gross
Minnetonka Middle School West
Chaska, Minnesota

Cynthia Gore
Castillero Middle School
San Jose, California

Tom Harris
Oak Park Middle School
Leesburg, Florida

Valerie Hill
Gaston Middle School
Dallas, Texas

Robert Jones
Perry Junior High School
New Hartford, New York

Marilyn Kretzer
Johnston Middle School
Houston, Texas

Janie Maldanado
Lanier High School
Austin, Texas

Barbara Mayo
Program Facilitator
Austin Independent School District
Austin, Texas

Steve Munzel
Jane Lathrop Stanford Middle School
Palo Alto, California

Milt Perlman
Junior High School 185
Flushing, New York

Pat Tobbe
Newburg Middle School
Louisville, Kentucky

Helen Webb
Wynn Seale Middle School
Corpus Christi, Texas

George Wood
Gregory-Portland Junior High School
Portland, Texas

Field Test Teachers

Sandra Poe Borowiecki
New Hartford Perry Junior High
School
New Hartford, New York

Mary Beth Breshears
Wood Middle School
Fort Leonard Wood, Missouri

Richard J. Giannicchi
West Seneca Junior High School
West Seneca, New York

Kim Gravell
Dripping Springs Middle School
Dripping Springs, Texas

Deborah K. Lofton
Charles F. Blackstock Junior High
School
Port Hueneme, California

Stan Mendenhall
Broadmoor Junior High School
Pekin, Illinois

Daniel Murray
Hackett Middle School
Albany, New York

Martha Potter
John Jay Middle School
Katonah, New York

Linda B. Rothrock
Harlandale Middle School
San Antonio, Texas

Amy Thompson
Union Middle School
San Jose, California

It's All About

YOUNG PEOPLE IN HISTORY uses stories of America's young heroes and their important roles in the development of our nation to draw your students into history and help them make connections.

The first step to success in the social studies classroom is capturing and sustaining the interest of your students. *HOLT CALL TO FREEDOM* is designed to be open and friendly to all students, so that they develop an enthusiasm for learning and an appreciation for the past.

HOLT CALL TO FREEDOM **offers**
- **Built-in Reading Support**
- **Technology with Instructional Value**
- **Standardized Testing and Skill Building**
- **The Best Teacher Management System in the Industry**

RELEVANCE

CNN fyi.com™ is a site designed to give students in grades 6–12 access to people, places, and environments around the globe while offering "real-world" articles, career and college resources, and online activities.

IN-TEXT FEATURES THAT PUT HISTORY INTO PERSPECTIVE

- Biographies
- Citizenship and You
- Connecting to Geography
- Connecting to Literature
- Connecting to Math
- Connecting to Science, Technology, and Society
- Connecting to the Arts
- Daily Life
- Global Connections

- If You Were There
- Interpreting the Visual Record
- Linking Past to Present
- Political Cartoons
- Presidential Profiles
- That's Interesting!
- Why it Matters Today
- Young People in History

Reading for

At Holt, we don't assume that students know how or have any desire to make sense of what they're reading, and we develop our programs based on that assumption. We don't just ask students questions about content, we give them strategies to get to that content. Through design, research, and the help of experts like Dr. Judith Irvin, we make sure students' reading needs are covered with our programs.

Helping Students Make Sense of What They're Reading

An Essay by Dr. Judith Irvin, Ph.D.

Who in middle and high schools helps students become more successful at reading and writing informational text? When I ask this question of a school faculty, the Language Arts/English teachers point to the social studies and science teachers because they are the ones with this type of textbook. The social studies and science teachers point to the Language Arts/English teachers because they are the ones that "do" words.

I advocate teachers taking an active role in helping students learn how to use text structure and context to understand what they read. Through consistent and systematic instruction that includes modeling of effective reading behavior, teachers can assist students in becoming better readers while at the same time helping them learn more content material.

The strategies in this book are designed to assist students with getting started, maintaining focus with reading, and organizing information for later retrieval. They engage students in learning material, provide the vehicle for them to organize and reorganize concepts, and extend their understanding through writing.

When teachers combine the teaching of reading and the teaching of content together into meaningful, systematic, and corrected instruction, students can apply what they have learned to understanding increasingly more difficult and complex texts as they progress through the school years.

READING STRATEGIES FOR THE SOCIAL STUDIES CLASSROOM

by Dr. Judith Irvin, Ph.D. Reading Education

Reading Strategies for the Social Studies Classroom
Dr. Judith Irvin

ADDITIONAL READING SUPPORT

- Main Idea Activities
- Graphic Organizer Activities
- Audio CD Program
- Guided Reading Activities
- Vocabulary Activities

MEANING

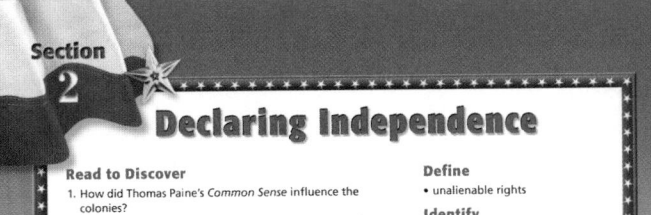

Section 2

Declaring Independence

Read to Discover
1. How did Thomas Paine's *Common Sense* influence the colonies?
2. What were the main ideas stated in the Declaration of Independence?
3. How did Americans react to the Declaration of Independence?

WHY IT MATTERS TODAY

The Declaration of Independence established the basic principles of our individual freedoms. Use CNNfyi.com or other current events sources to find an example of how we experience these freedoms today. Record your findings in your journal.

Define
• unalienable rights

Identify
• Common Sense
• Thomas Paine
• Thomas Jefferson
• Declaration of Independence
• Patriots
• Loyalists
• Abigail Adams

Thomas Paine became well known throughout the colonies for his political pamphlet Common Sense.

The Story Continues

On January 9, 1776, a 47-page pamphlet hit the streets of Philadelphia. The author was 38-year-old Thomas Paine, a self-educated British Quaker. About two years before, Paine had met Benjamin Franklin in London and impressed the colonist with his sharp mind. Franklin had helped Paine come to Philadelphia, where Paine became the editor of the *Pennsylvania Magazine*. Then in 1776 Paine produced a work that changed the course of American history.

☆ Paine's *Common Sense*

In his pamphlet *Common Sense*, **Thomas Paine** argued for breaking away from Great Britain. News of the work spread through the thirteen colonies, and it eventually sold some 500,000 copies. *Common Sense* became popular because of its message and style. Most pamphlets of the time were written by lawyers in a style that only well-educated people could understand. Paine wrote as a common person speaking to common people, which allowed him to reach a wider audience.

Paine stated in *Common Sense* that the system of monarchy in countries such as Britain was not fair. He said that the people, not kings and

queens, should make the laws. "A government of our own is our natural right," he wrote. At a time when monarchs ruled most countries of the world, this was a fairly new idea. Paine said that the colonies should demand their independence.

Paine's *Common Sense* helped change the way many colonists viewed Britain. With war now under way, the idea of independence gained more and more supporters.

✔ **Reading Check: Identifying Points of View** How did many colonists react to the ideas Thomas Paine expressed in *Common Sense*?

☆ Declaring Independence

Many colonial leaders agreed with Paine that the colonies should be free. In June 1776 the Second Continental Congress created a committee to write a document declaring the colonies' independence. The committee members were John Adams, Benjamin Franklin, **Thomas Jefferson**, Robert R. Livingston, and Roger Sherman. Jefferson was the main author of the document.

The **Declaration of Independence** expresses three main ideas. First, Jefferson argued that all men possess **unalienable rights**. He stated that these basic rights include "life, liberty, and the pursuit of happiness." The writings of Enlightenment philosophers such as John Locke inspired the idea of unalienable rights.

Jefferson's second point was that King George III had violated the colonists' rights. Like Thomas Paine, he charged the king with passing unfair laws and interfering with colonial self-government. He also accused the king of taxing colonists without their consent. In addition, the presence of a large British army in the colonies upset Jefferson.

". . . life, liberty, and the pursuit of happiness."

Interpreting the Visual Record

Independence Delegate Thomas Jefferson and the other members of his committee present the Declaration of Independence before the Second Continental Congress. Who are some of the colonial leaders shown in this image?

190   Chapter 7

191

Successful Readers must have:

AN ENGAGING NARRATIVE

Great care is taken in selecting and presenting content in a way that students will find motivating and engaging. Features such as **Young People in History** help students connect their own lives to those who have played a role in the development of our nation.

A FORECAST OF WHAT THEY WILL LEARN

Read to Discover questions give students insight into the content they will cover in the chapter to come. In features such as **If You Were There,** students are encouraged to give their opinions, thus helping them develop an ownership of the material.

OPPORTUNITIES TO ACTIVATE PRIOR KNOWLEDGE

In the pre-reading features **Build on What You Know** and **You Be the Historian,** students are encouraged to

connect content they have covered in previous chapters or other courses to the material they will learn about in the upcoming chapter.

VOCABULARY DEFINED IN CONTEXT

Important new terms are identified at the beginning of every section and are defined in context so students will develop an understanding of the contextual meaning of all terms.

STRATEGIES FOR UNDERSTANDING WHAT THEY READ

Through the design of the text, students are led through the content using built-in reading strategies. For example, **Reading Checks** in the text are used as a comprehension tool. The checks remind students to stop and engage with what they have read, functioning as a "Tutor in the Text."

M3

Get Your Students

Your students love activities that get them involved with the content. That's why Holt offers active-learning resources that link directly to program content and provide a multitude of different lessons for large-group, small-group, and individual projects.

CREATIVE TEACHING STRATEGIES

These innovative teaching strategies can be utilized at various points in your lesson. The wide range of cooperative-learning activities, including learning stations and simulations, motivate your students and help them develop critical-thinking skills.

CITIZENSHIP SIMULATIONS AND CASE STUDIES

Your students will explore issues about U.S. citizenship with this resource. These creative, hands-on activities encourage students to explore their rights and roles in their community by putting them in decision-making positions for Supreme Court cases, having them write a presidential magazine article, and more.

HANDS-ON HISTORY ACTIVITIES: CLASSROOM TO COMMUNITY

This resource will get your students out of their seats for group-oriented, active-learning projects. Chapter content, historical research, and student creativity blend together and bring the focus of your lessons to specific links between history and your local community.

Involved in Learning

Joining Forces

CNN PRESENTS AMERICA: YESTERDAY AND TODAY

to Enrich your Classroom

CNNfyi.com

At **CNNfyi.com**, students will love exploring news stories written by experienced journalists as well as student bureau reporters complete with links to homework help and lesson plans.

CNN PRESENTS VIDEO LIBRARY

The **CNN PRESENTS** video collection tackles the issue of making content relevant to students head on. Real-world news stories enable students to see the connections between classroom curriculum and today's issues and events around the nation and the world.

CNN PRESENTS...

- **America: Yesterday and Today, Beginnings to 1914**
- **America: Yesterday and Today, 1850 to Present**
- **America: Yesterday and Today, Modern Times**
- **Geography: Yesterday and Today**
- **World Cultures: Yesterday and Today**
- **American Government**
- **Economics**

Holt is proud to team up with CNN/TURNER LEARNING to provide you and your students with exceptional current and historical news videos and online resources that add depth and relevance to your daily instruction. This information collection takes your classroom to the far corners of the globe without students ever leaving their desks!

Your Multi-talented Classroom

Developed by the Association of American Geographers

ACTIVITIES AND READINGS IN THE GEOGRAPHY OF THE UNITED STATES

Integrate real geography into the topic you're studying with *Activities and Readings in the Geography of the United States (ARGUS).* This CD-ROM features 26 American history case studies with a multitude of activities that focus around geographical themes, population geography, economic geography, political geography, and environmental issues. Case studies will help teachers address the National Geography standards.

HOLT RESEARCHER: AMERICAN HISTORY CD-ROM

This CD-ROM contains a fully researchable database, including biographies, state and nation profiles, Supreme Court cases, statistics, and more. This outstanding research tool comes with an easy-to-use search engine, an Internet link to **www.hrw.com**, and powerful graphing capabilities.

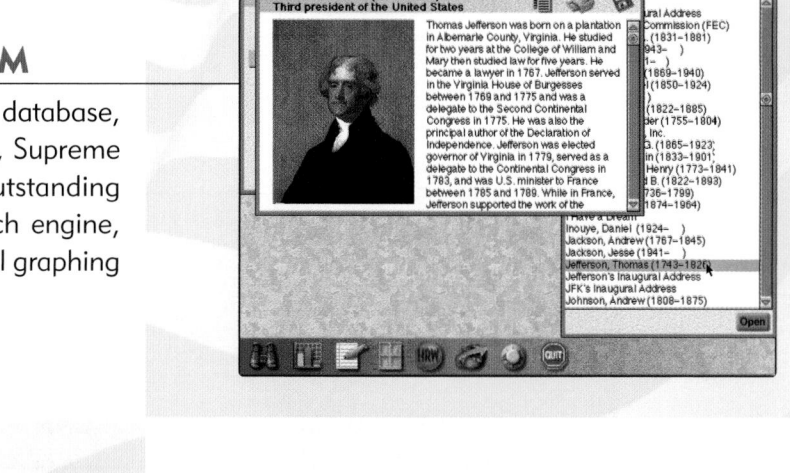

AMERICAN HISTORY SIMULATIONS CD-ROM

What was it like to be a miner during the gold rush? How many acres of land do you have to buy to make a profit on cotton? All of these questions and more will be answered on this CD-ROM that allows your students to role-play as important decision-makers in our history.

needs Multimedia Tools

AMERICAN HISTORY INTERACTIVE MAPS CD-ROM

The maps, audio and video clips, text, and illustrations on this powerful tool provide hands-on activities for your students to examine geographic and economic issues. Interactive strategies ask students to collect and analyze data about the importance of the people, places, and events that affected our nation's past.

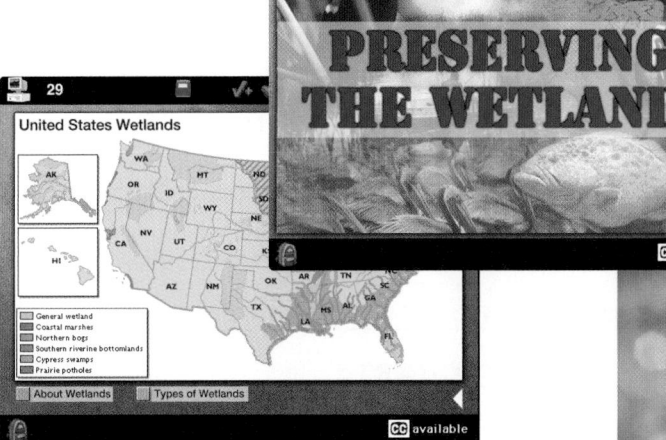

EXPLORING AMERICA'S PAST VIDEO PROGRAM

This video resource highlights key events, people, and ideas in American history. Each segment helps students understand important themes and serves as a stimulus for class discussion.

OTHER MULTIMEDIA PRODUCTS

- **American Music Audio CD**
- **Global Skill-Builder CD-ROM**
- **Chapter Summary Audio CD Program in English and Spanish**
- **Holt Researcher: American History CD-ROM**
- **Holt Researcher: Economy and Government CD-ROM**
- **The American Nation Video Program**

Technology with

go.hrw.com for Teachers

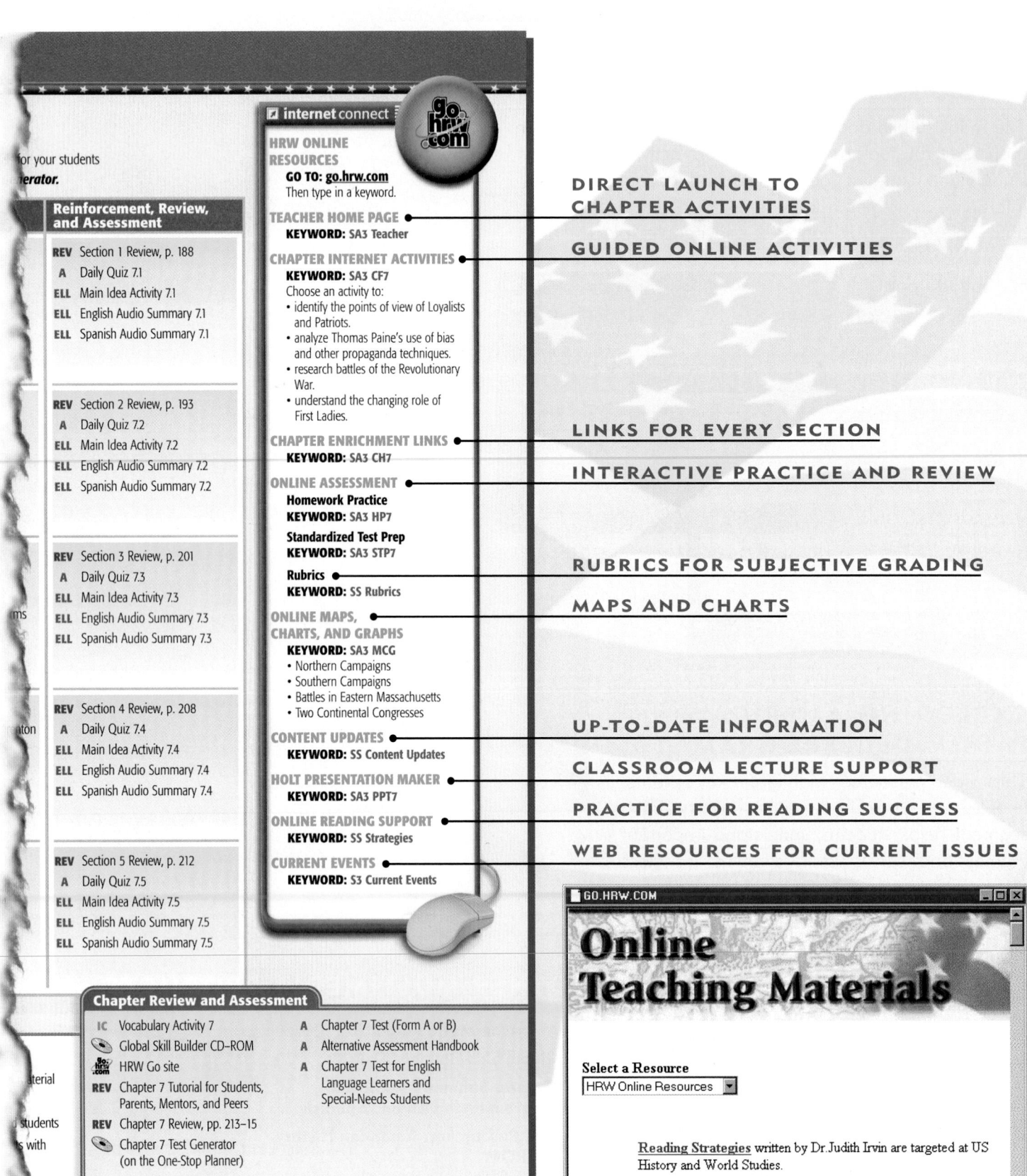

for your students
...erator.

Reinforcement, Review, and Assessment

REV	Section 1 Review, p. 188
A	Daily Quiz 7.1
ELL	Main Idea Activity 7.1
ELL	English Audio Summary 7.1
ELL	Spanish Audio Summary 7.1
REV	Section 2 Review, p. 193
A	Daily Quiz 7.2
ELL	Main Idea Activity 7.2
ELL	English Audio Summary 7.2
ELL	Spanish Audio Summary 7.2
REV	Section 3 Review, p. 201
A	Daily Quiz 7.3
ELL	Main Idea Activity 7.3
ELL	English Audio Summary 7.3
ELL	Spanish Audio Summary 7.3
REV	Section 4 Review, p. 208
A	Daily Quiz 7.4
ELL	Main Idea Activity 7.4
ELL	English Audio Summary 7.4
ELL	Spanish Audio Summary 7.4
REV	Section 5 Review, p. 212
A	Daily Quiz 7.5
ELL	Main Idea Activity 7.5
ELL	English Audio Summary 7.5
ELL	Spanish Audio Summary 7.5

✓ internet connect

HRW ONLINE RESOURCES
GO TO: go.hrw.com
Then type in a keyword.

TEACHER HOME PAGE
KEYWORD: SA3 Teacher

CHAPTER INTERNET ACTIVITIES
KEYWORD: SA3 CF7
Choose an activity to:
• identify the points of view of Loyalists and Patriots.
• analyze Thomas Paine's use of bias and other propaganda techniques.
• research battles of the Revolutionary War.
• understand the changing role of First Ladies.

CHAPTER ENRICHMENT LINKS
KEYWORD: SA3 CH7

ONLINE ASSESSMENT
Homework Practice
KEYWORD: SA3 HP7

Standardized Test Prep
KEYWORD: SA3 STP7

Rubrics
KEYWORD: SS Rubrics

ONLINE MAPS, CHARTS, AND GRAPHS
KEYWORD: SA3 MCG
• Northern Campaigns
• Southern Campaigns
• Battles in Eastern Massachusetts
• Two Continental Congresses

CONTENT UPDATES
KEYWORD: SS Content Updates

HOLT PRESENTATION MAKER
KEYWORD: SA3 PPT7

ONLINE READING SUPPORT
KEYWORD: SS Strategies

CURRENT EVENTS
KEYWORD: S3 Current Events

DIRECT LAUNCH TO CHAPTER ACTIVITIES

GUIDED ONLINE ACTIVITIES

LINKS FOR EVERY SECTION

INTERACTIVE PRACTICE AND REVIEW

RUBRICS FOR SUBJECTIVE GRADING

MAPS AND CHARTS

UP-TO-DATE INFORMATION

CLASSROOM LECTURE SUPPORT

PRACTICE FOR READING SUCCESS

WEB RESOURCES FOR CURRENT ISSUES

Chapter Review and Assessment

IC	Vocabulary Activity 7	A	Chapter 7 Test (Form A or B)
	Global Skill Builder CD-ROM	A	Alternative Assessment Handbook
	HRW Go site	A	Chapter 7 Test for English Language Learners and Special-Needs Students
REV	Chapter 7 Tutorial for Students, Parents, Mentors, and Peers		
REV	Chapter 7 Review, pp. 213–15		
	Chapter 7 Test Generator (on the One-Stop Planner)		

GO.HRW.COM

Online Teaching Materials

Select a Resource
[HRW Online Resources ▼]

<u>Reading Strategies</u> written by Dr. Judith Irvin are targeted at US History and World Studies.

<u>HRW's State Handbooks</u> provide state-specific links and activities at the click of a mouse button.

material
...students
...s with

Instructional Value

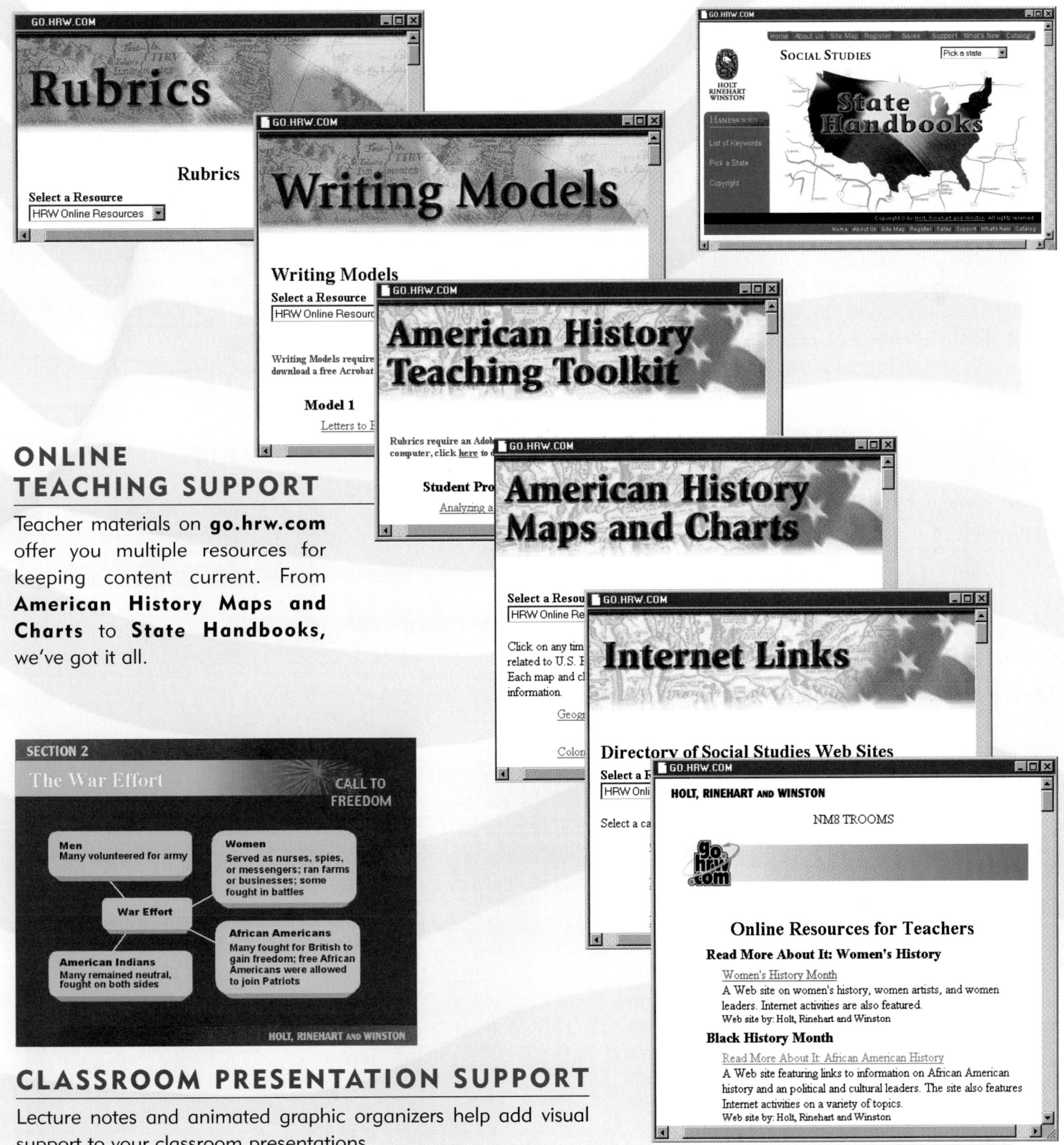

ONLINE TEACHING SUPPORT

Teacher materials on **go.hrw.com** offer you multiple resources for keeping content current. From **American History Maps and Charts** to **State Handbooks,** we've got it all.

CLASSROOM PRESENTATION SUPPORT

Lecture notes and animated graphic organizers help add visual support to your classroom presentations.

Technology that

go.hrw.com for Students

GEOMAPS

When you visit **go.hrw.com**, you can access **GeoMaps** which provides a unique opportunity to examine satellite maps that explore a region's land, water, places, and people.

ONLINE TEMPLATES

Your students can use these interactive templates to create newspapers, travel brochures, postcards, journals, creative works, and more. The instructional design of this tool allows students to do something with the content they have learned.

HOMEWORK PRACTICE

This helpful tool allows students to practice and review content by chapter anywhere there is a computer.

ONLINE HISTORICAL MAPS

These maps provide fascinating visual "snapshots" of the past. Students will relish the chance to explore medieval European trade routes, explorers' routes, ancient African kingdoms, and more.

HRW ONLINE ATLAS

This helpful online tool contains over 300 well-rendered and clearly labeled country and state maps. The clean design and easy-to-use navigational tools make accessing information simple. These maps are continually updated so you can rest assured that you and your students have the latest and most accurate geographical content available. Maps are available in English and Spanish.

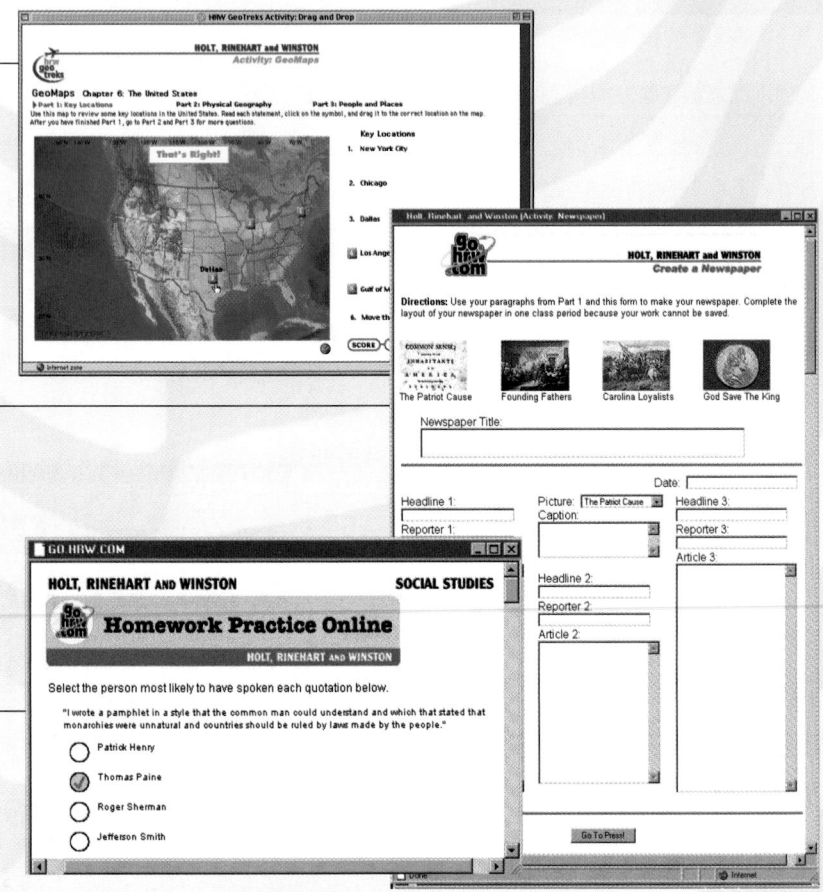

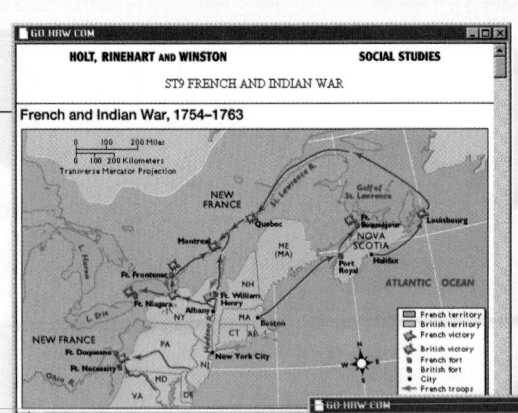

Delivers Content

NEW ONLINE TEXTBOOK

You'll know what to do when you see it!
Finally, an online textbook that takes full advantage of Web technology
in a way that makes sense—*HOLT CALL TO FREEDOM ONLINE EDITION.*

- **Entire student edition online formatted to match printed text**
- **User-friendly navigation**
- **Hot links to interactive activities, practice, and assessment**
- **Student Notebook for online responses**

Unique Teacher's

In-Text Chapter Planning

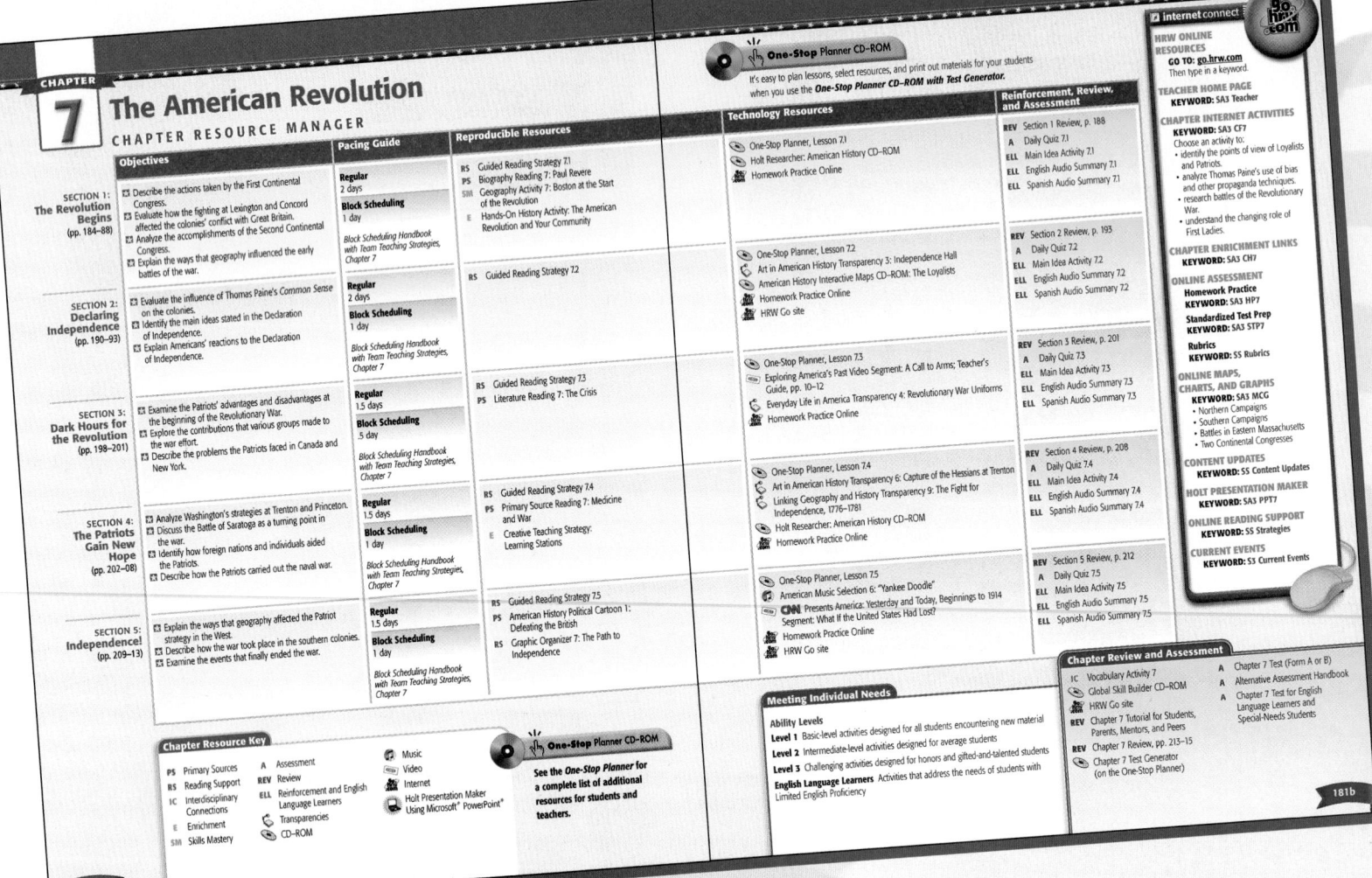

Program Resources at Your Fingertips

Reading Support
- **Graphic Organizer Activities**
- **Guided Reading Strategies**
- **Main Idea Activities for English Language Learners and Special-Needs Students**
- **Reading Strategies for the Social Studies Classroom**
- **Vocabulary Activities**
- **Writing About American History**

Active-Learning Support
- **Block Scheduling Handbook with Team-Teaching Strategies**
- **Citizenship Simulations and Case Studies**
- **Creative Teaching Strategies**
- **Hands-On History Activities: Classroom to Community**

Primary Sources
- **American History Political Cartoons**
- **American History Visual Resources**
- **Art in American History Transparencies**
- **The Constitution: Past, Present, and Future**
- **American History Document-Based Questions Activities**
- **Readings and Activities**
- **Eyewitnesses and Others: Readings in American History**

Geography Support
- **American History Outline Maps**
- **The Complete School Atlas**
- **Geography Activities**

Review and Assessment
- **Daily Quizzes**
- **Alternative Assessment Handbook**
- **Chapter Tutorials for Students, Parents, Mentors, and Peers**
- **Chapter and Unit Tests**
- **Chapter and Unit Tests for English Language Learners and Special-Needs Students**
- **Answer Key for Geography Activities, Guided Reading, and Vocabulary Activities**
- **Social Studies Skills Review**
- **Standardized Test Practice Handbook**

Management System

Everything you need is on one disc!

ONE-STOP PLANNER CD-ROM WITH TEST GENERATOR

Holt brings you the most user-friendly management system in the industry with the **One-Stop Planner CD-ROM with Test Generator.** Plan and manage your lessons from this single disc containing all the teaching resources for **Holt Call to Freedom,** valuable planning and assessment tools, and more.

- **Editable lesson plans**
- **Classroom Presentations**
- **Easy-to-use test generator**
- **Previews of all teaching and video resources**
- **Easy printing feature**
- **Direct launch to go.hrw.com**

BLOCK-SCHEDULING HANDBOOK WITH TEAM TEACHING STRATEGIES

This is more than a pacing guide—it provides daily lesson plans that suggest practical ways to cover more than one textbook section in an extended class period and ways to make interdisciplinary connections.

M15

Energize

PRESENTATIONS THAT BENEFIT LEARNING

Classroom presentations and lecture notes can be accessed with ease when you use Holt's **Presentation** tool found on the *One-Stop Planner CD-ROM.* This resource helps you spice up your presentations and gives you ideas to build on. You'll find Microsoft® PowerPoint® presentations that include lecture notes and animated graphic organizers for each chapter and section of your text.

Your Classroom Presentations

OBJECTIVE-BASED LESSON CYCLE

With lively activities and presentation strategies such as **Let's Get Started, Building Vocabulary,** and **Graphic Organizers,** your step-by-step lesson cycle makes planning your lessons easy and productive.

Section 3

OBJECTIVES

- Examine the Patriots' advantages and disadvantages at the beginning of the Revolutionary War.
- Explore the contributions that various groups made to the war effort.
- Describe the problems the Patriots faced in Canada and New York.

LET'S GET STARTED!

As students enter the classroom, tell them to read the Literature Reading *The Crisis.* Have students evaluate in writing the main idea of the piece. *(Students' responses will vary but should mention that it was written to rally the troops.)* Explain to students that at the beginning of the Revolutionary War, Great Britain seemed to have a huge advantage over the colonies but that as the war went on, the new nation was able to win some surprising victories. Tell students that in Section 3 they will learn more about the opening months of the Revolutionary War.

TEACH

Have students read Section 3 and complete Guided Reading Strategy 7.3. Choose one or more of the following activities to explore the section content with students. For further suggestions on block scheduling or team teaching, see the *Block Scheduling Handbook with Team Teaching Strategies.*

LEVEL 1: Have pairs of students create a graphic organizer that compares the Patriots' battles in Canada and New York. Students' graphic organizers should include information related to the problems that the Patriots faced in Canada and New York. *(Students' graphic organizers should include: in Canada the Patriots were far from home and faced poor weather; in New York they were outnumbered and out-maneuvered.)* **ENGLISH LANGUAGE LEARNERS , COOPERATIVE LEARNING**

HOMEWORK Tell students to imagine that they are Patriot soldiers fighting in Canada and New York. Have each student write a letter to a friend or family member back home that describes the problems he or she is facing.

ALL LEVELS: Copy the graphic organizer on the following page onto the chalkboard, omitting the italicized answers. Use it to help students explore the contributions of various groups to the war effort. **ENGLISH LANGUAGE LEARNERS**

| Men | | Women |
| many volunteered for army | | served as nurses, spies, or messengers; ran farms or businesses; some fought in battles |

War Effort

| American Indians | | African Americans |
| fought on both sides but many remained neutral | | many fought for British to gain freedom; free African Americans were allowed to join Patriots |

LEVEL 3: Have students create Patriot recruitment posters to encourage enlistment in the Continental Army. The recruitment posters should include information and images that reflect the Patriots' advantages and disadvantages at the beginning of the Revolutionary War. Have volunteers present their posters to the class.

CLOSE

Arrange a debate or panel discussion on each of the following topics: a)Resolved: That the Patriot army was at a strong disadvantage at the beginning of the Revolutionary War; and b) Resolved: That the Patriot army should not have invaded British Canada. Have students present their debates to the class. **COOPERATIVE LEARNING**

REVIEW AND ASSESS

Have students complete the **Section 3 Review** on p. 201. Then have students complete **Daily Quiz 7.3.** As **Alternative Assessment,** you may want to use the war effort graphic organizer or recruitment posters in this section's lessons.

RETEACH

Have students complete **Main Idea Activity for English Language Learners and Special-Needs Students 7.3.** Then ask students to write a question and answer that addresses the main idea for each subsection in the section. Have volunteers read their questions to the class. Have the class try to answer each question. **ENGLISH LANGUAGE LEARNERS**

EXTEND

Organize students into groups. Have each group find the names of five people from different backgrounds who contributed to the Revolutionary War effort. Tell students to use the library or other available resources to write a brief biographal sketch for each of their chosen people that describes his or her contributions to the Revolutionary War effort. Ask volunteers to share their sketches with the class. **COOPERATIVE LEARNING , BLOCK SCHEDULING**

TEACHER TO TEACHER

These strategies are offered in the columns of your *Annotated Teacher's Edition* and provide you with valuable, classroom-tested ideas and activities that have been developed and successfully applied by your peers.

SIDE-COLUMN ANNOTATIONS THAT SPARK CURIOSITY

- **Across the Curriculum**
- **Biographies and Presidential Profiles**
- **Citizenship and You**
- **Connecting to the Arts**
- **Connecting to Geography**
- **Connecting to Literature**
- **Connecting to Math**
- **Connecting to Science, Technology, and Society**
- **Daily Life**
- **Global Connections**
- **Linking Past to Present**
- **People in History**
- **That's Interesting!**
- **Young People in History**

Assessment for

Section 5 Review

1 Define and explain:
- guerrilla warfare

2 Identify and explain:
- George Rogers Clark
- Battle of Vincennes
- Horatio Gates
- Francis Marion
- Comte de Rochambeau
- Battle of Yorktown
- Treaty of Paris of 1783

3 Sequencing Copy the graphic organizer below. Use it to list the major events that led to the end of the Revolutionary War.

1. _____
2. _____
3. _____

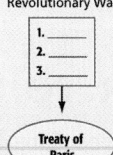

Treaty of Paris

4 Finding the Main Idea
a. How did geography affect the Patriot strategy on the western frontier?
b. How did the war progress in the southern colonies up to Washington's victory at Yorktown?

5 Writing and Critical Thinking
Summarizing Imagine that you are a colonial diplomat. Create a pamphlet announcing the war's end. Your pamphlet should include a summary of the war's final events.
Consider the following:
- the Battle of Yorktown
- the terms of the Treaty of Paris 1783
- how you think the United States will fare after the war

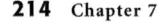

M18

Chapter 7 Review

The Chapter at a Glance
Examine the visual summary of the chapter below. Use it to help you create a five-question quiz that you might give to a classmate.

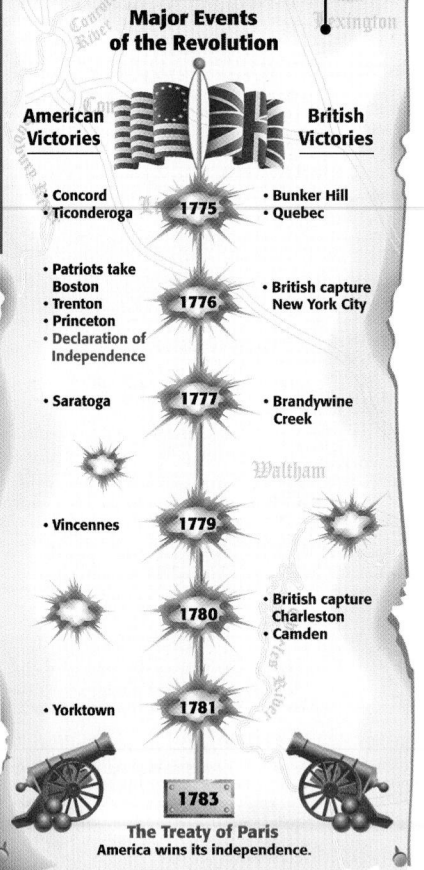

Major Events of the Revolution

American Victories | **British Victories**

1775
- Concord
- Ticonderoga
- Bunker Hill
- Quebec

1776
- Patriots take Boston
- Trenton
- Princeton
- Declaration of Independence
- British capture New York City

1777
- Saratoga
- Brandywine Creek

1779
- Vincennes

1780
- British capture Charleston
- Camden

1781
- Yorktown

1783

The Treaty of Paris
America wins its independence.

Identifying People and Ideas
Use the following terms or people in historically significant sentences.
1. minutemen
2. George Washington
3. *Common Sense*
4. Thomas Jefferson
5. Declaration of Independence
6. Abigail Adams
7. Marquis de Lafayette
8. John Paul Jones
9. Battle of Yorktown
10. Treaty of Paris of 1783

Understanding Main Ideas
Section 1 (Pages 184–189)
1. How did the fighting at Lexington and Concord affect the relationship between the colonies and Great Britain?
2. What did the First and Second Continental Congresses achieve?

Section 2 (Pages 190–193)
3. What effect did Thomas Paine's *Common Sense* have on colonial attitudes toward Britain?

Section 3 (Pages 198–201)
4. What advantages and disadvantages did the Patriots have when the Revolutionary War began?

Section 4 (Pages 202–208)
5. How did Washington defeat the British at Trenton and Princeton?
6. Why was the Battle of Saratoga important?

Section 5 (Pages 209–213)
7. How did the Patriots fight the war in the West and in the South?

You Be the Historian— Reviewing Themes
1. **Citizenship** Why did the colonies declare their independence from Britain?
2. **Constitutional Heritage** What are three rights that all men have according to the Declaration of Independence?
3. **Global Relations** Why did some foreign countries help the Patriots, and what role did Patriots such as Benjamin Franklin play in gaining this support?

Thinking Critically
1. **Supporting a Point of View** Did the Patriots' belief in their cause make up for their lack of supplies? Explain your answer.
2. **Summarizing** What key events occurred in 1776?
3. **Drawing Inferences and Conclusions** What do you think were the most significant causes of the American Revolution? Explain your answer.

214 Chapter 7

Every Student

Social Studies Skills Workshop

Interpreting Charts

Study the chart below. Then use the information on the chart to help you answer the questions that follow.

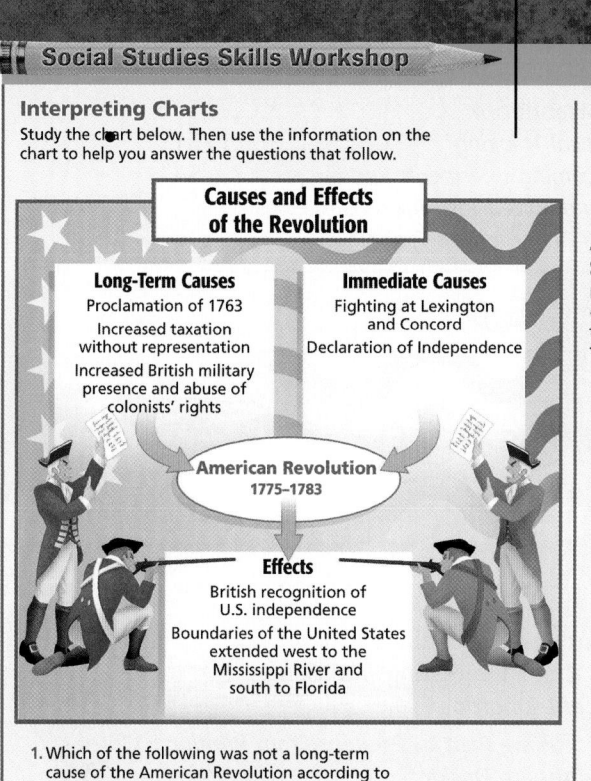

Causes and Effects of the Revolution

Long-Term Causes
Proclamation of 1763
Increased taxation without representation
Increased British military presence and abuse of colonists' rights

Immediate Causes
Fighting at Lexington and Concord
Declaration of Independence

American Revolution 1775–1783

Effects
British recognition of U.S. independence
Boundaries of the United States extended west to the Mississippi River and south to Florida

1. Which of the following was not a long-term cause of the American Revolution according to the chart?
   a. the Proclamation of 1763
   b. taxation without representation
   c. abuse of colonial rights
   d. French attacks on the colonies

2. Based on the chart and your knowledge of the period, how do you think the long-term causes of the Revolution contributed to the immediate causes of the war?

Analyzing Primary Sources

Read the following excerpt from *Common Sense* by Thomas Paine, then answer the questions that follow.

“A government of our own is our natural right; and when a man seriously reflects on the precariousness [uncertainness] of human affairs, he will become convinced that it is infinitely [completely] wiser and safer to form a constitution of our own in a cool deliberate manner, while we have it in our power, than to trust such an interesting event to time and chance.”

3. Which of the following best describes Paine's viewpoint?
   a. Americans should rush to form a new nation.
   b. Americans would be better off independent.
   c. Americans should remain British citizens.
   d. It is best to take risks.
4. Why do you think that Paine's message was popular with many colonists?

Alternative Assessment

Building Your Portfolio

American History

Linking to Community
John Paul Jones was a hero of the American Revolution. Present an oral report on a war hero from your community. This hero can be someone living in your community today or someone who lived there in the past. If the person still lives in your community, you may want to interview the individual for your report.

internet connect

go.hrw.com

Internet Activity: go.hrw.com
keyword: SA3 CF7
Access the Internet through the HRW Go site to conduct research on the differing viewpoints of Loyalists and Patriots. Then create a newspaper that shows bias to the Loyalist or Patriot position on the Revolution. Make sure you use at least three examples of biased reporting in your newspaper. On a separate sheet of paper, explain where the bias occurs and why it is biased.

The American Revolution **215**

ACCESS ONLINE RUBRICS FOR GRADING PROJECTS AND PORTFOLIO ASSIGNMENTS

STANDARDIZED TEST PRACTICE HANDBOOK

This resource helps your students gear up for future standardized tests. Content-specific practice exposes them to a variety of question types—like multiple choice and short answer—commonly found in today's standardized assessments.

Standardized Test Practice Handbook with Answer Key

HOLT CALL TO FREEDOM
Beginnings to 1877

HOLT, RINEHART AND WINSTON

ADDITIONAL PRINT AND TECHNOLOGY ASSESSMENT RESOURCES

- **Alternative Assessment Handbook**
- **Audio CD Program**
- **Chapter and Unit Tests**
- **Chapter and Unit Tests for English Language Learners and Special-Needs Students**
- **Chapter Tutorials for Students, Parents, Mentors, and Peers**
- **Daily Quizzes**
- **Document-Based Questions Activities**
- **Main Idea Activities**
- **Test Generator (located on the One-Stop Planner with Test Generator)**

Call to Freedom
Beginnings to 1877

CONTENTS

*Pottery made by
Native Americans*

Colonists build their first settlement in New England.

Benjamin Franklin

A cannon from the American Revolution

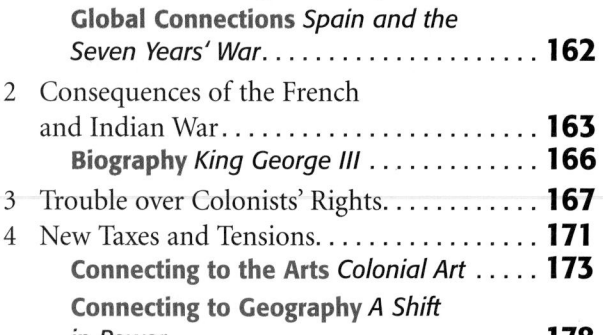

*During the Boston Tea Party,
colonists dumped boxes of tea
off of several ships.*

Washington's cabinet

Sequoya

First Lady Dolley Madison had to flee Washington when the British burned it during the War of 1812.

*Cotton bolls and a
southern plantation*

U.S. troops enter Mexico City.

An illustration of manifest destiny, an idea that led many settlers to move west

A Civil War soldier and his family

THE GRANGER COLLECTION, NEW YORK

Abraham Lincoln

Primary Sources

The bald eagle

History Makers Speak

Abigail Adams

Primary Sources, *continued*

Frederick
Douglass

Primary Sources

Historical Documents

The Emancipation Proclamation

Political Cartoons

History and Your World

National Guard members helping a community

A quill pen from the 1700s

Supreme Court justice Ruth Bader Ginsburg speaking to a group of students

Young People
IN HISTORY

LINKING
PAST to ★ PRESENT ★

Citizenship ★★★★★ ★★★★★ and You

Interdisciplinary Activities

Historical Highlights

Early pioneers used wagons such as this one to settle the frontier.

THE GRANGER COLLECTION, NEW YORK

Technology Activities

Research on the R⊙M

internet connect gohrw.com

Skill-Building Activities

Social Studies Skills WORKSHOPS

History in Action UNIT SIMULATIONS

Skill-Building Activities, continued

MAPS

An astrolabe

THE GRANGER COLLECTION, NEW YORK

GRAPHS AND CHARTS

TIME LINES ➡

VISUALIZING HISTORY

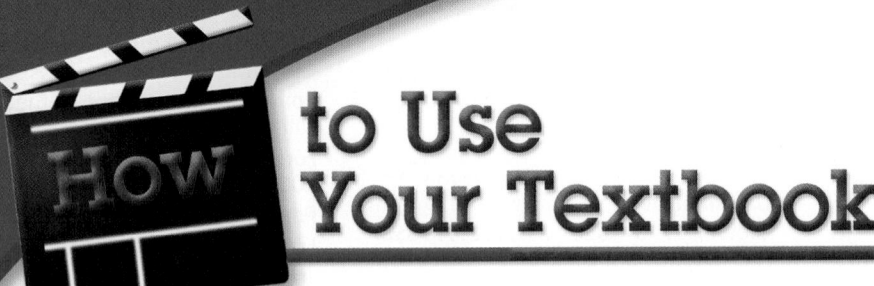

How to Use Your Textbook

Use the chapter opener to get an overview of the time period.

The Chapter Time Line shows you a comparison of U.S. and global events.

CHAPTER

19 The Civil War
(1861–1865)

The fierce fighting at the First Battle of Bull Run surprised many Americans who had expected the war to be over swiftly.

UNITED STATES

1861 Confederate guns open fire on Fort Sumter in South Carolina on April 12.

1861 Confederate forces win the first battle of the Civil War on July 21 at Bull Run Creek in Virginia.

1862 The Monitor fights the Virginia on March 9.

1862 On December 13 General Robert E. Lee wins a major victory at Fredericksburg, Virginia.

1863 The Emancipation Proclamation goes into effect on January 1.

1863 Union forces capture Vicksburg, Mississippi, on July 4. That same day, General Lee's forces retreat after losing the Battle of Gettysburg in Pennsylvania.

1863 On November 19 President Lincoln delivers the Gettysburg Address.

1864 Union general William T. Sherman takes Atlanta on September 2.

1865 General Lee surrenders to General Grant at Appomattox Courthouse on April 9.

When Lee surrendered to Grant, the Union commander agreed to treat the defeated Confederate troops with dignity.

This sword belonged to Robert E. Lee.

1861 **1862** **1863** **1864** **1865**

1861 On March 17 nationalist leader Giuseppe Garibaldi declares Victor Emmanuel II king of Italy.

1862 Jean-Henri Dunant of Switzerland proposes the creation of the International Red Cross.

1863 On June 7, French forces capture Mexico City.

1864 The Taiping Rebellion in China ends after the capture of Nanjing in July.

WORLD

Together, Giuseppe Garibaldi and Victor Emmanuel II helped unify Italy.

This medal was used by the International Red Cross.

If you were there . . . Would you support or oppose secession?

Build on What You Know

In the 1850s the North and the South were strongly divided over the issue of slavery. The election of Republican Abraham Lincoln as president in 1860 led 11 southern states to leave the Union. When the North refused to accept this secession, the opposing views of each side soon led to a terrible civil war between North and South.

You Be the Historian

What's Your Opinion? Do you **agree** or **disagree** with the following statements? Support your point of view in your journal.

- **Science, Technology & Society** New technology always makes wars easier to win.
- **Economics** Wars are bad for a nation's economy.
- **Citizenship** All citizens have a duty to support their government during a war.

578 Chapter 19

579

Build on What You Know bridges the material you have studied in previous chapters with the material you are about to begin. As you read the Build on What You Know feature, take a few minutes to think about the topics that might apply to the chapter you are starting.

You Be the Historian puts you in the place of a historian looking at the past. In this feature you will be asked to respond to three general statements about the chapter. Each statement is tied to one of the key themes of the program. You should respond based on your own knowledge and then record your responses in your journal. There are no right or wrong answers, just your informed opinion.

Use these built-in tools to read for understanding.

Read to Discover questions begin each section of *Call to Freedom*. These questions serve as your guide as you read through the section. Keep them in mind as you explore the section content.

Why It Matters Today is an exciting way for you to make connections between what you are reading in your history book and the world around you. In each section you will be invited to explore a topic that is relevant to our lives today by using **CNNfyi.com** connections.

History Makers Speak quotations appear frequently throughout the book. These exciting primary source quotations give you a glimpse into the lives of actual people who made history. Many of these quotations are accompanied by an Analyzing Primary Sources question to help you better interpret the sources and draw inferences about their importance.

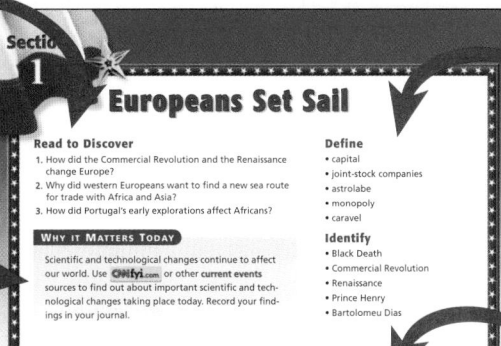

Section 1

Europeans Set Sail

Read to Discover
1. How did the Commercial Revolution and the Renaissance change Europe?
2. Why did western Europeans want to find a new sea route for trade with Africa and Asia?
3. How did Portugal's early explorations affect Africans?

WHY IT MATTERS TODAY

Scientific and technological changes continue to affect our world. Use **CNNfyi.com** or other **current events** sources to find out about important scientific and technological changes taking place today. Record your findings in your journal.

Define
- capital
- joint-stock companies
- astrolabe
- monopoly
- caravel

Identify
- Black Death
- Commercial Revolution
- Renaissance
- Prince Henry
- Bartolomeu Dias

A trade union in the Netherlands used this seal.

The Story Continues

In 1299 the city of Arras in present-day France was famous for its wealthy merchants. The powerful Crespin family was so rich that it loaned money to cities, bishops, and even monarchs. Some people worried about this new interest in money. "Money is too much worshipped here," wrote poet Adam de la Halle about Arras. Others welcomed the changing economy. They thought it provided ways for workers to make money and improve their social status. When Baude Crespin died in 1316 his tombstone read, "Pray for his immortal spirit then, Laborers and working men."

★ The European Economy Grows

Europe's wealth and population grew steadily during the late Middle Ages. Then, in the mid-1300s Europe suffered a terrible blow. Some ships belonging to Italian merchants returned from Asia carrying rats infected with bubonic plague, a deadly disease. The plague led to an epidemic called the **Black Death**, which swept through Europe from about 1348 to 1350. The epidemic killed as many as 30 million people, about

32 Chapter 2

These leaders had not signed any treaties with Britain and would not give up their land because of an agreement between Britain and France. Chippewa leader Minavavana expressed this view to a trader in 1761. "Englishman, although you have conquered the French, you have not yet conquered us!"

In the 1760s American Indian tribes began to join together to resist the British. Chief Pontiac of the Ottawa led forces that included the Delaware, Huron, Miami, Ottawa, and Shawnee peoples. Pontiac followed the teachings of the so-called Delaware Prophet. This leader called on Indians to drive out the white settlers and give up all European practices. In 1763 Pontiac shared these ideas with a gathering of American Indians.

Interpreting the Visual Record

Fort Detroit *Pontiac's forces tried for months to capture Fort Detroit from the British. What in the image suggests the difficulties of attacking the fort?*

History Makers Speak "How comes it that you suffer the whites on your lands? Can't you do without them? You might live wholly [completely] as you did before you knew them. . . . Those who come to trouble your country, drive them out, make war [on] them! . . . They are my enemies and the enemies of your brothers!"

—Pontiac, quoted in *The World Turned Upside Down*, edited by Colin G. Calloway

Analyzing Primary Sources
Identifying Points of View How does Pontiac describe white settlers?

Pontiac's Rebellion began in May 1763 when American Indians attacked British forts on the frontier. Within a month Pontiac's forces had destroyed or captured seven forts. Pontiac then led the attack on Fort Detroit, Britain's political and trading center in the Great Lakes area. Despite the best efforts of Pontiac and his allies, the British held out for months. The American Indians following Pontiac grew tired of attacking the fort and returned to their villages. An Indian attack on the important British position at Fort Pitt also failed. Both sides suffered many casualties. As more Indians left Pontiac, he surrendered in 1766.

✔ **Reading Check: Identifying Cause and Effect** Why did Pontiac and his followers fight the British, and what happened as a result?

Conflicts in the Colonies **165**

Define and Identify terms are introduced at the beginning of each section. The terms will be defined in context.

The Story Continues features an interesting episode from American history that shows you that history is not just a collection of facts but a blend of many individual stories and adventures.

Interpreting the Visual Record features accompany many of the book's rich images. Pictures are one of the most important primary sources historians can use to help analyze the past. These features invite you to examine the images and to interpret their content.

Reading Check questions appear throughout the book to allow you to check your comprehension while you are reading. As you read each section, pause for a moment to consider each Reading Check. If you have trouble answering the question, go back and examine the material you just read.

Use these review tools to pull together all the information you have learned.

Graphic Organizers will help you review important information from the section. You can complete the graphic organizer as a study tool to prepare for a test or writing assignment.

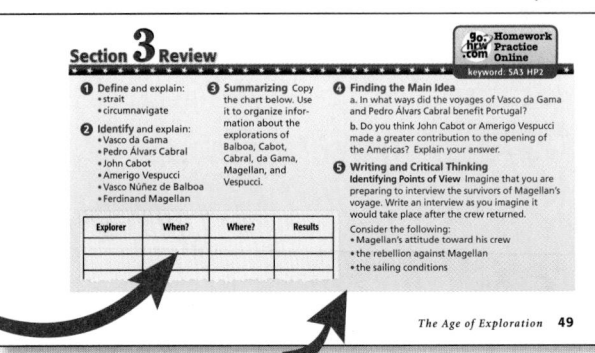

Homework Practice Online lets you log on to the go.hrw.com Web site to complete an interactive self-check of the material covered in the section.

Writing and Critical Thinking activities allow you to explore a section topic in greater depth and to build your skills.

The Chapter at a Glance is an interesting visual summary of the main ideas of the chapter.

Social Studies Skills Workshop is a way for you to build your skills at analyzing information and to practice answering standardized-test questions.

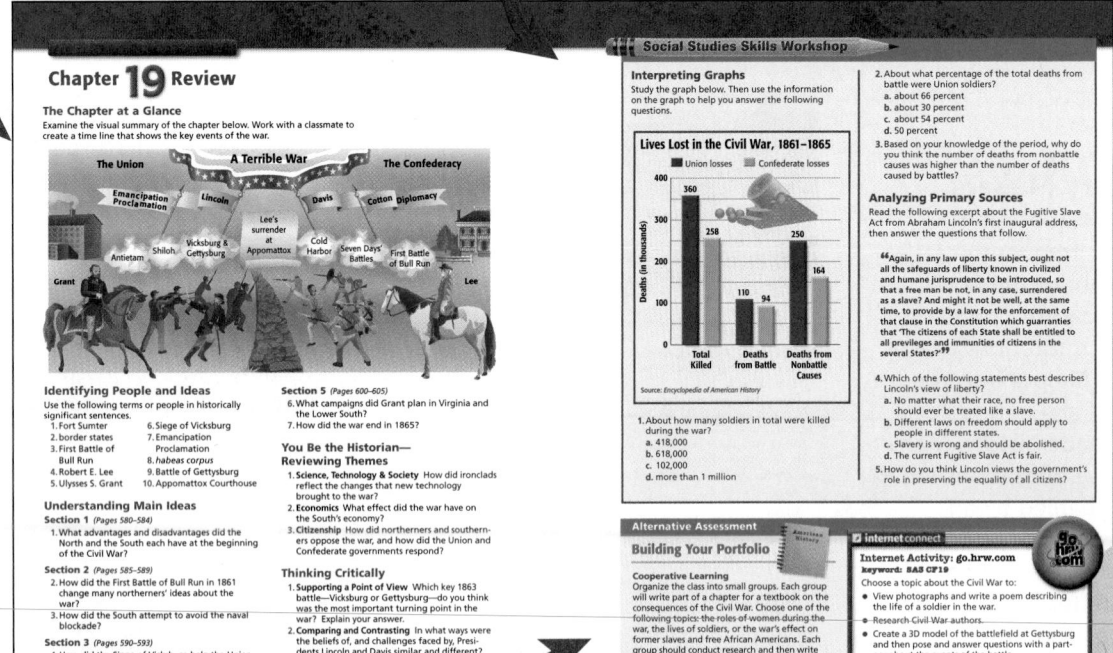

Thinking Critically questions ask you to use the information you have learned in the chapter to extend your knowledge. You will be asked to analyze information by using your critical thinking skills.

Building Your Portfolio is an exciting and creative way to demonstrate your understanding of history.

Use these online tools to review and complete online activities.

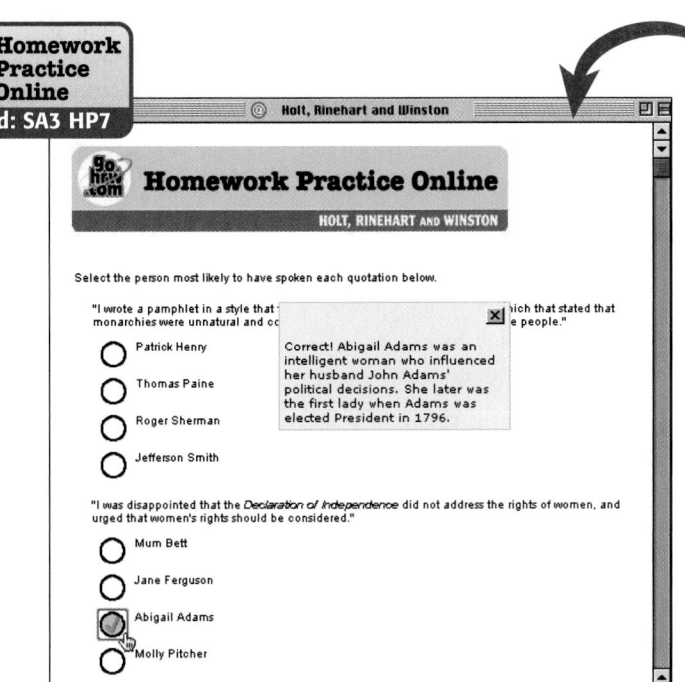

go.hrw.com Homework Practice Online

keyword: SA3 HP7

Homework Practice Online

HOLT, RINEHART AND WINSTON

Holt, Rinehart and Winston

Select the person most likely to have spoken each quotation below.

"I wrote a pamphlet in a style that [ ] hich that stated that monarchies were unnatural and co [ ] e people."

○ Patrick Henry

○ Thomas Paine

○ Roger Sherman

○ Jefferson Smith

Correct! Abigail Adams was an intelligent woman who influenced her husband John Adams' political decisions. She later was the first lady when Adams was elected President in 1796.

"I was disappointed that the *Declaration of Independence* did not address the rights of women, and urged that women's rights should be considered."

○ Mum Bett

○ Jane Ferguson

◉ Abigail Adams

○ Molly Pitcher

Homework Practice Online lets you log on for review anytime.

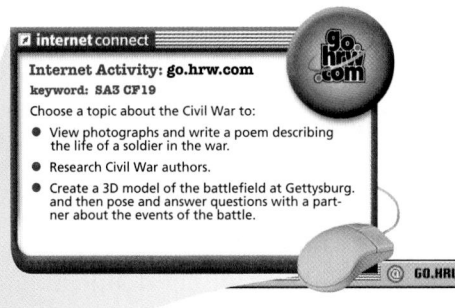 

📶 internet connect

Internet Activity: go.hrw.com

keyword: SA3 CF19

Choose a topic about the Civil War to:
- View photographs and write a poem describing the life of a soldier in the war.
- Research Civil War authors.
- Create a 3D model of the battlefield at Gettysburg, and then pose and answer questions with a partner about the events of the battle.

GO.HRW.COM

HOLT, RINEHART AND WINSTON   **SOCIAL STUDIES**

SA3 CF19

HOLT **CALL TO FREEDOM**

The Civil War

To learn more about the Civil War, click on the activities below.

Internet Activities

Civil War Authors
Research the viewpoints of writers covering the Civil War and create a biography.

Poetry and Photography
View Civil War photographs online and research the lives of soldiers. Then create a poem that expresses the content and emotional mood of the photographs.

Geography of Gettysburg
Research the battle and geography of the battle site. Then create a 3D map of the battlefield.

Internet Resources

Maps and Charts
Explore these additional resources to find out about Union and Confederate soldiers.

Chapter Enrichment Links
Learn more about the Civil War.

go.hrw.com For more information about keywords or about the go.hrw.com Web site, click the icon on the left.

● Internet zone

Internet Connect activities are just one part of the world of online learning experiences that awaits you on the go.hrw.com Web site. By exploring these online activities, you will take a journey through some of the richest American history materials available on the World Wide Web. You can then use these resources to create real-world projects, such as newspapers, brochures, reports, and even your own Web site!

Why History Matters Today

> "**H**istory and destiny have made America the leader of the world that would be free. And the world that would be free is looking to us for inspiration."
>
> **—Colin Powell**

Right now at this very second, somewhere in the United States, someone is making history. It is impossible to know whom or in what way, but the actions of people today may become the history of tomorrow.

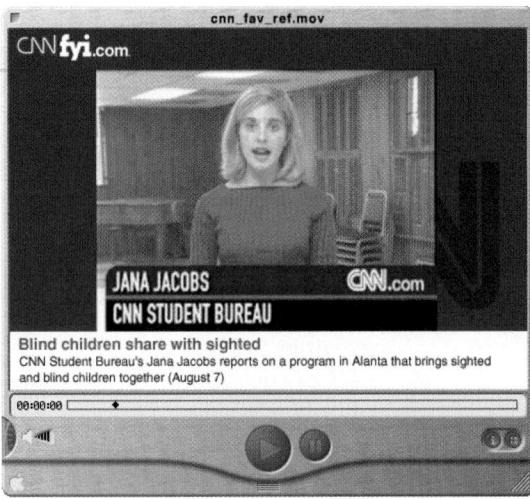

CNNfyi.com

JANA JACOBS
CNN STUDENT BUREAU

Blind children share with sighted
CNN Student Bureau's Jana Jacobs reports on a program in Alanta that brings sighted and blind children together (August 7)

00:00:00

@CNNfyi.com

CNNfyi.com >News for students, resources for teachers

SEARCH
GO
Select a section:
FYI MAIN PAGE
TEACHER RESOURCES
EDUCATION NEWS
HOW TO USE THIS SITE
BACK TO CNN.com
CNN NEWSROOM

• Daily guide
• Guide Archives
• Transcript
• Program Calender
• Enroll now

CNN Newsroom is a commercial-free TV program for classrooms. It airs at 4:30 a.m. ET Monday-Friday on CNN TV

In partnership with: **Harcourt**   **Riverdeep**

August 22, 2001 -- Updated 05:10 PM EDT

Big ball would make Mars study a breeze
A spherical probe as tall as a house could use the natural winds on Mars to propel itself around the red planet, rolling like a giant tumbleweed over boulders instead of sidestepping them like conventional rovers, according to NASA scientists.

Tax credit helps parents save for school expenses
✓ Lesson plan

Wind chill factor gets new formula
✓ Lesson plan

Education effort follows West Nile death
✓ Lesson plan

Weekly Activities:
Updated August 16, 2001

Who Am I?
Answer questions to discover my identity

XTRA! XTRA! XTRA!

Internet zone

History and Your World

All you need to do is watch or read the news to see history unfolding. How many news stories do you see or hear about ordinary people doing extraordinary things? The Why It Matters Today feature beginning every section of *Call to Freedom* invites you to use the vast resources of **CNNfyi.com** or other current events sources to examine the links between past and present. Through this feature you will be able to draw connections between what you are studying in your history book and the events that are taking place today.

Anyone Can Be a History Maker

When you think of the word *history,* what comes to mind? Do you picture politicians sitting around a table deciding the future of the nation? Or do you see a long list of dates and boring facts to be memorized? Of course, politicians, dates, and facts are part of history, but there is actually much more to understanding and exploring our past. Our nation has developed through the efforts of many different people, from all backgrounds and walks of life. Many of them were teenagers like yourself. Did you know that teenagers helped settle the West? It's true. For example, teenager Nancy Kelsey was among the first pioneers to arrive in California in 1841.

Student reporters contribute to CNNfyi.com.

History Makes Us Who We Are

There is no one single "story" in history. Instead, the combined experiences of millions of people across time have come together to form the foundation of American society today.

Student visiting the Vietnam Veterans Memorial

"So when someone asks you 'Why does history matter today?' you might answer, 'Because in our past, we see a reflection of ourselves.'"

Teenagers also played a role in the Civil War. Thousands of soldiers, like 15-year-old Thomas Galway, fought in this bloody conflict, which shaped the nation's future. You might also be interested to know that young Americans in the Civilian Conservation Corps played a key role in keeping the nation going during the darkest hours of the Great Depression. These are just a few of the many examples of how people about the same age as yourself have helped shape our nation's past. What contributions do you think your generation will make to our national history?

These young people are participating in a reenactment to celebrate the unveiling of the African American Civil War Memorial at Arlington National Cemetery.

Themes in American History

Call to Freedom begins every chapter with a set of theme statements under the heading "You Be the Historian." These statements are drawn from several broad themes central to American history: Geography; Economics; Government; Citizenship; Culture; Science, Technology & Society; Constitutional Heritage; and Global Relations. As you begin each chapter of *Call to Freedom*, you will be asked to respond to the theme statements in a general way, based on your own knowledge. At the end of the chapter, you will be asked to respond to more specific questions about the themes, based on the chapter content.

Geography

The Geography theme explores ways in which the nation's vast and diverse geography has played an important role in American history. The theme examines how the development of the nation's resources has helped shape its economy, society, and politics. In addition, the Geography theme traces how public and government attitudes about resources and the environment have changed over time.

Economics

President Calvin Coolidge once said that "the business of America is business." The Economics theme asks you to explore the relationship between history and economics in the United States. The theme traces the changing relationship between government, business, and labor in America. It examines how the growth of a strong national free-enterprise economic system has influenced the country's domestic and global politics as well as individual lives and American society.

Catalogs display hundreds of goods for consumers.

Government

Even before the nation had won its independence from Great Britain in the Revolution, the Founding Fathers saw the need to establish a national government. The Government theme asks you to explore the workings of the American system of government—from the Articles of Confederation up to the present. This theme also examines the relationships between federal, state and local governments and how the system is designed to serve the people.

The American West

Scientists such as these underwater archaeologists search for clues about the distant past.

Citizenship

Throughout our history, Americans have struggled to define, possess, and protect individual rights and personal freedoms, such as the freedoms of speech and of religion, the right to vote, and the right to privacy. Americans have also worked to uphold the responsibilities of citizenship that accompany participation in our democracy. The Citizenship theme explores how changing social, economic, and political conditions have influenced the theory and practices of these rights, freedoms, and responsibilities. This theme also examines the many conflicts that have arisen over these democratic values as well as Americans' attempts to resolve these conflicts.

Science, Technology & Society

From the building of the transcontinental railroad and the construction of skyscrapers during the Second Industrial Revolution, to the computers that help you with your school assignments and personal projects today, science and technology have influenced every aspect of our culture and society. The Science, Technology & Society theme explores scientific and technological developments and their influence on the U.S. economy and life.

Articles of Confederation
Weak central government

Achievements
Northwest Ordinance
Northwest Territory

Problems
Poor international trade
Poor foreign relations
Weak economy
Shays's Rebellion

Constitution
Strong central government

Compromises
Great Compromise
Three-Fifths Compromise
Slave trade

Structure
Legislative branch
Executive branch
Judicial branch
Checks and balances

Problems
Struggle over ratification

Bill of Rights
The first 10 amendments
Passed to protect individual rights and freedoms

Immigrants to the United States take an oath to become citizens.

The Constitution

Culture

Our nation's rich and unique cultural heritage comes from its many ethnic, racial, and religious groups. The Culture theme examines the influences of diverse culture groups, from before the time of the European explorers to recent immigrants from around the world.

Constitutional Heritage

No study of American history would be complete without examining the U.S. Constitution, the document that provides the legal framework for our democratic government. The Constitutional Heritage theme will help you understand the Constitution's origins and how it has evolved through constitutional amendments, Supreme Court rulings, and congressional action. This theme also explores how individuals and different groups in the nation's history have influenced the Constitution.

Global Relations

Since the first Asian nomads crossed a land bridge to this continent thousands of years ago, America has been involved in global events. The Global Relations theme invites you to trace ways in which our nation's political, social, and economic development has affected—and been affected by—other countries and their people.

International Red Cross medal

xxxii   Themes in American History

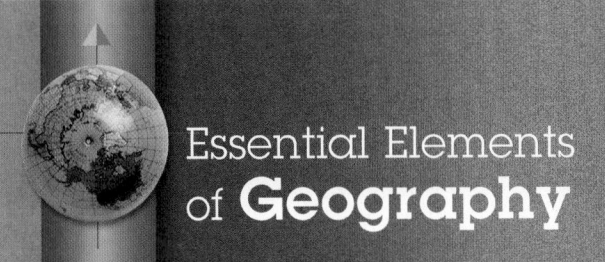

Essential Elements of Geography

History and geography share many elements. History describes important events that have taken place from ancient times until the present day. Geography describes how physical environments affect human events. It also examines how people's actions influence the environment around them. One way to look at geography is to identify essential elements of its study. The following six essential elements, developed from the National Geography Standards, will be used throughout Call to Freedom.

The World in Spatial Terms
This essential element refers to the way geographers view the world. They look at where things are and how they are arranged on Earth's surface. For example, geographers might be interested to learn why certain cities developed where they did.

Places and Regions
Geographers often focus on the physical and human characteristics that make particular parts of Earth special. A region is an area with common characteristics that make it different from surrounding areas. People create regions as a convenient way to study the world. Regions can be large, like North America, or small like a neighborhood.

Physical Systems
Geographers study the physical processes and interactions between four physical systems— Earth's atmosphere, land, water, and life. Physical processes shape and change Earth's physical features and environments.

Human Systems
As with physical systems, studying human systems can tell geographers much about the world around us. For example, studying population growth, distribution, and movement helps in understanding human events and their effects on the environment.

Environment and Society
One of the most important topics in geography is how people interact with the environment. People depend on the environment's natural resources for survival. However, human activities can have both positive and negative effects on Earth's environment.

The Uses of Geography
Historians use geography to understand the past. They look not only at when things happened but where and why they happened. But geography is important to the present as well as the past. People use geography every day to explore how to use Earth's limited resources, such as water and minerals, more effectively and in a way that ensures the success of future generations.

Anasazi homes were built of stone and sun-dried clay bricks. Some were built in openings in high cliffs.

Skills Handbook

The first battle of the American Revolution took place in Lexington.

Critical Thinking

Throughout *Call to Freedom*, you will be asked to think critically about the events and issues that have shaped U.S. history. Critical thinking is the reasoned judgment of information and ideas. The development of critical thinking skills is essential to effective citizenship. Such skills empower you to exercise your civic rights and responsibilities. Helping you develop critical thinking skills is an important goal of *Call to Freedom*. The following critical thinking skills appear in the section reviews and chapter reviews of the book.

1 Analyzing Information is the process of breaking something down and examining the relationships between its parts. Analyzing enables you to better understand the whole. For example, to analyze the outcome of the 1876 presidential election, you might study how, since the election results were disputed, both sides had to come to an agreement before Rutherford B. Hayes could become president.

2 Sequencing is the process of placing events in correct chronological order to better understand the historical relationships be-tween the events. You can sequence events in two basic ways: according to absolute or relative chronology. Absolute chronology means that you pay close attention to the exact dates on which events took place. Placing events on a time line would be an example of absolute chronology. Relative chronology refers to the way events relate to one another. To put events in relative order, you need to know which one happened first, which came next, and so forth.

Coat of arms granted to Christopher Columbus

3 Categorizing is the process by which you group things together by the characteristics they have in common. By putting things or events into categories, it is easier to make comparisons and see differences among them.

4 Identifying Cause and Effect is a part of interpreting the relationships between historical events. A *cause* is an action that leads to an event. The outcome of the action is an *effect*. To explain historical events, historians often point out multiple causes and effects. For example, economic and politi-cal differences between the North and South, as well as the issue of slavery, brought about the Civil War—which in turn had many far-reaching effects.

Emancipation Proclamation

5 Comparing and Contrasting is examining events, situations, or points of view for their similarities and differences. *Comparing* focuses on both the similari-ties and the differences. *Contrasting* focuses only on the differences. For example, a comparison of early Irish and Chinese immigrants to the United States shows that both groups were recruited to help build railroads and that both groups faced discrimination. In contrast, language and racial barriers generally proved more of a problem for Chinese immigrants.

6 **Finding the Main Idea** is combining and sifting through information to determine what is most important. Historical writing often uses many examples and details to support the author's main ideas. Throughout *Call to Freedom,* you will find numerous Reading Checks and questions in section reviews to help you focus on the main ideas in the text.

7 **Summarizing** is the process of taking a large amount of information and boiling it down into a short and clear statement. Summarizing is particularly useful when you need to give a brief account of a longer story or event. For example, the story of the Battle of Gettysburg during the Civil War is an exciting but detailed one. Many different events came together to make up this story. You could summarize these events by saying something like, "In 1863 General Lee led his army north into Pennsylvania where he met the Union forces under General Meade at Gettysburg. After several days of bloody fighting, Lee was forced to retreat. Lee's defeat at Gettysburg was a major turning point in the war."

Lee's surrender at Appomattox Courthouse

8 **Making Generalizations and Predictions** is the process of interpreting information to form more general statements and to guess about what will happen next. A *generalization* is a broad statement that holds true for a variety of historical events or situations. Making generalizations can help you see the "big picture" of historical events, rather than just focusing on details. It is very

important, however, that when making generalizations you try not to include situations that do not fit the statement. When this occurs, you run the risk of creating a stereotype, or overgeneralization. A *prediction* is an educated guess about an outcome. When you read history, you should always be asking yourself questions like, "What will happen next? If this person does this, what will that mean for . . . ?", and so on. These types of questions help you draw on information you already know to see patterns throughout history.

9 **Drawing Inferences and Conclusions** is forming possible explanations for an event, a situation, or a problem. When you make an *inference,* you take the information you know to be true and come up with an educated guess about what else you think is true about that situation. A *conclusion* is a prediction about the outcome

Women's suffrage supporter

of a situation based on what you already know. Often, you must be prepared to test your inferences and conclusions against new evidence or arguments. For example, a historian might conclude that women's leadership roles in the abolition movement led to the development of the early women's movement. The historian would then organize the evidence needed to support this conclusion and challenge other arguments.

10 **Identifying Points of View** is the process of identifying factors that influence the outlook of an individual or group. A person's point of view includes beliefs and attitudes that are shaped by factors such as age, gender, religion, race, and economic status. This critical thinking skill helps you examine why people see things as they do, and it reinforces the realization that people's views may change over time or with a change in circumstances.

S2 **Skills Handbook**

11 Supporting a Point of View involves choosing a viewpoint on a particular event or issue and arguing persuasively for that position. Your argument should be well organized and based on specific evidence that supports the point of view you have chosen. Supporting a point of view often involves working with controversial or emotional issues. For example, you might consider the points of view involved in the struggles between labor unions and businesses in the late 1800s. Whether you choose a position in favor of unions or in favor of businesses, you should state your opinion clearly and give reasons to defend it.

Labor union booklet

12 Identifying Bias is the process of evaluating the opinions of others about events or situations. Bias is an opinion based on prejudice or strong emotions, rather than on fact. It is important to identify bias when looking at historical sources, because biased sources often give you a false sense of what really happened. When looking at both primary and secondary sources, it is always important to keep the author's or speaker's point of view in mind and to adjust your interpretation of the source when you detect any bias.

13 Evaluating is assessing the significance or overall importance of something, such as the success of a reform movement, the actions of a president, or the results of a major conflict. You should base your judgment on standards that others will understand and are likely to share. For example, you might consider the outcome of the Mexican War and evaluate its importance to U.S. politics and expansion. You could also evaluate the effect of the war on the peoples already living in the West.

14 Problem Solving is the process by which you pose workable solutions to difficult situations. The first step in the process is to identify a problem. Next you will need to gather information about the problem, such as its history and the various factors that contribute to the problem. Once you have gathered information, you should list and consider the options for solving the problem. For each of the possible solutions, weigh their advantages and disadvantages and, based on your evaluation, choose and implement a solution. Once the solution has been tried, go back and evaluate the effectiveness of the solution you selected.

15 Decision Making is the process of reviewing a situation and then making decisions or recommendations for the best possible outcome. To complete the process, first identify a situation that requires a solution. Next, gather information that will help you reach a decision. You may need to do some background research to study the history of the situation. Once you have done your research, identify options that might resolve the situation. For each option, predict what the possible consequences might be if that option were followed. Once you have identified the best option, take action by making a recommendation and following through on any tasks that option requires.

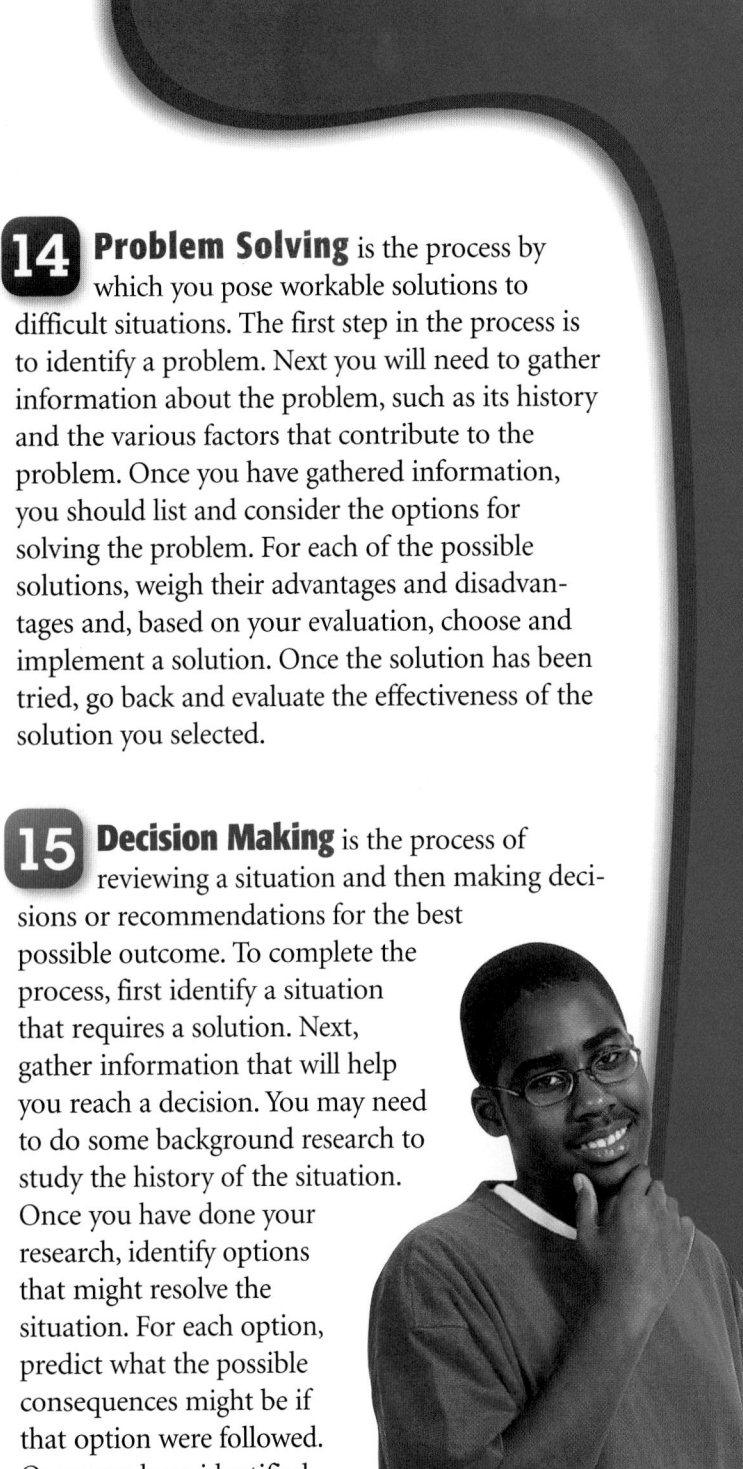

Becoming a Strategic Reader

by Dr. Judith Irvin

Everywhere you look, print is all around us. In fact, you would have a hard time stopping yourself from reading. In a normal day, you might read cereal boxes, movie posters, notes from friends, T-shirts, instructions for video games, song lyrics, catalogs, billboards, information on the Internet, magazines, the newspaper, and much, much more. Each form of print is read differently depending on your purpose for reading. You read a menu differently from the way you read poetry, and a motorcycle magazine is read differently than a letter from a friend. Good readers switch easily from one type of text to another. In fact, they probably do not even think about it, they just do it.

When you read, it is helpful to use a strategy to remember the most important ideas. You can use a strategy before you read to help connect information you already know to the new information you will encounter. Before you read, you can also predict what a text will be about by using a previewing strategy. During the reading you can use a strategy to help you focus on main ideas, and after reading you can use a strategy to help you organize what you learned so that you can remember it later. *Call to Freedom* was designed to help you more easily understand the ideas you read. Important reading strategies employed in *Call to Freedom* include the following:

1 Methods to help you **anticipate** what is to come

2 Tools to help you **preview and predict** what the text will be about

3 Ways to help you **use and analyze visual information**

4 Ideas to help you **organize the information** you have learned

1. Anticipate Information

How Can I Use Information I Already Know to Help Me Understand What a New Chapter Will Be About?

Anticipating what a new chapter will be about helps you connect the upcoming information to what you already know. By drawing on your background knowledge, you can build a bridge to the new material.

1 Each chapter of *Call to Freedom* asks you to explore the main themes of the chapter before you start reading by forming opinions based on your current knowledge.

> ### You Be the Historian
>
> **Themes Journal** **What's Your Opinion?** Do you **agree** or **disagree** with the following statements? Support your point of view in your journal.
>
> - **Science, Technology & Society** New technology always makes wars easier to win.
> - **Economics** Wars are bad for a nation's economy.
> - **Citizenship** All citizens have a duty to support their government during a war.

Create a chart like this one to help you analyze the statements.

A Before Reading Agree/Disagree		B After Reading Agree/Disagree
2	New technology always makes wars easier to win.	**4**
	Wars are bad for a nation's economy.	
	All citizens have a duty to support their government during a war.	

3 Read the text and discuss your answers with classmates.

5 You can also refine your knowledge by answering the You Be the Historian—Reviewing Themes questions in the chapter review.

Anticipating Information

▶ **Step ❶** Identify the major concepts of the chapter. In *Call to Freedom*, these are presented in the **You Be the Historian** feature at the beginning of each chapter.

▼

Step ❷ Agree or disagree with each of the statements and record your opinions in your journal.

▼

Step ❸ Read the text and discuss your responses with your classmates.

▼

Step ❹ After reading the chapter, revisit the statements and respond to them again based on what you have learned.

▼

Step ❺ Go back and check your knowledge by answering the You Be the Historian—Reviewing Themes questions in the chapter review.

You Be the Historian— Reviewing Themes

1. **Science, Technology & Society** How did ironclads reflect the changes that new technology brought to the war?
2. **Economics** What effect did the war have on the South's economy?
3. **Citizenship** How did northerners and southerners oppose the war, and how did the Union and Confederate governments respond?

2. Preview and Predict

How Can I Figure out What the Text Is about before I Even Start Reading a Section?

Previewing and Predicting

▶ **Step ❶** Identify your purpose for reading. Ask yourself what will you do with this information once you have finished reading.

▼

Step ❷ Ask yourself what the main idea of the text is and what key vocabulary words you need to know.

▼

Step ❸ Use signal words to help identify the structure of the text.

▼

Step ❹ Connect the information to what you already know.

Previewing and **predicting** are good methods to help you understand the text. If you take the time to preview and predict before you read, the text will make more sense to you during your reading.

❶ Usually, your teacher will set the purpose for reading. After reading some new information, you may be asked to write a summary, take a test, or complete some other type of activity.

"After reading about the Civil War, you will work with a partner to create a historical museum exhibit describing…"

❷ As you preview the text, use *graphic signals* such as headings, subheadings, and boldfaced type to help you determine what is important in the text. Each section of *Call to Freedom* opens by giving you important clues to help you preview the material.

Looking at the section's **main heading** and **subheadings** can give you an idea of what is to come.

Read to Discover questions give you clues as to the section's main ideas.

Define and Identify terms let you know the key vocabulary you will encounter in the section.

The War in the East

Read to Discover

1. What battles did the Confederates win in Virginia, and why were they important?
2. What stopped the northward advance of the Confederate army?
3. What was the significance of the *Monitor* and the *Virginia*?

WHY IT MATTERS TODAY

During the Civil War, powerful new types of warships were developed. Use **CNNfyi.com** or other **current events** sources to find out about the types of ships used by the U.S. Navy today. Record your findings in your journal.

Define

• ironclad

Identify

• Thomas "Stonewall" Jackson
• First Battle of Bull Run
• George B. McClellan
• Robert E. Lee
• Seven Days' Battles
• Second Battle of Bull Run
• Battle of Antietam

3 Other tools that can help you in previewing are **signal words**. These words prepare you to think in a certain way. For example, when you see words such as *similar to, same as,* or *different from,* you know that the text will probably compare and contrast two or more ideas. Signal words indicate how the ideas in the text relate to each other. Look at the list below of some of the most common signal words grouped by the type of text structures they indicate.

Signal Words

Cause and Effect	Compare and Contrast	Description	Problem and Solution	Sequence or Chronological Order
• because • since • consequently • this led to...so • if... then • nevertheless • accordingly • because of • as a result of • in order to • may be due to • for this reason	• different from • same as • similar to • as opposed to • instead of • although • however • compared with • as well as • either...or • but • on the other hand • unless	• for instance • for example • such as • to illustrate • in addition • most importantly • another • furthermore • first, second...	• the question is • a solution • one answer is	• not long after • next • then • initially • before • after • finally • preceding • following • on (date) • over time • today • when

4 Learning something new requires that you connect it in some way with something you already know. This means you have to think before you read and while you read. You may want to use a chart like this one to remind yourself of the information already familiar to you and to come up with questions you want answered in your reading. The chart will also help you organize your ideas after you have finished reading.

What I know	What I want to know	What I learned

3. Use and Analyze Visual Information

How Can All the Pictures, Maps, Graphs, and Time Lines with the Text Help Me Be a Stronger Reader?

Analyzing Visual Information

▶ **Step 1** As you preview the text, ask yourself how the visual information relates to the text.

▼

Step 2 Generate questions based on the visual information.

▼

Step 3 After reading the text, go back and review the visual information again.

▼

Step 4 Make connections to what you already know.

Using visual information can help you understand and remember the information presented in *Call to Freedom*. Good readers form a picture in their minds when they read. The pictures, charts, graphs, cartoons, time lines, and diagrams that occur throughout *Call to Freedom* are placed strategically to increase your understanding.

1 You might ask yourself questions like:

> Why did the author include this information with the text? What details about this visual are mentioned in the text?

After you have read the text, see if you can answer your own questions.

2

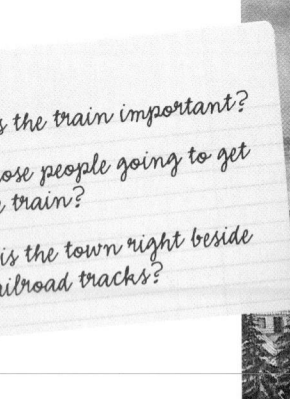

Why is the train important?
Are those people going to get on the train?
Why is the town right beside the railroad tracks?

3 After reading, take another look at the visual information.

4 Try to make connections to what you already know.

4. Organize Information
Once I Learn New Information, How Do I Keep It All Straight So That I Will Remember It?

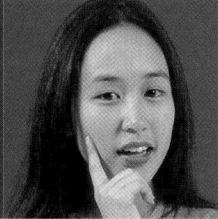

To help you remember what you have read, you need to find a way of **organizing information**. Two good ways of doing this are by using graphic organizers and concept maps. **Graphic organizers** help you understand important relationships—such as cause-and-effect, compare/contrast, sequence of events, and problem/solution—within the text. **Concept maps** provide a useful tool to help you focus on the text's main ideas and organize supporting details.

Identifying Relationships

Using graphic organizers will help you recall important ideas from the section. They are also study tools you can use to prepare for a quiz or test or to help with a writing assignment. Some of the most common types of graphic organizers are shown below.

▶ Cause and Effect

Events in history cause people to react in certain ways. Cause-and-effect patterns show the relationship between results and the ideas or events that made the results occur. You may want to represent cause-and-effect relationships as one cause leading to multiple effects,

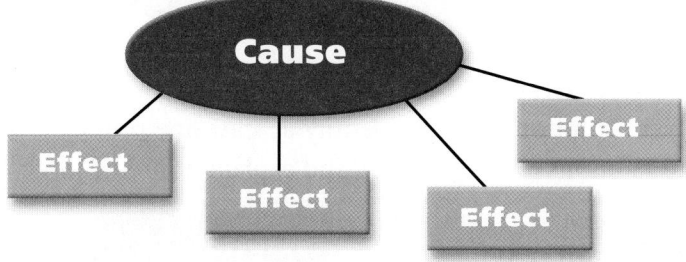

or as a chain of cause-and-effect relationships.

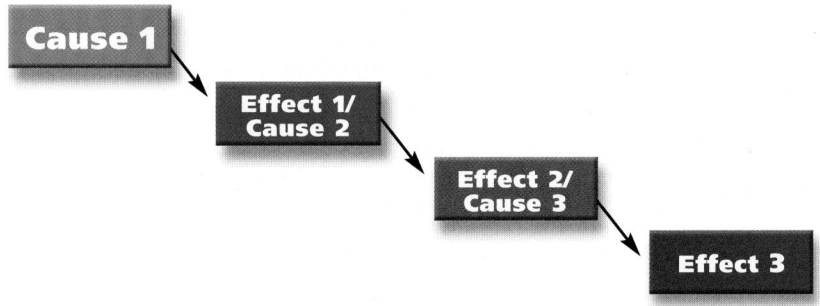

Constructing Graphic Organizers

▶ **Step 1** Preview the text, looking for signal words and main ideas.

▼

Step 2 Form a hypothesis as to which type of graphic organizer would work best to display the information presented.

▼

Step 3 Work individually or with your classmates to create a visual representation of what you read.

Comparing and Contrasting

Graphic organizers are often useful when you are comparing or contrasting information. Compare-and-contrast diagrams point out similarities and differences between two concepts or ideas.

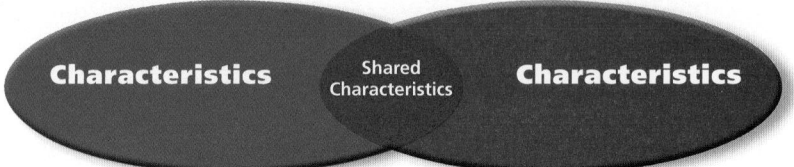

Sequencing

Keeping track of dates and the order in which events took place is essential to understanding history. Sequence or chronological-order diagrams show events or ideas in the order in which they happened.

Problem and Solution

Problem/solution patterns identify at least one problem, offer one or more solutions to the problem, and explain or predict outcomes of the solutions.

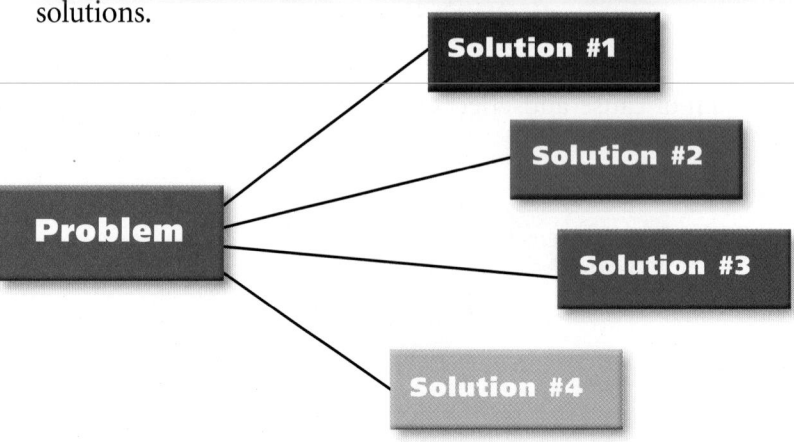

Identifying Main Ideas and Supporting Details

One special type of graphic organizer is the concept map. A concept map, sometimes called a semantic map, allows you to zero in on the most important points of the text. The map is made up of lines, boxes, circles, and/or arrows. It can be as simple or as complex as you need it to be to accurately represent the text.

Here are a few examples of concept maps you might use.

Constructing Concept Maps

▶ **Step 1** Preview the text, looking for what type of structure might be appropriate to display a concept map.

▼

Step 2 Taking note of the headings, boldfaced type, and text structure, sketch a concept map you think could best illustrate the text.

▼

Step 3 Using boxes, lines, arrows, circles, or any shapes you like, display the ideas of the text in the concept map.

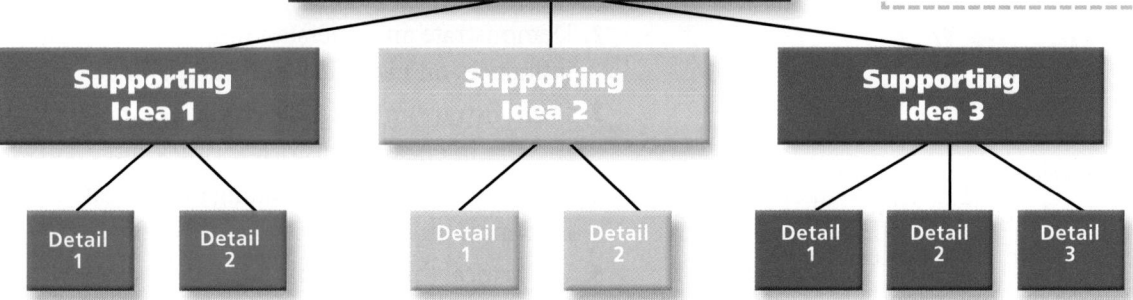

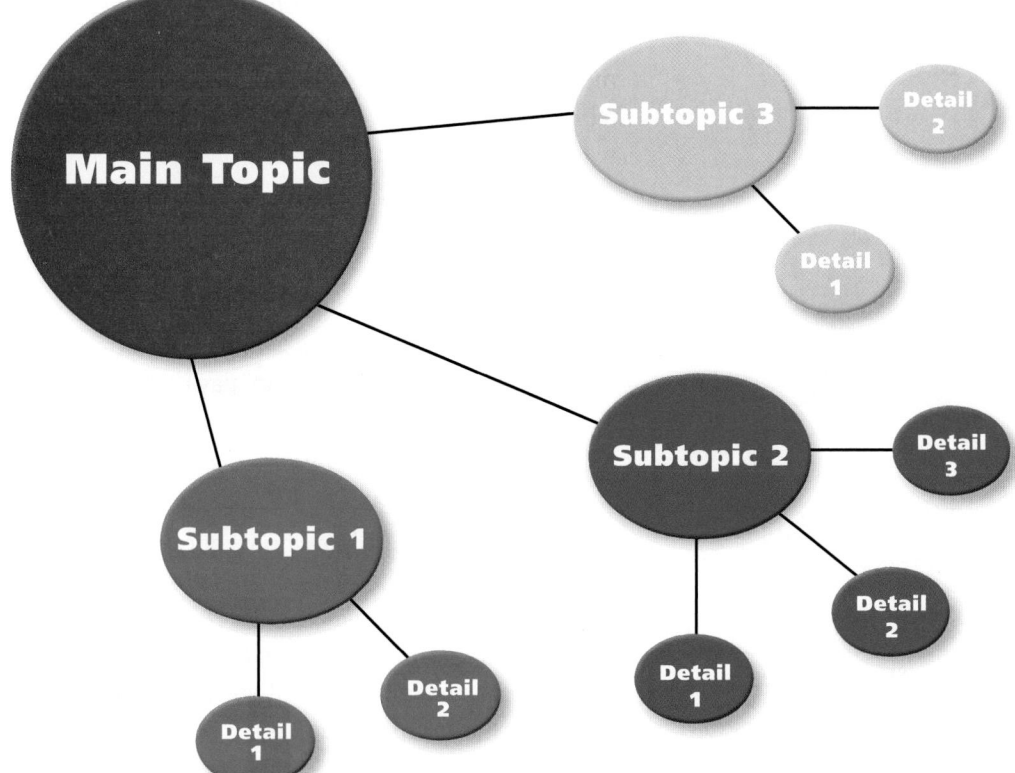

Standardized Test–Taking Strategies

A number of times throughout your school career, you may be asked to take standardized tests. These tests are designed to demonstrate the content and skills you have learned. It is important to keep in mind that in most cases the best way to prepare for these tests is to pay close attention in class and to take every opportunity to improve your general social studies, reading, writing, and mathematical skills.

Tips for Taking the Test

1. Be sure that you are well rested.
2. Be on time and be sure that you have the necessary materials.
3. Listen to the instructions of the teacher.
4. Read directions and questions carefully.
5. **DON'T STRESS!** Just remember what you have learned in class, and you should do well.

▶ **Practice the strategies at go.hrw.com.**

go.hrw.com
Standardized Test–Prep Online
keyword: SA3 STP

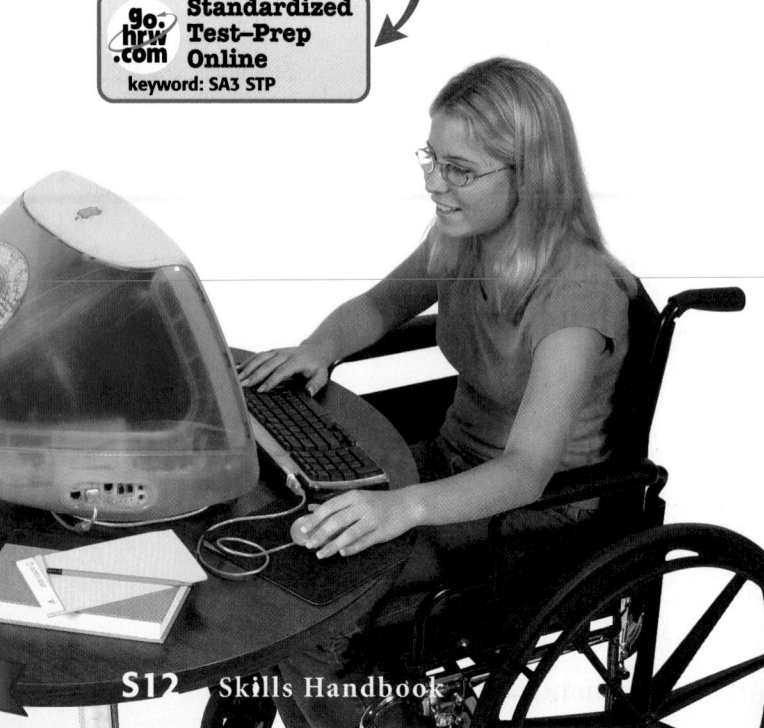

Tackling Social Studies

The social studies portions of many standardized tests are designed to test your knowledge of the content and skills that you have been studying in one or more of your social studies classes. Specific objectives for the test vary, but some of the most common include the following:

1. Demonstrate an understanding of issues and events in history.
2. Demonstrate an understanding of geographic influences on historical issues and events.
3. Demonstrate an understanding of economic and social influences on historical issues and events.
4. Demonstrate an understanding of political influences on historical issues and events.
5. Use critical thinking skills to analyze social studies information.

Standardized tests usually contain multiple-choice and, sometimes, open-ended questions. The multiple-choice items will often be based on maps, tables, charts, graphs, pictures, cartoons, and/or reading passages and documents.

Tips for Answering Multiple-Choice Questions

1. If there is a written or visual piece accompanying the multiple-choice question, pay careful attention to the title, author, and date.
2. Then read through or glance over the content of the piece accompanying the question.
3. Next, read the multiple-choice question for its general intent. Then reread it carefully, looking for words that give clues. For example, words such as *most* or *best* tell you that there may be several correct answers, but you should look for the most appropriate answer.

4. Always read all of the possible answer choices, even if the first one seems like the correct answer. There may be a better choice farther down in the list.

5. Reread the accompanying information (if any is included) carefully to determine the answer to the question. Again, note the title, author, and date of primary-source selections. The answer will rarely be stated exactly as it appears in the primary source, so you will need to use your critical thinking skills to read between the lines.

6. Use your knowledge of the time in history or person involved to help limit the answer choices.

7. Finally, reread the question and selected answer to be sure that you made the best choice and that you marked it correctly on the answer sheet.

Strategies for Success

There are many strategies you can use to help you feel more confident about answering questions on social studies standardized tests. Here are a few suggestions:

1. Adopt an acronym—a word formed from the first letters of other words—that you will always use for analyzing a document or visual that might accompany a question.

Helpful Acronyms

For a document, use **SOAPS**, which stands for

S	Subject
O	Occasion
A	Audience
P	Purpose
S	Speaker/author

For a picture, cartoon, map, or other visual piece of information, use **OPTIC**, which stands for

O	Overview
P	Parts (labels or details of the visual)
T	Title
I	Interrelations (how the different parts of the visual work together)
C	Conclusion (what the visual means)

2. Form visual images of maps and try to draw them from memory. The standardized test will most likely include important maps from the time period and subjects you have been studying. For example, in early U.S. history, be able to see in your mind's eye such things as where the New England, middle, and southern colonies were located, what land the Louisiana Purchase and Mexican Cession covered, and the dividing line for slave and free states. Know major physical features, such as the Mississippi River, the Appalachian and Rocky Mountains, the Great Plains, and the various regions of the United States, and be able to place them on a map.

3. When you have finished studying any historical era, try to think of who or what might be important enough for the test. You may want to keep your ideas in a notebook to refer to when it is almost time for the test.

4. Pay particular attention to the Constitution and its development. Many standardized tests contain questions about this all-important document and the period during which it was written. Questions may include Magna Carta, the English Bill of Rights, the Declaration of Independence, and *Common Sense*, as well as many other important historical documents.

5. For the skills area of the tests, practice putting major events and personalities in order in your mind. Sequencing people and events by dates can become a game you play with a friend who also has to take the test. Always ask yourself why this event is important.

6. Follow the tips under "Ready for Reading" on the next page when you encounter a reading passage in social studies, but remember that what you have learned about history can help you in answering reading-comprehension questions.

Ready for Reading

The main goal of the reading sections of most standardized tests is to determine your understanding of different aspects of a reading passage. Basically, if you can grasp the main idea and the author's purpose, then pay attention to the details and vocabulary so that you are able to draw inferences and conclusions, you will do well on the test.

Tips for Answering Multiple-Choice Questions

1. Read the passage as if you were not taking a test.
2. Look at the big picture. Ask yourself questions like, "What is the title?", "What do the illustrations or pictures tell me?", and "What is the author's purpose?"
3. Read the questions. This will help you know what information to look for.
4. Reread the passage, underlining information related to the questions.

Types of Multiple-Choice Questions

1. **Main Idea** This is the most important point of the passage. After reading the passage, locate and underline the main idea.
2. **Significant Details** You will often be asked to recall details from the passage. Read the question and underline the details as you read. But remember that the correct answers do not always match the wording of the passage precisely.
3. **Vocabulary** You will often need to define a word within the context of the passage. Read the answer choices and plug them into the sentence to see what fits best.
4. **Conclusion and Inference** There are often important ideas in the passage that the author does not state directly. Sometimes you must consider multiple parts of the passage to answer the question. If answers refer to only one or two sentences or details in the passage, they are probably incorrect.

5. Go back to the questions and try to answer each one in your mind before looking at the answers.
6. Read all the answer choices and eliminate the ones that are obviously incorrect.

Tips for Answering Short-Answer Questions

1. Read the passage in its entirety, paying close attention to the main events and characters. Jot down information you think is important.
2. If you cannot answer a question, skip it and come back later.
3. Words such as *compare, contrast, interpret, discuss,* and *summarize* appear often in short-answer questions. Be sure you have a complete understanding of each of these words.
4. To help support your answer, return to the passage and skim the parts you underlined.
5. Organize your thoughts on a separate sheet of paper. Write a general statement with which to begin. This will be your topic statement.
6. When writing your answer, be precise but brief. Be sure to refer to details in the passage in your answer.

Targeting Writing

On many standardized tests, you will occasionally be asked to write an essay. In order to write a concise essay, you must learn to organize your thoughts before you begin writing the actual composition. This keeps you from straying too far from the essay's topic.

Tips for Answering Composition Questions

1. Read the question carefully.
2. Decide what kind of essay you are being asked to write. Essays usually fall into one of the following types: persuasive, classificatory, compare/contrast, or "how to." To determine the type of essay, ask yourself questions like, "Am I trying to persuade my audience?", "Am I comparing or contrasting ideas?", or "Am I trying to show the reader how to do something?"
3. Pay attention to key words, such as *compare, contrast, describe, advantages, disadvantages, classify,* or *speculate.* They will give you clues as to the structure that your essay should follow.
4. Organize your thoughts on a separate sheet of paper. You will want to come up with a general topic sentence that expresses your main idea. Make sure this sentence addresses the question. You should then create an outline or some type of graphic organizer to help you organize the points that support your topic sentence.
5. Write your composition using complete sentences. Also, be sure to use correct grammar, spelling, punctuation, and sentence structure.
6. Be sure to proofread your essay once you have finished writing.

Gearing up for Math

On most standardized tests you will be asked to solve a variety of mathematical problems that draw on the skills and information you have learned in class. If math problems sometimes give you difficulty, use the tips below to help yourself work through the problems.

Tips for Solving Math Problems

1. Decide what the goal of the question is. Read or study the problem carefully and determine what information must be found.
2. Locate the factual information. Decide what information represents key facts—the ones you must use to solve the problem. You may also find facts you do not need to reach your solution. In some cases, you may determine that more information is needed to solve the problem. If so, ask yourself, "What assumptions can I make about this problem?" or "Do I need a formula to help solve this problem?"
3. Decide what strategies you might use to solve the problem, how you might use them, and what form your solution will be in. For example, will you need to create a graph or chart? Will you need to solve an equation? Will your answer be in words or numbers? By knowing what type of solution you should reach, you may be able to eliminate some of the choices.
4. Apply your strategy to solve the problem and compare your answer to the choices.
5. If the answer is still not clear, read the problem again. If you had to make calculations to reach your answer, use estimation to see if your answer makes sense.

The Geographer's Tool Kit

A map is an illustration drawn to scale of all or part of Earth's surface. Knowing how to read and interpret maps is one of the most valuable tools you can use to study history.

Types of Maps

Types of maps include physical maps, political maps, and thematic (special-purpose) maps.

▶ **Physical maps** illustrate the natural landscape of an area—the landforms that mark Earth's surface. Physical maps often use shading to show relief—the existence of mountains, hills, and valleys—and colors to show elevation, or height above sea level. The map of the United States on pages A2–A3 is strictly a physical map.

▶ **Political maps** illustrate political units, such as states and nations, and use color variations and lines to mark boundaries, dots for major cities, and stars or stars within circles for capitals. Political maps show information such as territorial changes or military alliances. The map of the United States on page A1 is a political map.

The United States in 1860

▶ **Thematic (special-purpose) maps** present specific information, such as the routes of explorers or the outcome of an election. Both the maps shown on these two pages are thematic maps.

Map Features

Most maps have some features in common. Familiarity with these elements makes reading maps easier.

▶ **Titles, legends, and labels** A map's title tells you what the map is about, what areas are shown, and usually what time period is represented. The legend, or key, explains any special symbols, colors, or shadings used on the map. Labels designate political and geographic place-names as well as physical features like mountain ranges and rivers.

▶ **The global grid** The absolute location of any place on Earth is given in terms of latitude (degrees north or south of the equator) and longitude (degrees east or west of the prime meridian). The symbol for a degree is °. Degrees are divided into 60 equal parts called minutes, which are represented by the symbol ′. The global grid is created by the intersecting lines of latitude (parallels) and lines of longitude (meridians). Lines of latitude and longitude may sometimes be indicated by tick marks near the edge of a map or by lines across an entire map.

▶ **Directions and distance** Most maps in *Call to Freedom* have a compass rose, or directional indicator. The compass rose indicates the four cardinal points—*N* for north, *S* for south, *E* for east, and *W* for west. You can also find intermediate directions—northeast, southeast, southwest, and northwest—using the compass rose. This helps in describing the relative location of a place. (If a map has no compass rose, assume that north is at the top, east is to the right, and so on.) Many maps in this textbook include a scale, showing both miles and kilometers, to help you relate distances on the map to actual distances on Earth's surface.

Map projections Because Earth is a sphere, it is best represented by a three-dimensional globe. Although a flat map is an imperfect representation of Earth's surface, mapmakers have devised various ways of showing Earth two dimensionally. These different flat views of Earth's surface are called projections.

Every map projection, and therefore every map, distorts to some extent at least one of the following aspects: (1) the shape of land areas, (2) their relative sizes, (3) directions, or (4) distances. Mapmakers choose the projection that least distorts what they wish to show. For example, an equal-area projection shows the relative sizes of different countries or continents quite accurately but distorts shapes somewhat.

How to Read a Map

1. **Determine the focus of the map.** Read the map's title and labels to determine the map's focus—its subject and the geographic area it covers.

2. **Study the map legend.** Read the legend and become familiar with any special symbols, lines, colors, and shadings used on the map.

3. **Check directions and distance.** Use the directional indicator and scale as needed to determine direction, location, and distance between various points on the map.

4. **Check the grid lines.** Refer to lines of longitude and latitude or to a locator map to place the area on the map in a larger context.

5. **Study the map.** Study the map's basic features and details, keeping its purpose in mind. If it is a special-purpose map, study the specific information being presented.

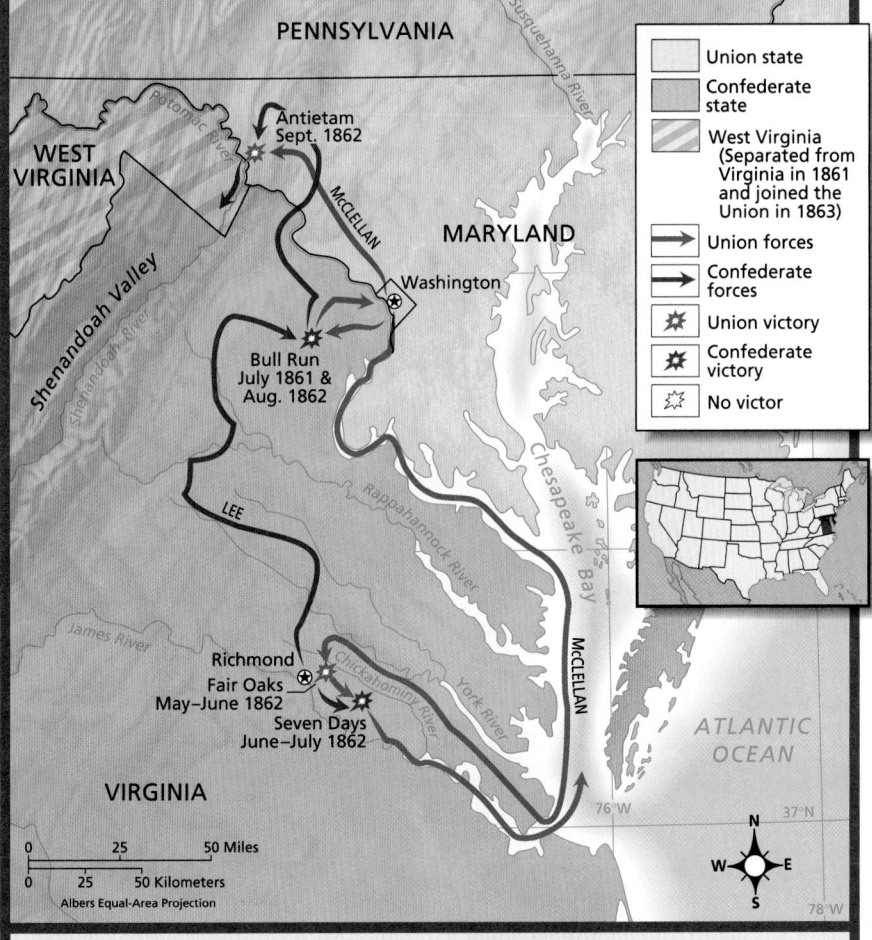

Legend:
- Union state
- Confederate state
- West Virginia (Separated from Virginia in 1861 and joined the Union in 1863)
- Union forces
- Confederate forces
- Union victory
- Confederate victory
- No victor

The War in the East, 1861–1862

Interpreting Maps One Union objective was to capture the Confederate capital of Richmond.

Skills Assessment Locate What battle took place in Maryland? What was the outcome?

ATLAS

United States of America: Political

Strait of Juan de Fuca

Puget Sound

Seattle
Tacoma
Olympia ★

WASHINGTON

Spokane

Franklin D. Roosevelt Lake
Pend Oreille
Flathead Lake

Portland
Columbia River

★ Salem

Eugene

OREGON

PACIFIC OCEAN

Goose Lake

Cape Mendocino

Shasta Lake

Sacramento River

Pyramid Lake

Reno
Carson City ★
Lake Tahoe

Berkeley
Oakland
San Francisco
San Francisco Bay

San Jose

Monterey Bay

San Joaquin River

NEVADA

CALIFORNIA

Fresno

Santa Barbara
Ventura
Channel
Los Angeles
Long Beach
Anaheim
Santa Ana
Islands
Riverside
Palm Springs

San Diego

Salton Sea

Colorado River

Las Vegas

Lake Mead

IDAHO

★ Boise
Sun Valley

Pocatello

Snake River

Great Falls

Helena ★

MONTANA

Billings

Yellowstone River
Yellowstone Lake

Fort Peck Lake

Missouri River

Ogden

Great Salt Lake
Salt Lake City ★
Utah Lake
Provo

UTAH

Green River

Lake Powell

Flagstaff

ARIZONA

Phoenix

Casa Grande

Tucson

Gila River

WYOMING

Cheyenne ★

Boulder
Vail
Denver

Aspen

COLORADO

Colorado Springs
Pueblo

Taos

Santa Fe ★

Albuquerque

NEW MEXICO

Las Cruces

El Paso

NORTH DAKOTA

Lake Sakakawea

Grand Forks

★ Bismarck

Fargo

Lake Oahe

SOUTH DAKOTA

Pierre ★

Rapid City

Sioux Falls

Sioux City

NEBRASKA

Platte River

Omaha
Lincoln ★

Minnesota

Topeka ★

KANSAS

Wichita

Canadian River

Keystone Lake

Tulsa

OKLAHOMA

Amarillo

Oklahoma City ★

Eufaula Lake

Lawton

Lake Texoma

Lubbock

Abilene

Fort Worth
Dallas

Midland
Odessa

Pecos River

TEXAS

Brazos River

Waco

Colorado River

Austin

Rio Grande

Amistad Reservoir

San Antonio

Houston

Laredo

Corpus Christi

PADRE ISLAND

GULF OF CALIFORNIA

To understand the relative locations of Alaska and Hawaii, as well as the vast distances separating them from the rest of the United States, see the world map.

KAUAI
NIIHAU
OAHU
Honolulu
MOLOKAI
MAUI
HAWAII
LANAI
KAHOOLAWE
Hilo
HAWAII

PACIFIC OCEAN

0   75   150 Miles
0   75   150 Kilometers

ARCTIC OCEAN

RUSSIA

Arctic Circle

Bering Strait

Nome

ST. LAWRENCE ISLAND

ST. MATTHEW ISLAND

Yukon River

Fairbanks

CANADA

ALASKA

Anchorage
Valdez

Skagway

Juneau ★

Gulf of Alaska

ALEXANDER ARCHIPELAGO

BERING SEA

ATTU ISLAND

NUNIVAK ISLAND

KODIAK ISLAND

MEXICO

PACIFIC OCEAN

ALEUTIAN ISLANDS

0   250   500 Miles
0   250   500 Kilometers
Projection: Albers Equal Area

CANADA

MINNESOTA
• Duluth
• Superior
• Marquette   • Sault Ste. Marie
• Minneapolis
★ St. Paul
WISCONSIN
• Green Bay
• Madison ★
• Milwaukee

MICHIGAN
• Grand Rapids
• Saginaw
★ Lansing
• Ann Arbor
• Detroit

IOWA
• Cedar Rapids
• Davenport
★ Des Moines
• Rockford
• Chicago
• Gary
• South Bend
• Fort Wayne
• Peoria

ILLINOIS
INDIANA
★ Indianapolis
• Springfield ★
• St. Louis
• East St. Louis
Kansas City
Kansas City

MISSOURI
• Springfield
★ Jefferson City
Lake of the Ozarks

OHIO
• Toledo
• Cleveland
• Youngstown
• Akron
★ Columbus
• Dayton
• Cincinnati

Lake Erie

PENNSYLVANIA
• Pittsburgh
★ Harrisburg

WEST VIRGINIA
★ Charleston

KENTUCKY
• Louisville
• Evansville
★ Frankfort
• Lexington
Lake Barkley
Kentucky Lake

NEW YORK
• Buffalo
• Rochester
• Syracuse
• Albany ★

Lake Ontario

VERMONT / VT
★ Montpelier
• Burlington
Lake Champlain

NH
★ Concord
• Manchester

MAINE
★ Augusta
• Portland

MA
• Springfield
★ Boston
• Worcester
• Providence RI
★ Hartford CT
• New Haven
• Bridgeport
Cape Cod
LONG ISLAND
Long Island Sound

• Yonkers
• Newark
• New York City
• Jersey City
NJ
• Allentown
★ Trenton
• Camden
• Philadelphia
• Atlantic City

• Baltimore
MD ★ Annapolis
DE
★ Dover
DELAWARE BAY
⊛ Washington, D.C.
CHESAPEAKE BAY

VIRGINIA
★ Richmond
• Newport News
• Norfolk
• Virginia Beach
Cape Hatteras

NORTH CAROLINA
• Greensboro
• Durham
★ Raleigh
• Winston-Salem
• Charlotte

TENNESSEE
★ Nashville
• Knoxville
• Asheville
• Chattanooga
• Memphis

ARKANSAS
• Fayetteville
★ Little Rock
• Pine Bluff

MISSISSIPPI
• Vicksburg
• Meridian
★ Jackson

ALABAMA
• Huntsville
• Birmingham
★ Montgomery
• Columbus
• Mobile

GEORGIA
★ Atlanta
• Macon
• Savannah

SOUTH CAROLINA
★ Columbia
• Greenville
• Charleston

SEA ISLANDS
Savannah River
Chattahoochee River

LOUISIANA
• Shreveport
• Beaumont
★ Baton Rouge
• New Orleans
• Biloxi
CHANDELEUR ISLANDS
Galveston

Red River

GULF OF MEXICO

FLORIDA
• Pensacola
★ Tallahassee
• Jacksonville
• Gainesville
• Orlando
Cape Canaveral
• Tampa
• St. Petersburg
Lake Okeechobee
• Fort Myers
• Fort Lauderdale
• Miami
Cape Sable
FLORIDA KEYS
Straits of Florida

THE BAHAMAS

CUBA

ATLANTIC OCEAN

St. Lawrence River
Lake Superior
Lake Michigan
Lake Huron
Illinois River
Mississippi River
Ohio River
Susquehanna River
Hudson River
Connecticut River

50° N   60° W   65° W
45° N
40° N   65° W
35° N
30° N   70° W
25° N   75° W
90° W   85° W   80° W

Legend

⊛ National capital
★ State capitals
• Other cities

Inset globe

ARCTIC OCEAN
NORTH AMERICA
EUROPE
ASIA
AFRICA
ATLANTIC OCEAN
PACIFIC OCEAN
SOUTH AMERICA
INDIAN OCEAN
AUSTRALIA
Equator
ANTARCTICA
Robinson Projection

Scale

0   250   500 Miles
0   250   500 Kilometers
Projection: Albers Equal Area

N
W   E
S

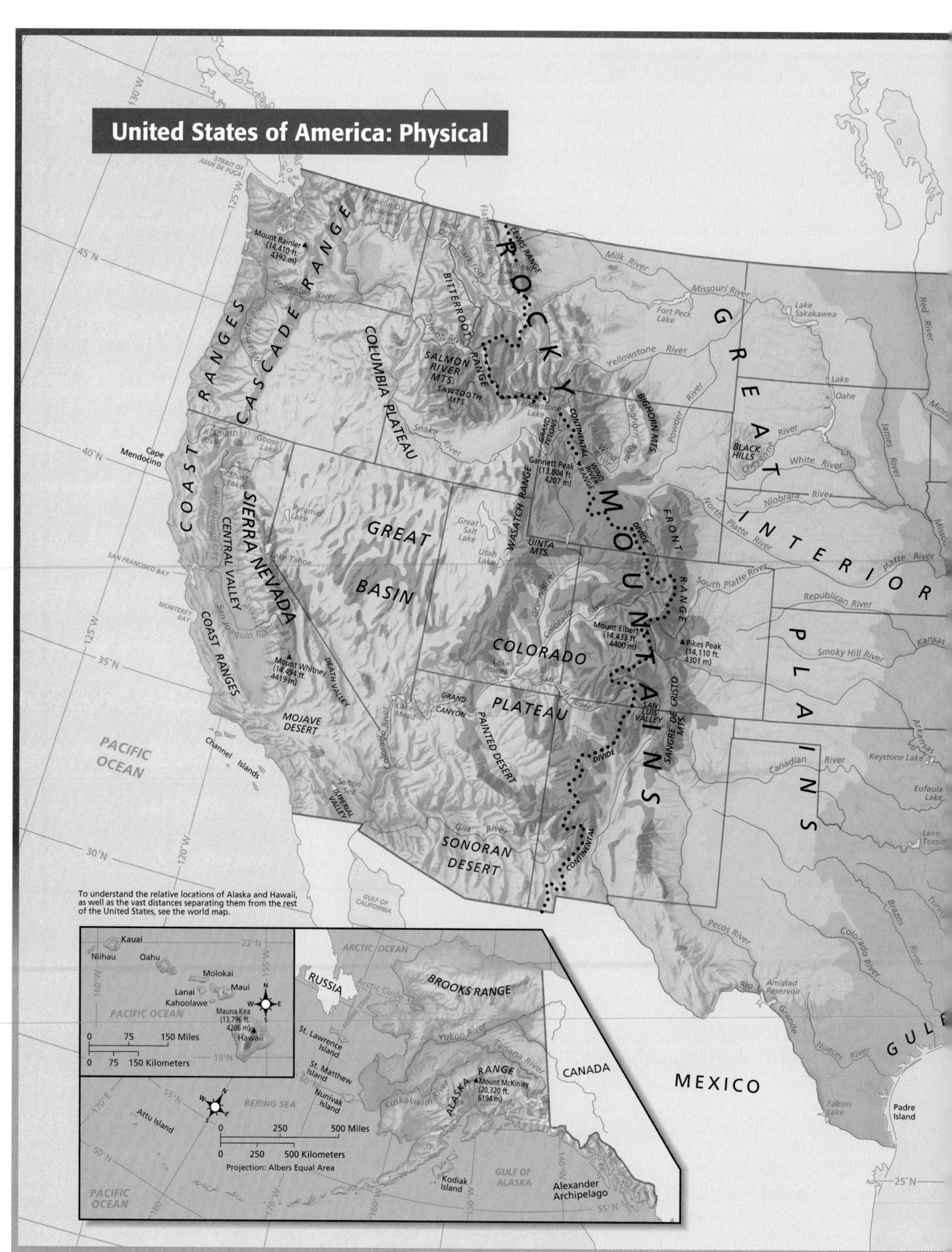

United States of America: Physical

STRAIT OF JUAN DE FUCA

Mount Rainier ▲ (14,410 ft. 4392 m)

Columbia River

COAST RANGES

CASCADE RANGE

COLUMBIA PLATEAU

Franklin D. Roosevelt Lake

Pend Oreille

Clark Fork

Flathead Lake

BITTERROOT RANGE

SALMON RIVER MTS.

Salmon River

SAWTOOTH MTS.

Snake River

LEWIS RANGE

ROCKY

Milk River

Fort Peck Lake

Yellowstone River

Yellowstone Lake

GRAND TETONS

CONTINENTAL

WIND RIVER RANGE

Gannett Peak (13,804 ft. 4207 m)

BIGHORN MTS.

Bighorn River

Powder River

Missouri River

Lake Sakakawea

Lake Oahe

Minn

Red River

BLACK HILLS

Cheyenne River

White River

James River

GREAT INTERIOR PLAINS

Klamath River

Shasta Lake

Goose Lake

Pyramid Lake

Lake Tahoe

SIERRA NEVADA

CENTRAL VALLEY

San Joaquin River

COAST RANGES

Cape Mendocino

SAN FRANCISCO BAY

MONTEREY BAY

GREAT

BASIN

Great Salt Lake

Utah Lake

WASATCH RANGE

UINTA MTS.

Green River

Lake Powell

Colorado River

Lake Mead

MOUNTAINS

DIVIDE

FRONT RANGE

Mount Elbert (14,433 ft. 4400 m)

San Luis River

SAN LUIS VALLEY

SANGRE DE CRISTO MTS.

DIVIDE

Pikes Peak (14,110 ft. 4301 m)

North Platte River

South Platte River

Platte River

Republican River

Smoky Hill River

Niobrara River

Kansas

PLAINS

Mount Whitney (14,494 ft. 4419 m)

DEATH VALLEY

COLORADO

PLATEAU

GRAND CANYON

PAINTED DESERT

MOJAVE DESERT

PACIFIC OCEAN

Channel Islands

Salton Sea

IMPERIAL VALLEY

Gila River

SONORAN DESERT

CONTINENTAL

GULF OF CALIFORNIA

Canadian River

Keystone Lake

Eufaula Lake

Arkansas River

Lake Texoma

Pecos River

Colorado River

Rio Grande

Amistad Reservoir

Nueces River

Brazos

GULF

MEXICO

Falcon Lake

Padre Island

To understand the relative locations of Alaska and Hawaii, as well as the vast distances separating them from the rest of the United States, see the world map.

Kauai

Niihau

Oahu

Molokai

Lanai

Maui

Kahoolawe

PACIFIC OCEAN

Mauna Kea (13,796 ft. 4206 m)

Hawaii

0   75   150 Miles

0   75   150 Kilometers

ARCTIC OCEAN

Arctic Circle

RUSSIA

BROOKS RANGE

Yukon River

St. Lawrence Island

St. Matthew Island

Nunivak Island

BERING SEA

Attu Island

Kuskokwim River

ALASKA RANGE

Mount McKinley (20,320 ft. 6194 m)

Tanana River

CANADA

Kodiak Island

GULF OF ALASKA

Alexander Archipelago

0   250   500 Miles

0   250   500 Kilometers

Projection: Albers Equal Area

PACIFIC OCEAN

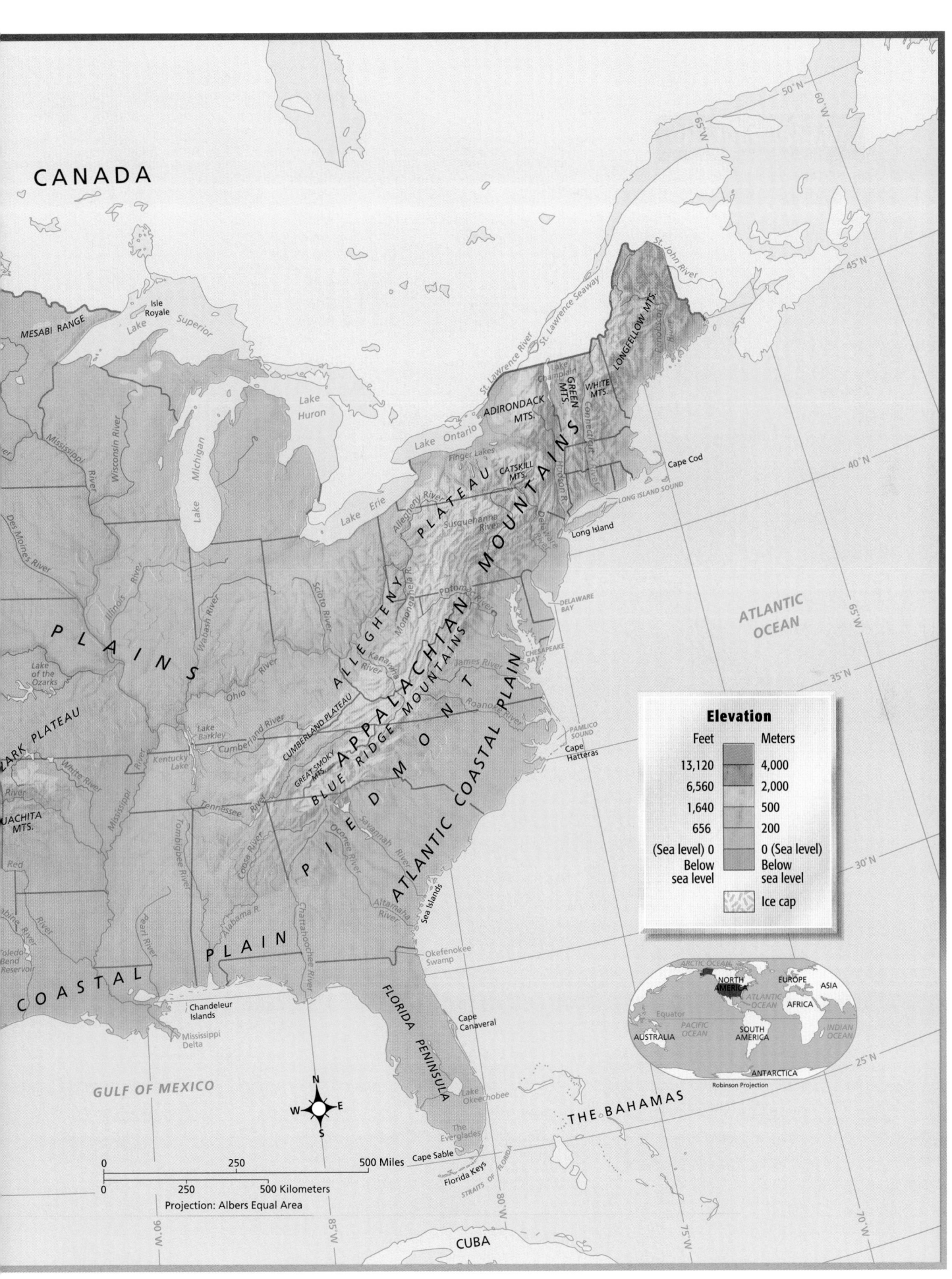

CANADA

MESABI RANGE

Isle Royale

Lake Superior

Lake Michigan

Lake Huron

Lake Ontario

Lake Erie

Finger Lakes

St. Lawrence River

St. Lawrence Seaway

Lake Champlain

ADIRONDACK MTS.

CATSKILL MTS.

GREEN MTS.

WHITE MTS.

LONGFELLOW MTS.

St. John River

Cape Cod

LONG ISLAND SOUND

Long Island

ALLEGHENY PLATEAU

APPALACHIAN MOUNTAINS

Allegheny River

Susquehanna River

Hudson R.

Delaware R.

Connecticut R.

DELAWARE BAY

CHESAPEAKE BAY

PAMLICO SOUND

Cape Hatteras

Potomac River

Monongahela R.

Kanawha River

James River

Roanoke River

PIEDMONT

BLUE RIDGE MOUNTAINS

CUMBERLAND PLATEAU

GREAT SMOKY MTS.

ATLANTIC COASTAL PLAIN

ATLANTIC OCEAN

PLAINS

Mississippi River

Des Moines River

Wisconsin River

Illinois River

Wabash River

Scioto River

Ohio River

Cumberland River

Kentucky River

Tennessee River

White River

Lake of the Ozarks

Lake Barkley

Kentucky Lake

OZARK PLATEAU

OUACHITA MTS.

Red River

Tombigbee River

Coosa River

Alabama R.

Pearl River

Chattahoochee River

Flint River

Oconee River

Ocmulgee River

Savannah River

Altamaha River

Sea Islands

Toledo Bend Reservoir

COASTAL PLAIN

Chandeleur Islands

Mississippi Delta

GULF OF MEXICO

Okefenokee Swamp

FLORIDA PENINSULA

Cape Canaveral

Lake Okeechobee

The Everglades

Cape Sable

Florida Keys

STRAITS OF FLORIDA

THE BAHAMAS

CUBA

Elevation

Feet		Meters
13,120		4,000
6,560		2,000
1,640		500
656		200
(Sea level) 0		0 (Sea level)
Below sea level		Below sea level

Ice cap

ARCTIC OCEAN

NORTH AMERICA

EUROPE

ASIA

ATLANTIC OCEAN

AFRICA

Equator

PACIFIC OCEAN

SOUTH AMERICA

AUSTRALIA

INDIAN OCEAN

ANTARCTICA

Robinson Projection

N E S W

0   250   500 Miles

0   250   500 Kilometers

Projection: Albers Equal Area

50° N
45° N
40° N
35° N
30° N
25° N

60° W
65° W
70° W
75° W
80° W
85° W
90° W

65° W

World: Political

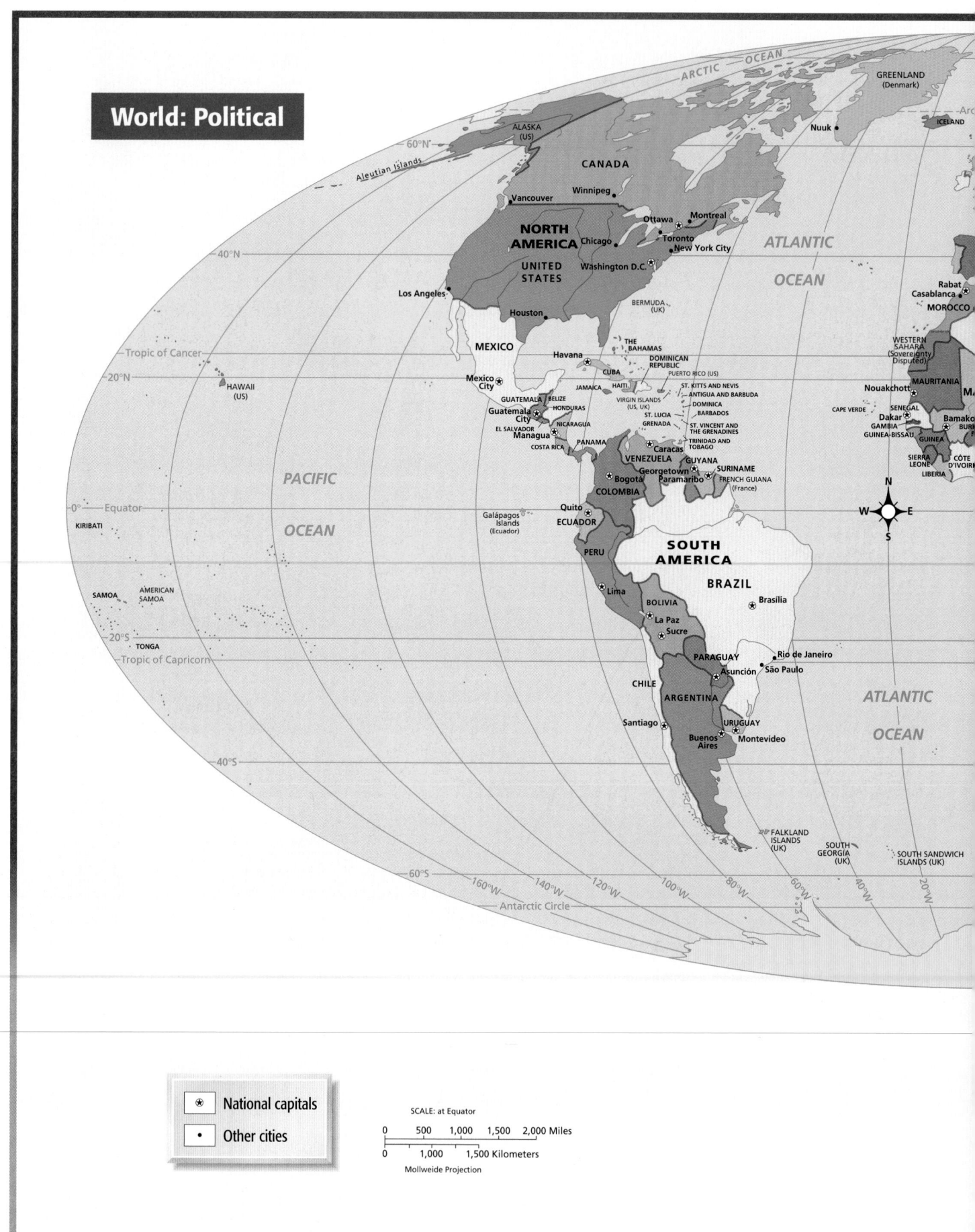

National capitals ⊛

Other cities •

SCALE: at Equator

0   500   1,000   1,500   2,000 Miles

0   1,000   1,500 Kilometers

Mollweide Projection

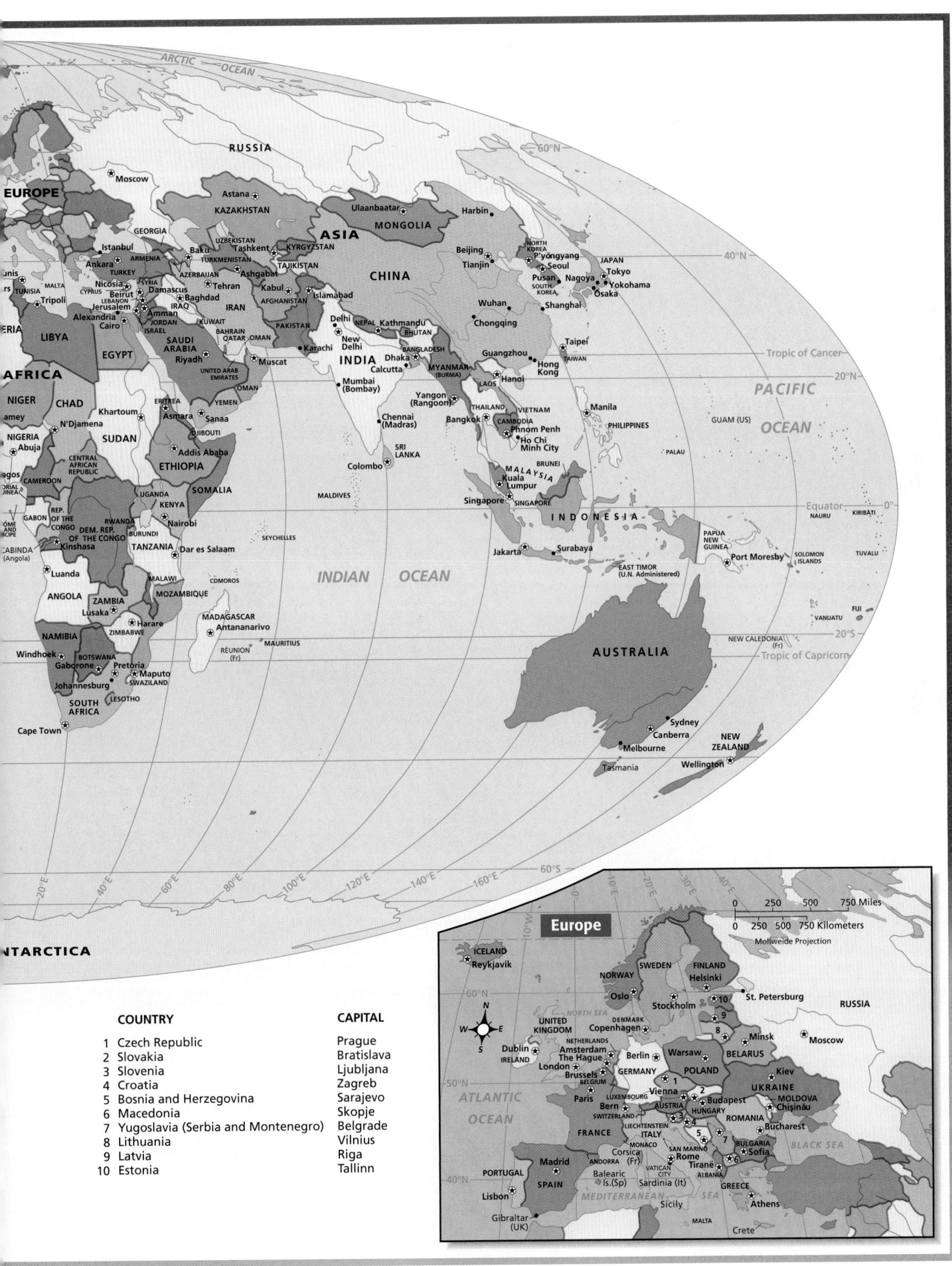

ARCTIC OCEAN

RUSSIA

EUROPE

Moscow

Astana
KAZAKHSTAN

Ulaanbaatar
MONGOLIA

Harbin

ASIA

GEORGIA

Istanbul

UZBEKISTAN
Tashkent
KYRGYZSTAN

Beijing

NORTH
KOREA
P'yongyang Seoul
Pusan
SOUTH
KOREA

JAPAN
Tokyo
Nagoya Yokohama
Osaka

Ankara
TURKEY
ARMENIA
Baku
AZERBAIJAN
TURKMENISTAN
Ashgabat
TAJIKISTAN

CHINA

Tianjin

Tunis

MALTA
CYPRUS
Nicosia
LEBANON
Beirut
Damascus
SYRIA
Tehran
Kabul
Islamabad

Wuhan

Shanghai

Tripoli
Jerusalem
ISRAEL
Amman
JORDAN
Baghdad
IRAQ
KUWAIT
IRAN
AFGHANISTAN

Delhi
New
Delhi
NEPAL
Kathmandu
BHUTAN

Chongqing

Taipei
TAIWAN

Alexandria
Cairo

BAHRAIN
QATAR
OMAN

PAKISTAN

BANGLADESH
Dhaka

Guangzhou
Hong
Kong

Tropic of Cancer

ERIA

LIBYA

EGYPT

SAUDI
ARABIA

Riyadh

UNITED ARAB
EMIRATES

Muscat

Karachi

INDIA

Mumbai
(Bombay)

Calcutta
MYANMAR
(BURMA)

Hanoi

LAOS

PACIFIC

20°N

AFRICA

NIGER

CHAD

Khartoum

ERITREA
Asmara
YEMEN
Sanaa

OMAN

Yangon
(Rangoon)

THAILAND

VIETNAM
CAMBODIA
Phnom Penh

Manila

PHILIPPINES

GUAM (US)

OCEAN

amey

N'Djamena

DJIBOUTI

Chennai
(Madras)

Bangkok

Ho Chi
Minh City

NIGERIA
Abuja

SUDAN

Addis Ababa

SRI
LANKA

BRUNEI

PALAU

CENTRAL
AFRICAN
REPUBLIC

ETHIOPIA

SOMALIA

Colombo

MALAYSIA
Kuala
Lumpur

CAMEROON

UGANDA
KENYA

MALDIVES

Singapore
SINGAPORE

ORIAL
UINEA

GABON
REP.
OF THE
CONGO

RWANDA
BURUNDI

Nairobi

INDONESIA

PAPUA
NEW
GUINEA

SOLOMON
ISLANDS

NAURU

KIRIBATI

Equator
0°

ME
CIPE
CABINDA
(Angola)

DEM. REP.
OF THE CONGO
Kinshasa

TANZANIA
Dar es Salaam

SEYCHELLES

Jakarta
Surabaya

Port Moresby

TUVALU

Luanda

ANGOLA

ZAMBIA
Lusaka

MALAWI

MOZAMBIQUE

COMOROS

INDIAN

OCEAN

EAST TIMOR
(U.N. Administered)

VANUATU

FIJI

Harare
ZIMBABWE

MADAGASCAR
Antananarivo

MAURITIUS

NEW CALEDONIA
(Fr)

20°S

NAMIBIA

Windhoek
BOTSWANA
Gaborone
Pretoria

RÉUNION
(Fr)

AUSTRALIA

Tropic of Capricorn

Johannesburg
Maputo
SWAZILAND

SOUTH
AFRICA
LESOTHO

Cape Town

Sydney
Canberra

NEW
ZEALAND

Melbourne

NTARCTICA

Tasmania

Wellington

20°E
40°E
60°E
80°E
100°E
120°E
140°E
160°E
60°S

COUNTRY	CAPITAL
1 Czech Republic	Prague
2 Slovakia	Bratislava
3 Slovenia	Ljubljana
4 Croatia	Zagreb
5 Bosnia and Herzegovina	Sarajevo
6 Macedonia	Skopje
7 Yugoslavia (Serbia and Montenegro)	Belgrade
8 Lithuania	Vilnius
9 Latvia	Riga
10 Estonia	Tallinn

Europe

0   250   500   750 Miles
0   250   500   750 Kilometers
Mollweide Projection

ICELAND
Reykjavik

SWEDEN
FINLAND
Helsinki

NORWAY
Oslo

St. Petersburg

RUSSIA

Stockholm
10
9

NORTH
SEA

DENMARK
Copenhagen

8

Minsk

UNITED
KINGDOM

Moscow

N
W   E
S

NETHERLANDS
Amsterdam
The Hague

Berlin

Warsaw

BELARUS

Dublin
IRELAND

London
BELGIUM
Brussels

GERMANY

POLAND

Kiev

UKRAINE

ATLANTIC

Paris

LUXEMBOURG

Vienna
1

Budapest

MOLDOVA
Chişinău

OCEAN

Bern
SWITZERLAND

AUSTRIA
2

HUNGARY

ROMANIA

Bucharest

LIECHTENSTEIN

3
4

FRANCE

MONACO

5

7

BULGARIA
Sofia

BLACK SEA

SAN MARINO
(Fr)
VATICAN
CITY
Rome
Tirane
ALBANIA

6

Madrid

Corsica
(Fr)

ANDORRA

Sardinia (It)

GREECE

PORTUGAL

SPAIN

Balearic
Is.(Sp)

ITALY

MEDITERRANEAN
SEA

Sicily

Athens

Lisbon

Gibraltar
(UK)

MALTA

Crete

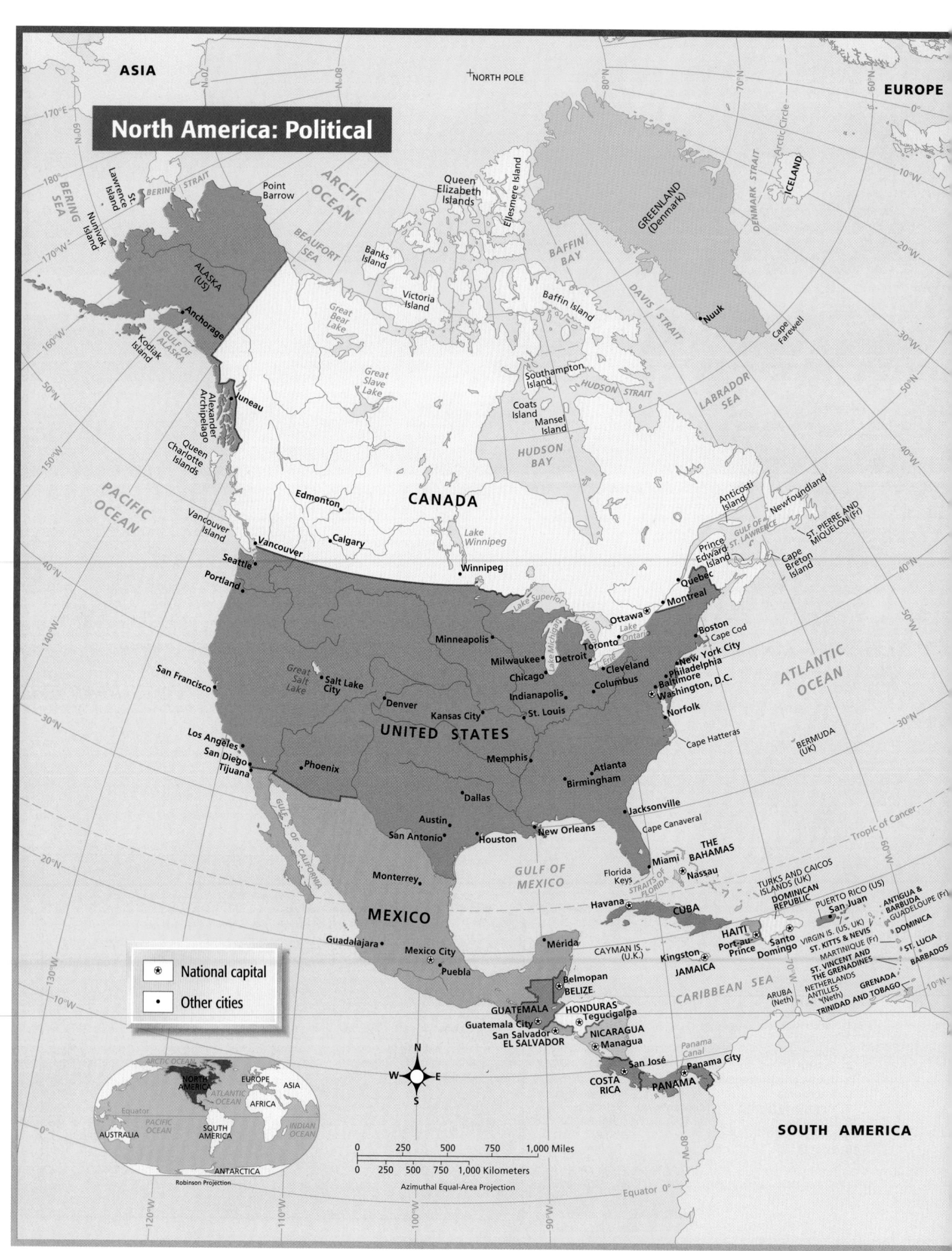

North America: Political

ASIA

EUROPE

NORTH POLE

ARCTIC OCEAN

BERING STRAIT

BERING SEA

St. Lawrence Island

Nunivak Island

Point Barrow

BEAUFORT SEA

Banks Island

Victoria Island

Great Bear Lake

Queen Elizabeth Islands

Ellesmere Island

GREENLAND (Denmark)

DENMARK STRAIT

ICELAND

Arctic Circle

BAFFIN BAY

Baffin Island

Nuuk

Cape Farewell

DAVIS STRAIT

LABRADOR SEA

ALASKA (US)

Anchorage

GULF OF ALASKA

Kodiak Island

Juneau

Alexander Archipelago

Queen Charlotte Islands

Great Slave Lake

Southampton Island

Coats Island

Mansel Island

HUDSON STRAIT

HUDSON BAY

CANADA

Anticosti Island

Newfoundland

ST. PIERRE AND MIQUELON (Fr)

PACIFIC OCEAN

Vancouver Island

Vancouver

Edmonton

Calgary

Seattle

Portland

Winnipeg

Lake Winnipeg

Lake Superior

Quebec

Montreal

Prince Edward Island

GULF OF ST. LAWRENCE

Cape Breton Island

Ottawa

Lake Huron

Lake Michigan

Toronto

Lake Ontario

Lake Erie

Boston

Cape Cod

Minneapolis

Milwaukee

Detroit

Cleveland

New York City

Philadelphia

Chicago

Columbus

Baltimore

Washington, D.C.

ATLANTIC OCEAN

San Francisco

Great Salt Lake

Salt Lake City

Denver

Indianapolis

St. Louis

Kansas City

Norfolk

UNITED STATES

Los Angeles

San Diego

Tijuana

Phoenix

Memphis

Dallas

Atlanta

Birmingham

Cape Hatteras

BERMUDA (UK)

Austin

San Antonio

Houston

New Orleans

Jacksonville

Cape Canaveral

GULF OF CALIFORNIA

Monterrey

GULF OF MEXICO

Florida Keys

Miami

THE BAHAMAS

Nassau

Tropic of Cancer

TURKS AND CAICOS ISLANDS (UK)

MEXICO

Guadalajara

Mexico City

Puebla

Mérida

Havana

CUBA

STRAITS OF FLORIDA

CAYMAN IS. (U.K.)

DOMINICAN REPUBLIC

PUERTO RICO (US)

San Juan

ANTIGUA & BARBUDA

GUADELOUPE (Fr)

HAITI

Port-au-Prince

Santo Domingo

VIRGIN IS. (US, UK)

ST. KITTS & NEVIS

DOMINICA

Kingston

JAMAICA

MARTINIQUE (Fr)

ST. VINCENT AND THE GRENADINES

ST. LUCIA

BARBADOS

Belmopan

BELIZE

NETHERLANDS ANTILLES (Neth)

GRENADA

GUATEMALA

HONDURAS

Tegucigalpa

CARIBBEAN SEA

ARUBA (Neth)

TRINIDAD AND TOBAGO

Guatemala City

San Salvador

EL SALVADOR

NICARAGUA

Managua

Panama Canal

San José

Panama City

COSTA RICA

PANAMA

SOUTH AMERICA

★ National capital

• Other cities

ARCTIC OCEAN

NORTH AMERICA

EUROPE

ASIA

ATLANTIC OCEAN

AFRICA

Equator

PACIFIC OCEAN

SOUTH AMERICA

INDIAN OCEAN

AUSTRALIA

ANTARCTICA

Robinson Projection

| 0 | 250 | 500 | 750 | 1,000 Miles |

| 0 | 250 | 500 | 750 | 1,000 Kilometers |

Azimuthal Equal-Area Projection

Equator 0°

South America: Political

CENTRAL
AMERICA

CARIBBEAN SEA

Barranquilla
Cartagena

Caracas

VENEZUELA

Lake Maracaibo

Medellín

⊛ Bogotá

COLOMBIA

Cali

Orinoco River

Georgetown
Paramaribo

GUYANA

Cayenne

SURINAME

FRENCH
GUIANA
(Fr)

Malpelo
Island
(Colombia)

Río Negro

Amazon River

Equator 0°

⊛ Quito

ECUADOR

Amazon River

Belém

Guayaquil

Galápagos
Islands
(Ecuador)

0° Equator

PERU

Marañón River

Ucayali River

BRAZIL

Trujillo

Recife

Callao ⊛ Lima

10°S

PACIFIC
OCEAN

Arequipa

Lake
Titicaca

BOLIVIA

La Paz

São Francisco River

⊛ Brasília

Salvador

Lake
Poopó

⊛ Sucre

Belo Horizonte

20°S

Paraná River

PARAGUAY

Campinas

São Paulo

Tropic of Capricorn

San Ambrosio
Island
(Chile)

Asunción ⊛

Paraguay River

Curitiba

Rio de Janeiro

Tropic of Capricorn

San Félix Island
(Chile)

Paraná River

CHILE

N

W ⊕ E

S

Juan Fernández
Islands
(Chile)

Córdoba

Pôrto Alegre

URUGUAY

30°S

ATLANTIC
OCEAN

Valparaíso
Santiago ⊛

Rosario

Buenos Aires
Morón
San Justo
Lomas de Zamora

Montevideo ⊛

RIO DE LA PLATA

ARGENTINA

⊛	National capital
•	Other cities

ARCTIC OCEAN

NORTH
AMERICA

EUROPE

ASIA

ATLANTIC
OCEAN

AFRICA

Equator

PACIFIC
OCEAN

SOUTH
AMERICA

INDIAN
OCEAN

AUSTRALIA

ANTARCTICA

Robinson Projection

0	250	500	750	1,000 Miles
0	250	500	750	1,000 Kilometers

Azimuthal Equal-Area Projection

STRAIT OF
MAGELLAN

FALKLAND
ISLANDS (UK)

Tierra del
Fuego

SOUTH GEORGIA
ISLAND
(UK)

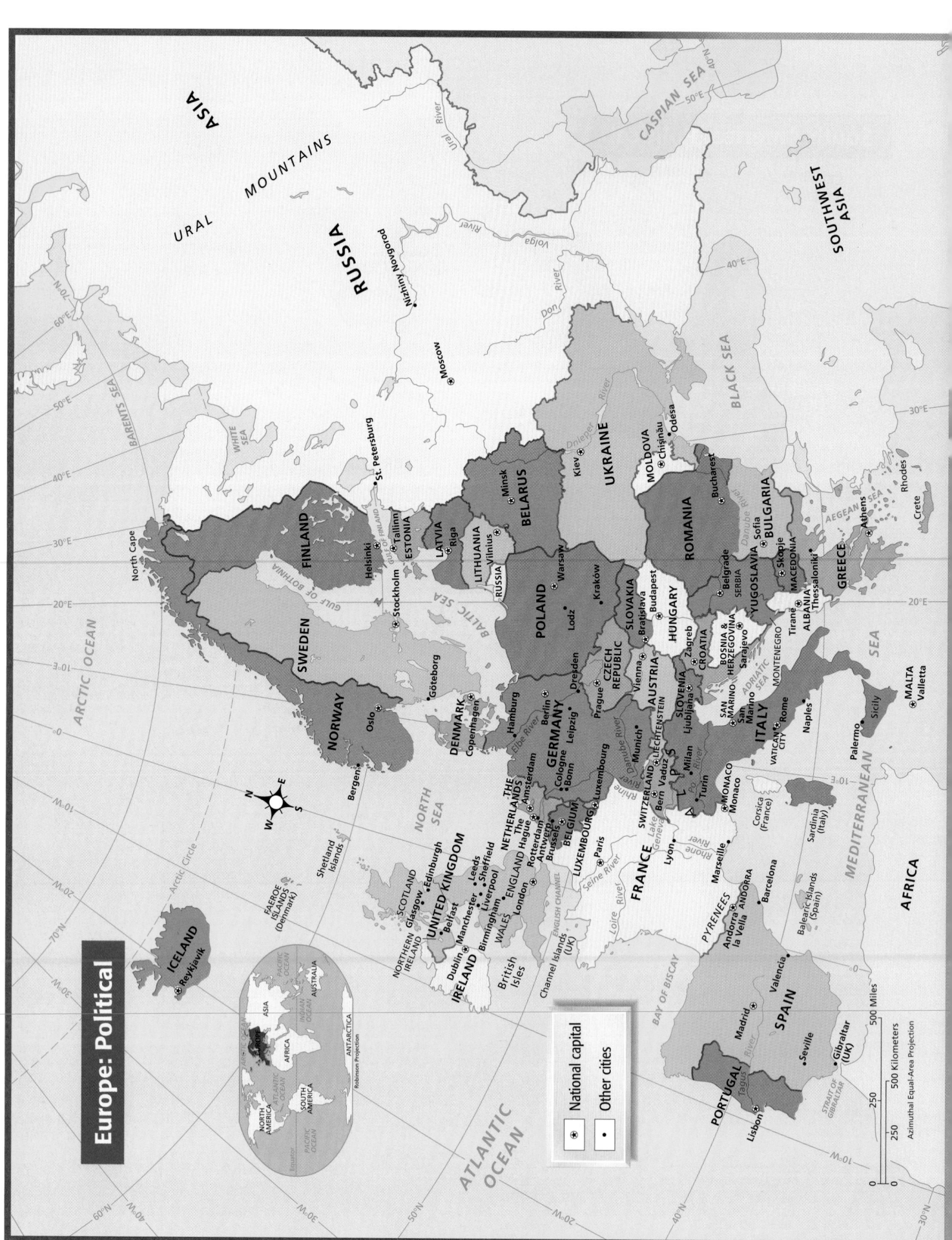

Europe: Political

National capital ⊛

Other cities •

ASIA

URAL MOUNTAINS

RUSSIA

Nizhniy Novgorod •

• Moscow

CASPIAN SEA

SOUTHWEST ASIA

Ural River

Volga River

Don River

BARENTS SEA

WHITE SEA

St. Petersburg •

BLACK SEA

North Cape

FINLAND

Helsinki ⊛

Tallinn ⊛ **ESTONIA**

Riga ⊛ **LATVIA**

Vilnius ⊛ **LITHUANIA**

Minsk ⊛ **BELARUS**

Kiev ⊛

UKRAINE

Dnieper River

MOLDOVA

Chişinău ⊛ • Odesa

Bucharest •

ROMANIA

Belgrade ⊛

SERBIA

Sofia ⊛ **BULGARIA**

Skopje ⊛ **MACEDONIA**

YUGOSLAVIA

Danube River

Rhodes

AEGEAN SEA

Athens ⊛

GREECE

Thessaloniki •

Crete

ARCTIC OCEAN

GULF OF BOTHNIA

SWEDEN

Stockholm ⊛

Göteborg •

BALTIC SEA

POLAND

Warsaw ⊛

Kraków •

Lodz •

SLOVAKIA

Bratislava ⊛

HUNGARY

Budapest ⊛

Zagreb ⊛ **CROATIA**

BOSNIA & HERZEGOVINA

Sarajevo ⊛

MONTENEGRO

ALBANIA

Tiranë ⊛

ADRIATIC SEA

NORWAY

Oslo ⊛

Bergen •

DENMARK

Copenhagen ⊛

Hamburg •

Berlin ⊛

Dresden •

Leipzig •

GERMANY

Prague ⊛ **CZECH REPUBLIC**

Vienna ⊛ **AUSTRIA**

SLOVENIA

Ljubljana ⊛

SAN MARINO

San Marino ⊛

VATICAN CITY

Rome ⊛

ITALY

Naples •

Palermo •

Sicily

MALTA

Valletta ⊛

NORTH SEA

Shetland Islands

FAEROE ISLANDS (Denmark)

SCOTLAND

Edinburgh • Glasgow •

ICELAND

Reykjavik ⊛

UNITED KINGDOM

Belfast •

NORTHERN IRELAND

IRELAND

Dublin ⊛

Manchester •

Leeds •

Sheffield •

Liverpool •

Birmingham •

WALES

ENGLAND

London ⊛

British Isles

Elbe River

Munich •

Cologne •

Bonn •

NETHERLANDS

Amsterdam ⊛

The Hague

Rotterdam •

Antwerp •

BELGIUM

Brussels ⊛

LUXEMBOURG

Luxembourg ⊛

Paris ⊛

Vaduz ⊛ **LIECHTENSTEIN**

SWITZERLAND

Bern ⊛

Geneva •

Lake Geneva

MONACO

Monaco ⊛

Milan •

Turin •

Po River

Rhine River

Danube River

A L P S

FRANCE

Lyon •

Marseille •

Rhône River

Seine River

Loire River

Corsica (France)

Sardinia (Italy)

MEDITERRANEAN SEA

AFRICA

English Channel

Channel Islands (UK)

BAY OF BISCAY

PYRENEES

ANDORRA

Andorra la Vella ⊛

Barcelona •

Balearic Islands (Spain)

SPAIN

Madrid ⊛

Valencia •

Seville •

PORTUGAL

Lisbon ⊛

Tagus River

Gibraltar (UK)

STRAIT OF GIBRALTAR

ATLANTIC OCEAN

NORTH AMERICA

SOUTH AMERICA

ASIA

AUSTRALIA

AFRICA

ANTARCTICA

EUROPE

ATLANTIC OCEAN

PACIFIC OCEAN

INDIAN OCEAN

Equator

Robinson Projection

N E W S

0 250 500 Miles

0 250 500 Kilometers

Azimuthal Equal-Area Projection

Arctic Circle

70°N

60°N

50°N

40°N

30°N

10°E

20°E

30°E

40°E

50°E

60°E

10°W

20°W

30°W

0°

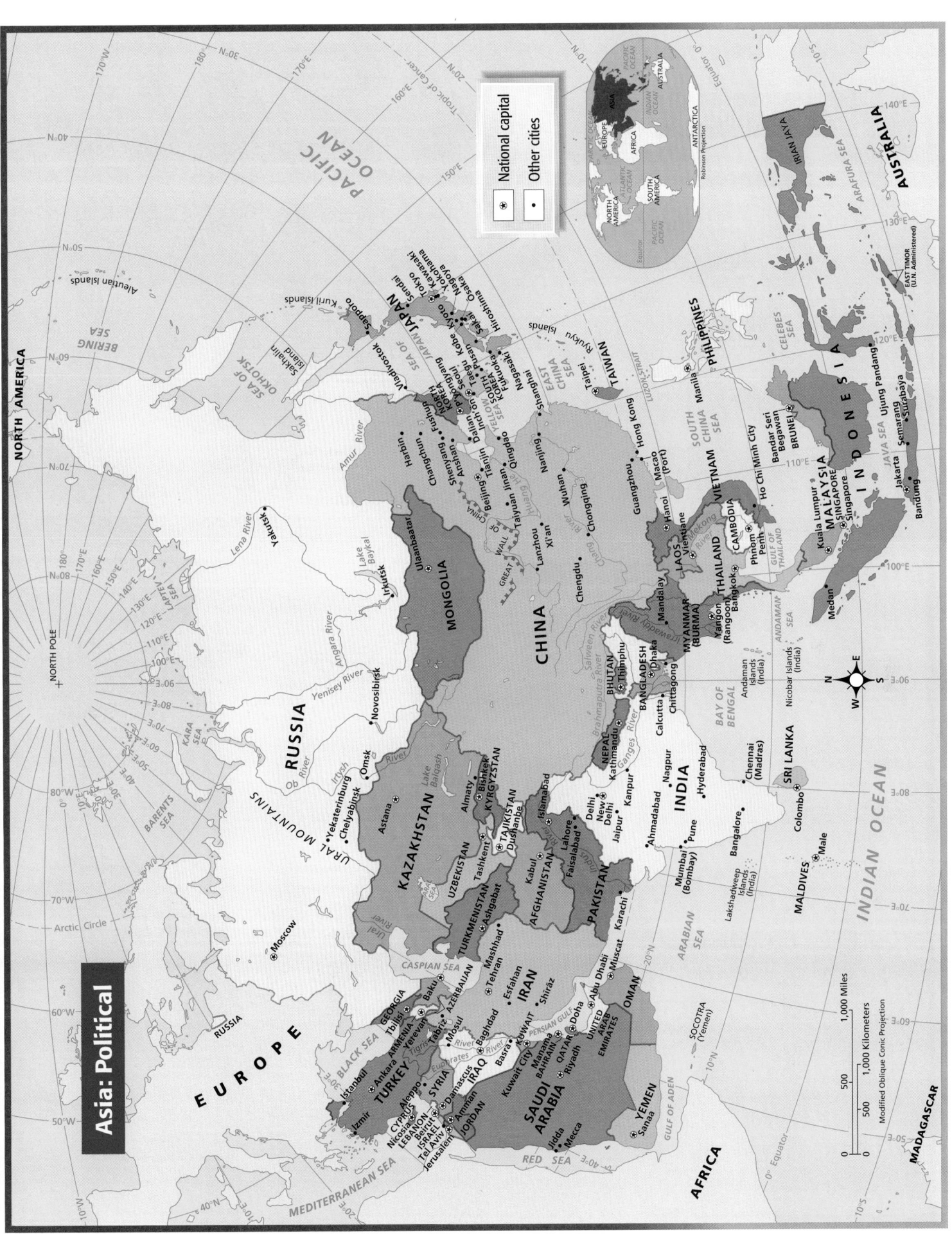

Asia: Political

National capital ⊛
Other cities •

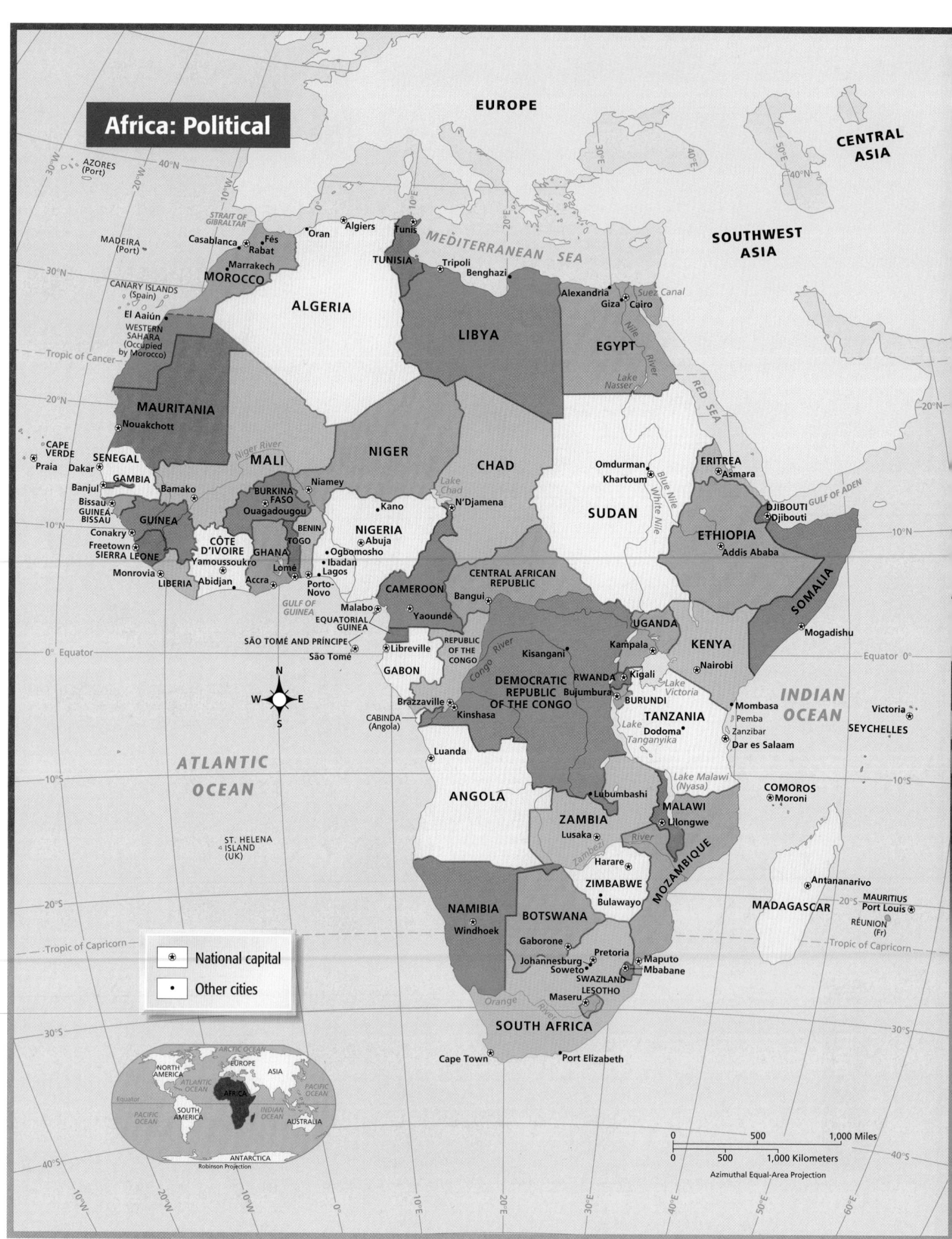

Africa: Political

EUROPE

CENTRAL ASIA

SOUTHWEST ASIA

MEDITERRANEAN SEA

AZORES (Port)

MADEIRA (Port)

STRAIT OF GIBRALTAR

Casablanca • Fés • Oran ⊛ Algiers ⊛ Tunis
Rabat
Marrakech
MOROCCO
CANARY ISLANDS (Spain)
El Aaiún
WESTERN SAHARA (Occupied by Morocco)

TUNISIA
⊛ Tripoli
Benghazi

Alexandria
Giza • ⊛ Cairo

Suez Canal

Lake Nasser

Nile River

RED SEA

GULF OF ADEN

Tropic of Cancer

ALGERIA

LIBYA

EGYPT

MAURITANIA
⊛ Nouakchott

CAPE VERDE
Praia ⊛ • Dakar ⊛
SENEGAL
Banjul ⊛ **GAMBIA**
Bissau ⊛ **GUINEA-BISSAU**
GUINEA
Conakry ⊛
Freetown ⊛
SIERRA LEONE
Monrovia ⊛
LIBERIA

MALI
Bamako ⊛
BURKINA FASO
Ouagadougou ⊛
Niamey ⊛
Kano •

NIGER

CHAD
N'Djamena ⊛

Niger River

Lake Chad

Omdurman •
Khartoum ⊛

ERITREA
⊛ Asmara

DJIBOUTI
⊛ Djibouti

Blue Nile
White Nile

SUDAN

ETHIOPIA
⊛ Addis Ababa

SOMALIA
⊛ Mogadishu

BENIN
TOGO
GHANA
Yamoussoukro ⊛
CÔTE D'IVOIRE
Abidjan •
Accra ⊛
Lomé ⊛
Porto-Novo ⊛
NIGERIA
⊛ Abuja
Ogbomosho •
Ibadan •
Lagos •

CENTRAL AFRICAN REPUBLIC
Bangui ⊛

CAMEROON
Yaoundé ⊛

UGANDA
Kampala ⊛
KENYA
Nairobi ⊛

Malabo ⊛
EQUATORIAL GUINEA

SÃO TOMÉ AND PRÍNCIPE
São Tomé •

0° Equator

REPUBLIC OF THE CONGO
⊛ Libreville
GABON
Brazzaville ⊛
CABINDA (Angola)

Kisangani •
Congo River

DEMOCRATIC REPUBLIC OF THE CONGO
Kinshasa ⊛
Luanda ⊛

RWANDA Kigali ⊛
Bujumbura ⊛
BURUNDI
Lake Victoria

TANZANIA
Dodoma ⊛
Zanzibar •
Dar es Salaam •
Lake Tanganyika

Mombasa •
Pemba •

Equator 0°

INDIAN OCEAN

Victoria ⊛
SEYCHELLES

ATLANTIC OCEAN

ST. HELENA ISLAND (UK)

ANGOLA

Lubumbashi •

Lake Malawi (Nyasa)

COMOROS
⊛ Moroni

ZAMBIA
Lusaka ⊛

MALAWI
Lilongwe ⊛

Zambezi River

MOZAMBIQUE

Harare ⊛
ZIMBABWE
Bulawayo •

⊛ Antananarivo

MADAGASCAR

MAURITIUS
Port Louis ⊛
RÉUNION (Fr)

Tropic of Capricorn

NAMIBIA
Windhoek ⊛

BOTSWANA
Gaborone ⊛

Pretoria ⊛
Johannesburg •
Soweto •
SWAZILAND
Maseru ⊛
LESOTHO
Maputo ⊛
Mbabane ⊛

Orange River

SOUTH AFRICA

Cape Town • • Port Elizabeth

⊛ National capital
• Other cities

ARCTIC OCEAN
NORTH AMERICA
EUROPE
ASIA
ATLANTIC OCEAN
PACIFIC OCEAN
AFRICA
Equator
PACIFIC OCEAN
SOUTH AMERICA
INDIAN OCEAN
AUSTRALIA
ANTARCTICA
Robinson Projection

| 0 | 500 | 1,000 Miles |
| 0 | 500 | 1,000 Kilometers |

Azimuthal Equal-Area Projection

Pacific Islands: Political

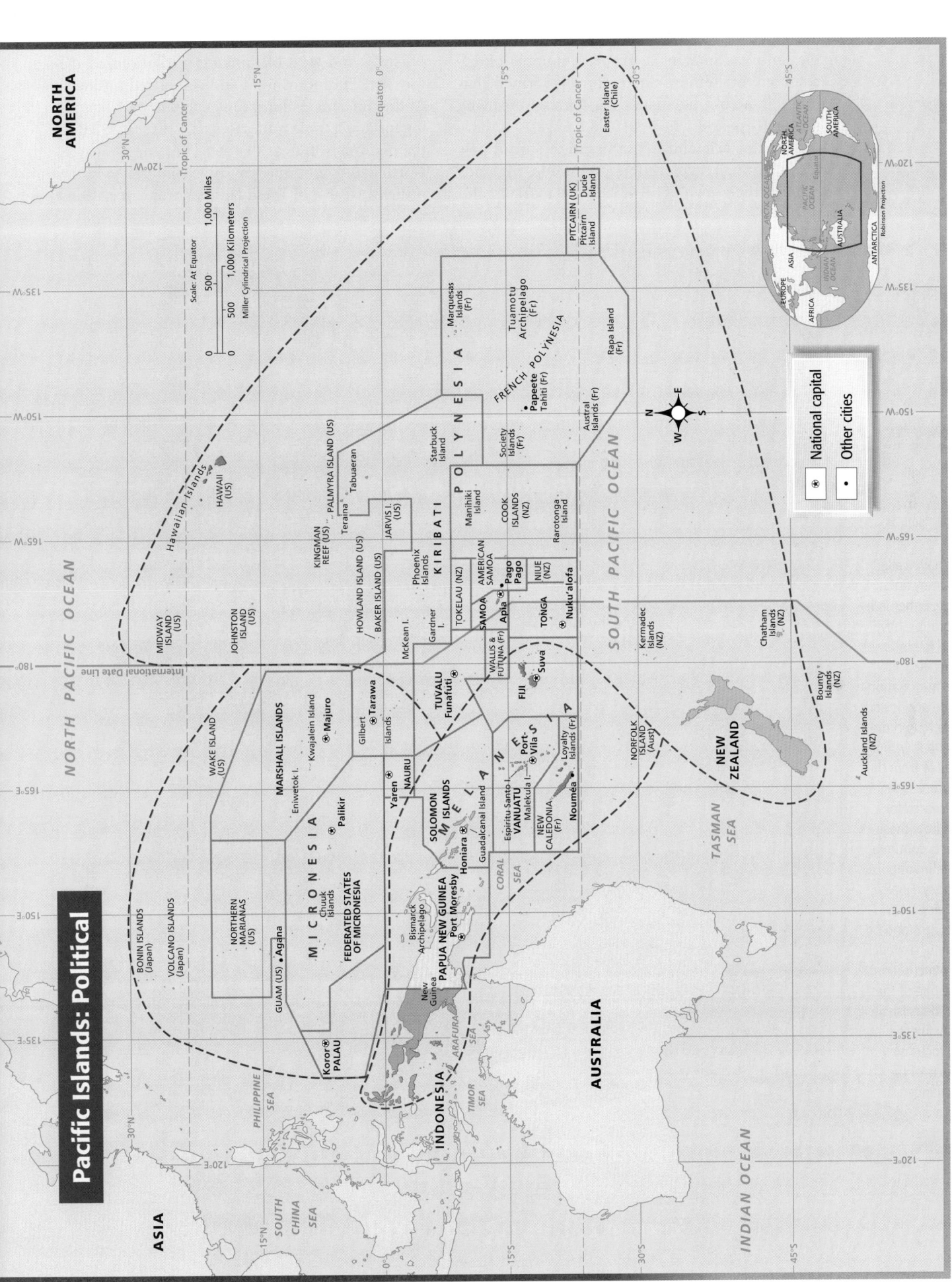

ASIA

NORTH AMERICA

NORTH PACIFIC OCEAN

SOUTH PACIFIC OCEAN

PHILIPPINE SEA

SOUTH CHINA SEA

INDONESIA

New Guinea

AUSTRALIA

TIMOR SEA

ARAFURA SEA

CORAL SEA

TASMAN SEA

INDIAN OCEAN

NEW ZEALAND

Scale: At Equator
Miller Cylindrical Projection
0   500   1,000 Miles
0   500   1,000 Kilometers

National capital ⊛
Other cities •

Equator 0°
Tropic of Cancer
Tropic of Cancer
International Date Line

BONIN ISLANDS (Japan)
VOLCANO ISLANDS (Japan)
NORTHERN MARIANAS (US)
GUAM (US) • Agaña
Koror ⊛ PALAU
FEDERATED STATES OF MICRONESIA
MICRONESIA
Chuuk Islands
Palikir ⊛
WAKE ISLAND (US)
MARSHALL ISLANDS
Eniwetok I.
Kwajalein Island
Majuro ⊛
Gilbert Islands
Tarawa ⊛
NAURU
Yaren ⊛
Palikir
MIDWAY ISLAND (US)
JOHNSTON ISLAND (US)
Hawaiian Islands
HAWAII (US)
KINGMAN REEF (US)
PALMYRA ISLAND (US)
Teraina
Tabuaeran
JARVIS I. (US)
HOWLAND ISLAND (US)
BAKER ISLAND (US)
McKean I.
Gardner I.
Phoenix Islands
KIRIBATI
Manihiki Island
Starbuck Island
POLYNESIA
Marquesas Islands (Fr)
Tuamotu Archipelago (Fr)
FRENCH POLYNESIA
Papeete
Tahiti (Fr)
Society Islands (Fr)
COOK ISLANDS (NZ)
Rarotonga Island
Austral Islands (Fr)
Rapa Island (Fr)
PITCAIRN (UK)
Pitcairn Island
Ducie Island
Easter Island (Chile)
TOKELAU (NZ)
AMERICAN SAMOA
Pago Pago •
SAMOA
Apia ⊛
WALLIS & FUTUNA (Fr)
NIUE (NZ)
TONGA
Nuku'alofa ⊛
TUVALU
Funafuti ⊛
FIJI
Suva •
Kermadec Islands (NZ)
Chatham Islands (NZ)
Bounty Islands (NZ)
Auckland Islands (NZ)
MELANESIA
SOLOMON ISLANDS
Honiara ⊛
Guadalcanal Island
Bismarck Archipelago
PAPUA NEW GUINEA
Port Moresby ⊛
Espiritu Santo I.
Malekula I.
VANUATU
Port-Vila ⊛
NEW CALEDONIA (Fr)
Nouméa •
Loyalty Islands (Fr)
NORFOLK ISLAND (Aus)

PACIFIC OCEAN
Robinson Projection
EUROPE
ASIA
AFRICA
INDIAN OCEAN
NORTH AMERICA
ATLANTIC OCEAN
SOUTH AMERICA
AUSTRALIA
ANTARCTICA
Equator

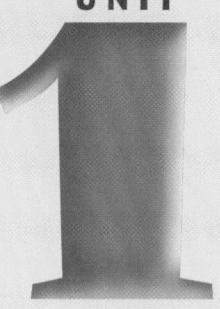
⭐ CHAPTER 1
The World before the Opening of the Atlantic

According to many scientists, humans migrated across a land bridge from Asia to North America during the last Ice Age. As they spread throughout the Americas, humans developed a number of different cultural groups and eventually formed civilizations. Across the Atlantic, Europeans were living through a period called the Middle Ages, and civilizations in Asia and Africa began to spread new ideas through exploration and trade in lands beyond their own. The search for markets and products to trade eventually led Europeans to search for new routes to Asia.

⭐ CHAPTER 2
The Age of Exploration

During the 1400s and 1500s, changes in business practices and ways of thinking revolutionized the way that Europeans lived and conducted business. At the time, many European explorers were searching for direct trade routes to Asia. This search led to the discovery of areas that later became known as North and South America. Largely interested in the mineral wealth of these lands, European nations

Internet Activity

The Columbian Exchange Today

🖥 internet connect

go.hrw.com

TOPIC: The Columbian Exchange
GO TO: go.hrw.com
KEYWORD: SA3 Columbian Exchange

Some scholars have called Columbus's journey an ongoing voyage. Either individually or in groups, have students search the Internet through the HRW Go site to obtain more information about new trade goods and new ideas that crossed the Atlantic from either Europe to the Americas or from the Americas to Europe. Then have students search for information on how these ideas or products continue to be part of life in America or in Europe today. Finally, have students prepare a short report, using standard grammar, spelling, sentence structure, and punctuation, describing how one of these trade goods or ideas is still important today. These reports should focus on the lasting effects of the Columbian Exchange.

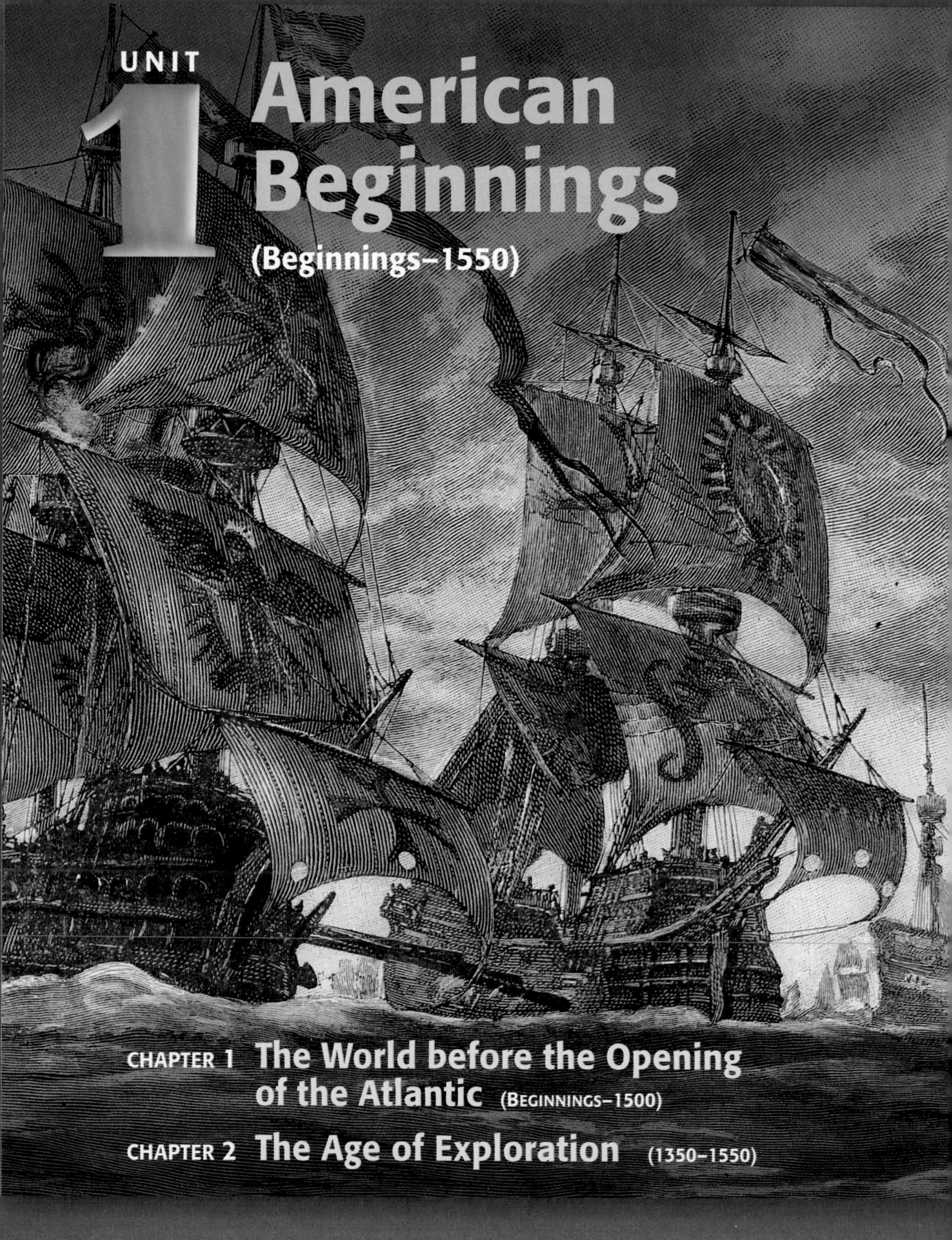

UNIT 1
American Beginnings
(Beginnings–1550)

CHAPTER 1 The World before the Opening of the Atlantic (BEGINNINGS–1500)

CHAPTER 2 The Age of Exploration (1350–1550)

competed for trade routes and territory in these areas. Trade with these lands led to an enormous exchange of goods across the Atlantic. Unfortunately, this trade also brought devastating diseases to the people of the Americas.

★ UNIT MOTIVATOR

Share the information in the chapter overview with students. Write each of the unit's chapter titles as headings on the chalkboard. Have students brainstorm what things and ideas might have been different before the opening of the Atlantic and during the age of exploration. Use the two headings to create a comparison chart of what the students think might have changed. Next have students use these ideas to speculate on how life in the United States might change if we were to discover complex civilizations on another planet. Have students work in groups to create sample conversations that might occur between two people from Earth discussing the newly discovered civilization. Call on volunteers to act out their conversations. Later, when you have finished the unit, come back to these conversations and have students evaluate how closely their ideas about how Americans might respond to contact with different civilizations mirrored the actual responses that Europeans had to American Indian civilizations.

Young People
IN HISTORY
Young Sailors

During the early days of European exploration, sailors kept track of time with sand-filled hourglasses. They turned them over every half hour. On Spanish ships, some crew members would stand watch, or serve as lookouts. As they did, a young boy would announce that watch's eighth turning of the glass.

> *"Good is that which passeth,*
> *better that which cometh,*
> *seven is past and eight floweth,*
> *more shall flow if God willith."*

The boys who sang these verses were sailors-in-training called *gromets*. These boys often served as cabin boys and pages on their first voyages. The youngest ones helped with the ship's religious ceremonies. They sang the blessing every morning and led the hymns.

Gromets also helped take care of the ship. They maintained the ship's compass and made materials to help keep water out of the ship. *Gromets* also swept the decks and served as lookouts. Late at night, when the sea was calm and there was little danger, *gromets* could take the ship's steering wheel. Although some *gromets* were too small to see over the ship's railing, they learned to keep a steady course for the ship.

On his first voyage to the Americas, Christopher Columbus gave orders not to allow *gromets* to steer. He believed that it was too risky. The ships, he felt, were too far from home and in unknown waters. Not all the sailors followed these orders. Columbus reported in his log on December 25, 1492, that there had been an accident involving the *Santa María*, his flagship. "The sailor who was steering the ship decided to go away to sleep and left the [steering] to a ship's boy. . . . The currents of water carried the ship upon one of those banks [coral reefs]." Soon after that collision, the *Santa María* sank.

After a crew mutiny in 1611, explorer Henry Hudson, his young son, and seven others were set adrift in a small boat.

If You Were There *How would you contribute as a crew member on a sailing ship?*

LEFT PAGE: *The Spanish fleet arrives in the English Channel in the late 1500s.*

★ **Using Visual Resources**

International Trade. The engraving of the Spanish Armada on the opposite page shows the size and beauty of the period's sailing ships. Although these ships were Spanish, they contained materials from every region of Europe, including English tin, Hungarian copper, and German and Italian gunpowder. In addition, artisans from many different countries had a hand in building this huge fleet. For example, the Spanish hired expert Genoese carpenters and caulkers. The Spanish king had to hire Protestant Germans to forge the cannons that the ships carried, even though he planned to use the Armada to wage war against Protestants. In fact, many worried that the labor and ideas that British craftspeople had exported to Spain would strengthen the Catholic nation enough that it could conquer England.

CRITICAL THINKING

Why might Spain have needed to rely on the skills and products of so many countries to build the Armada?

ANSWER: Students might suggest that for such a huge undertaking, Spain would have wanted to find the best materials and workers.

1

The World before the Opening of the Atlantic

CHAPTER RESOURCE MANAGER

Objectives	Pacing Guide	Reproducible Resources
SECTION 1: The Earliest Americans (pp. 4–9) ⭐ Explain how the first people arrived in the Americas. ⭐ Describe why the development of agriculture was important. ⭐ Identify some aspects of early Mesoamerican cultures. ⭐ Analyze early societies in North America and their accomplishments.	**Regular** 1.5 days **Block Scheduling** .75 days *Block Scheduling Handbook with Team Teaching Strategies, Chapter 1*	**RS** Guided Reading Strategy 1.1 **SM** Geography Activity 1: The Maya Empire **E** Creative Teaching Strategy: Webbing
SECTION 2: Cultural Areas in North America (pp. 10–16) ⭐ Explain how the environment influenced Native American cultures in North America. ⭐ Describe the types of housing built by Native Americans. ⭐ Examine the various traits of Native Americans in different culture areas.	**Regular** 1.5 days **Block Scheduling** .75 days *Block Scheduling Handbook with Team Teaching Strategies, Chapter 1*	**RS** Guided Reading Strategy 1.2 **RS** Graphic Organizer 1: Native American Groups **PS** Primary Source Reading 1: Iroquois Creation Legend **E** Hands-On History Activity: Native American Cultures of Your Region
SECTION 3: Europe during the Middle Ages (pp. 17–22) ⭐ Identify the new lands that Vikings explored. ⭐ Describe society and daily life during the Middle Ages. ⭐ Examine the role of the Catholic Church in people's lives during the Middle Ages. ⭐ Analyze events that brought about major change in the late Middle Ages.	**Regular** 1.5 days **Block Scheduling** .75 days *Block Scheduling Handbook with Team Teaching Strategies, Chapter 1*	**RS** Guided Reading Strategy 1.3 **PS** Biography Reading 1: Christine de Pisan **PS** Literature Reading 1: *Song of Roland*
SECTION 4: Trade across Continents (pp. 23–27) ⭐ Describe how Islam affected the Mediterranean region. ⭐ Examine the causes that led the Chinese to join in and then withdraw from international trade. ⭐ Explain how trade influenced African kingdoms.	**Regular** 1.5 days **Block Scheduling** .75 days *Block Scheduling Handbook with Team Teaching Strategies, Chapter 1*	**RS** Guided Reading Strategy 1.4

Chapter Resource Key

PS Primary Sources	**A** Assessment	Music
RS Reading Support	**REV** Review	Video
IC Interdisciplinary Connections	**ELL** Reinforcement and English Language Learners	Internet
E Enrichment	🖐 Transparencies	💻 Holt Presentation Maker Using Microsoft® PowerPoint®
SM Skills Mastery	💿 CD-ROM	

 One-Stop Planner CD–ROM

See the *One-Stop Planner* for a complete list of additional resources for students and teachers.

One-Stop Planner CD-ROM

It's easy to plan lessons, select resources, and print out materials for your students when you use the **One-Stop Planner CD-ROM with Test Generator.**

Technology Resources	Reinforcement, Review, and Assessment

 One-Stop Planner, Lesson 1.1
 Linking Geography and History Transparency 1: Americas Landscape Map
 Art in American History Transparency 1: Mesa Verde
 CNN Presents America: Yesterday and Today, Beginnings to 1914 Segment: Preserving the Past
 Holt Researcher: American History CD–ROM
 Homework Practice Online
 HRW Go site

REV Section 1 Review, p. 9
A Daily Quiz 1.1
ELL Main Idea Activity 1.1
ELL English Audio Summary 1.1
ELL Spanish Audio Summary 1.1

 One-Stop Planner, Lesson 1.2
 American Music Selection 1: "Stomp Dance"
 Linking Geography and History Transparency 3: Native American Culture Areas
 Art in American History Transparency 2: Kachina Dolls
 Holt Researcher: American History CD–ROM
 Homework Practice Online
HRW Go site

REV Section 2 Review, p. 16
A Daily Quiz 1.2
ELL Main Idea Activity 1.2
ELL English Audio Summary 1.2
ELL Spanish Audio Summary 1.2

 One-Stop Planner, Lesson 1.3
 Holt Researcher: American History CD–ROM
 Homework Practice Online

REV Section 3 Review, p. 22
A Daily Quiz 1.3
ELL Main Idea Activity 1.3
ELL English Audio Summary 1.3
ELL Spanish Audio Summary 1.3

 One-Stop Planner, Lesson 1.4
 Holt Researcher: American History CD–ROM
 Homework Practice Online

REV Section 4 Review, p. 26
A Daily Quiz 1.4
ELL Main Idea Activity 1.4
ELL English Audio Summary 1.4
ELL Spanish Audio Summary 1.4

internet connect

HRW ONLINE RESOURCES
GO TO: go.hrw.com
Then type in a keyword.

TEACHER HOME PAGE
KEYWORD: SA3 Teacher

CHAPTER INTERNET ACTIVITIES
KEYWORD: SA3 CF1
Choose an activity to:
• learn about Maya Mathematics.
• research Paleolithic culture at Clovis.
• learn about modern Africa and Asia.

CHAPTER ENRICHMENT LINKS
KEYWORD: SA3 CH1

ONLINE ASSESSMENT
Homework Practice
KEYWORD: SA3 HP1

Standardized Test Prep
KEYWORD: SA3 STP1

Rubrics
KEYWORD: SS Rubrics

ONLINE MAPS, CHARTS, AND GRAPHS
KEYWORD: SA3 MCG
• Medieval Manor
• Medieval Trade Routes
• A Monks Day
• Printing Centers in Europe Before 1500
• Medieval Technology

CONTENT UPDATES
KEYWORD: SS Content Updates

HOLT PRESENTATION MAKER
KEYWORD: SA3 PPT1

ONLINE READING SUPPORT
KEYWORD: SS Strategies

CURRENT EVENTS
KEYWORD: S3 Current Events

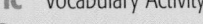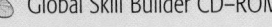
Chapter Review and Assessment

IC Vocabulary Activity 1
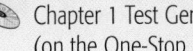 Global Skill Builder CD–ROM
HRW Go site
REV Chapter 1 Tutorial for Students, Parents, Mentors, and Peers
REV Chapter 1 Review, pp. 27–29
Chapter 1 Test Generator (on the One-Stop Planner)
A Chapter 1 Test (Form A or B)

A Alternative Assessment Handbook
A Chapter 1 Test for English Language Learners and Special-Needs Students

---

Meeting Individual Needs

Ability Levels

Level 1 Basic-level activities designed for all students encountering new material

Level 2 Intermediate-level activities designed for average students

Level 3 Challenging activities designed for honors and gifted-and-talented students

English Language Learners Activities that address the needs of students with Limited English Proficiency

Build on What You Know

If You Were There...

Ask students to answer the following question:

What part of the world would you choose to visit in the early 1000s?

Consider:

- the geographic location of new continents
- types of resources to be found in new lands

You Be the Historian

What's Your Opinion?

To help students create their **Themes** Journal entries, provide the following examples of appropriate **agree**/**disagree** statements.

EXPLORING THE TIME LINE

AMERICAN EVENTS

internet connect

TOPIC: Maya Civilization
GO TO: go.hrw.com
KEYWORD: SA3 CF1

Have students access the Internet through the HRW Go site to research Maya glyphs, the counting system that provided the mathematical basis for constructing buildings and keeping track of agriculture and commerce. Students should use the printable activity chart to take notes, and then they should create a model of the Maya mathematical system by solving a math problem using Maya glyphs.

CHAPTER 1

The World before the Opening of the Atlantic
(Beginnings–1500)

The Maya created many complex wall carvings.

Maize was an important crop for many early Americans.

UNITED STATES

c. 38,000–10,000 B.C. Paleo-Indians migrate to the Americas.	**c. 5000 B.C.** Communities in Mexico cultivate corn.	**c. 1200 B.C.** The Olmec civilization appears in Mesoamerica.	**c. A.D. 300** The Maya civilization begins a period of great development in Mesoamerica.

10,000 B.C.   5000 B.C.   1 B.C. / A.D. 1

WORLD

c. 8000 B.C. The Ice Age ends.	**c. 2600 B.C.** The Great Pyramid is built at Giza, Egypt, as the tomb for the pharaoh Cheops.	**509 B.C.** The Roman Republic is established.	**A.D. 800s** Vikings invade England, France, Iceland, and Ireland.

The Egyptian pyramids were considered wonders of the ancient world.

The Romans built aqueducts like this one to carry water to their towns.

Build on What You Know

Native Americans lived in the Americas for thousands of years before the first Europeans arrived after A.D. 1000. During this time, merchants and adventurers around the world traveled great distances in search of land and riches. Trade brought many different cultures into contact with one another.

Culture

Agree The environment creates situations that culture groups within it must respond to.

Disagree Many aspects of a culture group, such as marriage ceremonies, are independent of the environment.

Geography

Agree A group cannot survive if it is unable to grow what it needs to eat.

Disagree A group's survival is dependent upon its knowledge.

Global Relations

Agree Nations that do not trade with other countries cannot survive.

Disagree A nation's strength is determined by its own resources.

This Inca knife is made of gold.

Tenochtitlán was the capital of the mighty Aztec Empire.

A.D. 1100 The Anasazi people begin moving into protected cliff dwellings.

C. A.D. 1250 The ceremonial center of the Mississippi culture in North America begins to decline.

C. A.D. 1325 The Aztec build the great city of Tenochtitlán in Mesoamerica.

C. A.D. 1400 The Inca begin expanding in South America.

| A.D.**1000** | A.D.**1100** | A.D.**1200** | A.D.**1300** | A.D.**1400** |

A.D. 1066 William the Conqueror wins the Battle of Hastings.

A.D. 1099 The crusaders capture Jerusalem.

A.D. 1215 England's King John agrees to Magna Carta—one of the first documents to protect individuals' rights.

A.D. 1368 The Ming dynasty begins in China.

C. A.D. 1400 The African kingdom of Mali breaks apart.

If you were there . . .

What part of the world would you choose to visit in the early 1000s?

You Be the Historian

Themes Journal

What's Your Opinion? Do you **agree** or **disagree** with the following statements? Support your point of view in your journal.

- **Culture** A group's culture is heavily influenced by its environment.
- **Geography** A group's survival depends on its ability to adjust to its environment.
- **Global Relations** Trade is the cause of most contact between cultures.

EXPLORING THE TIME LINE

GLOBAL EVENTS

Constitutional Heritage

Magna Carta. Magna Carta, the document that limited the power of the monarch and promised to protect the rights of citizens, was originally issued in 1215. However, it was updated several times. In 1264 the charter was reissued for the fourth and last time by King John's son, Henry III. The charter was reissued each time in an attempt to keep it up-to-date. However, by the end of the 1200s it became apparent that this process was not practical. In 1297 King Edward I only inspected the charter rather than reissuing it. From that point on, it was clear that Magna Carta was to be only a basis for laws, not a statement of current laws. Magna Carta continued to play an important role in government, serving as a model for many future governments, including that of the United States.

CRITICAL THINKING

What aspects of Magna Carta are reflected in our system of government today?

ANSWER: Students might mention the limited power of the president and the protection of certain rights.

Section 1

OBJECTIVES

* Explain how the first people arrived in the Americas.
* Describe early societies in North America and their accomplishments.
* Identify some aspects of early Mesoamerican culture.
* Analyze why the development of agriculture was important.

Section 1

The Earliest Americans

Read to Discover

1. How did the first people arrive in the Americas?
2. Why was the development of agriculture important?
3. What were some aspects of early Mesoamerican cultures?
4. What early societies existed in North America, and what were their accomplishments?

WHY IT MATTERS TODAY

People continue to move to new places in search of better living conditions. Use CNNfyi.com or other **current events** sources to identify a group that is currently migrating to a new home. Record your findings in your journal.

Define

* archaeology
* artifacts
* migration
* hunter-gatherers
* environments
* societies
* culture
* domestication
* maize
* glyphs

Identify

* Paleo-Indians

The Story Begins

When the world was young, there were only "the trees, the moon, the sun, water, and a few animals." So begins the creation story told by some northwestern Native Americans. In this emptiness, the Raven walked along the beach. The lonely bird wished for company. To Raven's surprise, a clam rose up from the sand. The clam opened and out came a crowd of tiny people. Raven "sang a beautiful song of great joy." He was happy because "he had brought the first people to the world." This story is just one of many different ways that Native Americans explain their origins.

The Raven was an important figure in some Native American myths.

The First Migration to the Americas

Many scientists believe that people first arrived in North America during the last Ice Age. At the start of the Ice Age, the world grew colder. Water froze into huge moving ice sheets called glaciers, which locked up large amounts of water. As a result, ocean levels dropped more than 300 feet lower than they are today. When the water level fell, a land bridge appeared between northeastern Asia and present-day Alaska. Geographers call this landmass Beringia.

Have students read Section 1 and complete Guided Reading Strategy 1.1. Choose one or more of the following activities to explore the section content with students. For further suggestions on block scheduling or team teaching, see the *Block Scheduling Handbook with Team Teaching Strategies*.

LEVEL 1: Pair students. Then have each pair to pose questions to his or her partner about the first Americans, focusing on their route to the Americas and the estimated dates of their arrival. *(Students' answers should indicate that the first Americans were hunter-gatherers from Asia who crossed Beringia into present-day Alaska between 50,000 and 10,000 B.C.)* Provide students with an outline map of Asia and North America. Have pairs draw the routes that the first Americans took from Asia across Beringia into North America.
ENGLISH LANGUAGE LEARNERS , COOPERATIVE LEARNING

No one knows exactly when people crossed into North America. The travelers from Asia left no written records. Instead, historians rely on **archaeology**—the study of the unwritten past. Archaeologists look at **artifacts**, or remains of objects made by humans. Artifacts suggest that **Paleo-Indians**, or the first Americans, crossed into Alaska sometime between 38,000 and 10,000 B.C.

This **migration**—a movement of people from one region to another—took place over a long period of time. Most archaeologists believe the Paleo-Indians first crossed over the land bridge in search of animals to hunt. One archaeologist described what the land crossing might have looked like.

History Makers Speak

❝The low lying land bridge was no landscape of gently waving grass. . . .[it] was a treeless, arctic land, covered with a patchwork of very different types of vegetation.❞

—Brian M. Fagan, *Ancient North America*

Analyzing Primary Sources

Drawing Inferences and Conclusions What does this quote suggest about the harshness of the journey across the Beringia land bridge? The journey was probably difficult because of the barren environment.

Most Paleo-Indians and their descendants traveled into present-day Canada, the United States, and Mexico. Eventually their descendants reached as far as the tip of South America. The Paleo-Indians were **hunter-gatherers**. They lived by hunting animals and gathering wild plants. They also made stone tools to hunt large animals such as mammoths.

✔ **Reading Check: Finding the Main Idea** When and how did the first people come to the Americas? between 38,000 and 10,000 B.C.; across the Beringia between northeastern Asia and present-day Alaska

☐ internet connect

TOPIC: Archaeology in North America
GO TO: go.hrw.com
KEYWORD: SA3 CF1

Have students access the Internet through the HRW Go site to research Paleolithic cultures in North America. Then have students take notes on cultural artifacts and tools found at Clovis, New Mexico. Ask students to draw an artifact found at the Clovis site. Students should label their drawings and explain how the artifact represents Paleolithic humans.

Visual Record Answer

1. *Asia*
2. *Students' answers will vary.*

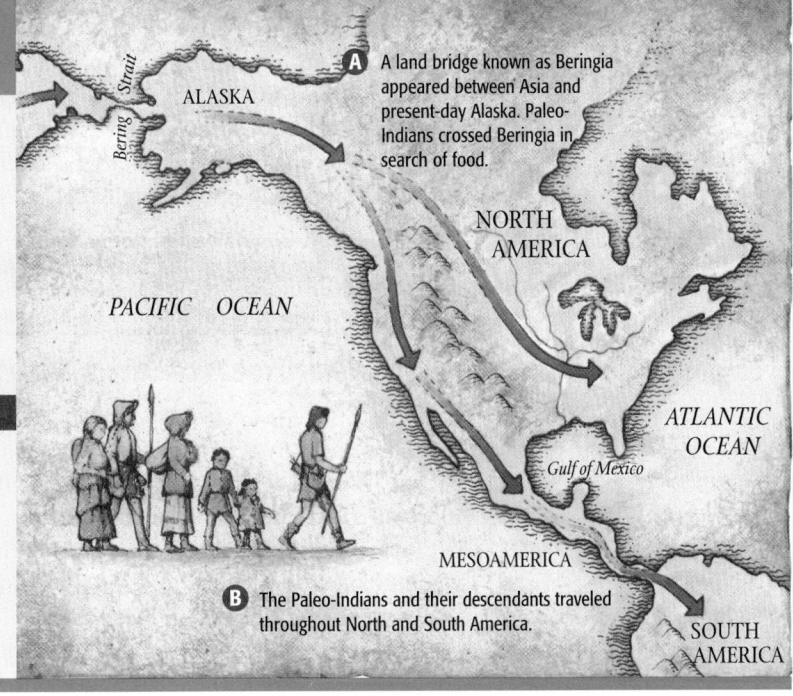

Migration to the Americas

During the Ice Age much of the world grew very cold. Water froze into huge moving ice sheets called glaciers. Ocean levels dropped more than 300 feet lower than they are today.

Visualizing History

1. **Geography** Where did the Paleo-Indians come from?

2. **Connecting to Today** What methods do people use to come to the Americas today?

Ⓐ A land bridge known as Beringia appeared between Asia and present-day Alaska. Paleo-Indians crossed Beringia in search of food.

ALASKA

Bering Strait

NORTH AMERICA

PACIFIC OCEAN

ATLANTIC OCEAN

Gulf of Mexico

MESOAMERICA

Ⓑ The Paleo-Indians and their descendants traveled throughout North and South America.

SOUTH AMERICA

ALL LEVELS: Tell students to imagine that they are Paleo-Indians who have recently arrived in the Americas. Have each student create a series of cave drawings illustrating the journey. Then tell students to imagine that they are modern-day archaeologists. Have students create captions explaining their cave drawings. **ENGLISH LANGUAGE LEARNERS**

Note: For an additional teaching idea, see the Chapter 1 Webbing activity in the **Creative Teaching Strategies** handbook.

 ALL LEVELS: Copy the following graphic organizer onto the chalkboard, omitting the italicized answers. Ask students to complete the organizer by providing the appropriate effects of the development of agriculture. Then lead a class discussion on the effects of the development of agriculture on societies. **ENGLISH LANGUAGE LEARNERS**

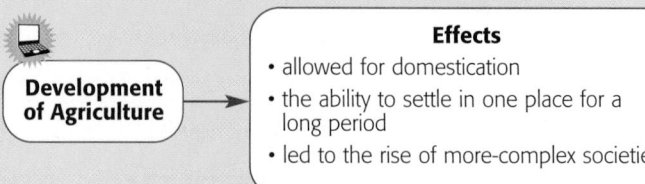

Development of Agriculture →
Effects
• allowed for domestication
• the ability to settle in one place for a long period
• led to the rise of more-complex societies

Using Visual Resources

Maya Glyphs. Scientists struggled for years to decipher the glyphs, like the ones on the artifact pictured on page 7, found at Maya sites. Finally, in the 1970s a small group of scholars combined several different theories and determined that the glyphs were not just pictoral representations of historical events. They actually represented a spoken language. Although interpretations of the glyphs have met with controversy, it is known that Maya writing was very complex and was used for much more than just to record events. Carved into buildings and tombs and written on bark paper, the glyphs are thought to have been used to teach history, describe rituals, and to dedicate buildings.

CRITICAL THINKING

Why would deciphering the Maya writings have been so important for scientists?

ANSWER: Students might suggest that scientists could learn much more about the true Maya history if they could understand their written language.

CONNECTING TO SCIENCE AND TECHNOLOGY ANSWER

Since they know half the carbon 14 decays in 50,000 years, scientists can measure the amount of carbon 14 left in a dead object to figure out its age.

 CONNECTING TO SCIENCE AND TECHNOLOGY

Discovering the Distant Past

Archaeologists use scientific tests to determine the age of artifacts. In 1949 Willard Libby developed carbon-14 dating. This highly accurate test measures the amount of carbon 14—a form of carbon atom—that exists in an artifact. Before the use of carbon-14 dating, archaeologists used unreliable methods to guess the age of artifacts.

Scientists know that half the carbon 14 in a dead plant or animal decays about every 5,000 years. After 50,000 years almost all the carbon 14 is gone. Knowing this, archaeologists measure the amount of carbon 14 in a fossil or artifact. This measurement is then used to figure out its age. Today scientists can also use other advanced methods to date objects older than 50,000 years. How do scientists use carbon 14 to determine the age of artifacts?

⭐ Adapting to a New Climate

When the Ice Age ended about 8000 B.C., the world's climate changed. Rising temperatures melted glaciers. The oceans rose, covering Beringia with water. As late as 1000 B.C. people continued to come to North America using small boats.

The warmer weather at the end of the Ice Age created many new **environments**—climates and landscapes that surround living things. Short grasses replaced the taller grasses that had fed giant animals such as the mammoth. These animals either died out naturally or were hunted to extinction by Native Americans. However, large herds of smaller animals such as buffalo and deer ate the new short grasses. Paleo-Indians adapted to the changes by hunting these animals. People also ate more berries, roots, and seeds.

Different environments influenced the development of Native American **societies**. A society is a group that shares a common **culture**—a set of common values and traditions. These traits include language, government, and family relationships. Like all societies, Native American groups changed over time.

The earliest farming societies in the Americas began in Mesoamerica, or Middle America, and South America. Mesoamerica includes southern Mexico and northern Central America. People in this region learned to breed and grow wild plants to create food crops. This process of breeding plants or animals to meet human needs is called **domestication**.

Archaeologists in Mexico have found signs of the first **maize**, or corn, grown by people. People in Mesoamerica also grew beans and peppers. In eastern North America, Native Americans domesticated plants by about 2000 B.C. In the Southwest, agricultural methods were introduced from Mesoamerica between 1000 and 750 B.C. Agriculture allowed many Native American groups to settle in villages. It thus led to the rise of larger and more complex societies.

✔ **Reading Check: Analyzing Information** How did the end of the Ice Age help make the rise of civilizations in North America possible?
allowed domestication, the development of agriculture, and the ability to settle in one place for a long period and to build complex societies

⭐ Mesoamerica and South America

Some of the earliest American civilizations developed in Mesoamerica. The Olmec society was one of the first. It has been called the "mother culture" because it highly influenced most later civilizations in Mesoamerica. The Olmec developed along the Mexican Gulf Coast between about 1200 and 400 B.C. During that time Olmec priests created number and calendar systems. They invented a method of writing that used **glyphs**, or symbols that represent ideas.

The Maya civilization thrived in southeastern Mesoamerica from about A.D 300 to 900. The Maya built many large stone temples, palaces, and bridges. The city of Tikal was an important Maya center. The Maya created several calendars. They also studied mathematics and astronomy. By about A.D. 900 the Maya civilization started to decline. Historians are not sure why this took place.

About A.D. 1200, Aztec invaders came south and occupied the central valley of Mexico. The center of Aztec civilization was Tenochtitlán (tay-nawch-teet-LAHN). Present-day Mexico City was built on the site of this ancient city. Tenochtitlán stood in the middle of a huge lake, with raised highways connecting the city to the shore. It is thought that as many as 300,000 people may have lived in this great capital.

The Aztec created a large empire by conquering most of their neighbors. The empire had a vast trading network involving goods such as cocoa, gold, and jade. However, the Aztec knew that their success might not last. They expressed this idea in their poetry.

Primary Sources

❝Truly do we live on earth?
Not forever on earth; only a little
    while here.
Although it be jade, it will be
    broken,
Although it be gold, it is
    crushed. . . .
Not forever on earth; only a little
    while here.❞

—King Nezahualcóyotl, quoted in
Aztec Thought and Culture by Miguel León-Portilla

While the Aztec were thriving in Mexico, the Inca created their own civilization in South America. The Inca civilization began high in the Andes. In the A.D. 1400s they started to conquer surrounding lands. Eventually, the Inca ruled an area stretching from present-day Ecuador to central Chile. Across this empire the Inca built a network of roads some 25,000 miles long. These roads let armies and messengers move quickly. The Inca built palaces and temples in their capital city of Cuzco (KOO-skoh). Decorated with gold and silver, the palaces had beautiful gardens and bathrooms with running water. Most Inca subjects lived in villages. They were allowed to keep their own land and many of their customs. But families did have to dig canals and grow crops to help feed the Inca Empire.

✔ **Reading Check: Comparing** List some cultural developments of the Mesoamerican and South American civilizations. Olmec: architecture, number and calendar systems, writing system; Inca: transportation network, architecture, irrigation system; Maya: stone temples, palaces, bridges, calendars, mathematics, and astronomy; Aztec: large capital, empire, and trading network.

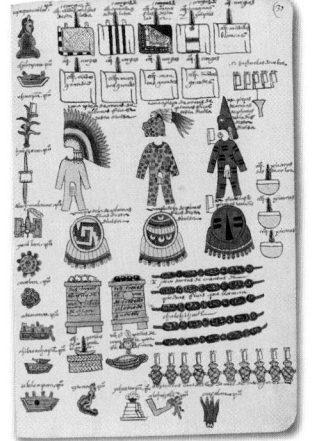

The Aztec used tax records like this one to keep track of their wealth.

⭐ CLOSE

Ask students to list all of the early American societies discussed in this section. After the list is completed, organize the class into small groups. Provide each group with colored note cards so each group has a different color. Assign each group one of the societies students listed. Then have each group develop a list of questions about the assigned society and its contributions to the development of civilization. Ask students to write each question on one side of a note card and the answer to that question on the other side of the note card, until all of the questions have been answered. Group members should take turns quizzing one another on the questions they created.
COOPERATIVE LEARNING

⭐ Early North American Societies

Although less populated than South America and Mesoamerica, North America had several farming cultures. These cultures had to adapt to very different environments. For example, in the southwestern region of the present-day United States there was little rainfall for farming. As a result, Native Americans created irrigation systems to bring water to crops, allowing groups to build permanent settlements.

The Anasazi (ah-nuh-SAH-zee) lived in the Four Corners region, where present-day Arizona, Colorado, New Mexico, and Utah meet. They built their pueblos, or villages, among high hills and deep canyons. Anasazi pueblos were made mostly of cut stone or adobe—sun-baked clay and straw. Many pueblos were multistory buildings with ladders connecting the different levels. Pueblo Bonito in New Mexico's Chaco Canyon has five stories and 800 rooms.

The Anasazi built their early pueblos on mesas, or flat-topped hills. Later, about A.D. 1100, they began building their homes into cliffsides for defense. By A.D. 1300, some Anasazi began to leave the larger pueblos. Drought or war may have driven them away.

In eastern and midwestern North America, advanced cultures developed between 1000 B.C. and A.D. 1250. The Hopewell culture arose between 300 and 200 B.C. The Hopewell lived along the Mississippi,

Interpreting the Visual Record

Mesa Verde *Southwestern Indians built cliff dwellings, like this one in Mesa Verde, to protect themselves from harsh weather and enemy attacks.* **Why would the location of these buildings have offered protection?**

★ REVIEW AND ASSESS

Have students complete the **Section 1 Review** on p. 9. Then have students complete **Daily Quiz 1.1**. As **Alternative Assessment**, you may want to use the outline map or agriculture graphic organizer in this section's lessons.

★ RETEACH

Have students complete **Main Idea Activity for English Language Learners and Special-Needs Students 1.1**. Then organize students into small groups. Assign each group a subsection. Tell groups to develop five questions about the main ideas in the assigned subsections. Then have groups exchange questions until all groups have answered all other groups'

questions. Go over the questions and answers with the class to ensure that students have given the correct answers.

ENGLISH LANGUAGE LEARNERS, **COOPERATIVE LEARNING**

★ EXTEND

Organize the class into small groups. Assign each group one specific Native American culture—the Olmec, Maya, Toltec, Aztec, Inca, Anasazi, Adena, or Hopewell. Have each group research the region in which the assigned culture lived and the ways in which geography influenced each of the following: food, clothing, shelter, transportation, and defense. Have each group share its findings with the class.

COOPERATIVE LEARNING, **BLOCK SCHEDULING**

Interpreting the Visual Record

Burial mounds *The ancient mound builders constructed the Great Serpent Mound near what is now Hillsboro, Ohio.* **How do you think this mound got its present name?**

Ohio, and lower Missouri River valleys. They built large burial mounds, some 30 feet tall, to honor their dead. The Hopewell supported their large populations with agriculture and trade. However, by about A.D. 400, the Hopewell no longer dominated the region. Archaeologists have yet to discover why the Hopewell culture declined.

The Mississippians were another widespread farming culture that relied on trade. Like the Hopewell, the Mississippians also had religious practices honoring the dead. From about A.D. 700 to the early 1500s, the Mississippian people lived along the Ohio and Mississippi Rivers. Mississippians built pyramid mounds out of solid earth. Religious ceremonies were held on top of these pyramids. The largest of these is Monks Mound, near Cahokia (kuh-HOH-kee-uh), Illinois. Monks Mound covers 16 acres and stands 98 feet tall.

✔ **Reading Check: Summarizing** What were some features of early North American cultures? Anasazi—multistory adobe dwellings on mesas and cliff-sides; Hopewell—mound building to honor dead; Mississippians—earth pyramids

Section 1 Review

go.hrw.com **Homework Practice Online**
keyword: SA3 HP1

1 Define and explain:
• archaeology
• artifacts
• migration
• hunter-gatherers
• environments
• societies
• culture
• domestication
• maize
• glyphs

2 Identify and explain:
• Paleo-Indians

3 Summarizing Copy the chart below. Use it to identify the early societies in the Americas, where they were located, and one major accomplishment of each society.

Early American Societies	Location	Accomplishments

4 Finding the Main Idea
a. What events made it possible for Paleo-Indians to migrate to North America?

b. Why do you think that growing crops such as maize was important to many early Native American civilizations?

5 Writing and Critical Thinking
Analyzing Information Imagine that you are a visitor to one of the early Mesoamerican cultures. Write a letter to a friend describing the society you encounter.

Consider the following:
• the time period of the culture
• the location and physical environment of the society
• the society's cultural accomplishments

★ ★ ★ ★ ★ ★ ★
Section 1 Review
ANSWERS

1 Define
• archaeology, p. 5
• artifacts, p. 5
• migration, p. 5
• hunter-gatherers, p. 5
• environments, p. 6
• societies, p. 6
• culture, p. 6
• domestication, p. 6
• maize, p. 6
• glyphs, p. 6

2 Identify
• Paleo-Indians, p. 5

3 Olmec—Mexican Gulf Coast, calender, glyphs; Maya—southeastern Mesoamerica, mathematics, astronomy; Aztec—central Mexico, trade; Inca—Ecuador to central Chile, roads, canals, crops; Anasazi—Four Corners, pueblos; Hopewell—Mississippi, Ohio, and Missouri River valleys, burial mounds; Mississippian—Ohio and Mississippi Rivers, pyramid mounds

4 a. glaciers locked up large amounts of water, causing sea levels to drop and exposing the Beringia land bridge
b. such crops provided a staple food source allowing people to settle one area for a long time

5 Students letters will vary but should include the following: Olmec—between about 1200 and 400 B.C., Mexican Gulf Coast, number and calendar systems, writing system using glyphs; Maya—about A.D. 300 to about A.D. 900, great stone temples, palaces, and bridges, calendars, mathematical and astronomical systems; Aztec—about A.D. 1200, central Mexico, great capital Tenochtitlán, a large empire, a vast trading network

Section 2

OBJECTIVES

* Explain how the environment influenced Native American cultures in North America.
* Describe the types of housing built by Native Americans.
* Examine the various traits of Native Americans in different culture areas.

LET'S GET STARTED!

Write the word *culture* on the chalkboard. As students enter the classroom, have them write their own definitions of this word. Then ask students to explain what characteristics define a culture. Write their responses on the chalkboard. (*Students' responses may include food, language, customs, economy, hobbies, agriculture, music, and so on.*) Explain to students that in Section 2 they will learn about several Native American cultures and how the regions in which these culture groups lived influenced their daily lives.

Section 2

Cultural Areas in North America

Read to Discover

1. How did the environment influence Native American cultures in North America?
2. What types of housing did Native Americans build?
3. What were various traits of Native Americans in different culture areas?

WHY IT MATTERS TODAY

Many Native Americans still practice ancient cultural traditions. Use CNNfyi.com or other **current events** sources to find out about a Native American tradition being followed today. Examples might include storytelling, art, or dance. Record your findings in your journal.

Define

* kayaks
* igloos
* totems
* potlatches
* kivas
* wigwams
* longhouses

Identify

* Iroquois League

Southwestern Native Americans often decorated their pottery with animal symbols.

The Story Continues

Native Americans developed customs based on their close ties to the land. Many tribes in the American Southwest held dances that celebrated the importance of the Sun and rain. One Native American song called the Southwest "a House Made of Dawn . . . made of pollen and of rain." The Inuit of the Far North lived on land too cold to grow crops. They held ceremonies to help them hunt wild game. Native Americans across the continent adapted their lifestyles to their surroundings.

⭐ The Far North

Researchers use culture areas—the geographic locations that influenced societies—to help them describe ancient Native American peoples. The Far North of North America is divided into the Arctic and Subarctic culture areas. Few plants grow in the Arctic because the ground is always frozen. The Aleut and the Inuit adapted to these harsh conditions. The Inuit lived in present-day northern Alaska and Canada, and the Aleut lived in western Alaska. The two groups shared many cultural traits,

★ TEACH

⏱ Have students read Section 2 and complete Guided Reading Strategy 1.2. Choose one or more of the following activities to explore the section content with students. For further suggestions on block scheduling or team teaching, see the *Block Scheduling Handbook with Team Teaching Strategies.*

Note: To help students make meaningful connections between events in American history and those in their own hometown, use the Chapter 1 **Hands-On History** activity, Native American Cultures of Your Region.

LEVEL 1: Write the name of each North American region on a slip of paper and put the slips in a hat. Organize the class into small groups and have each group choose a slip of paper. Provide each group with a sheet of butcher paper and colored pencils. Then have each group draw a scene that illustrates the lifestyle of the people in the region that was chosen. Have students refer to the text and class notes to find information about the area they were assigned. Encourage students to include details such as primary food sources, housing styles, climate, and landscape. Display illustrations around the classroom and have students compare the different lifestyles of each region. **ENGLISH LANGUAGE LEARNERS** , **COOPERATIVE LEARNING**

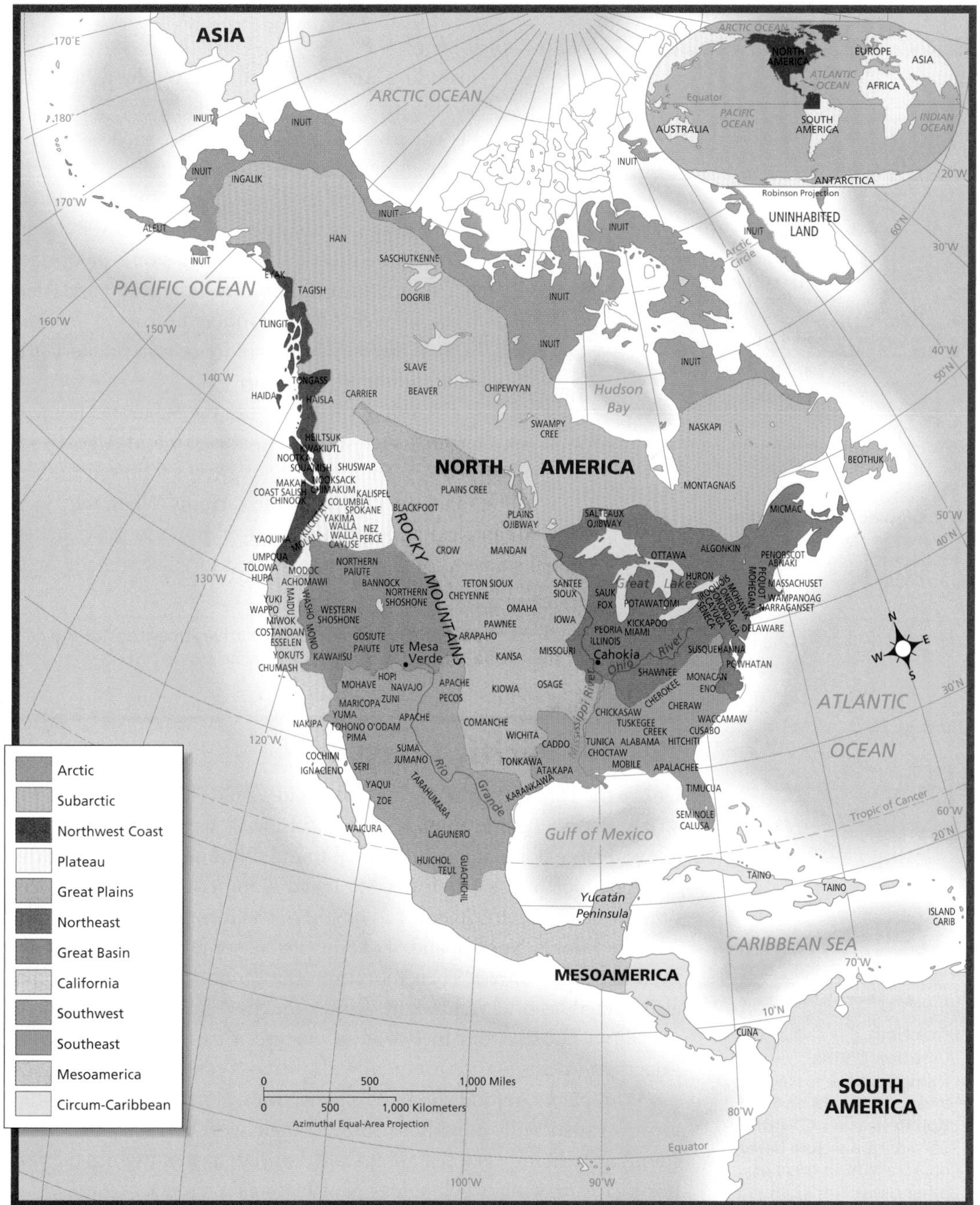

Native American Culture Areas

Interpreting Maps Various Native American cultures inhabited the Americas. These cultures adapted to a wide range of climatic and geographic regions.

Skills Assessment Environment and Society How might the geography and climate of an area influence the culture that develops there?

Interdisciplinary Connection

▶Science◀

Snowshoes and Toboggans. Subarctic peoples lived on snow-covered land for a large part of the year. To better survive in such a harsh climate, they developed snowshoes— oval or round bent-wood frames with webbing like a tennis racket's—to allow people to walk on snow without sinking. They also developed toboggans, which are long flat sleds. Toboggans could be loaded with supplies and pulled with relative ease by dogs or humans.

CRITICAL THINKING

Why do you think snowshoes were a particularly important development?

ANSWER: Students might say that snowshoes allowed people to travel more quickly and more safely and that they kept people's feet out of the snow.

Technology Resources

 Linking Geography and History Transparency 3: Native American Culture Areas

MAP ANSWER

Cultures must adapt their ways of gathering food, establishing communities, and building shelter to the environment in which they live.

Types of Houses					
	igloos	wood	animal skins	wigwams	longhouses
Inuit	X	X			
Aleut	*X*	*X*			
Athabascan		*X*	*X*		
Algonquian		*X*	*X*		
Tlingin		*X*			
Nootka		*X*			
Skokomish		*X*			
Comanche			*X*		
Blackfoot			*X*		
Teton Sioux			*X*		
Arapaho			*X*		
Wampanoag				*X*	
Pequot				*X*	
Iroquois					*X*

The Inuit used kayaks to cross icy waters in the Arctic. They also made carvings from walrus bones.

including language. Both survived by fishing and by hunting large mammals. They also both depended on dogs for many tasks, such as hunting and pulling sleds.

In addition to dogsleds, the Inuit and Aleut used **kayaks**, or one-person canoes covered with skins. Some Inuit built earthen, stone, or wooden houses partly underground. Other Inuit and Aleut built aboveground wooden houses. The Inuit sometimes used blocks of ice or other materials to build **igloos** for housing.

South of the Arctic lies the Subarctic, home to groups such as the Athabascan and Algonquian peoples. Each year these groups followed the seasonal migrations of the caribou. When they went on a hunt, the Athabascan and Algonquian lived in temporary shelters made of animal skins. At other times they lived in villages made up of log houses.

✔ **Reading Check: Summarizing** How did the Native Americans of the Far North get their food? *fishing, hunting large mammals*

⭐ The Pacific Coast

Unlike the Far North, the Pacific Coast had a mild climate. The area had a rich supply of game animals, sea life, and wild plants. These resources allowed large populations to develop that did not need to rely on farming. The Northwest Coast area stretched along the shoreline between present-day southern Alaska and northern California.

The Tlingit, Nootka, and Skokomish were some of the peoples who lived in the Northwest. Their most important food was salmon, but they also hunted sea otters and whales from large canoes. People in the Northwest built houses from the wood of evergreen trees. They also carved images of **totems**—ancestor or animal spirits—on tall wooden poles.

With plenty of food and building materials, Northwest Coast culture groups prospered. Individuals showed their wealth and earned social standing by holding special events called **potlatches**. At these gatherings hosts gave away many belongings in order to gain respect.

Farther south along the coast was the California region, which had several climates. Native Americans living in this area had many food sources available year-round, so farming was not necessary. Their major food plant was acorns, which they ground into a flour. They also fished and hunted deer and other game. Most Native Americans in the California region lived in isolated groups of families. Each of these groups had

LEVEL 2: Explain to students that the environment influenced the way each Native American culture developed. For example, the Inuit of the Far North lived in the Arctic culture area and survived by fishing and hunting large animals. Write the following culture areas and environment descriptions on the chalkboard. Have students use their textbooks to match the culture areas with the appropriate environment. Then have students write one way a Native American group in each culture area had to adapt to its environment. (*Students' answers should indicate culture areas—Arctic and Subarctic; Northwest Coast; California; West; Southwest;* *Great Basin; Great Plains; Southeast; Northeast. Environmental characteristics include the following: few plants, frozen ground; mild climate, rich supply of game and wild plants; several climates, plentiful supply of food; less rainfall than Pacific Coast, fewer resources; dry climate, varied landscape from deserts to forests; dry climate, small animals; grasslands with millions of buffalo and other herd animals; rich in sources of food and shelter, mainly forests, large rivers and swamps; Great Lakes, cold winters.*) The culture areas and descriptions are listed in correct matching order. Be sure to scramble the order of the listed items before writing them on the chalkboard.

a small population of only 50 to 300. Among these Native Americans—which included the Pomo, Hupa, and Yurok—more than 100 different languages were spoken.

✔ **Reading Check: Finding the Main Idea** How did the environment influence the food sources for Native Americans in the California and Northwest Coast regions? The mild climate allowed for a plentiful supply of game, which meant they did not have to rely on agriculture.

★ The West and Southwest

The West and Southwest of the present-day United States received less rain than the Far West. As a result, the people had fewer resources than their neighbors on the Pacific Coast. Although they did not practice agriculture, groups in the dry Columbia Plateau region lived in permanent villages. Native Americans living near rivers fished for salmon, hunted small game, and gathered plants. These groups included the Flathead, Modoc, and Nez Percé.

Native Americans faced more difficulties surviving in the much drier Great Basin region. They adapted to the dry climate by gathering seeds, digging roots, and trapping small animals for food. They also ate ants, crickets, lizards, and rabbits. Rabbits were highly valued because they provided meat as well as fur and skins for blankets and clothing. Most Native Americans of the Great Basin lived in small family groups that moved often in search of food. Most groups in this region spoke variations of the same language. These groups included the Paiute, Shoshone, and Ute.

Native Americans of the Southwest also had to adapt to a dry climate. This region's landscape varied from deserts to evergreen forests. Southwestern culture groups included the Apache, Navajo, and Pueblo. The

---

CONNECTING TO

THE ARTS

Totems In parts of Alaska and British Columbia, Native Americans practice a unique and striking ancient tradition. Artists carve images of ravens, bears, fish, and human beings into towering totem poles. The Tlingit, Nootka, and other groups have long used these poles to tell important stories.

To create the poles, the artist first listens to the story that the purchaser wants to have shown. These tales can be personal, family, or tribal stories. Then the artist designs and carves the work. After the totem pole's completion, the buyer hosts a potlatch to dedicate it and raise it into place. During the potlatch, singers and actors often perform the pole's story. **How do totem poles reflect the relationship between people in the Northwest Coast culture area and their environment?**

Games. The Native Americans of the California cultural area were passionate game players. Their many games of chance and skill were popular with children and adults alike. Games included attempting to catch a hoop on a stick, ball games similar to soccer, and counting and guessing games. Women often played counting games using sticks, shells, or pebbles, while men usually played guessing games involving objects hidden in a person's hands.

CRITICAL THINKING

Why do you think games were so popular among many American Indian peoples?

ANSWER: Students might suggest that playing games helped people to relax and enjoy each other's company. Students might also suggest that these American Indian peoples valued skill, whether in games or serious pursuits.

CONNECTING TO THE ARTS ANSWER
Poles are made of trees—an abundant resource in the Northwest. Totems are images of local wildlife.

HOMEWORK Have students design a book jacket for a book about houses built by various Native American culture groups. The book jacket should include the title, a cover illustration, and a brief summary of the book's content. The summary of the book should include the various types of houses Native Americans built, which groups built each type of house, and why certain groups built specific types of houses.

LEVELS 2 AND 3: Write the following Native American group names on the chalkboard: *Inuit, Algonquian, Pomo, Nez Percé, Ute, Pueblo, Mandan,* and *Iroquois.* Ask students to choose two of the groups and have them write an outline for a documentary film about their groups. Outlines should address the types of housing each group had, its methods for gathering food, and any other significant cultural trait associated with each group.

Linking Past to Present

Religious Rituals. Many ancient Native American rituals and ceremonies were passed down from generation to generation. Some have even been preserved, at least in part, to the present day. In the Southwest, Navajo and Pueblo Indians still perform the elaborate rituals of their ancestors. The Pueblo, for example, still perform the ceremonies representing the cycles of the year with dances, songs, and prayers.

CRITICAL THINKING

Why have some Native American religious rituals endured?

ANSWER: Students might suggest that religion was probably central to most cultures; so passing on the sacred rituals would have been of primary importance.

Technology Resources
Art in American History
Transparency 2:
Kachina Dolls

Technology Resources
American Music
Selection 1:
"Stomp Dance"

Visual Record Answer

Students might suggest that certain aspects of the costumes are similar, while the faces appear to be different.

Interpreting the Visual Record

Kachinas *Southwestern Native Americans such as the Zuni believed in ancestral spirits called kachinas, who were often represented in ceremonies by costumed dancers. This wooden doll is a model of a kachina dancer. Sandpaintings also had important ceremonial uses. This Navajo blanket was based on a sandpainting design.* **What is similar and different about the figures shown in these two images?**

Pueblo were farmers who irrigated their land to grow crops. Other tribes, such as the Apache, hunted game and gathered plants for food. These groups also raided the villages of farming groups such as the Pueblo.

The Pueblo people had many religious festivals. These rituals focused on the two key areas of Pueblo life—rain and maize. Pueblo religious activities were held in **kivas**—round ceremonial rooms.

 Reading Check: Finding the Main Idea How did Native Americans adapt to the dry environment of the West and Southwest? by using a variety of methods to obtain food, such as hunting, irrigation, agriculture, and raiding other villages

★ The Great Plains

The huge Great Plains region stretches south from Canada into Texas. This culture area is bounded by the Mississippi Valley on the east and the Rocky Mountains on the west. The Plains were mainly grassland, on which millions of buffalo and other game grazed in herds. The Mandan lived in the northern Plains, while the Pawnee lived on the central Plains. Both groups grew crops such as beans, maize, and squash. Like some other Native American groups, the Pawnee society was matrilineal. This means that people traced their ancestry through their mothers, rather than through their fathers. In addition, when a couple married, the husband moved into the wife's home.

Several Native American groups, such as the Apache, lived in the southern Plains. People in this area hunted buffalo on foot and gathered berries, nuts, and vegetables. Some groups grew to depend largely on the buffalo for clothing, food, and shelter.

Many other Native Americans lived on the eastern or western borders of the Plains. These groups included the Arapaho, Blackfoot, Comanche, and Teton Sioux. Hunters among the Blackfoot sometimes killed huge numbers of buffalo by chasing the animals over steep cliffs.

14

★ The East

Unlike the Great Plains, eastern North America was rich in sources for food and shelter. The East was mainly forest. The Mississippi River and the Everglades—a huge swamp in what is now Florida—also provided many resources.

Native Americans of the Southeast included the Cherokee, Creek, Natchez, and Seminole. The Natchez were direct descendants of the ancient Mississippian people. Most southeastern groups lived in villages along river valleys. They relied mainly on farming but also hunted game, gathered plants, fished, and traded. Each of these groups was led by a village council.

Northeastern tribes lived in a broad area stretching west from the Atlantic Ocean to the Mississippi Valley. This area extended north to the Great Lakes region and south into present-day Virginia and North Carolina. The Algonquian and Iroquois peoples were the two main groups of the Northeast. Some Algonquian peoples lived north of the Great Lakes. These groups could not farm all year-round because the climate in this northern region was too cold. They survived by hunting and by gathering edible plants.

Other Algonquian peoples, including the Wampanoag and Pequot, lived farther south. In the warmer areas they farmed, hunted, gathered plants, and fished in rivers and the ocean. These groups lived in

Daily Life

Hunting buffalo Buffalo are large, powerful animals that once roamed the Great Plains in huge herds. Hunting these creatures was not an easy task for early Native Americans. But the buffalo could provide for so many needs, including food and clothing, that it was worth the risk to hunt them. Here two Native American hunters wearing wolf skins try to get close enough to bring down a buffalo. **Why do you think these hunters are wearing wolf skins?**

★ REVIEW AND ASSESS

Have students complete the **Section 2 Review** on p. 16. Then have students complete **Daily Quiz 1.2**. As **Alternative Assessment**, you may want to use the housing graphic organizer or the documentary film outline in this section's lessons.

★ RETEACH

Have students complete **Main Idea Activity for English Language Learners and Special-Needs Students 1.2**. Then have students create an outline of the most important information from the section. Ask them to leave some of the categories incomplete and then have students exchange outlines and fill in the missing information. **ENGLISH LANGUAGE LEARNERS , COOPERATIVE LEARNING**

★ EXTEND

Have students use the library or search the Internet through the HRW Go site to obtain information about one of the types of Native American housing discussed in this section. Then have each student construct a scale model of the type of housing that he or she researched. Encourage students to incorporate materials that Native Americans used if possible. Have students show their models to the class and explain how they built them. After the presentations, lead a class discussion comparing and contrasting the various types of housing. **BLOCK SCHEDULING**

Section 2 Review
ANSWERS

❶ Define
- kayaks, p. 12
- igloos, p. 12
- totems, p. 12
- potlatches, p. 12
- kivas, p. 14
- wigwams, p. 16
- longhouses, p. 16

❷ Identify
- Iroquois League, p. 16

❸ Far North—extreme cold, few plants and animals, hunters and fishers, built houses of wood, earth, or ice; Southwest—dry environment with relatively few resources, irrigated crops and hunted; East—abundant resources, practiced agriculture, as well as hunting and fishing, built permanent housing structures such as longhouses, out of wood

❹ a. Far North: housing—wooden, stone, or earthen houses partially underground, above-ground wooden houses, igloos; food sources—hunting large mammals, fishing. Southwest: housing—adobe pueblos; food sources—irrigated crops, hunting, gathering, raiding
b. Students may suggest that following herds for hunting prevented permanent settlements.

❺ Students' paragraphs will vary but should consider how food is obtained, the type of shelter, and other cultural traits particular to the chosen tribe.

Iroquois warriors such as the one shown here had great success in warfare.

permanent villages. Some built large multifamily lodges, while others lived in small **wigwams**, or round huts.

To the east of the Algonquian lived the Iroquois. Unlike other Native American women, Iroquois women controlled the material goods of their people. They also oversaw most parts of community life. The Iroquois relied mostly on farming for food, although they also hunted and traded with other tribes. Men were responsible for hunting and trading. Women grew and harvested crops.

The Iroquois lived in **longhouses**, or rectangular homes made from logs and bark. Longhouses ranged from 50 to 100 feet long and housed 8 to 10 families each. Fences of pointed stakes surrounded longhouses for defense. Neighboring tribes feared the military skills of the Iroquois.

The Iroquois also developed the **Iroquois League**. This political confederation was made up of the Cayuga, Mohawk, Oneida, Onondaga, and Seneca. The League was responsible for waging war and making peace with non-Iroquois peoples. Women selected the male members of the League council. Women could overrule decisions made by the council and could remove its members. The League helped the Iroquois become one of the most powerful peoples in North America.

✔ **Reading Check: Comparing and Contrasting** What were some of the similarities and differences between the cultures of Native Americans in the Great Plains and the East? similarities: agriculture, hunting and gathering, high status of women; differences: buffalo vital on Plains; fixed settlements, power of Iroquois women in East

go. hrw .com **Homework Practice Online**
keyword: SA3 HP1

Section 2 Review

❶ Define and explain:
- kayaks
- igloos
- totems
- potlatches
- kivas
- wigwams
- longhouses

❷ Identify and explain:
- Iroquois League

❸ Identifying Cause and Effect Copy the graphic organizer below. Use it to show how the environments of the Far North, the Southwest, and the East affected the cultures of the Native Americans who lived in each area.

Far North
Environment
Food   Homes

Southwest
Environment
Food   Homes

East
Environment
Food   Homes

❹ Finding the Main Idea
a. Compare and contrast the major cultural traits of the Far North and the Southwest culture groups.

b. Why do you think that Native Americans who practiced agriculture were more likely than hunter-gatherers to establish permanent homes?

❺ Writing and Critical Thinking
Summarizing Imagine that you are living in an early Native American society. Write a paragraph describing your life as a member of this group.

Consider the following:
- how you obtain your food
- the type of shelter in which you live
- other cultural traits your group shares

Section 3

OBJECTIVES

⭐ Identify the new lands that Vikings explored.

⭐ Describe society and daily life during the Middle Ages.

⭐ Examine the role of the Catholic Church in people's lives during the Middle Ages.

⭐ Analyze events that brought about major change in the late Middle Ages.

Section 3

Europe during the Middle Ages

Read to Discover

1. What new lands did the Vikings explore?
2. What were society and daily life like during the Middle Ages?
3. How did the Catholic Church affect people's lives during the Middle Ages?
4. What events brought about major change in the late Middle Ages?

WHY IT MATTERS TODAY

A person who rules over a kingdom or empire is known as a monarch. Use **CNNfyi.com** or other **current events** sources to find information about a country that has a monarch today. Record your findings in your journal.

Define

- feudalism
- manors

Identify

- Leif Eriksson
- Middle Ages
- Eleanor of Aquitaine
- William of Normandy
- King John
- Magna Carta

The Story Continues

The bold Vikings described their adventures in sagas—long, heroic stories that mixed myth and fact. "Erik's Saga" tells how Leif Eriksson heard tales of a land across the sea. Seeking fame and fortune, he went in search of the mysterious land. Eriksson and his crew were tossed by the seas as they set sail from his home in Iceland. According to the saga, the Vikings eventually "came upon lands whose existence he [Eriksson] had never suspected." They saw "fields of flowing wheat there, and vines" with wild grapes. Eriksson, who had landed on the shore of North America, called this place Vinland.

This replica of a Viking ship shows the unique design used.

⭐ The Viking Explorations

The Vikings were from Scandinavia, which includes the present-day countries of Denmark, Norway, and Sweden. The Vikings were skilled sailors who developed a new style of ship that curved up at both ends. These ships traveled on the rough North Atlantic seas better than

★ **TEACH**

Have students read Section 3 and complete Guided Reading Strategy 1.3. Choose one or more of the following activities to explore the section content with students. For further suggestions on block scheduling or team teaching, see the *Block Scheduling Handbook with Team Teaching Strategies.*

 LEVEL 1: Discuss society and daily life during the Middle Ages with students. Organize the class into several small groups. Give each group a large sheet of butcher paper. Have students create an organizational chart describing society and daily life during the Middle Ages. Students should draw arrows from one class of people to another and label them with interactions that would occur between the classes. For example, an arrow going from lords to peasants could indicate that lords provided land for peasants to farm, while the arrow going from peasants to lords could indicate that the peasants tilled the lords' fields. Have each group share its chart with the class. **ENGLISH LANGUAGE LEARNERS , COOPERATIVE LEARNING**

Interdisciplinary Connection

▶Science◀

Knights' Armor. Knights wore plate armor, either at vulnerable points or over the entire body, to protect them from enemy blows. When enemies could not penetrate the armor, they aimed at the knight's horse, so the horses were soon armored as well.

CRITICAL THINKING

What parts of the body were most likely protected by armor?

ANSWER: Students might suggest that knights protected their heads, necks, and midsection.

Vikings led by Leif Eriksson attack a Native American camp in Vinland.

★★★★★★★★★★★★
That's Interesting!
★★★★★★★★★★★★

Fire and Ice Did you know that Iceland has more than 200 volcanoes? That's right! While icy glaciers cover one tenth of the island, large numbers of volcanoes erupt from the island's surface. There are also many geysers and hot springs, which supply energy used today to heat homes. And despite being located just south of the Arctic Circle, Iceland's average daily temperatures are only slightly below freezing in the winter. Iceland's unusually fair weather made it an inviting spot for the Vikings to start a settlement.

earlier designs. The Vikings raided and traded throughout Europe. Evidence shows that the Vikings reached the British Isles, the northern European coast, and as far away as the Mediterranean and the Black Sea. In many places their raids caused great fear. "Never before had such a terror appeared in Britain," noted Anglo-Saxon scholar Alcuin in A.D. 793.

Eventually the Vikings sailed west into the North Atlantic. Much of what historians know about these explorations comes from Viking stories called sagas. According to the sagas, the Vikings founded a settlement on the island of Iceland about A.D. 874. More than 100 years later, the Viking Erik the Red left Iceland to settle Greenland.

Leif Eriksson, son of Erik the Red, shared his father's love of adventure. About A.D. 1000 he gathered a crew and launched his own expedition, sailing west from Greenland. After a difficult journey, they reached North America, landing on Labrador Peninsula and the island of Newfoundland in present-day Canada. This landing represented the first time Europeans made contact with the North American continent. The Vikings then sailed farther south, perhaps as far as what is now New England. According to the sagas, they saw forests, meadows, and rivers that held "larger salmon than they had ever seen."

Eriksson settled in a coastal area he called Vinland. The Vikings left Vinland after only a few years, however. As one Viking reported, "they would always live in dread" of attacks by Native Americans. Vinland may also have simply been too far from other Viking settlements to be supported. In the 1400s the Vikings left Greenland as well. The settlers remained in Iceland, however.

✔ **Reading Check: Sequencing** What were the stages of Viking exploration that led to their landing in North America, and when did the landing take place? the discovery of Iceland, Greenland, then finally Vinland; landed about A.D. 1000

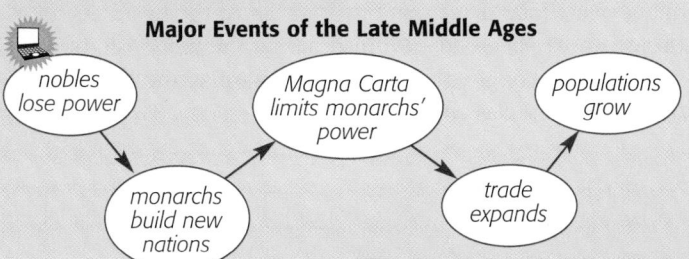
⭐ The Middle Ages

While the Vikings were exploring, Europe was struggling through a difficult period. Beginning in the late A.D. 300s, the Roman Empire had suffered serious political and economic problems. The vast empire soon crumbled under continued invasion by groups such as the Huns. The fall of the Roman Empire marked the beginning of Europe's **Middle Ages**. This historical period lasted roughly from A.D. 500 to 1500. During the Middle Ages, trade and communication were limited. City populations also dropped as people moved into the countryside.

During the Middle Ages a new system of government called **feudalism** emerged. Under this system people known as vassals pledged their loyalty to a lord in exchange for land. Acquiring land was an important step to achieving power and wealth in the Middle Ages. The lord benefited by gaining the military services of his vassals. These vassals often included mounted warriors called knights. Feeding knights and their horses and equipping them with weapons and armor was expensive. However, nobles needed knights to defend their **manors**, or large estates, against attack. The feudal system relied on the loyalty of vassals.

Unlike the nobility, peasants—free tenants and serfs—farmed the land. Tenants rented land from lords and could leave when their rental agreements were over. In contrast, serfs lived on one manor for life, farming the lord's land or performing other services. In return they received the protection of the lord. The degree of personal freedom enjoyed by serfs varied in different parts of Europe. In addition to peasants, there were a small number of slaves in Europe.

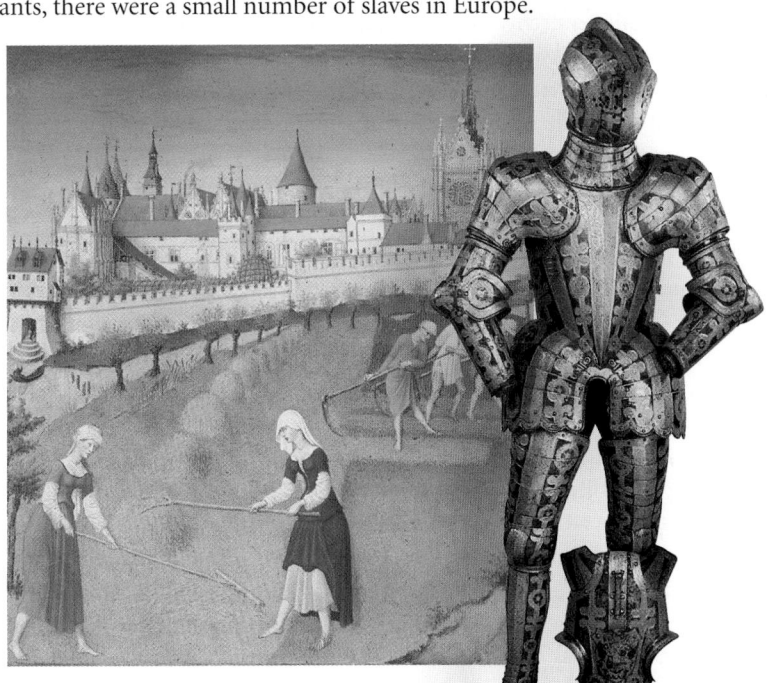

Interpreting the Visual Record

Society in the Middle Ages *While peasants such as those shown here working in the fields had few belongings, wealthy nobles might own fine goods such as this beautifully decorated suit of armor.* **What types of buildings can be seen behind the peasants?**

★ Historical Sidelight

Saint Benedict of Nursia.
Saint Benedict, who founded the monastery of Monte Cassino in Italy in about A.D. 529, drew up a set of rules that described how monks should behave. He believed that monks should live secluded lives of prayer and manual labor. The monasteries that followed this set of rules came to be known as the Benedictine Order. Later, under Pope Gregory VII, some monks became scholars and teachers, and thus helped to preserve a great deal of classical learning.

CRITICAL THINKING

Why do you think Saint Benedict ordered that monks should limit their lives to prayer and labor?

ANSWER: Students might say that Saint Benedict believed this would be the best way to dedicate one's life to God.

Visual Record Answer

Students' answers will vary, but they might suggest that the cathedral's size and beauty are impressive.

Interpreting the Visual Record

Medieval architecture *This French cathedral built in the 1200s reflects the beauty of medieval architecture.* **How might the design of such a building have affected those who worshiped there?**

★ Life on a Manor

Manors provided most of what their inhabitants needed to live. Lords ruled their manors with little interference. Lords and their families lived in large wooden or stone houses or castles. These were often surrounded by water-filled trenches—called moats—and high walls for defense. Noblemen spent their time ruling, fighting in battles, and managing their farmland. Noblewomen usually ran the home and raised children. Noblemen and noblewomen also spent a large amount of time carrying out their duties as Christians. For example, women often prayed daily for the well-being of the household. In 1190 Richard of Devizes listed some of the qualities of **Eleanor of Aquitaine**, whom he considered an ideal noblewoman. He described her as "beautiful yet virtuous [moral], powerful yet gentle, humble yet keenwitted [intelligent]."

Life for peasants was very different. Whole families often slept and ate in a single room. Women and men worked in the fields from before sunrise until after sunset. From an early age, children were also expected to work. Children grew up knowing that they would have little chance to move ahead in life. Under feudalism, a person's birth usually determined his or her place in society.

✔ **Reading Check: Contrasting** How did daily life differ for nobles and peasants during the Middle Ages? nobles—had large homes, fought battles, managed manors, fulfilled Christian duties; peasants—had small homes, long workdays farming for nobles, few opportunities to move ahead

★ The Catholic Church

The Catholic Church was the center of religious and social life in the Middle Ages. Both peasants and nobles attended church services led by the local priest. Priests also cared for the sick and poor, counseled the rich, and taught the young. Frequent religious festivals offered everyone a chance to celebrate.

Many religious groups existed during the Middle Ages, but most Europeans were Roman Catholic. Christianity influenced culture and politics across Europe. By the late 800s, the Church owned large amounts of land. In addition, church leaders often advised rulers on important matters. The Catholic Church paid for many art and architecture projects. One example is the Notre Dame cathedral in Paris, France.

Monasteries were important during the early Middle Ages. These were religious communities in which men called monks devoted their lives to practicing Christianity. Monks gave up all personal possessions, but monasteries themselves often owned large estates. Monasteries became centers of learning, and some produced books.

Similar religious centers for women were called convents. The women who lived in these convents were known as nuns. Nuns spent most of their time running convent lands, reading religious texts, and writing. They also created works of art and earned money selling crafts

LEVEL 3: Write the following words on the chalk-board: *Viking explorations.* Ask students to share their knowledge of the topic. *(Students' responses will vary.)* Write students' responses on the chalkboard and discuss them. Then explain that each student must write a Viking saga about the Vikings exploration of North America. Remind students that a saga is a heroic story mixing fact and fiction. Ask volunteers to read their sagas to the class. Conclude the lesson by discussing why the Vikings were able to dominate early sea exploration.

LEVEL 3: Have students imagine that they are clergy members of the Catholic Church during the Middle Ages. Then have each student write three journal entries

from a typical week of a clergy member. *(Students' entries should include leading a church service, caring for the sick, teaching students, writing and studying texts, or working on art.)*

★ CLOSE

Remind students that many significant historical developments during the Middle Ages took place in Europe. Give students blank maps of Europe. Have them use the map to locate places of historical significance that are mentioned in the section. You may wish to create a list of places to locate. Then ask students to identify at least one important historical event that occurred at each location on the map.

such as woven goods. Many women joined convents because they wanted to devote their lives to learning and prayer. Convents gave women an alternative to getting married and having children. In other cases, families encouraged elderly or unmarried women to become nuns.

Convents offered women a rare chance to pursue an education. Some nuns wrote history, poetry, and plays. Others even advised leaders. Saint Hilda, who founded a religious community, received praise from an early historian of England.

> ❝So great was her prudence [good judgment] that not only ordinary folk, but kings and princes used to come and ask her advice in their difficulties and take it.❞
>
> Bede, *A History of the English Church and People*

✔ **Reading Check: Analyzing Information** What role did the Catholic Church play in people's lives during the Middle Ages? Most Europeans were Catholics. The church took part in arts and politics. Monasteries and convents were centers of education.

★ The Rise of Nations

During the mid- and late Middle Ages, some nobles began losing power to growing kingdoms. These kingdoms, including England and France, became some of the first nations in the world. In 1066 **William of Normandy** conquered England. (Normandy is an area in present-day France.) He later ordered a survey of the entire kingdom. The result was the enormous Domesday Book, or Day of Judgment Book. A writer recorded the process used to collect the information.

> ❝William, king of the English, sent [his men] through all the provinces of England and caused it to be inquired [asked] . . . how much the king had in lands and cattle and livestock in each province. . . . And so thoroughly was all this carried out that there did not remain in the whole of England . . . an ox or cow or a pig which was not written in that return [document]. And all the writings of all these things were brought back to the king.❞
>
> —Anonymous, quoted in *English Historical Documents, 1042–1189*, edited by David C. Douglas and George W. Greenaway

BIOGRAPHY

William of Normandy
(c. 1028–1087)

William of Normandy, also known as William the Conqueror, was born in what is now France. When the English king Edward the Confessor died in 1066, Duke William invaded England. He fought and defeated the new English king, Harold, at the Battle of Hastings.

William brought many changes to English society. He and his nobles established the feudal system in England and built the first English castles. William's court also introduced the English to French customs, laws, and language. What were some of the ways that William changed English society?

Analyzing Primary Sources
Making Generalizations and Predictions Why would the information from this survey have been important to the king? to determine the amount of tax that should be collected

The Bayeux Tapestry shows the Norman invasion of England.

★★★★★★★★★★★★
That's Interesting!
★★★★★★★★★★★★

William of Normandy was only eight years old when his father, Duke Robert I, died. In the period of lawlessness that followed, an attempt was made on William's life, and three of his closest guardians were murdered. His mother was one of the people who protected him through the most dangerous period of his youth.

BIOGRAPHY ANSWER
He established the feudal system in England and built the first English castles. William's court also introduced the English to French art, customs, and language.

★ REVIEW AND ASSESS

Have students complete the **Section 3 Review** on p. 22. Then have students complete **Daily Quiz 1.3**. As **Alternative Assessment**, you may want to use the society and daily life organizational chart or the Viking saga in this section's lessons.

★ RETEACH

Have students complete **Main Idea Activity for English Language Learners and Special-Needs Students 1.3**. Then pair students. Have each student write a short summary of Section 3 for his or her partner. Encourage students to take notes from each other's summary.

ENGLISH LANGUAGE LEARNERS , COOPERATIVE LEARNING

★ EXTEND

Remind students that in 1215 King John signed Magna Carta, which essentially forced monarchs to abide by laws, while granting certain legal rights and liberties to English citizens. Have students work in small groups to write their own Magna Carta for the school (or the classroom). Encourage students to find a copy of the text of Magna Carta to serve as a model for their project. Explain that their Magna Carta needs to follow the organizational structure that is already in effect in the school. Once students have completed this document, lead a discussion about the importance of citizens' rights in society.

COOPERATIVE LEARNING , BLOCK SCHEDULING

Section 3 Review
ANSWERS

❶ Define
- feudalism, p. 19
- manors, p. 19

❷ Identify
- Leif Eriksson, p. 18
- Middle Ages, p. 19
- Eleanor of Aquitane, p. 20
- William of Normandy, p. 21
- King John, p. 22
- Magna Carta, p. 22

❸ peasants: work—farmed the land for nobles; housing—one large room where the family ate and slept; nobles: work—ruling the manor, fighting in battles, managing the farmland, or carrying out their duties as Christians; housing—large wooden or stone houses

❹ a. superior shipbuilding; colonies on Iceland, Greenland, and North America
b. most Europeans were Roman Catholic; priests tended to villagers and nobles; the Church sponsored religious festivals and was involved in arts and politics and owned land; monasteries and convents were centers of education and provided opportunities for noblemen and women

❺ Students' paragraphs will vary, but they should mention that Magna Carta limited monarchs' power and protected some individual rights, trade expanded and led to growth in cities, and that agricultural innovations led to population growth.

As trade brought greater riches to Europe, wealthy couples could enjoy fine weddings such as the one shown here.

During the rule of William's great-great-grandson **King John**, the nobles rebelled against his misuse of royal power. In 1215 they forced John to agree to **Magna Carta**, or the Great Charter. The charter addressed the land rights of nobles. It also required the king to gain the agreement of the nobility before raising new taxes. In addition, Magna Carta was one of the first documents to protect some of the rights of free people.

The early 1200s brought other major changes to Europe. Trade greatly increased. One major cause for this was that Italian cities began expanding their trade connections. Eventually Italian merchants were trading regularly with nations around the Mediterranean Sea and northern Europe.

Across Europe, advances in farming led to increased food production and rising populations. Farmers began using horses instead of oxen to pull plows. They also learned to fertilize soil and to rotate crops. As the population grew, landowners cleared more land for farming. Many people began using new technology, such as windmills and watermills. These devices provided power for grinding grain, working with metals, and pumping water.

More people and more trade meant new towns and larger cities. With the growth of technology, trade, and kingdoms, by 1500 Europe's Middle Ages were drawing to a close.

✔ **Reading Check: Summarizing** How did countries change in the late Middle Ages? nobles lost power; monarchs built new nations; Magna Carta limited English monarchs' power and protected some individual rights; trade expanded; cities grew; agricultural innovations led to population growth

Section 3 Review

go.hrw.com **Homework Practice Online** keyword: SA3 HP1

❶ Define and explain:
- feudalism
- manors

❷ Identify and explain:
- Leif Eriksson
- Middle Ages
- Eleanor of Aquitaine
- William of Normandy
- King John
- Magna Carta

❸ Comparing and Contrasting Copy the diagram below. Use it to explain the similarities and differences between peasants' and nobles' daily lives under feudalism.

Peasants — Similarities — Nobles

❹ Finding the Main Idea
a. What technology enabled the Vikings to explore new lands, and what were the results of their explorations?

b. How did the Catholic Church influence daily life and culture during the Middle Ages?

❺ Writing and Critical Thinking
Identifying Cause and Effect Imagine that you are a monk or a nun during the Middle Ages and you are recording the history of your time. Write a paragraph explaining the major changes of the late Middle Ages and their effects.

Consider the following:
- the significance of Magna Carta
- the expansion of trade
- advances in agricultural technology

Section 4

OBJECTIVES

⭐ Describe how Islam affected the Mediterranean region.

⭐ Examine the causes that led the Chinese to join in and then withdraw from international trade.

⭐ Explain how trade influenced African kingdoms.

🔊 **LET'S GET STARTED!**

As students enter the classroom have them list as many items as possible that are made in other countries. Ask for volunteers to share their lists. *(Students' responses may mention electronic devices, cars, clothing, and so on.)* Explain to students that global trading is an important part of the economy. Then tell students that in Section 4 they will learn about the early effects of global trading between the Mediterranean region, Asia, and Africa.

Section 4

Trade across Continents

Read to Discover

1. How did Islam affect the Mediterrean region?
2. What led the Chinese to join in and then withdraw from international trade?
3. How did trade influence African kingdoms?

WHY IT MATTERS TODAY

Trade remains an important way for cultures around the world to interact with one another. Use CNN**fyi**.com or other **current events** sources to find information about some of the products that the United States trades with other countries. Record your findings in your journal.

Identify

• Muhammad
• Islam
• Crusades
• Kublai Khan
• Silk Road
• Zheng He
• Mansa Musa

SECTION 4 RESOURCES

REPRODUCIBLE

▸ Guided Reading Strategy 1.4

TECHNOLOGY

▸ One-Stop Planner, Lesson 1.4
▸ Holt Researcher: American History CD–ROM
▸ Homework Practice Online

REINFORCEMENT, REVIEW, AND ASSESSMENT

▸ Section 4 Review, p. 27
▸ Daily Quiz 1.4
▸ Main Idea Activity 1.4
▸ English Audio Summary 1.4
▸ Spanish Audio Summary 1.4

The Story Continues

The city of Mecca, in what is now Saudi Arabia, was a thriving trade center. One of its residents was Muhammad, a successful Arab merchant. In A.D. 610 Muhammad's life changed dramatically. That year he recorded having a vision of an angel, who ordered him to teach the word of God, or Allah. Muhammad dedicated his life to this task, spreading his faith first in Mecca and later in other communities. He overcame many obstacles and founded the religion known as Islam.

This Turkish miniature shows an Islamic scene.

⭐ The Spread of Islam

Muhammad devoted his life to preaching the messages of Allah. After his death, Muhammad's followers wrote these messages in the Qur'an (kuh-RAN), the holy book of **Islam**. Islam gained many followers, called Muslims, who swiftly spread their faith. Muslims took Jerusalem, Syria, the Persian Empire, and Egypt. Once they held the seaports of Syria and Egypt, Muslims built a powerful navy. By the late 600s they dominated the eastern Mediterranean Sea. Before long, North Africa, Sicily, and much of present-day Spain had come under Muslim control.

Have students read Section 4 and complete Guided Reading Strategy 1.4. Choose one or more of the following activities to explore the section content with students. For further suggestions on block scheduling or team teaching, see the *Block Scheduling Handbook with Team Teaching Strategies.*

LEVEL 1: Lead a class discussion on trade between Asia and Africa and how trade influenced African kingdoms. Be sure to discuss the goods that were most commonly traded as well as the goods that were most sought after. *(Students' discussions should include traded goods such as silk from China and ivory and gold from Africa.)* Then organize the class into groups. Have each group use newspapers, magazines, and art supplies to create a collage depicting trade between Asia and the Africa kingdom. Ask each group to present its project to the class. Display projects throughout the classroom in a Trade Goods Exhibition.

ENGLISH LANGUAGE LEARNERS , COOPERATIVE LEARNING

★ Linking Past to Present

Islam. In A.D. 630 Muhammad and his followers took over the city of Mecca, which to this day is the religious center of Islam. Many Muslims pray facing Mecca five times daily, and each Muslim is encouraged to make a pilgrimage to Mecca at least once in a lifetime. The Qur'an, published after Muhammad's death, is a compilation of all the religious beliefs that the Prophet proclaimed during his lifetime.

ACTIVITY: Have students investigate Islamic cultures and list five ways in which the culture of American muslims is similar to or different from Muslim cultures in other countries.

Visual Record Answer

Students might suggest that it took a good number of people and provisions to complete the trip.

Muslim traders helped spread Islam. Trade also allowed people to exchange new ideas. Muslims valued learning highly. Muslim mathematicians adopted a numeral system from India, including the concept of zero. Using this system, they developed algebra. Muslim scholars also studied medicine, philosophy, astronomy, and physics. Some of this they learned from ancient Greek writings. Muslim doctors improved surgical methods and the understanding of diseases. One teacher gave the following advice to young students. "He who has not endured the stress of study will not taste the joy of knowledge."

✔ **Reading Check: Drawing Inferences and Conclusions** Besides the spread of knowledge, in what other ways do you think the Muslim empire benefited from trade? Answers will vary but should include wealth, power/influence, and the spread of Islam.

★ The Crusades

Like Jews and Christians, Muslims showed their faith by visiting the Holy Land. This area included the city of Jerusalem and the land surrounding it. Muslims conquered Jerusalem in 637 but continued to let people of other religions visit. However, about 1077 the Seljuk Turks, who were also Muslims, took over the city and began to prevent Christians from visiting holy places. In 1095 Pope Urban II called on all Christians to start a holy war to seize control of Jerusalem.

Interpreting the Visual Record

Crusaders A group of crusaders is preparing to travel to the Holy Land. The banners of different noble families fly above the ships. *What does this image suggest about the difficulty of reaching the Holy Land?*

History Makers Speak

❝Jerusalem is the center of the earth; the land is fruitful above all others, like another paradise of delights. . . . This royal city . . . is now held captive by the enemies of Christ. . . . When an armed attack is made upon the enemy, let this one cry be raised by all the soldiers of God: it is the will of God! It is the will of God!❞

Pope Urban II, quoted in *The Medieval Reader,* edited by Norman Cantor

Deborah Lofton of Blackstock, California, suggested the following activity:

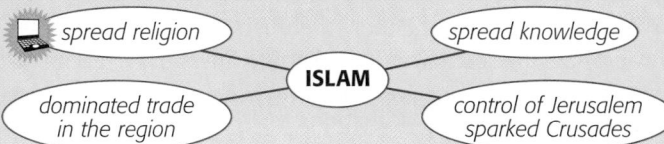

ALL LEVELS: Organize students into groups. Have each group develop a board game based on the Silk Road. The game should focus on the long distances traveled, the items that were traded, and the dangers along the way. The object of the game should be to transport goods from Europe to China and return safely to Europe with profitable Chinese merchandise. Once each group has finished developing its game have students play each other's games. Conclude the lesson with a discussion on what events led China to withdraw from international trade. **ENGLISH LANGUAGE LEARNERS , COOPERATIVE LEARNING**

ALL LEVELS: Copy the following graphic organizer onto the chalkboard, omitting the italicized answers. Ask students to complete the organizer by providing information on how Islam influenced the Mediterranean region. **ENGLISH LANGUAGE LEARNERS**

- *spread religion*
- *spread knowledge*
- **ISLAM**
- *dominated trade in the region*
- *control of Jerusalem sparked Crusades*

With these words, the pope asked Christians across Europe to take back the Holy Land. The resulting military expeditions to the Holy Land, which continued off and on for more than 150 years, were called the **Crusades**. Many knights, soldiers, and nobles joined the holy wars. According to William of Malmesbury, the Crusades greatly changed the European population. The "lands were deserted of their husbands-men, houses of their inhabitants, even whole cities migrated."

The crusaders captured Jerusalem in 1099 and controlled it for nearly 90 years. However, in 1187 Saladin, a Muslim sultan, arrived with a massive army. At the end of the battle that followed, the city was back in Muslim hands. Future Crusades were unable to recapture Jerusalem.

✔ **Reading Check: Finding the Main Idea** Why did the Crusades take place? Christians wanted to take the Holy Land from Muslims

★ Empires in Asia

While fighting continued in the Holy Land, China faced an invasion by the Mongols of Central Asia. Chinese emperors had built the Great Wall—which stretched some 4,500 miles—to defend against such attacks. But Mongol leader Genghis Khan could not be stopped. By 1279 his grandson **Kublai Khan** (koo-bluh-KAHN) ruled an Asian empire that stretched to the Black Sea from China's southern coast. Kublai Khan used his large navy to expand trade. In addition, merchants used the **Silk Road**, an overland trade route running from China to the Black Sea.

In 1368 the Ming dynasty overthrew the Mongol Empire in China. Zhu Di seized the Ming throne in 1402. He soon built a large fleet of ships. This fleet allowed China to exchange silk and porcelain for spices and other goods. China established new trade with India and Arabia. Admiral **Zheng He** commanded the fleet's 317 brightly painted ships and more than 27,000 men. His expeditions brought wealth and knowledge of other cultures to China.

After Zheng He's death, the Ming dynasty reduced its long-distance ocean trade. By the mid-1400s, China had abandoned its command of the seas. Political conflicts, piracy, a lack of tax money, and other events led the country to refocus on internal affairs.

✔ **Reading Check Summarizing** What role did China play in international trade between the 1200s and 1400s? Kublai Khan used his navy to expand trade and used the Silk Road to reopen trade westward to Europe. Zhu Di developed a naval fleet that increased trade with other Asian lands.

★ African Trading Kingdoms

Well before Chinese merchants established trade contacts with East Africa, several African kingdoms had grown wealthy from long-distance trade. The Aksum kingdom began in present-day Ethiopia. Aksum gained much of its wealth by trading with Egypt and ports in the Indian Ocean.

GLOBAL CONNECTIONS

The Silk Road

In the 100s B.C. Chinese emperor Wu Di opened up China's western trade routes. Chinese merchants began sending goods to Central Asia along a great highway known as the Silk Road. It eventually stretched about 5,000 miles from eastern China to the Black Sea. Harsh weather and bandits made the Silk Road dangerous.

The promise of wealth kept traders on the Silk Road. By A.D. 100, large caravans made regular journeys from western China. Chinese merchants carried furs, ceramics, jade, cinnamon, and silk. Caravans returning to China carried valuables like gold, glass, and linen fabrics.

Trade along the Silk Road slowed in the 800s, renewed in the 1300s, and then ended. Today, adventurers explore parts of what was once the Silk Road. **Why was the Silk Road important?**

Global Relations

Marco Polo. Descriptions of Kublai Khan's court can be found in the stories of Marco Polo, a merchant from Venice who visited the East with his father and uncle. Marco Polo's family visited the court of Kublai Khan twice, spending a total of 17 years there. They returned to Europe with gems, silks, spices, and other goods that stunned Europeans. Marco Polo described their adventures in the Far East, recounting the conditions in China and telling how he served Kublai Khan by governing a Chinese province. Many of Marco Polo's contemporaries questioned the truth of his account, as have modern historians. However, research has proven that some portions of the story are true.

ACTIVITY: Have students find out more about Marco Polo's adventures in the Far East. Encourage them to form an opinion about the degree of truthfulness of his account.

GLOBAL CONNECTIONS ANSWER
It provided a link for trade between Europe and Asia.

HOMEWORK Provide students with an outline map
of Europe or the Mediterranean region. Then have
them take home the map and shade in areas that were
dominated by Muslims during the Middle Ages and identify the
areas of military conquest that are discussed in the text. Also,
ask students to mark trade routes that connected Muslim cities
to other parts of the world.

LEVEL 3: Have students assume the role of panel
members engaged in a discussion on trade during the
Middle Ages. Panel members should be either
European, Chinese, African, or Islamic traders. Have each student develop questions and concerns that traders might have
about commerce during the Middle Ages. Finally, have students

participate in the panel discussion by asking and answering the
questions.

★ CLOSE

Organize the class into three groups, assigning each group one
of the following topics: 1) the importance of the Silk Road to
the early Chinese economy, 2) the effects of Islam on the
Mediterranean region, or 3) how East African kingdoms were
influenced by trade. Have each group create a study guide for its
assigned topic. Upon completion, each group should distribute
photocopies of its study guide to the rest of the class.
COOPERATIVE LEARNING

MAP ANSWERS
1. gold and salt
2. Mali

Section 4 Review
ANSWERS

❶ Identify
- Muhammad, p. 23
- Islam, p. 23
- Crusades, p. 25
- Kublai Khan, p. 25
- Silk Road, p. 25
- Zheng He, p. 25
- Mansa Musa, p. 27

❷ Africa: traded with —China
and Arab traders; benefits—
wealth, knowledge of other religions; China: traded with —Africa,
India, and Arab traders; benefits—
wealth, influence, knowledge of
other cultures; Islamic Empires:
trader with—China, India, and
Africa; benefits—wealth, rare
goods, knowledge, spread
of Islam

❸ a. Islam spread through
Muslim conquest of the Middle
East, North Africa, Sicily, and much
of present-day Spain
b. expanded under the leadership
of Kublai Khan in the A.D. 1200s.
Political conflicts, lack of money,
and other problems led the Ming
dynasty to focus on internal affairs
by the mid-1400s

❹ Students speeches will vary, but
supporters of the Crusades should
note that Jerusalem is a holy city
for Christians and that the Muslim
states are wealthy and could be
conquered. Dissenters will note
the risks of such a long journey
and fighting an enemy on their
own lands.

Research on the ROM

Free Find:
Two Views of Africa
After reading al-Mas'udi's
and Ibn Battuta's accounts
of traveling in Africa on
the **Holt Researcher
CD–ROM**, create a travel
guide to these areas dur-
ing the times the authors
were there.

African Trading Kingdoms

Interpreting Maps The African trade routes allowed the exchange of goods between regions and cultures.

Skills Assessment
1. **Places and Regions** According to the map, what products came from the African region south of the equator?
2. **Comparing** Which African kingdom was larger: Ghana, Mali, or Songhai?

Important port cities were built along the Red Sea, which separates Africa
from Southwest Asia. Aksum's most valuable trade good was ivory. Many
Aksumites converted to Christianity after North African and Middle Eastern Christians introduced the religion.

Farther down the East African coast, Arab traders came into contact
with Bantu-speaking peoples. They traded in market centers that grew
into about 30 separate city-states. Each competed for control of the
trade in gold, ivory, and slaves in southern Africa. Among the most
important city-states were Mogadishu (moh-guh-DEE-shoo), Mombasa
(mohm-BAH-sah), and Kilwa. Bantu and Arab influences in the region
combined to create a unique culture. The people shared a common religion, Islam, and a new language, Swahili (swah-HEE-lee).

Long-distance trading networks also developed in West Africa.
Traders eventually used camels to carry goods across the desert. These
nomads from North Africa and the northern Sahara—called Berbers—
brought salt south and gold north. Several kingdoms and empires grew
wealthy and powerful from this trade. Ghana (GAH-nuh) ruled an area
between the Niger (NY-juhr) and Senegal Rivers to the south and the

Sahara to the north. Most of Ghana's wealth came from trading gold. Berber merchants carried the gold north to the Mediterranean.

Mali emerged in the early 1200s, long after Ghana had collapsed. Mali stretched more than 1,000 miles inland from Africa's west coast. The empire of Mali included the important trading city of Timbuktu (tim-buhk-TOO). The Muslim traveler Ibn Battuta described the empire.

History Makers Speak
"[The Malians] are seldom unjust, and have a greater horror of injustice than other people. Their [ruler] shows no mercy to anyone who is guilty of the least act of it. There is complete security in their country. Neither traveler nor inhabitant in it has anything to fear from robbers or men of violence."

Ibn Battuta, quoted in *A Short History of Africa*, by Roland Oliver and J. D. Fage

This mosque in Timbuktu, Mali, dates from the early 1300s.

In the mid-1200s North African traders brought Islam to Mali. Traders also introduced Islam to the large eastern region of the Sudan. Mali's emperors became Muslim, and Timbuktu became a center of Islamic culture and learning. **Mansa Musa** was one of the greatest Malian leaders. He made a pilgrimage to the Islamic holy city of Mecca in 1324. Arabs in Mecca were impressed with the African emperor's wealth and power.

The large Songhai (SAWNG-hy) Empire also had great influence in the region. Songhai's Muslim rulers encouraged the spread of Islamic culture throughout their vast territory. The Songhai Empire remained powerful until the late 1500s.

✔ **Reading Check: Summarizing** What effect did trade have on different empires in Africa? Trade brought great wealth to some and spread culture; Aksum traded with India and converted to Christianity; Bantu and Arab traders on the East Coast of Africa created a unique culture including Islam and Swahili; West African kingdoms—Ghana, Mali, Songhai—traded north to the Mediterranean; Mali was strongly influenced by Islam.

Section 4 Review

go.hrw.com Homework Practice Online
keyword: SA3 HP1

❶ Identify and explain:
• Muhammad
• Islam
• Crusades
• Kublai Khan
• Silk Road
• Zheng He
• Mansa Musa

❷ Summarizing Copy the chart below. Use it to list the benefits of global trade for Africa, China, and the Muslim empire.

	Traded with	Benefits
Africa		
China		
Muslim empire		

❸ Finding the Main Idea
a. How was Islam spread through much of the Mediterranean region?

b. When did China reopen trading networks with other countries, and what led to the decline of Chinese participation in international trade?

❹ Writing and Critical Thinking
Supporting a Point of View Imagine that you are a noble lord in Europe at the time of the first Crusades. Write a speech to give to your vassals explaining why you think joining the Crusade is or is not a good idea.
Consider the following:
• Pope Urban's call to protect Jerusalem
• the risks of war so far from home
• the potential benefits of occupying the Holy Land

CHAPTER

1

REVIEW AND ASSESSMENT RESOURCES

REPRODUCIBLE
▶ Vocabulary Activity 1

TECHNOLOGY
▶ Chapter 1 Test Generator
(on the One-Stop Planner)
▶ Global Skill Builder
CD–ROM
▶ HRW Go site

**REINFORCEMENT,
REVIEW, AND
ASSESSMENT**
▶ Chapter 1 Review,
pp. 27–29
▶ Chapter 1 Tutorial for
Students, Parents,
Mentors, and Peers

▶ Chapter 1 Test
(Form A or B)
▶ Alternative Assessment
Handbook
▶ Chapter 1 Test for English
Language Learners and
Special-Needs Students

★ REVIEW
Have students complete the
Chapter 1 Review on pages
28–29.

★ ASSESS
Use one of the chapter tests to
assess students' understanding
of the content. For **Alternative
Assessment**, see the **Alternative
Assessment Handbook**.

Understanding Main Ideas

1. by hunting smaller animals, domesticating plants and animals (developing agriculture), and creating complex civilizations

2. Olmec—number and calendar systems, glyphs; Maya—stone structures, calendars, math and astronomical systems, Aztec—Tenochtitlán, vast trading network

3. Cold weather in the Far North restricted Native Americans to hunting and fishing. In the Southwest dry weather and limited resources required irrigated farming. In the Northwest and Northeast resources were abundant and many different ways of gathering food could be practiced.

4. a political federation of the Seneca, Oneida, Mohawk, Cayuga, and Onondaga peoples responsible for waging war and making peace; included a council made up of male members selected by Iroquois women

5. influenced daily life, culture, politics; provided centers of education in monasteries and convents

6. a series of holy wars; launched in 1095 when Pope Urban II urged Christians to recapture the holy city of Jerusalem from Muslim control.

7. Aksum, East Coast city-states (including Mogadishu, Mombasa, and Kilwa), Ghana, Mali, Songhay

You Be the Historian— Reviewing Themes

1. housing, language, method of obtaining food

Chapter **1** Review

The Chapter at a Glance

Examine the visual summary of the chapter below. Then use it to create a graphic organizer covering the chapter's main ideas that you might give to a classmate.

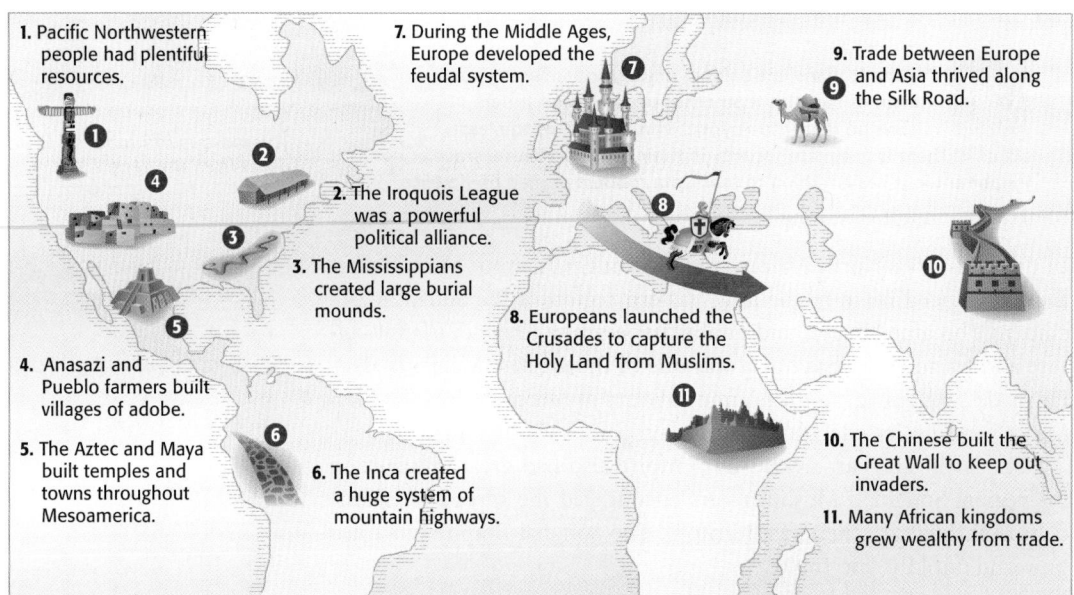

1. Pacific Northwestern people had plentiful resources.
2. The Iroquois League was a powerful political alliance.
3. The Mississippians created large burial mounds.
4. Anasazi and Pueblo farmers built villages of adobe.
5. The Aztec and Maya built temples and towns throughout Mesoamerica.
6. The Inca created a huge system of mountain highways.
7. During the Middle Ages, Europe developed the feudal system.
8. Europeans launched the Crusades to capture the Holy Land from Muslims.
9. Trade between Europe and Asia thrived along the Silk Road.
10. The Chinese built the Great Wall to keep out invaders.
11. Many African kingdoms grew wealthy from trade.

Identifying People and Ideas

Use the following terms and people in historically significant sentences.
1. archaeology
2. domestication
3. totems
4. Leif Eriksson
5. feudalism
6. Eleanor of Aquitaine
7. Magna Carta
8. Crusades
9. Silk Road
10. Zheng He

Understanding Main Ideas

Section 1 *(Pages 4–9)*
1. How did Paleo-Indians adapt to the widespread environmental changes caused by the end of the Ice Age?
2. What were some of the major achievements of Mesoamerican civilizations?

Section 2 *(Pages 10–16)*
3. How did the different environments in North America affect the ways that Native Americans gained food?
4. What was the Iroquois League?

Section 3 *(Pages 17–22)*
5. What role did the Catholic Church play in the Middle Ages?

Section 4 *(Pages 23–27)*
6. What were the Crusades, and why did they take place?
7. What were some of Africa's major kingdoms?

You Be the Historian— Reviewing Themes

1. **Culture** In what ways were Native American societies in the same region often similar?
2. **Geography** What types of housing did Native Americans build and why?
3. **Global Relations** How did trade networks benefit civilizations in Africa, Asia, and Europe?

Thinking Critically

1. **Comparing and Contrasting** How were the early Native American groups in the Northwest and Northeast culture areas similar and different?
2. **Finding the Main Idea** How did the development of agriculture change the way Native Americans lived?
3. **Supporting a Point of View** Do you think that all members of European society benefited from the feudal system during the Middle Ages? Explain your answer.

★ RETEACH

Organize the class into four groups. Tell each group to create a comic book that describes one of the chapter's sections. The comic book should provide answers to each of the section's Read to Discover questions. Encourage students to be creative, while maintaining historical accuracy. Once groups have finished, have them take turns reading each other's comic books, until each group has read all of them.

ENGLISH LANGUAGE LEARNERS ,
COOPERATIVE LEARNING

Portfolio Extensions

1. Interdisciplinary Connection to Literature Tell students that in Section 1 they read a brief creation story that explains how the first people came to the world. Have students write their own such story on one of the topics described in this chapter. Students might choose to write on how people first came to the Americas, how different customs were developed, how glyphs were created, and so on. They should illustrate their story with a drawing or picture.

2. Linking to Community Have students write a report on one of the Native American groups who lived in the geographic region where they live today. Students should describe the time period in which the Native Americans lived in this region and their daily life. Students should also investigate the ways that this group influenced culture in the region today. For example, the name of the Cuyahoga River is Indian, in the southwest many people live in adobe-style houses, and moccasin are popular in the Midwest.

Social Studies Skills Workshop

Interpreting Maps

Study the map below. Then use the information on the map to help you answer the questions that follow.

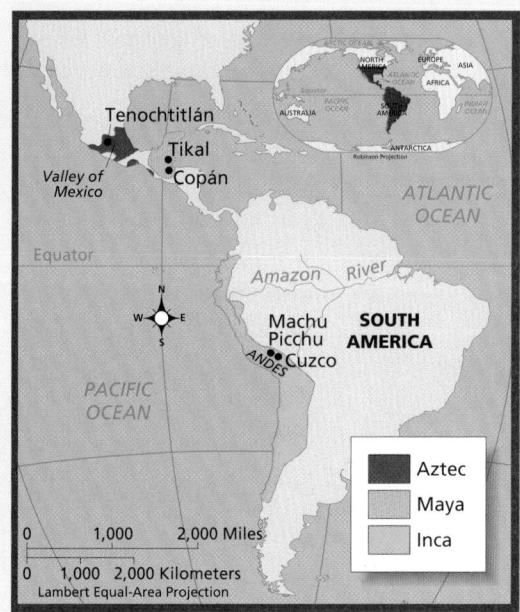

1. Which of the following is a fair statement based on the information provided on the map?
   a. The Maya Empire developed along the Pacific Coast.
   b. The Inca Empire developed along the Amazon River.
   c. Tenochtitlán was the capital of the Maya Empire.
   d. The Inca Empire controlled more land than the Aztec or Maya Empires.

2. Using the map, locate and identify the major geographic features within the Aztec and Inca Empires. How might these different environments have led to differences between the two civilizations?

Analyzing Primary Sources

Read the following pledge of loyalty by the knight Bernard Atton, then answer the questions.

> ❝I swear upon these four gospels of God that I will always be a faithful vassal to thee and to thy successors . . . in all things in which a vassal is required to be faithful to his lord; and I will defend thee, my lord, and all thy successors . . . and the castles and manors and all your men and their possessions against all malefactors [criminals] and invaders, of my own free will.❞

3. Which of the following best sums up what Bernard Atton is promising?
   a. to provide land and money to his lord
   b. to protect the lord and his possessions
   c. to be faithful to the Church
   d. to capture criminals

4. Whom does Atton promise to serve?
   a. only his lord
   b. his lord and the king
   c. his lord and the Catholic Church
   d. his lord and all his lord's successors

5. Historians carefully examine the historical context in which a source was written. Why might a ruler during Europe's Middle Ages have needed the services of a knight like Bernard Atton?

Building Your Portfolio

Cooperative Learning
Complete the following activity in small groups. Your group is responsible for creating a detailed map of a manor during the Middle Ages. Assign each group member the role of one of the following members of feudal society: lord, vassal, peasant, or church official. Each member should study his or her role and make suggestions for how it should be represented on the map. Your map should show where different groups lived, public buildings such as a church, and images of daily activity.

☑ internet connect

Internet Activity: go.hrw.com
keyword: SA3 CF1

Choose a topic about the World before the Opening of the Atlantic:
● Model Maya mathematics by solving a math problem.
● Learn about Paleolithic culture at the Clovis site.
● Research modern Africa and Asia.

---

2. Anasazi—multistory mesa and cliff dwellings; Aleut and Inuit—underground and above-ground houses, igloos; East—multifamily lodges, wigwams, longhouses; the type of housing determined by environment

3. African civilizations gained wealth and power by trading goods such as gold and ivory, helping them create trade centers. China gained wealth, exotic goods, and knowledge of foreign lands when it opened up sea trade routes and reopened the Silk Road. Muslim trade brought new ideas and knowledge to Europe, as well as rare spices, silk, and other goods from Asia.

Thinking Critically
1. Similarities might include that both hunted and fished, gathered plants for food, and lived in wooden houses. Differences might include the agriculture they developed, the holding of potlatches, and role of women.

2. It allowed them to stay in one place and establish permanent communities.

3. Students' responses will vary but should note the differences between the lives of peasants and nobles.

Skills Workshop
1. d
2. Students might suggest that the Inca developed along the Andes while the Aztec developed around a valley.
3. b
4. d
5. Students might suggest that a ruler is always in need of a loyal subject.

2

The Age of Exploration

CHAPTER RESOURCE MANAGER

	Objectives	Pacing Guide	Reproducible Resources
SECTION 1: **Europeans Set Sail** (pp. 32–37)	⚹ Explain how the Commercial Revolution and the Renaissance changed Europe. ⚹ Analyze the reasons why western Europeans sought a new sea route for trade with Africa and Asia. ⚹ Evaluate the effects *or* "the consequences of . . . *for* Africans" of early Portuguese exploration on Africans.	**Regular** 1.5 days **Block Scheduling** .75 day *Block Scheduling Handbook with Team Teaching Strategies, Chapter 2*	**RS** Guided Reading Strategy 2.1 **PS** Literature Reading 2: Marco Polo in China **E** Hands-On History Activity: Looking at Your Region for the First Time
SECTION 2: **Voyages to the Americas** (pp. 38–43)	⚹ Discuss Christopher Columbus's goal. ⚹ Identify what Columbus did during his explorations in the Americas. ⚹ Describe Portugal's reaction to news of Columbus's discoveries.	**Regular** 1.5 days **Block Scheduling** .75 day *Block Scheduling Handbook with Team Teaching Strategies, Chapter 2*	**RS** Guided Reading Strategy 2.2 **RS** Graphic Organizer 2: The Voyages of Christopher Columbus **PS** Primary Source Reading 2: First Impressions of the New World
SECTION 3: **The Race for Trade Routes** (pp. 44–49)	⚹ Discuss the areas that Vasco da Gama and Pedro Álvars Cabral explored and the results of their voyages for Portugal. ⚹ Analyze the achievements of John Cabot and Amerigo Vespucci. ⚹ Evaluate the importance of Ferdinand Magellan's voyage.	**Regular** 1.5 days **Block Scheduling** .75 day *Block Scheduling Handbook with Team Teaching Strategies, Chapter 2*	**RS** Guided Reading Strategy 2.3 **E** Creative Teaching Strategy: Collage
SECTION 4: **The Opening of the Atlantic** (pp. 50–53)	⚹ Analyze the effects of new trade routes on Portugal and Spain. ⚹ Evaluate how the Columbian Exchange affected Europeans and American Indians. ⚹ Identify reasons why some countries were searching for a Northwest Passage.	**Regular** 1.5 days **Block Scheduling** .75 day *Block Scheduling Handbook with Team Teaching Strategies, Chapter 2*	**RS** Guided Reading Strategy 2.4 **PS** Biography Reading 2: Cabeza de Vaca **SM** Geography Activity 2: Crossing the Atlantic

Chapter Resource Key

PS	Primary Sources	**A**	Assessment	Music	
RS	Reading Support	**REV**	Review	Video	
IC	Interdisciplinary Connections	**ELL**	Reinforcement and English Language Learners	Internet	
E	Enrichment		Transparencies	Holt Presentation Maker Using Microsoft® PowerPoint®	
SM	Skills Mastery		CD–ROM		

 One-Stop Planner CD-ROM

See the *One-Stop Planner* for a complete list of additional resources for students and teachers.

One-Stop Planner CD–ROM

It's easy to plan lessons, select resources, and print out materials for your students when you use the *One-Stop Planner CD–ROM with Test Generator.*

Technology Resources	Reinforcement, Review, and Assessment

 One-Stop Planner, Lesson 2.1
 Holt Researcher: American History CD–ROM
 Homework Practice Online
 HRW Go site

REV Section 1 Review, p. 37
A Daily Quiz 2.1
ELL Main Idea Activity 2.1
ELL English Audio Summary 2.1
ELL Spanish Audio Summary 2.1

 One-Stop Planner, Lesson 2.2
 Linking Geography and History Transparency 4: The World Atlas Circa 1500
 Exploring America's Past Video Segment: Visions of Adventure; Teacher's Guide, pp. 2–3
 Holt Researcher: American History CD–ROM
 CNN Presents America: Yesterday and Today, Beginnings to 1914 Segment: Columbus's Voyage–Then and Now
 Homework Practice Online
 HRW Go site

REV Section 2 Review, p. 43
A Daily Quiz 2.2
ELL Main Idea Activity 2.2
ELL English Audio Summary 2.2
ELL Spanish Audio Summary 2.2

 One-Stop Planner, Lesson 2.3
 Homework Practice Online

REV Section 3 Review, p. 49
A Daily Quiz 2.3
ELL Main Idea Activity 2.3
ELL English Audio Summary 2.3
ELL Spanish Audio Summary 2.3

 One-Stop Planner, Lesson 2.4
 Linking Geography and History Transparency 2: World Domestication
 American History Interactive Maps CD–ROM: The Columbian Exchange
Homework Practice Online

REV Section 4 Review, p. 53
A Daily Quiz 2.4
ELL Main Idea Activity 2.4
ELL English Audio Summary 2.4
ELL Spanish Audio Summary 2.4

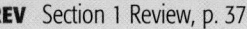

internet connect

HRW ONLINE RESOURCES
GO TO: go.hrw.com
Then type in a keyword.

TEACHER HOME PAGE
KEYWORD: SA3 Teacher

CHAPTER INTERNET ACTIVITIES
KEYWORD: SA3 CF2
Choose an activity to:
• research the history and impact of the printing press.
• learn about the life and work of Da Vinci.
• research Columbus' voyages to America.

CHAPTER ENRICHMENT LINKS
KEYWORD: SA3 CH2

ONLINE ASSESSMENT
Homework Practice
KEYWORD: SA3 HP2

Standardized Test Prep
KEYWORD: SA3 STP2

Rubrics
KEYWORD: SS Rubrics

ONLINE MAPS, CHARTS, AND GRAPHS
KEYWORD: SA3 MCG
• Empires of the Americas
• De Soto's Explorations
• Treasure from the Americas

CONTENT UPDATES
KEYWORD: SS Content Updates

HOLT PRESENTATION MAKER
KEYWORD: SA3 PPT2

ONLINE READING SUPPORT
KEYWORD: SS Strategies

CURRENT EVENTS
KEYWORD: S3 Current Events

Meeting Individual Needs

Ability Levels

Level 1 Basic-level activities designed for all students encountering new material

Level 2 Intermediate-level activities designed for average students

Level 3 Challenging activities designed for honors and gifted-and-talented students

English Language Learners Activities that address the needs of students with Limited English Proficiency

Chapter Review and Assessment

IC Vocabulary Activity 2
 Global Skill Builder CD–ROM
HRW Go site
REV Chapter 2 Tutorial for Students, Parents, Mentors, and Peers
REV Chapter 2 Review, pp. 54–55
 Chapter 2 Test Generator (on the One-Stop Planner)

A Chapter 2 Test (Form A or B)
A Alternative Assessment Handbook
A Chapter 2 Test for English Language Learners and Special-Needs Students

Build on What You Know

If You Were There...

Ask students to answer the following question:

Would you be interested in exploration?

Consider:

- the advantages of trade with other countries
- natural resources found in other countries

You Be the Historian

What's Your Opinion?

*To help students create their **Themes** Journal entries, provide the following examples of appropriate **agree**/**disagree** statements.*

EXPLORING THE TIME LINE

GLOBAL EVENTS

internet connect

TOPIC: The Printing Press
GO TO: go.hrw.com
KEYWORD: SA3 CF2

Have students access the Internet through the HRW Go site to research the history and impact of the printing press over time. Then have students create a 3D model that reflects the change in printing press technology as well as the change in its social influence. Their model can be abstract or symbolic, and it should be constructed out of everyday household materials.

CHAPTER

2 The Age of Exploration
(1350–1550)

Columbus encountered the Taino Indians when he reached the Americas.

This ancient manuscript shows the Aztec people and their gods.

UNITED STATES

1428 The Aztec Empire is founded.

1492 Christopher Columbus and his crew reach the Americas on October 12.

1497 John Cabot reaches the coast of North America.

1350	1400	1450	1490

c. 1350 The Black Death ends in Europe.

1440s Johannes Gutenberg invents a printing press that uses movable type, making it much easier to print books.

1492 The *Reconquista* ends when the Muslim kingdom of Granada surrenders to Ferdinand and Isabella.

1495 Leonardo da Vinci begins painting his masterpiece *The Last Supper*.

WORLD

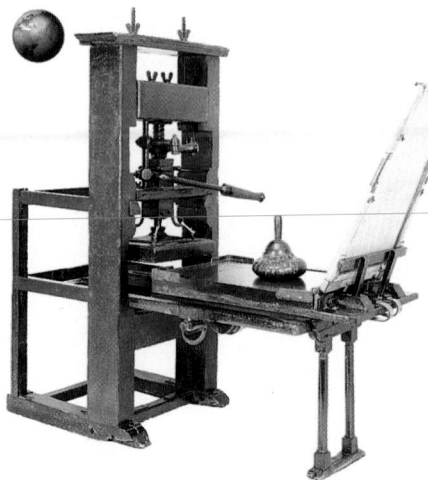

The invention of the printing press aided the spread of ideas during the Renaissance.

Build on What You Know

During the Middle Ages communication and trade between Europe and other areas slowed. By the 1300s, however, Europeans had formed trading relationships with merchants from Africa and Asia. During the Renaissance, Europeans began to explore and seek out new sea routes to Asia. While trying to find a new route, Christopher Columbus reached the Americas in 1492.

Global Relations

Agree Europeans as well as Native Americans benefitted from European explorations.

Disagree Native American cultures were destroyed during European exploration.

Economics

Agree Trading with other countries leads to new alliances.

Disagree Trading with other countries takes away resources needed by your own country.

Science, Technology & Society

Agree With each new invention some aspect of exploration was improved.

Disagree New inventions encouraged explorers to venture farther from home and safety.

This map from the 1540s shows French explorations and settlements in North America. The map shows Canada at the bottom and Florida in the upper-right corner.

1500 Columbus is removed as governor of Spanish territories in the Americas.

1513 Vasco Núñez de Balboa is the first European to see the Pacific Ocean.

1535 Jacques Cartier sails up the St. Lawrence River to the site of present-day Montreal.

1500 **1510** **1520** **1530** **1540**

1500 Portuguese explorer Pedro Álvars Cabral lands in South America.

1522 Survivors of Ferdinand Magellan's expedition complete the first voyage around the world.

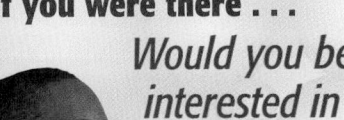

If you were there . . .
Would you be interested in exploration?

You Be the Historian

What's Your Opinion? Do you **agree** or **disagree** with the following statements? Support your point of view in your journal.

- **Global Relations** Exploration is good for all peoples involved.
- **Economics** Global trade makes a nation stronger.
- **Science, Technology, & Society** New inventions usually take much of the risk out of exploration.

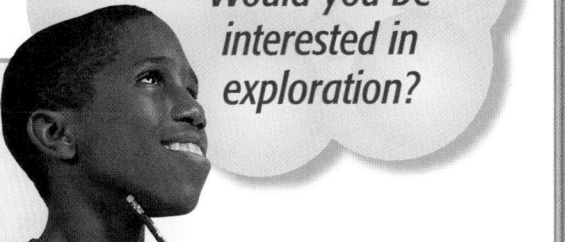

★ Biography

Vasco Núñez de Balboa.
The story of the untimely death of Spanish explorer Vasco Núñez de Balboa, the first European to see the Pacific Ocean, is full of intrigue and betrayal. After returning from his "discovery" of the Pacific Ocean, Balboa was confronted by the new governor of Panama, Pedro Arias Dávila, usually known as Pedrarias. Pedrarias and Balboa had an uneasy relationship. While Pedrarias was away further exploring the Pacific, he discovered that Balboa and others had been sending the king complaints about his conduct. Pedrarias learned that he was going to be replaced and put under investigation for his conduct. Fearing that Balboa's testimony might contribute to his downfall, Pedrarias had him arrested on various charges including rebellion and treason. After being tried by Pedrarias' chief justice, Balboa was found guilty, sentenced to death, and beheaded in 1519.

CRITICAL THINKING

What might have been a cause of tension between Balboa and Pedrarias?

ANSWER: Students might suggest that both men wanted to govern Panama, or that Pedrarias might have been jealous of Balboa's success as an explorer.

Section 1

OBJECTIVES

★ Explain how the Commercial Revolution and the Renaissance changed Europe.

★ Analyze the reasons why western Europeans sought a new sea route for trade with Africa and Asia.

★ Evaluate the effects of early Portuguese exploration on Africans.

SECTION 1 RESOURCES

REPRODUCIBLE
▶ Guided Reading Strategy 2.1
▶ Literature Reading 2: Marco Polo in China

TECHNOLOGY
▶ One-Stop Planner, Lesson 2.1
▶ Holt Researcher: American History CD–ROM
▶ Homework Practice Online
▶ HRW Go site

REINFORCEMENT, REVIEW, AND ASSESSMENT
▶ Section 1 Review, p. 37
▶ Daily Quiz 2.1
▶ Main Idea Activity 2.1
▶ English Audio Summary 2.1
▶ Spanish Audio Summary 2.1

Section 1

Europeans Set Sail

Read to Discover

1. How did the Commercial Revolution and the Renaissance change Europe?
2. Why did western Europeans want to find a new sea route for trade with Africa and Asia?
3. How did Portugal's early explorations affect Africans?

WHY IT MATTERS TODAY

Scientific and technological changes continue to affect our world. Use CNNfyi.com or other **current events** sources to find out about important scientific and technological changes taking place today. Record your findings in your journal.

Define
• capital
• joint-stock companies
• astrolabe
• monopoly
• caravel

Identify
• Black Death
• Commercial Revolution
• Renaissance
• Prince Henry
• Bartolomeu Dias

A trade union in the Netherlands used this seal.

The Story Continues

In 1299 the city of Arras in present-day France was famous for its wealthy merchants. The powerful Crespin family was so rich that it loaned money to cities, bishops, and even monarchs. Some people worried about this new interest in money. "Money is too much worshipped here," wrote poet Adam de la Halle about Arras. Others welcomed the changing economy. They thought it provided ways for workers to make money and improve their social status. When Baude Crespin died in 1316 his tombstone read, "Pray for his immortal spirit then, Laborers and working men."

★ The European Economy Grows

Europe's wealth and population grew steadily during the late Middle Ages. Then, in the mid-1300s Europe suffered a terrible blow. Some ships belonging to Italian merchants returned from Asia carrying rats infected with bubonic plague, a deadly disease. The plague led to an epidemic called the **Black Death**, which swept through Europe from about 1348 to 1350. The epidemic killed as many as 30 million people, about

Have students read Section 1 and complete Guided Reading Strategy 2.1. Choose one or more of the following activities to explore the section content with students. For further suggestions on block scheduling or team teaching, see the *Block Scheduling Handbook with Team Teaching Strategies.*

Note: To help students make meaningful connections between events in American history and those in their own hometown, use Chapter 2 **Hands-On History** activity, Looking at Your Region for the First Time.

LEVEL 1: Have students list the major events and developments discussed in this section. *(Students' lists should include the Black Death, the Commercial Revolution, creation of joint-stock companies, the Renaissance, trade networks, and exploration.)* Then give students an outline map of the world. Have each student create a content map that shows where each of the events occurred. Have students start with the subsection entitled The European Economy Grows and finish with Bartholomeu Dias's exploration around the Cape of Good Hope. Once students have finished, discuss the cause-and-effect sequence of events that led Europeans to seek a water route around the southern tip of Africa.
ENGLISH LANGUAGE LEARNERS

one third of Europe's population. One Italian man described the horror of the scene. "Great pits were dug and piled deep with the multitude [large numbers] of dead." The man continued, "I . . . buried my five children with my own hands."

Eventually Europe recovered from the Black Death and the shortage of workers it created. In the 1200s Europe had begun to experience the **Commercial Revolution**, a period of great change in the European economy. During this time, the way people did business changed dramatically. Throughout most of the Middle Ages, merchants had set their prices based on what the local community agreed was fair. During the Commercial Revolution, however, merchants and craftspeople became more aggressive about making a profit. Landlords encouraged farmers on rented lands to grow crops that could be sold at market for profit. Many cities grew rich, often from specializing in certain crafts. For example, the Italian city of Florence became famous for dyeing cloth. Venice, on the other hand, was known for its glassmaking. Venice and many other cities also began dealing in rare goods brought from faraway lands. In this way they became rich trading centers.

Wealthy people in European society began to gain greater status and power. Spanish poet Juan Ruiz described this trend in the mid-1300s.

This French tombstone showed the effect of the Black Death.

> **History Makers Speak** "Money can do much; it should be held in high esteem [regard]. It turns a tramp into a respected and honorable man. . . . The more money a man has, the more worthy he becomes, while the man who is penniless cannot call himself his own master. . . . Money makes hard things easy."

—Juan Ruiz, quoted in *The Medieval Reader*, edited by Norman Cantor

Merchant families in Europe wanted to get **capital**—money or property that is used to earn more money. The Medici (MED-ee-chee) family of Florence opened banks that made loans to monarchs, nobles, and other merchants. The borrowers repaid these loans with interest, which earned more money for the bankers. As a result of their wealth, the Medici and other bankers gained increasing influence in Europe. Merchants also created **joint-stock companies**. These are businesses in which a group of people invest together. The investors then share in the companies' profits and losses. Forming joint-stock companies helped merchants raise money while reducing the individual risk of starting a business for each investor.

✔ **Reading Check: Analyzing Information**
What effect did the Commercial Revolution have on Europe's economy? more focus on expanding trade, making profits, and raising capital

Interpreting the Visual Record

Trade and finance *European moneylenders gained more influence as monarchs, nobles, and merchants sought loans.* **How does this image depict the demand for moneylenders?**

★ **Economics**

Amsterdam and the Grain Trade. The Dutch city of Amsterdam made itself the grain capital of Europe. As Europe's population recovered following the Black Death, most countries could no longer produce enough grain to feed their people. These countries began importing it from elsewhere. The Dutch acquired grain from the Baltic ports and brought it to Amsterdam, where they re-exported it to Europe. Amsterdam became a storehouse for many goods because it was a convenient trading spot.

CRITICAL THINKING

Why might Europeans have bought their grain from the Dutch rather than go straight to the Baltic ports themselves?

ANSWER: Students might say that it was more convenient to get it from Amsterdam than to travel around gathering grain from many different ports.

Visual Record Answer

Students might suggest that there appear to be many people waiting to borrow money.

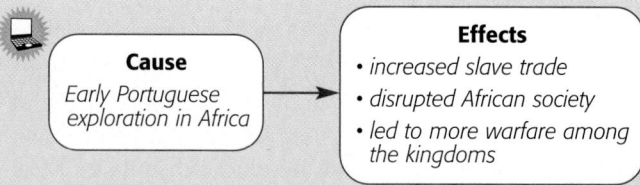

Cause
Early Portuguese exploration in Africa

Effects
- *increased slave trade*
- *disrupted African society*
- *led to more warfare among the kingdoms*

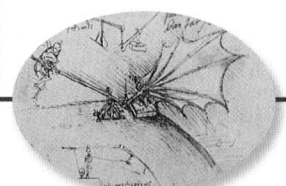

☆ The Renaissance

Some Europeans used their new wealth to support education and the arts. This change helped start the **Renaissance**, a rebirth of the arts and learning of ancient Greece and Rome. The Renaissance began in the 1300s in Italy and spread across Europe. It lasted into the 1600s.

During the Renaissance the interest in ancient Greek and Roman works mixed with new ideas about art, society, science, and technology. The translation of Arabic writings into Latin also shaped the Renaissance. Teachers taught students both the ideas of classical scholars and good morals. In his *Book of the Courtier*, Baldassare Castiglione (kahs-teel-YOH-nay) wrote that an ideal gentleman should know Greek and Latin. He should also "be very well acquainted with the poets, . . . and also skilled at writing both verse and prose."

Wealthy merchants and public officials supported artists, writers, musicians, and poets. Italian artist Leonardo da Vinci (lay-oh-NAHR-doh dah VEEN-chee), who painted the *Mona Lisa*, had many talents. He studied architecture, astronomy, biology, geology, and machinery. "A painter is not admirable unless he is universal," he wrote. Michelangelo Buonarroti (mee-kay-LAHN-jay-loh bwaw-nahr-RAW-tee) was another gifted Italian artist. He carved the sculpture *David* and also painted the ceiling of the Sistine Chapel at the Vatican in Rome.

Johannes Gutenberg made a major contribution to the Renaissance in the 1440s. He invented movable type for printing presses. The printing press made it much easier and less expensive to make many copies of a book. By 1500, European printers had printed between 15 and 20 million books. As one Italian writer said, "What did the Greeks and Romans ever invent that could be compared to the printing press?" Access to books helped spread the science and literature of the Renaissance across Europe.

Interpreting the Visual Record

Raphael *The Renaissance artist Raphael painted the fresco* School of Athens, *for Pope Julius II. The philosophers Aristotle and Plato stand at the center of the painting.* **How does this painting suggest the value that the Renaissance placed on Greek and Roman learning?**

LEVELS 1 AND 2: Have students create a drawing or a cartoon that depicts a change that occurred as a result of the Commercial Revolution or the Renaissance in Europe. For example, students can draw a cartoon that features people in Florence dyeing cloth and people in Venice trading rare goods, or artists painting and books being printed on a printing press. Once students have finished, have them present their work to the class. Finally, discuss the changes in Europe that resulted from the Commercial Revolution and the Renaissance.

HOMEWORK Have students imagine that they are explorers in the 1400s. Ask them to write a letter to Prince Henry of Portugal seeking navigational advice on sailing to Asia and Africa. Letters should focus on why they are interested in exploration and what help Prince Henry could offer. *(Students' letters should include looking for a better trade route to Asia, possibly around Africa. Students should also mention the various ways Prince Henry encouraged and aided sea exploration.)*

During the Renaissance many people believed that human beings were superior to all living creatures. "To you is given a body more graceful than other animals . . . to you wit, reason, [and] memory," wrote one teacher. Some people believed that human beings could achieve anything, which encouraged Europeans to explore the rest of the world.

Technological advances also led to exploration. Sailors began to make use of important developments. They used ancient astronomical knowledge and tools such as the magnetic compass and the **astrolabe**. The astrolabe allowed navigators to learn their ship's location by charting the position of the stars. Better charts and instruments let sailors travel the sea without needing landmarks to guide them.

✔ **Reading Check: Finding the Main Idea** What were the major achievements of the Renaissance? interest in arts, scientific development, and learning

⭐ Trade with Africa and Asia

Much of the wealth of the Commercial Revolution was created through trade. The greatest profits came from trading with distant lands such as Africa and Asia. From Africa came gold, ivory, salt, and slaves. Salt was used to preserve foods. From Asia came silk and spices. Skilled European tailors used silk fabric to sew fancy clothing, and cooks used expensive spices to flavor food. An old English recipe for fruit pie used "powdered pepper, cinnamon, cloves, mace, powdered ginger, pines, raisins or currants, saffron, and salt." Most of these spices grew only in Asia.

Goods usually traveled long overland routes to reach Europe. The Silk Road, for example, stretched several thousand miles westward from China. These journeys were very dangerous for traders because of possible attacks from bandits. Still, many merchants risked the trip because they could earn huge profits. Along the way, each merchant raised the price of the goods when selling to the next trader. By the time the goods arrived in Europe, their prices had risen greatly.

Some countries in western Europe wanted to find a new sea route to Africa and Asia. English, French, Portuguese, and Spanish merchants had many reasons for wanting such a route. First, they did not want to depend on others for the goods they needed. Merchants in Venice had a **monopoly** on the Asian products that reached the Mediterranean. This meant they had sole economic control of these goods. Instead of paying third parties, merchants wanted to make their own money from trade. In addition, by 1400 overland trade routes had become less reliable. Political changes in Asia and a growing threat of bandit raids made it more difficult to use the Black Sea route to bring goods from Asia to Europe. At the same time, ship designs had improved.

Meanwhile, many educated Europeans had become interested in Asian cultures. Marco Polo's book about his travels in Asia remained

THE GRANGER COLLECTION, NEW YORK

The Portuguese used astrolabes like this one to navigate at sea.

LINKING PAST to PRESENT ★

From Printing Press to Desktop

The printing press was a remarkable invention. The mass production of books spread new ideas across Europe. In the late 1800s inventors made an exciting new advance. They invented machines that made it easier for printers to set type.

In the mid-1980s printing and publishing again went through important changes. Desktop publishing became possible for anyone with access to a computer, a laser printer, and the right software. Today people print newsletters, magazines, and even books in their own homes or offices. One reporter for the *New York Times* described the change. "Armed with a few articles [and] a desktop publishing program . . . almost anyone can become a publisher." **What benefits and drawbacks does desktop publishing have for us today?**

Interdisciplinary Connection

▶**Art**◀

Renaissance Art. Florence, Italy, was one of the most dynamic art centers during the Renaissance. Florence established itself as an artistic center partly because its society allowed free discourse among classes and disciplines, unhampered by government or church restriction. In many cases, wealthy bankers and poor artisans sat together as equals to discuss such issues as cathedral construction and politics. This freedom of creative spirit provided an environment in which artists and writers thrived.

CRITICAL THINKING
Why was the free discussion of ideas important to the development of great art?

ANSWER: Students might suggest that it allowed the open exchange of ideas among people who ordinarily would not have reason to share their thoughts.

LINKING PAST TO PRESENT ANSWER
Students might mention that sharing ideas and information has become easier, but so has producing inaccurate information.

LEVEL 3: **LEVEL 3:** Organize the class into three groups. Have one group cover the Commercial Revolution, another group the Renaissance, and the third group trade with the East. Have each group prepare an issue of a magazine consisting of articles on important events and developments of the period; interviews with people from the period; and visuals that illustrate significant events, trends, people, or ideas. Have each student in each group be responsible for preparing one contribution to his or her group's magazine.

COOPERATIVE LEARNING

☆ CLOSE

Discuss with students the significance of the Commercial Revolution and the Renaissance to the European economy. Then ask each student to write a paragraph from the perspective of a European traveler who has recently been introduced to new products and changes in society that resulted from the growth in trade. Ask students to describe these new products or new ways of doing business and to offer their opinions about the positive and negative aspects of each change.

★ Geography

Mapmaking. Like the arts, the science of mapmaking, called cartography, experienced a rebirth during the 1400s. This happened when an ancient book of maps drawn by Ptolemy, an Alexandrian astronomer and geographer who lived during the A.D. 100s, was brought to Constantinople. Ideas presented in the book, including a scheme of longitude and latitude lines previously unknown to Europeans, revived an interest in cartography. The Portuguese took a special interest in the ideas presented in the text, particularly the latitude and longitude markings, which provided an easy universal frame of reference for mapmakers and navigators. As traders and explorers ventured farther from home, the maps grew to include new and amazing lands, peoples, and resources. As the maps grew, Europeans' view of the world expanded to include new possibilities and ideas.

CRITICAL THINKING

Why were latitude and longitude markings so important to trade and exploration?

ANSWER: As explorers found and described new trade routes, other explorers were able to retrace and extend their routes based on this universal frame of reference.

MAP ANSWER

Students might suggest that land travel may be difficult.

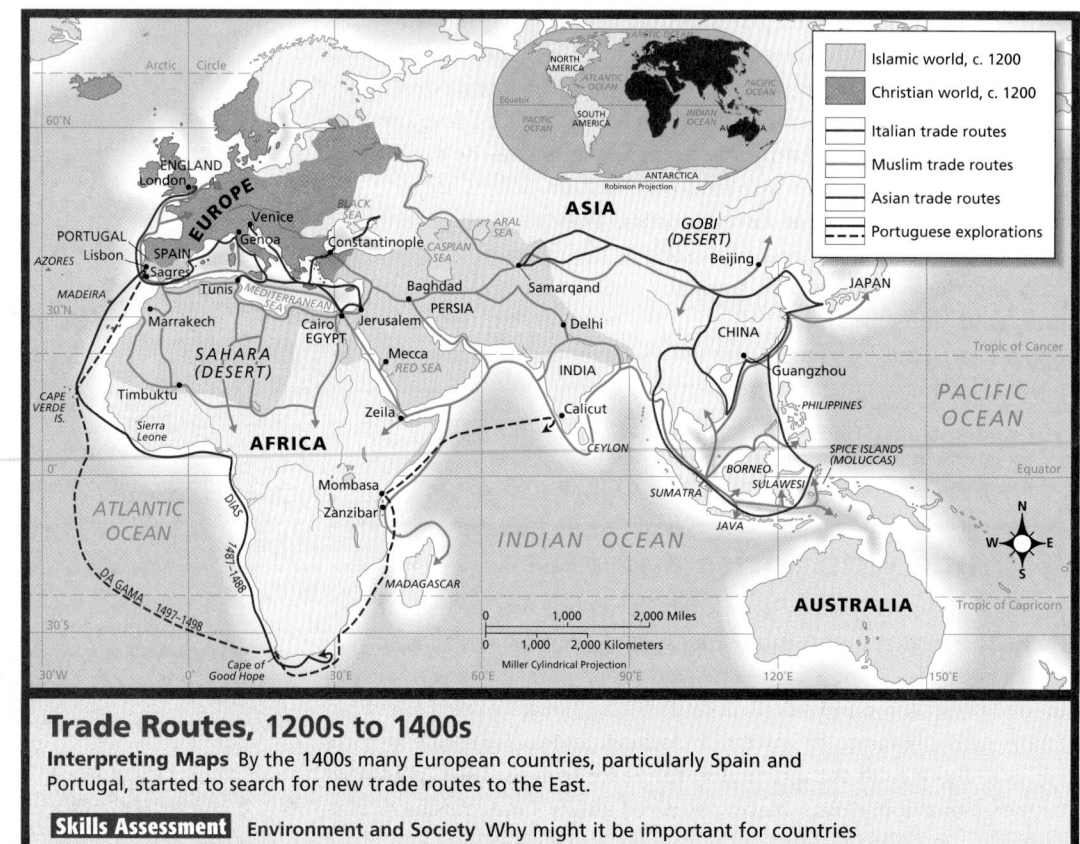

Trade Routes, 1200s to 1400s

Interpreting Maps By the 1400s many European countries, particularly Spain and Portugal, started to search for new trade routes to the East.

Skills Assessment Environment and Society Why might it be important for countries such as Portugal to find new trade routes to the East?

popular in Europe long after his death in 1324. Many Europeans hoped to learn more about these wondrous lands. Other Europeans hoped to spread Christianity. All of these factors encouraged Europeans to explore the Atlantic Ocean in search of new trade routes to Asia and Africa.

✔ **Reading Check: Summarizing** Why did Europeans want to trade directly with Asian and African merchants? to earn more money, to ensure they could get trade goods, to learn about other cultures

Research on the R⊙M

Free Find:
Henry the Navigator
After reading information about Prince Henry on the **Holt Researcher CD–ROM,** imagine what he studied. Make a list of classes that students hoping to become explorers would need to take.

☆ The Portuguese Explore Africa

Portugal became one of the leaders in exploration in the early 1400s. **Prince Henry,** known as the Navigator, greatly aided Portugal's efforts. Henry gathered together the finest mapmakers, sailors, and shipbuilders in the town of Sagres (SAH-greesh). He helped improve navigational instruments, such as the compass. His designers developed the **caravel,** a small ship built to move quickly and handle well. One Italian called caravels "the best ships that sailed the seas." Henry also paid for expeditions to explore the west coast of Africa. One observer wrote that Prince

Henry believed if he did not send explorers to this area, "no mariners [sailors] or merchants would ever dare to attempt it."

In 1487–88 Portuguese navigator **Bartolomeu Dias** led an expedition southward along the African coast. A storm blew the ships out to sea. When Dias sighted land again, he discovered that his ships had safely passed the southern tip of Africa! This point became known as the Cape of Good Hope. Dias wanted to continue the voyage, but his crew did not. According to Dias, his men were "terrified by the great seas through which they had passed . . . [and demanded] that they proceed no farther." They also were running low on supplies, so Dias returned to Portugal.

The Portuguese explored all along the west coast of Africa and established small trading posts to supply their ships. They also bargained with local rulers and merchants for gold, ivory, and slaves. The slave trade that developed had a terrible effect on African communities. It led to more warfare among the kingdoms of West Africa and broke up many families. In 1444 a Portuguese record keeper reported what he saw in Africa.

This bronze statue of a flute player came from what is now Benin, in West Africa.

History Makers Speak

❝Mothers would clasp [hold] their infants in their arms, and throw themselves on the ground to cover them with their bodies . . . so that they could prevent their children from being separated from them.❞

—Gomes Eanes de Zurara, from *The Chronicles of the Discovery and Conquest of Guinea*

Analyzing Primary Sources
Identifying Points of View
How do you think the speaker feels about what he sees? Explain your answer.
Answers may vary, but students should note the emotions and reactions that the speaker is describing.

The Portuguese sent many enslaved Africans to other Portuguese colonies. The Africans were forced to work hard and endured terrible living conditions.

✔ **Reading Check: Identifying Cause and Effect** Why did the Portuguese explore Africa, and how did they affect many African people? for trade and to supply their ships; they contributed to slave trade, which disrupted African communities and families

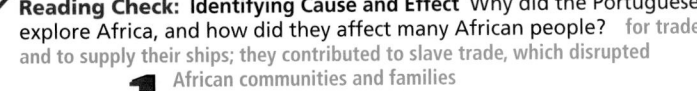

Section 1 Review

go.hrw.com Homework Practice Online
keyword: SA3 HP2

❶ **Define and explain:**
• capital
• joint-stock companies
• astrolabe
• monopoly
• caravel

❷ **Identify and explain:**
• Black Death
• Commercial Revolution
• Renaissance
• Prince Henry
• Bartolomeu Dias

❸ **Identifying Cause and Effect** Copy the graphic organizer below. Use it to show why the Portuguese began to explore Africa and how their actions affected Africans.

Causes → Portuguese Exploration → Effects

❹ **Finding the Main Idea**
a. How were the effects of the Commercial Revolution and the Renaissance similar and different?

b. What characteristics did most Renaissance artists, thinkers, and scientists share?

❺ **Writing and Critical Thinking**
Supporting a Point of View Imagine that you are a Portuguese merchant. Write a letter to other merchants persuading them that Portugal must find new sea routes for trading with Asia.

Consider the following:
• the wealth to be earned from trade
• the lure of other cultures
• recent technological accomplishments

Section 2

OBJECTIVES

⭐ Discuss Christopher Columbus's goal.

⭐ Identify what Columbus did during his explorations in the Americas.

⭐ Describe Portugal's reaction to news of Columbus's discoveries.

SECTION 2 RESOURCES

REPRODUCIBLE

▶ Guided Reading Strategy 2.2

▶ Graphic Organizer 2: The Voyages of Christopher Columbus

▶ Primary Source Reading 2: First Impressions of the New World

TECHNOLOGY

▶ One-Stop Planner, Lesson 2.2

▶ Linking Geography and History Transparency 4: The World Atlas Circa 1500

▶ Exploring America's Past Video Segment: Visions of Adventure; Teacher's Guide pp. 2–3

▶ Holt Researcher: American History CD–ROM

▶ CNN Presents America: Beginnings to 1914 Segment: Columbus's Voyage—Then and Now

▶ Homework Practice Online

▶ HRW Go site

REINFORCEMENT, REVIEW, AND ASSESSMENT

▶ Section 2 Review, p. 43

▶ Daily Quiz 2.2

▶ Main Idea Activity 2.2

▶ English Audio Summary 2.2

▶ Spanish Audio Summary 2.2

 **LET'S GET STARTED!**

Make three columns on the chalkboard. Label one *Facts you are positive you know about Columbus,* the second *Facts you think you know about Columbus,* and the third *Facts you want to find out about Columbus.* As students enter the classroom, ask them to write facts and ideas in the three categories. Allow time for students' responses. Then tell students that the purpose of studying Section 2 will be to check their knowledge of Columbus, to modify it by correcting errors, and to add to it by answering questions they have raised. Tell students that they will use these lists later on in this section.

Section 2

Voyages to the Americas

Read to Discover

1. What was Christopher Columbus's goal?
2. What did Columbus do on his explorations in the Americas?
3. How did Portugal react to news of Columbus's discoveries?

WHY IT MATTERS TODAY

Christopher Columbus was the first European to explore the Caribbean. Today many Caribbean nations have a mix of European, Native American, and African cultures. Use **CNNfyi.com** or other **current events** sources to learn about some of the food, languages, music, or sports that are common in the Caribbean today. Record your findings in your journal.

Define

• viceroy
• convert

Identify

• Christopher Columbus
• King Ferdinand
• Queen Isabella
• *Reconquista*
• Line of Demarcation
• Treaty of Tordesillas

The Story Continues

In 1488 Christopher Columbus traveled to Portugal to meet with King John II. The Italian explorer hoped to reach Asia by sailing across the Atlantic Ocean. He hoped that the king would give him money and ships to achieve his dream. King John had called Columbus "a big talker . . . full of fancy and imagination." However, he was still interested in Columbus's idea. Just as Columbus arrived in Lisbon, Bartolomeu Dias returned with news of sailing around the tip of Africa. King John decided that reaching Asia by way of Africa was the best idea. Columbus left Portugal without support for his plan.

Columbus was inspired by travelers' tales, such as Marco Polo's Description of the World.

⭐ Columbus's Bold Idea

Christopher Columbus was a sailor from Genoa, Italy. As a young man he sailed to Iceland and to West Africa. Stories of fabulous kingdoms and wealth in the Indies—a common European name for Asia—captured Columbus's imagination. He became convinced that he could reach Asia by sailing west across the Atlantic Ocean.

TEACH

Have students read Section 2 and complete Guided Reading Strategy 2.2. Choose one or more of the following activities to explore the section content with students. For further suggestions on block scheduling or team teaching, see the *Block Scheduling Handbook with Team Teaching Strategies.*

 LEVEL 1: Ask students why a person would have been skeptical about sponsoring Columbus's journey. *(Students' responses should include the high cost of sponsoring such a trip, the belief that it was 10,000 miles across the ocean to Asia, and a lack of knowledge about the existence of North and South America.)* Have students create a want ad written by Christopher Columbus seeking financial backers for his exploration. The want ads should explain why Columbus thought such a journey would be possible.

Columbus's plan was very risky at the time. No one knew the size of the great ocean to the west of Europe. Some people claimed that more than 10,000 miles separated Europe from the Indies. Traveling such a long distance seemed impossible. Navigating the open sea was hard, and crews would need enough food and water to last for months. Columbus believed such a voyage was possible. He was convinced that the Atlantic Ocean was much smaller than commonly thought.

Columbus went to Spain to ask **King Ferdinand** and **Queen Isabella** for help. Spain was fighting the kingdom of Granada, which was held by the Moors. These North African Muslims had conquered the area in the early Middle Ages. Ferdinand and Isabella did not answer Columbus for six years because they were trying to capture Granada. In the meantime, he failed to get support from other European leaders.

Finally, in January 1492 Spain won Granada, and the *Reconquista* (re-kawng-KEE-stah)—the ongoing struggle to drive the Moors from Spain—ended. Ferdinand and Isabella agreed to pay for Columbus's trip. They hoped that Columbus would find a new sea route to the Indies so that Spain could better compete with Portugal.

Ferdinand and Isabella ordered Columbus to bring back any "Pearls, Precious Stones, Gold, Silver, Spiceries, and other Things and Merchandise of whatever kind, name or description that may be." They told him to claim for Spain any lands he explored. They promised to reward Columbus with some of the gold he sent back to Spain and with profits from any trading. In addition, he would become **viceroy**, or royal governor, of the lands he explored.

✔ **Reading Check: Summarizing** What did King Ferdinand and Queen Isabella hope to gain from Columbus's trip? wealth, goods, new land, a trade route to Asia

---

★ Crossing the Ocean

On August 3, 1492, just before sunrise, Columbus's three ships set sail. The *Niña* and the *Pinta* were caravels. Columbus sailed in the larger *Santa María.* The cramped ships were crewed by some 90 sailors in all and carried a year's worth of supplies.

Columbus sailed for the Canary Islands off the west coast of Africa. From there he caught a wind that blew his ships west across the Atlantic Ocean. The tiny fleet made good progress. Soon, the ships passed the limits of Columbus's maps. They were sailing into unknown waters. The crew grew more and more worried after a month passed with no sight of land. "Here the people could stand it no longer, and complained of the long voyage," wrote Columbus in his journal.

Just a few days later, the crew began to see signs that land was near. Columbus promised a reward "to him who first sang out that he saw land." On October 12, 1492, a lookout cried "Land! Land!" The journey from the Canary Islands had taken 33 days.

BIOGRAPHY

Queen Isabella

1451–1504

Queen Isabella was the daughter of the ruler of the powerful kingdom of Castile (ka-STEEL). At the age of 18, she married Ferdinand. He was the heir to the throne of Aragon, which was another powerful Spanish kingdom. Their marriage united the houses of Aragon and Castile. Isabella became queen of Castile in 1474.

During her reign, Isabella financed and helped direct Castile's military operations. When Christopher Columbus came to the royal court, Isabella's support proved essential to his cause. When she died in 1504, Spain was about to become one of the most powerful nations on Earth. **How did Queen Isabella strengthen Spain's power?**

Interdisciplinary Connection

▶Literature◀

Columbus's Log.
Columbus wrote a detailed journal covering the events of his first voyage to the Americas. His log remained in his family for two generations before it became lost. The only reliable sources for some of the details of Columbus's original journal are excerpts and abstracted material recorded by Bartolomé de las Casas, a Dominican friar. Las Casas was a friend of the Columbus family, and he apparently borrowed their copy of the log before it disappeared—a fortunate circumstance for historians.

CRITICAL THINKING

Why is Las Casas's version of Columbus's journal so important to modern historians?

ANSWER: Students should point out that with each copy and translation, errors and changes can be introduced. Las Casas's version is now the best source available because it was derived directly from the original.

BIOGRAPHY ANSWER
Students might suggest that the Queen's support of a strong nation expanded Spain's borders by encouraging exploration.

ALL LEVELS: Copy the following flowchart onto the chalkboard, omitting the italicized answers. Have students complete the flowchart to show how Portugal reacted to news of Columbus's voyages. After students have completed their flowcharts, discuss with students Portugal's reaction to the news of Columbus's discoveries.

ENGLISH LANGUAGE LEARNERS

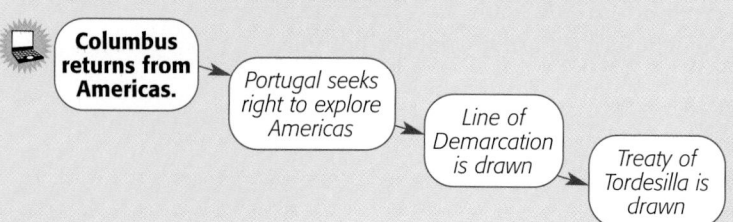

LEVEL 2: Lead a class discussion on the significance of Columbus's first journey. Have students use the textbook to write entries in the ship's logs for either the *Niña, Pinta,* or the *Santa María.* Ask students to begin their entries on the day that the ships left Spain and to make their final entry for the day that Columbus returned to Spain. Entries should describe the journey's progress and the crew's feelings. Encourage volunteers to share their entries with the class. Finally, discuss the range of emotions that Columbus's crew must have felt at different stages of the journey.

That's Interesting!

During his third voyage to the Americas, Columbus and his brothers were removed as the governors of the islands and brought back to Spain in shackles. Humiliated by this turn of events, Columbus refused to have his chains removed during the entire return trip. During this voyage Columbus also suffered from sleeplessness, eyestrain, and a form of rheumatoid arthritis.

Technology Resources

Exploring America's Past Video Segment: Visions of Adventure; Teacher's Guide, pp. 2–3

Search 1821, Play to 6472
Videodisc Red Side A
See *Teacher's Guide* for Spanish barcode.

Research on the R✺M

Free Find:
Columbus and the Taino
After reading the letter in which Columbus describes his contact with the Taino on the **Holt Researcher CD–ROM**, imagine that you are a Taino. Create a story describing your thoughts when you saw Columbus for the first time.

⭐ Columbus's First Explorations

The ships landed on an island in the Bahamas. Columbus called the island San Salvador, which means "Holy Savior." Columbus thought that he was near the coast of China or the islands of Japan. He did not realize that he had reached a different continent entirely.

Columbus searched for riches on other islands, including one he called Hispaniola. There he met the Taino (TY-noh). He called these people Indians because he believed that he had landed in the fabled Indies. The Taino lived in small, peaceful farming villages. Columbus described them as "very well built, with very handsome bodies and very good faces." He also noted that the Taino were "so generous . . . that no one would believe it who has not seen it. They never refuse [to give] anything which they possess, if it be asked of them."

Columbus had little desire to learn about the Taino's culture. He and his crew were more interested in discovering gold. "There may be many things that I don't know," he wrote in his journal. "But I do not wish to delay but to discover and go to many islands to find gold." Columbus and his search parties explored several islands. They asked the Taino if they knew of any wealthy rulers, gold mines, or great palaces. They collected little gold but saw many natural wonders. Columbus described these sights in a letter.

History Makers Speak
❝All [these islands] are beautiful, of a thousand shapes, and all are accessible [reachable] and filled with trees of a thousand kinds and tall, and they seem to touch the sky.❞

—Christopher Columbus, from *The Four Voyages of Columbus,* edited by Cecil Jane

Columbus spent more than two months exploring. Then he decided that he had found enough gold and local treasures to return to Spain. Before he and his men left, however, the *Santa María* struck a coral reef and sank. There was not enough room for all of the sailors on the *Niña* and *Pinta.* Instead, Columbus and his men built a small colony on the north coast of Hispaniola. They called it La Navidad, the Spanish word for Christmas. Columbus left about 40 of his men at La Navidad and promised to return for them soon. He then boarded the *Niña* and set sail for Spain in January of 1493.

Columbus's small fleet faced great risks on its voyage across the Atlantic Ocean.

✔**Reading Check: Finding the Main Idea** What interested Columbus most on his first voyage to the Americas? finding gold and treasure

LEVEL 3: Organize the class into three groups. Have one group represent Spain, another group represent Portugal, and the third group represent the Pope. Ask each group to prepare for a debate over the control of exploration in the Americas. The groups representing Spain and Portugal should focus on the economic advantages of controlling exploration in the Americas, while the group representing the Pope should focus on achieving a compromise. Have groups present their arguments and lead a class discussion on what might be the best solution. **COOPERATIVE LEARNING**

 HOMEWORK Ask students to imagine that they are television reporters covering Columbus's explorations. Have students prepare a report explaining what Columbus did on his explorations in the Americas. Have volunteers present their reports to the class.

★ CLOSE

Have students refer to the three lists created during the *Let's Get Started!* activity. Review the information in each column with students. Then call on volunteers to correct errors, modify information, or confirm facts found in the lists.

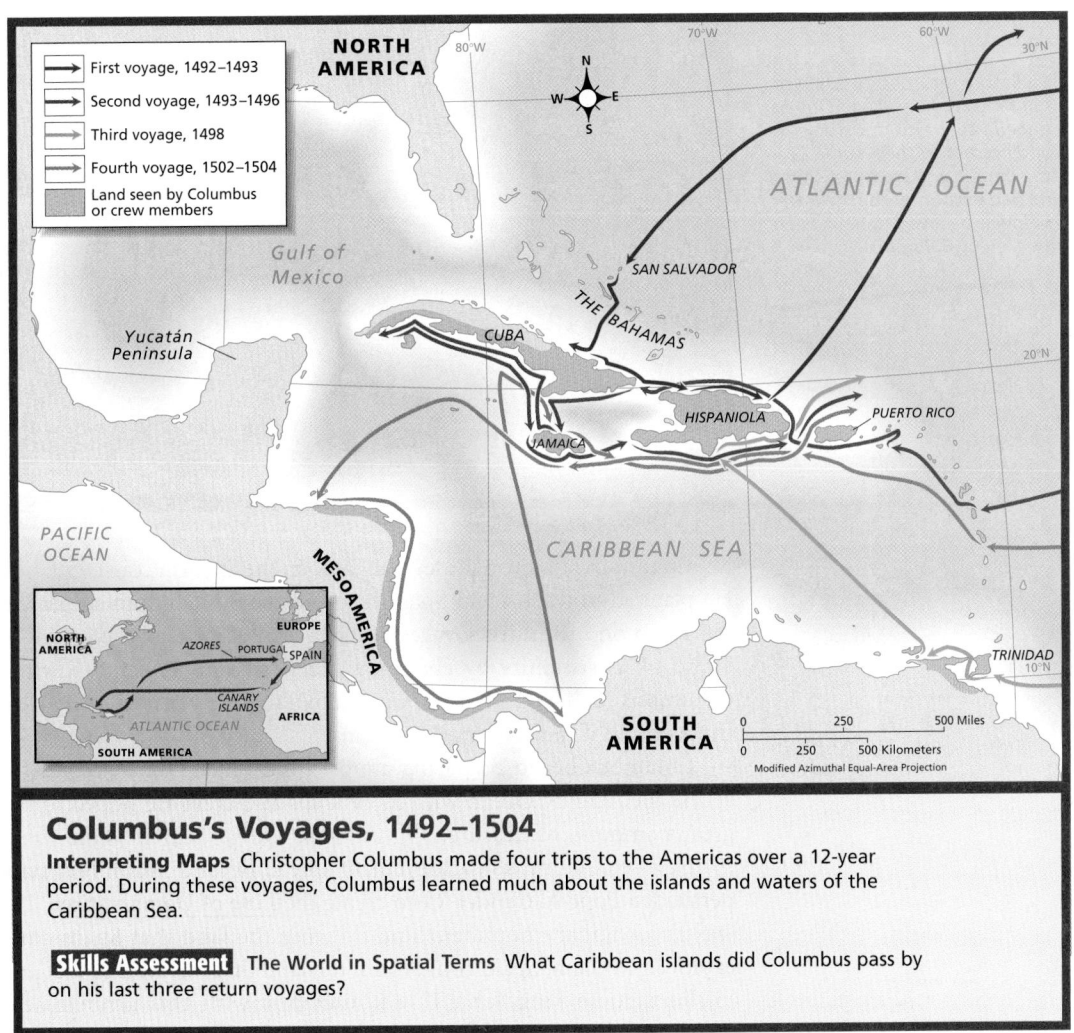

Columbus's Voyages, 1492–1504

Interpreting Maps Christopher Columbus made four trips to the Americas over a 12-year period. During these voyages, Columbus learned much about the islands and waters of the Caribbean Sea.

Skills Assessment The World in Spatial Terms What Caribbean islands did Columbus pass by on his last three return voyages?

★ Europe Learns of Columbus's Voyage

After a stormy return trip, Columbus finally reached Spain. He wrote a letter to King Ferdinand and Queen Isabella boasting of the wealth that lay across the ocean. The king and queen were excited by Columbus's news. They were even more pleased when he brought them gold nuggets and rare treasures. As a reward for his discoveries, Ferdinand and Isabella made Columbus an admiral and a governor.

 History Makers Speak ❝We, considering the risk and danger to which you have exposed yourself for our service . . . [award you] the said offices of Admiral of the said Ocean Sea, . . . and of viceroy and governor of the said islands and mainland.❞

—King Ferdinand and Queen Isabella, quoted in *The Conquest of Paradise*, by Kirkpatrick Sale

Analyzing Primary Sources
Identifying Points of View
Why did Ferdinand and Isabella believe that Columbus deserved a reward? He had gone on a dangerous journey for them.

Spotlight on Columbus's Explorations

Organize the class into four groups. Have each group use information from this section to create an act of a play based on the life of Christopher Columbus. Each act should be based on one of the following topics: 1) Columbus's appeal to Isabella and Ferdinand for support for his first voyage (explaining his goals, his promises to Ferdinand and Isabella, and their promises to him); 2) Columbus's description of his first voyage (of the journey itself, of the people he met, and of the goods he brought back to Europe); 3) Isabella's and Ferdinand's reaction to Columbus's voyage (including their thoughts regarding his efforts, the goods he brought back, and his treatment of the Taino); or 4) Columbus's description of his later journeys and life. Allow time for the class to act out the play. Once students have completed their presentation, discuss each of the acts and give feedback regarding the historical accuracy of each.

BLOCK SCHEDULING , **COOPERATIVE LEARNING**

★ Daily Life

Columbus's Second Voyage. The people responsible for supplying Columbus's ships for his second voyage to the Americas sacrificed quality to keep the price of provisions low. They used cheap barrels that allowed water to leak and wine to sour. Once Columbus's ships hit land, the tropical climate molded and dampened the hardtack biscuits that were a staple of ocean travel. This caused weevils to infest the food. The sailors were forced to eat new and unfamiliar foods, such as iguanas and pancakes made of cassava roots, which they learned about from the American Indians.

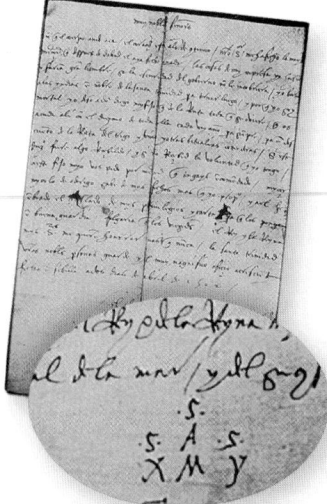

Columbus returned to Spain to tell King Ferdinand and Queen Isabella about his discovery and present to them some of the people and treasures that he had encountered. The letter below is believed to have been written by Columbus.

THE GRANGER COLLECTION

Columbus also brought several Taino to the Spanish court with him. He planned to teach them Spanish so they could help him speak with the Taino on his future voyages. Isabella wanted priests to **convert** the Taino to Christianity by changing their religious beliefs. However, Columbus believed that it was acceptable to enslave American Indians even if they became Christians.

Columbus began preparing almost immediately for a second trip across the Atlantic Ocean with more ships and crew. He hoped to find greater amounts of treasure.

News of Columbus's achievement spread beyond Spain. Ferdinand persuaded Pope Alexander VI to create the **Line of Demarcation.** This was an imaginary boundary line showing the land that Spain could explore and claim. Spain could claim the land that was west of this line.

Portuguese king John II was unhappy with this arrangement, which he felt favored Spain. To prevent conflict, the leaders of the two nations chose to compromise. Spain and Portugal signed the **Treaty of Tordesillas** (tawr-day-SEEL-yahs) in June 1494, which moved the Line of Demarcation some 800 miles farther west. This gave Portugal more opportunity to claim lands unexplored by other Europeans.

✔ **Reading Check: Analyzing Information** What was done in response to Portugal's unhappiness with the Line of Demarcation? A treaty moving the line west was signed.

★ Columbus's Later Voyages

Columbus returned to La Navidad in 1493 on his second voyage. He found that the colony had been destroyed and that all the sailors had been killed. Columbus was disappointed but began building new settlements on the islands. In 1498 Columbus became the first European explorer to see South America. He then returned to Hispaniola.

☆ REVIEW AND ASSESS

Have students complete the **Section 2 Review** on p. 43. Then have students complete **Daily Quiz 2.2**. As **Alternative Assessment**, you may want to use the ship's log entries or want-ads exercises in this section's lessons.

☆ RETEACH

Have students complete **Main Idea Activity for English Language Learners and Special-Needs Students 2.2**. Then ask students to write the section's heading and subheadings on a sheet of paper, leaving spaces between each. Then have each student list the main ideas of the subheadings in the appropriate spaces. Pair students and have them compare their main ideas. **ENGLISH LANGUAGE LEARNERS , COOPERATIVE LEARNING**

☆ EXTEND

Using biographies about Christopher Columbus, excerpts from his writings, and other research materials, have students write reports on the areas he explored. Have students describe the people, potential wealth, and resources of the areas Columbus explored. Encourage volunteers to discuss their findings with the class. **BLOCK SCHEDULING**

Although Columbus was the governor of these new Spanish territories, he spent his time exploring. The living conditions in the colonies grew poor, partly because the Spaniards had difficulty growing crops in the tropical climate. Columbus fought many small battles with the Taino. He enslaved the Taino he defeated despite Isabella's instructions not to do so.

These problems made Ferdinand and Isabella unhappy with Columbus. In 1500 they removed him from his post as governor. When he returned to Spain, Columbus pleaded to make one last voyage to the Americas. They agreed, and he set sail in 1502. The ships ran into bad weather off the coast of Central America and they wrecked on the Caribbean island of Jamaica. There Columbus wrote in his journal that the sailors had "nothing to look forward to but death." They spent a year on Jamaica before being rescued by Spanish colonists from Hispaniola. In 1504 Columbus returned to Spain a broken man.

Columbus lived for two more years in very poor health. His share of the royal income from the Caribbean had made him wealthy. However, he was too sick to participate in the royal court. Columbus often complained to family and friends that those he had served had forgotten him. In 1506 he died "unnoticed and unsung," according to one modern historian. It would be years before Europeans realized the impact of Columbus on their world.

THE GRANGER COLLECTION

Interpreting the Visual Record

A royal gift *Columbus was granted this coat of arms for his achievements.* **What do you think the different images on the coat of arms represent?**

✔ **Reading Check: Drawing Inferences and Conclusions** Why were the later voyages of Columbus less successful than his first? He did not govern his colonies well, and he was shipwrecked.

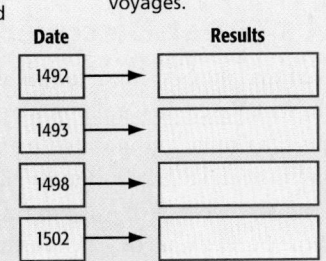

Section 2 Review

go.hrw.com **Homework Practice Online**
keyword: SA3 HP2

1 Define and explain:
• viceroy
• convert

2 Identify and explain:
• Christopher Columbus
• King Ferdinand
• Queen Isabella
• *Reconquista*
• Line of Demarcation
• Treaty of Tordesillas

3 Sequencing Copy the graphic organizer below. Use it to organize the information you have learned about Columbus's four voyages.

Date	Results
1492	
1493	
1498	
1502	

4 Finding the Main Idea
a. Do you think Columbus's voyages succeeded or failed? Explain your answer.

b. What do you think would have happened in the Spanish settlements if Isabella and Ferdinand had not removed Columbus from his post as viceroy?

5 Writing and Critical Thinking
Identifying Cause and Effect Imagine that you are an adviser to the Portuguese king in 1493. Prepare a short report describing the reasons for and effects of the voyage Columbus has just made.

Consider the following:
• Europeans' goal of finding a new sea route to Asia
• the people and gold Columbus encountered in the Americas
• the Line of Demarcation

Visual Record Answer

Students might suggest that each panel depicts an image representing either Spain or Columbus's voyages.

Section 2 Review
ANSWERS

1 Define
• viceroy, p. 39
• convert, p. 42

2 Identify
• Christopher Columbus, p. 38
• King Ferdinand, p. 39
• Queen Isabella, p. 39
• *Reconquista*, p. 39
• Line of Demarcation, p. 42
• Treaty of Tordesillas, p. 42

3 1492; San Salvador, Bahamas; met Taino, collected gold and treasures; 1493; La Navidad destroyed; created new settlements; 1498; South America; explored; 1502; Caribbean; got shipwrecked

4 a. Students might suggest that they were successful because they opened up new territory for settlement or because Columbus found gold and treasures. Others might suggest that they were unsuccessful because he mistreated the American Indians and was a poor governor.
b. Students might suggest that the Spanish settlers would have run out of food or gotten into more fights with the Taino.

5 Students' reports will vary but should consider the need for finding a new route to Asia, what Columbus encountered in the Americas, and the Line of Demercation.

Section 3

OBJECTIVES

✪ Discuss the areas that Vasco da Gama and Pedro Álvars Cabral explored and the results of their voyages for Portugal.

✪ Analyze the achievements of John Cabot and Amerigo Vespucci.

✪ Evaluate the importance of Ferdinand Magellan's voyage.

SECTION **3** RESOURCES

REPRODUCIBLE
► Guided Reading Strategy 2.3

TECHNOLOGY
► One-Stop Planner, Lesson 2.3
► Homework Practice Online

REINFORCEMENT, REVIEW, AND ASSESSMENT
► Section 3 Review, p. 49
► Daily Quiz 2.3
► Main Idea Activity 2.3
► English Audio Summary 2.3
► Spanish Audio Summary 2.3

LET'S GET STARTED!

As students enter the classroom have them identify Columbus's major goal for exploration. (*Students' responses should indicate he wanted to sail across the Atlantic Ocean to find a new sea route to Asia.*) Allow time for students to write their response. Then ask students if Columbus really achieved his major goal. (*Students' answers will vary but should indicate that Columbus's voyages did gain some success.*) Explain to students that in Section 3 they will learn how and why other explorers continued to search for a water route to Asia. Tell them that they will also learn about the areas these explorers visited and the importance of Magellan's voyage.

Section 3

The Race for Trade Routes

Read to Discover

1. Where did Vasco da Gama and Pedro Álvars Cabral explore, and what was the result of these voyages for Portugal?
2. What did John Cabot and Amerigo Vespucci achieve?
3. Why was Ferdinand Magellan's voyage important?

WHY IT MATTERS TODAY

Instead of sea exploration, today some countries are interested in exploring space. Use **CNN fyi.com** or other **current events** sources to find stories related to recent space explorations and the people involved in these projects. Record your findings in your journal.

Define
• strait
• circumnavigate

Identify
• Vasco da Gama
• Pedro Álvars Cabral
• John Cabot
• Amerigo Vespucci
• Vasco Núñez de Balboa
• Ferdinand Magellan

The Story Continues

Christopher Columbus always believed that he had landed just off the coast of China. He knew, however, that many people did not believe his claims. "Because everything [the wealth of the Indies] did not appear immediately, I was held up to abuse," he wrote. King Manuel had become ruler of Portugal in 1495. Manuel was one of those who thought that an eastern sea route to Asia, not Columbus's proposed western route, made more sense.

Chinese porcelain was a highly valued trade item in Europe.

⭐ Portugal's Great Discoveries

King Manuel believed that the best route to Asia was around the southern tip of Africa. He sent **Vasco da Gama** on an expedition around the Cape of Good Hope. Da Gama, a minor noble and skilled sailor, spent two years preparing his fleet. He left Lisbon in July 1497 and arrived in southwestern India in May 1498. Two Muslim traders greeted da Gama when he sailed into the port of Calicut. They cried out in Portuguese, "A lucky venture, a lucky venture! Plenty of rubies, plenty of emeralds!

TEACH

Have students read Section 3 and complete Guided Reading Strategy 2.3. Choose one or more of the following activities to explore the section content with students. For further suggestions on block scheduling or team teaching, see the *Block Scheduling Handbook with Team Teaching Strategies.*

 LEVEL 1: On an outline map of the world, ask students to trace the exploration routes described in this section. Ask students to create a key identifying each explorer by color. Have students refer to the textbook for help with labeling the locations reached by each explorer. After students have completed their maps, discuss the results and significance of these explorations.
ENGLISH LANGUAGE LEARNERS

ALL LEVELS: Tell students that the survivors of Magellan's crew were the first known people to circumnavigate Earth. Have students use details from this section of the textbook to write a dialogue between a survivor of Magellan's voyage and one of the financial backers. *(Students' dialogues will vary but should incorporate details from the textbook.)* Ask students to describe the conditions endured by the crew during the journey and the significance of proving that an all-water route between Europe and Asia existed.
ENGLISH LANGUAGE LEARNERS

You owe great thanks to God, for having brought you to a country holding such riches!" The king of Calicut even became angry with da Gama for not bringing the traditional gifts. One of da Gama's crew members wrote, "We never expected to hear our language spoken so far away from Portugal."

The Portuguese soon realized that the Indians had been trading with Muslim and Italian merchants for many years. Da Gama made two more trips back to India. He governed a small Portuguese colony there. As a result of his efforts, Portugal had won the European race for a new sea route to the wealth of Asia.

Another Portuguese explorer, **Pedro Álvars Cabral**, made his discovery by accident. He was leading a fleet along da Gama's route down the west coast of Africa. A terrible storm blew the ships far off course. Cabral's ships drifted westward for weeks. In 1500 Cabral finally reached South America. He landed somewhere along the coast of what is now Brazil. He claimed the land for Portugal, not knowing at the time that he had landed on the coast of a continent rather than a large island. Brazil's eastern shore was on Portugal's side of the Line of Demarcation, so Cabral was able to claim this land for his country. Portugal eventually founded forts, trading posts, and settlements in Brazil.

✔ **Reading Check: Summarizing** Explain da Gama's and Cabral's important accomplishments. Da Gama found an eastern trade route to Asia, and Cabral claimed land in South America for Portugal.

⭐ Cabot and Vespucci Explore

Like Christopher Columbus, other Italian explorers sailed for other nations, looking for wealth, knowledge, and adventure. Giovanni Caboto, called **John Cabot** by the English, also wanted to find a sea route to Asia. He knew that King Henry VII of England was interested in controlling such a route. Cabot offered to pay for his own expedition. He asked only that the king grant him a royal charter to any lands he found. The king agreed, and Cabot made voyages in 1497 and 1498.

King Henry told Cabot "to seek out, discover, and finde . . . countreyes, regions or provinces . . . whiche before this time have beene unknowen to all Christians." Cabot hoped to sail farther north than Columbus and continue on to Asia. Instead, Cabot found North America. Cabot left very few records of his journey, but it is believed that he traveled along the coast of present-day Newfoundland in Canada. Although Cabot did not find a passage to the Indies, his voyages were successful. They became the basis of England's claim to land in North America. Henry VII rewarded Cabot and then sent him out again to find a way to Asia. Cabot and his fleet disappeared mysteriously on this expedition. Historian Polydore Vergil wrote at the time of Cabot's journey. "[Cabot] found his new lands only in the ocean's bottom, to which he and his ship are thought to have sunk."

Interpreting the Visual Record

India *Vasco da Gama and his crew arrived on the southwest coast of India in 1498.* **What parts of this image suggest that da Gama had encountered a powerful kingdom?**

ALL LEVELS: Take an outline map of the world and fill in the names of countries and geographic features discussed in this section. Next to each of these names, have students identify the first explorer to travel to the area, the name of the country the explorer sailed for, and the year that the explorer arrived in the new area. For example, if the map showed the eastern portion of Brazil, students should indicate that Cabral was the first explorer to arrive there, that he sailed for the Portuguese, and that he arrived there in 1500. **ENGLISH LANGUAGE LEARNERS**

Note: For an additional teaching idea, see the Chapter Collage activity in the **Creative Teaching Strategies** handbook.

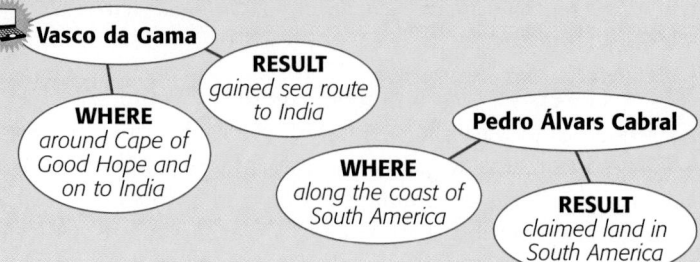 **ALL LEVELS:** Copy the following graphic organizer onto the chalkboard, omitting the italicized answers. Have students complete the organizer to learn more about the explorations of Vasco da Gama and Pedro Álvars Cabral. **ENGLISH LANGUAGE LEARNERS**

- **Vasco da Gama**
  - **RESULT** *gained sea route to India*
  - **WHERE** *around Cape of Good Hope and on to India*
- **Pedro Álvars Cabral**
  - **WHERE** *along the coast of South America*
  - **RESULT** *claimed land in South America*

★ Geography

Map of La Cosa. Before the Waldseemüller map became popular, the la Cosa map was one of Europe's only sources of geographic information about the Americas. Juan de la Cosa, who had sailed with Columbus, became intrigued with exploration of the Americas. He returned to explore the Caribbean in 1499. Using the information he had gathered as well as that of other European voyagers, La Cosa created the first map showing both the Eastern and Western Hemispheres. It was crudely drawn and not very accurate, but it was nonetheless a milestone in Europeans' understanding of Earth's geography.

ACTIVITY Provide students with or have them find an image of the la Cosa map. Have them compare it to a modern, accurate map and point out the similarities and differences between the two.

CONNECTING TO THE ARTS ANSWER
Students might suggest that the proportions on the map are wrong, and that Antarctica's location and size are incorrect.

CONNECTING TO
THE ARTS

Images of the Americas In the 1500s few Europeans had the chance to visit the Americas. Instead they relied on illustrated maps. Such maps often recorded where explorers went and what they found. The map of North and South America shown here is surrounded by pictures of explorers such as Columbus. As well as land masses and names of places, the map includes decorations such as a sea monster. These early maps were often not very accurate, but they helped feed people's curiosity about new lands. What major geographic errors can you find on this early map of the Americas?

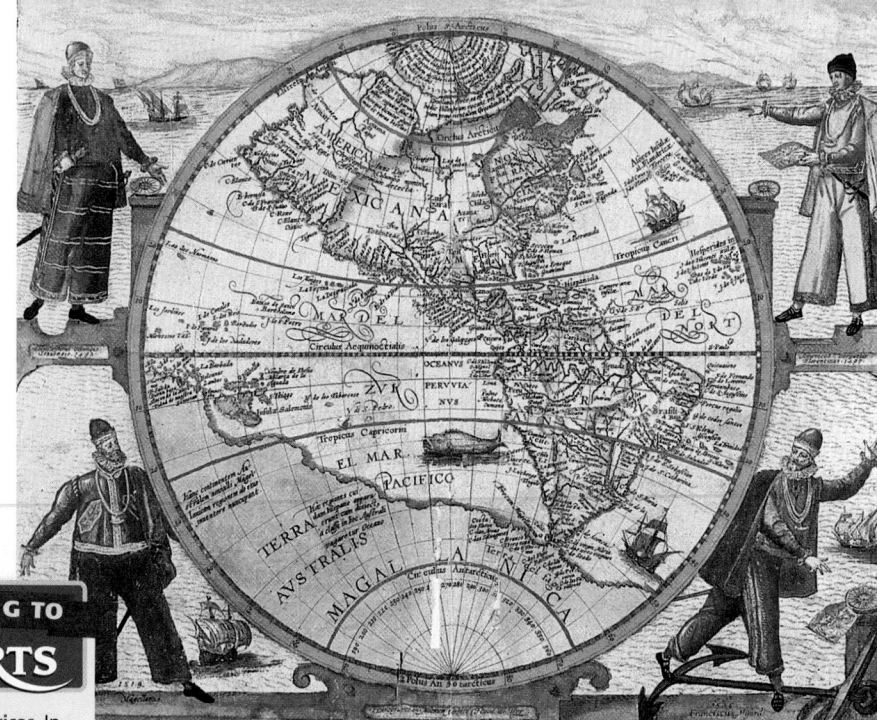

The Italian explorer **Amerigo Vespucci** (ve-SPOO-chee) led Spanish ships on a westward voyage. Vespucci had worked as a business agent for the powerful Medici family. When the Medici were forced to leave Florence in 1494, Vespucci went to Spain. In 1501 he sailed with a fleet that reached the coast of present-day South America. Vespucci was amazed by the animals he saw. They were quite different from those in Europe.

 History Makers Speak ❝What should I tell of the multitude of wild animals, the abundance of pumas, of panthers, of wild cats not like those of Spain . . .; of so many wolves, red deer, monkeys . . . and many large snakes?❞

—Amerigo Vespucci, quoted in *The Discoverers*, by Daniel J. Boorstin

Vespucci and his crew also met American Indians. He wrote many exaggerated letters about them, which captured the imaginations of European readers.

Martin Waldseemüller (VAHLT-zay-mool-uhr), a German mapmaker, published some of Vespucci's letters in a book and printed a large map. He labeled the continents across the Atlantic Ocean "America" in honor of Vespucci. The book and map became popular throughout Europe. As a result, Europeans soon began using the names North America and South America for the new lands.

✔ **Reading Check: Contrasting** Contrast Cabot's and Vespucci's voyages to the Americas. Cabot explored the coast of North America and claimed land for England; Vespucci explored South America and shared his discoveries with other Europeans.

★ Balboa Reaches the Pacific

Europeans came to understand that the Americas were a pair of continents. They realized that Columbus had not found a sea route to Asia after all. Some Spanish explorers began to search for a water passage around or through the American lands.

One of these explorers was **Vasco Núñez de Balboa** (NOON-yays day bahl-BOH-uh). Balboa had failed as a farmer in a Spanish colony in the Caribbean. After arriving at a new settlement in present-day Panama, he took control. Balboa improved the living conditions of the colonists. Using a combination of force and trade, he also made alliances with local American Indians. Peter Martyr was a historian from the time. He wrote that the son of an American Indian leader shared with the Spaniards some fascinating news.

 History Makers Speak 66 I will shewe [show] you a region flowing with golde, where you may satisfie your ravening [hungry] appetites. . . . When you are passing over [the] mountains . . . you shall see another sea, where they sayle [sail] with shippes as bigge as yours. 99

—Anonymous, quoted in *The Discoverers*, by Daniel J. Boorstin

Balboa wanted to know if such stories were true. He went with about 200 of his men and some American Indian guides to search for this ocean. The men traveled for weeks through thick jungle and across deadly swamps. The journey was tiring and dangerous. The group fought with Indians along the way. In 1513 Balboa finally reached the top of a mountain near the coast. From there he saw a great blue sea stretching out as far as his eyes could see. "Behold the much-desired ocean!" he exclaimed. Balboa named these waters the South Sea.

There was no way for ships to cross Panama to reach these waters. However, Balboa's report offered hope that Spain might find a way into the South Sea. Balboa decided to build a fleet to explore the area around the coast. His ships had to be transported piece by piece across the mountains to the South Sea. However, Balboa's success threatened some Spanish authorities, including the governor of Panama. Balboa's enemies charged him with treason and executed him in 1519.

✔ **Reading Check: Finding the Main Idea** Why was Balboa's discovery of the South Sea important to Spain? It offered new hope of finding a western sea route to Asia.

Analyzing Primary Sources
Identifying Points of View What does this statement show about the American Indians' knowledge of the Europeans? Students might suggest that they understand that the Europeans want to find gold and other treasures.

Interpreting the Visual Record

The South Sea *This detail from an early map shows Balboa claiming the South Sea for Spain.* **What does this illustration suggest about how Balboa's group was equipped and the terrain it had to cross?**

LEVEL 3: Organize the class into groups, and have each group design the front page of a newspaper detailing Magellan's voyage. Students' articles for the front page should discuss the reasons for the voyage, the hardships faced along the way, and the importance of the trip. Encourage groups to include illustrations and maps to enhance the articles. Display newspapers around the classroom, and discuss the overall significance of Magellan's voyage. **COOPERATIVE LEARNING**

LEVEL 3: Pair students and assign one partner the role of John Cabot and the other partner the role of Amerigo Vespucci. Have each partner research their explorer as well as develop questions to ask about the other

explorer. Allow time for partners to interview each other. Finally, lead a discussion on the importance of the two explorers. **COOPERATIVE LEARNING**

☆ CLOSE

Place an outline map of the world on the overhead projector. (If a projector is not available, you can simply use a large world map.) On the overhead projector, highlight one of the exploration routes discussed in this section. Ask students to identify the explorer whose route is indicated. Add one route after another until you have covered all of the journeys described in this section.

★ Historical Sidelight

The Death of Magellan.
Antonio Pigafetta, one of the few survivors of the first voyage around the world, described Magellan's death as a hero's passing. Pigafetta explained how Magellan had been wounded several times in a battle with Philippine islanders but was still fighting his way back to the longboats when an enemy struck his leg with a bladed weapon. "That caused the captain to fall face downward, when immediately they rushed upon him with iron and bamboo spears and with their cutlasses, until they killed our mirror, our light, our comfort, and our true guide." Pigafetta states that in the captain's dying moments, after falling under a swarm of warriors, Magellan glanced back several times to make sure his crew had made it safely to the boats.

CRITICAL THINKING
Why do you think Pigafetta admired Magellan so much?

ANSWER: Students might suggest Pigafetta saw Magellan fight bravely against great odds, that he saw the captain's concern for his crew, and that he was impressed with Magellan's navigation and leadership.

MAP ANSWER
the Pacific Ocean

Ferdinand Magellan

The Voyage of Magellan and Elcano, 1519–1522
Interpreting Maps After Ferdinand Magellan died, Juan Sebastián de Elcano became the fleet's leader.

Skills Assessment The World in Spatial Terms What is the last ocean Magellan crossed?

★ Sailing Around the Globe

News of Balboa's discovery interested other European explorers who were looking for a sea route to the Indies. **Ferdinand Magellan** (muh-JEL-uhn) was one sailor who believed he could sail to Asia through this South Sea.

Magellan was a Portuguese captain who had spent many years sailing to Africa and India. Antonio Pigafetta was an Italian adventurer who sailed along with Magellan. Pigafetta later wrote that Magellan "was always the most constant [dependable] in greatest adversity [danger]."

Magellan believed there was a sea passage through South America. Magellan had been accused of treason in Portugal, so he took his idea to Spain. At first, the Spanish did not trust the Portuguese sailor. Magellan's experience and confidence convinced the royal advisers to send him, however. Spain provided him with five ships for the trip.

Magellan set sail in September 1519. From the start he had many problems. Several of his captains did not trust or respect him. Magellan also made his officers angry by refusing to tell them where they were headed. When asked, he shouted, "Follow me and don't ask questions!" Magellan did not find the sea passage where he expected it. He traveled south, searching desperately for a channel through the continent. The weather grew colder, and supplies began to run low. At the same time, Magellan and his supporters had to put down a rebellion led by the Spanish officers.

Then the fleet of ships found a **strait**—a narrow, winding sea passage—between the coastal cliffs. It took them more than a month to pass through the strait. Along the way they battled fierce winds and avoided jagged rocks. Finally, as Pigafetta wrote, "The men . . . reported that they had seen the cape and the open sea. The captain-general [Magellan] wept for joy." The passageway at the southern tip of South America became known as the Strait of Magellan. By then Magellan had lost two of his five ships. He and the other captains thought that they could reach Asia in a few weeks. Instead, the journey took another 100 days. The ships quickly ran out of supplies. The conditions were terrible.

Analyzing Primary Sources
Making Generalizations and Predictions How do you think sailors would react to such conditions? Students might suggest that they would mutiny or demand better food.

History Makers Speak
❝We were three months and twenty days without getting any kind of fresh food. We ate . . . powder of biscuit swarming with worms. We drank yellow water that had been putrid [spoiled] for many days. . . . Often we ate sawdust.❞

—Antonio Pigafetta, from *Magellan's Voyage, a Narrative Account of the First Circumnavigation*, edited by R. A. Skelton

☆ **REVIEW AND ASSESS**

Have students complete the **Section 3 Review** on p. 49. Then have students complete **Daily Quiz 2.3**. As **Alternative Assessment**, you may want to use the dialogue exercise or the explorers graphic organizer in this section's lessons.

☆ **RETEACH**

Have students complete **Main Idea Activity for English Language Learners and Special-Needs Students 2.3**. Then ask each student to write 10 questions about the material in Section 3. Have students exchange questions, write answers, and return them to the writer for grading. Have students share

the most difficult questions in a classroom discussion.
ENGLISH LANGUAGE LEARNERS , COOPERATIVE LEARNING

☆ **EXTEND**

Ask students to develop a crossword puzzle based on the explorers discussed in this section. The questions used in the puzzle should be based on significant points related to each explorer and his voyage. Each question should require a one-word answer. Finally, have each student exchange his or her crossword puzzle with another student. **BLOCK SCHEDULING**

The weather, however, was calm during the entire trip. The crew decided to rename the South Sea, calling it the Pacific, or peaceful, Ocean.

Magellan navigated the unknown waters using instinct and skill. His ships crossed the world's largest ocean and reached the Indies. Then he searched for islands that Portugal had not claimed. While doing so, Magellan landed in the present-day Philippines. There he was killed in a battle with a Philippine kingdom.

Magellan's crew wanted to return to Spain. Led by officer Juan Sebastián de Elcano (el-KAHN-oh), they decided to continue sailing west through unfamiliar waters. Along the way they had to avoid Portuguese seaports and pirate ships. In September 1522 one of the three remaining ships arrived in Spain, carrying a cargo of cloves. The sale of the cloves paid for the cost of the entire voyage and even earned a profit. However, only 18 of the fleet's approximately 250 original crew members and one of the fleet's five ships survived the long journey. These 18 sailors were the first people to **circumnavigate,** or sail completely around, the world. Their 40,000-mile voyage had taken them across three oceans. They had finally found the western route to Asia for which Columbus and others had been searching since 1492.

One member of Magellan's crew sketched this scene of two crew members sailing a boat, off the present-day island of Guam, in March 1521.

✔ **Reading Check: Sequencing** Describe the important events that took place on the first sea voyage around the world in their proper order.
the ships passed through a strait at the southern tip of South America and entered the Pacific Ocean; they sailed across the unknown ocean for more than three months; they landed in the Indies; Magellan was killed; the remaining ships sailed west to return to Spain; only one ship reached Spain.

Section 3 Review

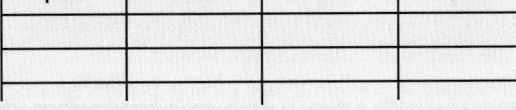

go.hrw.com Homework Practice Online
keyword: SA3 HP2

❶ **Define** and explain:
• strait
• circumnavigate

❷ **Identify** and explain:
• Vasco da Gama
• Pedro Álvars Cabral
• John Cabot
• Amerigo Vespucci
• Vasco Núñez de Balboa
• Ferdinand Magellan

❸ **Summarizing** Copy the chart below. Use it to organize information about the explorations of Balboa, Cabot, Cabral, da Gama, Magellan, and Vespucci.

Explorer	When?	Where?	Results

❹ **Finding the Main Idea**
a. In what ways did the voyages of Vasco da Gama and Pedro Álvars Cabral benefit Portugal?

b. Do you think John Cabot or Amerigo Vespucci made a greater contribution to the opening of the Americas? Explain your answer.

❺ **Writing and Critical Thinking**
Identifying Points of View Imagine that you are preparing to interview the survivors of Magellan's voyage. Write an interview as you imagine it would take place after the crew returned.

Consider the following:
• Magellan's attitude toward his crew
• the rebellion against Magellan
• the sailing conditions

Section 3 Review
ANSWERS

❶ **Define**
• strait, p. 48
• circumnavigate, p. 49

❷ **Identify**
• Vasco da Gama, p. 44
• Pedro Álvars Cabral, p. 45
• John Cabot, p. 45
• Amerigo Vespucci, p. 46
• Vasco Núñez de Balboa, p. 47
• Ferdinand Magellan, p. 48

❸ Balboa—1513; South America; encouraged other explorers to look for a sea route to Asia once he saw the Pacific; Cabot—1497, 1498; North America; gave England claim to land there; Cabral—1500; South America; claimed land for Portugal; Magellan—1519–22; circumnavigated Earth and showed an all-water route to Asia existed; Vespucci—1501; North America; North and South America named for him

❹ a. These voyages gave Portugal the first sea route to Asian trading regions and allowed Portugal to claim land in South America.
b. Students might suggest Cabot because he established future land claims for England. Students might answer Vespucci because he stimulated a greater interest in the Americas among Europeans.

❺ Students' interviews will vary but should include the following information: Magellan's attitude toward his crew, the rebellion against Magellan, and the sailing conditions.

Section 4

OBJECTIVES

- ★ Analyze the effects of new trade routes on Portugal and Spain.
- ★ Evaluate how the Columbian Exchange affected Europeans and American Indians.
- ★ Identify reasons why some countries were searching for a Northwest Passage.

SECTION 4 RESOURCES

REPRODUCIBLE

- ▶ Guided Reading Strategy 2.4
- ▶ Biography Reading 2: Cabeza de Vaca
- ▶ Geography Activity 2: Crossing the Atlantic

TECHNOLOGY

- ▶ One-Stop Planner, Lesson 2.4
- ▶ Linking Geography and History Transparency 2: World Domestication
- ▶ American History Interactive Maps CD–ROM: The Columbian Exchange
- ▶ Homework Practice Online

REINFORCEMENT, REVIEW, AND ASSESSMENT

- ▶ Section 4 Review, p. 53
- ▶ Daily Quiz 2.4
- ▶ Main Idea Activity 2.4
- ▶ English Audio Summary 2.4
- ▶ Spanish Audio Summary 2.4

Technology Resources

Linking Geography and History Transparency 2: World Domestication

---

🎙 LET'S GET STARTED!

As students enter the classroom, ask them to list the types of changes that have resulted or may result from such developments as nuclear power, computers, or the ability to clone animals. *(Students' responses may include either positive or negative results.)* After students have written their responses, ask volunteers to share their ideas. Explain to students that the effects of such knowledge, whether positive or negative, cannot be reversed. Tell students that in Section 4 they will learn about the effects, both positive and negative, of knowledge gained from European expansion during the 1500s.

Section 4

The Opening of the Atlantic

Read to Discover

1. How did new trade routes affect Portugal and Spain?
2. How did the Columbian Exchange affect Europeans and American Indians?
3. Why were some countries searching for a Northwest Passage?

Identify

- Columbian Exchange
- Northwest Passage
- Jacques Cartier
- Samuel de Champlain
- Henry Hudson

WHY IT MATTERS TODAY

The opening of the Atlantic allowed goods and crops to be traded between Europe and the Americas. Today, countries around the world trade with each other. Use **CNNfyi.com** or other **current events** sources to learn about some of the items from faraway places that you use every day. Record your findings in your journal.

At different periods in history, saffron—a spice made from flowers such as these—has been worth much more than its weight in gold.

the true Saffron

The Story Continues

The voyages of Christopher Columbus, Vasco da Gama, Ferdinand Magellan, and others changed the way Europeans looked at the world. The Atlantic Ocean was transformed into the gateway to Africa, India, and the Americas. Exploration changed world trade patterns. It also greatly changed the nations of western and northern Europe. One Spaniard explained the change. "Formerly we were at the end of the world; now we are in the middle of it, with an unprecedented [never-before-experienced] change in our fortunes."

★ A Shift in Trade

In the 1500s Europe turned to the Atlantic Ocean for trading routes. Portuguese ships traveled to India, around Africa, and across the Atlantic. Spanish ships went to Asia across the Atlantic and Pacific Oceans. These new routes made traditional overland trade routes less important. Venice lost its monopoly on trade with Asia and grew weaker.

Spanish and Portuguese traders made greater profits because they no longer dealt with third parties such as Muslim traders. Portugal came

Have students read Section 4 and complete Guided Reading Strategy 2.4. Choose one or more of the following activities to explore the section content with students. For further suggestions on block scheduling or team teaching, see the *Block Scheduling Handbook with Team Teaching Strategies.*

LEVEL 1: Have students develop a *Before* and *After* chart for Spain and Portugal. The *Before* side of the chart should focus on Spain and Portugal's roles in global trading before the explorations of Columbus and da Gama. *(Students' charts should indicate that both countries had* to pay middlemen and follow overland trade routes.) The *After* side of the chart should focus on Spain and Portugal's roles after new trade routes and the Americas were discovered. (Students' charts should indicate that Spain and Portugal saved money and made large profits. Both countries became more powerful.)

ENGLISH LANGUAGE LEARNERS

HOMEWORK Have students conduct research to find common words that are of American Indian origin. Encourage students not only to look for place-names, but also for words that described events unfamiliar to the European explorers, such as *hurricane* from the Taino.

---

to control as much as 75 percent of the spice trade between Europe and Asia. Investors made great profits of nearly 90 percent on each voyage. Spain established an outpost in the Philippines to trade with China. As a result of their explorations, Portugal and Spain gained influence in European affairs. Other European nations also wanted to profit from this rich trade. Countries such as England, France, and the Netherlands began to explore the Atlantic. Each hoped to find its own sea route to Asia.

Around this time Europeans also began to see the Atlantic Ocean as more than just a path to Africa and Asia. The Americas promised to be full of wealth. Christopher Columbus and Amerigo Vespucci had said that the Americas were full of lush forests, clear streams, and many natural resources. In the 1500s some Europeans already were using some of these resources. For example, Spanish, Portuguese, English, and French fishermen traveled across the Atlantic to catch cod near present-day Canada.

✔ **Reading Check: Finding the Main Idea** Why did Spain and Portugal become stronger in the 1500s? They had sea trade routes to Asia and controlled much of the trade with Europe.

★ The Columbian Exchange

Explorers carried plants, animals, and diseases to the "New World" of the Americas. They also brought back plants and animals to the "Old World"—Asia, Africa, and Europe. This transfer became known as the **Columbian Exchange** because it resulted from Columbus's explorations. The Columbian Exchange dramatically changed the world.

European explorers in the Americas found many plants and animals that were unlike any seen back home. "All the trees were as different from ours as day from night," Columbus noted in his journal. These American plants proved valuable and useful. Explorers introduced corn to Europe for use as animal food. Many Europeans began to cook with tomatoes, particularly in Mediterranean countries. In the late 1600s some Europeans began to grow potatoes, which were from South America. Later, European settlers brought potatoes to North America. Europeans also saw American Indians using tobacco and cocoa, which became luxury items in Europe.

Settlers and explorers also brought plants and animals to the American continents. European horses, cattle, and pigs soon ran wild there. American Indians came to use these animals for transportation and to improve their diet. They also started to farm European grains, such as wheat and barley. These grains grew well in cool climates. Rice and bananas grew well in warmer parts of the Americas.

The explorers also unintentionally introduced deadly diseases. Measles, smallpox, and typhus were common in Europe. As a result, most adult Europeans had developed some degree of immunity, or natural resistance, to them. American Indians, however, had never been

★★★★★★★★★★★★
That's Interesting!
★★★★★★★★★★★★

"Golden Apples" Did you know that for many years some Europeans thought tomatoes were poisonous? It's true! Tomatoes originated in South America and later spread to Mesoamerica. The word *tomato* comes from the Aztec word *tomatl.* Tomatoes were first brought back to Europe by Spanish explorers. Northern Europeans grew tomato plants for decoration but were not sure that eating them was safe. In Italy and Spain, however, people soon began cooking with the new fruits. The Italians called tomatoes "golden apples," perhaps because some of the early varieties were yellow. Many years later European settlers brought tomatoes back across the Atlantic Ocean to North America.

⭐ Daily Life

Pigs in the Americas.
One of the animals introduced to the Americas through the Columbian Exchange was the pig. Columbus brought eight pigs to Hispaniola in 1493. The pigs' willingness to eat almost anything and ability to adapt to varied climates allowed them to multiply and spread across the American continent amazingly quickly. Wild descendants of these original pigs apparently reached the Pacific coast of Guatemala even before the Spaniards did. Today pigs are important in the diet of people throughout the Americas.

ACTIVITY: Have students obtain information about another plant or animal that made its way to the Americas through the Columbian Exchange. Ask them to write a paragraph or two explaining what role that plant or animal plays in the Americas today. Remind students to use standard grammar, spelling, sentence structure, and punctuation.

Technology Resources
 American History Interactive Maps CD–ROM: The Columbian Exchange

ALL LEVELS: Copy the following graphic organizers onto the chalkboard, omitting the italicized answers. Have students complete the charts to show how the Columbian Exchange affected Europeans and American Indians. **ENGLISH LANGUAGE LEARNERS**

POSITIVE EXCHANGES

Plants and Animals from The Americas	Plants and Animals from Europe
corn, tomatoes, tobacco, potatoes and cocoa	*horses, cattle, pigs, wheat, barley, rice, and bananas*

NEGATIVE EXCHANGES

Diseases from Europe	Effects on American Indians
measles, smallpox, typhus	*thousands die; weakens groups*

LEVEL 3: Have students write a monologue of an explorer asking for funding for a journey to find the Northwest Passage. Students should state the advantages of finding a passage to Asia, the failed attempts of other explorers, and the various countries staking claims in North America.

★ CLOSE

Assign each student one of the following topics: European balance of power; competition between Europeans for control of new lands; changes in diet and health; or geographic knowledge of the world and its resources. Ask students to find information in the text on the influence new trade had on their assigned topic, and prepare a *Before* and *After* illustration depicting the change that occurred. **COOPERATIVE LEARNING**

Visual Record Answer

Students might suggest that many American Indians were exposed to new diseases and became very ill or died.

★ ★ ★ ★ ★ ★ ★ ★ ★

Section 4 Review
ANSWERS

❶ Identify
• Columbian Exchange, p. 51
• Northwest Passage, p. 52
• Jacques Cartier, p. 52
• Samuel de Champlain, p. 52
• Henry Hudson, p. 53

❷ Europe—cocoa, corn, potatoes, tobacco, wealth through trade; Spain— trade with China; grew stronger; Portugal—controlled much of the spice trade; grew stronger; France—land claims in North America

❸ a. it helped Europeans because they obtained new crops and animals; American Indians obtained new crops and animals as well, it was more harmful to them because they were killed by European diseases
b. Spain and Portugal's growing strength in Europe as well as their dominance of trade with Asia was a problem; other countries found their own sea routes to Asia so to benefit from trade

❹ Students' petitions will vary but should consider the following information: a sea route to Asia, the opportunity to lay claim to new lands in North America, which the French are already doing, and the failures of Yerrezano, Cartier, Champlain, and Hudson.

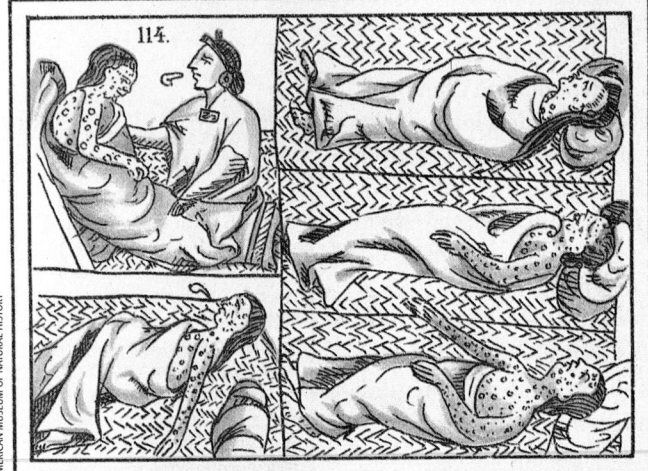

AMERICAN MUSEUM OF NATURAL HISTORY

Interpreting the Visual Record

Deadly diseases *This illustration from a history of Spanish settlement in the Americas written in the 1500s shows the effects of smallpox on the Aztec of Mexico.* **What happened to many of the American Indians who came into contact with European explorers?**

Analyzing Primary Sources
Identifying Points of View
Why does Champlain support European exploration? It makes European countries wealthy and spreads Christianity.

exposed to such diseases. They had no immunity to them. As a result, many American Indians became terribly sick after the first encounters with Europeans took place. Hundreds of thousands of American Indians died.

No one knows how many American Indians died from European diseases, but the loss of life was staggering. Spanish author Fernández de Oviedo reported in 1548 about the destruction of the American Indians of Hispaniola. He reported that of the estimated 1 million American Indians who had lived on the island in 1492, "there are not now believed to be at the present time . . . five hundred persons [left]."

✔ **Reading Check: Drawing Inferences and Conclusions** What were some of the long-term benefits and drawbacks of the Columbian Exchange? benefits: introduction of new plants and animals; drawback: deadly diseases that weakened groups and killed individuals

★ The Search for a Northwest Passage

Spain and Portugal were busy exploring Central and South America. Therefore, other European nations turned to North America. They hoped to find a path around or through the continent. A **Northwest Passage** through North America would allow ships to sail from the Atlantic to the Pacific.

In 1524 France sent Italian captain Giovanni da Verrazano (vayr-raht-SAHN-oh) to find the Northwest Passage. Verrazano sailed along the coast of North America from present-day North Carolina to Maine. **Jacques Cartier** (kahr-TYAY), a French sailor, led France's next major exploration of North America. He made two trips to what is now Canada in 1534 and 1535. He sailed into the St. Lawrence River and traveled all the way to present-day Montreal. Cartier's crew spent the winter near what is now Quebec. On these journeys, Cartier encountered the Huron Indians and strange animals such as polar bears.

Nearly 70 years later French sailor **Samuel de Champlain** began exploring North America. Champlain recorded his ideas about European exploration in his journal.

History Makers Speak

❝Through [exploration] we gain knowledge of different countries, regions and kingdoms; through it we attract and bring into our countries all kinds of riches; through it . . . Christianity [is spread] in all parts of the earth.❞

—Samuel de Champlain, quoted in *The Canadian Frontier, 1534–1760,* by W. J. Eccles

☆ REVIEW AND ASSESS

Have students complete the **Section 4 Review** on p. 53. Then have students complete **Daily Quiz 2.4**. As **Alternative Assessment**, you may want to use the before and after chart or the Columbian exchange graphic organizer in this section's lessons.

☆ RETEACH

Have students complete **Main Idea Activity for English Language Learners and Special-Needs Students 2.4**. Then organize students into three groups, assigning each group one of the three subheads in Section 4. Have each group review its assigned material and lead a class discussion on its main points.
ENGLISH LANGUAGE LEARNERS , COOPERATIVE LEARNING

☆ EXTEND

Organize a debate on the question of whether the European "discovery" of the Americas has been helpful or harmful to humankind. Encourage students to consider the short- and long-term effects of European exploration, not only for Europeans, but also for American Indians, Africans, and others.
BLOCK SCHEDULING

Champlain followed Cartier's old paths. Over the years he made many journeys along the St. Lawrence River. He also visited the Great Lakes in 1615, led by Huron guides. Champlain founded a small colony on the St. Lawrence River that he named Quebec. His explorations became the basis of France's claim to much of Canada.

The Dutch hired English captain **Henry Hudson** to enter the race to find a Northwest Passage. Hudson first sailed to present-day New York in 1609. The following year Hudson returned to North America. This time he sailed under the English flag. He traveled far to the north. Eventually he reached a strait that he hoped would lead to the Pacific Ocean. Instead, it led into a huge bay, later named Hudson Bay.

Hudson and his crew spent a hungry, freezing winter there. "The cold was so extreme that it lamed [crippled] most of our company," wrote a member of Hudson's crew. Hudson wanted to continue exploring in the spring, but some of his crew rebelled. They put Hudson and his followers into a small boat and set it adrift. Some of his crew remained in the area for a day or so, "in all which time we saw not the [boat]," said one crewman, "nor ever saw her after." Hudson did not return.

Neither Verrazano, Cartier, Champlain, nor Hudson ever found a Northwest Passage. Their explorations, however, increased European interest in North America.

In 1609 Henry Hudson sailed the ship Half Moon *to present-day New York.*

✔ **Reading Check: Finding the Main Idea** Why did European explorers seek a Northwest Passage, and how successful were their efforts?
They wanted a new sea route to Asia, but failed to find a Northwest Passage.

Section 4 Review

go. hrw .com **Homework Practice Online**
keyword: SA3 HP2

❶ **Identify** and explain:
• Columbian Exchange
• Northwest Passage
• Jacques Cartier
• Samuel de Champlain
• Henry Hudson

❷ **Comparing** Copy the web diagram below. Use it to show how explorations benefited Europe. In the smaller circles, list the key benefits of exploration to Spain, Portugal, and France. In the center circle, list the general benefits to Europe.

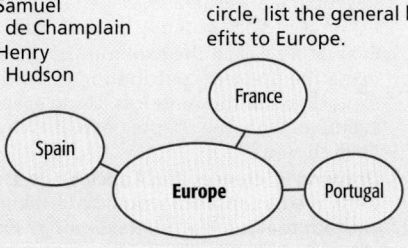

❸ **Finding the Main Idea**
a. Do you think that the Columbian Exchange helped or harmed Europeans? American Indians? Explain your answers.

b. What problems did Spain's and Portugal's discoveries cause for other western European nations?

❹ **Writing and Critical Thinking**
Supporting a Point of View Imagine that you are asking the king of England to finance a journey to find the Northwest Passage. Write a petition asking for the money you need.

Consider the following:
• the benefits of a sea route to Asia
• the failures of Verrazano, Cartier, Champlain, and Hudson
• France's claim to land in North America

CHAPTER 2 REVIEW ANSWERS

The Chapter at a Glance
Students' quizzes will vary but should include information about Spanish, Portuguese, English, and French explorations to the Americas.

Identifying People and Ideas
Students' sentences should indicate an understanding of the following definitions:

1. chart the positions of the stars in order to calculate their positions on Earth

2. greatly aided Portugal's exploration efforts

3. the first European explorer to land in the Americas

4. imaginary line of demarcation some 800 miles west with all lands found west and south belonging to Spain and those north and east belonging to Portugal (1494)

5. the first European to reach Asia by sailing around the Cape of Good Hope

6. the first Europeans to circumnavigate the world

7. a narrow passage of water joining two larger bodies of water

8. the transfer of plants and animals between the "New World" of Americas and the "Old World" of Africa, Asia, and Europe

9. a passage that would allow ships to sail from the Atlantic Ocean to the Pacific Ocean through North America

10. explored the St. Lawrence River and the Great Lakes for France

REPRODUCIBLE
► Vocabulary Activity 2

TECHNOLOGY
► Chapter 2 Test Generator
  (on the One-Stop Planner)
► Global Skill Builder
  CD–ROM
► HRW Go Site

**REINFORCEMENT,
REVIEW, AND
ASSESSMENT**
► Chapter 2 Review,
  pp. 54–55
► Chapter 2 Tutorial for
  Students, Parents,
  Mentors, and Peers
► Chapter 2 Test
  (Form A or B)

► Alternative Assessment
  Handbook
► Chapter 2 Test for English
  Language Learners and
  Special-Needs Students

★ REVIEW
Have students complete the
Chapter 2 Review on pages
54–55.

★ ASSESS
Use one of the chapter tests to
assess students' understanding
of the content. For **Alternative
Assessment**, see the **Alternative
Assessment Handbook**.

**Understanding
Main Ideas**

1. changed the way that people did business, and the Renaissance changed people's ideas about art, education, learning, and culture

2. to conduct direct trade with Asia for Asian goods

3. hoped to find a sea route to Asia; his voyages were unsuccessful in that he never reached Asia, but he did succeed in opening up new territory to Europe

4. gave Portugal a sea route to Asia, as well as a claim to land in South America

5. plants, gold and pearls, animals

6. to find a way for ships to sail from the Atlantic to the Pacific

**You Be The Historian—
Reviewing Themes**

1. plants and animals were exchanged between the Old World and the New World; many American Indians died from European diseases

2. they became more powerful and more important in European affairs

3. it made navigation easier and safer; better able to sail rough seas

Chapter 2 Review

The Chapter at a Glance

Examine the visual summary of the chapter below. Use the summary to create a five-question quiz covering the chapter's main ideas that you might give to a classmate.

England
• John Cabot; 1497, 1498; Newfoundland
• Henry Hudson, 1609, Hudson Bay

Portugal
• Vasco da Gama, 1498, India
• Pedro Álvars Cabral, 1500, Brazil

Spain
• Christopher Columbus, 1492, Hispaniola (North America)
• Vasco Núñez de Balboa, 1513, Panama coast on Pacific Ocean
• Ferdinand Magellan, 1519–1520, Strait of Magellan

France
• Jacques Cartier; 1534, 1535; St. Lawrence River
• Samuel de Champlain, 1615, Great Lakes

Identifying People and Ideas

Use the following terms or people in historically significant sentences.

1. astrolabe
2. Prince Henry
3. Christopher Columbus
4. Treaty of Tordesillas
5. Vasco da Gama
6. Ferdinand Magellan
7. strait
8. Columbian Exchange
9. Northwest Passage
10. Samuel de Champlain

Understanding Main Ideas

Section 1 *(Pages 32–37)*
1. What effects did the Commercial Revolution and the Renaissance have on Europe?
2. Why did Portugal search for a new sea route to Asia?

Section 2 *(Pages 38–43)*
3. What did Christopher Columbus hope to achieve when he set out on his first journey in 1492, and how successful were his four voyages?

Section 3 *(Pages 44–49)*
4. How did Vasco da Gama's and Pedro Álvars Cabral's discoveries help Portugal?

Section 4 *(Pages 50–53)*
5. What types of goods were exchanged between Europe and the Americas?

6. Why were England, France, and the Netherlands interested in finding a Northwest Passage?

You Be the Historian—
Reviewing Themes

1. **Global Relations** What were the positive and negative effects of the Columbian Exchange?
2. **Economics** What effect did their increased global trade have on the economic development of Spain and Portugal?
3. **Science, Technology & Society** How did technological developments help make it possible for Europeans to explore new lands?

Thinking Critically

1. **Summarizing** Why did John Cabot, Amerigo Vespucci, and Ferdinand Magellan set out on explorations across the Atlantic Ocean?
2. **Evaluating** Select the explorer that you think made the greatest contribution to European exploration in the Americas. Using specific examples from the chapter, explain why you have chosen this explorer.
3. **Drawing Inferences and Conclusions** Do you think the Renaissance would have taken place without the Commercial Revolution? Explain your answer.

RETEACH

Organize students into four groups and assign each group one of the chapter's sections. Have members of each group create a television news broadcast that highlights the main ideas of the section. Groups may tape and then play the broadcasts for the class or present a live broadcast to the class. Encourage students to use visual aids to clarify or emphasize important information from the section.

ENGLISH LANGUAGE LEARNERS ,
COOPERATIVE LEARNING

Portfolio Extensions

American History

1. Cooperative Learning
Have students complete the following activity in small groups. Instruct half of the members of each group to conduct research to compile a list of 10 goods that the United States buys from other countries. Then have the other half of each group conduct research to find out 10 goods that the United States sells to other nations. Finally, prepare a map of the world that shows trade patterns between the United States and other countries.

2. Interdisciplinary Connection to Art
Ask students to imagine that they are crewmembers on one of the European explorers' journeys to the Americas. Have them create an illustrated map to show the people at home the landforms, people, plants, and animals that they encountered. Locations on students' maps should be labeled, and legends should be included, as necessary.

Social Studies Skills Workshop

Analyzing Primary Sources

Read the following quote from Bartolomé de Las Casas, a Spanish priest who wrote about Columbus's journey to the Americas, and then answer the following questions.

> ❝The Admiral [Columbus] cheered them [his crew] as best he could, holding out good hope of the benefits they would have. And he added that it was useless to complain since he had come to find the Indies, and so had to continue until he found them.❞

1. Which of the following statements best describes Columbus's point of view?
   a. He was worried about where he was going.
   b. He was willing to give up if difficulties arose.
   c. He did not care how his crew felt.
   d. He was determined to find the Indies.

2. What sort of benefits might Columbus have promised his crew if their journey was successful?

Interpreting Charts

Study the chart below. Then use the information on the chart to help you answer the following questions.

3. Which of the following inventions were important to sea travel?
   a. the astrolabe and the compass
   b. the heavy plow and the horse collar
   c. paper and the printing press
   d. none of the above

4. Using the information from the chart and your knowledge of the time period, create a list of changes made possible by the introduction of paper and the printing press.

Technology of the Middle Ages

INVENTION	PLACE OF ORIGIN	BENEFIT TO EUROPE
Astrolabe	Europe	Enabled sailors to determine their north-south position on Earth—that is, their degree of latitude—by using the location of the stars
Compass	China	Enabled people to determine their direction of travel even when the stars were hidden
Heavy plow	Europe	Enabled farming in the hard soils of northern Europe
Horse collar	Central Asia	Enabled horses to pull the heavy plow
Paper	China	Served as a cheap replacement for parchment
Printing	China	Johannes Gutenberg later developed his own printing techniques in Europe, which allowed the quick and cheap printing of large quantities of material.

Alternative Assessment

American History

Building Your Portfolio

Linking to Community
Trading was one way that businesspeople in the 1300s through the 1500s earned money. Use your local library and primary and secondary sources or interview several people to find out the three most important economic activities in your community. Create a chart listing these three activities and explaining why they are important to your community.

⧉ internet connect

go.hrw.com

Internet Activity: go.hrw.com
keyword: SA3 CF2

Choose a topic about the Age of Exploration:
- Trace the history and impact of the printing press.
- Commemorate the life and work of Leonardo da Vinci.
- Follow Columbus's explorations of the Americas.

Thinking Critically

1. wanted to gain wealth and find sea routes to Asia

2. Answers will vary

3. Some students will say no, because the Commercial Revolution made some people wealthier, and these people began to use their wealth to pursue education and the arts. Some students will say yes, because the Renaissance came about from new ideas and from inventions that did not have wealth as their basis.

Skills Workshop

1. D

2. Students' answers will vary, but students should consider options such as land, wealth, titles, and so forth.

3. A

4. Students' answers will vary, but students should include a reduced cost and greater number of books and the wider spread of information.

LET'S GET STARTED!

As students enter the classroom ask them to describe the ingredients in spaghetti. *(Students' answers will vary, but students will probably identify at least the following ingredients: pasta and tomato sauce.)* Then ask them to identify the ethnic origin of the dish. Explain to students that many foods that we identify with European countries actually contain ingredients that were not native to those nations. Tell students that tomatoes, which are an ingredient in spaghetti sauce are native to the Americas and were introduced to Europe through the Columbian Exchange.

☆ TEACH

Have students read the Connecting to Geography lesson. Choose one or more of the following activities to explore the Connecting to Geography content with students.

★ Linking Past to Present

The Chocolate War. In the past few years chocolate, a product of the Columbian Exchange, has created debate among members of the European Union. Some European counties, such as Britain and Denmark, regularly add vegetable fats, such as palm oil, to their chocolate. In other countries, such as Belgium and France, chocolate is made from pure cocoa butter, a much more expensive method, but also considered the "purists's" chocolate. These chocolate makers argue that adding vegetable oils to chocolate makes it less expensive to produce and that the purists may be driven out of the market as a result. After months of arguments, the European Parliament voted that the vegetable-fat chocolate makers are in fact not really producing "chocolate" at all.

CRITICAL THINKING

What is one way that the two sides might resolve their differences?

ANSWER: Students might suggest that chocolate makers be required to state on their product labels if their chocolate is made out of pure cocoa butter or contains vegetable fat.

Connecting to Geography

The Columbian Exchange

 On the morning of October 12, 1492, a lookout aboard the Pinta, one of three ships in Christopher Columbus's fleet, sighted land. That day Columbus and his crew landed on an island in the Bahamas, starting the European settlement of the Americas. Columbus's landing also started a long process known today as the Columbian Exchange.

In this process, explorers brought plants and animals from Europe, Africa, and Asia to the Americas. They often returned home with American plants and animals. These plants and animals were later spread throughout the Eastern Hemisphere.

Origins of Food Crops

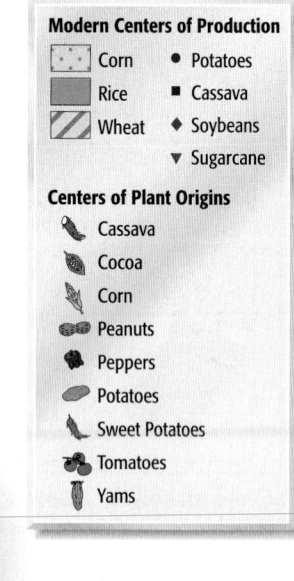

When Columbus returned to the Americas in 1493, he brought with him a number of plants, including wheat. European explorers also took home some plants raised by American Indians, such as corn, potatoes, and tomatoes.

Origins and Production Areas of Food Crops

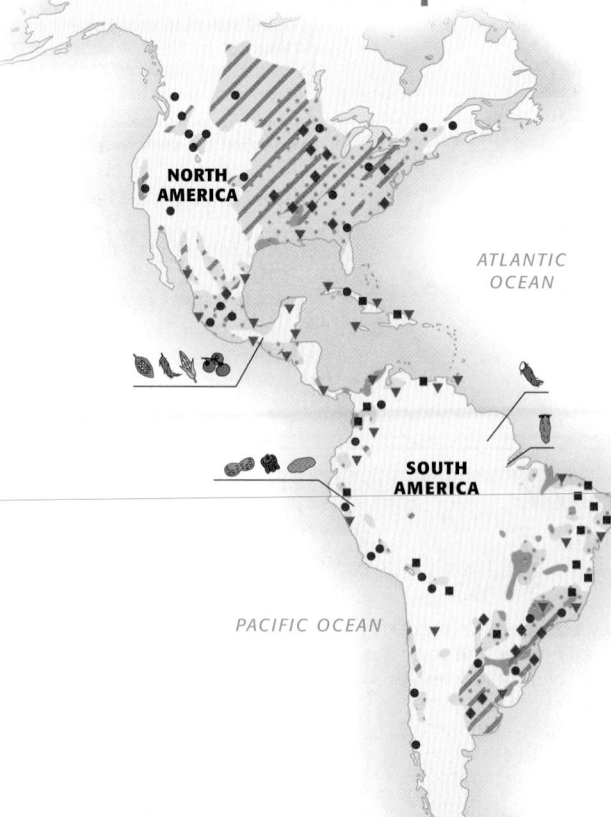

Modern Centers of Production

- ⠿ Corn
- ▦ Rice
- ▨ Wheat
- ● Potatoes
- ■ Cassava
- ◆ Soybeans
- ▼ Sugarcane

Centers of Plant Origins

- Cassava
- Cocoa
- Corn
- Peanuts
- Peppers
- Potatoes
- Sweet Potatoes
- Tomatoes
- Yams

NORTH AMERICA

ATLANTIC OCEAN

SOUTH AMERICA

PACIFIC OCEAN

Origins and Production Areas of Food Crops

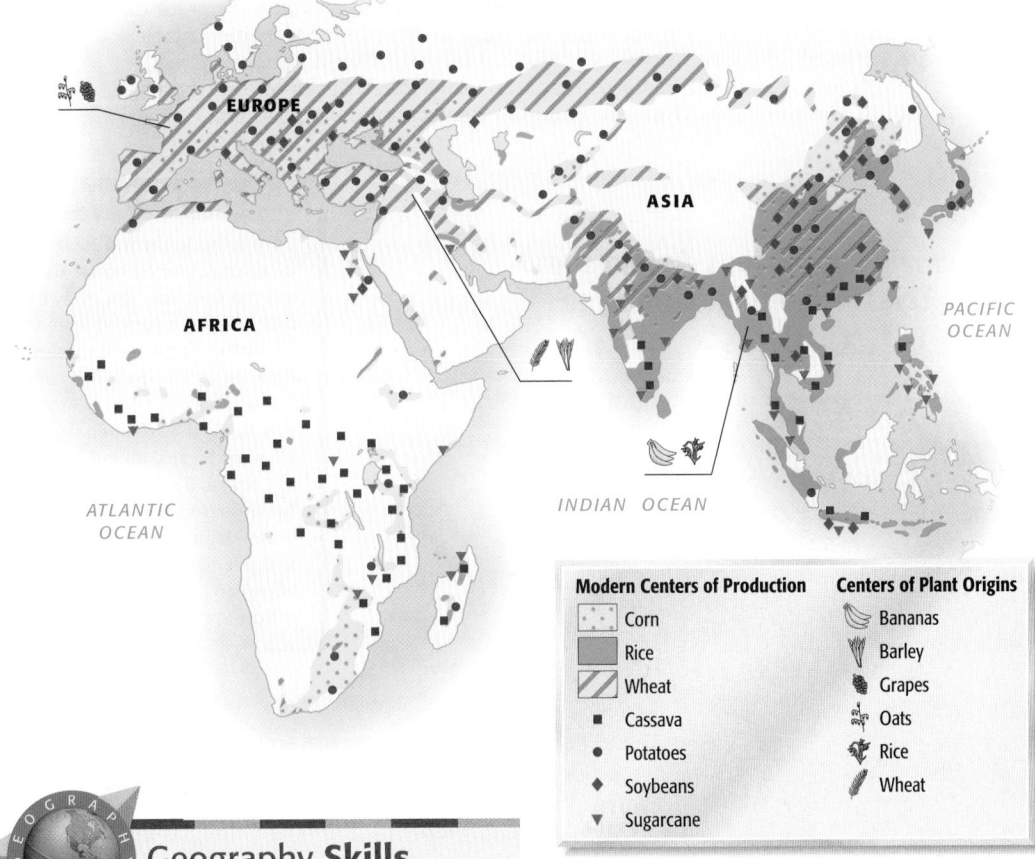

EUROPE

ASIA

AFRICA

PACIFIC
OCEAN

ATLANTIC
OCEAN

INDIAN OCEAN

Modern Centers of Production

- Corn
- Rice
- Wheat
- ▪ Cassava
- ● Potatoes
- ◆ Soybeans
- ▼ Sugarcane

Centers of Plant Origins

- Bananas
- Barley
- Grapes
- Oats
- Rice
- Wheat

Geography **Skills**
Interpreting Thematic Maps

1. Where did rice and oats originate?
2. Where did corn and potatoes originate?
3. **Places and Regions** What crop grown throughout South America is not widely grown in the United States?
4. **Environment and Society** Which continent has the least amount of land dedicated to growing cereal grains? Which continent has the most areas of potato production?
5. **Contrasting** What cereal crops are most common in Europe and Asia?

Europeans brought tomatoes back from the Americas.

LEVEL 3: Tell students that sometimes you can determine where a person has traveled by what he or she has seen on the trip. Have students review the routes traveled by famous explorers found in Chapter 2. Then have students look at the maps found in the textbook on pages 56–59 to determine what plants and animals the explorers may have encountered on their voyages. Ask students to create a short story describing one of these explorers' journeys to the Americas. The story should identify areas to which the explorer traveled and the crops and animals that he may have encountered along the journey.

☆ CLOSE

Organize the class into several small groups and assign each group a continent. Have groups imagine that they were alive before the Columbian Exchange took place. Give each group a shopping list consisting of crops or animal products mentioned in this unit. Then have each group use information from the maps on pages 56–59 to determine if people living in the assigned continent would have been able to obtain the product without leaving their continent. Have groups present their information to the class. **COOPERATIVE LEARNING**

Origins of Animals

On his second voyage to the Americas in 1493, Columbus brought many kinds of domesticated animals. Among these animals were dogs, horses, pigs, cattle, chickens, sheep, and goats. North and South America offered Europe, Africa, and Asia fewer types of animals. The animals that these areas offered included the turkey and the llama. Such animals had less economic importance.

Origins of Various Animals and Livestock Production Areas

NORTH AMERICA

ATLANTIC OCEAN

PACIFIC OCEAN

SOUTH AMERICA

Modern Centers of Livestock Production
- Cattle
- Sheep
- Pigs
- Poultry

Centers of Animal Origins
- Guinea pig
- Llama
- Turkey

History Note 1

During the 1500s and 1600s, Spanish colonists raised horses throughout the Americas. Runaway horses multiplied and formed wild herds. Gradually, horse herds spread throughout the grasslands of central and northern South America. Eventually they roamed from the plains of Mexico all the way north to Canada. By the early 1700s American Indians of the western Great Plains had learned to train and ride these horses. They made horses an important part of their culture.

Geography **Skills**
Interpreting Thematic Maps

1. Which types of animals are most common to the southern tip of South America?
2. **The World in Spatial Terms** In what part of the world did turkeys originate?
3. **Drawing Inferences and Conclusions** Why do you think settlers from Europe brought their own livestock, seeds, and plant clippings to the Americas?

History Note 2

Pigs had the easiest time adapting to the hot wet climate of the Caribbean and present-day southeastern United States. It even became common practice for explorers to leave pigs behind on islands as food for future expeditions.

★ REVIEW AND ASSESS

Have students review the information in the Connecting to Geography Unit 1. Then have students complete Geography and History Quiz 1.

★ RETEACH

Have students imagine that they are traveling around the world sampling cuisine from each continent that was involved in the Columbian Exchange. Then ask students to create postcards to send back to the United States from each continent. Each postcard should identify the continent that the student is visiting and contain a brief message identifying foods he or she has eaten that were introduced to the continent during the Columbian Exchange. **ENGLISH LANGUAGE LEARNERS**

★ EXTEND

Provide students with copies of three recipes that contain ingredients from the maps in this unit, or have them use the library to obtain information about three dishes from various countries around the world. Then instruct students to review information from the maps in this unit to determine whether the main ingredients in each dish were available in the country that is associated with that dish prior to Columbus's voyages. If the ingredients were found there, have students write the recipe on a note card identifying the ingredients found in that country of origin. If the ingredients were not available, have students indicate that as well.

BLOCK SCHEDULING

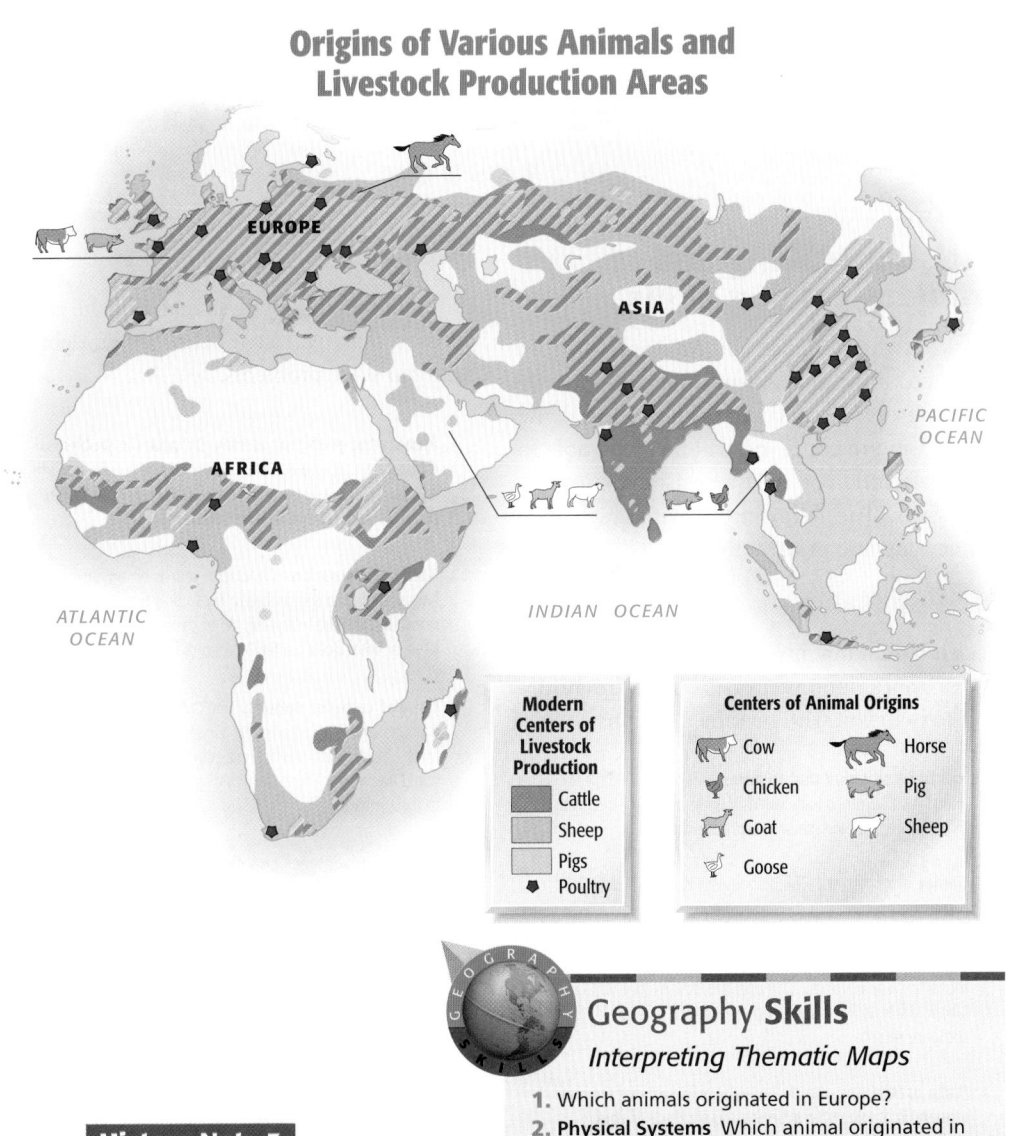

Origins of Various Animals and Livestock Production Areas

EUROPE

ASIA

PACIFIC OCEAN

AFRICA

ATLANTIC OCEAN

INDIAN OCEAN

Modern Centers of Livestock Production
- ▨ Cattle
- ▨ Sheep
- ☐ Pigs
- ◆ Poultry

Centers of Animal Origins
- Cow
- Horse
- Chicken
- Pig
- Goat
- Sheep
- Goose

Geography **Skills**
Interpreting Thematic Maps

1. Which animals originated in Europe?
2. **Physical Systems** Which animal originated in both Europe and Asia?
3. **Summarizing** What are the geographic origins of the plants and animals involved in the Columbian Exchange? Create a chart or table that will help a fellow student organize this information. Then exchange charts with a partner and fill them in using the information in your textbook and notes.

History Note 3

The Africanized, or "killer," bee is an example of how intercontinental exchanges continue in modern times. In the 1950s research scientists brought African honeybees to Brazil. African bees accidentally escaped from Brazilian laboratories and mixed with South American bees to produce the so-called killer bee. These bees then began to spread north. Today swarms of killer bees live in both Texas and California.

★ Economics

Africanized Bees. If the Africanized bee population in the United States continues to rise as is predicted, it could have serious effects on U.S. agricultural production. More Africanized bees in the United States may reduce the population of domestic honey bees, which pollinate many crops. A leading U.S. agricultural university has said that such an increase in Africanized bees could lead to a decline in honey production as well as that of other crops, such as almonds, apples, berries, cantaloupes, and cucumbers.

CRITICAL THINKING

How can nature's unpredictability affect people's economic development?

ANSWER: Students might suggest that people's livelihood can be harmed by nature's unpredictability.

SKILL ANSWERS

1. the cow, horse, and the pig
2. the pig
3. Students' charts or tables should reflect the information found in this unit.

NEW Y

★ TEACH

ALL LEVELS: Organize students into groups to practice their decision-making and problem-solving skills by choosing a current issue debated within their community. You may want to assign a specific issue to each group. Then have each group address this issue by writing an outline incorporating the steps included on this page. Groups should begin by identifying the problem or situation and should conclude their outline with a resolution. Have a volunteer from each group present his or her group's outline to the class. **ENGLISH LANGUAGE LEARNERS , COOPERATIVE LEARNING**

LEVELS 2 AND 3: Pair students. Ask pairs to do a role-playing exercise. One student should assume the role of a city councilperson and the other student should assume the role of a newspaper reporter. Pairs should then address a current issue that has come before the council. The reporter should ask specific questions about the issue, and the councilperson should present his or her viewpoints and present the plans that are being put into motion to solve the problem. Ask volunteers to present their role-playing exercise to the class. **COOPERATIVE LEARNING**

DECISION MAKING AND PROBLEM SOLVING

Ask students to apply the decision-making or problem-solving skills to an ongoing issue within their school. Students should draw a graphic organizer to illustrate either the decision-making or problem-solving process.

SKILLS ANSWERS

1. Students' decisions will vary, but they should be able to defend their process and decisions.
2. Students' solutions will vary, but they should incorporate problem-solving skills into their solutions.

Social Studies Skills
WORKSHOP

Decision-Making and Problem-Solving Skills

Like you, many figures in American history have faced difficult problems and decisions. By using appropriate skills such as problem solving and decision making, you will be better able to choose a solution or make a decision on important issues. The following activities will help you develop and practice these skills.

Decision Making

Decision making involves choosing between two or more options. Listed below are guidelines to help you with making decisions.

1. **Identify a situation that requires a decision.** Think about your current situation. What issue are you faced with that requires you to take some sort of action?

2. **Gather information.** Think about the issue. Examine the causes of the issue or problem and consider how it affects you and others.

3. **Identify your options.** Consider the actions that you could take to address the issue. List these options so that you can compare them.

4. **Make predictions about consequences.** Predict the consequences of taking the actions listed for each of your options. Compare these possible consequences. Be sure the option you choose produces the results you want.

5. **Take action to implement a decision.** Choose a course of action from your available options, and put it into effect.

Problem Solving

Problem solving involves many of the steps of decision making. Listed below are guidelines to help you solve problems.

1. **Identify the problem.** Identify just what the problem or difficulty is that you are facing. Sometimes you face a difficult situation made up of several different problems. Each problem may require its own solution.

2. **Gather information.** Conduct research on any important issues related to the problem. Try to find the answers to questions like the following: What caused this problem? Who or what does it affect? When did it start?

3. **List and consider options.** Look at the problem and the answers to the questions you asked in Step 2. List and then think about all the possible ways in which the problem could be solved. These are your options—possible solutions to the problem.

4. **Examine advantages and disadvantages.** Consider the advantages and disadvantages of all the options that you have listed. Make sure that you consider the possible long-term effects of each possible solution. You should also determine what steps you will need to take to achieve each possible solution. Some suggestions may sound good at first but may turn out to be impractical or hard to achieve.

5. **Choose and implement a solution.** Select the best solution from your list and take the steps to achieve it.

6. **Evaluate the effectiveness of the solution.** When you have completed the steps needed to put your plan into action, evaluate its effectiveness. Is the problem solved? Were the results worth the effort required? Has the solution itself created any other problems?

Practicing the Skill

1. Chapter 2, Section 4: The Opening of the Atlantic, describes the search for a Northwest Passage to Asia. Imagine that you are an explorer who is aware of the failed attempts to find this passage. Use the decision-making guidelines to help you decide whether to continue searching for such a passage. Be prepared to defend your decision.

2. Identify a similar problem discussed in Chapters 1 or 2 and apply the problem-solving process to come up with a solution.

LEVEL 3: Have students review the problem in the History in Action Simulation. Then have each student prepare an oral request to present to the monarch in which they seek exploration funding. Remind students to incorporate the problem-solving skills outlined in the simulation into their pleadings. Have volunteers present their pleading to the class as they would to the monarch. Ask the audience to imagine that they are the monarch and encourage them to ask probing questions of the petitioner.

LEVEL 3: Bring several newspapers to class. Have students read selected articles pertaining to state news and issues. Then ask each student to choose a state issue currently in the news and to write a letter to their governor or congressperson addressing that issue. Students should recommend steps that can be taken to solve the problem as well as an effective resolution. Ask volunteers to present their letters to the class.

History in Action

UNIT 1 SIMULATION

You Solve the Problem . . .

How Do You Convince a Monarch to Finance Your Expedition?

Complete the following activity in small cooperative groups. It is the era of exploration, 1492–1534. You and your crew wish to petition your country's monarch for more funds to further explore distant lands. Your group is not the only one that would like more money. The monarch does not want only personal presentations. He or she has requested that a brochure be submitted also. The ship that will transport the brochure to the monarch leaves with the next tide. Follow these steps to solve your problem.

 **1. Gather Information.** Use your textbook and other resources to find information that might influence your plan of action for developing a brochure. Be sure to use what you learned from this unit's Skills Workshop on Decision Making and Problem Solving to help you find an effective solution to this problem. You may want to divide different parts of the research among group members.

2. List and Consider Options. After reviewing the information you have gathered, list and consider the options you might use as justifications for your request that the monarch fund further explorations. Your final solution to the problem may be easier to reach if you consider as many options as possible. Be sure to record your possible options for the preparation of your brochure.

 3. Consider Advantages and Disadvantages. Now consider the advantages and disadvantages of taking each option. Ask yourselves questions like: "Will this information convince the monarch that your expedition will benefit his or her country?" Once you have considered the advantages and disadvantages, record them as notes for use in preparing your brochure.

4. Choose, Implement, and Evaluate a Solution. After considering the advantages and disadvantages, you should plan and create your brochure. Be sure to make your proposal very clear. You will need to support your reasons for exploration by including information you gathered and by explaining why you rejected other options or reasons for exploration. Your brochure needs to be visually appealing to attract the attention of the monarch. When you are ready, decide which group members will present the brochure, and then take yourbrochure to the monarch (the rest of the class). Good luck!

History in Action Ask students to conduct research at the library to learn how people in history have used problem-solving or decision-making skills. For example, students might show how some Americans organized to peacefully protest civil rights abuses during the 1960s. These Americans recognized a problem, arrived at a plan of action, (bus boycotts, sit-ins, and so on), and implemented their plan. Then using standard grammar, spelling, sentence structure, and punctuation, students should write a how-to paper showing the steps of the problem-solving process and incorporating an effective solution if one was not met in their chosen historical issue.

★ CHAPTER 3
New Empires in the Americas

In the 1500s Spain sent soldiers and explorers to America to explore and conquer the lands there. After Spain conquered the Aztec and Inca Empires, it established a system of colonial government to rule these new territories. Spanish settlers grew wealthy in the new world, often by using American Indians or Africans as slave laborers. However, Spain's defeat in religious wars in Europe led to a decline in its power. France, England, Sweden, and the Netherlands also hoped to create their own empires in the Americas and began to establish colonies at this time.

★ CHAPTER 4
The English Colonies

In April 1607 a group of English colonists established the first English settlement in Virginia, hoping to find wealth. Later colonists, such as the Puritans, Catholics, and Quakers, came to America seeking religious and political freedom. Throughout the colonies, these new settlers had to adapt to different environments with a variety of crops and varied ways of life.

Internet Activity

Everyday Life in Colonial America

☑ internet connect

TOPIC: Colonial Towns
GO TO: go.hrw.com
KEYWORD: SA3 Colonial Towns

Either individually or in groups, have students search the Internet through the HRW Go site for sites relating to historical re-creation of colonial towns such as Plimoth Plantation, Colonial Williamsburg, or Old Sturbridge Village. Have students use the information at these sites to design an advertisement for the chamber of commerce in a colonial town. Ask them to describe the business and social opportunities that they think might attract potential settlers to their area. In addition, students should remember to make their advertisements as persuasive and eye-catching as possible.

UNIT 2 Colonies in the Americas
(1500–1760)

CHAPTER 3 **New Empires in the Americas** (1500–1700)

CHAPTER 4 **The English Colonies** (1605–1735)

CHAPTER 5 **Life in the English Colonies** (1630–1760)

Life in the English Colonies

Each of the English colonies had its own form of government and operated independently from the other colonies. The colonies were bound together by an extensive trade network, however, which extended from the colonies to the West Indies to Great Britain. The goods that the colonies produced for trade varied from region to region according to geography and climate. In addition to increased trade, the early 1700s brought a revival of faith known as the Great Awakening, and the ideas of the Enlightenment changed much of everyday colonial life.

★ UNIT MOTIVATOR

Share the information in the Unit Overview with students. Write each of the unit chapter titles as headings on the chalkboard. Have the students use what they know about exploration to brainstorm what differences might exist between the English and Spanish colonies. List the characteristics that the students expect under the appropriate heading. Next ask students to imagine that they are advisers to the rulers of either England or Spain and to create a plan describing best ways to develop their new colonies. Later, when you have finished the unit, come back to these plans and have students evaluate how closely their plans for colonization coincided with the actual events of colonization.

Young People

IN HISTORY

Young American Indians

Many different American Indian peoples lived in the eastern woodlands region of North America. Teenagers from the various peoples shared similar responsibilities and experiences. Girls learned how to grow and harvest beans, corn, and squash in their own gardens and also in larger community fields. Girls also collected wild plants for food and medicine. They took care of household chores, such as collecting firewood and making clothes. Boys learned how to hunt and fish for survival. The Delaware people, who lived in what is now New York, required their teenage boys to stay alone in the woods for several days. These boys depended on their hunting and woodcraft skills to find food and build shelters.

Life for young American Indians was not all about work, however. Many peoples in eastern North America played ball games similar to lacrosse and soccer. The Cherokee of the Southeast liked to play a game called *anetsa*. In this rough physical game, players used netted sticks to carry a ball and throw it toward a goal. Only the most athletic young men played *anetsa,* and many suffered broken bones. Every Cherokee village had a team. The Cherokee believed that great honor and good fortune would come to the winner.

By their early teenage years most American Indians were considered adults. Among the Powhatan, who lived around Chesapeake Bay, boys took part in a special coming-of-age ritual. This ceremony required boys between the ages of about 10 and 15 to live in the woods for several months. They were tested with hardships and fasting. Those boys who proved their strength and bravery were declared worthy as future leaders. Virginia colonist Robert Beverly explained that the intention of the ritual was educational. The ritual encouraged the boys' progress into adulthood. Beverly observed, "Thus they unlive their former lives, and [become] men, by forgetting that they ever have been boys."

Young American Indians, like this boy, often played sports similar to some of those played today, such as lacrosse.

If You Were There *How would you survive on your own in the woods?*

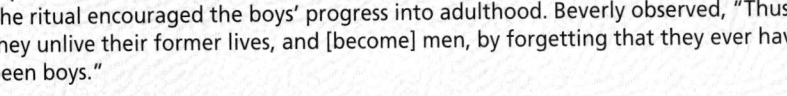

LEFT PAGE: *In October 1764, British colonists met with American Indian leaders in what is now Ohio.*

★ Using Visual Resources

Engraving. During the 1700s, American engravers, like many American artists, became more interested in using scenes and details that were native to America, rather than focusing on English models and forms. Engraving was a popular art form during the colonial period, and colonists depended on engravers to depict current events accurately. American artists thus began to put models to work in new settings and situations to create artwork that more clearly reflected everyday life in America.

CRITICAL THINKING

What elements of this engraving reflect the artist's focus on tangible American details?

ANSWER: Students might suggest that the artist represents American Indians, exact military uniforms, native plants, and a log cabin.

	Objectives	Pacing Guide	Reproducible Resources
SECTION 1: **The Conquistadores** (pp. 66–71)	⊡ Compare Hernán Cortés's conquest of the Aztec to Francisco Pizarro's conquest of the Inca in Peru. ⊡ Explain the reasons for Spanish exploration of Florida and the American Southwest.	**Regular** 1.5 days **Block Scheduling** 1 day *Block Scheduling Handbook with Team Teaching Strategies, Chapter 3*	**RS** Guided Reading Strategy 3.1 **SM** Geography Activity 3: Cortés Conquers Mexico
SECTION 2: **Spanish America** (pp. 72–77)	⊡ Describe how Spain organized and governed its empire in the Americas. ⊡ Analyze the structure of New Spain's economy and society. ⊡ Explain why the Spanish settled in the borderlands.	**Regular** 1.5 days **Block Scheduling** .5 day *Block Scheduling Handbook with Team Teaching Strategies, Chapter 3*	**RS** Guided Reading Strategy 3.2 **PS** Literature Reading 3: Through the Eyes of a Spanish Missionary-Explorer **E** Hands-On History Activity: Memorializing the Founders of Your Town
SECTION 3: **Religious and Political Changes in Europe** (pp. 78–82)	⊡ Define the Protestant Reformation and explain how it changed Europe. ⊡ Discuss the reasons why Spain and England went to war in the late 1500s. ⊡ Analyze what led to the end of Spain's Golden Age.	**Regular** 1.5 days **Block Scheduling** 1 day *Block Scheduling Handbook with Team Teaching Strategies, Chapter 3*	**RS** Guided Reading Strategy 3.3 **PS** Biography Reading 3: Martin Luther
SECTION 4: **The Race for Empires** (pp. 83–87)	⊡ Analyze the reasons for French, Dutch, and English interest in colonizing North America. ⊡ Identify the common problems faced by French, Dutch, and Swedish colonies. ⊡ Describe what happened to the first English settlements in North America.	**Regular** 1.5 days **Block Scheduling** .5 day *Block Scheduling Handbook with Team Teaching Strategies, Chapter 3*	**RS** Guided Reading Strategy 3.4 **PS** Primary Source Reading 3: France and the New World **RS** Graphic Organizer 3: European Presence in the Americas **E** Creative Teaching Strategy: Daily Journal Writing

Chapter Resource Key

PS	Primary Sources	**A**	Assessment
RS	Reading Support	**REV**	Review
IC	Interdisciplinary Connections	**ELL**	Reinforcement and English Language Learners
E	Enrichment		Transparencies
SM	Skills Mastery		CD-ROM

 Music

 Video

 Internet

Holt Presentation Maker Using Microsoft® PowerPoint®

 One-Stop Planner CD–ROM

See the *One-Stop Planner* for a complete list of additional resources for students and teachers.

One-Stop Planner CD–ROM

It's easy to plan lessons, select resources, and print out materials for your students when you use the **One-Stop Planner CD–ROM with Test Generator.**

Technology Resources	Reinforcement, Review, and Assessment

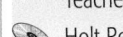 One-Stop Planner, Lesson 3.1

Exploring America's Past Video Segment 3: The Serpent God; Teacher's Guide, pp. 4–5

 Holt Researcher: American History CD–ROM

Homework Practice Online

REV Section 1 Review, p. 71
A Daily Quiz 3.1
ELL Main Idea Activity 3.1
ELL English Audio Summary 3.1
ELL Spanish Audio Summary 3.1

 One-Stop Planner, Lesson 3.2

 American Music Selection 3: "Alabado"

 Everyday Life in America Transparency 2: Religious Folk Art in the Spanish Colonies

CNN. Presents America: Yesterday and Today, Beginnings to 1914 Segment: Mission Bells in California

Homework Practice Online

REV Section 2 Review, p. 77
A Daily Quiz 3.2
ELL Main Idea Activity 3.2
ELL English Audio Summary 3.2
ELL Spanish Audio Summary 3.2

 One-Stop Planner, Lesson 3.3

Homework Practice Online

HRW Go site

REV Section 3 Review, p. 82
A Daily Quiz 3.3
ELL Main Idea Activity 3.3
ELL English Audio Summary 3.3
ELL Spanish Audio Summary 3.3

 One-Stop Planner, Lesson 3.4

 Linking Geography and History Transparency 3: Native American Culture Areas

Homework Practice Online

HRW Go site

REV Section 4 Review, p. 86
A Daily Quiz 3.4
ELL Main Idea Activity 3.4
ELL English Audio Summary 3.4
ELL Spanish Audio Summary 3.4

---

internet connect

HRW ONLINE RESOURCES
GO TO: go.hrw.com
Then type in a keyword.

TEACHER HOME PAGE
KEYWORD: SA3 Teacher

CHAPTER INTERNET ACTIVITIES
KEYWORD: SA3 CF3
Choose an activity to:
- learn about the settlement of St. Augustine.
- research the role of Spanish missions in the New World.
- research French settlement in North America.

CHAPTER ENRICHMENT LINKS
KEYWORD: SA3 CH3

ONLINE ASSESSMENT
Homework Practice
KEYWORD: SA3 HP3

Standardized Test Prep
KEYWORD: SA3 STP3

Rubrics
KEYWORD: SS Rubrics

ONLINE MAPS, CHARTS, AND GRAPHS
KEYWORD: SA3 MCG
- Exploration in the New World
- Europe and West Africa in the 15th Century
- Settling New England

CONTENT UPDATES
KEYWORD: SS Content Updates

HOLT PRESENTATION MAKER
KEYWORD: SA3 PPT3

ONLINE READING SUPPORT
KEYWORD: SS Strategies

CURRENT EVENTS
KEYWORD: S3 Current Events

Meeting Individual Needs

Ability Levels

Level 1 Basic-level activities designed for all students encountering new material

Level 2 Intermediate-level activities designed for average students

Level 3 Challenging activities designed for honors and gifted-and-talented students

English Language Learners Activities that address the needs of students with Limited English Proficiency

---

Chapter Review and Assessment

IC Vocabulary Activity 3
Global Skill Builder CD–ROM
HRW Go site
REV Chapter 3 Tutorial for Students, Parents, Mentors, and Peers
REV Chapter 3 Review, pp. 87–89
Chapter 3 Test Generator (on the One-Stop Planner)
A Chapter 3 Test (Form A or B)

A Alternative Assessment Handbook
A Chapter 3 Test for English Language Learners and Special-Needs Students

63b

Build on What You Know

If You Were There...

Ask students to answer the following question:

How would you react to the arrival of strangers in your land?

Consider:

- the fear that European settlers might have caused
- the hope for new allies against other American Indian enemies

You Be the Historian

What's Your Opinion?

To help students create their **Themes** Journal entries, provide the following examples of appropriate **agree**/disagree statements.

EXPLORING THE TIME LINE

AMERICAN EVENTS

internet connect

go.hrw.com

TOPIC: St. Augustine
GO TO: go.hrw.com
KEYWORD: SA3 CF3

Have students access the Internet through the HRW Go site to research the settlement of St. Augustine. Ask students to write a journal entry using standard grammar, spelling, sentence structure, and punctuation to describe the settlement and its people, and then have them create a line drawing model of The Castillio de San Marcos.

CHAPTER

3 New Empires in the Americas

(1500–1700)

Spanish explorer Juan Ponce de León was unable to found a settlement in Florida.

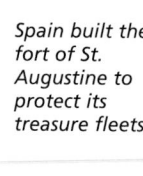

Spain built the fort of St. Augustine to protect its treasure fleets.

UNITED STATES

1513 Juan Ponce de León lands in Florida.

1542 Spanish explorer Álvar Núñez Cabeza de Vaca publishes an account of his travels in North America.

1565 Spain founds the first permanent European settlement in the present-day United States, at St. Augustine, Florida.

1585 Sir Walter Raleigh sends an expedition to found an English colony on Roanoke Island in North America.

1500	**1520**	**1540**	**1560**	**1580**

1517 Reformer Martin Luther posts his 95 Theses criticizing the Catholic Church.

1521 Hernán Cortés captures the Aztec capital of Tenochtitlán in present-day Mexico.

1531 Francisco Pizarro invades the Inca Empire in the Andes of South America.

1558 Elizabeth I becomes queen of England.

1571 A European fleet defeats the Ottoman navy at the Battle of Lepanto.

1588 The English navy defeats the Spanish Armada.

WORLD

Francisco Pizzaro was a ruthless military leader.

Build on What You Know

By 1500, Europeans had begun crossing the Atlantic Ocean in search of wealth, glory, and converts to the Christian faith. Spain established a large colonial empire in North and South America. The Spanish were soon followed by explorers seeking to establish colonies for other European nations.

Global Relations

Agree   Larger forces always have the advantage in warfare.

Disagree   Superior weapons and tactics will always win regardless of the number of soldiers.

Geography

Agree   Natural resources are the only reason for exploration.

Disagree   Nations should not explore in the hopes of gaining natural resources.

Economics

Agree   A colony only provides economic benefits for its mother country.

Disagree   A mother country should not depend on the economic benefits of its colonies.

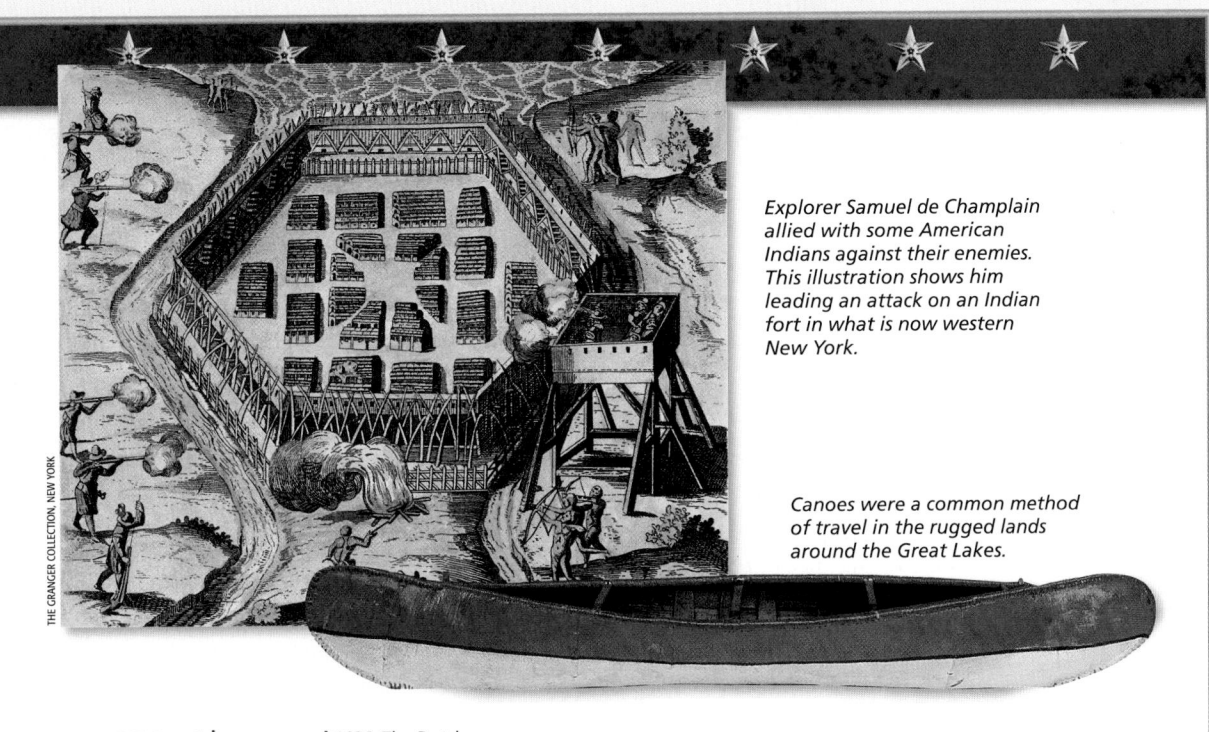

THE GRANGER COLLECTION, NEW YORK

Explorer Samuel de Champlain allied with some American Indians against their enemies. This illustration shows him leading an attack on an Indian fort in what is now western New York.

Canoes were a common method of travel in the rugged lands around the Great Lakes.

1615 French explorer Samuel de Champlain reaches the Great Lakes.

1626 The Dutch found New Amsterdam on the site of present-day New York City.

1655 The Dutch take control of New Sweden in North America.

1680 Pueblo Indians revolt in New Mexico.

1600   1620   1640   1660   1680

1611 William Shakespeare's play *The Tempest* is first performed.

1636 The Manchu establish the Qing Dynasty in Manchuria, later extending it into China.

1652 The Dutch establish a colony near the Cape of Good Hope in southern Africa.

EXPLORING THE TIME LINE
GLOBAL EVENTS

Tenotchtitlán. The Spanish capture of the Aztec capital of Tenochtitlán was not an easy task for Cortés and his troops. Cortés and the Spanish controlled Tenochtitlán for about six months before the Aztec rebelled against them. In an effort to drive the conquistadores out of their city, the Aztec destroyed bridges and forced the Spanish into the many canals located in the city. Weighted down with armor and stolen gold, many of the Spanish drowned in the canals. In the end, however, the weapons of the Aztec proved to be no match for the iron and steel weapons of the Spanish.

CRITICAL THINKING

Why might the Aztec have rebelled after six months of rule by the Spanish?

ANSWER: Students might suggest that the Aztec were probably frightened or in awe of the Spanish at first, but as time went on they began to resent the Spanish presence.

You Be the Historian

Themes Journal

What's Your Opinion? Do you **agree** or **disagree** with the following statements? Support your point of view in your journal.

- **Global Relations** A large population defending its homeland will always defeat a smaller invading army.
- **Geography** Nations establish settlements in other lands in order to take advantage of their natural resources.
- **Economics** Establishing colonies always benefits a nation economically.

If you were there . . .
How would you react to the arrival of strangers in your land?

Section 1

OBJECTIVES

★ Compare Hernán Cortés's conquest of the Aztec to Francisco Pizarro's conquest of the Inca in Peru.

★ Explain the reasons for Spanish exploration of Florida and the American Southwest.

 **LET'S GET STARTED!**

Write the following question on the chalkboard: *How would you react if aliens from outer space came to the United States?* Have students write their responses and then share them with the class. *(Students' responses will vary but will most likely include some description of being afraid.)* Explain to students that the native people of North America were sometimes angry with or confused by the Europeans who came to explore and settle it. Explain to the class that in Section 1 they will learn about the fall of the Aztec and Inca empires, the Spanish conquistadores in Florida, and the reasons for Spanish exploration in the American Southwest.

Section 1

The Conquistadores

Read to Discover

1. How was Hernán Cortés's conquest of the Aztec similar to Francisco Pizarro's conquest of the Inca in Peru?
2. Why did the Spanish explore Florida and the American Southwest?

WHY IT MATTERS TODAY

People from different cultures sometimes fight against each other because their beliefs are different. Use **CNNfyi.com** or other **current events** sources to learn about a world conflict involving cultures with different beliefs. Record your findings in your journal.

Define

• conquistadores

Identify

• Hernán Cortés
• Moctezuma II
• Malintzin
• Francisco Pizarro
• Atahualpa
• Juan Ponce de León
• Álvar Núñez Cabeza de Vaca
• Hernando de Soto
• Francisco Vásquez de Coronado
• Juan Rodríguez Cabrillo

The Story Continues

During the *Reconquista* there was constant warfare in Spain, creating a class of Spanish warriors that had little land or money. After the *Reconquista* these soldiers lacked work. Military leader Hernán Cortés explained the problem. "Since this harsh land will yield us no living, we must rely on our swords and lances. For the same reason, we must move on." In the 1500s many Spanish soldiers chose to "move on" to the Americas to seek their fortunes.

Hernán Cortés came to the Americas as a young man hoping to gain wealth and power.

★ Cortés and the Aztec

Conquistadores (kahn-kees-tuh-DAWR-eez) were Spanish soldiers who led military expeditions in the Americas. The governor of Cuba sent conquistador **Hernán Cortés** to present-day Mexico in 1519. Cortés heard stories of a wealthy land to the west ruled by a king named **Moctezuma II** (mawk-tay-SOO-mah). "I decided to go and see him [Moctezuma] wherever he might be," wrote Cortés. "I would take him alive in chains or make him subject to [the King of Spain]." To prevent his soldiers from turning back, Cortés ordered their ships sunk. He then marched inland in search of Moctezuma and riches.

Have students read Section 1 and complete Guided Reading Strategy 3.1. Choose one or more of the following activities to explore the section content with students. For further suggestions on block scheduling or team teaching, see the *Block Scheduling Handbook with Team Teaching Strategies.*

LEVEL 1: Have students create a matching activity that focuses on the achievements of Cortés and Pizarro. *(Students' activities should focus on Cortés's conquests in Mexico and Pizarro's conquests in South America.)* On the left-hand side of the page, have students list the name of each conquistador and leave a blank space next to it for the letters of the descriptions that apply to him. On the right-hand side of the page, have students write descriptions of significant events that apply to the conquistadores. Tell students to place these descriptions in random order and to identify each statement with a letter in alphabetical order. Ask students to exchange their activities with another student. Have each student complete the activity and give it back to its creator for grading.

ENGLISH LANGUAGE LEARNERS, **COOPERATIVE LEARNING**

Moctezuma's kingdom was the Aztec Empire. The Aztec ruled several million people and had a rich civilization. They had thousands of warriors. In contrast, Cortés had only about 600 soldiers, 16 horses, and some guns. Cortés hoped that his superior weapons would bring him victory. In addition, the Aztec had never before seen horses and found them frightening. "These 'horses' . . . make a loud noise when they run . . . as if stones were raining on the earth," Aztec messengers told Moctezuma. Cortés received help from an American Indian woman named **Malintzin** (mah-LINT-suhn), also known as Malinche. She acted as an interpreter and advised him about the Aztec and their many enemies. These enemies allied with Cortés against the Aztec.

Moctezuma sent Cortés gifts of gold and other valuables, hoping to keep him away from the Aztec capital, Tenochtitlán. These signs of great wealth only encouraged Cortés. He and his men arrived in the capital in November 1519. Conquistador Bernal Díaz recorded his first impressions of the city, which sat in the middle of a great lake.

History Makers Speak

❝We were astounded [amazed]. These great towns and temples and buildings rising from the water, all made of stone, seemed like an enchanted vision.❞

—Bernal Díaz, quoted in *Cortés and the Downfall of the Aztec Empire*, by Jon Manchip White

Moctezuma was friendly to the Spanish, but Cortés was suspicious and took him prisoner. While Cortés was away, the Aztec rebelled and took back their city. The outnumbered Spanish who remained in the city fought their way out with heavy losses. Moctezuma was wounded during the battle and died soon after. Refusing to accept defeat, Cortés returned and fought the Aztec for several months. He then gathered thousands of soldiers from other American Indian groups and built a small fleet armed with cannons. This army attacked Tenochtitlán again. After three weeks of fighting, the city lay in ruins.

The battle for Tenochtitlán destroyed much of the city. After Cortés and his forces won, an Aztec poet wrote, "The houses are roofless now, and the walls are red with blood."

★★★★★★★★★★★★★
That's Interesting!
★★★★★★★★★★★★★

Mistaken Identity Can you imagine arriving in a new land and having strangers treat you like a legendary king? Indeed, some of the Aztec treated Cortés this way. Their reaction was based on Aztec legends about Quetzalcoatl (kwet-suhl-kuh-WAH-tuhl). In some Aztec historians' accounts, this being was a god who would return from beyond the sea. In other stories he was a powerful king. Images of him showed a man with pale skin and dark hair. Aztec historians wrote that when Moctezuma first heard of Cortés, "it was as if he thought the new arrival was our prince Quetzalcoatl."

Moctezuma II

Interdisciplinary Connection

▶**Literature**◀

Francisco López de Gómara. When studying historical literature, it is important to pay attention to the source and context of the text. Francisco López de Gómara, for example, is one of the most frequently cited authors of the conquest period. As Hernán Cortés's personal secretary, Gómara had first-hand knowledge of Cortés's personality and inspiration. Yet because Gómara was not a part of Cortés's mission, and thus all of his knowledge is derived from secondary sources and Cortés's own accounts.

ACTIVITY: Ask students to imagine that they were on the expedition with Cortés and then have them write journal entries that provide an account of their journeys. Remind students to use standard grammar, spelling, sentence structure, and punctuation. Then ask them why a personal account of the expedition might be more accurate than Gómara's second-hand account.

MAP ANSWER
(for p. 68)
Cortés

ALL LEVELS: Explain to students that conquistadores originally believed that they would find plentiful amounts of gold when they reached Florida and the American Southwest. What they found, however, were American Indian tribes that were sometimes hostile to the conquistadores' presence. Have students work in small groups to create an illustrated time line of the significant events that occurred in the Spanish conquistadores' explorations of Florida and the American Southwest. *(Students' time lines should include Ponce de Leon and de Soto's explorations of Florida, Cabeza de Vaca and Estevanico's explorations in the Southwest, Coronado's explorations, and Cabrillo's explorations along the California coast.)* The time line should include illustrations describing each of the major events. Provide each group with a large sheet of butcher paper and art supplies to create its time line. Once students have finished, ask them to explain the events they illustrated to the class.

ENGLISH LANGUAGE LEARNERS ,
COOPERATIVE LEARNING

HOMEWORK Tell students to imagine that they are Spanish conquistadores who have been asked to create a ship's log that describes their encounter with the Aztec or the Inca. Tell students to describe the events that led to the fall of each empire.

Peruvian Indians. The Inca Empire originated from a small tribe of Quechua-speaking Indians who lived in the Andes in what is now Peru. In approximately A.D. 1400 the Inca began to expand their territory. They eventually ruled an empire that included some 10 million people, which was later conquered by the Spanish. Today, Quechua-speaking Indians still live in Peru. They number approximately 6 million and continue to follow many of the ancient traditions of their ancestors.

CRITICAL THINKING

Why might some Quechua speakers continue to follow their ancestors' traditions?

ANSWER: Students might suggest that they may do it as a way of remembering their history and showing respect for their ancestors.

Technology Resources

Exploring America's Past Video Segment: The Serpent God; Teacher's Guide pp. 4–5

Search 6477, Play to 13038
Videodisc Red Side A
See *Teacher's Guide* for Spanish barcode.

Spanish Exploration and Conquests, 1513–1542

Interpreting Maps Spanish explorers claimed a tremendous amount of land in the Americas.

Skills Assessment The World in Spatial Terms Which of the explorers shown traveled the shortest distance?

Other Aztec towns soon fell to Cortés as well. The Aztec also suffered terribly from diseases that the Spanish introduced to Mexico. Illnesses such as smallpox caused hundreds of thousands of deaths in a very short time, hastening the fall of the Aztec Empire.

✔ **Reading Check: Identifying Cause and Effect** How was Cortés able to conquer the Aztec at Tenochtitlán, and how did this defeat affect the Aztec Empire? Cortés had superior weapons, horses, and American Indian allies; the fall of the Aztec capital led to the defeat of other Aztec communities.

★ Pizarro's Conquest of the Inca

Cortés had conquered a territory larger than Spain. His success brought him fame back home and inspired other conquistadores. Among these was **Francisco Pizarro** (pee-SAHR-roh), who had traveled with the explorer Nuñez de Balboa. Pizarro heard rumors of golden cities in the mountains of South America. In late 1531 Pizarro landed with a small army on the coast of what is now Peru. After marching for several weeks, he reached the Inca Empire.

The Inca ruled a huge region that stretched from present-day Chile to Colombia. The Inca ruler, **Atahualpa** (ah-tauh-WAHL-pauh), heard about the Spanish invaders, but he was not worried. Fewer than 200 strangers did not seem much of a threat. Like the Aztec, however, the Inca had no weapons to match the conquistadores' swords and guns. The Inca had also been weakened by smallpox, which had killed tens of thousands of people. In addition, Atahualpa faced an ongoing civil war with his half-brother.

After reaching the Andes, Pizarro arranged a meeting with Atahualpa. He then kidnapped the Inca ruler. Atahualpa promised to fill a large room with gold and silver in return for his freedom. The Inca delivered 24 tons of gold and silver. Pizarro killed Atahualpa instead of freeing him, however. The Spaniard then joined with several powerful Inca rebel leaders. By 1534 he and his local American Indian allies had conquered the Inca Empire. The second great empire of the Americas had fallen.

✔ **Reading Check: Summarizing** Explain how Pizarro was able to defeat the Inca. Atahualpa underestimated the Spanish, his people were weakened by smallpox, and Pizarro was able to use Atahualpa's enemies against him.

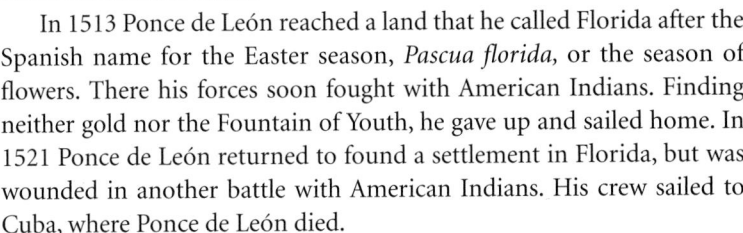

⭐ Conquistadores in Florida

The hope of finding another rich empire lured many other conquistadores to the Americas. One of these was **Juan Ponce de León** (PAWN-say day lay-AWN). King Ferdinand of Spain had given Ponce de León the right to settle the mainland of North America. According to legend, Ponce de León heard American Indian stories about a magic spring that "makes old men young again." This mythical spring became known as the Fountain of Youth.

In 1513 Ponce de León reached a land that he called Florida after the Spanish name for the Easter season, *Pascua florida*, or the season of flowers. There his forces soon fought with American Indians. Finding neither gold nor the Fountain of Youth, he gave up and sailed home. In 1521 Ponce de León returned to found a settlement in Florida, but was wounded in another battle with American Indians. His crew sailed to Cuba, where Ponce de León died.

Despite Ponce de León's failure, the Spanish remained interested in Florida. In 1528 Pánfilo de Narváez (PAHM-fee-loh day nahr-BAH-ays) arrived from Spain to explore Florida's western coast. Narváez split his forces. He sent the ships ahead to explore and led about 300 soldiers north through the inland swamps. This move proved to be a mistake. The ships lost contact with Narváez and had to return home.

Narváez and his conquistadores faced illness, hostile American Indians, and bad weather. They were starving and desperate. Finally they built simple boats and tried to sail west across the Gulf of Mexico. Most of the boats sank or wrecked, and Narváez died.

Among the few survivors were **Álvar Núñez Cabeza de Vaca** (kay-BAY-sah day BAH-kah) and a Moor named Estevanico (e-stay-bah-NEE-koh). In 1528 the survivors reached the coast of what is now Texas. They were captured by local American Indians but managed to escape. The group began a journey across Texas to what is now New Mexico. Cabeza de Vaca recalled this time as "years during which I wandered lost and naked through many and very strange lands." He and his companions survived by their wits and luck.

For eight years Cabeza de Vaca lived with various American Indian tribes while searching for a Spanish settlement. He worked as a servant, trader, and healer. During this time he gained fame and respect from the Pueblo Indians. Finally, in 1536 Cabeza de Vaca met a group of Spanish

Interpreting the Visual Record

The Fountain of Youth
Legends of a Fountain of Youth may have drawn Ponce de León and other explorers to Florida. This illustration shows a group of happy conquistadores supposedly finding the miraculous fountain. **In what ways do you think the actual experiences of conquistadores would have differed from the scene shown here?**

Robert Jones of New Hartford, New York, suggested the following activity:

 **LEVEL 2:** Organize the class into small groups. Then have each group create a graphic organizer that identifies significant conquistadores, key events that happened on their voyages, the dates of their journeys, and reasons for their exploration. Then give each group a blank outline map of the Americas. Have each group create a color-coded key that identifies each conquistador with a specific color. Tell students to use the appropriate color to highlight the exploration route of each conquistador on the list. Ask students to label the location where each significant event occurred. Next to the location, students should write a sentence or two explaining the reasons for exploration. **COOPERATIVE LEARNING**

☆ CLOSE

Tell students that the Spanish conquistadores achieved both successes and failures on their journeys. Have students create two outlines, one describing the successes that Spanish conquistadores encountered and another describing their failures. Once students are finished, have them identify the events they placed in each category. Create a chart on the chalkboard that correctly identifies each success or failure.

De Soto's Camp. Located near present-day Tallahassee, Florida, Hernando de Soto's winter camp is the oldest known European building site on the North American mainland. The structure was supported by 8-inch square vertical beams spaced 10 to 11 feet apart. Twigs and vines were woven between smaller vertical beams and then covered with mud to form the walls. The structure was sheltered by a palm-thatched roof.

ACTIVITY: Have students construct models of what they imagine de Soto's winter camp looked like.

Visual Record Answer

Students might suggest that Coronado needed many people to aid him in his conquests.

Research on the R◉M

Free Find:
El Dorado
After reading about El Dorado on the **Holt Researcher CD–ROM**, draw a picture of the ceremony described by the Spanish author.

Interpreting the Visual Record

In search of gold *Coronado and his conquistadores traveled throughout the Southwest but never found the treasure they sought.* **What does this image suggest about the size and power of Coronado's expedition?**

soldiers "who were thunderstruck to see me so strangely dressed and in the company of Indians." Cabeza de Vaca traveled on with the soldiers to Mexico. In 1542 after returning to Spain, he published the story of his travels as *The Narrative of Álvar Núñez Cabeza de Vaca.*

✔ **Reading Check: Comparing and Contrasting** What were the similarities and differences between the explorations of Ponce de León and Cabeza de Vaca? *Both started in Florida. Ponce de León sought the Fountain of Youth and hoped to found a settlement. Cabeza de Vaca was trying to return home. Cabeza de Vaca had better relations with American Indians.*

☆ The Quest for Gold

While in Spain, Cabeza de Vaca described his adventures to **Hernando de Soto**. De Soto, who had fought for Pizarro in Peru, became convinced that Florida held a kingdom as rich as the Inca Empire. Arriving in Florida in 1539, de Soto led some 600 conquistadores north in search of gold. Once he reached what is now North Carolina, de Soto traveled west to present-day Arkansas. He became the first European to cross the Mississippi River. An expedition member described the river as "half a league [more than a mile] wide . . . of great depth and of very strong current."

De Soto encountered American Indian cultures that had rich farms and large populations. Ignoring chances for trade or settlement, de Soto kept moving. He stole food and fought American Indians as he went. One conquistador wrote about de Soto.

> **History Makers Speak** ❝His object [being] to find another treasure like that of [Atahualpa], . . . [he] would not be content with good lands nor pearls, even though many of them were worth their weight in gold.❞
>
> —The Gentleman of Elvas, "The Narrative of the Expedition of Hernando de Soto"

De Soto was worn down from battle and upset at his failure to find riches. At last, in 1542 he decided to return home. De Soto fell ill on the way, however, and died near the mouth of the Mississippi River. The other conquistadores reached Spanish settlements in Mexico the next year.

Meanwhile, Cabeza de Vaca's fellow adventurer, Estevanico, returned to New Mexico in 1539. He was part of a group led by Fray Marcos de Niza. The conquistadores' goal was to find the legendary Seven Cities of Cíbola, which were said to hold great wealth. After Estevanico was killed by Zuni Indians, the expedition returned to Mexico. There Fray Marcos claimed that he had seen the Seven Cities of Cíbola. He said that they were full of gold and gems.

These reports brought the conquistador **Francisco Vásquez de Coronado** to New

☆ REVIEW AND ASSESS

Have students complete the **Section 1 Review** on p. 71. Then have students complete **Daily Quiz 3.1**. As **Alternative Assessment**, you may want to use the matching activity or conquest graphic organizer in this section's lessons.

☆ RETEACH

Have students complete **Main Idea Activity for English Language Learners and Special-Needs Students 3.1**. Have students work in pairs to write short summaries of each of the subsections of Section 1. Then group each pair with another pair and ask the foursome to review each other's summaries,

looking for key points that may have been missed.
ENGLISH LANGUAGE LEARNERS , COOPERATIVE LEARNING

☆ EXTEND

Tell students to choose a conquistador to research. Have students create a resumé for the conquistador that describes significant accomplishments of his journey(s). Remind students that resumés should include a purpose statement (describing the conquistador's goals), a summary of current and past jobs (describing the conquistador's significant explorations), and reference section (including names of other famous conquistadores). **BLOCK SCHEDULING**

Mexico in 1540. Coronado captured a Zuni town called Cíbola. Zuni legends later described the Spanish. "They wore coats of iron . . . and carried for weapons short canes that spit fire and made thunder." Instead of gold, Coronado found only adobe buildings and bushels of corn. However, he continued to search for the Seven Cities. One of his scouting groups even reached the Grand Canyon.

Traveling northeast, Coronado met Zuni and other Pueblo Indians, such as the Hopi. His demands for food and clothing angered the Pueblo, who drove him away. Coronado traveled all the way to present-day Kansas. There he discovered that his American Indian guide had tricked him. "[The guide took] us to a place where we and our horses would starve to death." But, Coronado and his conquistadores survived, only to return home in 1542 without any treasure.

That same year, Portuguese explorer **Juan Rodríguez Cabrillo** (kah-BRE-yoh) set sail under the Spanish flag. He sailed 1,200 miles along the coast of present-day California. Cabrillo was looking for gold and a new sea route to China. Bartolomé Ferrer, a crew member, described the northern coast. "There are mountains which seem to reach the heavens. . . . It appears as though they would fall on the ships." Cabrillo heard strange stories from American Indians. "Men like us [other Europeans] were traveling about, bearded, clothed, and armed." Cabrillo never returned from his voyage. He died during the winter in 1543, having failed to find wealth. However, his journey gave Spain a claim to the Pacific coast of North America.

THE GRANGER COLLECTION, NEW YORK

After his travels with Cabeza de Vaca, Estevanico returned to the Southwest.

✔ **Reading Check: Sequencing** Create a time line listing the explorations of de Soto, Estevanico, Coronado, and Cabrillo. Note when they began and ended their journeys and what happened to them. De Soto—set out in 1539, died near Mississippi River in 1542, soldiers returned home in 1543; Estevanico—set out in 1539, died in New Mexico; Coronado—set out in 1540, returned home empty-handed in 1542; Cabrillo—set out in 1542, died in 1543

go.hrw.com Homework Practice Online
keyword: SA3 HP3

Section 1 Review

1 Define and explain:
• conquistadores

2 Identify and explain:
• Hernán Cortés
• Moctezuma II
• Malintzin
• Francisco Pizarro
• Atahualpa
• Juan Ponce de León
• Álvar Núñez Cabeza de Vaca
• Hernando de Soto
• Francisco Vásquez de Coronado
• Juan Rodríguez Cabrillo

3 Summarizing Copy the chart below. Use it to link the conquistadores described in this section to the places they explored or to the people they conquered.

Conquistador	Place Explored or People Conquered

4 Finding the Main Idea
a. Compare Cortés's conquest of the Aztec Empire with Pizarro's conquest of the Inca Empire.

b. Why did conquistadores such as Ponce de León, de Soto, and Coronado explore the Americas, and what did they achieve?

5 Writing and Critical Thinking
Analyzing Information Imagine that you are an adviser to Atahualpa. Prepare a report that suggests how to deal with Pizarro's Spanish forces, which have just entered the Inca Empire.

Consider the following:
• the advantages and disadvantages the Inca have in comparison to the Spanish
• Pizarro's motives for coming to the Inca Empire
• civil conflict in the Inca Empire

★ Section 1 Review ANSWERS

1 Define
• conquistadores, p. 66

2 Identify
• Hernán Cortés, p. 66
• Moctezuma II, p. 66
• Malintzin, p. 67
• Francisco Pizarro, p. 68
• Atahualpa, p. 68
• Juan Ponce de León, p. 69
• Álvar Núñez Cabeza de Vaca, p. 69
• Hernando de Soto, p. 70
• Francisco Vásquez de Coronado, p. 70
• Juan Rodríguez Cabrillo, p. 71

3 Cortés—Aztec; Pizarro—Inca; Ponce de León—Florida; Coronado—the American Southwest

4 a. Answers may vary but should note that both men conquered large and powerful empires with the help of superior technology, American Indian allies, and the effects of disease on American Indian populations. Both gained great wealth for Spain as well.
b. Answers will vary but should note that most of these conquistadores were looking for treasure like that gained by Cortés and Pizarro. None found this treasure, but they explored much of North America while searching.

5 Students' reports may vary but should include the following: The Inca greatly outnumbered the Spanish, but the Inca were politically divided, ravaged by disease, and lacked the superior weapons of the Spanish. Atahualpa may not be able to rely on other Inca leaders for assistance. Pizarro appears to be interested in conquest and treasure.

Section 2

OBJECTIVES

★ Describe how Spain organized and governed its empire in the Americas.

★ Analyze the structure of New Spain's economy and society.

★ Explain why the Spanish settled in the borderlands.

SECTION 2 RESOURCES

REPRODUCIBLE

▶ Guided Reading Strategy 3.2

▶ Literature Reading 3: Through the Eyes of a Spanish Missionary-Explorer

TECHNOLOGY

▶ One-Stop Planner, Lesson 3.2

▶ American Music Selection 3: "Alabado"

▶ Everyday Life in America Transparency 2: Religious Folk Art in the Spanish Colonies

▶ Holt Researcher: American History CD–ROM

▶ CNN Presents America: Beginnings to 1914 Segment: Mission Bells in California

▶ Homework Practice Online

REINFORCEMENT, REVIEW, AND ASSESSMENT

▶ Section 2 Review, p. 77

▶ Daily Quiz 3.2

▶ Main Idea Activity 3.2

▶ English Audio Summary 3.2

▶ Spanish Audio Summary 3.2

🔊 LET'S GET STARTED!

Write the following terms on the chalkboard: *missions, plantations,* and *pueblos.* Ask students to list possible words that they associate with each of these terms. *(Students' responses might include American Indians, churches, or slavery).* Allow time for students to write their responses. Ask students to identify which culture they believe introduced these concepts to the Americas. Explain to them that Spanish settlements had significant cultural effects on the Americas, including the introduction of missions, plantations, and pueblos. Tell students that in Section 2 they will learn about the economies, government, and societies of the Spanish, and why Spanish settlers chose to settle in the borderlands.

Section 2

Spanish America

Read to Discover

1. How did Spain organize and govern its empire in the Americas?
2. How were the economy and society of New Spain structured?
3. Why did the Spanish settle in the borderlands?

WHY IT MATTERS TODAY

Women in many countries must often still fight for equal rights. Use **CNNfyi.com** or other **current events** sources to identify women in some part of the world who are struggling for equality. Record your findings in your journal.

Define

- pueblos
- missions
- presidios
- *encomienda* system
- plantations
- borderlands

Identify

- Council of the Indies
- Bartolomé de Las Casas
- Juan de Oñate
- Popé
- El Camino Real

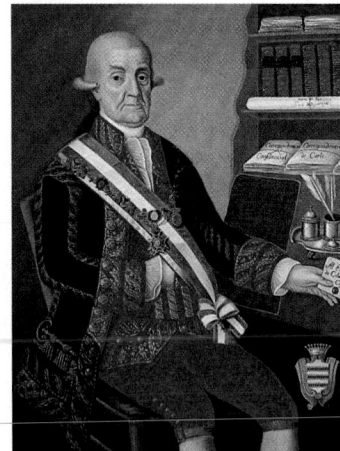

Matias de Gálvez, was one of many viceroys of New Spain during Spanish rule.

The Story Continues

Conquistadores such as Hernán Cortés and Francisco Pizarro conquered a huge territory for Spain. By the mid-1500s Spain's American empire was larger than that of any other European nation. However, the challenge for Spain had changed. A Spanish official described the problem. "Without settlement there is no good conquest." Spain had to somehow settle and control an empire many times its size from across the ocean.

★ The Spanish Empire

Spain ruled its large American empire through a system of royal officials. At the top was the **Council of the Indies**, formed in 1524 to govern the Americas from Spain. The Council wrote laws, selected officials, and judged legal cases. The Council appointed two viceroys, or royal governors. One governor oversaw the Viceroyalty of Peru, which included most of South America. The other ruled the Viceroyalty of New Spain. This area included Central America, Mexico, and the southern part of what is now the United States. Each governor chose his local officials.

★ ★

GRAPHIC ORGANIZER : POSSIBLE SOLUTION

The Path to Independence

Fill in the following cause-and-effect chart with information about events that took place during the American Revolution.

Cause	Effect
Colonists and British troops exchange fire at Lexington and Concord.	The rebellion against Britain begins.
Thomas Paine publishes his pamphlet *Common Sense*.	*Many colonists support colonial protests against Britain and want independence.*
Colonial leaders sign the Declaration of Independence.	*This act broke all ties to the British crown.*
The Declaration of Independence includes the statement that "all men are created equal."	Some colonists point out that the document does not include women or slaves.
The royal governor of Virginia promises freedom to any slave who fights for the British.	Many slaves join the British troops.
British general William Howe decides to give his troops a break for the holidays in the winter of 1776–77.	*General George Washington and his troops make a surprise attack on Trenton, New Jersey, and are victorious.*
France and Britain were longtime enemies.	France secretly aids the Patriots.
Prussian army officer Baron Friedrich von Steuben comes to General George Washington's aid in 1778.	*Von Steuben transforms the disorganized Continental Army into a finely tuned fighting force.*
George Rogers Clark organizes a series of meetings with Indian leaders in the West.	*The Indians agree to remain neutral in the war.*
The Patriots' southern army is destroyed in the attack on Camden, South Carolina.	The Patriots switch to guerrilla warfare to fight the British in the South.
The Patriots prepare to attack British troops at Yorktown, Virginia.	*British general Charles Cornwallis surrenders, and the Patriots win the American Revolution.*

Have students read Section 2 and complete Guided Reading Strategy 3.2. Choose one or more of the following activities to explore the section content with students. For further suggestions on block scheduling or team teaching, see the *Block Scheduling Handbook with Team Teaching Strategies.*

Note: To help students make meaningful connections between events in American history and in their own home towns, use the Chapter 3 **Hands-On History** activity, Memorializing the Founders of Your Town.

LEVEL 1: Have students work in groups to create the front page of a newspaper from a Spanish settlement in the borderlands. Students should include headlines that describe the Spanish settlement's organization and government, drawing or picture depicting an aspect of the settlement, and the publication date. *(Students' drawings may include a mission or a presidio.)* Once groups are finished, have each group present its newspaper to the class.
ENGLISH LANGUAGE LEARNERS , COOPERATIVE LEARNING

All officials in Spanish America had a great deal of independence. The empire was too large for the governors to know everything that was going on. Spain was so far away that the governors themselves could often ignore royal laws without being caught. One worried Spaniard wrote about this issue.

History Makers Speak
❝Our people, transported across an ocean . . . leave [Spain] meeker than lambs, [but] change as soon as they arrive there [America] into wild wolves, forgetting all the royal commands.❞

—Angeleria, quoted in *A Violent Evangelism,* by Luis N. Rivera

Most people in Spanish America lived in the former Aztec and Inca Empires. These lands were rich with gold and silver mines. From 1503 to 1660, Spanish treasure fleets carried 200 tons of gold and 18,600 tons of silver to Spain. Thus Spain's American colonies helped make the country very wealthy. The people of Mexico and Peru also grew food to help support Spain's growing empire.

✔ **Reading Check: Summarizing** Explain the system of royal officials that Spain used to control its growing empire in the Americas. Council of Indies; viceroys of New Spain and Peru appointed by Council; local officials appointed by viceroys

⭐ Ruling New Spain

The Spanish established three kinds of settlements in New Spain. These settlements filled economic, religious, or military roles. **Pueblos** served as trading posts and sometimes as centers of government. Many pueblos were formed on the sites of American Indian villages. Priests started **missions** to convert local American Indians to Catholicism. Each mission community was built around a church. The Spanish built **presidios**, or military forts, to protect towns and missions. Many of these forts were built in frontier areas, such as present-day Florida and Texas.

The Catholic Church played an important part in ruling New Spain. King Philip II issued the Royal Orders for New Discoveries in 1573. In them he declared that spreading Christianity was the main reason for founding new settlements. The Royal Orders commanded priests to teach American Indians about Christianity. Missions were also to teach

---

CONNECTING TO MATH

Just the Facts

Imported Treasure from the Americas to Spain, 1506–1645
(in pesos)

20-Year Period	Total Treasure
1506–1525	3,139,158
1526–1545	11,580,568
1546–1565	34,580,779
1566–1585	72,668,380
1586–1605	117,849,324
1606–1625	113,056,467
1626–1645	72,143,787

Using Mathematical Skills

1. What was the value of treasure imported from 1506 to 1545?
2. Create a graph that shows the value of total treasure in 20-year periods from 1506 to 1645.
3. Imagine that you are an adviser to the Spanish government in 1645. Prepare a report that describes the trends in treasures imported from the Americas to Spain.

San José Mission was established in 1720 in present-day Texas.

Missions. The friars who lived in missions like the one shown here were often the only Europeans in the area. Missions were built to be independent economic, political, and social units. Although their primary purpose was to provide areas for religious celebrations, missions also had to serve many different functions, such as providing education or producing food. This is a mission in San Antonio, Texas.

CRITICAL THINKING

Why do you think so many statues might be used to decorate the missions?

ANSWER: Students might suggest that these statues might have helped American Indians to understand the religious values of the friars even though the Indians did not speak Spanish.

Technology Resources

American Music
Selection 3: "Alabado"

CONNECTING TO MATH ANSWERS

1. 14,719,726
2. Graphs should correlate to the information from the chart.
3. All reports should use statistics from the chart to verify the explanation of the trends.

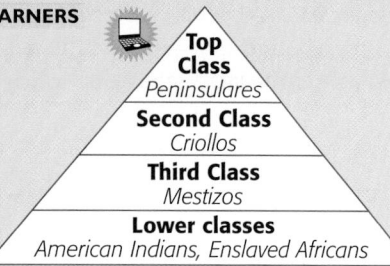

Top Class
Peninsulares

Second Class
Criollos

Third Class
Mestizos

Lower classes
American Indians, Enslaved Africans

The priest Bartolomé de Las Casas tried to get the Spanish government to treat American Indians more fairly.

Analyzing Primary Sources

Drawing Inferences and Conclusions Why do you think Las Casas criticized the treatment of American Indians under the *encomienda* system? Students might say he believed the system violated the natural rights of Indians, which they shared with all other humans.

American Indians "the use of . . . bread, silk, linen, horses, cattle, tools, and weapons, and all the rest that Spain has had." Some American Indians accepted this new way of life, combining Spanish customs with their own. Others rejected Spanish ideas completely.

✔ **Reading Check: Categorizing** What types of communities did the Spanish establish in New Spain? Pueblos served as trading posts or seats of government, missions were religious centers for conversion of American Indians, and presidios were military forts to protect other settlements.

★ The Economy of New Spain

Many settlers in New Spain depended on the labor of American Indians. One viceroy complained that "no one comes to the Indies to plow and sow, but only to eat and loaf." To reward settlers for their service to the Crown, Spain established the ***encomienda*** (en-koh-mee-EN-duh) **system**. It gave Spanish settlers known as *encomenderos* (en-koh-muhn-DE-rohs) the right to tax local American Indians or to make them work. In exchange, these settlers were supposed to protect and teach local American Indians. *Encomenderos* were also expected to convert the Indians to Christianity. Most Spanish treated the Indians like slaves, forcing them to grow crops, to work in mines, and to herd cattle. The working conditions were very hard. Many American Indians died of disease and exhaustion.

Some settlers spoke out against this unjust treatment. **Bartolomé de Las Casas** was an *encomendero* who later became a priest. He protested the *encomienda* system and defended American Indians' rights.

 66The natural laws and rules and rights of men are common to all nations . . . whatever their sect [religious faith], law, state, color, and condition, without any difference.**99**

—Bartolomé de Las Casas, quoted in *The Conquest of America,* by Tzvetan Todorov

Las Casas wrote books and letters calling for an end to the *encomienda* system. He was not able to change the laws, however. Many settlers continued to force Indians to work for them.

In the Caribbean, American Indians resisted the *encomienda* system. In addition, many American Indians died from European diseases. These factors led the Spanish to start bringing enslaved Africans to New Spain in 1501. Thousands of these slaves worked on **plantations**—large farms that grew just one kind of crop. For example, sugar plantations were very common on the Caribbean islands. These plantations could make huge profits for their owners. At first, even Las Casas favored using enslaved Africans rather than American Indians for plantation labor. After watching the slave trade grow and seeing its harsh conditions, he changed his mind. Las Casas wrote in his *History of the Indies* that Africans were "unjustly and tyrannically [ruthlessly] reduced to slavery." The African slave trade continued despite the protests.

✔ **Reading Check: Finding the Main Idea** Why did the Spanish establish plantations and the *encomienda* system? primarily for economic reasons—provided a profitable system of cheap labor for Spanish settlers

LEVEL 2: Lead a discussion on the organization of Spanish government in the Americas. Explain to the class that Spain ruled its colonies through a system of royal officials. Ask students to create an organizational chart that depicts how Spain ruled its colonies in the Americas. *(Students' charts should include the Council of the Indies, viceroys, appointed officials, and the role of the church.)* Under each level of organization, students should write a sentence that describes its responsibilities. Allow time for students to complete their charts; be sure to offer assistance to those that need help.

LEVEL 3: Tell students that the Spanish utilized three types of settlements in the territories of New Spain. Explain to them that these were based on economic, military, and religious concerns. Tell students that the Council of the Indies wants them to write a description of each type of settlement and of the economic organization of New Spain. Have students work in small groups to create these descriptions. Be sure to tell students to include descriptions of missions, presidios, and pueblos. Also, have students include a description of the *encomienda* system and explain how it eventually led to the creation of plantations and the use of slave labor. Encourage students to develop visual aids to help describe each type of settlement. Ask volunteers to share their descriptions and visual aids with the class. Then lead a discussion on the economic system of New Spain. **COOPERATIVE LEARNING**

⭐ Expanding into the Borderlands

Most colonists in New Spain settled where they could gain the most wealth. Few lived in the **borderlands** on the outer reaches of the empire. This region included northern Mexico, Florida, and parts of present-day Arizona, California, New Mexico, and Texas. Spanish settlement of the borderlands took place over several hundred years.

Several explorers had died in Florida, and none had found great wealth. The Spanish government began to wonder if Florida was worth the risk. This view changed when the French settled on Florida's east coast. Spain's King Philip II sent Pedro Menéndez de Avilés (may NAYN-days day ah-bee-LAYS) to "cast them out by the best means . . . possible." In 1565 Menéndez de Avilés destroyed a French town. He then founded the fort of St. Augustine. From this base, the Spanish hoped to protect their treasure fleets.

The first mission established in California was the Mission San Diego de Alcalá, created July of 1769. Over the next 54 years, a total of 21 missions were built in California, all of which are still standing today.

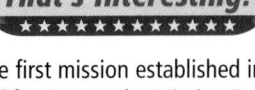

TOPIC: Missions
GO TO: go.hrw.com
KEYWORD: SA3 CF3

Have students use the library or search the Internet through the HRW Go site for information on Spanish missions. Ask students to prepare an oral report with the information they find.

Spanish America, c. 1650

Interpreting Maps The Spanish built many towns and settlements and established missions to convert American Indians to Christianity.

Skills Assessment

1. **Locate** What were the capitals of the two viceroyalties?
2. **Analyzing Information** What type of Spanish settlement was most common in Florida and New Mexico?

Technology Resources

CNN. Presents America: Beginnings to 1914 Segment: Mission Bells in California

MAP ANSWERS

1. Mexico City and Lima
2. missions

La Conquistadora upon her altar at St. Francis Cathedral, Santa Fe

HOMEWORK Have students write a poem or song
that describes the class system of New Spain and
explains why a person who was designated as being in
one of its lower classes might wish to change the system.
Encourage students to share their poems or songs with the rest
of the class.

☆ CLOSE

Write the following terms on the chalkboard: *African
Americans, American Indians, criollos, vestizos, peninsulares,* and
women. Explain to students that all of these groups played a role
in the class structure created by the Council of the Indies. Have
students create a hierarchical chart describing the class system
of New Spain. Next to each term, students should write a brief
description of the types of jobs that people in that class usually
performed. *(Students' descriptions should include slavery for
African Americans, laborers for American Indians, plantation owners for crillos, laborers or craftspeople for mestizos, high government
positions for peninsulares, and a variety of jobs for women.)* Finally,
lead a class discussion about the problems of having a class
structure based on race and sex.

Father Junípero Serra.
Father Serra was as determined
to spread Christianity as the
explorers were to find land and
riches. For every fort built to defend
the coastline, Father Serra built a
mission. Traveling an estimated
4,000 to 5,000 miles up and
down the California coastline on
an infected foot that he refused
to stop and treat, Father Serra
provided an example of dedication
that later priests followed.

CRITICAL THINKING

Why did Father Serra establish a
mission for every fort?

ANSWER: Students might suggest
that he probably wanted to provide
a balance between military and
religious influences.

**CONNECTING TO
LITERATURE ANSWER**
She has chosen to be a thought-
ful, intelligent person, rather
than being overly concerned with
worldly things.

CONNECTING TO *Literature*

"World, in Hounding Me"

Sor Juana Inés de la Cruz

*The nun Sor Juana Inés de la Cruz
spoke out on a woman's right to
education and independence. In
the following poem she defends her
choice to defy the traditional role of
women in New Spain.*

World, in hounding me, what do you gain?
How can it harm you if I choose, **astutely**[1],
rather to stock my mind with things of beauty,
than waste its stock on every beauty's claim?

Costliness and wealth bring me no
   pleasure;
the only happiness I care to find
derives from setting treasure in my mind,
and not from mind that's set on winning
   treasure.

I prize no **comeliness**[2].
All fair things pay to time, the victor, their
   appointed fee and
treasure cheats even the practiced eye.
Mine is the better and truer way:
to leave vanities of life aside,
not to throw my life away on vanity.

[1] **astutely:** wisely   [2] **comeliness:** beauty

Understanding What You Read

Literature and History What choices has the poet
made in her life that were unusual for her time?

The first effort to settle New Mexico came
in 1598. **Juan de Oñate** (ohn-YAH-tay) set out
from Mexico City to explore and to start a
colony. After fighting the Pueblo Indians,
Oñate helped found the town of Santa Fe about
1609–10. Santa Fe soon became a trade center
and the most important Spanish settlement in
New Mexico. Other Spanish settlements in the
area included missions founded by priests.

Spanish settlements depended on food and
labor provided by the Pueblo Indians. Beginning in 1660 the Pueblo experienced crop
failures and raids by other American Indians.
Spanish abuses finally pushed the Pueblo to
revolt in 1680. Led by Pueblo medicine man
Popé (poh-PAY), some Pueblo came together
and drove the Spanish out of New Mexico.
Popé could not keep the Pueblo united, however. In 1692 the Spanish regained control.

Many Spanish survivors of the Pueblo
Revolt had fled to what is now Texas. The first
major Spanish settlement in Texas was founded
in 1682 near the site of present-day El Paso. In
the 1700s the Spanish learned that the French
were building forts in Louisiana. Official
Francisco Hidalgo warned the viceroy of New
Spain. "[The French] are slipping behind our
backs in silence, but God sees their intentions."
The Spanish responded by building more missions and forts of their own. Father Eusebio
Kino (yoo-SAYB-yoh KEE-noh) helped establish
many missions in present-day Arizona.

To connect the scattered communities of
New Spain, Spanish settlers built **El Camino Real**, or "the Royal Road."
This network of trails ran for hundreds of miles. It eventually reached
settlements in California, one of the last borderland areas settled by the
Spanish. In the late 1760s missionary Junípero Serra (hoo-NEE-pay-roh
SER-rah) traveled to California. Serra wanted to spread Christianity to
the Indians in the area. He helped persuade the viceroy of New Spain to
support further expansion. Serra led his friars and local Indians in
founding San Francisco and eight other missions along the Pacific coast.
Most Spanish settlers saw better opportunities in Mexico and Peru,
however. Fewer than 1,000 Spanish had settled in California by 1790.

✔ **Reading Check: Identifying Cause and Effect** What factors led to Popé's
revolt against the Spanish in New Mexico, and what was the result?
Crop failures, American Indian raids, and Spanish abuses led to the revolt; the
Spanish were temporarily driven out of the area, but the Pueblo alliance collapsed, and the Spanish regained control.

☆ **REVIEW AND ASSESS**

Have students complete the **Section 2 Review** on p. 77. Then have students complete **Daily Quiz 3.2**. As **Alternative Assessment**, you may want to use the newspaper exercise or Spanish society graphic organizer in this section's lessons.

☆ **RETEACH**

Have students complete **Main Idea Activity for English Language Learners and Special-Needs Students 3.2**. Then organize students into groups of three. Have each group make an annotated outline of the section with brief summaries of each subsection. **ENGLISH LANGUAGE LEARNERS** , **COOPERATIVE LEARNING**

☆ **EXTEND**

Organize the class into several small groups. Assign each group to research settlements in California, Florida and Georgia, and the Southwest. Have each group compare and contrast what daily life was like in each of these areas. Tell each group to make a list of the similarities of life in the three areas and a list of the differences in the areas. Once all groups have finished, create two lists on the chalkboard—one describing the similarities and one the differences. Have students share ideas from their group's lists and write them under the appropriate list on the chalkboard. **COOPERATIVE LEARNING** , **BLOCK SCHEDULING**

☆ Colonial Society

By 1650 the Spanish Empire in the Americas had between 3 and 4 million people. American Indians made up about 80 percent of the population. The rest were whites, Africans, and people of mixed racial background. Spanish law divided society into classes based on birthplace and race. The *peninsulares* (pay-neen-soo-LAHR-ays) were white Spaniards born in Spain. They usually held the highest government offices in Spanish America. Just below them in status were the criollos (kree-OH-yohs), people born in the Americas to Spanish parents. Next came the mestizos (me-STEE-zohs), who had both Spanish and American Indian parents. Mestizos made up the largest part-European group in Spanish America. They often worked for criollos as laborers or craftspeople. American Indians had only limited rights. Enslaved Africans had little or no legal protection.

Women from all the social classes typically had fewer rights than men. In New Spain the high death rates for men often left female family members with added work. Married women in New Spain could own property and pass it on to their children. This was not the case in most European countries. Neither men nor women received much education. However, upper-class children were given some education.

Skilled artisans among the Pueblo Indians made beautifully decorated blankets and pottery.

✔ **Reading Check: Categorizing** Describe the major social classes that existed in Spanish America. *peninsulares* —white Spaniards born in Spain, held the highest government offices in Spanish America; criollos—Spanish people born in the Americas; mestizos—people of both Spanish and American Indian descent, the largest group of European descent in Spanish America; American Indians and enslaved Africans

Section 2 Review

go. **Homework** hrw **Practice** .com **Online**
keyword: SA3 HP3

① **Define and explain:**
• pueblos
• missions
• presidios
• *encomienda* system
• plantations
• borderlands

② **Identify and explain:**
• Council of the Indies
• Bartolomé de Las Casas
• Juan de Oñate
• Popé
• El Camino Real

③ **Categorizing** Copy the graphic organizer below. Use it to identify and describe the major institutions created by the Spanish to govern New Spain and Peru. Include a sentence describing each institution.

Council of the Indies

④ **Finding the Main Idea**
a. What were the advantages and disadvantages for Spain of having such a large empire in the Americas?

b. Why did the Spanish establish settlements in the borderlands?

⑤ **Writing and Critical Thinking**
Evaluating Imagine that you are an adviser to the Council of the Indies. Prepare an official report that describes the *encomienda* system and the Spanish colonial class structure.

Consider the following:
• the benefits of the *encomienda* system
• the drawbacks of the system
• the social structure of New Spain

Section 3

OBJECTIVES

★ Define the Protestant Reformation, and explain how it changed Europe.

★ Discuss the reasons Spain and England went to war in the late 1500s.

★ Analyze what led to the end of Spain's Golden Age.

Section 3

Religious and Political Changes in Europe

Read to Discover

1. What was the Protestant Reformation, and how did it change Europe?
2. Why did Spain and England go to war in the late 1500s?
3. What led to the end of Spain's Golden Age?

WHY IT MATTERS TODAY

In many countries today, religion plays a key role in political issues and events. Use **CNN fyi**.com or other **current events** sources to learn about the influence of religion on a key present-day political issue or event. Record your findings in your journal.

Define
• sea dogs
• inflation

Identify
• Martin Luther
• Protestant Reformation
• Protestants
• Henry VIII
• Philip II
• Elizabeth I
• Francis Drake
• Spanish Armada

Martin Luther helped begin a major change in European religion.

The Story Continues

On October 31, 1517, a priest named Martin Luther nailed an important paper to the door of Castle Church in Wittenberg, Germany. The paper listed 95 theses about the Catholic Church. Luther charged that the church was too wealthy. He also thought the church abused its power. Charles V, emperor of the Holy Roman Empire, asked Luther to give up his views. Luther replied, "I cannot and will not." He added, "On this I take my stand. I can do no other."

★ The Protestant Reformation

Martin Luther was a Catholic priest in Germany. He became well known for protesting the policies of the Catholic Church. In 1517 Luther started the **Protestant Reformation**. This was a religious movement that began as an effort to reform the church. It spread through German towns in the 1520s and then to other parts of Europe. The reformers became known as **Protestants** because they protested the Catholic Church's practices. Many Protestants believed that the Bible intended for religion to be simple. They

Have students read Section 3 and complete Guided Reading Strategy 3.3. Choose one or more of the following activities to explore the section content with students. For further suggestions on block scheduling or team teaching, see the *Block Scheduling Handbook with Team Teaching Strategies*.

LEVEL 1: Explain to students that the Protestant Reformation began as an attempt to reform the Catholic Church, but it eventually led to the creation of the Protestant Church and war in Europe. After students have read through this section of the text, ask them to identify the most important events that are covered. Write their responses on the chalkboard. Have students create an annotated time line that includes the dates of each of these events and a brief description of the event's significance. (*Students' time lines should include Luther nailing his paper to the Castle Church in 1517, fighting between French Catholics and Protestants in the late 1500s, King Henry of England founding the Anglican Church in 1534, and King Philip II of Spain leading the Catholic Reformation in the late 1500s.*) After students have finished, review the dates for and the importance of each of the events listed on the chalkboard.

ENGLISH LANGUAGE LEARNERS

THE GRANGER COLLECTION, NEW YORK

Interpreting the Visual Record

A religious war *Spain sent the Duke of Alba to take control of the Netherlands, where he was soon feared for his cruel punishments of Dutch Protestants.* **How do the people shown here appear to be treating the Duke?**

thought the Catholic Church had too many rules. Protestants also objected to the great power held by the pope.

The printing press helped spread the ideas of the Reformation. Protestants printed large numbers of Bibles as well as short essays explaining their ideas. This let more people read and think about the Bible on their own, rather than relying on the teachings of a priest.

Confrontations between Catholics and Protestants took place throughout Europe, often leading to violence. During the late 1500s French Catholics fought French Protestants, known as Huguenots (HYOO-guh-nahts). Other parts of Europe also suffered violence and destruction. Political issues mixed with religious struggles. In 1534 King **Henry VIII** founded the Church of England, or the Anglican Church. This was a Protestant church that observed many Catholic ceremonies, such as mass. By making himself the head of the Anglican Church, Henry defied the authority of the pope. His actions angered English Catholics.

✔ **Reading Check: Identifying Cause and Effect** What issues led to the Protestant Reformation, and what effect did it have on Europe? conflicting interpretations of the Bible and of the power of the pope; fighting between Protestants and Catholics

★ Conflict between Spain and England

In the late 1500s King **Philip II** used Spain's great wealth to lead a Catholic Reformation against the Protestant movement. Philip sent troops to fight Protestants in the Netherlands. He also hoped to drive the Protestants out of England, just as Ferdinand and Isabella had driven the Moors out of Spain. Standing in his way was Queen **Elizabeth I**, the daughter of Henry VIII. A Protestant, Elizabeth wanted peace between England's Protestants and Catholics. She opposed Spain's treatment of Protestants in the Netherlands, but feared supporting them openly because of Spain's power.

GLOBAL CONNECTIONS

War in the Netherlands

In the mid-1500s fighting broke out in the Netherlands between Protestants and Catholics. At the time Spain, a Catholic nation, ruled the Netherlands. Some Dutch people became Calvinists—followers of Protestant leader and writer John Calvin. Spain responded by persecuting Protestants and trying to enforce Catholic beliefs. The Spanish also passed strict new laws and raised taxes. Protestants soon rebelled. In 1609 the civil war finally ended. The Dutch Protestants had won, but thousands of lives had been lost. **How did Philip II try to maintain control of the Netherlands?**

★ Historical Sidelight

John Calvin. John Calvin, a French lawyer and humanist, is perhaps the most noted contributor to the Protestant Reformation. At age 27, Calvin traveled to Geneva, where he published his ideas about reforming the Christian religion, established a loyal following, and eventually came to control the local government. Calvin's beliefs incorporated the idea that people's destinies were predetermined by God before they were born. He sought to reform not only the church, but also society as a whole. In doing so, he made Geneva the most famous and influential city of the Reformation movement.

🖳 **internet** connect

TOPIC: John Calvin
GO TO: go.hrw.com
KEYWORD: SA3 CF3

Have students use the library or search the Internet through the HRW Go site to obtain more information on John Calvin. Then have them write a brief biographical sketch about his life using standard grammar, spelling, sentence structure, and punctuation. Encourage students to reference primary and secondary sources in their sketch.

ALL LEVELS: Copy the following graphic organizer onto the chalkboard, omitting the italicized answers. Have students complete the organizer to show the steps in the decline of Spain's Golden Age.

ENGLISH LANGUAGE LEARNERS

 Spain's Golden Age

Inflation resulted from American silver imports.

Defeat of the Spanish Armada weakened Spain's dominance of the Americas and opened the way for other European countries.

THE STEPS IN THE DECLINE OF SPAIN'S GOLDEN AGE

End of Spain's Golden Age

★ Biography

Sir John Hawkins. One of Queen Elizabeth's most daring sea dog captains was Sir John Hawkins. The cousin of Sir Francis Drake, Hawkins spent several years running slave trade ships before spending 20 years in the queen's service. He was knighted for the gallantry he demonstrated in the great sea battle of 1588. In an attempt to rescue his only son, Richard, who was being held captive by the Spanish in Peru, Hawkins joined Drake for what would be their final voyage. Both died on the journey.

ACTIVITY: Have students write an entry from the ship's log of a sea dog expedition using standard grammar, spelling, sentence structure, and punctuation.

BIOGRAPHY ANSWER
She led her country through many troubled years.

Visual Record Answer

(for p. 79)

Students might suggest that the people appear to be treating the Duke with respect and honor because they are kneeling before him.

BIOGRAPHY

Elizabeth I

(1533–1603)

Elizabeth was an intelligent and well-educated leader. She could read Greek and speak French, Italian, and Latin. Elizabeth was just 25 years old when she became queen of England in 1558. Many people did not want a woman to rule England, no matter how gifted she was. Despite such prejudices, Elizabeth became one of England's most popular rulers. After gaining the throne, Elizabeth led her country through many troubled years. By the time her long reign ended in 1603, England had become a world power. **What did Elizabeth I accomplish as queen?**

To fight Spain without going to war, Elizabeth made use of the **sea dogs**. These were veteran English sailors whom she encouraged to raid Spanish treasure ships. The raids hurt Spain's economy, and the sea dogs gained treasure for themselves. When Philip protested, Elizabeth pretended that her government had nothing to do with the raids.

The most successful sea dog was the daring Sir **Francis Drake**. In 1578 he sailed through the Strait of Magellan and attacked the west coast of Peru and New Spain. The Spanish were caught off guard by Drake's daring raids. They had not expected any English ships to pass through the strait. In addition to his raids, Drake sailed north and explored part of California's coast. He landed near present-day San Francisco. Turning west, he sailed back to England. Drake and his crew thus became the first English people to sail around the world.

✔ **Reading Check: Drawing Inferences and Conclusions** Why might Elizabeth have pretended that she did not ask sea dogs to attack Spanish treasure ships? Students might suggest that she knew the raids hurt Spain, but she feared Spanish power and hoped to avoid war.

★ The Spanish Armada

King Philip was angered by the English attacks. He also feared England's ability to help the Protestants in the Netherlands. He decided to solve both problems by gathering a huge fleet known as the **Spanish Armada**. The Armada had about 130 ships and some 27,000 sailors and soldiers. This mighty fleet was sent to invade England. Philip hoped to overthrow both Queen Elizabeth and the Anglican Church.

From the beginning the Spanish had problems. The Armada's leader, the Duke of Medina-Sidonia, was a poor sailor who did not know how to run the fleet. Then, while the ships were in the Spanish port of Cádiz (KAH-dees), Drake raided their supplies. The attack delayed the Armada for several months.

Despite delays and poor leadership, the Armada was a strong fighting force. In contrast, England's navy had fewer than 40 ships. To try to even the odds, sea dogs, merchants, and fishermen added their ships to England's defense. The English ships had the advantages of speed, greater mobility, and better cannons. They could outmaneuver the larger Spanish vessels while firing on them from a distance. The Spanish, on the other hand, had to attempt to sail close to English ships and then board them with soldiers.

In late July 1588 the Armada and the English fleet finally met off the coast of England, in the English Channel. In a series of battles, the quicker English ships damaged but could not destroy the Armada. Then the English surprised the Spanish at night by sending ships loaded with explosives into the Spanish fleet. These fire ships exploded in the middle of the Armada, causing the Spanish to scatter. The next day the English fleet defeated the Armada in a huge battle.

THE GRANGER COLLECTION, NEW YORK

The defeat of the Armada was a disaster for Spain.

News of the Armada's defeat did not reach England immediately. Queen Elizabeth gave a stirring speech to an army of English soldiers preparing to face the Spanish.

History Makers Speak

❝I know I have but the body of a weak and feeble woman; but I have the heart and stomach of a King, and a King of England, too; and I think it foul scorn [pride] that . . . Spain . . . should dare to invade the borders of my realm.❞

—Queen Elizabeth I, quoted in *Armada,* by Duff Hart-Davis

Analyzing Primary Sources
Drawing Inferences and Conclusions What do you think was the purpose of Elizabeth's speech? to inspire her men to fight for England

While the soldiers cheered for their queen, the Armada struggled home to Spain. Storms sank many of the surviving ships. Only about half made it back safely to Spain. Philip's attempt to conquer England had failed.

✔ **Reading Check: Summarizing** Explain why England was able to defeat the larger Spanish Armada. Though England had fewer ships than Spain did, English ships were faster, more mobile, had improved weapons, and were commanded by experienced sailors like Drake.

★ The Decline of the Spanish Empire

The Armada's defeat shocked Spain. As Spain's power and wealth had grown, the country had enjoyed a Golden Age. Spain made great strides in the arts. King Philip oversaw the building of the Escoriala, a huge palace that included its own monastery. Religious art was particularly valued in Spain. El Greco, a Greek artist living in Spain, became famous for his religious paintings in the late 1500s.

✪ REVIEW AND ASSESS

Have students complete the **Section 3 Review** on p. 82. Then have students complete **Daily Quiz 3.3**. As **Alternative Assessment**, you may want to use the annotated timeline or Spain's golden age graphic organizer in this section's lessons.

✪ RETEACH

Have students complete **Main Idea Activity for English Language Learners and Special-Needs Students 3.3**. Then organize the class into small groups and assign to each group one of the section objectives. Have each group prepare two or three newspaper headlines capturing the main ideas of its assigned section. Ask each group to share its headlines with

the class. Invite students to comment on the accuracy and insight of the headlines. **ENGLISH LANGUAGE LEARNERS** , **COOPERATIVE LEARNING**

✪ EXTEND

Have students use their textbooks, the library, or search the Internet through the HRW site to find information regarding the significance of the invention of the printing press. Ask them to write a short report about the printing press that compares and contrasts the spread of information before and after its invention. Encourage students to analyze the importance of the printing press in spreading the ideas of the Reformation. **BLOCK SCHEDULING**

✦ Section 3 Review
ANSWERS

❶ **Define**
• sea dogs, p. 80
• inflation, p. 82

❷ **Identify**
• Martin Luther, p. 78
• Protestant Reformation, p. 78
• Protestants, p. 78
• Henry VIII, p. 79
• Philip II, p. 79
• Elizabeth I, p. 79
• Francis Drake, p. 80
• Spanish Armada, p. 80

❸ Protestant Reformation; conflict between England and Spain; decline of the Spanish Empire

❹ **a.** Luther protested the practices and corruption of the Catholic Church and the power of the pope. Christian Europe divided between Protestants and Catholics. Conflict led to war and civil unrest.
b. Philip was a devout Catholic who started a Catholic Reformation to rid Europe of Protestants. Elizabeth encouraged sea dogs to make raids against Philip's treasure ships returning from the Americas.

❺ Students' poems will vary but should include the following: the reign of King Philip II and the vast amounts of treasures gained from the Americas; the crushing defeat of the Spanish Armada by the English; and the massive inflation and economic problems that led to the decline of Spain's Golden Age.

Causes and Effects of Spain's Golden Age

Long-Term Causes
Columbus's landing in the Caribbean

Spanish exploration and conquest

Founding of colonies in North and South America

Immediate Causes
Conquest of the Aztec by Cortés, 1521

Conquest of the Inca by Pizarro, 1534

Spanish treasure fleets from the Americas

Spain's Golden Age 1492 to mid-1600s

Effects
Rise in Spanish wealth and influence

Increase in the prices of Spanish goods because of high inflation caused in part by American silver and gold

Spain's dependence on imported goods

Spain also had many poets and playwrights. One was Lope de Vega, who had sailed with the Armada. Many Spanish authors wrote romantic novels about the courage of Spanish nobles and conquistadores. Author Miguel de Cervantes made fun of such stories in his novel *Don Quixote*. In this novel the aging knight Don Quixote and his companion Sancho Panza have many comical adventures.

Economic problems helped bring Spain's Golden Age to an end. The large amounts of gold and silver that Spain took from the Americas contributed to high **inflation**. Inflation is a rise in the amount of money in use and thus in the price of goods. Rather than buying local items made expensive by inflation, Spaniards bought cheaper goods from other countries. This further weakened Spain's economy.

England's defeat of the Spanish Armada showed that Spain's navy could be beaten. The weakened navy could no longer protect Spain's distant empire in the Americas. This led countries such as England, France, and the Netherlands to challenge Spanish power overseas.

✔ **Reading Check: Evaluating** What led to the decline of the Spanish Empire? defeat of the Armada, inflation, dependence on imports

go. **hrw** **.com** | Homework Practice Online
keyword: SA3 HP3

Section **3** Review

❶ **Define and explain:**
• sea dogs
• inflation

❷ **Identify and explain:**
• Martin Luther
• Protestant Reformation
• Protestants
• Henry VIII
• Philip II
• Elizabeth I
• Francis Drake
• Spanish Armada

❸ **Sequencing** Copy the graphic organizer below. Use it to show religious and political events leading to the defeat of the Spanish Armada and to show how the defeat affected Spain.

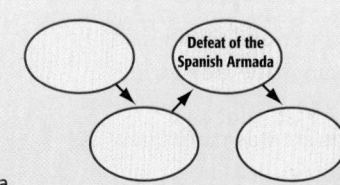
Defeat of the Spanish Armada

❹ **Finding the Main Idea**
a. Why did the Protestant Reformation take place, and how did it influence Europe?
b. Why did Philip II of Spain want to drive Protestants out of England, and how did Elizabeth I respond to Spain's aggression?

❺ **Writing and Critical Thinking**
Sequencing Imagine that you are a poet in Spain in 1700. Write a poem of 6 to 10 lines about the events that led to the end of Spain's Golden Age.

Consider the following:
• the defeat of the Spanish Armada
• economic problems in Spain

Section 4

OBJECTIVES

★ Analyze the reasons for French, Dutch, and English interest in colonizing North America.

★ Identify the common problems faced by French, Dutch, and Swedish colonies.

★ Describe what happened to the first English settlements in North America.

((•)) LET'S GET STARTED!

Write the following statement on the chalkboard: *List possible conditions that the first European settlers who came to the Americas might have faced.* Allow time for students to write their responses. *(Students' responses might include a lack of food or encountering opposition from American Indians.)* Ask volunteers to share their answers. Explain to the class that conditions were often very difficult and that settlers were frequently undersupplied and unprepared for the conditions they encountered. Tell students that in Section 4 they will learn more about these early settlements, including the lost colony of Roanoke.

Section 4

The Race for Empires

Read to Discover

1. Why were the French, Dutch, and English interested in colonizing North America?
2. What common problems did the French, Dutch, and Swedish colonies face?
3. What happened to the first English settlements in North America?

WHY IT MATTERS TODAY

The urge to explore remains strong today. Use **CNNfyi**.com or other **current events** sources to learn how people continue to explore our world. Record your findings in your journal.

Define
- charter

Identify
- René-Robert de La Salle
- Peter Minuit
- Walter Raleigh

SECTION 4 RESOURCES

REPRODUCIBLE
▶ Guided Reading Strategy 3.4
▶ Primary Source Reading 3: France and the New World
▶ Graphic Organizer 3: European Presence in the Americas

TECHNOLOGY
▶ One-Stop Planner, Lesson 3.4
▶ Linking Geography and History Transparency 3: Native American Culture Areas
▶ Homework Practice Online
▶ HRW Go site

REINFORCEMENT, REVIEW, AND ASSESSMENT
▶ Section 4 Review, p. 87
▶ Daily Quiz 3.4
▶ Main Idea Activity 3.4
▶ English Audio Summary 3.4
▶ Spanish Audio Summary 3.4

The Story Continues

When French explorer Jacques Cartier sailed to North America in 1534, he witnessed many strange sights. He saw walruses and thousands of seabirds. He said these birds covered islands "as a field is covered with grass." However, one of the most unexpected sights was a French fishing boat! French fishermen had begun traveling to the north coast of North America in the early 1500s. Cartier soon saw why. There were so many fish that he and his crew could catch about 100 cod in an hour. Some of the fishermen had built temporary settlements to trade with local American Indians.

French explorer Jacques Cartier

★ Early French Settlement

France built its first North American settlement in Florida. French Huguenots started a few small colonies there in 1564. The Spanish soon destroyed these settlements and drove out the French. Religious wars in France slowed further French efforts to colonize North America. When the fighting ended, the French renewed efforts to settle present-day eastern Canada. The explorations of Jacques Cartier and Samuel de Champlain had given France a claim to this region.

Have students read Section 4 and complete Guided Reading Strategy 3.4. Choose one or more of the following activities to explore the section content with students. For further suggestions on block scheduling or team teaching, see the *Block Scheduling Handbook with Team Teaching Strategies.*

LEVEL 1: Pair students and have them create a children's book describing what happened to the first English settlements in the Americas. Have students write an age-appropriate story and create drawings to illustrate it.

ENGLISH LANGUAGE LEARNERS , COOPERATIVE LEARNING

HOMEWORK Have students find pictures that show the reasons for European settlement of North America and the conditions settlers faced. *(Students' pictures might show people hunting or people in snowy conditions.)* Ask students to organize these pictures into a collage. Have students label each picture to show which country's colonies were settled for that reason or faced that condition.

Note: For an additional teaching idea, see the Chapter 3 Daily Journal Lesson in the **Creative Teaching Strategies** handbook.

☑ internet connect

TOPIC: French Exploration
GO TO: go.hrw.com
KEYWORD: SA3 CF3

Have students access the Internet through the HRW Go site to research French exploration in North America. Then have students create an illustrated report on an explorer, a settlement, or an aspect of French exploration of their choice. Students should use standard grammar, spelling, sentence structure, and punctuation in their report. They should also cite where they found the their information and whether it is a primary or secondary source.

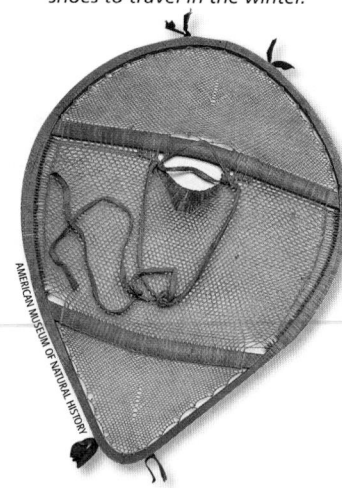

American Indians in cold northern regions taught Europeans how to make and use snowshoes to travel in the winter.

AMERICAN MUSEUM OF NATURAL HISTORY

Analyzing Primary Sources

Identifying a Point of View How do you think this observer viewed the French traders he describes? He seems to admire their perseverance and their ability to overcome harsh conditions.

In 1604 the French settled in a region they called Acadia. This area included what is now Nova Scotia, New Brunswick, and parts of Maine. There they formed small trading communities and fishing villages. Champlain founded Port Royal on the coast of Nova Scotia, then headed west. He reached the St. Lawrence River and the Great Lakes. He founded the town of Quebec on the St. Lawrence in 1608. He also explored areas in present-day New York and Vermont, where Lake Champlain was named after him.

The Great Lakes region proved valuable to France because of the fur trade. Europeans used animal furs, particularly beaver pelts, to make expensive hats. The French traded tools, jewelry, and cloth with American Indians in exchange for furs. Merchants then shipped the furs back to France. Founded in 1642, Montreal became a center for the fur trade.

Fur traders often had to travel deep into the wilderness to meet with their American Indian trading partners. The traders usually traveled by river, braving the dangers of white-water rapids. French traders used Indian birch-bark canoes, which were light enough to carry. Fur traders lived far from French settlements for long periods of time. Many of them adopted local American Indians' clothing and customs to survive. One observer in the mid-1700s described the life of a fur trader.

History Makers Speak ❝It is inconceivable [unbelievable] what hardships the people of Canada must undergo on their hunting journeys. . . . They often suffer hunger, thirst, heat, and cold, and are bitten by . . . dangerous animals and insects. . . . None of them fears danger or hardships. Many of them settle among the Indians far from Canada, marry Indian women, and never come back again.❞

—Peter Kalm, quoted in *The Canadian Frontier, 1534–1760*, by W. J. Eccles

✔ **Reading Check: Finding the Main Idea** Why did the French move inland from the coast of North America? to establish trade with American Indians

★ The Expansion of the French Empire

In the late 1600s the French began spreading out from the Great Lakes region. Fur traders, explorers, and missionaries were all on the move. Many headed south, toward New Spain. In the 1650s French missionaries heard stories about "a beautiful river, large, broad, and deep." In 1673 the explorer Louis Jolliet (jahl-ee-et) and the missionary Jacques Marquette set out to find this great river, the Mississippi. They reached the river and traveled down it as far as present-day Arkansas. Finally they turned back to avoid encountering the Spanish. Nine years later, **René-Robert de La Salle** followed the Mississippi River to the Gulf of Mexico. He claimed the Mississippi Valley for King Louis XIV of France. To honor the king, La Salle named the region Louisiana.

The French called their North American territory New France. France had trouble building up the number of settlers in this territory, which had

ALL LEVELS: Copy the following graphic organizer onto the chalkboard, omitting the italicized answers (shown in the graphic organizer as check marks). Have students complete the organizer to compare the reasons for European settlement in North America and conditions faced by settlers from each country. Have students label each column with various reasons for colonization and conditions that were faced in the Americas. For each country, have students place a check mark in each square that corresponds to the conditions faced by the country and its reasons for choosing to settle.

ENGLISH LANGUAGE LEARNERS

Country	wealth	missionary work	fur trade	few settlers	traded with American Indians
France	✓	✓	✓	✓	✓
The Netherlands	✓	✓	✓	✓	✓
England		✓			✓

THE GRANGER COLLECTION, NEW YORK

only about 12,000 French settlers by 1688. In the late 1600s and early 1700s the French built new outposts, including Detroit on the Great Lakes and New Orleans along the Mississippi River. For a time the French government also helped pay the travel costs for interested colonists.

New France's small population and the value of the fur trade led French settlers to ally with the Algonquian and Huron Indians. As a result, they became enemies of the Iroquois. In general, the French treated American Indians with more respect than did other Europeans.

⭐ New Netherland and New Sweden

Europeans were drawn to America by the promise of good farmland and the fur trade. The Dutch, who had merchant fleets around the world, came to America in search of trade. Explorer Henry Hudson's first voyage to North America gave the Dutch a claim to the land between the Delaware and Hudson Rivers. The Dutch called this area New Netherland. This region included parts of what are now New Jersey, New York, Connecticut, and Delaware. In 1624 the newly formed Dutch West India Company sent about 30 families to settle in New Netherland. Two years later **Peter Minuit** bought Manhattan Island from local American Indians. There he founded the town of New Amsterdam.

To bring more settlers to America, the Dutch West India Company decided to let other Europeans settle in New Netherland. To attract colonists, the Dutch practiced religious toleration. In 1646 missionary Isaac Jogues (zhawg) described the people of New Amsterdam. "There may well be four or five hundred men of different sects [religious groups] and nations."

Daily Life

Louisiana Robert de La Salle claims Louisiana for France in this painting. The French did not begin settling Louisiana until the early 1700s. The city of New Orleans was founded in 1718, and Louisiana became a royal colony of France in 1731. At that time the colony's population of settlers and slaves was still fairly small, numbering some 8,000 people. **Why would a city with access to the Mississippi River be valuable to France?**

⭐ **Linking Past to Present**

Manhattan. Peter Minuit gave the Wappinger 60 guilders (approximately $24 in U.S. dollars) in 1626 for the island of Manhattan. Although these American Indians believed that they had been paid to share the land, the Dutch considered the transaction a sale and took possession of the area for the establishment of settlements. Today, the five boroughs of New York City—Brooklyn, the Bronx, Manhattan, Staten Island, and Queens—have a combined population of 7,300,000, making New York the largest city in the United States and one of the largest in the world.

ACTIVITY: Have students imagine that they are an early settler of Manhattan Island who has traveled to the future and is observing modern-day New York City. Ask them to write a diary entry describing their reactions to the city using standard grammar, spelling, sentence structure, and punctuation.

Technology Resources

 Linking Geography and History Transparency 3: Native American Culture Areas

DAILY LIFE ANSWER
Students might suggest that the French would want access for transportation and trade.

LEVEL 3: Explain to students that historical events are often viewed by various groups of people differently. To many Europeans, the Americas offered a variety of goods to trade and markets to control, but to American Indians, the land was sacred and so were its creatures. Tell students to review the section to identify the reasons that the French, Dutch, and English came to settle in North America and the common problems faced by French, Dutch, and Swedish settlers. Have students imagine that they are American Indians observing the European settlers who recently came to North America. Tell students to create an oral history from an American Indian's perspective explaining the effects of the actions of the strangers. Students should pretend that the settlers have shared with them their reasons for being in North America, and they should use arguments against their reasons as part of their oral histories. Encourage volunteers to share their oral histories with the class.

★ CLOSE

Lead a class discussion about the first English settlements. Then ask each student to create a poster illustrating the common problems faced by European colonies and what happened to the first English settlements in the Americas.

Section 4 Review
ANSWERS

❶ **Define**
• charter, p. 87

❷ **Identify**
• René-Robert de La Salle, p. 84
• Peter Minuit, p. 85
• Walter Raleigh, p. 87

❸ England—Newfoundland, North Carolina, Roanoke Island, Virginia. France—eastern Canada, Florida, Maine, Mississippi Valley. The Netherlands—parts of Connecticut, Delaware, New Jersey, New York, and Manhattan Island. Sweden—Delaware River.

❹ a. Europeans were attracted by the possibilities of wealth gained from the resources of North America.
b. Each settlement attracted few settlers; the French made enemies of the Iroquois; the Dutch and the Swedes fought each other with the Swedes losing their colony.

❺ Students' reports will vary but should include the following: the fighting that might have occurred between the settlers and American Indians, the previous failures to start colonies, and the possible significance of the word *CROATOAN* carved into a tree.

Minuit left the Dutch West India Company and helped Swedish settlers found New Sweden along the Delaware River. He also helped them choose the site for Fort Christina, which was built in 1638. There the Swedish farmed and traded with local American Indians for furs. Swedish settlers were among the first in North America to build log cabins. The Swedish settlement was small, but the Dutch felt that it threatened Dutch lands and fur trading. The two sides fought a series of battles. Finally the governor of New Netherland, Peter Stuyvesant (STY-vi-suhnt), conquered New Sweden in 1655.

✔ **Reading Check: Comparing** How were French, Dutch, and Swedish settlements similar? They all hoped to exploit the fur trade and to trade with American Indians; none were able to attract large numbers of settlers.

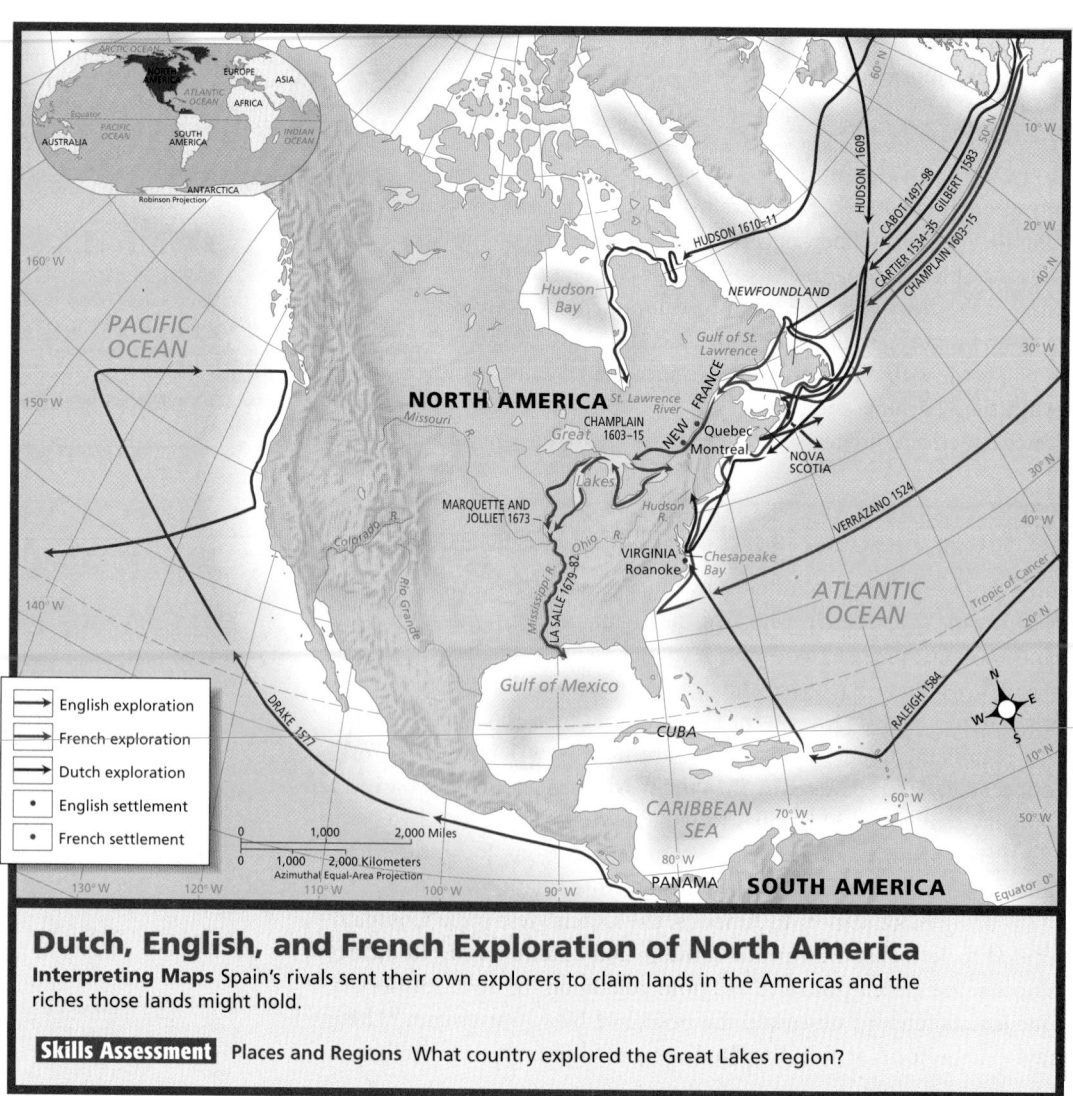

Dutch, English, and French Exploration of North America
Interpreting Maps Spain's rivals sent their own explorers to claim lands in the Americas and the riches those lands might hold.

Skills Assessment Places and Regions What country explored the Great Lakes region?

☆ REVIEW AND ASSESS

Have students complete the **Section 4 Review** on p. 87. Then have students complete **Daily Quiz 3.4**. As **Alternative Assessment**, you may want to use the children's book exercise or the colonization graphic organizer in this section's lessons.

☆ RETEACH

Have students complete **Main Idea Activity for English Language Learners and Special-Needs Students 3.4**. Then assign each student one of the subsections in Section 4. Have students write four questions about the material in their subsections. Then distribute the questions to students, and ask them to answer the questions. Have students return their

questions to the author, who should check them and correct them, if necessary. **ENGLISH LANGUAGE LEARNERS** ⭐ 8.31D

☆ EXTEND

Tell the class to conduct research on the routes traveled by the explorers mentioned in this section. Give students an outline map of North America, and have them fill in the map so that it identifies the first few colonies established by each nation and the areas that each nation's explorers reached. Tell students to create a color-coded key that identifies which country each color represents. In the areas representing each colony, have students identify the products that the home nation was trying to obtain from the colony. **BLOCK SCHEDULING** ⭐ 8.2A, 8.10A, 8.31D

★ English Settlements

In the late 1500s England decided to start its own North American colony. In 1578 Sir Humphrey Gilbert received a patent, or **charter**, a document giving him royal permission to start a colony. Gilbert sent an expedition to Newfoundland, which England claimed as a result of John Cabot's explorations. Gilbert's efforts to found a colony failed, and he drowned at sea in 1583. His half-brother, Sir <u>Walter Raleigh</u>, soon led a new effort.

Raleigh paid for an expedition that landed in present-day Virginia and North Carolina. He named the entire area Virginia. In 1585 he sent another group to found a colony on Roanoke Island. The English colonists found life hard. They fought with local American Indians and had trouble finding and growing food. In 1586 Sir Francis Drake stopped at Roanoke after a raid on New Spain. He offered to take the remaining settlers home to England.

John White resettled the Roanoke colony in the spring of 1587. White's granddaughter, Virginia Dare, was the first English child born in the present-day United States. White returned to England at the end of the summer and did not come back until 1590. He found the colony's buildings still standing but deserted. Carved into a post was the word *CROATOAN*. This may have been the name of a nearby island inhabited by American Indians. White searched for the settlers and his granddaughter. Years later he recalled his efforts. "And thus we [stopped] seeking our Colony, that was never any of them found, nor seen to this day." Historians are not certain just what happened to the colony.

John White painted many American plants and animals. His works are among the earliest known European pictures of North American wildlife.

Reading Check: Summarizing Explain the reasons for and the results of England's first attempts to colonize North America. The English wanted to establish colonies to compete with the growing colonial empires of France, Spain, and other European countries. Both efforts failed. Gilbert drowned, and Roanoke disappeared mysteriously. [⭐ 8.2A, 8.30B]

Section 4 Review

⭐ TEKS Questions 3, 4a

go.hrw.com Homework Practice Online
keyword: SA3 HP3

★ ★

❶ Define and explain:
• charter

❷ Identify and explain:
• René-Robert de La Salle
• Peter Minuit
• Walter Raleigh

❸ Summarizing Copy the graphic organizer below. Use it to list the European nations that established colonies in North America during the 1500s and 1600s. Include the location of these colonies.

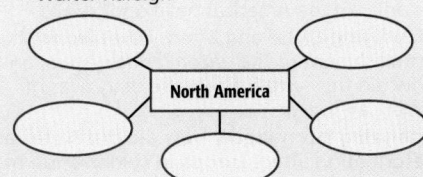

North America

❹ Finding the Main Idea
a. What motivated France, England, and the Netherlands to establish settlements in North America?
b. What problems did the French, Dutch, and Swedish settlements face?

❺ Writing and Critical Thinking
Drawing Inferences and Conclusions Imagine that you are a sailor on John White's resupply expedition to Roanoke. Prepare a brief report to Queen Elizabeth explaining what might have happened to the missing settlers.

Consider the following:
• relations between American Indians and Europeans
• the word carved into the post at Roanoke

THE GRANGER COLLECTION, NEW YORK

REPRODUCIBLE
▶ Vocabulary Activity 3

TECHNOLOGY
▶ Chapter 3 Test Generator (on the One-Stop Planner)
▶ Global Skill Builder CD–ROM
▶ HRW Go site

REINFORCEMENT, REVIEW, AND ASSESSMENT
▶ Chapter 3 Review, pp. 87–89
▶ Chapter 3 Tutorial for Students, Parents, Mentors, and Peers

▶ Chapter 3 Test (Form A or B)
▶ Alternative Assessment Handbook
▶ Chapter 3 Test for English Language Learners and Special-Needs Students

★ REVIEW

Have students complete the **Chapter 3 Review** on pages 88–89.

★ ASSESS

Use one of the chapter tests to assess students' understanding of the content. For **Alternative Assessment,** see the **Alternative Assessment Handbook.**

Understanding Main Ideas

1. both men conquered large and powerful empires with the help of superior technology, American Indian allies, the effects of disease on American Indian populations and both gained great wealth for Spain

2. viceroys of New Spain and Peru; pueblos, missions, and presidios

3. Philip was a devout Catholic who started a Catholic Reformation to rid Europe of Protestants. Elizabeth encouraged sea dogs to make raids against Philip's treasure ships from the Americas.

4. each was founded to compete with Spain for control of the Americas, each attracted few settlers, French made enemies of the Iroquois, Dutch and Swedes fought each other, with the Swedes losing their colony

5. Spain declined in power after the defeat of the Spanish Armada. Europeans were attracted by the possibilities of wealth gained from the resources of North America.

You Be the Historian— Reviewing Themes

1. superior Spanish technology, American Indian enemies who allied with the Spanish, and the spread of new diseases

2. hoped to acquire treasure, to open or find new trade routes, and to expand their power

3. contributed great wealth to Spain, but also inflation—when treasure began to run out, Spain's economy was in trouble

Chapter 3 Review

The Chapter at a Glance

Examine the visual summary of the chapter below. Prepare a poster that illustrates each of the main ideas contained in the boxes representing each section. Use facts and ideas from the chapter to prepare your poster. Present your poster to the class.

Spain conquered powerful American Indian empires and searched for treasure in the Americas.

Spain's colonial empire used new institutions to rule conquered American Indians. Spain gained great wealth.

The Protestant Reformation caused great conflict in Europe, leading to England's defeat of the Spanish Armada.

As Spain's power weakened, other European nations began founding colonies in North America.

Identifying People and Ideas

Use the following terms or people in historically significant sentences.
1. conquistadores
2. Council of the Indies
3. *encomienda* system
4. Bartolomé de Las Casas
5. plantations
6. Protestant Reformation
7. Elizabeth I
8. Spanish Armada
9. inflation
10. Walter Raleigh

Understanding Main Ideas

Section 1 *(Pages 66–71)*
1. How was Cortés's conquest of the Aztec Empire similar to Pizarro's conquest of the Inca Empire?

Section 2 *(Pages 72–77)*
2. What institutions did the Spanish establish in order to govern the vast territories under their control?

Section 3 *(Pages 78–82)*
3. What led to conflict between Spain and England?

Section 4 *(Pages 83–87)*
4. How were the French, Dutch, and English settlements different from and similar to each other?

5. What motivated other European nations to challenge Spain and to establish settlements of their own in North America?

You Be the Historian— Reviewing Themes

1. **Global Relations** Why were the Aztec and Inca unable to defeat the smaller invading armies led by conquistadores?
2. **Geography** Why did the Spanish and the French establish settlements in the Americas?
3. **Economics** How did having colonies in the Americas affect Spain's economy?

Thinking Critically

1. **Finding the Main Idea** What effect did its colonies in the Americas have on Spain?
2. **Identifying Cause and Effect** What led to the establishment of the *encomienda* system, and how did this system affect the daily lives of American Indians?
3. **Analyzing Information** How did the Protestant Reformation affect European colonization of the Americas in the 1600s?

★ RETEACH

Organize the class into several small groups. Tell each group to review material from this chapter that compares and contrasts the colonization efforts of the nations mentioned in the chapter. Have students create a chapter of a book that analyzes colonization efforts in the Americas. Encourage them to use illustrations.

**ENGLISH LANGUAGE LEARNERS ,
COOPERATIVE LEARNING**

Portfolio Extensions

1. Interdisciplinary Connection to the Arts Ask students to create a bulletin board display of artistic and cultural achievements in Spain or New Spain during the Golden Age. Have them select one painter, poet, playwright, and writer who was popular in Spain or New Spain. Encourage students find or re-create examples of each person's work to put in their display. Finally, have them write a biographical sketch of each person to accompany his or her work.

2. Linking to Community Tell students that in his *History of the Indies*, Bartolomé de Las Casas criticized the effects of Spanish rule on enslaved Indians and Africans. Have students present an oral report on a member of their community who is well known as a social activist against injustice. The person they select may be living in the community today or may have lived there in the past.

Social Studies Skills Workshop

Interpreting Maps

Study the map below. Then use the information on the map to help you answer the questions that follow.

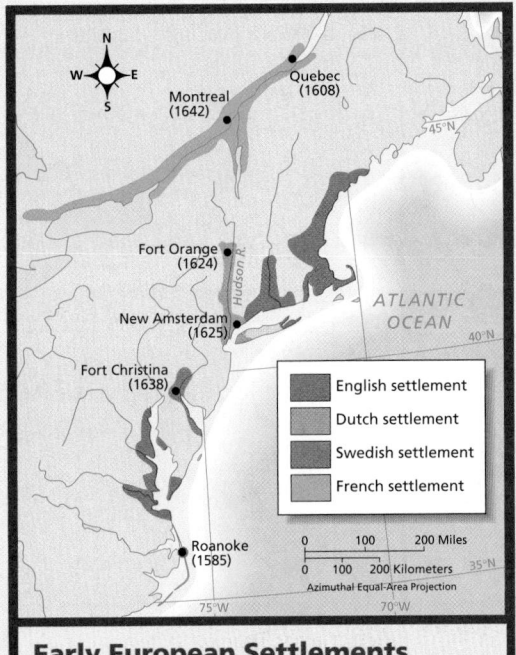

Early European Settlements

1. What is the earliest settlement shown on the map?
   a. Quebec
   b. New Amsterdam
   c. Roanoke
   d. Fort Christina

2. Using the map and your knowledge of the period, what European nations appear to have the most powerful settlements?

Analyzing Primary Sources

Read the following quote by Bartolomé de Las Casas, a Spanish priest commenting on the conquest of the lands that became New Spain, then answer the questions.

❝Any reasonable person who knows something . . . of rights and of civil law can imagine for himself what the likely reaction would be of any people living peaceably within their own frontiers, unaware that they owe allegiance to anyone save their natural lords, were a stranger suddenly to issue a demand along the following lines: 'You shall henceforth obey a foreign king, whom you have never seen nor ever heard of and, if you do not, we will cut you to pieces'—Especially when they discover that these strangers are indeed quite prepared to carry out this threat to the letter.❞

3. Which of the following statements best describes the author's point of view?
   a. Europeans had a legal right to conquer American Indians.
   b. American Indians were probably happy to become subjects of European empires.
   c. American Indians had a right to resist when Europeans took their lands.
   d. Nobody can guess how American Indians felt when they first met Europeans.

4. Based on your knowledge of the period, how did American Indians in different parts of the Americas respond to European settlers?

Thinking Critically

1. helped create a Golden Age for Spain by expanding its imperial power and bringing in treasure; made Spain a target for other European nations wanting to create their own colonies

2. system was needed to reward settlers for their service to the Crown. In general it had a negative effect. Some American Indians learned skills. The majority were subjected to harsh labor conditions and treated like slaves. Many died from disease.

3. led to war between England and Spain and to the defeat of the Spanish Armada, which weakened Spain's power in the Americas and encouraged other countries to colonize there

Skills Workshop

1. c

2. France and England

3. c

4. Students should note that in some places American Indians fought fiercely against Europeans, while in others they were sometimes helpful to the early colonists.

Alternative Assessment

American History

Building Your Portfolio

Cooperative Learning
Complete the following activity in small groups. Create a newspaper titled *Settling the Americas*. Devote one page each to the colonies of Spain, France, Sweden, and the Netherlands. Your newspaper should have thematic maps, a chart listing each of the colonies, a feature story, a biography of an important person, and quotations from people who were involved in the establishment of the colonies. Each group should present its newspaper to the class.

🖳 internet connect

Internet Activity: go.hrw.com
keyword: SA3 CF3

Choose a topic about new empires in the Americas to:
- Learn about the settlement of St. Augustine.
- Research the role of Spanish Missions in the New World.
- Follow the French Explorers of the New World.

The English Colonies

CHAPTER RESOURCE MANAGER

Objectives	Pacing Guide	Reproducible Resources
SECTION 1: **The Virginia Colony** (pp. 92–97) ★ Explain why people in England were interested in founding Jamestown, and when the colony was established. ★ Analyze how the Jamestown colonists interacted with the local American Indians. ★ Analyze how the English plantation system began. ★ Examine the role indentured servants and enslaved Africans played in Virginia's economy.	**Regular** 1 day **Block Scheduling** .5 day *Block Scheduling Handbook with Team Teaching Strategies, Chapter 4*	**RS** Guided Reading Strategy, 4.1 **E** Hands-On History Activity: Holidays, Festivals, and Celebrations in Your Community
SECTION 2: **The Pilgrims' Experience** (pp. 98–102) ★ Explain why the Pilgrims came to America. ★ Define the Mayflower Compact, and explain why it was important. ★ Describe life in the Plymouth colony.	**Regular** 1 day **Block Scheduling** .5 day *Block Scheduling Handbook with Team Teaching Strategies, Chapter 4*	**RS** Guided Reading Strategy 4.2 **PS** Primary Source Reading 4: Journal of Sarah Kemble Knight **PS** Biography Reading 4: Squanto
SECTION 3: **The New England Colonies** (pp. 103–108) ★ Explain the Great Migration and why it occurred. ★ Analyze the role that religion and the church played in the Massachusetts Bay Colony. ★ Describe how the Puritans responded to dissenters.	**Regular** 1.5 day **Block Scheduling** 1 day *Block Scheduling Handbook with Team Teaching Strategies, Chapter 4*	**RS** Guided Reading Strategy 4.3 **PS** Literature Reading 4: Mary Rowlandson's Captivity **E** Creative Teaching Strategy: Role Playing
SECTION 4: **The Southern and Middle Colonies** (pp. 109–115) ★ Discuss the role religion played in the founding and development of Maryland. ★ Explain how the Carolinas were established and how their economies developed. ★ Describe how the middle colonies were founded.	**Regular** 1 day **Block Scheduling** .5 day *Block Scheduling Handbook with Team Teaching Strategies, Chapter 4*	**RS** Guided Reading Strategy 4.4 **SM** Geography Activity 4: The Settling of the Colonies **RS** Graphic Organizer 4: English Colonial Settlements

Chapter Resource Key

PS Primary Sources
RS Reading Support
IC Interdisciplinary Connections
E Enrichment
SM Skills Mastery

A Assessment
REV Review
ELL Reinforcement and English Language Learners
 Transparencies
 CD-ROM

 Music
 Video
 Internet
 Holt Presentation Maker Using Microsoft® PowerPoint®

 One-Stop Planner CD-ROM

See the *One-Stop Planner* for a complete list of additional resources for students and teachers.

One-Stop Planner CD–ROM

It's easy to plan lessons, select resources, and print out materials for your students when you use the *One-Stop Planner CD–ROM with Test Generator.*

☑ **internet** connect

HRW ONLINE RESOURCES
GO TO: go.hrw.com
Then type in a keyword.

Technology Resources	Reinforcement, Review, and Assessment
One-Stop Planner, Lesson 4.1 American History Simulations CD–ROM: Building a Colony Holt Researcher: American History CD–ROM Homework Practice Online HRW Go site	**REV** Section 1 Review, p. 97 **A** Daily Quiz 4.1 **ELL** Main Idea Activity 4.1 **ELL** English Audio Summary 4.1 **ELL** Spanish Audio Summary 4.1
One-Stop Planner, Lesson 4.2 **CNN** Presents America: Yesterday and Today, Beginnings to 1914 Segment: A Visit to Colonial America Homework Practice Online	**REV** Section 2 Review, p. 102 **A** Daily Quiz 4.2 **ELL** Main Idea Activity 4.2 **ELL** English Audio Summary 4.2 **ELL** Spanish Audio Summary 4.2
One-Stop Planner, Lesson 4.3 Everyday Life in America Transparency 3: Gravestone Styles in the English Colonies American Music Selection 3: London Tune: Psalm 19 Holt Researcher: American History CD–ROM Homework Practice Online	**REV** Section 3 Review, p. 108 **A** Daily Quiz 4.3 **ELL** Main Idea Activity 4.3 **ELL** English Audio Summary 4.3 **ELL** Spanish Audio Summary 4.3
One-Stop Planner, Lesson 4.4 Exploring America's Past Video Segment: Diary of a Young Girl; Teacher's Guide, pp. 6–7 Homework Practice Online HRW Go site	**REV** Section 4 Review, p. 114 **A** Daily Quiz 4.4 **ELL** Main Idea Activity 4.4 **ELL** English Audio Summary 4.4 **ELL** Spanish Audio Summary 4.4

TEACHER HOME PAGE
KEYWORD: SA3 Teacher

CHAPTER INTERNET ACTIVITIES
KEYWORD: SA3 CF4
Choose an activity to:
• organize,interpret, and graphically represent information in a database.
• construct a scale model of a colonial house.
• learn about colonial food.

CHAPTER ENRICHMENT LINKS
KEYWORD: SA3 CH4

ONLINE ASSESSMENT
Homework Practice
KEYWORD: SA3 HP4

Standardized Test Prep
KEYWORD: SA3 STP4

Rubrics
KEYWORD: SS Rubrics

ONLINE MAPS, CHARTS, AND GRAPHS
KEYWORD: SA3 MCG
• The Great Migration
• British Imports
• French and Dutch Imports
• Settling New England

CONTENT UPDATES
KEYWORD: SS Content Updates

HOLT PRESENTATION MAKER
KEYWORD: SA3 PPT4

ONLINE READING SUPPORT
KEYWORD: SS Strategies

CURRENT EVENTS
KEYWORD: S3 Current Events

Meeting Individual Needs

Ability Levels

Level 1 Basic-level activities designed for all students encountering new material

Level 2 Intermediate-level activities designed for average students

Level 3 Challenging activities designed for honors and gifted-and-talented students

English Language Learners Activities that address the needs of students with Limited English Proficiency

Chapter Review and Assessment

IC Vocabulary Activity 4
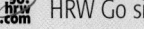 Global Skill Builder CD–ROM
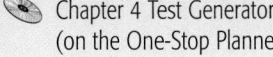 HRW Go site
REV Chapter 4 Tutorial for Students, Parents, Mentors, and Peers
REV Chapter 4 Review, pp. 115–17
Chapter 4 Test Generator (on the One-Stop Planner)
A Chapter 4 Test (Form A or B)

A Alternative Assessment Handbook
A Chapter 4 Test for English Language Learners and Special-Needs Students

4

Build on What You Know

If You Were There...

Ask students to answer the following question:

What factors would lead you to settle in a new country?

Consider:

• seeking adventure

• escaping problems in your homeland

You Be the Historian

What's Your Opinion?

To help students create their **Themes** Journal entries, provide the following examples of appropriate **agree**/**disagree** statements.

EXPLORING THE TIME LINE

AMERICAN EVENTS

internet connect

go.hrw.com

TOPIC: Jamestown
GO TO: go.hrw.com
KEYWORD: SA3 CF4

Have students access the Internet through the HRW Go site to gather data related to settlement in the early English colonies, particularly Jamestown in 1607. Students should then input the data into the Holt grapher database and represent their data in at least two different forms. Students should write a brief explanation of how the information is represented in each graph.

CHAPTER

4 The English Colonies
(1605–1735)

John Smith was an early leader at Jamestown.

THE GRANGER COLLECTION, NEW YORK

Puritan colonists built their first settlement in New England.

UNITED STATES

1607 English colonists found the Jamestown settlement in present-day Virginia.

1619 The first representative assembly in North America is formed in Virginia.

1620 The Pilgrims sign the Mayflower Compact.

1630 Puritans found the Massachusetts Bay Colony.

1639 Thomas Hooker helps draft the Fundamental Orders of Connecticut.

1610	**1620**	**1630**	**1640**

1611 The first edition of the King James Version of the Bible is published.

WORLD

1630s The Great Migration begins as thousands of people leave England to settle in colonies or other European countries.

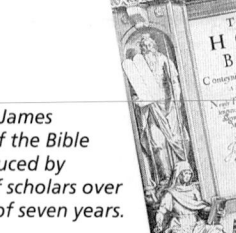

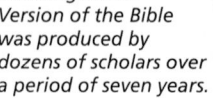

The King James Version of the Bible was produced by dozens of scholars over a period of seven years.

Build on What You Know

By the early 1600s, European exploration of the Americas had led to great interest in colonization. At first, the English wanted to colonize North America because they hoped to have a better quality of life there. However, many English colonists quickly found that merely surviving in their harsh new environment took most of their efforts.

Geography

Agree Cooperative weather ensures a successful harvest.

Disagree Through hard work and determination, people can overcome geographical hardships and be successful.

Economics

Agree A colony must have money to meet its basic needs.

Disagree A colony that provides for its basic needs will survive.

Culture

Agree The new colonies would not have survived without religious freedom.

Disagree Religious freedom should be fought for at all costs.

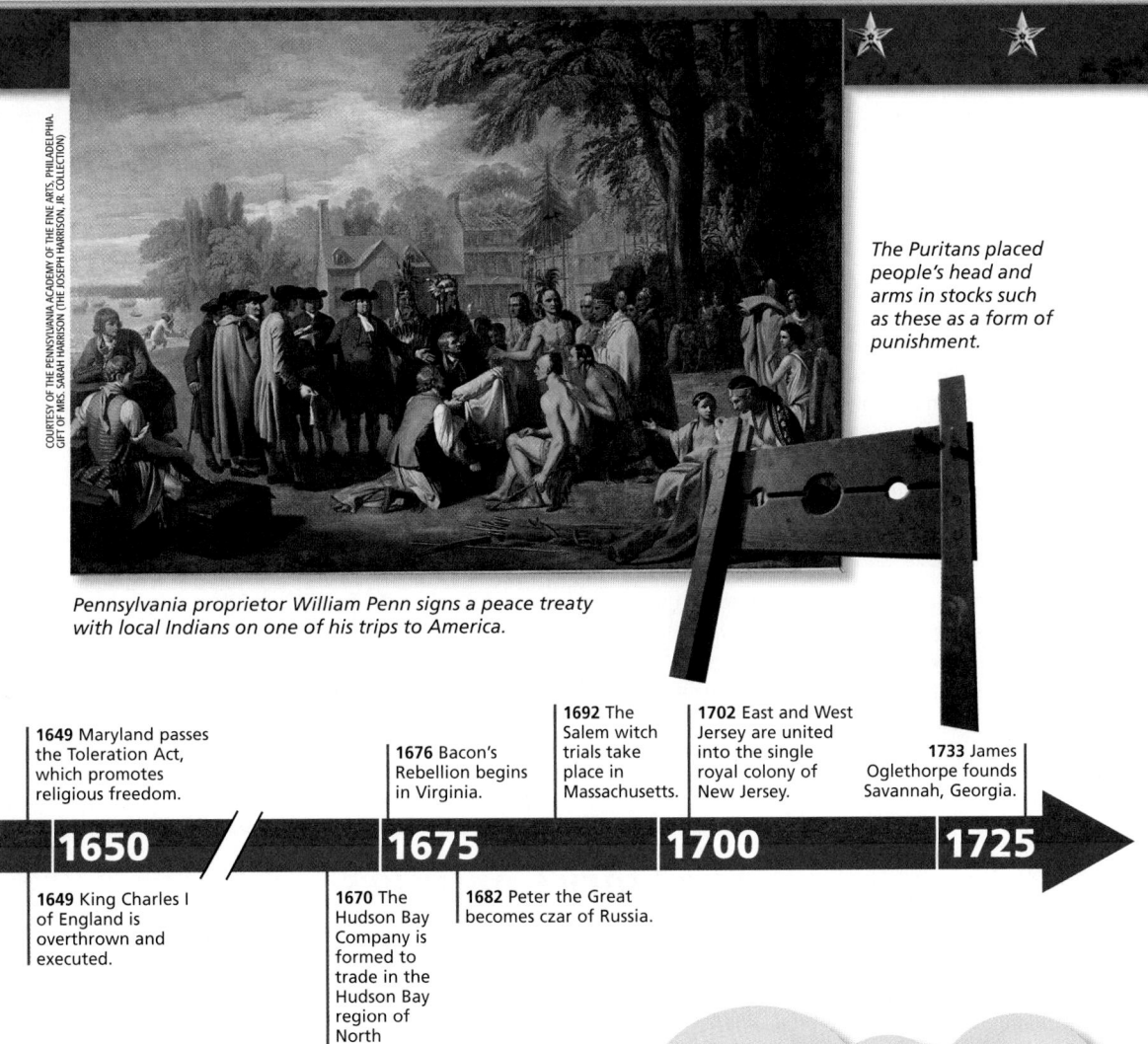

COURTESY OF THE PENNSYLVANIA ACADEMY OF THE FINE ARTS, PHILADELPHIA. GIFT OF MRS. SARAH HARRISON (THE JOSEPH HARRISON, JR. COLLECTION)

The Puritans placed people's head and arms in stocks such as these as a form of punishment.

Pennsylvania proprietor William Penn signs a peace treaty with local Indians on one of his trips to America.

1649 Maryland passes the Toleration Act, which promotes religious freedom.

1676 Bacon's Rebellion begins in Virginia.

1692 The Salem witch trials take place in Massachusetts.

1702 East and West Jersey are united into the single royal colony of New Jersey.

1733 James Oglethorpe founds Savannah, Georgia.

1650 **1675** **1700** **1725**

1649 King Charles I of England is overthrown and executed.

1670 The Hudson Bay Company is formed to trade in the Hudson Bay region of North America.

1682 Peter the Great becomes czar of Russia.

If you were there . . .
What factors would lead you to settle in a new country?

You Be the Historian

Themes Journal

What's Your Opinion? Do you **agree** or **disagree** with the following statements? Support your point of view in your journal.

- **Geography** Weather and geography determine a people's way of life—how they work, where they live, and how wealthy they can become.
- **Economics** A colony cannot survive unless the colonists find a way to make money.
- **Culture** Religious freedom is a basic right of all people.

The Great Migration.
In contrast to the Pilgrims, most Puritans remained in England and did not leave the Anglican Church. These religious dissenters hoped to reform the church from within. The crown, however, opposed reform. James I feared that Puritan demands would lead to political unrest. In addition, the English Puritans faced economic difficulties. During the early 1600s England's population had dramatically increased, but employment had not. Land was scarce, and the money needed to purchase an acre or two in England would purchase several hundred acres in America. To escape both religious persecution and economic ruin, many Puritans decided to risk a move to the colonies. Beginning in 1630, some 60,000 people left England for the Americas in what became known as the Great Migration. Although most of the people settled in the West Indies, 10,000 to 20,000 settled in Massachusetts.

ACTIVITY: Have students imagine that they are teenagers whose parents have decided to colonize the Americas. Then using standard grammar, spelling, sentence structure, and punctuation, ask them to write diary entries about their feelings and fears about moving so far away from home.

Section 1

OBJECTIVES

★ Explain why people in England were interested in founding Jamestown and when the colony was established.

★ Analyze how the Jamestown colonists interacted with local American Indians.

★ Analyze how the English plantation system began.

★ Examine the role indentured servants and enslaved Africans played in Virginia's economy.

SECTION 1 RESOURCES

REPRODUCIBLE

▶ Guided Reading Strategy, 4.1

TECHNOLOGY

▶ One-Stop Planner, Lesson 4.1
▶ American History Simulations CD–ROM: Building a Colony
▶ Holt Researcher: American History CD–ROM
▶ Homework Practice Online
▶ HRW Go site

REINFORCEMENT, REVIEW, AND ASSESSMENT

▶ Section 1 Review, p. 97
▶ Daily Quiz 4.1
▶ Main Idea Activity 4.1
▶ English Audio Summary 4.1
▶ Spanish Audio Summary 4.1

LET'S GET STARTED!

Write the following statement on the chalkboard: *Imagine that you are setting out on an expedition to a place you know little about.* As students enter the classroom, ask them to write down what and who they would want to take along. Also ask them what their goals might be. *(Students' responses will vary.)* Tell students that the English expedition to Jamestown faced similar issues. Have volunteers share their responses with the class. Tell students that in Section 1 they will learn why people came to Jamestown, how they responded to American Indians, and how the settlers made their colony a success.

Section 1

The Virginia Colony

Read to Discover

1. Why were people in England interested in founding Jamestown, and when was the colony established?
2. How did the Jamestown colonists interact with local American Indians?
3. How did the English plantation system begin?
4. What role did indentured servants and enslaved Africans have in Virginia's economy?

WHY IT MATTERS TODAY

Many important historical places in the United States have been protected and preserved. Use **CNNfyi.com** or other **current events** sources to find out about a historical site in the United States today. Record your findings in your journal.

Define

• headright
• indentured servants
• planters

Identify

• John Smith
• Powhatan Confederacy
• John Rolfe
• Pocahontas
• Nathaniel Bacon
• Bacon's Rebellion

NOVA BRITANNIA.
OFFERING MOST Excellent fruites by Planting in VIRGINIA.

Exciting all such as be well affected to further the same.

LONDON
Printed for SAMVEL MACHAM, and are to be sold at his Shop in Pauls Church-yard, at the Signe of the Bul-head.
1609.

THE GRANGER COLLECTION, NEW YORK

Posters like this one promoted the opportunities that were to be found in the colonies.

The Story Continues

In 1605 a company of English merchants asked the Crown for the right to found a new settlement in North America. They asked to settle in a region called Virginia. At the time, Virginia extended from present-day Maine to South Carolina. In 1606 King James I granted the request. He promised the London Company the rights to "all the lands . . . rivers . . . [and] commodities [goods]" along part of the Virginia coast. The company's efforts, wrote King James, "may in time bring . . . a settled and quiet government."

★ Settlement in Jamestown

The members of the London Company knew about the Roanoke colony's failure. They wanted to start a settlement without depending on the wealth of just one person. Instead, investors formed a joint-stock company, which allowed a group to share the cost and risk of founding a colony. Colonies formed in this way were called company colonies. To attract investors and settlers, the London Company printed advertisements praising Virginia.

Have students read Section 1 and complete Guided Reading Strategy 4.1. Choose one or more of the following activities to explore the section content with students. For further suggestions on block scheduling or team teaching, see the *Block Scheduling Handbook with Team Teaching Strategies.*

 LEVEL 1: Copy the following graphic organizer onto the chalkboard, omitting the italicized answers. Have each student complete the chart by providing the high and low points of relations between American Indians and the Jamestown settlers. As a class, discuss the significance of the events that they listed on their organizers in terms of maintaining relations and interaction between the colonists and the American Indians. **ENGLISH LANGUAGE LEARNERS**

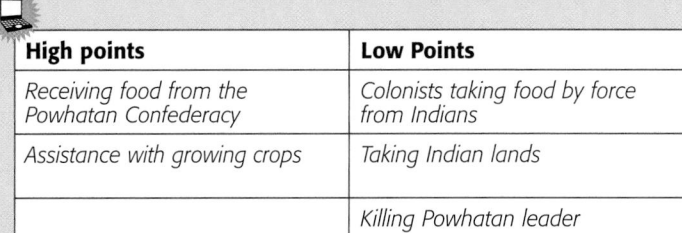

High points	Low Points
Receiving food from the Powhatan Confederacy	*Colonists taking food by force from Indians*
Assistance with growing crops	*Taking Indian lands*
	Killing Powhatan leader

History Makers Speak

❝The land yields . . . [an] abundance of fish, infinite store [endless supply] of deer, and hares, with many fruits and roots. . . . There are hills and mountains making a sensible proffer [offer] of hidden treasure, never yet searched.❞

—The Virginia Company of London, quoted in *Ordinary Americans,* edited by Linda R. Monk

Analyzing Primary Sources
Identifying Bias What might this report have left out of its description of Virginia?
Students may suggest difficult living conditions such as climate, or difficult relationships with local American Indians.

The promise of such wealth attracted adventurers and people who were suffering economic hardship in England.

On April 26, 1607, the first three ships sent by the London Company arrived off the Virginia coast. The fleet brought 105 male colonists to found a settlement. The ships sailed into Chesapeake Bay and up the James River. About 40 miles upstream, the colonists founded their first settlement, named Jamestown after the English king.

The men who came to Jamestown were poorly prepared to start a settlement. Most were adventurers interested in making their fortune and returning to England. One of the colonists, Captain **John Smith**, complained that "ten good workmen would have done more substantial work in a day than ten of these [colonists] in a week." In fact, very few colonists had farming experience or useful skills such as carpentry. Jamestown was also a poor site for a settlement. The settlement was surrounded by marshes full of disease-carrying mosquitoes. In addition, the river water was too salty to drink safely. These conditions proved deadly. By the time winter arrived, two thirds of the original colonists had died. The few survivors were hungry and sick. The situation temporarily improved after Smith took control of the colony in September 1608. He forced the settlers to work and to build better housing. This reduced the number of deaths from starvation and exposure.

April 26, 1607
The London Company founds Jamestown.

Interpreting the Visual Record

Jamestown *The settlers at Jamestown settled close by the James River.* **Why do you think the colonists built their settlement in the manner shown here?**

COLONIAL WILLIAMSBURG FOUNDATION

Daily Life

Early Housing. Jamestown colonists described their first homes as wigwams, although they were modeled after English shacks, not American Indian huts. Their homes were so flimsy that in bad weather they sought protection under a rotten old tent. The houses shocked early visitors to the colony. One visitor wrote that they were worse than the shacks on which they had been modeled.

🖥 **internet** connect

TOPIC: Colonial Housing
GO TO: go.hrw.com
KEYWORD: SA3 CF4

Have students access the Internet through the HRW Go site to research housing in Colonial America. Students should then construct a scale model of a colonial home. Remind students to base the scale of their model on information from their research. Students should also be prepared to discuss the materials used to build a typical colonial house.

Visual Record Answer

Students might suggest that the fort gives the settlement protection and the location provides easy access to water.

ALL LEVELS: Copy the following graphic organizer onto the chalkboard, omitting the italicized answers. Have each student complete the organizer to explain how the English plantation system began.
ENGLISH LANGUAGE LEARNERS

The English Plantation System

↓

Plantations (large farms) grew out of the headright system. Under this system colonists who paid their own way to Virginia received 50 acres of land. A colonist could earn 50 acres more for every additional person brought from England. Thus, many people were eager to come to America and begin a new life.

TEACHER TO TEACHER

James Pyne of Flossmoor, Illinois, suggested the following activity:

 ALL LEVELS: Organize students into groups. Ask students to imagine that they work in the advertising department of the London Company. Have them prepare pamphlets to promote English settlement in the new colony at Jamestown. Encourage groups to consider conditions in England and the goals of the company. (*Students' pamphlets might include: disappearing farmland for tenant farmers, increased population, and rising unemployment levels; students*)

★ Historical Sidelight

The Saga of Jamestown. Misfortune loomed before the 105 men who settled an area they called Jamestown on the Chesapeake Bay in 1607. Unfortunately, Jamestown was not the paradise they sought. The initial settlers (mostly aristocracy and unskilled laborers) were ill equipped to sustain a community. This fact, combined with an unhealthy marshland environment that bred disease, spelled disaster for the colonists. Only 38 of the original settlers survived the first year. The survivors owed their lives to Captain John Smith who took charge of the settlement and concentrated on survival. The colony managed to survive thanks to the leadership of the new governor Thomas West in 1610. Profits from tobacco also caused the colony's prospects to improve greatly.

ACTIVITY: Have students research the establishment of other colonies. Then have students make a chart comparing and contrasting the political, economic, and social reasons the other colonies were founded with the reasons Jamestown was established.

Technology Resources
 American History Simulations CD–ROM: Building a Colony

Analyzing Primary Sources
Identifying Points of View
How does Wahunsonacock describe his people's view of the colonists? They are willing to be friendly to the colonists if the colonists themselves are friendly.

Research on the R⚫M

Free Find:
Pocahontas
After reading about Pocahontas on the **Holt Researcher CD–ROM**, write a short essay describing the way the Powhatan treated the English settlers of Jamestown.

★ The Powhatan Confederacy

The colonists also received help from the powerful **Powhatan Confederacy**. Wahunsonacock (wah-hoohn-SUH-nuh-kahk) led this alliance of Algonquian Indians. At times, the Powhatan brought food to aid the colonists. The Powhatan also taught them how to grow corn.

The relationship between the Powhatan and the Virginia colonists was not entirely peaceful, however. The colonists at times took food from the Powhatan by force. These actions led Wahunsonacock to say:

 History Makers Speak ❝Why will you take by force what you may obtain by love? Why will you destroy us who supply you with food? What can you get by war? . . . We are unarmed, and willing to give you what you ask, if you come in a friendly manner.❞

—Wahunsonacock, quoted in *The Portable North American Indian Reader*, edited by Frederick W. Turner III

In 1609 some 400 more settlers arrived in Jamestown. An injury from an accident forced John Smith to return to England, leaving the settlers without a strong leader. That winter, disease and famine once again hit the colony. The colonists called this period the "starving time." By the spring of 1610, only 60 colonists were still alive.

Because the colony struggled to survive, Jamestown failed to make a profit for the London Company. Colonist **John Rolfe** helped solve this problem in 1612. Smoking tobacco had been a favorite pastime in England since the 1560s. Tobacco grew well in Virginia. However, the local variety grown by the Powhatan was too bitter for European tastes, so Rolfe introduced a sweeter West Indian variety. Soon the colonists were able to export tobacco to England successfully. As Virginia colonist John Pory wrote in 1619, "All our riches for the present doe consiste in [come from] Tobacco." Another important change in the colony was a shift in land ownership from the London Company to individual colonists. The possibility of owning land attracted new settlers and thus helped the colony survive.

✔ **Reading Check: Finding the Main Idea** When did English settlers arrive in Virginia, and what challenges did they face? 1607; poor organization, lack of skills, lack of food and shelter, conflict with the Powhatan

★ War in Virginia

John Rolfe married **Pocahontas**, Wahunsonacock's daughter, in 1614. Their marriage helped the Jamestown colony form more peaceful relations with the Powhatan. However, in 1617 Pocahontas died while visiting England, and Wahunsonacock died the next year. By that time, the colonists no longer depended on the Powhatan for food. They lost interest in allying with their American Indian neighbors. Many colonists also wanted to grow tobacco on American Indian lands. As the colony grew, the Powhatan and the Virginia colonists came into greater conflict.

should suggest that the London Company offered new opportunities for the growing numbers of homeless and unemployed people.) Have each group present its pamphlet to the class, and have the class decide which pamphlet would most likely have the greatest appeal. **ENGLISH LANGUAGE LEARNERS**, **COOPERATIVE LEARNING**

LEVEL 2: Ask students to imagine that they are indentured servants living in Virginia in the 1600s. Then have them write a letter home describing their experiences. The letter should include their motives for leaving home, descriptions of the headright system, their contract, and the conditions under which they work. *(Students' letters will vary but should include examples from the text.)* Call on volunteers to read their letters to the class.

LEVEL 3: Discuss with students why and when Jamestown was colonized, the demographics of the colonists, the early challenges settlers faced, and how they met those challenges. Ask students to prepare reports supporting an argument for the early success or failure of the colony. Then have volunteers present their findings to the class.

Note: To help students make meaningful connections between events in American history and those in their own hometown, use the Chapter 4 **Hands-On History** activity, Holidays, Festivals, and Celebrations in Your Community.

In 1622, colonists killed a Powhatan leader. Opechancanough (OH-puh-chan-kuh-noh), the brother of Wahunsonacock, responded by attacking the Virginia settlers later that year. The Powhatan killed about 350 men, women, and children. Among the dead was John Rolfe. Angry survivors then burned American Indian villages. Fighting between the colonists and the Powhatan continued for the next 20 years.

The war in Virginia showed that the London Company could not help its colonists. Settlers were running short of supplies and were angry that the Company failed to send them any military support. These problems persuaded the English Crown to cancel the London Company's charter in 1624. Virginia became a royal colony under the authority of a governor chosen by the king.

✔ **Reading Check: Sequencing** List the events that marked the Jamestown colonists' changing relationship with American Indians in the proper sequence. marriage of Rolfe and Pocahontas, peace and cooperation; colonists stole food, tried to expand; war for 20 years; colony charter revoked

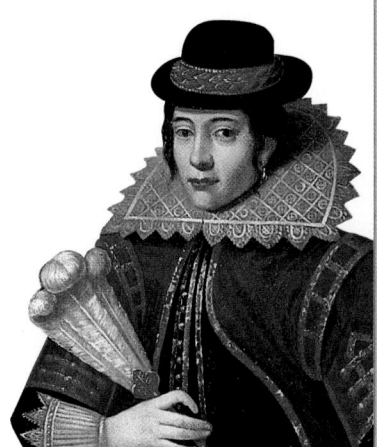

Pocahontas had this portrait painted when she visited England with John Rolfe in 1616.

Daily Life in Virginia

In early Virginia, people lived on scattered farms rather than in towns. Tobacco farmers soon began founding large farms called plantations. These plantations were made possible in part by use of the **headright** system. Under this system, colonists who paid their own way to Virginia received 50 acres of land. A colonist could earn 50 acres more for every

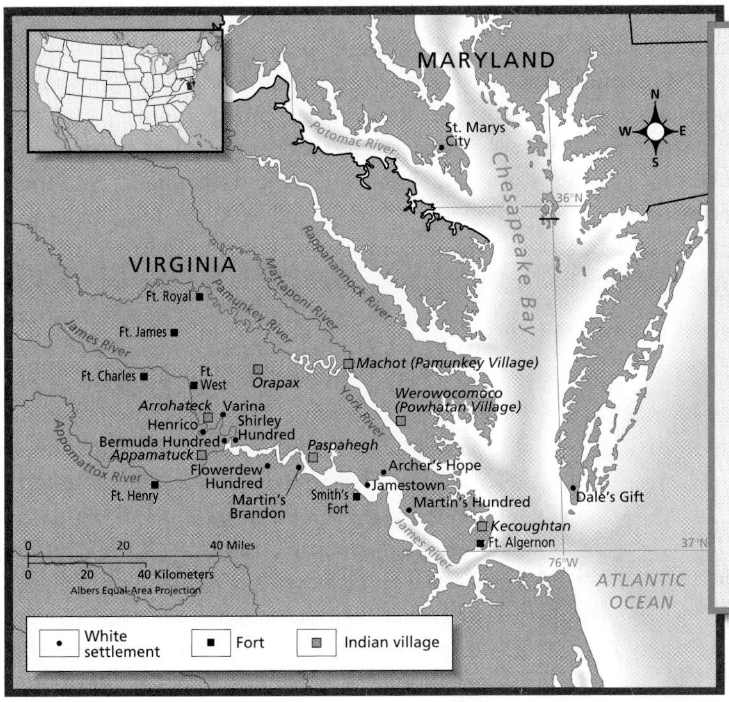

MARYLAND
VIRGINIA
St. Marys City
Potomac River
Chesapeake Bay
Rappahannock River
Mattaponi River
Pamunkey River
James River
York River
Appomattox River
Ft. Royal
Ft. James
Ft. Charles
Ft. West
Orapax
Machot (Pamunkey Village)
Werowocomoco (Powhatan Village)
Arrohateck
Varina
Henrico
Shirley Hundred
Bermuda Hundred
Appamatuck
Paspahegh
Flowerdew Hundred
Ft. Henry
Martin's Brandon
Smith's Fort
Archer's Hope
Jamestown
Martin's Hundred
Dale's Gift
Kecoughtan
Ft. Algernon
36°N
37°N
76°W
ATLANTIC OCEAN
N
S
E
W
0 20 40 Miles
0 20 40 Kilometers
Albers Equal-Area Projection
White settlement
Fort
Indian village

English Settlement in the Chesapeake Region, 1607–1675

Interpreting Maps English colonies in the Chesapeake Bay area were often located near American Indian villages. The contact between the two cultures was sometimes cooperative but often turned violent.

Skills Assessment

1. **The World in Spatial Terms** What Indian villages were located on the York River?
2. **Analyzing Information** Near what geographic features were most English settlements located? Why do you think settlers chose these areas?

Biography

Smith and the Algonquian Indians. Algonquian Indians captured Captain John Smith and brought him to the Powhatan capital, Werowocomoco. Smith later wrote in his *Generall Historie of Virginia* that they had set him before an altar stone to be killed when the 13-year-old Pocahontas threw herself over his body, saving his life.

CRITICAL THINKING

Why do you think some historians doubt Smith's story about Pocahontas?

ANSWER: Students might suggest that it is unlikely that Pocahontas would have gone to such lengths to save a stranger.

MAP ANSWERS

1. Werowocomoco, Machot
2. rivers or coastlines; waterways provided transportation for colonists

LEVEL 3: Have students prepare a one-page essay on how plentiful land and scarce labor in Virginia affected the headright system, the growth of the plantation system, and the replacement of indentured servitude with slavery. *(Students' essays should include the fact that landowners were eager to bring as many passengers as possible to the Americas in order to secure the largest acreages possible. The profitable tobacco crop required large plots of land—plantations. Thus the need for more servants to work the land grew. Landowners felt it was inefficient to replace servants every 4–7 years, therefore slavery began to replace indentured servitude.)* Once students have finished, ask each student to give a three-minute presentation on his or her essay.

HOMEWORK Ask students to imagine that they were poor colonists in the late 1600s. Have them write a diary entry detailing the events leading up to Bacon's Rebellion. They should also describe the confrontation itself as well as the aftermath.

☆ CLOSE

Ask each student to list the successes and failures of the Jamestown colonists. Lead a class discussion on why students categorized the factors as they did.
ENGLISH LANGUAGE LEARNERS

additional person brought from England. Rich colonists brought servants or relatives to Virginia and gained large amounts of land.

Those who brought relatives to Virginia found that raising a family was difficult. Loved ones often died of deadly diseases, such as malaria. The London Company tried to bring women to the colony by offering promises of marriage. However, during the early years of the settlement men outnumbered women seven to one. Colonial families in Virginia focused on providing the basic necessities for themselves. Most colonists provided their own food and shelter. They also made eating utensils, tools, furniture, and clothing by hand. Parents gave lessons in reading and religion at home because there were no schools and few churches.

✔ **Reading Check Summarizing** How and why did the plantation system develop in the South? The headright system gave large amounts of land to wealthy colonists who brought servants and/or relatives.

★ Labor in Virginia

Colonists in Virginia faced a hard life. They suffered very high death rates, which led to labor shortages in the colony. More laborers were needed to work on plantations and farms. The majority of these workers were **indentured servants**. These colonists signed a contract to work from four to seven years for those who paid their ship fare to America. Of the early Virginia colonists, some 75 percent arrived as indentured servants. In one such contract, Margarett Williams promised to work for plantation owner Richard Smyth for four years. Smyth agreed "to pay for her [ocean] passing, and to find and allow [provide] her meate, drinke, apparel [clothes] and lodging."

Living conditions were poor, and sickness was common. As a result, many indentured servants died before their term had ended. One servant wrote to his parents: "I have eaten more in a day at home than I have [had] here for a week." However, servants who survived their period of indenture gained their freedom and were able to claim land.

Not all laborers in Virginia came from Europe. The first Africans came to Virginia on a Dutch ship in 1619. Some Africans were indentured servants. Others had been enslaved. African indentured servants worked and lived side by side with white indentured servants and had similar contracts. Some of them became successful farmers when their contracts ended.

At first, indentured servants were more common than slaves in Virginia. These servants were clearly less expensive to bring to the colonies than slaves. However, the demand for workers was greater than the supply of people willing to work as indentured servants under the harsh conditions. Over time the cost of slaves fell.

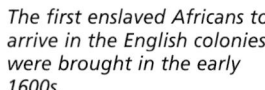

The first enslaved Africans to arrive in the English colonies were brought in the early 1600s.

COLONIAL WILLIAMSBURG FOUNDATION

✭ REVIEW AND ASSESS

Have students complete the **Section 1 Review** on p. 97. Then have students complete **Daily Quiz 4.1**. As **Alternative Assessment**, you may want to use the pamphlet exercise or graphic organizer activity in this section's lessons.

✭ RETEACH

Have students complete **Main Idea Activity for English Language Learners and Special-Needs Students 4.1**. Then assign each student a subsection of Section 1. Ask students to prepare a summary of his or her subsection. Have volunteers share their summaries with the class. Use these summaries to compile a master section summary on the chalkboard. **ENGLISH LANGUAGE LEARNERS**

✭ EXTEND

Have students work in teams to gather statistics on population growth, voluntary and involuntary immigration, and gender ratios in the early decades of Virginia's history. Have them prepare graphic organizers to illustrate their findings, draw inferences or conclusions from the data about growth and immigration, and prepare oral reports to explain their research to the class. **BLOCK SCHEDULING**

These factors led some colonists, particularly **planters**—wealthy farmers with large plantations—to turn to slave labor. By the late 1600s most Africans in Virginia were being kept in lifelong slavery. The widespread use of slave labor helped some tobacco plantation owners become rich. However, this wealth came at a great cost in human life and liberty.

✭ Bacon's Rebellion

During the mid-1600s many colonists grew increasingly unhappy with conditions in the colony. They were angered by the governor's tight control over the colony and his refusal to call elections. Poor colonists also believed that members of Virginia's assembly were ignoring their concerns. They complained about higher taxes and the lack of available farmland. Many of them began farming on land belonging to American Indians. In doing so, they ignored treaties between the government and local American Indians.

In 1676 a group of former indentured servants attacked some peaceful American Indians. These angry colonists were led by **Nathaniel Bacon**, a wealthy frontier planter and a relative of the governor. When the governor tried to stop Bacon, he and his followers attacked and burned Jamestown. The uprising was known as **Bacon's Rebellion**. At one point Bacon controlled much of the colony. After he died of fever, however, the rebellion soon ended, and 23 of the remaining rebels were eventually hanged. Following the rebellion, the Virginia colonists found it difficult to make peace with American Indians. In addition, fears of future uprisings by former indentured servants led some planters in Virginia to depend more on slavery.

✔ **Reading Check: Analyzing Information** What factors led to the increased use of slave labor in Virginia? The cost of slaves fell, and Bacon's Rebellion and fear of future rebellions by former servants led some farmers to use more slave labor.

Interpreting the Visual Record

Bacon's Rebellion *This scene shows a confrontation between Nathaniel Bacon at the right and Governor William Berkeley on the left.* **What is threatening about Bacon's appearance in this image?**

Visual Record Answer

Students might suggest that Bacon is holding a sword and warding off the man in front of him.

Section 1 Review

go.hrw.com **Homework Practice Online**
keyword: SA3 HP4

❶ Define and explain:
• headright
• indentured servants
• planters

❷ Identify and explain:
• John Smith
• Powhatan Confederacy
• John Rolfe
• Pocahontas
• Nathaniel Bacon
• Bacon's Rebellion

❸ Summarizing Copy the graphic organizer below. Use it to explain the reasons people from England decided to establish the Jamestown colony in 1607.

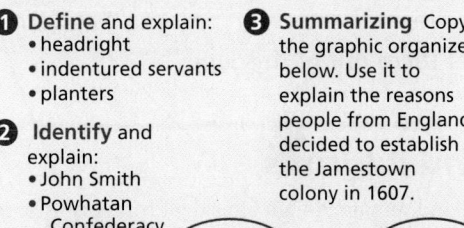

Problems in England → Jamestown Colony, 1607 ← Advantages of America

❹ Finding the Main Idea
a. Provide examples of the cooperation and conflict between American Indians and Virginia colonists.

b. Why did the plantation system develop in Virginia, and what economic role did tobacco play?

❺ Writing and Critical Thinking
Supporting a Point of View Imagine that you are a wealthy planter in colonial Virginia. Create a pamphlet for investors in England explaining why indentured servants and enslaved Africans are important for the colonial economy.

Consider the following:
• the headright system
• the development of tobacco plantations
• high death rates in the colony

Section 1 Review ANSWERS

❶ Define
• headright, p. 95
• indentured servants, p. 96
• planters, p. 97

❷ Identify
• John Smith, p. 93
• Powhatan Confederacy, p. 94
• John Rolfe, p. 94
• Pocahontas, p. 94
• Nathaniel Bacon, p. 97
• Bacon's Rebellion, p. 97

❸ England—economic hardships; America—promise of land and wealth for colonists

❹ a. Cooperation—Powhatan supply colonists with food; teach colonists how to grow crops; John Rolfe marrying Pocahontas Conflict—colonists steal food from Powhatan; murder by both groups; 20 year war
b. headright system—gave large amounts of land to colonists who brought servants; tobacco production—required many laborers, and was the colony's most important crop

❺ Students' pamphlets will vary but should note that the headright system encouraged the development of plantations. The labor intensive growing of tobacco and the high death rate in the colony caused labor shortages that were most easily filled through the use of the indentured servants or enslaved Africans.

Section 2

OBJECTIVES

* ❇ Explain why the Pilgrims came to America.
* ❇ Define the Mayflower Compact and explain why it was important.
* ❇ Describe life in the Plymouth colony.

Section 2

The Pilgrims' Experience

Read to Discover

1. Why did the Pilgrims come to America?
2. What was the Mayflower Compact, and why was it important?
3. What was life like in the Plymouth colony?

WHY IT MATTERS TODAY

Religious intolerance is still present in many parts of the world. Use **CNNfyi.com** or other **current events** sources to identify a religious group that recently faced intolerance. Record your findings in your journal.

Define

* sect
* immigrants

Identify

* Puritans
* Separatists
* Pilgrims
* William Bradford
* Mayflower Compact
* Squanto

The Story Continues

England's King James I held a conference in 1604 to meet with Protestant leaders. They wanted to reform the Church of England, also known as the Anglican Church. The leaders criticized the power held by Anglican bishops. As they talked, the king grew restless. Finally, he interrupted one of the reformers and began shouting furiously. "While I am in England I will have bishops to govern the Church." The king had plans for those who asked for reform, too. James stated, "I will make them conform themselves [become Anglicans] or I will harry [drive] them out of this land."

King James I disagreed with many proposed Puritan religious reforms.

★ Puritans and Pilgrims

Religious tension in England remained high after the Protestant Reformation. A Protestant group called the **Puritans** wanted to reform, or purify, the Church of England. The Puritans thought that bishops and priests had too much power over church members. They believed that the Bible was the most reliable source of authority. The most extreme **sect**, or religious group, of Puritans wanted to separate from the Church of England. These **Separatists** formed their own churches and cut all ties with the Church of England. In response, English leaders began to punish Separatists.

★ TEACH

Have students read Section 2 and complete Guided Reading Strategy 4.2. Choose one or more of the following activities to explore the section content with students. For further suggestions on block scheduling or team teaching, see the *Block Scheduling Handbook with Team Teaching Strategies.*

LEVEL 1: Have students review the excerpt from the Mayflower Compact. Organize students into small groups, and ask each group to imagine that it was a part of that first Mayflower voyage. Ask each group to list reasons why it would need to draft the Compact. *(Students' lists will vary but might include: to keep order in the colony, to establish a means of planning the goals of the colony, or to put into place a governing body.)* Ask volunteers to share their lists with the class. **ENGLISH LANGUAGE LEARNERS**

HOMEWORK Have students read the excerpt from the Mayflower Compact. Have them write a short article like one that might have appeared in a Massachusetts newspaper in 1670. This article should commemorate the 50th anniversary of the signing of the Mayflower Compact by explaining its importance to the colony.

One group of Separatists who faced such treatment became known as the **Pilgrims**. In 1608 the Pilgrims left England to escape this persecution and moved to the Netherlands. The Pilgrims were **immigrants**—people who came to a new country after leaving the land of their birth. Dutch officials welcomed the Pilgrims and allowed them to practice their religion freely.

The Pilgrims were glad to be able to practice their faith. They were not happy, however, that their children were learning the Dutch language and culture. The Pilgrims feared that their children would forget their English traditions. They were also disappointed by the types of jobs available to them. These concerns led the Pilgrims to leave the Netherlands. First, they formed a joint-stock company with some merchants. Then, they returned to England to apply for permission to settle in Virginia.

✔ **Reading Check: Summarizing** What factors led the Pilgrims to leave England and come to America? religious intolerance in England and desire to preserve their English traditions

DETAIL, COURTESY OF THE PILGRIM SOCIETY, PLYMOUTH, MASSACHUSETTS

Interpreting the Visual Record

Plymouth Rock *After the Pilgrims arrived at Plymouth Rock, their ship, the Mayflower, stayed with them as they struggled through the winter to build their settlement.* **What does this image suggest about the condition of the Pilgrims when they arrived in America?**

★ The Founding of Plymouth

On September 16, 1620, a ship called the *Mayflower* left England with more than 100 men, women, and children aboard. Not all of these colonists were Pilgrims. However, Pilgrim leaders such as **William Bradford** were in charge. The Pilgrims also hired Captain Miles Standish to help organize the defense of their colony.

After two months of rough ocean travel, the Pilgrims sighted land. Soon they realized that they were far north of present-day Virginia. The Pilgrims realized that they were outside the boundaries of their English charter. They decided to establish basic laws and social rules to govern their colony. On November 21, 1620, 41 of the male passengers on board the *Mayflower* signed a legal contract. They called this contract the **Mayflower Compact**. In it they agreed to have fair laws to protect the general good. This was one of the first attempts at self-government in the English colonies.

In late 1620 the Pilgrims landed at Plymouth Rock in present-day Massachusetts. Bradford described the scene. "They [the Pilgrims] fell upon their knees and blessed the God of Heaven who had brought them over the vast and furious ocean." As they struggled to build the Plymouth settlement, nearly half the tired Pilgrims died from cold and sickness during the first winter.

✔ **Reading Check: Finding the Main Idea** Why was the Mayflower Compact created, and why is it significant? It represents one of the first attempts at self-government in the colonies.

ALL LEVELS: Copy the following graphic organizer onto the chalkboard, omitting the italicized answers. Have students assess the new rights women discovered they held in Plymouth. Then, ask students to supply the answers that belong in the circles. **ENGLISH LANGUAGE LEARNERS**

Pilgrim women could sign contracts.

They cold bring cases before local courts.

New Rights for Pilgrim Women

Widows could own property.

Married and widowed women gained licenses to run inns & sell liquor.

Occasionally, women's business talents were recognized by the community.

LEVELS 2 AND 3: Ask students to review the subsection on Puritans and Pilgrims. Then tell them to make a bulleted list that describes these groups' complaints against the Church of England. *(Students' lists might include: the Church keeping too many Catholic traditions, the leaders of the Church having too much power over members, and the Bible not being the main source of authority within the church.)* When students have completed their lists, have them write a paragraph in which they describe the Puritans' solutions to the problems they had with the Church of England. They should also explain how the Puritans' grievances led to their voyage to America. Have volunteers read their paragraphs to the class.

★ Citizenship

The Mayflower Compact.

William Bradford reported that some people on board the *Mayflower* made "discontented and mutinous speeches" as soon as they realized they were no longer under the jurisdiction of the Virginia Company. Fearing disorder, the leaders on the ship quickly drew up a document for all the men on board to sign. The 41 men who signed the Mayflower Compact included the reasonably wealthy stockholders as well as the crew members and indentured servants. The 41 signers became the colony's first citizens and had the right to elect its leaders.

CRITICAL THINKING

How could the Mayflower Compact influence the signers to maintain its provisions?

ANSWER: Students might suggest that to keep order in their small community, the Pilgrims knew that they would need all members—from wealthy stockholders to servants—to agree and cooperate.

ANALYZING PRIMARY SOURCES ANSWERS

1. Students may suggest that the distance from England prompted the colonists to write their own laws.
2. Answers will vary, but students should note that the document created something of a model for independent governments in the Americas.

Historical Document

THE MAYFLOWER COMPACT

In November 1620, the Pilgrim leaders aboard the *Mayflower* drafted the Mayflower Compact. This was the first document in the English colonies to establish guidelines for self-government. This excerpt from the Mayflower Compact describes the principles of the Pilgrim colony's government.

The Pilgrims arrived in the Mayflower.

THE GRANGER COLLECTION, NEW YORK

We whose names are underwritten, . . . having undertaken, for the glory of God, and advancement of the Christian faith, and the honour of our King and country, a voyage to plant the first colony in the northern parts of Virginia, do by these **presents**[1] solemnly and mutually in the presence of God, and one of another, **covenant**[2] and combine ourselves together into a civil body **politic**[3] for our better ordering and preservation and furtherance of the ends **aforesaid**[4]; and by **virtue**[5] hereof, to enact, constitute, and frame such just and equal laws, **ordinances**[6], acts, constitutions, and offices . . . as shall be thought most **meet**[7] and convenient for the general good of the colony unto which we promise all due . . . obedience. In witness whereof, we have . . . subscribed our names at Cape Cod, the eleventh of November, 1620.

Analyzing Primary Sources

1. Why do you think the colonists felt the need to establish a government for themselves?
2. How do you think the Mayflower Compact influenced later governments in America?

[1] **by these presents:** by this document
[2] **covenant:** promise
[3] **civil body politic:** group organized for government
[4] **aforesaid:** mentioned above
[5] **virtue:** authority
[6] **ordinances:** regulations
[7] **meet:** fitting

"such just and equal laws . . . as shall be thought most . . . convenient for the general good of the colony . . ."

★ Pilgrims and American Indians

European fishing boats had already visited the Plymouth area before the Pilgrims' arrival. These European fishermen brought new diseases to the region. These sicknesses killed most of the local American Indians, such as the Patuxet. For some time the Pilgrims met no American Indians. Occasionally they came across deserted American Indian villages and empty cornfields. The Pilgrims used these empty fields in the spring to plant their crops.

Then, according to Bradford, in March 1621 an American Indian walked boldly into the settlement. He "spoke to them in broken English, which they could well understand, but marveled at it." The man's name was Samoset. He came from a Pemaquid tribe that lived in the area. Samoset had learned some English from the crews of fishing boats. He gave the Pilgrims useful information about the peoples and places surrounding Plymouth. Later he introduced them to a Patuxet Indian named **Squanto**.

LEVEL 2: Ask each student to imagine that he or she is a Pilgrim composing a letter home to a relative remaining in England. The letter should detail the interactions between the American Indians and the Pilgrims, as well as the various ways in which the Indians helped the colonists. *(Students' letters might include: geographical information, planting, fishing, and farming advice, and establishing peaceful relations between Pilgrims and other American Indian nations.)* Then, pair students and have them exchange and read the letters.

COOPERATIVE LEARNING

 LEVEL 3: Write the following headline on the chalkboard: *Church of England Oppresses Citizens!* Ask each student to imagine that he or she is a Pilgrim living in the 1600s. Then have each student write an article to accompany the headline. Students' articles should explain the numerous grievances that the Pilgrims had against the church. Encourage volunteers to read their articles to the class.

★ CLOSE

Have each student compare the circumstances that compelled the Pilgrims to move from England with those possible circumstances cited by the class in the *Let's Get Started!* activity. Have each student prepare a one paragraph summary of the differences between the two. Have volunteers read their paragraphs to the class.

Squanto had lived in Europe and spoke English. He was a great help to the colonists. Bradford described Squanto's contributions.

 History Makers Speak ❝Squanto continued with them and was their interpreter. . . . He directed them how to set [plant] corn, where to take [catch] fish, and procure [get] other commodities [goods], and was also their pilot [guide] to bring them to unknown places.❞

—William Bradford, *History of Plymouth Plantation*

From Squanto the Pilgrims learned to fertilize the soil on their farms with fish remains. Squanto also helped the Pilgrims establish relations with Massasoit, the chief of the local Wampanoag Indians.

Conditions in the Plymouth colony began to improve. William Bradford described the Pilgrims' first harvest.

 History Makers Speak ❝They began now to gather in the small harvest that they had, and to fit up their houses and dwellings against winter, being all well recovered in health and strength and had all things in good plenty.❞

—William Bradford, *History of Plymouth Plantation*

The Pilgrims invited Chief Massasoit and 90 other Wampanoag guests to celebrate their harvest. This feast, held to thank God, became known as the first Thanksgiving. For the event, the Pilgrims killed wild turkeys. For three days the two groups feasted with each other. This event marked the survival of the Pilgrims in the new colony.

✔ **Reading Check: Summarizing** What was the relationship like between Pilgrims and American Indians, and what did this mean for the colony?
helpful, peaceful, cooperative; helped the colony survive and prosper

★ The Pilgrim Community

Although the Pilgrims overcame many problems, their small settlement still struggled. Most Pilgrims tried farming, but the farmland around their settlement was poor. They had hoped to prosper by trading furs and by fishing. Unfortunately, fishing and hunting conditions were not good in their area. Some colonists traded corn with American Indians for beaver furs. The Pilgrims were not wealthy but were able to form a strong community. The colony began to grow stronger in the mid-1620s after new settlers arrived and, as in Jamestown, colonists began to have more rights to farm their own land.

The Pilgrim settlement was different from Virginia in that families were common there. Most people hoped to have many children, who were needed to help with the work. If parents died, Pilgrim families quickly adopted children left behind. They raised them as their own. The Pilgrims taught their children to read and offered some education to their indentured servants. The family served as the center of religious life, health care, and community well-being. All family members worked together to survive during the early years of the colony. Women generally cooked, spun

Analyzing Primary Sources
Identifying Points of View
How did Bradford regard Squanto? Squanto was a talented and valuable ally—he "continued with" the Pilgrims, acted as an interpreter and guide, and taught them how to obtain food.

★ ★ ★ ★ ★ ★ ★ ★ ★ ★
That's Interesting!
★ ★ ★ ★ ★ ★ ★ ★ ★ ★

Squanto's Journey Did you know that Squanto had traveled even farther than the Pilgrims when they first met in America? It's true! Squanto had been kidnapped by English explorers in 1605. He lived in England until 1614, when he returned to New England. Squanto was captured once again in 1615 and sold into slavery in Spain. He managed to escape the Spanish and make his way to England, returning to New England in 1619. When Squanto finally reached his home, however, he discovered that his tribe had been wiped out by disease. He then lived with the Wampanoag until Samoset introduced him to the Pilgrims.

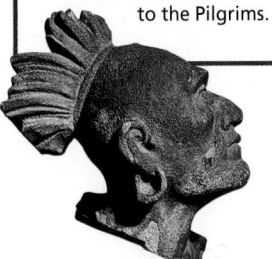

★ Global Relations

Hobomok. A Wampanoag named Hobomok also befriended the Pilgrims. After he alerted the Pilgrims that Chief Corbitant had captured Squanto and was threatening to kill him, Hobomok joined the party sent to free Squanto. Eventually, Hobomok moved onto Miles Standish's farm, where he lived until his death in 1642.

CRITICAL THINKING
How do you know that the Pilgrims thought highly of Hobomok?

ANSWER: Students might suggest that they trusted him to help free their friend Squanto, and that Hobomok also formed a close friendship with Miles Standish.

★ ★ ★ ★ ★ ★ ★ ★ ★ ★
That's Interesting!
★ ★ ★ ★ ★ ★ ★ ★ ★ ★

Thanksgiving did not become a fixed annual holiday until many years after the first Thanksgiving. The colonists celebrated Thanksgiving intermittently—some years they did not celebrate at all and some years they celebrated several times. Thanksgiving was held to celebrate events such as victory over the American Indians, suppression of pirates, the success of Protestants in Germany, or the end of an epidemic.

☆ REVIEW AND ASSESS

Have students complete the **Section 2 Review** on p. 102. Then have students complete **Daily Quiz 4.2**. As **Alternative Assessment**, you may want to use either the newspaper article or rights for Pilgrim women graphic organizer in this section's lessons.

☆ RETEACH

Have students complete **Main Idea Activity for English Language Learners and Special-Needs Students 4.2**. Then assign students one of the section objectives. Have each student write four or five questions with answers related to his or her

objective. Ask volunteers to share their questions and answers with the class. **ENGLISH LANGUAGE LEARNERS**

☆ EXTEND

Ask each student to prepare a crossword puzzle and clues for 10 events, key developments, people, or terms discussed in this section. Then pair students and have them complete their partner's puzzle. Have students return the puzzles to their creators for grading. **COOPERATIVE LEARNING** , **BLOCK SCHEDULING**

Visual Record Answer

Students might suggest that women performed tasks related to the home such as spinning and cooking as seen here.

★ ★ ★ ★ ★ ★ ★ ★ ★ ★

Section 2 Review
ANSWERS

❶ Define
• sect, p. 98
• immigrants, p. 99

❷ Identify
• Puritans, p. 98
• Separatists, p. 98
• Pilgrims, p. 99
• William Bradford, p. 99
• Mayflower Compact, p. 99
• Squanto, p. 100

❸ England—persecuted for separating from the Church of England, left for the Netherlands; The Netherlands—children losing English culture and language, traveled to America; America—founded Plymouth Colony

❹ a. created a family-centered community that included women and children, centered on a strong faith that provided stability
b. through cooperation, peaceful relations, and by teaching them agricultural techniques

❺ Students' essays will vary but should note that the colony was outside the jurisdiction of the Virginia Company, that the adult males signed the agreement, and that it was the first step toward representative government in the colonies.

THE GRANGER COLLECTION, NEW YORK

Interpreting the Visual Record

Homework *This woman works a spinning wheel in her kitchen. Colonial women made the family's clothing, often including shoes.* **What can you learn from the image about the different jobs that women had to do?**

and wove wool, and sewed clothing. They also made soap and butter, carried water, dried fruit, and cared for livestock. Men spent most of their time repairing tools and working in the fields. They also chopped wood and built shelters.

In Plymouth, women had more legal rights than they did in England. In England women were not allowed to make contracts, to sue, or to own property. In America, Pilgrim women had the right to sign contracts and to bring certain cases before local courts. Widows could also own property. A widow often received one third of her husband's land and belongings. In addition, married and widowed women could get licenses to run inns and to sell liquor.

From time to time, local courts recognized the ways women helped the business community. Widow Naomi Silvester received a large share of her husband's estate. The court called her "a frugal [thrifty] and laborious [hardworking] woman in the providing of the said estate." Widow Elizabeth Warren's business ability convinced colonial leaders to make her a purchaser for the colony. She took the place of her late husband. The hard work of such women helped the Plymouth colony to survive.

✔ **Reading Check: Analyzing Information** How did the Pilgrims view the importance of women and children to the colony? Evidence suggests that they valued them: children were educated and needed to help with daily work; women had more legal rights than in England and were recognized for their economic contributions; families were the center of the community.

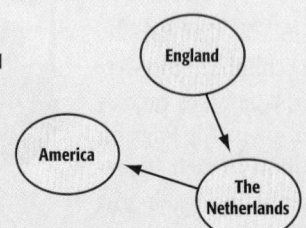
go. Homework
hrw Practice
.com Online
keyword: SA3 HP4

Section 2 Review

★ ★

❶ Define and explain:
• sect
• immigrants

❷ Identify and explain:
• Puritans
• Separatists
• Pilgrims
• William Bradford
• Mayflower Compact
• Squanto

❸ Identifying Cause and Effect Copy the web diagram below. Use it to describe the problems that the Pilgrims faced in Europe, and explain how they responded to these problems.

England → America → The Netherlands

❹ Finding the Main Idea
a. How were family relations and religion important to the Plymouth colony?

b. How did American Indians help the Plymouth colonists survive the early years?

❺ Writing and Critical Thinking
Summarizing Imagine that you are Pilgrim leader William Bradford. Write an essay describing the Mayflower Compact to place in the official records of the Plymouth colony.

Consider the following:
• why the Compact was necessary
• who signed the document
• the influence of the document on government

Section 3

OBJECTIVES

- ⭐ Explain the Great Migration and why it occurred.
- ⭐ Analyze the role that religion and the church played in the Massachusetts Bay Colony.
- ⭐ Describe how the Puritans responded to dissenters.

📻 LET'S GET STARTED!

Write the following question on the chalkboard: *What is the value or importance of religious freedom and how would your life change if there were just one religion to which you had to belong?* As students enter the classroom, ask volunteers to share their thoughts with the class. *(Students' responses will vary.)* Tell students that in Section 3 they will learn about how Puritans migrated from England in part to escape religious persecution, and that once here they struggled with religious dissent within their colony.

Section 3

The New England Colonies

Read to Discover

1. What was the Great Migration, and why did it occur?
2. What role did religion and the church play in the Massachusetts Bay Colony?
3. How did the Puritans respond to dissenters?

WHY IT MATTERS TODAY

The Puritans made education an important part of their community. Many colleges founded in colonial times still operate today. Use **CNNfyi.com** or other **current events** sources to identify ways in which colleges and universities affect our lives today. Record your findings in your journal.

Define
- dissenters
- covenant

Identify
- Great Migration
- John Winthrop
- Thomas Hooker
- Fundamental Orders of Connecticut
- Roger Williams
- Anne Hutchinson

SECTION 3 RESOURCES

REPRODUCIBLE
▶ Guided Reading Strategy 4.3
▶ Literature Reading 4: Mary Rowlandson's Captivity

TECHNOLOGY
▶ One-Stop Planner, Lesson 4.3
▶ Everyday Life in America Transparency 3: Gravestone Styles in the English Colonies
▶ American Music Selection 3: London Tune: Psalm 19
▶ Holt Researcher: American History CD–ROM
▶ Homework Practice Online

REINFORCEMENT, REVIEW, AND ASSESSMENT
▶ Section 3 Review, p. 108
▶ Daily Quiz 4.3
▶ Main Idea Activity 4.3
▶ English Audio Summary 4.3
▶ Spanish Audio Summary 4.3

The Story Continues

In the early 1600s John Winthrop wrote to his wife, Margaret. He worried that "this land [England] grows weary of her inhabitants." As an Englishman, John Winthrop was fond of his country. As a Puritan, however, he believed that the members of his church were no longer welcome in England. Winthrop believed that the time was coming when they would have to leave their comfortable life behind. He later wrote that the Puritans would have to seek a new home to "be better preserved from the common corruptions [sins] of this evil world."

John Winthrop was one of many Puritans who left England in search of religious freedom.

THE GRANGER COLLECTION, NEW YORK

⭐ The Massachusetts Bay Colony

Beginning about 1620, England experienced an economic downturn, costing many people their jobs. Charles I, who became king in 1625, made the situation worse by raising taxes. This unpopular act led to a political crisis. At the same time, the Church of England began to punish Puritans because they were **dissenters**—people who disagree with official opinions. Charles I refused to allow Puritans to criticize Church actions.

Have students read Section 3 and complete Guided Reading Strategy 4.3. Choose one or more of the following activities to explore the section content with students. For further suggestions on block scheduling or team teaching, see the *Block Scheduling Handbook with Team Teaching Strategies.*

LEVEL 1: Lead students in a discussion of the things that new colonists in Massachusetts would need to know about their church and community upon arriving in America. *(Students' responses might include: who would lead the community, the climate of the region, etc.)* Make a list on the chalkboard and assign each student an item from that list.

Have students create a page for a picture book that illustrates these items for new colonists. **ENGLISH LANGUAGE LEARNERS**

ALL LEVELS: Have students compose a bulleted list of factors that illustrate why the Great Migration occurred. *(Students' lists might include: economic hardships in England, increasingly higher taxes, dissolution of the legislature, targeting of religious dissenters, and harsh punishments exacted for writings against the Church of England.)* Have volunteers write their lists on the chalkboard. As a class, discuss the lists and why the Great Migration occurred.
ENGLISH LANGUAGE LEARNERS

★ Citizenship

The First Plan to Settle Massachusetts. Most royal charters required the governing body to meet in London. However, the Puritan lawyer who wrote the charter for the lands in New England did not specify where the governors would meet, allowing them to meet in the colonies.

CRITICAL THINKING

How would meeting in the colonies influence the governors?

ANSWER: Students might suggest that they would be more responsive to the colonists' needs than governors meeting in England.

Analyzing Primary Sources
Identifying Points of View
What did Winthrop believe should be the focus of the Puritan colony?
their community

Religious services were a key part of community life for both the Pilgrim and Puritan colonies in New England.

These economic, political, and religious problems in England led to the **Great Migration**. Between 1630 and 1640 tens of thousands of English men, women, and children left England. More than 40,000 English emigrants moved to colonies in the Caribbean and New England. In 1629 a group of Puritans and merchants began planning a Puritan colony in North America. King Charles I granted the group a charter, allowing its members to establish a colony in the area known as New England. They formed the Massachusetts Bay Company.

In 1630 a fleet of ships carrying Puritan colonists left England for Massachusetts. There they hoped to have the freedom to practice their religion freely. While on board the flagship, *Arbella*, the colony's governor, **John Winthrop**, wrote about the Puritans' goals.

History Makers Speak ❝We must delight in each other, make others' conditions our own and rejoice together, mourn together, labor and suffer together, always having before our eyes . . . our community . . . . For we must consider that we shall be like a City upon a Hill; the eyes of all people are on us.❞

—John Winthrop, quoted in *The Annals of America*

Winthrop's speech reflected the Puritans' belief that they had made a **covenant** with God. Under this covenant, or sacred agreement, Puritans agreed to build an ideal Christian community.

The Puritans arrived in New England well prepared to start their colony. They brought large numbers of tools and livestock. Trade with the colony of Plymouth helped them too. Like the Pilgrims, the Puritans faced little resistance at first from local American Indians. In addition, the Massachusetts region, unlike coastal Virginia, had a healthy climate. Thus, few Puritans died from sickness. All of these factors helped the Puritan colony do well.

THE GRANGER COLLECTION, NEW YORK

ALL LEVELS: Copy the following graphic organizer onto the chalkboard, omitting the italicized answers. Ask students to complete the organizer by listing factors that illustrate the role that religion and the church played in the Massachusetts Bay Colony.

ENGLISH LANGUAGE LEARNERS

Note: For an additional teaching idea, see the Chapter 14 Role Playing activity in the **Creative Teaching Strategies** handbook.

Religion and the Church in the Massachusetts Bay Colony
Ministers and church members were often government leaders.
Puritans gathered weekly to listen to sermons that brought all members of the community together.
As a result of shared beliefs and the presence of family, the community was more stable than those in Virginia.

By the end of 1630, about 1,000 more men, women, and children had joined the first settlers. These immigrants established the towns of Salem, Mystic, Newton, Watertown, and Dorchester. In addition, they built Boston, which became the colony's chief city and capital. Colonists also settled to the north, in present-day New Hampshire. In 1679 New Hampshire became a royal colony.

✔ **Reading Check: Summarizing** In what ways was religion an important factor in the establishment of the Massachusetts Bay Colony? Religious persecution contributed to the Great Migration; Puritans believed they had a covenant with God to establish an ideal Christian community.

⭐ Church and State in New England

According to its company charter, Massachusetts was subject to English laws. However, the company charter provided more independence than did the royal charter of Virginia. The company charter created a General Court to help run the colony. The Puritan colonists turned this court into a type of self-government that tried to represent the needs of the people. Each town sent two or three delegates to the Court. After John Winthrop served as the first governor of Massachusetts, the General Court elected the governor and his assistants. In 1644 the General Court became a two-house legislature. This meant that the lawmaking body had two groups, and all decisions required a majority in each house.

Politics and religion were closely linked in Puritan New England. Government leaders were also church members. Although ministers were not political officials, they often had a great deal of power in Puritan communities. Male church members were the only colonists who could vote. Colonists became full members in the church by becoming what the Puritans called God's "elect," or chosen. Reaching this status was a difficult process. Individuals had to pass a public test to prove that their faith was strong.

In 1636 minister **Thomas Hooker** and his followers decided to leave Massachusetts to help found Connecticut, another New England colony. In 1639 Hooker helped draft the **Fundamental Orders of Connecticut**, a set of principles that made Connecticut's government more democratic. For example, the Orders allowed men who were not church members to vote. As a result of his role, some historians have called Hooker "the father of American democracy." The Fundamental Orders of Connecticut also outlined the powers of the general courts.

"General courts . . . shall have power to make laws or repeal them, to grant levies, to admit . . . freemen, dispose of [distribute] lands undisposed of to several towns or persons."

—The Fundamental Orders of Connecticut

✔ **Reading Check: Finding the Main Idea** What was distinctive about Connecticut's government? Connecticut had the Fundamental Orders of Connecticut, which allowed more people to vote and made the government more representative.

FUNDAMENTAL ORDERS OF CONNECTICUT

This excerpt describes the structure of the government adopted by the citizens of Connecticut in 1639. The Fundamental Orders are an example of the development of representative democracy in the colonies.

It is ordered . . . that there shall be yearly two general assemblies or courts: . . . The first shall be called the Court of Election, wherein shall be yearly chosen . . . public officers . . . which choice shall be made by all that are admitted freemen and have taken the oath of **fidelity**[1]. . . . It is ordered . . . that . . . [each town] shall have power . . . to send four of their freemen as their deputies to every general court; . . . which deputies shall have the power . . . to give their votes . . . as may be for the public good, and unto which the said towns are to be bound.

[1] **fidelity:** faithfulness

Analyzing Primary Sources

1. Who elected the public officials in Connecticut?
2. How are the people represented in the General Court?

⭐ Citizenship

Public Schools. The law that dictated that towns with 50 or more households provide a schoolteacher also stated that any community with more than 100 families needed to maintain a grammar school. Obeying the law was expensive—one city paid its school teacher £25 a year. The General Court could fine towns that ignored this law, and within less than a decade it had raised the fine from £10 to £20. In 1718 the fine was raised again.

CRITICAL THINKING

Why might the General Court raise the fine for maintaining a grammar school?

ANSWER: Students might suggest that the General Court may have wished to show how important education was to the colonies, but it might also have raised the fine because towns had found that it was previously cheaper to pay the fine than to hire a teacher.

ANALYZING PRIMARY SOURCES ANSWERS

1. all admitted freemen who took an oath of fidelity
2. each town was represented by four freemen who voted on their behalf in the General Court

Technology Resources

Everyday Life in America Transparency 3: Gravestone Styles in the English Colonies

LEVEL 2: Organize students into small groups, and have each group create a covenant for a new town it was founding. Ask group members to consider the reasons behind their migration to the American colonies. (*Students' responses might include: the search for better economic conditions, escaping religious persecution, or a desire for a new life elsewhere.*) Groups' covenants should reflect these experiences and values. Call on groups to read their covenants and explain how they arrived at the various segments of the covenants.

COOPERATIVE LEARNING

HOMEWORK Have students imagine that they are reporters for a Massachusetts newspaper during the 1600s. Ask them to write an article describing the events surrounding the forced exile of Anne Hutchinson and Roger Williams. Tell students that in their articles they should mention the ideas of Hutchinson and Williams, how the community reacted to their ideas, and what happened as a result.

★ Daily Life and Customs

New England colonists' lives centered around religion, family duties, and public work. Puritan religion strongly shaped everyday life in colonial New England. On Sundays, Puritans often heard two sermons. These weekly church meetings brought all members of the community together. In general, community life was more stable than in Virginia. Colonists in Virginia tended to be either wealthy or poor. Most colonists who immigrated to New England, however, were somewhere in between. Many New England colonists were skilled workers, and some were experienced farmers. Others had success with fishing enterprises or fur trading.

New England farmers grew food mainly for their own use rather than crops like tobacco for sale. Most New England farms were owned and run entirely by families. These small farms did not bring great wealth to their owners but also did not need as many laborers as did southern plantations. New England thus had little need for indentured servants or slaves.

Most colonists came to New England in family groups. As the colony grew, couples often had many children, who helped run the family farm. Parents helped choose their children's marriage partners in colonial New England in part because marriage involved a transfer of property from one family to another. Puritans believed that women had three main duties to fulfill in marriage. They had to obey their husbands, have children, and run the household. Husbands were expected in turn to treat their wives "with the greatest love, gentleness, kindness, [and] tenderness."

Education was an important part of New England society, largely because mothers and fathers wanted their children to be able to read the Bible. The Massachusetts Bay Colony passed some of the first laws requiring parents to provide instruction for their children. In 1636 John Harvard and the General Court founded Harvard College. Harvard taught ministers and met the colony's need for higher education. By 1700 about 70 percent of the men and 45 percent of the women in New England could read and write. Figures for literacy were much lower in Virginia.

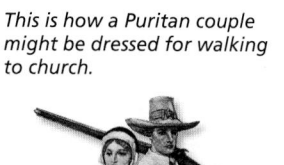

This is how a Puritan couple might be dressed for walking to church.

NEW FRANCE

Land claimed by New York and New Hampshire.

MASSACHUSETTS

Penobscot River

St. Lawrence River

Lake Champlain

Lake Ontario

Connecticut River

44°N

NEW HAMPSHIRE
Portsmouth 1623

Annexed by Massachusetts in 1652.

Hudson River

NEW YORK   MASSACHUSETTS   Salem 1626
Boston 1630   *Massachusetts Bay*   42°N

Hartford 1636   Plymouth 1620
CONNECTICUT   Providence 1636

PENNSYLVANIA   New Haven 1638   RHODE ISLAND   ATLANTIC OCEAN

NEW JERSEY   LONG ISLAND   72°W   70°W   68°W

0   100   200 Miles
0   100   200 Kilometers
Albers Equal-Area Projection

The New England Colonies

Intrepreting Maps Many groups seeking religious freedom settled in New England.

Skills Assessment Human Systems What New England settlement was founded in 1630?

✔ **Reading Check: Contrasting** In what ways were the Massachusetts Bay Colony and the Virginia colony different? family farms vs. plantations; many families, many children vs. fewer families and children; high literacy rate vs. lower emphasis on education

LEVEL 3: Pair students and ask each pair to take the role of either a Puritan official or a religious dissenter in Massachusetts. Then have each pair prepare a two-part written statement of why the official is within their right to banish the dissenter from the colony, and why the dissenter believes he or she should be allowed to stay. *(Students' statements might include: colonists felt dissenters threatened the colony, dissenters' teachings went against church doctrine, religious freedom, the court was overstepping its authority.)* Have volunteers debate their arguments for the class. **COOPERATIVE LEARNING**

☆ CLOSE

Have students write a short story based on either daily life in the Massachusetts Bay Colony or on the problems that the colony experienced during the mid- to late 1600s. Students' stories should be as historically accurate as possible and should include major events from this section.

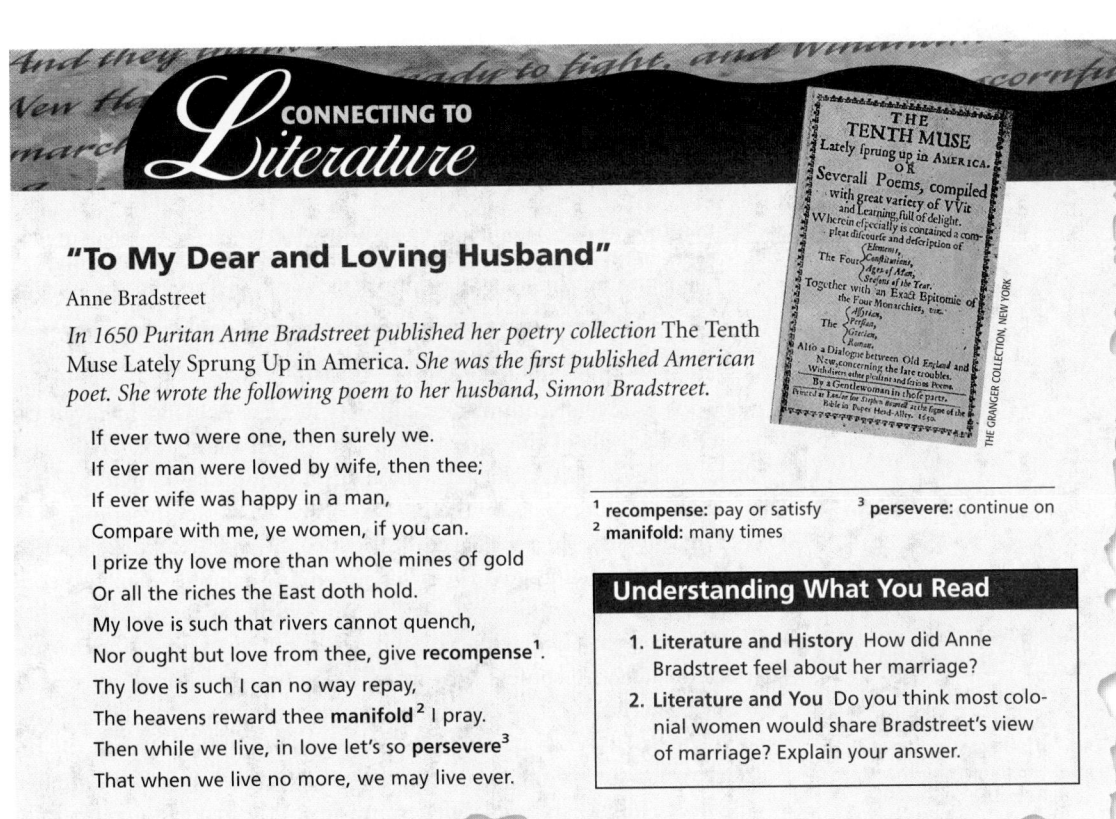

CONNECTING TO *Literature*

"To My Dear and Loving Husband"

Anne Bradstreet

In 1650 Puritan Anne Bradstreet published her poetry collection The Tenth Muse Lately Sprung Up in America. *She was the first published American poet. She wrote the following poem to her husband, Simon Bradstreet.*

If ever two were one, then surely we.
If ever man were loved by wife, then thee;
If ever wife was happy in a man,
Compare with me, ye women, if you can.
I prize thy love more than whole mines of gold
Or all the riches the East doth hold.
My love is such that rivers cannot quench,
Nor ought but love from thee, give **recompense**[1].
Thy love is such I can no way repay,
The heavens reward thee **manifold**[2] I pray.
Then while we live, in love let's so **persevere**[3]
That when we live no more, we may live ever.

THE GRANGER COLLECTION, NEW YORK

[1] **recompense:** pay or satisfy
[2] **manifold:** many times
[3] **persevere:** continue on

Understanding What You Read

1. **Literature and History** How did Anne Bradstreet feel about her marriage?

2. **Literature and You** Do you think most colonial women would share Bradstreet's view of marriage? Explain your answer.

☆ Dissent in Massachusetts

Not all Puritans shared the same religious views. Minister **Roger Williams** did not agree with the leadership of Massachusetts. He called for his church to separate completely from the other New England congregations. Williams also criticized the General Court for taking land from American Indians without paying them.

Puritan leaders worried that Williams's ideas might hurt the colony and made him leave Massachusetts forever. Williams took his supporters to southern New England where they formed a new settlement called Providence. This settlement later became the colony of Rhode Island. Williams received a charter for his small settlement in 1644. In Providence, Williams supported the separation of the church from politics and promoted religious tolerance for all members of the community. In addition, he wanted to deal with American Indians fairly.

In Boston, **Anne Hutchinson** angered Puritan church leaders by publicly discussing religious ideas that some leaders thought radical. For example, Hutchinson believed that God speaks directly to people, apart from the bible. A group of important community members often met at her home for religious discussions.

Interdisciplinary Connection

▶Literature◀

Anne Bradstreet. *The Tenth Muse Lately Sprung Up in America* was published without Bradstreet's knowledge. Although she was embarrassed to see her work in print, she did not stop writing. Her poems show her initial difficulties with life in Massachusetts but also demonstrate her religious faith and her faith in her new home. Today Bradstreet is most admired for the poems that portray domestic life, describing her feelings for her husband and children.

ACTIVITY: Have students conduct research to obtain information about more of Anne Bradstreet's work. Then citing references and using standard grammar, spelling, sentence structure, and punctuation, have them write an essay about how she supported her family.

CONNECTING TO LITERATURE ANSWERS
1. She loves her husband deeply and treasures their marriage.
2. Students' answers will vary, but should support their arguments.

Technology Resources

American Music Selection 3: London Tune: Psalm 19

★ REVIEW AND ASSESS

Have students complete the **Section 3 Review** on p. 108. Then have students complete **Daily Quiz 4.3.** As **Alternative Assessment,** you may want to use either the class meeting or covenant exercise in this section's lessons.

★ RETEACH

Have students complete **Main Idea Activity for English Language Learners and Special-Needs Students 4.3.** Then ask each student to create a "hidden words" puzzle that includes all the key terms and key people in Section 3. Have students exchange and solve their puzzles.
ENGLISH LANGUAGE LEARNERS

★ EXTEND

Ask students to imagine other alternatives open to Puritans considering immigration in the 1620s and to make a list of those alternatives. *(For example, students might mention rebellion against persecutors.)* Then have students research the history of the Puritans' experience in England and the advantages and disadvantages of one of these options by using the library or other resources. Have students report their findings to the class and hold a discussion in which students decide whether immigration to Massachusetts was the best option available and explain why. **BLOCK SCHEDULING**

Section 3 Review
ANSWERS

❶ **Define**
• dissenters, p. 103
• covenant, p. 104

❷ **Identify**
• Great Migration, p. 104

• John Winthrop, p. 104
• Thomas Hooker, p. 105
• Fundamental Orders of Connecticut, p. 105
• Roger Williams, p. 107
• Anne Hutchinson, p. 107

❸ Massachusetts Bay—Puritans led by John Winthrop; religious freedom, representative assembly/ courts; Providence—Roger Williams; religious freedom; Connecticut—Thomas Hooker; more open voting, representative government

❹ **a.** Puritans believed they had a covenant to create an ideal community; government leaders were church members, ministers had great authority in the community; and only male church members could vote
b. banished them for publicly disagreeing with Puritan beliefs

❺ Students' letters will vary, but should note the struggle between the king and Parliament, the growing oppression of Puritans in England, the poor English economy, and the 40,000 English colonists already coming to the Caribbean and North America.

Anne Hutchinson's beliefs led to her exile from Massachusetts.

Research on the R⊙M

Free Find:
Anne Hutchinson
After reading about Anne Hutchinson on the **Holt Researcher CD–ROM,** create a news report that explains both sides of her conflict with religious leaders.

Hutchinson's views alarmed Puritan leaders such as John Winthrop. Puritan officials therefore put Hutchinson on trial for her ideas. The court decided to force Hutchinson out of the colony. With a group of followers, Hutchinson helped found the new colony of Portsmouth on Aquidneck Island (Rhode Island).

✔ **Reading Check: Identifying Cause and Effect** What led to religious disagreements among the Puritans, and what was the result? Williams and Hutchinson both challenged the power of the church. They were banished and founded separate colonies.

★ The Salem Witch Trials

Perhaps the worst community conflicts in New England involved the witchcraft trials of the early 1690s. The largest number of trials were held in Salem, Massachusetts. In Salem a group of girls had accused people of casting spells on them. Most of the accused were women. The community formed a special court to judge the witchcraft cases. During the trials the young girls often screamed and fainted when someone accused of witchcraft entered the room. Witnesses reported they had seen witches speaking with the devil. The court often pressured the suspected witches to confess. One woman accused of witchcraft protested, "There was no other way to save our lives . . . but by our confessing."

The Salem witch trials led to 19 people being put to death. By the next year, many of the local officials and clergymen involved regretted their acts. Judge Samuel Sewall became one of the first to apologize publicly for his role in the wrongs committed by the Salem court.

✔ **Reading Check: Drawing Inferences and Conclusions** What effect do you think the witch trials had on Puritan communities? Students may answer that the witch trials harmed community trust by setting neighbor against neighbor, or they may answer that the community members who agreed with each other came together to get rid of those with different views.

Section **3** Review

go.hrw.com Homework Practice Online
keyword: SA3 HP4

❶ **Define** and explain:
• dissenters
• covenant

❷ **Identify** and explain:
• Great Migration
• John Winthrop
• Thomas Hooker
• Fundamental Orders of Connecticut
• Roger Williams
• Anne Hutchinson

❸ **Summarizing** Copy the chart below. Use it to show how religious beliefs influenced the founding of various New England colonies and their systems of government.

Colony	Founded By	Reason for Founding	Form of Government

❹ **Finding the Main Idea**
a. How did religion and the church influence the government and daily life of the Massachusetts Bay Colony?

b. How did Puritan leaders treat dissenters such as Roger Williams and Anne Hutchinson?

❺ **Writing and Critical Thinking**
Analyzing Information Imagine that you are a Dutch citizen living in London during the time of the Great Migration. Write a letter to your friends in the Netherlands describing the Great Migration and why it is taking place.

Consider the following:
• freedom of religion
• economic and political unrest in England
• the number of English citizens leaving for the Americas

Section 4

OBJECTIVES

⭐ Discuss the role religion played in the founding and development of Maryland.

⭐ Explain how the Carolinas were established and how their economies developed.

⭐ Describe how the middle colonies were founded.

📻 **LET'S GET STARTED!**

Write the following question on the board? *What circumstances might prompt you to create a colony of your own?* As students enter the classroom, have them use what they have already learned about England to create a list of reasons for forming new colonies. *(Students' lists might include: religious reasons, seeking fortune, desire for a different or better life elsewhere.)* Tell students that in Section 4 they will be learning about several new colonies established in the century following the Great Migration, many of which were founded for special purposes.

Section 4

The Southern and Middle Colonies

Read to Discover

1. What role did religion play in the founding and development of Maryland?
2. How were the Carolinas established, and how did their economies develop?
3. How were the middle colonies founded?

WHY IT MATTERS TODAY

The United States continues to receive thousands of immigrants each year. Use **CNNfyi.com** or other **current events** sources to find information on one or more groups of immigrants coming to the United States today. Record your findings in your journal.

Define

• proprietors

Identify

• Cecilius Calvert
• Toleration Act of 1649
• Peter Stuyvesant
• Quakers
• William Penn
• James Oglethorpe

SECTION 4 RESOURCES

REPRODUCIBLE

▶ Guided Reading Strategy 4.4
▶ Geography Activity 4: The Settling of the Colonies
▶ Graphic Organizer 4: English Colonial Settlements

TECHNOLOGY

▶ One-Stop Planner, Lesson 4.4
▶ Exploring America's Past Video Segment: Diary of a Young Girl; Teacher's Guide, pp. 6–7
▶ Homework Practice Online
▶ HRW Go site

REINFORCEMENT, REVIEW, AND ASSESSMENT

▶ Section 4 Review, p. 115
▶ Daily Quiz 4.4
▶ Main Idea Activity 4.4
▶ English Audio Summary 4.4
▶ Spanish Audio Summary 4.4

The Story Continues

The English ship the *Ark* sailed into Chesapeake Bay. As it did, one passenger, Father Andrew White, looked out in wonder. He called the Potomac the "greatest river I have seene, so that the Thames is but a little finger to it." The *Ark* and its sister ship, the *Dove*, landed along the banks of the Potomac in March 1634. Most of the colonists on board were Catholic. On the riverbank, the colonists made a cross out of a large tree to celebrate their first Catholic mass in the new colony.

Maryland's St. Ignatius Church was established in 1641.

⭐ Tolerant Maryland

Many English Catholics came to America for the same reason that many Puritans did. They wanted to escape religious persecution. English Catholics had long been against England's separation from the Roman Catholic Church. For this reason, they were not allowed by the Church of England to worship freely. England's leaders also feared that English

✪ TEACH

Have students read Section 4 and complete Guided Reading Strategy 4.4. Choose one or more of the following activities to explore the section content with students. For further suggestions on block scheduling or team teaching, see the *Block Scheduling Handbook with Team Teaching Strategies*.

LEVEL 1: Organize the class into groups and ask each group to create a bulleted list about life in Maryland. *(Students' lists might include: why the colony developed; employment opportunities; the role Lord Baltimore played in its founding; or points about lifestyle, religion, and other opportunities in the colony.)* Have volunteers present their lists to the class.

ENGLISH LANGUAGE LEARNERS , COOPERATIVE LEARNING

★ Economics

Lord Baltimore's Original Plan. Lord Baltimore planned a development of great estates called honours or baronies in the colonies. Each new baron was to settle his manor with peasants who would work the land and receive enough food and shelter to assure their survival. The baron's rule would only be subject to the rule of the lord proprietor.

ACTIVITY: Have students write a letter to Lord Baltimore from a person in Virginia, explaining why this plan might not be feasible in the American colonies.

Technology Resources

Exploring America's Past Video Segment: Diary of a Young Girl; Teacher's Guide, pp. 6–7

Search 13041, Play to 19806
Videodisc Red Side A
See *Teacher's Guide* for Spanish barcode.

Cecilius Calvert never visited the colony that he founded.

Analyzing Primary Sources

Drawing Inferences and Conclusions What historical events in Europe might have caused Lord Baltimore to introduce the Toleration Act? Students might mention religious wars and persecution of religious groups in some countries

Catholics would aid Catholic countries, such as France and Spain. In 1632 King Charles I gave **Cecilius Calvert** a charter to found a new colony. Also known as Lord Baltimore, Calvert intended the colony to be a refuge for English Catholics. He named the southern colony Maryland in honor of England's queen, Henrietta Maria.

Maryland was a proprietary colony. This meant that **proprietors**, or owners, controlled the government. Maryland was located just north of Virginia in the Chesapeake Bay area. In 1634 about 200 colonists arrived in Maryland to start a settlement.

Settlers in Maryland benefited from the lessons learned by the Jamestown colonists. They spent their time raising corn, cattle, and hogs. This way they would have enough to eat. Before long, however, many colonists turned their energies to growing tobacco for profit. Most of the colonists were men, and there were few families in Maryland at first.

Although Catholics founded Maryland, a growing number of Protestants began moving there in the 1640s. Soon religious conflicts between the two groups arose. To reduce tensions, Lord Baltimore presented a bill to the colonial assembly that became known as the **Toleration Act of 1649**. It made restricting the religious rights of Christians a crime. This act was one of the first laws supporting religious tolerance passed in the English colonies.

 ❝No person or persons whatsoever within this province . . . professing [claiming] to believe in Jesus Christ shall . . . be any way troubled, molested [persecuted], or . . . any way compelled [forced] to the belief or exercise of any other religion against his or her consent.❞

—Lord Baltimore, quoted in *Colonial America*, by Richard Middleton

The Toleration Act did not put an end to all religious conflict. However, it did show that the government wanted to offer some religious freedom and to protect the rights of minority groups.

✔ **Reading Check: Finding the Main Idea** How did religion shape the Maryland colony? Religious persecution of Catholics in England led to the establishment of the colony; religious conflicts led to the Toleration Act of 1649, which promoted religious tolerance.

★ The Carolinas

In 1663 Charles II gave much of the land between Virginia and Spanish Florida to eight of his supporters. These colonial proprietors named the new southern colony Carolina, which is a Latin form of the name *Charles*. For many years Carolina was a single colony. However, the settlements within the colony were widely divided, making it hard for leaders to govern them all. Finally, in 1712 North and South Carolina became separate colonies. Most of the colonists in North Carolina were farmers who had moved south from Virginia. Unlike Virginia, North Carolina had few plantations. The colony had no towns and few churches until the early 1700s.

	Founded by	Types of Colonists	Major Events
New York	*originally founded by Dutch and called New Netherland*	*mainly fur traders and farmers*	*an Englishman, the Duke of York, challenged the Dutch to the claim of the colony and prevailed*
New Jersey	*proprietors Sir John Carteret and Lord John Berkeley from England*	*Dutch, Swedes, Finns, and Scots*	*eventually divided into an eastern and western province until England united East and West NJ into a single colony in 1702*
Pennsylvania	*William Penn who sought religious freedom and just government*	*Quakers, Welsh, Irish Quakers, Germans (Pennsylvania Dutch)*	*colony grew rapidly because Penn advertised throughout Europe for colonists and offered religious freedom*

Colonial settlement in South Carolina began in 1670. That year three ships arrived from London with about 100 settlers. The colonists founded the port of Charles Town, which later became Charleston. Colonists who paid their own way to South Carolina received large grants of land. South Carolina drew many settlers from other English colonies, particularly from the British West Indies. These Caribbean colonists brought enslaved Africans with them. Because of this, South Carolina became one of the first colonies to depend mainly on the work of slaves.

Some colonists thought that rice might grow well in South Carolina's lowland swamps. However, they had little experience growing the crop. Many historians believe that African laborers taught the colonists how to raise rice in the 1690s. By the mid-1700s South Carolina's royal governor James Glen saw a change. He reported that "the only Commodity of Consequence [importance] produced in South Carolina is Rice."

Rice production required many workers, and plantation owners chose to meet their growing labor needs by using slaves. By 1730 about 20,000 enslaved Africans were living in the colony, compared to half as many white settlers. South Carolina was the only mainland colony with a higher population of enslaved Africans than free whites.

The proprietors' poor management of the Carolinas displeased the colonists. In 1719 the British government bought South Carolina from the original proprietors. The Crown then bought North Carolina in 1729, making it a royal colony as well.

✔ **Reading Check: Analyzing Information** How was South Carolina different from the other colonies, and why was this the case? had a mainly black population; Caribbean colonists brought slaves to South Carolina, rice production needed many workers

Daily Life

Charleston Charleston was the commercial, political, and social center of South Carolina. Because of the city's climate and location, many planters and officials chose to make it home. Soon, the wealth of merchants and planters helped build Charleston's cultural life. Cultural attractions included the city's library society and one of two newspapers published in the southern colonies. Over the years, Charleston's architecture has become another famous feature. Instead of using official buildings, government officials met in the large private homes of political leaders. **What features do you see in the image that might have drawn people to Charleston?**

THE GRANGER COLLECTION, NEW YORK

★ **Constitutional Heritage**

The Carolina Constitution. In 1699 the Earl of Shaftesbury wrote the Fundamental Constitutions for the Carolina colony. In them he divided the land between estates for proprietors, large blocks for colonial nobility, and smaller pieces for farmers. This plan never took effect because it was too complicated.

CRITICAL THINKING
How do you think settlers might have reacted to the plan that Shaftesbury presented?

ANSWER: Students might suggest that small farmers may have liked it because it guaranteed them land, but others may not have wanted to restrict land ownership.

DAILY LIFE ANSWER
Students might suggest that Charleston appears to be a busy trading port and that there is easy access to the water.

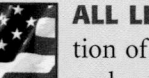
⭐ Diversity in New York and New Jersey

The Dutch founded New Netherland on the Hudson River in 1613 as a trading post for exchanging furs with the Iroquois. The town of New Amsterdam became the center of the fur trade in New Netherland. This settlement was founded on Manhattan Island. Most colonists in New Amsterdam were fur traders and farmers. Generous land grants and religious tolerance soon brought Jews, French Huguenots, Puritans, and others to the colony. Director General **Peter Stuyvesant** took control of the colony beginning in 1647. Stuyvesant was an experienced soldier with a wooden leg who ruled the colony as a dictator.

In 1664 the English took control of New Netherland when an English fleet captured New Amsterdam without a shot. New Netherland became an English colony and was renamed New York, the first of the middle colonies. Many Dutch settlers remained in the colony, shaping colonial life in different ways. For example, the Dutch contributed words such as *boss*, *cookie*, and *stoop* to the English language.

Soon after the conquest in 1664, the Duke of York made Sir George Carteret and John Lord Berkeley proprietors of New Jersey. This colony occupied lands between the Hudson and Delaware Rivers. It had a diverse population, including Dutch, Swedes, Finns, and Scots.

The fur trade remained important to New York's economy, and overseas trade grew over time. Both New York and New Jersey also produced large amounts of wheat.

✔ **Reading Check: Sequencing** List in their proper order the steps that established the colonies of New York and New Jersey. See text above for proper sequence.

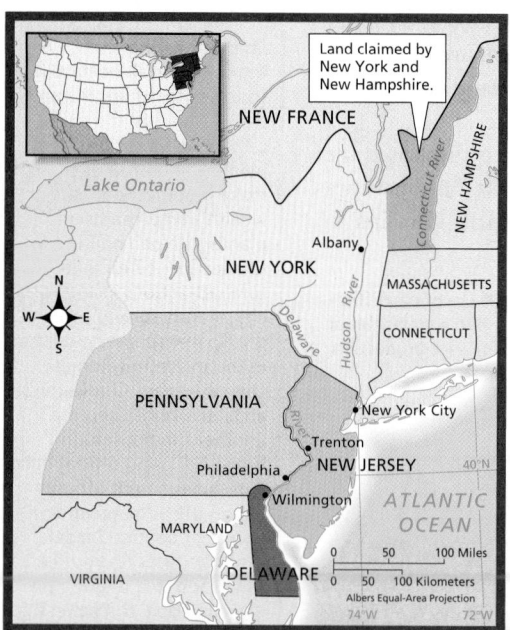

Land claimed by New York and New Hampshire.

NEW FRANCE

Lake Ontario

Albany

NEW YORK

MASSACHUSETTS

CONNECTICUT

PENNSYLVANIA

New York City

Trenton

Philadelphia

NEW JERSEY

Wilmington

MARYLAND

VIRGINIA

DELAWARE

ATLANTIC OCEAN

0   50   100 Miles
0   50   100 Kilometers
Albers Equal-Area Projection

The Middle Colonies

Interpreting Maps The middle colonies were formed from land grants given by King Charles II.

Skills Assessment The World in Spatial Terms What river connects major cities in Delaware, New Jersey, and Pennsylvania?

After the English captured New Amsterdam, they renamed it New York, in honor of the Duke of York.

THE GRANGER COLLECTION, NEW YORK

LEVEL 2: Ask each student to write a paragraph summarizing how the middle colonies were founded. *(Students' paragraphs will vary but should include information on New York, New Jersey, and Pennsylvania.)* Encourage students to reference the section for their paragraphs. Assign each student a partner. Then have partners exchange paragraphs, read them, and evaluate the summaries presented.

COOPERATIVE LEARNING

LEVEL 3: Locate the Rhode Island Charter (1663) and the Pennsylvania Charter of Privileges (1701) and select excerpts from each that show the degree of religious toleration permitted in each colony. Also refer to the excerpt from the Toleration Act of 1649 quoted on textbook page 110. Have students read and analyze the three sources. Then discuss the varying levels of freedom permitted in the three colonies. Encourage students to think of explanations for the differences in the levels of freedom each document permitted.

THE GRANGER COLLECTION, NEW YORK

★ The Pennsylvania Experiment

The Society of Friends, or the **Quakers**, made up one of the largest religious groups in New Jersey. The Quakers were a Protestant sect founded by George Fox in the mid-1600s in England. Quakers believed that all people had an "inner light" that could help them experience God. They rejected formal religious practices and dressed plainly. The Quakers supported nonviolence as well as religious tolerance for all peoples. Such views differed from those of many Christians. As a result, Quakers were persecuted in both England and the American colonies.

One proprietor of the New Jersey colony was a Quaker named **William Penn**. Penn wished to found a larger colony under his own control that would provide a safe home for Quakers. In 1681 King Charles II agreed to grant Penn a charter to begin a colony west of New Jersey.

Known as Pennsylvania, this middle colony grew rapidly. Penn tried to create a government that was fair to all its people. He limited his own powers so that "the will of one man may not hinder [harm] the good of a whole country." He also provided a means of changing the colony's laws to reflect the will of the people. Penn sold land to colonists at low prices, and he also promised religious freedom to all Christians. In addition, Penn said that the government would care for the poor. His work

Interpreting the Visual Record

Quaker meeting *Many of the colonists in Pennsylvania were farmers and helped create a peaceful and stable society there.* **What does this image suggest about life in Pennsylvania?**

★ Biography

Education in Pennsylvania. In 1749 Benjamin Franklin wrote a book entitled *Proposals Relating to the Education of Youth in Pennsylvania.* He believed that school should emphasize self-expression, and that children should not only learn to write, but that they should also write what they learned in their own words and create their own stories. Franklin believed that their studies should be led by a schoolteacher who did not rely on rote memorization but instead could explain what children needed to know.

CRITICAL THINKING

What do Franklin's ideas from his book show about his beliefs regarding educating children?

ANSWER: Students might suggest that Franklin believed that children would learn more if they were allowed to be creative and use their own reason.

Visual Record Answer

Students might suggest that life appears to be tranquil and orderly.

BIOGRAPHY ANSWER
(for p. 114)
He insisted on fair dealings with local American Indians, welcomed immigrants, promised religious toleration, and did not require settlers to serve in a colonial militia.

LEVEL 3: Explain to students that the Toleration Act of 1649 made it a crime to restrict the religious rights of Christians. Tell them that Lord Baltimore presented the bill to the colonial assembly and that it was eventually made into law. Ask students to write an essay explaining why Lord Baltimore and the colonial assembly would have wanted such a law. Encourage students to consider that Maryland had a population consisting of both Catholics and Protestants. Ask volunteers to explain their reasoning to the class.

★ CLOSE

Have each student select a colony discussed in this section and then prepare a picture-postcard with a message to a friend or relative that briefly describes the immigrant's experience in the colony and the items for which the colony is known. "Send" the postcards to other members of the class, and invite comment by the recipient on the accuracy of the picture and its message.

★ ★ ★ ★ ★ ★ ★ ★ ★ ★ ★ ★

Section 4 Review
ANSWERS

❶ Define
• proprietors, p.110

❷ Identify
• Cecilius Calvert,
  p. 110
• Toleration Act of 1649,
  p. 110
• Peter Stuyvesant,
  p. 112
• Quakers, p. 113
• William Penn,
  p. 113
• James Oglethorpe,
  p. 114

❸ MD—religious freedom; proprietary; tobacco farming; NC—political, proprietary, small farms; SC—economic, proprietary, rice plantations; NY—political, royal; NJ—political, proprietary; PA—religious/political, proprietary, farming; GA—political, proprietary, small farms and then plantations

❹ a. Catholics settled to escape religious persecution; Toleration Act of 1649 provided some religious freedom and protection for minority groups.
b. 1663; poor farmers and few plantations in North Carolina, large plantations, rice, and slave labor in South Carolina

❺ Students' pamphlets will vary but they should include the following: New Netherland captured from the Dutch; William Penn's role and the middle colonies' economy.

BIOGRAPHY

William Penn

(1644–1718)

William Penn was born in London, the son of a wealthy admiral. Penn joined the Quakers in 1666 and became an active preacher and writer of religious works. He supported toleration for dissenters. In 1681 he received a charter to establish a new colony called Pennsylvania. There Penn put his beliefs into practice. He insisted on fair dealings with local American Indians, welcomed immigrants, and promised religious toleration. Because he believed in nonviolence, he did not require settlers to serve in a colonial militia.

Although Penn played a major role in establishing Pennsylvania, he lived there only a few years. **How did William Penn put his Quaker beliefs into practice when he founded Pennsylvania?**

made Pennsylvania a key example of representative self-government in the colonies. Some of the largest groups to arrive in the colony were Welsh and Irish Quakers, and Germans. After arriving, many became farmers. These groups helped create a peaceful and stable society in Pennsylvania. Penn described one type of colonist he was seeking.

History Makers Speak

❝Another sort of person [who is] . . . necessary in the colonies is the person of universal spirits. These people are concerned about the future. They both understand and promote good discipline and just government. Such persons . . . may find a place in the colonies for their good advice. These people deserve our esteem and should be encouraged to settle here.❞

—William Penn, "Some Account of the Province of Pennsylvania in America"

Penn named the capital of his colony Philadelphia, or the City of Brotherly Love. Penn designed the city himself. He laid it out in a checkerboard pattern that became a model for city planners in other colonies. Pennsylvania grew a great deal in 1682. That year the Duke of York sold Penn a region to the south of Pennsylvania. This area, called Delaware, remained part of Pennsylvania until 1776.

✔ **Reading Check: Finding the Main Idea** Why did William Penn establish Pennsylvania, and how did he influence its government? safe haven for Quakers; promoted religious freedom, established an example of fair, representative self-government

★ The Ideal of Georgia

The English also founded the southern colony of Georgia. In 1732 King George II granted a charter to **James Oglethorpe** and other trustees. They received permission to start a colony for poor English citizens. Among the group were people who had been jailed for unpaid debts. The king hoped that Georgia would also serve as a shield between South Carolina and Spanish Florida.

In 1733 Oglethorpe and 120 other English colonists founded the city of Savannah on the coast of Georgia. Many of the early colonists were German, Swiss, and Welsh Protestants. Jewish settlers also moved to Savannah. Oglethorpe had high hopes for the Georgia settlement.

History Makers Speak

❝The examples of other colonies suggest that the new colony will succeed. . . . Georgia is even more likely to succeed than either Virginia or Pennsylvania were.❞

James Oglethorpe, quoted in *Voices of America*, edited by Thomas R. Frazier

Oglethorpe wanted his colony to be different from the other southern colonies. He did not want Georgia to have large plantations ruled by a few wealthy individuals. He hoped that the colony would draw small farmers and avoid the rise of a class of wealthy planters. To reach this goal, Oglethorpe outlawed slavery and limited the size of land grants. He also gave poor colonists free passage to Georgia. Colonists received cattle, land, and food until they could provide their own. Soon, however,

✪ REVIEW AND ASSESS

Have students complete the **Section 4 Review** on p. 115. Then have students complete **Daily Quiz 4.4**. As **Alternative Assessment**, you may want to use either the map or chart exercise in this section's lessons.

✪ RETEACH

Have students complete **Main Idea Activity for English Language Learners and Special-Needs Students 4.4**. Then organize students into groups of three. Have each group make an annotated outline of the section with brief summaries of each subsection. **ENGLISH LANGUAGE LEARNERS**

✪ EXTEND

Organize the class into several groups, assigning each group an English colonial proprietor discussed in this section. Have each group prepare an oral presentation on the assigned proprietor. Encourage students to use charts, maps, pictures, and other illustrations. Finally, have groups make their presentations to the class. **BLOCK SCHEDULING**

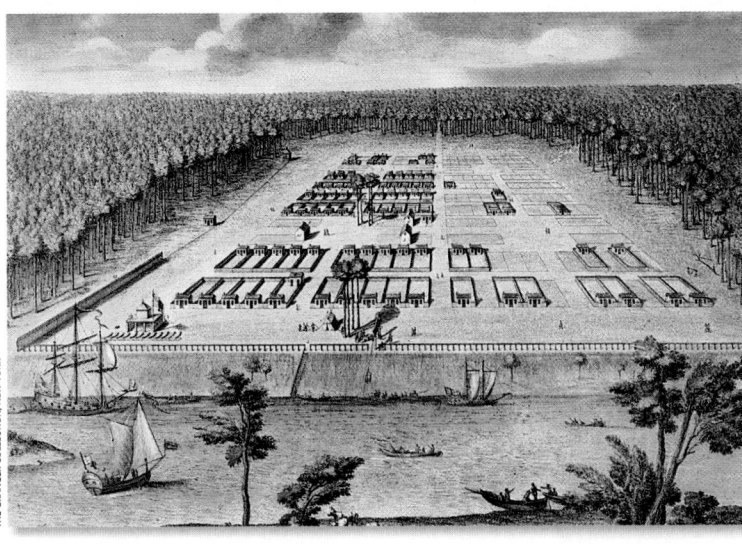

THE GRANGER COLLECTION, NEW YORK

Interpreting the Visual Record

An orderly community *James Oglethorpe carefully planned the town of Savannah, Georgia.* **What suggests that this town has been planned?**

the settlers grew unhappy with Oglethorpe's strict rules. For example, many settlers wanted to allow slavery. They also wanted to have larger farms.

Finally, in 1752 the trustees of Georgia gave up their charter. The English government then made Georgia a royal colony with new laws. Coastal Georgia was soon filled with large rice plantations worked by thousands of slaves.

✔ **Reading Check: Analyzing Information** How did James Oglethorpe hope to make Georgia's population different from the other colonies? Oglethorpe wanted to provide opportunities for poor English citizens, including jailed debtors. To achieve this, he and his backers tried to limit the size of farms and help pay the way for poor immigrants.

Section 4 Review

go.hrw.com **Homework Practice Online**

keyword: SA3 HP4

❶ Define and explain:
• proprietors

❷ Identify and explain:
• Cecilius Calvert
• Toleration Act of 1649
• Peter Stuyvesant
• Quakers
• William Penn
• James Oglethorpe

❸ Comparing and Contrasting Copy the chart below. Use it to compare and contrast the reasons why each of the colonies discussed in this section was founded. Include the type of charter given to each colony and its main economic pursuit.

Colony	Reason for Founding	Type of Charter	Economic Pursuit
MD			
NC			
SC			
NY			
NJ			
PA			
GA			

❹ Finding the Main Idea
a. In what ways did religion affect settlement and law in the Maryland colony?

b. When were the Carolinas founded, and how were their economies different from each other?

❺ Writing and Critical Thinking
Summarizing Imagine that you are a colonial historian. Create a pamphlet describing the founding and development of the middle colonies.

Consider the following:
• the capture of New Netherland
• the role of William Penn
• the economies of the middle colonies

Visual Record Answer

Students might suggest that the grid arrangement suggests a planned community.

CHAPTER 4 REVIEW ANSWERS

The Chapter at a Glance
Students' charts should list the following: Economic—Jamestown, New Hampshire, New York, Carolinas, Delaware; Political—Plymouth, Massachusetts Bay, Connecticut, Maryland, Rhode Island, New Jersey, Pennsylvania; Social—Georgia

Identifying People and Ideas
Students' sentences should indicate an understanding of the following definitions:

1. Bacon led a group of slaves, freed slaves, and former servants in an attack against some American Indians, and then they attacked and burned Jamestown in protest against rising taxes and lack of farmland.

2. extreme Separatist sect of Puritans who wanted to develop their own church and cut all ties with the Church of England

3. a legal contract in which 41 male passengers of the *Mayflower* agreed to create laws for the good of the community

4. Pawtuxet who taught the Pilgrims how to plant and fish, was their guide, and worked out a peace treaty with the Wampanoag.

5. governor of the Massachusetts Bay Colony

CHAPTER

4

REVIEW AND ASSESSMENT RESOURCES

REPRODUCIBLE
▶ Vocabulary Activity 4

TECHNOLOGY
▶ Chapter 4 Test Generator (on the One-Stop Planner)
▶ Global Skill Builder CD–ROM
▶ HRW Go Site

REINFORCEMENT, REVIEW, AND ASSESSMENT
▶ Chapter 4 Review, pp. 115–17
▶ Chapter 4 Tutorial for Students, Parents, Mentors, and Peers

▶ Chapter 4 Test (Form A or B)
▶ Alternative Assessment Handbook
▶ Chapter 4 Test for English Language Learners and Special-Needs Students

★ REVIEW
Have students complete the **Chapter 4 Review** on pages 116–17.

★ ASSESS
Use one of the chapter tests to assess students' understanding of the content. **For Alternative Assessment**, see the **Alternative Assessment Handbook**.

6. solemn promise

7. set of principles which defined the powers of the Connecticut government

8. banished from Massachusetts because she claimed to speak directly to God

9. Maryland law that made persecution of other Christians a crime

10. a Quaker who founded Pennsylvania where he offered religious freedom to all Christians

Understanding Main Ideas

1. poor preparation, lack of skilled workers, poor location, conflicts with Powhatan

2. Samoset shared useful information; Squanto taught agricultural practices

3. they fought for religious freedom

4. North Carolina—poor farmers from Virginia, few plantations; South Carolina—wealthy colonists, some from the British West Indies who brought enslaved Africans with them, large plantations; Georgia—poor English citizens including debtors, small land grants, no slavery

Chapter **4** Review

The Chapter at a Glance

Examine the visual summary of the chapter below. Use the visual summary to create a chart comparing the thirteen colonies that shows which were founded for economic, political, or social reasons. If a colony was founded for more than one reason, list it in all appropriate columns on the chart.

New England Colonies

Massachusetts: Founded for religious freedom; Plymouth, 1620; Massachusetts Bay, 1630
New Hampshire: Founded for farming in 1623
Connecticut: Founded for political and religious freedom in 1635
Rhode Island: Founded for religious freedom in 1636

Middle Colonies

New York: Originally New Netherland; captured by England in 1664
New Jersey: Founded for farming and trade in 1664
Pennsylvania: Founded for religious freedom in 1682
Delaware: Established in 1776

Southern Colonies

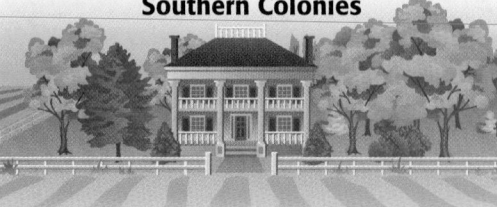

Virginia: Jamestown founded in 1607 to find wealth
Maryland: Founded in 1634 for religious freedom
North and South Carolina: Founded in 1670 for farming and trade; divided into two colonies in the 1700s
Georgia: Founded in 1733 to provide relief for poor and protection from Spanish Florida

Identifying People and Ideas

Use the following terms or people in historically significant sentences.
1. Bacon's Rebellion
2. Pilgrims
3. Mayflower Compact
4. Squanto
5. John Winthrop
6. covenant
7. Fundamental Orders of Connecticut
8. Anne Hutchinson
9. Toleration Act of 1649
10. William Penn

Understanding Main Ideas

Section 1 *(Pages 92–97)*
1. What factors made it difficult for the Jamestown settlement to survive?

Section 2 *(Pages 98–102)*
2. In what ways did American Indians help the Pilgrims survive in Plymouth?

Section 3 *(Pages 103–108)*
3. How did Puritan dissenters such as Roger Williams contribute to the development of self-government in the colonies?

Section 4 *(Pages 109–115)*
4. Contrast the founding and settlement of the Carolinas, Georgia, and Maryland.

You Be the Historian— Reviewing Themes

1. **Geography** How did climate and geography affect the colonies' development?
2. **Economics** Why were indentured servants and enslaved Africans more important to the southern colonies' economies than to New England's?
3. **Culture** Why did Catholics, Puritans, and Quakers immigrate to America, and what colonies did they establish?

Thinking Critically

1. **Evaluating** Why was it important for members of colonial families to support each other?
2. **Comparing and Contrasting** Compare and contrast the economic reasons for founding each of the thirteen colonies.
3. **Categorizing** What were the social differences between the colonies at Jamestown and Plymouth, and what caused those differences?

★ RETEACH

★ RETEACH

Ask students to make lists of circumstances that (a) *pushed* English people away from England and that (b) *pulled* them specifically toward either Virginia, the New England colonies, the middle colonies, or the southern colonies.

ENGLISH LANGUAGE LEARNERS

Portfolio Extensions

1. Cooperative Learning

Have students complete the following activity in small groups. Ask them to imagine that their group is an English company responsible for putting together a group of colonists to settle in America. Have students decide how many people to take with them, what kinds of occupations they should have, and where to settle. Then have them write a short skit about their first month in the settlement.

2. Linking to Community Tell students that William Penn's ideas about government significantly influenced the success of Pennsylvania and its capital city, Philadelphia. Then ask them to prepare an oral report on the founder(s) of their community or those of a nearby community. Students should use the local library and both primary and secondary sources for their research. Remind students to explain how the founders influenced the development of the community.

Social Studies Skills Workshop

Interpreting Maps

Study the map below. Then use the information on the map to help you answer the questions that follow.

The Thirteen Colonies

1. Using your knowledge of the period, explain why it would have been important for major towns to be located along rivers or along the coast.

2. Which colonies were known as the middle colonies?
   a. Georgia, Maryland, North Carolina, South Carolina, and Virginia
   b. Connecticut, Massachusetts, New Hampshire, and Rhode Island
   c. Delaware, New Jersey, New York, and Pennsylvania
   d. New Hampshire and New York

Analyzing Primary Sources

Read the following quotation by a woman accused of witchcraft in Massachusetts, and then answer the questions that follow.

❝There was no other way to save our lives, . . . but by our confessing. . . . Indeed, that confession, that it is said we made, was no other than what was suggested to us by some gentlemen, they telling us that we were witches, and they knew it and we knew it, which made us thinking that it was so. . . . Some time after, when we were better composed, they telling us what we had confessed, we did profess that we were innocent and ignorant of such things.❞

3. Which of the following statements best describes the claim being made by the accused woman?
   a. She and her friends are now convinced that they are witches.
   b. She and her friends confessed out of confusion and to save their lives.
   c. The confessions were given freely and fairly.
   d. There was a lot of evidence to back up the confessions.

4. Based on the information in this quote, do you think the woman and her friends received a fair trial? Explain your answer.

Alternative Assessment

Building Your Portfolio

Interdisciplinary Connection to Geography

Imagine that you are an English merchant traveling through the thirteen colonies to find new trade goods. Create a travel journal of your trip through the colonies. Include a map showing your route and descriptions of the people, places, and types of goods you encounter. Your journal should have at least one entry for each of the thirteen colonies.

🖳 internet connect

Internet Activity: go.hrw.com
keyword: SA3 CF4

Choose a topic about the English Colonies to:

● Research settlement in Jamestown and create a graph to illustrate your information.
● Construct a scale model of a colonial home.
● Learn about colonial cuisine.

You Be the Historian— Reviewing Themes

1. affected the health and life span of the colonists, determined the agriculture and economy of the colony

2. southern economy was based on large crops such as tobacco and rice which required many workers

3. religious persecution in England; Maryland, Massachusetts Bay, Pennsylvania

Thinking Critically

1. the labor of all family members was important to the survival of small farms and the creation of stable communities.

2. Students should refer to their textbook for answers.

3. reasons for immigrating, goals for the colony, relationship with American Indians; Jamestown had fewer families, less education; Plymouth was a family-centered community

Skills Workshop

1. to provide access for easier transportation and trade

2. c

3. b

4. Students may note that this woman and her friends appear to have been forced to confess under duress.

5 Life in the English Colonies

CHAPTER RESOURCE MANAGER

Objectives	Pacing Guide	Reproducible Resources
SECTION 1: **Forms of Government** (pp. 120–25) ★ Describe how representative government developed in the colonies. ★ Explain how the colonists influenced the rulings of colonial courts. ★ Evaluate how the Dominion of New England affected the New England colonies. ★ Analyze how the English Bill of Rights influenced colonists.	**Regular** 1.5 days **Block Scheduling** 1 day *Block Scheduling Handbook with Team Teaching Strategies, Chapter 5*	**RS** Guided Reading Strategy 5.1
SECTION 2: **The Growth of Trade** (pp. 126–30) ★ Evaluate the effects the Navigation Acts had on colonial economies. ★ Describe the types of trade that took place in the colonies during the 1700s. ★ Analyze why the colonies participated in the slave trade.	**Regular** 1.5 days **Block Scheduling** .5 day *Block Scheduling Handbook with Team Teaching Strategies, Chapter 5*	**RS** Guided Reading Strategy 5.2 **PS** Literature Reading 5: Narrative of the Life of Olaudah Equiano **E** Hands-On History Activity: Religions in Your Community
SECTION 3: **The Colonial Economy** (pp. 131–35) ★ Explain why enslaved Africans were the main workforce in the southern colonies. ★ Identify how New England's economic activities were different from those of the southern colonies. ★ Describe how the middle colonies combined economic aspects of the southern and New England colonies.	**Regular** 2 days **Block Scheduling** 1 day *Block Scheduling Handbook with Team Teaching Strategies, Chapter 5*	**RS** Guided Reading Strategy 5.3 **SM** Geography Activity 5: Agriculture in the Colonies
SECTION 4: **The Great Awakening** (pp. 136–39) ★ Analyze the message of the Great Awakening. ★ Describe how the Great Awakening changed colonial religious organizations and leaders. ★ Explain how the Great Awakening changed colonial society.	**Regular** 1.5 days **Block Scheduling** .5 day *Block Scheduling Handbook with Team Teaching Strategies, Chapter 5*	**RS** Guided Reading Strategy 5.4 **PS** Primary Source Reading 5: "Sinners in the Hands of an Angry God"
SECTION 5: **American Culture** (pp. 140–45) ★ Explain how both the Scientific Revolution and the Enlightenment reflected new ways of thinking. ★ Describe education during colonial times. ★ Identify Benjamin Franklin's key achievements. ★ Analyze contributions that were made to American culture in the 1700s.	**Regular** 2 days **Block Scheduling** 1 day *Block Scheduling Handbook with Team Teaching Strategies, Chapter 5*	**RS** Guided Reading Strategy 5.5 **PS** Biography Reading 5: Benjamin Banneker **RS** Graphic Organizer 5: Colonial Life **E** Creative Teaching Strategy: Resource Speaker

Chapter Resource Key

PS Primary Sources	**A** Assessment	Music	
RS Reading Support	**REV** Review	Video	
IC Interdisciplinary Connections	**ELL** Reinforcement and English Language Learners	Internet	
E Enrichment	🖳 Transparencies	Holt Presentation Maker Using Microsoft® PowerPoint®	
SM Skills Mastery	💿 CD–ROM		

 One-Stop Planner CD–ROM

See the *One-Stop Planner* for a complete list of additional resources for students and teachers.

One-Stop Planner CD–ROM

It's easy to plan lessons, select resources, and print out materials for your students when you use the *Texas One-Stop Planner CD–ROM with Test Generator.*

Technology Resources	Reinforcement, Review, and Assessment
Texas One-Stop Planner, Lesson 5.1 Homework Practice Online	**REV** Section 1 Review, p. 125 **A** Daily Quiz 5.1 **ELL** Main Idea Activity 5.1 **ELL** English Audio Summary 5.1 **ELL** Spanish Audio Summary 5.1 ⭐ TAKS Every Day!
Texas One-Stop Planner, Lesson 5.2 Linking Geography and History Transparency 5: The Slave Trade, 1451–1870 Holt Researcher: American History CD–ROM **CNN** Presents America: Yesterday and Today, Beginnings to 1914 Segment: Two Stories of Slavery Homework Practice Online HRW Go site	**REV** Section 2 Review, p. 130 **A** Daily Quiz 5.2 **ELL** Main Idea Activity 5.2 **ELL** English Audio Summary 5.2 **ELL** Spanish Audio Summary 5.2 ⭐ TAKS Every Day!
Texas One-Stop Planner, Lesson 5.3 Linking Geography and History Transparency 7: Major Colonial Economies Homework Practice Online	**REV** Section 3 Review, p. 135 **A** Daily Quiz 5.3 **ELL** Main Idea Activity 5.3 **ELL** English Audio Summary 5.3 **ELL** Spanish Audio Summary 5.3 ⭐ TAKS Every Day!
Texas One-Stop Planner, Lesson 5.4 Everyday Life in America Transparency 3: Gravestone Styles in the English Colonies Holt Researcher: American History CD–ROM Homework Practice Online	**REV** Section 4 Review, p. 139 **A** Daily Quiz 5.4 **ELL** Main Idea Activity 5.4 **ELL** English Audio Summary 5.4 **ELL** Spanish Audio Summary 5.4 ⭐ TAKS Every Day!
 Texas One-Stop Planner, Lesson 5.5 Exploring America's Past Video Segment: Made in America; Teacher's Guide, pp. 8–9 American Music Selection 4: "Springfield Mountain" Homework Practice Online HRW Go site	**REV** Section 5 Review, p. 144 **A** Daily Quiz 5.5 **ELL** Main Idea Activity 5.5 **ELL** English Audio Summary 5.5 **ELL** Spanish Audio Summary 5.5 ⭐ TAKS Every Day!

internet connect

HRW ONLINE RESOURCES
GO TO: go.hrw.com
Then type in a keyword.

TEACHER HOME PAGE
KEYWORD: SA3 Teacher

CHAPTER INTERNET ACTIVITIES
KEYWORD: SA3 CF5
Choose an activity to:
• explore the impact of the Zenger case on press freedom.
• understand theories and concepts of the Scientific Revolution.
• learn about modern trade in the original 13 colonies.

CHAPTER ENRICHMENT LINKS
KEYWORD: SA3 CH5

ONLINE ASSESSMENT
Homework Practice
KEYWORD: SA3 HP5

TAKS Prep
KEYWORD: SA3 T5

Rubrics
KEYWORD: SS Rubrics

ONLINE MAPS, CHARTS, AND GRAPHS
KEYWORD: SA3 MCG
• German and Scotch-Irish Settlements in Colonial British America
• Colonial and Overseas Trade
• African American Population in Colonial British America

CONTENT UPDATES
KEYWORD: SS Content Updates

HOLT PRESENTATION MAKER
KEYWORD: SA3 PPT5

ONLINE READING SUPPORT
KEYWORD: SS Strategies

CURRENT EVENTS
KEYWORD: S3 Current Events

TEXAS ONLINE RESOURCES
KEYWORD: S3 TX

Meeting Individual Needs

Ability Levels

Level 1 Basic-level activities designed for all students encountering new material

Level 2 Intermediate-level activities designed for average students

Level 3 Challenging activities designed for honors and gifted-and-talented students

English Language Learners Activities that address the needs of students with Limited English Proficiency

Chapter Review and Assessment

IC Vocabulary Activity 5
Global Skill Builder CD–ROM
HRW Go site
REV Chapter 5 Tutorial for Students, Parents, Mentors, and Peers
REV Chapter 5 Review, pp. 145–47
Chapter 5 Test Generator (on the One-Stop Planner)

A Chapter 5 Test (Form A or B)
A Alternative Assessment Handbook
A Chapter 5 Test for English Language Learners and Special-Needs Students

5

Build on What You Know

If You Were There...

Ask students to answer the following question:

What occupation would you choose as a colonist?

Consider:

- the different occupations and trades appropriate to colonial times
- the type of work and time commitment involved for each profession

You Be the Historian

What's Your Opinion?

To help students create their **Themes** Journal entries, provide the following examples of appropriate **agree**/**disagree** statements.

EXPLORING THE TIME LINE

AMERICAN EVENTS

internet connect

TOPIC: Freedom of the Press
GO TO: go.hrw.com
KEYWORD: SA3 CF5

Have students access the Internet through the HRW Go site to research the trial of John Peter Zenger and other landmark cases related to freedom of the press. Then have them choose one of the cases and use standard grammar, spelling, sentence structure, and punctuation, to create a newspaper article that describes the following information about the case: the issues presented by both sides, the main facts of the case, and its effect on the concept of a free press.

---

5 Life in the English Colonies
(1630–1770)

This scene shows Harvard College in Cambridge, Massachusetts, some 100 years after it was founded.

Puritan leaders of the Massachusetts Bay Colony had the Bay Psalm Book printed.

UNITED STATES

1636 Harvard College, located in Massachusetts, is the first college in the colonies.

1640 The *Bay Psalm Book* is the first book published in the English colonies.

1661 Virginia passes an act recognizing African slavery.

1686 The Dominion of New England is founded.

1630	1650	1670	1690

1648 Work is finished on India's Taj Mahal.

1653 Oliver Cromwell becomes Lord Protector of England.

1660 King Charles II is crowned as ruler of England.

1687 Sir Isaac Newton publishes the first volume of *Principia*, a new theory of physics.

WORLD

The crowning of Charles II was known as the Restoration because it returned the English monarchy to power.

Build on What You Know

English colonists began settling in North America in the 1600s. Some people came to America hoping to make their fortunes. Others came to escape religious persecution. Each region of the colonies developed its own economy. All of the colonies were still closely tied to England, but a unique colonial culture also began to develop.

Economics

Agree   Colonies should be required to provide economic benefits to their homeland.

Disagree   Colonies are economically independent and should not be indebted to their mother country.

Geography

Agree   Natural resources are the key to a successful colony.

Disagree   A colony's success depends on the resourcefulness of the settlers.

Science, Technology & Society

Agree   All scientific discoveries have benefited society.

Disagree   Scientific discoveries benefit some people more than others.

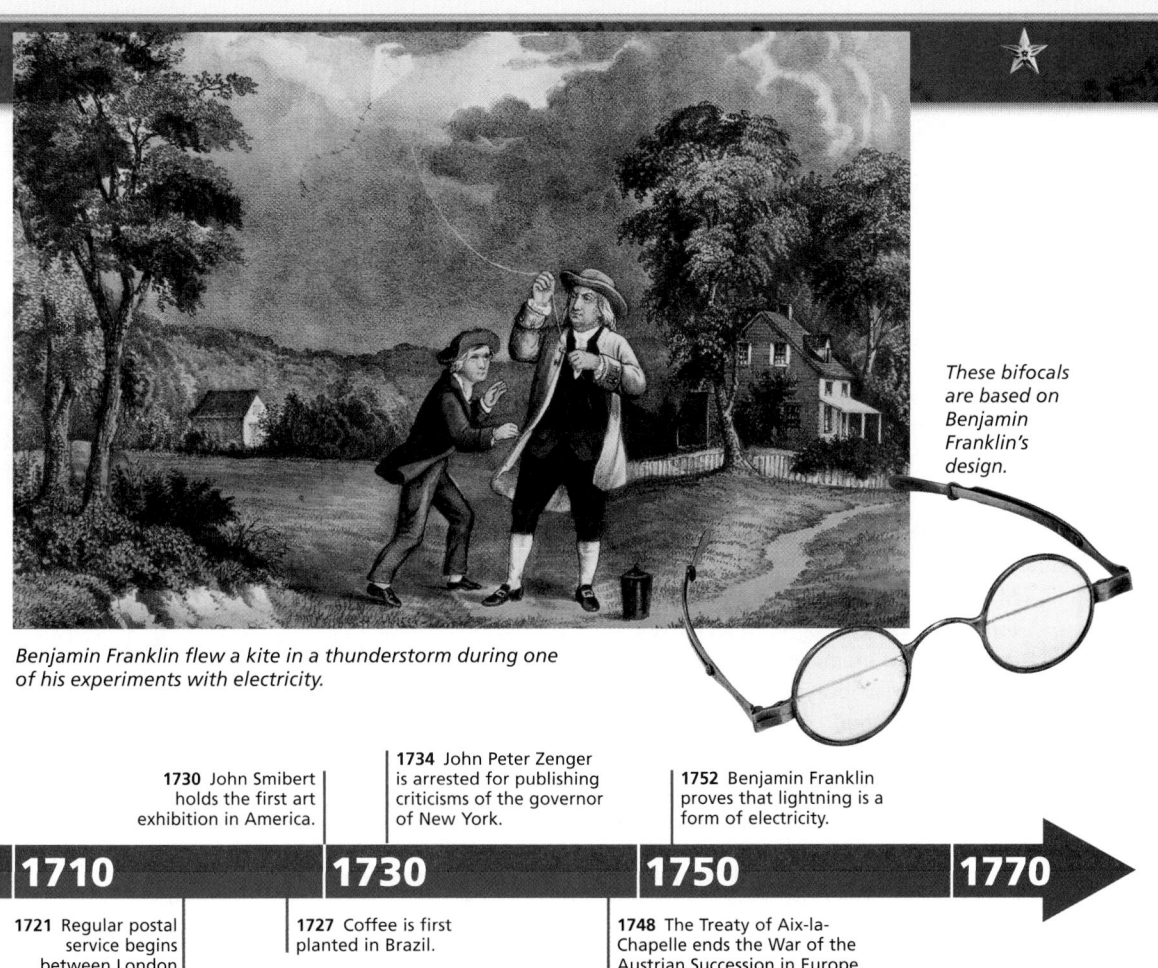

These bifocals are based on Benjamin Franklin's design.

Benjamin Franklin flew a kite in a thunderstorm during one of his experiments with electricity.

1730 John Smibert holds the first art exhibition in America.

1734 John Peter Zenger is arrested for publishing criticisms of the governor of New York.

1752 Benjamin Franklin proves that lightning is a form of electricity.

1710   1730   1750   1770

1721 Regular postal service begins between London and New England.

1727 Coffee is first planted in Brazil.

1748 The Treaty of Aix-la-Chapelle ends the War of the Austrian Succession in Europe.

If you were there . . .

What occupation would you choose as a colonist?

You Be the Historian

What's Your Opinion? Do you **agree** or **disagree** with the following statements? Support your point of view in your journal.

- **Economics** Colonies should trade only with their home country.
- **Geography** A colony must have good weather and many natural resources to be successful.
- **Science, Technology & Society** Scientific discoveries are always good for everyone.

Section 1

OBJECTIVES

* ★ Describe how representative government developed in the colonies.
* ★ Explain how the colonists influenced the rulings of colonial courts.
* ★ Evaluate how the Dominion of New England affected the New England colonies.
* ★ Analyze how the English Bill of Rights influenced colonists.

 **LET'S GET STARTED!**

Write the following scenario on the chalkboard: *You are playing a game with a group of friends when suddenly in the middle of the game the rules change. Then you begin to lose to the other players. How would you feel about the rules changing with little or no warning?* As students enter the classroom, have them write down their responses. *(Students' responses will vary, but students might suggest that they would feel confused or cheated.)* Explain to students that the English colonists experienced similar difficulties as they were forced to follow England's new rules while attempting to manage everyday affairs in the colonies. Explain to students that in Section 1 they will learn about the changes in English rule in the colonies and how the colonists controlled their own local governments.

SECTION 1 RESOURCES

REPRODUCIBLE
▶ Guided Reading Strategy 5.1

TECHNOLOGY
▶ One-Stop Planner, Lesson 5.1
▶ Homework Practice Online

REINFORCEMENT, REVIEW, AND ASSESSMENT
▶ Section 1 Review, p. 125
▶ Daily Quiz 5.1
▶ Main Idea Activity 5.1
▶ English Audio Summary 5.1
▶ Spanish Audio Summary 5.1

Section 1

Forms of Government

Read to Discover

1. How did representative government develop in the colonies?
2. How did colonists influence the rulings of colonial courts?
3. How did the Dominion of New England affect the New England colonies?
4. How did the English Bill of Rights influence colonists?

WHY IT MATTERS TODAY

Many citizens participate in their local governments today. Use **CNN fyi.com** or other **current events** sources to find examples of ways citizens voice their opinions to their local governments. Record your findings in your journal.

Define
* bicameral legislature
* town meeting
* libel

Identify
* Privy Council
* Parliament
* House of Burgesses
* John Peter Zenger
* Dominion of New England
* Edmund Andros
* Glorious Revolution
* English Bill of Rights

The Story Continues

The colonial Capitol Building in Williamsburg, Virginia, still stands.

One September morning, William Byrd II rose at 5 A.M. to begin the business of running his Virginia plantation. After a few hours, he met Colonel Bassett, and the two men rode into Williamsburg. In the busy colonial capital, Byrd met with several members of the Council of State. These men were an important part of the colony's government. That day he was sworn in as a member of the Council—a major step in his political career. He wrote in his diary, "God grant I may distinguish myself with honor and good conscience."

★ Colonial Governments

The English colonies in America all had their own governments when they were first founded. Each government was given power by a charter. The three charter types were proprietary—meaning that one or more individuals had authority over the colony—company, and royal. The English monarch owned all of the colonies and had the sole power to grant charters. A group of royal advisers called the **Privy Council** set English policies in the colonies. However, the Privy Council allowed

★ TEACH

Have students read Section 1 and complete Guided Reading Strategy 5.1. Choose one or more of the following activities to explore the section content with students. For further suggestions on block scheduling or team teaching, see the *Block Scheduling Handbook with Team Teaching Strategies.*

LEVEL 1: Have students work in pairs to make a **before** and **after** chart displaying three ways the Glorious Revolution and the English Bill of Rights influenced the colonists. *(Students' charts might include the following: Before—New England colonies were under the Dominion of New England; After—they formed assemblies Before—Governor*

Andros passed laws without the colonies' approval; After— colonies elected representatives to decide local issues; Before— English monarchy had tremendous power; After—power of the monarchy declined, and Parliament's power increased.)

ENGLISH LANGUAGE LEARNERS , COOPERATIVE LEARNING

ALL LEVELS: Ask students to imagine that the classroom is a small New England community in the early 1600s. Inform them that it is time for a town meeting to take place. Have students elect representatives to run the meeting. Have students create a list of issues that the community would like to address. In a town meeting format, have students discuss and resolve each issue.

ENGLISH LANGUAGE LEARNERS

most colonies to run their own affairs. For example, Rhode Island's 1644 charter stated that all of the colony's laws should agree with those of England. At the same time, the charter stated that the colonists had "full Power and Authority to rule themselves."

Each colony had a governor who served as head of the government. Most governors were assisted by an advisory council. In royal colonies the English king or queen selected the governor and the council members. In proprietary colonies the proprietors chose all of these officials. In a few colonies, such as Connecticut, the people elected the governor. No matter who chose them, governors often possessed significant powers. It was their job to carry out the policies set by England.

✔ **Reading Check: Summarizing** What were the three types of colonial charters? company, proprietary, and royal

★ Colonial Assemblies

In the colonies the people also elected representatives to help make laws and set policy. These officials served in assemblies. Colonists based their assemblies on **Parliament**, England's national legislature, or lawmaking body. Parliament is a **bicameral legislature**—a lawmaking body made up of two houses, or groups. Colonial assemblies worked like the lower house of Parliament. They had the power to raise taxes and organize local governments. They also shared control of the military with the governor. The laws passed by each assembly had to be approved first by the advisory council and then by the governor. Then the Privy Council reviewed the colonial laws to make sure that they followed English laws.

Interpreting the Visual Record

Virginia's assembly *This scene shows an early meeting of Virginia's legislature.* **What does this image suggest about the wealth and social status of these representatives? Explain your answer.**

★ Citizenship

Colonial Governments.
Before about 1720, the colonial governors and assemblies held the political power in the colonies, but, in many ways, they were weak and ineffectual. There were few full-time, paid public officials. Most officials were community members who donated their time to serve in local government. Likewise, military groups tended to be temporary because local taxes were low and budgets were small. Moreover, laws were sometimes difficult to enforce in the widespread communities. In addition, colonists, who were extremely independent anyway, expected little from their governments.

CRITICAL THINKING

What do you think this situation indicates about citizens' participation in politics?

ANSWER: Students will probably suggest that most individuals were largely uninvolved in politics.

Visual Record Answer

Students' responses might indicate that because of their dress, the attendees seem to come from the upper classes.

Development of Representative Government

Types	How chosen	Function
governors	*elected by people*	*approved legislature, carried out policies*
assemblies	*elected by people*	*made laws, set policy, controlled the military*
town meetings	*representatives from the town*	*determined support of local schools, regulated land usage*

★ Citizenship

Congregationalist Church. The Congregationalist Church in New England differed from the Church of England in many ways. One of the most important differences was that it accorded all power—religious and civil—to the members of the church. Each congregation wrote its own covenant. As a result, each church was "a city, compact within itself." The town meeting was often the congregation of the church, which met together to manage the town's affairs.

CRITICAL THINKING

How might the Congregationalist Church reflect the development of representation in America?

ANSWER: Students might suggest that it allowed members to govern themselves in both religious and civic matters.

CITIZENSHIP AND YOU ANSWER

Students' responses will vary, but they should support their answers to indicate why they think meetings may or may not be a good way for people to participate in government.

Citizenship and You

Town Meetings

atertown, Massachusetts, is known as the "cradle of the town meeting." It held its first town meeting in the 1630s. In colonial times, the town meeting was the preferred form of local government in New England. Today any gathering open to the public to discuss community issues may be called a town meeting. The U.S. government has held such meetings so that citizens can discuss issues ranging from nuclear science to ways to improve neighborhoods.

Presidential candidates also have held town meetings to let voters ask questions and make their views known. Historian John Hope Franklin declared, "The town meeting movement seems to me a magnificent opportunity to catch the whole country up in a common effort." Do you think town meetings are a good way for people to participate in government? Explain your answer.

A town meeting in Hebron, Massachusetts

Virginia's assembly, founded in Jamestown in 1619, was the first colonial legislature in North America. At first it met as a single body, but it was later split into two houses. The first house was known as the Council of State. The governor's advisory council and the Virginia Company selected its members. The **House of Burgesses** was the assembly's second house. The members of this house were elected by colonists to represent Virginia's plantations and towns.

Sometimes assemblies and governors disagreed. In such cases the governor had the final say on whether a law was passed. But assemblies could influence governors' actions by refusing to pay their salaries. William Byrd II described the relationship between the House of Burgesses and the royal governor of Virginia.

 History Makers Speak
"Our government . . . is so happily constituted [designed] that a governor must first outwit us before he can oppress [subdue] us. And if he ever squeezes money out of us he must first take care to deserve it."
—William Byrd II, quoted in *Albion's Seed*, by David Hackett Fischer

Legislatures were not the only important political bodies in the colonies. The center of New England politics was the **town meeting**. In town meetings people talked about and decided issues of local interest, such as paying for schools. They also regulated other important issues, including the ownership and use of unsettled lands. The men in the community met one or more times every year. They would also select the group of officials who would carry out the town's decisions.

In the southern colonies people typically lived farther away from one another. Therefore, many decisions were made at the county level. The middle colonies used a combination of county meetings and town meetings in their local governments.

✔ **Reading Check: Analyzing Information** Why were colonial assemblies and town meetings created, and what did they do? to provide representative government; assemblies: raised taxes, organized local governments, controlled the military; town meetings: handled local issues

★ Colonial Courts

Colonial courts made up another important part of colonial governments. Royal officials could have a strong influence on the courts. Whenever possible, however, colonists used the courts to control local affairs. In general, the courts supported the interests and ideas of their communities. For example, many laws in Massachusetts enforced the Puritans' religious views.

Sometimes colonial courts also protected individual freedoms. For example, the court case of **John Peter Zenger** dealt with the issue of freedom of the press. In 1733 Zenger began criticizing the royal governor of New York in his newspaper. Officials charged him with committing **libel** against a public official. They accused him of printing a false

LEVEL 2: Organize the class into groups of four. Assign two students in each group the roles of colonial judges, and the other two students the roles of either an accusing settler or a royal official. Present to each group the following case: *A settler has accused a royal official of taking bribes, and the royal official denies the charge.* The two judges in each group should listen to other students' arguments as to the guilt or innocence of the royal official. Have the judges consider the following questions: Did the royal official accept bribes? Is it appropriate for a settler to accuse an official of such a crime? Is the royal official being accused simply because he/she is an official and not a common settler? What obligation do the judges have to the royal official? Finally, have the judges make a decision about the official's guilt or innocence. Allow each group time to discuss its decision and the reasons for its decision. Conduct a discussion and ask students to identify how or if the colonists influenced the rulings of colonial courts.

COOPERATIVE LEARNING

HOMEWORK Have students write a five-question quiz about the development of representative government in the colonies. Students may exchange and answer quizzes in the following class period.

THE GRANGER COLLECTION, NEW YORK

written statement that damaged the governor's reputation. Zenger was arrested in 1734.

Andrew Hamilton served as Zenger's attorney at the trial. He said that Zenger could publish whatever he wished as long as it was true. Even damaging facts could be printed, Hamilton said. The chief justice of the court did not agree with this view. He explained his opinion to the jury. "Nothing can be worse to any government than to have people attempt to create distrust and dislike of the management of it." The jury, however, found Zenger not guilty. The jury's decision showed its dislike of the royal governor. The jury's agreement with Hamilton's argument also reflected their support for the idea that colonists had a right to express their views openly.

✔ **Reading Check: Finding the Main Idea** Why might colonists support freedom of the press? Freedom of the press allowed colonists to voice their opinions about their government and its leaders.

⭐ The Dominion of New England

In 1685 James II became king of England. He was determined to take more control over the English government, both in England and in the colonies. James believed that the northern colonies were too independent. He wanted them to be more connected to each other and to England. In 1686 James united the northern colonies under one government called the **Dominion of New England**. The Dominion eventually included the colonies of Connecticut, Maine, Massachusetts, New Hampshire, New Jersey, New York, and Rhode Island. James appointed Sir **Edmund Andros** as royal governor of the Dominion. James also chose a royal council for the Dominion.

Interpreting the Visual Record

Freedom of the Press *Attorney Andrew Hamilton argued that John Peter Zenger could publish the truth even if it offended people.* **In what ways does this courtroom scene look different from the trial system used in the United States today?**

Controlling the Colonies. The English government was alarmed by evidence of colonial chaos, including Bacon's Rebellion, an unauthorized Indian war (King Philip's War), and unsupervised trade with the Dutch and other European powers. The English government under Charles II, therefore, began trying to control the colonies even before James II established the Dominion. England instituted a colonial office and sent agents to America to enforce the Navigation Acts, while Parliament continued to pass new acts to better regulate colonial trade. In addition, royal governors were encouraged to use force if necessary to raise tax revenues in their colonies.

CRITICAL THINKING

How do you think the colonists responded to these early efforts by the English government to bring them under control?

ANSWER: Students might suggest that some colonists submitted more or less willingly out of loyalty to the Crown, while others simply ignored such actions.

Visual Record Answer

Students' responses might indicate that there appear to be three judges, versus the one that presides over a courtroom today, and the room is filled with men only.

LEVEL 3: Remind students that Sir Edmund Andros —whom James II appointed as governor in chief of the Dominion of New England—was disliked by many of the colonists because of his desire to exert control over and impose laws on the colonies. Have students imagine that they are colonists living under the governorship of Sir Edmund Andros. Ask them to write a letter to a friend living in another part of the colonies describing how life has changed since the Dominion of New England was established. *(Students' letters might mention that the colonies' charters have been suspended, and that Andros has raised taxes and limited the powers of the town meeting.)*

★ CLOSE

Have students work in groups to create a graphic organizer illustrating the structures of the colonial governments. Tell students to include the different types of governments, the duties involved in the various government positions, differences between the assemblies and the governors, and the effectiveness of these governments. Encourage students to assign roles within each group so that each group member contributes to the final project. **COOPERATIVE LEARNING**

★ Global Relations

The Glorious Revolution.
The Glorious Revolution of 1688, also known as the Bloodless Revolution, was a significant turning point in the role of the monarchy. With James II refusing to change his pro-Catholic stance, and the birth of a son to his Catholic queen, many Anglican Church leaders sought help from abroad. They invited William of Orange from the Netherlands to bring his army to England to help address the concerns of the people. William's arrival and slow march to London showed James II that his support was fading. With the departure of his daughter Anne to William's camp, James II escaped to France. Soon after, William and his wife Mary were offered the Crown. The entire change from one monarchy to a new one was without any fighting, hence the name the Bloodless Revolution. This revolution not only changed the ruling family of England but also altered the power and role of the English monarchy forever.

CRITICAL THINKING

What might have happened if James II had not fled to France?

ANSWER: Students might suggest that the conflict could have continued and that William and James II probably would have fought for control of England resulting in a great loss of life.

The Dominion government took the place of the northern colonies' original charters. The king's actions greatly upset many of the colonists. As one colonist grumbled, the Dominion was "without any liberty for an Assembly."

In December 1686 Sir Edmund Andros arrived in Boston. Andros was a former governor of New York. The colonists disliked him, as one pamphlet writer explained.

Analyzing Primary Sources
Identifying Points of View
Why does the speaker think the colonists dislike Andros?
He raised taxes and brought soldiers to enforce the new laws he had made without their consent.

 History Makers Speak ❝Sir Edmund Andros arrived as our governor; who besides his power, with the advice and consent of his Council, to make laws and raise taxes as he pleased, had also authority by himself to muster [gather for military duty] and employ all persons residing in the territory. . . . And several companies of soldiers were now brought from Europe to support what was to be imposed upon us.❞

—"A. B.," quoted in *The Annals of America*

In 1687 many residents of Ipswich, Massachusetts, protested Andros's taxation policy. Five were arrested and jailed. To prevent further protests, Andros used his royal authority to limit the powers of town meetings in 1688.

✔ **Reading Check: Summarizing** How did James II and Governor Andros limit New England colonists' participation in government? James II forced colonies to unite under one government; Andros passed laws without their approval and limited the powers of town meetings.

★ The Glorious Revolution

The new policies of James II were unpopular in England as well as in the colonies. Parliament felt threatened when he tried to change England from a Protestant country back to a Catholic one. To stop the king, leaders of Parliament asked James's Protestant daughter, Mary, and her husband, William of Orange, to rule England. William, the leader of the Netherlands, landed in England with his army in the fall of 1688. James left the country. The overthrow of James II became known as the **Glorious Revolution**.

Protestant colonists celebrated the crowning of King William and Queen Mary with songs and pictures.

THE GRANGER COLLECTION, NEW YORK

When residents of the Dominion first learned about the Glorious Revolution in 1689, they removed Andros as governor. The delighted colonists sent Andros to England to answer for his actions. The individual colonies left the Dominion and quickly formed new assemblies. They then sent declarations of support for William and Mary. In time, William and Mary replaced the canceled colonial charters. The new charters were like the original ones, except in Massachusetts. The colonists there had originally elected the governor. However, the Crown now chose this person. In addition, men no longer had to be full church members to vote. Instead, they had to own a certain amount of property. Massachusetts also grew in size with the addition of Plymouth and Maine to its territory.

The political ideas of the Glorious Revolution led Parliament to pass the **English Bill of Rights** in 1689. Under this act, the powers of the English monarchy were reduced. At the same time, Parliament gained power. American colonists were greatly interested in this shift in power from the monarch to a representative governing body. As time went on, the colonists valued their own right to elect the representatives that governed them. (See pages 228–29.)

THE GRANGER COLLECTION, NEW YORK

The English Bill of Rights gave greater powers to Parliament, shown here meeting in London's Westminster Hall about 1700.

✔ **Reading Check: Finding the Main Idea** How did the Glorious Revolution and the English Bill of Rights affect the political views of colonists?
Colonists were interested in the shift of power to a representative governing body.

Section 1 Review

go.hrw.com **Homework Practice Online**
keyword: SA3 HP5

❶ **Define and explain:**
• bicameral legislature
• town meeting
• libel

❷ **Identify and explain:**
• Privy Council
• Parliament
• House of Burgesses
• John Peter Zenger
• Dominion of New England
• Edmund Andros
• Glorious Revolution
• English Bill of Rights

❸ **Contrasting** Copy the chart below. Use it to compare and contrast the powers that different institutions of colonial government held.

Privy Council	
Governors	
Assemblies	
Town Meetings	
Courts	

❹ **Finding the Main Idea**
a. Provide at least two examples of how colonists began to develop representative governments.

b. Make a time line that describes the creation of the Dominion of New England, its actions and their effects on the colonies, and the Dominion's end.

❺ **Writing and Critical Thinking**
Making Generalizations and Predictions
Imagine that you publish a colonial newspaper. Write an editorial announcing the passage of the English Bill of Rights and predicting its effect on the colonies.

Consider the following:
• reaction to the Glorious Revolution
• the shift toward representative government in England
• the document's guarantee of rights

Life in the English Colonies **125**

125

Section 2

OBJECTIVES

- Evaluate the effects the Navigation Acts had on the colonial economy.
- Describe the types of trade that took place in the colonies during the 1700s.
- Analyze why the colonies participated in the slave trade.

LET'S GET STARTED!

Write the following statement and question on the chalkboard: *Write down a time when you wanted to trade a possession for something that someone else owned. What were the risks and benefits involved in such a trade?* As students enter the classroom, allow time for them to respond. *(Students' responses might include the risk of getting an unfair trade or the benefit of trading for something of more value.)* Lead a class discussion on what constitutes fair trade and the limits that should be placed on trading. Explain to students that in Section 2 they will learn about the positive and negative effects of colonial trade.

SECTION 2 RESOURCES

REPRODUCIBLE

- Guided Reading Strategy 5.2
- Literature Reading 5: Narrative of the Life of Olaudah Equiano

TECHNOLOGY

- One-Stop Planner, Lesson 5.2
- Linking Geography and History Transparency 5: The Slave Trade, 1451–1870
- Holt Researcher: American History CD–ROM
- CNN Presents America: Beginnings to 1914 Segment: Two Stories of Slavery
- Homework Practice Online
- HRW Go site

REINFORCEMENT, REVIEW, AND ASSESSMENT

- Section 2 Review, p. 130
- Daily Quiz 5.2
- Main Idea Activity 5.2
- English Audio Summary 5.2
- Spanish Audio Summary 5.2

Section 2

The Growth of Trade

Read to Discover

1. What effects did the Navigation Acts have on colonial economies?
2. What types of trade took place in the colonies during the 1700s?
3. Why did the colonies participate in the slave trade?

Define

- mercantilism
- balance of trade
- imports
- exports
- duties
- free enterprise
- triangular trade

Identify

- Navigation Acts
- Middle Passage
- Olaudah Equiano

WHY IT MATTERS TODAY

Many countries around the world have formed trading networks. Use CNNfyi.com or other **current events** sources to identify a trading network involving the United States. Record your findings in your journal.

The Story Continues

The beat of a drum began trade at the slave market. African slaves stood terrified as buyers rushed in to make their choices. Cries were heard from people who were separated from their family and friends. Such scenes led Olaudah Equiano (oh-LOW-duh ek-wee-AHN-oh), once a slave himself, to ask, "Why are parents to lose their children, brothers their sisters, or husbands their wives?" The answer was money and greed. The slave trade had become an important part of the colonial economy.

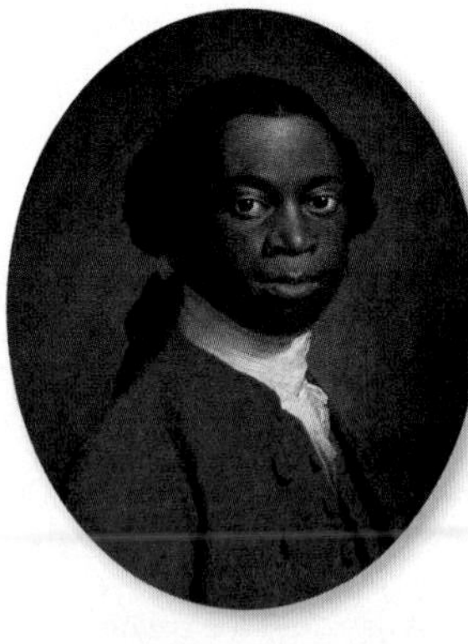

After gaining his freedom, Olaudah Equiano spoke out against slavery and published an account of his life.

English Trade Laws

Trade was one of England's main reasons for founding its American colonies. In 1689 an English official pointed out that the colonies made up "a full third part of the whole Trade and Navigation of England." In the late 1600s England, like most western European nations, practiced **mercantilism.** Using this economic system, nations created and maintained wealth by carefully controlling trade. A nation could be self-sufficient if it had a good **balance of trade.** This meant a country had fewer **imports**—goods bought from other countries—than **exports**—goods sold to other countries. Between 1650 and 1696 Parliament passed

Have students read Section 2 and complete Guided Reading Strategy 5.2. Choose one or more of the following activities to explore the section content with students. For further suggestions on block scheduling or team teaching, see the *Block Scheduling Handbook with Team Teaching Strategies.*

LEVEL 1: Have students create graphic organizers illustrating the Navigation Acts' effect on the colonial economies. Conduct a class discussion and ask students to identify and compare imports and exports before and after the Navigation Acts. Tell students to create two separate organizers: one depicting the colonies' imports and exports before the Navigation Act of 1660, the other after the Navigation Acts were passed. *(Students' organizers illustrating the time before the Navigation Acts might include goods from countries other than Britain, while imports and exports after the Navigation Acts might include only British imports and exports of enumerated articles.)* **ENGLISH LANGUAGE LEARNERS**

a series of **Navigation Acts**. These acts required colonists to do the bulk of their trading with England. The Navigation Acts also set **duties**, or import taxes, on some trade products.

England claimed that the Navigation Acts were good for the colonies. After all, the colonies had a steady market in England for their goods. But not everyone agreed. Many colonists wanted more freedom to buy or sell goods in whatever markets offered the best prices. Within the colonies many merchants practiced **free enterprise**—economic competition with little government control. But local demand for colonial goods was small compared to foreign demand for colonial products. English laws limited free enterprise by preventing colonists from selling or buying goods directly to or from many foreign countries. This led to an unfavorable balance of trade for the colonies.

✔ **Reading Check: Analyzing Information** In what ways did mercantilism and the Navigation Acts limit free enterprise in the colonies? restricted colonial trade partners, set duties on goods, kept colonists from getting best prices for goods

Mercantilism and the Colonies

Under the system of mercantilism, nations such as England tried to control what goods were traded to and from their colonies.

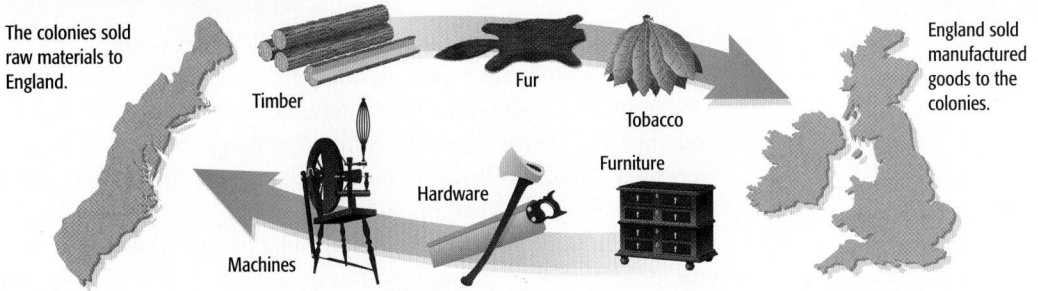

The colonies sold raw materials to England.

Timber
Fur
Tobacco
Furniture
Hardware
Machines

England sold manufactured goods to the colonies.

Colonists were not allowed to trade many of these goods with other countries. They had to buy from and sell only to England.

The colonies
Tobacco
Cotton
Navigation Acts
Fabric
France

Visualizing History

1. **Economics** What were some of the disadvantages that colonists experienced under mercantilism?

2. **Connecting to Today** Do you think American businesses would support such a system today? Why or why not?

The Hat Act. One of the more unusual restrictive acts that the British government passed was the Hat Act, which prohibited the sale of hats among the colonies and required a seven-year apprenticeship for anyone who wished to become a hat-maker. Parliament passed this act in response to pressure from London felt makers who wanted to protect their industry from competition.

ACTIVITY: Ask students to create a political cartoon or to use standard grammar, spelling, sentence structure, and punctuation to write a newspaper editorial protesting the British government's Hat Act.

VISUALIZING HISTORY ANSWER
1. Students' responses might suggest that other nations tried to control goods traded to and from the colonies.
2. Students' responses will vary.

ALL LEVELS: Copy the following graphic organizer onto the chalkboard, omitting the italicized answers. Have students complete the organizer to describe the types of trade that took place in the colonies during the 1700s. Then lead a discussion, asking students to describe the characteristics of each type of trade.
ENGLISH LANGUAGE LEARNERS

Types of Trading
• *smuggling*
• *triangular trade*
• *slave trade*

TRADING IN THE COLONIES

 LEVEL 2: Organize students into small groups. Have students work together to create a poster reflecting the various types of colonial trade. *(Students' posters will vary but should include depictions of the following: smuggling, triangular trade, and the slave trade.)* Ask groups to share their work with the class. **COOPERATIVE LEARNING**

internet connect

go.hrw.com

TOPIC: Trade in Modern times
GO TO: go.hrw.com
KEYWORD: SA3 CF5

Have students access the Internet through the HRW Go site to research modern trade in the states that made up the original thirteen colonies. Divide the states among the class and have each group research the principal trade goods or commodities produced in their assigned state. Then instruct them to create a map of their state and to mark the goods produced in that state with special symbols. Finally, have each group submit a paragraph that explains how trade has changed or remained the same since the colonial period.

Visual Record Answer

Students' responses may indicate that the factory might be hot and dirty.

Technology Resources

 Linking Geography and History Transparency 5: The Slave Trade, 1451–1870

⭐ Colonial Trade

Despite colonial complaints, trade restrictions continued into the 1700s. In 1733 Parliament passed the Molasses Act, which placed duties on sugar, molasses, and rum. In response, some colonists began to bring these goods into the colonies illegally, a practice known as smuggling. However, British officials rarely punished these smugglers. One colonial official in Massachusetts complained that he could only enforce the law "with great delay and too many difficulties."

Legal trade was much more significant than smuggling. By the early 1700s the newly unified kingdom of Great Britain was trading around the world. Most American merchants traded directly with Britain or with its colonies in the West Indies. The West Indies produced large amounts of sugar. Writer and economist Adam Smith commented on the wealth that the sugar trade brought to the British West Indies.

Analyzing Primary Sources

Supporting a Point of View Why does Smith suggest that sugar plantations are particularly important? they produce especially high profits

 History Makers Speak "The profits of a [sugar] plantation in any of our West Indian colonies are generally much greater than those of any other cultivation [crop] that is known either in Europe or America."

—Adam Smith, *The Wealth of Nations*

Some merchants also took part in the **triangular trade,** which could follow several different routes. In one route the colonies sold goods like fish, grain, beef, and horses to plantation owners in the West Indies. In exchange, merchants received sugar and molasses. Some of these goods were then shipped to Britain. This was just one example of how colonial merchants sought the best markets for their products. This colonial participation in trade all across the Atlantic Ocean was an early form of free enterprise.

✔ **Reading Check: Finding the Main Idea** In what ways were colonists beginning to practice free enterprise? They took the goods they could produce best and tried to find the best markets to sell them in.

Interpreting the Visual Record

Sugar refining *Slaves in the West Indies refined sugar by boiling sugarcane and drying the sugar in bins.* **What do you think working conditions in such a refinery would be like?**

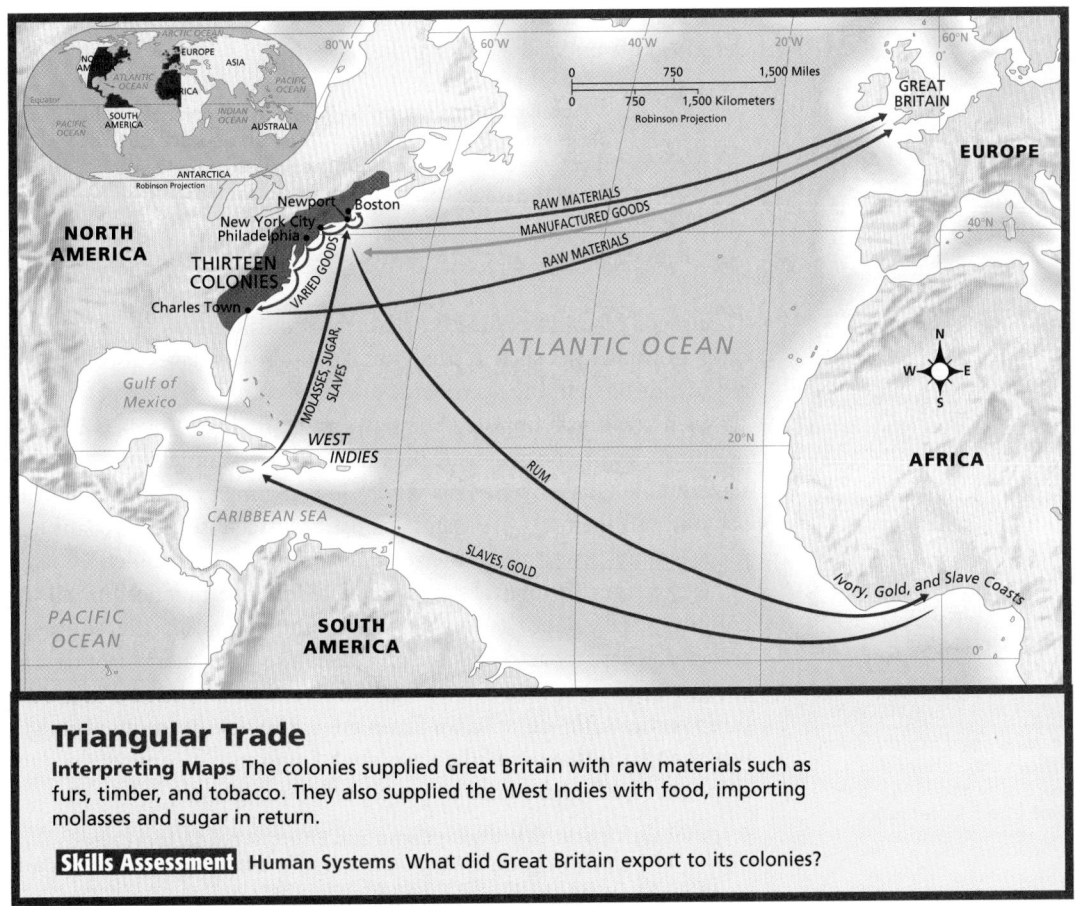

Triangular Trade

Interpreting Maps The colonies supplied Great Britain with raw materials such as furs, timber, and tobacco. They also supplied the West Indies with food, importing molasses and sugar in return.

Skills Assessment Human Systems What did Great Britain export to its colonies?

☆ The Middle Passage

One version of the triangular trade had a much greater cost in human suffering. It began with New England traders exchanging rum for slaves on the West African coast. The traders then sold the enslaved Africans in the West Indies for molasses or brought them back to sell in the mainland American colonies.

The slave trade brought around 10 million Africans across the Atlantic Ocean. This terrifying and often deadly voyage was called the **Middle Passage**. The journey could last as long as three months. Enslaved Africans were chained by the neck and legs. They lived between the upper and lower decks of the ship, in spaces just a few feet high. Even the sailors remarked on the terrible conditions enslaved Africans faced on the voyage. "They [the Africans] had not so much room as a man in his coffin," wrote one slave ship captain. Slave traders carried as many slaves as possible so they could earn greater profits when they sold their human cargo in North or South America.

⭐ REVIEW AND ASSESS

Have students complete the **Section 2 Review** on p. 130. Then have students complete **Daily Quiz 5.2**. As **Alternative Assessment**, you may want to use the types of trade graphic organizer or the fair trade handbook of guidelines from this section's lessons.

⭐ RETEACH

Have students complete **Main Idea Activity for English Language Learners and Special-Needs Students 5.2**. Ask each student to write 10 questions about the material in Section 2. Have students exchange questions, write answers to the questions

they receive, and return the completed set of questions to the writer for grading. Have students share their most difficult question in a classroom discussion.
ENGLISH LANGUAGE LEARNERS

⭐ EXTEND

Ask students to use the library to research the amount of goods and number of slaves exchanged in the triangular trade. Have students create bar graphs depicting the changes in the number of both goods and slaves exchanged in the triangular trade from 1700 to 1800. **BLOCK SCHEDULING**

Section 2 Review
ANSWERS

❶ Define
- mercantilism, p. 126
- balance of trade, p. 126
- imports, p. 126
- exports, p. 126
- duties, p. 127
- free enterprise, p. 127
- triangular trade, p. 128

❷ Identify
- Navigation Acts, p. 127
- Middle Passage, p. 129
- Olaudah Equiano, p. 130

❸ Colonies—tobacco, cotton, furs, lumber, fish, grain, beef, horses, rum; West Africa—enslaved Africans, gold; Great Britain—hardware, machinery, furniture, fabric; West Indies—sugar, molasses, slaves; arrows should connect the colonies, West Indies, and West Africa as well as the colonies, West Indies, and Britain

❹ a. because it brought them great profits.
b. Students might suggest that customs officers be made to arrest smugglers, that duties be lifted, or that the Navigation Acts be revoked.

❺ Students' handbills will vary, but students should note that the Navigation Acts restricted colonial trade by preventing colonists from selling to foreign countries despite strong overseas demand for many colonial products and that Britain benefited heavily from the trade between itself and the colonies.

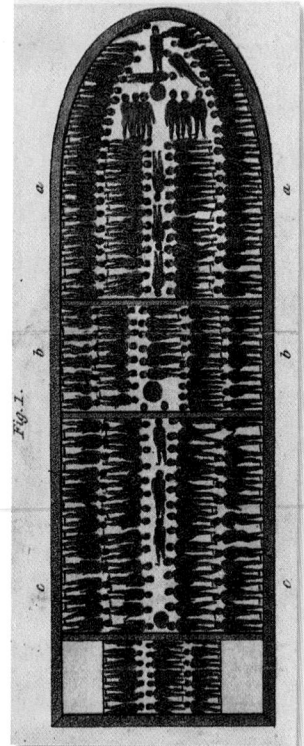

On slave ships like this, each African was confined in a space only about 16 inches wide and 5 ½ feet long.

Olaudah Equiano was sold into slavery when he was about 11. He described life under the decks of the slave ships.

❝I received such a salutation [smell] in my nostrils, as I had never experienced in my life; . . . I became so sick and low that I was not able to eat. . . . The groans of the dying rendered [made] the whole a scene of horror almost inconceivable [unbelievable].❞

—Olaudah Equiano, *The Interesting Narrative of the Life of Olaudah Equiano, or Gustavus Vassa, the African*

Thousands of captives died on slave ships during the Middle Passage, often from diseases such as smallpox. Thousands of slaves also committed suicide by jumping overboard.

Some colonists opposed the slave trade. In 1688 Quakers in Germantown, Pennsylvania, made the first recorded colonial protest against slavery. One Quaker stated his view: "To bring men hither [here], or to rob and sell them . . . we stand against." Massachusetts merchant and judge Samuel Sewall also criticized slavery in a 1700 pamphlet.

Despite such protests, slavery continued to be practiced in all the colonies. Slave labor was particularly important in the southern colonies, where tobacco and rice production required many workers. As southern farmers relied increasingly on slave workers instead of indentured servants, the demand for slaves grew. The slave trade also brought wealth to areas that used little slave labor. For example, some of the slave ships were built and owned by people in New England.

✔ **Reading Check: Identifying Cause and Effect** What factors caused the slave trade to grow, and how did this affect conditions on the Middle Passage? slave labor and slave trade were important parts of the colonial economy; slave traders' desire for profits led to horrible conditions on slave ships

Section 2 Review

go. hrw .com **Homework Practice Online**
keyword: SA3 HP5

❶ Define and explain:
- mercantilism
- balance of trade
- imports
- exports
- duties
- free enterprise
- triangular trade

❷ Identify and explain:
- Navigation Acts
- Middle Passage
- Olaudah Equiano

❸ Summarizing Copy the web diagram below. Fill in each circle with goods and people that came from that region. Use arrows to show what goods were exchanged between the four regions.

The Colonies — Atlantic Ocean — Great Britain
West Indies
West Africa

❹ Finding the Main Idea
a. Why did colonists participate in the slave trade?

b. Imagine that you are a British official. How would you address the problem of colonial smuggling?

❺ Writing and Critical Thinking
Supporting a Point of View Imagine that you are a New England merchant who supports a freer market in the colonies. Create a handbill that explains the Navigation Acts and mercantilism and that calls for an end to both. Consider the following:
- the economic effects of the Navigation Acts
- the overseas demand for colonial products
- the benefits of free enterprise

Section 3

OBJECTIVES

- ★ Explain why enslaved Africans were the main workforce in the southern colonies.
- ★ Identify how New England's economic activities were different from those of the southern colonies.
- ★ Describe how the middle colonies combined economic aspects of the southern and New England colonies.

🔊 LET'S GET STARTED!

Write the following statement on the chalkboard: *Identify your favorite winter and summer activities.* As students enter the classroom, have them write their responses to the statement. *(Students' responses will vary.)* Lead a discussion on the ways that the environment affects the different summer or winter activities. Explain to students that this was also the case in colonial America. Colonists in the North engaged in different activities, held different jobs, and harvested different crops than people in the middle or southern colonies. Tell students that in Section 3 they will learn about colonial economies, sources of labor, and women's economic roles.

Section 3

The Colonial Economy

Read to Discover

1. Why were enslaved Africans the main workforce in the southern colonies?
2. How were New England's economic activities different from those of the southern colonies?
3. How did the middle colonies combine economic aspects of the southern and New England colonies?

WHY IT MATTERS TODAY

The different parts of the United States still have different economies. Use **CNNfyi.com** or other **current events** sources to find out about the major economic activities of a region of the United States. Record your findings in your journal.

Define

- cash crops
- slave codes
- apprentices
- staple crops

Identify

- Eliza Lucas Pinckney

SECTION 3 RESOURCES

REPRODUCIBLE

- ▶ Guided Reading Strategy 5.3
- ▶ Geography Activity 5: Agriculture in the Colonies

TECHNOLOGY

- ▶ One-Stop Planner, Lesson 5.3
- ▶ Linking Geography and History Transparency 7: Major Colonial Economies
- ▶ Homework Practice Online

REINFORCEMENT, REVIEW, AND ASSESSMENT

- ▶ Section 3 Review, p. 135
- ▶ Daily Quiz 5.3
- ▶ Main Idea Activity 5.3
- ▶ English Audio Summary 5.3
- ▶ Spanish Audio Summary 5.3

The Story Continues

In 1647 Leonard Calvert, the governor of Maryland, lay dying. He asked that Margaret Brent be brought to his bedside. Brent had left England in 1638 to escape religious persecution. She now owned a Maryland plantation. Before witnesses, Governor Calvert said to Brent, "I make you my sole executrix [woman who carries out a will]. Take all and pay all." Brent was well known for her business skills and the management of her plantation. Calvert trusted her to handle his estate wisely.

Leonard Calvert was sent by his older brother, Cecilius Calvert, to rule the Maryland colony.

★ Agriculture in the Southern Colonies

The economies of the southern colonies depended on agriculture. They also exported materials for building ships, such as wood and tar. Some colonies also traded with local American Indians for deerskins to sell.

The colonies had many small farms and some large plantations. Farms did well because the South enjoyed a warm climate and long growing season. Many farms grew **cash crops** that were sold for profit. Tobacco, rice, and indigo—a plant used to make blue dye—were the

Life in the English Colonies **131**

Have students read Section 3 and complete Guided Reading Strategy 5.3. Choose one or more of the following activities to explore the section content with students. For further suggestions on block scheduling or team teaching, see the *Block Scheduling Handbook with Team Teaching Strategies.*

LEVEL 1: Tell students to imagine that they are southern farmers. Have them write a letter to the editor of their local newspaper describing why the southern colonies enslaved Africans to work. **ENGLISH LANGUAGE LEARNERS**

Jeri Goodspeed-Gross of St. Paul, Minnesota, suggested the following activity:

 ALL LEVELS: Using a blank outline map of the United States, have students label each of the colonial regions discussed in this section. Then have students put symbols in each region representing the products produced by its residents. Finally, lead a discussion comparing ways that each region's climate and geography influenced and affected products. **ENGLISH LANGUAGE LEARNERS**

★ Historical Sidelight

Colonial Slave Rebellions. Two significant slave rebellions took place during the colonial era. In 1712 about 25 slaves set fire to some New York City houses and killed nine whites who tried to stop them. They were in turn killed or captured and executed by soldiers sent to stop the rebellion. The second rebellion occurred in 1739 in Stono, South Carolina, when about 80 slaves armed themselves and attempted to reach Spanish Florida. They were overtaken by their pursuers. More than 40 escapees and 20 whites were killed.

CRITICAL THINKING

How do you think southern communities reacted to such rebellions?

ANSWER: Students might suggest that they tightened security on slaves and harshly punished those who participated.

DAILY LIFE ANSWER

Students might suggest that it appears to be a time-consuming process.

Daily Life

Tobacco industry Many of the slaves in the Chesapeake Bay area worked on tobacco plantations, as shown in this 1670 painting. The tremendous demand for tobacco led planters to increase greatly their production. By the early 1700s the American colonies were exporting millions of pounds of tobacco to Europe. The demand for slave labor also increased. The growing slave trade led to more slave auctions such as the one listed on the poster above. What does this image suggest about the effort it took to produce tobacco?

most important cash crops. Virginia specialized in tobacco, and South Carolina specialized in rice and indigo. Eliza Lucas (later **Eliza Lucas Pinckney**) introduced indigo to the colony after she learned how to grow it on her family's plantation.

Crops such as indigo and rice required many workers to grow and harvest. By the 1700s the indentured servants who had first done this labor had been largely replaced by enslaved Africans. Unlike indentured servants, slaves and their children had to work for life.

Slaves performed most of the plantation labor. In his diary, William Byrd II described his daily life as a plantation owner.

 History Makers Speak
❝I said my prayers and ate milk for breakfast. I walked out to see my people [slaves] at work at the ditch. I read a little geometry. I ate mutton [sheep] for dinner. I walked to the ditch again. In the evening I said my prayers.❞
—William Byrd II, *The Secret Diary of William Byrd of Westover, 1709–1712*

When a job was finished, slaves might be allowed to do their own work. A few slaves were able to earn enough money to buy their freedom.

Most of the southern colonies passed **slave codes**, or laws to control slaves. Colonies with large numbers of slaves had the most extensive slave codes. South Carolina's slaveholders feared that slaves would revolt. As a result, South Carolina's code said slaves could not hold meetings or own weapons. Some colonies did not allow slaveholders to free their slaves. The Virginia Assembly claimed that runaway slaves committed "injuries to the inhabitants of this dominion [colony]." Assembly members passed a law allowing people to kill a runaway slave who resisted capture.

✔ **Reading Check: Summarizing** What role did slavery play in the southern plantation economy, and how was slavery regulated? slave labor kept the plantations running; slaves were controlled by slave codes

Economic Activities	New England	Middle	Southern
Grew Cash Crops			X
Participated in Slave Trade		X	*X*
Had Small Family Farms	X		
Fishing	*X*		
Shipbuilding	*X*		
Exported Local Products	*X*	*X*	
Grew Staple Crops		*X*	

⭐ Industry and Trade in New England

Connecticut, Massachusetts, New Hampshire, and Rhode Island were very different from the southern colonies. The often harsh climate and rocky soil meant that few New England farms grew cash crops. They had little demand for large numbers of farm laborers. Although some people held slaves, slavery did not become as important to this region.

Trade was vital to New England's economy. New England entrepeneurs—people who undertake new businesses to make a profit—traded goods locally, with other colonies, and overseas. Many entrepeneurs traded local products such as furs, pickled beef, and pork.

Fishing and shipbuilding became two of the region's leading industries. One of the earliest settlers in Massachusetts exclaimed, "Here is a good store of fish, if we had boats to go 8 or 10 leagues [about 25 to 30 miles] to sea to fish in." Merchants exported dried fish. Whaling provided valuable oil for lighting. In addition, whale meat became an important part of the colonial diet.

The shipbuilding industry prospered in New England for several reasons. The region had plenty of forests and the local fishing industry needed ships. In addition, as trade in the New England seaports grew, more merchant ships were built. Shipyards throughout New England towns made high-quality, valuable vessels. Shipowners sometimes even told their captains to sell the ship along with the cargo when they reached their destination.

The diverse economy of New England needed skilled craftspeople. Families often sent younger sons off to learn skilled trades such as blacksmithing, weaving, shipbuilding, and printing. The young boys who learned skilled trades were known as **apprentices**. They lived with a master craftsman and learned from him. In exchange, the boys performed simple tasks. Gabriel Ginings was an apprentice in Portsmouth, Rhode Island. He received "sufficient food and raiment [clothing] suitable for such an apprentice," as his 1663 contract stated.

✔ **Reading Check: Contrasting** How were New England's economic activities different from those in the southern colonies, and why was this the case? *lack of cash crops, more trade, a diverse economy with industries; climate, local resources*

Indigo Dye

During colonial times, the finest blue dyes came from an Asian plant called indigo. Indigo was not grown in the American colonies, however, until the mid-1700s. In 1740 Eliza Lucas (later Eliza Lucas Pinckney) began growing indigo on her family's plantation in South Carolina.

Removing the blue compounds from indigo was hard work. Skilled workers—usually slaves—had to soak, whip, and strain the plants for many hours. It took around 100 pounds of indigo plants to make a single four-ounce indigo bar!

By 1747 South Carolina was exporting more than 135,000 pounds of indigo each year. Today artificial indigo dye is used to color clothes such as blue jeans. How did Eliza Lucas Pinckney contribute to indigo production?

Tremendous labor went into building sailing ships such as these three vessels in a New England shipyard.

⭐ Economics

Indigo Bounties. The indigo market benefited from British trade controls. The British, whose textile industry was booming, set a bounty, or an incentive to produce a certain product, for the production of indigo. So not only did producers enjoy free shipment to Britain, they were paid extra (by the pound) to do so.

CRITICAL THINKING

Why might Britain have refrained from taxing indigo exports?

ANSWER: Students might suggest that the British textile industry needed indigo, so the government did not want to discourage its production in the colonies.

CONNECTING TO SCIENCE AND TECHNOLOGY ANSWER
She learned how to grow and process it, and she shared her knowledge and seeds with other people.

Technology Resources

Linking Geography and History Transparency 7: Major Colonial Economies

134

HOMEWORK Have students imagine that they are farmers in either the New England, middle, or southern colonies. Ask them to write journal entries describing the kind of farm that they work on, the types of crops that they grow, and the amount of help that they have.

LEVEL 3: Provide each student with a sheet of poster board. Then have students make a visual summary illustrating how the middle colonies combined economic aspects of the southern and New England colonies. Encourage students to include brief written explanations to accompany their drawings. Have volunteers present their visual summaries to the class.

★ CLOSE

Remind students of the triangular trade, discussed in the previous section, in which goods and slaves were traded among the colonies, England, and the West Indies. Have students create a flowchart depicting trade that students would expect to see between the southern, middle, and New England colonies. Encourage students to discuss the crops, food products, and raw materials that might have been traded between these colonial regions. Have volunteers present their flowcharts to the class.

★ Economics

The Prosperous Middle Colonies. The Middle Colonies incorporated the best features of their northern and southern neighbors. The fertile coastal and valley plains of Pennsylvania, New Jersey, and New York provided these regions with the optimum climate in which to grow staple crops. The cities there also produced extensive commercial activity. In fact, by 1750 the middle colonies became the most economically dynamic region of all the North American regions, with their food supply exceeding the needs of the local population by as much as 50 percent.

CRITICAL THINKING

Why do you think that neither the New England nor the southern colonies were as economically productive as the Middle Colonies?

ANSWER: Students might suggest that neither region was able to benefit from both an agriculturally rich climate as well as a commercially diverse economy.

CONNECTING TO MATH ANSWERS

1. about 4 percent; 20 percent
2. Line graphs should accurately display the statistics from the chart.
3. Pamphlets will vary but should use various statistics to support their arguments.

★ The Middle Colonies

The middle colonies—Delaware, Pennsylvania, New Jersey, and New York—combined qualities of the New England and southern colonies. With a good growing season and rich land, farmers there could grow large amounts of food. The middle colonies grew **staple crops,** or crops that are always needed. Some of these crops were wheat, barley, and oats. Farmers also raised and sold livestock.

Slaves were more important to the middle colonies than they were to New England. They worked in cities as skilled laborers, such as blacksmiths and carpenters. Other slaves also worked on farms, in dockyards, on board ships, and in the growing shipbuilding industry. However, indentured servants largely filled the middle colonies' growing labor needs. Between 1700 and 1775 about 135,000 indentured servants came to the middle colonies from Britain and Germany. About half of them moved to Pennsylvania. By the mid-1700s Philadelphia had become one of the largest British colonial cities. Other cities in the middle colonies, such as New York City, also grew quickly.

Trade and free enterprise were important to the economy of the middle colonies. Merchants in Philadelphia and New York City exported colonial goods to markets in Britain and the West Indies. These products included wheat from New York. Colonial merchants also sold wheat and flour from Pennsylvania and New Jersey. Through hard work, they could make a comfortable living. A Philadelphia merchant noted this in a letter he wrote in 1768. He said that he was able "to live well, but [I] have not been able to lay up such a Stock, as would maintain me without daily labor."

✔ **Reading Check: Comparing** How did geography factors affect agriculture in each colonial region? M: good climate/soil, many big farms; S: good climate, many plantations; NE: poor climate/soil, smaller farms

---

CONNECTING TO MATH

Just the Facts

African American Population in the American Colonies

Year	Population of African Ancestry	Total Population
1660	2,920	75,058
1680	6,971	151,507
1700	27,817	250,888
1720	68,839	466,185
1740	150,024	905,563
1760	325,806	1,593,625
1780	575,420	2,780,369

Using Mathematical Skills

1. About what percent of the colonial population in 1660 were people of African ancestry? About what percent were they in 1760?
2. Create a line graph showing these population figures.
3. Imagine that you are a colonial Quaker who opposes slavery. Prepare a pamphlet attacking the rise of slavery in the colonies, using these statistics to support your argument.

Philadelphia was a major center of colonial trade.

RARE BOOK DEPARTMENT, THE FREE LIBRARY OF PHILADELPHIA

★ Women and the Economy

Throughout the colonies, women made important contributions to the economy. They ran farms and businesses, such as clothing and grocery stores, bakeries, and drugstores. A few female shopkeepers used their business success to call for a voice in colonial politics. One group of women wrote to a New York newspaper in 1733.

History Makers Speak
❝We are House keepers, Pay our taxes, carry on Trade, and most of us are the Merchants, and as we in some measure contribute to the Support of Government, we ought to be Intitled to some of the Sweets of it.❞

—New York shopkeepers, quoted in *Colonial Women of Affairs*, by Elisabeth Anthony Dexter

MARYLAND HISTORICAL SOCIETY, BALTIMORE

Plantation manager Margaret Brent—shown here speaking to colonial officials—was respected for her business skills.

Some women also practiced medicine, often as nurses and midwives. However, colonial laws and customs limited women's economic activities. Typically, a married woman could not work outside the home without her husband's permission. A husband also had the right to keep the money his wife earned.

Most colonial women worked in the home. Married women managed households and raised children. Sometimes they earned money for their families by washing clothes or selling products such as butter. Many women made items that their family needed, such as clothing.

✔ **Reading Check: Finding the Main Idea** How did women play important roles in the colonial economy? *They performed many jobs, such as running homes, farms, and businesses, and practicing medicine.*

Section **3** Review

go.hrw.com Homework Practice Online
keyword: SA3 HP5

❶ Define and explain:
• cash crops
• slave codes
• apprentices
• staple crops

❷ Identify and explain:
• Eliza Lucas Pinckney

❸ Comparing and Contrasting Copy the graphic organizer below. Use it to compare and contrast the characteristics of the economies of the three major colonial regions.

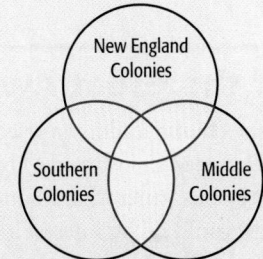
New England Colonies
Southern Colonies
Middle Colonies

❹ Finding the Main Idea
a. Why was slavery common on southern plantations, and how did it affect laws in the southern colonies?

b. What types of contributions did women make to the colonial economy?

❺ Writing and Critical Thinking
Summarizing Imagine that you are going to participate in a debate about the different colonial economic regions. Write a speech explaining how and why the middle colonies are similar to and different from the southern and New England colonies.

Consider the following:
• the economic activities of each region
• the labor required by each region
• the physical features of each region

Section 4

OBJECTIVES

★ Analyze the message of the Great Awakening.

★ Describe how the Great Awakening changed colonial religious organizations and leaders.

★ Explain how the Great Awakening changed colonial society.

SECTION 4 RESOURCES

REPRODUCIBLE

▶ Guided Reading Strategy 5.4

▶ Primary Source Reading 5: "Sinners in the Hands of an Angry God"

TECHNOLOGY

▶ One-Stop Planner, Lesson 5.4

▶ Everyday Life in America Transparency 3: Gravestone Styles in the English Colonies

▶ Holt Researcher: American History CD–ROM

▶ Homework Practice Online

REINFORCEMENT, REVIEW, AND ASSESSMENT

▶ Section 4 Review, p. 139

▶ Daily Quiz 5.4

▶ Main Idea Activity 5.4

▶ English Audio Summary 5.4

▶ Spanish Audio Summary 5.4

Section 4

The Great Awakening

Read to Discover

1. What was the message of the Great Awakening?
2. How did the Great Awakening change colonial religious organizations and leaders?
3. How did the Great Awakening change colonial society?

WHY IT MATTERS TODAY

In some countries religious differences have led to conflict. Use CNNfyi.com or other **current events** sources to find out about a country where groups with different religious beliefs are either involved in or resolving a conflict. Record your findings in your journal.

Define

• revivals

Identify

• Great Awakening
• Jonathan Edwards
• George Whitefield
• Gilbert Tennent

The Story Continues

One morning a Connecticut farmer and his wife heard that George Whitefield would be preaching in a nearby town. They quickly dropped their work. As fast as they could, they rushed to make the 12-mile journey. Still several miles from the meeting site, the couple met a line of horses carrying fellow travelers. To the farmer, each horse appeared "to go with all his might to carry his rider to hear news from heaven for the saving of souls." After hearing Whitefield's message, the inspired farmer joined others who had religious conversions. "I was born on Feb 15th 1711 and born again Octo 1741," he later wrote in the first line of his autobiography.

A beautifully decorated colonial Bible like this one would have been a prized possession.

★ Words of the Great Awakening

In the early 1700s many church leaders worried that colonists were losing their religious faith. These leaders wanted to bring back the sense of religious duty held by previous generations. Some believed that emotional and inspiring sermons would revive interest in religion. Several ministers in the middle colonies began holding **revivals**, emotional gatherings where people came together to hear sermons and declare their faith.

Have students read Section 4 and complete Guided Reading Strategy 5.4. Choose one or more of the following activities to explore the section content with students. For further suggestions on block scheduling or team teaching, see the *Block Scheduling Handbook with Team Teaching Strategies.*

LEVEL 1: Ask students to imagine that they have just heard a sermon by one of the following people: George Whitefield, Charles Chauncy, Jonathan Edwards, or Gilbert Tennent. Have students write a letter to a friend that explains the concept of the sermon, depicts the speaker's stance regarding revivals and the Great Awakening ideas, and illustrates the energy and persuasiveness used in the sermons of the period. Ask volunteers to read their letters to the class.

ENGLISH LANGUAGE LEARNERS

HOMEWORK Have students write a brief resumé for one of the influential individuals of the Great Awakening. Ask them to examine the effect their subject had on religion in the colonies and to include the works of their chosen individual as well in the resumé.

Because of these ministers' work, many colonists experienced "a great awakening" in their religious lives. This **Great Awakening** reached its height in the 1730s and 1740s. It was a widespread Christian movement involving sermons and revivals that emphasized faith in God. The Great Awakening changed not only colonial religion but also social and political life. **Jonathan Edwards** was one of the most important leaders of the Great Awakening. He was a pastor of the Congregational Church in Northampton, Massachusetts. Edwards's dramatic sermons urged sinners to seek forgiveness for their sins or face punishment in Hell forever.

In 1739 British minister **George Whitefield** made the second of his seven trips to America. On this visit he held revivals from Georgia to New England. Whitefield became one of the most popular ministers of the Great Awakening. Because of Whitefield, thousands of colonists found new faith in Christianity. New England farmer Nathan Cole was one of many people who found Whitefield's message inspiring.

Interpreting the Visual Record

Revival The Great Awakening preacher George Whitefield could draw crowds of thousands to his outdoor revival meetings. **How does this image suggest the power of Whitefield's preaching?**

 History Makers Speak

❝When I saw Mr. Whitefield come upon the scaffold [platform], he looked almost angelical [like an angel]. . . . And my hearing how God was with him everywhere as he came along, it solemnized [made serious] my mind and put me into a trembling fear before he began to preach; for he looked as if he was clothed with authority from the Great God . . . and my hearing him preach gave me a heart wound.❞

—Nathan Cole, quoted in *The Great Awakening,* edited by Alan Heimert and Perry Miller

Analyzing Primary Sources
Identifying Points of View
Why does Cole feel that Mr. Whitefield's words are important? He believes that Whitefield speaks with authority from God.

The ministers of the Great Awakening preached that all people were born sinners who could only be saved by the will of God. However, the opportunity to be saved was available to all—rich and poor alike—who confessed their sins and accepted God's grace. This message brought hope to many people. However, the ministers of the Great Awakening could use a threatening tone. Jonathan Edwards's 1741 sermon *Sinners in the Hands of an Angry God* called up frightening images. "God . . . holds you over the pit of hell, much as one holds a spider, or some loathsome [disgusting] insect over the fire."

✔ **Reading Check: Finding the Main Idea** What did preachers of the Great Awakening and their followers believe? All people were sinners. Salvation came only through confession, accepting God's grace, and contrition.

Biography

Jonathan Edwards. One of Jonathan Edwards's most controversial opinions was his belief that humans had free will. The traditional church taught that God controls every aspect of life, predetermining who would be saved. Edwards believed that humans could determine their own actions and save themselves.

CRITICAL THINKING

Why do you think so many people liked Edwards's assertion about free will?

ANSWER: Students might suggest that people may have wanted a greater sense of control over their destinies and the ability to determine their own salvation.

Visual Record Answer

Students might suggest that the number of people kneeling and praying indicates his power.

★ Constitutional Heritage

Separation of Church and State. The years following the Great Awakening movement brought a new trend toward the separation of church and state. This movement for complete religious freedom gained momentum leading up to and following the American Revolution. Eventually, the Constitution of the new nation would guarantee the separation of church and state.

Minister Jonathan Edwards was known for sermons such as Sinners in the Hands of an Angry God.

★ Old and New Lights

THE GRANGER COLLECTION, NEW YORK

Not all colonists believed in these new religious ideas. Eventually, some church congregations divided because of disagreements. There were traditionalists and those who followed the new ministers. In New England the traditionalists were called the "Old Lights." The followers of the Great Awakening were called the "New Lights."

Old Light ministers did not believe that the enthusiasm of the Great Awakening could truly awaken one's spirituality. Charles Chauncy of Boston's First Church agreed with this view. He stated that anyone who took part in such revivals was "under no other influence than that of an over-heated imagination." Chauncy thought that this excited form of religion was not a proper way to try to save one's soul.

The Great Awakening also changed the Presbyterian Church in the middle colonies. Presbyterian minister **Gilbert Tennent** was a leader of the new movement. His sermons attacked the traditionalists. As a result of Tennent's efforts, the Presbyterian Church split into two groups with opposing views on the revival movement. These became known as the "Old Side" and the "New Side."

In the middle and southern colonies, particularly Virginia, the Great Awakening greatly increased church membership. Much of this growth took place among the Baptists and Methodists. The Great Awakening was also influential on the frontier, where traveling preachers held revivals in small towns. There were few churches on the frontier. Therefore, these ministers were important to settlers.

Traditional and new ideas were in conflict even in these distant areas, however. Frontier missionary Charles Woodmason tried to oppose the changes brought about by the Great Awakening. He expressed his frustration.

 History Makers Speak **"If I give out [announce] to be at such a Place at such a Time, three or four of these fellows [Great Awakening ministers] are constantly at my Heels—They either get there before me, and hold forth—or after I have finish'd, or the next Day, or for days together. Had I a hundred Tongues, or as many Pairs of Legs, I could not singly [alone] oppose such a Numerous Crew."**

—Charles Woodmason, quoted in *The Power of Words,* edited by T. H. Breen

✔ **Reading Check: Identifying Cause and Effect** What conflicts did the Great Awakening cause, and what were some of the effects of these conflicts? The Great Awakening caused divisions within religious groups. Religious leaders responded by speaking out against each other, as well as by attempting to convert colonists to their beliefs.

⭐ The Great Awakening and Society

The Great Awakening attracted people of different classes and races. Women, members of minority groups, and poor people often took part in services. Women in particular welcomed the message of the Great Awakening. Many women sought spiritual renewal around the time of childbirth. They were interested in part because their lives were at risk during this time. One woman explained that her faith "would wear off again 'till the time of my first Lying in [labor]; and then I was . . . brought to the very brink of eternity." Both free and enslaved African Americans were drawn to the Great Awakening's message of acceptance and spiritual equality. Despite the stated belief in equality, however, some revivals were separated by race.

Before the Great Awakening, there was little communication between people living in different colonies. This changed as ministers began moving about and exchanging ideas. Educational opportunities also improved as many colleges were founded to provide religious instruction. Such efforts helped bring together the different colonial regions.

The Great Awakening promoted ideals that may also have affected colonial politics. Sermons about the spiritual equality of all people led some colonists to begin demanding more political equality. Revivals became popular places to talk about political and social issues. As a result of sharing new ideas, some colonists began to question the authority of existing institutions.

This illustration shows the First Baptist Church of Providence, Rhode Island. Baptist congregations were among those that grew rapidly during the Great Awakening.

✔ **Reading Check: Summarizing** How did the Great Awakening change colonial communities and society? It improved communication between the colonies and led to more discussion of political and social issues and may have contributed to colonists' later demands for political equality.

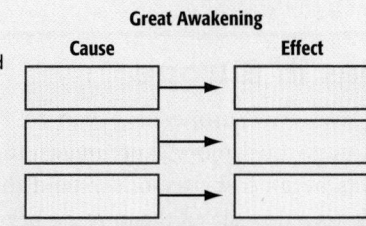

Section 4 Review

go.hrw.com **Homework Practice Online**
keyword: SA3 HP5

❶ **Define** and explain:
• revivals

❷ **Identify** and explain:
• Great Awakening
• Jonathan Edwards
• George Whitefield
• Gilbert Tennent

❸ **Identifying Cause and Effect** Copy the cause-and-effect chart below. Fill in at least three causes and effects relating to why the Great Awakening came about and how it affected society.

Great Awakening

Cause		Effect
	→	
	→	
	→	

❹ **Finding the Main Idea**
a. What message did preachers of the Great Awakening tell their followers?

b. Why might the teachings of the Great Awakening have led to a movement for greater democracy?

❺ **Writing and Critical Thinking**
Analyzing Information Imagine that you are a leader of a church that has become divided between New Lights and Old Lights. Write a story to share with church members that describes the problems faced by churches such as yours.

Consider the following:
• the beliefs of the Old Lights and New Lights
• religion on the frontier
• the splitting of some religious groups

Section 5

OBJECTIVES

✪ Explain how both the Scientific Revolution and the Enlightenment reflected new ways of thinking.
✪ Describe education during colonial times.
✪ Identify Benjamin Franklin's key achievements.
✪ Analyze contributions that were made to American culture in the 1700s.

📻 LET'S GET STARTED!

Write the following statement on the chalkboard: *Make a list of historical figures who have influenced today's world.* As students enter the classroom, have them prepare their lists. Then discuss how the inventions and/or teachings of these people have affected modern society. Explain that the Enlightenment was a period in which great thinkers came up with ideas that changed society in various ways and that these ideas influenced modern society. Tell students that in Section 5 they will learn how Enlightenment thinkers borrowed ideas from the Scientific Revolution, what education was like in the colonies, and about the contributions by colonial writer, scientists, and artists.

Section 5

American Culture

Read to Discover

1. How did both the Scientific Revolution and the Enlightenment reflect new ways of thinking?
2. What was education like during colonial times?
3. What were Benjamin Franklin's key achievements?
4. What contributions were made to American culture in the 1700s?

WHY IT MATTERS TODAY

Scientists are always making new, important discoveries. Use **CNN fyi.com** or other **current events** sources to learn more about a new scientific discovery. Think about fields such as medicine or computer science. Record your findings in your journal.

Define

• scientific method

Identify

• Scientific Revolution
• Galileo Galilei
• Isaac Newton
• Enlightenment
• David Rittenhouse
• Benjamin Banneker
• Benjamin Franklin
• Anne Bradstreet
• Phillis Wheatley

Galileo built and decorated his first telescope by hand.

The Story Continues

Night after night in 1610 Italian scientist Galileo Galilei looked up at the sky. People had long believed that Earth was the center of the universe. Galileo, however, began to doubt this idea. He used his newly built telescope to view Jupiter and observed small moons around this planet. This discovery told him that not everything in the universe moved around Earth. Other scientists began to share Galileo's views. They thought that many other ideas about the natural world also needed to be reconsidered.

⭐ New Ideas in Europe

During the 1600s Western Europeans began to re-examine their world. As scientists performed more experiments, they made exciting discoveries. Scientists began to better understand the basic laws that govern nature. Their new ideas about the universe began what is known as the **Scientific Revolution**. This revolution began in mathematics and astronomy, but it later changed all areas of natural science.

★ TEACH

Have students read Section 5 and complete Guided Reading Strategy 5.5. Choose one or more of the following activities to explore the section content with students. For further suggestions on block scheduling or team teaching, see the *Block Scheduling Handbook with Team Teaching Strategies.*

Note: For an additional teaching idea, see the Chapter 5 Resource Speaker activity in the **Creative Teaching Strategies** handbook.

LEVEL 1: Have students create a headline announcing one of the following events: Galileo's discovery that small moons orbited Jupiter; Newton's discovery of the law of gravity; or Franklin's discovery that lightning is a form of electricity. Have volunteers present their headlines to the class. Then lead a class discussion on ways the Scientific Revolution and the Enlightenment reflected new ways of thinking.

ENGLISH LANGUAGE LEARNERS

Galileo Galilei was one of the leading figures in the Scientific Revolution. He demonstrated that the planets revolve around the Sun. In the late 1600s Sir **Isaac Newton** explained how objects on Earth and in the sky behaved. His theories proved that the same laws of physics govern both. He also developed much of the **scientific method** used today. The scientific method requires that scientists carefully study natural events. Scientists then form theories based on their observations and experiments. These ideas can be used to predict other behaviors or events. Scientists then test their theories as they learn new facts.

The Scientific Revolution also began changing the way people viewed human actions. This change in thought is often called the Age of Reason, or the **Enlightenment.** The Enlightenment took place during the 1700s. Enlightenment philosophers used reason and logic, much as scientists were doing. These thinkers, however, studied human nature and suggested ways to improve their world. Jean-Jacques Rousseau (roo-SOH), Voltaire, and Baron de Montesquieu (mohn-tes-kyoo) all formed ideas about how government should work to best serve the people.

Some Enlightenment thinkers believed that there was a social contract between government and citizens. With this contract, rulers needed the consent of the governed. Philosophers such as John Locke believed that people had natural rights such as equality and liberty. Locke stated that people should obey their rulers only if the state protected their life, liberty, and property. Eventually the ideas of the Scientific Revolution and the Enlightenment began to influence some colonial leaders.

✔ **Reading Check: Summarizing** What changes in ways of thinking took place in the 1600s and 1700s in Europe? The Scientific Revolution changed the way people viewed the natural world. The Enlightenment changed the way people viewed human activity.

★ Colonial Education

In the colonies few people could afford a formal education. The availability of schooling also varied widely in the colonies. For example, there were more schools in New England than in the southern and middle colonies. New England colonists particularly valued the ability to read the Bible. They also wanted to make sure future generations had educated ministers. Therefore, communities founded and paid for town schools. Schoolchildren often used the *New England Primer,* which had characters and stories from the Bible. They learned to read at the same time that they learned about the community's religious values. In the middle and southern colonies, most children lived far from towns. They had to be taught by their parents or private tutors.

Most colonial children stopped their education after the elementary grades. Many went to work, either on the family farm or away from home. Some boys became apprentices. In New England and in the middle colonies, some girls became servants for other families.

LINKING PAST to PRESENT

Public Schools

Today most Americans consider public education to be a basic right. This was not the case in colonial America. In many places children received little or no formal education. Pennsylvania and most New England colonies were exceptions to this rule. In 1642 Massachusetts passed one of the first public education laws in Europe or the Americas. In 1683, Quaker officials passed laws requiring all children in Pennsylvania to learn how to read and write. Quaker leaders also decided to offer free schooling for poor children. In both Massachusetts and Pennsylvania male and female children received instruction. **How does current education compare with colonial public education? Use examples to support your answer.**

A page from the *New England Primer,* a colonial schoolbook

☑ internet connect

TOPIC: The Scientific Revolution
GO TO: go.hrw.com
KEYWORD: SA3 CF5

Have students access the Internet through the HRW Go site to research the theories and discoveries of a prominent individual of the Scientific Revolution. Then have students represent this individual's discovery by constructing a model or demonstration of it.

LINKING PAST TO PRESENT ANSWER
Students might suggest that colonial education was not available to all children, in many communities education was religious based, or many children quit school after the elementary grades.

ALL LEVELS: Copy the following graphic organizer onto the chalkboard, omitting the italicized answers. Have students complete the organizer by listing contributions to the American culture during the 1700s.

ENGLISH LANGUAGE LEARNERS

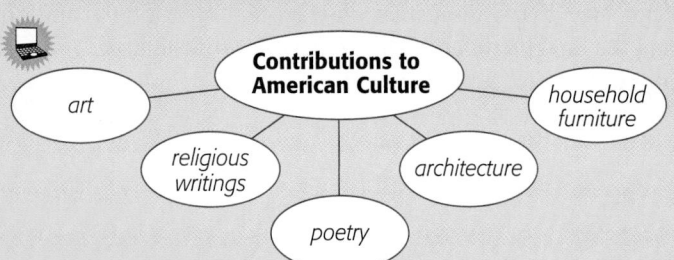

Contributions to American Culture
- art
- religious writings
- poetry
- architecture
- household furniture

LEVEL 2: Discuss with students the availability of and types of education that existed in colonial times. Have students write an encyclopedia entry about educational opportunities in the colonies. Ask students to answer the following questions in their entries: Did the availability of education vary from region to region. If so, how? Did boys and girls have the same opportunities for education? What were the opportunities for higher education? Finally, have students present their entries to the class.

Interdisciplinary Connection

▶Science◀

Early American Science. American scientists during the 1700s pursued a variety of studies, ranging from astronomy to zoology and physics to mathematics. Many published highly original work in European scientific journals.

ACTIVITY: Have students use the library to find information on one of the following American scientists: Cadwallader Colden, Paul Dudley, James Logan, Cotton Mather, David Rittenhouse, or Thomas Robie. Ask them to create a visual montage that is representative of the life and work of the individual and to show the effects their innovations had on society.

Technology Resources

Exploring America's Past Video Segment: Made in America; Teacher's Guide, pp. 8–9

Search 19815, Play to 24570
Videodisc Red Side A
See *Teacher's Guide* for Spanish barcode.

Yale College, in New Haven, Connecticut, was founded in 1701.

★★★★★★★★★★★★
That's Interesting!
★★★★★★★★★★★★

Banneker's Clock Did you know that Benjamin Banneker was the first colonist to build a clock? It's true! He did this even though he had never seen one before. In his early twenties, Banneker, who only had a few years of formal education, designed and built a clock. He used only a picture of a clock from an English journal and a geometry book for help. The clock kept time with great accuracy. His clock is said to have run for over 40 years.

A growing number of young men did attend universities. In 1636 colonists in Massachusetts founded Harvard College. Colonists went on to establish nine colleges, most of which were in the middle colonies and in New England. The classes at many of these colleges focused on religion. Some young men also went to English universities to study the sciences or law. Others studied at a colonial college and then trained with a professional in their field.

✔ **Reading Check: Contrasting** How did education in the New England colonies compare to schooling in the middle and southern colonies?
Schools were more common in New England, though there were some colleges in the middle colonies.

★ Colonial Scientists

Although few schools taught science, there were several talented scientists in the colonies. These scientists taught themselves by observing the world around them. In 1743 the American Philosophical Society was founded in Philadelphia for the study of science. Its members also wanted to improve communication among colonial scientists. **David Rittenhouse**, the society's second president, designed mathematical and astronomical instruments. Thomas Jefferson thought Rittenhouse was "second to no astronomer living."

Rittenhouse admired the astronomer and surveyor **Benjamin Banneker**, a free African American who lived in Maryland. In 1789 Banneker predicted a solar eclipse—when the Moon passes in front of the Sun. Banneker published his work in an almanac.

Botanist John Bartram was also self-taught. He traveled throughout the colonies studying plants and founded a botanical garden. Bartram also exchanged plants and information with scientists in Britain.

HOMEWORK Ask students to write a brief description of their school day. Then have students describe how school was different in colonial times than it is today. Have them compare the different subjects studied, who their teacher might be, and their future educational opportunities.

 LEVEL 3: Ask each student to imagine that he or she is Benjamin Franklin. Tell the students that Benjamin Franklin has applied to be a teacher at their school. Have students write a letter from Franklin in which he details his key achievements and the reasons why he would make a good teacher. Remind them that Franklin was an inventor, printer, statesman, and writer. Ask volunteers to present their letters to the class.

★ CLOSE

Explain to students that the Scientific Revolution and the Enlightenment were periods in which significant discoveries and creative thinking changed the way people viewed the world. Ask students to think about the decade of the 1990s. Then discuss scientific experiments, new technologies, or new ways of thinking that were developed during the 1990s and how they might affect future generations.

★ Benjamin Franklin

Perhaps the most famous colonial scientist was **Benjamin Franklin**. A man with many interests, Franklin was one of the most important thinkers of his time. He was born in Boston in 1706 and worked first in his father's candle and soap shop. Later he became an apprentice in his brother's printing shop. In 1723 Franklin moved to Philadelphia. In his mid-20s, he started a newspaper, which quickly became the most successful paper in the colonies. Franklin published *Poor Richard's Almanack* between 1732 and 1757. He wrote the almanac under the made-up name of Richard Saunders. Franklin came up with sayings that are still used today, including "Early to Bed, and early to rise, makes a Man healthy, wealthy and wise." Poor Richard offered much additional advice.

History Makers Speak 66If you would be wealthy, think of Saving as well as of Getting: The Indies have not made Spain rich, because her Outgoes [expenses] are greater than her Incomes.99

—Poor Richard (Benjamin Franklin), quoted in *Anthology of American Literature, Volume I*, 2nd edition

Franklin believed that reason could be used to make life better for people. During his life, he invented many useful devices. The lightning rod reduced the risk of fire started by electrical storms. The Franklin stove heated homes better than previous stoves had. Franklin also invented bifocals, eyeglasses with lenses that correct for both far- and nearsightedness. Franklin once said he was "glad of an opportunity to serve others" through his inventions. He did not take out patents on his work because he wanted all people to benefit from his good ideas.

Franklin also conducted many scientific experiments. He flew a kite during a thunderstorm in 1752 as an experiment to prove lightning is a form of electricity. He also found the positive and negative charges in electricity. These discoveries made him well known in the colonies and in Europe. Thomas Jefferson even boasted:

History Makers Speak 66We [Americans] have produced a Franklin, than whom no one of the present age has made more important discoveries, nor has enriched philosophy [improved scientific knowledge] with more, or more ingenious [clever] solutions of the phaenomena [events] of nature.99

—Thomas Jefferson, quoted in *The Americans: The Colonial Experience*, by Daniel J. Boorstin

Franklin helped people in other ways as well. He started the first subscription library in the colonies, and opened an academy that later became the University of Pennsylvania. In addition, Franklin founded the American Philosophical Society.

✔ **Reading Check: Drawing Inferences and Conclusions** How are Franklin's many accomplishments alike? Students might suggest that many of Franklin's accomplishments benefited others.

Analyzing Primary Sources
Identifying Points of View
What does Franklin advise a person to do in order to get rich? spend less than is earned

Benjamin Franklin served as the first president of the American Philosophical Society, which he helped found.

Technology Resources
 American Music Selection 4: "Springfield Mountain"

BIOGRAPHY ANSWER
(for p. 144)
Students might suggest that she grew up a slave but was educated and published poetry.

Have students complete the **Section 5 Review** on p. 144. Then have students complete **Daily Quiz 5.5**. As **Alternative Assessment**, you may want to use the press release exercise or cultural contributions graphic organizer in this section's lessons.

☆ RETEACH

Have students complete **Main Idea Activity for English Language Learners and Special-Needs Students 5.5.** Then organize students into five groups and assign each group one of the subsections in Section 5. Have each group develop a detailed outline of its subsection. Then ask each group to exchange its outline with another group and then write five questions and accompanying answers on that group's outline. Collect the questions and use them to quiz the class.

ENGLISH LANGUAGE LEARNERS , **COOPERATIVE LEARNING**

☆ EXTEND

Have students research colonial inventions that affected people's lives. Have students list the inventions and describe how they changed people's lives. Then have students investigate some modern inventions to determine how they affected people's lives. Have students write song lyrics comparing the influence of the inventions from the two periods. Ask volunteers to share their lyrics with the class. **BLOCK SCHEDULING**

★★★★★★★★★★★★★★★★★★

Section 5 Review
ANSWERS

❶ **Define**
• scientific method, p. 141

❷ **Identify**
• Scientific Revolution, p. 140
• Galileo Galilei, p. 141
• Sir Isaac Newton, p. 141
• Enlightenment, p. 141
• David Rittenhouse, p. 142
• Benjamin Banneker, p. 142
• Benjamin Franklin, p. 143
• Anne Bradstreet, p. 144
• Phillis Wheatley, p. 144

❸ Science—new astronomical discoveries, new inventions, better understanding of electricity; Writing—use of artistic language, poetry that celebrated family and religion, new American style of preaching, history of Virginia, *Poor Richard's Almanack*; Art—development of the fine arts, improved architecture, improved household furnishings, first art exhibition

❹ a. reason and logic were used to understand the natural world and human behavior
b. there are more schools and colleges today, that education is available for all children, that more subjects are taught, or that religion plays a lesser role

❺ Students' letters will vary, but should detail all of his achievements.

BIOGRAPHY

Phillis Wheatley
c. 1753–1784

Phillis Wheatley was one of the first African Americans to be published. She was educated by the Boston family that bought her as a slave in 1761. Wheatley began writing poetry while still a teenager. Her first poem was published in 1770. In 1773 the Wheatleys freed Phillis so that she could go to England. While there she published a book of poetry. After both of the Wheatleys died, Phillis married John Peters. What is remarkable about Phillis Wheatley's career?

★ Colonial Writers and Artists

Self-taught writers and artists also contributed to colonial American culture. Religious speech and writing changed the colonies in many ways. Ministers such as John Cotton, Jonathan Edwards, and Cotton Mather developed a new American way of preaching, revealed in their dramatic sermons.

New England poet **Anne Bradstreet** wrote about her love for her family and her faith. Her poetry was published in *The Tenth Muse* in London in 1650. **Phillis Wheatley** also used religious language and imagery in her poetry. In "On Being Brought from Africa to America," Wheatley described how Christianity changed her life.

In the early 1700s the fine arts began to grow in the colonies. A few European artists came to America to paint and teach. British-born painter John Smibert held the first art exhibition in the English colonies in Boston in 1730. His pupil, American-born portrait artist Robert Feke, became a widely admired painter. Most colonial artists painted portraits because they were popular with colonists.

Colonial architecture and household furniture also improved in style and quality. The houses of the richest colonists were often made of brick, not wood, and were often built in fancy British styles. Inside these homes beautiful furniture showed the talents of highly skilled local carpenters and cabinetmakers. These changes reflected the general improvement in the colonists' lives.

✔ **Reading Check: Analyzing Information** What areas of the arts did colonists begin to pursue, and how did interest in the arts change over time in the colonies? Colonists created literature, art, and new styles of architecture and furniture. Colonists gradually became more involved in the fine arts.

Section 5 Review

★★★★★★★★★★★★★★★★★★★★★★★★★★★★★★★★

**go. Homework
hrw. Practice
.com Online**
keyword: SA3 HP5

❶ **Define and explain:**
• scientific method

❷ **Identify and explain:**
• Scientific Revolution
• Galileo Galilei
• Sir Isaac Newton
• Enlightenment
• David Rittenhouse
• Benjamin Banneker
• Benjamin Franklin
• Anne Bradstreet
• Phillis Wheatley

❸ **Summarizing** Copy the table below. Use it to list three important achievements made during colonial times for each category.

Science		
Writing		
Art		

❹ **Finding the Main Idea**
a. What new ways of thinking resulted from the Scientific Revolution and the Enlightenment?
b. How does education in colonial times compare with modern schooling?

❺ **Writing and Critical Thinking**
Supporting a Point of View Imagine that you are a teenager living in colonial Philadelphia. You would like to serve as an apprentice to Benjamin Franklin. Write a letter to Franklin explaining why you would like to study with him and what you hope to learn.

Consider the following:
• Franklin's inventions and scientific experiments
• Franklin's writings
• Franklin's contributions to his community

Have students conduct research on Benjamin Franklin's *Poor Richard's Almanack* and his autobiography. Ask students to identify any recurring themes in both Franklin's autobiography and *Poor Richard's Almanack*. Have students develop a chart that outlines the differences and similarities between the two books. *(Possible similarities could be the practical advice given in each book. Possible differences could be that* Poor Richard's Almanack *does not contain biographical information about Franklin.)* **BLOCK SCHEDULING**

CONNECTING TO
Literature

Benjamin Franklin's *Autobiography*

Benjamin Franklin's Autobiography *was not published until the year after his death. Many people believe Franklin's* Autobiography *to be a classic of American literature. Franklin's simple, clear writing influenced and inspired many American readers. The success of the* Autobiography *popularized the autobiography as a literary form.*

The Autobiography *also emphasized one of the values closely associated with the American character—self-reliance. In the following passage, Franklin shares his strategy for leading a successful life.*

Benajmin Franklin's Autobiography was full of advice for readers.

It was about this time that I **conceiv'd**[1] the bold and **arduous**[2] Project of arriving at moral Perfection. . . . As I knew, or thought I knew, what was right and wrong, I did not see why I might not always do the one and avoid the other. But I soon found I had undertaken a Task of more Difficulty than I have imagined. . . . I therefore **contriv'd**[3] the following Method. . . . I proposed to myself, for the sake of clearness, to use rather more names with fewer ideas **annexed**[4] to each than a few names with more ideas, and I included after . . . Names of Virtues all that at that time occurr'd to me as necessary or desirable, and annex'd to each a short **Precept**[5] . . . .

1. **Temperance** Eat not to Dulness. Drink not to Elevation.
2. **Silence** Speak not but what may benefit others or yourself. Avoiding **trifling**[6] Conversation.
3. **Order** Let all your Things have their Places. Let each Part of your Business have its Time.
4. **Resolution** Resolve to perform what you ought. Perform without fail what you resolve.
5. **Frugality** Make no Expense but to do good to others or yourself: **i.e.**[7], Waste nothing.
6. **Industry** Lose no Time. Be always employ'd in something useful. Cut off all unnecessary Actions.
7. **Sincerity** Use no hurtful Deceit. Think innocently and justly; and, if you speak, speak accordingly.
8. **Justice** Wrong none by doing Injuries or omitting the Benefits that are your Duty.
9. **Moderation** Avoid extremes. **Forbear**[8] resenting Injuries so much as you think they deserve.
10. **Cleanliness** Tolerate no Uncleanness in Body, Clothes or **Habitation**.[9]
11. **Tranquility** Be not disturbed at trifles or at accidents common or unavoidable.

Understanding What You Read

1. **Literature and History** What similarities exist among the virtues that Franklin lists?
2. **Literature and You** Do you think the virtues described by Franklin represent universal themes that still matter today? Explain your answer.

---

[1] **conceiv'd:** thought up
[2] **arduous:** difficult
[3] **contriv'd:** developed
[4] **annexed:** attached
[5] **precept:** rule
[6] **trifling:** unimportant
[7] **i.e.:** that is
[8] **forbear:** keep from
[9] **habitation:** home

CONNECTING TO LITERATURE ANSWERS
1. They all emphasize fairness, order, organization, and self-control.
2. Students' answers will vary.

CHAPTER 5 REVIEW ANSWERS

The Chapter at a Glance
Students' summaries will vary but should include colonial events and achievements.

Identifying People and Ideas
Students' sentences should indicate an understanding of the following definitions:

1. Virginia's second legislative house
2. reduced English monarchy's power and increased the power of Parliament
3. a method by which nations created wealth through careful control of trade
4. terrifying and often deadly voyage of slave ships across the Atlantic
5. crops grown mainly to be sold for profit
6. laws to control slaves
7. first to introduce indigo into South Carolina
8. widespread religious movement involving sermons and revivals
9. colonial scientist, inventor, and one of the most significant thinkers of his time
10. colonial poet

REPRODUCIBLE
▶ Vocabulary Activity 5

TECHNOLOGY
▶ Chapter 5 Test Generator
(on the One-Stop Planner)
▶ Global Skill Builder
CD–ROM
▶ HRW Go site

REINFORCEMENT, REVIEW, AND ASSESSMENT
▶ Chapter 5 Review,
pp. 145–47
▶ Chapter 5 Tutorial for
Students, Parents,
Mentors, and Peers
▶ Chapter 5 Test
(Form A and B)

▶ Alternative Assessment
Handbook
▶ Chapter 5 Test for English
Language Learners and
Special-Needs Students

★ REVIEW

Have students complete the **Chapter 5 Review** on pages 146–47.

★ ASSESS

Use one of the chapter tests to assess students' understanding of the content. For **Alternative Assessment**, see the **Alternative Assessment Handbook**.

Understanding Main Ideas

1. Governors approved legislation and carried out policies; assemblies organized local governments and controlled certain local issues; courts often extended control over local affairs; and town meetings determined local issues.

2. took power away from the monarch and gave it to a representative governing body

3. Trade restrictions kept merchants and farmers from selling their goods to the country that would pay the highest price.

4. rum and molasses

5. New England relied on commerce; the southern colonies relied on agriculture and slave labors; the middle colonies

6. led to a renewal of religious beliefs, a split in some religious bodies, and greater communication among the colonies.

7. Students' answers will vary.

You Be the Historian— Reviewing Themes

1. to force the colonies to do most of their trading with England

2. southern colonies and the middle colonies both had good soil and a good climate for agriculture; shipbuilding and fishing became important because New England had a lot of forests and rich fishing waters

Chapter 5 Review

The Chapter at a Glance

Examine the visual summary of the chapter below. Create a written summary of colonial events and achievements based on the drawing.

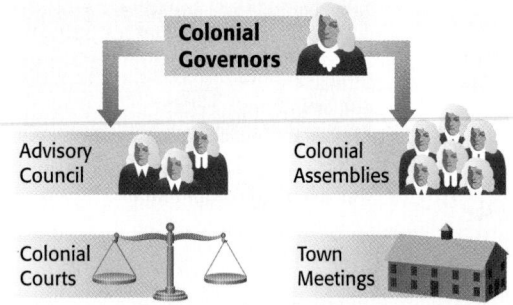

Government

Colonial Governors

Advisory Council

Colonial Assemblies

Colonial Courts

Town Meetings

Economy

New England
Fishing, Manufacturing, Small Farms, Trade

Middle Colonies
Large Farms, Staple Crops, Trade

Southern Colonies
Cash Crops, Plantations, Slave System

Society

The Great Awakening

Colonial Culture

Identifying People and Ideas

Use the following terms or people in historically significant sentences.
1. House of Burgesses
2. English Bill of Rights
3. mercantilism
4. Middle Passage
5. cash crops
6. slave codes
7. Eliza Lucas Pinckney
8. Great Awakening
9. Benjamin Franklin
10. Anne Bradstreet

Understanding Main Ideas

Section 1 *(Pages 120–125)*
1. What roles did governors, assemblies, courts, and town meetings play in local governments?
2. Why were colonists interested in the Glorious Revolution and the English Bill of Rights?

Section 2 *(Pages 126–130)*
3. Why did mercantilism and English trade laws upset colonial merchants and farmers?
4. What items were part of the triangular trade?

Section 3 *(Pages 131–135)*
5. How did the economies of the New England, middle, and southern colonies differ?

Section 4 *(Pages 136–139)*
6. How did the Great Awakening change colonial society?

Section 5 *(Pages 140–144)*
7. Who were the most important writers and artists of the colonial period, and what were some of their accomplishments?

You Be the Historian— Reviewing Themes

1. **Economics** Why did England pass the Navigation Acts?
2. **Geography** How was the economy of each colonial region affected by its geography?
3. **Science, Technology & Society** In what ways did Benjamin Franklin's scientific discoveries and inventions benefit the colonies?

Thinking Critically

1. **Analyzing Information** Why did colonists begin thinking about representative government and political equality?
2. **Drawing Inferences and Conclusions** Why did much of the slave trade take place in northern ports?
3. **Evaluating** In what ways did the colonists practice free enterprise, and how did this benefit the colonies?

Organize the class into five groups and assign each group a section of the chapter. Have students design a mock Go site dealing with material from the section. Have students decide what information to include on the home page. (This should include brief descriptions of topics found in the site and links to other sites.)

ENGLISH LANGUAGE LEARNERS,
COOPERATIVE LEARNING

Portfolio Extensions

1. Cooperative Learning

Divide students into small groups. Ask them to imagine that they are a group of colonists preparing a time capsule to be opened 400 years later. What would they put in the time capsule? Have students create a list of items and artifacts to place in your capsule that would best represent colonial economy and society. Then assign one of the colonial regions to each person in the group. Then compile individual ideas into one final list to share with the class.

2. Interdisciplinary Connection to Science and Technology
Tell students that people today still wear bifocals, like the ones Benjamin Franklin invented hundreds of years ago. Have students obtain information about other inventions from the colonial period that are still in use in the modern world. Have students create a chart of their findings.

Social Studies Skills Workshop

Interpreting Graphs

Study the graph below. Then use the information in the graph to help you answer the following questions.

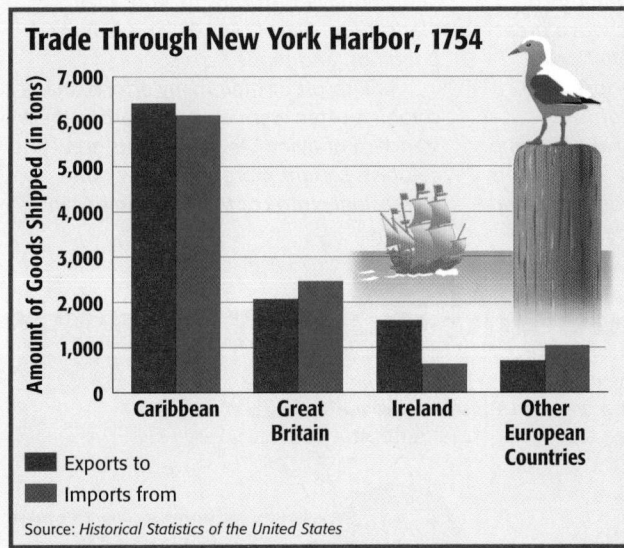

Trade Through New York Harbor, 1754

Y-axis: Amount of Goods Shipped (in tons), 0 to 7,000

X-axis: Caribbean, Great Britain, Ireland, Other European Countries

■ Exports to
■ Imports from

Source: *Historical Statistics of the United States*

1. About how many tons of goods did the American colonies export to Great Britain through New York Harbor?
   a. less than 1,000
   b. more than 6,000
   c. about 4,400
   d. about 2,000

2. Based on your knowledge of the period, why do you think the amount of trade with the Caribbean was so much higher than with other areas?

Analyzing Primary Sources

Read the following quote about the rules of Harvard College written by the clergymen Hugh Peter and Thomas Weld. Then answer the questions that follow.

❝Studiously redeem [make use of] the time, observe the general hours appointed for all the students, and the special hours for their own classes, and then diligently attend the lectures without any disturbance by word or gesture. . . . Every scholar shall be present in his tutor's chamber at the seventh hour in the morning, immediately after the sound of the bell . . . so also at the fifth hour at night, and then give account of his own private reading . . . and constantly attend lectures in the hall at the hours appointed.❞

3. Which of the following statements best describes the schedule of the Harvard students?
   a. They could attend classes whenever they pleased and study on their own time.
   b. They had to report to tutors in the morning and evening and also go to other classes.
   c. They had to go to class from seven in the morning till five at night.
   d. Students had to attend classes regularly and were expected to ask many questions during lectures.

4. How do these requirements compare to a typical day at your school?

---

3. the Franklin stove provided good heating, the lightning rod helped prevent fires, and bifocals helped people with poor vision see better

Thinking Critically

1. because the passage of the English Bill of Rights gave greater power to a representative governing body and the Great Awakening, because its message was that all people were equal and also people discussed politics at revivals

2. there were more ports, shipbuilders, and trading merchants

3. smugglers ignored trade restrictions and sold their goods to whoever paid the highest price.

Skills Workshop

1. d

2. Students might suggest that the Caribbean was closer to the colonies and that it was an important part of the triangular trade pattern

3. b

4. Answers will vary.

Alternative Assessment

Building Your Portfolio

Linking to Community
Private citizens still play an important part in local government. Using newspapers and other resources, find out about an issue in your community that has been raised at a town meeting or a council meeting. Learn about different opinions on the issue as well as what actions were taken. Then write a dramatization of the meeting showing the views of all the participants. Perform the dramatization with some of your classmates.

⧉ internet connect

Internet Activity: go.hrw.com
keyword: SA3 CF5

Choose a topic about life in the English colonies to:
● Analyze the impact of the Zenger case on the concept of freedom of the press.
● Create a model of a concept or theory from the Scientific Revolution.
● Explore modern trade in the original thirteen colonies and create a map.

LET'S GET STARTED!

As students enter the classroom, ask them what types of items that the United States sells to other nations. *(Students' responses will vary, but students should identify various types of mineral and agricultural products as well as consumer goods.)* Then ask students how a map can help a person hypothesize about the products a city or region might sell. Tell students that they will learn more about interpreting maps, charts, and graphs in the unit.

★ TEACH

Have students read the Connecting to Geography lesson. Choose one or more of the following activities to explore the Connecting to Geography content with students.

★ Linking Past to Present

New York City. Today New York City, shown as a colonial city on the map on this page, is known for different products than it was in the 1700s. Many advertising and publishing companies as well as television and radio networks make their headquarters in New York. Almost all of the major publishing companies in the country are based in Manhattan, and the publishing industry continues to grow. The city can certainly be called the mass media capital of the United States.

ACTIVITY: Have students conduct research to find out about the current economy of the other cities shown on the map on p. 148.

SKILLS ANSWERS
1. Portsmouth
2. middle and southern regions near Jamestown, Norfolk, and New Bern
3. These port cities were alive with commercial activity. The exchange of goods through the ports of these cities were part of a trade network created between the colonies and other parts of the world.

Connecting to Geography

Colonial Economies

Many settlers came to the American colonies for economic opportunities. For example, there was a great demand in Europe for furs from North America. Europeans explored north and west looking for new sources of furs.

As the colonies grew, they also became a rich source of farm products. The colonies exported tobacco, rice, and wheat to Great Britain. Plantation owners expanded agricultural production in the southern colonies. As they did so, they imported many enslaved Africans to work their plantations. Slaves cleared land, put up buildings, and tended crops.

As a result of their many efforts, many colonists often were able to improve their standard of living. As settlements grew and colonists sought more land, they came increasingly into conflict with American Indians.

Colonial Trade and Industry

The British colonies produced a variety of goods for sale around the world. Most exports went to Britain, but markets in the West Indies and Europe were also important shipping destinations.

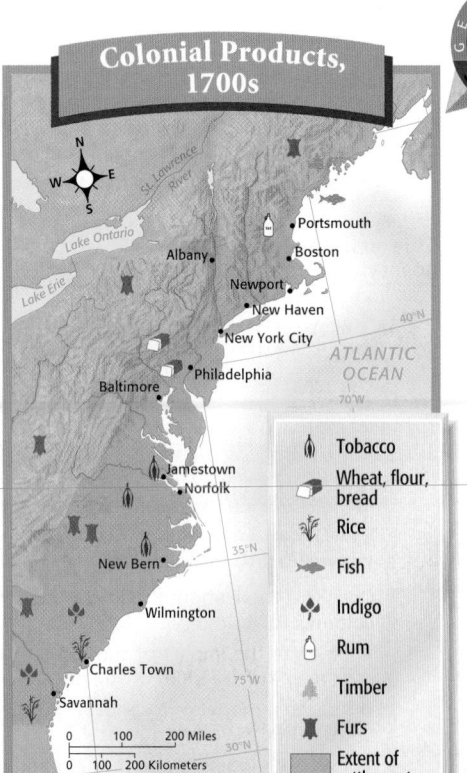

Colonial Products, 1700s

- Tobacco
- Wheat, flour, bread
- Rice
- Fish
- Indigo
- Rum
- Timber
- Furs
- Extent of settlement

0   100   200 Miles
0   100   200 Kilometers
Albers Equal-Area Projection

Geography Skills

Interpreting Thematic Maps

1. Where was fish an important colonial product?
2. **Places and Regions** In what area of the colonies was tobacco an important product?
3. **Drawing Inferences and Conclusions** Why do you think the towns shown on the map were important to colonial trade?

Colonial Boston Harbor

LEVEL 1: Tell students to pretend that they have been chosen by the administrators to welcome new students to the school. Then organize students into groups. Give groups a map of the school and instruct each group that as part of its duties it must draw a map for the new students to assist them in finding their way around the school. Groups' maps should show the main office, the gymnasium, the cafeteria, classrooms and any other areas that are important. Have members of each group pose questions to the other members about which areas of the school are most important, what the quickest routes from one point to another might be, and so on. Group members should answer these questions to ascertain what information the new students should know. Then give each group an imaginary schedule from which they must write directions for the new

students to navigate the school to get to their classes.
ENGLISH LANGUAGE LEARNERS , COOPERATIVE LEARNING

ALL LEVELS: Explain to the class that charts, graphs, and maps can sometimes be illustrated in different ways to emphasize specific aspects of the information presented. Point out the map on p. 151 to students. Ask students what information the map provides. *(Students' answers will vary, but students should state that the map shows from where the slaves were taken and to where they were brought.)* Tell students to draw a chart or pie graph in order to graphically organize information about the percentage of slaves taken to each area. Finally, lead a class discussion on the information given in the chart.
ENGLISH LANGUAGE LEARNERS

British Colonial Exports, 1770

Percentage of total value of exports from the British colonies by destination*

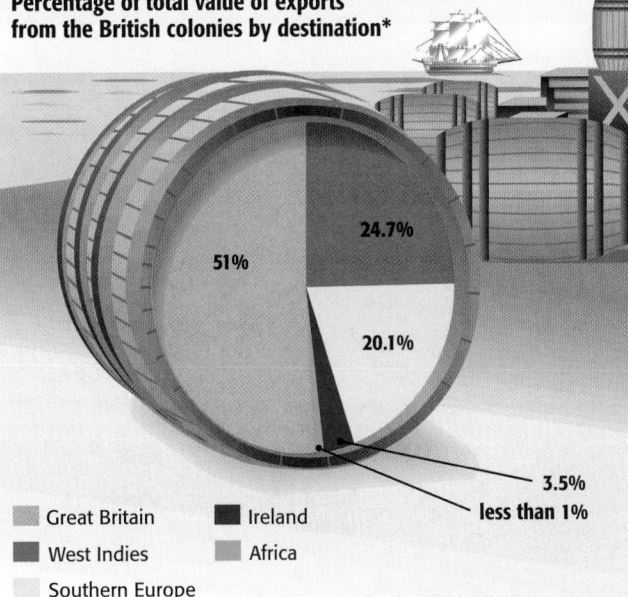

- 24.7%
- 51%
- 20.1%
- 3.5%
- less than 1%

- ■ Great Britain
- ■ West Indies
- ■ Southern Europe
- ■ Ireland
- ■ Africa

*Includes Bahamas, Bermuda, and Newfoundland

Source: *Historical Statistics of the United States*

History Note 1

In the 1700s, most exports from the thirteen colonies went to Great Britain. In recent years, however, most U.S. trade has stayed closer to home. Canada and Mexico are now major markets for U.S. exports. The United States also imports many goods from these two neighboring nations.

Many colonial goods were shipped in barrels.

Geography **Skills**
Interpreting Pie Graphs

1. What percentage of the total value of British exports from colonies in North America went to Britain in 1770?
2. **Human Systems** Which destination received the smallest percentage of the value of colonial exports?
3. **Analyzing Information** Rank each of the destinations shown on the pie graph in order of their importance to the colonial economy. Show your list to a fellow student. Ask him or her to explain why the colonists traded the most with the top two destinations on the list.

History Note 2

Which colony's settlers were the wealthiest? One way to address this question is to compare the average net worth per person in each area. Net worth equals the total value of a person's property, cash, and all other possessions of value minus the debts that they owe. In 1774 a free settler in the southern colonies had more than twice the net worth of a free settler in the middle colonies. A southern settler's net worth was about four times that of a free settler in New England.

★ Economics

Social Classes in Colonial America. Colonial America had a variety of socio-economic classes. At the bottom were people who were legally not free—mainly African American slaves and white indentured servants. Free wage earners ranked above this group. They ranged from unskilled laborers to skilled workers, such as cabinetmakers or tailors. Farmers with smaller parts of land were usually considered on the same level as these urban workers. Large landowners, wealthy merchants, and professional workers ranked at the top of society.

CRITICAL THINKING

Into what class would a shoemaker fall?

ANSWER: Students should suggest that a shoemaker is a skilled worker.

SKILLS ANSWERS
1. 51 percent
2. Africa
3. Great Britain, West Indies, Southern Europe, Ireland, Africa; Great Britain was the mother country, and the West Indies was a British colony.

LEVELS 2 AND 3: Ask students why it might be difficult to judge the distance of the trading routes found on the map on p. 150. *(Students' answers will vary, but students should suggest that the distances are hard to measure because the routes do not follow a straight path.)* Tell students to follow these steps to measure the distance of each route: (a) pin the end of a string to the route's starting point, (b) run the string along the route and mark its endpoint, (c) measure the length of string needed to cover the route, (d) divide the length of the route by the length of the map's scale, (e) and multiply the total from step (d) by the distance per unit given on the scale. For example, if the string measures 9 inches and the scale shows that every 1.5 inches of the map represent 500 miles, students would divide 9 by 1.5, which equals 6. They would then multiply 6 by 500, which equals 3,000. This shows that the route was 3,000 miles long. Have students calculate the length of each route on the map in both miles and kilometers. Allow students time in class to work and have them finish their calculations as home.
ENGLISH LANGUAGE LEARNERS

★ CLOSE

Remind students that line graphs can frequently be used to depict the same information as pie graphs. Show students the pie graph that details British colonial exports found on p. 149. Have students transfer data from the pie graph to a line graph. You may wish to have students draw the graphs on graph paper. Encourage students to use 5 percent intervals on the horizontal axis and to place the names of the countries on the vertical axis.

★ Historical Sidelight

French Fur Traders.
French fur traders, called *coureurs de bois,* lived among American Indians for months at a time to acquire furs. They went to distant places to set their traps, traveling by foot and by canoe. From Indians they learned valuable lessons about survival and trapping animals.

CRITICAL THINKING

Why would living with American Indians of the region have benefited French fur traders?

ANSWER: Students might suggest that the Indians had lived in the region all of the lives, and were able to teach the traders how to live off the land and to trap animals.

SKILLS ANSWERS

1. Great Britain

2. New Orleans; Charles Town

3. Students' answers may vary, but students should note that New Orleans had access to the interior of America by its location near the mouth of the Mississippi River and the Gulf of Mexico and to France by way of sea. Charles Town's location gave the British access to the southeastern colonies and to Britain by sea.

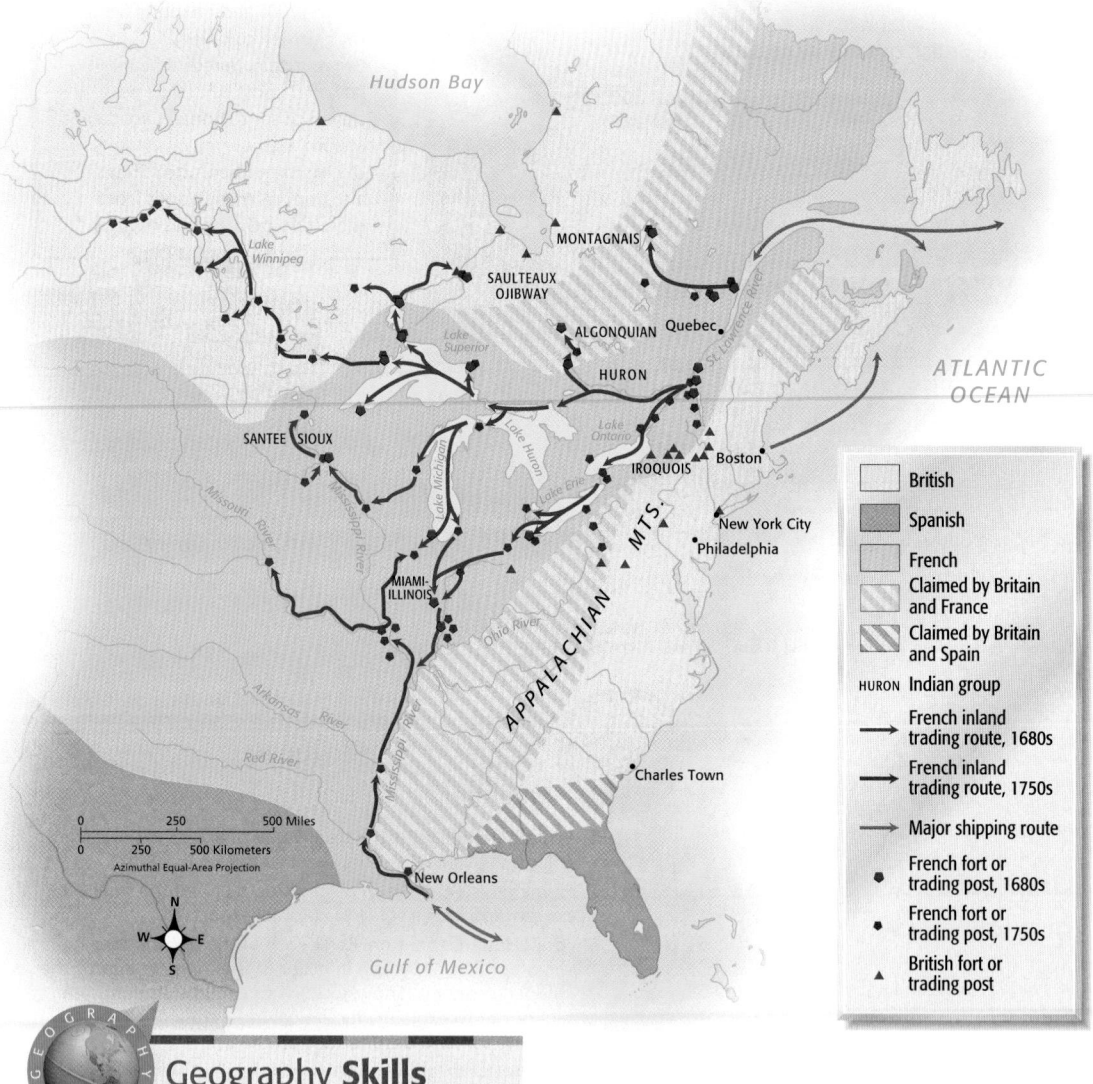

The Growth of the Fur Trade in North America

Geography **Skills**
Interpreting Thematic Maps

1. Which nation's trading posts were located farthest north?
2. **Human Systems** What French town was located farthest south? What British town was located farthest south?
3. **Evaluating** How would the location of these two southern towns have made them important to the French and the British?

History Note 3

The fur trade was very important to French Canada. The French built trading forts along rivers west of the British colonies to protect the fur trade. The thirteen colonies concentrated more on agriculture, although some British colonists traded in furs.

★ **REVIEW AND ASSESS**

Have students review the information in the Connecting to Geography Unit 2. Then have students complete Geography and History Quiz 2.

★ **RETEACH**

Lead a class discussion that reviews how to determine direction by looking at a compass rose on a map and how to judge distances traveled. Have students examine the map on p. 151. Instruct them to describe the general routes that ships traveling to each area followed and the approximate distances of each journey. Ask volunteers to share their findings with the class.
ENGLISH LANGUAGE LEARNERS

★ **EXTEND**

Have students choose a trade route from the map on p. 150. Then have them use the library or other resources to obtain information about the areas located along the route. Have students create a journal that someone who travels along that route today might write. Tell students to include information about the cities, industries, and natural areas that a traveler might encounter as well as facts about the climate and geography of the areas along the route. Remind students to consider the transportation methods used by the traveler when estimating the travel time between areas. Have volunteers read their journal entries to the class. **BLOCK SCHEDULING**

The Slave Trade

Colonial settlers in the Americas imported many enslaved Africans to clear land and plant crops. Slaves were particularly important in the southern British colonies. In these colonies tobacco, rice, and indigo were often grown on large plantations.

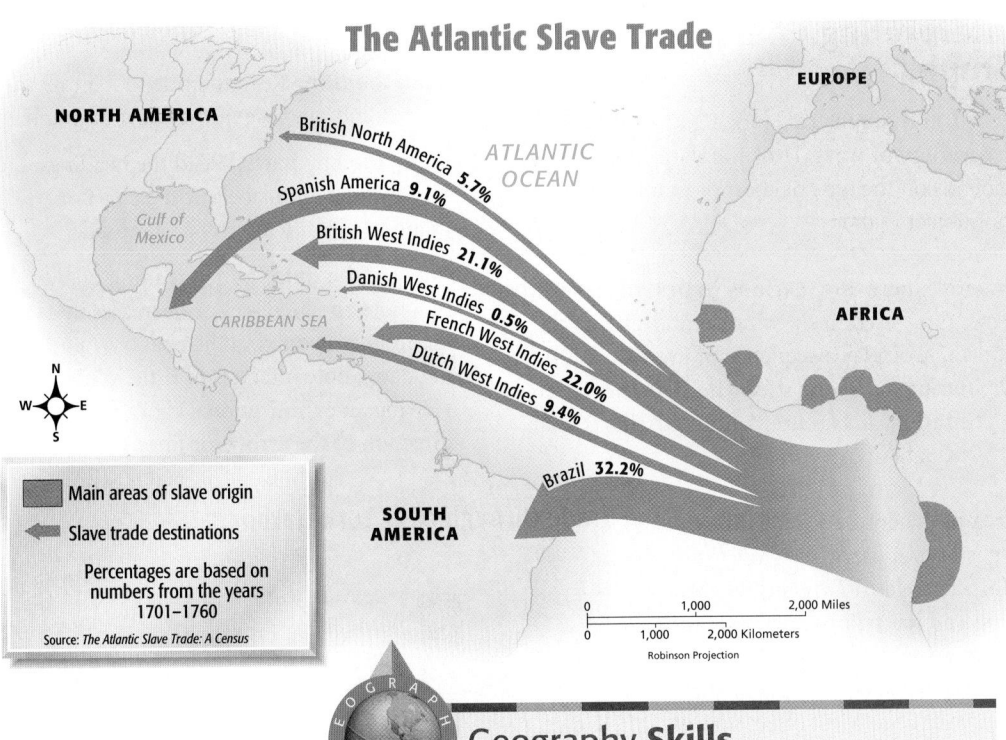

The Atlantic Slave Trade

NORTH AMERICA

British North America 5.7%
Spanish America 9.1%
ATLANTIC OCEAN
EUROPE
British West Indies 21.1%
Danish West Indies 0.5%
French West Indies 22.0%
Dutch West Indies 9.4%
Gulf of Mexico
CARIBBEAN SEA
AFRICA
Brazil 32.2%
SOUTH AMERICA

Main areas of slave origin

Slave trade destinations

Percentages are based on numbers from the years 1701–1760

Source: *The Atlantic Slave Trade: A Census*

```
0        1,000      2,000 Miles
0    1,000   2,000 Kilometers
       Robinson Projection
```

Geography **Skills**

Interpreting Thematic Maps

1. In what part of Africa did most slave trading take place?
2. **Human Systems** What percentage of slaves went to British North America during this period?
3. **Summarizing** Which destination received the highest percentage of slaves? Create a pie graph showing how the percentage of slaves brought across the Atlantic Ocean was divided among the regions shown on the map.

African slave market

History Note 4

Millions of Africans were taken to the Americas as slaves between the 1500s and 1800s. Enslaved Africans were the main labor force for large plantations in North America, South America, and the West Indies. Opposition to slavery grew gradually in the mid-1700s. Great Britain, once one of the world's largest traders in slaves, abolished the slave trade in 1807.

★ **Economics**

Indigo. Indigo has been used in different parts of the world for more than 2,000 years. It was first brought to Europe in the 1500s and then was introduced into North America. By the mid-1700s it was the most important crop of South Carolina. In colonial times, about 1 million pounds of indigo a year were exported to England from the colonies. In later years, however, England began to import indigo from East India.

CRITICAL THINKING

Why might England have turned to East India to supply its indigo needs?

ANSWER: Students might suggest that East India may have provided cheaper or better indigo.

SKILLS ANSWERS
1. along the southwestern coast
2. 5.7 percent
3. Brazil; Students' graphs will vary but should reflect information from the map.

NEW YO

★ TEACH

ALL LEVELS: Explain that charts and graphs can often convey information more efficiently and clearly than detailed explanations. Ask students to identify which type of graph or chart could best present the following type of information: methods of getting to school, who makes up the school administration, the number of students in the class born in a certain month, the number of hours students spend on their homework now compared to the number they spent three years ago, students' favorite TV shows, and students' heights. Then organize students into groups, assigning each group one of the topics above. Ask groups to create a graph and encourage them to provide a title, labels for the axis, and any other information a reader might need to understand the information that they are presenting.

ENGLISH LANGUAGE LEARNERS , COOPERATIVE LEARNING

INTERPRETING CHARTS AND GRAPHS

Have students bring in a newspaper or magazine article that discusses an opinion poll. Then have students find at least two ways to make a chart or graph representing the statistics that the article presents. Remind students to label and title their charts or graphs. Have volunteers interpret their charts or graphs for the class.

SKILLS ANSWERS

1. The labels Caribbean, Great Britain, Ireland, and Other European Countries comprise the horizontal axis. The vertical axis refers to the amount of goods shipped in tons in increments of 1,000—beginning with 0 and ending with 7,000.

2. about 20,000 tons

3. Students might suggest that the vast majority of trade through New York harbor in 1754 was with the Caribbean.

Social Studies Skills
WORKSHOP

Interpreting Charts and Graphs

Charts and graphs categorize and display data in a variety of ways. How the data is displayed depends on the type of chart or graph used and the subject matter.

Charts There are various types of charts. *Flowcharts,* used to show cause-and-effect relationships, display a sequence of events or steps. *Organizational charts* show the structure of an organization. *Tables* are columned charts that present data in categories.

Graphs There are several different types of graphs. A *line graph* often plots changes in quantities over time and has a horizontal axis and a vertical axis. A *bar graph* can also be used to display changes in quantities over time. Most often, however, bar graphs compare quantities within categories. A *pie graph,* or *circle graph,* shows sections of a whole graph as if they were slices of a pie. Taken together, all the sections of this circular graph total 100 percent.

How to Read a Chart or Graph

1. **Read the title.** Read the title to identify the subject and purpose of the chart or graph.

2. **Study the key parts.** Read the headings, subheadings, and labels of the chart or graph to identify the categories used.

3. **Analyze the data.** When reading quantities, note any increases or decreases in amounts presented in the chart. When reading dates, note intervals of time. When viewing an organizational chart, follow the direction of the arrows or lines.

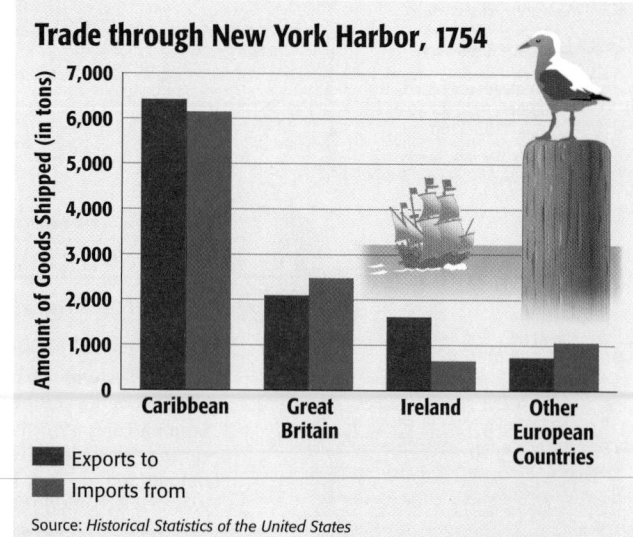

Trade through New York Harbor, 1754

Amount of Goods Shipped (in tons)

Caribbean · Great Britain · Ireland · Other European Countries

■ Exports to
■ Imports from

Source: *Historical Statistics of the United States*

Practicing the Skills

Study the graph above. Then answer the following questions.

1. What labels are used for each axis?
2. What was the total amount of goods shipped through New York Harbor in 1754?
3. Using the information in this graph, what generalizations or conclusions can you draw about colonial trade in 1754?

LEVELS 2 AND 3: Have students review the problem in the History in Action Simulation. Then organize the class into five groups. Ask groups to prepare a written proposal to the king, recommending which colonies are the most important to Great Britain and therefore should continue to receiving funding. Along with the proposal, groups should prepare various charts and graphs to support their recommendations. **COOPERATIVE LEARNING**

LEVEL 3: Organize students into groups. Ask groups to imagine that they are residents of a colony that has been denied further financial assistance from Great Britain. Have groups prepare a persuasive speech to present to Parliament arguing for a reversal of that decision. Ask groups to present their speeches to the class. **COOPERATIVE LEARNING**

History in Action

UNIT 2 SIMULATION

You Make the Decision . . .

Which Colonies Should Receive Financial Support from Great Britain?

Complete the following activity in small cooperative groups. It is 1755. George II is king of England. Britain and France are fighting each other for control of North American colonies and trade routes in the French and Indian War. In order to increase the cash flow for his country, King George II has to cut finances to the colonies. Your group has been asked to help the king decide which colonies Britain should not continue funding. Follow these steps to reach your decision.

1. Gather Information. Use your textbook and other resources to find information that might help you decide which colonies are least valuable to Great Britain. These colonies will not continue to receive financial assistance. Be sure to use what you learned from this unit's Skills Workshop on Interpreting Charts and Graphs to help you make an informed decision. For example, you might refer to charts on colonial exports. You may want to divide different parts of the research among group members.

2. Identify Options. After reviewing the information you have gathered, consider the options you might recommend to the king about which colonies should not get financial assistance. Your final decision may be easier to reach if you consider as many options as

possible. Be sure to record your possible options for your presentation.

3. Predict Consequences. Now take each option you and the members of your group came up with and consider what might be the outcome of each course of action. Ask yourselves questions like: "How will not giving financial support to the colony affect Great Britain?" Once you have predicted the consequences, record them as notes for your presentation.

4. Take Action to Implement Your Decision. After you have considered your options, you should create your presentation. Be sure to make your decision on which colonies should receive financial aid very clear. You will need to support your decision by including information you gathered and by explaining why you rejected other options. Your presentation needs to be visually appealing to convince the king. When you are ready, decide which group members will make each part of the presentation, and then take your decision to the king (the rest of the class). Good luck!

History in Action Ask students to conduct research at the library to investigate how people in history have used decision-making skills with some form of statistical data. For example, students might show how the U.S. government allocated money to fund a war. Then have students represent their findings in a chart, graph, or map illustrating the results of their research. Ask volunteers to present their completed lessons to the class and to explain both the statistical data and the decisions that were made to support that data.

VALUE OF COLONIAL GOODS
- PRODUCT 1
- PRODUCT 2
- PRODUCT 3
- PRODUCT 4
- PRODUCT 5

★ CHAPTER 6
Conflicts in the Colonies

As Britain's colonists in North America continued to push farther west, they came into conflict with American Indians and French settlers. Tensions came to a head in 1754 with the outbreak of the French and Indian War. Britain's victory in the war in 1763 put an end to France's empire in North America. After the war, Parliament became determined to make the American colonists pay for their defense. Claiming that this was "taxation without representation," colonists began to launch angry protests against the British.

★ CHAPTER 7
The American Revolution

Great Britain's continued taxation of the colonies led to open conflict in 1775 at the Battle of Lexington and Concord. In 1776 the Second Continental Congress decided to draft the Declaration of Independence, declaring the United States of America an independent nation. American forces had to fight many long and difficult battles and face numerous hardships before finally winning a decisive victory at Yorktown, which ended the war. The colonists were aided in their struggle by France and Spain, longtime enemies of Britain. In the Treaty of

Internet Activity

Revolutionary War Art Gallery

Have students search the Internet through the HRW Go site to obtain pictures of paintings or sculptures about the American Revolution era or to obtain information about these works or their artists. Next, have students use sheets of posterboard to design their own Web page and to title it Revolutionary War Art Gallery. The posters should provide potential visitors some information about the subject. Remind students that Web sites should be exciting and eye-catching.

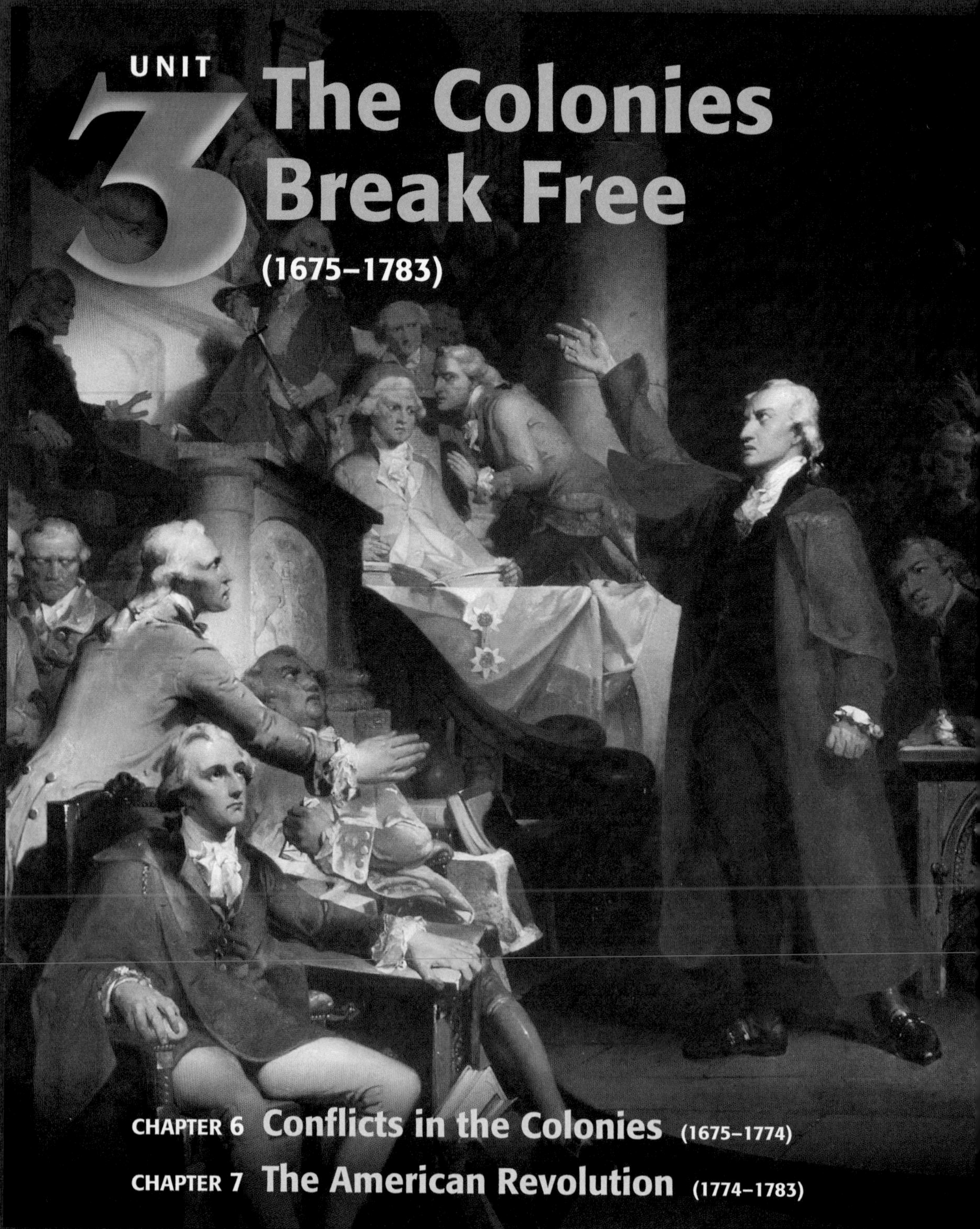

UNIT 3
The Colonies Break Free
(1675–1783)

CHAPTER 6 **Conflicts in the Colonies** (1675–1774)

CHAPTER 7 **The American Revolution** (1774–1783)

Paris of 1783, Parliament recognized U.S. independence and agreed to boundaries for the new nation.

★ UNIT MOTIVATOR

Share the information in the chapter overviews with students. Write each of the unit's chapter titles as headings on the chalkboard. Then lead a brainstorming session about the ideas and topics that students think might be discussed in each of the chapters. Write students' responses under the appropriate headings. Next, have students use these ideas as clues to draw a picture that could be used to illustrate the content of each chapter. Remind students to include captions explaining their pictures. Call on volunteers to present their pictures to the class. After you have finished the unit, refer to the students' pictures and have them evaluate how closely they reflect the content of the chapters.

Young People
IN HISTORY
Young Patriots

Jonathan Nickerson had quite a story to tell. At age 14 he volunteered to join the Continental Army during the Revolutionary War. Years after serving his country, he told of an event that happened outside of White Plains, New York. The year was 1782. About 80 British cavalrymen rode up to a group of American soldiers, including Nickerson. The British demanded, "Surrender, you . . . rebels, surrender!" Outnumbered, Nickerson and several American Patriots laid down their muskets to surrender. However, the British wanted blood and attacked the unarmed men. Nickerson was knocked to the ground and trampled by a horse. Then the British struck him repeatedly in the head and body with a sword. He recalled a soldier asking, "Shall we kill him?" The British commander replied, "No, let him alone. He will die soon himself." Nickerson proved the British captain wrong. He recovered from his wounds and lived to tell about his dramatic brush with death.

Among those who bravely contributed to the revolutionary struggle was 16-year-old Sybil Ludington. In April 1777, Luddington rode some 40 miles through the night to warn American colonists that British forces had landed at Danbury, Connecticut.

Young battlefield drummers, like the boy shown on the left, helped boost soldiers' morale during the Revolutionary War.

Another teenager to fight for American independence was 16-year-old Michael Smith. Smith's regiment served on a gunboat on the Hudson River in New York. The gunboat crew was ordered to protect Americans living in the area from British raiding parties. When a British warship approached the shore to land its raiding party, the gunboat's crew opened fire. The cannon shots that Smith and two of his fellow crew members fired successfully turned the British away. Smith and his crewmates were declared heroes.

If You Were There *How would you help the Patriots?*

LEFT PAGE: *Patrick Henry spoke before the Virginia legislature in favor of American independence.*

★ Using Visual Resources

Historical Art. Years after the event took place, artist Peter Rothermel painted the picture on the opposite page of Patrick Henry's famous speech to the Virginia House of Burgesses. Henry made the speech in 1765 to convince the Virginia legislators to draft a resolution protesting the actions of the British Parliament and King George III. Parliament had recently passed the Stamp Act, which forced all American colonies to pay taxes on printed materials in the colonies. Henry, who was accused of treason for his beliefs, replied "If this be treason, make the most of it!"

CRITICAL THINKING

Judging from the expressions of the people in the painting, how do you think the legislators reacted to Patrick Henry's remarks? Why might they have responded this way?

ANSWER: Students might suggest anger, disbelief, or other descriptions of strong emotion. Henry's beliefs were very revolutionary for the time. Few people dared to openly criticize the government's actions.

	Objectives	Pacing Guide	Reproducible Resources
SECTION 1: **Trouble on the Frontier** (pp. 158–62)	✪ Describe how the English colonists and American Indians viewed each other. ✪ Identify wars that the English colonists fought against other European colonists. ✪ Explain how the French and Indian War affected the British colonies.	**Regular** 1.5 days **Block Scheduling** .5 day *Block Scheduling Handbook with Team Teaching Strategies, Chapter 6*	**RS** Guided Reading Strategy 6.1 **RS** Graphic Organizer 6: Early Conflicts in North America **PS** Primary Source Reading 6: The Outbreak of War **E** Creative Teaching Strategy: Learning Stations
SECTION 2: **Consequences of the French and Indian War** (pp. 163–66)	✪ Explain why many colonists moved to the frontier. ✪ Identify the factors that lead to Pontiac's Rebellion. ✪ Describe the Proclamation of 1763, and analyze its effectiveness.	**Regular** 1.5 days **Block Scheduling** .5 day *Block Scheduling Handbook with Team Teaching Strategies, Chapter 6*	**RS** Guided Reading Strategy 6.2 **SM** Geography Activity 6: Colonial Settlements in the Backcountry
SECTION 3: **Trouble over Taxes** (pp. 167–70)	✪ Explain why Great Britain created new taxes for the colonies. ✪ Explore the reasons that colonists disliked the new tax laws. ✪ Analyze the ways that colonists challenged these new taxes.	**Regular** 2 days **Block Scheduling** 1 day *Block Scheduling Handbook with Team Teaching Strategies, Chapter 6*	**RS** Guided Reading Strategy 6.3
SECTION 4: **New Taxes and Tensions** (pp. 171–75)	✪ Describe colonists' responses to the Townshend Acts. ✪ Analyze why the Boston Massacre and the Boston Tea Party were significant events. ✪ Explain the purpose of the Intolerable Acts.	**Regular** 2 days **Block Scheduling** 1 day *Block Scheduling Handbook with Team Teaching Strategies, Chapter 6*	**RS** Guided Reading Strategy 6.4 **PS** Biography Reading 6: Mercy Otis Warren **PS** Literature Reading 6: Patrick Henry: The Voice of Freedom **E** Hands-On History Activity: Taxing and Spending

Chapter Resource Key

PS Primary Sources
RS Reading Support
IC Interdisciplinary Connections
E Enrichment
SM Skills Mastery

A Assessment
REV Review
ELL Reinforcement and English Language Learners
🖎 Transparencies
💿 CD-ROM

 Music
 Video
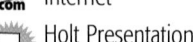 Internet
 Holt Presentation Maker Using Microsoft® PowerPoint®

 🖑 **One-Stop** Planner CD-ROM

See the *One-Stop Planner* for a complete list of additional resources for students and teachers.

One-Stop Planner CD–ROM

It's easy to plan lessons, select resources, and print out materials for your students when you use the **One-Stop Planner CD–ROM with Test Generator.**

Technology Resources

 One-Stop Planner, Lesson 6.1

 Linking Geography and History Transparency 8: North America in 1754, 1763, and 1783

 Holt Researcher: American History CD–ROM

 Homework Practice Online

 One-Stop Planner, Lesson 6.2

 Homework Practice Online

 HRW Go site

 One-Stop Planner, Lesson 6.3

 CNN. Presents America: Yesterday and Today, Beginnings to 1914 Segment: Boycotts, Boycotts, Boycotts

Homework Practice Online

 One-Stop Planner, Lesson 6.4

 Holt Researcher: American History CD–ROM

American Music Selection 5: "The Liberty Song"

Homework Practice Online

Reinforcement, Review, and Assessment

REV	Section 1 Review, p. 162
A	Daily Quiz 6.1
ELL	Main Idea Activity 6.1
ELL	English Audio Summary 6.1
ELL	Spanish Audio Summary 6.1

REV	Section 2 Review, p. 166
A	Daily Quiz 6.2
ELL	Main Idea Activity 6.2
ELL	English Audio Summary 6.2
ELL	Spanish Audio Summary 6.2

REV	Section 3 Review, p. 170
A	Daily Quiz 6.3
ELL	Main Idea Activity 6.3
ELL	English Audio Summary 6.3
ELL	Spanish Audio Summary 6.3

REV	Section 4 Review, p. 175
A	Daily Quiz 6.4
ELL	Main Idea Activity 6.4
ELL	English Audio Summary 6.4
ELL	Spanish Audio Summary 6.4

internet connect

HRW ONLINE RESOURCES
GO TO: go.hrw.com
Then type in a keyword.

TEACHER HOME PAGE
KEYWORD: **SA3 Teacher**

CHAPTER INTERNET ACTIVITIES
KEYWORD: **SA3 CF6**
Choose an activity to:
• research battles of the French and Indian War and create a map of the major engagements.
• examine the fur trade in New France and create a pamphlet on settlements.
• research the life of Daniel Boone and write a biography.

CHAPTER ENRICHMENT LINKS
KEYWORD: **SA3 CH6**

ONLINE ASSESSMENT
Homework Practice
KEYWORD: **SA3 HP6**

Standardized Test Prep
KEYWORD: **SA3 STP6**

Rubrics
KEYWORD: **SS Rubrics**

ONLINE MAPS, CHARTS, AND GRAPHS
KEYWORD: **SA3 MCG**
• Pontiac's Rebellion
• Victories of John Paul Jones
• Battle of Saratoga
• Two Continental Congresses

CONTENT UPDATES
KEYWORD: **SS Content Updates**

HOLT PRESENTATION MAKER
KEYWORD: **SA3 PPT6**

ONLINE READING SUPPORT
KEYWORD: **SS Strategies**

CURRENT EVENTS
KEYWORD: **S3 Current Events**

Meeting Individual Needs

Ability Levels

Level 1 Basic-level activities designed for all students encountering new material

Level 2 Intermediate-level activities designed for average students

Level 3 Challenging activities designed for honors and gifted-and-talented students

English Language Learners Activities that address the needs of students with Limited English Proficiency

Chapter Review and Assessment

IC	Vocabulary Activity 6
	Global Skill Builder CD–ROM
	HRW Go site
REV	Chapter 6 Tutorial for Students, Parents, Mentors, and Peers
REV	Chapter 6 Review, pp. 176–77
	Chapter 6 Test Generator (on the One-Stop Planner)

A	Chapter 6 Test (Form A or B)
A	Alternative Assessment Handbook
A	Chapter 6 Test for English Language Learners and Special-Needs Students

Build on What You Know

If You Were There...

Ask students to answer the following question:

How would you respond to British efforts to increase control of the colonies?

Consider:

- political and economic problems that might arise
- the fear of losing colonies to Great Britain

You Be the Historian

What's Your Opinion?

*To help students create their **Themes** Journal entries, provide the following examples of appropriate **agree**/**disagree** statements.*

EXPLORING THE TIME LINE

GLOBAL EVENTS

internet connect

go.hrw.com

TOPIC: The Battle of Quebec
GO TO: go.hrw.com
KEYWORD: SA3 CF6

Have students access the Internet through the HRW Go site to research the Battle of Quebec. Students should then create a thematic map that shows the British troop movements and major engagements of the battle. Students should create a legend for their map and also write short captions that explain the importance of the battle, a brief description of it, and identify General Wolfe's overall strategy.

CHAPTER 6 Conflicts in the Colonies
(1675–1774)

The Stamp Act required colonists to display stamps such as this one on nearly all paper documents.

THE GRANGER COLLECTION, NEW YORK

George Washington served as a member of the Virginia militia.

UNITED STATES

1676 King Philip's War ends.

1754 George Washington's surrender of Fort Necessity marks the beginning of the French and Indian War.

1763 Pontiac's Rebellion begins in March.

In October King George III issues the Proclamation of 1763, limiting western expansion.

1765 Parliament passes the Stamp Act to raise revenue in the colonies.

1767 Parliament passes the Townshend Acts, which place import duties on many everyday items.

1675 / **1760** **1765**

WORLD

1759 The British capture Quebec from the French.

1763 The Treaty of Paris ends the Seven Years' War.

1764 The British East India Company takes control of Bengal in India.

Colonial artist Benjamin West painted this scene of the Battle of Quebec entitled The Death of Wolfe.

Build on What You Know

A series of wars beginning in the late 1600s between France and Britain left the British as the major European power in eastern North America. As colonists began to move to the frontier, tensions rose between the settlers and American Indians. New British tax laws also upset the colonists.

Global Relations

Agree Colonies should always support their homeland.

Disagree Colonies are not bound to fight the enemies of their mother country.

Geography

Agree Nations always compete with each other for land and territory.

Disagree A nation's expansion or growth never infringes on another nation's territory.

Economics

Agree Lack of representation is the price people must pay in order to be well protected.

Disagree Protection from enemies is a right, not a privilege, and people should not have to sacrifice representation for it.

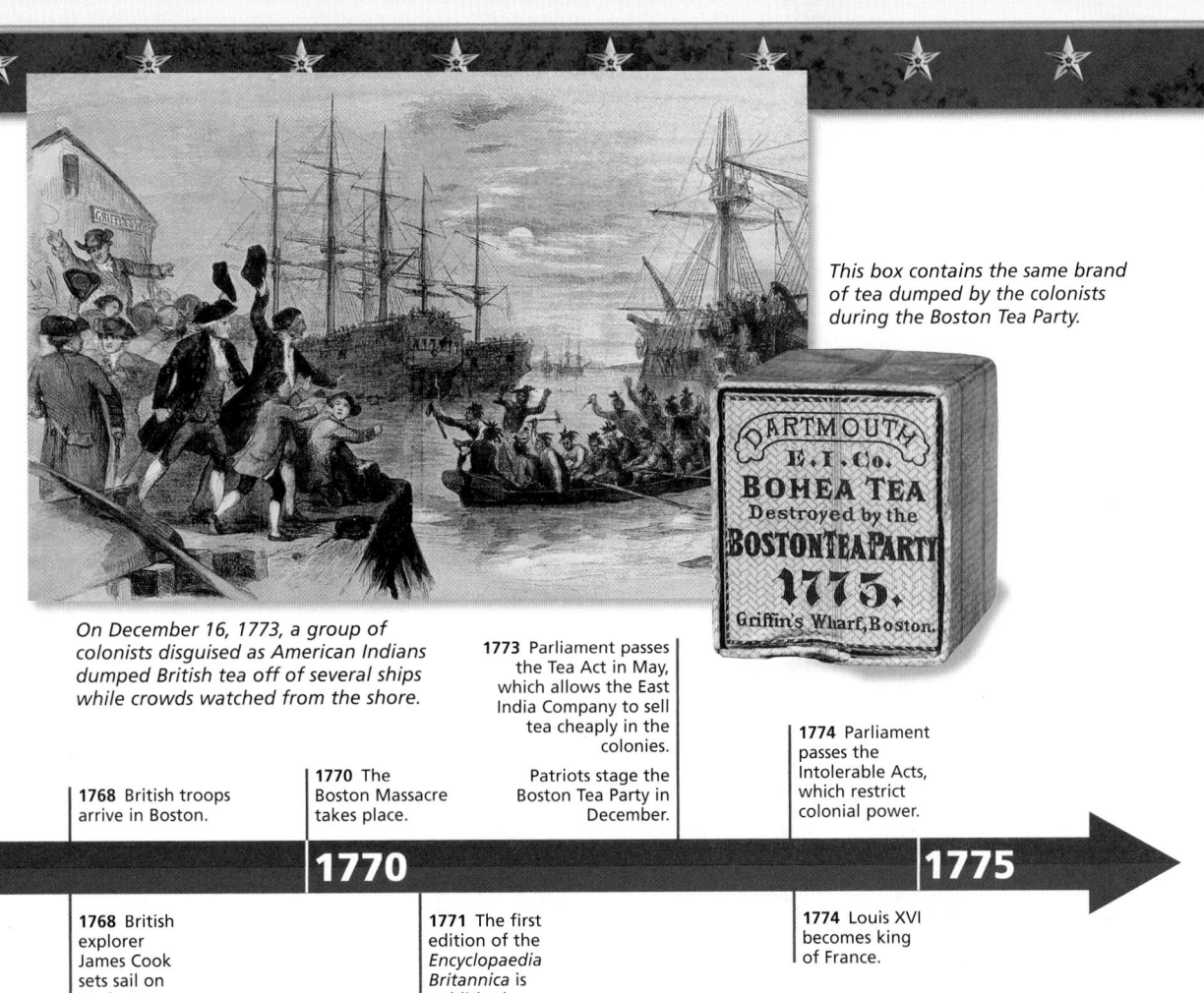

This box contains the same brand of tea dumped by the colonists during the Boston Tea Party.

On December 16, 1773, a group of colonists disguised as American Indians dumped British tea off of several ships while crowds watched from the shore.

1768 British troops arrive in Boston.

1768 British explorer James Cook sets sail on his first trip to the South Pacific.

1770 The Boston Massacre takes place.

1771 The first edition of the *Encyclopaedia Britannica* is published.

1773 Parliament passes the Tea Act in May, which allows the East India Company to sell tea cheaply in the colonies.

Patriots stage the Boston Tea Party in December.

1774 Parliament passes the Intolerable Acts, which restrict colonial power.

1774 Louis XVI becomes king of France.

1770

1775

★ Historical Sidelight

Boston Massacre Martyr. One of the first victims of the American Revolution was Crispus Attucks. A sailor and a former slave, Attucks was one of the first colonists killed in the Boston Massacre on March 5, 1770. As a crowd of colonists gathered around British soldiers, tensions mounted. When a soldier was struck, the other soldiers opened fire on the crowd. Attucks and four others were killed. His body was carried to Faneuil Hall and kept there until all five victims were buried in a common grave. Today Attucks remains a symbol of the beginning of the struggle for Independence. He was the only victim of the Boston Massacre whose name is widely remembered.

ACTIVITY: From the point of view of a colonist sympathetic to independence, have students write a eulogy for Crispus Attucks. Remind them to use standard grammar, spelling, sentence structure, and punctuation.

If you were there . . .
How would you respond to British efforts to increase control of the colonies?

You Be the Historian

Themes Journal

What's Your Opinion? Do you **agree** or **disagree** with the following statements? Support your point of view in your journal.

- **Global Relations** A nation's colonies should fight on its behalf.
- **Geography** The growth of one nation will cause conflict with other nations.
- **Economics** People who are not represented in government will gladly pay taxes if they are protected from their enemies.

Section 1

OBJECTIVES

- ✪ Describe how the English colonists and American Indians viewed each other.
- ✪ Identify wars that the English colonists fought against other European colonists.
- ✪ Explain how the French and Indian War affected the British colonies.

🔊 LET'S GET STARTED!

Write the following question on the chalkboard: *Why did the Europeans want to establish colonies in the Americas?* As students enter the classroom, have them write their responses to the question. *(Students' responses will vary but should include Europeans' desire for land, religious freedom, and economic opportunities).* Explain to the class that when European settlement began in the Americas, it caused conflicts between American Indians and colonists, as well as among European nations. Explain to students that in Section 1 they will learn about relations between English colonists and American Indians, why French and English colonists were frequently at war, and how the French and Indian War affected the English colonies.

Section 1

Trouble on the Frontier

Read to Discover

1. How did English colonists and American Indians view each other?
2. What wars did the English colonists fight against other European colonists?
3. How did the French and Indian War affect the British colonies?

WHY IT MATTERS TODAY

Nations still struggle against each other to control areas of the world. Use CNNfyi.com or other **current events** sources to find out where modern nations are in conflict over land or resources. Record your findings in your journal.

Define

- militia
- casualties

Identify

- Metacomet
- Albany Plan of Union
- Edward Braddock
- Treaty of Paris

Metacomet opposed further colonial expansion onto American Indian lands.

The Story Continues

Chief Massasoit of the Wampanoag made a peace agreement with the Pilgrims in 1621. The agreement lasted his entire life. However, by the 1670s, Massasoit's son Metacomet had begun to distrust and dislike the English colonists. He said that they treated their Wampanoag neighbors poorly and were greedy for more land. Metacomet wanted the colonial leaders to treat him with respect. He finally told the colonists, "Your governor is but a subject. I shall treat [negotiate] only with my brother [equal], King Charles of England."

✪ Colonists' Relations with American Indians

English settlers called **Metacomet** King Philip because he had compared himself to King Charles II. Metacomet opposed the colonists' efforts to take his people's land. At the same time, the colonists were afraid that Metacomet wanted to destroy them. In 1675 these tensions finally erupted into a conflict called King Philip's War. The colonial **militia**—civilians serving as soldiers—fought American Indian warriors.

Have students read Section 1 and complete Guided Reading Strategy 6.1. Choose one or more of the following activities to explore the section content with students. For further suggestions on block scheduling or team teaching, see the *Block Scheduling Handbook with Team Teaching Strategies.*

LEVEL 1: Write the following two headings on the chalkboard: *American Indians* and *English Colonists.* Ask students to describe how these groups interacted, and write the students' responses on the chalkboard, under the correct heading. (*Students' responses might include that the American Indians had their land taken by colonists while some*

colonists and Indians coexisted peacefully.) Then lead a discussion further exploring how American Indians and English colonists viewed each other. **ENGLISH LANGUAGE LEARNERS**

ALL LEVELS: Organize the class into two groups. Have one group use the textbook to conduct research on English colonies in North America. Have the other group research American Indian tribes located near English settlements. Then have each group produce a map representing its topic with either the English colonies or American Indian settlements labeled. Lead a class discussion on how they viewed each other. **ENGLISH LANGUAGE LEARNERS , COOPERATIVE LEARNING**

Both sides also attacked each other's settlements, killing men, women, and children. The fighting finally ended in 1676, but only after about 600 colonists and some 3,000 Indians had been killed, including Metacomet.

Some American Indians allied with the colonists to fight against Metacomet's forces. This alliance was based on trade. Indian leaders wanted tools, weapons, and other goods that Europeans could provide. In exchange, the colonists wanted furs, which they sold for large profits in Europe. As a result, each side came to depend upon the other.

French colonists traded and allied with the Algonquian and Huron. English colonists traded and allied with the Iroquois League. This powerful group united American Indians from six different tribes. Many American Indians trusted the French more than they did the English. This was in part because the smaller French settlements were less threatening to Indians than the rapidly growing English colonies. No matter who their allies were, American Indian leaders took care to protect their people's independence.

History Makers Speak 66We are born free. We neither depend upon [the governor of New France] nor [the governor of New York]. We may go where we please, and carry with us whom we please, and buy and sell what we please.99

—Garangula, an Iroquois leader, quoted in *The World Turned Upside Down,* edited by Colin G. Calloway

✔ **Reading Check: Finding the Main Idea** Why did some American Indians join Europeans in wars against other Indians? to protect trade alliances on which Indians had become dependent

Interpreting the Visual Record

Raiding party *During King Philip's War, colonists and American Indians raided each other's towns and forts.* **Who are the defenders in this image, and what difficulties are the attackers facing?**

★ **Global Relations**

William Johnson. British fur trader William Johnson was at least partly responsible for forging a cooperative relationship between the British and the Iroquois. Upon settling in the Mohawk Valley, Johnson became a fast friend of the Iroquois. By 1746 Johnson had forged such a strong relationship with the Iroquois that the British eventually placed him in charge of the British Crown's northern American Indian affairs. He lived off large grants given to him by the Six Nations and became the owner of some of the most extensive lands in colonial America.

CRITICAL THINKING

What benefits might the British government have hoped to gain by endorsing Johnson's relationship with the Iroquois?

ANSWER: Students might suggest that as an ally of the American Indians, Johnson could promote communication and cooperation between the Iroquois and the British.

Visual Record Answer

Students should suggest that the Indians are the defenders and the attacking colonists have to fight their way uphill as well as being easier targets for the Indians.

ALL LEVELS: Copy the following graphic organizer onto the chalkboard, omitting the italicized answers. Have students complete the chart to identify the effects of the French and Indian War on the British colonies.
ENGLISH LANGUAGE LEARNERS

Cause	Effects
French and Indian War	• British colonies grew in size.
	• Britain became a dominant power in the Americas.
	• Spain grew in power in the Americas.

HOMEWORK Have students create a 10-question quiz that asks questions about the various wars that Britain and the colonies participated in. Students should exchange their quizzes with another student to answer.

LEVEL 3: Organize the class into three groups. Have one group review the material on King Philip's War, another Queen Anne's War, and the final group the French and Indian War. Have each group make a list summarizing the causes and results of the wars that the English colonists fought against other European colonists. Give each group several sheets of poster board and instruct them to design a Web site that outlines the history of the war.
COOPERATIVE LEARNING

★ Geography

Building Fort Duquesne.
The French decided to build their primary northern fort at the fork of the Monongahela River and the Allegheny, which they called "La Belle Rivière"—the Beautiful River. The fortress would be named Fort Duquesne in honor of the man who recommended building it. The plan for its construction looked simple on a map. Execution of the plan, however, would prove tremendously difficult. Almost all building materials had to be transported into the region, forcing the builders to cross vast areas of wilderness. The crossing from Lake Erie to French Creek, which led to La Belle Rivière, was 20 miles. Some 2,000 men had to carry 20,000 pieces of baggage over this route. Every survivor of the expedition recounted losing friends on the unmerciful trail. Even the group's first leader, Paul Marin, died early in the expedition.

CRITICAL THINKING
Given the difficulty of its construction, why did the French think it was so important that they build Fort Duquesne?

ANSWER: Students might mention that it was an important site for continuing the French advance because it involved controlling two important rivers.

★★★★★★★★★★★
That's Interesting!
★★★★★★★★★★★

Following Orders Could you stand still while people shot at you? That's how the British and other Europeans fought during the 1600s and 1700s. Their old muskets were not very accurate. Soldiers were told to get close to the enemy, stand in one place, and shoot as quickly as possible. It could take dozens of shots to hit one enemy soldier! American colonists were not used to this style of fighting, and many had difficulty adjusting to it.

Research on the R⊙M

Free Find:
Iroquois Great Law of Peace
After reading about the Iroquois on the **Holt Researcher CD–ROM**, create a version of the Great Law of Peace for you and your classmates.

★ Conflicts with France

In the late 1600s France and England each wanted control over both Europe and North America. This conflict caused a series of wars between the two empires. The first, King William's War, lasted from 1689 to 1697 but did not change colonial boundaries in North America. Queen Anne's War began in 1702, with England fighting both France and Spain. In the colonies, English and French forces each had American Indian allies who raided the other side's frontier towns. English forces gained the upper hand in the war when they captured French Canada's Port Royal. Later they burned the Spanish settlement of St. Augustine in Florida. In 1713 a treaty ended Queen Anne's War. This time, Great Britain received what are now Hudson Bay, Newfoundland, and Nova Scotia from France. King George's War, fought against France in the 1740s, had little lasting effect on the colonies.

After King George's War, Great Britain and France were still competing for the Ohio Valley and the Great Lakes. British colonists wanted to settle the region. The French believed this settlement would harm their valuable fur trade with American Indians in the area. To protect their interests, the French built three forts in the Ohio Valley, on land claimed by the colony of Virginia. The British colonists felt that the French were keeping them from expanding west. In 1753 Virginia demanded that France give up its forts. When French officers refused, another war seemed likely.

British colonists knew that they were poorly organized and that fighting the French would be dangerous. In 1754 seven colonies sent delegates to Albany, New York. Colonial leaders wanted to make a treaty with the powerful Iroquois League. Soon the colonists were also talking about ways that the colonies could work together. Pennsylvania delegate Benjamin Franklin helped write the **Albany Plan of Union**, which called for all the colonies except Georgia to unite. Franklin based much of the proposal on the example of unified government that the Iroquois League represented.

History Makers Speak ❝It would be a strange thing if Six Nations [of American Indians] should be capable of such a scheme [plan] for such a union, and be able to execute it in such a manner as that it has subsisted [lasted] ages . . . and yet that a like union should be impracticable [not practical] for ten or a dozen English colonies.❞

—Benjamin Franklin, quoted in
From Colonies to Country, by Joy Hakim

However, the colonial governments did not want to give up their individual authority to form a union. They rejected the Albany Plan, as did Parliament.

✔ **Reading Check: Comparing and Contrasting** How were British and French goals for the Ohio Valley similar and different? Both wanted to control the region. The French wanted to protect their fur trade; the British wanted to settle the region.

TEACHER TO TEACHER

Robert Jones of New Hartford, New York, suggested the following activity:

ALL LEVELS: Lead a class discussion about the similarities and differences between French and British colonies in North America. Organize the class so that each student has a partner. Have each pair create a graphic organizer that compares and contrasts the French and British colonies. The vertical axis should contain the following heading: *British Colonies* and *French Colonies*. The horizontal axis should include the following headings: *Size of Colonies, Government Structure,* and

Relationship with American Indians. Have each pair complete the organizer by writing a sentence or two for each category. Finally, discuss the organizers with the class.

ENGLISH LANGUAGE LEARNERS , COOPERATIVE LEARNING

★ CLOSE

Tell students to imagine that they are American Indians who have interacted with settlers who want their lands and furs. Ask each student to create a series of at least three drawings depicting American Indians' responses to the settlers. Have students write captions for their drawings, and then display finished drawings around the classroom.

★ The French and Indian War

While the delegates were meeting in Albany, the British had begun building a fort along the Ohio River. However, the French drove them off and built Fort Duquesne (dooh-KAYN) on the site. A young Virginian named George Washington arrived with more soldiers and built a simple fort, which he named Fort Necessity. The French attacked, causing many **casualties**—killed, injured, or captured soldiers—and forcing Washington to surrender. Washington's defeat in 1754 was the start of the French and Indian War, between Britain and France. In 1756 fighting also began in Europe and elsewhere. This worldwide conflict was called the Seven Years' War.

King George II sent General **Edward Braddock** to command British forces in North America. Braddock knew little about frontier fighting, which led to disaster when he decided to attack Fort Duquesne in 1755. His forces marched straight into a forest ambush

This medallion commemorates the British victory at Quebec.

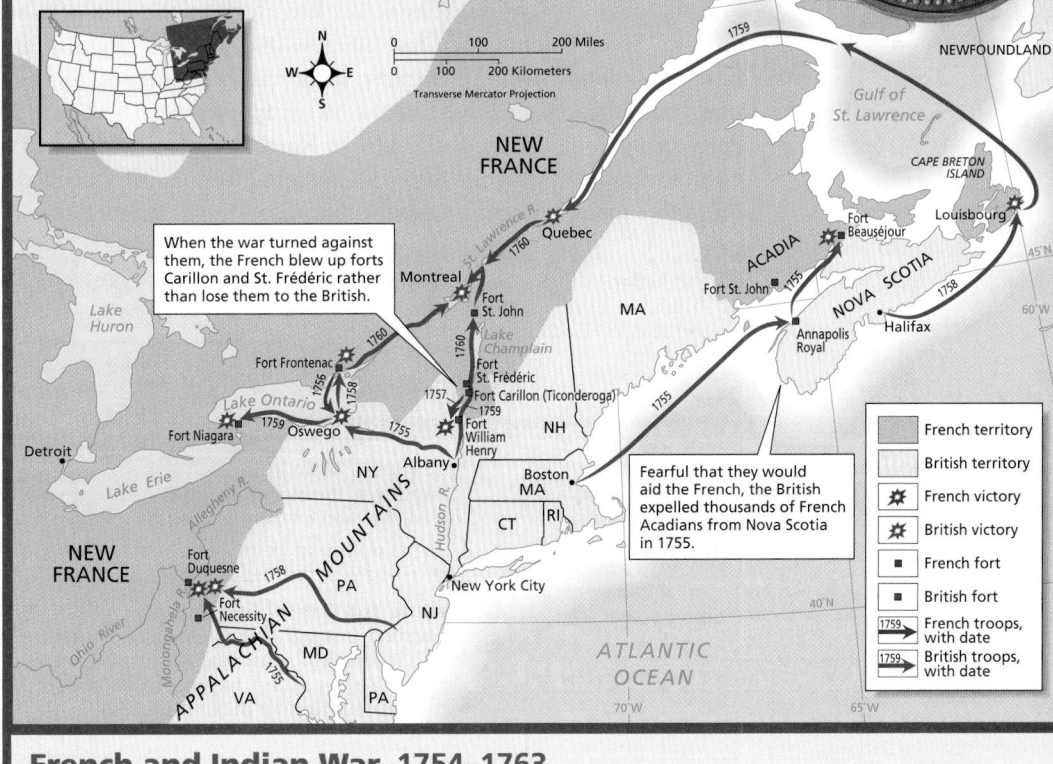

When the war turned against them, the French blew up forts Carillon and St. Frédéric rather than lose them to the British.

Fearful that they would aid the French, the British expelled thousands of French Acadians from Nova Scotia in 1755.

	French territory
	British territory
☼	French victory
☼	British victory
■	French fort
■	British fort
1759 ➤	French troops, with date
1759 ➤	British troops, with date

French and Indian War, 1754–1763

Interpreting Maps Great Britain gained most of France's North American lands at the end of the French and Indian War.

Skills Assessment The World in Spatial Terms Which French fort was located near Lake Erie?

★ REVIEW AND ASSESS

Have students complete the **Section 1 Review** on p. 162. Then have students complete **Daily Quiz 6.1.** As **Alternative Assessment,** you may want to use the settlements map or the graphic organizer depicting the contrasts between the French and British colonies in this section's lessons.

★ RETEACH

Have students complete **Main Idea Activity for English Language Learners and Special-Needs Students 6.1.** Ask students to list specific examples from the section of how European establishment of colonies led to conflicts with American Indians and among European nations.

ENGLISH LANGUAGE LEARNERS

★ EXTEND

Have students research one of the wars covered in this section. Ask them to choose an individual who had a significant influence on the outcome of war. Then have students research and write a brief biography of the subject. Have volunteers present their biographies to the class. Encourage students to ask questions about each individual's involvement in the war.

BLOCK SCHEDULING

Note: As an additional teaching idea, see the Chapter 6 Learning Stations activity in the **Creative Teaching Strategies** handbook.

GLOBAL CONNECTIONS

Spain and the Seven Years' War

During the 1700s, kings from the Bourbon family ruled both France and Spain. These nations signed the Family Compact of 1761, which stated that "whoever attacked one crown, attacked the other." This Family Compact drew Spain into the conflict between France and Great Britain. Spain paid a high price for joining the war. In the Treaty of Paris, Britain gained control of Florida. Britain had become Spain's main enemy in North America. **Why did Spain enter the Seven Years' War?**

by French and American Indian troops. As one survivor explained, "The Enemy kept behind Trees, and cut down our Troops." The surprised British soon retreated. The British suffered almost 500 casualties, including Braddock himself, but the French and American Indians lost just 50.

The turning point of the war came in 1759, when British general James Wolfe captured Quebec, the capital of New France. Both Wolfe and the French commander were killed in the battle. Although fighting continued until 1763, Britain won most of the important battles.

★ The Treaty of Paris

Finally, in 1763 Great Britain and France signed the **Treaty of Paris,** officially ending the war. The treaty stated that the war "had spread trouble in the four parts of the world." Now the two sides wanted peace. In the process of ending their conflict, Britain and France redrew the political map of North America.

The terms of the treaty gave Canada to Britain, which also gained all French lands east of the Mississippi River except the city of New Orleans. From Spain, which had allied with France in 1762, Britain received Florida. (In an earlier treaty, Spain received Louisiana, the land that France had claimed west of the Mississippi River.) The Treaty of Paris changed the balance of power in North America. Britain had a claim to almost all land east of the Mississippi River. Spain was now the only other major European nation with lands in North America.

✔ **Reading Check: Identifying Cause and Effect** What caused the French and Indian War, and how did it affect North America? France captured a British fort; Britain gained Canada, all French lands east of the Mississippi River, and Spanish Florida.

Section 1 Review

go.hrw.com **Homework Practice Online**
keyword: SA3 HP6

❶ **Define and explain:**
• militia
• casualties

❷ **Identify and explain:**
• Metacomet
• Albany Plan of Union
• Edward Braddock
• Treaty of Paris

❸ **Summarizing** Copy the table below. Use it to explain how each of the five wars that British colonists fought against Europeans and American Indians affected the American colonies.

War	Opponent	Effect on Colonies

❹ **Finding the Main Idea**
a. What was the main cause of the French and Indian War, and how did it affect the colonies?

b. What do you think might have happened if France had won the French and Indian War?

❺ **Writing and Critical Thinking**
Evaluating Imagine that you are an American Indian leader living near the British and French colonies. Write a speech for your council that expresses your feelings about the British colonists.

Consider the following:
• worries about British expansion
• the value of trade with the British
• actions of the French compared to the British

Section 2

OBJECTIVES

⭐ Explain why many colonists moved to the frontier.

⭐ Identify the factors leading to Pontiac's Rebellion.

⭐ Describe the Proclamation of 1763, and analyze its effectiveness.

📀 LET'S GET STARTED!

Write the following statement on the chalkboard: *Define the term* **backcountry**. As students enter the classroom, allow them time to respond. *(Students' responses will vary, but students should identify backcountry as a thinly settled rural area.)* Ask students if there are still areas in the United States that could be described as backcountry. *(Students' responses will vary but students should mention that such areas do exist.)* Explain to students that in the 1760s, the United States had a significant amount of backcountry in the area between the coastal settlements and the Appalachian Mountains. Explain to students that in Section 2 they will learn about the reasons for expansion onto the frontier and the problems associated with it.

Section 2

Consequences of the French and Indian War

Read to Discover

1. Why did many colonists move to the frontier?
2. What factors led to Pontiac's Rebellion?
3. What was the Proclamation of 1763, and how effective was it?

WHY IT MATTERS TODAY

Great Britain tried to tell its colonists where they could and could not live. Use **CNNfyi.com** or other **current events** sources to find an area that a modern government has made off-limits to growth. Record your findings in your journal.

Define
- backcountry
- pioneers

Identify
- Pontiac's Rebellion
- King George III
- Proclamation of 1763

SECTION 2 RESOURCES

REPRODUCIBLE
▶ Guided Reading Strategy 6.2
▶ Geography Activity 6: Colonial Settlements in the Backcountry

TECHNOLOGY
▶ One-Stop Planner, Lesson 6.2
▶ Homework Practice Online
▶ HRW Go site

REINFORCEMENT, REVIEW, AND ASSESSMENT
▶ Section 2 Review, p. 166
▶ Daily Quiz 6.2
▶ Main Idea Activity 6.2
▶ English Audio Summary 6.2
▶ Spanish Audio Summary 6.2

The Story Continues

In 1759 British minister Andrew Burnaby decided to visit the American colonies to learn about their culture. He found life on the frontier interesting and kept a journal of his travels. To Burnaby, Americans seemed to want more and more new land. He wrote that families "will gradually retire [move] westward and settle upon fresh land."

Early pioneers used wagons such as this one to settle the frontier.

THE GRANGER COLLECTION, NEW YORK

⭐ The Frontier

Colonists set up most of the early settlements along the eastern coast or by major rivers. To the west was a huge frontier. Fur traders and a few forts were often the only signs of Europeans in this area. Yet European settlers slowly moved into the Virginia and Carolina **backcountry**. The backcountry was a thinly populated frontier area between the coastal settlements and the Appalachian Mountains. The first Europeans to settle the frontier were called **pioneers**. They risked attacks from American Indians who resisted this settlement on their land. There was little colonial settlement in what is now Tennessee and Kentucky until the 1770s.

Have students read Section 2 and complete Guided Reading Strategy 6.2. Choose one or more of the following activities to explore the section content with students. For further suggestions on block scheduling or team teaching, see the *Block Scheduling Handbook with Team Teaching Strategies.*

LEVEL 1: Write the following question on the chalkboard: *What were the causes of Pontiac's Rebellion?* Ask students to identify the reasons. Then write their responses on the chalkboard under the question. *(Students' responses should include: the British ban on gifts to the American*

Indians and the movement of British settlers onto American Indian lands). **ENGLISH LANGUAGE LEARNERS** ,
COOPERATIVE LEARNING

ALL LEVELS: Give students a blank outline map that features the eastern half of the United States after 1763. Have them identify the areas where colonists settled on the frontier after 1763. **ENGLISH LANGUAGE LEARNERS**

HOMEWORK Ask students to write a proposal to King George III which would solve the problems between the settlers and American Indians other than issuing the Proclamation of 1763.

★ Geography

The Appalachian Mountains. Stretching in a series of almost continuous mountain ranges from the Canadian province of Newfoundland to central Alabama, the Appalachians served as a formidable border between eastern colonial settlements and the West. The range, though quite long, is actually very narrow, rarely exceeding 100 miles wide. The mountains of the range vary in height, with the highest peak—Mount Mitchell in North Carolina—reaching 6,684 feet above sea level. The range's lowest areas are located in Massachusetts and Connecticut.

CRITICAL THINKING

Why do you think settlements originally stopped at the base of the Appalachian Mountains?

ANSWER: Students might suggest that early settlers traveled by horse and wagon, so it was difficult to cross the mountains, and they feared American Indian attacks.

MAP ANSWERS

1. Fort Detroit, Fort Sandusky, Fort Presque Isle
2. Fort Detroit

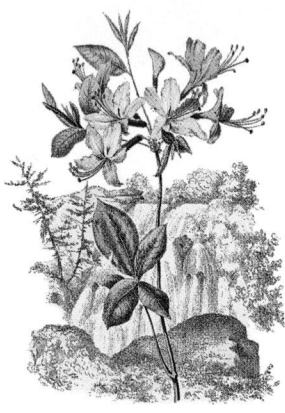

Wild honeysuckle was one of the many colorful plants that pioneers encountered in the Ohio Valley.

Some pioneers crossed the Appalachians farther to the north. They moved into the forested lands along the Ohio River in the 1750s. Pioneers found that the soil in the Ohio River valley was good for farming, and the valley was full of wild game such as turkey and deer. Although these were good conditions, fears of American Indian attacks kept British settlements small and isolated. However, this worry eased after the British won the French and Indian War. Then settlers began crossing the Appalachian Mountains in greater numbers.

✔ **Reading Check: Summarizing** When and why did pioneers begin settling in large numbers beyond the Appalachian Mountains? after the British victory in the French and Indian War; reduced colonists' fears of Indian raids and renewed their interest in western land

★ Conflict in the Ohio River Valley

After the Treaty of Paris, Great Britain replaced France as the European power in the Ohio River valley. The British believed they were entitled to the land that France had controlled. This area included all of the American Indian lands in the Ohio River valley and the Great Lakes region. Unlike the French, the British wanted to build settlements in the area. This new policy led to problems between the British and American Indian leaders who opposed an increase in British settlements.

Pontiac's Rebellion

Interpreting Maps American Indians under the leadership of the Ottawa chief Pontiac won early battles, but their inability to capture key forts eventually doomed their rebellion.

Skills Assessment

1. **Locate** What British forts lay along Lake Erie?
2. **Analyzing Information** What British fort was not captured despite many nearby American Indian victories?

Chief Pontiac

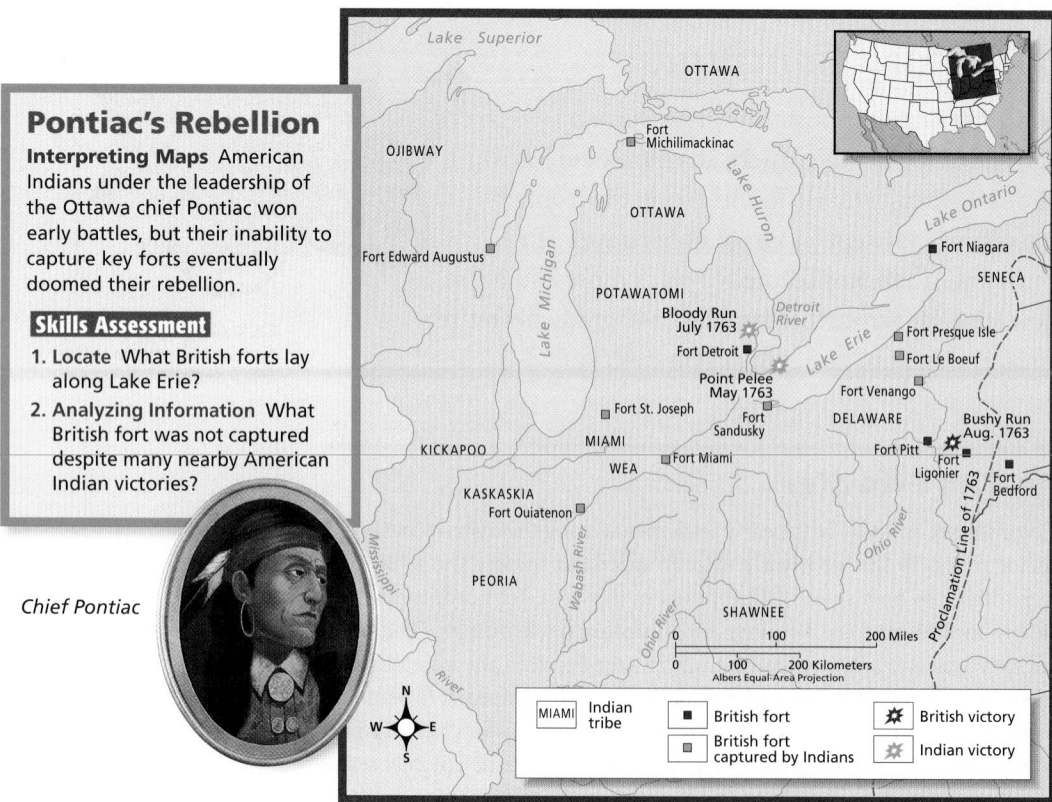

THE GRANGER COLLECTION, NEW YORK

These leaders had not signed any treaties with Britain and would not give up their land because of an agreement between Britain and France. Chippewa leader Minavavana expressed this view to a trader in 1761. "Englishman, although you have conquered the French, you have not yet conquered us!"

In the 1760s American Indian tribes began to join together to resist the British. Chief Pontiac of the Ottawa led forces that included the Delaware, Huron, Miami, Ottawa, and Shawnee peoples. Pontiac followed the teachings of the so-called Delaware Prophet. This leader called on Indians to drive out the white settlers and give up all European practices. In 1763 Pontiac shared these ideas with a gathering of American Indians.

> **History Makers Speak** ❝How comes it that you suffer the whites on your lands? Can't you do without them? You might live wholly [completely] as you did before you knew them. . . . Those who come to trouble your country, drive them out, make war [on] them! . . . They are my enemies and the enemies of your brothers!❞
>
> —Pontiac, quoted in *The World Turned Upside Down*, edited by Colin G. Calloway

Pontiac's Rebellion began in May 1763 when American Indians attacked British forts on the frontier. Within a month Pontiac's forces had destroyed or captured seven forts. Pontiac then led the attack on Fort Detroit, Britain's political and trading center in the Great Lakes area. Despite the best efforts of Pontiac and his allies, the British held out for months. The American Indians following Pontiac grew tired of attacking the fort and returned to their villages. An Indian attack on the important British position at Fort Pitt also failed. Both sides suffered many casualties. As more Indians left Pontiac, he surrendered in 1766.

✔ **Reading Check: Identifying Cause and Effect** Why did Pontiac and his followers fight the British, and what happened as a result? British encroached on their land; Pontiac's forces destroyed several British forts but were defeated.

Interpreting the Visual Record

Fort Detroit *Pontiac's forces tried for months to capture Fort Detroit from the British.* **What in the image suggests the difficulties of attacking the fort?**

Analyzing Primary Sources

Identifying Points of View How does Pontiac describe white settlers? as enemies of the Indians who should be driven off Indian lands

☆ REVIEW AND ASSESS

Have students complete the **Section 2 Review** on p. 166. Then have students complete **Daily Quiz 6.2**. As **Alternative Assessment**, you may want to use the parliamentary committee cooperative learning activity or the Proclamation of 1763 graphic organizer activity in this section's lessons.

☆ RETEACH

Have students complete **Main Idea Activity for English Language Learners and Special-Needs Students 6.2**. Ask students to write a brief summary of the events that led to the Proclamation of 1763 from the perspective of an American Indian. Have students include in the summary the goal and the effectiveness of the Proclamation.

ENGLISH LANGUAGE LEARNERS

☆ EXTEND

Have students use the library to locate information on the American Indian nations they studied in this section and the treaties that were made with them. Ask students to compare the terms of treaties established with at least two different nations. Then have them create a list of similarities and differences between the treaties. Have volunteers share their lists with the class, and then lead a class discussion on the treaties.

BLOCK SCHEDULING

BIOGRAPHY ANSWER
He wanted to maintain control of the colonies.

★ ★ ★ ★ ★ ★ ★ ★

Section 2 Review
ANSWERS

❶ **Define**
- backcountry, p. 163
- pioneers, p. 163

❷ **Identify**
- Pontiac's Rebellion, p. 165
- King George III, p. 166
- Proclamation of 1763, p. 166

❸ Causes—settlers moved onto Indian land; Pontiac's Rebellion took place on the frontier; Proclamation of 1763—banned settlement beyond the Appalachians, orders colonists in the upper Ohio River valley to leave; Effect—many ignore the ban

❹ a. British victory in the French and Indian War reduced the risk of Indian attacks
b. the British wanted to settle the region and were moving onto Indian lands—the British were therefore seen as a threat

❺ Students' letters will vary but should address the following: feel safer on the frontier with the British victory in the French and Indian War, Pontiac's Rebellion and poor relations with American Indians worry them, some students might make fun of the Proclamation of 1763 while others might say it bothers them to be breaking the law.

THE GRANGER COLLECTION, NEW YORK

BIOGRAPHY

King George III
(1738–1820)

George III became king of Great Britain in 1760. King George had many rigid views. He wanted to assert his royal power and keep a strict rule over the colonies. But the economic and political changes that took place during his rule were beyond his control, and his harsh measures could not keep the Thirteen colonies loyal. In 1788 King George began to show signs of mental illness, and by 1811 his son had to rule as king until George's death in 1820. **What did King George III hope to achieve?**

☆ The Proclamation of 1763

Tensions with American Indians worried officials in the British government. Leaders feared that more fighting would take place on the frontier if colonists kept moving onto American Indian lands. These conflicts would disrupt trade in the region and force Britain to spend more money on defense. To avoid these problems, Britain's **King George III** issued the **Proclamation of 1763**. This law banned the British from settling west of the Appalachian Mountains. The Proclamation created a border between colonial and American Indian lands. King George stated his position.

History Makers Speak
❝It is just and reasonable and essential to our interest and the security of our colonies that the several nations or tribes of Indians with whom we are connected, and who live under our protection should not be . . . [attacked] or disturbed.❞

—Proclamation of 1763, from *The Annals of America*

The Proclamation also ordered colonists in the upper Ohio River valley "to remove themselves from such settlements." Many colonists defied the Proclamation. Some felt that Britain should allow the colonies to grow rapidly following France's defeat.

The Proclamation proved difficult to enforce. Most people who wanted to settle or trade in the Ohio River valley ignored it. As explorers like Daniel Boone led people west of the Appalachians, colonial settlement expanded. The colonists' disregard for the Proclamation showed their increasing unhappiness with British attempts to control them.

✔ **Reading Check: Summarizing** Why did King George III issue the Proclamation of 1763, and how did colonists respond to it? to prevent conflict with Indians; colonists opposed it, because they wanted to settle western lands

go. hrw .com
Homework Practice Online
keyword: SA3 HP6

Section 2 Review

★ ★

❶ **Define and explain:**
- backcountry
- pioneers

❷ **Identify and explain:**
- Pontiac's Rebellion
- King George III
- Proclamation of 1763

❸ **Identifying Cause and Effect** Copy the diagram below. Use it to show the reasons that Great Britain issued the Proclamation of 1763 and how it affected the colonies.

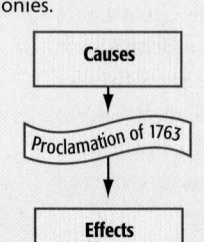

Causes

↓

Proclamation of 1763

↓

Effects

❹ **Finding the Main Idea**
a. Why did colonists move west of the Appalachians?

b. Why did American Indians in the Ohio River valley unite and join Pontiac to fight the British?

❺ **Writing and Critical Thinking**
Supporting a Point of View Imagine that you are a settler on the frontier in the 1760s. Write a letter to relatives back East explaining what you do or do not like about living on the frontier.

Consider the following:
- relations between pioneers and American Indians
- the British victory in the French and Indian War
- the Proclamation of 1763

Section 3

OBJECTIVES

⭐ Explain why Great Britain created new taxes for the colonies.

⭐ Explore the reasons colonists disliked the new tax laws.

⭐ Analyze the ways that colonists challenged the new taxes.

 **LET'S GET STARTED!**

Write the following question on the chalkboard: *What would you do if your favorite type of clothing suddenly cost three times as much as it did the last time you bought it?* As students enter the classroom, allow them time to write their responses. *(Students' responses will vary, but students might reply that they would try to find it somewhere else for a better price or wait until it went on sale.)* Tell students that this situation is similar to what happened to colonists when England established a series of new taxes. Explain to students that in Section 3 they will find out why Britain created these new taxes, what the colonists disliked about them, and how the colonists protested them.

Section 3

Trouble over Colonists' Rights

Read to Discover

1. Why did Great Britain create new taxes for the colonies?
2. Why did colonists dislike the new tax laws?
3. How did colonists challenge these new taxes?

WHY IT MATTERS TODAY

Colonists formed organizations to protest British abuses of colonial rights. Use **CNNfyi.com** or other **current events** sources to research a modern organization that protests violations of certain rights. Record your findings in your journal.

Define

- boycott
- repeal

Identify

- George Grenville
- Sugar Act
- James Otis
- Samuel Adams
- Committees of Correspondence
- Stamp Act
- Sons of Liberty
- Patrick Henry

SECTION 3 RESOURCES

REPRODUCIBLE

▶ Guided Reading Strategy 6.3

TECHNOLOGY

▶ One-Stop Planner, Lesson 6.3

▶ **CNN** Presents America: Beginnings to 1914 Segment: Boycotts, Boycotts, Boycotts

▶ Homework Practice Online

REINFORCEMENT, REVIEW, AND ASSESSMENT

▶ Section 3 Review, p. 170

▶ Daily Quiz 6.3

▶ Main Idea Activity 6.3

▶ English Audio Summary 6.3

▶ Spanish Audio Summary 6.3

The Story Continues

Great Britain had heavy debts from its recent war against France. Prime Minister and Lord of the Treasury George Grenville set out to pay these debts. After taking office in 1763, he spared no one in his search for money. Grenville turned his attention to the American colonists.

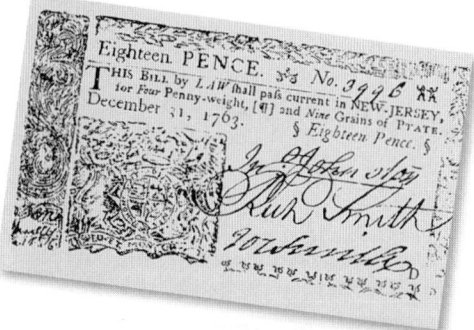

The colonies used bills such as this New Jersey 18-pence note for currency.

⭐ Raising Taxes

Great Britain had won the French and Indian War, but Parliament still had to pay for it. In addition, Britain kept an army in North America to protect the colonists against American Indian attacks. To help pay for this standing army, Prime Minister **George Grenville** asked Parliament to tax the colonists. In 1764 Parliament passed the **Sugar Act**. This law set duties, or taxes, on molasses and sugar imported by colonists. This was the first act passed specifically to raise money in the colonies, rather than to regulate trade.

In addition to passing new taxes, the British would not let the colonies print their own money. Parliament also made life much harder for

Have students read Section 3 and complete Guided Reading Strategy 6.3. Choose one or more of the following activities to explore the section content with students. For further suggestions on block scheduling or team teaching, see the *Block Scheduling Handbook with Team Teaching Strategies.*

LEVEL 1: Organize the class into small groups. Ask each group to imagine that it is living in the colonies shortly after the imposition of new taxes by the British government. Have each group discuss its options regarding the new taxes *(Students' discussions might include the following: pay the tax, protest and pay the tax, refuse to pay, boycott British goods, or destroy British goods.)* Tell members of each group to make a list of the arguments for and against each option and to vote on which option they support. Finally, lead a class discussion about the methods that colonists actually used when faced with these new taxes.* **ENGLISH LANGUAGE LEARNERS , COOPERATIVE LEARNING**

 HOMEWORK Have students prepare a flyer that calls for colonists to boycott British goods. Students should note why the boycott is necessary, who should participate in the boycott, and what the organizers hope to accomplish with their boycott.

☆ Government

The Sugar Act. Many colonists were angry over the passage of the Sugar Act because it took away rights that they had previously enjoyed. Persons accused of violating the act would now be tried in faraway Halifax, Nova Scotia instead of local courts. This meant that the accused would most likely not have a speedy trial. The vice-admiralty courts established by the act also violated colonists' rights to a trial by jury. In addition, the Sugar Act denied the accused the right to sue for false seizure of goods and placed the burden of proof on the accused, rather than on the government.

CRITICAL THINKING

Why would colonists have viewed the Sugar Act as both an economic, and political threat?

ANSWER: Answers might include that the act would cost the accused money to defend themselves and that it violated colonists' traditional rights.

VISUALIZING HISTORY ANSWERS

1. by taking their goods and ships from them
2. the government receives an income from trash goods

Parliament's New Tax Policies

Parliament made great efforts to force colonists to obey mercantile laws and pay the new taxes.

Colonial merchants had to give royal officials a list of all the trade goods on their ships. This made it hard for traders to avoid paying duties.

The British also began to stop and search ships for smuggled goods.

Traders caught smuggling could have their goods and ships taken from them.

Visualizing History

1. **Government** How did the British punish smugglers?

2. **Connecting to Today** Why is it important for a government to stop smugglers?

Samuel Adams encouraged colonists to protest the new British taxes.

DEPOSITED BY THE CITY OF BOSTON, COURTESY, MUSEUM OF FINE ARTS BOSTON

smugglers by giving the vice-admiralty courts greater powers. These courts had no juries, and their judges treated suspected smugglers as guilty until proven innocent. In regular British courts, accused persons were treated as innocent until proven guilty. In addition, trial by jury was a recognized right of British citizens.

✔ **Reading Check: Finding the Main Idea** In what ways did Parliament's new laws increase British control of the American colonies? tax and currency regulations; crackdown on smugglers; use of vice-admiralty courts

☆ Taxation without Representation

Parliament's actions upset many colonists who had grown used to being independent. Merchants thought the taxes were unfair and hurt business. **James Otis**, a lawyer from Boston, was one of the first colonists to protest taxation by Parliament. Otis argued that Parliament could not "take from any man any part of his property, without his consent in person or by representation." No one in Britain had asked the colonists if they wanted to be taxed. The colonists had no direct representatives in Parliament. In addition, colonial assemblies had little influence on Parliament's decisions. Therefore, Otis said, the tax was unfair and violated colonists' rights.

At a Boston town meeting in May 1764, leader **Samuel Adams** agreed with Otis. He believed that Parliament could not tax the colonists without their consent and said that agreeing to the tax would be dangerous.

ALL LEVELS: Copy the following graphic organizer onto the chalkboard, omitting the italicized answers. Use it to identify the reasons that the colonists disliked the new laws. **ENGLISH LANGUAGE LEARNERS**

NEW TAXES

Reasons Colonists Disliked the Taxes:

1. *taxation without representation*
2. *reflected British efforts to gain more control*
3. *challenged the colonists' efforts to be more autonomous*
4. *hurt colonial economy*

LEVEL 3: Organize the class into small groups. Have each group create a British proclamation that announces new taxes for the colonies. Ask the students to ensure that their proclamations include a description of the new taxes, as well as the reasons the taxes are being created. **COOPERATIVE LEARNING**

★ CLOSE

Tell students to imagine that they live in Boston at the time of the Stamp Act. Have each student write a diary entry describing everyday life in Boston after the Stamp Act went into effect. Diary entries should explain the purpose of the new taxes and colonists' feelings about them.

History Makers Speak

❝For if our trade may be taxed, why not our lands? Why not the produce of our lands and, in short, everything we possess or make use of?❞

—Samuel Adams, quoted in *Patriots,* by A. J. Langguth

The ideas of Otis and Adams helped spread the slogan "No Taxation without Representation" throughout the colonies.

Adams also helped found the **Committees of Correspondence**, groups that contacted other towns and colonies. They shared ideas and information about the new British laws and ways to challenge them. A popular protest method was the **boycott**, in which people refuse to buy certain goods. In many homes women made substitutes for British goods. The boycott began in Massachusetts and soon spread to other colonies. Colonists hoped such efforts would hurt the British economy, perhaps convincing Parliament to end the new taxes.

✔ **Reading Check: Analyzing Information** How did Samuel Adams and James Otis influence colonial protests against new taxes? They argued for no taxation without representation, and Adams helped form Committees of Correspondence to organize protests.

★ The Stamp Act

By early 1765 Prime Minister Grenville had heard the complaints about the Sugar Act. He asked the colonists if they had a better plan for paying their share of military costs. Some colonists suggested taxing themselves, but Grenville rejected the idea. Grenville then proposed the **Stamp Act**, which Parliament passed in March 1765. This act affected most colonists. It required them to pay for an official stamp, or seal, whenever they bought paper items. The tax had to be paid on legal documents, licenses, newspapers, pamphlets, and even playing cards. Colonists who refused to buy stamps could be fined or sent to jail.

Grenville thought this tax was fair. After all, in Britain people already paid similar taxes. But colonists saw it differently. The Stamp Act was Parliament's first effort to raise money by taxing them directly. Protests against the Stamp Act began almost immediately.

In places such as New York and Massachusetts, colonists formed secret societies called the **Sons of Liberty**. Samuel Adams helped organize the Sons of Liberty in Boston. These groups sometimes used violence to frighten tax collectors. They told tax collector Andrew Oliver that "his house would be destroyed and his life [would be] in continual danger" unless he quit his job. Oliver quit. Many colonial courts shut down because people refused to buy the stamps required for legal documents. Businesses openly ignored the law by refusing to buy stamps.

In May 1765 **Patrick Henry** presented a series of resolutions to the House of Burgesses in Virginia. These resolutions stated that the Stamp Act violated the rights of the colonists as British citizens. In addition to taxation without representation, the Stamp Act denied the accused trial

Analyzing Primary Sources
Identifying Points of View
What did Adams fear would happen if Americans did not protest the new British taxes? that everything would eventually be taxed

"No Taxation without Representation"

This teapot was one of many ways in which the colonists opposed the Stamp Act.

No Stamp Act.

COLONIAL WILLIAMSBURG FOUNDATION

Interdisciplinary Connection

▶Language Arts◀

Poor Richard's Almanack.
When the boycott of British goods began, the colonists had to live less extravagantly than they had before. For many people, Benjamin Franklin's *Poor Richard's Almanack* became a guidebook for their efforts. The *Almanack* was a testament to living economically, and it provided colonists with not only a calendar but also a humorous collection of anecdotes, moral advice, and satire. Franklin's advice ranged from the economic: "Keep thy shop and thy shop will keep thee" to the practical: "Early to bed and early to rise makes a man healthy, wealthy, and wise."

ACTIVITY: Have students use the library to locate an edition of *Poor Richard's Almanack.* Ask each student to choose a quotation that they particularly enjoy and to prepare an explanation of how it may have helped the colonists survive the boycott and why the quotation is or is not still practical advice today.

Technology Resources
 CNN Presents America: Beginnings to 1914 Segment: Boycotts, Boycotts, Boycotts

Interpreting the Visual Record

The end of the Stamp Act *This cartoon shows members of Parliament giving a funeral for the Stamp Act.* **Do you think the artist was pleased or upset at the repeal of the act? Explain your answer.**

by jury. The leader of the House, John Robinson, interrupted Henry's speech by crying, "Treason! Treason!" "If this be treason," replied Henry, "make the most of it!" Henry's speech convinced the assembly to support some of his ideas.

★ Repealing the Stamp Act

Word of Virginia's action reached Boston. There the members of the Massachusetts legislature called for a Stamp Act Congress. In October 1765, delegates from nine colonies met in New York. They issued a declaration that the Stamp Act violated their rights and liberties. They then asked Parliament to **repeal**, or end, the act.

Pressure to repeal the Stamp Act began to grow. A group of London merchants said that their trade suffered from the colonial boycott and asked Parliament to repeal the Stamp Act. Benjamin Franklin, serving as an official agent for Pennsylvania, spoke before Parliament. Repeal the stamp tax, he said, and colonists would buy British goods again. William Pitt, an important member of Parliament, also believed that the Stamp Act was unfair. Pitt led Parliament in repealing the act in 1766.

The members of Parliament were still upset that colonists had challenged their authority. Thus, Parliament issued the Declaratory Act, which stated that Parliament had the power to make laws for the colonies "in all cases whatsoever." In other words, Parliament made the rules, not the colonists.

✔ **Reading Check: Summarizing** What methods did the colonists use to protest the Sugar and Stamp Acts, and what were the results of their efforts? boycotts, intimidation, breaking the law; Stamp Act repealed

Section **3** Review

go. hrw .com Homework Practice Online
keyword: SA3 HP6

★ ★

❶ **Define and explain:**
• boycott
• repeal

❷ **Identify and explain:**
• George Grenville
• Sugar Act
• James Otis
• Samuel Adams
• Committees of Correspondence
• Stamp Act
• Sons of Liberty
• Patrick Henry

❸ **Summarizing** Copy the graphic organizer below. Use it to show why the British taxed the American colonists, what the British tax laws were, and how the colonists responded.

Reasons for Taxation → British Tax Laws
1._____
2._____
→ Colonial Response

❹ **Finding the Main Idea**
a. Why did colonists dislike the Sugar Act, the vice-admiralty courts, and the Stamp Act?

b. Compare and contrast the ways in which colonists challenged new taxes.

❺ **Writing and Critical Thinking**
Supporting a Point of View Imagine that you are a colonist upset by new taxes. Write a newspaper editorial persuading colonists to protest these new taxes.

Consider the following:
• reasons for British taxes
• ideas of James Otis and Samuel Adams
• Benjamin Franklin's testimony before Parliament

Section 4

OBJECTIVES

⭐ Describe colonists' reactions to the Townshend Acts.

⭐ Analyze how the Boston Massacre and the Boston Tea Party were significant events.

⭐ Explain the purpose of the Intolerable Acts.

 **LET'S GET STARTED!**

Write the following terms on the chalkboard: *boycotts, hunger strikes, marches, petitions, rallies, sit-ins,* and *strikes.* As students enter the classroom, ask them to write down what these terms have in common. *(Students' answers will vary but should note that they are all forms of peaceful protest.)* Lead a class discussion about successful protests for women's suffrage and boycotts against South Africa's apartheid system. Explain to the class that the Boston Tea Party is an example of what can happen when people's peaceful protests go unanswered. Tell students that in Section 4 they will learn how colonists reacted to the Townshend Acts, why the Boston Massacre and Boston Tea Party were significant, and the purpose of the Intolerable Acts.

Section 4

New Taxes and Tensions

Read to Discover

1. How did colonists respond to the Townshend Acts?
2. Why were the Boston Massacre and the Boston Tea Party significant events?
3. What was the purpose of the Intolerable Acts?

WHY IT MATTERS TODAY

The British government taxed the colonies to pay for the French and Indian War. Today our government uses taxes to pay for many services. Use **CNNfyi.com** or other **current events** sources to learn about a U.S. government program that uses tax dollars. Record your findings in your journal.

Define

- writs of assistance
- propaganda

Identify

- Townshend Acts
- Daughters of Liberty
- Boston Massacre
- Tea Act
- Boston Tea Party
- Intolerable Acts
- Mercy Otis Warren

SECTION 4 RESOURCES

REPRODUCIBLE

▶ Guided Reading Strategy 6.4
▶ Biography Reading 6: Mercy Otis Warren
▶ Literature Reading 6: Patrick Henry: The Voice of Freedom

TECHNOLOGY

▶ One-Stop Planner, Lesson 6.4
▶ Holt Researcher: American History CD–ROM
▶ American Music Selection 5: "The Liberty Song"
▶ Homework Practice Online

REINFORCEMENT, REVIEW, AND ASSESSMENT

▶ Section 4 Review, p. 175
▶ Daily Quiz 6.4
▶ Main Idea Activity 6.4
▶ English Audio Summary 6.4
▶ Spanish Audio Summary 6.4

The Story Continues

People in cities across the colonies celebrated the repeal of the Stamp Act with fireworks. In Boston the people built a giant pyramid lit by 280 lamps. The Massachusetts legislature thanked King George III and promised to be loyal to him. However, Parliament and the colonies still disagreed on many issues.

Colonial lanterns and lamps were often lit by candles or oil.

⭐ The Townshend Acts

In June 1767 Parliament passed the **Townshend Acts**, which placed duties on imported glass, lead, paint, paper, and tea. The money from these duties paid for military costs and the salaries of colonial governors. These payments violated the guarantee of having no standing army in peacetime without the colonists' consent. To enforce the Townshend Acts, British officials used **writs of assistance**. These special forms allowed tax collectors to search for smuggled goods. Colonists hated the new laws because they violated colonists' constitutional rights.

The colonists responded to the Townshend Acts by once again boycotting British goods. Women calling themselves the **Daughters of Liberty** supported the boycott. One leader explained their actions.

Have students read Section 4 and complete Guided Reading Strategy 6.4. Choose one or more of the following activities to explore the section content with students. For further suggestions on block scheduling or team teaching, see the *Block Scheduling Handbook with Team Teaching Strategies*.

LEVEL 1: Organize students into three groups. Assign each group either the Boston Massacre, the Boston Tea Party, or the Intolerable Acts. Have each group discuss and take notes on its assigned topic and analyze how these were significant events. *(Students' notes will vary but should include that killings at the Boston Massacre outraged colonists and led to a trial of the soldiers who fired into the crowd. The Boston Tea Party outraged Parliament and led to the passage of the Intolerable Acts. The Intolerable Acts were passed by Parliament in 1774 as the Coercive Acts, and were designed to be a punishment for the Boston Tea Party.)* Have a volunteer from each group summarize the group's discussion. As a class, discuss the significance of the events and point out any pertinent information that was missed during the group work. **ENGLISH LANGUAGE LEARNERS**, **COOPERATIVE LEARNING**

★ Citizenship

The Town Meeting. The town meeting was an essential part of colonial political life and, as such, something that the British tried to thwart. Boston's Old South Meeting House was a popular gathering place for colonists opposed to British practices. One night, British officials heard that Bostonians were holding a meeting there to protest British colonial policy. In an attempt to stop the protest, British officials packed the meeting house with British soldiers. However, the speaker, Joseph Warren, climbed through a window and over the podium to take his place. The window is still known as Warren's Window.

CRITICAL THINKING

Why do you think British officials were so anxious to stop the town meetings?

ANSWER: Students might mention that town meetings were a means of generating political and social unrest.

Technology Resources

 American Music Selection 5: "The Liberty Song"

Analyzing Primary Sources
Identifying Points of View
How did this leader view the Townshend Acts? as an insult to the colonists

The Sons of Liberty displayed posters like this one calling for a boycott against a Boston merchant.

WILLIAM JACKSON,
an *IMPORTER*; at the
BRAZEN HEAD,
North Side of the TOWN-HOUSE,
and Opposite the Town-Pump, in
Corn-hill, BOSTON.

It is desired that the Sons and DAUGHTERS of *LIBERTY*, would not buy any one thing of him, for in so doing they will bring Disgrace upon *themselves*, and their *Posterity*, for ever and ever, AMEN
PROSCRIBING AN IMPORTER!

Research on the ROM

Free Find:
Samuel Adams
After reading about Samuel Adams on the **Holt Researcher CD–ROM**, imagine that you are a reporter for a Boston newspaper. Write a set of questions you might ask Adams about British treatment of the colonies. Include the answers you think Adams would give.

 History Makers Speak **❝I hope [we] would sooner wrap ourselves in sheep and goatskin than buy English goods of a people who have insulted us in such a scandalous [shocking] way.❞**

—Anonymous Daughter of Liberty, quoted in
A History of Women in America, by Carol Hymowitz and Michaele Weissman

Colonial legislatures also protested the Townshend Acts. In February 1768 Samuel Adams wrote a letter stating that the acts violated the legal rights of the colonists. The Massachusetts legislature sent this letter to other colonies, asking for their help. In a few months several legislatures voted to join the protest against the Townshend Acts.

At the same time, tax collectors in Massachusetts seized the ship *Liberty* on suspicion of smuggling. This action angered the ship's owner, Boston merchant John Hancock, who accused the tax collectors of punishing him because he opposed the Townshend Acts. The Sons of Liberty supported Hancock. They began to attack the houses of customs officials in protest. In response, Governor Francis Bernard broke up the Massachusetts legislature. He also asked troops to restore order. British soldiers arrived in Boston in October 1768.

✔ **Reading Check: Sequencing** What series of events led to the arrival of British troops in Boston in 1768? Townshend Acts; boycott; crackdown on smugglers; disbanding the Massachusetts legislature

---

★ The Boston Massacre

Many Bostonians believed that the British government had sent the troops to silence its critics. Local leader Samuel Adams declared, "I look upon [British soldiers] as foreign enemies." Both sides disliked each other—name-calling and fights between locals and the soldiers were common.

The tension exploded on March 5, 1770, when a lone British soldier standing guard got into a fight with a colonist. A crowd gathered around the soldier, throwing snowballs and shouting insults. Soon a small group of troops arrived. The mob grew louder and angrier by the moment. Suddenly, the soldiers fired into the crowd killing several colonists.

Samuel Adams and others used the event as a form of **propaganda**—information giving only one side in an argument—against the British. Colonists called the shootings the **Boston Massacre**. The soldiers and their officer, Thomas Preston, were charged with murder. Two Boston lawyers, Josiah Quincy and John Adams—Samuel Adams's cousin—agreed to defend the soldiers. They argued that the troops had acted in self-defense. The Boston jury agreed. The jury found Preston and six soldiers not guilty. Two soldiers were convicted of killing people in the crowd by accident. These men were branded on the hand and then released. The trial helped calm people down, but many colonists were still angry at the British.

✔ **Reading Check: Contrasting** How did Samuel Adams and John Adams differ in their response to the Boston Massacre? Samuel used it as propaganda against the British; John defended the soldiers accused of murdering innocent civilians.

THE INTOLERABLE ACTS

Causes	Purpose	Results
• *continued protests by the colonists* • *Boston Tea Party*	• *to force the colonists to submit to British authority* • *prevent any further protests*	• *closed Boston Harbor* • *Massachusetts's charter canceled* • *royal officials allowed to be tried in Britain* • *Quartering Act established for Boston* • *General Thomas Gage new governor of Massachusetts*

The BLOODY MASSACRE perpetrated in King—Street BOSTON on March 5th 1770 by a party of the 29th REGt.

CONNECTING TO THE ARTS

Colonial Art Colonial artists often tried to show what daily life was like. Some used art to make a political point. Paul Revere's engraving of the Boston Massacre was one example. The picture shows British soldiers attacking unarmed colonists. The *Boston Gazette* advertised it as "A Print . . . of the late horrid [terrible] Massacre in King St." Revere's engraving sold many copies. It became a symbol of Great Britain's injustice toward the colonies. **How does Paul Revere's picture reveal changing colonial attitudes toward the British?**

☆ A Tax on Tea

To reduce tensions in the colonies, Parliament repealed almost all of the Townshend Acts—but it kept the tax on tea. British officials knew that the colonial demand for tea was high despite the boycott. But the colonies were smuggling most of this imported tea and paying no duty on it. The British East India Company offered Parliament a solution. If allowed to sell its tea directly to the colonies, the Company could charge low prices and still profit. Cheaper tea might lead to less smuggling and the collection of more money in taxes.

Parliament agreed and passed the **Tea Act** in 1773. Many colonial merchants and smugglers feared that cheap British tea would put them out of business. Other colonists worried that the British East India Company would monopolize—or gain complete control of—the tea trade. Other British companies might follow its example and threaten colonial businesses. As a result, colonists united against the Tea Act.

A ship carrying British tea arrived in Boston Harbor in November 1773. Two other tea ships soon joined it. The Sons of Liberty demanded that the ships leave immediately. But Thomas Hutchinson, governor of Massachusetts since 1771, would not let the ships leave without paying

LEVEL 3: Explain to students that Parliament responded to the Boston Tea Party by passing the Intolerable Acts (Coercive Acts). Tell them that Parliament justified these acts based on colonists' previous actions, but colonists found the acts intolerable. Assign one of the Intolerable Acts to each student and have students write two or three paragraphs supporting the act (British point of view) and two or three paragraphs objecting to the act.

HOMEWORK Have students imagine that they are supportive of the British soldiers' actions during the Boston Massacre. Ask them to write a letter to a friend explaining why the soldiers were justified in the actions that they took and how their punishment was too severe for their actions.

★ CLOSE

Have students create a flowchart that describes the relationship between events and laws covered in this section. Tell them to use the following headings to create an outline for their charts: *the Townshend Acts, the Boston Massacre, the Boston Tea Party,* and *the Intolerable Acts.* Then ask students to fill in their flow charts with other significant details. Ask volunteers to share their charts with the class. Finally, lead a discussion on the cause-and-effect sequence of events covered in this section.

Battling British Acts

ACT	COLONIAL RESPONSE	BRITISH REACTION
The **Sugar Act (1764)** replaced the Molasses Act and was aimed specifically at raising revenues from the colonies.	Colonists protested the act and called for a boycott on items with duties.	After asking colonists for a plan to pay military expenses and not receiving a satisfactory one, the prime minister proposed the Stamp Act.
The **Stamp Act (1765)** required colonists to purchase a stamp for newspapers, pamphlets, legal documents, and other items.	Colonists formed the Sons of Liberty, boycotted goods, and used violence to frighten tax collectors; Stamp Act Congress asked Parliament to repeal the act.	Parliament repealed the Stamp Act in March 1766, then issued the Declaratory Act.
The **Townshend Acts (1767)** placed duties on imported glass, lead, paint, paper, and tea and made it easier for tax collectors to get writs of assistance.	Colonists used boycotts, colonial legislatures circulated a letter protesting the acts, and the Sons of Liberty attacked homes of tax collectors.	Soldiers were sent to Boston in October 1768; colonists were killed in the Boston Massacre on March 5, 1770; most of the acts were repealed by Parliament; troops were removed from Boston.
The **Tea Act (1773)** kept in place duties on imported tea and allowed the British East India Company to export directly to the colonies.	Colonists used boycotts and propaganda, held the Boston Tea Party, and destroyed tea shipments in some colonies.	Parliament passed the Coercive Acts, also called the Intolerable Acts by colonists.
The **Intolerable Acts (1774)** closed Boston Harbor, canceled the Massachusetts charter, moved trials of colonial officials to Britain, allowed quartering of British troops in all colonies, and gave Canada control of the Ohio region.	Colonists called for large-scale boycotts, published propaganda, and convened the First Continental Congress.	King George III rejected the suggestions of the First Continental Congress.

the tea duty. On the night of December 16, colonists disguised as American Indians snuck onto the three tea-filled ships. One participant recalled his experience.

Analyzing Primary Sources
Drawing Inferences and Conclusions Based on George Hewes's statement, how organized does the Boston Tea Party seem? Explain your answer. Well organized—in three hours groups on different ships destroyed the tea chests and dumped the tea.

 History Makers Speak 66In about three hours from the time we went on board, we had thus broken and thrown overboard every tea chest to be found in the ship, while those in the other ships were disposing of the tea in the same way, at the same time. . . . No attempt was made to resist us.99

—George Hewes, quoted in *The Spirit of 'Seventy-Six,* edited by Henry Steele Commager and Richard B. Morris

After dumping 342 tea chests into Boston Harbor, the colonists headed home to remove their disguises. Word of this **Boston Tea Party** spread. Soon the streets echoed with shouts of "Boston harbour [is] a teapot tonight!"

✔ **Reading Check: Finding the Main Idea** Why did colonists oppose the Tea Act? Merchants feared the act would put them out of business; others feared a monopoly for the East India Company would lead to other monopolies that would threaten colonial businesses in the future.

✪ REVIEW AND ASSESS

Have students complete the **Section 4 Review** on p. 175. Then have students complete **Daily Quiz 6.4**. As **Alternative Assessment**, you may want to use the Intolerable Acts graphic organizer or the Townshend Acts letters to the editor activity in this section's lessons.

✪ RETEACH

Have students complete **Main Idea Activity for English Language Learners and Special-Needs Students 6.4**. Ask students to create crossword puzzles using the key terms at the beginning of the section. Tell students to use the definitions as clues and the terms as answers. Have students exchange their crossword puzzles and tell them to fill in the puzzle and return it to its author for grading.

ENGLISH LANGUAGE LEARNERS

EXTEND

Ask students to conduct research on the Sons or Daughters of Liberty. Then have them create a newsletter describing the organization's purpose and its actions. The newsletter should also seek to recruit new members and solicit donations to help fund the organization. Encourage students to explain their newsletter to the class. (You may wish to make photocopies of students' newsletters so that other students can read them.)

BLOCK SCHEDULING

✪ The Intolerable Acts

Lord North, the new British prime minister, was furious when he heard about the Boston Tea Party. "Can we remain in this situation long?" he asked Parliament. Parliament decided to punish Massachusetts. In the spring of 1774 Britain passed the Coercive Acts, which colonists called the <u>Intolerable Acts</u>. The acts had several effects.

1. Boston Harbor was closed until Boston paid for the lost tea.
2. The Massachusetts charter was canceled. The governor decided if and when the legislature could meet.
3. Royal officials accused of crimes were sent to Britain for trial. This let them face a more friendly judge and jury.
4. The Quartering Act forced colonists to quarter, or house and supply, British soldiers.
5. General Thomas Gage became the new governor of Massachusetts.

The British hoped that these steps would bring back order in the colonies by making an example of Massachusetts. But the acts simply made more people angry. The acts went against many of the traditional rights of British citizens, such as freedom of travel in peacetime and no quartering of troops in private homes. Some colonists wrote essays and poems critical of the British government's actions. <u>Mercy Otis Warren</u> wrote plays such as *The Group* and *The Blockheads*. In *The Group*, Warren gave British supporters names such as Hum Humbug to make them look foolish.

Colonial leaders in Boston proposed a boycott of all British goods in the colonies. They also tried to bring together leaders from each colony to decide the best way to respond to Britain's abuses of colonial rights.

BEQUEST OF WINSLOW WARREN, COURTESY MUSEUM OF FINE ARTS, BOSTON MA

Playwright Mercy Otis Warren was the daughter of James Otis and a friend of John Adams and Abigail Adams.

✔ **Reading Check: Summarizing** What were the major effects of the Intolerable Acts, and what methods did colonists use to protest them? See list above. Colonists supported new boycotts and wrote critiques of the British.

go.
hrw
.com
Homework Practice Online
keyword: SA3 HP6

Section 4 Review

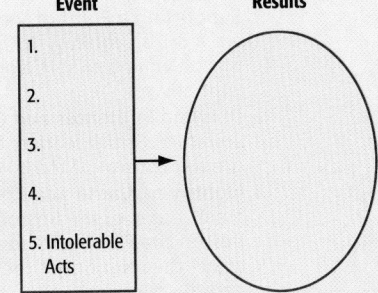

❶ Define and explain:
• writs of assistance
• propaganda

❷ Identify and explain:
• Townshend Acts
• Daughters of Liberty
• Boston Massacre
• Tea Act
• Boston Tea Party
• Intolerable Acts
• Mercy Otis Warren

❸ Sequencing Copy the graphic organizer below. Use it to explain the sequence of major events that led to the Intolerable Acts of 1774.

Event	Results
1.	
2.	
3.	
4.	
5. Intolerable Acts	

❹ Finding the Main Idea
a. In what ways did colonists react to the Townshend Acts?
b. How did the Boston Massacre and the Boston Tea Party affect relations between Great Britain and the colonies?

❺ Writing and Critical Thinking
Evaluating Imagine that you are a colonist. Write a brief pamphlet explaining what you think Parliament hopes to achieve with the Intolerable Acts.

Consider the following:
• the Boston Tea Party
• the writings of Mercy Otis Warren
• colonial boycott efforts

★★★★★★★★★★★★★★★
Section 4 Review
ANSWERS

❶ Define
• writs of assistance, p. 171
• propaganda, p. 172

❷ Identify
• Townshend Acts, p. 171
• Daughters of Liberty, p. 171
• Boston Massacre, p. 172
• Tea Act, p. 173
• Boston Tea Party, p. 174
• Intolerable Acts, p. 175
• Mercy Otis Warren, p. 175

❸ Event—Townshend Acts, Boston Massacre, Tea Act, Boston Tea Party, Intolerable Acts; Results—students should examine each event in detail, and should note that with each event colonists became angered and alienated and sought both peaceful and aggressive forms of response

❹ a. began another boycott, colonial legislatures made formal protests, and the Sons of Liberty began attacking customs officials
b. killings at the Boston Massacre outraged colonists and led to a trial of the soldiers who fired into the crowd; the Boston Tea Party outraged Parliament and led to the passage of the Intolerable Acts

❺ Students' pamphlets will vary but they should note that Parliament wanted to make an example out of Massachusetts for other colonies and to prevent further colonial protests of British policies.

REPRODUCIBLE
▶ Vocabulary Activity 6

TECHNOLOGY
▶ Chapter 6 Test Generator (on the One-Stop Planner)
▶ Global Skill Builder CD–ROM
▶ HRW Go site

REINFORCEMENT, REVIEW, AND ASSESSMENT
▶ Chapter 6 Review, pp. 176–77
▶ Chapter 6 Tutorial for Students, Parents, Mentors, and Peers

▶ Chapter 6 Test (Form A or B)
▶ Alternative Assessment Handbook
▶ Chapter 6 Test for English Language Learners and Special-Needs Students

⭐ **REVIEW**
Have students complete the **Chapter 6 Review** on pages 176–77.

⭐ **ASSESS**
Use one of the chapter tests to assess students' understanding of the content. For **Alternative Assessment**, see the **Alternative Assessment Handbook**.

CHAPTER 6 REVIEW ANSWERS

The Chapter at a Glance
Students' paragraphs will vary.

Identifying People and Ideas
Students' sentences should indicate an understanding of the following definitions:

1. plan designed to unite the colonies for the first time

2. first Europeans to settle the frontier

3. king of England who issued the Proclamation of 1763

4. banned colonial settlement west of the Appalachians

5. colonist who helped start the slogan "No taxation without representation"

6. groups formed to share information about new British laws and devise ways to challenge them

7. British act requiring that a stamp be purchased whenever paper items were sold to colonists

8. presented a series of resolutions saying that the Stamp Act violated colonists' rights

9. special search warrants allowing tax collectors to search for smuggled goods

10. colonist who wrote plays critical of the British government

Understanding Main Ideas
1. French built forts in the Ohio River valley, Fort Necessity captured by French

Chapter 6 Review

The Chapter at a Glance
Examine the visual summary of the chapter below. Write a one-paragraph summary of the main ideas covered in the chapter. Share your summary with a classmate to compare and contrast your ideas.

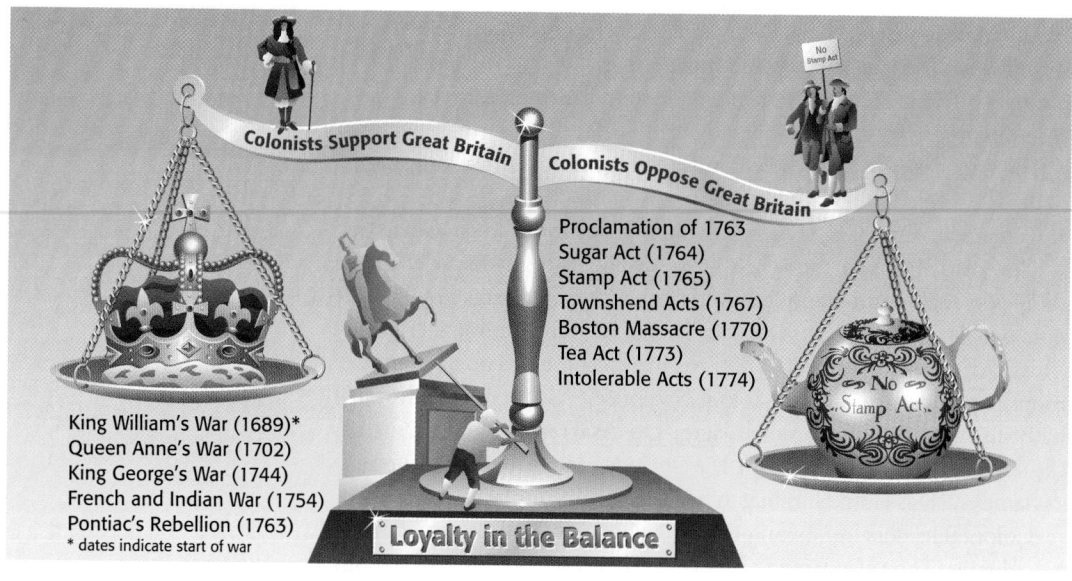

Colonists Support Great Britain

Colonists Oppose Great Britain
Proclamation of 1763
Sugar Act (1764)
Stamp Act (1765)
Townshend Acts (1767)
Boston Massacre (1770)
Tea Act (1773)
Intolerable Acts (1774)

King William's War (1689)*
Queen Anne's War (1702)
King George's War (1744)
French and Indian War (1754)
Pontiac's Rebellion (1763)
* dates indicate start of war

Loyalty in the Balance

Identifying People and Ideas
Use the following terms or people in historically significant sentences.
1. Albany Plan of Union
2. pioneers
3. King George III
4. Proclamation of 1763
5. Samuel Adams
6. Committees of Correspondence
7. Stamp Act
8. Patrick Henry
9. writs of assistance
10. Mercy Otis Warren

Understanding Main Ideas
Section 1 *(Pages 158–162)*
1. What events led to the French and Indian War?
2. What were the terms of the Treaty of Paris?

Section 2 *(Pages 163–166)*
3. Why and how did King George III and Parliament try to limit colonial expansion?

Section 3 *(Pages 167–170)*
4. Why did colonists oppose new taxes?
5. How did colonists try to change the new taxes?

Section 4 *(Pages 171–175)*
6. How did colonists view the Townshend Acts?
7. Why did Parliament pass the Intolerable Acts?

You Be the Historian—Reviewing Themes
1. **Global Relations** How did the wars between France and Great Britain affect the British colonists in North America?
2. **Geography** What region did American pioneers settle during the 1760s, and what happened as a result?
3. **Economics** How did Americans react when they were taxed by Parliament, in which they were not represented?

Thinking Critically
1. **Supporting a Point of View** Imagine that you are a British colonist during the 1760s. Would you be willing to settle on the frontier? Explain your answer.
2. **Drawing Inferences and Conclusions** Why do you think British leaders felt the need to take greater control of the colonies?
3. **Identifying Cause and Effect** What were the main causes of the Boston Massacre and the Boston Tea Party, and how did these two events affect the relationship between Great Britain and the colonies?

Organize students into four groups and assign each group one of the chapter's sections. Give each group a large sheet of butcher paper and have them illustrate the major events covered in the section it was assigned. Tell students to include captions for each illustration. Have members of each group present their work to the class.

ENGLISH LANGUAGE LEARNERS ,

COOPERATIVE LEARNING

Portfolio Extensions
American History

1. Connection to Government
Ask students to imagine that they are members of a colonial legislature in the 1770s. Tell students that Parliament's new laws have upset them. Then have students create a political cartoon to illustrate one example of colonial protest against British laws or actions. Have them include a brief paragraph that explains your cartoon.

2. Linking to Community
Tell students that Samuel Adams helped organize Committees of Correspondence to discuss and protest British laws. Then have students prepare an oral report on a national organization that has a local branch in their community. Students should explain what the group's goals are and what it does locally. They may interview someone or use the local library, local newspaper, or other sources to obtain this information.

Social Studies Skills Workshop

Interpreting Graphs
Study the graph below. Then use the information on the graph to help you answer the questions that follow.

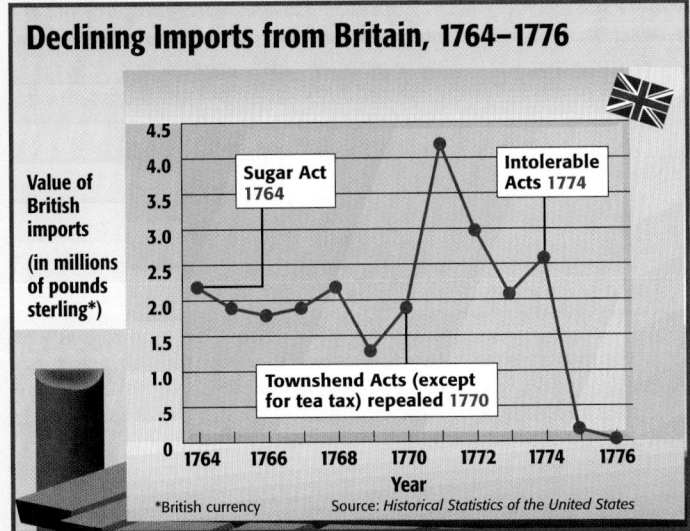

Declining Imports from Britain, 1764–1776

Value of British imports (in millions of pounds sterling*)

Sugar Act 1764

Intolerable Acts 1774

Townshend Acts (except for tea tax) repealed 1770

Year

*British currency   Source: *Historical Statistics of the United States*

1. What happened to the value of British imports in the colonies between 1770 and 1771 and 1774 and 1775?
   a. Imports increased during both periods.
   b. Imports decreased during both periods.
   c. Imports fell in 1771 and rose in 1775.
   d. Imports rose in 1775 and fell in 1771.

2. Based on the graph and your knowledge of the period, do you think that the colonial boycotts against British goods were effective? Explain your answer.

Analyzing Primary Sources
Read the following quote by colonial militia member David Perry, and then answer the questions that follow.

❝We had proceeded but a short distance into the woods before we were met by the enemy. . . . It was the first engagement I had ever seen, and the whistling of balls [bullets] and roar of musquetry [guns] terrified me not a little. At length our regiment formed among the trees, behind which the men kept stepping from their ranks for shelter. Colonel Preble, who, I well remember, was a harsh man, swore he would knock the first man down who should step out of his ranks, which greatly surprised me, to think that I must stand still to be shot at.❞

3. Which of the following statements best describes Perry's reaction to this style of fighting?
   a. He was pleased that the militia was allowed to take cover behind trees.
   b. He was frightened by the fighting and confused by his orders.
   c. He was eager to fight against the French and American Indians.
   d. He was angry that Colonel Preble knocked him down.

4. What would be some of the disadvantages of the style of fighting described by Perry?

2. Britain gained Canada & all French lands east of the Mississippi River and received Florida from Spain.

3. to prevent conflict between settlers & American Indians, by issuing the Proclamation of 1763

4. Parliament was trying to gain more control

5. boycotted British goods, refused to buy stamps, intimidated tax collectors

6. unfair & extreme taxes

7. to make an example out of Massachusetts

You Be the Historian— Reviewing Themes
1. got them directly involved in the fighting, limited western settlement, brought a lot of land to the colonies

2. settled in the Ohio River valley & the backcountry, coming into conflict with Indians

3. arranged boycotts & demanded repeals

Thinking Critically
1. Answers will vary.

2. British needed to raise more money from the colonies.

3. British occupation of Boston, Tea Act and colonial fears of British trade monopolies worsened relationships

Skills Workshop
1. d

2. Answers will vary.

3. b

4. Answers will vary.

Alternative Assessment
American History

Building Your Portfolio

Cooperative Learning
Complete this activity in small groups. Imagine that you are attending a meeting of the Sons of Liberty after the Stamp Act has been passed. Write a skit that explains why you are upset with the British government and what actions you might take. Have at least one character in the skit urge the group to proceed with caution. Perform your skit for the class.

⌨ internet connect

Internet Activity: go.hrw.com
keyword: SA3 CF6

Choose an activity on Conflict in the Colonies to:
- Research battles of the French and Indian War, and create a map of the major engagements.
- Examine the fur trade in New France, and create a pamphlet on settlements.
- Research the life of Daniel Boone, and write a biography.

go.hrw.com

LET'S GET STARTED!

Ask students to identify the nations that claimed large areas of land in North America. (*Students' answers will vary, but students should identify England, France, Spain, and Russia.*) Then ask students to identify who was living on the land when these nations claimed it. (*Student' responses should indicate that the land was home to American Indians.*) Explain to students that as settlers arrived from other countries, they became involved in disagreements over land with American Indians. Tell students that they will study maps and graphs that present information about the changing population and the conflicts that took place in North America between 1660 and 1763 in this unit.

★ TEACH

Have students read the Connecting to Geography lesson. Choose one or more of the following activities to explore the Connecting to Geography content with the students.

★ Historical Sidelight

Massasoit and Metacomet. Massasoit, the chief of the Wampanoag, established peaceful relations with the English settlers. He taught them how to plant, fish, and cook in their new environment. When Massasoit fell ill in the winter of 1632, the Pilgrims helped him regain his health. The leader of the Pilgrim's colony, Governor Edward Winslow, is reported to have traveled miles through the snow with broth for Massasoit to help his recovery. When Massasoit died, his son Metacomet became the Wampanoag chief. Metacomet believed that the settlers did not treat the Indians fairly, and within a decade he had become the Pilgrim's bitter enemy.

CRITICAL THINKING

Why do you think Metacomet and the settlers did not get along as well as Massasoit and the settlers did?

ANSWER: Students might suggest that as increased numbers of settlers came to North America, American Indians were unhappy about losing more of their land.

SKILLS ANSWERS

1. 1660–1670
2. Students may suggest that King Philip's War may have turned future colonists away from the New World.

Connecting to Geography

A Shift in Power

The British colonies in North America grew rapidly in the late 1600s and 1700s. New France grew more slowly. Yet the French were still a significant threat to British expansion. This was particularly true in Canada and the area west of the thirteen colonies. The two colonial powers fought a number of wars during this period. Britain's victories gave the British control over much of North America by the late 1700s.

During this same time, another shift in power was taking place. American Indians were gradually losing their lands to European colonists. As more Europeans settled in North America, American Indians found themselves being pushed westward.

Conflict with American Indians

Like other parts of colonial America, the population of New England grew rapidly. Chief Metacomet of the Wampanoag Indians, called King Philip by the settlers, led a war against colonists in New England in 1675. Such conflicts slowed colonial growth, but did not stop it.

Rate of New England Population Growth, 1660–1750

Source: *Historical Statistics of the United States*

Geography **Skills**
Interpreting Bar Graphs

1. **Human Systems** During what 10-year period was New England's percentage of population growth the greatest?
2. **Drawing Inferences and Conclusions** What might have accounted for the drop in population growth from 1670 to 1680?

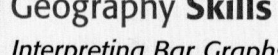

LEVEL 1: Pair students and have them study the maps on pp. 180–181 that reflect the changing American empire. Have pairs imagine that they are Spanish rulers in 1754 who want to increase their territory in North America. As students to refer to the map, ask them to prioritize five reasons that they want to acquire more land in the North American empire.

ENGLISH LANGUAGE LEARNERS , COOPERATIVE LEARNING

 ALL LEVELS: Explain to students that the population of the New England colonies grew rapidly between 1660 and 1750. Then have students review information from the bar graph on p. 178. Ask students to determine how many 10-year periods had a population increase of 50 percent,

of 40 to 49 percent, of 30 to 39 percent, of 20 to 29 percent, of 10 to 19 percent, and of 0 to 9 percent. Then have students choose a color to represent each range of population increase and create a key identifying the color that represents each range. Finally, have students create a pie graph that shows the information that they gathered. Tell them to be sure to include a key identifying the colors and what they represent.

ENGLISH LANGUAGE LEARNERS

 LEVEL 2: Have students study the map about King Philip's War on p. 179. Then have them create flashcards. Students should write questions on note cards (one question per card) about the location, date of occurrence, and victor of each of the battles depicted on the map. Then

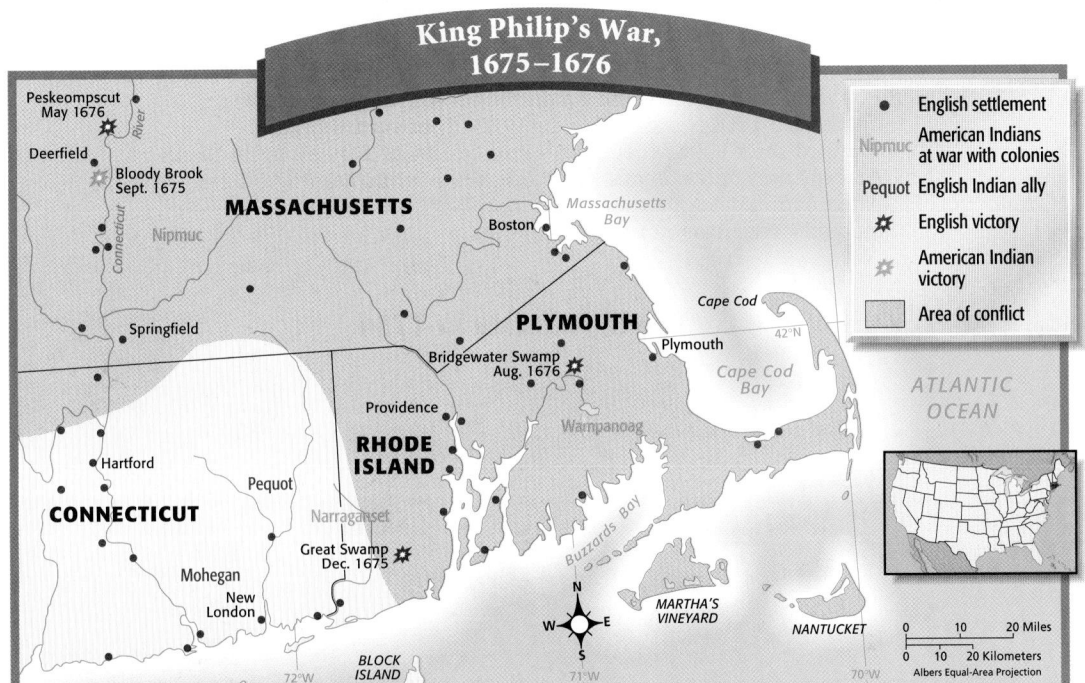

King Philip's War, 1675–1676

- English settlement
- *Nipmuc* American Indians at war with colonies
- *Pequot* English Indian ally
- ☼ English victory
- ☼ American Indian victory
- Area of conflict

Geography **Skills**

Interpreting Thematic Maps

1. **The World in Spatial Terms** Locate the settlements of Boston and Plymouth. Which battle in the war was closest to these towns?
2. **Summarizing** Which colonies were involved in the conflict?

Metacomet, also known as King Philip

History Note 1

Historians have made widely varying estimates of the American Indian population in North America when the first Europeans arrived. Some researchers have put the number as low as 1 million. Others have placed the American Indian population as high as 18 million. Experts believe that both European diseases and wars with European settlers greatly reduced the American Indian population. By 1890 there were only some 250,000 American Indians.

History Note 2

In 1675, disagreements between the Wampanoag, and the growing number of New England colonists led to war. Many people on both sides were killed in the conflict, known as King Philip's War. The defeated American Indians had to accept colonial authority and the loss of more of their land.

★ **Linking Past to Present**

American Indian Populations Today. A little less than half of the 2 million American Indians in the United States today live on or near the country's more than 250 Indian reservations. Each year the Indian population continues to grow. Of the total number of American Indians, the majority live west of the Mississippi River; particularly in Arizona, California, New Mexico, Oklahoma, and South Dakota.

CRITICAL THINKING

Why do you think the majority of American Indians live west of the Mississippi?

ANSWER: Students might suggest that the colonists first settled on the East Coast, and thus most Indians were pushed off eastern lands.

SKILLS ANSWERS
1. Bridgewater Swamp, August 1676
2. Connecticut, Massachusetts, Plymouth, Rhode Island

have students refer to the map to determine the answer to each question and write it on the opposite side of the appropriate note card. Finally, pair students and have them quiz each other about the battles of King Philip's War. **COOPERATIVE LEARNING**

LEVEL 3: Explain to students that conflicts between the English and American Indians led to King Philip's War. Have students review information from the map on p. 179 and use that information to write a fictional short story based on events depicted on the map. Have students work the following information into their stories: the dates and locations of significant battles, the approximate distance between battles, the direction traveled from one battle to another, and the side that won each of the battles. To help students see other ways they could have used the data from the map, have them read at least one other student's story.

⭐ CLOSE

Have students look at the map on p.180 and compare it to a map of the contemporary United States. Instruct students to create a list of each country claiming land in North America. The list should identify which states or portions of states have been formed from the land claimed by each nation in 1754. Then have students repeat the process with the map on p. 181. Finally, lead a class discussion comparing information contained in the lists for 1754 and 1763.

⭐ Culture

When Two Cultures Meet.

The Cheyenne had a relatively beneficial relationship with the Spanish, French, and American traders who entered their territory in the 1700s. Long accustomed to the give and take of trade, the Cheyenne managed to successfully incorporate European technology into their society. They used horses to hunt buffalo, guns to attack their enemies, and metal to make stronger sharper arrow tips. At the same time, however, the Cheyenne worried that these elements might erode their culture. Horses, for example, allowed greater independence, threatening the Cheyenne's traditional cohesiveness.

CRITICAL THINKING

How might the Cheyenne have countered these negative cultural affects?

ANSWER: Some students might suggest that the Cheyenne could have stressed the importance of traditional culture.

SKILLS ANSWERS

1. Students' maps should accurately reflect the locations.

2. France and Spain

3. three regions—territory between New France and British territory in northern Canada, territory to the west of the thirteen colonies, and territory in what is now the southeastern United States.

Changing Empires

France, Great Britain, and Spain fought a series of wars beginning in the late 1600s and ending in 1763. These wars greatly changed their colonial empires. France lost almost all of its North American colonies. Spain lost some lands while gaining others. After winning the French and Indian War, Britain gained a huge amount of territory in North America.

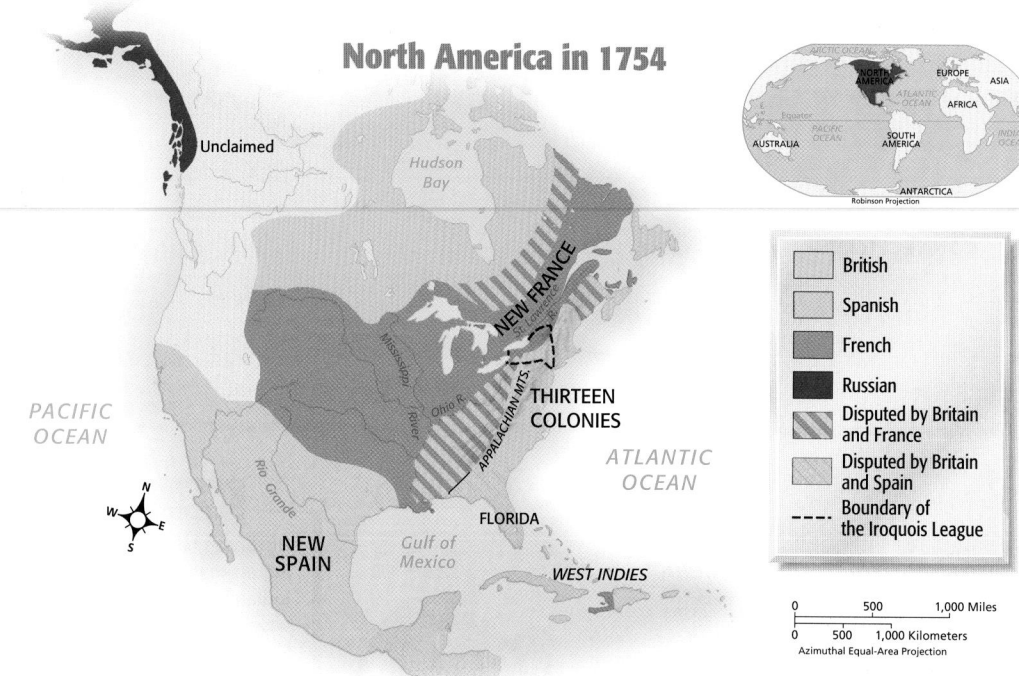

North America in 1754

Legend:
- British
- Spanish
- French
- Russian
- Disputed by Britain and France
- Disputed by Britain and Spain
- Boundary of the Iroquois League

0   500   1,000 Miles
0   500   1,000 Kilometers
Azimuthal Equal-Area Projection

Geography **Skills**

Interpreting Political Maps

1. Trace this map on a separate sheet of paper and ask a fellow student to fill in the general locations of each of the European colonial empires in North America in 1754.

2. **The Uses of Geography** Which European powers appeared to control the largest parts of the present-day United States in 1754?

3. **Analyzing Information** Over which areas of North America did European powers dispute control?

History Note 3

Many modern U.S. place-names reflect the colonial influence of France and Spain. The name of Terre Haute, Indiana, means "high land" in French. Des Moines, Iowa, comes from the French for "some monks." Louisiana was named after French king Louis XIV. Florida is Spanish for "flowered." Spanish names in the Southwest include Rio Grande, or "great river," and Las Cruces, New Mexico, which means "the crosses."

180

180   Unit 3   Connecting to Geography

★ REVIEW AND ASSESS

Have students review the information in Connecting to Geography Unit 3. Then have students complete Geography and History Quiz 3.

★ RETEACH

Refer students to the maps on pp. 180–181 that compare North America in 1754 to North America 1763. Then ask them to make a bulleted list of the differences between these two maps. Finally, lead a class discussion about the shifts in power that took place in North America during the late 1600s to mid-1700s.

ENGLISH LANGUAGE LEARNERS

★ EXTEND

Have students use the library or other resources to obtain information about the population growth in England, France, Spain, and Russia from 1660 to 1780. Then instruct students to create a graph that plots data about population growth in each of the nations they researched and also in the North American colonial settlements. Tell students to choose a color for each nation or colony and then to create a map key explaining what each color represents. Finally, lead a class discussion comparing and contrasting the population growth of each nation and colony on the graph. **BLOCK SCHEDULING**

North America in 1763

History Note 5

By the late 1700s there were about 20,000 Spanish-speaking settlers living in New Mexico. Still, the population of the Spanish Southwest never approached the size of the growing British colonies in the east.

Map legend:
- British
- Spanish
- French
- Russian
- Disputed by Britain, Russia, and Spain

Geography Skills
Interpreting Political Maps

1. Which areas in North America did each European power hold in 1763?
2. **Places and Regions** What areas of North America were disputed or unclaimed?
3. **Contrasting** Compare the map of North America in 1754 with the map of North America in 1763. Then create a map of North America in 1763 that shows which parts of the territories controlled by Britain and Spain were once held by France.

History Note 4

France gave Louisiana to Spain in 1762. But the Spanish never really had full control over most of this huge territory. French influence remained strong in the area, and Louisiana was returned to French control in 1800.

Fort St. Marie de Gannentaha, Lake Onondaga, New York

★ Culture

Immigrants in Louisiana. Although New Orleans is often associated with French culture, people of many backgrounds lived in this area in the early 1700s. Early French leaders allowed about 2,000 Catholics from Switzerland and the Rhineland to settle near New Orleans around 1720. Jews also numbered among Louisiana's earliest arrivals, but their settlement was forbidden after 1723. Several waves of Germans came in the 1700s. By the end of the century, the so-called German coast was the most thickly settled part of the province.

ACTIVITY: Have students conduct research and report on the trends in immigration of another large U.S. region.

SKILLS ANSWERS

1. Britain controlled most of eastern North America, Spain controlled most of central and southwestern North America, Russia controlled parts of present-day Alaska, and France controlled part of what is now Haiti.

3. disputed—a region along the Pacific Ocean between British, Spanish, and Russian claims; unclaimed—large area of northwestern North America, including much of the interior of present-day Alaska

3. Students' maps should accurately reflect the territories.

7 The American Revolution

CHAPTER RESOURCE MANAGER

Objectives	Pacing Guide	Reproducible Resources
SECTION 1: **The Revolution Begins** (pp. 184–88) ★ Describe the actions taken by the First Continental Congress. ★ Evaluate how the fighting at Lexington and Concord affected the colonies' conflict with Great Britain. ★ Analyze the accomplishments of the Second Continental Congress. ★ Explain the ways that geography influenced the early battles of the war.	**Regular** 2 days **Block Scheduling** 1 day *Block Scheduling Handbook with Team Teaching Strategies, Chapter 7*	**RS** Guided Reading Strategy 7.1 **PS** Biography Reading 7: Paul Revere **SM** Geography Activity 7: Boston at the Start of the Revolution **E** Hands-On History Activity: The American Revolution and Your Community
SECTION 2: **Declaring Independence** (pp. 190–93) ★ Evaluate the influence of Thomas Paine's *Common Sense* on the colonies. ★ Identify the main ideas stated in the Declaration of Independence. ★ Explain Americans' reactions to the Declaration of Independence.	**Regular** 2 days **Block Scheduling** 1 day *Block Scheduling Handbook with Team Teaching Strategies, Chapter 7*	**RS** Guided Reading Strategy 7.2
SECTION 3: **Dark Hours for the Revolution** (pp. 198–201) ★ Examine the Patriots' advantages and disadvantages at the beginning of the Revolutionary War. ★ Explore the contributions that various groups made to the war effort. ★ Describe the problems the Patriots faced in Canada and New York.	**Regular** 1.5 days **Block Scheduling** .5 day *Block Scheduling Handbook with Team Teaching Strategies, Chapter 7*	**RS** Guided Reading Strategy 7.3 **PS** Literature Reading 7: The Crisis
SECTION 4: **The Patriots Gain New Hope** (pp. 202–08) ★ Analyze Washington's strategies at Trenton and Princeton. ★ Discuss the Battle of Saratoga as a turning point in the war. ★ Identify how foreign nations and individuals aided the Patriots. ★ Describe how the Patriots carried out the naval war.	**Regular** 1.5 days **Block Scheduling** 1 day *Block Scheduling Handbook with Team Teaching Strategies, Chapter 7*	**RS** Guided Reading Strategy 7.4 **PS** Primary Source Reading 7: Medicine and War **E** Creative Teaching Strategy: Learning Stations
SECTION 5: **Independence!** (pp. 209–13) ★ Explain the ways that geography affected the Patriot strategy in the West. ★ Describe how the war took place in the southern colonies. ★ Examine the events that finally ended the war.	**Regular** 1.5 days **Block Scheduling** 1 day *Block Scheduling Handbook with Team Teaching Strategies, Chapter 7*	**RS** Guided Reading Strategy 7.5 **PS** American History Political Cartoon 1: Defeating the British **RS** Graphic Organizer 7: The Path to Independence

Chapter Resource Key

PS Primary Sources	**A** Assessment	Music	**One-Stop** Planner CD–ROM
RS Reading Support	**REV** Review	 Video	
IC Interdisciplinary Connections	**ELL** Reinforcement and English Language Learners	 Internet	**See the *One-Stop Planner* for a complete list of additional resources for students and teachers.**
E Enrichment	Transparencies	 Holt Presentation Maker Using Microsoft® PowerPoint®	
SM Skills Mastery	CD–ROM		

One-Stop Planner CD–ROM

It's easy to plan lessons, select resources, and print out materials for your students when you use the **One-Stop Planner CD–ROM with Test Generator.**

Technology Resources	Reinforcement, Review, and Assessment

 One-Stop Planner, Lesson 7.1
 Holt Researcher: American History CD–ROM
 Homework Practice Online

- **REV** Section 1 Review, p. 188
- **A** Daily Quiz 7.1
- **ELL** Main Idea Activity 7.1
- **ELL** English Audio Summary 7.1
- **ELL** Spanish Audio Summary 7.1

 One-Stop Planner, Lesson 7.2
 Art in American History Transparency 3: Independence Hall
American History Interactive Maps CD–ROM: The Loyalists
 Homework Practice Online
 HRW Go site

- **REV** Section 2 Review, p. 193
- **A** Daily Quiz 7.2
- **ELL** Main Idea Activity 7.2
- **ELL** English Audio Summary 7.2
- **ELL** Spanish Audio Summary 7.2

 One-Stop Planner, Lesson 7.3
 Exploring America's Past Video Segment: A Call to Arms; Teacher's Guide, pp. 10–12
 Everyday Life in America Transparency 4: Revolutionary War Uniforms
 Homework Practice Online

- **REV** Section 3 Review, p. 201
- **A** Daily Quiz 7.3
- **ELL** Main Idea Activity 7.3
- **ELL** English Audio Summary 7.3
- **ELL** Spanish Audio Summary 7.3

 One-Stop Planner, Lesson 7.4
 Art in American History Transparency 6: Capture of the Hessians at Trenton
Linking Geography and History Transparency 9: The Fight for Independence, 1776–1781
 Holt Researcher: American History CD–ROM
 Homework Practice Online

- **REV** Section 4 Review, p. 208
- **A** Daily Quiz 7.4
- **ELL** Main Idea Activity 7.4
- **ELL** English Audio Summary 7.4
- **ELL** Spanish Audio Summary 7.4

 One-Stop Planner, Lesson 7.5
 American Music Selection 6: "Yankee Doodle"
 CNN. Presents America: Yesterday and Today, Beginnings to 1914 Segment: What If the United States Had Lost?
 Homework Practice Online
HRW Go site

- **REV** Section 5 Review, p. 212
- **A** Daily Quiz 7.5
- **ELL** Main Idea Activity 7.5
- **ELL** English Audio Summary 7.5
- **ELL** Spanish Audio Summary 7.5

internet connect

go.hrw.com

HRW ONLINE RESOURCES
GO TO: go.hrw.com
Then type in a keyword.

TEACHER HOME PAGE
KEYWORD: SA3 Teacher

CHAPTER INTERNET ACTIVITIES
KEYWORD: SA3 CF7
Choose an activity to:
- identify the points of view of Loyalists and Patriots.
- analyze Thomas Paine's use of bias and other propaganda techniques.
- research battles of the Revolutionary War.
- understand the changing role of First Ladies.

CHAPTER ENRICHMENT LINKS
KEYWORD: SA3 CH7

ONLINE ASSESSMENT
Homework Practice
KEYWORD: SA3 HP7

Standardized Test Prep
KEYWORD: SA3 STP7

Rubrics
KEYWORD: SS Rubrics

ONLINE MAPS, CHARTS, AND GRAPHS
KEYWORD: SA3 MCG
- Northern Campaigns
- Southern Campaigns
- Battles in Eastern Massachusetts
- Two Continental Congresses

CONTENT UPDATES
KEYWORD: SS Content Updates

HOLT PRESENTATION MAKER
KEYWORD: SA3 PPT7

ONLINE READING SUPPORT
KEYWORD: SS Strategies

CURRENT EVENTS
KEYWORD: S3 Current Events

Meeting Individual Needs

Ability Levels

Level 1 Basic-level activities designed for all students encountering new material

Level 2 Intermediate-level activities designed for average students

Level 3 Challenging activities designed for honors and gifted-and-talented students

English Language Learners Activities that address the needs of students with Limited English Proficiency

Chapter Review and Assessment

- **IC** Vocabulary Activity 7
- 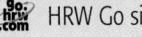 Global Skill Builder CD–ROM
- HRW Go site
- **REV** Chapter 7 Tutorial for Students, Parents, Mentors, and Peers
- **REV** Chapter 7 Review, pp. 213–15
- Chapter 7 Test Generator (on the One-Stop Planner)

- **A** Chapter 7 Test (Form A or B)
- **A** Alternative Assessment Handbook
- **A** Chapter 7 Test for English Language Learners and Special-Needs Students

CHAPTER

7

Section 1   The Revolution Begins

Section 2   Declaring Independence

Section 3   Dark Hours for the Revolution

Section 4   The Patriots Gain New Hope

Section 5   Independence!

Build on What You Know

If You Were There...

Ask students to answer the following question:

Would you support the Revolution?

Consider:

- the risks associated with rebellion
- the loyalty of colonists to the king

You Be the Historian

What's Your Opinion?

To help students create their **Themes** Journal entries, provide the following examples of appropriate **agree**/disagree statements.

EXPLORING THE TIME LINE
AMERICAN EVENTS

internet connect

TOPIC: The Revolutionary War
GO TO: go.hrw.com
KEYWORD: SA3 CF7

Have students access the Internet through the HRW Go site to conduct research on the differing viewpoints of the Loyalists and Patriots during the Revolutionary War. Then have students use our interactive writing template to compose an informative essay that explains the reasons why one might choose to be a Loyalist or Patriot and the risks of choosing one side or the other. Remind students to use standard grammar, spelling, sentence structure, and punctuation. They should also cite evidence from their research in their report.

CHAPTER

7 The American Revolution
(1774–1783)

Colonial minutemen were outnumbered by British soldiers at the Battle of Lexington in Massachusetts.

Patriot Thomas Jefferson was the author of the Declaration of Independence.

UNITED STATES

1774 The First Continental Congress meets.

1775 On April 19 the Revolutionary War begins with the fighting at Lexington and Concord.

1776 On July 4 the thirteen colonies issue the Declaration of Independence and break away from Great Britain.

1776 On December 26 General George Washington wins the Battle of Trenton.

1777 On October 17 a British army surrenders to the Patriots after the Battle of Saratoga.

1778 The Continental Army suffers through the end of a harsh winter while stationed at Valley Forge, Pennsylvania.

| 1774 | 1775 | 1776 | 1777 | 1778 |

WORLD

1776 Scottish economist Adam Smith writes *The Wealth of Nations* about open economic markets and competition.

1778 France allies with the Americans and joins the war against Great Britain.

A gold British guinea coin

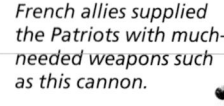

French allies supplied the Patriots with much-needed weapons such as this cannon.

Build on What You Know

By 1774 many colonists were angry with the British government. These colonists believed that Parliament had repeatedly violated their rights. Eventually their protests led to battles with British troops and a war for independence from Great Britain. The American Revolution marked the birth of the United States of America.

Citizenship

Agree   Citizens should be responsible for determining how their government is run.

Disagree   Citizens have an obligation to obey the laws of their government.

Constitutional Heritage

Agree   Slavery violated natural rights and therefore should be abolished.

Disagree   Slavery was a necessary evil because of the needs of society.

Global Relations

Agree   The Spanish had the right to spread their religion and language among the American Indians.

Disagree   American Indians should not have been forced to follow European customs and culture.

George Washington looks on as American forces accept the British surrender at Yorktown, Virginia.

The early U.S. flag had a star and a stripe for each state.

COLONIAL WILLIAMSBURG FOUNDATION

1779 Patriot George Rogers Clark and his forces recapture Vincennes.

1780 The British defeat the southern Patriot army at Camden, South Carolina.

1781 On October 19 the British surrender to George Washington at Yorktown, securing the American victory in the Revolutionary War.

1783 The Treaty of Paris is signed, ending the war.

1779   1780   1781   1782   1783

1779 Spain declares war on Britain.

1780 Great Britain declares war on the Netherlands.

1783 Great Britain agrees to return Florida to Spain.

If you were there . . .
Would you support the Revolution?

You Be the Historian

Themes Journal

What's Your Opinion? Do you **agree** or **disagree** with the following statements? Support your point of view in your journal.

- **Citizenship** Citizens have the right to rebel against an unjust government.
- **Constitutional Heritage** All human beings possess certain natural rights that should be protected.
- **Global Relations** A powerful nation will always defeat a weaker country in war.

EXPLORING THE TIME LINE
GLOBAL EVENTS

★ Global Relations

The Franco-American Alliance. A turning point of the War for Independence occurred when France declared war on Great Britain in February 1778, and joined the colonies in their fight against Britain. The French had remained bitter over the loss of their North American holdings after the French and Indian War, and therefore they were eager to subvert Britain's position in the colonies. The French and Americans signed two treaties. The first treaty officially recognized the new country and encouraged trade, and the second treaty provided for the military alliance against Great Britain and required recognition of complete independence for the United States as a condition of peace. During the war, the French proved to be an indispensable asset in the Patriot victory at the Battle of Yorktown, which ended the war.

CRITICAL THINKING

Do you think the Patriots could have won the war without aid of the French?

ANSWER: Some students might suggest "no" since the French brought much-needed manpower and supplies to the Patriots.

Section 1

OBJECTIVES

- ★ Describe the actions taken by the First Continental Congress.
- ★ Evaluate how the fighting at Lexington and Concord affected the colonies' conflict with Great Britain.
- ★ Analyze the accomplishments of the Second Continental Congress.
- ★ Explain the ways that geography influenced the early battles of the war.

📻 LET'S GET STARTED!

Write the following question on the chalkboard: *What are some of the British laws that American colonists thought were unfair?* As students enter the classroom, have them write a brief description of each law. *(Students' descriptions might include the Stamp Act, the Tea Act, or the Intolerable Acts.)* Have volunteers share their responses with the class. Remind students that the colonists felt that Britain was ignoring their rights by passing unjust laws and taxing them without representation. Tell students that in Section 1 they will learn that this treatment eventually led to the Revolutionary War.

Section 1

The Revolution Begins

Read to Discover

1. What actions did the First Continental Congress take?
2. How did the fighting at Lexington and Concord affect the colonies' conflict with Great Britain?
3. What did the Second Continental Congress accomplish?
4. How did geography influence the early battles of the war?

WHY IT MATTERS TODAY

At times Americans still have to defend their liberties. Sometimes the United States also helps protect the freedoms of people in other countries. Use **CNNfyi.com** or other **current events** sources to find a country in which the United States is helping to protect basic human rights. Record your findings in your journal.

Define

- minutemen
- siege

Identify

- First Continental Congress
- Thomas Gage
- Redcoats
- Second Continental Congress
- Continental Army
- George Washington
- Olive Branch Petition
- Battle of Bunker Hill

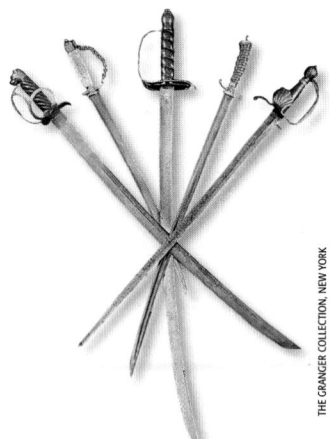

THE GRANGER COLLECTION, NEW YORK

This is a collection of swords used during the Revolutionary War.

The Story Continues

By the fall of 1774 the colonists had to do something about their problems with Great Britain. Cousins John and Samuel Adams were part of the debate. Samuel Adams was the rebel who had organized the Boston Tea Party. John Adams had defended the British soldiers who took part in the Boston Massacre. Both cousins thought that colonial leaders needed to respond to British acts. They agreed to represent Massachusetts at a colonial assembly taking place in Philadelphia.

★ The First Continental Congress

In September 1774 the **First Continental Congress** met in Philadelphia. The Congress had 56 colonial delegates, including John and Samuel Adams. Georgia was the only colony that did not send representatives. The delegates at the meeting debated the best way to respond to the crisis taking place in Boston. Delegate John Dickinson thought that the colonists should make peace with Great Britain. Delegate Patrick Henry said that there was no way to avoid a fight. "Arms [weapons] are a resource to which we shall be forced," he declared.

Have students read Section 1 and complete Guided Reading Strategy 7.1. Choose one or more of the following activities to explore the section content with students. For further suggestions on block scheduling or team teaching, see the *Block Scheduling Handbook with Team Teaching Strategies.*

LEVEL 1: Work with students to create a list of the actions taken by the First Continental Congress against Great Britain. *(Students' lists should include the following: recommended that colonists continue to boycott British goods and that they warn their militias to be prepared in case violence broke out, assembled a carefully worded list of 10 resolutions—the*

Declaration of Resolves—*to present to King George III, and agreed to meet again in May 1775 if the king did not acknowledge these rights.)* Then ask students to explain the results of these actions. *(Students should note that King George III refused to consider the colonists' demands, and instead ordered troops in the colonies to prepare to seize the colonial militias' weapons.)* Encourage students to take notes. **ENGLISH LANGUAGE LEARNERS**

HOMEWORK Have students prepare a handbill explaining actions taken by the first Continental Congress. Handbills should be created so that they develop public support for the actions to be taken against Great Britain.

In the end, the delegates reached a compromise. They recommended that colonists continue to boycott British goods but also warned colonial militias to be prepared to fight. Meanwhile, they assembled a list of 10 resolutions to present to King George III. This Declaration of Rights listed freedoms that the delegates believed colonists should possess, including the right to "life, liberty, and property." The delegates agreed to meet again in May 1775 if the king did not agree.

✔ **Reading Check: Summarizing** Describe the accomplishments of the First Continental Congress. Declaration of Rights; advised militias to prepare for a fight; continued boycotts

---

★ The "Shot Heard round the World"

Tensions remained high in Boston. Local militia members began calling themselves **minutemen** because they were ready to fight on a minute's notice. In April 1775 British general **Thomas Gage** decided to take away the minutemen's weapons and ammunition. These weapons were stored in Concord, a town about 20 miles west of Boston.

The Sons of Liberty learned of the British plan. On the evening of April 18, 1775, spies brought serious news to Paul Revere and William Dawes. British troops were heading toward Concord. The two men raced on their horses through the countryside, warning minutemen that the British were coming! Isaac Davis was one of the minutemen who heard the warning. His wife later described his response to Revere's call.

> **History Makers Speak** ❝The alarm was given early in the morning, and my husband lost no time in making ready to go to Concord with his company . . . [he] said but little that morning. He seemed serious and thoughtful; but never seemed to hesitate. . . . He only said, 'Take good care of the children.'❞
>
> —Mrs. Isaac Davis, quoted in *From Colonies to Country,* by Joy Hakim

On the morning of April 19, fewer than 70 minutemen gathered at the Lexington village green, near Concord. There they met a much larger force of British troops. The colonial commander shouted to his soldiers,

GIFT OF JOSEPH W. REVERE, WILLIAM B. REVERE, AND EDWARD H.R. REVERE, COURTESY, MUSEUM OF FINE ARTS, BOSTON

Paul Revere's heroic ride helped warn the Patriots of the British advance toward Concord.

Interpreting the Visual Record

The first battle *The fighting at Lexington was fierce but brief. The colonists suffered their first casualties of the war.* **What differences does this image show between the fighting style of the minutemen and that of the British regular troops?**

THE GRANGER COLLECTION, NEW YORK

★ Citizenship

The First Continental Congress. Georgia was the only colony not to send a representative to the First Continental Congress. Of the 55 delegates from the other 12 colonies, few had much experience in politics. Among them, however, were people whose services would later be important to the United States—Roger Sherman, John and Samuel Adams, John Jay, Patrick Henry, and George Washington.

CRITICAL THINKING

Why might Georgia have not sent a delegate to the First Continental Congress?

ANSWER: Students might suggest that most of the conflicts occurred farther north and that Georgia may not have felt involved enough to send delegates.

Visual Record Answer

Students might suggest that minutemen engaged in hand-to-hand combat.

ALL LEVELS: Copy the following graphic organizer onto the chalkboard, omitting the italicized answers. Have each student evaluate the fighting at Lexington and Concord by completing the web diagram with key people, dates, and events associated with each location. Use students' completed diagrams to discuss how the fighting at Lexington and Concord affected the colonies' dispute with Britain. *(Students should suggest that many colonists were shocked and angry. They prepared to defend themselves.)*

ENGLISH LANGUAGE LEARNERS

Note: To help students make meaningful connections between events in American history and those in their own hometown, use the Chapter 7 **Hands-On History** activity, The American Revolution and Your Community.

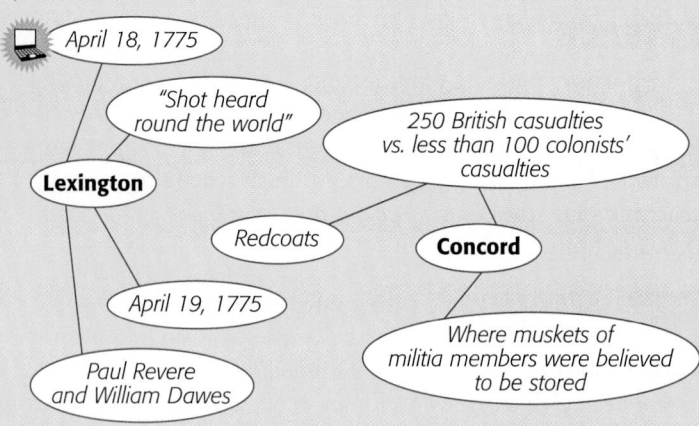

April 18, 1775

"Shot heard round the world"

250 British casualties vs. less than 100 colonists' casualties

Lexington

Redcoats

Concord

April 19, 1775

Where muskets of militia members were believed to be stored

Paul Revere and William Dawes

After the battles at Lexington and Concord, some 10,000 Patriot civilians moved out of Boston as the town became a base for British troops. The number of British troops grew to 13,500 by July 1775.

★ Economics

Funding the Revolution.
When the Second Continental Congress raised the Continental Army, it was reluctant to impose a new tax on the already tax-weary colonists. Thus, the Second Continental Congress printed and issued a new national currency. It was expected that individual colonies would eventually collect an equivalent amount in taxes. Because Congress had no authority to force the states to tax their residents, however, its demands went largely ignored. This created a significant national debt. To raise money, Congress then borrowed money from France, sold government bonds, and issued soldiers IOUs in lieu of pay.

CRITICAL THINKING
What advantages might a national government have over a state-centered government?

ANSWER: Students might suggest that a national government is better able to collect taxes and regulate an economy.

Analyzing Primary Sources
Identifying Bias Do you think Dr. Thacher supports the minutemen or the Redcoats? Why? Answers will vary. Most students should be able to determine that Dr. Thacher is talking about the countryside resisting the British, indicating his pro-minutemen sentiments.

George Washington had fought in the French and Indian War.

"Don't fire unless fired upon. But if they mean to have a war, let it begin here!" Suddenly a shot rang out. No one knows who fired this "shot heard round the world"—but once the soldiers heard it, the fight began. The battle ended in minutes. When the smoke cleared, the badly outnumbered colonists had suffered 8 dead and 10 wounded.

The British marched on to Concord, where they found few weapons because the colonists had already removed them. In anger, British troops set fire to a few buildings. One of the colonists shouted, "Will you let them burn the town down?" In response, the minutemen charged forward.

As the British retreated back to Boston, the minutemen fired upon them from behind trees and buildings. The British soldiers' bright red uniforms made easy targets. The colonists called the British soldiers **Redcoats** because of these uniforms. By the time the British reached Boston, they had suffered more than 250 casualties. Fewer than 100 colonists were killed or wounded. Isaac Davis was among those who died that day.

Word of the fighting at Lexington and Concord spread. Many people responded with shock and anger. Dr. James Thacher noted the effect on one Massachusetts town.

 History Makers Speak ❝This tragical event seems to have electrified all classes of people. . . . The sword is now unsheathed [drawn], and our friends are slaughtered by our cruel enemies. Expresses [messengers] are hastening from town to town, in all directions through the country . . . rousing the people To Arms! To Arms!❞

—Dr. James Thacher, quoted in *Military Journal of the American Revolution*

✔ **Reading Check: Identifying Cause and Effect** What led to the fighting at Lexington and Concord, and how did it affect the colonies' conflict with Great Britain? The British wanted to disarm the minutemen. The battles were the start of open warfare with the British.

★ The Second Continental Congress

In May 1775, representatives from 12 of the colonies met in the city of Philadelphia for the **Second Continental Congress**. The leaders of the Congress had to decide how to react to the fighting. They decided not to break away from Great Britain. The Congress did make plans to create a **Continental Army** to defend the colonies and chose Virginian **George Washington** to command this army.

As Washington began gathering his troops, the Congress tried one last time to keep the peace. On July 5 the delegates signed the **Olive Branch Petition**. This petition was so named because the olive branch is a symbol of peace. In November the colonists learned that King George III had angrily rejected the peace offer. By that time the fighting in the colonies had spread.

✔ **Reading Check: Drawing Inferences and Conclusions** Why do you think King George III rejected the Olive Branch Petition? Answers will vary, but students may say the king thought the colonies were being disrespectful.

LEVELS 2 AND 3: Organize students into small groups. Have half of the groups design the front page of a colonial newspaper writing headlines and articles that focus on the actions taken by the First Continental Congress. *(See the Level 1 Lesson for actions taken by the First Continental Congress.)* Have the other half of the groups design front pages that focus on the actions taken by the Second Continental Congress. *(These actions should include: decided not to break away from Great Britain, made plans to organize and fund the Continental Army, chose George Washington to lead the Continental Army, and signed the Olive Branch Petition)* Conduct a discussion and ask students to identify the events that made these two front pages so different.

COOPERATIVE LEARNING

LEVEL 3: Ask students to write an essay describing the early battles of the American Revolution and the ways that geography influenced the early battles. *(Students' essays should include the fact that the colonists positioned themselves at high elevations so that they could fire down on the British.)*

★ CLOSE

Discuss with students the significance of the battles at Breed's Hill, Bunker Hill, Concord, Dorchester Heights, Fort Ticonderoga, and Lexington. Then have students work in groups to prepare a protest sign indicating how these battles related to the start of the Revolution.

★ Early Battles

While the Second Continental Congress was meeting, some colonists were striking at the British. Their target was Fort Ticonderoga in northern New York. This fort guarded access to Lake Champlain, a key waterway. Colonel Benedict Arnold joined Ethan Allen, from present-day Vermont, to lead the effort. On May 10, 1775, the colonists surprised the British by attacking during an early morning storm. They quickly took the fort and its large supply of weapons, including cannons.

Back in Massachusetts, minutemen held Boston under **siege**—a situation in which soldiers surround a city or fort. In mid-June 1775 the British prepared to take Charlestown, an area that overlooks Boston from the north. Warned of the plan, colonial forces rushed to build defenses on nearby Bunker Hill and Breed's Hill. The British were surprised when they saw the colonial soldiers already on the hills. Still, the Redcoats tried to capture the colonists' positions. The colonial forces were well protected from attack, but they were low on gunpowder. The colonial commander ordered his troops not to fire on the Redcoats "until you see the whites of their eyes."

Research on the ROM

Free Find:
George Washington
After reading about George Washington on the **Holt Researcher CD–ROM**, list the information you think led the Second Continental Congress to select him to command the Continental Army.

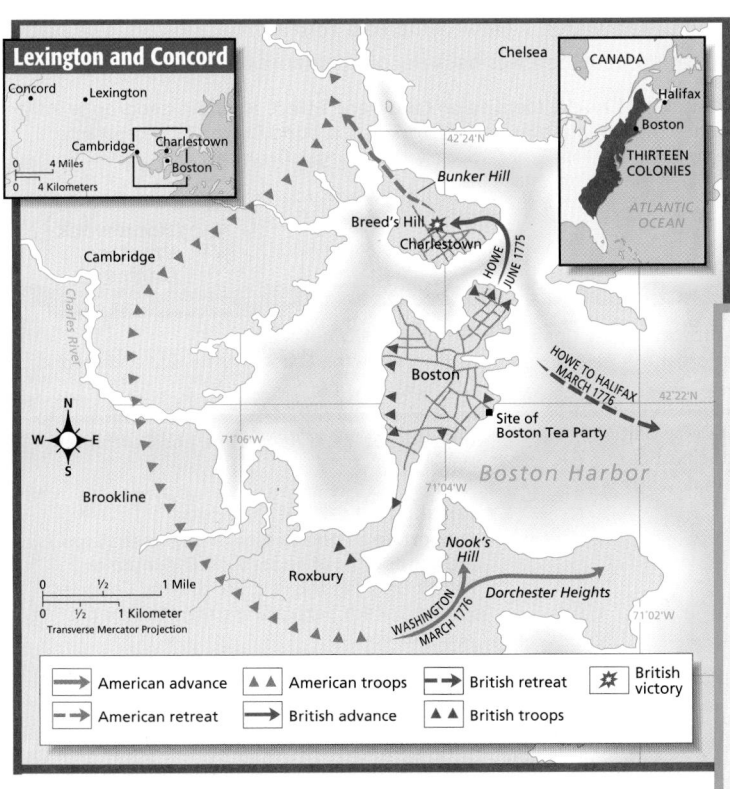

Lexington and Concord

Concord • Lexington
Cambridge • Charlestown
Boston
0 4 Miles
0 4 Kilometers

CANADA
Chelsea
Halifax
42°24'N
Boston
THIRTEEN COLONIES
ATLANTIC OCEAN

Bunker Hill
Breed's Hill
Charlestown
Cambridge
Charles River
HOWE JUNE 1775
HOWE TO HALIFAX MARCH 1776
42°22'N

Boston
Site of Boston Tea Party
71°06'W
71°04'W
Boston Harbor

Brookline
Nook's Hill
Roxbury
Dorchester Heights
WASHINGTON MARCH 1776
71°02'W

N W E S

0 ½ 1 Mile
0 ½ 1 Kilometer
Transverse Mercator Projection

→ American advance   ▲▲ American troops   ⇢ British retreat   ✳ British victory
⇢ American retreat   ⟹ British advance   ▲▲ British troops

The Siege of Boston, 1775–1776

Interpreting Maps After the fighting at Lexington and Concord, the British retreated to the safety of Boston. It was not long, however, before the American forces moved closer to threaten the British positions.

Skills Assessment
1. **Locate** Find the location of Boston, Breed's Hill, and Bunker Hill on the map.
2. **Drawing Inferences and Conclusions** Why do you think the British did not retreat by land?

THE GRANGER COLLECTION, NEW YORK

As the British attacked Breed's Hill, Bostonians climbed onto city rooftops to watch the battle unfold.

Most of the fighting took place on Breed's Hill. The outnumbered colonists turned back several assaults. Yet, they eventually ran out of ammunition and had to retreat. The British suffered more than 1,000 casualties, compared to about 400 for the colonists. The **Battle of Bunker Hill** showed the colonists that they could hold their own against the British.

General Washington soon arrived to command the siege of Boston. To drive out the British, Washington needed the cannons from Fort Ticonderoga. In November he gave the task of transporting these guns to officer Henry Knox. Knox managed to haul the guns 300 miles in the middle of winter.

In March 1776 Washington used the cannons to fire on the British from Dorchester Heights, a hill overlooking southern Boston. The British were in trouble. The situation astonished British general William Howe. "The rebels have done more in one night than my whole army could do in months," he declared. On March 7 Howe ordered a retreat from Boston. The birthplace of the rebellion was back in colonial hands.

✔ **Reading Check: Identifying Cause and Effect** How did geography influence the early battles in New York and around Boston? The geographic importance of Fort Ticonderoga made it a target. Occupying the hills near Boston helped the Patriots retake the city.

Section 1 Review

go.hrw.com **Homework Practice Online**
keyword: SA3 HP7

❶ Define and explain:
• minutemen
• siege

❷ Identify and explain:
• First Continental Congress
• Thomas Gage
• Redcoats
• Second Continental Congress
• Continental Army
• George Washington
• Olive Branch Petition
• Battle of Bunker Hill

❸ Analyzing Information Copy the graphic organizer below. Use it to describe some of the factors that led to the start of the American Revolution, including the battles of Lexington and Concord.

Causes

Revolution

❹ Finding the Main Idea
a. How were the actions of the First and Second Continental Congresses similar and different?

b. How did the colonial forces use geography to their advantage at Bunker Hill and Dorchester Heights?

❺ Writing and Critical Thinking
Supporting a Point of View Imagine that you are a supporter of either John Dickinson or Patrick Henry at the First Continental Congress. Write a speech persuading others to support your position.

Consider the following:
• the abuses committed by British authorities
• the colonies' economic and social ties to Great Britain
• the risks of fighting against the British

SPOTLIGHT
on *My Brother Sam is Dead*

Have students obtain a copy of *My Brother Sam is Dead*. Organize students into small groups and have each group act out a short scene from the book. Groups should create appropriate props and develop a script for their presentation. Have groups present their scenes to the class. After each performance, have students discuss the different viewpoints of the characters about the Revolutionary War.

BLOCK SCHEDULING , **COOPERATIVE LEARNING**

SPOTLIGHT
on Decision-Making

In *My Brother Sam is Dead*, Tim Meeker has to deal with a war that has divided his family. Ask students to imagine that they are in a similar situation to Tim Meeker and that they too have family members with different opinions about supporting a war. Have them use the decision-making process to identify a possible situation that your family might be facing. Using *My Brother Sam is Dead* and other related sources, have students identify options that they and their family might use to resolve the situation, predicting possible consequences of each option. Finally, specifically identify possible actions that can be taken to implement a decision. **BLOCK SCHEDULING**

CONNECTING TO *Literature*

My Brother Sam Is Dead

James Collier and Christopher Collier

James and Christopher Collier describe the Revolutionary War in their book My Brother Sam Is Dead. *They write from the viewpoint of young Connecticut colonist Timmy Meeker. Tim's father is a Loyalist, or Tory, but his older brother Sam has joined the Patriots. In the following excerpt, Tim and Sam talk with Betsy Read about the possibility of war between the Americans and the British.*

Tim Meeker's family is divided by the Revolutionary War.

"Is your grandfather going to fight the Lobster-backs [Redcoats]?"

"I don't think so," Betsy said. "He's too old. He said he would probably resign his **commission**[1] to some younger man. Anyway he doesn't think we ought to fight unless we really have to. He says there ought to be some way of working it out with the King and Parliament without having to fight."

"There isn't any way to work it out," Sam said. "The British government is determined to keep us their slaves. We're going to fight."

"A lot of people aren't going to fight," I said.

"Around here they aren't. This is Tory country. Father, Mr. Beach, the Lyons, the Couches—most of them in our church are Tories. And they think it's the same everywhere, but it isn't. Down in New Haven they're ready to fight, and Windham's already marched their militia to Boston." He was being **scornful**.[2] Sam always got scornful when other people disagreed with him, because he always thought he was right, although to be honest, a lot of the time he was right, because of being so smart. But still it was hard for me to think that Father was wrong.

"Sam, Father says for most people it isn't being free, it's only a few **pence**[3] in taxes."

"That's Father for you, it's the money that counts. There are principles involved, Tim. Either you live up to your principles or you don't and maybe you have to take a chance on getting killed."

"Who wants to get killed?"

"Nobody *wants* to get killed," Sam said. "But you should be willing to die for your principles."

"That's right," Betsy said.

"But Betsy, you don't have to take a chance on getting killed," I said.

"I'd fight if I could," she said.

I hated arguing about it. "Well maybe the King will change his mind and get the Lobsterbacks out."

Sam shook his head. "He won't. He thinks he's going to teach us a lesson. But we're going to teach him one. We already taught him one at Lexington."

"That's what I mean," I said. "Maybe he'll give up now."

Betsy shook her head. "He won't. Not according to my father."

Everybody was quiet for a minute. Then Sam said, "There's going to be war. Which side are you going to be on?"

I couldn't answer. . . .

Understanding What You Read

1. **Literature and History** Why does Sam believe the colonists should fight the British?
2. **Literature and You** Why do you think Tim cannot say which side he will be on? Which side would you choose?

[1] **commission:** rank [2] **scornful:** insulting [3] **pence:** pennies

Interdisciplinary Connection

▶**Language Arts**◀

Word Origins. The origin of the term *Tories* is not certain, but according to the *Oxford University Dictionary*, "Tory" is thought to be the Anglicized spelling of an Irish word meaning "pursuer." The term referred to Irish outlaws who preyed on English settlers and soldiers.

ACTIVITY: Have students find the origins of other terms in the chapter, such as musket, Minutemen, and Redcoats.

CONNECTING TO LITERATURE ANSWERS

1. Sam feels that the British are trying to make slaves out of the colonists and that the colonies must fight for their freedom.
2. Students might suggest that he may not be sure whether he agrees more with his father or with his brother. Or Tim may be unwilling to tell his brother Sam that he thinks fighting is a bad idea.

Section 2

OBJECTIVES

⭐ Evaluate the influence of Thomas Paine's *Common Sense* on the colonies.

⭐ Identify the main ideas stated in the Declaration of Independence.

⭐ Explain Americans' reactions to the Declaration of Independence.

 **LET'S GET STARTED!**

Write the following instructions on the chalkboard: *Imagine a situation in which people are unhappy with their system of government or with their political leaders.* As students enter the classroom, ask them to think about what set of circumstances would make it appropriate for people to overthrow a government and create a new one. *(Students' responses will vary.)* Have students write down their thoughts in brief sentences. Have volunteers share their responses with the class. Tell students that in Section 2 they will learn how and why the colonists declared independence from Great Britain.

SECTION 2 RESOURCES

REPRODUCIBLE

▶ Guided Reading Strategy 7.2

TECHNOLOGY

▶ One-Stop Planner, Lesson 7.2
▶ Art in American History Transparency 3: Independence Hall
▶ American History Interactive Maps CD–ROM: The Loyalists
▶ Homework Practice Online
▶ HRW Go site

REINFORCEMENT, REVIEW, AND ASSESSMENT

▶ Section 2 Review, p. 193
▶ Daily Quiz 7.2
▶ Main Idea Activity 7.2
▶ English Audio Summary 7.2
▶ Spanish Audio Summary 7.2

Technology Resources

Art in American History Transparency 3: Independence Hall

Technology Resources

American History Interactive Maps: CD–ROM: The Loyalists

Section 2

Declaring Independence

Read to Discover

1. How did Thomas Paine's *Common Sense* influence the colonies?
2. What were the main ideas stated in the Declaration of Independence?
3. How did Americans react to the Declaration of Independence?

WHY IT MATTERS TODAY

The Declaration of Independence established the basic principles of our individual freedoms. Use **CNN fyi.com** or other **current events** sources to find an example of how we experience these freedoms today. Record your findings in your journal.

Define
• unalienable rights

Identify
• *Common Sense*
• Thomas Paine
• Thomas Jefferson
• Declaration of Independence
• Patriots
• Loyalists
• Abigail Adams

Thomas Paine became well known throughout the colonies for his political pamphlet Common Sense.

The Story Continues

On January 9, 1776, a 47-page pamphlet hit the streets of Philadelphia. The author was 38-year-old Thomas Paine, a self-educated British Quaker. About two years before, Paine had met Benjamin Franklin in London and impressed the colonist with his sharp mind. Franklin had helped Paine come to Philadelphia, where Paine became the editor of the *Pennsylvania Magazine.* Then in 1776 Paine produced a work that changed the course of American history.

⭐ Paine's *Common Sense*

In his pamphlet ***Common Sense***, **Thomas Paine** argued for breaking away from Great Britain. News of the work spread through the thirteen colonies, and it eventually sold some 500,000 copies. *Common Sense* became popular because of its message and style. Most pamphlets of the time were written by lawyers in a style that only well-educated people could understand. Paine wrote as a common person speaking to common people, which allowed him to reach a wider audience.

Paine stated in *Common Sense* that the system of monarchy in countries such as Britain was not fair. He said that the people, not kings and

★ **TEACH**

Have students read Section 2 and complete Guided Reading Strategy 7.2. Choose one or more of the following activities to explore the section content with students. For further suggestions on block scheduling or team teaching, see the *Block Scheduling Handbook with Team Teaching Strategies.*

LEVEL 1: Pair students and have them imagine that they are colonists who were influenced by *Common Sense.* Have each pair create a flyer advertising *Common Sense* and supporting Thomas Paine's ideas. Students' flyers

should identify what the ideas were and explain how these ideas influenced them. (*Students' flyers should address the following ideas: breaking away from Great Britain; the system of monarchy in European countries was unnatural and wrong; and countries should be ruled by laws made by the people.*)

ENGLISH LANGUAGE LEARNERS , COOPERATIVE LEARNING

 HOMEWORK Have students write a few stanzas of a song or a short poem describing the main ideas expressed in the Declaration of Independence.

queens, should make the laws. "A government of our own is our natural right," he wrote. At a time when monarchs ruled most countries of the world, this was a fairly new idea. Paine said that the colonies should demand their independence.

Paine's *Common Sense* helped change the way many colonists viewed Britain. With war now under way, the idea of independence gained more and more supporters.

✔ **Reading Check: Identifying Points of View** How did many colonists react to the ideas Thomas Paine expressed in *Common Sense*? The ideas inspired many colonists to support independence and democracy.

★ Declaring Independence

Many colonial leaders agreed with Paine that the colonies should be free. In June 1776 the Second Continental Congress created a committee to write a document declaring the colonies' independence. The committee members were John Adams, Benjamin Franklin, **Thomas Jefferson**, Robert R. Livingston, and Roger Sherman. Jefferson was the main author of the document.

The **Declaration of Independence** expresses three main ideas. First, Jefferson argued that all men possess **unalienable rights**. He stated that these basic rights include "life, liberty, and the pursuit of happiness." The writings of Enlightenment philosophers such as John Locke inspired the idea of unalienable rights.

Jefferson's second point was that King George III had violated the colonists' rights. Like Thomas Paine, he charged the king with passing unfair laws and interfering with colonial self-government. He also accused the king of taxing colonists without their consent. In addition, the presence of a large British army in the colonies upset Jefferson.

". . . life, liberty, and the pursuit of happiness."

Interpreting the Visual Record

Independence *Delegate Thomas Jefferson and the other members of his committee present the Declaration of Independence before the Second Continental Congress.* **Who are some of the colonial leaders shown in this image?**

ALL LEVELS: Copy the following graphic organizer onto the chalkboard, omitting the italicized answers. Have students complete the organizer to help them identify the main ideas stated in the Declaration of Independence.
ENGLISH LANGUAGE LEARNERS

Declaration of Independence, July 4th 1776

- **colonists' rights**—*the colonists have unalienable rights*
- **actions of King George III**—*King George violated these unalienable rights*
- **actions of colonists**—*because King George violated these rights, the colonists have the right to be independent*

 LEVELS 2 AND 3: Have students draw political cartoons that indicate either the colonists' support or opposition to the Declaration of Independence. *(Students' cartoons in support will take the Patriots' point of view. Students' cartoons in opposition will take the Loyalists' point of view.)* Have students write caption paragraphs to accompany their cartoons. Ask volunteers to present their cartoons to the class.

✖ CLOSE

Ask students after reviewing this section, to consider whether the colonists were justified in declaring independence. Lead a class discussion on the issue.

Interdisciplinary Connection

▶**Language Arts**◀

The Declaration of Independence. There was both criticism and praise for the language of the Declaration of Independence. Some newspapers pointed out the irony of such statements as "all men are created equal" in a slave-holding nation. One newspaper in South Carolina noted that as a clergyman read the Declaration aloud, a slave held a parasol over the clergyman's head and fanned his face.

CRITICAL THINKING

Why was it important that the Declaration state that all men are created equal?

ANSWER: Students responses will vary.

internet connect

TOPIC: First Ladies
GO TO: go.hrw.com
KEYWORD: SA3 CF7

Have students conduct an Internet search through the HRW Go site for information on more recent first ladies. Ask students to write a paragraph describing how the role of first lady has changed over time using standard grammar, spelling, sentence structure, and punctuation.

July 4, 1776
The United States of America is formed.

Interpreting the Visual Record

Rebellion *Patriots pull down a statue of King George III in New York.* **How do you think these colonists feel about King George and Great Britain?**

Third, Jefferson argued that the colonies had the right to break away from Great Britain. Jefferson was influenced by the Enlightenment idea of the social contract, which states that rulers should protect the rights of their citizens. In exchange, the people agree to be governed. Jefferson said that because King George III had broken the social contract, the colonists need no longer obey him.

On July 4, 1776, the Continental Congress approved the Declaration of Independence. This act broke all ties to the British Crown. The United States of America was born.

✔ **Reading Check: Finding the Main Idea** What are the key ideas stated by Jefferson in 1776 in the Declaration of Independence? The colonists have unalienable rights, which King George has violated. So the colonists have the right to be independent.

★ Choosing Sides

Colonists who chose to fight for independence became known as **Patriots**. Those who remained loyal to Great Britain were called **Loyalists** or Tories. Many other colonists remained neutral, choosing neither side. People on both sides often felt very strongly about their views. In March 1775, before the fighting had even started, Patriot Patrick Henry spoke before the Virginia House of Burgesses.

 History Makers Speak ❝Is life so dear or peace so sweet as to be purchased at the price of chains and slavery? Forbid it, Almighty God! I know not what course others may take; but as for me, give me liberty, or give me death!❞

—Patrick Henry, quoted in *The Annals of America*

Once the Declaration of Independence was signed, Loyalists became targets of abuse by Patriots. It is estimated that more than 100,000 Loyalists fled the colonies during the Revolution. Most of them went to Canada.

Many Loyalists shared the feelings of Samuel Curwen of Massachusetts. He was a merchant who believed that the colonies did not need independence. To Curwen, British rule was the best way to maintain peace and prosperity in the colonies. He refused to blame the fighting at Lexington and Concord entirely on the British. Patriot neighbors called him a Tory. Curwen had to flee his home to escape "the looks, words, and actions of the mad rabble [masses]."

The divisions caused by the war also affected some key Patriot leaders. For example, Thomas Fairfax, one of George Washington's closest friends, fled to Britain because he was a Loyalist. Even the great Patriot Benjamin Franklin had a Loyalist son, William.

✔ **Reading Check: Identifying Points of View** Why did some colonists remain Loyalists? They believed the colonies were not ready for independence, or they felt a duty to obey their king.

☆ **REVIEW AND ASSESS**

Have students complete the **Section 2 Review** on p. 193. Then have students complete **Daily Quiz 7.2**. As **Alternative Assessment**, you may want to use the advertising flyer or political cartoon exercises in this section's lessons.

☆ **RETEACH**

Have students complete **Main Idea Activity for English Language Learners and Special-Needs Students 7.2**. Then have students write the section's headings and subheadings on a sheet of paper, leaving a space between each. Ask students to list the main ideas of each heading and subheading in the appropriate space. **ENGLISH LANGUAGE LEARNERS**

☆ **EXTEND**

Organize students into groups. Have each group use the library or other available resources to find examples of organizations that used the Declaration of Independence to promote reform or liberation movements. Ask volunteers to present their findings in brief reports to the class. **COOPERATIVE LEARNING ,**
BLOCK SCHEDULING

★ Other Reactions to the Declaration

Some people pointed out that the Declaration ignored many colonists. Although many women were Patriots, the Declaration did not address their rights. The phrase "all men are created equal" failed to mention women at all. This issue worried **Abigail Adams**, the wife of John Adams. In a letter she asked her husband to protect the rights of women.

> "In the new code of Laws which I suppose it will be necessary for you to make I desire you would Remember the Ladies. . . . If particular care and attention is not paid to the Ladies we . . . will not hold ourselves bound by any Laws in which we have no voice, or Representation."

—Abigail Adams, quoted in *Notable American Women*

In addition, the Declaration did not recognize the rights of enslaved African Americans. In July 1776 slavery was legal in all the colonies. In his first draft of the Declaration, Thomas Jefferson—a slaveholder himself—had included a passage that attacked the slave trade. However, southern delegates insisted that the passage be removed.

The Revolution raised questions about whether slavery should exist in a land that valued liberty. Some Patriots had compared living under British rule to living as slaves. These writers could not ignore the difference between the ideals of liberty and the practice of slavery. Some colonists wanted the principle "all men are created equal" to apply to all people. Massachusetts abolished slavery in 1783, and by 1784 the rest of New England also had taken steps to end slavery. Even so, the conflict over slavery continued long after the Revolutionary War had ended.

✔ **Reading Check: Finding the Main Idea** What groups felt ignored by the Declaration of Independence? Some women and African Americans felt overlooked by the Declaration.

BIOGRAPHY

Abigail Adams
(1744–1818)

Abigail Adams was born in Massachusetts in 1744. Educated at home by her parents, she developed a great love of reading and writing. She married John Adams in 1764, and they raised five children. Abigail Adams ran most of the family's businesses and advised her husband on political issues. Many of her letters to family and friends were saved long after her death in 1818. Some historians have called her "one of the great letter writers of all time." How have historians been able to learn about the life of Abigail Adams?

**Section 2 Review
ANSWERS**

❶ **Define**
• unalienable rights, p. 191

❷ **Identify**
• *Common Sense*, p. 190
• Thomas Paine, p. 190
• Thomas Jefferson, p. 191
• Declaration of Independence, p. 191
• Patriots, p. 192
• Loyalists, p. 192
• Abigail Adams, p. 193

❸ argument for independence— violation of rights by King George; arguments against independence— colonists not ready for independence, duty to obey the king

❹ a. Paine spoke in plain language, and many agreed with his criticisms of the British government.
b. it was the year colonists declared independence; Second Continental Congress met, Declaration written

❺ Students' essays will vary, but they should address the views of the Loyalists and the Patriots, the contributions of women to society, and the meaning of the phrase "all men are created equal."

Section 2 Review

go.hrw.com **Homework Practice Online**
keyword: SA3 HP7

❶ **Define and explain:**
• unalienable rights

❷ **Identify and explain:**
• *Common Sense*
• Thomas Paine
• Thomas Jefferson
• Declaration of Independence
• Patriots
• Loyalists
• Abigail Adams

❸ **Comparing** Copy the graphic organizer below. Use it to compare the arguments that colonists offered for and against independence, including Thomas Jefferson's arguments in the Declaration of Independence.

Arguments for Independence		Arguments against Independence
	VS.	

❹ **Finding the Main Idea**
a. Why did colonists find Thomas Paine's arguments in *Common Sense* so persuasive?
b. Why was 1776 significant for the colonies, and what major events took place that year?

❺ **Writing and Critical Thinking**
Identifying Points of View Imagine that you are living in the colonies in 1776. Write an essay explaining how colonists reacted to the Declaration of Independence.

Consider the following:
• the views of Loyalists and Patriots
• the contributions of women to society
• the meaning of the phrase "all men are created equal"

193

Exploring the Document

Thomas Jefferson wrote the first draft of the Declaration in a little more than two weeks. **How is the Declaration's idea about why governments are formed still important to our country today?**

[1] **impel:** force

[2] **endowed:** provided

[3] **usurpations:** wrongful seizures of power

[4] **evinces:** clearly displays

[5] **despotism:** unlimited power

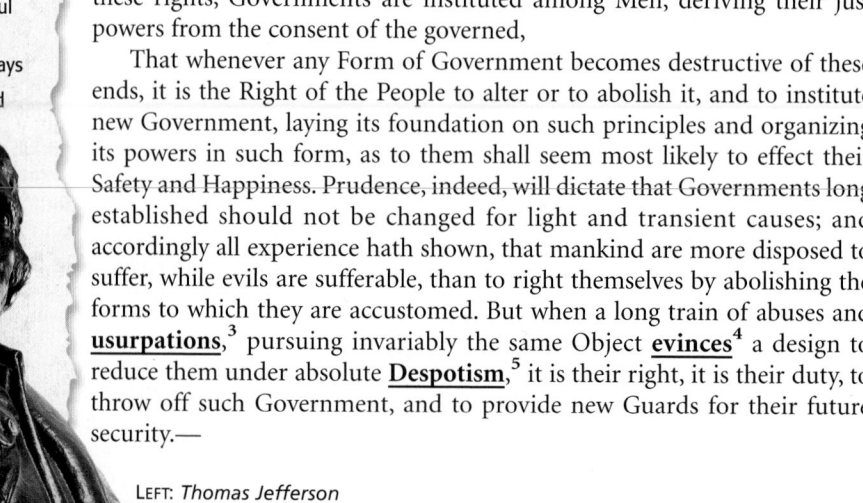

THE DECLARATION *of* INDEPENDENCE

In Congress, July 4, 1776
The unanimous Declaration of the thirteen
united States of America,

When in the Course of human events, it becomes necessary for one people to dissolve the political bands which have connected them with another, and to assume among the Powers of the earth, the separate and equal station to which the Laws of Nature and of Nature's God entitle them, a decent respect to the opinions of mankind requires that they should declare the causes which **impel**[1] them to the separation.

Natural Rights

We hold these truths to be self-evident, that all men are created equal, that they are **endowed**[2] by their Creator with certain unalienable Rights, that among these are Life, Liberty, and the pursuit of Happiness. That to secure these rights, Governments are instituted among Men, deriving their just powers from the consent of the governed,

That whenever any Form of Government becomes destructive of these ends, it is the Right of the People to alter or to abolish it, and to institute new Government, laying its foundation on such principles and organizing its powers in such form, as to them shall seem most likely to effect their Safety and Happiness. Prudence, indeed, will dictate that Governments long established should not be changed for light and transient causes; and accordingly all experience hath shown, that mankind are more disposed to suffer, while evils are sufferable, than to right themselves by abolishing the forms to which they are accustomed. But when a long train of abuses and **usurpations**,[3] pursuing invariably the same Object **evinces**[4] a design to reduce them under absolute **Despotism**,[5] it is their right, it is their duty, to throw off such Government, and to provide new Guards for their future security.—

LEFT: *Thomas Jefferson*

Colonists' Complaints against the King

Such has been the patient sufferance of these Colonies; and such is now the necessity which constrains them to alter their former Systems of Government. The history of the present King of Great Britain is a history of repeated injuries and usurpations, all having in direct object the establishment of an absolute **Tyranny**[6] over these States. To prove this, let Facts be submitted to a **candid**[7] world.

He has refused his Assent to Laws, the most wholesome and necessary for the public good.

He has forbidden his Governors to pass Laws of immediate and pressing importance, unless suspended in their operation till his Assent should be obtained; and when so suspended, he has utterly neglected to attend to them.

He has refused to pass other Laws for the accommodation of large districts of people, unless those people would **relinquish**[8] the right of Representation in the Legislature, a right **inestimable**[9] to them and **formidable**[10] to tyrants only.

He has called together legislative bodies at places unusual, uncomfortable, and distant from the depository of their Public Records, for the sole purpose of fatiguing them into compliance with his measures.

He has dissolved Representative Houses repeatedly, for opposing with manly firmness his invasions on the rights of the people.

He has refused for a long time, after such dissolutions, to cause others to be elected; whereby the Legislative Powers, incapable of **Annihilation**,[11] have returned to the People at large for their exercise; the State remaining in the mean time exposed to all the dangers of invasion from without, and **convulsions**[12] within.

He has endeavored to prevent the population of these States; for that purpose obstructing the Laws of **Naturalization of Foreigners**;[13] refusing to pass others to encourage their migration hither, and raising the conditions of new **Appropriations of Lands**.[14]

He has obstructed the Administration of Justice, by refusing his Assent to Laws for establishing Judiciary Powers.

He has made Judges dependent on his Will alone, for the **tenure**[15] of their offices, and the amount and payment of their salaries.

He has erected **a multitude of**[16] New Offices, and sent hither swarms of Officers to harass our people, and eat out their substance.

He has kept among us, in times of peace, Standing Armies without the Consent of our legislature.

He has affected to render the Military independent of and superior to the Civil Power.

He has combined with others to subject us to a jurisdiction foreign to our constitution, and unacknowledged by our laws; giving his Assent to their Acts of pretended legislation:

[6]**tyranny:** oppressive power exerted by a government or ruler

[7]**candid:** fair

Exploring the Document

Here the Declaration lists the charges that the colonists had against King George III. **How might the language and content of the list appeal to people's emotions?**

[8]**relinquish:** release, yield

[9]**inestimable:** priceless

[10]**formidable:** causing dread

[11]**annihilation:** destruction

[12]**convulsions:** violent disturbances

[13]**naturalization of foreigners:** the process by which foreign-born persons become citizens

[14]**appropriations of land:** setting aside land for settlement

[15]**tenure:** term

[16]**a multitude of:** many

The Signers. The 56 signers of the Declaration of Independence shared many characteristics—almost all were Protestant white males and were fairly wealthy. Forty-eight of the signers were born in America.

CRITICAL THINKING

How might the fact that 48 of the signers were born in America have influenced their decision to declare independence?

ANSWER: Students might suggest that these signers might have felt less loyalty to Great Britain and more loyalty to the colonies.

EXPLORING THE DOCUMENT ANSWER

Students might point to words such as *absolute despotism, repeated injuries and usurpations, tyranny, refused, forbidden,* and *obstructed* and mention that these words convey a sense of injustice that Jefferson and the other members of the Continental Congress felt the colonists had suffered at the hands of Great Britain.

EXPLORING THE DOCUMENT ANSWER

(for p. 197)
without representation they were angry they were being taxed

[17]**quartering:** lodging, housing

Exploring the Document

Colonists had been angry over British tax policies since just after the French and Indian War. **Why were the colonists protesting British tax policies?**

[18]**arbitrary:** not based on law

[19]**render:** make

[20]**abdicated:** given up

[21]**foreign mercenaries:** soldiers hired to fight for a country not their own

[22]**perfidy:** violation of trust

[23]**insurrections:** rebellions

[24]**petitioned for redress:** asked formally for a correction of wrongs

[25]**unwarrantable jurisdiction:** unjustified authority

[26]**magnanimity:** generous spirit

[27]**conjured:** urgently called upon

[28]**consanguinity:** common ancestry

[29]**acquiesce:** consent to

For **quartering**[17] large bodies of armed troops among us:

For protecting them, by a mock Trial, from Punishment for any Murders which they should commit on the Inhabitants of these States:

For cutting off our Trade with all parts of the world:

For imposing taxes on us without our Consent:

For depriving us in many cases, of the benefits of Trial by Jury:

For transporting us beyond Seas to be tried for pretended offences:

For abolishing the free System of English Laws in a neighboring Province, establishing therein an **Arbitrary**[18] government, and enlarging its Boundaries so as to **render**[19] it at once an example and fit instrument for introducing the same absolute rule into these Colonies:

For taking away our Charters, abolishing our most valuable Laws, and altering fundamentally the Forms of our Governments:

For suspending our own Legislature, and declaring themselves invested with Power to legislate for us in all cases whatsoever.

He has **abdicated**[20] Government here, by declaring us out of his Protection and waging War against us.

He has plundered our seas, ravaged our Coasts, burnt our towns, and destroyed the lives of our people.

He is at this time transporting large armies of **foreign mercenaries**[21] to complete the works of death, desolation and tyranny, already begun with circumstances of Cruelty & **perfidy**[22] scarcely paralleled in the most barbarous ages, and totally unworthy the Head of a civilized nation.

He has constrained our fellow Citizens taken Captive on the high Seas to bear Arms against their Country, to become the executioners of their friends and Brethren, or to fall themselves by their Hands.

He has excited domestic **insurrections**[23] amongst us, and has endeavored to bring on the inhabitants of our frontiers, the merciless Indian Savages, whose known rule of warfare, is an undistinguished destruction of all ages, sexes and conditions.

In every stage of these Oppressions We have **Petitioned for Redress**[24] in the most humble terms: Our repeated Petitions have been answered only by repeated injury. A Prince, whose character is thus marked by every act which may define a Tyrant, is unfit to be the ruler of a free People.

Nor have We been wanting in attention to our British brethren. We have warned them from time to time of attempts by their legislature to extend an **unwarrantable jurisdiction**[25] over us. We have reminded them of the circumstances of our emigration and settlement here. We have appealed to their native justice and **magnanimity**,[26] and we have **conjured**[27] them by the ties of our common kindred to disavow these usurpations, which, would inevitably interrupt our connections and correspondence. They too have been deaf to the voice of justice and of **consanguinity**.[28] We must, therefore, **acquiesce**[29] in the necessity, which denounces our Separation, and hold them, as we hold the rest of mankind, Enemies in War, in Peace Friends.

An Independent and United Nation

We, therefore, the Representatives of the united States of America, in General Congress, Assembled, appealing to the Supreme Judge of the world for the **rectitude**[30] of our intentions, do, in the Name, and by Authority of the good People of these Colonies, solemnly publish and declare, That these United Colonies are, and of Right ought to be Free and Independent States; that they are Absolved from all Allegiance to the British Crown, and that all political connection between them and the State of Great Britain, is and ought to be totally dissolved; and that as Free and Independent States, they have full Power to levy War, conclude Peace, contract Alliances, establish Commerce, and to do all other Acts and Things which Independent States may of right do. And for the support of this Declaration, with a firm reliance on the Protection of Divine Providence, we mutually pledge to each other our Lives, our Fortunes and our sacred Honor.

[30]**rectitude:** rightness

John Hancock
President of Massachusetts

GEORGIA
Button Gwinnett
Lyman Hall
George Walton

NORTH CAROLINA
William Hooper
Joseph Hewes
John Penn

SOUTH CAROLINA
Edward Rutledge
Thomas Heyward, Jr.
Thomas Lynch, Jr.
Arthur Middleton

MARYLAND
Samuel Chase
William Paca
Thomas Stone
Charles Carroll of Carrollton

VIRGINIA
George Wythe
Richard Henry Lee

Thomas Jefferson
Benjamin Harrison
Thomas Nelson, Jr.
Francis Lightfoot Lee
Carter Braxton

PENNSYLVANIA
Robert Morris
Benjamin Rush
Benjamin Franklin
John Morton
George Clymer
James Smith
George Taylor
James Wilson
George Ross

DELAWARE
Caesar Rodney
George Read
Thomas McKean

NEW YORK
William Floyd
Philip Livingston
Francis Lewis
Lewis Morris

NEW JERSEY
Richard Stockton
John Witherspoon
Francis Hopkinson
John Hart
Abraham Clark

NEW HAMPSHIRE
Josiah Bartlett
William Whipple
Matthew Thorton

MASSACHUSETTS
Samuel Adams
John Adams
Robert Treat Paine
Elbridge Gerry

RHODE ISLAND
Stephen Hopkins
William Ellery

CONNECTICUT
Roger Sherman
Samuel Huntington
William Williams
Oliver Wolcott

Exploring the Document

On July 4, 1776, Congress adopted the final draft of the Declaration of Independence. A formal copy written on parchment paper was signed on August 2, 1776. **From whom did the Declaration's signers receive their authority to declare independence in 1776?**

Exploring the Document

The following is part of a passage that the Congress removed from Jefferson's original draft: "He has waged cruel war against human nature itself, violating its most sacred rights of life and liberty in the persons of a distant people who never offended him, captivating and carrying them into slavery in another hemisphere, or to incur miserable death in their transportation thither." **Why do you think the Congress deleted this passage?**

Section 3

OBJECTIVES

★ Examine the Patriots' advantages and disadvantages at the beginning of the Revolutionary War.

★ Explore the contributions that various groups made to the war effort.

★ Describe the problems the Patriots faced in Canada and New York.

Section 3

Dark Hours for the Revolution

Read to Discover

1. What were the Patriots' advantages and disadvantages at the beginning of the Revolutionary War?
2. How did different groups contribute to the war effort?
3. What problems did the Patriots face in Canada and New York?

WHY IT MATTERS TODAY

When the colonies rebelled against Britain, they did not have a navy and a professional army. Today U.S. leaders consider it vital to have a well-equipped and prepared military. Use CNNfyi.com or other **current events** sources to learn where U.S. military forces are serving today. Record your findings in your journal.

Define

• mercenaries

Identify

• Lord Dunmore's Proclamation
• Thayendanegea
• Molly Pitcher
• William Howe

During the winters, Martha Washington joined her husband wherever his army was camped.

The Story Continues

General George Washington faced a challenging task when he took command of the Continental Army. The Patriots were up against a mighty enemy in Britain. Washington wrote to his wife, Martha, that he did not know if he could build a strong enough army. "I shall hope that my undertaking is designed to answer some good purpose," he said. He did not know what to expect when he led his men into the field.

★ Comparing Strengths and Weaknesses

At the beginning of the war, the British seemed much stronger than the Patriots. Great Britain had more money and resources than the colonies. Britain also had a powerful military. Its navy was the largest in the world. British soldiers were mostly well-trained professionals. In contrast, when the war began, the colonists had no navy at all. The colonial army was made up of poorly trained local militias. Few of these groups had ever fought together.

TEACH

Have students read Section 3 and complete Guided Reading Strategy 7.3. Choose one or more of the following activities to explore the section content with students. For further suggestions on block scheduling or team teaching, see the *Block Scheduling Handbook with Team Teaching Strategies.*

 LEVEL 1: Have pairs of students create a graphic organizer that compares the Patriots' battles in Canada and New York. Students' graphic organizers should include information related to the problems that the Patriots faced in Canada and New York. *(Students' graphic organizers should include: in Canada the Patriots were far from home and* faced poor weather; in New York they were outnumbered and out-maneuvered.) **ENGLISH LANGUAGE LEARNERS ,** **COOPERATIVE LEARNING**

 HOMEWORK Tell students to imagine that they are Patriot soldiers fighting in Canada and New York. Have each student write a letter to a friend or family member back home that describes the problems he or she is facing.

ALL LEVELS: Copy the graphic organizer on the following page onto the chalkboard, omitting the italicized answers. Use it to help students explore the contributions of various groups to the war effort. **ENGLISH LANGUAGE LEARNERS**

However, the colonists did have some advantages. Many Americans supported the Revolution. As a result, the British army often had to deal with hostile citizens. The British also had to ship their supplies across the Atlantic Ocean. This process slowed down their war effort. Finally, the Patriots were fighting for a cause in which they believed. On the other hand, some British soldiers were **mercenaries**, or hired foreign soldiers.

✔ **Reading Check: Categorizing** What advantages and disadvantages did the Patriots have when the war began? The Patriots fought on their own soil and had the courage of their convictions. They faced a richer nation that had a stronger military.

Colonial soldiers often used horns such as this one to store their gunpowder.

⭐ A Call to Arms

General Washington's first task was to organize and raise more troops for the Continental Army. During the course of the war, more than 230,000 soldiers served in the Continental Army. Another 145,000 Americans joined local militias. These volunteers came from many backgrounds. Many were teenagers, such as 14-year-old James Forten, who served in the Continental Navy. Some officers had fought in the French and Indian War, but few of the volunteers had combat experience. General Charles Lee hoped that their courage would be enough.

 History Makers Speak ❝They are admirable—young, stout, healthy, zealous [eager], good-humored and sober [serious]. . . . I really believe a very little time and pains would render [make] 'em the most invincible [unbeatable] army that have appeared.❞

—General Charles Lee, quoted in *Voices of 1776*, by Richard Wheeler

One question facing Washington was whether to recruit African Americans. Many African Americans, including some slaves, were already serving in local militias. African Americans like Peter Salem and Salem Poor had already fought in battles. But many southerners did not want the American forces to include black soldiers. Washington soon banned African Americans from serving in the army.

The British reacted quickly. Lord Dunmore, Virginia's governor, issued a proclamation on November 7, 1775. **Lord Dunmore's Proclamation** promised freedom to any slave who fought for the British. Thousands of slaves agreed. In response, the Continental Army began allowing free African Americans to enlist, and eventually some 5,000 joined.

⭐ Other Sources of Help

American Indian groups fought on both sides during the war. The British had many Indian allies. One of Great Britain's key allies was Mohawk leader **Thayendanegea** (thah-yuhn-dah-ne-GAY-uh), also known as Joseph Brant. He persuaded many of the Iroquois to support the British. However, the Patriots worked hard just to keep American Indians neutral. This effort was very important on the frontier.

CONNECTING TO SCIENCE AND TECHNOLOGY

The Long Rifle

Many Patriots from the frontier used a gun known as the long rifle or Kentucky rifle. A rifle is a type of gun with a grooved barrel. The grooves spin the ball, or bullet, as it is shot. Compared to a musket, a long rifle can shoot a ball farther and with greater accuracy. However, soldiers could fire and reload muskets faster than rifles. Rifles also lacked bayonets for use in hand-to-hand combat.

General Washington used rifle units for special missions such as sharpshooting and scouting. These groups impressed the British with their accuracy at long range. By the end of the war, the long rifle was well known. Over time, it became one of the most common weapons in North America. How were rifles different from muskets?

Interdisciplinary Connection

▶**Math**◀

Pay and Rations. Each soldier in the Second Regiment was paid $6.67 monthly. Rations consisted of a pound of beef or pork; a pound of bread or flour a day; a few vegetables when available; four ounces of rum or whiskey a day; and a small quantity of vinegar, salt, soap, and candles a week.

ACTIVITY: Have students use the library to obtain information on the monthly salary and rations of a soldier in the U.S. Army today. Then ask students to figure the percentage increase in pay and rations from then until today.

Technology Resources

 Exploring America's Past Video Segment: A Call to Arms; Teacher's Guide, pp. 10–12

Search 24575, Play to 31727
Videodisc Red Side A
See *Teacher's Guide* for Spanish barcode.

CONNECTING TO SCIENCE AND TECHNOLOGY ANSWER
They had a grooved barrel and could shoot farther with more accuracy, while muskets could be fired faster and could use bayonets.

```
┌─────────────────────┐          ┌─────────────────────────────┐
│        Men          │          │          Women              │
│  many volunteered   │          │  served as nurses, spies, or │
│     for army        │          │ messengers; ran farms or     │
└─────────────────────┘          │ businesses; some fought in   │
                                 │         battles             │
         ┌──────────────┐        └─────────────────────────────┘
         │  War Effort  │
         └──────────────┘
┌─────────────────────┐          ┌─────────────────────────────┐
│  American Indians   │          │      African Americans      │
│ fought on both sides but │     │ many fought for British to gain │
│ many remained neutral │        │ freedom; free African Americans │
└─────────────────────┘          │ were allowed to join Patriots │
                                 └─────────────────────────────┘
```

LEVEL 3: Have students create Patriot recruitment posters to encourage enlistment in the Continental Army. The recruitment posters should include information and images that reflect the Patriots' advantages and disadvantages at the beginning of the Revolutionary War. Have volunteers present their posters to the class.

★ CLOSE

Arrange a debate or panel discussion on each of the following topics: a)Resolved: That the Patriot army was at a strong disadvantage at the beginning of the Revolutionary War; and b) Resolved: That the Patriot army should not have invaded British Canada. Have students present their debates to the class.
COOPERATIVE LEARNING

★ Citizenship

African Americans and the War. African Americans fought on both sides during the Revolutionary War. Historians estimate that around 10,000 served in some capacity for the British forces, while around 5,000 fought with the Patriots. One of the most notable African American contributions to the Patriot war effort came in August 1778 at the Battle of Rhode Island. There, the First Rhode Island, a nearly all-black regiment composed of free African Americans, held off British attacks to allow other Continental forces time to escape. The commander of Continental forces in the battle, General John Sullivan, reported that the First Rhode Island was "entitled to a proper share of the day's honors." Later abolitionists looked back on the regiment's accomplishments with pride, calling their actions, "deeds of desperate valor."

CRITICAL THINKING

Why do you think African Americans joined the Patriot cause?

ANSWER: Many probably hoped that if the Patriots were successful, African Americans who helped in the victory might achieve more freedom and rights in society.

Technology Resources

 Everyday Life in America Transparency 4: Revolutionary War Uniforms

THE GRANGER COLLECTION, NEW YORK

This painting shows Molly Pitcher fighting alongside other Patriots at the Battle of Monmouth.

Analyzing Primary Sources
Summarizing How are women supporting the war effort according to this speaker? by making ammunition and encouraging soldiers

Many women also helped the Patriot cause. Women often ran farms and businesses while men served as soldiers. Other women helped support the army by raising money for supplies or joining sewing groups to make uniforms.

 "At every house Women and children [are] making Cartridges, running Bullets . . . and at the same time animating [encouraging] their Husbands and Sons to fight."

—Anonymous, quoted in *Born for Liberty,* by Sara M. Evans

Some women served as messengers, nurses, or spies. A few women, such as Deborah Sampson, even disguised themselves as men to fight in the war. The woman who perhaps became best known for her wartime service was Mary Ludwig Hays. She earned the nickname **Molly Pitcher** by bringing water to thirsty Patriot troops. When her husband was wounded in a 1778 battle, she quickly took his place loading cannons.

✔ **Reading Check: Summarizing** How did different groups living in the colonies contribute to the war effort? Many white men, some African American men, and a few women served in the Army. Many women aided the war effort. Many slaves fought for the British to gain freedom.

★ British Victories

Many Patriot leaders favored fighting a defensive war. This would help the army's limited supplies last longer. However, other, more aggressive leaders wanted to make British-controlled Canada the "fourteenth colony." In November 1775, Patriot troops led by General Richard Montgomery took the town of St. John's, Canada. Shortly afterward Montgomery captured the nearby town of Montreal.

The next major target was the well-defended city of Quebec. General Benedict Arnold led his troops on a long march north through what is now Maine. When Arnold's forces reached Quebec, he waited for Montgomery's troops to arrive. Together, the commanders planned their attack. The American troops were cold and far from home. Many of the soldiers also had enlistments that would soon end. This meant that the Patriots had to act quickly, but the Americans had no cannons to knock down Quebec's walls. Arnold and Montgomery decided to wait for a snowstorm. They hoped the storm would provide cover while the Patriots got close to the city's defenses.

During a fierce blizzard on New Year's Eve, the Patriots attacked Quebec. The Americans suffered a crushing defeat. General Montgomery was killed early in the battle. More than half of the American troops were captured, killed, or wounded. Patriots' hopes of taking Canada soon faded.

Farther south, General Washington had moved his troops to New York. In early July 1776, Patriots spotted a large fleet of British ships nearing New York Bay. Led by General **William Howe**, the British drove the Continental Army off of Long Island. Washington's troops retreated to Manhattan Island. The British force was much larger and better equipped than that of the Patriots. Washington had to use all his leadership skills just to save his outnumbered army. In a series of battles, Howe forced the Continental Army to keep retreating. The Redcoats captured many Patriots as well as valuable supplies. After several months they pushed Washington out of New York. Howe's revenge for his defeat at Boston was complete.

Soldiers in the Continental Army (left) often wore the tricornered hat shown here.

British soldiers (below) were nicknamed Redcoats because of their uniforms.

COLLECTION OF THE NEW YORK HISTORICAL SOCIETY

✔ **Reading Check: Contrasting** Describe the different problems faced by the Continental Army in Canada and New York. In Canada the Patriots were in a hurry and far from home. In New York they were outnumbered and outmaneuvered.

Section 3 Review

go.hrw.com Homework Practice Online
keyword: SA3 HP7

1 Define and explain:
• mercenaries

2 Identify and explain:
• Lord Dunmore's Proclamation
• Thayendanegea
• Molly Pitcher
• William Howe

3 Comparing Copy the chart below. Use it to compare the military advantages of the British and the Patriots.

British Advantages	Patriots' Advantages

4 Finding the Main Idea
a. Explain the roles that some young white men, African Americans, American Indians, and women played in supporting the Patriots during the American Revolution.
b. Why did the American invasion of Canada fail while the British attack on New York succeeded?

5 Writing and Critical Thinking
Analyzing Information Imagine that you are a British officer on the frontier. Write a brief report to your commander explaining why you think that many American Indians will side with the British.

Consider the following:
• which side Indian leaders think will win the war
• conflicts on the frontier
• alliances between American Indians and the British

Section 4

OBJECTIVES

- ✪ Analyze Washington's strategies at Trenton and Princeton.
- ✪ Discuss the Battle of Saratoga as a turning point in the war.
- ✪ Identify how foreign nations and individuals aided the Patriots.
- ✪ Describe how the Patriots carried out the naval war.

SECTION 4 RESOURCES

REPRODUCIBLE

- ▶ Guided Reading Strategy 7.4
- ▶ Primary Source Reading 7: Medicine and War

TECHNOLOGY

- ▶ One-Stop Planner, Lesson 7.4
- ▶ Art in American History Transparency 6: Capture of the Hessians at Trenton
- ▶ Linking Geography and History Transparency 9: The Fight for Independence, 1776–1781
- ▶ Holt Researcher: American History CD–ROM
- ▶ Homework Practice Online

REINFORCEMENT, REVIEW, AND ASSESSMENT

- ▶ Section 4 Review, p. 208
- ▶ Daily Quiz 7.4
- ▶ Main Idea Activity 7.4
- ▶ English Audio Summary 7.4
- ▶ Spanish Audio Summary 7.4

LET'S GET STARTED!

Write the following statement on the chalkboard: *List different strategies that an army might use to defeat a more-powerful opponent.* As students enter the classroom, have them write down their responses to the statement. *(Students' lists might mention by trying to surprise the opponent or by using the terrain to gain an advantage, such as at the Battle of Bunker Hill and Dorchester Heights.)* Tell students that in Section 4 they will learn about how the victories in New Jersey and New York helped turn the tide of the war for the Patriots and how these victories helped gain new European allies for the colonists.

Section 4

The Patriots Gain New Hope

Read to Discover

1. What were Washington's strategies at Trenton and Princeton?
2. Why was the Battle of Saratoga a turning point in the war?
3. How did foreign nations and individuals aid the Patriots?
4. How did the Patriots carry out the naval war?

WHY IT MATTERS TODAY

Foreign allies helped the Patriots fight the Revolutionary War. The United States still has close alliances with many countries. Use **CNN fyi.com** or other **current events** sources to learn more about a nation that is a U.S. ally today. Record your findings in your journal.

Identify

- • Battle of Trenton
- • Battle of Princeton
- • John Burgoyne
- • Battle of Brandywine Creek
- • Battle of Saratoga
- • Bernardo de Gálvez
- • Marquis de Lafayette
- • Friedrich von Steuben
- • John Paul Jones

The Story Continues

General Howe was confident that the British would win the war quickly.

In November 1776 General Howe took the last Patriot fort on Manhattan Island. Patriot Alexander Graydon was among those captured. He later recalled a British officer warning the prisoners, "Young men, ye should never fight against your king!" Graydon and other Patriots like him survived their capture. But they began to fear that the British were getting close to complete victory in the war.

✪ Victory in New Jersey

General Howe sent troops to take New Jersey in November 1776. After the British victories in Canada and New York, Howe thought the war would be over soon. So he gave his troops a rest and settled in New York City for the winter. Howe left New Jersey in the hands of Hessians. These were German mercenaries, many from the state of Hesse, hired to fight for the British.

Howe's delay allowed Washington to gather reinforcements. The Patriots were still in trouble, however. Writer Thomas Paine described the difficult situation in the first of his *Crisis* papers. "These are the times that try men's souls," he wrote. Paine urged the Patriots to stay loyal to their cause.

Have students read Section 4 and complete Guided Reading Strategy 7.4. Choose one or more of the following activities to explore the section content with students. For further suggestions on block scheduling or team teaching, see the *Block Scheduling Handbook with Team Teaching Strategies.*

 LEVEL 1: Draw two columns on the chalkboard. Title one *Army* and the other *Navy*. Call on students to identify the contributions each branch of the American military made to the Revolutionary War effort. As students give their answers, write them under the appropriate heading on the chalkboard. As a class, discuss with students how the Patriots carried out their naval war. (*Students' responses should include that John Paul Jones concentrated on capturing British merchant ships and that the Patriots fought one-on-one with British warships instead of choosing large engagements.*)

ENGLISH LANGUAGE LEARNERS

CONNECTING TO
THE ARTS

Crossing the Delaware
George Washington and his troops crossed the partially frozen Delaware River on the night of December 25, 1776. This daring act led to a key Patriot victory. German-American artist Emanuel Leutze created this famous painting of the event in 1851. *Washington Crossing the Delaware* now hangs in the Metropolitan Museum of Art in New York City. In 1999 Leutze's painting was used as the basis for the image on the back of the New Jersey state quarter. What feelings do you think Leutze wanted to inspire with this painting?

★ Culture

African Americans and the War. Two of the soldiers chosen by George Washington to take part in the crossing of the Delaware River on Christmas Day, 1776, were Oliver Cromwell and Prince Whipple. Both men were African Americans. They helped prepare the surprise attack on the Hessians at Trenton.

ACTIVITY: Ask students to prepare a bulletin-board display of the contributions that various groups in society made to the Revolutionary War effort.

Technology Resources
Art in American History Transparency 6: Capture of the Hessians at Trenton

CONNECTING TO
THE ARTS ANSWER
Students' answers will vary, but most students will probably see the painting as an effort to stir feelings of patriotism, courage, and pride.

Washington decided to attack the Hessians at Trenton, New Jersey. He believed he could take them by surprise while they celebrated the holiday. On Christmas night in 1776, Washington and 2,400 soldiers silently crossed the icy Delaware River. The troops were short on supplies—many had no shoes. But, they were ready to fight. After landing early on the morning of December 26, the Patriots marched to Trenton. The **Battle of Trenton** lasted less than an hour. The Patriot forces captured more than 900 Hessians with just five American casualties. The impressive victory boosted the Patriots' spirits.

Washington was not satisfied with only one victory. As British general Charles Cornwallis rushed to stop him, Washington marched to the town of Princeton, northeast of Trenton. Washington planned another surprise for the enemy. On the night of January 2, the Patriots kept their campfires burning for the British to see. Most of the Patriots then left camp under cover of darkness and circled behind the British troops. The Patriots attacked the next morning. An 85-year-old civilian described the battle.

History Makers Speak ❝The battle was plainly seen from our door . . . and the guns went off so quick and many together that they could not be numbered. We presently went down into the cellar to keep out of the way of the shot. There was a neighbor woman down in the cellar with us that was so affrighted [frightened]. . . . Almost as soon as the firing was over, our house was filled and surrounded with General Washington's men.❞

—Anonymous, quoted in *Voices of 1776,* by Richard Wheeler

The hard-fought **Battle of Princeton** ended in another victory for the Patriots. As he watched the Redcoats flee, Washington cheered, "It is a fine fox chase, my boys!"

✔ **Reading Check: Summarizing** Explain General Washington's strategy at Trenton and Princeton. Washington sought the element of surprise in both battles, catching the enemy off guard.

NATION/INDIVIDUAL		CONTRIBUTION
France and Spain	→ → →	*provided military supplies*
Bernardo de Gálvez	→ → →	*helped on western frontier*
Marquis de Lafayette	→ → →	*fought and provided money*
Tadeusz Kosciusko	→ → →	*brought engineering skills*
Kazimierz Pulaski	→ → →	*helped train cavalry units*
Friedrich von Steuben	→ → →	*taught basic military skills*

⭐ Biography

Benedict Arnold. Until 1779 Benedict Arnold served the Patriot cause with distinction and valor, participating in the attack on Quebec and leading troops in the Battle of Saratoga. In 1778 General Washington had even made Arnold the commander of Philadelphia. In Philadelphia, Arnold engaged in secret meetings with the British, ultimately planning to surrender West Point. When Arnold's plan was discovered he escaped on a British ship. In 1781 Arnold fled to Britain. Despite his service for their country, even the British reviled him as a traitor, and he died an outcast. Ever since, the name Benedict Arnold has been used as a synonym for traitor.

CRITICAL THINKING

How might Arnold's behavior compare with that of hired mercenaries?

ANSWER: Students might point out that if Arnold was motivated by money or prestige, then he acted much like hired mercenaries.

Visual Record Answer

Burgoyne is handing his sword over to the Americans.

Technology Resources

Linking Geography and History Transparency 9: The Fight for Independence, 1776–1781

Research on the R◉M

Free Find:
Battle of Saratoga
After reading about the Battle of Saratoga on the **Holt Researcher CD–ROM**, create a fictional account of how the British might have won the battle.

THE GRANGER COLLECTION, NEW YORK

Interpreting the Visual Record
Patriot victory *British general John Burgoyne surrenders his army to American Patriot general Horatio Gates at Saratoga, New York, on October 17, 1777.* **What is Burgoyne handing over to the Americans?**

⭐ Turning Point at Saratoga

The defeats at Trenton and Princeton embarrassed the British. In the spring of 1777, they decided to strike back. They planned to cut New England off from the rest of the colonies. The plan called for British troops in Canada to take back Fort Ticonderoga. General **John Burgoyne** would lead this effort. He would then march south. Meanwhile, a second force would march east from Lake Ontario. Finally, General Howe's troops in New York City would move north. All three groups would come together at Albany, New York.

Burgoyne recaptured Fort Ticonderoga by early July. However, his route across New York cut through thick forests. Colonists chopped down large trees across his path to slow his progress. Another problem with the plan soon arose. General Howe decided to attack Philadelphia before marching to Albany. Washington raced to stop Howe, and the two sides met at the **Battle of Brandywine Creek**. On September 11, 1777, Howe's forces won a convincing victory. The Patriots suffered almost twice as many casualties as the British. Howe probably could have crushed the Continental Army completely, but he allowed many soldiers to escape.

Burgoyne did not know that Howe and the force from western Canada were both late. As a result, when Burgoyne neared Albany he found his army badly outnumbered by Patriot troops. At the **Battle of Saratoga** Burgoyne suffered a major defeat. Patriot troops led by General Horatio Gates drove back a British attack. American officer Benedict Arnold then led a bold charge that forced the British to retreat. Burgoyne soon found himself surrounded. On October 17, 1777, he surrendered to General Gates. The Patriots captured Burgoyne's entire army.

The victory at Saratoga was the greatest win yet for the American forces. It greatly boosted morale and led to increased foreign support for the Patriots. Patriot James Thacher wrote, "This event will make one of the most brilliant pages of American history."

✔ **Reading Check: Finding the Main Idea** Why was the Battle of Saratoga a turning point in the war for the Patriots? It was a major victory over a large British force that improved morale and helped the United States gain foreign allies.

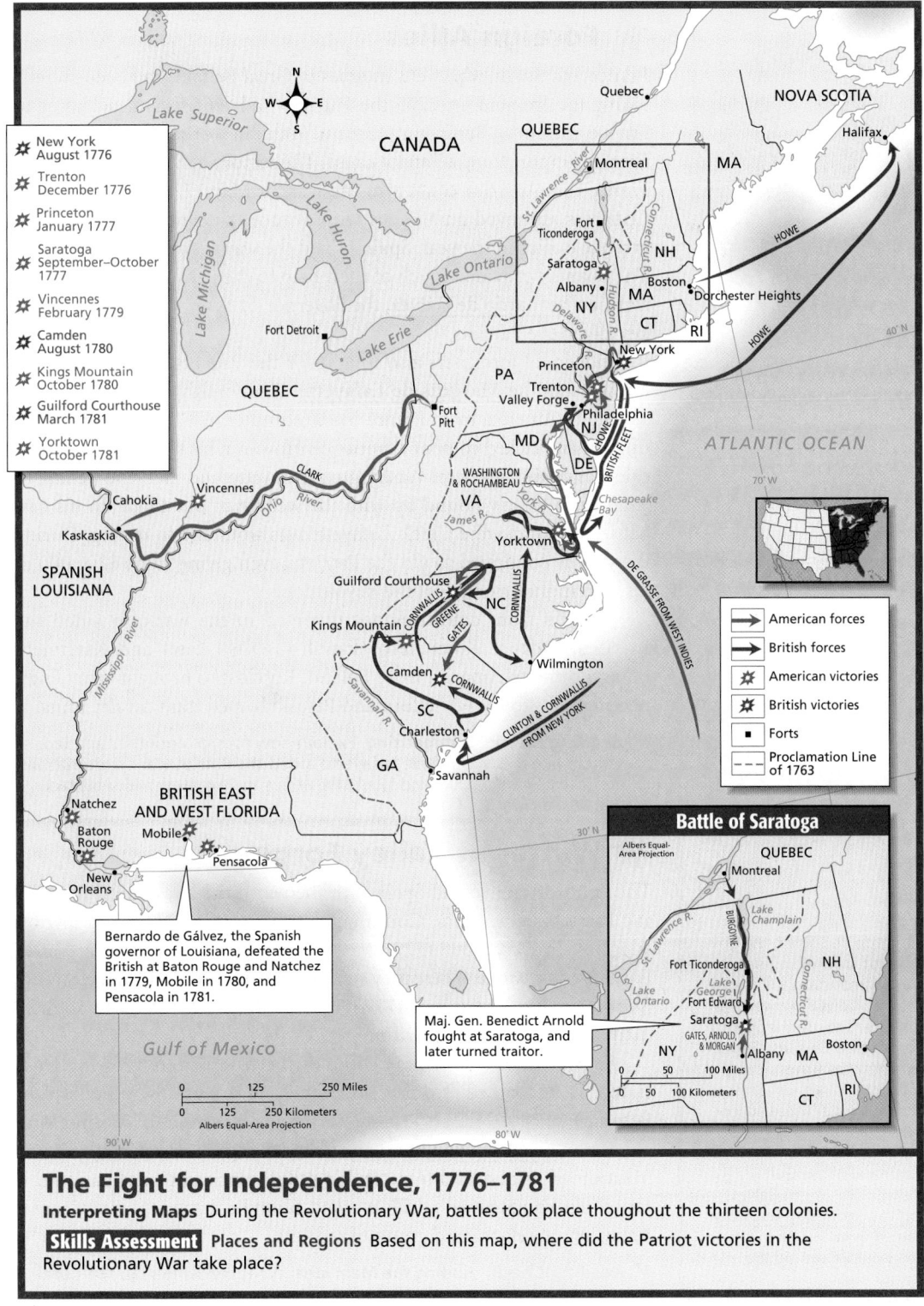

HOMEWORK Have students design a commemorative stamp honoring a foreign country or individual that aided the Patriots during the war. Stamps should also include an explanation of how their subject helped the Patriots.

LEVEL 2: Have students create a cause and effect chart illustrating the effect of the Battle of Saratoga as a turning point in the war. Remind students to include the effect the Battle had on the Patriots. Then ask students to annotate their chart with footnotes identifying ways that foreign aid changed the course of the war.

New York
August 1776

Trenton
December 1776

Princeton
January 1777

Saratoga
September–October
1777

Vincennes
February 1779

Camden
August 1780

Kings Mountain
October 1780

Guilford Courthouse
March 1781

Yorktown
October 1781

Bernardo de Gálvez, the Spanish governor of Louisiana, defeated the British at Baton Rouge and Natchez in 1779, Mobile in 1780, and Pensacola in 1781.

Maj. Gen. Benedict Arnold fought at Saratoga, and later turned traitor.

American forces
British forces
American victories
British victories
Forts
Proclamation Line of 1763

Battle of Saratoga

The Fight for Independence, 1776–1781

Interpreting Maps During the Revolutionary War, battles took place thoughout the thirteen colonies.

Skills Assessment Places and Regions Based on this map, where did the Patriot victories in the Revolutionary War take place?

Interdisciplinary Connection

▶**Art**◀

Art in the Capitol. John Trumbull is best known for his depictions of Revolutionary War battles. In 1814 he proposed that Congress buy his series of 12 epic paintings, in the hopes that they would become centerpieces of a national gallery. Congress accepted only four—including *The Surrender of Burgoyne*, shown on page 204—which were placed in the rotunda of the new Capitol building. However, the paintings were so neglected that they started to mildew in the humidity of Washington, D.C.

CRITICAL THINKING

Why might Congress have selected these paintings to place in the Capitol?

ANSWER: Students might suggest that the paintings commemorated important battles and represented American heroism.

MAP ANSWER

Trenton, Princeton, Saratoga, Vincennes, Kings Mountain, Yorktown, Natchez, Baton Rouge, Mobile, Pensacola

LEVELS 2 AND 3: Organize the class into small groups and assign each group one of the following battles: the Battle of Trenton, the Battle of Princeton, the Battle of Brandywine Creek, or the Battle of Saratoga. Have members of each group use their textbooks to draw a map showing what plans for the battle might have looked like. Have students include a legend identifying troop movements and distinguishing Patriot and British forces. Then have them write a paragraph on one of the following related topics: explain the outcome and significance of their group's battle; analyze General Washington's strategies at Trenton and Princeton; or discuss the Battle of Saratoga as a turning point in the war.
COOPERATIVE LEARNING

LEVEL 3: Organize the class into small groups. Have group members write a one-act play involving three soldiers at Valley Forge. Tell them to set the play in the late spring of 1778 and to have soldiers discuss hardships they faced and how circumstances have changed in recent weeks. Have groups perform their plays for the rest of the class.
COOPERATIVE LEARNING

Note: For an additional teaching idea, see the Chapter 6 Learning Stations activity in the **Creative Teaching Strategies** handbook.

★ Global Relations

Aid from Abroad.
Thousands of Europeans— including French, Germans, and Irish—came to the Americans' aid during the Revolutionary War. Some 700 free black Haitians— members of what was known as the Fontages Legion—participated in the allied American and French siege of Savannah, Georgia, in 1779. Many of these fighters carried the seeds of revolution back to their homeland and were important in establishing the Haitian Republic.

CRITICAL THINKING
Why might Haitians have fought in the American Revolution?

ANSWER: Students might mention that Haitians could have believed they were fighting for the freedom of African Americans.

Technology Resources

Linking Geography and History Transparency 9: The Fight for Independence

GLOBAL CONNECTIONS ANSWER
Gálvez let the Americans use the port of New Orleans. He also attacked British forts.

The Marquis de Lafayette was an important ally of the Patriots.

GLOBAL CONNECTIONS

Bernardo de Gálvez

Bernardo de Gálvez, the governor of Spanish Louisiana, was an important ally to the Patriots. Gálvez allowed the Americans to use the Spanish port of New Orleans. Gálvez also attacked British forts along the Mississippi River and in Florida. These actions helped Patriots in the West. His efforts also kept Spain in command of the Gulf of Mexico. The city of Galveston in present-day Texas was named in his honor. **In what ways did Gálvez aid the Patriot cause?**

★ Foreign Allies

France and Spain, who were enemies of Great Britain, had been secretly aiding the Patriots. In 1776 the Patriots had sent several delegates to France, including Benjamin Franklin. Franklin worked hard to increase French support for the Patriot cause. The victory at Saratoga convinced France that America could win the war. In May 1778 the Continental Congress approved an alliance with France that Franklin had helped arrange earlier in the year. Spain joined the war against Britain in 1779. The Spanish provided much of their help to the Patriots on the western frontier. **Bernardo de Gálvez**, the governor of Spanish Louisiana, was a key ally to the Patriots.

Individual foreigners also fought for the Patriots. One of the best-known was the **Marquis de Lafayette**. The wealthy, young Lafayette arrived in America from France in the summer of 1777. He spoke little English and lacked combat experience. However, his belief in the Patriot cause impressed General Washington. Lafayette said that "the welfare of America is closely bound up with the welfare of mankind." In his first battle, at Brandywine Creek, Lafayette was wounded in the leg. During the war he continued to aid the Patriots, even giving some $200,000 of his own money to support the Revolution.

Officers from countries not involved in the war also aided the Patriots. Tadeusz Kościuszko (kawsh-CHOOSH-kaw) and Kazimierz Pulaski came to America from Poland. Kościuszko brought army engineering skills to the war effort, and Pulaski helped train cavalry units.

✔ **Reading Check: Summarizing** Explain how foreign countries and individuals like the Marquis de Lafayette aided the Patriot war effort. Nations provided military supplies and fought the British. Individuals provided military skills and money.

★ Winter at Valley Forge

The entry of France and Spain into the war came at a critical time for the Patriots because the Continental Army was running very low on supplies. In December 1777, Washington settled his troops at Valley Forge, Pennsylvania. There they suffered shortages of food and clothing. During the harsh winter of 1777–78, more than one fifth of the soldiers died of disease and malnutrition.

By the end of the winter, some of the troops were growing frustrated. They chanted "No pay, no clothes, no provisions [supplies]." In February 1778 a veteran Prussian army officer came to Washington's aid. Baron **Friedrich von Steuben** spoke no English. He led with a combination of respect and fear, teaching the American troops basic military skills. Von Steuben's drills worked. Soon he turned the Continental Army into a well-trained group of soldiers.

✔ **Reading Check: Finding the Main Idea** What challenges did the Continental Army face at Valley Forge? lack of food, clothing, and pay as well as cold weather

Milt Perlman of Flushing, New York, suggested the following activity:

LEVEL 3: Organize the class into small groups. Give each group a large sheet of butcher paper and have them create a map showing the major battles of the Revolutionary War. Ask students to leave a space large enough for a note card next to each battle. Have each group create a map legend indicating which side won the battle. Ask groups to mark each battle appropriately. Then ask each group to find more information about the battles, such as the dates they occurred, the number of troops that died on each side, and the number of prisoners taken by each side. Have groups write this information on a note card and place it next to the appropriate location on the map. **COOPERATIVE LEARNING**, **BLOCK SCHEDULING**

★ CLOSE

Have each student prepare a table of contents for a magazine about the Revolutionary War. Have students select events and people from the section to be the subjects of feature articles. Then ask students to create titles for the imaginary articles and describe each article's content. Display their tables of contents around the classroom, and have students view each other's work.

THE GRANGER COLLECTION, NEW YORK

★ The War at Sea

The Americans also faced difficult odds in the war at sea. The Continental Congress had created the Continental Navy and the marines in 1775. However, by February 1776, the navy had only eight fighting ships. This small fleet was no match for the much larger British one. The British navy could easily transport troops and attack American ports.

Instead of fighting large battles, the Patriots tried to attack individual British ships. The Patriots also attacked British supply ports and merchant ships. During the war the British lost hundreds of ships to small American raiding vessels. Many of these raiders were not officially part of the American navy. Their crews fought because they were allowed to sell any British cargo that they captured.

One of the most successful American captains was **John Paul Jones**. Jones was born John Paul in Scotland. He began working on ships at a young age. After accidentally killing the leader of a mutiny, he fled to America and added "Jones" to his name.

When the war broke out, Jones joined the newly created navy. He quickly established himself as a brave and clever sailor, capturing many British supply ships. The French greatly admired Jones. In 1779, French leaders gave him a small fleet of seven vessels to command. He named his flagship *Bonhomme Richard* ("Gentleman Richard") in honor of Benjamin Franklin's *Poor Richard's Almanack*.

One of Jones's most famous victories came against the British warship *Serapis* on September 23, 1779. Early in the battle, the British did heavy damage to the *Bonhomme Richard*. Captain Richard Pearson of the *Serapis* then called out to Jones, "Has your ship struck [surrendered]?" Jones replied, "I have not yet begun to fight!" More than two hours later, the British surrendered. Captain Pearson described the battle.

Daily Life

Valley Forge Soldiers in the Continental Army had to deal with many shortages throughout the Revolutionary War. They went for long periods of time without pay and often lacked needed supplies. Some of the most difficult conditions they faced came during the harsh winter of 1777–78 at Valley Forge, Pennsylvania. Short on food, clothing, and shelter, about 2,500 of Washington's soldiers died in the camp. How does this picture show the hardships faced by soldiers at Valley Forge?

The Naval Battles. The Continental and state navies did not commission more than 100 ships during the war, yet Great Britain increased its fleet from 270 to 468 ships, 174 of which carried 60 more guns. Nevertheless, American frigates either sank or captured almost 200 British ships. Great Britain lost more ships to privateers. The Royal Navy performed miserably under a succession of incompetent admirals. These actions, combined with Britain's foolish reluctance to support its army forces in America, resulted in the defeat of Great Britain's war efforts.

CRITICAL THINKING

Why might Great Britain strengthen its naval forces at the expense of its army?

ANSWER: Students might suggest that Britain felt it had more of a chance of military success at sea than on land with its ground troops.

DAILY LIFE ANSWER

Students should note the heavy snow and the poor clothing worn by the soldiers, who are huddling around a fire to stay warm.

★ REVIEW AND ASSESS

Have students complete the **Section 4 Review** on p. 208. Then have students complete **Daily Quiz 7.4**. As **Alternative Assessment,** you may want to use the graphic organizer or the map exercise in this section's lessons.

★ RETEACH

Have students complete **Main Idea Activity for English Language Learners and Special-Needs Students 7.4**. Then tell each student to create an annotated time line of the Revolutionary War battles. Ask volunteers to present their time lines to the class. **ENGLISH LANGUAGE LEARNERS**

★ EXTEND

Encourage students to obtain more information about Valley Forge by writing to the Valley Forge National Historical Park, P.O. Box 953, Valley Forge, Pennsylvania, 19482. Then have them use the materials they obtain to create a bulletin-board display about Valley Forge. **BLOCK SCHEDULING**

Section 4 Review
ANSWERS

❶ Identify
- Battle of Trenton, p. 203
- Battle of Princeton, p. 203
- John Burgoyne, p. 204
- Battle of Brandywine Creek, p. 204
- Battle of Saratoga, p. 204
- Bernardo de Gálvez, p. 206
- Marquis de Lafayette, p. 206
- Friedrich von Steuben, p. 206
- John Paul Jones, p. 207

❷ morale—victories greatly improved Patriot morale; Allies—Saratoga helped convince foreign nations such as France to ally with the Patriots; victory—each battle was a convincing victory over British forces that weakened the British militarily and showed the improved fighting abilities of the Continental Army

❸ a. used surprise to overcome the enemy
b. by raiding British shipping and by fighting smaller battles rather than confronting the larger British fleet in major battles

❹ Students' letters will vary, but students might mention being an enemy of the British or believing in the Patriot cause as well as any contribution they feel they could make.

The Bonhomme Richard *defeated the* Serapis *in a long and bloody battle.*

THE GRANGER COLLECTION, NEW YORK

DONT TREAD ON ME

Ships of the Continental Navy flew this flag during the war.

Analyzing Primary Sources
Drawing Inferences and Conclusions According to the British captain, why did the Americans win the battle?
because of John Paul Jones's courage and determination

History Makers Speak
❝Long before the close of the action, it became clearly apparent that the American ship was dominated by a command will . . . and there could be no doubt that the intention of her commander was, if he could not conquer, to sink alongside.❞
—Captain Richard Pearson, quoted in *Voices of 1776,* by Richard Wheeler

The Continental Navy used fewer than 100 ships during the war. Yet the British navy lost almost 200 ships to the small but effective American naval forces.

✔ **Reading Check: Making Generalizations and Predictions** How did the achievements of John Paul Jones demonstrate the Patriots' naval strategy?
Jones captured British merchant ships and avoided large battles with British warships.

go.hrw.com Homework Practice Online
keyword: SA3 HP7

Section 4 Review

❶ Identify and explain:
- Battle of Trenton
- Battle of Princeton
- John Burgoyne
- Battle of Brandywine Creek
- Battle of Saratoga
- Bernardo de Gálvez
- Marquis de Lafayette
- Friedrich von Steuben
- John Paul Jones

❷ Summarizing Copy the graphic organizer below. Use it to explain why the battles at Trenton, Princeton, and Saratoga helped turn the tide for the Patriots in the Revolutionary War.

Morale → Allies
Battles
Victory

❸ Finding the Main Idea
a. What was Washington's strategy for capturing Trenton and Princeton?
b. Explain how the achievements of John Paul Jones demonstrated the ways in which American captains fought the war at sea.

❹ Writing and Critical Thinking
Supporting a Point of View Imagine that you are a foreign officer like the Marquis de Lafayette who has come to assist the Patriots against the British. Write a letter home explaining to a friend how and why you have chosen to help the Patriot cause.

Consider the following:
- your military experience
- your belief in the Patriot cause
- any economic help you might be able to provide

Section 5

OBJECTIVES

⭐ Explain the ways that geography affected the Patriot strategy in the West.

⭐ Describe how the war took place in the southern colonies.

⭐ Examine the events that finally ended the war.

📻 **LET'S GET STARTED!**

As students enter the classroom, ask them to discuss what happens at the end of a war between two nations. *(Students' responses might include that the two nations usually sign a peace treaty.)* Then ask students to discuss what a country must do after it gains independence. *(Students might mention that the winning nation must devise a plan of government.)* Tell students that in Section 5 they will learn about the events leading up to the end of the Revolutionary War.

Section 5

Independence!

Read to Discover

1. How did geography affect the Patriot strategy in the West?
2. How did the war take place in the southern colonies?
3. What events finally ended the war?

WHY IT MATTERS TODAY

The United States has grown from a small country to one of the most powerful nations in the world. Use **CNNfyi.com** or other **current events** sources to find an example that illustrates the strength of the United States today. Record your findings in your journal.

Define

• guerrilla warfare

Identify

• George Rogers Clark
• Battle of Vincennes
• Horatio Gates
• Francis Marion
• Comte de Rochambeau
• Battle of Yorktown
• Treaty of Paris of 1783

SECTION 5 RESOURCES

REPRODUCIBLE
▶ Guided Reading Strategy 7.5
▶ American History Political Cartoon 1: Defeating the British
▶ Graphic Organizer 7: The Path to Independence

TECHNOLOGY
▶ One-Stop Planner, Lesson 7.5
▶ American Music Selection 6: "Yankee Doodle"
▶ CNN Presents America: Beginnings to 1914 Segment: What If the United States Had Lost?
▶ Homework Practice Online
▶ HRW Go site

REINFORCEMENT, REVIEW, AND ASSESSMENT
▶ Section 5 Review, p. 213
▶ Daily Quiz 7.5
▶ Main Idea Activity 7.5
▶ English Audio Summary 7.5
▶ Spanish Audio Summary 7.5

The Story Continues

Eventually the Revolutionary War reached the western frontier. Most of the fighting consisted of small battles between colonists and Britain's Indian allies. This situation changed when a young Virginian named George Rogers Clark stepped forward. Though only 24 years old at the time, Clark was a natural leader. His intelligence and forceful personality gained him the trust of men ranging from frontier fighters to Patriot Patrick Henry. Even the Indian leaders on the frontier viewed Clark with respect.

George Rogers Clark was a key American leader in the West.

⭐ The War in the West

George Rogers Clark had spent years exploring and mapping the frontier, and he had a plan for capturing some small forts and Indian villages. Clark's goal was to build an army while weakening the British. He traveled across the frontier, gathering soldiers from small towns. Clark's first target was the British trading village of Kaskaskia, located along the Mississippi River. Clark thought the small post had great strategic value, which he explained to his superiors.

★ **TEACH**

Have students read Section 5 and complete Guided Reading Strategy 7.5. Choose one or more of the following activities to explore the section content with students. For further suggestions on block scheduling or team teaching, see the *Block Scheduling Handbook with Team Teaching Strategies.*

LEVEL 1: Ask students to select the main events described in Section 5 that finally ended the war. List them on the chalkboard. *(Students' lists should include: the role geography played in the West, the Battle of Vincennes, the major events of the war in the South, guerrilla warfare, the Battle of Yorktown, and the Treaty of Paris of 1783.)* Then ask students to develop newspaper headlines that could be used to describe each event. Write these headlines on the chalkboard. Work with students to develop a list of details that might appear in articles accompanying each headline. **ENGLISH LANGUAGE LEARNERS**

★ Culture

American Indians and the War. The Revolutionary War was costly to many American Indians. The war divided Indian nations and confederacies, as illustrated by the Oneidas and Tuscaroras. These American Indians split from the Loyalist nations in the Iroquois League to assist the Patriots. In addition, Iroquois and Cherokee homelands suffered devastating invasions by both armies. In 1782 some 100 Moravian Delaware Indians were killed by a mob of soldiers seeking revenge for losses in the Revolutionary War.

CRITICAL THINKING

Why do you think the war divided tribes and Indian confederacies?

ANSWER: Students might mention that tribes were trying to protect their land and their way of life and that they wanted to support the side that would benefit them the most.

Technology Resources

American Music Selection 6: "Yankee Doodle"

Visual Record Answer

Students might suggest that the Patriots had to make their way through dense forests and to cross bodies of water to continue their fight.

★★★★★★★★★★★★
That's Interesting!
★★★★★★★★★★★★

Solar Eclipse Can a solar eclipse affect people's lives? You bet it can. George Rogers Clark was an experienced frontiersman. He knew that the route he had chosen to Kaskaskia would be difficult. But not even he expected the surprise his troops received on June 26, 1778. While crossing river rapids they viewed a total eclipse of the Sun! Clark guided his soldiers safely through the dangerous rapids and told them that the eclipse was a good sign. A week later his troops captured Kaskaskia without firing a shot.

History Makers Speak

❝The remote situation of this town . . . enables [the British] to . . . keep up a strict friendship with the Indians. . . . If it was in our possession it would distress the garrison [soldiers] at Detroit for provisions [supplies], it would fling [throw] the command of the two great rivers [Mississippi and Ohio] into our hands.❞

—George Rogers Clark, quoted in *Encyclopedia of the American Revolution,* by Mark M. Boatner III

In June 1778 Clark and 175 soldiers set out toward Kaskaskia. To surprise the enemy, they took a difficult route. Clark's troops had to cross river rapids before marching more than 120 miles through thick forests and open prairies. The plan worked. On July 4, 1778, the surprised leaders of Kaskaskia surrendered to Clark without a fight.

News of Clark's achievement spread, and the town of Vincennes on the Wabash River also surrendered to the Patriots. Clark then organized meetings with American Indian leaders on the frontier. He persuaded some of them to be temporarily neutral in the war. During this period the British recaptured Vincennes. Clark's forces returned and took back the town at the **Battle of Vincennes** in late February 1779. Clark was never able to capture Fort Detroit, Britain's major base on the frontier, but his efforts greatly weakened the British army in the West.

✔ **Reading Check: Finding the Main Idea** Explain how geography affected Clark's campaign in the West. Clark chose targets based on their locations, and he overcame difficult terrain to reach those targets before being detected.

★ The War in the South

After the American victory at Saratoga, the British focused more of their efforts on the southern colonies. General Henry Clinton led their campaign. The British strategy of freeing slaves who joined them worked well in the South. In Georgia a slave named Quamino Dolly showed the British a secret trail to the port city of Savannah. The British used the trail to surprise the Patriots and capture the city. The next major

Interpreting the Visual Record

Guerrilla war *A band of southern Patriots crosses a river in South Carolina.* **How does this image show the difficult conditions that Patriots fought under in the South?**

THE GRANGER COLLECTION, NEW YORK

southern city to fall to the British was the port of Charleston, South Carolina. Following months of hard-fought battles, the Patriots there surrendered on May 12, 1780. The British took more than 5,000 prisoners of war.

As the British marched through the South, they destroyed Patriot property. For example, in South Carolina they seized the plantation of indigo developer Eliza Lucas Pinckney. They stole her valuables, destroyed her crops, and killed her farm animals.

One of the most serious Patriot defeats was at Camden, South Carolina. In August 1780, Patriot forces led by **Horatio Gates** tried to drive out the British. The attack was poorly planned, however. Gates had only half as many soldiers as he first thought. In addition, most of his troops were hungry and tired from the march. In an attempt to raise their spirits, Gates fed the troops large amounts of molasses and cornmeal. This effort backfired, however, when the food made many of the troops sick.

When the weakened Patriots faced the British at Camden, a large group of Americans panicked and ran. The Patriot attack quickly fell apart. By the time the fighting ended, the British army had crushed Gates's forces. Only about 700 of approximately 4,000 American troops made it to safety. The Patriots had lost their southern army.

The southern Patriots did not stop fighting. Instead, they switched to **guerrilla warfare**—swift, hit-and-run attacks. No Patriot was better at this style of fighting than **Francis Marion**. He organized Marion's Brigade, a group of guerrilla soldiers that used surprise attacks to destroy British communications and supply lines. Despite great effort by the British, they could not catch Marion and his men. One frustrated British general claimed, "As for this . . . old fox, the devil himself could not catch him." From that point on, Marion was known as the Swamp Fox.

✔ **Reading Check: Sequencing** Describe the events of the war in the southern colonies in their proper order. The Patriots lost the major battles, and the southern army was destroyed at Camden. Still, Patriots using guerrilla tactics kept harassing the British.

⭐ Victory at Yorktown

In early 1781 the war was going badly for the Patriots. They were low on money to pay soldiers and buy supplies. The entry of their foreign allies had not ended the war quickly. The army's morale took a blow when Benedict Arnold, one of America's most gifted officers, turned traitor. Arnold felt that the Continental Congress had treated him poorly and that Britain would reward his treachery. In addition to these problems, the British controlled most of the South.

British general Charles Cornwallis wanted to tighten his hold on the southern colonies. He therefore moved his forces into Yorktown, Virginia. Yorktown lies on a peninsula bounded by the Chesapeake Bay and the James and York Rivers. There Cornwallis prepared to attack a small Patriot force led by the Marquis de Lafayette.

CONNECTING TO
MATH

Just the Facts

American and British Troops in Battle

Year	American	British
1775	9,173	7,555
1776	47,993	78,918
1777	67,790	67,737
1778	19,922	21,159
1779	14,682	8,575
1780	16,652	27,089
1781	35,829	28,590
Total	**212,041**	**239,623**

Using Mathematical Skills

1. How many more British troops than American troops served in 1776?
2. Create a graph comparing the number of American and British forces during each year of the war.
3. Imagine that you are a Continental Army officer in 1776. Write a letter using these statistics to argue that the Continental Congress needs to raise a larger army.

LEVEL 3: Organize the class into two groups. Have one group imagine they are military leaders stationed in the West during the Revolutionary War and the other group imagine that it is a military leader stationed in the South. Ask each group to prepare a report on the progress of the war effort in its assigned area. Encourage students to report on the colonists' progress, and to identify factors that either benefited or hurt their efforts. For example, the military leader stationed in the West should discuss ways that geography affected his strategy in the West; the military leader stationed in the South should detail how the war progressed in the southern colonies. *(Students' reports should include that geography allowed the colonists to surprise the British in the West; in the South, the British captured Savannah and Charleston, defeated* *the Patriots at Camden, and controlled the South. Also in the South, the Patriots adopted guerrilla warfare tactics and won a victory at Yorktown.)* **COOPERATIVE LEARNING**

HOMEWORK Ask students to imagine that they are organizing a rally to celebrate the Treaty of Paris of 1783. Have students create banners or write poems or songs commemorating independence and the Patriot victory.

★ CLOSE

Ask students to write a journal entry on the following question: *How is the Revolutionary War relevant to us today?* Encourage students to consider the political principles for which the American Revolution was fought.

MAP ANSWERS
1. Spain
2. Spain, the United States, and the British

★ ★ ★ ★ ★ ★ ★ ★

Section 5 Review
ANSWERS

❶ Define
• guerrilla warfare, p. 211

❷ Identify
• George Rogers Clark, p. 209
• Battle of Vincennes, p. 210
• Horatio Gates, p. 211
• Francis Marion, p. 211
• Comte de Rochambeau, p. 212
• Battle of Yorktown, p. 212
• Treaty of Paris of 1783, p. 213

❸ French supplied troops; victory at Yorktown; negotiations

❹ a. William Rogers Clark chose his targets based on their ability to control the Mississippi River; he chose a difficult route so that he could surprise the enemy
b. Patriots lost major battles at Charleston and at Camden, where the southern Patriot army was destroyed; however, a combined French and American army was able to trap Cornwallis at Yorktown and to defeat him

❺ Students' pamphlets will vary, but they should include the appropriate information.

During the siege at Yorktown, the Patriots made a daring attack that captured part of the British fortifications.

Meanwhile, General Washington was in New York. There he planned strategy with a French general, the **Comte de Rochambeau** (roh-shhn-boh). Rochambeau had recently arrived in New York with a large French army. A French fleet commanded by the naval officer Comte de Grasse was also sailing from the West Indies to aid the Patriots and challenge the mighty British navy. It could also prevent any British ships from entering Chesapeake Bay to bring reinforcements to Yorktown.

Washington saw a chance to trap Cornwallis. As the French fleet was taking control of Chesapeake Bay, Washington and Rochambeau moved their troops south. They surrounded Cornwallis with a Patriot army of some 16,000 soldiers. This was more than twice the size of Cornwallis's own forces. Suddenly the Patriots had the upper hand.

For weeks the Patriots held Yorktown under siege. During the **Battle of Yorktown** the Patriots steadily wore down the British defenses. The British navy tried to rescue Cornwallis's army, but the French fleet drove them away. In early October Washington prepared for a major attack on the weakened British troops. Fearing a defeat, Cornwallis surrendered. After negotiating for several days, the two sides agreed to terms of surrender for Cornwallis and his troops. The British marched out of Yorktown in defeat on October 20, 1781. Lord North, the British prime minister, received word of the Yorktown surrender in November. In shock he declared, "It is all over!"

✔ **Reading Check: Finding the Main Idea** How did Washington win the Battle of Yorktown? He used the aid of the French army and navy to surround and outnumber Cornwallis, forcing him to surrender his army.

North America in 1783

Interpreting Maps The Treaty of Paris officially marked the end of the Revolutionary War and granted the United States its independence as well as large areas of land to the West.

Skills Assessment
1. **Places and Regions** What nation controlled most of the present-day western United States in 1783?
2. **Analyzing Informaton** What three countries controlled most of the land shown on the map in 1783?

★ **REVIEW AND ASSESS**

Have students complete the **Section 5 Review** on p. 217. Then have students complete **Daily Quiz 7.5.** As **Alternative Assessment,** you may want to use the newspaper headline exercise or the graphic organizer in this section's lessons.

★ **RETEACH**

Have students complete **Main Idea Activity for English Language Learners and Special-Needs Students 7.5.** Then pair students and assign each pair a subsection. Ask each pair to write three true-or-false statements about the material in its assigned subsection. Collect these statements and use them to

quiz the class. **ENGLISH LANGUAGE LEARNERS ,**
COOPERATIVE LEARNING

★ **EXTEND**

Have students conduct research on a city that the British occupied during the Revolutionary War. (Some possible cities include Charleston or Camden, South Carolina, and New York City.) Ask students to use the library, primary and secondary sources, or other available resources to research life in that city during British occupation and life in that city today. Suggest that students present their findings in a brief, illustrated report.

BLOCK SCHEDULING

★ The Treaty of Paris

At Yorktown the Patriots captured the largest British army in America. Only a few small battles took place afterward. In June 1781 a committee from the Continental Congress began peace negotiations with the British. The American delegates were John Adams, Benjamin Franklin, John Jay, and Henry Laurens. Franklin had played a key role in gaining French aid during the war. He was also influential in the peace talks. He expressed his feelings in a letter to a British friend.

 History Makers Speak ❝Let us now forgive and forget. . . . America will, with God's blessing, become a great and happy Country; and England, if she has at length gained Wisdom, will have gained something.❞

—Benjamin Franklin, from *The Autobiography and Other Writings,* edited by L. Jesse Lemisch

The delegates took more than two years to come to an agreement, but in the **Treaty of Paris of 1783** Great Britain recognized the independent United States. The treaty also set the new nation's borders. The Great Lakes bounded the north. The Mississippi River served as the western border. A line at 31° north latitude formed the southern border. The British also accepted American rights to settle and trade west of the original thirteen colonies. With the war over, Patriot soldiers returned to their homes and families. The courage of soldiers and civilians had made America's victory possible. As the Continental Army's soldiers returned home, General Washington reflected on the triumph of his new country. "The citizens of America," he said, "are . . . acknowledged to be possessed of absolute freedom and independency."

✔ **Reading Check: Summarizing** Explain how the Revolutionary War finally ended. *Students should summarize the events leading up to and including the Battle of Yorktown and the conditions of the Treaty of Paris.*

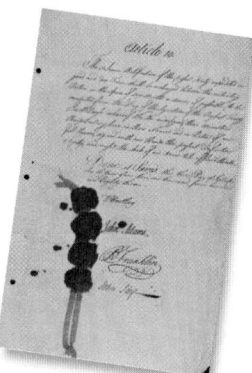

This is a signed copy of the Treaty of Paris.

Analyzing Primary Sources
Identifying Points of View
How did Franklin think Great Britain and America should treat each other after the war? *forgive and forget; pursue their own interests*

CHAPTER 7 REVIEW ANSWERS

The Chapter at a Glance
Students' quizzes will vary but should test information on the major battles of the Revolution.

Identifying People and Ideas
Students' sentences should indicate an understanding of the following definitions:

1. local Boston militia men

2. commanded Continental Army, leading it to victory

3. pamphlet by Thomas Paine that caused many colonists to support the impending war

4. supported the idea that government had to be formed on the basis of liberty—if the rulers governed unjustly, the people had the right to overthrow them

5. document that declared the colonies' independence from Great Britain

6. wife of John Adams; wrote letter urging her husband and the other Declaration signers to protect the rights of women

Section 5 Review

go.hrw.com **Homework Practice Online**
keyword: SA3 HP7

❶ **Define** and explain:
• guerrilla warfare

❷ **Identify** and explain:
• George Rogers Clark
• Battle of Vincennes
• Horatio Gates
• Francis Marion
• Comte de Rochambeau
• Battle of Yorktown
• Treaty of Paris of 1783

❸ **Sequencing** Copy the graphic organizer below. Use it to list the major events that led to the end of the Revolutionary War.

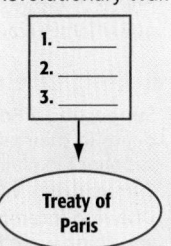

1. _____
2. _____
3. _____

↓

Treaty of Paris

❹ **Finding the Main Idea**
a. How did geography affect the Patriot strategy on the western frontier?

b. How did the war progress in the southern colonies up to Washington's victory at Yorktown?

❺ **Writing and Critical Thinking**
Summarizing Imagine that you are a colonial diplomat. Create a pamphlet announcing the war's end. Your pamphlet should include a summary of the war's final events.

Consider the following:
• the Battle of Yorktown
• the terms of the Treaty of Paris of 1783
• how you think the United States will fare after the war

REPRODUCIBLE
▶ Vocabulary Activity 7

TECHNOLOGY
▶ Chapter 7 Test Generator (on the One-Stop Planner)
▶ Global Skill Builder CD–ROM
▶ HRW Go site

REINFORCEMENT, REVIEW, AND ASSESSMENT
▶ Chapter 7 Review, pp. 213–15
▶ Chapter 7 Tutorial for Students, Parents, Mentors, and Peers

▶ Chapter 7 Test (Form A or B)
▶ Alternative Assessment Handbook
▶ Chapter 7 Test for English Language Learners and Special-Needs Students

★ **REVIEW**
Have students complete the **Chapter 7 Review** on pages 214–15.

★ **ASSESS**
Use one of the chapter tests to assess students' understanding of the content. For **Alternative Assessment**, see the **Alternative Assessment Handbook**.

7. French citizen helped the Patriot cause

8. captain in U.S. Navy who captured numerous British supply ships

9. where British surrendered to Americans, ending the war

10. peace treaty between Great Britain and the United States

Understanding Main Ideas

1. turned political conflict into open military conflict

2. First—Declaration of Resolves, encouraged colonies to prepare their militias; Second—Olive Branch Petition, formed the Continental Army

3. encouraged many colonists to support independence

4. advantages—fighting on home soil, believed in their cause; disadvantages—British had more money and a bigger military

5. Trenton—Patriots silently crossed Delaware River at night to surprise Hessian soldiers on Christmas; Princeton—Patriots secretly moved army at night, attacked from the rear

6. great victory for the Patriots; convinced France and Spain to officially support the Americans

7. mostly small unit actions, frontier raids and guerrilla warfare

Chapter 7 Review

The Chapter at a Glance

Examine the visual summary of the chapter below. Use it to help you create a five-question quiz that you might give to a classmate.

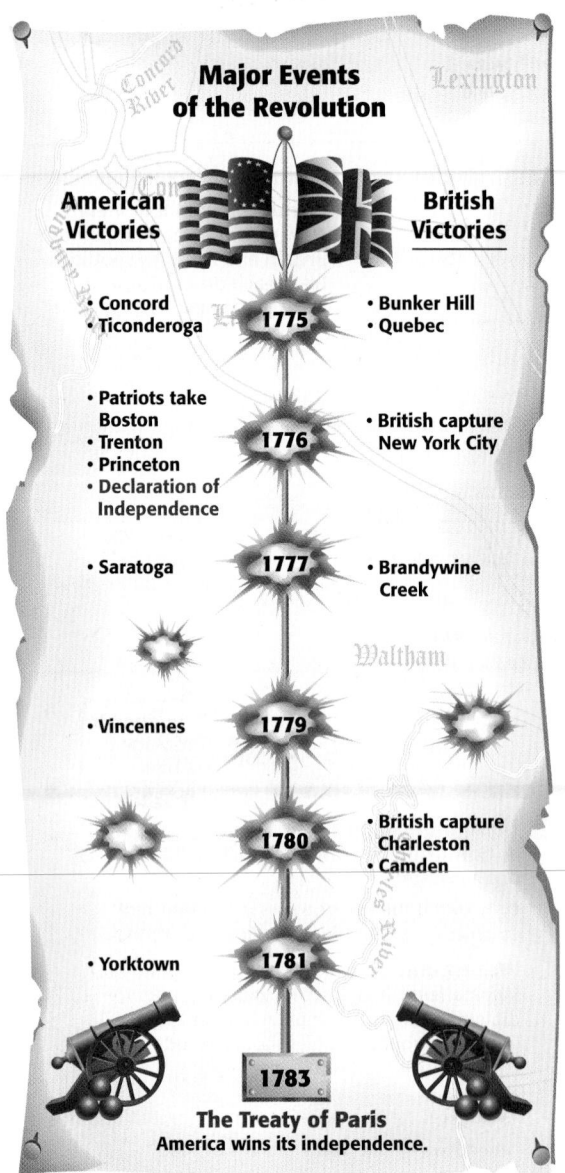

Major Events of the Revolution

American Victories		British Victories
• Concord • Ticonderoga	**1775**	• Bunker Hill • Quebec
• Patriots take Boston • Trenton • Princeton • Declaration of Independence	**1776**	• British capture New York City
• Saratoga	**1777**	• Brandywine Creek
• Vincennes	**1779**	
	1780	• British capture Charleston • Camden
• Yorktown	**1781**	

1783

The Treaty of Paris
America wins its independence.

Identifying People and Ideas

Use the following terms or people in historically significant sentences.

1. minutemen
2. George Washington
3. *Common Sense*
4. Thomas Jefferson
5. Declaration of Independence
6. Abigail Adams
7. Marquis de Lafayette
8. John Paul Jones
9. Battle of Yorktown
10. Treaty of Paris of 1783

Understanding Main Ideas

Section 1 *(Pages 184–189)*
1. How did the fighting at Lexington and Concord affect the relationship between the colonies and Great Britain?
2. What did the First and Second Continental Congresses achieve?

Section 2 *(Pages 190–193)*
3. What effect did Thomas Paine's *Common Sense* have on colonial attitudes toward Britain?

Section 3 *(Pages 198–201)*
4. What advantages and disadvantages did the Patriots have when the Revolutionary War began?

Section 4 *(Pages 202–208)*
5. How did Washington defeat the British at Trenton and Princeton?
6. Why was the Battle of Saratoga important?

Section 5 *(Pages 209–213)*
7. How did the Patriots fight the war in the West and in the South?

You Be the Historian— Reviewing Themes

1. **Citizenship** Why did the colonies declare their independence from Britain?
2. **Constitutional Heritage** What are three rights that all men have according to the Declaration of Independence?
3. **Global Relations** Why did some foreign countries help the Patriots, and what role did Patriots such as Benjamin Franklin play in gaining this support?

Thinking Critically

1. **Supporting a Point of View** Did the Patriots' belief in their cause make up for their lack of supplies? Explain your answer.
2. **Summarizing** What key events occurred in 1776?
3. **Drawing Inferences and Conclusions** What do you think were the most significant causes of the American Revolution? Explain your answer.

★ **RETEACH**

Organize students into five groups and assign each group one of the chapter's sections. Have members of each group create maps or diagrams illustrating the main events in their assigned section. Ask them to illustrate each event and to include any relevant dates and captions. Have each group present its work to the class.

ENGLISH LANGUAGE LEARNERS ,
COOPERATIVE LEARNING

Portfolio Extensions

1. Cooperative Learning Have students complete the following activity in small groups. Ask each person in the group to assume the role of a soldier or sailor fighting with one or more of the following four groups: (a) George Washington's army in the Northeast, (b) George Rogers Clark's troops in the West, (c) Francis Marion's brigade in the South, or (d) John Paul Jones's forces at sea. Then have students create a journal describing the experiences of the people in their group throughout the war.

2. Interdisciplinary Connection to Music Ask students to imagine that they are the leader of a civilian organization that wants to aid the war effort. Have students write a short song to inspire colonists to help the Patriot cause. Their song should explain why the colonies are fighting Britain. Remind them to include information that would attract support from people of various nationalities and backgrounds.

Social Studies Skills Workshop

Interpreting Charts

Study the chart below. Then use the information on the chart to help you answer the questions that follow.

Causes and Effects of the Revolution

Long-Term Causes
Proclamation of 1763
Increased taxation without representation
Increased British military presence and abuse of colonists' rights

Immediate Causes
Fighting at Lexington and Concord
Declaration of Independence

American Revolution
1775–1783

Effects
British recognition of U.S. independence
Boundaries of the United States extended west to the Mississippi River and south to Florida

1. Which of the following was not a long-term cause of the American Revolution according to the chart?
   a. the Proclamation of 1763
   b. taxation without representation
   c. abuse of colonial rights
   d. French attacks on the colonies

2. Based on the chart and your knowledge of the period, how do you think the long-term causes of the Revolution contributed to the immediate causes of the war?

Analyzing Primary Sources

Read the following excerpt from *Common Sense* by Thomas Paine, then answer the questions that follow.

❝A government of our own is our natural right; and when a man seriously reflects on the precariousness [uncertainness] of human affairs, he will become convinced that it is infinitely [completely] wiser and safer to form a constitution of our own in a cool deliberate manner, while we have it in our power, than to trust such an interesting event to time and chance.❞

3. Which of the following best describes Paine's viewpoint?
   a. Americans should rush to form a new nation.
   b. Americans would be better off independent.
   c. Americans should remain British citizens.
   d. It is best to take risks.

4. Why do you think that Paine's message was popular with many colonists?

Alternative Assessment

Building Your Portfolio

Linking to Community
John Paul Jones was a hero of the American Revolution. Present an oral report on a war hero from your community. This hero can be someone living in your community today or someone who lived there in the past. If the person still lives in your community, you may want to interview the individual for your report.

🖳 **internet** connect

Internet Activity: go.hrw.com
keyword: **SA3 CF7**
Access the Internet through the HRW Go site to conduct research on the differing viewpoints of Loyalists and Patriots. Then create a newspaper that shows bias to the Loyalist or Patriot position on the Revolution. Make sure you use at least three examples of biased reporting in your newspaper. On a separate sheet of paper, explain where the bias occurs and why it is biased.

You Be the Historian—Reviewing Themes

1. They wanted to be free of British rule.

2. life, liberty, and the pursuit of happiness

3. France and Spain were long-time enemies of Great Britain. Franklin worked to increase French support.

Thinking Critically

1. Some students will agree, mentioning that the Patriots continued to fight despite the harsh winters and their supplies ran low.

2. Patriots take Boston, Trenton, Princeton; British take New York City; the Declaration of Independence

3. Students' answers will vary.

Skills Workshop

1. d

2. Students' answers will vary, but they might note the growing colonist frustration and anger.

3. b

4. Answers will vary, but students should note that Paine's appeal to natural rights, his warning about the potential danger of future abuses, and his call for a carefully made constitution would all appeal to colonists tired of British actions.

⚙ TEACH

ALL LEVELS: Tell students that you are going to read a list of phrases that deal with the same topic and that will all fit into one of three related subtopics. Ask students to copy the list you read and then to write each term under the appropriate category heading. Read this list: *brush your teeth, go to homeroom, eat breakfast, wait for the bus, get dressed, choose a seat, get on the bus, take a shower, enter the* *school, make the bed, go to your locker, get off the bus, get the books you will need.* Tell students that the main idea is going to school. Ask students to identify the three subtopics. Explain to them that the categories you had intended were getting ready for school, traveling to school, and getting to class. Then ask students to sequence and organize information that describes outlining a report, preparing a recipe, building a birdhouse, and so on. **ENGLISH LANGUAGE LEARNERS**

READING SKILLS

Have students apply their reading skills to either a short story that you assign or one of their choosing. Then ask students to use standard grammar, spelling, sentence structure, and punctuation to write a report summarizing the main idea and sequencing the events or information found in the story.

SKILLS ANSWERS

1. Students' summaries will vary.
2. Students might mention the following events: Proclamation of 1763, Pontiac's Rebellion, Sugar Act, Committees of Correspondence, Stamp Act, Townshend Acts, Boston Massacre, the Tea Tax, Boston Tea Party, Intolerable Acts, First Continental Congress, Battles of Lexington and Concord, Second Continental Congress, Battle of Bunker Hill, *Common Sense,* Declaration of Independence, Battle of Trenton, Battle of Princeton, Battle of Brandywine Creek, Battle of Saratoga, winter at Valley Forge, victory at Yorktown, and the Treaty of Paris.

Social Studies Skills
WORKSHOP

Reading Skills

One of the biggest challenges you face in learning history is understanding what you read. By using appropriate Reading Skills, you will be able to understand more of what you read. Two important Reading Skills are Finding the Main Idea and Sequencing Information. The following activities will help you develop and practice these skills.

Finding the Main Idea

The main idea statement summarizes the most important point of a reading section. The main idea of a reading section is usually supported by sentences that provide details. Listed below are guidelines that will help you find the main idea of any reading assignment.

1. **Preview the material.** Read the title, introduction, and any other study clues that the assignment provides. These will often point to the main ideas being covered.

2. **Keep questions in mind.** Read the study questions that accompany the text. If the assignment does not provide study questions, create your own. Keeping these questions in mind will help you focus your reading.

3. **See how ideas are arranged.** Pay attention to the headings, subheadings, and opening paragraphs. Major ideas are often introduced in such material.

4. **Look for conclusions.** As you read, try to separate sentences that supply details from sentences that make general statements. Often a string of sentences providing detailed information leads to a conclusion that expresses a main idea.

Sequencing Information

Sequencing involves trying to determine the order in which certain events occurred. Specific dates and words related to time or time periods can provide clues for use in determining the proper sequence of certain events. For example, suppose you were asked to explain how the colonists declared their independence from Great Britain. You might come up with ideas that you place in the following:

> Parliament taxed the colonists without their consent.
>
> Colonists held protests, such as the Boston Tea Party.
>
> British troops clashed with colonists at Lexington and Concord.
>
> The Second Continental Congress drafted the Declaration of Independence.

Practicing the Skills

1. In Chapter 7, The American Revolution, look at the section entitled The Patriots Gain New Hope. Read the Turning Point at Saratoga subsection. Write four sentences that summarize the material in that subsection. Then condense your sentences into a single sentence that states the main idea of the subsection.

2. Brainstorm some important events that took place in America from 1763 to 1783. Then place these events in their proper sequence from first to last.

LEVEL 2: Explain to students that an important step of democratic decision making can be the polling of the voting public to determine their position concerning a critical issue. Organize students into four groups and tell them that they have been selected as members of a subcommittee to the special committee, designed by the French government, to determine France's position in the American Revolution.

Instruct students that their assignment is to poll the French public by developing a series of questions to determine whether France should assist the Patriots in their fight against the British or should remain neutral. Groups should conclude their polling exercises with a recommendation on the issue.
COOPERATIVE LEARNING

History in Action

UNIT 3 SIMULATION

You Make the Decision . . .

Should France Help the Patriots Fight the British?

Complete the following activity in small cooperative groups. The year is 1778. You and your associates are a special committee of French government officials. Your assignment is to decide whether France should join the Patriots in their fight against Great Britain. Because your king has asked you to make a formal presentation of your answer to him very soon, you need to come to a decision quickly. Follow these steps to reach your decision.

1. Gather Information. Use your textbook and other resources to find information that might help you decide whether to support the Patriots. Be sure to use what you learned from this unit's Skills Workshop on Finding the Main Idea and Sequencing Information to help you focus on key points in your research. You may want to divide different parts of the research among group members.

2. Identify Options. After reviewing the information you have gathered, consider the options you might recommend to the king. Your final decision may be easier to reach if you consider as many options as possible. For example, you might think of ways to help the Patriots without joining the war against Britain directly. Be sure to record your possible options for your presentation.

3. Predict Consequences. Now take each option your associates came up with and consider what might be the outcome of each course of action. Ask yourselves questions like: "How might France benefit from doing this?" Once you have predicted the consequences, record them as notes for your presentation.

4. Take Action to Implement Your Decision. After you have considered your options, you should plan and create your presentation. Be sure to make your decision on whether to support the Patriots very clear. You will need to support your decision by including information you gathered and by explaining why you rejected other options. Your presentation needs to be visually appealing to convince the king. When you are ready, decide which group members will make each part of the presentation, and then take your decision to the king (the rest of the class). Good luck!

★ **CHAPTER 8**

Forming a Government

American colonists formed state and federal governments based on English laws, Enlightenment ideas, and American political traditions. The government formed under the Articles of Confederation lacked sufficient power to rule effectively. To remedy the problems of the Articles, American leaders wrote a new constitution that created a more powerful central government. Eventually, the required nine states ratified the Constitution.

★ **CHAPTER 9**

Citizenship and the Constitution

The framers of the Constitution developed a system of checks and balances that divides power among the legislative, executive, and judicial branches of government. To address concerns about individual rights, the First Congress added 10 amendments—known as the Bill of Rights—to the Constitution. The Constitution specifies the rights of U.S. citizens and the responsibilities of the federal and state governments.

Internet Activity

Constitutional Amendments

☑ internet connect

TOPIC: Constitutional Amendments
GO TO: go.hrw.com
KEYWORD: SA3 Amendments

Have students search the Internet through the HRW Go site for information on amendments to the U.S. Constitution that were added after the Bill of Rights. Have them create a chart that shows the number of the amendment, its subject matter, and the date it was ratified. Then have volunteers present their charts to the class.

UNIT

4

A New American Nation
(1777–1800)

CHAPTER 8 **Forming a Government** (1777–1791)

CHAPTER 9 **Citizenship and the Constitution** (1787–PRESENT)

CHAPTER 10 **Launching the Nation** (1789–1800)

After the states ratified the Constitution, the leaders of the United States set about creating a government for the new nation. These leaders faced numerous challenges, including how to pay off the national debt, how to respond to threats from overseas, and how to resolve internal conflicts. Although President Washington had warned against them, political parties developed during this time.

Share the information in the chapter overviews with students. Ask them to brainstorm a list of challenges that any new government might face. Have students rank the answers they suggested in order of importance. Organize students into groups and give each group one of the problems that the class decided was among the most important. Have groups come up with at least three solutions that a government might use to meet this challenge. Later, when you have finished the unit, revisit these solutions and have students evaluate how closely their ideas about how a new government might meet challenges mirror the actual responses that U.S. leaders had at the Constitutional Convention.

Young People

IN HISTORY

Young Americans

Several things shaped the lives of young citizens of the newly independent United States. Where these young people lived and what their parents did for a living often determined what they would do with their lives.

Young people growing up on the frontier could expect a life of hard work. This work included planting and harvesting crops, tending the farm animals, or helping to keep the house in order. Many young people on the frontier spent little or no time in school each year. In the early United States there were few free public schools. Most families could not afford to send their children to a private school. Most parents believed that the purpose of education was to teach young people how to work. This training helped young people support their families. Boys of six or seven worked with their fathers after they exchanged their infant clothes for breeches, or pants, like their fathers wore.

Children from wealthy families could expect to receive a more formal education. Boys usually received more education than girls. A girl was expected to learn reading, writing, and some basic math. Any well-educated boy also learned Greek and Latin.

Most African American youths, particularly in the South, could expect to spend their lives working as slaves or house servants. Enslaved children also helped support their families. They tended the family garden and gathered berries, herbs, and nuts for cooking.

Almost all teenagers, from whatever region or social background, spent some time at play. Sometimes they flew kites, or played leapfrog and marbles. In some places, young people played tag—the same game played today. One teacher during this time period described how his students played. "They all find places of Rendezvous [meeting places] so soon as the Beell [bell] rings, and all seem to choose different sports!" In addition, many young Americans spent their time looking after their pets, which ranged from squirrels to dogs and cats.

THE GRANGER COLLECTION, NEW YORK

This illustration shows two girls from the early American republic studying geography.

If You Were There *How would you spend your time in the early United States?*

LEFT PAGE: *In September 1787, delegates at the Constitutional Convention signed the final draft of the Constitution.*

Historical Paintings.
Howard Chandler Christy, whose painting shown on the opposite page depicts the signing of the Constitution, was best known as an illustrator. He began work for *Scribner's Magazine* in 1898, illustrating current-events articles and stories. He also traveled to Cuba and Puerto Rico to provide the magazine with firsthand illustrations of the Spanish-American War. His illustrations eventually appeared on World War I recruitment posters. Christy began creating large oil paintings of historical scenes late in his life. The painting on the opposite page is huge—20 feet by 30 feet. It is now located above the grand staircase in the Capitol in Washington, D.C.

CRITICAL THINKING
In this picture, how does Christy show the importance of the signing of the Constitution?

ANSWER: Students might suggest the serious expressions on the faces, the noble stance of George Washington, the light falling on the document, and the grandeur of the room and the clothes.

8 Forming a Government

CHAPTER RESOURCE MANAGER

Objectives	Pacing Guide	Reproducible Resources
SECTION 1: **The Articles of Confederation** (pp. 222–27) ⊡ Describe the ideas and documents that shaped American beliefs about government. ⊡ Evaluate how state constitutions contributed to the development of representative government. ⊡ List the powers held by the central government under the Articles of Confederation. ⊡ Explain what the Northwest Ordinance accomplished.	**Regular** 1.5 days **Block Scheduling** 1 day *Block Scheduling Handbook with Team Teaching Strategies, Chapter 8*	**RS** Guided Reading Strategy 8.1 **PS** Primary Source Reading 8: Iroquois Great Law of Peace **E** Creative Teaching Strategy: Quick Survey **E** Hands-On History Activity: Statehood
SECTION 2: **Problems in the New Nation** (pp. 230–35) ⊡ Describe how other nations treated the new U. S. government. ⊡ Examine the economic problems that arose under the Articles of Confederation. ⊡ Analyze the causes and consequences of Shays's Rebellion.	**Regular** 1.5 days **Block Scheduling** .5 day *Block Scheduling Handbook with Team Teaching Strategies, Chapter 8*	**RS** Guided Reading Strategy 8.2 **PS** Literature Reading 8: A View of America
SECTION 3: **The Constitution** (pp. 236–41) ⊡ Explain why delegates met for the Constitutional Convention. ⊡ Examine some of the main issues debated and compromises that were reached at the Constitutional Convention. ⊡ Describe how the federal government is balanced under the U.S. Constitution.	**Regular** 2 days **Block Scheduling** 1 day *Block Scheduling Handbook with Team Teaching Strategies, Chapter 8*	**RS** Guided Reading Strategy 8.3 **RS** Graphic Organizer 8: Comparing Systems of Government
SECTION 4: **Ratification of the Constitution** (pp. 242–47) ⊡ Explain why some people were against the new Constitution. ⊡ Examine the *Federalist Papers'* arguments for the Constitution. ⊡ Describe when and how the Constitution was ratified. ⊡ Identify the reasons some people wanted a bill of rights, and explain how it was added to the Constitution.	**Regular** 1.5 days **Block Scheduling** .5 day *Block Scheduling Handbook with Team Teaching Strategies, Chapter 8*	**RS** Guided Reading Strategy 8.4 **PS** Biography Reading 8: George Mason **SM** Geography Activity 8: Ratification of the Constitution **PS** American History Political Cartoon 2: Ratifying the Constitution

Chapter Resource Key

PS	Primary Sources	**A**	Assessment
RS	Reading Support	**REV**	Review
IC	Interdisciplinary Connections	**ELL**	Reinforcement and English Language Learners
E	Enrichment		Transparencies
SM	Skills Mastery		CD–ROM

 Music

Video

Internet

Holt Presentation Maker Using Microsoft® PowerPoint®

One-Stop Planner CD-ROM

See the *One-Stop Planner* for a complete list of additional resources for students and teachers.

One-Stop Planner CD–ROM

It's easy to plan lessons, select resources, and print out materials for your students when you use the *One-Stop Planner CD–ROM with Test Generator.*

Technology Resources	Reinforcement, Review, and Assessment

 One-Stop Planner, Lesson 8.1
 Holt Researcher: American History CD–ROM
Homework Practice Online

REV Section 1 Review, p. 227
A Daily Quiz 8.1
ELL Main Idea Activity 8.1
ELL English Audio Summary 8.1
ELL Spanish Audio Summary 8.1

 One-Stop Planner, Lesson 8.2
Homework Practice Online
HRW Go site

REV Section 2 Review, p. 235
A Daily Quiz 8.2
ELL Main Idea Activity 8.2
ELL English Audio Summary 8.2
ELL Spanish Audio Summary 8.2

 One-Stop Planner, Lesson 8.3
 American History Simulations CD–ROM: The Democracy Project
CNN Presents America: Yesterday and Today, Beginnings to 1914 Segment: Our Most Important Papers
Homework Practice Online
HRW Go site

REV Section 3 Review, p. 241
A Daily Quiz 8.3
ELL Main Idea Activity 8.3
ELL English Audio Summary 8.3
ELL Spanish Audio Summary 8.3

 One-Stop Planner, Lesson 8.4
Holt Researcher: American History CD–ROM
Homework Practice Online

REV Section 4 Review, p. 246
A Daily Quiz 8.4
ELL Main Idea Activity 8.4
ELL English Audio Summary 8.4
ELL Spanish Audio Summary 8.4

internet connect

HRW ONLINE RESOURCES
GO TO: go.hrw.com
Then type in a keyword.

TEACHER HOME PAGE
KEYWORD: SA3 Teacher

CHAPTER INTERNET ACTIVITIES
KEYWORD: SA3 CF8
Choose an activity to:
• make a global connection to the music of Mozart
• examine world trade then and now.
• research the leaders of the Constitutional convention.
• explore the political ideals of Alexander Hamilton and James Madison.

CHAPTER ENRICHMENT LINKS
KEYWORD: SA3 CH8

ONLINE ASSESSMENT
Homework Practice
KEYWORD: SA3 HP8

Rubrics
KEYWORD: SS Rubrics

ONLINE MAPS, CHARTS, AND GRAPHS
KEYWORD: SA3 MCG
• Federalist/Antifederalist
• Two Continental Congresses
• The Federal System

CONTENT UPDATES
KEYWORD: SS Content Updates

HOLT PRESENTATION MAKER
KEYWORD: SA3 PPT8

ONLINE READING SUPPORT
KEYWORD: SS Strategies

CURRENT EVENTS
KEYWORD: S3 Current Events

Meeting Individual Needs

Ability Levels

Level 1 Basic-level activities designed for all students encountering new material

Level 2 Intermediate-level activities designed for average students

Level 3 Challenging activities designed for honors and gifted-and-talented students

English Language Learners Activities that address the needs of students with Limited English Proficiency

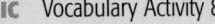
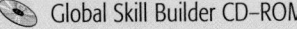
Chapter Review and Assessment

IC Vocabulary Activity 8
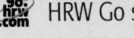 Global Skill Builder CD–ROM
HRW Go site
REV Chapter 8 Tutorial for Students, Parents, Mentors, and Peers
REV Chapter 8 Review, pp. 247–49
Chapter 8 Test Generator (on the One-Stop Planner)

A Chapter 8 Test (Form A or B)
A Alternative Assessment Handbook
A Chapter 8 Test for English Language Learners and Special-Needs Students

Build on What You Know

If You Were There...

Ask students to answer the following question:

How would you help create a new government?

Consider:

• Americans' complaints with the colonial system of government

• ideas expressed in the Declaration of Independence

You Be the Historian

What's Your Opinion?

To help students create their **Themes** Journal entries, provide the following examples of appropriate **agree**/**disagree** statements.

EXPLORING THE TIME LINE
AMERICAN EVENTS

internet connect

TOPIC: Wolfgang Amadeus Mozart
GO TO: go.hrw.com
KEYWORD: SA3 CF8

Have students access the Internet through the HRW Go site to research the life and accomplishments of Wolfgang Amadeus Mozart. Then, using standard grammar, spelling, sentence structure, and punctuation, they should write a biography of Mozart from the point of view of his rival Antonio Salieri. Students should include information on the musical structure of Mozart's music. Remind students that they are writing from a biased point of view, so their presentation of the information should be slanted accordingly.

CHAPTER

8 Forming a Government
(1777–1791)

Members of the Second Continental Congress knew that the former colonies needed to create a central government.

States such as New York minted their own coins.

UNITED STATES

1777 The Continental Congress approves the Articles of Confederation on November 15.

1781 On March 1 the Articles of Confederation go into effect after being ratified by all 13 states.

1777	1779	1781	1783

WORLD

Early hot-air balloons, which were often decorated, delighted crowds in the late 1700s.

1781 German philosopher Immanuel Kant publishes his *Critique of Pure Reason,* a major theoretical work.

1782 Spain completes its conquest of British Florida.

1783 The Montgolfier brothers of France make the first flight in a hot-air balloon.

Build on What You Know

The United States declared its independence in 1776. But then Americans were faced with the difficult task of forming a new government. After a first attempt at national government failed to solve many of the nation's problems, many Americans wanted a change. In 1787, leaders from around the country came to Philadelphia to find a solution.

Global Relations

Agree New nations are not strong.

Disagree A country's strength is not determined by its age.

Citizenship

Agree People have certain natural rights that should never be taken away.

Disagree The government should be able to choose which rights citizens have.

Constitutional Heritage

Agree A state government should be stronger than the federal government.

Disagree A strong federal government creates a more powerful country.

A signed copy of the Constitution

VIRGINIA MUSEUM OF FINE ARTS, RICHMOND, VA. DETAIL OF WASHINGTON ADDRESSING THE CONSTITUTIONAL CONVENTION BY JUNIUS BRUTUS STEARNS. GIFT OF EDGAR WILLIAM AND BERNICE CHRYSLER GARBISCH. PHOTO: RON JENNINGS ©2000 VIRGINIA MUSEUM OF FINE ARTS

George Washington served as president of the Constitutional Convention.

1785 The United States begins using the dollar currency.

1786 Shays's Rebellion breaks out in Massachusetts.

1787 On May 14, state delegates begin to arrive at the Constitutional Convention in Philadelphia.

Congress passes the Northwest Ordinance on July 13.

The final draft of the Constitution is signed on September 17.

1789 James Madison submits possible amendments to the Constitution.

1790 Rhode Island becomes the final state to ratify the Constitution.

1791 The Bill of Rights is ratified by the states in December.

1785   1787   1789   1791

1786 Mennonites from central Europe settle in Canada.

1787 The Ottoman Empire declares war on Russia.

1791 Austrian composer Wolfgang Amadeus Mozart dies.

If you were there . . .
How would you help create a new government?

You Be the Historian

Themes Journal

What's Your Opinion? Do you **agree** or **disagree** with the following statements? Support your point of view in your journal.

- **Global Relations** New nations will be taken advantage of by other countries.
- **Citizenship** Governments must protect certain rights of their citizens.
- **Constitutional Heritage** The power of the government must be limited.

Science, Technology & Society

A Break at the Constitutional Convention. Some of the delegates at the Constitutional Convention took some time off to observe a new invention. In August of 1787, John Fitch launched his new steamboat, carrying members of Congress and the American flag across the Delaware River. Fitch's boat was harnessed to a steam engine that turned six paddles and caused the boat to travel at about three miles an hour.

CRITICAL THINKING

Why do you think Fitch demonstrated his new boat for the delegates?

ANSWER: Students might suggest that he hoped the new government or individuals would give him financial backing, or that he wanted to impress the most powerful people of the country.

Section 1

OBJECTIVES

- ✯ Describe the ideas and documents that shaped American beliefs about government.
- ✯ Evaluate how state constitutions contributed to the development of representative government.
- ✯ List the powers held by the central government under the Articles of Confederation.
- ✯ Explain what the Northwest Ordinance accomplished.

LET'S GET STARTED!

Write the following question on the chalkboard: *What were some of the reasons that the colonists sought independence from Britain?* As students enter the classroom, allow time for them to respond. *(Students' responses might mention unfair taxes, a lack of representation and a desire for greater personal freedom.)* After discussing students' responses, tell them that the desire to be represented fairly and equally in the lawmaking process was probably the most important issue for the former colonists. Tell students that in Section 1 they will learn about the first government of the United States under the Articles of Confederation.

Section 1

The Articles of Confederation

Read to Discover

1. What ideas and documents shaped American beliefs about government?
2. How did state constitutions contribute to the development of representative government?
3. What powers did the central government have under the Articles of Confederation?
4. What did the Northwest Ordinance accomplish?

WHY IT MATTERS TODAY

Many countries have modeled their political systems on American and European ideas of representative government. Use **CNN fyi.com** or other **current events** sources to learn about how a foreign nation elects its leaders. Record your findings in your journal.

Define

- constitution
- republicanism
- limited government
- suffrage
- ratification

Identify

- Virginia Statute for Religious Freedom
- Articles of Confederation
- Land Ordinance of 1785
- Northwest Ordinance of 1787
- Northwest Territory

The Story Continues

In 1776 a short essay by an unknown author appeared. The essay called for the newly independent states to take great care when building their new governments. "They [the people] are now planting a seed," it stated. The author predicted that the seed would grow into a tree, whose branches would "shelter the liberty of succeeding ages." Many Americans agreed with this idea. They hoped that a strong republic could be formed in America.

The bald eagle is one of the symbols of the United States.

✯ Ideas about Government

The American colonies had taken a bold step in declaring their independence from Great Britain in July 1776. Their next political goal was to form new governments. To do so, the American people drew from a wide range of political ideas.

Have students read Section 1 and complete Guided Reading Strategy 8.1. Choose one or more of the following activities to explore the section content with students. For further suggestions on block scheduling or team teaching, see the *Block Scheduling Handbook with Team Teaching Strategies.*

LEVEL 1: Lead a class discussion on the Articles of Confederation. Then pair students and ask each pair to list the powers that the Articles of Confederation granted to the national government. *(Students' responses should include that Congress could coin and borrow money, negotiate and make treaties with foreign nations and with American Indians, and resolve conflicts between the states.)* Then ask students to note the possible advantages and disadvantages of the provisions. *(Students' lists might suggest that the advantages were the power to coin and borrow money, conduct foreign affairs, set policy toward American Indians, and settle disputes between the states. The disadvantages might be that the government could not force the states to contribute soldiers or money to the federal government, and the government essentially had limited authority.)*

ENGLISH LANGUAGE LEARNERS , COOPERATIVE LEARNING

Note: For an additional teaching idea, see the Chapter 8 Quick Survey activity in the **Creative Teaching Strategies** handbook.

Interpreting the Visual Record

The Enlightenment *During the Enlightenment, philosophers often discussed their ideas at elegant social gatherings. British philosopher John Locke was widely respected.* **How does the painting suggest the interest that the wealthy had in Enlightenment ideas?**

One source of inspiration was English law. England had limited the power of its kings and queens in two documents—Magna Carta and the English Bill of Rights. Magna Carta, signed by King John in 1215, required the king to follow the rule of law like other English people. The English Bill of Rights, passed in 1689, kept the king or queen from passing new taxes or changing laws without Parliament's approval. As a result, the people's representatives had a stronger voice in government.

Americans were also influenced by the Enlightenment. Writers of that period had called for the use of reason and expressed a belief in human goodness. Enlightenment philosopher John Locke believed that a social contract, or agreement, existed between political leaders and the people they ruled. One side of this contract was the government's duty to protect the people's unalienable rights. The rule of law, wrote Locke, was more important than the authority of any individual.

History Makers Speak "Whosoever in authority exceeds the power given him by the law . . . may be opposed as any other man who by force invades the right of another."

—John Locke, *Two Treatises on Government*

Locke stated that leaders who broke the law or lost the approval of the people should be replaced.

Naturally American leaders looked to their own political traditions, such as the New England town meeting. At these meetings, townspeople addressed important issues in their community. Americans also looked to their own legislative assemblies, such as the Virginia House of Burgesses. These bodies offered models of representative governments. Christian traditions, such as the Great Awakening, may have also inspired colonists to question existing political institutions and look for more local control.

Analyzing Primary Sources
Identifying Points of View
To whom does Locke compare a ruler who breaks the law? to someone who uses force to violate someone's rights

Interdisciplinary Connection

▶Literature◀

The Enlightenment. Many Enlightenment thinkers argued that an informed public would bring about social change. For example, British writer Joseph Addison coauthored hundreds of essays in the early 1700s for the periodical *The Spectator.* He hoped that by introducing the middle class to ideas in philosophy and literature, he would promote a more enlightened world.

ACTIVITY: Have students research an American Enlightenment writer such as Benjamin Franklin. Have them use standard grammar, spelling, sentence structure, and punctuation to write a paragraph about that person's Enlightenment ideas.

Visual Record Answer

Students might suggest that the wealthy are indicated by their dress and the decorations in the room.

Interpreting the Visual Record

Female voters *The only state to give voting rights to women was New Jersey, though it took that right away in 1807.* **From the way these women voters are dressed, do you think that they are property owners? Why or why not?**

THE GRANGER COLLECTION, NEW YORK

Americans also had written documents supporting the principles of self-government. In 1620 the Pilgrims had agreed to govern themselves at Plymouth colony by signing the Mayflower Compact. In 1639 the people of Connecticut had drawn up the Fundamental Orders of Connecticut. This plan was widely considered to be the first written **constitution** in the English colonies. A constitution is a set of basic principles and laws that state the powers and duties of the government. Finally, the Declaration of Independence clearly set forth the ideas on which Americans thought government should be based.

✔ **Reading Check: Summarizing** What influenced American ideas of government? Magna Carta, English Bill of Rights, Enlightenment, John Locke, town meetings, House of Burgesses, Mayflower Compact, Fundamental Orders of Connecticut, Declaration of Independence

★ The State Constitutions

All of these political ideas were quickly put into practice after the United States declared independence. During the American Revolution nearly every colony wrote a new state constitution. These constitutions showed a belief in **republicanism**—that is, support for a system of government called a republic. In such a system, citizens elect representatives who are responsible to the people. Most Americans wanted to keep individual leaders from gaining too much power. Thus, each state constitution created a **limited government**. In a limited government all leaders have to obey the laws and no one has total power. For example, many states placed their courts outside of the governor's control.

Most state constitutions protected the individual rights of citizens. For example, George Mason wrote the Virginia Declaration of Rights. Some of the rights it defended were trial by jury, freedom of the press, and private ownership of property. In 1786 Thomas Jefferson's support for freedom of religion was included in the **Virginia Statute for Religious Freedom**. This law promoted the separation of church and state in Virginia. Other states soon followed, and by 1833 there were no state governments that supported an official church.

In addition, many state constitutions expanded **suffrage**, or voting rights. As one Virginian wrote, "The spirit of independence was converted into equality." Some states allowed any white man who was a taxpaying citizen to vote. Other states gave the vote only to white men who owned property. In most states people had to own property to hold an elected office. Seven of the first state constitutions gave voting rights to free African American men. However, by the 1860s these rights had been taken away or greatly limited by high property or residency requirements.

✔ **Reading Check: Analyzing Information** How did the first state constitutions promote the growth of democracy? organized the state government like a republic; protected religious freedom; protected natural rights with a bill of rights; expanded voting rights

LEVELS 2 AND 3: Have students imagine that they are living in the United States in 1787. Then ask them to write a letter to a friend living in the Ohio Territory. Have students explain in their letters why the friend should be pleased that Congress passed the Northwest Ordinance. Instruct students to include the process that the ordinance established for admitting new states, its rules regarding slavery in the territory, and its provisions for public education. Then have students exchange letters and write a brief response to the author. **COOPERATIVE LEARNING**

Note: To help students make meaningful connections between events in American history and those in their own hometown, use the Chapter 8 **Hands-On History** activity, Statehood.

 LEVEL 3: Organize the class into three groups. Have students discuss within their groups which ideas and documents shaped American beliefs about government. Then have each group decide which document had the greatest influence and was the most important in the development of the American representative government. Each group should build a debate around that premise, with one side arguing the merits and influence of the document, and the other side arguing the flaws and weaknesses of the document. Then have each group perform its debate for the class.

COOPERATIVE LEARNING

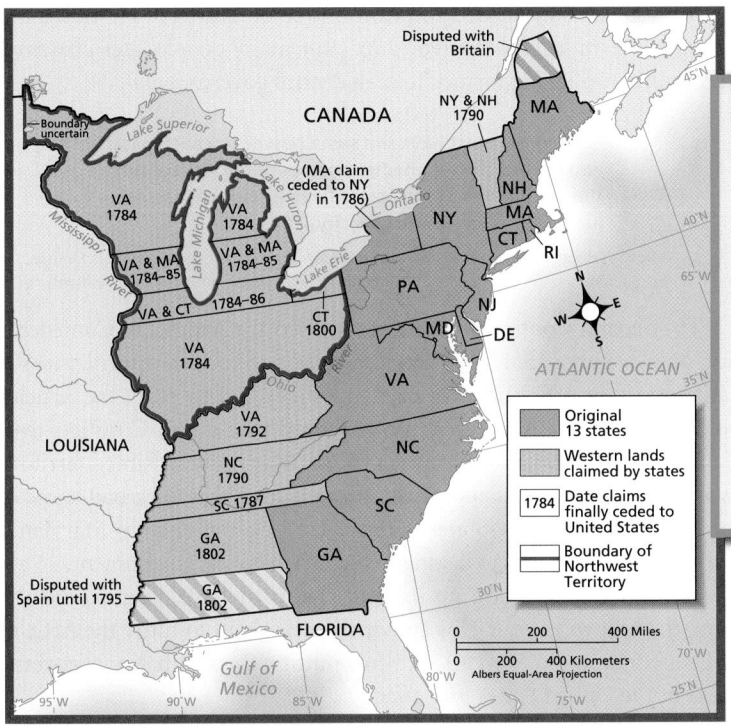

Western Land Claims, 1781–1802

Interpreting Maps Many of the original 13 states had claims to western lands that dated back to their colonial charters. It took several years for all the states to cede these lands to the United States.

Skills Assessment

1. **Places and Regions** What states claimed land within the boundaries of what became the Northwest Territory?
2. **Summarizing** Which states had no land claims?

★ Forming a Union

To many members of the Second Continental Congress, it was not enough for each state to have its own government. They believed that a national government was necessary in order to hold the country together. Some leaders of the Revolution disagreed. They worried that a new central government would be too powerful. After all, they were rebelling against Great Britain in part because of Parliament's abuse of authority.

On June 12, 1776, the Congress appointed a Committee of Thirteen, made up of one member from each colony. This group was assigned to create a national constitution. Committee members met for a month to discuss and draft the new document, called the **Articles of Confederation**. Under the Articles of Confederation, a new Confederation Congress would become the central national government. Each state would have one vote in the Congress. The national government did not have a president or a court system.

The Confederation Congress had only limited powers. It could make coins and borrow money. It could negotiate and make treaties with other countries and with American Indians. Congress also could settle conflicts between the states and could ask states for money and soldiers. However, Congress could not force the states to provide money or troops, even in an emergency.

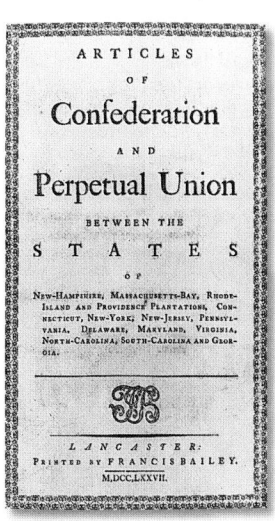

The Articles of Confederation created a central government with limited powers.

Constitutional Heritage

The Limits of the Articles of Confederation. Under the Articles of Confederation, the states did not always respond to the requests of Congress. The legislative body did not even meet on a regular basis, and between 1783 and 1785 it met in four different cities. Members also did not attend every meeting. It took a great deal of effort to get enough members gathered to ratify the Treaty of Paris.

CRITICAL THINKING

Why would such organizational problems make it difficult to run a country?

ANSWER: Students might suggest the lack of support weakened Congress' authority.

MAP ANSWERS

1. Connecticut, Massachusetts, and Virginia
2. Delaware, Maryland, New Jersey, Pennsylvania, and Rhode Island

Organize students into groups. Tell students to create a set of rules that would apply to everyone in the school, students, teachers, and workers alike. These rules must be fair to everyone, deal with all matters related to school, and be designed so that the school would run efficiently and everyone would accept them. Tell students that only after everyone in their group has agreed to the set of the rules can any specific rule take effect. When all groups have finished, write each group's rules on the chalkboard and discuss them. Then have the class create one set of rules from all the rules on the chalkboard. These rules will go into effect only if the entire class has accepted all of them. After a final set of rules has been decided on, ask students what problems they encountered in the rule-making process. *(Students' answers will probably mention problems coming to agreement on rules.)* Ask them if they think their process might be similar to the process that American leaders responsible for creating a new government experienced.

BLOCK SCHEDULING , COOPERATIVE LEARNING

★ CLOSE

Ask students to make a series of posters. Have them include in each poster a power of the federal government that was included in the Articles of Confederation and where the philosophical basis of the idea originated. Encourage volunteers to present their posters to the class.

Even after the Revolutionary War many westerners, who could not elect their highest officials without federal supervision, saw themselves as "colonists" —with the federal government, rather than Great Britain, being their mother country. In part to alleviate these complaints, the Northwest Ordinance offered clear steps to political statehood and equality.

★ Government

The National Seal. Soon after its formation under the Articles of Confederation, Congress adopted an official seal for the United States. This seal remains in use today. An eagle— a symbol of imperial Rome— centers the seal. A constellation of 13 stars hovers over its head, and a shield with 13 vertical stripes covers its breast. A ribbon bearing the words *E Pluribus Unum* extends from its beak, and it grasps an olive branch with one talon and a sheath of arrows with the other.

CRITICAL THINKING

What might the olive branch and the sheath of arrows in the national seal symbolize?

ANSWER: Students might suggest that the olive branch symbolizes peace, while the sheath of arrows symbolizes war.

Analyzing Primary Sources
Drawing Inferences and Conclusions Why might Webster have held this view? Students might suggest that Webster believed that the state governments were good models for a central government.

Research on the R◉M

Free Find:
Schooling
After reading about public schools on the **Holt Researcher CD–ROM,** imagine that you attend a public school in the late 1780s. Write a short account of your experiences.

Surveyors used tools like these to help them determine property boundaries.

John Dickinson headed the Committee of Thirteen. He called the Articles "a firm league of friendship." But many people later criticized the Articles for having formed a weak central government.

> **History Makers Speak** ❝Congress must have the same power to enact [pass] laws and compel [force] obedience throughout the continent, as the legislatures of the States have in their respective jurisdictions [areas of authority].❞
>
> —Noah Webster, quoted in *The Growth of the American Republic*, by Samuel Eliot Morison, Henry Steele Commager, and William E. Leuchtenburg

The Second Continental Congress passed the Articles of Confederation on November 15, 1777. Then it sent them to each state legislature for **ratification**, or official approval. All 13 states had to ratify the Articles before the new national government could take effect. Conflicts over claims to western lands slowed the process. Many states claimed territory as far west as the Mississippi River. Virginia and New York had some of the largest land claims. States without land claims, such as Maryland, wanted these territories to belong to the new national government.

New York finally gave up its land claims in 1780. Virginia did the same the following year. This convinced Maryland to ratify the Articles of Confederation in March 1781, thus putting the first national government of the United States into effect.

✔ **Reading Check: Finding the Main Idea** What powers did the national government have under the Articles of Confederation? coining and borrowing money; negotiating treaties; settling interstate conflicts; asking for troops from the states

★ The Northwest Territory

The new central government had to decide what to do with the western lands now under its control. It also had to raise money to pay war debts. The Confederation Congress hoped to solve both problems by selling western land to the public. It passed the **Land Ordinance of 1785**, which set up a system for surveying and dividing the public territory. First the land was split into townships of 36 square miles. Each township was divided into 36 lots of 640 acres each. One lot was set aside for a public school, with another 4 lots saved for Revolutionary War veterans. The remaining lots were for sale to the public.

To form a political system for the region north of the Ohio River, Congress passed the **Northwest Ordinance of 1787**. The ordinance created the **Northwest Territory**, which included the area that is now Illinois, Indiana, Michigan, Ohio, and Wisconsin.

The Northwest Ordinance also created a system for bringing new states into the Union. Congress agreed to divide the Northwest Territory into several smaller territories, each of which had a governor appointed by Congress. When the population of a territory reached 60,000, its settlers could draft their own constitution. The people could then ask Congress for permission to join the Union as a state.

★ REVIEW AND ASSESS

Have students complete the **Section 1 Review** on p. 227. Then have students complete **Daily Quiz 8.1.** As **Alternative Assessment**, you may want to use the students' editorials or posters in this section's lessons.

★ RETEACH

Have students complete **Main Idea Activity for English Language Learners and Special-Needs Students.** Then write Define and Identify words from the section opener on the chalkboard as headings. Have students list three facts about each key term. Then have them share their ideas with the class. Write students' ideas under the appropriate heading on the

chalkboard. Then lead a class discussion on how the ideas that are listed under each heading relate to the term.
ENGLISH LANGUAGE LEARNERS

★ EXTEND

Have students work in small groups to create a brochure that urges people to move to the Northwest Territory following passage of the Land Ordinance of 1785 and the Northwest Ordinance of 1787. Ask students to appeal to either merchants or small farmers. Encourage students to include testimonials by citizens who have already moved to the Northwest Territory, as well as illustrations. **BLOCK SCHEDULING** ,
COOPERATIVE LEARNING

In addition, the ordinance had a bill of rights. It also required that public education be provided for the citizens of the region. Finally, the Northwest Ordinance stated that "there shall be neither slavery nor involuntary servitude [forced labor] in the . . . territory." This last condition, based on a proposal by Thomas Jefferson, banned slavery in the Northwest Territory. However, the question of slavery would become more controversial as other new territories were formed.

✔ **Reading Check: Summarizing** How did the new Congress organize the nation's western lands? The Land Ordinance of 1785 divided the lands into lots for sale to the public. The Northwest Ordinance created a system for admitting new states, required public education, and outlawed slavery.

Daily Life

Moving West After the Revolutionary War Americans began heading west in greater numbers. Thousands of people settled in the lands of the Northwest Territory. Many of these people were farmers from New England, where good farmland was scarce. As the population of the Northwest Territory grew and the region was divided into states, more settlers came from throughout the nation and from overseas. Why do you think settlers would travel in a large group as shown here?

Section 1 Review

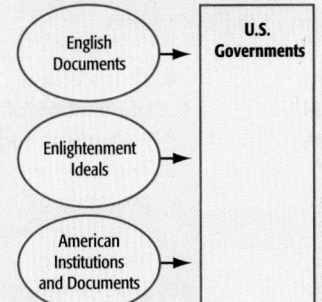

go.hrw.com
Homework Practice Online
keyword: SA3 HP8

1 Define and explain:
• constitution
• republicanism
• limited government
• suffrage
• ratification

2 Identify and explain:
• Virginia Statute for Religious Freedom
• Articles of Confederation
• Land Ordinance of 1785
• Northwest Ordinance of 1787
• Northwest Territory

3 Summarizing Copy the graphic organizer below. Use it to identify the ideas and documents that influenced the U.S. state and national governments.

English Documents → U.S. Governments
Enlightenment Ideals →
American Institutions and Documents →

4 Finding the Main Idea
a. In what ways did the first state constitutions support the growth of representative government?

b. Why did Congress pass the Northwest Ordinance, and what did it achieve?

5 Writing and Critical Thinking
Analyzing Information Imagine that you are a member of the Committee of Thirteen. Write a brief report for the states describing the powers given to the central government under the Articles of Confederation.

Consider the following:
• the structure of the national government
• what the Confederation Congress could and could not do

**Section 1 Review
ANSWERS**

1 Define
• constitution, p. 224
• republicanism, p. 224
• limited government, p. 224
• suffrage, p. 224
• ratification, p. 226

2 Identify
• Virginia Statute for Religious Freedom, p. 224
• Articles of Confederation, p. 225
• Land Ordinance of 1785, p. 226
• Northwest Ordinance of 1787, p. 226
• Northwest Territory, p. 226

3 English documents—Magna Carta, English Bill of Rights; Enlightenment ideals—use of reason, belief in human goodness, rule of law; American institutions—New England town meeting, Virginia House of Burgesses; American documents—Mayflower Compact, Fundamental Orders of Connecticut; Declaration of Independence

4 a. organizing the state government like a republic, protecting religious freedom, creating a limited government, expanding voting rights
b. established a political structure for the region, provided for the admission of new states, included a bill of rights, required public education in the region, and outlawed slavery in the area

5 Students' reports will vary.

Read with the class the principles of Magna Carta. Discuss what these principles imply about the acts of the English king prior to the signing of Magna Carta. List students' suggestions on the chalkboard. (*Students' responses might include that the king unfairly taxed citizens, deprived them of liberties, imprisoned them unfairly, or otherwise treated them unfairly.*) Then have students create a scene of a play showing a possible way that the king may have abused or misused English subjects. **BLOCK SCHEDULING**

SPOTLIGHT
on Magna Carta

Ask students to rephrase the five given principles of Magna Carta in everyday language. Then have them rank these principles in the order that they consider to be the most important to least important, and how Magna Carta may have influenced those forming the new U.S. government. Have volunteers share their lists with the class and explain why they ranked the principles as they did. **BLOCK SCHEDULING**

Global Relations

The French Declaration of the Rights of Man and of the Citizen. France's Constituent Assembly adopted the Declaration of the Rights of Man and of the Citizen in 1789. It outlined the principles of the French Revolution, which began that same year. The Declaration described the rights of freedom and equality that should belong to French citizens, and it was similar to both the English and the U.S. Bill of Rights. Among the important principles were the citizen's right to elect a government, to think and speak freely, and to vote on new taxes.

CRITICAL THINKING

Why do you think the Declaration was influenced by the U.S. Bill of Rights?

ANSWER: Students should note that the French Revolution began only a few years after the American Revolution, and leaders probably looked to the United States for inspiration.

ANALYZING PRIMARY SOURCES ANSWERS

1. by requiring the "common council of our kingdom" to approve taxes for military purposes
2. Students may suggest all of them; however, the most accurate answers are 38, 39, and 40.

Historical Documents

MAGNA CARTA

A copy of Magna Carta

England's King John angered many people with high taxes. In 1215 a group of English nobles joined the archbishop of Canterbury to force the king to agree to sign Magna Carta. This document stated that the king was subject to the rule of law, just as other citizens of England were. It also presented the ideas of a fair and speedy trial and due process of law. These principles are still a part of the U.S. Bill of Rights.

1. That the English Church shall be free, and shall have her whole rights and her liberties **inviolable.**[1] . . .

12. No **scutage**[2] nor aid shall be imposed in our kingdom, unless by the common council of our kingdom. . . .

38. No **bailiff,**[3] for the future, shall put any man to his law upon his own simple **affirmation,**[4] without **credible**[5] witnesses **produced for that purpose.**[6] . . .

39. No freeman shall be seized, imprisoned, **dispossessed,**[7] outlawed, or **exiled,**[8] or in any way destroyed; nor will we proceed against or prosecute him except by the lawful judgment of his **peers,**[9] or by the law of the land.

40. To none will we sell, to none will we deny, to none will we delay right or justice. . . .

Analyzing Primary Sources

1. How does Magna Carta allow for fair taxation?
2. Which of these rights supports the ideas of a fair trial and due process of law?

[1] **inviolable:** safe from sudden change
[2] **scutage:** tax for military purposes
[3] **bailiff:** sheriff
[4] **affirmation:** testimony
[5] **credible:** believable
[6] **produced for that purpose:** brought forward to testify
[7] **dispossessed:** deprived of his land
[8] **exiled:** forced to leave the country
[9] **peers:** equals

THE ENGLISH BILL OF RIGHTS

The seal of the House of Commons in Parliament

After the Glorious Revolution, Parliament passed the English Bill of Rights, which ensured that Parliament would have supreme power over the monarchy. The bill also protected the rights of English citizens.

1. That the pretended power of suspending of laws or the execution of laws by **regal**[1] authority without consent of Parliament is illegal; . . .

4. That **levying money**[2] for or to the use of the crown by pretense of **prerogative**[3] without grant of Parliament . . . is illegal;

5. That it is the right of the subjects to petition the king, and all commitments and prosecutions for such petitioning are illegal.

8. That election of members of Parliament ought to be free;

9. That the freedom of speech and debates or proceedings in Parliament ought not to be . . . questioned in any court or place out of Parliament;

10. That excessive bail ought not to be required, nor excessive fines imposed, nor cruel and unusual punishments inflicted.

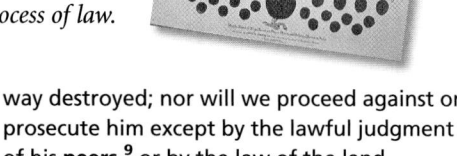

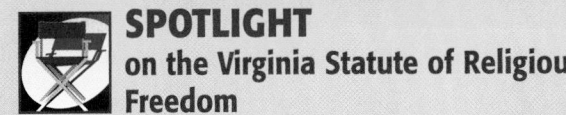
11. That jurors ought to be duly **impaneled**.[4] . . .
13. And that, for **redress of**[5] all grievances and for the amending, strengthening, and preserving of the laws, Parliaments ought to be held frequently.

---

[1] **regal:** royal
[2] **levying money:** raising taxes
[3] **prerogative:** right
[4] **impaneled:** selected
[5] **redress of:** to make up for

Analyzing Primary Sources

1. What parts of this document describe the rights and powers of Parliament, and what are those rights and powers?
2. What parts of this document do you think Americans would want to use in their government?

VIRGINIA STATUTE FOR RELIGIOUS FREEDOM

Thomas Jefferson wrote the Virginia Statute for Religious Freedom. Jefferson hoped that by separating church and state, Virginians could practice their religion—whatever it might be—freely.

I. Well aware that Almighty God has created the mind free; . . . that to **compel**[1] a man to **furnish contributions**[2] of money for the **propagation**[3] of opinions which he disbelieves is sinful and **tyrannical**;[4] that even . . . forcing him to support this or that teacher of his own religious **persuasion**[5] is depriving him of the comfortable liberty. . . . And, finally, that truth is great and will **prevail**[6] if left to herself . . . and has nothing to fear.

II. Be it **enacted**[7] by the General Assembly that no man shall be compelled to frequent or support any religious worship, place, or ministry whatsoever, nor shall be enforced, restrained, **molested**,[8] or burdened in his body or goods, nor shall otherwise suffer on account of his religious opinions or belief; but that all men shall be free to profess, and by argument to maintain, their opinion in matters of religion, and that the same shall in no wise **diminish**,[9] enlarge, or affect their civil capacities.

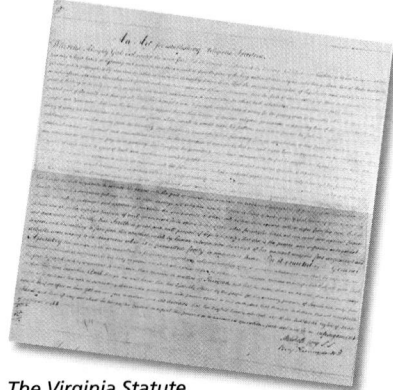

The Virginia Statute for Religious Freedom

III. And though we well know that this assembly . . . [has] no power to restrain the acts of succeeding assemblies . . . we are free to declare, and do declare, that the rights hereby **asserted**[10] are of the natural rights of mankind, and that if any act shall hereafter be passed to repeal the present or to narrow its operation, such act will be an **infringement**[11] of natural rights.

Analyzing Primary Sources

1. How does this document protect freedom of religion?
2. Why do you think section III was included?

---

[1] **compel:** force
[2] **furnish contributions:** pay
[3] **propagation:** spreading
[4] **tyrannical:** unjust
[5] **persuasion:** belief
[6] **prevail:** win
[7] **enacted:** decided
[8] **molested:** injured
[9] **diminish:** reduce
[10] **asserted:** stated
[11] **infringement:** violation

Section 2

OBJECTIVES

* Describe how other nations treated the new U.S. government.
* Examine the economic problems that arose under the Articles of Confederation.
* Analyze the causes and consequences of Shays's Rebellion.

 **LET'S GET STARTED!**

As students enter the classroom, ask them to write a brief overview of what they consider to be the three most powerful countries in the world today. *(Students' responses will vary.)* Write on the chalkboard the names of the nations that students have listed and record the number of times each nation is mentioned. Explain to students that although many (if not all of them) picked the United States, it has not always been considered a powerful nation. Tell students that in Section 2 they will learn about the foreign and domestic problems that faced the United States in its early years.

Section 2

Problems in the New Nation

Read to Discover

1. How did other nations treat the new government of the United States?
2. What economic problems arose under the Articles of Confederation?
3. What were the causes and consequences of Shays's Rebellion?

WHY IT MATTERS TODAY

The United States today has a powerful central government. Use **CNNfyi.com** or other **current events** sources to learn about a way in which the U.S. government regulates business or trade. Record your findings in your journal.

Define

* tariffs
* interstate commerce
* inflation
* debtors
* creditors
* depression

Identify

* Shays's Rebellion
* Daniel Shays

The Story Continues

Merchants relied on barrels to ship many kinds of goods by land, river, and sea.

On June 7, 1786, Thomas Amis sailed his ship down the Mississippi River. He was carrying trade goods, as he had done many times before. This day was different, however. Amis's trip broke a new Spanish law, which greatly limited U.S. citizens' navigation rights along the lower part of the river. The Spanish troops at the town of Natchez—in present-day Mississippi—captured Amis. Then the Spanish stripped him of all his cargo, including 50 barrels of flour.

★ A Lack of Respect

Congress could do little to protect citizens like Thomas Amis against foreign threats. Under the Articles of Confederation, Congress could not force states to provide soldiers for an army. Without an army, the national government found it difficult to protect its citizens. It was also difficult to enforce the terms of international treaties. For example, Congress could do little to enforce the Treaty of Paris of 1783. The treaty called for the British to turn over "with all convenient speed" their forts on the U.S. side of the Great Lakes, but Great Britain was slow to leave these positions.

Have students read Section 2 and complete Guided Reading Strategy 8.2. Choose one or more of the following activities to explore the section content with students. For further suggestions on block scheduling or team teaching, see the *Block Scheduling Handbook with Team Teaching Strategies.*

LEVEL 1: List the following weaknesses of the Articles of Confederation on the chalkboard: *Congress had no power to force states to provide soldiers for an army; Congress had no power to pass tariffs; Congress had no power to regulate trade between states;* and *States had power to print their own money.* Have students examine some specific economic problems that arose under the Articles of Confederation. (*Students' responses might include that the United States could not make Spain reopen the lower Mississippi River to U.S. shipping; the United States could not set tariffs on British imports; trade was difficult for merchants whose businesses crossed state lines; states printed large amounts of paper money, which led to inflation.*) Then ask students to imagine that they are colonial citizens who want to protest the Articles of Confederation. Give each student a sheet of poster board and have them prepare protest signs addressing a specific economic problem related to the Articles of Confederation. **ENGLISH LANGUAGE LEARNERS**

CONNECTING TO
THE ARTS

American Painters Artists John Singleton Copley, Gilbert Stuart, and Benjamin West all earned great success during the late 1700s. West was one of the most influential artists. Beginning his career as a portrait painter in America, West later moved to Britain and helped found the Royal Academy of Arts. West became known for his historical paintings, which showed people dressed in modern clothing instead of classical styles. West had to leave this painting of the signing of the Treaty of Paris unfinished when the British delegates refused to pose. **How is this unfinished painting symbolic of the relations between Britain and the United States?**

Spain also took advantage of the weakness of the United States. In 1784, Spanish officials closed the lower Mississippi River to U.S. shipping. Westerners who used the Mississippi to send goods to eastern markets were furious. But Spain refused to reopen the river to U.S. merchants.

Many state leaders began to criticize the weak Confederation Congress. Representatives from Rhode Island wrote to Congress. They said, "Our federal government is but a name; a mere shadow without substance [meaning]." Critics believed that a strong military would help the United States put pressure on Spain to open the Mississippi. For these political leaders, this failure showed that the national government needed to have more power.

✔ **Reading Check: Finding the Main Idea** How did the weaknesses of the Articles of Confederation affect U.S. relations with other countries?
The United States had no army and could not enforce treaties.

★ Trouble with Trade

The United States also faced economic problems involving Great Britain. Before the Revolutionary War, colonial ships had traded a great deal with the British West Indies. But after the Treaty of Paris was signed, Britain closed many of its ports to American ships. In addition to shutting down this trade, Britain forced American merchants to pay high duties on U.S. exports. The tariffs applied to goods such as rice, tar, and tobacco, which colonial merchants wanted to sell in Britain.

★ Linking Past to Present

Trade Regulations. International trade has changed a great deal since the 1780s. Today countries are working to make trade easier. In 1993, for example, the United States and 116 other nations expanded on an earlier trade agreement to form the World Trade Organization (WTO). Members of the WTO, which came into effect on January 1995, agreed to cut tariffs and eliminate manufacturing quotas.

🖥 **internet** connect

TOPIC: WTO
GO TO: go.hrw.com
KEYWORD: SA3 CF9

Have students access the Internet through the HRW Go site to find information regarding the WTO and global trade issues. Then create a mind map that illustrates the advantages and disadvantages of increased global trade. Create a legend for your mind map that explains it.

CONNECTING TO THE ARTS ANSWER because the British would not pose, it is symbolic of the strained relationships

ALL LEVELS: Copy the following graphic organizer onto the chalkboard, omitting the italicized answers. Have students complete the chart to show the causes and consequences of Shays's Rebellion.
ENGLISH LANGUAGE LEARNERS

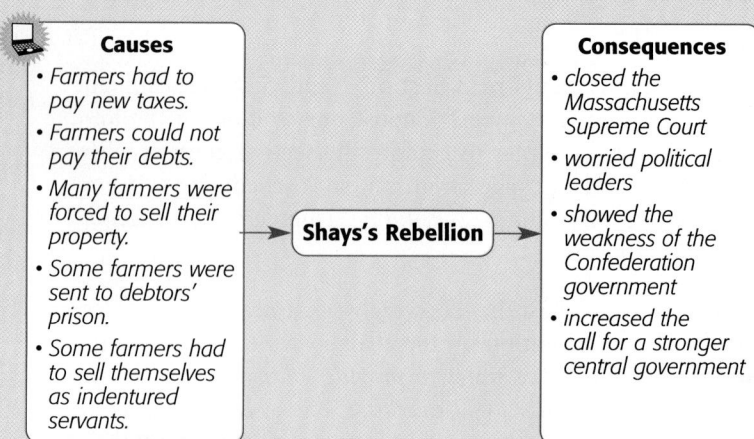

Causes
- *Farmers had to pay new taxes.*
- *Farmers could not pay their debts.*
- *Many farmers were forced to sell their property.*
- *Some farmers were sent to debtors' prison.*
- *Some farmers had to sell themselves as indentured servants.*

→ Shays's Rebellion →

Consequences
- *closed the Massachusetts Supreme Court*
- *worried political leaders*
- *showed the weakness of the Confederation government*
- *increased the call for a stronger central government*

★ Economics

Trade with China. In 1785 the ship *Empress of China* returned from China to New York. The ship's owners had traded more than 40 tons of ginseng for tea and other Chinese products. Many hoped that this success at opening trade with China would mean the United States would not have to rely so much on trade with Europe.

CRITICAL THINKING

Why do you think colonists had not attempted to trade with Asian nations before 1784?

ANSWER: Students might suggest that the restrictive trade laws of Britain and the distance to Asia may have prevented Americans from trading there.

Analyzing Primary Sources
Evaluating How did the end of the Revolutionary War affect the free enterprise system in the United States? The United States was unable to trade with the West Indies, and international trade in general suffered.

★ ★ ★ ★ ★ ★ ★ ★ ★ ★ ★
That's Interesting!
★ ★ ★ ★ ★ ★ ★ ★ ★ ★ ★

Talking Turkey Did you know that Benjamin Franklin wanted the turkey, not the bald eagle, to be the national bird of the United States? It's true! He thought that the bald eagle was "a Bird of bad moral Character." He had more respect for the wild turkey. He lost his argument, and the bald eagle became an American symbol. But the turkey did not lose out completely. In the late 1900s Alabama, Massachusetts, Oklahoma, and South Carolina adopted the turkey as their official state game bird. Alabama recognized the turkey as "undoubtedly the most noble of all game birds upon the North American Continent."

The loss of trade with the British shook the U.S. economy. James Madison of Virginia wrote about the crisis.

 History Makers Speak
❝The Revolution has robbed us of our trade with the West Indies . . . without opening any other channels to compensate [make up] for it. In every point of view, indeed, the trade of this country is in a deplorable [terrible] condition.❞
—James Madison, quoted in *Independence on Trial,* by Frederick W. Marks III

Farmers could no longer export their goods to the British West Indies. They also had to hire British ships to carry their goods to British markets, which was very expensive. Samuel Adams wrote about this to his cousin John Adams, "Our merchants are complaining bitterly that Great Britain is ruining their trade and there is good reason to complain." American exports dropped. At the same time, British goods flowed freely into the United States. This unequal trade caused serious economic problems for the new nation. British merchants could sell manufactured products in the United States at much lower prices than locally made goods. This competition hurt American businesses.

The Confederation Congress could not fix the problem because it did not have the power to pass **tariffs**—taxes on imports or exports. The states could offer little help. If one state passed a tariff, the British could simply sell their goods in another state. Most states did not cooperate when passing tariffs. Instead, each looked only to improve its own trade. In 1785 the situation led a British magazine to call the new nation the "Dis-United States." As a result of the trade problems with Britain, American merchants began looking for other new markets. Such new markets included China, France, and the Netherlands. Despite these attempts, Britain remained the most important trading partner of the United States.

✔ **Reading Check: Summarizing** What trade problems did the United States face with Great Britain, and why did these occur? loss of British West Indies markets, high British tariffs; weak government, lack of state unity

★ Economic Problems at Home

In addition to international trade issues, trade among the states became a major problem. The Confederation Congress had no power to regulate **interstate commerce**—trade between two or more states. Without such regulation, states followed their own commercial interests. As a result, trade laws differed from state to state. This situation made trade difficult for merchants whose businesses crossed state lines.

The ability of the states to print their own money caused more problems. After the Revolutionary War, most states had a hard time paying off war debts. They also struggled to collect overdue taxes. To ease economic hardships, some states at times printed large amounts of paper money. The result was **inflation**—increased prices for goods and

ALL LEVELS: Organize the class into small groups. Have students imagine that they are writing an advice column for American readers in the 1780s. Ask each group to create four or five questions that address economic issues of concern that arose under the Articles of Confederation. Then have groups write answers on how to establish a stable economic system. **ENGLISH LANGUAGE LEARNERS ,**
COOPERATIVE LEARNING

LEVEL 2: Organize the class into small groups and ask students to imagine that they are newspaper publishers who must determine the headlines for the next issue of their paper. Have groups write a headline and several subheads for each of the following topics: treatment of the United States by other governments; problems associated with tariffs; economic problems that arose under the Articles of Confederation; and the consequences of Shays's Rebellion. Then have each group place its headline and subheads on poster board.
COOPERATIVE LEARNING

LEVEL 2: Pair students. Assign one student in each pair to be an American political leader and assign the other student to be either a British or a Spanish political leader. Then have each pair write a dialogue about the problems that the two countries are facing and how other nations treated the U.S. government. **COOPERATIVE LEARNING**

---

services combined with the reduced value of money. Congress had no power to stop states from issuing more paper money. Thus, it could do little to stop inflation.

Inflation woes soon forced planters in North Carolina to sell tobacco to the state government in exchange for paper money. This money was worth almost nothing. In Rhode Island a similar problem arose. The state legislature printed large amounts of paper money worth very little. This made **debtors**—people who owe money—quite happy. They could pay back their debts with paper money worth less than the coins they had borrowed. However, **creditors**—people who lend money—were upset by the prospect of being paid back with worthless money. Similar situations took place in many states.

The rising inflation faced by the states combined with the loss of trade with Great Britain to cause a **depression**. A depression is a period of low economic activity combined with a rise in unemployment.

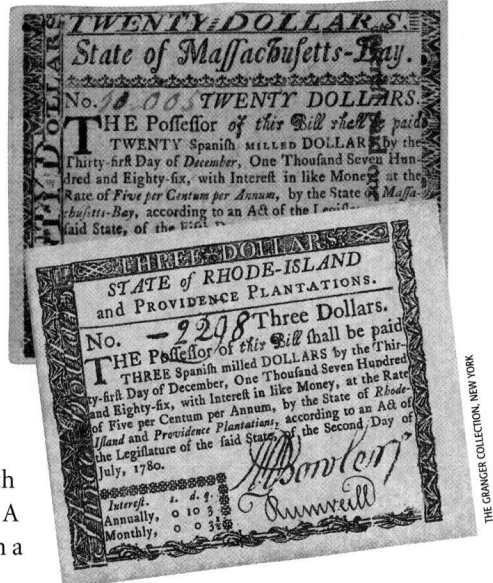

THE GRANGER COLLECTION, NEW YORK

The states of Massachusetts and Rhode Island both suffered economic problems related to their currency policies.

✔ **Reading Check: Identifying Cause and Effect** What led to the economic differences between the states, and how did this affect the national economy? Each state pursued its own economic policy, set its own tariffs, and printed its own money. This hurt trade, brought inflation, and contributed to a depression.

⭐ Debt in Massachusetts

Each state handled its economic problems differently. Massachusetts refused to print paper money and tried to pay its war debts by collecting taxes on land.

The state's economic policy hit farmers particularly hard. As landowners, they had to pay the new taxes. With little gold or silver and no paper money, however, farmers had trouble paying their debts. When people could not pay their debts, the Massachusetts courts began forcing them to sell their property. Some farmers also had to serve terms in debtors' prison. Some even had to sell themselves as indentured servants. People soon began calling for change.

History Makers Speak ❝We beg leave to inform your Honors that unless something takes place more favorable to the people, in a little time at least, one half of our inhabitants [people living in the state] in our opinion will become bankrupt [financially ruined] . . . . Sirs, in this situation what have we to live on—no money to be had; our estates [lands] daily posted and sold.❞

—Petition from a rural town, quoted in *The Growth of the American Republic*, by Samuel Eliot Morison, Henry Steele Commager, and William E. Leuchtenburg

Analyzing Primary Sources
Identifying Points of View
What worries did farmers have? that they would go bankrupt and lose their lands

However, many government leaders in Massachusetts had little sympathy for the problems of poor farmers. In some cases, farmers actually owed these politicians money.

⭐ Historical Sidelight

Jay on Interstate Relations. Many of the Founders worried about the worsening relations between the states. In 1786 John Jay wrote in a letter to George Washington that selfishness and greed had taken priority over the public good. "Personal rather than national interests," he said, seemed to be the states' guiding motives.

ACTIVITY: Have students imagine that they are John Jay and ask them to complete the letter that Jay wrote to Washington in 1786, using standard grammar, spelling, sentence structure, and punctuation. Make sure that they use examples from the chapter in their letters.

HOMEWORK Have students think about possible solutions to the economic problems caused by the weaknesses of the Articles of Confederation. Then have each student write a petition to the members of the Confederation Congress asking for specific changes to the Articles and explaining how the changes would improve the U.S. economy.

LEVEL 3: Assign to students one of the following categories: western merchant who sends items back East, eastern farmer who exports goods to British markets, North Carolina tobacco planter, Rhode Island creditor, or Massachusetts farmer. Have each student write a series of journal entries about the economic problems that he or she faces when conducting business.

⊠ CLOSE

Have each student make a list of the advantages and disadvantages of rebelling against a government for economic reasons. Lead a class discussion about ways that these advantages or disadvantages applied to Shays's Rebellion.

★ Citizenship

Responses to Shays's Rebellion. One of the American leaders who condemned Shays's Rebellion was Alexander Hamilton, who believed that democracy was dangerous. "Can a democratic assembly who annually revolve in the mass of the people be supposed steadily to pursue the public good? Nothing but a permanent body can check the imprudence of democracy."

CRITICAL THINKING

Have students read Jefferson's response to Shays's Rebellion in this section. Why did Jefferson and Hamilton disagree?

ANSWER: Students should note that Jefferson's quote shows that he thinks people ought to revolt against authority, while Hamilton seems to feel that people do not make sound political judgments and ought to be lead by a permanent authority.

Visual Record Answer

Students might suggest that they appear to be dangerous because they are carrying weapons.

Interpreting the Visual Record

Shays's Rebellion *The followers of Daniel Shays, shown above at left, took possession of a Massachusetts courthouse during their rebellion.* **Do you think this image portrays the rebels as dangerous? Why or why not?**

THE GRANGER COLLECTION, NEW YORK

★ Shays's Rebellion

In September 1786, farmers in three western Massachusetts counties began a revolt. Bands of angry citizens armed with pitchforks and other farm tools closed down courts in the western part of the state. Their reasoning was simple—with the courts shut down, no one's property could be taken. This uprising became known as **Shays's Rebellion**. A poor farmer and Revolutionary War veteran named **Daniel Shays** was its main leader. The state government ordered the farmers to stop the revolt and threatened death to any captured rebel. However, these threats only made Shays and his followers more determined. Shays asked other citizens to join the rebellion. He signed a document stating, "The seeds of war are now sown. . . . Our cause is yours. Don't give yourself a rest and let us die here."

In September the rebels forced the state supreme court in the town of Springfield to close. Shays's forces returned to Springfield the next month, hoping to capture a federal weapons storehouse. This time, state troops defeated the rebels in a short battle in January 1787. By February many rebels had surrendered or been arrested. During their trials, 14 leaders were sentenced to death. However, the state soon freed most of the rebels, including Shays. State officials knew that many citizens in Massachusetts agreed with the rebels and their motives.

The rebellion greatly upset many political leaders. George Washington exclaimed, "I am mortified [embarrassed] beyond expression." He feared that the United States must look "ridiculous . . . in the eyes of all Europe." Not everyone saw the rebellion this way, however. Thomas Jefferson, serving as ambassador to France, also responded to the event. He said, "A little rebellion, now and then, is a good thing. . . . The tree of liberty must be refreshed from time to time with the blood of patriots and tyrants."

⭐ REVIEW AND ASSESS

Have students complete the **Section 2 Review** on p. 235. Then have students complete **Daily Quiz 8.2**. As **Alternative Assessment**, you may want to use the students' newspaper headlines, journal entries, or petitions in this section's lessons.

⭐ RETEACH

Have students complete **Main Idea Activity for English Language Learners and Special-Needs Students 8.2**. Draw students' attention to the British periodical quotation in this section that calls the United States the "Dis-United States." Have students create two lists. Instruct the class to label the first list *United States* and have them include in their list examples from

this section that show that the states were united. Tell students to label the second list *Dis-United States* and to include examples showing that the states were disunited.
ENGLISH LANGUAGE LEARNERS

⭐ EXTEND

Have students conduct research to find examples of other revolts that had economic origins, particularly unjust taxation or restriction of trade. (Tell students not to research the American Revolution.) Have each student make a chart comparing and contrasting those revolts to Shays's Rebellion. Charts should include information about causes, actions, and consequences. Ask volunteers to present their charts to the class. **BLOCK SCHEDULING**

In the end, Shays's Rebellion helped reveal the weakness of the Confederation government. It led some Americans to admit that the Articles of Confederation were not working. When Massachusetts had asked the national government to help put down Shays's Rebellion, Congress could offer little help. More Americans began calling for a stronger central government. They wanted leaders who would be able to protect the nation in times of crisis.

✔ **Reading Check: Finding the Main Idea** What was Shays's Rebellion, and why was it important? an uprising of farmers who closed down courts in western Massachusetts; demonstrated weaknesses of Articles of Confederation

⭐ A Push for Change

In 1786 the Virginia legislature called for a national conference to talk about changing the Articles of Confederation. The meeting took place in Annapolis, Maryland, in September 1786. Only five states sent delegates to the Annapolis Convention, however. The New England states, the Carolinas, and Georgia were not represented. Even Maryland hesitated to send delegates.

James Madison and Alexander Hamilton attended the Annapolis Convention. At their urging, the Annapolis delegates called on all 13 states to send delegates to a Constitutional Convention at Philadelphia, in May 1787. They hoped this Convention would improve the national government. They wanted to make "the constitution of the Federal Government adequate to the exigencies [needs] of the Union."

✔ **Reading Check: Analyzing Information** How did the states address the problems of the central government? Some states sent delegates to the Annapolis Convention. Some delegates called for a new constitutional convention.

Alexander Hamilton was a lawyer with considerable influence in New York politics.

Section 2 Review

go.hrw.com Homework Practice Online
keyword: SA3 HP8

❶ **Define and explain:**
• tariffs
• interstate commerce
• inflation
• debtors
• creditors
• depression

❷ **Identify and explain:**
• Shays's Rebellion
• Daniel Shays

❸ **Categorizing** Copy the graphic organizer below. Use it to identify the domestic and international problems that arose under the Articles of Confederation.

Domestic Problems	International Problems

Articles of Confederation

❹ **Finding the Main Idea**
a. In what ways did Great Britain and Spain take advantage of the weaknesses of the United States under its new government?
b. Why did Massachusetts's farmers take part in Shays's Rebellion, and what was the result of the rebellion?

❺ **Writing and Critical Thinking**
Supporting a Point of View Imagine that you are a delegate to the Annapolis Convention. Write a letter to the states not attending the convention that explains why they should attend the next convention in Philadelphia.

Consider the following:
• economic problems under the Articles of Confederation
• problems with defining the authority of the central government
• social problems under the Articles of Confederation

Section 2 Review ANSWERS

❶ **Define**
• tariffs, p. 232
• interstate commerce, p. 232
• inflation, p. 232
• debtors, p. 233
• creditors, p. 233
• depression, p. 233

❷ **Identify**
• Shays's Rebellion, p. 234
• Daniel Shays, p. 234

❸ international problems—U.S. could not enforce Treaty of Paris and could not protect U.S. citizens when Spain closed the lower Mississippi to U.S. shipping; Britain closed ports to U.S. shipping and charged American merchants high tariffs; domestic problems—Confederation Congress could not regulate interstate commerce and could not address problem of inflation and economic depression; Congress could not send troops to put down Shays's Rebellion

❹ a. Britain cut off trade to the West Indies and refused to withdraw quickly from the Great Lakes region, Spain closed the lower Mississippi to U.S. shipping
b. farmers were upset by the state's economic policies and wanted to prevent the courts from taking their property; they were defeated by the state militia but were freed; the rebellion convinced many people that the Articles of Confederation were too weak.

❺ Students' letters will vary but should focus on the need for the Philadelphia convention.

Section 3

OBJECTIVES

⭐ Explain why delegates met at the Constitutional Convention.

⭐ Examine the main issues debated and the compromises that were reached at the Constitutional Convention.

⭐ Describe how the federal government is balanced under the U.S. Constitution.

SECTION 3 RESOURCES

REPRODUCIBLE

▶ Guided Reading Strategy 8.3

▶ Graphic Organizer 8: Comparing Systems of Government

TECHNOLOGY

▶ One-Stop Planner, Lesson 8.3

▶ American History Simulations CD–ROM: The Democracy Project

▶ CNN Presents America: Beginnings to 1914 Segment: Our Most Important Papers

▶ Homework Practice Online

▶ HRW Go site

REINFORCEMENT, REVIEW, AND ASSESSMENT

▶ Section 3 Review, p. 241

▶ Daily Quiz 8.3

▶ Main Idea Activity 8.3

▶ English Audio Summary 8.3

▶ Spanish Audio Summary 8.3

Technology Resources

 American History Simulations CD–ROM: The Democracy Project

🎵 LET'S GET STARTED!

As students enter the classroom, ask them to imagine that they are delegates to the Constitutional Convention. Ask each student to write a brief list of problems that the Articles of Confederation failed to solve. (*Students' lists might include excessive taxation, lack of representation in government, failure to respect natural rights, or other logical answers.*) Explain to the students that if the new U.S. government was going to survive, the problems they mentioned had to be solved. Tell students that in Section 3 they will learn about how political leaders created a new system of government for the United States.

Section 3

The Constitution

Read to Discover

1. Why did the delegates meet for the Constitutional Convention?
2. What were some of the main issues debated and compromises reached at the Constitutional Convention?
3. How is the federal government balanced under the U.S. Constitution?

WHY IT MATTERS TODAY

Debate and compromise are still an important part of government in the United States. Use CNN**fyi**.com or other **current events** sources to learn about a recent political debate in the U.S. Congress. Record your findings in your journal.

Define
- popular sovereignty
- federalism
- legislative branch
- executive branch
- judicial branch
- checks and balances

Identify
- Constitutional Convention
- James Madison
- Virginia Plan
- William Paterson
- New Jersey Plan
- Great Compromise
- Three-Fifths Compromise

The Story Continues

In 1786 a Pennsylvania newspaper printed an article about the U.S. government stating that the government could not afford to pay ambassador John Adams. The newspaper's editors were shocked. "Ought we not to blush . . . that the ambassadors of the states are . . . depending on foreign charity for their support?" John Adams's wife, Abigail, agreed. She felt that this was an embarrassment. She noted that "with the present salary and the present temper of the English no one need envy the [American] embassy." Such problems led some Americans to seek a more powerful national government.

John Adams served as U.S. ambassador to Great Britain.

⭐ The Constitutional Convention

By the mid-1780s most political leaders agreed that it was time to change the Articles of Confederation. In February 1787 the Confederation Congress invited each state to send delegates to a convention in Philadelphia. The delegates planned to discuss ways to improve the

★ TEACH

Have students read Section 3 and complete Guided Reading Strategy 8.3. Choose one or more of the following activities to explore the section content with students. For further suggestions on block scheduling or team teaching, see the *Block Scheduling Handbook with Team Teaching Strategies*.

LEVEL 1: As a class, read the section entitled The Constitutional Convention. Ask students why the Confederation Congress invited state delegates to attend the Constitutional Convention and what the Congress hoped to accomplish. *(Students' responses should mention that the delegates planned to discuss ways to change the Articles of Confederation.)* Then have students create a persuasive invitation to send to proposed delegates explaining the Convention's purpose. **ENGLISH LANGUAGE LEARNERS**

Articles of Confederation. The **Constitutional Convention** was held in May 1787 in Philadelphia's State House, now called Independence Hall. It was in this same building that Americans had officially declared their independence. Twelve states sent a total of 55 delegates to the Convention. Only Rhode Island refused to send a delegation.

The delegates were a remarkable group. Most were well educated, and many of them had served in state legislatures or the Confederation Congress. Benjamin Franklin of Pennsylvania was the oldest delegate. **James Madison** proved to be one of the most important delegates to the Convention. Madison took good notes and joined many talks during the Convention. Revolutionary War hero George Washington was part of the Virginia delegation and was soon elected president of the whole Convention.

Several important American political leaders did not attend the Convention. John Adams and Thomas Jefferson were serving as ambassadors. Others, like Revolutionary hero Patrick Henry, chose not to attend because they were against such a meeting. The states did not choose any women, African Americans, or American Indians as delegates to the Convention. Members of these groups did not yet have the rights of full citizens. Thus, the Convention's leaders believed they could not represent other citizens in government.

✔ **Reading Check: Finding the Main Idea** Who were some of the delegates at the Constitutional Convention, and what did they hope to accomplish? Answers might include James Madison and George Washington. They hoped to change the Articles of Confederation.

★ The Great Compromise

Several issues divided the delegates to the Constitutional Convention. Some members wanted only to make small changes to the Articles of Confederation, while others wanted to rewrite the Articles. But the delegates who wanted major changes in the Articles had different goals. For example, small and large states had different concerns about representation. States also had different views about regional issues such as slavery. Economic issues such as tariffs also divided northerners from southerners. In addition, there was disagreement over how strong to make the national government.

After the delegates had met for four days, Edmund Randolph of Virginia presented the **Virginia Plan**. James Madison wrote most of this plan, also called the large-state plan. It offered a new federal constitution that would give sovereignty, or supreme power, to the central government. The Virginia Plan divided the national government into three branches: executive, judicial, and legislative.

★★★★★★★★★★★★★
That's Interesting!
★★★★★★★★★★★★★

A "Heated" Debate Can you imagine sitting in a very hot room wearing a heavy suit and stockings? How about doing so in the middle of the summer with no air conditioning? That's what the framers of the Constitution did when they met in Philadelphia in 1787. Although it was hot, they kept the windows closed to keep out flies and so no one in the streets could hear their discussions. Despite the discomfort, the Founders were able to write a new Constitution for their country.

THE GRANGER COLLECTION, NEW YORK

Delegates from 12 of the 13 states gathered at Philadelphia's Independence Hall to revise the Articles of Confederation.

Interdisciplinary Connection

▶**Literature**◀

Preparing to Write the Constitution. James Madison began preparing for the Constitutional Convention in the fall of 1786 by rereading political history, works of classical republicanism, and works of modern political theory. With Thomas Jefferson's help, Madison had acquired a small library of the social and economic philosophies of the Enlightenment, including the 37-volume set of Denis Diderot's *Encyclopédie*, a compilation of knowledge and Enlightenment thought. In addition, Madison prepared two papers—one on the weaknesses of modern and ancient confederacies, and another entitled "Vices of the Political System of the United States," which outlined the political philosophy that he applied when creating the Constitution.

CRITICAL THINKING

How did Madison's preparation help the delegates to the Constitutional Convention?

ANSWER: Students might suggest that Madison's reading provided delegates with inspirational new ideas and that his writing analyzed previous political situations.

Visual Record Answer

(for p. 238)

Students might suggest that they are huddled together as if they are working with one another.

ALL LEVELS: Copy the following graphic organizer onto the chalkboard, omitting the italicized answers. Have students complete the chart with at least five delegates who took part in the Convention. Students should then identify each delegate's individual positions and contributions. As a class, discuss why delegates met at the Constitutional Convention.

ENGLISH LANGUAGE LEARNERS

Delegate	Positions and Contributions
James Madison	took good notes, joined many talks, wrote most of the Virginia Plan
George Washington	elected president of the Convention
Edmund Randolph	presented the Virginia Plan
William Paterson	presented the New Jersey Plan
Gouverneur Morris	spoke strongly against counting slaves in determining congressional representation
George Mason/John Dickinson	wanted to stop the slave trade
John Rutledge	supported the slave trade
Elbridge Gerry/ Edmund Randolph/ George Mason	refused to sign the Constitution

★ Global Relations

Hamilton on Government. Amidst the dispute over state representation, Alexander Hamilton gave one of the longest speeches at the Constitutional Convention. He was a strong supporter of the British government and urged delegates to create one like it. He advised that the presidency should be a lifetime job and even offered his own plan for the government—one modeled on Britain's. It seems that the rest of the delegates simply ignored Hamilton's suggestions and returned to discussion of the New Jersey Plan.

internet connect

TOPIC: Alexander Hamilton
GO TO: go.hrw.com
KEYWORD: SA3 CF8

Have students search the Internet through the HRW Go site to find more information about Alexander Hamilton's political beliefs. Have students use standard grammar, spelling, sentence structure, and punctuation to write an article summarizing some of his beliefs.

Visual Record Answer

(for p. 239)
She is offering books.

This engraving advised women that their proper place was in the home. Such attitudes were one reason that no female delegates were sent to the Constitutional Convention.

Interpreting the Visual Record

Constitutional compromises The delegates at the Constitutional Convention had to compromise to make progress. **How does this sculpture show delegates working together to address issues?**

The legislature in this plan would be a bicameral, or two-house, legislature. This arrangement was similar to that used by several state assemblies. Representatives in the legislature would be chosen on the basis of state populations. Larger states would thus have more representatives than smaller states. Delegates from the smaller states did not like the Virginia Plan. They argued that it would give too much power to the larger states.

The delegates debated about the Virginia Plan for two weeks. New Jersey delegate **William Paterson** then presented the small-state or **New Jersey Plan**. This plan proposed keeping Congress's structure the same. It called for a unicameral, or one-house, legislature. In this case each state would have an equal number of votes, giving the smaller states an equal voice in the national government. The New Jersey Plan proposed that all acts passed by Congress "shall be the supreme law of the respective States." The plan gave the central government the power to tax citizens in all states. It also allowed the government to regulate commerce. Delegates from the large states were against the New Jersey Plan, which would give smaller states more influence.

After a month of debate, the delegates were still unable to agree. The Convention formed a committee to determine how states should be represented. The committee proposed a compromise—an agreement in which both sides give up some of their demands so that other demands can be met. Some historians call this agreement at the Convention the **Great Compromise**. Every state, regardless of its size, would have an equal vote in the upper house of the legislature. This would satisfy supporters of the New Jersey Plan. In the lower house, each state would have a number of representatives based on its population. This proposal would please those who liked the Virginia Plan. The delegates passed the Great Compromise, but there were still problems to settle.

✔ **Reading Check: Contrasting** What were the differences between the Virginia Plan and the New Jersey Plan, and how were these resolved? Congress based on population versus equal representation; Great Compromise based lower house on population, upper house on equal representation

NEBRASKA STATE HISTORICAL SOCIETY

★ The Three-Fifths Compromise

The debate over representation also involved some regional differences. Southern delegates wanted slaves to be counted as part of their state populations. This way they would have more representatives in Congress. Northerners disagreed. They wanted the number of slaves to determine taxes but not representation.

To resolve this problem, some delegates proposed counting three fifths of the slaves in each state as part of its population. This number would then decide how many representatives a state would have in the lower house. New York delegate Gouverneur Morris spoke with much emotion against this idea.

History Makers Speak ❝The admission of slaves into the Representation . . . comes to this: that the inhabitant of [a state] who goes to the coast of Africa and . . . tears away his fellow creatures from their dearest connections and damns them to the most cruel bondage [slavery], shall have more votes in a Government [established] for protection of the rights of mankind.❞

—Gouverneur Morris, quoted in *Founding the Republic*, edited by John J. Patrick

However, the delegates voted to accept the so-called **Three-Fifths Compromise**. Under this agreement each slave would, in effect, be counted as three fifths of a person when determining representation.

Another major issue was the foreign slave trade. Some of the delegates wanted the federal government to end the slave trade. These people included George Mason of Virginia and John Dickinson of Delaware. Others said that the southern states' economies needed the slave trade. South Carolina delegate John Rutledge noted, "The people of these States will never be such fools as to give up so important an interest." Some of these southern delegates even threatened to leave the Union if the Constitution immediately ended the slave trade.

Worried delegates reached another compromise. Northern delegates agreed to wait 20 years before seeking to end the slave trade. Southern delegates agreed to stop insisting that laws in Congress be passed with a two-thirds majority vote. Oliver Ellsworth summed up the view of many delegates. He said, "The morality or wisdom of slavery . . . are considerations belonging to the states themselves."

✔ **Reading Check: Finding the Main Idea** What key compromises did delegates make about slavery at the Constitutional Convention? Three-Fifths Compromise; North—postponed its demands to ban the slave trade; South—gave up the demand that Congress pass all laws by a two-thirds majority vote

THE LIBRARY COMPANY OF PHILADELPHIA

Interpreting the Visual Record

Liberty *This antislavery painting shows a woman representing Liberty offering to aid freed slaves.* **What does Liberty offer to the freed slaves in the painting?**

Forming a Government **239**

LEVEL 3: Select six volunteers to participate in a debate. Have three students represent the large states and the other three represent the small states. Have the group representing large states prepare arguments in favor of the Virginia Plan, and the group representing the small states prepare arguments supporting the New Jersey Plan. Moderate a debate between the two groups. Have the rest of the class represent other delegates who ask questions and challenge each group's position. Conclude by working out a compromise among the debaters and the class. Finally, review the terms of the Great Compromise with the class.
COOPERATIVE LEARNING

★ CLOSE

Remind students that the framers of the Constitution sought to create a balance of power not only among the three branches of government but also between the federal government and the state governments. Have students create a political cartoon describing the balance of power that was created by the Constitution. Ask students to provide captions for their cartoons, and then have students post their cartoons around the classroom for other students to examine.

Analyzing Primary Sources
Evaluating How does this quotation support the principle of federalism? It states that the Constitution and federal laws override conflicting state laws.

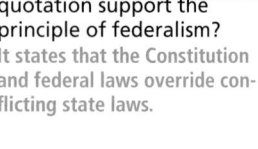

LINKING PAST to PRESENT ★

National Currency

The U.S. Constitution gives the federal government the sole power to issue legal currency, or money. Until the mid-1800s, however, many state banks could print banknotes. These notes could be exchanged at the bank that issued them for their value in gold or silver coins. However, banks often refused to accept notes from other banks, which interfered with trade. The federal government stopped the issuing of banknotes in the mid-1860s and created a national currency.

Recently, the Treasury has redesigned paper money to make it harder to copy. The U.S. Mint has also introduced new coins such as the state quarters and the Sacagawea gold dollar coin. **How does our national currency demonstrate the system of federalism?**

★ Our Living Constitution

Most of the convention delegates wanted a strong national government to replace the Articles of Confederation. At the same time they wanted to protect **popular sovereignty**—the idea that political authority belongs to the people. They also wanted to balance the power of the national government with the powers of the states. Therefore, the delegates looked to **federalism**, or the sharing of power between a central government and the states that make up a country.

In this system, the federal government has power to enforce its laws in the states. This idea is stated in Article VI of the Constitution.

 History Makers Speak "This Constitution and the Laws of the United States which shall be made in Pursuance thereof; and all Treaties made, or which shall be made, under the Authority of the United States, shall be the supreme Law of the Land; and the Judges in every State shall be bound thereby, any Thing in the Constitution or Laws of any State to the Contrary notwithstanding."

—The Constitution of the United States

Each state must obey the authority of the federal government. Article VI also notes that all state officials are required "by Oath . . . to support this Constitution." The federal government has the power to use the military to enforce its laws. These troops are under the command of the president.

Under the Constitution, states have control over government functions not specifically assigned to the federal government. For example, the states control local government, education, and the chartering of corporations. States also create and oversee civil and criminal law. States must also protect the welfare of their citizens.

✔ **Reading Check: Summarizing** What are some of the powers that belong to the states under the Constitution? controlling local government and education, the chartering of corporations, handling civil and criminal law, and protecting citizens' welfare

★ A Delicate Balance

The Constitution also balances the powers within the federal government. For this reason the federal government has three branches. Each is responsible for separate tasks. The first is the **legislative branch**, or Congress, which is responsible for proposing and passing laws. It is made up of two houses. The Senate, or upper house, has two members from each state, while in the House of Representatives, or lower house, each state is represented according to its population.

The second branch of the federal government is the **executive branch**. This branch includes the president and the departments that help run the government. The executive branch makes sure that laws are carried out. The third branch is the **judicial branch**, which is made up of all the national courts. This branch is responsible for interpreting laws,

☆ REVIEW AND ASSESS

Have students complete the **Section 3 Review** on p. 241. Then have students complete **Daily Quiz 8.3**. As **Alternative Assessment**, you may want to use the students' newspaper articles or political cartoons in this section's lessons.

☆ RETEACH

Have students complete **Main Idea Activity for English Language Learners and Special-Needs Students 8.3**. Then ask students to work with a partner to create a glossary for a new textbook about the Constitutional Convention. The glossary should include descriptions of each of the significant individuals,

major plans, significant compromises, and legal and governmental terms discussed in the section. Ask volunteers to share their work with the class. **ENGLISH LANGUAGE LEARNERS** , **COOPERATIVE LEARNING**

☆ EXTEND

Have students use the library to find pictorial representations of the events that took place at the Constitutional Convention. Then have students imagine the conversation that may have been talking place at that time. Students should then write a skit based on the selected image. **BLOCK SCHEDULING**

punishing criminals, and settling disputes between states. (*For the full text of the U.S. Constitution, see pages 264–83.*)

The framers of the Constitution created a system of **checks and balances** to keep any branch of government from becoming too powerful. For example, the framers gave Congress power to propose and pass legislation. The president has the power to veto, or reject, laws that Congress passes. However, Congress can override the president's veto with a two-thirds majority vote. Interpretation of the Constitution has provided the judicial branch with its own check. This check is the Supreme Court's power to review the laws passed by Congress. The Court may strike down a law that it finds unconstitutional—in violation of the Constitution.

The delegates knew that the Constitution was not a perfect document. They believed, however, that they had founded a strong government that still protected the ideas of republicanism. The long and difficult debates at the Constitutional Convention lasted 16 weeks. Finally, in September 1787 the delegates signed a final draft of the Constitution. Only three of the 42 delegates who remained refused to sign. These three were Elbridge Gerry of Massachusetts and Edmund Randolph and George Mason of Virginia. The delegates then sent the Constitution to Congress, which sent it to the states for ratification.

✔ **Reading Check: Summarizing** How was the government structured under the new Constitution, and how was power balanced? three branches—executive, legislative, and judicial; through checks and balances, and federal government's authority to enforce federal laws within states

This early draft of the Constitution shows corrections and comments by George Washington.

September 1787
The final draft of the Constitution is signed.

go. hrw .com Homework Practice Online
keyword: SA3 HP8

Section 3 Review

❶ **Define** and explain:
• popular sovereignty
• federalism
• legislative branch
• executive branch
• judicial branch
• checks and balances

❷ **Identify** and explain:
• Constitutional Convention
• James Madison
• Virginia Plan
• William Paterson
• New Jersey Plan
• Great Compromise
• Three-Fifths Compromise

❸ **Summarizing** Copy the graphic organizer below. Use it to explain the major compromises that took place at the Constitutional Convention.

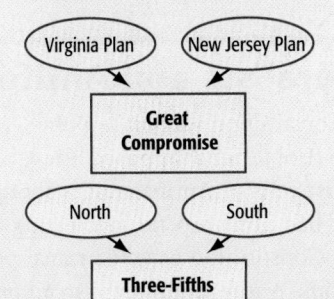

Virginia Plan → Great Compromise ← New Jersey Plan
North / South → Three-Fifths Compromise

❹ **Finding the Main Idea**
a. What was the original purpose of the Constitutional Convention?

b. How does the Constitution reflect the ideas of republicanism and limited government?

❺ **Writing and Critical Thinking**
Evaluating Imagine that you are a political scholar writing about the Constitutional Convention. Write an essay explaining how the actions of the Founding Fathers represented good citizenship.

Consider the following:
• the actions and beliefs of the Founding Fathers
• what it means to be a good citizen

Section 4

OBJECTIVES

✪ Explain why some people were against the new Constitution.

✪ Examine the *Federalist Papers'* arguments for the Constitution.

✪ Describe when and how the Constitution was ratified.

✪ Identify the reasons some people wanted a bill of rights, and explain how it was added to the Constitution.

SECTION 4 RESOURCES

REPRODUCIBLE

▶ Guided Reading Strategy 8.4

▶ Biography Reading 8: George Mason

▶ Geography Activity 8: Ratification of the Constitution

▶ American History Political Cartoon 2: Ratifying the Constitution

TECHNOLOGY

▶ One-Stop Planner, Lesson 8.4

▶ Holt Researcher: American History CD–ROM

▶ Homework Practice Online

REINFORCEMENT, REVIEW, AND ASSESSMENT

▶ Section 4 Review, p. 247

▶ Daily Quiz 8.4

▶ Main Idea Activity 8.4

▶ English Audio Summary 8.4

▶ Spanish Audio Summary 8.4

Section 4

Ratification of the Constitution

Read to Discover

1. Why were some people against the new Constitution?
2. What arguments for the Constitution did the *Federalist Papers* present?
3. When and how was the Constitution ratified?
4. Why did some people want a bill of rights, and how was it added to the Constitution?

WHY IT MATTERS TODAY

Debate still takes place over how much power the federal government has over the states. Use **CNNfyi.com** or other **current events** sources to study a recent dispute or legal case between a state and the federal government. Record your findings in your journal.

Define

• amendments

Identify

• Antifederalists
• George Mason
• Federalists
• *Federalist Papers*
• Bill of Rights

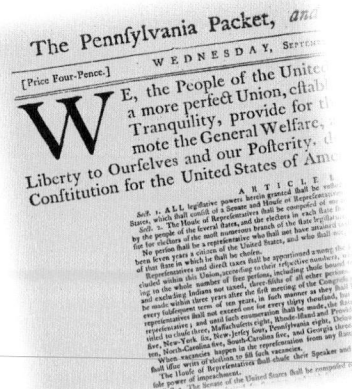

Newspapers supplied most Americans with their first look at the text of the Constitution.

The Story Continues

John Dunlap and David Claypoole stayed up well into the night on September 17, 1787. They reset type and filled all four pages of their Philadelphia newspaper. Dunlap and Claypoole had begun their work only hours after the end of the Constitutional Convention. The next morning, they presented the first printed copy of the U.S. Constitution.

✪ Federalists and Antifederalists

When the Constitution was made public, a great debate began among Americans. People who opposed the Constitution were known as **Antifederalists**. Some Antifederalists thought that the Constitutional Convention had gone too far in creating a new government. Others thought the Constitution gave too much power to the central government. For some Antifederalists, the main problem was that the Constitution did not include a bill of rights. Constitutional Convention delegate **George Mason** became an Antifederalist for this reason.

Have students read Section 4 and complete Guided Reading Strategy 8.4. Choose one or more of the following activities to explore the section content with students. For further suggestions on block scheduling or team teaching, see the *Block Scheduling Handbook with Team Teaching Strategies.*

 LEVEL 1: Lead a class discussion about the debate over adding a bill of rights to the Constitution. Ask students to imagine that they are businesspeople who want to take advantage of the debate concerning a bill of rights. Have them design banners or signs that give reasons for supporting or opposing a bill of rights. Encourage students to

review material from this section when developing slogans or symbols for their work. **ENGLISH LANGUAGE LEARNERS**

ALL LEVELS: Ask volunteers to list on the chalkboard the *Federalist Papers'* main arguments for the Constitution. (*Students' responses should include: the states would not be overpowered by the new federal government, and the diversity of the United States would prevent any single group from dominating the country.*) Have students work with a partner to create a dialog between two writers of the *Federalist Papers* who are developing an argument for a Constitution.
ENGLISH LANGUAGE LEARNERS , COOPERATIVE LEARNING

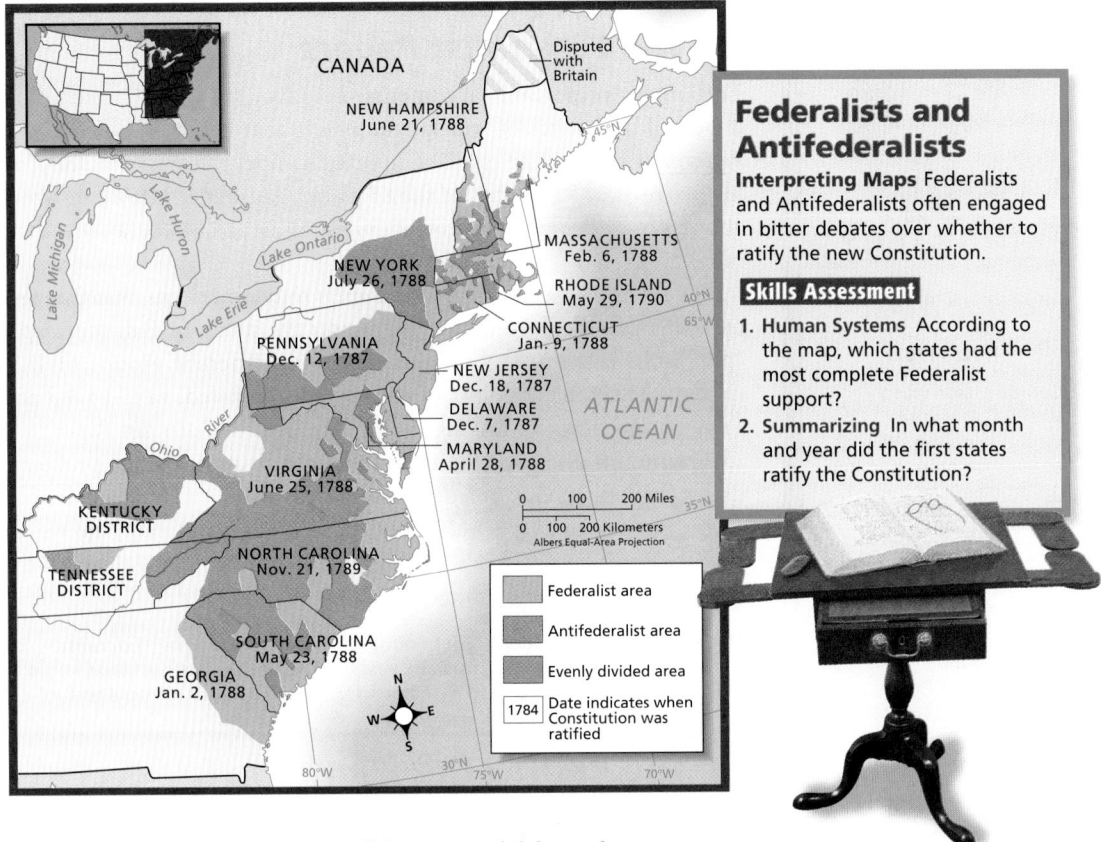

Federalists and Antifederalists

Interpreting Maps Federalists and Antifederalists often engaged in bitter debates over whether to ratify the new Constitution.

Skills Assessment

1. **Human Systems** According to the map, which states had the most complete Federalist support?
2. **Summarizing** In what month and year did the first states ratify the Constitution?

CANADA

Disputed with Britain

NEW HAMPSHIRE
June 21, 1788

MASSACHUSETTS
Feb. 6, 1788

NEW YORK
July 26, 1788

RHODE ISLAND
May 29, 1790

CONNECTICUT
Jan. 9, 1788

PENNSYLVANIA
Dec. 12, 1787

NEW JERSEY
Dec. 18, 1787

DELAWARE
Dec. 7, 1787

ATLANTIC OCEAN

MARYLAND
April 28, 1788

VIRGINIA
June 25, 1788

KENTUCKY DISTRICT

TENNESSEE DISTRICT

NORTH CAROLINA
Nov. 21, 1789

SOUTH CAROLINA
May 23, 1788

GEORGIA
Jan. 2, 1788

Lake Michigan · Lake Huron · Lake Ontario · Lake Erie · Ohio River

0   100   200 Miles
0 100   200 Kilometers
Albers Equal-Area Projection

Federalist area

Antifederalist area

Evenly divided area

1784 Date indicates when Constitution was ratified

The Fight in Virginia.
Patrick Henry repeatedly warned Virginia's ratifying convention of the horrors of federalism. At one point the scribe recording the convention, unable to keep up with Henry, wrote: "Here Mr. Henry strongly and pathetically expatiated [discussed] on the probability of the President's enslaving America, and the horrid consequences that must result."

CRITICAL THINKING
How might Henry's speech-making have hurt his cause?

ANSWER: Students might suggest that the other delegates may have taken Henry less seriously when they heard his exaggerations, or they might have come to dislike Henry.

MAP ANSWERS
1. Delaware and New Jersey (both are shaded completely Federalist)
2. December 1787

Many Antifederalists were small farmers and debtors, but some were wealthy. Some heroes of the American Revolution were also strong Antifederalists, such as Richard Henry Lee, Samuel Adams, and Patrick Henry. As the Constitution was debated in Virginia, George Mason warned against the power of a strong central government.

History Makers Speak ❝The very idea of converting [changing] what was formerly a confederation to a consolidated [united] government, is totally subversive of [against] every principle which has hitherto [before] governed us. This power is calculated to annihilate [destroy] totally the state governments.❞

—George Mason, quoted in *Great Issues in American History,* edited by Richard Hofstadter

Analyzing Primary Sources
Identifying Points of View
What did George Mason believe a strong central government would do to the states? completely destroy them

Antifederalists were challenged by many Americans who believed that the United States needed a stronger Constitution. Supporters of the Constitution called themselves **Federalists**. James Madison, George Washington, Benjamin Franklin, Alexander Hamilton, and John Jay were Federalists. Most Federalists believed that the Constitution offered a good balance of power. They thought it was a careful compromise between various political views.

✔ **Reading Check: Identifying Points of View** What were some of the Antifederalists' arguments against the Constitution? central government too powerful, no protection for individual rights, delegates exceeded authority

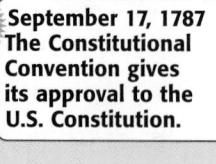 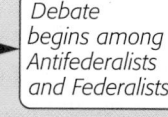 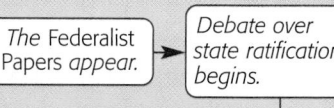
September 17, 1787 The Constitutional Convention gives its approval to the U.S. Constitution. → *Debate begins among Antifederalists and Federalists.* → The *Federalist Papers appear.* → *Debate over state ratification begins.*

Legislators create a list of 12 amendments to send to the states for ratification, which will add strength and flexibility to the Constitution. ← *In Congress's first session, Madison encourages legislators to put together a bill of rights.* ← *Rhode Island is the last state to ratify the Constitution.* ← *Delaware is the first state to ratify Constitution.*

December 1791 Three fourths of the states have ratified 10 of the proposed amendments as a bill of rights.

THE GRANGER COLLECTION, NEW YORK

BIOGRAPHY

George Mason
(1725–1792)

George Mason was a Virginia planter who turned to politics. He became devoted to limited government and the protection of human rights. His many speeches and writings greatly influenced the development of the U.S. government. One of his most important works was the Virginia Declaration of Rights, which served as a model for the bills of rights of many states. Although Mason served as a delegate to the Constitutional Convention, he refused to sign the Constitution because it did not include a bill of rights. **What role did George Mason play in shaping American government?**

★ The *Federalist Papers*

The most important arguments in favor of the Constitution appeared in a series of widely read essays that became known as the **Federalist Papers**. The essays were written under the name Publius, but historians now know that of the 85 essays, Alexander Hamilton wrote about 50. James Madison wrote about 30 essays, and John Jay wrote the other 5.

The authors of the *Federalist Papers* told Americans that the new federal government would not overpower the states. In *Federalist Paper* "No. 10," Madison wrote about the many different groups of U.S. citizens. Their many points of view, Madison stated, would keep any single group from controlling the government. In *Federalist Paper* "No. 15," Hamilton discussed the need to fix the country's many problems under the Articles of Confederation. "Let us make a firm stand for our safety, our tranquillity [peace], our dignity, our reputation," he wrote. The *Federalist Papers* were widely reprinted and strongly influenced the debate over the Constitution.

✔ **Reading Check: Identifying Points of View** How did the *Federalist Papers* defend the Constitution? reassured Americans that the states would not be overpowered, argued that diversity of the United States would protect democracy

★ The Ratification Fight

The true test of the Constitution's support came during the debate over state ratification, or approval. The Articles of Confederation had needed the approval of all 13 states to go into effect. However, the Constitution needed only 9 states to pass it. Each state except Rhode Island held special state conventions to give citizens the chance to discuss the Constitution. Then they could vote on whether the Constitution should be ratified.

Antifederalists also spoke out in state conventions. In New York one citizen said, "It appears that the government will fall into the hands of the few and the great." At the Virginia ratification convention, Patrick Henry spoke for many Antifederalists.

Analyzing Primary Sources
Identifying Points of View
What did Patrick Henry fear about the new form of government? that the government could not hold the states together and that there would be no real checks and balances

 History Makers Speak

❝If you make the citizens of this country agree to become the subjects of one great consolidated [united] empire of America, your government will not have sufficient energy to keep them together. . . . There will be no checks, no real balances, in this government.❞

—Patrick Henry, quoted in *Great Issues in American History*, edited by Richard Hofstadter

The Constitution had the support of heroes of the American Revolution such as Benjamin Franklin, Paul Revere, and George Washington. At the Massachusetts convention, Revere helped win the backing of other craftspeople.

Tom Harris of Leesburg, Florida, suggested the following activity:

 ALL LEVELS: Organize the class into groups. Explain to students that they are going to modernize the Bill of Rights. Have each group discuss concepts in the Bill of Rights that seem unclear or need to be written in a way that is easier to understand. Then have each group decide which amendments it would like to alter and what changes should be made. Ask students to rewrite the amendments. Have groups explain to the rest of the class the changes they made to the Bill of Rights. **ENGLISH LANGUAGE LEARNERS**

 LEVEL 2: Organize the class into small groups. Then give each group several sheets of poster board. Have groups create a design for a Web site that outlines the Federalists', Antifederalists', and *Federalist Papers'* arguments for ratification of the Constitution. Ask each group to design a home page that lists background information on the debate for ratification and why some were against this new Constitution. Remind students to include "links" (which students should make up) to a Federalist page or an Antifederalist page, as well as pages to key players in the ratification fight. **COOPERATIVE LEARNING**

On December 7, 1787, Delaware became the first state to ratify the Constitution. Throughout the rest of 1787 and the first half of 1788, eight other states ratified the Constitution. They did so in the following order: Pennsylvania, New Jersey, Georgia, Connecticut, Massachusetts, Maryland, South Carolina, and New Hampshire. The Constitution went into effect in June 1788 after New Hampshire became the ninth state to ratify it.

However, there was still debate in New York, North Carolina, Rhode Island, and Virginia. Political leaders across America knew the new government needed the support of Virginia and New York. Virginia had the largest population in the nation. New York was an important center for business and trade. Finally, James Madison and the other Virginia Federalists convinced Virginia to ratify the Constitution in late June 1788. In New York, Federalists John Jay and Alexander Hamilton said that New York City would break away and join the new government if the Constitution was not ratified. New York State finally ratified the Constitution in

June 1788
The Constitution goes into effect.

The Articles of Confederation and the Constitution

ARTICLES	CONSTITUTION
EXECUTIVE BRANCH	
No executive to administer and enforce legislation; Congress has sole authority to govern	President administers and enforces federal laws
Executive committee to oversee government when Congress is out of session	
LEGISLATIVE BRANCH	
A unicameral (one-house) legislature	A bicameral (two-house) legislature
Each state has one vote, regardless of population	Each state has equal representation in the Senate; each state is represented according to population in the House of Representatives
Nine votes (of the original 13) to enact major legislation	Simple majority to enact legislation
JUDICIAL BRANCH	
No national court system	National court system, headed by the Supreme Court
Congress to establish temporary courts to hear cases of piracy	Courts to hear cases involving national laws, treaties, and the Constitution as well as cases between states, between citizens of different states, or between a state and citizen of another state
OTHER MATTERS	
Admission to the Confederation by 9 votes (of 13)	Congress to admit new states; all must have a republican form of government
Amendment of the Articles by unanimous vote	Amendment of the Constitution by two-thirds vote of both houses of Congress or by national convention, followed by ratification by three fourths of the states
The states retain independence	The states accept the Constitution as the supreme law of the land

Interdisciplinary Connection

▶Literature◀

Debating the Ratification on Paper. Like the Federalists, the Antifederalists published hundreds of essays during the debate over ratification. Leading Antifederalist pamphlets included *Letters from the Federal Farmer to the Republican, Observations on the New Constitution . . . by a Columbian Patriot,* and the *Letters of Brutus.* Like Alexander Hamilton, James Madison, and John Jay, who all published under the name "Publius," many Antifederalist writers used names other than their own that were derived from classical Roman sources.

CRITICAL THINKING
Why might Federalist and Antifederalist writers have used pen names derived from classical sources?

ANSWER: Students might suggest that writers from both sides might have wanted to associate their work with the famous philosophers or writers of ancient Rome.

Interpreting the Visual Record

Political parade *Federalists held a parade to celebrate New York's ratification of the Constitution in July 1788.* **Whose name is on the float, and why do you think this person was chosen to represent the Federalist cause?**

THE GRANGER COLLECTION, NEW YORK

July 1788. North Carolina ratified the Constitution in November 1789. Rhode Island was the last state to ratify the Constitution in May 1790.

✔ **Reading Check: Sequencing** In what order did the states ratify the Constitution, and which states ratified the Constitution after it went into effect? order—DE, PA, NJ, GA, CT, MA, MD, SC, NH, VA, NY, NC, RI; after— VA, NC, NY, and RI

✪ Demanding a Bill of Rights

Several states ratified the Constitution only after they were promised that a bill of rights would be added to it. Many Antifederalists did not think that the Constitution would protect personal freedoms. The writer Mercy Otis Warren, an Antifederalist, expressed this concern in Boston's *Columbian Patriot.* "The whole constitution . . . appears a perversion [abuse] of the rights of particular states and of private citizens."

In the new Congress, some Federalists said that the nation did not need a federal bill of rights. They believed that state constitutions already promised these rights. Many Federalists also believed that the whole Constitution itself was a bill of rights. It was, they argued, written to protect the liberty of all U.S. citizens.

James Madison did not think that a bill of rights was necessary. However, he understood that the promise of such a bill had been key to ratification. He therefore wanted to make a bill of rights one of the new government's first priorities. Thomas Jefferson supported Madison's efforts. He wrote that "a bill of rights is what the people are entitled to against every government on earth, . . . and what no just government should refuse." In Congress's first session, Madison encouraged the legislators to put together a bill of rights. Then, the rights would be added to the Constitution as **amendments**—official changes, corrections, or

★ REVIEW AND ASSESS

Have students complete the **Section 4 Review** on p. 247. Then have students complete **Daily Quiz 8.4**. As **Alternative Assessment**, you may want to use the students' essays or Web sites activity in this section's lessons.

★ RETEACH

Have students complete **Main Idea Activity for English Language Learners and Special-Needs Students 8.4**. Then instruct the class to review the Read to Discover questions for this section. Have students create picture postcards that describe the establishment of the new government, along with captions. Encourage volunteers to present their postcards to the class. **ENGLISH LANGUAGE LEARNERS**

★ EXTEND

Explain to students that the U.S. Post Office occasionally issues special stamps to commemorate an individual or event. Have students design a series of commemorative stamps celebrating the Constitution. Encourage students to design stamps that represent the following: the Constitutional Convention and the creation of the Constitution, the battle over ratification between Federalists and Antifederalists, debate over inclusion of the Bill of Rights, and celebration over ratification. Have students reproduce the designs for one of their stamps on poster board, and display the posters around the classroom. **BLOCK SCHEDULING**

additions. In Article V of the Constitution, the Founders had provided a way to change the document. They believed amendments would be necessary to reflect the will of the people. They designed the process to be difficult, however. Proposed amendments must be approved by a two-thirds majority of both houses of Congress. Then they must be ratified by three fourths of the states before taking effect.

To create a list of possible amendments, the legislators took ideas from the state ratifying conventions. They also consulted the Virginia Declaration of Rights and the Declaration of Independence. Members of Congress worked to make sure that the abuses listed in the Declaration would be illegal under the new government. Congress debated the amendments for three months. Finally, in September 1789, Congress proposed 12 amendments, which were then sent to the states for ratification. By December 1791, the required three fourths of the states had ratified 10 of these proposed amendments. These first 10 amendments to the U.S. Constitution are known as the **Bill of Rights**. *(For a full discussion of the Bill of Rights, see Chapter 9.)*

These 10 amendments added to the strength and flexibility of the Constitution. The Bill of Rights also set a clear example of how to amend the Constitution to address the needs of the nation.

The Constitution is a remarkable document. It has clear guidelines and principles, yet can be changed to meet new challenges. The flexibility of the U.S. Constitution has allowed it to survive for more than 200 years. It is the world's oldest written national constitution.

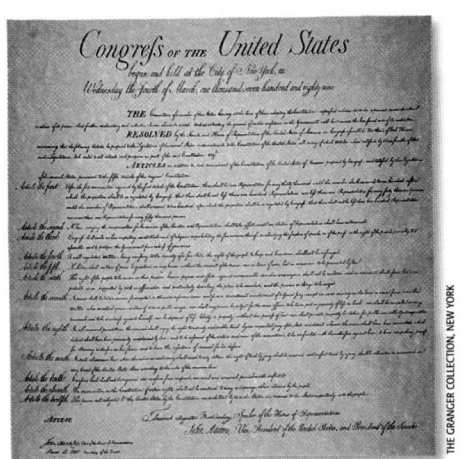

THE GRANGER COLLECTION, NEW YORK

The Bill of Rights assured many Americans that their new government would act to protect their liberties.

✔ **Reading Check: Analyzing Information** Why did some people feel a bill of rights was necessary, and how was it added to the Constitution? to protect individual liberties; through the amendment process

Section 4 Review

go.hrw.com Homework Practice Online

keyword: SA3 HP8

❶ **Define** and explain:
• amendments

❷ **Identify** and explain:
• Antifederalists
• George Mason
• Federalists
• *Federalist Papers*
• Bill of Rights

❸ **Contrasting** Copy the chart below. Use it to identify the arguments for and against the Constitution.

U.S. Constitution

Federalist Views	Antifederalist Views

❹ **Finding the Main Idea**
a. Who wrote the *Federalist Papers*, and what were their arguments?

b. How was the Constitution ratified, and when did it take effect?

❺ **Writing and Critical Thinking**
Summarizing Imagine that you are James Madison. Write an essay arguing why the Constitution should be amended with a bill of rights and explaining the amendment process.

Consider the following:
• the purpose of a Bill of Rights
• those who supported a Bill of Rights in the Constitution
• the process of amending the Constitution

CHAPTER 8 REVIEW ANSWERS

The Chapter at a Glance
Students' posters will vary but should include information about the key issues surrounding the Articles of Confederation, the Constitution, and the Bill of Rights.

Identifying People and Ideas
Students' sentences should indicate an understanding of the following definitions:

1. Virginia law that protected religious freedom

2. first constitution of the new Union; created a central government with limited powers and gave more power to the states

3. established a political system for the region north of the Ohio River; created the Northwest Territory and a system of limited self-government for settlers; also created a system for bringing new states into the union, and abolished slavery in the territory

4. the sharing of power between a central government and the states that make up a country

5. delegate to the Constitutional Convention; writer of the Virginia Plan

6. agreement that resolved the differences that arose over representation in VA & NJ Plans

7. proposal that declared that each slave would be counted as 3/5 of a person

REVIEW AND ASSESSMENT RESOURCES

REPRODUCIBLE

▶ Vocabulary Activity 8

TECHNOLOGY

▶ Chapter 8 Test Generator (on the One-Stop Planner)
▶ Global Skill Builder CD–ROM
▶ HRW Go site

REINFORCEMENT, REVIEW, AND ASSESSMENT

▶ Chapter 8 Review, pp. 247–49
▶ Chapter 8 Tutorial for Students, Parents, Mentors, and Peers

▶ Chapter 8 Test (Form A or B)
▶ Alternative Assessment Handbook
▶ Chapter 8 Test for English Language Learners and Special-Needs Students

★ REVIEW

Have students complete the **Chapter 8 Review** on pages 248–49.

★ ASSESS

Use one of the chapter tests to assess students' understanding of the content. For **Alternative Assessment**, see the **Alternative Assessment Handbook**.

---

8. Antifederalist who expressed concern over the lack of a bill of rights in the new Constitution

9. series of anonymous essays written in defense of the Constitution

10. official changes, corrections, or additions to the Constitution

Understanding Main Ideas

1. Magna Carta, English Bill of Rights, Mayflower Compact, Fundamental Orders of Connecticut, New England town meeting, Declaration of Independence

2. prepared public western lands for sale

3. created and contributed to an economic depression

4. every state would get two votes in the upper house, while each state would get representatives based on population in the lower house

5. into three branches: the legislative, executive, & judicial

6. Federalists—Articles of Confederation were too weak; stronger national government was needed; the Constitution needed for balance of power; Antifederalists—delegates had no right to replace the Articles; human rights would not be protected by the Constitution, and no real checks and balances

Chapter 8 Review

The Chapter at a Glance

Examine the visual summary of the chapter below. Then create a poster illustrating the chapter's main ideas that you might present to the class.

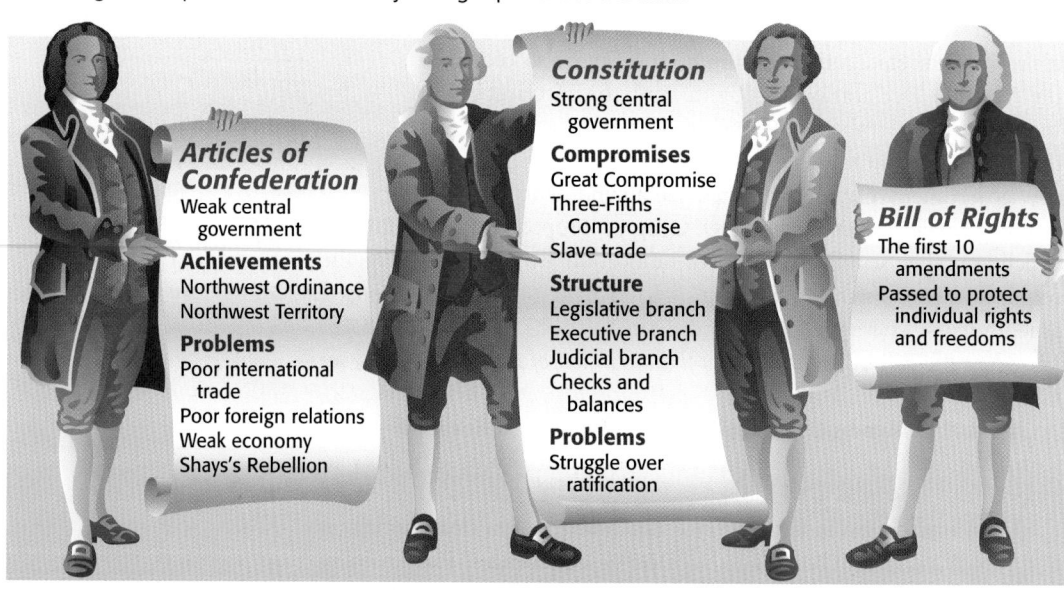

Articles of Confederation
Weak central government

Achievements
Northwest Ordinance
Northwest Territory

Problems
Poor international trade
Poor foreign relations
Weak economy
Shays's Rebellion

Constitution
Strong central government

Compromises
Great Compromise
Three-Fifths Compromise
Slave trade

Structure
Legislative branch
Executive branch
Judicial branch
Checks and balances

Problems
Struggle over ratification

Bill of Rights
The first 10 amendments
Passed to protect individual rights and freedoms

Identifying People and Ideas

Use the following terms or people in historically significant sentences.

1. Virginia Statute for Religious Freedom
2. Articles of Confederation
3. Northwest Ordinance of 1787
4. James Madison
5. Great Compromise
6. Three-Fifths Compromise
7. federalism
8. George Mason
9. *Federalist Papers*
10. amendments

Understanding Main Ideas

Section 1 *(Pages 222–227)*

1. What English and colonial examples of political ideas did Americans draw from when creating their new government?
2. What did the Northwest Ordinance of 1787 accomplish?

Section 2 *(Pages 230–235)*

3. How did a weak central government affect the American economy?

Section 3 *(Pages 236–241)*

4. What were the terms of the Great Compromise?
5. How is the federal government organized under the Constitution?

Section 4 *(Pages 242–247)*

6. What arguments did the Federalists and Antifederalists make regarding the Constitution?

You Be the Historian— Reviewing Themes

1. **Global Relations** How did the Articles of Confederation affect the new national government's ability to conduct foreign policy?
2. **Citizenship** Why did many Americans want a federal bill of rights?
3. **Constitutional Heritage** How does the Constitution guard against the misuse of power?

Thinking Critically

1. **Making Generalizations and Predictions** Without compromises, how do you think the Constitutional Convention would have turned out?
2. **Supporting a Point of View** Imagine that you are a delegate at a state ratifying convention. You have read the arguments made by Alexander Hamilton and Patrick Henry. Explain whose point of view you support and how you will vote.
3. **Drawing Inferences and Conclusions** In what ways did the Founding Fathers serve as examples of civic virtue?

Organize students into four groups, and assign each group one of the chapter's sections. Have each group make an annotated flowchart showing how the major events in each section are connected. Instruct students to create an annotation for each event that describes its significance. Display the flowcharts around the classroom, and ask volunteers from each group to present their flowcharts to the class.

ENGLISH LANGUAGE LEARNERS ,
COOPERATIVE LEARNING

Portfolio Extensions

1. Cooperative Learning
Complete the following activity in groups. Organize each group into three subgroups that represent each branch of government. Group members should clip articles and photographs from newspapers and magazines that illustrate the activities of their branch of the federal government. Return to the large group to create a bulletin board display that shows the issues that each branch of the government tackles

today. You may wish to present your group's display to the class.

2. Linking to Community
Conduct a poll with community members or students to determine your community's knowledge about the Constitution. As a class, design a questionnaire asking basic questions about the content of the Constitution. After you conduct the poll, compile the results in a brief report and evaluate your community's performance.

Social Studies Skills Workshop

Interpreting Charts
Study the chart below. Then use the information from the chart to help you answer the questions that follow.

Ratifying the Constitution

STATE	RATIFICATION DATE
Delaware	December 7, 1787
Pennsylvania	December 12, 1787
New Jersey	December 18, 1787
Georgia	January 2, 1788
Connecticut	January 9, 1788
Massachusetts	February 6, 1788
Maryland	April 28, 1788
South Carolina	May 23, 1788
New Hampshire	June 21, 1788
Virginia	June 25, 1788
New York	July 26, 1788
North Carolina	November 21, 1789
Rhode Island	May 29, 1790

1. About how many months passed between the time that the first and last states ratified the Constitution?
   a. 31
   b. 33
   c. 6
   d. 3

2. During which year did the most states ratify the Constitution?
   a. 1787
   b. 1788
   c. 1789
   d. 1790

3. Based on your knowledge of the period and the information presented on the chart, when did the Constitution go into effect? Why was the support of New York and Virginia important?

Analyzing Primary Sources
Read the following quote by Benjamin Franklin, and then answer the questions that follow.

❝Thus I consent, Sir, to this Constitution because I expect no better . . . I hope therefore that for our own sakes as a part of the people, and for the sake of posterity [future generations], we shall act heartily and unanimously in recommending this constitution . . . wherever our influence may extend, and turn our future thoughts and endeavors to the means of having it well administered.❞

4. Which of the following statements best describes Franklin's point of view?
   a. Future generations will like the Constitution more than the present one does.
   b. Americans should write a better constitution.
   c. The Constitution is as good as it can be, and the Founders should speak highly of it to Americans.
   d. The Constitution has broad influence.

5. Based on your knowledge of the period, do you think that Franklin's opinion would have been important to the other delegates at the Constitutional Convention? Explain your answer.

You Be the Historian—Reviewing Themes
1. Congress could not force the states to provide soldiers and thus it was difficult to enforce treaties with foreign nations.

2. felt the Constitution did not protect personal liberties

3. separates and balances power among three branches of government as well as the state and national governments

Thinking Critically
1. Students' answers will vary.

2. Students' answers will vary.

3. gave Congress the power to regulate interstate and foreign trade.

Skills Workshop
1. a

2. b

3. went into effect in June 1788; because they were 2 of the more economically powerful states

4. c

5. Students' answers will vary.

Alternative Assessment

Building Your Portfolio

Interdisciplinary Connection to Drama
Imagine that you are attending the Constitutional Convention. Think of an issue that was not addressed in the original Constitution (for example, suffrage for all Americans or the ending of slavery). Write a one-act play about the discussion that takes place at the Convention surrounding your issue. If possible, perform your play for the class using actors and appropriate props.

☑ internet connect

Internet Activity: go.hrw.com
keyword: SA3 CF8

Choose an activity about Forming a Government to:
- Use graphic organizers to display global trade issues.
- Research a significant delegate to the Constitutional Convention and write a biography.
- Explore the political ideas of Federalists and Antifederalists.

Ask students to identify a document that is more than 200 years old and still governs the lives of more than a quarter of a billion people of various races, religions, and ethnic backgrounds. If students have trouble identifying the document, tell them that it is the U.S. Constitution. Tell the class that although the Constitution was created more than 200 years ago, when the U.S. population was about 4 million people, it continues to govern successfully, despite the fact that the population now exceeds 260 million. Point out that the key to the Constitution's success has been both its strength and its flexibility to adapt to a constantly changing world. Tell students that in this activity they will learn more about the growth of the United States.

★ TEACH

Have students read the Connecting to Geography lesson. Choose one or more of the following activities to explore the Connecting to Geography content with students.

★ Constitutional Heritage

Rights in the Northwest Ordinance. The Northwest Ordinance included a bill of rights that applied to Americans who lived in the Northwest Territory. Among the protections included in the ordinance were the right to a trial by jury, a ban on cruel or unusual punishment, and a guarantee that government in the area would be representative. The ordinance also included a provision that protected private contracts from government interference. The contract clause later appeared in the U.S. Constitution.

CRITICAL THINKING

In what ways might the Northwest Ordinance have influenced the drafting of the U.S. Constitution?

ANSWER: The ordinance included a bill of rights and provisions such as the contract clause that later appeared in the Constitution.

SKILLS ANSWERS

1. When a state has 60,000 free inhabitants, it becomes eligible for statehood.
2. Congress
3. Ohio, 1803
   Indiana, 1816
   Illinois, 1818
   Michigan, 1837
   Wisconsin, 1848

Connecting to Geography

The Living Constitution

The United States is governed by the Constitution, which was adopted by the original 13 states in 1789. The Constitution established a government in which the people choose their leaders. These officials make the nation's laws and run the government.

The framers of the Constitution created a federal system that is strong enough to enforce its authority. The principles and methods of governing that are outlined in the Constitution, however, are quite flexible. This flexibility has allowed the federal government to adjust to great change over more than 210 years. For example, the original nation of 13 states had a population of less than 4 million. Today the United States has 50 states and more than 280 million people.

The Union

The Northwest Ordinance was passed by the Confederation Congress in 1787, before the Constitution was written. The Ordinance established a method for admitting new states to the Union. The last states admitted to the Union were Alaska and Hawaii in 1959.

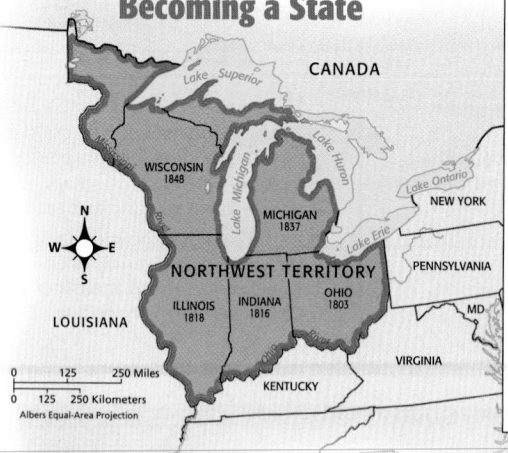

The Northwest Ordinance: Becoming a State

CANADA

Lake Superior

WISCONSIN 1848

Lake Michigan

Lake Huron

MICHIGAN 1837

Lake Ontario

NEW YORK

Lake Erie

NORTHWEST TERRITORY

PENNSYLVANIA

ILLINOIS 1818

INDIANA 1816

OHIO 1803

MD

LOUISIANA

VIRGINIA

KENTUCKY

N W E S

0 125 250 Miles
0 125 250 Kilometers
Albers Equal-Area Projection

STEPS TO STATEHOOD

Congress specifies that three to five territories will be carved out of the Northwest Territory.

For each territory, Congress appoints a governor, a secretary, and three judges.

When a territory's population reaches 5,000 free male inhabitants of voting age, it elects a territorial legislature and sends a nonvoting delegate to Congress.

Once a territory's population increases to 60,000 free inhabitants, it becomes eligible for statehood and can draft a state constitution.

Congress approves the state constitution, and the territory becomes a state.

Sources: *Record of America; The Oxford Companion to American History*

Geography **Skills**
Interpreting Political Maps

1. When is a territory eligible for statehood?
2. **Human Systems** Under the Northwest Ordinance, who, or what, approves a territory's proposed constitution before the territory becomes a state?
3. **Sequencing** When did each state of the Northwest Territory join the Union?

LEVEL 1: Explain to students that the map on p. 251 contains information about the order in which states were admitted to the Union and includes the date that each state either ratified the U.S. Constitution or was admitted to the Union. Have students write down the name of the state in which they were born or in which they live now, the order in which that state was admitted to the Union, and the date that it became a state. **ENGLISH LANGUAGE LEARNERS**

 ALL LEVELS: Have students create flashcards containing the information about the requirements of, term of, and method of selection for the federal office positions included in the chart on p. 252. Then have students take turns quizzing one another on the information found in the chart. **ENGLISH LANGUAGE LEARNERS**

 LEVEL 2: Have students create graphic organizers with the following horizontal headings: *State's Name and Date It Ratified the Constitution or Was Admitted to the Union.* Have students number the vertical axis 1 through 50. Then ask students to use the map on p. 251 to fill in each square with the appropriate information.

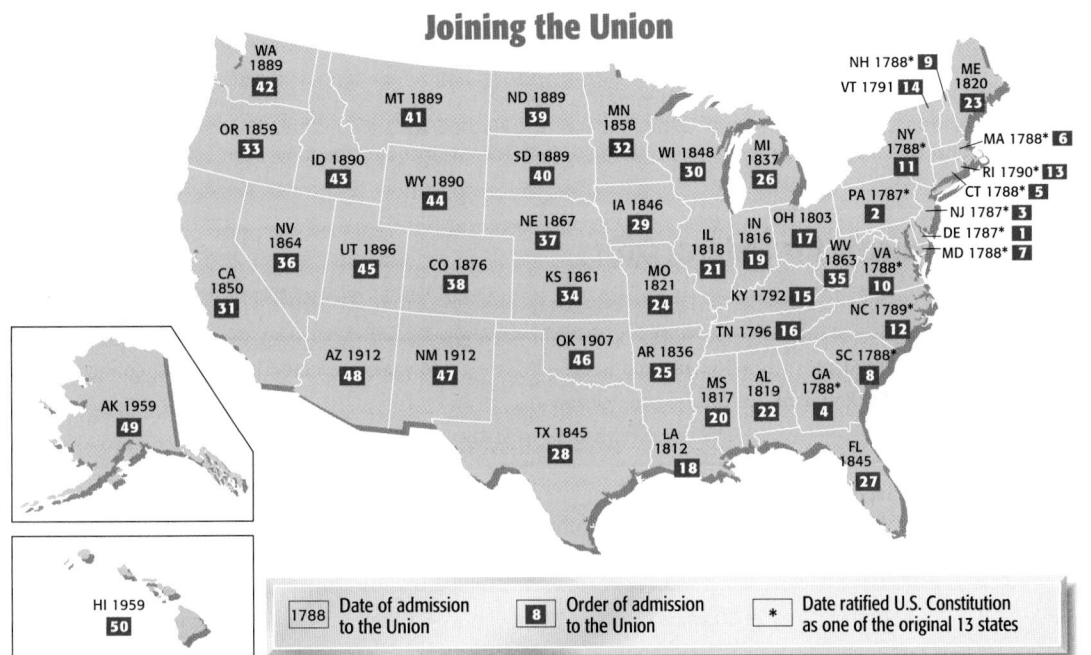

Joining the Union

1788	Date of admission to the Union
8	Order of admission to the Union
*	Date ratified U.S. Constitution as one of the original 13 states

Geography **Skills**

Interpreting Thematic Maps

1. Which three states ratified the Constitution first?
2. **Places and Regions** What were the original 13 states of the Union?
3. **Summarizing** What states were admitted to the Union in the 1900s? In what years during this period were more than one state admitted?

History Note 1

Congress established the method for admitting new states to the Union in the Northwest Ordinance of 1787. Before that, however, some people in what is now the state of Tennessee made the first attempt to create a new state. In 1784 North Carolina turned over the Tennessee territory to the new government of the United States. Residents in northeastern Tennessee applied to Congress to form a new state named "Franklin" after Benjamin Franklin. However, North Carolina reclaimed the region before Congress could decide the issue. Finally, in 1790 North Carolina again gave the territory to the federal government. In 1796 the proposed state of Franklin became part of the new state of Tennessee.

Rocky Mount was the capital for the first territorial government of Tennessee.

LEVEL 3: Review the Northwest Ordinance with the class, pointing out that the process of becoming a state has not changed since 1787. Ask students to state their opinions on the adequacy of these steps. Would today's American public be willing to admit a new state based on these requirements, or would they expect different standards to be met? Have students prepare an opinion survey by using the steps for applying for statehood as outlined in the Northwest Ordinance, which appears on p. 250. Their questions should be phrased to require a yes or no answer. Once students have created their surveys, instruct them to pose the questions to 10 adults. For each question, ask students who had an answer of yes to raise their hands and record the total number of positive and negative responses. Discuss the results with the class.

★ CLOSE

Give students a list consisting of imaginary people. That list should include information about each person's age, the number of years he or she has lived in the United States, and his or her citizenship status. For each person on the list, have students identify whether he or she meets the requirements for election or appointment to any of the following offices: president, Supreme Court justice, senator, or representative. For each person who does not meet a requirement, have students write an explanation of why he or she is not qualified for the position in question. Finally, as a class, review the positions each person is qualified to hold.

★ Constitutional Heritage

Presidential Qualifications.

Contemporary political concerns determined many of the qualifications for the presidency included in the U.S. Constitution. In an attempt to squelch the rumor that delegates to the Constitutional Convention intended to invite a foreign king to rule the country, the delegates themselves included the constitutional provision requiring he president to be a natural-born citizen. They chose a 14-year residency requirement to disqualify British Loyalists who had left during the American Revolution and later returned to the United States.

CRITICAL THINKING

What does the reasoning behind the presidential qualifications reveal about the drafting of the Constitution?

ANSWER: The delegates hoped to solve pressing political issues as well as to create a design for operating the country in the future.

SKILLS ANSWERS

1. president and vice president— 35; Supreme Court justice— none; senator—30; representative—25
2. yes
3. Supreme Court justice; Supreme Court justice

Elected Officials and Voters

The Constitution sets the requirements for federal officials. The president, vice president, and members of Congress are all elected by the people. The percentage of the U.S. population that is eligible to vote has increased greatly over time.

Requirements for Federal Office

	OFFICE	REQUIREMENTS	TERM	SELECTION
	President Vice President	• 35 years old • Natural-born citizen • Live in United States 14 years	4 years	Elected by electoral college
	Supreme Court Justice	• None	Life	Appointed by president and approved by Senate
	Senator	• 30 years old • U.S. citizen 9 years • Live in state where elected	6 years	Originally chosen by state legislature (per Constitution); Currently elected by voters of state (per Seventeenth Amendment)
	Representative	• 25 years old • U.S. citizen 7 years • Live in state where elected	2 years	Elected by voters of district

Geography **Skills**

Interpreting Charts

1. What are the age requirements for federal officials?
2. What are the terms of the federal officials listed?
3. **Comparing and Contrasting** Which federal office has the fewest requirements listed? Which position listed is not an elected office?

History Note 2

Franklin D. Roosevelt was the only president elected to more than two terms. He was elected president four times. In 1951 the Twenty-second Amendment was adopted, stating that no president can be elected more than twice. In 1995 the Supreme Court ruled that neither the states nor Congress could pass laws limiting the terms of members of Congress. A constitutional amendment that would allow term limits has been proposed. However, such an amendment has failed to pass in Congress.

The inauguration of President George W. Bush

★ **REVIEW AND ASSESS**

Have students review the information in Connecting to Geography Unit 4. Then have students complete Geography and History Quiz 4.

★ **RETEACH**

Have students review material from the graph and History Notes on p. 253. Ask them to use the information to identify the approximate increase in the eligible electorate that resulted from the ratification of the Fifteenth, Nineteenth, and Twenty-sixth Amendments. **ENGLISH LANGUAGE LEARNERS**

★ **EXTEND**

Tell students that in 1800 each congressional district represented approximately 20,000 to 25,000 people. Whereas, in 1995 each congressional district represented approximately 600,000 people. Provide each student with an outline map of the United States. Have students use the library to determine the number of House members for each state, both 50 years ago and today. Also, have them find each state's population for both time periods. For each of the time periods, have students divide each state's population by the number of House members from that state. This will show how many people each House member represented for both years. Instruct students to label their maps with each state's name and to fill in the number of people each House member represented, both 50 years ago and today. **BLOCK SCHEDULING**

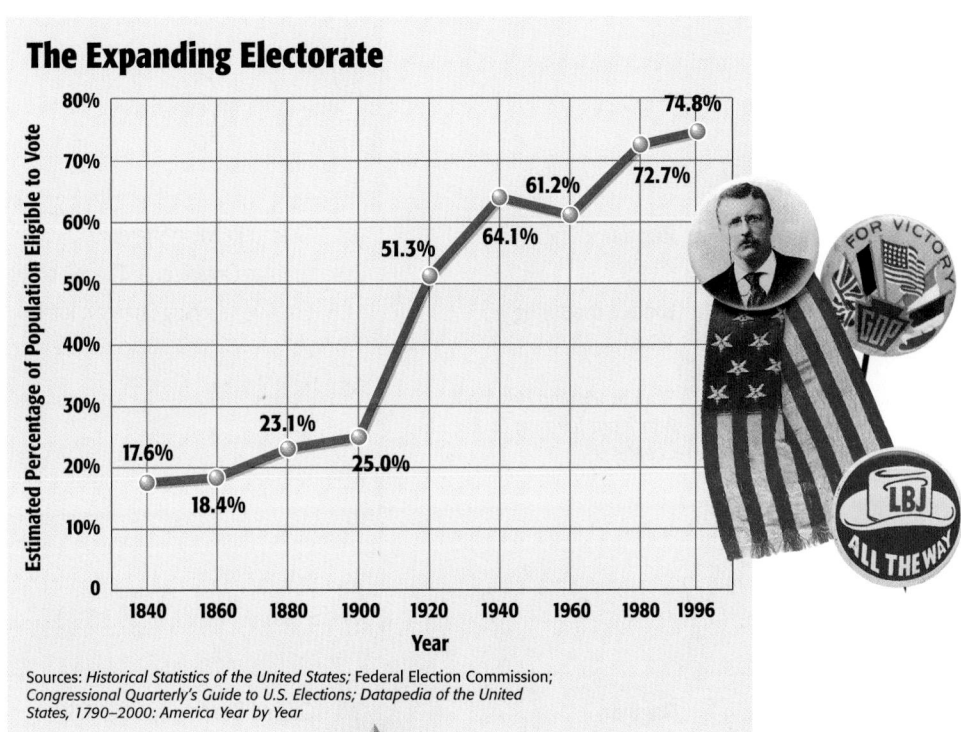

The Expanding Electorate

Estimated Percentage of Population Eligible to Vote

- 17.6%
- 18.4%
- 23.1%
- 25.0%
- 51.3%
- 64.1%
- 61.2%
- 72.7%
- 74.8%

Year: 1840 1860 1880 1900 1920 1940 1960 1980 1996

Sources: *Historical Statistics of the United States; Federal Election Commission; Congressional Quarterly's Guide to U.S. Elections; Datapedia of the United States, 1790–2000: America Year by Year*

Geography **Skills**
Interpreting Line Graphs

1. **Human Systems** What twenty-year interval on the graph shows the largest increase in the percentage of the U.S. population eligible to vote?
2. **Drawing Inferences and Conclusions** Show this graph to another student. Ask him or her to explain to you which amendments to the Constitution might account for the increases in voter eligibility seen in 1920 and 1980.

History Note 3

The power to decide who is eligible to vote is reserved to the states under the Tenth Amendment. However, later constitutional amendments have extended the right to vote to more and more people. The Fifteenth Amendment, ratified in 1870, protects the right of people of any race to vote. In 1920 the Nineteenth Amendment gave women the right to vote in all states. The Twenty-sixth Amendment, ratified in 1971, lowered the legal voting age from 21 to 18.

Presidential campaign buttons

★ **Constitutional Heritage**

Twenty-sixth Amendment.
As of 1970, four states had established a minimum voting age lower than 21. That year, Congress passed a law allowing citizens 18 and older to vote in federal elections. The Supreme Court found the law constitutional, but noted that Congress did not have the power to set the voting age in state elections. To remedy any conflicts between federal and state voting standards, Congress passed the Twenty-sixth Amendment, which established 18 as the minimum voting age in all elections in the United States. The amendment was quickly ratified.

CRITICAL THINKING

Why was it necessary to amend the Constitution to establish a national voting age of 18?

ANSWER: It was necessary to amend the Constitution because establishing voting ages in local elections was a power reserved to state governments.

SKILLS ANSWERS
1. 1900–1920
2. The Nineteenth Amendment, ratified in 1920, gave women the right to vote, and the Twenty-sixth Amendment, ratified in 1971, lowered the voting age to 18.

Citizenship and the Constitution

CHAPTER RESOURCE MANAGER

Objectives	Pacing Guide	Reproducible Resources
SECTION 1: Understanding the Constitution (pp. 256–61)	★ Explain how the framers of the Constitution tried to balance state and federal powers. ★ List the three branches of the federal government and describe the requirements for membership in each branch. ★ Analyze how power is divided between the three branches of government.	**Regular** 3 days **Block Scheduling** 2 days *Block Scheduling Handbook with Team Teaching Strategies, Chapter 9*	**RS** Guided Reading Strategy 9.1 **PS** Biography Reading 9: John Jay **PS** Primary Source Reading 9: Antifederalists **E** Hands-On History Activity: The Constitution: A Survey
SECTION 2: The Bill of Rights (pp. 284–89)	★ Discuss the main freedoms outlined within the First Amendment, and analyze why they are important. ★ Outline how the Bill of Rights addresses colonial grievances listed in the Declaration of Independence. ★ Examine the protections that the Bill of Rights gives to people accused of crimes.	**Regular** 2 days **Block Scheduling** 1.5 days *Block Scheduling Handbook with Team Teaching Strategies, Chapter 9*	**RS** Guided Reading Strategy 9.2 **RS** Graphic Organizer 9: The Bill of Rights **E** Creative Teaching Strategy: Ranking
SECTION 3: Rights and Responsibilities of Citizenship (pp. 290–95)	★ Describe how a person can become a U.S. citizen. ★ Identify some of the most important responsibilities of citizenship. ★ Evaluate why citizens should be involved with their community and government.	**Regular** 1.5 days **Block Scheduling** .5 day *Block Scheduling Handbook with Team Teaching Strategies, Chapter 9*	**RS** Guided Reading Strategy 9.3 **PS** Literature Reading 9: The Free Citizen **SM** Geography Activity 9: Changes in Electoral Votes

Chapter Resource Key

PS Primary Sources
RS Reading Support
IC Interdisciplinary Connections
E Enrichment
SM Skills Mastery

A Assessment
REV Review
ELL Reinforcement and English Language Learners
 Transparencies
 CD-ROM

 Music
 Video
 Internet
 Holt Presentation Maker Using Microsoft® PowerPoint®

One-Stop Planner CD-ROM

See the *One-Stop Planner* for a complete list of additional resources for students and teachers.

One-Stop Planner CD-ROM

It's easy to plan lessons, select resources, and print out materials for your students when you use the **One-Stop Planner CD-ROM with Test Generator.**

Technology Resources	Reinforcement, Review, and Assessment
One-Stop Planner, Lesson 9.1 Exploring America's Past Video Segment: Who Has the Power?; Teacher's Guide, pp. 52–55 Holt Researcher: American History CD–ROM Homework Practice Online HRW Go site	**REV** Section 1 Review, p. 261 **A** Daily Quiz 9.1 **ELL** Main Idea Activity 9.1 **ELL** English Audio Summary 9.1 **ELL** Spanish Audio Summary 9.1
One-Stop Planner, Lesson 9.2 CNN Presents America: Yesterday and Today, Beginnings to 1914, Segment: Remembering the Bill of Rights Exploring America's Past Video Segment: The Roles of a Citizen; Teacher's Guide, pp. 48–51 Homework Practice Online	**REV** Section 2 Review, p. 289 **A** Daily Quiz 9.2 **ELL** Main Idea Activity 9.2 **ELL** English Audio Summary 9.2 **ELL** Spanish Audio Summary 9.2
One-Stop Planner, Lesson 9.3 Exploring America's Past Video Segment: On the Campaign Trail; Teacher's Guide, pp. 60–63 Holt Researcher: American History CD–ROM Homework Practice Online HRW Go site	**REV** Section 3 Review, p. 294 **A** Daily Quiz 9.3 **ELL** Main Idea Activity 9.3 **ELL** English Audio Summary 9.3 **ELL** Spanish Audio Summary 9.3

Meeting Individual Needs

Ability Levels

Level 1 Basic-level activities designed for all students encountering new material

Level 2 Intermediate-level activities designed for average students

Level 3 Challenging activities designed for honors and gifted-and-talented students

English Language Learners Activities that address the needs of students with Limited English Proficiency

internet connect

HRW ONLINE RESOURCES
GO TO: go.hrw.com
Then type in a keyword.

TEACHER HOME PAGE
KEYWORD: SA3 Teacher

CHAPTER INTERNET ACTIVITIES
KEYWORD: SA3 CF9
Choose an activity to:
- write biographies of Sandra Day O'Connor and of First Ladies.
- analyze a Supreme Court case from the most recent term and write a concurring or dissenting opinion.
- interpret census information and databases regarding immigration.

CHAPTER ENRICHMENT LINKS
KEYWORD: SA3 CH9

ONLINE ASSESSMENT
Homework Practice
KEYWORD: SA3 HP9

Standardized Test Prep
KEYWORD: SA3 STP9

Rubrics
KEYWORD: SS Rubrics

ONLINE MAPS, CHARTS, AND GRAPHS
KEYWORD: SA3 MCG
- U.S. Regions, 1790
- The Federal System
- Amending the Constitution

CONTENT UPDATES
KEYWORD: SS Content Updates

HOLT PRESENTATION MAKER
KEYWORD: SA3 PPT9

ONLINE READING SUPPORT
KEYWORD: SS Strategies

CURRENT EVENTS
KEYWORD: S3 Current Events

Chapter Review and Assessment

IC Vocabulary Activity 9 Global Skill Builder CD-ROM HRW Go site **REV** Chapter 9 Tutorial for Students, Parents, Mentors, and Peers **REV** Chapter 9 Review, pp. 295–97 Chapter 9 Test Generator (on the One-Stop Planner) **A** Chapter 9 Test (Form A or B)	**A** Alternative Assessment Handbook **A** Chapter 9 Test for English Language Learners and Special-Needs Students

CHAPTER

9 Citizenship and the Constitution

(1787–Present)

Suffragists parade down a street in Washington, D.C.

THE GRANGER COLLECTION, NEW YORK

Congress sent the Constitution to the states for ratification in 1787.

THE GRANGER COLLECTION, NEW YORK

UNITED STATES

1791 The Bill of Rights becomes part of the Constitution on December 15.

1920 The Nineteenth Amendment gives women the right to vote.

1954 The Supreme Court rules that segregated public schools are unconstitutional.

| **1800** | **1920** | **1930** | **1940** | **1950** |

WORLD

1917 Mexico adopts a new constitution.

1930 Mohandas K. Gandhi leads acts of civil disobedience to protest British rule in India.

1945 Delegates from 50 nations meet in San Francisco to found the United Nations.

1948 The United Nations adopts the Universal Declaration of Human Rights.

Mohandas K. Gandhi (looking down at center) led many marches protesting British colonial rule in India.

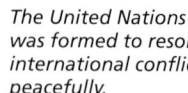

The United Nations was formed to resolve international conflicts peacefully.

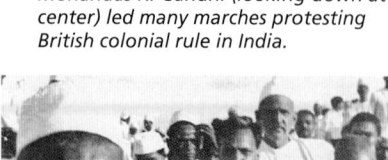

Build on What You Know

After much discussion, the states ratified the new Constitution. For over 200 years the Constitution has provided the foundation of American democracy and freedom. Throughout recent history this document has been an example for many nations and democratic movements around the world.

Constitutional Heritage

Agree A country's leader with too much power will become a dictator.

Disagree The leader of a country must have a great deal of power in order to run the government effectively.

Citizenship

Agree One vote cast out of millions of votes cannot affect a presidential election.

Disagree Past elections have shown that every American's vote counts.

Culture

Agree The rights of any group are more important than the interests of all people.

Disagree The rights and interests of all Americans should be protected equally.

Immigrants take an oath to become U.S. citizens.

Colin Powell led the organization America's Promise—The Alliance for Youth to promote volunteerism.

1967 Thurgood Marshall becomes the first African American justice on the Supreme Court.

1971 The Twenty-sixth Amendment is passed, giving the right to vote to all U.S. citizens aged 18 years or older.

1981 Sandra Day O'Connor becomes the first woman justice on the Supreme Court.

1990 The Americans with Disabilities Act is passed.

1997 Colin Powell starts a campaign for volunteerism.

1960 **1970** **1980** **1990** **2000**

1989 The East German government opens the Berlin Wall, allowing citizens of East Germany to travel to the West.

Demonstrators and celebrators gathered as the Berlin Wall was opened.

You Be the Historian

Themes Journal

What's Your Opinion? Do you **agree** or **disagree** with the following statements? Support your point of view in your journal.

- **Constitutional Heritage** The government should be set up to make sure that the president does not have too much power.
- **Citizenship** One person's vote is not important to the outcome of an election.
- **Culture** The government should protect the rights of minorities over the interests of the majority.

If you were there . . .
How would you educate Americans about their rights and responsibilities?

Constitutional Heritage

Freedom of Speech.
Seven years after the Bill of Rights was added to the Constitution, Congress passed the Sedition Act of 1798. This act seemed to abridge freedom of speech by making it a crime for a person to say or write anything "false, scandalous and malicious against the government." Ten people were imprisoned for breaking this law, but every justice of the Supreme Court, upheld the law's constitutionality. Historian Leonard Levy later explained how legal minds understood the issue. Levy noted that the government could not prevent people from speaking or writing against the government ahead of time, it could punish the speaker or writer afterward.

CRITICAL THINKING

Do you believe that people should be punished for speaking or writing against the government? Explain your answer.

ANSWER: Students might suggest that people should be punished because such statements could weaken the government. Students might also suggest that people should not be punished for exercising their freedom of speech.

Section 1

OBJECTIVES

★ Explain how the framers of the Constitution tried to balance state and federal powers.

★ List the three branches of the federal government and describe the requirements for membership in each branch.

★ Analyze how power is divided between the three branches of government.

SECTION 1 RESOURCES

REPRODUCIBLE

▶ Guided Reading Strategy 9.1
▶ Biography Reading 9: John Jay
▶ Primary Source Reading 9: Antifederalists

TECHNOLOGY

▶ One-Stop Planner, Lesson 9.1
▶ Exploring America's Past Video Segment: Who Has the Power?; Teacher's Guide, pp. 52–55
▶ Holt Researcher: American History CD–ROM
▶ Homework Practice Online
▶ HRW Go site

REINFORCEMENT, REVIEW, AND ASSESSMENT

▶ Section 1 Review, p. 261
▶ Daily Quiz 9.1
▶ Main Idea Activity 9.1
▶ English Audio Summary 9.1
▶ Spanish Audio Summary 9.1

LET'S GET STARTED!

Write the following question on the chalkboard: *What might happen if the president were the only person to make, enforce, and interpret the nation's laws?* As students enter the classroom, allow time for them to respond. *(Students' responses might mention that the president would be able to make laws that benefited his or her best interests or that punished people he or she disliked.)* Explain to students that in order to prevent any one person from gaining too much power, the framers of the Constitution created a government with three branches. Tell students that in Section 1 they will learn about how the framers of the Constitution addressed the division of power between the three branches of government.

Section 1

Understanding the Constitution

Read to Discover

1. How did the framers of the Constitution try to balance state and federal powers?
2. What are the three branches of the federal government, and what are the requirements for membership in each branch?
3. How is power divided between the three branches of government?

WHY IT MATTERS TODAY

The cabinet regularly advises the president on important issues. Use CNNfyi.com or other **current events** sources to identify a member of the presidential cabinet and read about some of the person's basic duties. Record your findings in your journal.

Define

- representative democracy
- delegated powers
- elastic clause
- reserved powers
- concurrent powers
- separation of powers
- apportionment
- impeach
- veto
- executive order
- pardon
- cabinet

Identify

- Thurgood Marshall
- Sandra Day O'Connor

The Department of Justice was established in 1870, with the attorney general as its head.

The Story Continues

A sign on the Justice Department Building in Washington, D.C., describes the role of the Constitution. It reads, "No Free Government Can Survive That Is Not Based on the Supremacy of Law." This idea is central to the Constitution of the United States. The laws of our nation protect the freedom and the rights of our citizens.

★ The Federal System

The United States is a **representative democracy**—a government led by officials who are chosen by the people. The Constitution created a federal system in which power is divided between the states and the federal government. The powers granted to the federal government are called **delegated powers**. Examples of these powers are coining money and regulating interstate and international trade. The federal government also runs the country's defense, declares war, and conducts diplomacy.

Have students read Section 1 and complete Guided Reading Strategy 9.1. Choose one or more of the following activities to explore the section content with students. For further suggestions on block scheduling or team teaching, see the *Block Scheduling Handbook with Team Teaching Strategies.*

Note: To help students make meaningful connections between events in American history and those in their own hometown, use the Chapter 9 **Hands-On History** activity, the Constitution: A Survey.

LEVEL 1: Write the following terms in a row on the chalkboard: *Judge, Member of the House, President, Senator.* In another row write the following: *25 years old, 30 years old, 35 years old.* In a third row write the following: *native-born U.S. citizen, citizen for 7+ years, citizen for 9+ years.* In a fourth row write the following: *live in United States 14+ years, live in the state where elected.* Ask volunteers to match up the age, citizenship, and residency requirements for each of these governmental positions. Lead a class discussion asking students which governmental position has no age, citizenship, or residency requirements. *(Students' answers should be judge.)* Ask students why they think this position is different from other important government positions.

ENGLISH LANGUAGE LEARNERS

Federalism

POWERS DELEGATED TO THE NATIONAL GOVERNMENT	POWERS SHARED BY NATIONAL AND STATE GOVERNMENTS	POWERS RESERVED TO THE STATES
Declare war	Maintain law and order	Establish and maintain schools
Maintain armed forces	Levy taxes	Establish local governments
Regulate interstate and foreign trade	Borrow money	Regulate business within the state
Admit new states	Charter banks	Make marriage laws
Establish post offices	Establish courts	Provide for public safety
Set standard weights and measures	Provide for public welfare	Assume other powers not delegated to the national government or not prohibited to the states
Coin money		
Establish foreign policy		
Make all laws necessary and proper for carrying out delegated powers		

★ Government

A Divided Senate.
The elections of 2000 led to a remarkable event: an even 50-50 split between Democratic and Republican members in the Senate. The last time the Senate was evenly divided was in 1880, when 37 members represented each major party. Despite the equal number of senators, the Republicans had an edge after the 2000 election, since Vice President Dick Cheney, a Republican, held the constitutional right to cast any tie-breaking votes. In 2001, however, a historic mid-year shift in Senate power occurred when Senator Jim Jeffords of Vermont left the Republican party to become an independent. This shifted the balance of power in the Senate to 50 Democrats to 49 Republicans, giving the Democrats control of the chamber.

CRITICAL THINKING
What did the results of the Senate races of 2000 reveal about the American voting population?

Answer: Students might suggest that American voters were evenly divided between Democrats and Republicans.

Sometimes, Congress has stretched its delegated powers to address new or unexpected issues. The "necessary and proper" clause of Article I, Section 8, of the Constitution makes this possible. The clause allows Congress to "make all Laws which shall be necessary and proper" for carrying out its duties. Because it provides flexibility for the government, this clause has become known as the **elastic clause**.

The powers kept by the state governments or by the citizens are **reserved powers**. These powers include creating local governments and holding elections. States also control education and trade within their borders. **Concurrent powers** are powers that the federal and state governments share. Taxing, borrowing money, enforcing laws, and providing for citizens' welfare are examples of these powers.

✔ **Reading Check: Categorizing** List at least two examples each of delegated, reserved, and concurrent powers. See the examples described above under each power.

★ The Legislative Branch

The federal government is divided into three separate branches, each with its own responsibilities and powers. This **separation of powers** is designed to balance each branch against the others. It keeps any single branch from becoming too powerful.

The legislative branch, or Congress, makes the nation's laws. "Members of Congress are the human connection between the citizen and . . . government," noted one member. Article I divides Congress into the House of Representatives and the Senate.

This is the seal of Congress, the lawmaking branch of the federal government.

ALL LEVELS: Copy the graphic organizer at the right onto the chalkboard, omitting the italicized answers. Lead a class discussion about the meanings of the terms *delegated powers, reserved powers,* and *concurrent powers.* Then have students suggest examples of each of these powers to fill in the graphic organizer. Use students' answers to begin a discussion about why they think the framers of the Constitution balanced state and federal powers. **ENGLISH LANGUAGE LEARNERS**

HOMEWORK Tell students that they have been assigned to describe the U.S. government to citizens of another country who are considering changing their nation's constitution. Have students create a diagram or graphic organizer that shows the role of each of the three

Delegated Powers
• coining money
• regulating interstate & international trade
• providing for the nation's defense
• declaring war
• conducting diplomacy

Concurrent Powers
• taxing
• borrowing money
• enforcing laws
• providing for citizens' welfare

Reserved Powers
• conducting elections
• regulating trade within each state
• establishing local governments
• regulating education

branches of the federal government and the interaction among the branches.

Interpreting the Visual Record

Federal Hall *The first Congress under the Constitution met in Federal Hall in New York City.* **Why might the Congress later need a new building?**

With 435 members, the House of Representatives is the larger of the two houses of Congress. The U.S. census, a population count taken every 10 years, decides the number of representatives for each state. To keep each state's total current, Congress uses **apportionment**, or planned distribution, of representatives. Under this system, no state can gain a representative unless another state loses one. House members represent a particular district of voters in a state. House members must be at least 25 years old, have been U.S. citizens for seven or more years, and be residents of the state in which they are elected. House members serve two-year terms.

The Senate is made up of two representatives, called senators, from each state. Senators represent the interests of their entire state. They must be at least 30 years old and have been U.S. citizens for nine or more years. Senators serve six-year terms and must be residents of the state they represent. The senator who has served longer is the state's senior senator. No law limits the number of times someone may be elected to either house of Congress.

The political party that has the most members in each house of Congress is called the majority party. The party with fewer members is the minority party. The leader of the House of Representatives is the Speaker of the House. House members select the Speaker, who is usually from the majority party. The vice president of the United States serves as the president of the Senate. The vice president does not join in Senate debates but can cast a vote to break a tie. When the vice president is absent, the president *pro tempore* leads the Senate.

Congress begins its regular session, or meeting, each year in the first week of January. Each house of Congress carries out most of its work in committees that specialize in certain types of bills, or proposed laws. For example, all bills about taxes begin in the House Ways and Means Committee.

✔ **Reading Check: Summarizing** What are the requirements and terms of office for members of the House and the Senate? See the first two paragraphs at the top of the page.

★ The Executive Branch

Article II of the Constitution specifies the powers of the executive branch. This branch enforces the laws that Congress passes. The president, as head of the executive branch, is the most powerful elected leader in the country. To become president, one must be a native-born U.S. citizen, at least 35 years old, and have been a U.S. resident for at least 14 years. The requirements are the same for the vice president.

Thus far, all U.S. presidents have been white men. In more-recent elections, candidates for the nation's highest offices have been

LEVEL 2: Ask students to create a three-column chart on a sheet of paper. Tell students to label each column with one of the three branches of the federal government. (*Students' columns should be labeled: Legislative Branch, Executive Branch, and Judicial Branch.*) Ask volunteers to identify the differences between the three branches of government, including powers, duties, and other characteristics. As students answer, have them fill in the answers on their chart. After students' charts are completed, lead a discussion about the ways in which the three branches of government interact.

LEVEL 3: Explain to students that one reason why the framers of the Constitution delegated some powers directly to the federal government—rather than reserving them for state governments—was to avoid creating situations that would make interactions between the states difficult. Organize the class into groups of five or six students. Have each group create and act out a short skit that highlights the confusion that might occur if a specific power that is now delegated to the national government were held by state governments. After each group has presented its skit, lead a class discussion about the importance of the division of powers in the Constitution. **COOPERATIVE LEARNING**

more diverse. African Americans such as Jesse Jackson and Alan Keyes have campaigned for nomination. In 1984 Geraldine Ferraro ran as the Democratic nominee for vice president. She was the first female candidate for a major political party. In 2000 Democrat Joseph Lieberman became the first Jewish nominee for vice president.

Every four years Americans elect a president and vice president. Franklin D. Roosevelt, who won four presidential elections, was the only president to serve more than two terms. Later, the Twenty-second Amendment limited presidents to two terms. If the president dies, resigns, or is removed from office, the vice president becomes president.

The House of Representatives can **impeach**, or vote to bring charges of "treason, bribery, or other high crimes and misdemeanors" against, a president. The Senate tries all impeachment cases. If a president is found guilty, Congress can remove him or her from office. In 1868 Andrew Johnson became the first president to be impeached. President Bill Clinton was impeached in 1998. In each case the Senate tried the president and found him not guilty. In 1974 President Richard Nixon resigned to avoid possible impeachment.

★ Working with Congress

The system of checks and balances often places the president against Congress. This problem is quite challenging when the president's party is different from that of the majority party in Congress. Despite their differences, the executive and legislative branches must cooperate. President Lyndon Johnson described the role Congress played in his work.

History Makers Speak

❝What a President says and thinks is not worth five cents unless he has the people and Congress behind him. Without the Congress I'm just a six-feet-four Texan. With Congress I'm President of the United States in the fullest sense.❞

—President Lyndon Johnson, from
The Macmillan Dictionary of Political Quotations

Although Congress passes laws, the president can ask members of Congress to pass or reject certain bills. The president also has the power to **veto**, or cancel, laws that Congress passes. Congress can override, or undo, a president's veto; however, doing so is very difficult. Overriding a veto requires a two-thirds majority vote. After Congress passes a law, federal agencies and departments often decide how to enforce it. In carrying out laws that affect parts of the Constitution, treaties, and statutes, the president may issue an **executive order**, a command that has the power of law. In an emergency the president might issue an executive order that stretches the definition of laws passed by Congress. The president also has the power to grant a **pardon**, or freedom from punishment. Pardons are sometimes given to persons convicted of federal crimes or who are facing criminal charges.

★★★★★★★★★★★★
That's Interesting!
★★★★★★★★★★★★

Electoral Oversights Did you know that the runner-up in a presidential election used to become vice president? It's true! Even if the top two finishers were from different policital parties, the candidate in second place served as vice president. To solve this problem, parties began choosing both a presidential and vice presidential candidate to run on the same ticket. But because electors cast only one ballot for both candidates, the two Democratic-Republican candidates in 1800 ended up tied with each other for president! In 1804, Congress passed the Twelfth Amendment, which directs electors to cast separate ballots for president and vice president.

Aaron Burr tied with Thomas Jefferson in the 1800 electoral vote.

THE GRANGER COLLECTION, NEW YORK

Analyzing Primary Sources

Drawing Inferences and Conclusions Why did President Johnson believe the support of Congress was important? Students might suggest that he needed the support of Congress to complete his responsibilities as president.

 **LEVEL 3:** Explain to students that some decisions of the courts, particularly the Supreme Court, have far-reaching implications. Assign small groups of students significant Supreme Court decisions to research. Have students write an article for a newspaper that includes a description of both sides of the argument in the case, a summary of the Court's decision and how it might affect other related cases, and students' own opinions about the significance of the case and its decision. Have students place their articles in a binder to serve as a classroom reference for information about these important decisions. **BLOCK SCHEDULING** , **COOPERATIVE LEARNING**

☆ CLOSE

Ask students to imagine that they are a member of the Constitutional Convention who wants to give an update to the people of his or her state about the convention. Have students write a letter that describes the reasons for the division of power between the federal government and state governments as well as how power is divided among the three branches of the federal government.

★ Biography

Sandra Day O'Connor. Supreme Court justice Sandra Day O'Connor has achieved several "firsts" in her legal career. By 1965 she had become the first female assistant attorney general in Arizona. In the Arizona senate, she held the position of majority leader for two years—the first woman to hold such a position in any U.S. state. When President Ronald Reagan appointed O'Connor to the Supreme Court, she was yet again the first woman to hold this position.

🖳 internet connect

TOPIC: Sandra Day O'Connor
GO TO: go.hrw.com
KEYWORD: SA3 CF9

Have students search the Internet through the HRW Go site to find more information on Sandra Day O'Connor. Then ask them to write brief biographies that expand on the information in the textbook.

BIOGRAPHY ANSWER

assistant attorney general and state legislator

Visual Record Answer

(for p. 261)
Students' answers will vary.

Research on the R⊙M

Free Find:
Pendleton Civil Service Act
After reading about the Pendleton Civil Service Act on the **Holt Researcher CD–ROM**, write an editorial describing why it is important to have civil service jobs that are not appointed positions.

BIOGRAPHY

Sandra Day O'Connor

1930–

Sandra Day O'Connor was born in El Paso, Texas, and attended law school at Stanford University in California. She served as Arizona's assistant attorney general and as a state legislator before becoming an Arizona state judge. In 1981 President Ronald Reagan chose O'Connor to serve on the Supreme Court. Although she was appointed by a conservative Republican president, at times O'Connor is often seen as a moderate justice. Her decisions show how Supreme Court justices can often be free from party politics. **What experience did O'Connor have before becoming a judge?**

The president is also commander in chief of the armed forces. In an emergency, the president can send in U.S. troops, but only Congress can declare war. Some other executive duties are foreign relations and arranging treaties. Currently, 14 executive departments do most of the executive branch's work. The president chooses the department heads, whom Congress must then approve. The **cabinet**, made up of these department secretaries, advises the president on important matters.

✔ **Reading Check: Comparing** What powers do the executive and legislative branches have over each other? The executive branch can veto legislation; the legislative branch can impeach the president.

★ The Judicial Branch

The third branch of the government is the judicial branch. This branch is made up of a system of federal courts headed by the U.S. Supreme Court. Article III of the Constitution outlines the courts' duties. As an implied part of these duties, a federal court can strike down a state or federal law. However, a court can only do this if it finds a law unconstitutional. If Congress desires, it can propose an amendment to the Constitution that would make the law constitutional.

The president makes all appointments to federal courts. These judges receive the appointment for life to ensure that they will not be influenced by political parties. The lower courts in the federal system are divided according to the types of cases over which they have jurisdiction, or authority. Each state has at least one district court to handle federal cases. States with higher populations often have more than one district court. Today there are 94 U.S. district courts and 13 courts of appeals that review lower-court decisions.

At times, someone convicted of a crime believes that the original trial was unfair. That person can appeal his or her case to the higher court. Each of these courts of appeals has a panel of judges who decide whether the lower court tried the original case properly. If the judges uphold, or accept, the lower court's decision, then the case's original outcome stands. If not, the case may go back to the lower court for a new trial.

✔ **Reading Check: Analyzing Information** What check does the judicial branch have over the legislative branch? It can declare a law to be unconstitutional.

★ The Supreme Court

After a case has been decided by the court of appeals, the losing side may appeal the decision to the Supreme Court. Thousands of cases are appealed to the Court each year. However, Supreme Court justices have time to review only about 100 of these cases. The justices carefully choose which cases to hear. Generally, cases that are chosen must involve

✪ REVIEW AND ASSESS

Have students complete the **Section 1 Review** on p. 261. Then have students complete **Daily Quiz 9.1**. As **Alternative Assessment**, you may want to use the government powers graphic organizer or the branches of government chart in this section's lessons.

✪ RETEACH

Have students complete **Main Idea Activity for English Language Learners and Special-Needs Students 9.1**. Then ask them to create a study guide for this section. Have students exchange guides with other students for review.

ENGLISH LANGUAGE LEARNERS , COOPERATIVE LEARNING

✪ EXTEND

Lead a class discussion that examines the differences between delegated, inherent, implied, and concurrent powers. Have students review old newspapers and magazines to find examples of the use of each of these types of powers. Then hang four large sheets of butcher paper around the classroom. Label each sheet of paper with the name of one of the types of powers. Have students tape copies of articles they have found onto the appropriate sheet of paper. When students have finished, lead a class discussion in which students explain why they classified the articles as they did. Reclassify any articles that have been placed in the wrong category. **BLOCK SCHEDULING**

an important constitutional or public interest issue. If the Court refuses to hear a case, the decision of the court of appeals is final. Most cases that are presented to the Supreme Court are review cases. However, some cases go directly to the Supreme Court. Some examples are cases that involve international diplomats or disputes between states.

Congress decides how many justices sit on the Court. Traditionally that number has been fixed at nine. The chief justice of the United States leads the Supreme Court. Unlike the president and members of Congress, Court justices do not have specific requirements set by the Constitution. So far, however, every justice has been an attorney.

In the past few decades the makeup of the Supreme Court has become more diverse. In 1967 **Thurgood Marshall** became the first African American justice, with Clarence Thomas becoming the second in 1991. Right now two women sit on the high court—Ruth Bader Ginsburg and **Sandra Day O'Connor**. O'Connor became the first female Court justice after her 1981 appointment by President Ronald Reagan.

Interpreting the Visual Record

The Supreme Court *Supreme Court justice Ruth Bader Ginsburg speaks to a group of students.* **What would you ask Justice Ginsburg if you were one of the students in the picture?**

✔ **Reading Check: Finding the Main Idea** What types of cases does the Supreme Court usually review? cases involving constitutional or public interest issues; cases involving international diplomats or disputes between states

Section 1 Review

go.hrw.com Homework Practice Online
keyword: SA3 HP9

❶ **Define** and explain:
• representative democracy
• delegated powers
• elastic clause
• reserved powers
• concurrent powers
• separation of powers
• apportionment
• impeach
• veto
• executive order
• pardon
• cabinet

❷ **Identify** and explain:
• Thurgood Marshall
• Sandra Day O'Connor

❸ **Categorizing** Copy the web diagram below. Use it to list the powers of the federal government's three branches.

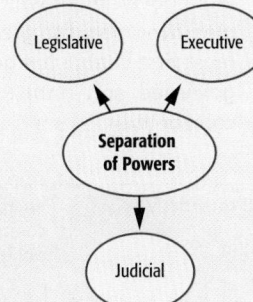

❹ **Finding the Main Idea**
a. What are the requirements for membership in the three branches of the federal government?
b. Do you think the three branches of government share power equally? Explain your answer.

❺ **Writing and Critical Thinking**
Summarizing Imagine that you are one of the framers explaining the Constitution to U.S. citizens. Design a poster that explains how the Constitution balances state and federal powers. Your poster should define each power and provide examples.
Consider the following:
• delegated powers
• reserved powers
• concurrent powers

Section 1 Review
ANSWERS

❶ **Define**
• representative democracy, p. 256
• delegated powers, p. 256
• elastic clause, p. 257
• reserved powers, p. 257
• concurrent powers, p. 257
• separation of powers, p. 257
• apportionment, p. 258
• impeach, p. 259
• veto, p. 259
• executive order, p. 259
• pardon, p. 259
• cabinet, p. 260

❷ **Identify**
• Thurgood Marshall, p. 261
• Sandra Day O'Connor, p. 261

❸ legislative: impeach president, override presidential veto, declare war, approve Supreme Court justices and department heads; judicial: declare a law unconstitutional; executive: veto laws passed by Congress, issue executive orders, appoint Supreme Court justices, grant pardons, handle foreign relations

❹ a. executive: 35 years old, native-born citizen, live in United States 14 years; judicial: none; legislative—senator: 30 years old, U.S. citizen 9 years, live in state where elected; representative: 25 years old, U.S. citizen 7 years, live in state where elected
b. Answers will vary.

❺ Students' posters will vary but should show the balance of powers.

James Madison

FEDERALIST PAPER "No. 51"

During the debates over the ratification of the Constitution, some New York newspapers printed essays favoring ratification. These essays answered Antifederalists' objections. The *Federalist Papers* were written by Alexander Hamilton, John Jay, and James Madison. In this excerpt from essay "No. 51," Madison describes the separation of powers. He also talks about how this separation would be preserved among the three branches of the government.

In order to lay a **due**[1] foundation for . . . the different powers of government, . . . it is evident that each department should have a will of its own; and consequently should be so **constituted**[2] that the members of each should have as little **agency**[3] as possible in the appointment of the members of the others. Were this principle **rigorously adhered to**,[4] it would require that all the appointments for the supreme executive, legislative, and judiciary **magistracies**[5] should be drawn from the same fountain of authority, the people, through channels having no communication whatever with one another. . . .

But the great security against a gradual concentration of the several powers in the same department [branch], consists in giving to those who administer each department the necessary constitutional means and personal motives to resist **encroachments**[6] of the others. The provision for defense must . . . be made **commensurate**[7] to the danger of attack. . . . It may be a reflection on human nature that such devices should be necessary to control the abuses of government. But what is government itself but the greatest of all

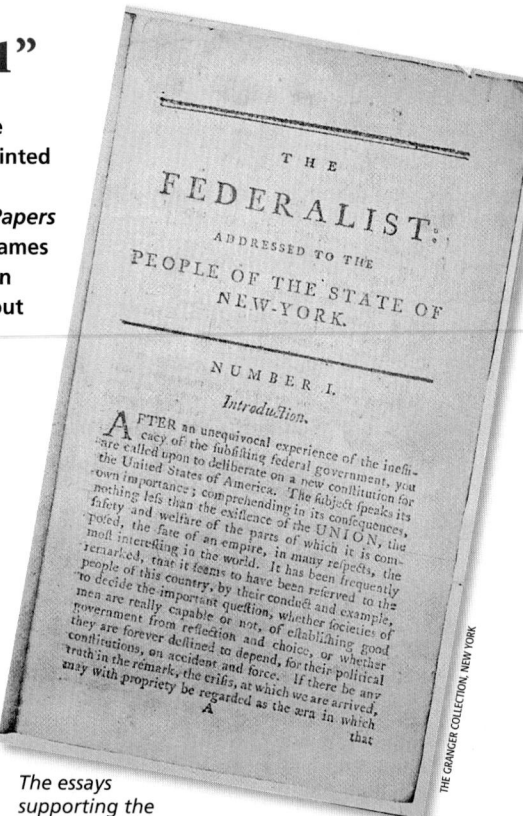

The essays supporting the Constitution appeared in a book called The Federalist *in 1788.*

THE GRANGER COLLECTION, NEW YORK

reflections on human nature? If men were angels, no government would be necessary. If angels were to govern men, neither external nor internal controls on government would be necessary. In framing a government which is to be administered by men over men, the great difficulty lies in this: you must first enable the government to control the governed; and in the next place **oblige**[8] it to control itself.

---

[1] **due:** proper
[2] **constituted:** set up
[3] **agency:** power

[4] **rigorously adhered to:** strictly followed
[5] **magistracies:** offices

[6] **encroachments:** improper advances
[7] **commensurate:** equal
[8] **oblige:** force

George Mason

"THE OBJECTIONS OF THE HON. GEORGE MASON TO THE PROPOSED FEDERAL CONSTITUTION"

George Mason played a behind-the-scenes role in the Revolutionary War and wrote Virginia's Declaration of Rights. He attended the Constitutional Convention in 1787. Mason criticized the proposed Constitution for allowing slavery, creating a strong central government, and lacking a Bill of Rights. As a result, he refused to sign the Constitution. However, after the Constitution was ratified, the government soon added a Bill of Rights. In addition to addressing Mason's concerns, the government used Virginia's Declaration of Rights as a model. In the following excerpt, George Mason explains why he will not sign the Constitution.

George Mason wanted the Constitution to include a Bill of Rights similar to Virginia's Declaration of Rights.

There is no declaration of rights: and the laws of the general government being **paramount**[1] to the laws and constitutions of the several states, the declarations of rights, in the separate states, are no security. Nor are the people secured even in the enjoyment of the benefit of the common law, which stands here upon no other foundation than its having been adopted by the respective acts forming the constitutions of the several states.

In the House of Representatives there is not the substance, but the shadow only of representation; which can never produce proper information in the legislature, or inspire confidence in the people. The laws will, therefore, be generally made by men little concerned in, and unacquainted with their effects and consequences. . . .

The President of the United States has no constitutional council. . . . He will therefore be unsupported by proper information and advice; and will generally be directed by **minions**[2] and favorites— or he will become a tool to the Senate. . . .

. . . There is no declaration of any kind for preserving the liberty of the press, the trial by jury in civil cases, nor against the danger of standing armies in time of peace. . . .

. . . [T]he general legislature is restrained from prohibiting the further importation of slaves for twenty odd years, though such importations render the United States weaker, more vulnerable, and less capable of defense.

Analyzing Primary Sources

1. How does Madison plan to "control the abuses of government"?
2. According to Mason, what rights were not protected by the Constitution?
3. In what ways do Madison and Mason agree?

---

[1] **paramount:** superior   [2] **minions:** servants

The weather in Philadelphia during the Constitutional Convention was very humid and extremely uncomfortable. One visitor to the city remarked: "At each inhaling of air, one worries about the next one. The slightest movement is painful." Most delegates from New England wore full woolen suits throughout the Convention, making the heat in the Pennsylvania State House even more oppressive.

ANALYZING PRIMARY SOURCES ANSWERS

1. by giving people in the government the means and the motive to resist the abuses of others, in short, through the system of checks and balances
2. freedom of the press, trial by jury in civil cases, and protection against standing armies in times of peace
3. They both recognize that there is a danger that officials will abuse the power of government.

THE CONSTITUTION

The Preamble. Although short, the Preamble was hotly debated in the state ratifying conventions. The phrase "We the People" was particularly contentious, since the delegates to the conventions had been appointed by states, rather than elected by the people. Patrick Henry challenged this phrase during the ratifying process in Virginia saying, "The people gave them [the delegates to the Constitutional Convention] no power to use their name. That they exceeded their power is perfectly clear."

CRITICAL THINKING

How might someone have countered Henry's argument?

ANSWER: Students might suggest that people gave the states the right to appoint the delegates, so the people did actually give them power.

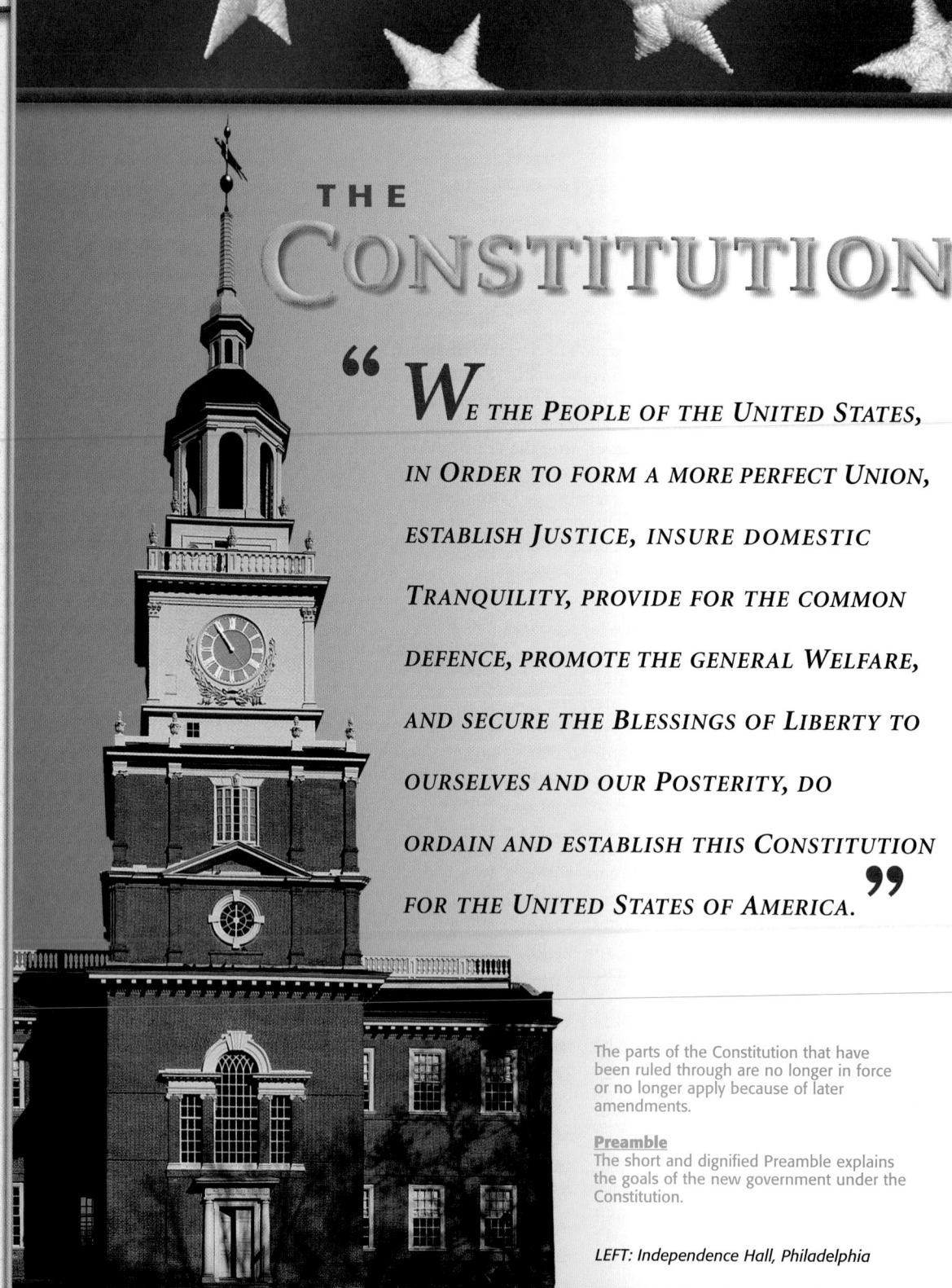

THE CONSTITUTION

"**W**E THE PEOPLE OF THE UNITED STATES, IN ORDER TO FORM A MORE PERFECT UNION, ESTABLISH JUSTICE, INSURE DOMESTIC TRANQUILITY, PROVIDE FOR THE COMMON DEFENCE, PROMOTE THE GENERAL WELFARE, AND SECURE THE BLESSINGS OF LIBERTY TO OURSELVES AND OUR POSTERITY, DO ORDAIN AND ESTABLISH THIS CONSTITUTION FOR THE UNITED STATES OF AMERICA."

The parts of the Constitution that have been ruled through are no longer in force or no longer apply because of later amendments.

Preamble
The short and dignified Preamble explains the goals of the new government under the Constitution.

LEFT: Independence Hall, Philadelphia

ARTICLE I

Section 1. All legislative Powers herein granted shall be vested in a Congress of the United States, which shall consist of a Senate and House of Representatives.

Section 2. The House of Representatives shall be composed of Members chosen every second Year by the People of the several States, and the Electors in each State shall have the Qualifications requisite for Electors of the most numerous Branch of the State Legislature.

No Person shall be a Representative who shall not have attained to the Age of twenty five Years, and been seven Years a Citizen of the United States, and who shall not, when elected, be an Inhabitant of that State in which he shall be chosen.

Representatives and direct Taxes shall be apportioned among the several States which may be included within this Union, according to their respective Numbers, which shall be determined by adding to the whole Number of free Persons, including **those bound to Service**[1] for a Term of Years, and excluding Indians not taxed, three fifths of **all other Persons**.[2] The actual **Enumeration**[3] shall be made within three Years after the first Meeting of the Congress of the United States, and within every subsequent Term of ten Years, in such Manner as they shall by Law direct. The Number of Representatives shall not exceed one for every thirty Thousand, but each State shall have at Least one Representative; and until such enumeration shall be made, the State of New Hampshire shall be entitled to chuse three; Massachusetts eight; Rhode Island and Providence Plantations one; Connecticut five; New York six; New Jersey four; Pennsylvania eight; Delaware one; Maryland six; Virginia ten; North Carolina five; South Carolina five; and Georgia three.

When vacancies happen in the Representation from any State, the Executive Authority thereof shall issue Writs of Election to fill such Vacancies.

The House of Representatives shall chuse their Speaker and other Officers; and shall have the sole Power of Impeachment.

Section 3. The Senate of the United States shall be composed of two Senators from each State, chosen by the Legislature thereof, for six Years; and each Senator shall have one Vote.

Immediately after they shall be assembled in Consequence of the first Election, they shall be divided as equally as may be into three Classes. The Seats of the Senators of the first Class shall be vacated at the Expiration of the second Year, of the second Class at the Expiration of the fourth Year, and of the third Class at the Expiration of the sixth Year, so that one third may be chosen every second Year; and if Vacancies happen by

---

Legislative Branch
Article I explains how the legislative branch, called Congress, is organized. The chief purpose of the legislative branch is to make the laws. Congress is made up of the Senate and the House of Representatives.

The House of Representatives
The number of members each state has in the House is based on the population of the individual state. In 1929 Congress permanently fixed the size of the House at 435 members.

[1] **those bound to Service:** indentured servants
[2] **all other Persons:** slaves
[3] **Enumeration:** census or official population count

★ Linking Past to Present

Income Tax. Although the Constitution gave Congress the right to raise revenue through taxes, the Constitution stood in the way of an income tax until the passage of the Sixteenth Amendment in 1913. The Union passed the first income tax during the Civil War to pay for maintaining the army. The minimum rate of this tax was 3 percent on income above $600, and the maximum rate was 5 percent on income above $10,000. This tax remained in effect until 1872. However, when Congress enacted an income tax in 1894, the Supreme Court ruled it unconstitutional for failing to apportion the tax burden fairly "among the several States." With the passage of the Sixteenth Amendment, the personal income tax became an increasingly important source of federal revenue. In the 2001 federal budget, it accounted for an estimated 48 percent of federal revenue.

ACTIVITY: Tell students to use the library or other resources to find information about the U.S. income tax. Have them create a chart that shows the percentage of federal revenues received from income tax at three points during the last 50 years.

Availability of Information. For many years, the best way for the public to learn about congressional proceedings was to consult the *Congressional Record*, a bulky set of printed volumes. With the increased availability of the Internet, tracking a congressperson's votes has become easier. The Library of Congress supports a Web site that covers many aspects of the government. In addition, independent organizations, such as Project Vote Smart, provide links to help track congressional votes.

internet connect

TOPIC: Library of Congress
GO TO: go.hrw.com
KEYWORD: SA3 CF9

Have students use the library or search the Internet through the HRW Go site to track a current piece of legislation. Ask them to find out how their congressperson voted.

EXPLORING THE DOCUMENT ANSWER
Students might suggest that it allows one branch of government to exert power over another branch of government.

The Vice President
The only duty that the Constitution assigns to the vice president is to preside over meetings of the Senate. Modern presidents have usually given their vice presidents more responsibilities.

4 pro tempore: temporarily
5 Impeachments: official accusations of federal wrongdoing

Exploring the Document

If the House of Representatives charges a government official with wrongdoing, the Senate acts as a court to decide if the official is guilty. **How does the power of impeachment represent part of the system of checks and balances?**

6 Quorum: the minimum number of people needed to conduct business
7 adjourn: to stop indefinitely

~~Resignation, or otherwise, during the Recess of the Legislature of any State, the Executive thereof may make temporary Appointments until the next Meeting of the Legislature, which shall then fill such Vacancies.~~

No Person shall be a Senator who shall not have attained to the Age of thirty Years, and been nine Years a Citizen of the United States, and who shall not, when elected, be an Inhabitant of that State for which he shall be chosen.

The Vice President of the United States shall be President of the Senate, but shall have no Vote, unless they be equally divided.

The Senate shall chuse their other Officers, and also a President **pro tempore**,[4] in the Absence of the Vice President, or when he shall exercise the Office of President of the United States.

The Senate shall have the sole Power to try all **Impeachments**.[5] When sitting for that Purpose, they shall be on Oath or Affirmation. When the President of the United States is tried, the Chief Justice shall preside: And no Person shall be convicted without the Concurrence of two thirds of the Members present.

Judgment in Cases of Impeachment shall not extend further than to removal from Office, and disqualification to hold and enjoy any Office of honor, Trust or Profit under the United States: but the Party convicted shall nevertheless be liable and subject to Indictment, Trial, Judgment and Punishment, according to Law.

Section 4. The Times, Places and Manner of holding Elections for Senators and Representatives, shall be prescribed in each State by the Legislature thereof; but the Congress may at any time by Law make or alter such Regulations, except as to the Places of chusing Senators.

~~The Congress shall assemble at least once in every Year, and such Meeting shall be on the first Monday in December, unless they shall by Law appoint a different Day.~~

Section 5. Each House shall be the Judge of the Elections, Returns and Qualifications of its own Members, and a Majority of each shall constitute a **Quorum**[6] to do Business; but a smaller Number may **adjourn**[7] from day to day, and may be authorized to compel the Attendance of absent Members, in such Manner, and under such Penalties as each House may provide.

Each House may determine the Rules of its Proceedings, punish its Members for disorderly Behaviour, and, with the Concurrence of two thirds, expel a Member.

Each House shall keep a Journal of its Proceedings, and from time to time publish the same, excepting such Parts as may in their Judgment require Secrecy; and the Yeas and Nays of the Members of either House on any question shall, at the Desire of one fifth of those Present, be entered on the Journal.

Neither House, during the Session of Congress, shall, without the Consent of the other, adjourn for more than three days, nor to any other Place than that in which the two Houses shall be sitting.

Section 6. The Senators and Representatives shall receive a Compensation for their Services, to be ascertained by Law, and paid out of the Treasury of the United States. They shall in all Cases, except Treason, Felony and Breach of the Peace, be privileged from Arrest during their Attendance at the Session of their respective Houses, and in going to and returning from the same; and for any Speech or Debate in either House, they shall not be questioned in any other Place.

No Senator or Representative shall, during the Time for which he was elected, be appointed to any civil Office under the Authority of the United States, which shall have been created, or the **Emoluments**[8] whereof shall have been encreased during such time; and no Person holding any Office under the United States, shall be a Member of either House during his **Continuance**[9] in Office.

Section 7. All **Bills**[10] for raising Revenue shall originate in the House of Representatives; but the Senate may propose or concur with Amendments as on other Bills.

Every Bill which shall have passed the House of Representatives and the Senate, shall, before it become a Law, be presented to the President of the United States; If he approve he shall sign it, but if not he shall return it, with his Objections to that House in which it shall have originated, who shall enter the Objections at large on their Journal, and proceed to reconsider it. If after such Reconsideration two thirds of that House shall agree to pass the Bill, it shall be sent, together with the Objections, to the other House, by which it shall likewise be reconsidered, and if approved by two thirds of that House, it shall become a Law. But in all such Cases the Votes of both Houses shall be determined by yeas and Nays, and the Names of the Persons voting for and against the Bill shall be entered on the Journal of each House respectively. If any Bill shall not be returned by the President within ten Days (Sundays excepted) after it shall have been presented to him, the Same shall be a Law, in like Manner as if he had signed it, unless the Congress by their Adjournment prevent its Return, in which Case it shall not be a Law.

Every Order, Resolution, or Vote to which the Concurrence of the Senate and House of Representatives may be necessary (except on a question of Adjournment) shall be presented to the President of the United States; and before the Same shall take Effect, shall be approved by him, or being disapproved by him, shall be repassed by two thirds of the Senate and House of Representatives, according to the Rules and Limitations prescribed in the Case of a Bill.

[8] **Emoluments:** salary

[9] **Continuance:** term

[10] **Bills:** proposed laws

Exploring the Document

The framers felt that because members of the House are elected every two years, representatives would listen to the public and seek its approval before passing taxes. **How does Section 7 address the colonial demand of "no taxation without representation"?**

Exploring the Document

The veto power of the president is one of the important checks and balances in the Constitution. **Why do you think the Founding Fathers included the ability of Congress to override a veto?**

Linking Past to Present

Veto Power. In 1996 Congress passed the line-item veto, which gave the president the power to cancel specific items in spending bills. Proponents of the law hoped that it would help stop wasteful spending by allowing the president to prevent spending that he considered unnecessary. However, almost immediately a group of lawmakers challenged the line-item veto on constitutional grounds. A federal court decided that the law was unconstitutional because it upset the system of checks and balances built into the Constitution. The judge claimed that the power to revoke spending appropriations once they are passed is a congressional one and "according to the [Constitution's] Framers' careful design, may not be delegated at all." In June 1998 the Supreme Court struck down the line-item veto, confirming the lower court's ruling that it was unconstitutional.

CRITICAL THINKING

Do you think the line-item veto would significantly change the system of checks and balances that the framers built into the Constitution?

ANSWER: Students' answers will vary, but some may suggest that it would grant the president too much power. Others may argue that it would be a useful way for the president to help Congress control spending.

11 Duties: tariffs

12 Imposts: taxes

13 Excises: internal taxes on the manufacture, sale, or consumption of a commodity

14 Rule of Naturalization: a law by which a foreign-born person becomes a citizen

15 Securities: bonds

16 Letters of Marque and Reprisal: documents issued by governments allowing merchant ships to arm themselves and attack ships of an enemy nation

The Elastic Clause
The framers of the Constitution wanted a national government that was strong enough to be effective. This section lists the powers given to Congress. The last sentence in Section 8 contains the so-called "elastic clause"—which has been stretched (like elastic) to allow Congress to meet changing circumstances.

Section 8. The Congress shall have Power To lay and collect Taxes, **Duties**,[11] **Imposts**[12] and **Excises**,[13] to pay the Debts and provide for the common Defence and general Welfare of the United States; but all Duties, Imposts and Excises shall be uniform throughout the United States;

To borrow Money on the credit of the United States;

To regulate Commerce with foreign Nations, and among the several States, and with the Indian Tribes;

To establish an uniform **Rule of Naturalization**,[14] and uniform Laws on the subject of Bankruptcies throughout the United States;

To coin Money, regulate the Value thereof, and of foreign Coin, and fix the Standard of Weights and Measures;

To provide for the Punishment of counterfeiting the **Securities**[15] and current Coin of the United States;

To establish Post Offices and post Roads;

To promote the Progress of Science and useful Arts, by securing for limited Times to Authors and Inventors the exclusive Right to their respective Writings and Discoveries;

To constitute Tribunals inferior to the supreme Court;

To define and punish Piracies and Felonies committed on the high Seas, and Offences against the Law of Nations;

To declare War, grant **Letters of Marque and Reprisal**,[16] and make Rules concerning Captures on Land and Water;

To raise and support Armies, but no Appropriation of Money to that Use shall be for a longer Term than two Years;

To provide and maintain a Navy;

To make Rules for the Government and Regulation of the land and naval Forces;

To provide for calling forth the Militia to execute the Laws of the Union, suppress Insurrections and repel Invasions;

To provide for organizing, arming, and disciplining, the Militia, and for governing such Part of them as may be employed in the Service of the United States, reserving to the States respectively, the Appointment of the Officers, and the Authority of training the Militia according to the discipline prescribed by Congress;

To exercise exclusive Legislation in all Cases whatsoever, over such District (not exceeding ten Miles square) as may, by Cession of particular States, and the Acceptance of Congress, become the Seat of the Government of the United States, and to exercise like Authority over all Places purchased by the Consent of the Legislature of the State in which the Same shall be, for the Erection of Forts, Magazines, Arsenals, dock-Yards, and other needful Buildings;—And

To make all Laws which shall be necessary and proper for carrying into Execution the foregoing Powers, and all other Powers vested by this

Constitution in the Government of the United States, or in any Department or Officer thereof.

Section 9. ~~The Migration or Importation of such Persons as any of the States now existing shall think proper to admit, shall not be prohibited by the Congress prior to the Year one thousand eight hundred and eight, but a Tax or duty may be imposed on such Importation, not exceeding ten dollars for each Person.~~

The Privilege of the **Writ of Habeas Corpus**[17] shall not be suspended, unless when in Cases of Rebellion or Invasion the public Safety may require it.

No **Bill of Attainder**[18] or **ex post facto Law**[19] shall be passed.

No **Capitation**,[20] or other direct, Tax shall be laid, unless in Proportion to the Census or Enumeration herein before directed to be taken.

No Tax or Duty shall be laid on Articles exported from any State.

No Preference shall be given by any Regulation of Commerce or Revenue to the Ports of one State over those of another: nor shall Vessels bound to, or from, one State, be obliged to enter, clear, or pay Duties in another.

No Money shall be drawn from the Treasury, but in Consequence of Appropriations made by Law; and a regular Statement and Account of the Receipts and Expenditures of all public Money shall be published from time to time.

No Title of Nobility shall be granted by the United States: And no Person holding any Office of Profit or Trust under them, shall, without the Consent of the Congress, accept of any present, Emolument, Office, or Title, of any kind whatever, from any King, Prince, or foreign State.

Section 10. No State shall enter into any Treaty, Alliance, or Confederation; grant Letters of Marque and Reprisal; coin Money; emit Bills of Credit; make any Thing but gold and silver Coin a Tender in Payment of Debts; pass any Bill of Attainder, ex post facto Law, or law impairing the Obligation of Contracts, or grant any Title of Nobility.

No State shall, without the Consent of the Congress, lay any Imposts or Duties on Imports or Exports, except what may be absolutely necessary for executing its inspection Laws: and the net Produce of all Duties and Imposts, laid by any State on Imports or Exports, shall be for the Use of the Treasury of the United States; and all such Laws shall be subject to the Revision and Controul of the Congress.

No State shall, without the Consent of Congress, lay any Duty of Tonnage, keep Troops, or Ships of War in time of Peace, enter into any Agreement or Compact with another State, or with a foreign Power, or engage in War, unless actually invaded, or in such imminent Danger as will not admit of delay.

[17] **Writ of Habeas Corpus:** a court order that requires the government to bring a prisoner to court and explain why he or she is being held

[18] **Bill of Attainder:** a law declaring that a person is guilty of a particular crime

[19] **ex post facto Law:** a law that is made effective prior to the date that it was passed and therefore punishes people for acts that were not illegal at the time

[20] **Capitation:** a direct uniform tax imposed on each head, or person

Exploring the Document

Although Congress has implied powers, there are also limits to its powers. Section 9 lists powers that are denied to the federal government. Several of the clauses protect the people of the United States from unjust treatment. **In what ways does the Constitution limit the powers of the federal government?**

The President. Initially, the writers of the Constitution agreed that the president would be chosen by the national legislature for a single, seven-year term. Many delegates opposed a strong executive branch. However, when the Constitution was turned over to the Committee on Style, Gouverneur Morris, who wanted a stronger executive, reworded the article outlining the role of the president. He shortened the length of the president's term, allowed the president to run for more than one term, and altered the method by which the president would be elected. These changes passed with little debate, partly because the delegates were ready to go home and partly because many members believed that George Washington would be the first president and felt that he would not abuse the power of the executive branch.

CRITICAL THINKING

Why might many of the delegates to the Constitutional Convention have opposed a one-person executive?

ANSWER: Students might suggest that they feared that they might create another monarchy.

EXPLORING THE DOCUMENT ANSWER

35 years old

Executive Branch
The president is the chief of the executive branch. It is the job of the president to enforce the laws. The framers wanted the president's and vice president's terms of office and manner of selection to be different from those of members of Congress. They decided on four-year terms, but they had a difficult time agreeing on how to select the president and vice president. The framers finally set up an electoral system, which varies greatly from our electoral process today.

Presidential Elections
In 1845 Congress set the Tuesday following the first Monday in November of every fourth year as the general election date for selecting presidential electors.

Exploring the Document

The youngest elected president was John F. Kennedy; he was 43 years old when he was inaugurated. (Theodore Roosevelt was 42 when he assumed office after the assassination of McKinley.) **What is the minimum required age for the office of president?**

ARTICLE II

Section 1. The executive Power shall be vested in a President of the United States of America. He shall hold his Office during the Term of four Years, and, together with the Vice President, chosen for the same Term, be elected, as follows.

Each State shall appoint, in such Manner as the Legislature thereof may direct, a Number of Electors, equal to the whole Number of Senators and Representatives to which the State may be entitled in the Congress: but no Senator or Representative, or Person holding an Office of Trust or Profit under the United States, shall be appointed an Elector.

The Electors shall meet in their respective States, and vote by Ballot for two Persons, of whom one at least shall not be an Inhabitant of the same State with themselves. And they shall make a List of all the Persons voted for, and of the Number of Votes for each; which List they shall sign and certify, and transmit sealed to the Seat of the Government of the United States, directed to the President of the Senate. The President of the Senate shall, in the Presence of the Senate and House of Representatives, open all the Certificates, and the Votes shall then be counted. The Person having the greatest Number of Votes shall be the President, if such Number be a Majority of the whole Number of Electors appointed; and if there be more than one who have such Majority, and have an equal Number of Votes, then the House of Representatives shall immediately chuse by Ballot one of them for President; and if no Person have a Majority, then from the five highest on the List the said House shall in like Manner chuse the President. But in chusing the President, the Votes shall be taken by States, the Representation from each State having one Vote; A quorum for this Purpose shall consist of a Member or Members from two thirds of the States, and a Majority of all the States shall be necessary to a Choice. In every Case, after the Choice of the President, the Person having the greatest Number of Votes of the Electors shall be the Vice President. But if there should remain two or more who have equal Votes, the Senate shall chuse from them by Ballot the Vice President.

The Congress may determine the Time of chusing the Electors, and the Day on which they shall give their Votes; which Day shall be the same throughout the United States.

No Person except a natural born Citizen, or a Citizen of the United States, at the time of the Adoption of this Constitution, shall be eligible to the Office of President; neither shall any Person be eligible to that Office who shall not have attained to the Age of thirty five Years, and been fourteen Years a Resident within the United States.

In Case of the Removal of the President from Office, or of his Death, Resignation, or Inability to discharge the Powers and Duties of the said Office, the Same shall devolve on the Vice President, and the Congress

may by Law provide for the Case of Removal, Death, Resignation or Inability, both of the President and Vice President, declaring what Officer shall then act as President, and such Officer shall act accordingly, until the Disability be removed, or a President shall be elected.

The President shall, at stated Times, receive for his Services, a Compensation, which shall neither be increased nor diminished during the period for which he shall have been elected, and he shall not receive within that Period any other Emolument from the United States, or any of them.

Before he enter on the Execution of his Office, he shall take the following Oath or Affirmation:—"I do solemnly swear (or affirm) that I will faithfully execute the Office of President of the United States, and will to the best of my Ability, preserve, protect and defend the Constitution of the United States."

Section 2. The President shall be Commander in Chief of the Army and Navy of the United States, and of the Militia of the several States, when called into the actual Service of the United States; he may require the Opinion, in writing, of the principal Officer in each of the executive Departments, upon any Subject relating to the Duties of their respective Offices, and he shall have Power to grant **Reprieves**[21] and **Pardons**[22] for Offenses against the United States, except in Cases of Impeachment.

He shall have Power, by and with the Advice and Consent of the Senate, to make Treaties, provided two thirds of the Senators present concur; and he shall nominate, and by and with the Advice and Consent of the Senate, shall appoint Ambassadors, other public Ministers and Consuls, Judges of the supreme Court, and all other Officers of the United States, whose Appointments are not herein otherwise provided for, and which shall be established by Law: but the Congress may by Law vest the Appointment of such inferior Officers, as they think proper, in the President alone, in the Courts of Law, or in the Heads of Departments.

The President shall have Power to fill up all Vacancies that may happen during the Recess of the Senate, by granting Commissions which shall expire at the End of their next Session.

Section 3. He shall from time to time give to the Congress Information of the State of the Union, and recommend to their Consideration such Measures as he shall judge necessary and expedient; he may, on extraordinary Occasions, convene both Houses, or either of them, and in Case of Disagreement between them, with Respect to the Time of Adjournment, he may adjourn them to such Time as he shall think proper; he shall receive Ambassadors and other public Ministers; he shall take Care that the Laws be faithfully executed, and shall Commission all the Officers of the United States.

Presidential Salary
In 1999 Congress voted to set future presidents' salaries at $400,000 per year. The president also receives an annual expense account. The president must pay taxes only on the salary.

Commander in Chief
Today, the president is in charge of the army, navy, air force, marines, and coast guard. Only Congress, however, can decide if the United States will declare war.

[21] **Reprieves:** delays of punishment
[22] **Pardons:** releases from the legal penalties associated with a crime

Appointments
Most of the president's appointments to office must be approved by the Senate.

The State of the Union
Every year the president presents to Congress a State of the Union message. In this message, the president introduces and explains a legislative plan for the coming year.

John Marshall. The Supreme Court was considered a fairly unimportant institution in its early years. When John Marshall was appointed chief justice in 1801, he and his colleagues had to meet in the basement of the Capitol because there wasn't a Supreme Court building. Having served in the Revolutionary War, Marshall was a committed nationalist. As chief justice, he established the Supreme Court as the final interpreter of the Constitution and made the Court into an important check on the power of the president and of Congress.

CRITICAL THINKING

How might Marshall's war time experiences have shaped his ideas about the Constitution?

ANSWER: Students might suggest that having fought to gain independence, he would be particularly committed to making sure that the constitutional system worked fairly.

EXPLORING THE DOCUMENT ANSWER

In vice-admiralty courts, colonists could not have a trial by jury.

Judicial Branch
The Articles of Confederation did not set up a federal court system. One of the first points that the framers of the Constitution agreed upon was to set up a national judiciary. In the Judiciary Act of 1789, Congress provided for the establishment of lower courts, such as district courts, circuit courts of appeals, and various other federal courts. The judicial system provides a check on the legislative branch: it can declare a law unconstitutional.

Exploring the Document

In the Declaration of Independence, the colonists accused the British king of not allowing them trial by jury. How does trial by jury differ from the vice-admiralty courts that colonists had faced?

[23] **Corruption of Blood:** punishing the family of a person convicted of treason

---

Section 4. The President, Vice President and all civil Officers of the United States, shall be removed from Office on Impeachment for, and Conviction of, Treason, Bribery, or other high Crimes and Misdemeanors.

ARTICLE III

Section 1. The judicial Power of the United States, shall be vested in one supreme Court, and in such inferior Courts as the Congress may from time to time ordain and establish. The Judges, both of the supreme and inferior Courts, shall hold their Offices during good Behaviour, and shall, at stated Times, receive for their Services, a Compensation, which shall not be diminished during their Continuance in Office.

Section 2. The judicial Power shall extend to all Cases, in Law and Equity, arising under this Constitution, the Laws of the United States, and Treaties made, or which shall be made, under their Authority;—to all Cases affecting Ambassadors, other public Ministers and Consuls;—to all Cases of admiralty and maritime Jurisdiction;—to Controversies to which the United States shall be a Party;—to Controversies between two or more States;— between a State and Citizens of another State;— between Citizens of different States;—between Citizens of the same State claiming Lands under Grants of different States, and between a State, or the Citizens thereof, and foreign States, Citizens or Subjects.

In all Cases affecting Ambassadors, other public Ministers and Consuls, and those in which a State shall be Party, the supreme Court shall have original Jurisdiction. In all the other Cases before mentioned, the supreme Court shall have appellate Jurisdiction, both as to Law and fact, with such Exceptions, and under such Regulations as the Congress shall make.

The Trial of all Crimes, except in Cases of Impeachment, shall be by Jury; and such Trial shall be held in the State where the said Crimes shall have been committed; but when not committed within any State, the Trial shall be at such Place or Places as the Congress may by Law have directed.

Section 3. Treason against the United States, shall consist only in levying War against them, or in adhering to their Enemies, giving them Aid and Comfort. No Person shall be convicted of Treason unless on the Testimony of two Witnesses to the same overt Act, or on Confession in open Court.

The Congress shall have Power to declare the Punishment of Treason, but no Attainder of Treason shall work **Corruption of Blood**,[23] or Forfeiture except during the Life of the Person attainted.

ARTICLE IV

Section 1. Full Faith and Credit shall be given in each State to the public Acts, Records, and judicial Proceedings of every other State. And the

Congress may by general Laws prescribe the Manner in which such Acts, Records and Proceedings shall be proved, and the Effect thereof.

Section 2. The Citizens of each State shall be entitled to all Privileges and Immunities of Citizens in the several States.

A Person charged in any State with Treason, Felony, or other Crime, who shall flee from Justice, and be found in another State, shall on Demand of the executive Authority of the State from which he fled, be delivered up, to be removed to the State having Jurisdiction of the Crime.

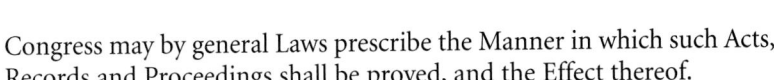

~~No Person held to Service of Labour in one State, under the Laws thereof, escaping into another, shall, in Consequence of any Law or Regulation therein, be discharged from such Service or Labour, but shall be delivered up on Claim of the Party to whom such Service or Labour may be due.~~

Section 3. New States may be admitted by the Congress into this Union; but no new State shall be formed or erected within the Jurisdiction of any other State; nor any State be formed by the Junction of two or more States, or Parts of States, without the Consent of the Legislatures of the States concerned as well as of the Congress.

The Congress shall have Power to dispose of and make all needful Rules and Regulations respecting the Territory or other Property belonging to the United States; and nothing in this Constitution shall be so construed as to Prejudice any Claims of the United States, or of any particular State.

Section 4. The United States shall guarantee to every State in this Union a Republican Form of Government, and shall protect each of them against Invasion; and on Application of the Legislature, or of the Executive (when the Legislature cannot be convened) against domestic Violence.

ARTICLE V

The Congress, whenever two thirds of both Houses shall deem it necessary, shall propose Amendments to this Constitution, or, on the Application of the Legislatures of two thirds of the several States, shall call a Convention for proposing Amendments, which, in either Case, shall be valid to all Intents and Purposes, as Part of this Constitution, when ratified by the Legislatures of three fourths of the several States, or by Conventions in three fourths thereof, as the one or the other Mode of Ratification may be proposed by the Congress; Provided that ~~no Amendment which may be made prior to the Year One thousand eight hundred and eight shall in any Manner affect the first and fourth Clauses in the Ninth Section of the first Article; and that~~ no State, without its Consent, shall be deprived of its equal Suffrage in the Senate.

Exploring the Document

The framers wanted to ensure that the citizens could determine how the state governments would operate. **How does the need to respect the laws of each state support the principle of popular sovereignty?**

The States

States must honor the laws, records, and court decisions of other states. A person cannot escape a legal obligation by moving from one state to another.

Exploring the Document

In a republic, voters elect representatives to act in their best interest. **How does Article IV protect the practice of republicanism in the United States?**

Exploring the Document

America's founders may not have realized how long the Constitution would last, but they did set up a system for changing or adding to it. They did not want to make it easy to change the Constitution. **By what methods may the Constitution be amended? Under what sorts of circumstances do you think an amendment might be necessary?**

★ Constitutional Heritage

Admission of New States. Although the framers of the Constitution wanted to allow new states to be admitted, many also wanted to preserve the power of the original states. One delegate suggested that the total number of representatives in the lower house from the new states should never exceed the total number from the original states.

CRITICAL THINKING

If this suggestion had become part of the Constitution, how might the current U.S. government be affected?

ANSWER: Students might suggest that states along the Atlantic would have a disproportionate amount of power.

EXPLORING THE DOCUMENT ANSWER

It allows the people, rather than the federal government, to determine the laws of each state.

EXPLORING THE DOCUMENT ANSWER

It guarantees that every state will have a representative government.

The Signers of the Constitution. At 27 years old, Jonathan Dayton was the youngest person to sign the Constitution. At 81, Benjamin Franklin was the oldest. Franklin's signature was particularly important. As one of the most renowned men in America, he lent respectability to the new document.

CRITICAL THINKING

Why might having people of varying ages draft the Constitution help create a lasting document?

ANSWER: Students might suggest that it brought different perspectives and experiences to their efforts.

EXPLORING THE DOCUMENT ANSWER
(for p. 273)

two-thirds of both Houses can propose Amendments, or two thirds of the states can propose amendments; students' responses will vary

National Supremacy
One of the biggest problems facing the delegates to the Constitutional Convention was the question of what would happen if a state law and a federal law conflicted. Which law would be followed? Who would decide? The second clause of Article VI answers those questions. When a federal law and a state law disagree, the federal law overrides the state law. The Constitution and other federal laws are the "supreme Law of the Land." This clause is often called the supremacy clause.

Ratification
The Articles of Confederation called for all 13 states to approve any revision to the Articles. The Constitution required that 9 out of the 13 states would be needed to ratify the Constitution. The first state to ratify was Delaware, on December 7, 1787. Almost two and a half years later, on May 29, 1790, Rhode Island became the last state to ratify the Constitution.

ARTICLE VI

All Debts contracted and Engagements entered into, before the Adoption of this Constitution, shall be as valid against the United States under this Constitution, as under the Confederation.

This Constitution, and the Laws of the United States which shall be made in Pursuance thereof; and all Treaties made, or which shall be made, under the Authority of the United States, shall be the supreme Law of the Land; and the Judges in every State shall be bound thereby, any Thing in the Constitution or Laws of any State to the Contrary notwithstanding.

The Senators and Representatives before mentioned, and the Members of the several State Legislatures, and all executive and judicial Officers, both of the United States and of the several States, shall be bound by Oath or Affirmation, to support this Constitution; but no religious Test shall ever be required as a Qualification to any Office or public Trust under the United States.

ARTICLE VII

The Ratification of the Conventions of nine States, shall be sufficient for the Establishment of this Constitution between the States so ratifying the Same.

Done in Convention by the Unanimous Consent of the States present the Seventeenth Day of September in the Year of our Lord one thousand seven hundred and Eighty seven and of the Independence of the United States of America the Twelfth. In witness whereof We have hereunto subscribed our Names,

George Washington—
President and deputy from Virginia

NEW HAMPSHIRE
John Langdon
Nicholas Gilman

DELAWARE
George Read
Gunning Bedford, Jr.
John Dickinson
Richard Bassett
Jacob Broom

MASSACHUSETTS
Nathaniel Gorham
Rufus King

MARYLAND
James McHenry
Daniel of St. Thomas Jenifer
Daniel Carroll

CONNECTICUT
William Samuel Johnson
Roger Sherman

NEW YORK
Alexander Hamilton

VIRGINIA
John Blair
James Madison, Jr.

NEW JERSEY
William Livingston
David Brearley
William Paterson
Jonathan Dayton

NORTH CAROLINA
William Blount
Richard Dobbs Spaight
Hugh Williamson

PENNSYLVANIA
Benjamin Franklin
Thomas Mifflin
Robert Morris
George Clymer

Thomas FitzSimons
Jared Ingersoll
James Wilson
Gouverneur Morris

SOUTH CAROLINA
John Rutledge
Charles Cotesworth
  Pinckney
Charles Pinckney
Pierce Butler

GEORGIA
William Few
Abraham Baldwin

Attest:
William Jackson, Secretary

THE AMENDMENTS

Articles in addition to, and Amendment of the Constitution of the United States of America, proposed by Congress, and ratified by the Legislatures of the several States, pursuant to the fifth Article of the original Constitution.

[The First through Tenth Amendments, now known as the Bill of Rights, were proposed to the states for ratification on September 25, 1789, and declared in force on December 15, 1791.]

First Amendment

Congress shall make no law respecting an establishment of religion, or prohibiting the free exercise thereof; or abridging the freedom of speech, or of the press; or the right of the people peaceably to assemble, and to petition the Government for a redress of grievances.

Second Amendment

A well regulated Militia, being necessary to the security of a free State, the right of the people to keep and bear Arms, shall not be infringed.

Third Amendment

No Soldier shall, in time of peace, be **quartered**[24] in any house, without the consent of the Owner, nor in time of war, but in a manner to be prescribed by law.

Fourth Amendment

The right of the people to be secure in their persons, houses, papers, and effects, against unreasonable searches and seizures, shall not be violated, and no **Warrants**[25] shall issue, but upon probable cause, supported by Oath or affirmation, and particularly describing the place to be searched, and the persons or things to be seized.

Fifth Amendment

No person shall be held to answer for a capital, or otherwise **infamous**[26] crime, unless on a presentment or **indictment**[27] of a Grand Jury, except in cases arising in the land or naval forces, or in the Militia, when in actual service in time of War or public danger; nor shall any person be subject for the same offence to be twice put in jeopardy of life or limb; nor shall be compelled in any criminal case to be a witness against himself, nor be deprived of life, liberty, or property, without due process of law; nor shall private property be taken for public use, without just compensation.

Sixth Amendment

In all criminal prosecutions, the accused shall enjoy the right to a speedy and public trial, by an impartial jury of the State and district wherein the

---

Bill of Rights
One of the conditions set by several states for ratifying the Constitution was the inclusion of a bill of rights. Many people feared that a stronger central government might take away basic rights of the people that had been guaranteed in state constitutions.

Exploring the Document

Freedom of Religion. The First Amendment forbids Congress from making any "law respecting an establishment of religion" or restraining the freedom to practice religion as one chooses. **Why is freedom of religion an important right?**

[24] **quartered:** housed

[25] **Warrants:** written orders authorizing a person to make an arrest, a seizure, or search
[26] **infamous:** disgraceful
[27] **indictment:** the act of charging with a crime

Rights of the Accused
The Fifth, Sixth, and Seventh Amendments describe the procedures that courts must follow when trying people accused of crimes.

Trials
The Sixth Amendment makes several guarantees, including a prompt trial and a trial by a jury chosen from the state and district in which the crime was committed.

Civil Liberties. Throughout the 1900s the Supreme Court extended the coverage of the civil liberties in the Bill of Rights. For some time, justices ruled that the Bill of Rights did not override state laws. Although the Fourteenth Amendment stated that the states could not deprive citizens of their constitutional rights, few justices changed their opinions. In the mid-1900s, Justice Hugo Black began to reinterpret the Fourteenth Amendment. He believed that the guarantees in the Bill of Rights were absolute. Most justices have since tempered this position, believing that these guarantees are constrained by competing social interests.

ACTIVITY: Have students bring in newspaper articles that deal with the exercise of civil liberties. Using these articles to start discussion, have students describe what they think are proper and improper limitations of civil liberties.

EXPLORING THE DOCUMENT ANSWER
They extend rights to the people and to the states.

[28] **ascertained:** found out

[29] **construed:** explained or interpreted

President and Vice President
The Twelfth Amendment changed the election procedure for president and vice president.

crime shall have been committed, which district shall have been previously **ascertained**[28] by law, and to be informed of the nature and cause of the accusation; to be confronted with the witnesses against him; to have compulsory process for obtaining witnesses in his favor, and to have the Assistance of Counsel for his defence.

Seventh Amendment

In Suits at common law, where the value in controversy shall exceed twenty dollars, the right of trial by jury shall be preserved, and no fact tried by a jury, shall be otherwise re-examined in any Court of the United States, than according to the rules of the common law.

Eighth Amendment

Excessive bail shall not be required, nor excessive fines imposed, nor cruel and unusual punishments inflicted.

Ninth Amendment

The enumeration in the Constitution, of certain rights, shall not be construed to deny or disparage others retained by the people.

Tenth Amendment

The powers not delegated to the United States by the Constitution, nor prohibited by it to the States, are reserved to the States respectively, or to the people.

Eleventh Amendment

[Proposed March 4, 1794; declared ratified January 8, 1798]
The Judicial power of the United States shall not be **construed**[29] to extend to any suit in law or equity, commenced or prosecuted against one of the United States by Citizens of another State, or by Citizens or Subjects of any Foreign State.

Twelfth Amendment

[Proposed December 9, 1803; declared ratified September 25, 1804]
The Electors shall meet in their respective states, and vote by ballot for President and Vice-President, one of whom, at least, shall not be an inhabitant of the same state with themselves; they shall name in their ballots the person voted for as President, and in distinct ballots the person voted for as Vice-President, and they shall make distinct lists of all persons voted for as President, and of all persons voted for as Vice-President, and of the number of votes for each, which lists they shall sign and certify, and transmit sealed to the seat of the government of the United States, directed to the President of the Senate;—The President of the Senate shall, in the presence of the Senate and House of Representatives, open all the certificates and the votes

shall then be counted;—The person having the greatest number of votes for President, shall be the President, if such number be a majority of the whole number of Electors appointed; and if no person have such majority, then from the persons having the highest numbers not exceeding three on the list of those voted for as President, the House of Representatives shall choose immediately, by ballot, the President. But in choosing the President, the votes shall be taken by states, the representation from each state having one vote; a quorum for this purpose shall consist of a member or members from two-thirds of the states, and a majority of all the states shall be necessary to a choice. ~~And if the House of Representatives shall not choose a President whenever the right of choice shall devolve upon them, before the fourth day of March next following, then the Vice-President shall act as President, as in the case of the death or other constitutional disability of the President.~~ The person having the greatest number of votes as Vice-President, shall be the Vice-President, if such number be a majority of the whole number of Electors appointed, and if no person have a majority, then from the two highest numbers on the list, the Senate shall Choose the Vice-President; a quorum for the purpose shall consist of two-thirds of the whole number of Senators, and a majority of the whole number shall be necessary to a choice. But no person constitutionally ineligible to the office of President shall be eligible to that of Vice-President of the United States.

Thirteenth Amendment

[Proposed January 31, 1865; declared ratified December 18, 1865]

Section 1. Neither slavery nor **involuntary servitude**,[30] except as a punishment for crime whereof the party shall have been duly convicted, shall exist within the United States, or any place subject to their jurisdiction.

Section 2. Congress shall have power to enforce this article by appropriate legislation.

Fourteenth Amendment

[Proposed June 13, 1866; declared ratified July 28, 1868]

Section 1. All persons born or naturalized in the United States, and subject to the jurisdiction thereof, are citizens of the United States and of the State wherein they reside. No State shall make or enforce any law which shall abridge the privileges or immunities of citizens of the United States; nor shall any State deprive any person of life, liberty, or property, without due process of law; nor deny to any person within its jurisdiction the equal protection of the laws.

Section 2. Representatives shall be apportioned among the several States according to their respective numbers, counting the whole number of per-

---

Abolishing Slavery
Although some slaves had been freed during the Civil War, slavery was not abolished until the Thirteenth Amendment took effect.

30 involuntary servitude: being forced to work against one's will

Protecting the Rights of Citizens
In 1833 the Supreme Court ruled that the Bill of Rights limited the federal government but not the state governments. This ruling was interpreted to mean that states were able to keep African Americans from becoming state citizens and keeping the Bill of Rights from protecting them. The Fourteenth Amendment defines citizenship and prevents states from interfering in the rights of citizens of the United States.

★ Citizenship

Postwar Amendments.
Three amendments—the Thirteenth, Fourteenth, and Fifteenth—were meant initially to respond to changes demanded by the northern victory in the Civil War. At the time it was passed, many southerners interpreted the Fourteenth Amendment as a way for the North to punish them for their rebellion by making the South extend civil rights to African Americans. Scholars have argued that the Fourteenth Amendment remains the most important addition to the Constitution since the Bill of Rights because of its inclusion of due process and equal protection clauses.

CRITICAL THINKING
Why might scholars feel the Fourteenth Amendment is so important?

ANSWER: Students might suggest that it redefined citizenship and for the first time appeared to guarantee African Americans their civil rights. It also made the Bill of Rights apply to state law.

Suffrage. The passage of the Fourteenth and Fifteen Amendments dramatically increased African Americans' political participation. Strikes broke out among African American workers throughout the South. The workers staged sit-ins on segregated carriages in Richmond, Virginia, and when police tried to stop their protests, angry crowds formed, demanding, "Let's have our rights." Almost every institution of black life, particularly the church, worked to mobilize the African American vote and to educate new voters. So many African American laborers attended the Republican state convention in Virginia that Richmond's tobacco factories had to close.

CRITICAL THINKING

Why might African Americans after the Civil War have found the vote to be so important?

ANSWER: Students might suggest that since African Americans had been denied any form of political participation, they hoped that the vote would help them become full citizens of the United States and accepted members of their communities.

EXPLORING THE DOCUMENT ANSWER

Students might suggest that in order to have equal representation under the law, all people need to have the right to vote.

Exploring the Document

The Fifteenth Amendment extended the vote to African American men. Why is the right to vote guaranteed by the Fifteenth Amendment important?

sons in each State, ~~excluding Indians not taxed~~. But when the right to vote at any election for the choice of electors for President and Vice President of the United States, Representatives in Congress, the Executive and Judicial officers of a State, or the members of the Legislature thereof, is denied to any of the ~~male~~ inhabitants of such State, ~~being twenty-one years of age,~~ and citizens of the United States, or in any way abridged, except for participation in rebellion, or other crime, the basis of representation therein shall be reduced in the proportion which the number of such ~~male~~ citizens shall bear to the whole number of ~~male~~ citizens ~~twenty-one years of age~~ in such State.

Section 3. No person shall be a Senator or Representative in Congress, or elector of President and Vice President, or hold any office, civil or military, under the United States, or under any State, who, having previously taken an oath, as a member of Congress, or as an officer of the United States, or as a member of any State legislature, or as an executive or judicial officer of any State, to support the Constitution of the United States, shall have engaged in insurrection or rebellion against the same, or given aid or comfort to the enemies thereof. But Congress may by a vote of two-thirds of each House, remove such disability.

Section 4. The validity of the public debt of the United States, authorized by law, including debts incurred for payment of pensions and bounties for services in suppressing insurrection or rebellion, shall not be questioned. But neither the United States nor any State shall assume or pay any debt or obligation incurred in aid of insurrection or rebellion against the United States, ~~or any claim for the loss of emancipation of any slave~~; but all such debts, obligations and claims shall be held illegal and void.

Section 5. The Congress shall have power to enforce, by appropriate legislation, the provisions of this article.

Fifteenth Amendment
   [Proposed February 26, 1869; declared ratified March 30, 1870]

Section 1. The right of citizens of the United States to vote shall not be denied or abridged by the United States or by any State on account of race, color, or previous condition of servitude.

Section 2. The Congress shall have power to enforce this article by appropriate legislation.

Sixteenth Amendment
   [Proposed July 12, 1909; declared ratified February 25, 1913]

The Congress shall have power to lay and collect taxes on incomes, from whatever source derived, without apportionment among the several States, and without regard to any census or enumeration.

Seventeenth Amendment

[Proposed May 13, 1912; declared ratified May 31, 1913]

The Senate of the United States shall be composed of two Senators from each State, elected by the people thereof, for six years; and each Senator shall have one vote. The electors in each State shall have the qualifications requisite for electors of the most numerous branch of the State legislatures.

When vacancies happen in the representation of any State in the Senate, the executive authority of such State shall issue writs of election to fill such vacancies: *Provided,* That the legislature of any State may empower the executive thereof to make temporary appointments until the people fill the vacancies by election as the legislature may direct.

~~This amendment shall not be so construed as to affect the election or term of any Senator chosen before it becomes valid as part of the Constitution.~~

Eighteenth Amendment

[Proposed December 18, 1917; declared ratified January 29, 1919; repealed by the Twenty-first Amendment December 5, 1933]

~~**Section 1.** After one year from the ratification of this article the manufacture, sale, or transportation of intoxicating liquors within, the importation thereof into, or the exportation thereof from the United States and all territory subject to the jurisdiction thereof for beverage purposes is hereby prohibited.~~

~~**Section 2.** The Congress and the several States shall have concurrent power to enforce this article by appropriate legislation.~~

~~**Section 3.** This article shall be inoperative unless it shall have been ratified as an amendment to the Constitution by the legislatures of the several States, as provided in the Constitution, within seven years from the date of the submission hereof to the States by the Congress.~~

Nineteenth Amendment

[Proposed June 4, 1919; declared ratified August 26, 1920]

The right of citizens of the United States to vote shall not be denied or abridged by the United States or by any State on account of sex.

Congress shall have power to enforce this article by appropriate legislation.

Twentieth Amendment

[Proposed March 2, 1932; declared ratified February 6, 1933]

Section 1. The terms of the President and Vice-President shall end at noon on the 20th day of January, and the terms of Senators and Representatives

---

Exploring the Document

The Seventeenth Amendment requires that senators be elected directly by the people instead of by the state legislature. **What principle of our government does the Seventeenth Amendment protect?**

Prohibition
Although many people believed that the Eighteenth Amendment was good for the health and welfare of the American people, it was repealed 14 years later.

Women's Suffrage
Abigail Adams and others were disappointed that the Declaration of Independence and the Constitution did not specifically include women. It took almost 130 years and much campaigning by groups before suffrage for women was finally achieved.

George W. Norris. During his long congressional career, George W. Norris not only created and worked to pass the Twentieth Amendment but also worked for the introduction of presidential primaries and for the direct election of senators. Though a Republican, Norris rarely voted along party lines. In defense of his independence, he claimed he "would rather be right than regular."

ACTIVITY: Have students find examples of recent political reforms. Then have them draft bills or constitutional amendments that could be used to enact these reforms.

EXPLORING THE DOCUMENT ANSWER
It had to be ratified by state conventions.

Taking Office
In the original Constitution, a newly elected president and Congress did not take office until March 4, which was four months after the November election. The officials who were leaving office were called lame ducks because they had little influence during those four months. The Twentieth Amendment changed the date that the new president and Congress take office. Members of Congress now take office during the first week of January, and the president takes office on January 20.

Exploring the Document

The Twenty-first Amendment was the first amendment not ratified by state legislatures. **According to the crossed-out text, what method was used to ratify the Twenty-first Amendment?**

at noon on the 3d day of January, of the years in which such terms would have ended if this article had not been ratified; and the terms of their successors shall then begin.

Section 2. The Congress shall assemble at least once in every year, and such meeting shall begin at noon on the 3d day of January, unless they shall by law appoint a different day.

Section 3. If, at the time fixed for the beginning of the term of the President, the President elect shall have died, the Vice-President elect shall become President. If a President shall not have been chosen before the time fixed for the beginning of his term, or if the President elect shall have failed to qualify, then the Vice-President elect shall act as President until a President shall have qualified; and the Congress may by law provide for the case wherein neither a President elect nor a Vice-President elect shall have qualified, declaring who shall then act as President, or the manner in which one who is to act shall be selected, and such person shall act accordingly until a President or Vice-President shall have qualified.

Section 4. The Congress may by law provide for the case of the death of any of the persons from whom the House of Representatives may choose a President whenever the right of choice shall have devolved upon them, and for the case of the death of any of the persons from whom the Senate may choose a Vice-President whenever the right of choice shall have devolved upon them.

~~**Section 5.** Sections 1 and 2 shall take effect on the 15th day of October following the ratification of this article.~~

~~**Section 6.** This article shall be inoperative unless it shall have been ratified as an amendment to the Constitution by the legislatures of three-fourths of the several States within seven years from the date of its submission.~~

Twenty-first Amendment
[Proposed February 20, 1933; declared ratified December 5, 1933]

Section 1. The eighteenth article of amendment to the Constitution of the United States is hereby repealed.

Section 2. The transportation or importation into any State, Territory, or possession of the United States for delivery or use therein of intoxicating liquors, in violation of the laws thereof, is hereby prohibited.

~~**Section 3.** This article shall be inoperative unless it shall have been ratified as an amendment to the Constitution by conventions in the several States, as provided in the Constitution, within seven years from the date of the submission hereof to the States by the Congress.~~

Twenty-second Amendment

[Proposed March 21, 1947; declared ratified February 26, 1951]

Section 1. No person shall be elected to the office of the President more than twice, and no person who has held the office of President, or acted as President, for more than two years of a term to which some other person was elected President shall be elected to the office of the President more than once. ~~But this Article shall not apply to any person holding the office of President when this Article was proposed by the Congress, and shall not prevent any person who may be holding the office of President, or acting as President, during the term within which this Article becomes operative from holding the office of President or acting as President during the remainder of such term.~~

~~**Section 2.** This article shall be inoperative unless it shall have been ratified as an amendment to the Constitution by the legislatures of three-fourths of the several States within seven years from the date of its submission to the States by the Congress.~~

Twenty-third Amendment

[Proposed June 16, 1960; ratified March 29, 1961]

Section 1. The District constituting the seat of Government of the United States shall appoint in such manner as the Congress may direct:

A number of electors of President and Vice-President equal to the whole number of Senators and Representatives in Congress to which the District would be entitled if it were a State, but in no event more than the least populous state; they shall be in addition to those appointed by the States, but they shall be considered, for the purposes of the election of President and Vice-President, to be electors appointed by a State; and they shall meet in the District and perform such duties as provided by the twelfth article of amendment.

Section 2. The Congress shall have power to enforce this article by appropriate legislation.

Twenty-fourth Amendment

[Proposed August 27, 1962; ratified January 23, 1964]

Section 1. The right of citizens of the United States to vote in any primary or other election for President or Vice-President, for electors for President or Vice-President, or for Senator or Representative in Congress, shall not be denied or abridged by the United States or any State by reason of failure to pay any poll tax or other tax.

Exploring the Document

From the time of President George Washington's administration, it was a custom for presidents to serve no more than two terms in office. Franklin D. Roosevelt, however, was elected to four terms. The Twenty-second Amendment restricted presidents to no more than two terms in office. Why do you think citizens chose to limit the power of the president in this way?

Voting Rights

Until the ratification of the Twenty-third Amendment, the people of Washington, D.C., could not vote in presidential elections.

Historical Sidelight

Woodrow Wilson.
Realization of the need for the Twenty-fifth Amendment began during Woodrow Wilson's term. In 1919 Wilson suffered a stroke and could not meet with his cabinet for seven months. While the president was ill, his vice president, Thomas Marshall, made it clear that he did not want to serve as president. Instead, the seriously ill Wilson conducted government affairs through his wife, Edith.

CRITICAL THINKING

How can the U.S. government continue to function even when the head of state is ill?

ANSWER: The Constitution divides decision making and provides a framework for government activity to continue.

Constitutional Heritage

Presidential Succession.
The rules for determining presidential succession have been amended, but the line of succession has never been tested past the vice president. Of the nine vice presidents who have succeeded presidents who have died or resigned, just four have been re-elected to a full term.

ACTIVITY: Have students research and draw a chart of the line of succession for the current presidency.

Presidential Disability
The illness of President Eisenhower in the 1950s and the assassination of President Kennedy in 1963 were the events behind the Twenty-fifth Amendment. The Constitution did not provide a clear-cut method for a vice president to take over for a disabled president or upon the death of a president. This amendment provides for filling the office of the vice president if a vacancy occurs, and it provides a way for the vice president—or someone else in the line of succession—to take over if the president is unable to perform the duties of that office.

Section 2. The Congress shall have power to enforce this article by appropriate legislation.

Twenty-fifth Amendment
[Proposed July 6, 1965; ratified February 10, 1967]

Section 1. In case of the removal of the President from office or of his death or resignation, the Vice-President shall become President.

Section 2. Whenever there is a vacancy in the office of the Vice-President, the President shall nominate a Vice-President who shall take office upon confirmation by a majority vote of both Houses of Congress.

Section 3. Whenever the President transmits to the President pro tempore of the Senate and the Speaker of the House of Representatives his written declaration that he is unable to discharge the powers and duties of his office, and until he transmits to them a written declaration to the contrary, such powers and duties shall be discharged by the Vice-President as Acting President.

Section 4. Whenever the Vice-President and a majority of either the principal officers of the executive departments or of such other body as Congress may by law provide, transmit to the President pro tempore of the Senate and the Speaker of the House of Representatives their written declaration that the President is unable to discharge the powers and duties of his office, the Vice-President shall immediately assume the powers and duties of the office as Acting President.

Thereafter, when the President transmits to the President pro tempore of the Senate and the Speaker of the House of Representatives his written declaration that no inability exists, he shall resume the powers and duties of his office unless the Vice-President and a majority of either the principal officers of the executive department or of such other body as Congress may by law provide, transmit within four days to the President pro tempore of the Senate and the Speaker of the House of Representatives their written declaration that the President is unable to discharge the powers and duties of his office. Thereupon Congress shall decide the issue, assembling within forty-eight hours for that purpose if not in session. If the Congress, within twenty-one days after receipt of the latter written declaration, or, if Congress is not in session, within twenty-one days after Congress is required to assemble, determines by two-thirds vote of both Houses that the President is unable to discharge the powers and duties of his office, the Vice-President shall continue to discharge the same as Acting President; otherwise, the President shall resume the powers and duties of his office.

Twenty-sixth Amendment

[Proposed March 23, 1971; ratified July 1, 1971]

Section 1. The right of citizens of the United States, who are eighteen years of age or older, to vote shall not be denied or abridged by the United States or by any State on account of age.

Section 2. The Congress shall have power to enforce this article by appropriate legislation.

Twenty-seventh Amendment

[Proposed September 25, 1789; ratified May 7, 1992]

No law, varying the compensation for the services of the Senators and Representatives, shall take effect, until an election of Representatives shall have intervened.

Expanded Suffrage
The Voting Act of 1970 tried to set the voting age at 18. However, the Supreme Court ruled that the act set the voting age for national elections only, not state or local elections. This ruling would make necessary several different ballots at elections. The Twenty-sixth Amendment gave 18-year-old citizens the right to vote in all elections.

Separation of Powers and Checks and Balances

LEGISLATIVE BRANCH (Congress)
writes the laws
confirms presidential appointments
approves treaties
grants money
declares war

may reject appointments
may reject treaties
may withhold funding for presidential initiatives
may impeach president
may override a veto

may propose constitutional amendments to overrule judicial decisions
may impeach Supreme Court justices
may reject appointments to the Supreme Court

may adjourn Congress in certain situations
may veto bills

may declare laws unconstitutional

EXECUTIVE BRANCH (President)
proposes laws
administers the laws
commands armed forces
appoints ambassadors and other officials
conducts foreign policy
makes treaties

may declare executive actions unconstitutional

appoints judges

JUDICIAL BRANCH (Supreme Court)
interprets the Constitution and other laws
reviews lower-court decisions

Section 2

OBJECTIVES

⭐ Discuss the main freedoms outlined within the First Amendment and analyze the importance of each.

⭐ Outline how the Bill of Rights addresses colonial grievances listed in the Declaration of Independence.

⭐ Examine the protections that the Bill of Rights gives to people accused of crimes.

SECTION 2 RESOURCES

REPRODUCIBLE

▶ Guided Reading Strategy 9.2
▶ Graphic Organizer 9: The Bill of Rights

TECHNOLOGY

▶ One-Stop Planner, Lesson 9.2
▶ CNN Presents America: Beginnings to 1914 Segment: Remembering the Bill of Rights
▶ Exploring America's Past Video Segment: The Roles of a Citizen; Teacher's Guide, pp. 48–51
▶ Homework Practice Online

REINFORCEMENT, REVIEW, AND ASSESSMENT

▶ Section 2 Review, p. 289
▶ Daily Quiz 9.2
▶ Main Idea Activity 9.2
▶ English Audio Summary 9.2
▶ Spanish Audio Summary 9.2

Section 2

The Bill of Rights

Read to Discover

1. What are the main freedoms outlined within the First Amendment, and why are they important?
2. How does the Bill of Rights address colonial grievances listed in the Declaration of Independence?
3. What protections does the Bill of Rights give to people accused of crimes?

WHY IT MATTERS TODAY

The Bill of Rights protects some of the basic rights that we enjoy in our daily lives. Not all countries let their citizens enjoy these same rights. Use **CNN fyi.com** or other **current events** sources to learn about people in another country who are trying to exercise some of the rights granted U.S. citizens in the Bill of Rights. Record your findings in your journal.

Define

• petition
• search warrant
• due process
• indict
• double jeopardy
• eminent domain

Identify

• James Madison

Quill pens like this one were used in the 1700s.

The Story Continues

James Madison was worried that the Constitution might not pass. The Antifederalists opposed it, and even Virginia, Madison's home state, was hesitating. Forceful speaker Patrick Henry wanted the Constitution to include a bill of rights before Virginia ratified it. The Virginia legislature rejected Henry's position and approved the Constitution on the condition that a bill of rights would be added later. At first, Madison had opposed amending the Constitution, but to satisfy the concerns of others, he put together a set of amendments.

⭐ The First Amendment

Federalist **James Madison** promised that a bill of rights would be added to the Constitution. With this promise, the Constitution was ratified. In 1789 Madison began narrowing down the huge list of proposed amendments. He then gave a shorter list of amendments to the House of Representatives. Of those, Congress approved 12 amendments. The

★ TEACH

Have students read Section 2 and complete Guided Reading Strategy 9.2. Choose one or more of the following activities to explore the section content with students. For further suggestions on block scheduling or team teaching, see the *Block Scheduling Handbook with Team Teaching Strategies.*

LEVEL 1: Lead a class discussion in which you ask students how the Bill of Rights addresses the colonial grievances outlined in the Declaration of Independence. (*Students' responses should note that under the Bill of Rights the* states can maintain militias; the military is prohibited from forcing citizens to house soldiers; no unreasonable searches or seizures are permitted; no one may be punished for a crime without due process; everyone has a right to a prompt, public trial; the Bill of Rights also establishes bail and the prohibition of cruel and unusual punishments.) Then organize students into small groups. Have students use their textbooks to create a set of drawings that show how these amendments protect citizens against the problems that existed before the Bill of Rights was written. **ENGLISH LANGUAGE LEARNERS ,**

COOPERATIVE LEARNING

states ratified 10. Those 10 amendments, called the Bill of Rights, protect U.S. citizens' individual liberties.

History Makers Speak
❝The safety and happiness of society are the objects at which all political institutions aim and to which all such institutions must be sacrificed.❞

—James Madison, from *The Macmillan Dictionary of Political Quotations*

The ideas within the First Amendment form the most basic rights of all U.S. citizens. These rights include freedom of religion, the press, speech, assembly, and to **petition**—make a request of the government. The First Amendment begins by stating that "Congress shall make no law respecting an establishment of religion, or prohibiting the free exercise thereof." In other words, the government cannot support or interfere with the practice of a religion. This amendment keeps the government from favoring any religion over others. When the Constitution was written, many countries had an official state religion. However, some Americans wanted to keep the government from establishing an official religion.

The First Amendment also guarantees freedom of speech and of the press. Americans have the right to express their own ideas and views and to hear the ideas and views of others. John Peter Zenger, the publisher of the *New York Weekly Journal,* was an example of why freedom of the press is important. Zenger had gone on trial in 1735 for criticizing New York's royal governor. The jury found Zenger not guilty because the statements he printed were true.

Freedom of speech does not mean that people can say anything they want to, however. The Constitution does not protect slander—false statements meant to damage someone's reputation. Libel, or intentionally publishing a lie that harms another person, is not protected either. The Supreme Court has also ruled that the First Amendment does not protect speech that endangers public safety. For example, Justice Oliver Wendell Holmes explained that falsely shouting "Fire!" in a crowded theater is not protected as free speech.

History Makers Speak
❝The question in every case is whether the words used are used in such circumstances and are of such a nature to create a clear and present danger that . . . Congress has a right to prevent.❞

—Oliver Wendell Holmes, quoted in *A March of Liberty,* by Melvin I. Urofsky

Americans also have freedom of assembly, or to hold meetings. Any group may gather to discuss issues or to conduct business. If those people gather peacefully and are not involved in any illegal activity, the government cannot interfere. Any American can present a petition to a government official. This right lets Americans show their dissatisfaction with a law, as well as suggest new laws.

✔ **Reading Check: Finding the Main Idea** What are the freedoms protected by the First Amendment? *freedom of assembly, the press, religion, speech, and to petition*

Analyzing Primary Sources
Identifying Points of View What does James Madison think the purpose of the government is? *Students might say to ensure the safety and happiness of society.*

THE GRANGER COLLECTION, NEW YORK

BIOGRAPHY

James Madison
(1751–1836)

James Madison was born in Virginia in 1751. He attended the College of New Jersey, now Princeton University, before entering politics in Virginia. Early in his career, Madison became a strong supporter of religious freedom. Madison served in Congress until 1797. He later influenced politics from his family plantation. There he remained a slaveholder despite his stated belief in individual liberty. In 1801 Madison became secretary of state and went on to serve two terms as president. Madison played a central role in framing the Constitution and adding the Bill of Rights. For these reasons, he is often called the Father of the Constitution. Why is Madison called the Father of the Constitution?

The English Bill of Rights.
The Bill of Rights in the U.S. Constitution has its origins in the English Bill of Rights of 1689. That document contained provisions, such as prohibiting "cruel and unusual punishments," that the framers of the Constitution adopted verbatim.

CRITICAL THINKING
Why were the framers of the Constitution influenced by British documents?

ANSWER: Students might suggest that the intellectual and legal heritage of the colonies was largely British.

BIOGRAPHY ANSWER
Students might suggest he played an important role in framing the Constitution and adding the Bill of Rights.

Technology Resources

CNN Presents America: Beginnings to 1914 Segment: Remembering the Bill of Rights

---

ALL LEVELS: Copy the following graphic organizer onto the chalkboard, omitting the italicized answers. Then have students identify the rights protected by the First Amendment. Underneath each right, have students provide examples of what citizens may or may not do according to the amendment. **ENGLISH LANGUAGE LEARNERS**

LEVEL 3: Ask students what the Fifth, Sixth, Seventh, and Eighth Amendments have in common. *(Students' responses should note that they all focus on protecting the rights of the accused.)* Then organize the class into small groups. Have each group create an advertisement for a law firm that specializes in protecting the rights of the accused. Advertisements should focus on scenarios in which the rights of the accused appear to have been violated. They may be designed for print, radio, television, or the Internet, depending on available resources. Have a volunteer from each group present his or her group's ads to the class. After each group finishes its presentation, have the class discuss the situation presented and identify the amendment or amendments that guard against that type of situation. **COOPERATIVE LEARNING**

Freedom of Religion
The country cannot have an official religion.

First Amendment

Freedom of the Press
People cannot libel or slander others.

Freedom of Speech
People cannot yell "Fire!" in a crowded theater.

Freedom to Petition
Any American can present a petition to a government official.

Freedom of Assembly
People can hold meetings.

Global Relations

Quartering Troops.

In 1689 Parliament passed an act that protected British citizens from having to house or quarter troops in their homes. The British law did not apply to America, and during the French and Indian War (1754–63), colonists discovered that they had no legal protection against the practice of quartering.

CRITICAL THINKING

Why did the colonists come to resent the practice of quartering?

ANSWER: Students might suggest that quartering troops was an invasion of their privacy and that feeding the British soldiers cost money.

CITIZENSHIP AND YOU ANSWER

Students' opinions will vary, but they should clearly explain their views.

Visual Record Answer

Students might suggest that they should work together to preserve their community.

Interpreting the Visual Record

Flood control *These members of the National Guard are helping local citizens prevent a river from flooding.* **Why do you think it is important for community members to join together in such efforts?**

Citizenship and You

Freedom of Assembly

When Congress first talked about what should be in the Bill of Rights, some members argued that people in power should not be able to stop rival groups from meeting. Thus, freedom of assembly became part of the First Amendment. Over the years Americans have gathered to privately and publicly express their views on issues ranging from civil rights to education.

Americans do not have an unlimited right of assembly, however. Citizens must follow rules that protect public safety. For example, parades usually require a local permit so that traffic flow can be managed during the parade time. Such restrictions cannot be used to keep people or groups with unpopular beliefs from publicly expressing their views. Should all groups have the same freedom of assembly? Explain your answer.

★ Protecting Citizens

The Second, Third, and Fourth Amendments all relate to colonial disputes with Great Britain before the Revolution. The Second Amendment deals with state militias. Colonial militias were vital to America's defense. The first battle of the Revolutionary War started when British troops tried to seize the Massachusetts militia's weapons. The framers believed that the states needed to keep their militias for emergencies. Today the National Guard has replaced state militias. National Guard members also serve in wars and help restore order during crises, such as natural disasters.

Some people believe that gun control laws violate the Second Amendment. This part of the Constitution states that "the right of the people to keep and bear arms shall not be infringed [violated]." In 1939 the Supreme Court passed rules for nonmilitary firearms. Years later, a U.S. court of appeals ruled that gun control laws do not violate the Second Amendment. The Supreme Court let that ruling stand in 1983.

The Third Amendment keeps the military from forcing citizens to give housing to soldiers. Before the Revolution, the British government pressured colonists to give food and shelter to its soldiers. British leaders also issued writs of assistance. These written orders let officials search any colonist's property for illegal goods. Anger over such actions led to the Fourth Amendment's rule against "unreasonable searches and seizures." Before authorities search someone's property, they must first get a **search warrant**, an order permitting them to look through someone's property. But authorities do not always need a warrant to conduct a search. Sometimes a suspect tries to destroy evidence or hide a weapon. When this happens, police can conduct an emergency search. This helps to protect both the officers and any evidence needed to prove criminal activity.

✔ **Reading Check: Contrasting** Contrast colonists' rights under British rule with the rights that Americans enjoy today under the Second, Third, and Fourth Amendments. Under colonial rule, the British government could search without a warrant and force civilians to provide food and shelter for soldiers. Today, the Third and Fourth Amendments protect us from this.

★ The Rights of the Accused

The Fifth, Sixth, Seventh, and Eighth Amendments provide guidelines for trying people accused of crimes. The framers designed these amendments to protect the rights of the accused. According to the Fifth Amendment, the government cannot punish anyone for a crime without **due process** of law. This means that the law should always be fairly applied. A grand jury decides if there is enough evidence to **indict**, or formally accuse, the person. Without an indictment, the court cannot try someone for a serious crime. The Fifth Amendment also protects people from being forced to testify in their own criminal trial. To keep from testifying, the defendant "takes the Fifth." Anyone found not guilty in a criminal trial cannot face **double jeopardy**. In other words, that person cannot be tried again for the same crime.

The final clause of the Fifth Amendment addresses property rights. It states that no one will have property taken "without due process of law." The one exception to this principle is the government's power of **eminent domain**—the power to take personal property to benefit the public. An example would be the taking of private lands to build a public road. The government must pay the owners a fair price for their property. However, if the property that is taken was gained through illegal activities, then the person is not paid.

The Sixth Amendment protects the rights of someone who is indicted for a crime. It states that the accused must have a quick public trial by a jury. The accused person has the right to know the charges against him or her. The accused can also hear and question the witnesses testifying against him or her. The accused has the right to an attorney. If the person cannot afford legal services, the government provides an attorney.

Sometimes the accused refuses his or her Sixth Amendment rights. For example, some defendants refuse the services of an attorney. Others choose to have a trial in front of a judge alone instead of before a jury. Defendants can bypass a trial by agreeing to a plea bargain. In these cases, the individual pleads guilty to a lesser charge. By plea bargaining, defendants avoid the risk of conviction of a crime that may carry a greater sentence.

The Seventh Amendment states that juries can decide civil cases. Sometimes an individual causes physical or financial harm to another person without committing a crime. In such cases the injured party may sue, or seek justice, in civil court. Civil cases usually involve disputes over money or property. For example, someone might bring a civil suit against an individual who refuses to pay back a debt.

✔ **Reading Check: Summarizing** What rights do Americans have under the Fifth, Sixth, and Seventh Amendments? See each amendment above for specific rights.

A judge may issue a search warrant when it seems likely that someone's property contains evidence relating to a crime.

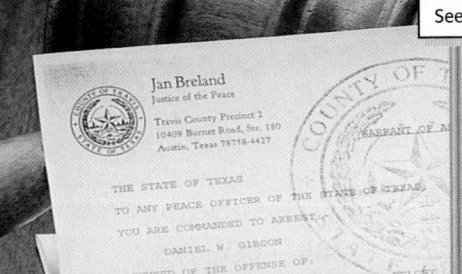

Organize the class into small groups. Have each group discuss and list the rights that it believes should be included in the Ninth Amendment. Have groups share their lists with the class. As a class, vote on whether or these suggested rights should be included. **COOPERATIVE LEARNING**

![director's chair icon] **SPOTLIGHT**
on Constitutional Amendments

Organize the class into small groups. Have each group use the library to research proposed amendments that were never ratified. Ask each group to identify an amendment that it believes should have been ratified. Then have groups write a petition to present the amendment to the government, explaining their opinion and asking the government to take action on the issue. Ask students in the class who agree with the idea to sign the petition. **COOPERATIVE LEARNING**

★ CLOSE

Have students write a poem or song about the Bill of Rights. Students should describe the protections provided by each amendment and the reasons why the colonists wanted to include each amendment in the Bill of Rights. Encourage students to share their songs or poems with the class.

★ Constitutional Heritage

Cruel and Unusual Punishment. The Supreme Court's 1972 ruling that the death penalty violated the constitutional guarantee against cruel and unusual punishment was based on the process that most states used for sentencing those convicted in death-penalty cases. The courts found the sentencing process unfair because it varied a great deal from state to state. In response to the Court's decision, most states immediately set new guidelines for death-penalty sentences. In 1976 a Georgia man convicted of murder was sentenced to death. The Supreme Court ruled that the new Georgia standards were not unfair and that the death penalty in this case was constitutional.

CRITICAL THINKING

Why did the Supreme Court require states to set strict guidelines for death-penalty sentences?

ANSWER: Students might suggest that the Supreme Court wanted to make the application of the death penalty as uniform as possible across the country.

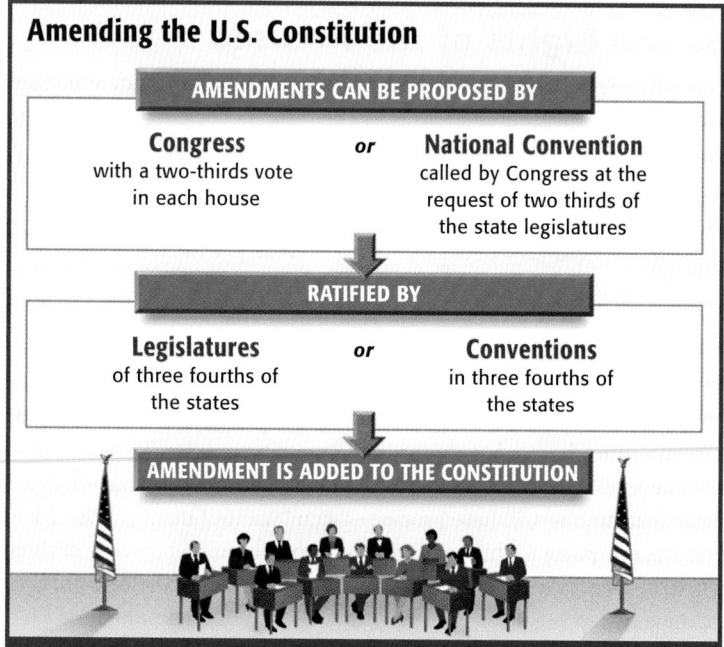

Amending the U.S. Constitution

AMENDMENTS CAN BE PROPOSED BY

Congress
with a two-thirds vote in each house

or

National Convention
called by Congress at the request of two thirds of the state legislatures

RATIFIED BY

Legislatures
of three fourths of the states

or

Conventions
in three fourths of the states

AMENDMENT IS ADDED TO THE CONSTITUTION

★ Bail and Punishment

The Eighth Amendment allows for defendants to post bail. Bail is money that defendants promise to pay the court if they do not appear in court at the proper time. Bail ensures that defendants do not have to stay in jail during the trial. Sometimes, a defendant does not show up for trial. If this happens, the court demands the bail money and issues a warrant for the defendant's immediate arrest. The Eighth Amendment prevents courts from setting unfairly high bail. However, the judge may refuse to set bail for individuals accused of very serious crimes or who the court believes may flee before trial.

The Eighth Amendment also bans "cruel and unusual punishments" of individuals convicted of a crime. For many years, Americans have debated exactly what this wording means. For example, in the 1972 case *Furman* v. *Georgia* the Supreme Court ruled that the methods by which most states carried out the death penalty were cruel and unusual. The Court also found that the processes used by many states to sentence people to death were unfair to the accused. As a result, executions were temporarily halted in those states that allowed the death penalty. However, in 1976 the Court ruled that not all executions are cruel and unusual. Today all states that allow the death penalty must establish guidelines to ensure that their methods are constitutional.

✔ **Reading Check: Finding the Main Idea** What rights does the Eighth Amendment protect? It establishes bail, prevents the courts from setting bail too high, and bans inflicting "cruel and unusual punishments."

★ **REVIEW AND ASSESS**

Have students complete the **Section 2 Review** on p. 289. Then have students complete **Daily Quiz 9.2**. As **Alternative Assessment**, you may want to use the First Amendment graphic organizer or groups' advertisements in this section's lessons.

★ **RETEACH**

Have students complete **Main Idea Activity for English Language Learners and Special-Needs Students 9.2**. Then ask students to create a five-question quiz focusing on the amendments and the rights discussed in this section. Pair students and have them exchange quizzes. After quizzes are complete, have each student return the quizzes to his or her partner for grading. **COOPERATIVE LEARNING** , **ENGLISH LANGUAGE LEARNERS**

★ **EXTEND**

Organize the class into small groups. Have students develop a list of rights they would like to include in a "Class Bill of Rights." Tell students that the document must clearly protect students' rights while focusing on creating an effective classroom. After all groups have finished, have volunteers present their groups' ideas to the class. Ask students to vote to determine which ideas to include in their official "Class Bill of Rights."
BLOCK SCHEDULING , **COOPERATIVE LEARNING**

★ The Rights of States and Citizens

The final two amendments in the Bill of Rights provide general protections for individual rights not addressed by the first eight amendments. The Ninth and Tenth Amendments also reserve some governmental powers for the states and people. The Ninth Amendment states that the rights listed in the Constitution are not the only rights citizens have. This amendment allows the courts and Congress to recognize other basic rights of citizens. For example, the Constitution does not address education, however most Americans believe education is a basic right. "Education is not just another consumer item. It is the bedrock [foundation] of our democracy," explained educational leader Mary Hatwood Futrell. Today state governments offer free public education—from elementary to high school—to all citizens.

The Tenth Amendment recognizes that the states and the people have additional powers beyond those specifically mentioned in the Constitution. These include any powers that the Constitution does not specifically grant to Congress or deny to the states. Thus, the last amendment in the Bill of Rights protects citizens' rights in addition to helping keep the balance of power between the federal and state governments.

These students benefit from free public education, which many Americans now consider a right of citizenship.

✔ **Reading Check: Analyzing Information** How do the Ninth and Tenth Amendments balance individual rights and governmental powers?
Ninth: listing specific rights in the Constitution does not mean that citizens do not have additional rights; Tenth: includes any powers not specifically given to Congress or prohibited from the states

Section 2 Review

go.hrw.com **Homework Practice Online**
keyword: SA3 HP9

❶ **Define and explain:**
• petition
• search warrant
• due process
• indict
• double jeopardy
• eminent domain

❷ **Identify and explain:**
• James Madison

❸ **Summarizing** Copy the chart below. Use it to list the rights guaranteed to citizens by the first 10 amendments.

Amendment	Right
1	
2	
3	
4	
5	
6	
7	
8	
9	
10	

❹ **Finding the Main Idea**
a. Why are the rights protected by the First Amendment significant?

b. How are the Constitution and the Bill of Rights related to the complaints against Great Britain made in the Declaration of Independence?

❺ **Writing and Critical Thinking**
Analyzing Information Imagine that you are a newspaper reporter covering a local trial. Write a brief article describing the rights of the accused as he or she faces trial.

Consider the following:
• due process
• trial by jury
• bail

Section 2 Review
ANSWERS

❶ **Define**
• petition. 285
• search warrant, p. 286
• due process, p. 287
• indict, p. 287
• double jeopardy, p. 287
• eminent domain, p. 287

❷ **Identify**
• James Madison, p. 284

❸ Students should refer to the Constitution in this chapter and section 2 for their answers.

❹ a. Answers will vary, but students should list all five of the First Amendment freedoms and support their answer.
b. it addresses the following: militias provide a defense against the British army; responds to British quartering of troops; reacts to the writs of assistance

❺ Students' articles will vary but should mention protections in the Bill of Rights.

Section 3

OBJECTIVES

- ⭐ Describe how a person can become a U.S. citizen.
- ⭐ Identify some of the most important responsibilities of citizenship.
- ⭐ Evaluate why citizens should be involved with their community and government.

🔊 LET'S GET STARTED!

Write the following question on the chalkboard: *What does it mean to be a U.S. citizen?* As students enter the classroom, allow them time to respond. *(Students' responses will vary, but students should point out that U.S. citizens have certain rights that are not necessarily protected in other countries.)* Explain to students that there is no correct answer but that many people associate U.S. citizenship with having choices and rights. Tell students that a U.S. citizen is guaranteed specific rights but also has certain responsibilities. Tell students that in Section 3 they will learn about the rights of U.S. citizenship and the responsibilities that come with those rights.

Section 3

Rights and Responsibilities of Citizenship

Read to Discover

1. How can a person become a U.S. citizen?
2. What are some of the most important responsibilities of citizenship?
3. Why should citizens be involved with their community and government?

Define

- naturalized citizen
- deport
- draft
- political action committees

WHY IT MATTERS TODAY

Taxes are the responsibility of all U.S. citizens. Taxes help pay for services like roads, salaries of government employees, and schools. Use **CNNfyi.com** or other **current events** sources to research a current or proposed use of tax dollars that affects your area. Record your findings in your journal.

The Story Continues

The Statue of Liberty is a symbol of freedom for many immigrants.

Patrick Henry argued that the United States should be open to all people who wanted to become citizens. "Let . . . Liberty stretch forth her fair hand toward the people of the old world," he said. "Tell them to come, and bid them welcome." Many people desiring liberty have become U.S. citizens. Jozef Patyna immigrated to the United States in the early 1980s. He wanted to leave an unjust government in Poland. "The idea of freedom and democracy is what the people have an instinctive need for," explained Patyna.

⭐ Becoming a U.S. Citizen

People can become U.S. citizens in several ways. Anyone born in the United States or a territory it controls is a citizen. For example, people born in Puerto Rico are citizens because that island is a commonwealth that is still a U.S. territory. When a person of foreign birth is granted full

LEVEL 1: Have students use information from the textbook to create a chart depicting the three ways that a person can become a U.S. citizen. Remind students to highlight the steps noncitizens must take to gain citizenship. Discuss these methods with the class. Then create various scenarios describing a person's background. Ask students to explain if the person in each scenario is automatically a U.S. citizen because of his or her circumstances of birth, if the person became a naturalized citizen, or if the person is not a U.S. citizen. **ENGLISH LANGUAGE LEARNERS**

citizenship, he or she has become a **naturalized citizen.** People born in a foreign country can become U.S. citizens if one of their parents is a U.S. citizen. Foreign-born people whose parents are not U.S. citizens must move to the United States if they want to become citizens. After completing a long process, they can apply for citizenship. The rights and responsibilities that naturalized citizens take on help create the sense of what it means to be an American.

People who permanently move to a new country are called immigrants. In the United States, legal immigrants have many of the same rights and responsibilities as citizens. They cannot vote or hold public office, however. The U.S. government can **deport**, or return to their country of origin, any immigrant who breaks the law. Only two differences between naturalized and native-born citizens exist. Naturalized citizens can lose their citizenship, and they cannot become president or vice president. Many famous Americans have been naturalized citizens, including scientist Albert Einstein and former secretary of state Madeleine Albright.

Legal immigrants who are older than 18 may petition for naturalization. However, they may do this only after living in the United States for five years. All legal immigrants must be able to support themselves financially. If they cannot do this, someone must sponsor them and assume that financial responsibility. The U.S. Immigration and Naturalization Service (INS) oversees the process of becoming a citizen and sets a hearing to test the person's qualifications. The immigrants must prove that they are law-abiding and of good moral character. In addition, they must take a series of tests to show that they can read, write, and speak English. They must also have a basic understanding of U.S. history and government. The INS also conducts a background check to ensure that the candidates for naturalization have not hidden any information about themselves.

When all these steps are complete, the candidates appear before a naturalization court. There they take an oath of allegiance to the United States. Finally, they receive their certificate of naturalization. At that point all minors of the newly naturalized citizens also become citizens. Becoming a naturalized citizen takes dedication and effort. A Japanese immigrant wrote a poem to celebrate her naturalization.

This immigrant and the people standing around her are taking the oath of allegiance to complete the process of becoming U.S. citizens.

Interdisciplinary Connection

▶**Math**◀

Immigration. The peak year for immigration to the United States was 1907, when 1,285,349 people arrived on U.S. shores. The lowest year was 1933, when just 23,068 immigrants arrived.

🖥 internet connect

TOPIC: U.S. Immigration
GO TO: go.hrw.com
KEYWORD: SA3 CF9

Have students search the Internet through the HRW Go site to determine the current annual immigration level for the United States. Then have them determine the percentage increase of immigration from its lowest level figure in the 1900s to its level today.

History Makers Speak

❝Going steadily to study English,
Even through the rain at night,
I thus attain [acquire],
Late in life,
American citizenship.❞

—Kiyoko Nieda, quoted in *Sounds from the Unknown*,
edited by Lucille Nixon and Tomoe Tana

Analyzing Primary Sources
Identifying Points of View
How do you think the author of this poem valued U.S. citizenship? Students might say very highly because the author discusses attending classes "steadily" and "even through the rain."

✔ **Reading Check: Identifying Cause and Effect** How does someone become a naturalized citizen, and what rights do they gain when they do? if a parent is a citizen or through naturalization; same rights as native-born citizens, but cannot become president or vice president and can lose their citizenship

Organization	Activities and Results
Citizens on Patrol and Neighborhood Watch	*patrol their neighborhood; report criminal activity to the police; help prevent crime; keep crime rates down in the neighborhood*
American Red Cross	*does jobs along with the government; helps citizens in times of natural disasters or emergencies*
Habitat for Humanity	*builds houses for low-income families*
Boy Scouts and Girl Scouts	*plan many projects for the community, such as planting trees*

ALL LEVELS: Copy the following graphic organizer onto the chalkboard, omitting the italicized answers. Ask students to name organizations that help make the community a better place to live in. List these groups on the chart. Discuss with students the variety of ways that these organizations and similar organizations affect the community and why citizens should be involved with their community and government. **ENGLISH LANGUAGE LEARNERS**

Organization	Activities and Results
Citizens on Patrol and Neighborhood Watch	*patrol their neighborhood; report criminal activity to the police; help prevent crime; keep crime rates down in the neighborhood*
American Red Cross	*does jobs along with the government; helps citizens in times of natural disasters or emergencies*
Habitat for Humanity	*builds houses for low-income families*
Boy Scouts and Girl Scouts	*plan many projects for the community, such as planting trees*

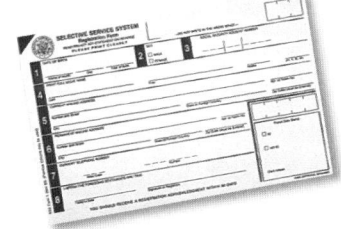

Upon turning 18, every male U.S. citizen must fill out a card like this one to register for a potential draft.

★ Duties of Citizens

In addition to having certain rights, U.S. citizens have responsibilities. These duties are to other citizens, their government, and themselves. For representative democracy to work, citizens must fulfill their civic responsibilities. Former Texas representative Barbara Jordan explained why these duties are important. "The stakes . . . are too high for government to be a spectator sport," she stated.

Citizens elect leaders to make laws for them. In turn, citizens must obey the laws those leaders pass. If citizens do not agree with a law, they can try to change it in several ways. They can speak with their local, state, or national representatives or petition elected leaders to change the law. Electing new leaders who might change the law is another option. Citizens can also challenge a law in court. Citizens have a duty to know what the laws are. Thus, citizens need to stay informed of changes to laws that affect them. Ignorance of a certain law will not keep a person from being punished for breaking it.

Citizens also have an obligation to respect people in authority and to respect the rights of others. People in authority include parents, police officers, and teachers. Such people have been trusted to protect the welfare of others. Parents have a responsibility to meet their children's basic needs for clothing, education, food, and shelter. In return, children have a responsibility to obey their parents. Government authorities may step in to protect any children whose parents do not take proper care of them.

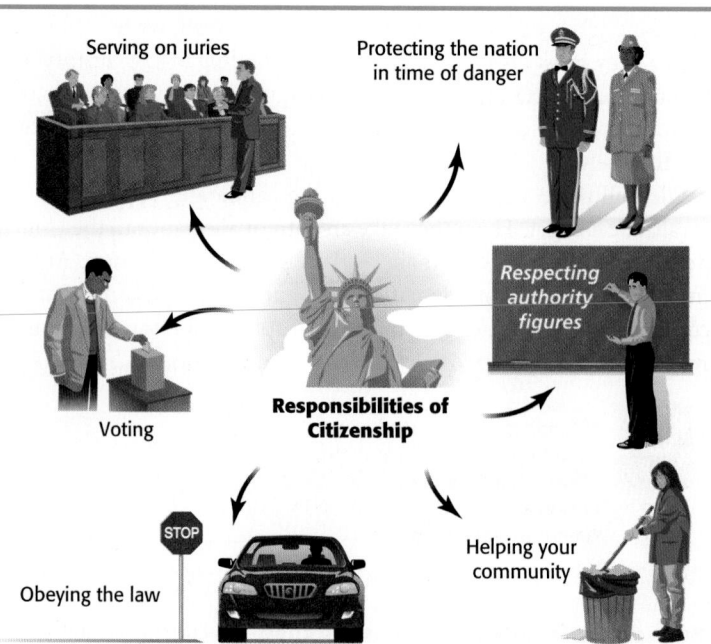

Responsibilities of Citizenship

In addition to having rights protected by the Constitution, citizens of the United States have important responsibilities to uphold.

Visualizing History

1. **Citizenship** Which of the responsibilities of citizenship are related to the legal system?
2. **Connecting to Today** What responsibilities of citizenship can you fulfill?

Serving on juries

Protecting the nation in time of danger

Respecting authority figures

Voting

Responsibilities of Citizenship

Obeying the law

Helping your community

Good citizenship also includes paying taxes. The government relies on taxes to pay for public roads, police and fire departments, and public schools. If Americans did not pay taxes, the government might be unable to provide these services. People pay many kinds of taxes, such as property taxes, sales taxes, and tariffs. For example, consumers often pay sales taxes when buying items at a store. Sales tax rates vary from place to place because state and local governments set and collect most sales taxes. People also pay a certain percentage of the value of their property to the government, called a property tax. Most school funding comes from property taxes.

April 15 of every year is income tax day. By that day all Americans who earned money the year before must pay a certain percentage of their income to the federal government. Some must pay their state government too. Income taxes are progressive—that is, the rate of income tax that people pay increases as their income level rises. Regressive taxes, such as city or state sales taxes, are applied equally to people regardless of income. Property taxes are based on the value of a person's property and may vary from area to area. Local governments gain much of their revenues from property taxes.

Citizens also have the duty to protect and defend the nation from harm. If a war breaks out, citizens should try to help in the war effort. In some war situations the federal government has set up a **draft**, or requirement of military service. A draft helps raise the needed number of soldiers. The United States has had all-volunteer armed forces since 1973. However, young men must register for the draft when they turn 18. This process gives the government a list of people who could be draftees if war were to break out. Women do not have to register for the draft, but many women serve in the armed forces.

All citizens can be called to serve on a jury. Jury duty involves listening to a court case and reaching a verdict on it. By serving as jurors, citizens help fulfill each person's Sixth Amendment right to a trial by jury. Americans also have a duty to testify in court if needed. For example, someone who witnesses a crime may be called to testify about it. Judges may issue subpoenas, or orders to appear in court, to force individuals to testify.

✔ **Reading Check: Summarizing** What are some of the responsibilities of citizenship? voting, paying taxes, serving on juries, and serving in the military

Daily Life

Political participation Even individuals who are not old enough to vote can find ways to join in the political process. These students are volunteering their time to help run a candidate's campaign in a local election. There are many ways in which students can assist public officials or express their own views on issues important to their community or nation. What do the students appear to be doing to participate in this local election?

Research on the RM

Free Find:
Taxes
After examining the Federal Budget Net Receipts from 1940 to 1995 on the **Holt Researcher CD-ROM**, create a bar graph that shows how much the federal government collected in taxes in the following years: 1940, 1950, 1960, 1970, 1980, and 1990.

Distribute a list of autobiographies or memoirs written by immigrants to the United States. Have students select one of the books from the list to read. Have students create a series of illustrations to accompany the text that shows the author's new life in the United States. You may want to display the illustrations around the classroom along with the book titles.

✭ CLOSE

On the chalkboard create a three-column chart. The first column should list the various rights and responsibilities of U.S. citizens, such as voting, paying taxes, signing up for the draft, and doing community service. Label the second column *Rights* and the third column *Responsibilities*. For each right or responsibility listed in the first column, have students identify which category it falls into and put a checkmark in the appropriate column. Have students explain why they classified each item as they did. **ENGLISH LANGUAGE LEARNERS**

These members of Students Against Driving Drunk visited Washington, D.C., to speak out against drinking and driving.

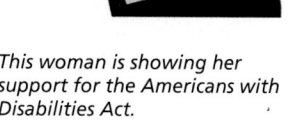

This woman is showing her support for the Americans with Disabilities Act.

Section 3 Review
ANSWERS

❶ Define
- naturalized citizen, p. 291
- deport, p. 291
- draft, p. 293
- political action committees, p. 294

❷ ways to become a citizen—be born in the United States or a U.S. territory; have a parent who is a U.S. citizen; go through the naturalization process; responsibilities—voting, serving on juries, serving in military, obeying the law, paying taxes, being involved in the community, and so on

❸ a. After living in the United States for five years, legal immigrants older than 18 petition for naturalization; the INS schedules a hearing to test the immigrants' qualifications; the immigrants must prove that they are law-abiding and that they support the U.S. Constitution; the immigrants take a series of tests to prove that they can read, write, and speak English, and that they have a basic understanding of U.S. history and government; the INS conducts a background check; the immigrants go before a naturalization court to take an oath of allegiance to the United States

b. taxes pay for government services; serving in the military helps defend the nation from harm; serving on juries guarantees citizens' Sixth Amendment right to a trial by a jury; voting maintains the democratic system.

❹ Students' poems will vary but should focus on the responsibilities of citizens.

✭ Citizens and Elections

Elections form the basis of representative democracy in the United States. Through free elections, citizens choose who will lead their government. Citizens should learn as much as they can about the issues and candidates before voting. Information is available through the Internet, newspapers, television, and other forms of media. However, voters should be beware of propaganda, or material that is biased deliberately to help or harm a cause.

In addition to voting, many Americans choose to campaign for a certain candidate or issue. Anyone can help campaign, even if he or she is not eligible to vote. Citizens can also give money to a candidate directly or through **political action committees** (PACs). These groups collect money to give to candidates who support certain issues.

To vote in the United States, one must be at least 18 years old. People younger than 18 can help campaigns by handing out pamphlets, making signs, or encouraging other citizens to vote. Many other members of political clubs get to know political leaders well. Some members stay active in politics as adults.

✭ Citizens and Government

When colonists protested British rule in the 1700s, they formed committees and presented their views to political leaders. Today, people can influence officials by letting them know what the citizens want done.

Some U.S. citizens join interest groups. These groups are formed to lobby, or try to influence, politicians on behalf of certain issues. Some groups hold demonstrations to show the government how they feel and to gather public support. In 2000, for example, mothers in favor of gun control gathered in Washington, D.C., on Mother's Day. They called this demonstration the Million Mom March. Donna Dees-Thomases planned the march. She explained that the movement "started in my family room and has grown . . . across the nation." Not everyone agreed with her group. On the day of the Million Mom March, the Second Amendment Sisters held their own demonstration calling for gun-safety and education programs instead of gun control.

Citizens do not have to join a group to influence political leaders. People can and should share their views with leaders by writing letters and attending public meetings. These activities are ways that Americans exercise their First Amendment rights. Political participation is an important duty for U.S. citizens and immigrants alike.

✔ **Reading Check: Drawing Inferences and Conclusions** How do you think the shared rights and responsibilities of citizenship help unite Americans who hold different views? Students may answer that even citizens of different views can respect the rights of other Americans and participate equally in carrying out the duties of good citizenship and participation in their government.

⭐ REVIEW AND ASSESS

Have students complete the **Section 3 Review** on p. 295. Then have students complete **Daily Quiz 9.3**. As **Alternative Assessment**, you may want to use the short stories or advertisement exercise in this section's lessons.

⭐ RETEACH

Have students complete **Main Idea Activity for English Language Learners and Special-Needs Students 9.3**. Then ask students to take one key term from this section and write a few sentences detailing important information they learned about it. As a class, review each of the terms by having students read their descriptions. **ENGLISH LANGUAGE LEARNERS**

⭐ EXTEND

Have students write to one or more of the community organizations discussed in this section of the textbook to obtain more information about the services provided by the organizations. Students should also inquire about volunteer opportunities with that organization. Have students use information from replies to their letters to create a bulletin board display that not only describes the various organizations' functions but also advertises actual volunteer opportunities.

BLOCK SCHEDULING

⭐ Community Service

Civic virtue, or the commitment to helping others, moves Americans to help their neighbors. Many of these Americans volunteer in community service groups. Some small communities rely on volunteers. These groups offer many public services, such as fire protection. Other volunteer groups help government-sponsored agencies, like police departments. For example, Citizens on Patrol and Neighborhood Watch are two groups that ask volunteers to walk their neighborhoods and report criminal activity. Neighborhoods with citizen patrols often have lower crime rates than other neighborhoods.

Other groups work along with the government. The American Red Cross aids citizens in times of natural disasters or other emergencies. Habitat for Humanity helps build houses for low-income families. The Boy Scouts and Girl Scouts plan many projects, such as planting trees to improve the environment.

Examples of community service could be found during the American Revolution, when patriotic women organized to make cloth and other goods for the colonists. Today the country's leaders want all citizens to serve others in their communities. Service projects can be simple acts like picking up trash or painting over graffiti.

Every day many Americans are in need. The nation is strengthened when all people do their part to help each other. Retired general Colin Powell, who was appointed secretary of state under President George W. Bush, launched a campaign in 1997 to promote volunteerism. He said, "This is the time for each and every one of us . . . to lift up a fellow American and put him on the road to success in this wonderful country of ours."

✔ **Reading Check: Finding the Main Idea** What are some of the benefits of community service? Student answers might include the following: it helps small communities that cannot afford public services; it makes neighborhoods safer and more attractive; and it helps citizens in need.

These volunteers are helping their neighbor by repainting a backyard fence.

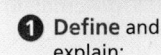

Section 3 Review

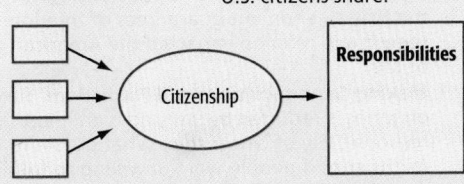

go.hrw.com **Homework Practice Online**
keyword: SA3 HP9

1 **Define** and explain:
• naturalized citizen
• deport
• draft
• political action committees

2 **Comparing and Contrasting** Copy the graphic organizer below. Use it to contrast the different ways that a person can become a U.S. citizen and to compare the responsibilities that all U.S. citizens share.

```
[  ]
       ↘
[  ] → ( Citizenship ) → [ Responsibilities ]
       ↗
[  ]
```

3 **Finding the Main Idea**
a. Describe the steps in the naturalization process.

b. How do responsibilities such as paying taxes, serving in the military, serving on juries, and voting help shape our national identity?

4 **Writing and Critical Thinking**
Supporting a Point of View Imagine that you will be making a presentation at an awards ceremony honoring volunteers in your community. Write a poem honoring the volunteers.

Consider the following:
• civic virtue and citizens' responsibilities
• how volunteerism benefits the community

CHAPTER 9 REVIEW ANSWERS

The Chapter at a Glance
Students' quizzes will vary but should include information on the branches of government, becoming a citizen, and the rights and responsibilities of U.S. citizens.

Identifying People and Ideas
Students' sentences should indicate an understanding of the following definitions:

1. government led by officials who are chosen by the people

2. balances each branch of the federal government against the others and keeps any single branch from becoming too strong

3. first female justice to serve on the U.S. Supreme Court

4. a Federalist who worked on the Bill of Rights

5. order issued by a judge giving authorities the permission to search through someone's property

6. fair application of the law

7. to be tried twice for the same crime

8. person of foreign birth who is granted full citizenship

9. requirement of military service

10. groups that collect money to give to candidates who support certain issues

REPRODUCIBLE

▶ Vocabulary Activity 9

TECHNOLOGY

▶ Chapter 9 Test Generator (on the One-Stop Planner)

▶ Global Skill Builder CD–ROM

▶ HRW Go site

REINFORCEMENT, REVIEW, AND ASSESSMENT

▶ Chapter 9 Review, pp. 295–97

▶ Chapter 9 Tutorial for Students, Parents, Mentors, and Peers

▶ Chapter 9 Test (Form A or B)

▶ Alternative Assessment Handbook

▶ Chapter 9 Test for English Language Learners and Special-Needs Students

★ REVIEW

Have students complete the **Chapter 9 Review** on pages 296–97.

★ ASSESS

Use one of the chapter tests to assess students' understanding of the content. For **Alternative Assessment,** see the **Alternative Assessment Handbook.**

Understanding Main Ideas

1. The legislative branch creates laws; the executive branch enforces laws; and judicial branch decides if the laws are constitutional

2. delegated—specifically granted to the federal government; reserved—belong to the state governments or to citizens; concurrent—granted to both the state and federal governments

3. 2nd, 3rd, & 4th amendments relate to colonial disputes with Great Britain

4. 5th—provides grand jury indictments for serious crimes, protects against self-incrimination, guarantees due process, prohibits double jeopardy; 6th—ensures right to a prompt public trial, right to know what one is accused of, right to hear & question prosecution witnesses, right to an attorney; 8th—ensures right to fair bail, prohibits cruel and unusual punishment

5. if one of their parents is a citizen or by going through the naturalization process

6. obeying authority, paying taxes, military service, jury duty, voting, community service

Chapter **9** Review

The Chapter at a Glance

Examine the visual summary of the chapter below. Using information in the chapter, create a five-question quiz for one of your classmates to complete.

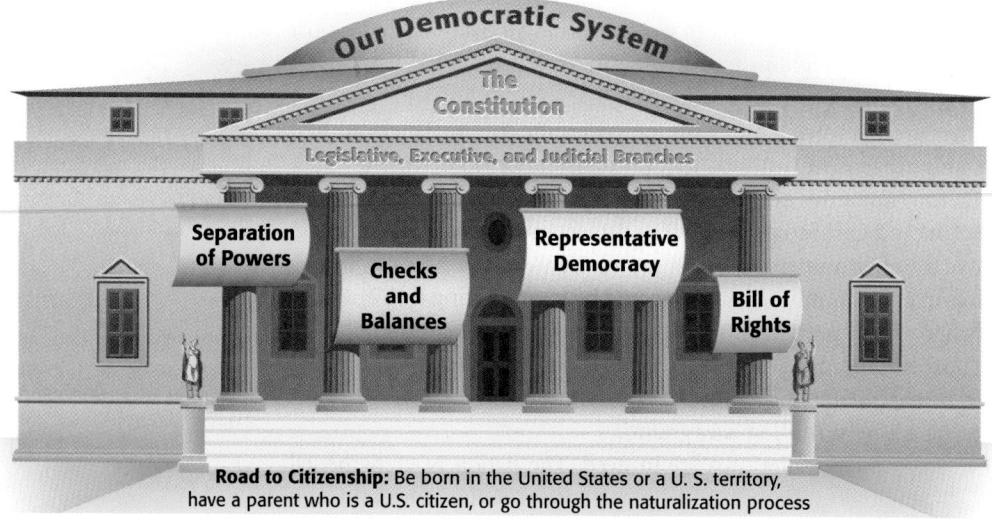

Our Democratic System

The Constitution

Legislative, Executive, and Judicial Branches

Separation of Powers

Checks and Balances

Representative Democracy

Bill of Rights

Road to Citizenship: Be born in the United States or a U. S. territory, have a parent who is a U.S. citizen, or go through the naturalization process

Identifying People and Ideas

Use the following terms or people in historically significant sentences.

1. representative democracy
2. separation of powers
3. Sandra Day O'Connor
4. James Madison
5. search warrant
6. due process
7. double jeopardy
8. naturalized citizen
9. draft
10. political action committees

Understanding Main Ideas

Section 1 *(Pages 256–261)*

1. What are the three branches of the federal government, and what are their primary responsibilities?
2. What are delegated powers, reserved powers, and concurrent powers?

Section 2 *(Pages 284–289)*

3. How did complaints against Great Britain made in the Declaration of Independence shape the Constitution and the Bill of Rights?
4. Which amendments focus on the rights of people accused of crimes, and what rights do these amendments guarantee?

Section 3 *(Pages 290–295)*

5. How does someone become a naturalized citizen?

6. What are the duties and responsibilities of citizenship?

You Be the Historian— Reviewing Themes

1. **Constitutional Heritage** How does the Constitution prevent any one branch of government from becoming too powerful? Be sure to consider all three branches of government.
2. **Citizenship** Why is voting an important responsibility in a representative democracy?
3. **Culture** In what ways does the U.S. government protect the rights of all Americans?

Thinking Critically

1. **Evaluating** How do you think the rights and duties of U.S. citizens reflect our identity as a nation?
2. **Drawing Inferences and Conclusions** How have the first amendment guarantees of freedom of speech and religion impacted the American way of life?
3. **Making Generalizations and Predictions** Serving on juries is required by law and is an important responsibility of citizenship. What problems might arise if people were unwilling to fulfill this responsibility?

Organize the class into several small teams to play "The Chapter Review Game." Each team should create 10 questions about the chapter. Have students write the questions on note cards and place the note cards in a large box. Take turns reading a question to each team and allowing them to answer.

ENGLISH LANGUAGE LEARNERS ,
COOPERATIVE LEARNING

Portfolio Extensions

1. Cooperative Learning. Ask students to complete the following activity in small groups. Groups should use the library or other primary and secondary sources to find out information about the nine Supreme Court justices sitting on the bench today. Have each person in the groups assume responsibility for one Supreme Court Justice. Then have groups create an annotated time line showing the names of each justice, what year he or she was confirmed, which president nominated him or her and brief biographical information on each justice.

2. Interdisciplinary Connection to Government Have students imagine that someone has written a book about the system of checks and balances that helps our government function. Ask students to design a cover for the book. Students should include illustrations as well as a summary of the book's content for the back cover.

Social Studies Skills Workshop

Interpreting Political Cartoons

Study the political cartoon below. Then use the information to help you answer the questions that follow.

FROM THE HERBLOCK GALLERY (SIMON & SCHUSTER, 1968)

1. What does the illustration suggest that President Johnson hopes to achieve by patting this Congressman on the back?
   a. Johnson wants the congressman to vote for his legislation.
   b. Johnson wants Congress to work harder.
   c. Johnson wants members of Congress to know how proud he is of their work.
   d. Johnson thinks Congress has too much power.

2. Based on your knowledge of the Constitution, why do you think President Johnson would find it necessary to encourage Congress to cooperate with him?

Analyzing Primary Sources

Read the following quote by President John F. Kennedy, and then answer the questions that follow.

❝The right to vote in a free American election is the most powerful and precious right in the world—and it must not be denied on the grounds of race or color. It is a potent [powerful] key to achieving other rights of citizenship. For American history—both recent and past—clearly reveals that the power of the ballot has enabled those who achieve it to win other achievements as well, gain a full voice in the affairs of their state and nation, and to see their interests represented in the governmental bodies which affect their future. In a free society, those with the power to govern are necessarily responsive to those with the right to vote.❞

3. Which of the following statements best describes Kennedy's point of view?
   a. The only way that people can influence their government is by writing letters to elected officials.
   b. You are not a citizen if you do not vote.
   c. Voting affects everyone's future.
   d. Government officials are more likely to respond to citizens if they know that citizens can vote them out of office.

4. Based on what you know about the Constitution of the United States, what amendment is President Kennedy probably referring to when he says that people of any race or color should not be denied the right to vote?

You Be the Historian— Reviewing Themes
1. by dividing the powers of government between the different branches

2. allows citizens to elect representatives who will serve their interests

3. through the Bill of Rights

Thinking Critically
1. Students answers will vary.

2. provides Americans with rights others do not have in some foreign countries

3. Students' answers will vary.

Skills Workshop
1. a

2. Congress had to pass legislation that Johnson proposed, and it also had the power to override the president's vetoes.

3. d

4. the Fifteenth Amendment

Alternative Assessment

American History

Building Your Portfolio

Linking to Community
Think about something in your community that is important to you, such as the creation of crosswalks or parks. Write a letter to a local official about this element of your community. Make sure the letter explains to the official who you are writing and what you want to be done. Then organize a campaign to get others to sign your letter. Support your campaign by creating signs, flyers, and other items.

🖉 **internet** connect

Internet Activity: go.hrw.com
keyword: **SA3 CF9**

Access the Internet through the HRW Go site to research Supreme Court cases heard during the recent term. Then write a brief summary that describes the main issues in the case, the Constitutional questions raised in the case, the Supreme Court's decision, and whether you agree with the Court's decision. Make sure your summary includes standard grammar, spelling, and punctuation.

	Objectives	Pacing Guide	Reproducible Resources
SECTION 1: **Laying the Foundations of Government** (pp. 300–03)	★ Explain why Americans elected George Washington as their first president. ★ Identify the expectations Americans had of their new government. ★ Describe the steps Congress and the president took to organize the new government.	**Regular** 2 days **Block Scheduling** 1 day *Block Scheduling Handbook with Team Teaching Strategies, Chapter 10*	**RS** Guided Reading Strategy 10.1 **PS** Primary Source Reading 10: Democracy in America **PS** Literature Reading 10: The Coquette **PS** Biography Reading 10: Judith Sargent Murray
SECTION 2: **Hamilton and National Finances** (pp. 304–09)	★ Identify the challenge Alexander Hamilton faced as secretary of the treasury and the issues his plans raised. ★ Describe the issues that Hamilton and Thomas Jefferson disagreed on, and explain their views. ★ Examine the questions that were raised when the Bank of the United States was founded, and examine the different views that Hamilton and Jefferson had concerning the Bank.	**Regular** 1.5 days **Block Scheduling** .5 day *Block Scheduling Handbook with Team Teaching Strategies, Chapter 10*	**RS** Guided Reading Strategy 10.2 **RS** Graphic Organizer 10: Hamilton and Jefferson **E** Hands-On History Activity: Your State Capital **E** Creative Teaching Strategy: Brainstorming
SECTION 3: **Troubles Abroad** (pp. 310–14)	★ Explain how Americans and President Washington responded to events in France. ★ Discuss the policy Washington followed toward foreign nations. ★ Describe how the United States settled its differences with Great Britain and Spain.	**Regular** 1.5 days **Block Scheduling** .5 day *Block Scheduling Handbook with Team Teaching Strategies, Chapter 10*	**RS** Guided Reading Strategy 10.3
SECTION 4: **Challenges at Home** (pp. 315–18)	★ Identify the domestic problems faced by the United States. ★ Explain the advice that Washington gave the nation in his Farewell Address.	**Regular** 1.5 days **Block Scheduling** 1 day *Block Scheduling Handbook with Team Teaching Strategies, Chapter 10*	**RS** Guided Reading Strategy 10.4 **SM** Geography Activity 10: Frontier Conflicts
SECTION 5: **John Adams's Presidency** (pp. 319–25)	★ Explain how political parties formed and the role they played in the presidential election of 1796. ★ Describe the problems with foreign nations that John Adams faced as president. ★ Describe the Alien and Sedition Acts and the Republicans' response to the Acts. ★ Analyze the main issues in the election of 1800 and identify some of its outcomes.	**Regular** 1.5 days **Block Scheduling** 1 day *Block Scheduling Handbook with Team Teaching Strategies, Chapter 10*	**RS** Guided Reading Strategy 10.5 **PS** American History Political Cartoon 3: Party Politics

Chapter Resource Key

PS	Primary Sources	**A**	Assessment		Music	
RS	Reading Support	**REV**	Review		Video	
IC	Interdisciplinary Connections	**ELL**	Reinforcement and English Language Learners		Internet	
E	Enrichment		Transparencies		Holt Presentation Maker Using Microsoft® PowerPoint®	
SM	Skills Mastery		CD-ROM			

One-Stop Planner CD-ROM

See the *One-Stop Planner* for a complete list of additional resources for students and teachers.

One-Stop Planner CD–ROM

It's easy to plan lessons, select resources, and print out materials for your students when you use the **One-Stop Planner CD–ROM with Test Generator.**

Technology Resources	Reinforcement, Review, and Assessment

 One-Stop Planner, Lesson 10.1
 Everyday Life in America Transparency 5: Education in Early America
Everyday Life in America Transparency 6: Frakturs: Folk Art in Federalist America
Homework Practice Online

REV Section 1 Review, p. 303
A Daily Quiz 10.1
ELL Main Idea Activity 10.1
ELL English Audio Summary 10.1
ELL Spanish Audio Summary 10.1

 One-Stop Planner, Lesson 10.2
 Exploring America's Past Video Segment: Building the Capital; Teacher's Guide, pp. 16–17
 Holt Researcher: American History CD–ROM
Homework Practice Online

REV Section 2 Review, p. 309
A Daily Quiz 10.2
ELL Main Idea Activity 10.2
ELL English Audio Summary 10.2
ELL Spanish Audio Summary 10.2

 One-Stop Planner, Lesson 10.3
 Exploring America's Past Video Segment: Time Travelers; Teacher's Guide, pp. 13–15
 Homework Practice Online
 HRW Go site

REV Section 3 Review, p. 314
A Daily Quiz 10.3
ELL Main Idea Activity 10.3
ELL English Audio Summary 10.3
ELL Spanish Audio Summary 10.3

 One-Stop Planner, Lesson 10.4
 Homework Practice Online

REV Section 4 Review, p. 318
A Daily Quiz 10.4
ELL Main Idea Activity 10.4
ELL English Audio Summary 10.4
ELL Spanish Audio Summary 10.4

 One-Stop Planner, Lesson 10.5
 Holt Researcher: American History CD–ROM
 CNN Presents America: Yesterday and Today, Beginnings to 1914 Segment: Sailing the *Constitution*
 Homework Practice Online

REV Section 5 Review, p. 324
A Daily Quiz 10.5
ELL Main Idea Activity 10.5
ELL English Audio Summary 10.5
ELL Spanish Audio Summary 10.5

---

internet connect

HRW ONLINE RESOURCES
GO TO: go.hrw.com
Then type in a keyword.

TEACHER HOME PAGE
KEYWORD: SA3 Teacher

CHAPTER INTERNET ACTIVITIES
KEYWORD: SA3 CF10
Choose an activity to:
- examine the connection between a free press and a democratic society in the context of the Alien and Sedition Acts and the Pentagon Papers case.
- research the American influences in the French Revolution.
- review the outcome of the last general election and compare it to the election of 1800.
- contrast today's Presidential cabinet to the cabinet during Washington's Presidency.

CHAPTER ENRICHMENT LINKS
KEYWORD: SA3 CH10

ONLINE ASSESSMENT
Homework Practice
KEYWORD: SA3 HP10
Standardized Test Prep
KEYWORD: SA3 STP10
Rubrics
KEYWORD: SS Rubrics

ONLINE MAPS, CHARTS, AND GRAPHS
KEYWORD: SA3 MCG
- Conflict in the Northwest Territory
- Ohio Valley, 1750-1811
- National Debt

CONTENT UPDATES
KEYWORD: SS Content Updates

HOLT PRESENTATION MAKER
KEYWORD: SA3 PPT10

ONLINE READING SUPPORT
KEYWORD: SS Strategies

CURRENT EVENTS
KEYWORD: S3 Current Events

Meeting Individual Needs

Ability Levels

Level 1 Basic-level activities designed for all students encountering new material

Level 2 Intermediate-level activities designed for average students

Level 3 Challenging activities designed for honors and gifted-and-talented students

English Language Learners Activities that address the needs of students with Limited English Proficiency

---

Chapter Review and Assessment

IC Vocabulary Activity 10
Global Skill Builder CD–ROM
HRW Go site
REV Chapter 10 Tutorial for Students, Parents, Mentors, and Peers
REV Chapter 10 Review, pp. 325–27
Chapter 10 Test Generator (on the One-Stop Planner)

A Chapter 10 Test (Form A or B)
A Alternative Assessment Handbook
A Chapter 10 Test for English Language Learners and Special-Needs Students

Build on What You Know

If You Were There...

Ask students to answer the following question:

What might your first actions be as part of this new government?

Consider:

- the peoples' complaints about England
- what people might need after a war

You Be the Historian

What's Your Opinion?

To help students create their **Themes** Journal entries, provide the following examples of appropriate **agree**/**disagree** statements.

EXPLORING THE TIME LINE

AMERICAN EVENTS

internet connect

TOPIC: The Whiskey Rebellion
GO TO: go.hrw.com
KEYWORD: SA3 CF10

Have students access the Internet through the HRW Go site to research the causes and effects of the Whiskey Rebellion. Then have the students create a political cartoon that supports the side of the western farmers or the Federal government. Students' cartoons should include historical references to the actual event.

CHAPTER

10 Launching the Nation

(1789–1800)

Angry farmers tar and feather a tax collector during the Whiskey Rebellion.

THE GRANGER COLLECTION, NEW YORK

President Washington with some members of his cabinet (left to right): Washington, Henry Knox, Alexander Hamilton, Thomas Jefferson, and Edmund Randolph

UNITED STATES

1789 George Washington is elected president on April 6.

1790 Washington is founded as the national capital.

1791 The Bank of the United States is formed.

1792 Kentucky becomes the 15th state.

1794 The Whiskey Rebellion begins in Pennsylvania.

1789   1791   1793

1789 The French Revolution begins.

1791 Thomas Paine defends the French Revolution in *Rights of Man.*

1792 Austrian and Prussian armies invade France to try to end the Revolution.

1793 French revolutionaries behead King Louis XVI.

WORLD

The citizens of Paris storm the prison known as the Bastille during the French Revolution.

Build on What You Know

The Constitution created a new system of government for the United States. This federal system divided power between the states and a strong central government. Yet there was still much work left for the nation's leaders to do. Americans chose George Washington and other Founding Fathers to lead the new nation.

Global Relations

Agree A new country should focus only on domestic issues.

Disagree A new country should quickly establish itself as a global power.

Constitutional Heritage

Agree The framers scripted a document that continues to suit the needs of the country.

Disagree The language used in the document is open to interpretation.

Economics

Agree A country should strengthen its own economy before it satisfies foreign debts.

Disagree It is vital to international relations to maintain good financial standing with other countries.

Mount Vernon, Washington's Virginia home, has been preserved as a historical landmark.

As first lady, Martha Washington tried to bring a sense of dignity and grace to the new government.

1795 American Indian leaders sign the Treaty of Greenville with the United States.

1796 Washington publishes his Farewell Address on September 19.

John Adams is elected president on December 7.

1798 Congress passes the Sedition Act on July 14.

1799 George Washington dies at Mount Vernon, Virginia, on December 14.

1795

1797

1799

1798 Agents of French foreign minister Talleyrand demand a bribe from U.S. diplomats, leading to the XYZ affair.

1799 The Rosetta Stone is discovered in Egypt. Inscriptions on the stone make it possible for researchers to read Egyptian hieroglyphics.

If you were there . . .

What might your first actions be as part of this new government?

You Be the Historian

Themes Journal

What's Your Opinion? Do you **agree** or **disagree** with the following statements? Support your point of view in your journal.

- **Global Relations** A new country must stay away from conflicts and alliances.
- **Constitutional Heritage** There is one correct way to interpret the U.S. Constitution.
- **Economics** Countries should invest their money at home before paying their foreign debts.

GLOBAL EVENTS

★ Global Relations

Thomas Paine and the People. Throughout his life, Thomas Paine put out many works and performed many actions in defense of peoples' rights interpreted through his ideal of justice. His widely read pamphlet *Common Sense* likely set the stage for the Declaration of Independence. In 1791, Thomas Paine published his *Rights of Man*, a work defending the French Revolution. Though he supported the movement to eliminate the monarchy, he fought to save the life of the monarch. When the French people sought to execute the king, Paine rallied for banishment instead. As this example shows, Paine remained true to his ideas in his actions.

CRITICAL THINKING

If Paine did not like the idea of a monarchy, why do you think he cared if the king lived?

ANSWER: Students might suggest that the king was a person, and Paine supported the rights of people. Since banishment would have been enough to end the monarchy, killing the man who acted as king likely seemed unnecessary to Paine.

Section 1

OBJECTIVES

☆ Explain why Americans elected George Washington as their first president.

☆ Identify the expectations Americans had of their new government.

☆ Describe the steps Congress and the president took to organize the new government.

SECTION 1 RESOURCES

REPRODUCIBLE

▶ Guided Reading Strategy 10.1

▶ Primary Source Reading 10: Democracy in America

▶ Literature Reading 10: The Coquette

▶ Biography Reading 10: Judith Sargent Murray

TECHNOLOGY

▶ One-Stop Planner, Lesson 10.1

▶ Everyday Life in America Transparency 5: Education in Early America

▶ Everyday Life in America Transparency 6: Frakturs: Folk Art in Federalist America

▶ Homework Practice Online

REINFORCEMENT, REVIEW, AND ASSESSMENT

▶ Section 1 Review, p. 303

▶ Daily Quiz 10.1

▶ Main Idea Activity 10.1

▶ English Audio Summary 10.1

▶ Spanish Audio Summary 10.1

🔔 LET'S GET STARTED!

Write the following question on the chalkboard: *What were the Constitution's purposes, as listed in the Preamble?* As students enter the classroom, have them write their responses. *(Students' responses might include the following: forming a more perfect union, establishing justice, insuring domestic tranquility, providing for the common defense, promoting the general welfare, and securing the blessings of liberty.)* Then ask students to identify steps that they think would be necessary in order for the new government to accomplish the goals listed in the Preamble. Tell students that in Section 1 they will learn more about the steps taken to accomplish the goals found in the preamble.

Section 1

Laying the Foundations of Government

Read to Discover

1. Why did Americans elect George Washington as their first president?
2. What did Americans expect of their new government?
3. What steps did Congress and the president take to organize the new government?

WHY IT MATTERS TODAY

Every day, leaders around the world try to serve their countries. Use CNNfyi.com or other **current events** sources to learn more about the president or leader of a country. Record your findings in your journal.

Define

• electoral college
• precedent

Identify

• George Washington
• Martha Washington
• Judiciary Act of 1789

COURTESY OF THE JOHN CARTER BROWN LIBRARY AT BROWN UNIVERSITY

This 1788 print shows George Washington surrounded by the seal of the United States and the seals of the 13 states.

The Story Continues

George Washington looked forward to retiring from public life once the states had ratified the Constitution. However, his friends had other plans for him. They soon drew him into politics as a presidential candidate. When Washington hesitated, politician Gouverneur Morris helped convince him. "Should the idea prevail [win] that you would not accept the presidency, it should prove fatal . . . to the new government." Morris ended confidently, "Of all men, you are the best fitted to fill that office."

☆ The First President

George Washington was concerned that his age and lack of political experience might make him a poor president. He also knew that he would have to deal with many difficult issues. Yet many Americans saw Washington as a great leader and hero of the Revolution. They believed that his strong character, honesty, and patriotism would make him an excellent leader. They thought he would be a model for all citizens.

Have students read Section 1 and complete Guided Reading Strategy 10.1. Choose one or more of the following activities to explore the section content with students. For further suggestions on block scheduling or team teaching, see the *Block Scheduling Handbook with Team Teaching Strategies.*

LEVEL 1: As a class, discuss expectations Americans had of their new government. *(Students' responses should include having the government protect their liberty and improving the national economy.)* Organize students into groups and have each group discuss which of these expectations is more important. Ask volunteers to present and explain their decision to the class.
ENGLISH LANGUAGE LEARNERS , COOPERATIVE LEARNING

 ALL LEVELS: Copy the graphic organizer on the following page onto the chalkboard, omitting the italicized answers. Have each student complete the organizer, which illustrates the structure of the national government as it was created by the Constitution. Then lead a discussion on the steps Congress and the president took to organize the new government. **ENGLISH LANGUAGE LEARNERS**

In January 1789 the 11 states that had passed the Constitution each sent electors to choose the first president. These delegates formed the **electoral college.** Each state legislature had chosen electors who would represent the popular vote in their states. However, electors could vote for different candidates if they felt the public had not chosen the right person. On April 6, 1789, Congress declared that the electoral college had selected Washington unanimously. John Adams became his vice president.

Washington accepted the presidency because he felt it was his duty "to render [give] service to my country in obedience to its call." He traveled to New York City to be sworn into office. Along the roads he traveled and in the city, Americans cheered him on and celebrated. Ships in New York Harbor flew colorful flags and fired their cannons.

The presidency brought many changes for the Washington family. **Martha Washington** had to entertain guests and attend social events with her husband. Two weeks after arriving in New York, Martha described the scene to her niece. "I have not had one half-hour to myself since the day of my arrival," she wrote. Martha Washington ran the presidential household with grace and style. Abigail Adams once wrote, "I found myself much more deeply impressed [by George and Martha Washington] than I ever did before their majesties of Britain."

Patriot and author Judith Sargent Murray hoped women would play a different role in the new nation. Murray declared in newspaper essays that young women needed to be educated. "I expect to see our young women forming a new era in female history," she wrote. Murray, Abigail Adams, and other women helped share the idea of Republican Motherhood. This was the idea that women played an important role because they taught their children to be good citizens. Still, most women lacked the opportunity to take part equally in society.

✔ **Reading Check: Analyzing Information** What qualities made George Washington a good candidate for president? He brought honesty, patriotism, and a sense of duty to the office of the president.

Cheering crowds greeted Washington as he traveled to his inauguration.

★ **Citizenship and You**

The Electoral College

Under the system established by the Constitution, American voters do not directly elect the president. Instead, each state is represented by a number of electors equal to the total number of representatives and senators it has in Congress.

Electors are sworn to represent the interests of the people of their state. In most cases the candidate who wins a state's popular vote receives all of that state's electoral votes. Electors meet in December in election years in the capital of their home state to cast their votes for president and vice president. If no candidate receives an electoral majority, the House of Representatives chooses the president and the Senate chooses the vice president. **Why do you think that most states award all their electoral votes to the winner of the popular vote?**

★ **Constitutional Heritage**

The First Presidential Election. Electors in the nation's first presidential election each cast two ballots. However, the ballots did not distinguish between the presidential and vice presidential candidates. Alexander Hamilton realized that if John Adams, whom he did not like, received as many ballots as George Washington, neither candidate would win the presidency. The election would have to be decided in the House of Representatives. Hamilton wrote to colleagues sympathetic with his concerns and plotted to make sure that some electors did not vote for Adams, thus ensuring that Washington would clearly win the election.

CRITICAL THINKING
How did the election actually turn out?

ANSWER: Washington won when he received the presidential vote of each of the electors.

CITIZENSHIP AND YOU ANSWER
Students might suggest that the states want to support the will of the people.

Technology Resources
 Everyday Life in America Transparency 5: Education in Early America

★ **Life in the New Republic**

Hard work lay ahead for the new government. Few Americans had ever thought of themselves as citizens of a united nation. They expected the federal government to protect their liberty and hoped it would improve the economy by providing stability. However, they did not want the government to restrict trade as the British Parliament had done.

In 1790 the United States was home to almost 4 million people. Most Americans lived in the countryside and worked on farms. Farmers wanted fair tax laws and the right to settle western lands. Other Americans worked in towns as craftspeople, laborers, or merchants. These people knew that Americans had begun buying and selling goods across the country and around the world. As a result, they became more interested in trade laws. Merchants wanted simpler trade laws

Branches Established	Parts of . . .
Executive	president, cabinet (dept. heads), departments (treasury, state, etc.)
Judicial	Supreme Court, court of appeals, state courts
Legislative	both houses of Congress

LEVEL 3: Have students create a resume for Washington as if he were applying for the job of president. Then discuss with the class why Americans elected Washington as their first president.

HOMEWORK Have each student write a letter to a relative living in a foreign country explaining how and why Washington was chosen as president and how living in America changed after he took office.

★ CLOSE

Ask students to write entries for Washington's memoirs, describing his thoughts about the developments of the early days of his presidency and how these developments affected the nation.

Like these women, many Americans worked on farms in the early republic.

established by a unified government. Manufacturers wanted laws to protect them from foreign competition.

Only New York City and Philadelphia had populations greater than 25,000. New York City was the first capital of the United States, and in many ways it represented the spirit of the new nation. Badly damaged during the Revolutionary War, the city had already begun recovering. Citizens got rid of the signs of British rule. They changed Crown Street to Liberty Street, for example. International trade became more active, and business activity increased. A French visitor noted the city's energy.

Analyzing Primary Sources
Drawing Inferences and Conclusions What does this quote tell you about New York City's economic activities? New York had an active, busy economy, and its merchants conducted overseas trade.

 History Makers Speak ❝Everything in the city is in motion; everywhere the shops resound [ring out] with the noise of workers. . . . One sees vessels arriving from every part of the world.❞

—A French visitor to New York, quoted in *New York in the American Revolution,* by Wilbur Abbott

By 1790 the city's population had topped 33,000 and was growing rapidly. Many leaders thought this lively community showed the country's potential. They believed it was a fitting place for the new administration to plan the country's future.

✔ **Reading Check: Finding the Main Idea** How did Americans expect the new government to help free enterprise? by providing stability and not interfering with trade and business as the British Parliament had done

★ Setting Precedents

The new federal government had to make important decisions about policies and procedures. President Washington noted this fact in a letter to James Madison. "The first of everything in our situation will serve to establish a precedent," he wrote. A **precedent** is an action or a decision that serves as an example for later generations.

Planning the government's executive branch was one of Congress's first tasks. Congress created several executive departments. Each department specialized in a different area of national policy, such as military affairs. Washington nominated the department heads, who required approval by the Senate. He picked Alexander Hamilton as secretary of the treasury and Thomas Jefferson as secretary of state. Washington began meeting with the department heads as a group, which became known as

★ REVIEW AND ASSESS

Have students complete the **Section 1 Review** on p. 303. Then have students complete **Daily Quiz 10.1**. As **Alternative Assessment**, you may want to use the governmental structure diagram or presidential memoirs exercises in this section's lessons.

★ RETEACH

Have students complete **Main Idea Activity for English Language Learners and Special-Needs Students 10.1**. Then ask them to write a letter to the editor of a newspaper in which

they address the problems faced by the new republic and how they should be handled. Call on volunteers to share their letters with the class. **ENGLISH LANGUAGE LEARNERS**

★ EXTEND

Have students use the library to find information about the growth of the president's cabinet. Tell students to prepare press releases describing the creation of cabinet positions and the people that Washington selected to fill those positions. **BLOCK SCHEDULING**

the cabinet. The cabinet members advised the president and talked about important issues. By 1792, cabinet meetings were common practice.

The judicial branch also needed organizing. The Constitution did not state the number or location of federal courts. In September 1789 Congress passed the **Judiciary Act of 1789**, which created a federal court system with three levels. It also outlined the powers of the federal courts and their relationship to the state courts. District courts were at the lowest level. Then came the courts of appeals, which reviewed district court decisions. At the top level was the Supreme Court, which had six justices.

The president nominated the candidates for federal judgeships at each level, who then needed congressional approval. John Jay served as the Supreme Court's first chief justice. Washington selected Edmund Randolph as attorney general. Washington wrote to the justices to explain the importance of their duties.

THE GRANGER COLLECTION, NEW YORK

Washington's cabinet members advised him on issues of national defense, diplomacy, and finance.

 History Makers Speak

❝I have always been persuaded that the stability and success of the national government, and consequently the happiness of the people of the United States, would depend in a considerable degree on the interpretation and execution of its laws. In my opinion, therefore, it is important that the judiciary system should not only be independent in its operations, but as perfect as possible in its formation.❞

—George Washington, from *The Real George Washington, Part 2,* edited by Andrew M. Allison, Jay A. Parry, and W. Cleon Skousen

With the parts of the federal government in place, leaders began addressing the problems that faced the country.

✔ **Reading Check: Summarizing** How did Washington and Congress set up the executive and judicial branches? Congress created several executive departments and Washington formed a cabinet. Congress created a three-level federal court system whose justices were nominated by the president and approved by the senate.

Section 1 Review

go.hrw.com Homework Practice Online
keyword: SA3 HP10

1 **Define and explain:**
• electoral college
• precedent

2 **Identify and explain:**
• George Washington
• Martha Washington
• Judiciary Act of 1789

3 **Summarizing** Copy the chart below. Use it to show how three important positions in the new U.S. government, such as the president or Supreme Court justices, were selected.

Position	How Selected
1.	
2.	
3.	

4 **Finding the Main Idea**
a. What did Americans want their government to do to help free enterprise?

b. What problems did Washington and Congress face in organizing the executive branch and the judicial branch, and how did they work together to solve these problems?

5 **Writing and Critical Thinking**
Supporting a Point of View Imagine that you are a member of the electoral college and that George Washington has not accepted his presidential nomination. Write a petition to persuade him to take office.
Consider the following:
• the needs of the nation
• the expectations Americans had of the new government
• Washington's civic and leadership qualities

Section 1 Review
ANSWERS

1 **Define**
• electoral college, p. 301
• precedent, p. 302

2 **Identify**
• George Washington, p. 300
• Martha Washington, p. 301
• Judiciary Act of 1789, p. 303

3 president: elected by the electoral college; electoral college: selected by the state legislatures; executive leaders: appointed by president; Supreme Court justices: appointed by president; attorney general: appointed by president

4 a. They wanted the government to develop a strong, stable economy, but they did not want the government to interfere in commerce. They wanted the government to make trade laws and laws that would protect them from foreign competition.
b. Both the executive and judicial branches needed organizing, and there were no precedents to follow. Congress created the executive departments, and Washington appointed their leaders. Congress passed the Judiciary Act, which organized the federal courts, and Washington appointed the Supreme Court justices.

5 Students' petitions will vary, but should note that the young nation needed a strong leader who believed in democracy, that Americans wanted stability and security, and that Washington had courage, patriotism, and a very strong sense of duty to his nation.

Section 2

OBJECTIVES

★ Identify the challenge Alexander Hamilton faced as secretary of the treasury and the issues his plans raised.

★ Describe the issues that Hamilton and Thomas Jefferson disagreed on, and explain their views.

★ Examine the questions that were raised when the Bank of the United States was founded, and examine the different views that Hamilton and Jefferson had concerning the Bank.

SECTION 2 RESOURCES

REPRODUCIBLE

▶ Guided Reading Strategy 10.2
▶ Graphic Organizer 10: Hamilton and Jefferson

TECHNOLOGY

▶ One-Stop Planner, Lesson 10.2
▶ Exploring America's Past Video Segment: Building the Capital; Teacher's Guide, pp. 16–17
▶ Holt Researcher: American History CD–ROM
▶ Homework Practice Online

REINFORCEMENT, REVIEW, AND ASSESSMENT

▶ Section 2 Review, p. 309
▶ Daily Quiz 10.2
▶ Main Idea Activity 10.2
▶ English Audio Summary 10.2
▶ Spanish Audio Summary 10.2

Section 2

Hamilton and National Finances

Read to Discover

1. What challenge did Alexander Hamilton face as secretary of the treasury, and what issues did his plans raise?
2. What issues did Hamilton and Thomas Jefferson disagree on, and what were their views?
3. What questions were raised when the Bank of the United States was founded, and what different views did Hamilton and Jefferson have concerning the Bank?

WHY IT MATTERS TODAY

The U.S. government still imposes tariffs on some foreign goods. Use **CNNfyi**.com or other **current events** sources to learn more about a tariff that is in place today. Record your findings in your journal.

Define

• national debt
• bonds
• speculators
• protective tariff
• loose construction
• strict construction

Identify

• Alexander Hamilton
• Thomas Jefferson
• Bank of the United States

Alexander Hamilton had served as an aide to George Washington during the Revolutionary War.

The Story Continues

President Washington was worried about how to solve the nation's money problems. "There is but one man in the United States who can tell you," his friend Robert Morris suggested. "That is Alexander Hamilton." Hamilton's impressive reputation helped him become secretary of the treasury. But his skills were quickly put to the test. Within days of his appointment, Congress directed him to prepare a plan to improve the national economy.

★ Settling the Debt

Alexander Hamilton had a strong interest in business matters. He grew up on the island of Nevis in the British West Indies. When he was just a teenager he had helped run a shipping company there. Because of his intelligence and hard work, family friends sent him to the American colonies for an education. Hamilton eventually married into a very wealthy New York family and began practicing law.

TEACH

Have students read Section 2 and complete Guided Reading Strategy 10.2. Choose one or more of the following activities to explore the section content with students. For further suggestions on block scheduling or team teaching, see the *Block Scheduling Handbook with Team Teaching Strategies.*

 LEVEL 1: Lead a class discussion regarding the challenges that Alexander Hamilton's plans raised. Have each student draw a political cartoon about one of the elements of Hamilton's financial program. Students' cartoons should either support or oppose an element of the plan.

ENGLISH LANGUAGE LEARNERS

TEACHER TO TEACHER

Jeri Goodspeed-Gross of St. Paul, Minnesota, suggested the following activity:

ALL LEVELS: Provide students with a historical and a current map of Washington, D.C. Have students identify changes that have occurred to the Mall over the years. Explain to students that besides being the nation's capital, Washington, D.C., has become a tourist attraction and that many of the changes to the Mall occurred as a result of promoting tourism. Then have students list the names of buildings that have been added to the Mall over the years.

As secretary of the treasury, Hamilton's biggest challenge was paying off the **national debt**. This was the amount of money owed by the United States to its lenders. Hamilton figured that the United States owed about $11.7 million to foreign countries such as France.

The United States also owed about $40.4 million to U.S. citizens. Some of the debt was in the form of **bonds**, or certificates that represent money owed. During the Revolutionary War the government sold bonds to raise money. Officials promised to buy back these bonds with interest, thus allowing buyers to make a profit. But the government had trouble keeping this promise. Eventually, bondholders began to doubt that the government would ever repay them. Many people sold their bonds for less than their original value to **speculators**. Speculators are people who buy items at low prices in the hope that the value will rise.

Hamilton wanted to put the federal government on a solid financial footing. He feared that otherwise the government would lose the trust of the American people. He also wanted to pay the country's foreign debt immediately and repay the full value of all bonds over time. This caused great argument among politicians, because paying full value would allow speculators to make a profit. Hamilton believed this was only fair. As he saw it, speculators "paid what the commodity [bond] was worth in the market and took the risks." **Thomas Jefferson** opposed Hamilton's plan. He thought that the idea cheated the original bondholders who had sold their bonds at low prices. Jefferson wrote, "Immense sums were thus filched [stolen] from the poor and ignorant." A majority in Congress agreed with Hamilton. In early 1790 the government started exchanging the old bonds for new, more reliable ones whose value was guaranteed by the federal government.

✔ **Reading Check: Finding the Main Idea** What domestic problem did Alexander Hamilton face, and how did he plan to solve it? The national debt was high. He wanted to pay back the foreign debt immediately and gradually pay back the full value of bonds.

★ The States' Debts

The states owed $25 million for Revolutionary War expenses. Hamilton wanted the federal government to pay for $21.5 million of this debt. Hamilton believed that this aid would increase support for the federal government. He also thought that paying the state debts would help the national economy. Debtor states would not have to spend so much on

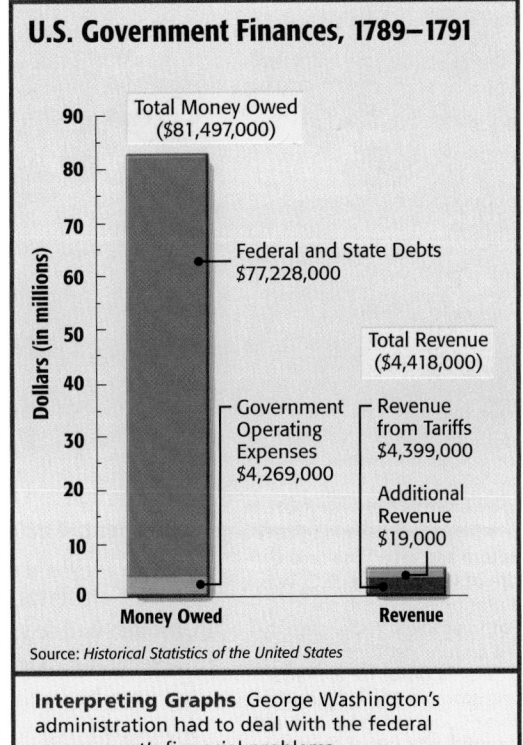

U.S. Government Finances, 1789–1791

Dollars (in millions)

Total Money Owed ($81,497,000)

Federal and State Debts $77,228,000

Total Revenue ($4,418,000)

Government Operating Expenses $4,269,000

Revenue from Tariffs $4,399,000

Additional Revenue $19,000

Money Owed — Revenue

Source: *Historical Statistics of the United States*

Interpreting Graphs George Washington's administration had to deal with the federal government's financial problems.

Skills Assessment Analyzing Information What were the government's operating expenses from 1789 to 1791?

The value of government bonds such as this one varied greatly before Alexander Hamilton's efforts.

★ Economics

The Confusing Debt.
When he accepted the position of treasury secretary, Alexander Hamilton faced a large and confusing national debt with several different creditors. The debt included IOUs written by the quartermaster, the officer in charge of army supplies; winning tickets from lotteries that the government had held to raise money and could not repay; and certificates that soldiers had received when the government had been unable to pay them for their military service. It was Hamilton's task to sort through this mass of paperwork in an attempt to reduce the debt.

CRITICAL THINKING
Why did the various types of government debt make Hamilton's job more difficult?

ANSWER: Students might suggest that he had to determine the size of the debt before he could make plans to reduce it.

GRAPH ANSWER
$4,269,000

Visual Record Answer

Students might suggest that Congress wanted the capital city to be associated only with the government.

ALL LEVELS: Copy the following graphic organizer onto the chalkboard, omitting the italicized answers. Have students complete the chart by listing arguments in support of Hamilton's and Jefferson's financial plans. Then lead a class discussion about the different views that Hamilton and Jefferson had concerning the Bank of the United States.

ENGLISH LANGUAGE LEARNERS

Hamilton	Jefferson
• *Paying speculators is fair because they took the risk.*	• *Paying speculators cheats the original bondholders.*
• *Aid to states would increase support for the federal government and strengthen the national economy.*	• *Jefferson agreed, and helped support the plan.*
• *Protective tariffs will cause Americans to buy U.S. goods.*	• *Lower tariffs are better for farmers, keeping import prices low.*
• *A national bank is "necessary and proper" for governing the nation.*	• *The elastic clause refers to necessity, not convenience.*

★ Geography

Sectional Tensions. The debate over Hamilton's economic plans revealed tensions between the northern and southern states. Many southerners pointed out that the bond payments would enrich speculators, most of whom lived in the North. In fact, speculators sent fast-sailing ships south from New York and Philadelphia in order to buy bonds before southerners learned of Hamilton's proposal. Virginians particularly hated Hamilton's programs. Virginia senator George Mason expressed his dismay over Hamilton's economic programs, saying that Hamilton had "done us more injury than Great Britain & all her fleets & armies."

CRITICAL THINKING

What does the speculators' attempt to deceive southerners reveal about communications in the early years of the United States?

ANSWER: Students might suggest that for most Americans, overseas routes were the quickest means of sending and receiving information.

Interpreting the Visual Record

Before and after *The future site of Washington, D.C., was a plot of land along the Potomac River. Today the city is a cultural center filled with treasured historical artifacts and monuments.* **Why do you think Congress chose to build a capital city rather than use an existing city for the national capital?**

THE GRANGER COLLECTION, NEW YORK

Research on the R◉M

Free Find:
Alexander Hamilton
After reading about Alexander Hamilton on the **Holt Researcher CD–ROM**, write a short essay explaining his contributions to the new government of the United States.

repayment. Therefore, Hamilton said, they would have resources to develop business and trade.

Not all states agreed. Southern states such as Virginia and North Carolina had few war debts. Their representatives did not want to help the federal government pay the debts of other states. Patrick Henry did not even believe that the Constitution gave Congress the power to pay state debts. Hamilton knew that he needed the help of southern representatives to get his plan approved.

He got this help because southern officials wanted a new national capital. Many southerners did not like having the capital in New York. They thought this gave the northern states too much influence over national policy. Hamilton, Jefferson, and Representative James Madison met in June 1790. Hamilton promised to convince northern members of Congress to move the capital. In exchange, Jefferson and Madison agreed to gather support in the South for Hamilton's debt payment plan.

The compromise worked. In July the House of Representatives approved the plan. They chose an area along the Potomac River for the new national capital. This site would become present-day Washington, D.C. Philadelphia served as the temporary capital while architects began designing the new capital city.

✔ **Reading Check: Summarizing** What compromise did Hamilton and Jefferson reach to allow Congress to repay the state debts? Hamilton helped move the national capital to present-day Washington, D.C., while Jefferson helped get southern states to support debt assumption.

★ Hamilton versus Jefferson

Hamilton and Jefferson did not cooperate for long. Instead, they began to disagree about how to define the authority of the central government. While Hamilton believed in a strong central government, Jefferson wanted to protect the powers of the states. Their conflict reflected basic differences in their opinions about democracy. Hamilton had little faith in the common person. He once said that "the people . . . seldom judge or determine [decide] right." He wanted a strong central government that balanced power between the "mass of the people" and wealthier citizens. He explained his beliefs.

 History Makers Speak ❝We must take man as we find him, and if we expect him to serve the public, [we] must interest his passions in doing so. A reliance on pure patriotism has been the source of many of our errors.❞

—Alexander Hamilton, quoted in *Odd Destiny: The Life of Alexander Hamilton,* by Marie B. Hecht

Hamilton believed that his approach would protect everyone's liberties while keeping the people from having too much power.

Jefferson disagreed strongly with Hamilton's views of the average citizen's ability. He did admit that "the people can not be all, and always, well informed." However, Jefferson firmly defended the right of the people to rule the country.

 History Makers Speak ❝It is my principle that the will of the Majority should always prevail [win]. . . . Above all things I hope the education of the common people will be attended to; [I am] convinced that on their good sense we may rely with the most security for the preservation of a due degree of liberty.❞

—Thomas Jefferson, quoted in *Thomas Jefferson,* edited by Joseph L. Gardner

Hamilton and Jefferson also argued over how the American economy should grow. Hamilton wanted new forms of economic growth. He also wanted to promote manufacturing and business. In a 1790 report he suggested that the government give prizes to certain American companies. These prizes would "reward some particular excellence or superiority" in the companies' products. In addition, Hamilton wanted to pass a higher tariff, or a tax on imported goods. Known as a **protective tariff**, this tax would raise the prices of foreign products. Hamilton hoped this would cause Americans to buy U.S. goods, which would protect American manufacturing from foreign competition.

Analyzing Primary Sources

Identifying Points of View Does Hamilton believe that people are naturally good citizens? Explain your answer. No. He believes that the government must lead them.

CONNECTING TO THE ARTS

American Architecture and Classical Revival After the Revolution, American architects began to create buildings in the classical style of ancient Greece and Rome. Many Americans admired these civilizations because they had some of the same democratic ideals as the new American nation.

Thomas Jefferson started this trend in 1785 when he designed Virginia's capitol building. It was inspired by Roman architecture's use of columns, domes, and white stone. Architects designed banks, churches, colleges, and even the new U.S. Capitol Building in the same style. Shown here is William Thornton's winning design for the outside of the building. **What view is shown by Americans' new interest in classical architecture?**

George Washington

Many people consider George Washington to be the Father of Our Country. He entered the presidency as one of the great heroes of the American Revolution. He felt a great sense of responsibility to the nation. He wanted to be a dignified leader who also listened to the needs of the people. Yet the pressure of other people's expectations often made life difficult for him. Washington was very sensitive to attacks made against him in the press. Thomas Jefferson wrote, "I think he feels those things [criticisms] more than any person I ever met."

Washington left politics in 1797 and returned to his home in Mount Vernon. He died just two years later. His image is carved into the national monument at Mount Rushmore, South Dakota. President's Day, a federal holiday, is held each year near his birthday, February 22. Why do you think George Washington has been called the "Father of Our Country"?

Jefferson, on the other hand, worried about depending too much on business and manufacturing. Jefferson believed that farmers were the most independent voters. They did not rely too much on other people's work to make a living. He wrote, "Our governments will remain virtuous [morally pure] for many centuries; as long as they are chiefly agricultural." Jefferson wanted lower tariffs, which would help farmers by keeping the price of imported goods low.

✔ **Reading Check: Comparing and Contrasting** Compare and contrast Hamilton's and Jefferson's ideas about government, the economy, and protective tariffs. Hamilton: strong central government, little faith in common people, favored trade, commerce, and tariffs; Jefferson: states' rights, strong belief in common people, favored agriculture and low tariffs

★ The Debate over the Bank

Hamilton's and Jefferson's differences came to the public's attention in early 1791. Hamilton wanted to start a national bank in which the government could safely deposit its money. The bank would also make loans to the government and businesses. Hamilton added that the United States should build a national mint—a place where coins are made. Then the country could begin issuing its own money. To limit the national bank's power, Hamilton asked for a 20-year charter. After this period of time, Congress could decide if it should extend the charter. Hamilton also asked each state to start its own bank so that the national bank would not have a monopoly.

The idea of establishing a national bank greatly worried both James Madison and Thomas Jefferson. They did not believe the U.S. Constitution gave Congress this power. In response, Hamilton and his supporters pointed to a clause in Article I, Section 8. This clause states that Congress has the power "to make all laws which shall be necessary and proper" for governing the nation. The passage later became known as the elastic clause because it has allowed the powers of the government to be stretched. Hamilton argued that this clause was meant to give the government the power to react to new situations. He saw the need for a national bank as an ideal example of such a situation. Hamilton's view became known as **loose construction** of the Constitution. According to loose construction, the federal government can take any reasonable actions that the Constitution does not specifically forbid it from taking.

Jefferson did not agree with Hamilton's argument. Jefferson believed that the "necessary and proper" clause should be used only in special cases. He wrote a letter explaining his view to President Washington. "The Constitution allows only the means which are 'necessary,' not those which are merely 'convenient.'" To Jefferson, the national bank was a convenience, not a necessity. Jefferson's view became known as **strict construction**. According to strict construction, the federal government should do only what the Constitution specifically says it can do.

☆ REVIEW AND ASSESS

Have students complete the **Section 2 Review** on p. 309. Then have students complete **Daily Quiz 10.2**. As **Alternative Assessment**, you may want to use the comparison chart or political cartoon exercise in this section's lessons.

☆ RETEACH

Have students complete **Main Idea Activity for English Language Learners and Special-Needs Students 10.2**. Then have them write an entry in Jefferson's journal explaining why he opposed the various parts of Hamilton's plan or an entry in Hamilton's journal explaining what he thought of Jefferson's criticisms. **ENGLISH LANGUAGE LEARNERS**

☆ EXTEND

Have students use the library to find information about the growth of the national debt during the 1900s and about current proposals to pay it off or to limit its growth. Have students create a two-column chart summarizing information about the plans. Instruct them to label one column *Hamilton* and the other column *Jefferson*. Then ask students to consider the arguments made for or against the plans and to decide whether Hamilton or Jefferson would have supported the arguments. Have students write the argument under the appropriate heading. **BLOCK SCHEDULING**

THE GRANGER COLLECTION, NEW YORK

Interpreting the Visual Record

National finance *Both the Bank of the United States, shown at the left, and the U.S. Mint, which issued the coins shown below, were projects of Alexander Hamilton.* **How are these two institutions similar?**

President Washington and Congress agreed with Hamilton. They hoped a bank would offer more security for the national economy. As a result, in February 1791 Congress chartered the **Bank of the United States**. The Bank helped offer stability during the next 20 years and played an important role in improving the U.S. economy.

✔ **Reading Check: Identifying Points of View** How did Hamilton interpret the Constitution during the Bank debate, and what problems did he face with this argument? Hamilton believed in loose construction, by which the federal government can take actions that the Constitution does not forbid. Jefferson, who favored strict construction, opposed him.

Section 2 Review

go.hrw.com Homework Practice Online
keyword: SA3 HP10

❶ Define and explain:
• national debt
• bonds
• speculators
• protective tariff
• loose construction
• strict construction

❷ Identify and explain:
• Alexander Hamilton
• Thomas Jefferson
• Bank of the United States

❸ Contrasting Copy the graphic organizer below. Use it to contrast the ideas that Hamilton and Jefferson held about the topics listed.

Hamilton		Jefferson
	Bonds	
	Democracy	
	Economy	
	Tariffs	
	National Bank	
	Constitution	

❹ Finding the Main Idea
a. What was Alexander Hamilton's biggest job, and what debate arose from his plans?

b. How did Hamilton win approval from Congress for the federal government to pay most of the states' war debts?

❺ Writing and Critical Thinking
Summarizing Imagine that you are a member of Congress during Washington's administration. Write a speech to be delivered to the people of your home state that explains the conflict over the creation of a national bank.

Consider the following:
• different interpretations of the Constitution
• political differences between Hamilton and Jefferson
• the benefits of a national bank

Section 3

OBJECTIVES

★ Explain how Americans and President Washington responded to events in France.

★ Discuss President Washington's foreign policy.

★ Describe how the United States settled its differences with Great Britain and Spain.

🔊 LET'S GET STARTED!

Write the following question on the chalkboard: *Should a nation's foreign policy be based on moral principle or self-interest?* As students enter the classroom, have them write their responses. Then ask them how and why these two methods of determining foreign policy might be in conflict with each other. (*Students' answers will vary but may include the choice to go to war with a democratic nation in order to protect a business interest that the country's economy depends upon.*) Tell the class that in Section 3 they will learn about conflicts in the early 1790s that forced the president and his advisers to create a foreign policy that would fulfill U.S. obligations without sacrificing the nation's self-interests.

Section 3

Troubles Abroad

Read to Discover

1. How did Americans and President Washington respond to events in France?
2. What policy did Washington follow toward foreign nations?
3. How did the United States settle its differences with Great Britain and Spain?

WHY IT MATTERS TODAY

The United States still signs treaties with other countries. Use **CNNfyi.com** or other **current events** sources to find out about an economic, military, or political treaty the United States has signed or considered signing in recent years. Record your findings in your journal.

Define

- privateers
- right of deposit

Identify

- French Revolution
- Neutrality Proclamation
- Edmond Genet
- John Jay
- Jay's Treaty
- Thomas Pinckney
- Pinckney's Treaty

THE GRANGER COLLECTION, NEW YORK

The fall of the Bastille is celebrated as a national holiday in France.

The Story Continues

On July 14, 1789, the citizens of Paris, France, challenged their corrupt government. Masses of people attacked the Bastille, a hated fortress and prison that held the enemies of the French Crown. Soldiers defending the walls were shocked. One of them described "the people . . . in a crowd, armed with muskets . . . swords . . . and shouting, 'We want the Bastille! Down with the troops.'" After hours of fighting, the crowd captured the fortress. The fall of this mighty symbol of royal power stunned the country.

★ The French Revolution

The storming of the Bastille was one of the first acts of the **French Revolution**. During this rebellion the French people overthrew their monarchy and created a republican government. The Declaration of the Rights of Man stated the French Revolution's principles: "liberty, equality, and fraternity [brotherhood]." As U.S. minister to France, Thomas Jefferson witnessed the early days of the Revolution. He wrote to friends back in America that the changes in France were "the first chapter of European liberty."

★ TEACH

Have students read Section 3 and complete Guided Reading Strategy 10.3. Choose one or more of the following activities to explore the section content with students. For further suggestions on block scheduling or team teaching, see the *Block Scheduling Handbook with Team Teaching Strategies.*

LEVEL 1: Lead a class discussion about how President Washington and Americans responded to events in France. Have students list actions taken by President Washington that were intended to protect or promote U.S. self-interests in its relations with France. *(Students' lists might include the following: he urged friendly and non partisan relations with both countries, issued the Neutrality Proclamation, and remained neutral in the war.)* List replies on the chalkboard. Call on volunteers to explain how one or more of the replies related to U.S. self-interests. **ENGLISH LANGUAGE LEARNERS**

In 1789 King Louis XVI addressed the members of the French Legislature. Four years later revolutionaries beheaded the king using a guillotine like the one below.

News of the French Revolution spread quickly, gaining the support of many Americans. They believed France was founding a democratic republic similar to the United States. These Americans celebrated French independence by burning huge bonfires and singing French songs. Jefferson wrote to a friend about the scene. He said that he was fortunate "to see in the course of fourteen years two such revolutions as were never before seen."

Some Americans were not as pleased. They were very worried about the French Revolution's violent riots. They also feared the many attacks on all forms of traditional authority. The revolutionaries shocked many Americans by beheading King Louis XVI in January 1793 and Queen Marie-Antoinette later that year.

✔ **Reading Check: Contrasting** What differing opinions did Americans hold about the French Revolution? Some supported it because they believed that France was establishing a republic. Others did not support it because of its violence.

★ U.S. Neutrality

A few months after the French Revolution started, France and Great Britain went to war. Some Americans backed the French, while others backed the British. The debate over U.S. foreign policy soon divided Congress and split President Washington's cabinet. After considering different arguments on the issue, Washington presented his own views to Congress on April 22, 1793.

> History Makers Speak
>
> ❝The duty and interest of the United States require that they should with sincerity and good faith adopt and pursue a conduct friendly and impartial [unbiased] towards the belligerent [fighting] powers.❞
>
> —Proclamation of Neutrality

★★★★★★★★★★★
That's Interesting!
★★★★★★★★★★★

"Let them eat cake." Maybe you've heard the saying "Let them eat cake." Many people believe that the French queen Marie-Antoinette said this. As the story goes, this was her reply when a large mob of hungry women stormed the palace demanding bread. The story of the queen's heartless attitude became quite popular. The queen was probably out of touch with the needs of poor French citizens. But many historians believe that the French philosopher Jean-Jacques Rousseau actually made up the story to make the French monarchy look bad.

★ Global Relations

American Influence.
French revolutionaries were influenced by the American Revolution. In August 1789 the French revolutionaries released the Declaration of the Rights of Man and of the Citizen, a document modeling the Declaration of Independence. In addition, the Marquis de Lafayette—a Frenchman who fought in the Revolutionary War alongside George Washington—sent the key of the Bastille to President Washington. The Bastille was a large royal fortress in Paris that the revolutionaries stormed and took over. Lafayette said to Washington "It is a tribute which I owe to you, as a son to my adoptive father, as an aide-de-camp to my General, as a Missionary of Liberty to its Patriarch."

🖥 **internet** connect

TOPIC: French Revolution
GO TO: go.hrw.com
KEYWORD: SA3 CF10

Have students use the library, search the Internet through the HRW Go site, or use primary and secondary sources to discover the grievances that the French had against their king. Have students make a chart comparing those grievances to the list of grievances in the Declaration of Independence.

ALL LEVELS: Copy the following graphic organizer onto the chalkboard, omitting the italicized answers. Then have students complete the organizer to illustrate how the United States settled its differences with Great Britain and Spain. **ENGLISH LANGUAGE LEARNERS**

HOMEWORK Have students prepare a time line of the events leading to Jay's and Pinckney's Treaties. Have students illustrate their time lines.

Jay's Treaty	Pinckney's Treaty
British concessions	**Spanish concessions**
• *Britain agreed to pay damages for U.S. ships seized.*	• *Spain agreed to change the Florida border.*
• *Britain abandoned forts on the Western frontier.*	• *Spain agreed to reopen the port of New Orleans to U.S. shipping and to provide right of deposit.*
• *Britain allowed small American merchant ships to continue trading certain items in Caribbean.*	

U.S. concessions
• *The United States promised to pay debts it owed to British merchants before the Revolution.*

Global Relations

The Neutrality Proclamation. Thomas Jefferson objected to the actual use of the word *neutrality* in the proclamation, arguing that using the word *neutral* would lead Great Britain to continue practices on the high seas that Americans opposed. George Washington agreed with Jefferson, and the word *neutrality* was removed from the proclamation.

CRITICAL THINKING

Do you think Jefferson was correct to object to the use of the word *neutrality*?

ANSWER: Students might argue that it made no difference because European nations considered it to be a neutrality proclamation.

GLOBAL CONNECTIONS ANSWER

They had been important figures in the Revolutionary War, and they believed in democratic rule and wanted to contribute to the French Revolution.

Visual Record Answer

(for p. 313)

Students should suggest that the figure represents John Jay.

GLOBAL CONNECTIONS

Patriots in France

The democratic goals of the French Revolution encouraged some former Patriots to take part. Two of the more well-known examples were Thomas Paine and the Marquis de Lafayette. Paine is shown above holding a copy of *Rights of Man,* which he wrote in support of the Revolution and the creation of democracies in Europe. When Paine went to France, however, he was jailed for protesting the new government's violent acts. In prison he wrote *The Age of Reason,* which attacked organized religion and cost him many of his supporters. The Marquis de Lafayette helped write the Declaration of the Rights of Man and the French Constitution of 1791. Lafayette then fled the country and took little part in French politics once Napoléon came to power. **How did Paine and Lafayette contribute to the French Revolution?**

This **Neutrality Proclamation** stated that the United States would not take sides with countries at war in Europe. Washington believed that this plan would be the safest and most reasonable. However, not everyone agreed. Some newspaper editors and members of Congress criticized him. James Madison questioned Washington's right to issue the proclamation without Congress's approval.

⭐ Citizen Genet

At this time **Edmond Genet** (zhuh-ne), France's new representative to the United States, arrived. Citizen Genet, as he was known, traveled across the country seeking American support for France. He found four sea captains who agreed to command **privateers**—private ships allowed by a country to attack its enemies. Washington warned Genet that recruiting privateers on American soil hurt U.S. neutrality. In response, Genet said he would ask the American people to overrule Washington. At that point, even pro-French Jefferson agreed that Genet should be sent back home.

Although he wanted Genet to be removed, Jefferson was still upset by the U.S. policy toward France. He also felt that pro-British Hamilton was influencing the president's foreign policy. Hamilton's influence interfered with Jefferson's duties as secretary of state. As a result, Jefferson eventually decided to leave Washington's cabinet. In December 1793 Jefferson resigned. This decision disappointed Washington, who had a high opinion of Jefferson's honesty and talent. Some 30 years after he resigned, Jefferson expressed his view of President Washington. Although he disagreed with some of Washington's policies, Jefferson had great respect for the president.

History Makers Speak

"**General Washington was himself sincerely a friend to the republican principles of our Constitution. . . . He repeatedly declared to me that he . . . would lose the last drop of his blood in its support.**"

—Thomas Jefferson, from *The Writings of Thomas Jefferson,* edited by Albert Ellery Bergh

✔ **Reading Check: Identifying Cause and Effect** What did President Washington do when France and Great Britain went to war, and how did Jefferson respond? Washington adopted a neutral stance. Jefferson resigned his position because he felt U.S. policy was pro-British.

⭐ Jay's Treaty

Washington experienced other threats to U.S. neutrality. In late 1793 the British began seizing all ships carrying food to the French West Indies. In the process, the British captured hundreds of neutral American merchant ships. Rumors also flew that British officers on the western frontier were encouraging American Indian uprisings. The British had never abandoned these frontier forts, as the Treaty of Paris required. Now it

LEVEL 3: Explain to students that the United States officially maintained a policy of neutrality in the war between France and England and that Edmond Genet's actions threatened to violate that neutrality. Tell students to imagine that they have been asked to spy on Genet in order to determine whether he presents a threat to national security and to see how U.S. citizens respond to his call to arms. Have students use information from this section to create a log of Genet's actions and citizens' responses to them. *(Student's logs will vary but should include information indicating that Genet went around the countryside trying to gain American support for the French Revolution, and that some Americans were ready to join his cause.)* After creating the log, students should offer written suggestions to President Washington about what to do concerning Genet's actions.

★ CLOSE

Have students prepare news releases from the French government to the United States. The releases should ask the United States to honor the treaty it signed with France in 1778 by providing food to French armies, by allowing French warships to use U.S. ports, and by helping to drive the French out of New Orleans. Then have students prepare a news release from the office of the president explaining his decision to proclaim neutrality in 1793. These releases should cite Washington's reasons for his decision.

---

looked as if the British might side with American Indians in a war against American settlers.

Even Alexander Hamilton recognized that the United States might be on the path to war. President Washington and Hamilton sent Chief Justice **John Jay** to London to work out a peaceful resolution. Jay's task was difficult. The British knew that the United States lacked a strong navy. Also, many American businesses relied on trade with Great Britain. However, the British did not want to fight another war in North America.

The two sides eventually reached an agreement in November 1794. **Jay's Treaty** was a compromise. The British agreed to pay damages for seized American ships. Small American merchant ships were allowed to continue trading certain items in the Caribbean. The British also said they would abandon their forts on the northwestern frontier. In exchange, the United States would pay the pre-Revolutionary debts it owed to British merchants.

Many congressional leaders argued that the treaty did not accomplish much. Critics pointed out that it ignored many important issues. The treaty did not prevent Britain from capturing large American ships or supporting American Indians on the frontier. It also did not make the British return slaves they had freed during the Revolutionary War. Although Washington disliked the treaty, he felt that it was the best that the United States could do. At his urging, the Senate approved the treaty.

THE GRANGER COLLECTION, NEW YORK

Interpreting the Visual Record

Protest *Some critics of Jay's Treaty were so angry that they protested in the streets.* **Whom does the figure being burned represent?**

✔ **Reading Check: Categorizing** Which aspects of Jay's Treaty benefited the United States, and which did not? The British would pay damages, abandon forts, and allow some trade ships in Caribbean. But the British kept taking U.S. ships, supporting Indians, and did not return slaves.

★ Pinckney's Treaty

Along the frontier with Spanish Florida and Louisiana, American settlers faced other problems. The Spanish disputed the border between the United States and Florida. As a result of this dispute, Spain closed the port of New Orleans to U.S. trade in 1784. New Orleans was an important port. All goods moving down the Mississippi to places in the East or overseas had to pass through the city. Closing the port separated settlers on the western frontier from their most important link with the outside world.

Washington asked U.S. ambassador **Thomas Pinckney** to help. Pinckney asked Spanish officials to reopen New Orleans to U.S. trade. Then he requested **right of deposit** at the port of New Orleans. This right would allow American boats to transfer their goods at New Orleans without paying fees on their cargo.

★ Economics

Trade with France. As one of his last acts as secretary of state, Jefferson sent a message to Congress saying that the United States should increase its trade with France and introduce restrictions on trade with Great Britain. Jefferson argued that this plan would decrease U.S. dependence on British imports.

CRITICAL THINKING

Why do you think Hamilton criticized Jefferson's proposal?

ANSWER: Students might suggest that Hamilton supported strong ties with Britain, not France.

Visual Record Answer

(for p. 314)

Students might suggest that people appear to be shipping and unloading goods.

Technology Resources

 Exploring America's Past Video Segment: Time Travelers; Teacher's Guide, pp. 13–15

Search 31731, Play to 36735 Videodisc Red Side A

See *Teacher's Guide* for Spanish barcode.

Have students complete the **Section 3 Review** on p. 314. Then have students complete **Daily Quiz 10.3**. As **Alternative Assessment**, you may want to use the time line or treaty graphic organizer in this section's lessons.

Have students use the library to obtain information about relations between Spain and the United States from the beginning of the Revolutionary War to the signing of Pinckney's Treaty. Have students prepare an outline for a book covering U.S.-Spanish relations. Outlines should explain why successful negotiations with Spain were important in satisfying the demands of citizens living in the western United States, in keeping the union together, and in defending the republic from nations like France and England once the war ended.

BLOCK SCHEDULING

★ **RETEACH**

Have students complete **Main Idea Activity for English Language Learners and Special-Needs Students 10.3**. Then organize the class into small groups. Ask each group to write down what its members consider to be the most important issue for each subsection and present that issue to the class.

ENGLISH LANGUAGE LEARNERS , COOPERATIVE LEARNING

Section 3 Review
ANSWERS

❶ Define
• privateers, p. 312
• right of deposit, p. 313

❷ Identify
• French Revolution, p. 310
• Neutrality Proclamation, p. 312
• Edmond Genet, p. 312
• John Jay, p. 313
• Jay's Treaty, p. 313
• Thomas Pinckney, p. 313
• Pinckney's Treaty, p. 314

❸ France: U.S. neutrality in war against Britain, Edmond Genet; Great Britain: U.S. neutrality in war against France, Jay's Treaty, John Jay; Spain: border disputes, loss of access to New Orleans, Pinckney's Treaty, Thomas Pinckney

❹ a. believed this was the safest and most reasonable course of action
b. Jay's Treaty negotiated because British seizing of U.S. ships and encouragement of American Indians to fight against American settlers; resulted in Great Britain paying damages for seized U.S. ships, some merchant trade in Caribbean, and promises to abandon frontier forts; Pinckney's Treaty negotiated because Spain and the U. S. had a border dispute over Florida, Spain's refusal to let U.S. use port of New Orleans; resulted in Spain's agreement to change Florida border, reopen the port at New Orleans, and provide right of deposit to American boats.

❺ Students' scripts will vary.

Interpreting the Visual Record

Western trade *The Mississippi River and the port of New Orleans were vital links to the wider world for settlers on the American frontier.* **What parts of this image show trade taking place?**

DETAIL FROM THE ORIGINAL, COURTESY OF THE HISTORIC NEW ORLEANS COLLECTION

Spanish minister Manuel de Godoy (goh-DOY) tried to delay reaching an agreement. He hoped that Pinckney would grow desperate and sign a treaty favorable to the Spanish. But Pinckney was patient. Godoy became worried that the United States and Great Britain might join against Spain after signing Jay's Treaty. So he agreed to **Pinckney's Treaty**, which was signed in October 1795. Under the treaty, Spain agreed to change the Florida border. Spain's government also reopened the port at New Orleans to American ships and gave them right of deposit. Because it opened the frontier to further expansion, Washington and most other Americans considered Pinckney's Treaty a success.

✔ **Reading Check: Analyzing Information** Why did most Americans believe Pinckney's Treaty was more successful than Jay's Treaty? The United States got all its requests met with Pinckney's Treaty, unlike with Jay's Treaty.

Section 3 Review

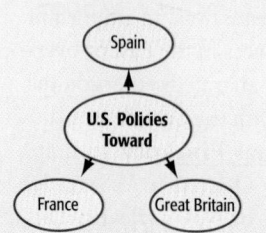

go. hrw .com **Homework Practice Online**

keyword: SA3 HP10

❶ Define and explain:
• privateers
• right of deposit

❷ Identify and explain:
• French Revolution
• Neutrality Proclamation
• Edmond Genet
• John Jay
• Jay's Treaty
• Thomas Pinckney
• Pinckney's Treaty

❸ Summarizing Copy the web diagram below. Use it to show the dealings the United States had with each country, as well as any important politicians involved.

Spain

U.S. Policies Toward

France   Great Britain

❹ Finding the Main Idea
a. Why did Washington want to pursue a policy of neutrality?
b. What problems led to Jay's Treaty and Pinckney's Treaty, and what were the results of these treaties?

❺ Writing and Critical Thinking
Analyzing Information Imagine that news of the French Revolution has reached the U.S. capital. Write a script for a short skit that describes how the president and other individuals react to the news.
Consider the following:
• pro-French attitudes
• pro-British attitudes
• Washington's views on foreign policy

Section 4

OBJECTIVES

⭐ Identify the domestic problems faced by the United States.

⭐ Explain the advice that Washington gave to the nation in his Farewell Address.

Section 4

Challenges at Home

Read to Discover

1. What domestic problems did the United States face?
2. What advice did Washington give the nation in his Farewell Address?

WHY IT MATTERS TODAY

George Washington helped our country in many ways. Use **CNNfyi.com** or other **current events** sources to find out about another U.S. citizen who has made important contributions to the country. Record your findings in your journal.

Identify

- Little Turtle
- Anthony Wayne
- Battle of Fallen Timbers
- Treaty of Greenville
- Whiskey Rebellion

The Story Continues

In November 1786 Mohawk leader Joseph Brant, or Thayendanegea, addressed a council of American Indian nations from the Ohio Valley. "The interests of any one [Indian] nation should be the welfare of all the others," he said. By uniting their efforts, they hoped to stop settlers from taking their land. Thayendanegea said that Indians must take action if they were to keep from being pushed farther west. The councilmembers agreed and formed a confederation of American Indian nations. The members promised to stop selling land to settlers and agreed to seek a new treaty from the U.S. government.

Thayendanegea had fought with the British against the United States in the Revolutionary War.

⭐ Conflict in the Northwest Territory

Despite the protests of American Indians, Americans continued to settle the Northwest Territory. Meetings between U.S. officials and American Indian leaders achieved little. Supplied with guns and ammunition by British traders, American Indians went to war. In 1790 and 1791 an American Indian confederation under Miami chief **Little Turtle** defeated U.S. forces. Washington then sent General **Anthony Wayne** to the frontier to take charge of the army.

Have students read Section 4 and complete Guided Reading Strategy 10.4. Choose one or more of the following activities to explore the section content with students. For further suggestions on block scheduling or team teaching, see the *Block Scheduling Handbook with Team Teaching Strategies.*

LEVEL 1: Ask volunteers to read George Washington's Farewell Address to the class. Lead a class discussion about the advice Washington gave to citizens in his address. Ask students to write a newspaper headline with two subheadlines covering key points of his address.

ENGLISH LANGUAGE LEARNERS

HOMEWORK Have students prepare an article for a magazine entitled *American Voices, American Perspectives.* Their articles should illustrate the ways that one of the following individuals viewed the domestic problems described in the section: Joseph Brant, Little Turtle, William Smith, George Washington, or Martha Washington. Compile all the articles into the magazine.

ALL LEVELS: Copy the graphic organizer on the next page onto the chalkboard, omitting the italicized answers. Have students complete the organizer by listing the domestic issues facing the United States and the key players involved in each of these issues.

ENGLISH LANGUAGE LEARNERS

★ Constitutional Heritage

The Whiskey Rebellion.
When the governor of Pennsylvania refused to enforce the federal tax on whiskey, President Washington requested that Congress exercise its power and raise a militia to enforce the law. Washington led this militia in a march across the Allegheny Mountains. Alexander Hamilton accompanied him, thus demonstrating that both the president and the secretary of the treasury believed that the federal government had the constitutional authority to put down an insurrection.

CRITICAL THINKING

What effect might Washington's and Hamilton's presence have had on the rebels?

ANSWER: Students might suggest that their presence could have convinced the rebels that victory was impossible.

Visual Record Answer

Students might suggest that the government wanted to remind the rebels of its authority.

Analyzing Primary Sources
Identifying Points of View
Why does Little Turtle give up the fight? The fight has already lasted a long time and caused much harm. There are also too many settlers to fight.

Interpreting the Visual Record

Whiskey Rebellion
Washington led an army into western Pennsylvania to put down the Whiskey Rebellion. **Why do you think the government felt it was necessary to send such a large force for this task?**

THE METROPOLITAN MUSEUM OF ART, GIFT OF EDGAR WILLIAM AND BERNICE CHRYSLER GARBISCH, 1963 (63.201.2)

Little Turtle asked his British allies for support, but they refused. He then quit his command and warned other American Indian leaders not to fight.

History Makers Speak
❝The trail has been long and bloody; it has no end. The [whites] come from where the sun rises, and they . . . are many. They are like the leaves of the trees. When the frost comes they fall and are blown away. But when the sunshine comes again they come back more plentiful than ever before.❞

—Little Turtle, quoted in *The Ohio Frontier,* by Douglas Hurt

American Indian forces and the U.S. Army fought the **Battle of Fallen Timbers** on August 20, 1794. The victory went to Wayne's troops, who then burned the American Indians' villages and fields. The frontier war soon ended. In August 1795, Indian leaders signed the **Treaty of Greenville**. This treaty gave the United States access to American Indian lands in the Northwest Territory and guaranteed the safety of U.S. citizens there. In exchange, Indians received $20,000 worth of goods and a formal acknowledgment of their claim to the lands they still held.

✔ **Reading Check: Sequencing** List the events in the Northwest Territory that affected U.S. national security in the order that they took place.
See text above for specific events and dates.

★ The Whiskey Rebellion

More conflicts arose on the frontier when Congress passed a tax on American-made whiskey in March 1791. Farmers who produced small amounts of whiskey for trade argued that they could not afford the tax. After being fined for not paying the tax, farmer William Smith wrote, "I felt my blood boil." What began as the complaints of a few turned into the **Whiskey Rebellion** in 1794. Protesters refused to pay the tax and even tarred and feathered tax collectors. Some called themselves the new Sons of Liberty.

President Washington saw the rebels as a threat to federal authority. Under the Constitution, Congress had the power to pass the tax. He assembled some 13,000 men from state militias. The army approached western Pennsylvania in November 1794. By this time, most of the rebels had fled, and the Whiskey Rebellion ended without a battle.

✔ **Reading Check: Finding the Main Idea** What did farmers say and do in response to the whiskey tax, and why did this response worry Washington?
that they could not afford the tax; refused to pay the tax and tarred and feathered some tax collectors; thought the rebellion was a threat to federal authority

Conflict in the Northwest Territory
• American Indians
• British Army
• Little Turtle
• General Anthony Wayne
• U.S. army

Whiskey Rebellion
• Congress
• Farmers
• Tax collectors
• President Washington
• State militias

LEVEL 3: Organize the class into several groups and assign each group the task of creating an oral history describing the American Indians' reasons for going to war against the United States. **COOPERATIVE LEARNING**

☆ CLOSE

Have the class review the section to find information about Washington's Farewell Address. Have students identify the key recommendations that Washington made regarding the U.S. government. Write these recommendations on the chalkboard. Then instruct each student to write a few sentences about each recommendation that explains whether the United States has followed the advice.

☆ Washington's Farewell Address

In 1796 Washington decided not to run for a third presidential term. He wrote that he was "tired of public life" and "devoutly [strongly] wished for retirement." He also believed that by stepping down he would remind Americans that he was only a president, not a king. The people were the country's true leaders.

With the help of Alexander Hamilton and James Madison, the president wrote his Farewell Address. In it he spoke about what he believed were the greatest dangers to the American republic. Among these were the dangers of foreign ties and political divisions at home. Washington

Historical Document

WASHINGTON'S FAREWELL ADDRESS

George Washington

On September 19, 1796, President George Washington's Farewell Address first appeared in a Philadelphia newspaper. In it, he wrote about the nation's economy, foreign policy, and political parties.

I have already **intimated**[1] to you the danger of [political] parties in the state, with particular reference to the founding of them on geographical discriminations. Let me now take a more **comprehensive**[2] view and warn you in the most solemn manner against the **baneful**[3] effects of the spirit of party generally. . . .

If, in the opinion of the people, the distribution or **modification**[4] of the constitutional powers be in any particular wrong, let it be corrected by an amendment. . . .

Promote, then, as an object of primary importance, institutions for the general **diffusion**[5] of knowledge. . . . As the structure of a government gives force to public opinion, it is essential that public opinion should be enlightened. . . .

[Avoid] likewise the accumulation of debt, . . . not ungenerously throwing upon **posterity**[6] the burden which we ourselves ought to bear. . . .

Observe good faith and justice toward all nations. **Cultivate**[7] peace and harmony with all. . . .

It is our true policy to steer clear of permanent alliances with any portion of the foreign world. . . . There can be no greater error than to expect, or **calculate**,[8] upon real favors from nation to nation. It is an illusion which experience must cure, which a just pride ought to discard.

[1]**intimated:** told
[2]**comprehensive:** complete
[3]**baneful:** destructive
[4]**modification:** change
[5]**diffusion:** spreading
[6]**posterity:** future generations
[7]**cultivate:** seek
[8]**calculate:** plan

Analyzing Primary Sources
1. Under what circumstances does Washington propose changing the Constitution, and how should this be done?
2. Do you think Washington's advice on political parties and foreign policy is still appropriate today? Explain your answer.

☆ Linking Past to Present

Presidential Communications.
President Washington sent the draft of his Farewell Address to David Claypoole, the publisher of the Philadelphia newspaper *American Daily Advertiser.* Because Claypoole reserved the front page for advertisements, he ran the address on the second and third pages. Other newspapers copied the story from the *Advertiser*, and Americans slowly learned about their president's farewell message. With the advent of modern communications devices such as the radio and television, people now learn about presidential messages immediately, instead of waiting weeks or months for word to spread.

CRITICAL THINKING

What problems might poor communications have caused for presidents in the 1700s and early 1800s?

ANSWER: Students' responses will vary.

ANALYZING PRIMARY SOURCES ANSWERS
1. The Constitution should be changed by amendment if the people believe the power it distributes is wrong.
2. Students' answers will vary but they should support their answer.

Have students complete the **Section 4 Review** on p. 319. Then have students complete **Daily Quiz 10.4**. As **Alternative Assessment**, you may want to use the magazine article or oral history exercises in this section's lessons.

★ RETEACH

Have students complete **Main Idea Activity for English Language Learners and Special-Needs Students 10.4**. Have each student create a crossword puzzle using key terms, significant events and locations, and important people mentioned in the section as answers to the clues they write. Then have

students exchange their puzzles and answer the questions. **ENGLISH LANGUAGE LEARNERS**

★ EXTEND

Organize the class into small groups and have each group prepare an encyclopedia entry for the Whiskey Rebellion. Each group's entries should include the following: a) the events leading up to the Whiskey Rebellion; b) the events occurring during the rebellion itself; c) how the Washington administration decided on its course of action regarding the rebellion; d) how the rebellion was finally suppressed; and e) what lessons may be drawn from a study of the rebellion and the government's response to it. **COOPERATIVE LEARNING , BLOCK SCHEDULING**

Section 4 Review
ANSWERS

❶ **Identify**
• Little Turtle, p. 315
• Anthony Wayne, p. 315
• Battle of Fallen Timbers, p. 316
• Treaty of Greenville, p. 316
• Whiskey Rebellion, p. 316

❷ 1790–91: U.S. forces defeated in the Northwest Territory; 1794: United States wins Battle of Fallen Timbers and the Whiskey Rebellion takes place; 1795: Treaty of Greenville; 1796: farewell address describes dangerous foreign alliances, domestic political divisions, and the public debt.

❸ a. As more American settlers moved to the frontier, more conflicts with American Indians arose. The U.S. Army defeated the American Indian confederation, and Indian leaders signed a treaty giving the United States access to American Indian land in the Northwest Territory and guaranteeing the safety of U.S. citizens there.
b. Students' answers will vary, but students should note that taxes were a key part of both protests.

❹ Students' entries will vary, but students will need to note Washington's warnings about having political parties, the need to keep a balanced budget, and the desire to avoid entanglements or long-term alliances with foreign nations.

Many Americans saw George Washington as a champion of liberty, represented by the woman standing by his statue.

also expressed his concerns about the public debt. He believed that the government should try not to borrow money. Such a policy would protect future generations from being saddled with debt.

Washington also wanted the country to be free from outside influences and to avoid diplomatic problems. He warned against forming permanent relationships, friendly or otherwise, with other countries.

History Makers Speak

❝The nation which indulges [allows] toward another an habitual [regular] hatred or an habitual fondness is in some degree a slave. It is a slave to its animosity [hate] or to its affection, either of which is sufficient [enough] to lead it astray from its duty and its interest.❞

—George Washington, quoted in *The Annals of America*

Washington believed that disagreements between political groups weaken government. He worried that regional differences could lead too easily to political conflict that would harm the nation. Political unity, he said, was key to national success. Thus, Washington left office telling the nation to work out its differences and protect its independence. He concluded his speech by looking forward to his retirement and praising his country. "I anticipate . . . the sweet enjoyment . . . of good laws under a free government, the ever favorite object of my heart."

✔ **Reading Check: Summarizing** What were the key points of Washington's Farewell Address? America should avoid debt and not borrow money; should remain neutral and not develop permanent ties; should work toward domestic political unity

Section 4 Review

❶ **Identify** and explain:
• Little Turtle
• Anthony Wayne
• Battle of Fallen Timbers
• Treaty of Greenville
• Whiskey Rebellion

❷ **Sequencing** Copy the graphic organizer below. Use it to describe, in order, the major domestic problems leading up to Washington's Farewell Address. Include Washington's views on the greatest threats that faced the United States.

1790–91 → 1794 → 1795 → 1796 Washington's Farewell Address

❸ **Finding the Main Idea**
a. What challenge did the United States face on the frontier, and what was its outcome?
b. Do you think that the farmers in the Whiskey Rebellion were really like the Sons of Liberty? Why or why not?

❹ **Writing and Critical Thinking**
Making Generalizations and Predictions Imagine that you are a historian reading George Washington's Farewell Address. Think about what the country would be like today if Washington's advice was followed strictly. Write a journal entry expressing your thoughts.
Consider the following:
• political divisions and parties
• the national debt
• alliances with foreign nations

go.hrw.com **Homework Practice Online**
keyword: SA3 HP10

Section 5

OBJECTIVES

★ Explain how political parties formed and the role they played in the presidential election of 1796.

★ Describe the problems with foreign nations that John Adams faced as president.

★ Describe the Alien and Sedition Acts and the Republicans' response to them.

★ Analyze the main issues in the election of 1800 and some of the outcomes of the election.

 *LET'S GET STARTED!*

Write the following question on the chalkboard: *In the next presidential election, what could happen if the candidate from the party currently holding the presidency is defeated by a candidate from another party?* As students enter the classroom, allow time for them to respond. *(Students' responses will vary, but students should describe a peaceful exchange of power.)* Explain to students that most Americans assume that peaceful transitions will occur. However, in the 1790s people were fearful that a change in power would not be peaceful. Tell students that in Section 5 they will learn about the growing tensions between the political parties during the late 1700s and early 1800s.

Section 5

John Adams's Presidency

Read to Discover

1. How did political parties form, and what role did they play in the presidential election of 1796?
2. What problems with foreign nations did John Adams face during his presidency?
3. What were the Alien and Sedition Acts, and how did Republicans respond to them?
4. What were the main issues in the election of 1800, and what were some of its outcomes?

WHY IT MATTERS TODAY

Today the United States has two main political parties. These are the Democratic Party and the Republican Party. Use **CNNfyi.com** and other **current events** sources to learn about how one party or the other has made the news recently. Record your findings in your journal.

Define

• political parties

Identify

• Federalist Party
• Democratic-Republican Party
• XYZ affair
• Alien and Sedition Acts
• Kentucky and Virginia Resolutions
• Twelfth Amendment

SECTION 5 RESOURCES

REPRODUCIBLE
▶ Guided Reading Strategy 10.5
▶ American History Political Cartoon 3: Party Politics

TECHNOLOGY
▶ One-Stop Planner, Lesson 10.5
▶ Holt Researcher: American History CD–ROM
▶ Homework Practice Online
▶ CNN Presents America: Beginnings to 1914 Segment: Sailing the *Constitution*

REINFORCEMENT, REVIEW, AND ASSESSMENT
▶ Section 5 Review, p. 325
▶ Daily Quiz 10.5
▶ Main Idea Activity 10.5
▶ English Audio Summary 10.5
▶ Spanish Audio Summary 10.5

The Story Continues

When two-term vice president John Adams learned that President Washington was retiring, he thought about running for office. He asked his wife, Abigail, what she thought. She answered, "I would be second unto no Man but Washington." She thought that Adams should either run for president or quit politics. He considered her advice and chose to run for the presidency.

Abigail Adams, a respected friend of several political figures, often gave her husband political advice.

THE GRANGER COLLECTION, NEW YORK

★ The Election of 1796

The election of 1796 began a new era in U.S. politics. For the first time, more than one candidate was running for president. **Political parties**, groups that help elect government officials and shape government policies, also had an important role. Two political parties had begun to form during Washington's presidency. Despite the warnings about party conflict given in Washington's Farewell Address, the rivalry between these two parties dominated the 1796 election.

Have students read Section 5 and complete Guided Reading Strategy 10.5. Choose one or more of the following activities to explore the section content with students. For further suggestions on block scheduling or team teaching, see the *Block Scheduling Handbook with Team Teaching Strategies.*

LEVEL 1: Call on volunteers to list the goals of the Alien and Sedition Acts. Write their responses on the chalkboard. Lead a class discussion about the Republican response to these acts. Ask students to share their feelings regarding the constitutionality of the acts. Finally, have students write paragraphs that describe the goals of the Alien and Sedition Acts. **ENGLISH LANGUAGE LEARNERS**

ALL LEVELS: Copy the following graphic organizer onto the chalkboard, omitting the italicized answers. Have students complete the organizer by listing the successes and failures of John Adams's presidency. **ENGLISH LANGUAGE LEARNERS**

Successes	Failures
• *increased the size of the U.S. military* • *Alien and Sedition Acts*	• *XYZ affair* • *Adams' refusal to ask Congress to declare war even though it was unofficially being waged*

★ Geography

The Federalist Party.
Support for the Federalist Party revealed divisions in American society between social classes and geographic regions. The Federalists were identified with the economic policies of party leader Alexander Hamilton. The party was popular in urban areas and among the elite, such as bankers and merchants, who stood to benefit from Hamilton's policies. The Federalists did not have much support in rural areas. Middle- and lower-class Americans viewed the Federalists as a party of people with aristocratic ambitions who were not committed to democratic ideals.

CRITICAL THINKING
How did the population distribution in the early United States work to the disadvantage of the Federalists?

ANSWER: Students might suggest that most Americans lived in rural areas where Federalist support was weaker and thus did not support Federalist policies.

Visual Record Answer
George Washington

THE PRESENT State of our COUNTRY.

Interpreting the Visual Record

Parties *This political cartoon shows members of the Federalist and Democratic-Republican Parties threatening to pull down the foundations of the government with their arguing.* **Who is the person watching the party members and criticizing their actions?**

Supporters of John Adams created this campaign button.

The **Federalist Party** wanted to make the federal government stronger and to promote industry and trade. This party was most popular in New England. Alexander Hamilton helped found the Federalist Party. However, he chose not to run for president. The Federalists chose former vice president John Adams and South Carolinian Thomas Pinckney as their candidates. Adams was not popular in the South or the West. But he and his wife Abigail hoped that voters would support him "as soon as they have had time to . . . consider and reflect [think about]" his years of loyal service to the nation.

The **Democratic-Republican Party** was started by such leaders as Thomas Jefferson and James Madison. The party's members were called Republicans. (This party is not related to the modern Republican Party.) Republicans wanted to limit the power of the federal government. The party was most popular in the South and along the western frontier. The Republicans chose former secretary of state Thomas Jefferson and New York politician Aaron Burr as their candidates.

Both sides attacked each other during the election. Republicans called the Federalists the British party. Campaign posters for Jefferson called Adams a "Royalist." The Federalists answered that the Republicans were influenced too greatly by the French. They also questioned Jefferson's political skills. One Federalist wrote that Jefferson was "fit to be a professor in a College, [or] President of a Philosophical Society . . . but certainly not" president. Abigail Adams wrote to her son about the style of the campaign. "I fear America will never go through another Election without Blood Shed. We have had a paper War for six weeks past."

Hamilton, who did not like Adams, complicated matters by trying to get Pinckney elected instead. The plan failed, and Adams only narrowly defeated Jefferson. At the time, the person who took second place in a presidential election became vice president. This happened even if that person was not of the same political party as the president. So after months of running against each other, Adams and Jefferson took office together.

✔ **Reading Check: Summarizing** Explain how the Federalist and the Democratic-Republican Parties formed in the mid-1790s. Both formed during Washington's presidency. The Federalists wanted stronger government, industry, and trade. The Republicans wanted limited government.

★ President Adams and the XYZ Affair

At first glance, John Adams did not appear well suited for the presidency. Adams had been a leading Patriot during the time of the American Revolution. He had later served as a foreign diplomat. Yet he lacked Washington's dignity, and most people saw him as a cold and distant person. Still, many people respected Adams—even his opponents. They recognized his hard work, honesty, and intelligence.

One of Adams's first goals as president was to improve relations between the United States and France. The French had been using privateers to attack American ships. In response, Adams sent U.S. diplomats Elbridge Gerry, John Marshall, and Charles C. Pinckney to Paris. Once in France, the diplomats learned that French foreign minister Charles-Maurice de Talleyrand-Périgord would not speak with them. Instead, three French agents paid them a secret visit. These agents said that Talleyrand would discuss a treaty only in exchange for a $250,000 bribe. The French government also wanted a loan of $12 million. The amazed diplomats refused this demand. In March 1798 President Adams told Congress that the peace-seeking mission had failed. He described the French terms, substituting the letters X, Y, and Z for the names of the French agents. Upon hearing the news, Federalists in Congress called for war with France.

Soon the story of the <u>XYZ affair</u>, as the requested bribe was called, spread across the country. "Millions for defense, but not one cent for tribute!" became the rallying cry of the American people. Fearing war, Adams asked Congress to expand the navy to a fleet of more than 30 ships. He also wanted to keep a peacetime army of several thousand troops. Congress approved both measures.

CONNECTING TO
MATH

Just the Facts

Building the National Defense

Year	Total Federal Budget (in dollars)	Defense Spending (in dollars)
1792	5,080,000	1,101,000
1793	4,482,000	1,130,000
1794	6,991,000	2,700,000
1795	7,540,000	2,892,000
1796	5,727,000	1,535,000
1797	6,134,000	1,422,000
1798	7,677,000	3,391,000*
1799	9,666,000	5,325,000
1800	10,786,000	6,010,000

*The Department of the Navy was created in 1798.

Using Mathematical Skills

1. How much did military spending decrease from 1795 to 1796? How much did the total federal budget increase from 1796 to 1800? How much of this increase was military spending?

2. Create a line graph that compares the total federal budget from 1792 to 1800 with defense spending for those same years.

3. Imagine that you are a Federalist or Republican in 1800. Use these statistics to write a speech for your presidential candidate. Make your speech either in favor of or against President Adams's spending policies.

LEVEL 2: Organize the class into small groups. Have each group prepare a pamphlet that includes drawings, pictures, quotations, or slogans supporting the election of Thomas Jefferson or John Adams in 1796. Then ask them to prepare a second pamphlet supporting their candidate during the election of 1800. Each election's key issues should be included in the pamphlets. Have each group present its two pamphlets to the class and analyze the issues involved in the presidential election of 1800 that led to its outcome.
COOPERATIVE LEARNING

LEVEL 3: Discuss the significance of the XYZ affair with the class. Tell students to imagine that they are official record keepers for Congress and are witnessing congressional debates about the XYZ affair. Have students write out the "official" record, including a time line of the actual events of the XYZ affair. Students should also include Americans' reaction to the affair as well as reasons for declaring war on France and reasons for avoiding war with France. Ask volunteers to present their work to the class.

★ Constitutional Heritage

Alien and Sedition Acts.
Most Republicans believed that the Sedition Act was unconstitutional and designed to destroy opposition to the Federalist Party. In fact, 25 people who were arrested for violations of the Sedition Act were Republican printers and publicists.

CRITICAL THINKING

Which constitutional amendment might the critics of the Sedition Act claim that it violated?

ANSWER: Students should suggest the First Amendment, which protects free speech.

Visual Record Answer

Students might suggest that the other representatives appear to be cheering on the fight.

Technology Resources

 CNN Presents America: Beginnings to 1914 Segment: Sailing the *Constitution*

However, Adams did not ask Congress to declare war and instead tried to reopen peace talks. He believed that many people in the United States and France were against war. Adams was also worried about the cost of a war. Despite his efforts, American and French ships began fighting each other in the Caribbean.

Adams's opposition to a war stunned many Federalists. Some insulted him in speeches or essays. Hamilton even worked to weaken the president's power, but Adams refused to change his mind. In 1800 the United States and France finally signed a treaty that stopped fighting between American and French ships. Adams then forced two members of his cabinet to resign for trying to block his peace efforts.

✔ **Reading Check: Analyzing Information** What problems arose between France and the United States, and how did President Adams try to solve them? The French attacked American ships. Efforts to negotiate led to the XYZ affair. Adams avoided war and pushed for a peace treaty, which was signed in 1800.

★ The Alien and Sedition Acts

Republicans criticized Adams for making the military stronger. They also attacked the Federalists for supporting war with France. Many Federalists saw these attacks as disloyal. They said that the country needed to be protected from Republican traitors.

Federalists in Congress passed the **Alien and Sedition Acts** in the summer of 1798. The Alien Act allowed the president to have foreign residents removed from the country. They could be removed if the president believed they were involved "in any treasonable or secret machinations [plots] against the government." The Sedition Act stated that U.S. citizens could not join any plots against the government's policies. The act also made it illegal to "write, print, utter or publish" any false or hostile words against the government or its policies.

Interpreting the Visual Record

Alien and Sedition Acts *In 1798 Federalist congressman Roger Griswald attacked Republican Matthew Lyon during an angry debate over the Alien and Sedition Acts.* **How are the other representatives responding to the fight?**

THE GRANGER COLLECTION, NEW YORK

These laws were applied mostly against Republican newspapers. In some cases the editors of newspapers were arrested. Federalists even had Republican representative Matthew Lyon arrested for speaking out against the government. French citizens living in the United States also began to leave the country.

Jefferson and Madison decided to strike back with the **Kentucky and Virginia Resolutions**. The states' legislatures passed these resolutions in 1798 and 1799. Madison wrote the Virginia Resolutions, and Jefferson wrote the Kentucky Resolutions.

They stated that the Alien and Sedition Acts were unconstitutional. Madison and Jefferson claimed that the federal government did not have the power to pass such laws and that the acts interferred with the state government. Jefferson explained their views. "Whensoever the general government assumes undelegated [unassigned] powers, its acts are unauthoritative [without authority], void, and of no force."

Madison and Jefferson said that state governments could ignore any federal laws that they found to be unconstitutional. To avoid such a conflict, they asked Congress to repeal the Alien and Sedition Acts. Congress refused. The acts remained in effect until a later Congress decided not to renew them. However, the resolutions had an important impact on the idea of states' rights. They gave support to the idea that state governments could challenge the federal government. This precedent would help other politicians who wanted to declare laws or actions of the federal government to be illegal.

✔ **Reading Check: Drawing Inferences and Conclusions** How did the Alien and Sedition Acts pose a threat to freedom of speech and freedom of the press, and why was this important? The acts made it illegal to criticize the government; this was important because freedom of speech and freedom of the press are guaranteed by the Bill of Rights.

CONNECTING TO
SCIENCE AND TECHNOLOGY

The USS *Constitution*

To protect American merchant ships, in 1794 Congress decided to create a small navy. The USS *Constitution* became the most famous ship of this first fleet. The ship's toughness in battle gained it the popular nickname Old Ironsides. When the *Constitution* became too old for active duty, the U.S. Navy preserved it for future generations. After 200 years it remains the world's oldest commissioned warship afloat. Tourists now visit Old Ironsides to touch a part of history. Why do you think Old Ironsides is respected today?

Spar deck: holds small cannons used for close-range fighting

Gun deck: holds main guns used for long-range fighting

Berthing deck: used as sailors' sleeping quarters

Hold: used to store supplies and ammunition

SPOTLIGHT
On Political Parties

Have each student to create a political cartoon illustrating the important differences between Federalists and Democratic-Republicans and each party's views on key issues. When students have completed their cartoons, state a significant issue mentioned in this section. Have volunteers declare each party's stance on the issue. **BLOCK SCHEDULING**

✖ CLOSE

Review with the class the advice Washington gave to the nation in his Farewell Address. Than ask students how well the United States followed Washington's advice during John Adams's presidency. Have students create a chart that identifies Washington's advice in the first column, states whether the United States followed that advice in the second column, and cites examples from this section to illustrate how the nation followed the advice in the third column, if the advice was followed. Encourage volunteers to share information from their charts with the class.

Section 5 Review
ANSWERS

❶ Define
• political parties, p. 319

❷ Identify
• Federalist Party, p. 320
• Democratic-Republican Party, p. 320
• XYZ affair, p. 321
• Alien and Sedition Acts, p. 322
• Kentucky and Virginia Resolutions, p. 322
• Twelfth Amendment, p. 324

❸ Federalist Party: wanted to strengthen the federal government; promote trade and industry; popular in New England; support the Alien and Sedition Acts; pro-British; most supported war with France; Republican Party: wanted to limit the power of the federal government; popular in the South and on the frontier; believed the Alien and Sedition Acts were unconstitutional; pro-French; against war with France; Both: criticized Adams for his dealings with France.

❹ a. tried to settle matter diplomatically
b. key issues were the Alien and Sedition Acts, creation of a permanent army, and the U.S. relationship with France; problems choosing a president led to the Twelfth Amendment

❺ Students' editorials will vary.

⭐ The Election Of 1800

Despite the problems his administration had faced, Adams decided to run for re-election. In the presidential election of 1800, Thomas Jefferson and Aaron Burr ran against Adams and Charles C. Pinckney. During the campaign the Republicans challenged the legality of the Alien and Sedition Acts. They criticized Adams's creation of a permanent army and the higher taxes needed to pay for it. In addition, Republicans said that Adams had hurt relations between France and the United States. The nation's leading Republican newspaper favored Jefferson.

Analyzing Primary Sources
Evaluating Sources Do you think the newspaper is making a fair statement? Explain your answer. Students should note that since the newspaper is Republican, it would support the Republican candidate. They should recall that Adams had worked hard to keep the United States out of war with France, so this statement is biased.

History Makers Speak 66The friends of *peace will vote for Jefferson*— the friends of war will vote for *Adams* or for *Pinckney.*99

—The *Philadelphia Aurora*, quoted in *In Pursuit of Reason*, by Noble E. Cunningham Jr.

The Federalists answered by calling Jefferson a pro-French revolutionary. If elected, they said, he would ruin the country. They also said that Jefferson, who was deeply interested in science and philosophy, was against organized religion. In response, Republicans reminded voters that Jefferson was the author of the Declaration of Independence. He could certainly be trusted to protect the liberties of all Americans.

Jefferson actively sought support, while Adams took little part in his own campaign. He believed that the people would judge him on his political record. Alexander Hamilton again worked against Adams, publishing a highly critical essay. By doing this, he caused further division among the Federalists.

⭐ A Narrow Republican Victory

Jefferson and Burr won 73 electoral votes each to 65 for Adams and 64 for Pinckney. The Republicans had won the election, but the tie caused a problem. At that time there were no votes for the vice president—the runner-up won this office. Both Jefferson and Burr were eligible for the presidency. The decision went to the House of Representatives.

The Federalists in the House refused to vote for Jefferson as president and tried to elect Burr. Meanwhile, the Republicans voted for Jefferson, resulting in another tie and another vote. This process was repeated more than 30 times. Finally, about half of the Federalists simply refused to vote for anybody. Because he trusted Jefferson more than Burr, Hamilton worked on Jefferson's behalf. The Republicans were thus able to elect Jefferson. The problems with the voting system led Congress to propose the **Twelfth Amendment** in 1803. This

Bitterness between Hamilton and Burr over the 1800 election and other issues eventually led to this duel, in which Burr killed Hamilton.

THE GRANGER COLLECTION, NEW YORK

---

amendment created a separate ballot for president and vice president. The states passed it in September 1804 before the next election.

Their loss in the presidential election weakened the Federalists, and Adams retired from public life. For many years following the election, Adams and Jefferson did not speak to each other. However, their respect for one another finally led them to renew their friendship.

Jefferson believed the transfer of power between parties showed the strengths of the U.S. system of government. Later, he wrote to a friend about the achievement that some Americans called the Revolution of 1800.

THE GRANGER COLLECTION, NEW YORK

This campaign banner was used by Jefferson's supporters in the election of 1800.

> **History Makers Speak**
> ❝[The election was] as real a revolution in the principles of our government as that of 1776 was in its form; not effected [caused] indeed by the sword, as that [was], but by the rational and peaceable instrument of reform, the suffrage [vote] of the people.❞
>
> —Thomas Jefferson, quoted in *In Pursuit of Reason*, by Noble E. Cunningham Jr.

To Jefferson, his victory was the triumph of the people. In addition, it proved that his faith in the intelligence of the everyday citizen was justified.

Analyzing Primary Sources

Identifying Points of View
Why did Jefferson think the election was revolutionary?
Answers will vary, but students should mention the fact that change was "rational and peaceable" and carried out by "suffrage [vote] of the people."

✔ **Reading Check: Finding the Main Idea** How did Jefferson win the presidency? He and Burr each received 73 electoral votes. The House had to choose the president. The Federalists tried to elect Burr, and the Republicans tried to elect Jefferson. After more than 30 ties, some Federalists refused to vote, allowing Jefferson to win.

go.hrw.com **Homework Practice Online**
keyword: SA3 HP10

Section 5 Review

1 Define and explain:
• political parties

2 Identify and explain:
• Federalist Party
• Democratic-Republican Party
• XYZ affair
• Alien and Sedition Acts
• Kentucky and Virginia Resolutions
• Twelfth Amendment

3 Identifying Cause and Effect Use the diagram to explain why the Federalist and Republican Parties were formed and how they influenced the 1796 presidential election.

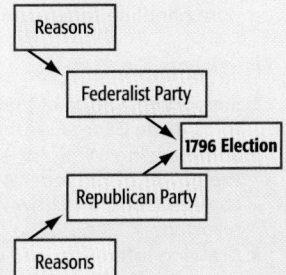

Reasons → Federalist Party → 1796 Election ← Republican Party ← Reasons

4 Finding the Main Idea
a. How did John Adams address U.S. problems with France?

b. What were the key issues of the election of 1800, and how did the outcome affect the political process?

5 Writing and Critical Thinking
Supporting a Point of View Imagine that you are a newspaper editor who does not belong to either the Federalist or Republican Party. Write an editorial in response to the Alien and Sedition Acts and the Kentucky and Virginia Resolutions.

Consider the following:
• the extent of the powers of the federal government
• how the Alien and Sedition Acts were used
• the constitutional right to freedom of speech and freedom of the press

---

CHAPTER 10 REVIEW ANSWERS

The Chapter at a Glance
Students' paragraphs will vary but they should address the challenges that faced the new nation.

Identifying People and Ideas
Students' sentences should indicate an understanding of the following definitions:

1. first president of the United States

2. created a federal court system with three levels

3. tax on an imported good that raises its price

4. national bank in which the government could safely deposit its money.

5. stated that the U.S. would not take sides with countries at war in Europe

6. compromise between U.S. and Britain to help deter a war between them

7. war leader of the Miamis who defeated St. Clair's army

8. frontier rebellion over tax on whiskey

9. groups that help elect government officials and shape government policies

10. bribe offer made by French officials to peace-seeking U.S. leaders

Understanding Main Ideas

1. organized executive and judicial branch, set precedents for the government, defined the powers of the federal courts

REVIEW AND ASSESSMENT RESOURCES

REPRODUCIBLE
▶ Vocabulary Activity 10

TECHNOLOGY
▶ Chapter 10 Test Generator (on the One-Stop Planner)
▶ Global Skill Builder CD–ROM
▶ HRW Go site

REINFORCEMENT, REVIEW, AND ASSESSMENT
▶ Chapter 10 Review, pp. 325–27
▶ Chapter 10 Tutorial for Students, Parents, Mentors, and Peers

▶ Chapter 10 Test (Form A or B)
▶ Alternative Assessment Handbook
▶ Chapter 10 Test for English Language Learners and Special-Needs Students

★ REVIEW
Have students complete the **Chapter 10 Review** on pages 326–27.

★ ASSESS
Use one of the chapter tests to assess students' understanding of the content. For **Alternative Assessment**, see the **Alternative Assessment Handbook**.

---

2. to promote economic stability; some did not believe that the Constitution gave Congress this authority

3. Jay's made Great Britain pay for damages for American ships attacked, Britain also agreed to leave its forts on the frontier. Pinckney's settled a new U.S.-Spain border in Florida, reopened the port of New Orleans, gave American boats the right of deposit

4. the farmers' actions threatened the strength and supremacy of the federal government

5. division caused by political parties, gathering of debt, and formation of alliances with foreign countries

6. formed during Washington's administration; Federalists wanted a strong Federal government and supported commerce and manufacturing; Republicans wanted to limit the federal government and supported agriculture

7. they responded with the Virginia and Kentucky Resolutions

You Be the Historian—Reviewing Themes
1. both tried to remain uninvolved in wars and sought to maintain peace

2. It created disagreements with Thomas Jefferson who thought that he Constitution did not give power to create the Bank

Chapter 10 Review

The Chapter at a Glance
Examine the visual summary of the chapter below. Write a paragraph describing the challenges that faced the new nation, leaving out the dates for key events. Have a classmate read the paragraph and fill in the missing dates.

Domestic Events
1789: Washington becomes president.
1790: The federal government assumes state debts. Washington is declared the U.S. capital.
1791: The Bank of the United States is established.
1794: U.S. troops win the Battle of Fallen Timbers. The Whiskey Rebellion takes place.
1796: Washington gives his Farewell Address. John Adams is elected president.
1798: Congress passes the Alien and Sedition Acts.
1800: Thomas Jefferson is elected president.

International Events
1789: The French Revolution begins.
1794: Jay's Treaty is signed by Britain and the United States.
1795: Pinckney's Treaty with Spain reopens the port of New Orleans.
1798: The XYZ affair takes place in France.

Identifying People and Ideas
Use the following terms or people in historically significant sentences.
1. George Washington
2. Judiciary Act of 1789
3. protective tariff
4. Bank of the United States
5. Neutrality Proclamation
6. Jay's Treaty
7. Little Turtle
8. Whiskey Rebellion
9. political parties
10. XYZ affair

Understanding Main Ideas
Section 1 *(Pages 300–303)*
1. Describe how Washington and the first Congress organized the government.

Section 2 *(Pages 304–309)*
2. Why did Congress create a national bank, and what challenges did it face in doing this?

Section 3 *(Pages 310–314)*
3. What did Jay's Treaty and Pinckney's Treaty achieve?

Section 4 *(Pages 315–318)*
4. Why was the Whiskey Rebellion significant?
5. What issues concerned Washington when he retired?

Section 5 *(Pages 319–325)*
6. When were the Federalist Party and the Democratic-Republican Party formed, and what were their policies?
7. What effect did the Alien and Sedition Acts have on the Republicans?

You Be the Historian—Reviewing Themes
1. **Global Relations** How did Presidents Washington and Adams address foreign-policy issues?
2. **Constitutional Heritage** What constitutional issues did Alexander Hamilton confront when he proposed the creation of a national bank?
3. **Economics** How did Alexander Hamilton propose handling federal and state debts, and why?

Thinking Critically
1. **Supporting a Point of View** What qualities do you think made George Washington a good leader?
2. **Summarizing** What issues led to debates over the power of the federal government in the early republic, and how were these issues resolved?
3. **Drawing Inferences and Conclusions** Why do you think the Republican Party was more popular in the South and along the western frontier?

Portfolio Extensions

American History

1. Cooperative Learning

Have students complete the following activity in small groups. Ask students to read over Washington's Farewell Address. Then have them create the front page of a newspaper. Their headlines, articles, and pictures should show what changes have occurred. [Examples might include headlines about how the United States has withdrawn from NATO and the UN, which are foreign alliances; articles about elections for Congress or the presidency in which there are no political parties, and so on.]

2. Linking to Community

Have students use local resources, such as the library, a news show, or the newspaper, to find out what political parties are most popular in their community. As a class, create a chart showing these parties, what representatives they have in public office, and what views they hold on community issues.

Social Studies Skills Workshop

Interpreting Political Cartoons

Study the political cartoon of the XYZ affair below. Then answer the questions that follow.

THE GRANGER COLLECTION, NEW YORK.

1. Which of the following statements best describes the main message of the cartoon?
   a. American diplomats are willing to take bribes and cannot be trusted.
   b. The Americans and the French were too different from each other to reach any kind of peace agreement.
   c. French officials are corrupt and dangerous but cannot frighten American officials.
   d. Americans should be willing to pay bribes to French agents if it will help achieve peace.

2. Why do you think the artist chose to portray the French agents as a many-headed monster? Do you think this cartoon supports going to war with France or not? Explain your answer.

Analyzing Primary Sources

Read the following quote by Secretary of the Treasury Alexander Hamilton, who argued that the Constitution allowed for the creation of a national bank. Then answer the questions that follow.

> ❝A bank has a direct relation to the [constitutional] power of borrowing money. . . . The essentiality of such an institution . . . is exemplified at this very moment. An Indian expedition is to be prosecuted [performed]. The only fund out of which the money can arise . . . is a tax, which only begins to be collected in July next. The preparations, however, are instantly to be made. The money must, therefore, be borrowed—and of whom could it be borrowed if there were no public banks? It happens that there are institutions of this kind, but if there were none, it would be indispensable [necessary] to create one.❞

3. Which of the following statements best describes the author's point of view?
   a. The Constitution gives the federal government the power to borrow money to pay for Indian expeditions.
   b. It would be easier to defend the United States if there were a national bank.
   c. A national bank is necessary because Congress might need to borrow money to provide for an emergency or for national defense.
   d. Congress has the power to collect taxes in July.

4. Why does Hamilton think that banks are important for the economy?

5. Based on what you know about the time, why might Congress need to use its constitutional power to borrow money?

3. proposed paying off the foreign federal debt immediately and paying off the national federal debt gradually; he believed that debtor states would then be more supportive of the government

Thinking Critically

1. Students' answers will vary.

2. the repayment of the debt, the creation of a national bank, the Alien and Sedition Acts; In some cases, politicians came to a compromise, in other cases, one political group prevailed

3. it supported agriculture over commerce and manufacturing, and these regions were more agricultural

Skills Workshop

1. a

2. to show them as difficult to deal with; students' answers will vary

3. c

4. Without banks there would be no way to borrow money for important and urgent causes.

5. Students might suggest that Congress would need to borrow money to pay the national debt, states or to regulate trade.

🔲 internet connect

**Internet Activity: go.hrw.com
keyword: SA3 CF10**

Access the Internet through the HRW Go site to locate primary and secondary sources such as databases and media and news services. Use these resources to learn about the Alien and Sedition Acts of 1798 and the Pentagon Papers case during the Vietnam War. Then use a computer word-processing program to write a report outlining the connection between a free and a democratic society.

☆ TEACH

ALL LEVELS: Explain to students that time lines are useful ways to keep events in order and to understand the relationship between them. Suggest that students make their own time lines as they read the chapters in the book. These time lines will help them draw connections between events, even when those events are in different sections of the book. Then ask each student to make a time line of his or her life. Ask them to start with their birth and include important dates, such as when they started school, moved, received pets, had important birthdays, met friends, learned to read, or started middle school. Students should also include any important news events they remember. Then organize students into pairs and have paired students exchange time lines. Have students place at least two of the events from their lives on their partner's time line, identify the framework their partner used in creating the time line, and describe two events on their partner's time line that may have a cause-and-effect relationship. Have students show their time lines to the class. Then discuss how these visual aids can help students link events and understand history.

ENGLISH LANGUAGE LEARNERS , COOPERATIVE LEARNING

INTERPRETING A TIME LINE.

Assign students one of the time lines for a chapter you have already covered. Ask students to find five events on the time line that are linked by cause and effect. Have students redraw the time line in their notebooks in a way that clarifies those cause-and-effect relationships.

SKILLS ANSWERS

1. 4 year intervals
2. almost 11 years
3. Students' time lines will vary.

Social Studies Skills
WORKSHOP

Interpreting a Time Line

Time lines display events in chronological order—the sequence in which the events occurred. Knowing the proper sequence of historical events helps you understand their significance. Time lines allow you to see relationships between events and help you to remember the dates of important events.

Sequence in a Time Line Time lines are meant to be read from left to right, with the oldest dates on the left. The lines of the time line mark the time period between each event. For example, the lines might mark 10-, 5-, or 1-year periods. Each entry on the time line lists an important event and when it took place. These entries provide you with a sequence of events and may suggest a relationship to one another.

B.C. and A.D. Sometimes a time line will contain the abbreviations B.C. and A.D. The abbreviation B.C. stands for "before Christ." A.D. stands for "anno Domini," which means "in the year of the Lord." The year 1 B.C. was followed by A.D. 1. There was no year "0." When you read dates marked B.C. or A.D., remember that the abbreviation B.C. appears after the year—for example, 100 B.C. The abbreviation A.D. appears before the year—for example, A.D. 100.

How to Read a Time Line

1. **Determine its framework.** Note the years covered and the intervals of time into which the time line is divided.

2. **Study the sequence of events.** Study the order of events on the time line and the length of time between events.

3. **Supply missing information.** Think about the people, places, and other events associated with each item on the time line.

4. **Note relationships.** Ask yourself how an event relates to earlier or later events. Look for cause-and-effect relationships and long-term developments.

1777 The Continental Congress approves the Articles of Confederation on November 15.	**1781** On March 1 the Articles of Confederation go into effect after being ratified by all 13 states.	**1787** On May 14, state delegates begin to arrive at the Constitutional Convention in Philadelphia. The final draft of the Constitution is signed on September 17.	**1788** On June 21 the Constitution is ratified by the required 9 out of 13 states.
1776	**1780**	**1784**	**1790**

Practicing the Skills

Study the time line above, which lists some important events in the history of the United States between 1776 and 1790. Then answer the following questions.

1. Into what periods is the time line divided?
2. How much time passed between the ratification of the Articles of Confederation and the ratification of the Constitution?
3. Create your own time line, listing several significant events in U.S. history that occurred during a span of at least five years.

ALL LEVELS: Explain to students that the debates over the Constitution did not end with ratification. Many of the factors that the Founders debated remained controversial throughout the early republic. Have students create mobiles to show how the factors that were debated at the Constitutional Convention became part of debates about how the United States would be governed in the early years of the Republic. For example, students might want to add Hamilton's ideas about the national bank to the arm that represents the discussion of centralized power. Students might also want to include the debate over the Alien and Sedition Acts on the arm where they weigh individual rights. Again ask students to balance their mobile to represent the relative weight different factors had. For example, on the arm for the Alien and Sedition Acts, students might show that the interests of the nation outweighed individual rights. Then students could add a paragraph to the corresponding their arm of the mobile explaining how this factor continued to be part of a national debate.

ENGLISH LANGUAGE LEARNERS

History in Action

UNIT 4 SIMULATION

You Solve the Problem . . .

How Should the President of the United States Be Selected?

Complete the following activity in small cooperative groups. It is early 1787. You are a delegate at the Constitutional Convention. The Convention has agreed upon the requirements for the candidates for the presidency: at least 35 years old, natural-born citizen, and a 14-year resident of the United States. Now you must give a presentation to the Constitutional Convention that suggests how the chief executive of the United States should be selected. Follow these steps to solve your problem.

1. Gather Information. Use your textbook and other resources to find information that might influence your plan of action for selecting a president. Be sure to use what you learned from this unit's Skills Workshop on Interpreting a Time Line to help you find an effective solution to the problem. For example, you might consider how often a new president should be selected. You may want to divide different parts of the research among group members.

2. List and Consider Options. Based on the information you have gathered, list and consider the options you might recommend for selecting a president. Your final solution to the problem may be easier to reach if you consider as many options as possible. Be sure to record your possible options for your presentation.

3. Consider Advantages and Disadvantages. Now consider the advantages and disadvantages of taking each option. Ask yourselves questions like: "Will all citizens be able to participate in the process?" Once you have considered the advantages and disadvantages, record them as notes for your presentation.

4. Choose, Implement, and Evaluate a Solution. After considering the advantages and disadvantages, you should plan and create a presentation. Be sure to make your proposal very clear. You will need to support your proposed method of selecting the president by including information you gathered and by explaining why you rejected other options. Your presentation needs to be visually appealing to the Constitutional Convention. When you are ready, decide which group members will make each part of the presentation, and then take your solution to Constitutional Convention (the rest of the class). Good luck!

History in Action Ask students to review the problem-solving activity on this page. Then have students conduct research at the library on the presidential elections of the last 100 years. Have students use their research and the steps outlined in the activity to determine if the requirements and selection process for the chief executive officeholder should be amended. Students should outline their reasoning and recommendations. Have students incorporate their analyses into a speech that they deliver before Congress (the class).

INTRODUCING UNIT 5

★ CHAPTER 11

The Expanding Nation

Thomas Jefferson's presidency marked several milestones in U.S. government. The Supreme Court strengthened its power by establishing the principle of judicial review, and the United States nearly doubled in size after the Louisiana Purchase. To explore these new lands, Jefferson sponsored expeditions to the West. In the early 1800s, under presidents Jefferson & Madison, the United States became involved in many conflicts, the most serious of which led to the War of 1812. During this war, the British attacked and burned Washington. However, neither side gained a clear advantage & the two nations signed a peace treaty.

★ CHAPTER 12

A New National Identity

James Monroe's presidency was known as the Era of Good Feelings because of the relative peace and development of national pride that the nation experienced at that time. However, disputes over westward expansion and slavery began to divide the nation. Growing in power, the people in the West helped elect Andrew Jackson to the presidency. Jackson endorsed the removal of American Indians

Internet Activity

Early American Maps

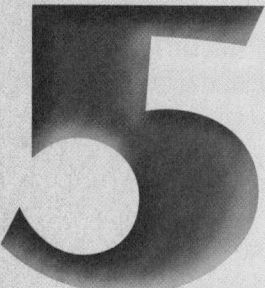

internet connect go.hrw.com

TOPIC: Early American Maps
GO TO: go.hrw.com
KEYWORD: SA3 U.S. Maps

Have students search the Internet through the HRW Go site for maps of North America created between 1800 and 1840. Compare the maps and discuss the fact that much of the Americas was unmapped during this period. Have students describe the difference in the maps. As students work through the unit, have them identify events that might account for those changes. In addition, use these maps to start a discussion of the geographic challenges that people settling the United States continued to face.

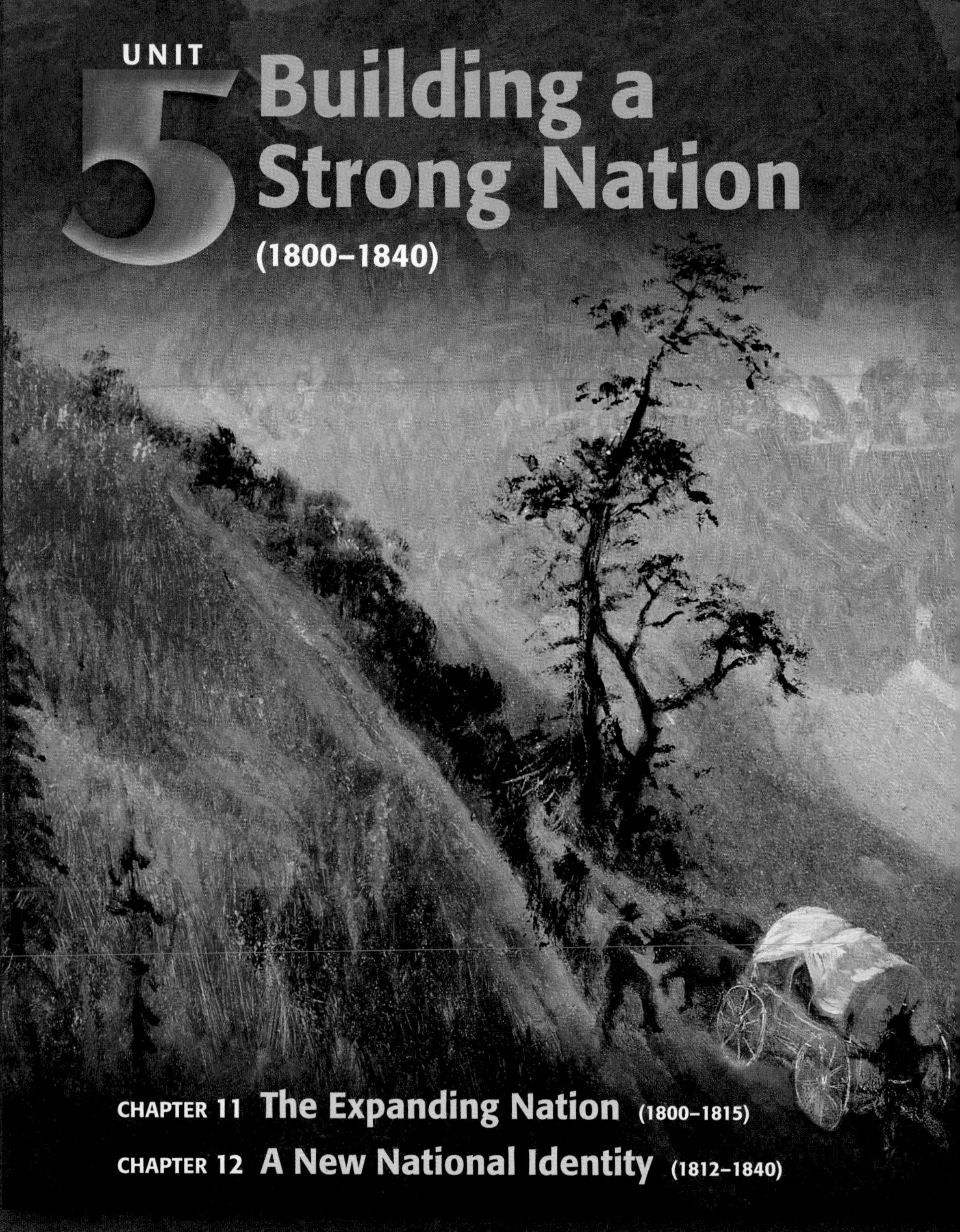

UNIT 5 Building a Strong Nation (1800–1840)

CHAPTER 11 **The Expanding Nation** (1800–1815)

CHAPTER 12 **A New National Identity** (1812–1840)

from their lands, a policy that led to much suffering for the Indians. During this period, Americans began to develop a national identity in the arts, as writers and artists turned to American stories and landscapes for inspiration.

★ **UNIT MOTIVATOR**

Share the information in the chapter overviews with students. Briefly discuss what the idea of national identity means. You may want to begin by having students describe what makes Americans different from people in other countries. Explain to students that during the early 1800s no one was certain what it meant to be an American because the country was so new. List the major events of this unit on the chalkboard (include the election of Thomas Jefferson, the Louisiana Purchase, the War of 1812,

and the election of Andrew Jackson.) Then give the students a brief preview of each event and have them suggest how the event might have shaped Americans' sense of identity. Then have students write a letter from a person in the early 1800s describing the American national identity. Later, when you have finished the unit, come back to these letters and have students evaluate how closely their ideas about American identity reflected the ideas that Americans developed in this time.

Young People

IN HISTORY

Young Explorers

In 1804 Meriwether Lewis and William Clark set out on an expedition to the western lands of the Louisiana Purchase. At age 18 George Shannon was the youngest member of their Corps of Discovery. Lewis described this group as the "best young woodsmen & Hunters in this part of the Countrey." Shannon excelled at his work and was put in charge of some expedition duties.

In late August 1804 Shannon failed to return after a day of hunting in Sioux Indian territory. Lewis and Clark sent out a search party, but it failed to find the young man, who had accidentally moved ahead of the group. Thinking he was actually behind the others, Shannon kept traveling westward as fast as he could.

Over time, he used all his bullets and was unable to hunt for food. He survived for a few weeks on plums and grapes. After becoming too weak to continue, Shannon sat down on a riverbank. He hoped that a trading boat might pass by. Instead, his friends rescued him! On September 11, 1804, the expedition rounded a bend in the Missouri River. To their surprise, they found an exhausted and hungry Shannon.

Shannon was one of many young adventurers who set their sights westward in the 1800s. William Swift and Titian Peale were two young men who accompanied Stephen Long on his expedition in 1819. Swift was 18 years old, and Peale was 19. They traveled along the Missouri River and into the western plains. Swift was hired to prepare a map of the territory, while Peale went along as an assistant naturalist.

Other teenagers explored the West as fur trappers. When he was about 18, Jim Bridger traveled to the upper Missouri River on a trapping expedition. Two years later, Bridger discovered what looked like a great shallow bay. Tasting the salty water, he reported he had found part of the Pacific Ocean. However, historians later determined that Bridger had actually seen the Great Salt Lake in what is now Utah.

Young frontiersmen, like those shown here, were an important part of the Lewis and Clark expedition.

If You Were There *What would you do if you got lost in the wilderness?*

LEFT PAGE: *Crossing the Rocky Mountains was one of the most difficult challenges facing western explorers.*

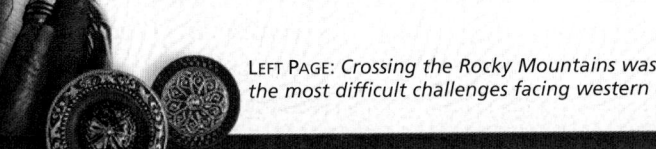

★ **Using Visual Resources**

Albert Bierstadt. Albert Bierstadt's grandiose western landscapes, like the one on the opposite page, were immensely popular. In 1863, banners were strung across Broadway in New York City to announce an exhibit of his paintings. In fact, Bierstadt could charge as much as $35,000 for a painting—the highest amount on record for any artist of his time. He began his career in 1858 as an artist working as part of Frederick W. Lander's overland wagon expedition to the Pacific Ocean. There he made sketches that he later turned into magnificent landscape paintings. Throughout his life, he continued to travel to the West and kept his studio filled with items he had collected on his trips.

CRITICAL THINKING

What do you think Bierstadt is trying to say about nature in this painting?

ANSWER: Students might suggest that the terrain was beautiful but difficult to cross, as it presented many natural barriers.

CHAPTER 11

The Expanding Nation
CHAPTER RESOURCE MANAGER

Objectives	Pacing Guide	Reproducible Resources
SECTION 1: **Jefferson as President** (pp. 334–37) ★ Analyze the views Thomas Jefferson expressed about political parties in his first inaugural address. ★ Identify the Republican policies Jefferson introduced and the Federalist policies that he accepted. ★ Evaluate the importance of *Marbury* v. *Madison* as an important court case.	**Regular** 1.5 days **Block Scheduling** 1 day *Block Scheduling Handbook with Team Teaching Strategies, Chapter 11*	**RS** Guided Reading Strategy 11.1 **PS** Primary Source Reading 11: Jefferson's Inaugural Address
SECTION 2: **The Louisiana Purchase** (pp. 338–43) ★ Describe how and why the Louisiana Purchase took place. ★ Explain what the Lewis and Clark expedition achieved. ★ Define the purpose of Pike's expedition.	**Regular** 2 days **Block Scheduling** 1 day *Block Scheduling Handbook with Team Teaching Strategies, Chapter 11*	**RS** Guided Reading Strategy 11.2 **PS** Biography Reading 11: Sacagawea **PS** American History Political Cartoon 4: The Louisiana Purchase **SM** Geography Activity 11: The French in North America **E** Hands-On History Activity: Trade with Canada
SECTION 3: **The Coming of War** (pp. 344–49) ★ Determine why the United States placed an embargo on France and Great Britain. ★ Explain what Tecumseh wanted to accomplish and how successful he was. ★ Analyze why the United States declared war on Great Britain in 1812.	**Regular** 2 days **Block Scheduling** 1 day *Block Scheduling Handbook with Team Teaching Strategies, Chapter 11*	**RS** Guided Reading Strategy 11.3 **PS** Literature Reading 11: A Shawnee Leader Seeks Allies
SECTION 4: **The War of 1812** (pp. 350–55) ★ Describe how the war progressed at sea and in the Great Lakes region. ★ Explain how actions by American Indians aided the British during the war. ★ Identify the strategy that the British pursued in the East. ★ Examine how the war came to an end.	**Regular** 2 days **Block Scheduling** 1 day *Block Scheduling Handbook with Team Teaching Strategies, Chapter 11*	**RS** Guided Reading Strategy 11.4 **RS** Graphic Organizer 11: The War of 1812 **E** Creative Teaching Strategy: Issue Strip

Chapter Resource Key

PS Primary Sources
RS Reading Support
IC Interdisciplinary Connections
E Enrichment
SM Skills Mastery

A Assessment
REV Review
ELL Reinforcement and English Language Learners
 Transparencies
 CD-ROM

 Music
 Video
Internet
Holt Presentation Maker Using Microsoft® PowerPoint®

 One-Stop Planner CD-ROM

See the *One-Stop Planner* for a complete list of additional resources for students and teachers.

One-Stop Planner CD–ROM

It's easy to plan lessons, select resources, and print out materials for your students when you use the *One-Stop Planner CD–ROM with Test Generator.*

Technology Resources	Reinforcement, Review, and Assessment

 One-Stop Planner, Lesson 11.1
 Art in American History Transparency 5: Monticello
 CNN Presents America: Yesterday and Today, Beginnings to 1914 Segment: White House Birthday
 Homework Practice Online
 HRW Go site

REV Section 1 Review, p. 337
A Daily Quiz 11.1
ELL Main Idea Activity 11.1
ELL English Audio Summary 11.1
ELL Spanish Audio Summary 11.1

 One-Stop Planner, Lesson 11.2
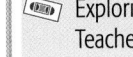 Exploring America's Past Video Segment: Blazing a Trail; Teacher's Guide, pp. 18–19
 Holt Researcher: American History CD–ROM
Homework Practice Online

REV Section 2 Review, p. 343
A Daily Quiz 11.2
ELL Main Idea Activity 11.2
ELL English Audio Summary 11.2
ELL Spanish Audio Summary 11.2

 One-Stop Planner, Lesson 11.3
 Homework Practice Online
 HRW Go site

REV Section 3 Review, p. 349
A Daily Quiz 11.3
ELL Main Idea Activity 11.3
ELL English Audio Summary 11.3
ELL Spanish Audio Summary 11.3

 One-Stop Planner, Lesson 11.4
 American Music CD Program: "The Star-Spangled Banner"
 Homework Practice Online
 HRW Go site

REV Section 4 Review, p. 354
A Daily Quiz 11.4
ELL Main Idea Activity 11.4
ELL English Audio Summary 11.4
ELL Spanish Audio Summary 11.4

▣ internet connect

HRW ONLINE RESOURCES
  GO TO: go.hrw.com
  Then type in a keyword.

TEACHER HOME PAGE
  KEYWORD: SA3 Teacher

CHAPTER INTERNET ACTIVITIES
  KEYWORD: SA3 CF11
  Choose an activity to:
  • explore the American West with Lewis and Clark.
  • research the causes and effects of the War of 1812 and lean about the roles of John Calhoun and Dolley Madison.
  • review the outcome of the last general election and compare it to the election of 1800.

CHAPTER ENRICHMENT LINKS
  KEYWORD: SA3 CH11

ONLINE ASSESSMENT
  Homework Practice
  KEYWORD: SA3 HP11

  Standardized Test Prep
  KEYWORD: SA3 STP11

  Rubrics
  KEYWORD: SS Rubrics

ONLINE MAPS, CHARTS, AND GRAPHS
  KEYWORD: SA3 MCG
  • Territorial Expansion
  • National Road
  • Transportation Methods

CONTENT UPDATES
  KEYWORD: SS Content Updates

HOLT PRESENTATION MAKER
  KEYWORD: SA3 PPT11

ONLINE READING SUPPORT
  KEYWORD: SS Strategies

CURRENT EVENTS
  KEYWORD: S3 Current Events

Meeting Individual Needs

Ability Levels

Level 1 Basic-level activities designed for all students encountering new material

Level 2 Intermediate-level activities designed for average students

Level 3 Challenging activities designed for honors and gifted-and-talented students

English Language Learners Activities that address the needs of students with Limited English Proficiency

Chapter Review and Assessment

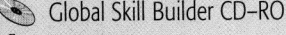

IC Vocabulary Activity 11
 Global Skill Builder CD–ROM
HRW Go site
REV Chapter 11 Tutorial for Students, Parents, Mentors, and Peers
REV Chapter 11 Review, pp. 355–57
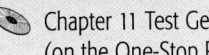 Chapter 11 Test Generator (on the One-Stop Planner)
A Chapter 11 Test (Form A or B)

A Alternative Assessment Handbook
A Chapter 11 Test for English Language Learners and Special-Needs Students

Build on What You Know

If You Were There...

Ask students to answer the following question:

How might you react to the election of Thomas Jefferson?

Consider:

• how Jefferson's victory represents the democratic system

• the effect on the Federalist Party's power

You Be the Historian

What's Your Opinion?

To help students create their **Themes** Journal entries, provide the following examples of appropriate **agree**/**disagree** statements.

EXPLORING THE TIME LINE

AMERICAN EVENTS

internet connect

TOPIC: Thomas Jefferson and Politics
GO TO: go.hrw.com
KEYWORD: SA3 CF11

Have students access the Internet through the HRW Go site to research the political thought of Thomas Jefferson and the concept of Jeffersonian Democracy. Then have students write a report in which they outline Jefferson's political viewpoint and how the concept of Jeffersonian Democracy has changed over the centuries citing at least one primary source. Instruct students to use standard grammar, spelling, sentence structure, and punctuation in their reports.

CHAPTER

11 The Expanding Nation

(1800–1815)

Explorers Lewis and Clark kept several journals, including this one bound in elk skin.

UNITED STATES

Sacagawea helped Lewis and Clark travel through the Rockies and on to the Pacific Northwest.

1801 Thomas Jefferson takes office as president.

1803 The U.S. Senate approves the Louisiana Purchase.

1804 Meriwether Lewis and William Clark set out to explore the Louisiana Territory.

1800	1802	1804	1806

WORLD

1803 France and Great Britain go to war.

1804 Napoléon becomes emperor of France.

1806 The Holy Roman Empire officially ends.

1807 The slave trade is abolished in the British Empire.

At the last minute, Napoléon took the crown from Pope Pius VII and placed it on his own head.

Build on What You Know

By 1800, Federalists knew they had lost control of both the presidency and Congress to their Republican rivals. During his presidency, Thomas Jefferson greatly expanded the size of the United States. The young nation also came into conflict with France and Great Britain.

Constitutional Heritage

Agree   All branches of government should have an equal balance of power.

Disagree The legislative and executive branches have more responsibilities and therefore should have more power.

Geography

Agree   Settlers will eventually move into new territories and begin exploration.

Disagree   A nation should explore new territories in order to establish relations with the people already living there.

Global Relations

Agree   The desire for more land will cause neighboring nations to fight.

Disagree   Nations along a common border will establish peaceful relations for trade and commerce.

Americans did not learn that the Treaty of Ghent had ended the War of 1812 until they had already fought the last battle.

British forces charged the walls built by General Andrew Jackson's troops in the Battle of New Orleans.

1811 William Henry Harrison's troops win the Battle of Tippecanoe against American Indian forces led by Tecumseh.

1814 On August 24, British soldiers burn the city of Washington.

Federalist delegates from New England hold the Hartford Convention on December 15.

1815 Andrew Jackson leads U.S. soldiers to victory over the British in the Battle of New Orleans.

1809 President Jefferson signs the Non-Intercourse Act.

1812 Congress declares war on Great Britain.

1808   1810   1812   1814

1808 Napoléon names his brother Joseph as king of Spain.

1811 Paraguay becomes the first Spanish colony in South America to gain independence.

1814 European nations meet at the Congress of Vienna to reorganize Europe after the fall of Napoléon.

If you were there . . .
How might you react to the election of Thomas Jefferson?

You Be the Historian

Themes Journal

What's Your Opinion? Do you **agree** or **disagree** with the following statements? Support your point of view in your journal.

- **Constitutional Heritage** The Supreme Court should have power equal to the president and Congress.

- **Geography** Nations do not need to explore new territories that they acquire.

- **Global Relations** Nations that share borders are likely to fight wars against each other.

Global Relations

The Fall of Napoléon. Napoléon's final defeat occurred near the village of Waterloo just south of Brussels, Belgium. Prior to this infamous battle, Napoléon managed to separate the much larger British and Prussian forces, but he was unable to completely destroy either army. In perhaps his worst tactical error in warfare, Napoléon delayed his attack on the British from morning until midday to allow the damp ground to dry. This delay was just long enough for the Prussians to regroup with the British and turn the tide of the battle against Napoléon.

CRITICAL THINKING

Why might Napoléon have wanted dry ground for his attack?

ANSWER: Students might suggest that a dry field of battle would allow his troops, cavalry, and artillery more mobility.

Section 1

OBJECTIVES

⭐ Analyze the views Thomas Jefferson expressed about political parties in his first inaugural address.

⭐ Identify the Republican policies Jefferson introduced and the Federalist policies that he accepted.

⭐ Evaluate the importance of *Marbury* v. *Madison* as an important court case.

SECTION 1 RESOURCES

REPRODUCIBLE

▶ Guided Reading Strategy 11.1
▶ Primary Source Reading 11: Jefferson's Inaugural Address

TECHNOLOGY

▶ One-Stop Planner, Lesson 11.1
▶ Art in American History Transparency 5: Monticello
▶ CNN Presents America: Beginnings to 1914 Segment: White House Birthday
▶ Homework Practice Online
▶ HRW Go site

REINFORCEMENT, REVIEW, AND ASSESSMENT

▶ Section 1 Review, p. 337
▶ Daily Quiz 11.1
▶ Main Idea Activity 11.1
▶ English Audio Summary 11.1
▶ Spanish Audio Summary 11.1

LET'S GET STARTED!

Write the following quote on the chalkboard: "His dress, was as usual, that of a plain citizen, without any distinctive badge of office." As students enter the classroom, ask them to explain the significance of Thomas Jefferson's clothing on the day of his inauguration. *(Students' responses will vary but should point out that his clothing symbolized the link between the president and all Americans.)* Tell students that in Section 1 they will learn how Jefferson's ideas on running the country differed from John Adams's and about the importance of the Supreme Court's decision in *Marbury* v. *Madison.*

Section 1

Jefferson as President

Read to Discover

1. What views did Thomas Jefferson express about political parties in his first inaugural address?
2. What Republican policies did Jefferson introduce, and which Federalist policies did he accept?
3. Why was *Marbury* v. *Madison* an important court case?

WHY IT MATTERS TODAY

Americans go to the polls to elect their president as well as many other officials. Use **CNNfyi.com** or other **current events** sources to learn about the policies of an elected official. Record your findings in your journal.

Define

• judicial review

Identify

• Thomas Jefferson
• William Marbury
• John Marshall
• *Marbury* v. *Madison*

COLLECTION OF THE AMERICAN NUMISMATIC SOCIETY

These coins celebrate Jefferson's inauguration.

The Story Continues

The day was March 4, 1801. Thomas Jefferson was about to become president of the United States. Washington and Adams had taken carriages to their inaugurations, or swearing-in ceremonies. Jefferson, however, chose to walk to the Capitol Building. Jefferson also decided not to wear fancy clothes. A reporter wrote, "His dress was, as usual, that of a plain citizen, without any distinctive badge of office."

⭐ The Republican Victory

A large crowd attended the inauguration of **Thomas Jefferson**, yet former president John Adams was absent. He was so upset by his defeat that he left the city. One observer who attended the inauguration called it "one of the most interesting scenes a free people can ever witness." The crowd was celebrating more than Jefferson's election. Along with his victory, the Republican Party had also won control of both houses of Congress. As a result, Jefferson would have the support of Congress for many of his plans. The inauguration marked the first time that one political party had replaced another in power in the United States. Many Americans saw the election of Jefferson as proof that the country could change leaders peacefully. That was a rare achievement for a government at the time.

Have students read Section 1 and complete Guided Reading Strategy 11.1. Choose one or more of the following activities to explore the section content with students. For further suggestions on block scheduling or team teaching, see the *Block Scheduling Handbook with Team Teaching Strategies.*

 LEVELS 1 AND 2: Discuss with students the importance of *Marbury* v. *Madison* as an important court case. (*Marbury v. Madison was brought forth by William Marbury, a judicial appointee whose commission was withheld by Secretary of State James Madison at Thomas Jefferson's request. In a ruling on this case, the Supreme Court established the principle of judicial review.*) Organize the class into two groups, one supporting William Marbury's position, the other supporting James Madison's position. Have groups petition the Supreme Court by listing on a sheet of paper arguments in support of their assigned positions. **ENGLISH LANGUAGE LEARNERS** , **COOPERATIVE LEARNING**

 ALL LEVELS: Copy the graphic organizer on the next page onto the chalkboard, omitting the italicized answers. Have students complete the flowchart by listing the Republican policies that Jefferson introduced and the Federalist policies that he accepted during his presidency. **ENGLISH LANGUAGE LEARNERS**

Interpreting the Visual Record

Monticello *Among his many talents, President Jefferson was a fine architect. He designed his magnificent home, Monticello.* **What does this image suggest about Jefferson's background?**

 **internet** connect

TOPIC: Election Results
GO TO: go.hrw.com
KEYWORD: SA3 CF11

Have students use the library or search the Internet through the HRW Go site to study the outcome of the most recent congressional or presidential elections and then determine which party controls the executive and legislative branches. Then lead a discussion on how the checks and balances system is in effect today.

Jefferson read his carefully written speech in a quiet voice. He wanted to make it clear that he supported the will of the majority. However, he did not favor mob rule, as some Federalists had claimed. In his speech, Jefferson tried to comfort the Federalists still in the government by promising to run the government fairly.

> **History Makers Speak**
> ❝We are all Republicans, we are all Federalists. . . . Let us, then, with courage and confidence pursue our . . . attachment to union and representative government.❞
> —Thomas Jefferson, First Inaugural Address

Analyzing Primary Sources

Drawing Inferences and Conclusions Why do you think Jefferson said "We are all Republicans, we are all Federalists"? Students might respond that he wanted to build unity after the bitter political battles of the 1790s.

After taking the oath of office, Jefferson walked back down New Jersey Avenue to his boardinghouse. There he met with supporters and friends.

✔ **Reading Check: Finding the Main Idea** What was significant about the Republican victory in 1800? It was the first time a political party had replaced another political party in power in the United States.

Jefferson in Office

President Jefferson faced the task of putting his Republican ideas into practice. First, he selected the members of his cabinet. He chose James Madison as secretary of state and Albert Gallatin as secretary of the treasury. Together they set new Republican policies. Jefferson lowered military spending, reducing the size of the army to about 3,200 troops. The navy was cut to seven active ships. Jefferson and Gallatin hoped that the money saved would allow the government to repay the national debt. Jefferson also asked Gallatin to find ways to get rid of domestic taxes, like the tax on whiskey. They even wanted to close down the government agency that collected such taxes. The Republican-led Congress passed the laws needed to carry out these policies.

Jefferson did keep some programs established by the Federalists. Even though he had opposed the Bank of the United States, he agreed to let the Bank continue as it had under the Federalists. Whatever its faults, the banking system created by Hamilton seemed practical to Jefferson.

Visual Record Answer

Students might suggest that he seems to have come from a wealthy background.

★★★★★★★★★★★
That's Interesting!
★★★★★★★★★★★

Capital under Construction Did you know that when Jefferson became president, the city of Washington was not even finished? It's true! The streets of Washington were muddy and filled with tree stumps. Some people complained that the city had only "a few bad houses, [and] extensive swamps." The weather was also hot and humid. During the summers most people, including President Jefferson, left the capital to avoid the danger of disease. However, Washington went on to become a large and impressive city. Jefferson later said that he was proud to be a part of building the new U.S. capital.

Technology Resources

 Art in American History Transparency 5: Monticello

HOMEWORK Have students prepare a report card for Jefferson's presidency. Students should grade Jefferson on the following categories: foreign and domestic relations, leadership, and popularity. In addition to a grade, have students provide two examples from the text to support the grade that was given.

LEVEL 3: Ask students to imagine that they are foreign dignitaries who have been asked to attend Jefferson's inauguration on behalf of their countries. Have students analyze the views Thomas Jefferson expressed about political parties in his inaugural address. Finally, lead a discussion about the significance of Jefferson's inauguration.

✪ CLOSE

Organize the class into two groups and hold a debate. Have one group argue in favor of changing government policy to match Jefferson's ideas. The other group should argue in favor of retaining Federalist policies. To conclude emphasize the need to compromise in order for the government to function efficiently.
COOPERATIVE LEARNING

★ Citizenship

Checks and Balances.
In the 1800 presidential election, the Democratic-Republican Party won 67 seats in the House of Representatives while the Federalists won only 39 seats. With Thomas Jefferson in the White House, the Democratic-Republican Party could at least potentially control both the executive and legislative branches of government. Bills based on Republican ideas were therefore more likely to be approved by Congress and to be signed into law by the president.

CRITICAL THINKING

Why do you think the checks and balances system is important?

ANSWER: Students' responses will vary but should indicate that the system should prevent one political party or interest group from dictating all public policy.

PRESIDENTIAL PROFILES ANSWER
Students should list his various government posts (delegate to the Constitutional Convention, ambassador to France, secretary of state, vice president, and president) in addition to his writing of the Declaration of Independence.

Technology Resources

CNN. Presents America: Beginnings to 1914
Segment: White House Birthday

Thomas Jefferson

Thomas Jefferson was born in 1743 to a family of Virginia plantation owners. He became a man of many talents. He attended private schools as a child and kept learning throughout his life. Jefferson loved architecture, art, farming, philosophy, and science. He put his studies to practical use. For example, he designed Monticello, his grand home on his Virginia plantation. Jefferson was a wealthy man who held more than 150 slaves. He became a member of the Virginia House of Burgesses in 1769. Jefferson was ambassador to France, secretary of state, and vice president before his two terms as president. Thomas Jefferson died on July 4, 1826, the 50th anniversary of the signing of the Declaration of Independence. In what ways did Thomas Jefferson serve his country?

This document presents the Supreme Court's decision in Marbury v. Madison.

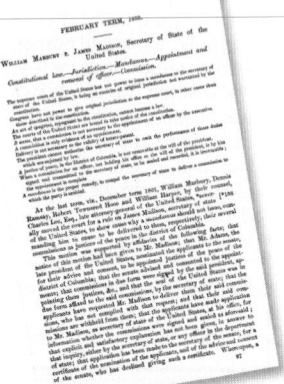

The president faced a difficult challenge soon after he was sworn into office. Jefferson had planned to keep many Federalists in their government jobs. However, many from his party expected the president to replace all Federalists with Republicans. The New York *American Citizen*, a pro-Republican newspaper, expressed this view. "If this should not be the case, for what . . . have we been contending [struggling]?" Federalists were equally unhappy with Jefferson. They complained that his military spending cuts put the country in danger.

Under pressure from both parties, Jefferson finally agreed to replace a number of Federalist officials with Republicans. However, he refused to replace them all. He also stuck to his ideas on government spending.

✔ **Reading Check: Summarizing** What problems did Jefferson face when he took office, and what Republican policies did Jefferson introduce to solve them? He needed to lower the debt and taxes. He replaced some Federalists in government, cut military spending to pay the debt, and ended some taxes set by Federalists.

★ *Marbury v. Madison*

Early in 1801, before Jefferson took office, Federalists in Congress passed a new law that created many new judgeships and other court offices. Before his term ended, President John Adams had appointed dozens of Federalists to fill these positions. Jefferson accused Adams of filling these positions "till 9 o'clock of the night, at 12 o'clock of which he was to go out of office." Other Republicans called the people chosen by Adams "midnight judges."

When Jefferson entered office on March 4, 1801, some Federalists chosen by Adams had not yet received their special commissions. Without these forms they could not begin working as judges. Jefferson took advantage of this fact. He ordered Secretary of State James Madison not to give out the papers. **William Marbury** was one of the people affected by this decision. He demanded that the Supreme Court force the executive branch to hand over his commission. The Court had never done such a thing. However, Marbury claimed that the Judiciary Act of 1789 gave the Supreme Court the right to do so.

The chief justice of the United States was **John Marshall**, a Federalist appointed by Adams. Marshall and President Jefferson disagreed about many political issues. When Marshall agreed to hear Marbury's case, Jefferson protested, complaining that the Federalists "have retired into the judiciary as a stronghold." He was concerned that Marshall would make sure that "all the works of republicanism are to be beaten down and erased."

The Supreme Court's decision in ***Marbury v. Madison*** surprised many people, including Jefferson. All the justices agreed that Marbury had been treated unfairly. But did the Supreme Court have the power to force Madison to give Marbury his commission? The Judiciary Act of 1789 said the Court did. Chief Justice Marshall said the Court did not.

★ REVIEW AND ASSESS

Have students complete the **Section 1 Review** on p. 337. Then have students complete **Daily Quiz 11.1**. As **Alternative Assessment**, you may want to use the Republican and Federalist policies graphic organizer or the Jefferson's inauguration lesson from this section.

★ RETEACH

Have students complete **Main Idea Activity for English Language Learners and Special-Needs Students 11.1**. Then ask students to create a two-column chart describing Jefferson's actions as president. Tell students to label the first column *Significant Points of Jefferson's Inaugural Address* and the second column *Actions Taken to Support Jefferson's Ideas*. Have students review the section to obtain information for the chart. **ENGLISH LANGUAGE LEARNERS**

★ EXTEND

Have students use the library to find Supreme Court decisions that have overturned an act of Congress based on its constitutionality. Tell students to describe the following concepts in their reports: the circumstances surrounding the case, the arguments made for the prosecution and the defense, the Court's decision regarding the case, and an explanation of how the decision was based on constitutionality. Ask volunteers to present their findings in written reports. **BLOCK SCHEDULING**

His reason was simple. He did not think that the Constitution allowed Congress to give the Supreme Court new powers. The Judiciary Act of 1789, he believed, had wrongly given the Court such a power. In other words, the act was unconstitutional—meaning it did something not allowed by the Constitution. Therefore, the Supreme Court did not have the power to force the federal government to give Marbury his commission.

Marshall seemed to be giving up a power of the Supreme Court. But he was really claiming a much greater power. Marshall's ruling established the power of **judicial review**. This power allows the Supreme Court to declare an act of Congress to be unconstitutional. Such a law is then no longer in force. Marshall strongly defended judicial review in his written decision.

> ❝It is, emphatically [absolutely], the province and duty of the Judicial Department to say what the law is. . . . The Constitution is superior to any ordinary act of the legislature.❞
>
> —John Marshall, *Marbury v. Madison*

Judicial review greatly increased the Supreme Court's legal authority. As a result, the Court became a much stronger branch within the national government.

✔ **Reading Check: Evaluating** What leadership qualities did Chief Justice John Marshall show in the *Marbury* v. *Madison* ruling? By ruling against Marbury, Marshall showed that he would not favor Federalists and established the Supreme Court's power of judicial review.

Interpreting the Visual Record

Chief Justice *John Marshall served as the first chief justice of the Supreme Court.* **Why was Marshall's ruling in the Marbury v. Madison** *case so significant?*

Section 1 Review

go.hrw.com Homework Practice Online
keyword: SA3 HP11

❶ **Define** and explain:
• judicial review

❷ **Identify** and explain:
• Thomas Jefferson
• William Marbury
• John Marshall
• *Marbury* v. *Madison*

❸ **Categorizing** Copy the chart below. Use it to show how President Jefferson continued some Federalist policies while introducing Republican policies.

Jefferson as President

Federalist Policies	Republican Policies

❹ **Finding the Main Idea**
a. What were the major issues Thomas Jefferson discussed in his First Inaugural Address?

b. What did Jefferson hope to accomplish by changing Federalist policies on military spending and taxes?

❺ **Writing and Critical Thinking**
Supporting a Point of View Imagine that you are a Supreme Court justice reviewing *Marbury* v. *Madison*. Write an opinion expressing your support for either Marbury or Madison.

Consider the following:
• "midnight judges"
• Judiciary Act of 1789
• judicial review

Section 2

OBJECTIVES

- ⭐ Describe how and why the Louisiana Purchase took place.
- ⭐ Explain what the Lewis and Clark expedition achieved.
- ⭐ Define the purpose of Pike's expedition.

📻 LET'S GET STARTED!

As students enter the classroom, ask them to write a brief overview of the reasons that Europeans, particularly the English, begin colonizing the Americas. (*Students' overviews should mention political, religious, and economic reasons for European colonization.*) After discussing their overviews, tell students that the big attraction was the large amount of land that was available. Explain that American Indians already lived on much of this land and that some areas had already been claimed. Tell students that in Section 2 they will learn how the United States doubled the size of its land holdings.

Section 2
The Louisiana Purchase

Read to Discover

1. How and why did the Louisiana Purchase take place?
2. What did the Lewis and Clark expedition achieve?
3. What was the purpose of Pike's expedition?

WHY IT MATTERS TODAY

People continue to explore Earth and beyond. Use **CNNfyi.com** or other **current events** sources to learn about one area being explored today. Record your findings in your journal.

Identify

- Napoléon Bonaparte
- Toussaint-Louverture
- Louisiana Purchase
- Meriwether Lewis
- William Clark
- Lewis and Clark expedition
- Sacagawea
- Zebulon Pike

The Story Continues

As Spain's rivals grew stronger, it struggled to hold on to its American empire. Spanish foreign minister Manuel de Godoy worried about how to keep American settlers out of the Spanish territory of Louisiana. "You can't put doors on open country," he said in despair. Years of effort failed to improve Spain's position. Under a secret treaty, Spain traded Louisiana to France, passing the problem on to someone else. One Spanish officer expressed his relief at leaving. "I can hardly wait to leave them [the Americans] behind me," he said.

The Spanish flag flew over New Orleans after Spain took control of the city in 1762.

⭐ French Louisiana

In 1800 France was led by General **Napoléon Bonaparte** (nuh-POH-lee-uhn BOH-nuh-pahrt). His political ambition and military skill caused fear across Europe. As he conquered neighboring countries, Napoléon also dreamed of rebuilding France's empire in North America. First, he wanted to send troops to Louisiana. Then France would replace Spain as the key European power in western North America.

Standing in the way of this plan was the former French colony of St. Domingue (present-day Haiti). The colony was located on the Caribbean island of Hispaniola. Enslaved Africans had gained their freedom by taking over the colony in the 1790s, and former slave

Have students read Section 2 and complete Guided Reading Strategy 11.2. Choose one or more of the following activities to explore the section content with students. For further suggestions on block scheduling or team teaching, see the *Block Scheduling Handbook with Team Teaching Strategies.*

Note: To help students make meaningful connections between events in American history and those in their own hometown, use the Chapter 11 **Hands-On History** activity, Trade with Canada.

LEVEL 1: Organize the class into two groups. Have one group research the Lewis and Clark expedition and the other Pike's expedition. Ask each group to create a mural identifying the purpose of the trip, the route traveled, geographic landmarks spotted, American Indian peoples encountered, and significant achievements of its assigned journey. Ask each group to present its mural to the class.

ENGLISH LANGUAGE LEARNERS , COOPERATIVE LEARNING

Toussaint-Louverture (too-san-loo-ver-toohr) ruled the island. Before sending troops to Louisiana, Napoléon needed to take back the island to use as a supply base. However, Toussaint's troops defeated the French forces sent to recapture St. Domingue in 1802. This defeat kept Napoléon from sending troops to Louisiana.

U.S. leaders became suspicious of Napoléon when they learned France once again owned Louisiana. President Jefferson knew that France could block the westward growth of the United States. The French could also interfere with American trade. Jefferson worried that from New Orleans, France could control American trade along the Mississippi River.

New Orleans was founded by the French in 1718 and came under Spanish rule in 1762. The city remained Spanish for some 40 years before returning to French control. Its busy docks were filled with settlers' farm products and valuable furs bought from American Indians. Many of these cargoes were then sent to Europe. At the same time, manufactured goods passed through the port on their way upriver. The city was also home to many languages and cultures, such as African, English, French, and Spanish. New Orleans soon became the focus of Jefferson's foreign policy.

THE GRANGER COLLECTION, NEW YORK

Toussaint-Louverture played a key role in the founding of the nation of Haiti.

✔ **Reading Check: Making Generalizations and Predictions** How do you think Napoléon's failure to regain control of Haiti would affect his plans for North America? Students might suggest that Haiti was needed as a base; failure to regain control weakened plans for a French empire.

★ The Louisiana Purchase

President Jefferson wanted to keep the French from controlling New Orleans, but he did not want to start a war. He hoped that the United States could find a peaceful answer.

Jefferson told the U.S. ambassador to France, Robert R. Livingston, to try to buy New Orleans and West Florida. Jefferson sent James Monroe to help Livingston. Livingston met with Talleyrand, the French foreign minister, to discuss the offer. Talleyrand said that without New Orleans "the rest [of Louisiana] would be of little value" to France. Then he asked what the United States would "give for the whole." The stunned Americans realized that France was offering to sell all of Louisiana.

Napoléon was willing to sell Louisiana for a number of reasons. France was about to go to war against Great Britain. Napoléon also did not want to fight the United States and Britain at once. In addition, the French still had no troops in Louisiana. Instead of more territory, Napoléon now wanted money to buy supplies for his armies in Europe. He also realized that if the United States owned Louisiana, it could challenge Britain's power in North America. "I have given England a rival who, sooner or later, will humble her pride," he boasted.

Livingston and Monroe were eager to take advantage of this sudden opportunity. Congress had only authorized them to offer $10 million. However, the ambassadors agreed to buy Louisiana from France for

ALL LEVELS: Ask students to imagine that they are accompanying Lewis and Clark on their expedition. Have them write journal entries describing the people, plants, and animals encountered; the land traveled; the dangers faced; and the travel conditions experienced by the explorers. Ask volunteers to read portions of their journal entries to the class. Finally, discuss the achievements of the Lewis and Clark expedition with the class. **ENGLISH LANGUAGE LEARNERS**

 ALL LEVELS: Copy the following graphic organizer onto the chalkboard, omitting the italicized answers. Have students complete the flowchart to explain how and why the Louisiana Purchase took place.
ENGLISH LANGUAGE LEARNERS

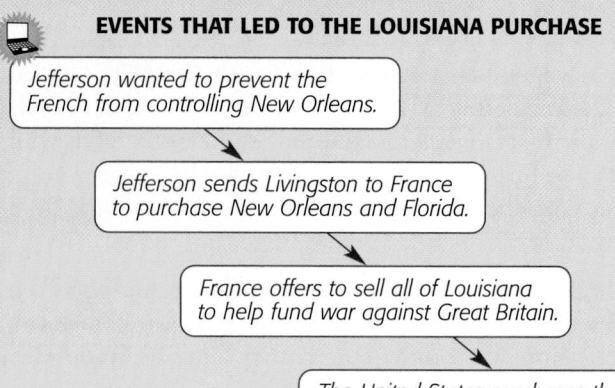

EVENTS THAT LED TO THE LOUISIANA PURCHASE

Jefferson wanted to prevent the French from controlling New Orleans.

Jefferson sends Livingston to France to purchase New Orleans and Florida.

France offers to sell all of Louisiana to help fund war against Great Britain.

The United States purchases the Louisiana Territory from France.

Interdisciplinary Connection

▶Math◀

Louisiana Purchase.
The United States purchased the Louisiana Territory for $15 million. The total area of the territory was 885,000 square miles. There are 640 acres per 1 square mile.

ACTIVITY: Ask students to determine how much the United States paid per square mile and per acre for the Louisiana Territory. *(Have students divide the total purchase price by the number of square miles in the purchase. They should calculate $16.95 per square mile. Then have students divide $16.95 by 640 to determine that the land of the Louisiana Territory cost the United States less than 3 cents per acre.)*

MAP ANSWER
St. Louis

October 20, 1803
The U.S. Senate approves the Louisiana Purchase.

This is what the Louisiana Purchase treaty and seals looked like.

about $15 million. They signed a treaty of purchase on May 2, 1803. Like Livingston and Monroe, Jefferson was pleased when he learned about the chance to buy all of Louisiana. But as a strict constructionist, Jefferson did not believe that the Constitution allowed him to buy the territory. However, Livingston and Monroe feared that the French might take back their offer, so they pushed the president to act quickly. Doing what he thought best for the country, Jefferson agreed to the purchase. On October 20, 1803, the Senate approved the treaty.

With the **Louisiana Purchase**, the size of the United States almost doubled. The Louisiana Territory was a huge region of land, stretching west from the Mississippi River all the way to the great Rocky Mountains. The exact boundaries of the territory were not yet clearly defined. President Jefferson was pleased that the land offered so much room for the United States to grow. He said proudly that the Louisiana Purchase expanded "the empire of liberty." He believed it would provide "a widespread field for the blessings of freedom."

✔ **Reading Check: Summarizing** What happened to U.S. territory in 1803, and why was this important to the future of the United States? The United States approved the Louisiana Purchase almost doubling the nation's size.

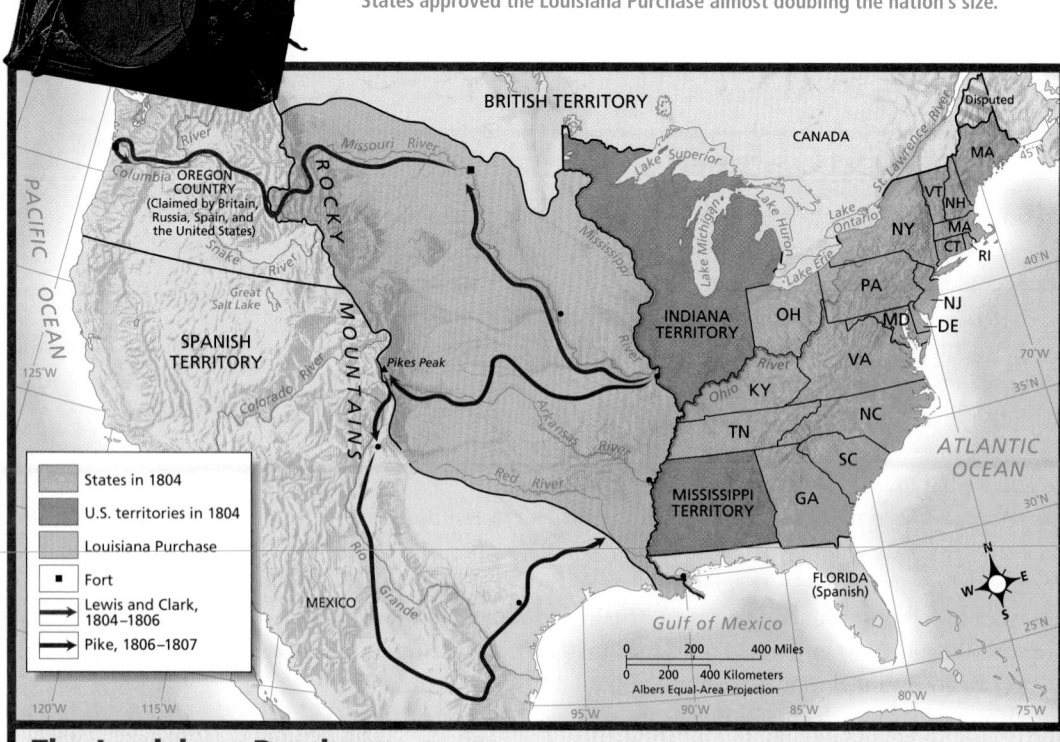

The Louisiana Purchase

Interpreting Maps Meriwether Lewis and William Clark, and later Zebulon Pike, led expeditions to explore the vast Louisiana Territory.

Skills Assessment The World in Spatial Terms From which city did both the Lewis and Clark and the Pike expeditions begin?

LEVEL 3: Have each student write a magazine article explaining why Napoléon was unable to reestablish France's North American empire and how this led to the sale of Louisiana. Ask students to discuss the following topics in their articles: rebellion in St. Domingue, possible ways that French control of Louisiana might have affected U.S. trade and westward expansion, and the French war with Britain. Students should end their articles with a conclusion about how and why the Louisiana Purchase took place. Encourage students to create illustrations for important information. After students have finished their articles, have volunteers read them to the class.

 **SPOTLIGHT**
on the Louisiana Purchase

Explain to students that the legality of the Louisiana Purchase was uncertain when Jefferson agreed to buy the land from France. Have students use information from the text to develop a survey that will show whether people agree or disagree with Jefferson's decision to purchase Louisiana. Have each student explain the circumstances surrounding the purchase to five adults and have adults complete the survey. Then discuss the results with the class and have students suggest explanations for their findings. **BLOCK SCHEDULING**

Interpreting the Visual Record

Lewis and Clark *Although Lewis and Clark tried to appear confident and powerful, they depended on the goodwill of American Indians they met.* **With what kinds of situations do you think the Indian guides in the picture might help Lewis and Clark?**

⭐ Mission of Discovery

Americans knew little about western American Indians or the lands they inhabited. Jefferson wanted to learn more about the people and land of the West. He also wanted to see if there was a river route that could be taken to the Pacific Ocean. In January 1803 the president asked Congress to fund a small western expedition. To lead it, he chose former army captain **Meriwether Lewis**. Lewis had served as his presidential assistant. Jefferson described Lewis as "brave, prudent [careful], habituated [used] to the woods, and familiar with Indian manners and character." Lewis chose Lieutenant **William Clark** to be the co-leader of the expedition. Jefferson told Lewis and Clark to explore the Missouri River. He wanted them to form peaceful relations with American Indians they met. Jefferson added a long list of other directions.

 History Makers Speak ❝The commerce which may be carried on with the people inhabiting the line you will pursue, renders [makes] a knowledge of these people important. . . . Other objects worthy of notice will be the soil and face of the country, its growth and vegetable productions . . . the animals of the country . . . mineral productions of every kind . . . [and the area's] climate.❞

—Thomas Jefferson, quoted in *The Journals of Lewis and Clark*, edited by Frank Bergon

To prepare for the journey, Lewis spent weeks studying with experts about botany, surveying, and other subjects. This knowledge would allow him to take careful notes on what he saw. He also gathered supplies for the journey. With Clark, Lewis carefully selected skilled frontiersmen for their Corps of Discovery.

Analyzing Primary Sources
Summarizing What kind of information did Jefferson want Lewis and Clark to collect on their journey? to learn about American Indian peoples in the region and all aspects of the local environment.

HOMEWORK Have students write a letter to Thomas Jefferson supporting or opposing the purchase of Louisiana. Students' letters should include reasons why the purchase is appropriate or why the purchase is not beneficial.

⭐ CLOSE

Write the following headings on the chalkboard: *Advantages* and *Disadvantages*. Then ask the class to identify the advantages and disadvantages of acquiring a vast new territory. Write students' responses under the appropriate heading. Then ask students to review material from this section to see which advantages and disadvantages apply to the Louisiana Purchase. Lead a class discussion on the importance of this acquisition to U.S. development.

William Clark's journal contained illustrations and written descriptions of his travels.

⭐ The Lewis and Clark Expedition

In May 1804 the **Lewis and Clark expedition** began its long journey. The group set out from St. Louis, in present-day Missouri. The Corps of Discovery traveled up the Missouri River to the lands of the Mandan and the Sioux. Lewis used interpreters to talk to the leaders of each of the peoples they met. He told them that the United States now owned the land on which the American Indians lived. **Sacagawea** (sak-uh-juh-WEE-uh), a Shoshone from the Rocky Mountains, proved to be very helpful. Sacagawea's husband, a French fur trader who lived with the Mandan, offered to guide the expedition across the Great Plains.

Lewis and Clark kept journals describing the people, places, and animals that they encountered. Their journal entries are filled with wonder at things they saw for the first time. On the Great Plains, Lewis saw huge herds "of Buffaloe, Elk, deer, and Antelopes feeding in one common and boundless pasture." Their journals also revealed the many dangers of the journey. They told stories of sickness and conflicts with American Indians. They also described natural hazards, such as high mountains, raging rivers, and terrible storms.

After Lewis and Clark crossed the Plains, they came to the Rocky Mountains. The sight of this giant snowcapped mountain range amazed and worried Lewis. Fortunately for the explorers, the leader of the Shoshone who lived in the area was Sacagawea's brother. He provided horses and a guide to lead the expedition across the mountains. The journey was dangerous and difficult. An exhausted Lewis wrote, "We suffered everything Cold, Hunger, and Fatigue could impart [give]."

Leaving the mountains behind, Lewis and Clark followed the Columbia River, which forms the border between what are now Oregon and Washington. Along the way they met the powerful and friendly Nez Percé. Like the Shoshone, the Nez Percé provided the expedition with food. On November 7, 1805, Clark saw the Pacific Ocean. He wrote in his journal, "*Ocean in view!* O! the joy." The expedition stayed in the Pacific Northwest during the rough winter. They traded with the Clatsop and explored the coast.

In March 1806 Lewis and Clark set out on the long trip home. The party arrived by canoe in St. Louis in late September 1806. Many people from the town lined up along the river to greet them. Clark happily wrote, "Every person . . . seemed to express great pleasure at our return."

Lewis and Clark had not found a river route across the West to the Pacific Ocean. Yet they learned much about western lands and paths across the Rockies. The explorers also established contact with many American Indian groups. They had also collected a great deal of valuable scientific information on western plants and animals.

✔ **Reading Check: Summarizing** What regions did Lewis and Clark cross, and why was their expedition important? Great Plains and Rocky Mountains; gained knowledge of Indian cultures, western environments, and paths across Rocky Mountains

★ REVIEW AND ASSESS

Have students complete the **Section 2 Review** on p. 343. Then have students complete **Daily Quiz 11.2.** As **Alternative Assessment**, you may want to use the Louisiana Purchase graphic organizer or survey lesson from this section.

★ RETEACH

Have students complete **Main Idea Activity for English Language Learners and Special-Needs Students 11.2.** Then organize students into groups and have them write a short story discussing how the United States changed after acquiring the Louisiana Territory. Have a volunteer from each group read his or her group's story to the class. Finally, lead a discussion comparing the stories. **ENGLISH LANGUAGE LEARNERS , COOPERATIVE LEARNING**

★ EXTEND

Have students use the library to find information on the natural resources found in the areas acquired in the Louisiana Purchase. Give students a blank outline map of the United States. Then have them fill in the map, using symbols to identify the natural resources in the states. Tell students to create a legend explaining their symbols. Finally, discuss the significance of acquiring these resources with the class. **BLOCK SCHEDULING**

★ Pike's Exploration

The year that Lewis and Clark returned home, young army officer **Zebulon Pike** was sent on another mission to the West. He was ordered to find the starting point of the Red River. This river runs through Louisiana and along some of the northern border of present-day Texas. The United States considered the Red River to be part of the Louisiana Territory's southwestern border with New Spain. Pike may also have had instructions to spy on Spanish outposts in the Southwest.

THE GRANGER COLLECTION, NEW YORK

Pike led his small expedition to the Rocky Mountains, in present-day Colorado. There he tried to climb the mountain known today as Pikes Peak. In 1807 he headed south with a few expedition members into present-day New Mexico. They struggled across mountains in the bitter winter before reaching a tributary of the Rio Grande.

Although he had passed into Spanish-held lands, Pike continued exploring. He followed the river until a group of Spanish cavalry arrested him. When stopped, Pike pointed to the Rio Grande. "What, is not this the Red River?" The Spanish were not fooled, however. They suspected Pike of being a spy and put him in jail. When he was finally released, he returned to the United States and reported on his trip. Despite his imprisonment, Pike thought there were good business opportunities for Americans in the Southwest.

✔ **Reading Check: Supporting a Point of View** What would you do if you were Zebulon Pike and found yourself in Spanish territory? Answers will vary. Students might say that if they had orders to spy on the Spanish they would have to continue their mission. If they feel that Pike was simply exploring, they might think it wise to turn back.

Interpreting the Visual Record

Zebulon Pike Explorer Zebulon Pike's report on his journey offered many Americans their first description of the Southwest. **What information do you think Pike's description contained?**

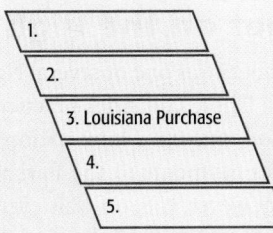

Section 2 Review

★ **Homework Practice Online** keyword: SA3 HP11

1 Identify and explain:
- Napoléon Bonaparte
- Toussaint-Louverture
- Louisiana Purchase
- Meriwether Lewis
- William Clark
- Lewis and Clark expedition
- Sacagawea
- Zebulon Pike

2 Sequencing Copy the graphic organizer below. Use it to show what events led to the Louisiana Purchase and what steps the United States took to learn about the Louisiana Territory afterward.

1.
2.
3. Louisiana Purchase
4.
5.

3 Finding the Main Idea
a. Why was France willing to sell Louisiana, and why did the United States purchase it?

b. What was the purpose of Pike's expedition, and where did he travel?

4 Writing and Critical Thinking
Summarizing Imagine that you are a soldier on the Lewis and Clark expedition. Write a diary entry describing a specific adventure on the trip.

Consider the following:
- the dangers faced on the journey
- the role of Sacagawea
- scientific knowledge gained on the expedition

Visual Record Answer

Students might suggest that Pike described mountainous terrain.

Section 2 Review
ANSWERS

1 Identify
- Napoléon Bonaparte, p. 338
- Toussaint Louverture, p. 339
- Louisiana Purchase, p. 340
- Meriwether Lewis, p. 340
- William Clark, p. 341
- Lewis and Clark expedition, p. 342
- Sacagawea, p. 342
- Zebulon Pike, p. 343

2 1. French fail to regain control of Haiti; 2. the United States offers to buy New Orleans; 4. U.S. government sends the Lewis and Clark expedition to explore the Louisiana Territory; 5. U.S. government sends the Pike expedition to explore the southern boundaries of the Louisiana Territory

3 a. it needed the money worse than the land, and the United States wanted to control New Orleans
b. to find the source of the Red River; Pike went to the Rocky Mountains, in present-day Colorado, and climbed the mountain known today as Pikes Peak, continued south into what is now New Mexico to the Rio Grande.

4 Students' diary entries will vary but should reflect an understanding of the hazards faced and different American Indian groups encountered.

Section 3

OBJECTIVES

- Determine why the United States placed an embargo on France and Great Britain.
- Explain what Tecumseh wanted to accomplish and how successful he was.
- Analyze why the United States declared war on Great Britain in 1812.

LET'S GET STARTED!

As students enter the classroom, tell them to imagine that they are the president of the United States. Ask each student to speculate, in writing, on the circumstances that justify a country declaring war on another nation. *(Students' writings will vary, but they might include that countries declare war to obtain more land, to protect their interests, or to defeat a threat to other people in the world.)* Tell students that in Section 3 they will learn about three wars the United States fought—one with the Barbary pirates, another one with American Indians, and the last one with Great Britain.

Section 3

The Coming of War

Read to Discover

1. Why did the United States place an embargo on France and Great Britain?
2. What did Tecumseh want to accomplish, and how successful was he?
3. Why did the United States declare war on Britain in 1812?

WHY IT MATTERS TODAY

Nations continue to use trade restrictions in their dealings with other countries. Use **CNNfyi.com** or other **current events** sources to learn more about an embargo—a government's refusal to buy another country's goods. Record your findings in your journal.

Define

- impressment
- embargo

Identify

- Embargo Act
- Non-Intercourse Act
- Tecumseh
- Battle of Tippecanoe
- War Hawks
- James Madison

The Barbary States were one of many threats to U.S. shipping in the late 1700s and early 1800s.

The Story Continues

In the fall of 1793 Samuel Calder wrote a desperate letter to the U.S. government. "I am very sorry to inform you of my present situation. . . . I was taken by an Algerian Cruzier [ship]." Calder went on to say that he and other Americans were being held prisoner by Algerian pirates. "We was immediately put into Chains and put to hard Labor," he wrote in despair. Calder begged for $100 so he could pay his ransom and be free again.

⭐ Danger on the High Seas

The state of Algiers was one of several North African lands known as the Barbary States. These countries practiced piracy and held foreign citizens captive for ransom. Many nations, including the United States, agreed to make payments to the Barbary States to protect their ships and citizens. However, U.S. officials eventually refused to pay any more and sent the U.S. Navy to end the pirate raids.

TEACH

Have students read Section 3 and complete Guided Reading Strategy 11.3. Choose one or more of the following activities to explore the section content with students. For further suggestions on block scheduling or team teaching, see the *Block Scheduling Handbook with Team Teaching Strategies.*

LEVEL 1: Pair students and have them make a list of the reasons why the United States issued the Embargo Act and the Non-Intercourse Act. Ask students to distinguish between British actions and French actions. *(Students'*

lists should mention the violation of U.S. neutrality at sea by both countries and the impressment of U.S. sailors by the British. Students should also mention that the embargoes hurt the U.S. economy more than the British and French economies.) Finally have them use their lists to determine how successful the embargoes were at punishing the British and French.

ENGLISH LANGUAGE LEARNERS , COOPERATIVE LEARNING

 HOMEWORK Ask students to write a song or poem depicting the issue of impressment and the conflict on the high seas.

However, the United States faced greater threats on the high seas. When Great Britain and France went to war in 1803, the United States was drawn into the conflict. Each country wanted to stop the United States from supplying goods and war materials to the other. In the early 1800s Britain passed a series of acts allowing the British navy to search and seize ships carrying war supplies to France. The French quickly struck back, declaring that no country could ship goods to Britain.

Many American merchants ignored these foreign laws. As a result, the British and French navies captured many American merchant ships headed for Europe. The British also searched these ships for sailors who had run away from the British navy. The British then made these people return to British warships. This practice of pressing, or forcing, people to serve in the army or navy was called **impressment**. Sometimes U.S. citizens suffered impressment by accident.

One widely publicized example of impressment took place in June 1807. The British ship *Leopard* stopped the U.S. Navy ship *Chesapeake* and tried to remove four of its sailors. When the *Chesapeake*'s captain refused, the British opened fire and took the sailors by force. The *Chesapeake* incident angered many Americans. Attorney General Caesar A. Rodney declared that it "has excited the spirit of '76 and the whole country is literally in arms."

✔ **Reading Check: Finding the Main Idea** How did Great Britain's actions affect its relationship with the United States? The British stopped and searched American ships and impressed some U.S. citizens. Such actions outraged Americans and hurt U.S.-British relations.

★ A Trade War

Debates raged about how the United States should respond to Great Britain's violations of U.S. neutrality. Some Americans wanted to go to war. Others favored an **embargo**, or the banning of trade, against Britain. A writer for the *Boston Chronicle* agreed. "Our trade is the most powerful weapon we can use in our defense."

Jefferson and the Republicans favored an embargo. In December 1807 Congress passed the **Embargo Act**. In effect, the law banned trade with foreign countries. Congress hoped to punish Britain and France and to protect American ships from capture. However, the act's main effect was to hurt American merchants. Without trade, they lost a great deal of money. The New England states and New York relied heavily on trade and were the most hard hit by the act.

The popularity of the Federalist Party rose, and Jefferson's support fell as the embargo continued. By December 1808 Jefferson had received 199 petitions asking him to repeal the Embargo Act. Meanwhile, the act had little effect on Britain or France. American merchants smuggled goods to Europe. The British also increased their trade with South America to replace lost U.S. trade. The U.S. minister in Paris noted that "here [the embargo] is not felt, and in England . . . it is forgotten."

GLOBAL CONNECTIONS

The Barbary Pirates

The small North African kingdoms of Algiers, Morocco, Tripoli, and Tunis—known as the Barbary States—operated pirate fleets. Like many European nations, the United States paid the Barbary States not to attack American ships. In 1801 Tripoli demanded a higher payment than normal. When the United States was slow to pay, Tripoli declared war. In response, Jefferson sent a small fleet to patrol the North African coast. Then in 1805, U.S. Marines and mercenaries marched across the desert to capture a Tripolitan town. Finally, the ruler of Tripoli signed a treaty and stopped attacks on American ships. The other Barbary States signed similar treaties in 1815. **How did the United States stop the Barbary pirates?**

On the High Seas. After the Revolutionary War, American merchant ships traveling through the Mediterranean were at the mercy of pirates. The small North African kingdoms of Algiers, Morocco, Tunis, and Tripoli—known as the Barbary States—operated these pirate fleets. The United States, like many European nations, had been paying the Barbary States a yearly fee to prevent them from capturing American ships. Thomas Jefferson opposed this arrangement, however, and refused to pay them their demanded tribute. Tripoli responded by declaring war on the United States. Jefferson then sent a small fleet of ships to patrol the Mediterranean and rescue a captured U.S. ship, the *Philadelphia*. Captain Stephen Decatur and his crew were able to board and destroy the pirated *Philadelphia* by posing as Maltese sailors who had lost their anchor. They boarded the ship, fending off resistance, and set fire to it. The whole escapade took only 20 minutes.

ACTIVITY: Have students write a scene for a movie about the experiences of American sailor.

GLOBAL CONNECTIONS ANSWER
Jefferson sent a fleet to patrol the Mediterranean and then sent troops to Tripoli.

★★★★★★★★★★★ That's Interesting! ★★★★★★★★★★★

Founded by Tecumseh and his brother, the Prophet, Tippecanoe Village was designed to be a national capital for united American Indian peoples. Established in 1808 on lands owned by the Potawatomi and Kickapoo nations, Tippecanoe Village served as a center to train as many as 1,000 American Indian troops in the spiritual and athletic arts.

CONNECTING TO MATH ANSWERS

1. $1.005 billion; $210 million; 21 percent
2. Students' graphs may vary but should include the appropriate information from the chart.
3. Students' presentations may vary but should provide information from the chart.

CONNECTING TO MATH

Just the Facts

American Exports, 1800–1815
(in millions of dollars)

Year	Total Value All U.S. Exports	Total Value U.S. Exports to Great Britain
1800	71	19
1801	93	31
1802	72	16
1803	56	18
1804	78	13
1805	96	15
1806	102	16
1807	108	23
1808	22	3
1809	52	6
1810	67	12
1811	61	14
1812	39	6
1813	28	---
1814	7	---
1815	53	18

Using Mathematical Skills

1. What was the total value of U.S. exports to Great Britain from 1800 through 1815?
2. Create a graph that shows the value of all U.S. exports and the value of U.S. exports to Britain from 1800 through 1815.
3. Imagine that you are an economic adviser to President Madison in 1812. Prepare a presentation to show how the American economy has been affected by U.S. efforts to force Britain to respect American trade rights.

Tecumseh hoped his union of American Indians might stop American settlers.

Congress replaced the unpopular law with the **Non-Intercourse Act** in 1809. This act banned trade only with Britain, France, and their colonies. It also stated that the United States would start trading with the first side that stopped violating U.S. neutrality. Congress wanted the new law to pressure Britain and France to stop taking American ships. In addition, Congress hoped that the Non-Intercourse Act would be less harmful to the nation's trade.

✔ **Reading Check: Comparing and Contrasting** How were the Embargo Act and the Non-Intercourse Act similar and different? Both asserted U.S. rights; Embargo Act banned trade; Non-Intercourse Act stopped trade only with only Britain and France.

★ The Rise of Tecumseh

Disagreements between Great Britain and the United States went beyond the neutrality issue. In the West, the British, American Indians, and American settlers again clashed. In the early 1800s, thousands of American settlers were entering the Northwest Territory. They started farms and settlements on what had once been American Indian lands. The United States had gained control of much of this land through the Treaty of Greenville. The loss of this land had upset many Indians whose leaders had not agreed to the treaty.

Britain wanted to contain the rapid western growth of the United States and to protect its interests in Canada. British leaders did not want to fight the United States, however. Instead, the British government gave military aid to American Indian nations in the Northwest Territory.

One of the most influential and talented American Indian leaders of this period was **Tecumseh**. A Shawnee chief, Tecumseh was a skilled military leader and a brilliant speaker. He warned other American Indians about the dangers they faced from settlers.

History Makers Speak ❝Where [today are] the Narranganset, the Mohican, the Pokanoket and many other once powerful tribes of our people? They have vanished before the avarice [greed] and oppression [domination] of the white man, as snow before a summer sun.❞

—Tecumseh, quoted in *Indian Wars*, by Robert M. Utley and Wilcomb E. Washburn

Tecumseh hoped to unite the American Indians of the Northwest Territory, the South, and the eastern Mississippi Valley. Aided by his brother, a religious leader called the Prophet, Tecumseh founded a village for his followers near the Wabash and Tippecanoe Rivers.

✔ **Reading Check: Analyzing Information** What was Tecumseh's goal? Tecumseh wanted to create a great union of American Indian peoples to resist American settlement.

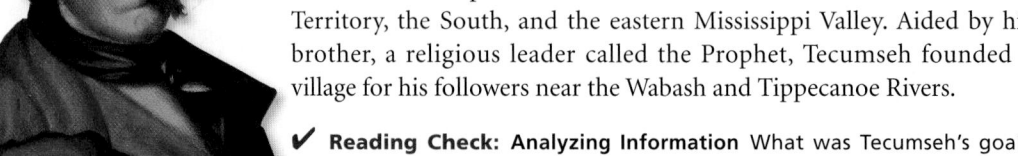

346

ALL LEVELS: Copy the following graphic organizer onto the chalkboard, omitting the italicized answers. Have students complete the organizer to help them identify why the United States declared war on Great Britain in 1812. **ENGLISH LANGUAGE LEARNERS**

```
                    REASONS FOR WAR

interference    impressment    military aid to    support of
with American   of American     American         War Hawks
   trade          sailors        Indians         for a war
```

LEVEL 2: Lead a class discussion about British impressment of American ships and the incident involving the *Chesapeake*. Explain to students that this event angered many U.S. citizens and became a cry for war. Ask students to imagine that they are going to march on the Capitol to encourage Congress to declare war on Great Britain. Have them create banners and signs denouncing Britain's actions and explaining why Congress should declare war against Great Britain. Ask volunteers to present their banners or signs to the class.

LEVEL 3: Have students imagine that they are American diplomats sent to meet with Tecumseh. Have each student write a report listing Tecumseh's goals and how he hoped to achieve them. Finally, have students conclude their reports by discussing how successful Tecumseh actually was at achieving his goals.

THE GRANGER COLLECTION, NEW YORK

Interpreting the Visual Record

Fighting on the frontier *The Battle of Tippecanoe broke the power of Tecumseh's American Indian confederation.* **What advantages does each side have in the battle as shown in the image?**

⭐ War on the Frontier

William Henry Harrison, the governor of the Indiana Territory, believed that Tecumseh was a serious threat to American power. Tecumseh met Harrison face to face in 1810. The governor urged him to follow the treaties that had been signed. Tecumseh replied, "The white people have no right to take the land from the Indians, because the Indians had it first." No single chief, he insisted, could sell land belonging to all American Indians who used it. In response, Harrison warned Tecumseh not to resist the power of the United States.

Tecumseh then traveled south to ask the Creek nation to join his forces. Harrison decided to attack while Tecumseh was gone. Harrison raised an army and then marched his troops close to the village of Tecumseh's followers. The **Battle of Tippecanoe** began when the Prophet ordered an attack on Harrison's camp early on November 7. Indian forces broke through the camp lines. Yet Harrison remained "calm, cool, and collected," according to one observer. During the all-day battle, Harrison's soldiers forced the American Indian forces to retreat. Then they destroyed Tecumseh's village. Chief Shabonee said, "With the smoke of that town and the loss of the battle, I lost all hope." Although Tecumseh was safe, he had lost much of his support.

✔ **Reading Check: Finding the Main Idea** Why were U.S. officials worried by Tecumseh's actions? They thought Tecumseh might unite many American Indian groups against the United States on the frontier.

Western politician Henry Clay was one of the leading War Hawks.

Analyzing Primary Sources
Identifying Points of View Why does Randolph oppose a war, and whom does he fear it would hurt? The people would suffer, and it would be costly.

★ The War Debate

The frontier fighting angered many Americans. A Republican newspaper declared, "The war on the Wabash [River] is purely BRITISH." Many Americans believed that Britain had encouraged Tecumseh to attack settlers in the West.

The **War Hawks** were members of Congress who favored war against Great Britain. They saw war as the only answer to Britain's insults. Led by members of Congress such as Henry Clay of Kentucky and John C. Calhoun of South Carolina, the War Hawks were strongest in the West and the South. "If we submit," Calhoun warned, "the independence of this nation is lost." Philadelphia newspaper editor John Binns agreed with Calhoun. He insisted that "the honor of the Nation . . . will be sacrificed if war be not declared."

Some War Hawks believed that war would give the United States a chance to expand. Speaking to the House, Tennessee representative Felix Grundy explained his views. "I . . . feel anxious [eager] not only to add the Floridas to the South, but the Canadas to the North of this empire."

The strongest opponents of the War Hawks were New England Federalists. British trade restrictions and impressment were hurting New England's economy. But people there wanted to renew friendly business ties with Britain instead of fighting another war. Other politicians, such as John Randolph of Virginia, argued that war was foolish. Standing up in Congress, Randolph challenged the War Hawks.

 History Makers Speak ❝But is war the true remedy? Who will profit by it? . . . A few lucky merchants . . . and contractors. Who must suffer by it? The people. It is their blood, their taxes, that must flow to support it.❞

—John Randolph, quoted in *Annals of America*

Other antiwar politicians feared that the United States was not yet ready to fight powerful Britain. Senator Obadiah German of New York observed that the U.S. Army and Navy were small and poorly equipped. German pleaded with Congress to be patient. "Prior to any declaration of war . . . my plan would be . . . to put the country in complete armor."

✔ **Reading Check: Contrasting** Contrast the arguments of the opposing sides in the war debate. War Hawks: war will bring expansion, protect American honor, and stop British aid to American Indians. War opponents: war is dangerous, unnecessary, and the nation is not ready.

★ A Declaration of War

President **James Madison**, a Republican elected in 1808, faced the difficulty of carrying on the trade war. He also felt growing pressure from the War Hawks. Speaking to Congress on June 1, 1812, Madison described Great Britain's conduct. He complained of Britain's impressment of American sailors and criticized Britain's continuing violation of

⭐ **REVIEW AND ASSESS**

Have students complete the **Section 3 Review** on p. 349. Then have students complete **Daily Quiz 11.3**. As **Alternative Assessment**, you may want to use the graphic organizer about why the United States declared war on Great Britain or the war debate lesson from this section.

⭐ **RETEACH**

Have students complete **Main Idea Activity for English Language Learners and Special-Needs Students 11.3**. Then have each student create a crossword puzzle using the terms and names in the Identify section of the Section 3 Review. Have students exchange their crossword puzzles and answer the

questions. When students have completed the puzzles, have them return the puzzles to their authors for grading. Finally, lead a class discussion on any terms or names that students had difficulty identifying. **ENGLISH LANGUAGE LEARNERS**

⭐ **EXTEND**

Assign each student one of the following conflicts: the Battle of Tippecanoe, the conflict with the Barbary pirates, or the War of 1812. Have students use their textbooks or the library to conduct research on their assigned conflict. Then have each student create a storyboard consisting of cartoons, drawings, or photographs that show the major events of the assigned conflict. **BLOCK SCHEDULING**

In 1812 the United States had only a small standing army to face its enemies.

U.S. neutrality. He concluded that Britain was in "a state of war against the United States." The president called on Congress to decide what the nation should do about this situation.

A few days later, representatives of southern and western states voted for war. Representatives of Delaware, the New England states, New Jersey, New York, and Pennsylvania voted for peace. When the votes were counted, the War Hawks had won. For the first time in U.S. history, Congress declared war. Months later, Madison was reelected. He would serve as commander in chief during the War of 1812.

✔ **Reading Check: Summarizing** Why did the United States declare war against Great Britain in 1812? British interference with American trade; impressment of American sailors; military aid to American Indians; support of the War Hawks for a war

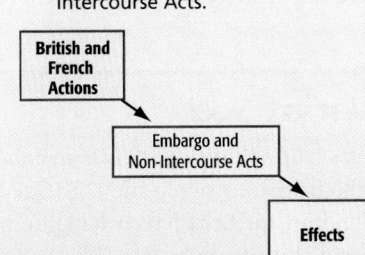

go.hrw.com **Homework Practice Online**
keyword: SA3 HP11

Section 3 Review

1 Define and explain:
• impressment
• embargo

2 Identify and explain:
• Embargo Act
• Non-Intercourse Act
• Tecumseh
• Battle of Tippecanoe
• War Hawks
• James Madison

3 Identifying Cause and Effect Copy the graphic organizer below. Use it to explain the causes and effects of the Embargo and Non-Intercourse Acts.

> British and French Actions → Embargo and Non-Intercourse Acts → Effects

4 Finding the Main Idea
a. What was Tecumseh's goal, and did he accomplish it?

b. What led the United States to declare war on Great Britain?

5 Writing and Critical Thinking
Analyzing Information Imagine that you are a reporter covering the War of 1812. Write an editorial on President Madison's foreign policy.

Consider the following:
• French and British interference with American ships
• fighting against American Indians on the frontier
• pressure from War Hawks

Section 3 Review
ANSWERS

1 Define
• impressment, p. 345
• embargo, p. 345

2 Identify
• Embargo Act, p. 345
• Non-Intercourse Act, p. 346
• Tecumseh, p. 346
• Battle of Tippecanoe, p. 347
• War Hawks, p. 348
• James Madison, p. 348

3 British actions—impressment of American sailors, the *Chesapeake* incident, and seizing of U.S. ships; French actions—seizing U.S. ships and violation of neutral rights; Effects—U.S. neutrality violated by Great Britain and France, a great deal of business lost by United States.

4 a. he hoped to establish an American Indian confederacy to stop the westward expansion of American settlers; the plan failed
b. British interference with American trade; impressment of American sailors; military aid to American Indians; support of the War Hawks for a war

5 Students' editorials will vary, but votes for declaring war should mention violation of neutrality and impressment.

Section 4

OBJECTIVES

✪ Describe how the war progressed at sea and in the Great Lakes region.

✪ Explain how actions by American Indians aided the British during the war.

✪ Identify the strategy the British pursued in the East.

✪ Examine how the war came to an end.

🎧 LET'S GET STARTED!

Write the following question on the chalkboard: *Have you ever received a message so late that the event it dealt with had already taken place?* As students enter the classroom, have them answer the question. *(Students' answers will vary, but students should state examples and describe what happened as a result.)* Then ask students if the use of any form of technology could have gotten the message through on time. *(Students' responses will vary but students might answer e-mail, phone calls, pagers, or any other modern communication technology.)* Explain to students that in Section 4 they will learn about the Battle of New Orleans, which was fought two weeks after a peace treaty ended the War of 1812.

Section 4

The War of 1812

Read to Discover

1. How did the war progress at sea and in the Great Lakes region?
2. How did actions by American Indians aid the British during the war?
3. What strategy did the British pursue in the East?
4. How did the war come to an end?

WHY IT MATTERS TODAY

The Federalists protested the War of 1812, even though Congress had the power to declare it. People today continue to disagree with actions of the government. Use **CNNfyi.com** or other **current events** sources to find a political issue over which people disagree. Record your findings in your journal.

Identify

• Oliver Hazard Perry
• Battle of Lake Erie
• Battle of the Thames
• Red Eagle
• Andrew Jackson
• Battle of Horseshoe Bend
• Battle of New Orleans
• Hartford Convention
• Treaty of Ghent

The Story Continues

On August 19, 1812, the USS *Constitution* met the British ship *Guerrière* off the coast of Nova Scotia. The crews on both ships scrambled across the decks as the vessels circled each other. An observer said the *Constitution*'s first cannon blast rocked the *Guerrière* like "the shock of an earthquake." When the British returned fire, a U.S. sailor saw a cannonball bounce off the side of the *Constitution*. "Huzza, her sides are made of iron!" he cried. Soon "Old Ironsides" won one of the first battles of the War of 1812.

This is the captain's wheel of the USS Constitution, *which fought one of the first battles of the War of 1812.*

⭐ The War at Sea

The *Constitution*'s triumph over the *Guerrière* shocked many observers who expected the British to sweep the U.S. Navy from the seas. When the War of 1812 began, the British navy had hundreds of ships stationed around the world. In contrast, the U.S. Navy had fewer than 20. Republican Adam Seybert declared, "We cannot contend [compete] with Great Britain on the ocean."

★ TEACH

Have students read Section 4 and complete Guided Reading Strategy 11.4. Choose one or more of the following activities to explore the section content with students. For further suggestions on block scheduling or team teaching, see the *Block Scheduling Handbook with Team Teaching Strategies.*

LEVEL 1: Lead a class discussion on the end of the war. Pair students and assign each pair one of the following topics: the Hartford Convention, the Treaty of Ghent, or the Battle of New Orleans. Have each pair write a newspaper headline and two subheadings illustrating why its topic was so instrumental in helping the end of the war.
ENGLISH LANGUAGE LEARNERS, COOPERATIVE LEARNING

Although outnumbered, the United States did have some advantages. The U.S. government licensed privately owned ships to attack British merchant ships. Equipping and operating these privateers cost less than building more naval ships. One Republican leader called the privateers "our cheapest & best Navy." The privateers captured hundreds of British ships. A London newspaper complained, "On the ocean, and even on our own coasts, we have been insulted."

Most of the British navy's ships were scattered around the globe and could not be called away to fight the United States. The U.S. Navy had well-trained sailors and new warships such as the *Constitution*. These well-built vessels carried more cannons than most British ships of the same size. U.S. captains proved their skill and the power of their ships early in the war, several times defeating British ships in one-on-one duels. These victories embarrassed the British and raised American morale. Eventually, the British brought more ships to the American coast. They began patrolling in large groups that the smaller U.S. Navy could not fight. The British blockaded American seaports and captured many American merchant ships.

✔ **Reading Check: Contrasting** What advantages did Great Britain and the United States have at the start of the war? Britain's navy was vastly superior, but scattered. The U.S. Navy was small, but supported by privateers, and its best ships were more powerful than British vessels.

The copper sheathing on the hull of the USS Constitution *was made by Patriot Paul Revere.*

The War of 1812

Interpreting Maps During the War of 1812 battles took place in several regions of the United States.

Skills Assessment
1. **Places and Regions** What battle took place in the state of New York?
2. **Drawing Inferences and Conclusions** Why do you think there were so many battles along the Canadian border?

An American cannon

Map legend:
- → Americans
- ✹ American victories
- → British
- ✹ British victories
- ▲▲ British blockade

0 150 300 Miles
0 150 300 Kilometers
Albers Equal-Area Projection

BRITISH TERRITORY
CANADA
Montreal
MASSACHUSETTS
Plattsburg Sept. 1814
Thames Oct. 1813
York
Fort Niagara
VT
NH
NEW YORK
Boston
MASSACHUSETTS
MICHIGAN TERRITORY
HARRISON
Fort Detroit Aug. 1812
CT
RI
Fort Dearborn
Battle of Lake Erie Sept. 1813
PENNSYLVANIA
New York City
NEW JERSEY
Philadelphia
ILLINOIS TERR.
INDIANA TERR.
OHIO
Baltimore Sept. 1814
Fort McHenry
DE
MD
Washington, D.C. Aug. 1814
VIRGINIA
Chesapeake Bay
KENTUCKY
TENNESSEE
NORTH CAROLINA
SOUTH CAROLINA
MISSISSIPPI TERRITORY
GEORGIA
Charleston
Savannah
LOUISIANA
JACKSON
New Orleans Jan. 1815
PAKENHAM
SPANISH TERRITORY
FLORIDA
Gulf of Mexico
ATLANTIC OCEAN

ALL LEVELS: Organize students into small groups and assign each group one of these two events: the Battle of the Thames or the Battle of Horseshoe Bend. Ask students to imagine that they are running a historical museum dedicated to their assigned topic. Have students create a museum brochure that includes a list of the museum's hours and entrance fees, its location, background information on how American Indians aided the British during the war, and descriptions and illustrations of the battles. Display brochures in the classroom and allow students the opportunity to view and discuss each group's brochure.

ENGLISH LANGUAGE LEARNERS , COOPERATIVE LEARNING

HOMEWORK Have students create a section study guide with questions on the important persons, places, and events discussed in the section.

Note: For an additional teaching idea, see the Chapter 11 Issue Strip activity in the **Creative Teaching Strategies** handbook.

★ Culture

French Canadians. French settlers founded the city of Montreal in 1657, which, along with Quebec City, remains one of French Canada's most important cities today. Unlike the British colonists, the French colonists came mostly for missionary reasons. Hoping to "convert" American Indians to Christianity, the French did not see Indians as enemies or rivals for land ownership.

▣ internet connect

TOPIC: Indian Relations
GO TO: go.hrw.com
KEYWORD: SA3 CF11

Have students use the library or search the Internet through the HRW Go site to find information about relations between American Indians living in Canada and British or French colonists. Then have students write a report on their findings, using standard grammar, spelling, sentence structure, and punctuation.

Visual Record Answer

Students might suggest that he is holding his weapon and is ready to take aim.

THE GRANGER COLLECTION, NEW YORK

Interpreting the Visual Record

The Battle of Lake Erie *Captain Oliver Hazard Perry was forced to abandon his damaged ship during the fighting and take command of a new one.* **How does this image display Captain Perry's determination to win the battle?**

★ The Canadian Border

Hoping to equal the early success of the U.S. Navy, American leaders planned to invade Canada with three separate armies. They expected French Canadians to welcome U.S. troops. Former president Thomas Jefferson thought that conquering Canada would be "a mere matter of marching [there]."

These hopes were soon dashed. In July 1812 the British joined with American Indians led by Tecumseh to defeat an American army and capture Fort Detroit. The other American forces had to retreat when militia members refused to cross the Canadian border. By the end of 1812, Britain controlled the strategic Great Lakes region. The situation worried Treasury Secretary Albert Gallatin.

History Makers Speak

❝The series of misfortunes exceeds [goes beyond] all anticipations made even by those who had least confidence in our inexperienced officers and undisciplined men.**❞**

—Albert Gallatin, quoted in *The War of 1812*, by Donald R. Hickey

In 1813, the United States struck back. In late April U.S. troops burned the Canadian capital, York. Then the United States moved to break Britain's control of Lake Erie. The navy gave the task to Captain **Oliver Hazard Perry**. After building a small fleet, Perry sailed out to meet the British on September 10, 1813. The **Battle of Lake Erie** lasted more than three hours, and both sides suffered heavy casualties. Finally, the British surrendered. Perry sent a message to General William Henry Harrison. "We have met the enemy and they are ours," he reported. Perry's victory forced the British to withdraw and gave the U.S. Army new hope.

 Reading Check: Finding the Main Idea Why was Perry's victory in the Battle of Lake Erie important to the U.S. war effort? forced the British to withdraw; improved American army's morale

★ The Frontier War

Harrison took advantage of Perry's victory by pursuing the British and their American Indian allies into Canada. General Harrison's forces caught up with the British by the Thames River in southern Canada in October 1813. In the **Battle of the Thames**, Harrison boldly ordered a cavalry charge directly into the British force. The British defenses broke apart, but the American Indian forces, led by Tecumseh, continued to fight. The Indian forces eventually retreated, but not before Tecumseh himself was killed. His death weakened the Indian-British alliance around the

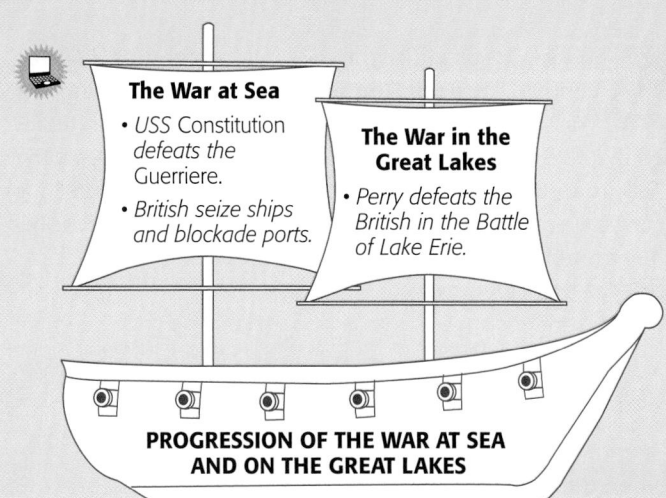

The War at Sea
• *USS* Constitution *defeats the Guerriere.*
• *British seize ships and blockade ports.*

The War in the Great Lakes
• *Perry defeats the British in the Battle of Lake Erie.*

PROGRESSION OF THE WAR AT SEA AND ON THE GREAT LAKES

Great Lakes. The U.S. victory in the Battle of the Thames broke British power on the Northwest frontier and secured the U.S. border with Canada.

Two years before his death, Tecumseh had tried to enlist the Creek Indians in his confederacy. In 1813 the Creek finally decided to take up arms against the United States. Led by Chief **Red Eagle**, Creek forces destroyed Fort Mims in present-day Alabama. Close to 250 of the fort's defenders were killed. **Andrew Jackson**, a general in the Tennessee militia, led his soldiers south to fight the Creek.

After several bloody battles, Jackson attacked the main Creek base in 1814. It was a small fort on the Tallapoosa River in what is now Alabama. The **Battle of Horseshoe Bend** was a convincing victory for Jackson and his troops. Days later, Red Eagle came into Jackson's camp and surrendered. Jackson's victory ended the Creek War and led to a treaty that forced the Creek to give up millions of acres of their land.

✔ **Reading Check: Summarizing** What major battles did the United States win in Canada and present-day Alabama? Battle of the Thames; Battle of Horseshoe Bend

★ The British on the Offensive

Despite U.S. success on the western and southern frontiers, the situation in the East grew worse. Having defeated France in April 1814, the British sent more troops to America. They also strengthened their blockade of Atlantic seaports. Now reinforced, the British moved to attack the U.S. capital. President Madison and most of his cabinet were forced to flee when the British broke through U.S. defenses. The British marched

Interpreting the Visual Record

Washington *First Lady Dolley Madison heard about the British advance on Washington. Despite the danger, she stayed and saved a famous portrait of George Washington before escaping.* **What threats would an American face trying to leave the capital?**

THE GRANGER COLLECTION, NEW YORK

LEVEL 3: Organize the class into two groups. Ask students to create an outline for a documentary on the War of 1812. Have one group address the strategies used by the British in the East during the War of 1812. Ask the other group to address the American Indian aid to the British during the war. Have a volunteer from each group present his or her group's documentary outline to the class.

COOPERATIVE LEARNING

☆ CLOSE

Organize students into several small groups. Have members of each group discuss what they think are the most significant events of the War of 1812. *(Students' responses will vary but might include the Battle of Lake Erie, the Battle of the Thames, the Hartford Convention, the Battle of New Orleans, or the Treaty of Ghent.)* Give each group several sheets of poster board, and have them create a series of commemorative stamps depicting the most significant events of the war. Have members of each group present their group's stamps and explain their choices of events to the class. **COOPERATIVE LEARNING**

CONNECTING TO THE ARTS ANSWER

Students might suggest that the song is appealing because it describes an important U.S. victory and celebrates our nation's bravery and freedom.

Visual Record Answer

Students might suggest that the men in this image are engaged in peaceful pursuits.

★ ★ ★ ★ ★ ★ ★ ★ ★

Section 4 Review ANSWERS

❶ **Identify**
• Oliver Hazard Perry, p. 352
• Battle of Lake Erie, p. 352
• Battle of the Thames, p. 352
• Red Eagle, p. 353
• Andrew Jackson, p. 353
• Battle of Horseshoe Bend, p. 353
• Battle of New Orleans, p. 354
• Hartford Convention, p. 355
• Treaty of Ghent, p. 355

❷ Battle of Lake Erie—Perry leads a small U.S. fleet to victory, gains control of Great Lakes region; Battle of the Thames—Harrison leads U.S. troops to victory over British & Tecumseh's American Indian forces, Tecumseh is slain, border with Canada is secured; Battle of Horseshoe Bend—Jackson leads U.S. troops to victory over the Creek in the South, ending the Creek War;

CONNECTING TO THE ARTS

The National Anthem In September 1814 American Francis Scott Key witnessed the British attack on Fort McHenry. Key could see the American flag flying over the fort as the battle began. He anxiously waited as the British fired their cannons throughout the night. At 7:00 A.M. the mist and smoke finally cleared. Key saw that the American flag still flew above the fort. The British had lost the battle. Key was so moved with joy that he wrote the words to "The Star-Spangled Banner," which became the national anthem in 1931. **Why do you think "The Star-Spangled Banner" became so popular?**

---

onward into the city setting fire to the White House and other government buildings.

This destruction was in response to the Americans' earlier burning of the British capital in Canada. After the British left the city, one observer surveyed the damage. All that was left of the president's home were "unroofed, marked walls, cracked, defaced [damaged], blackened with the smoke of fire." The British sailed on to Baltimore, Maryland, which was guarded by Fort McHenry. The British fleet shelled the fort and its defenders for 25 hours.

History Makers Speak
"The attack on Fort McHenry . . . was distinctly [clearly] seen from Federal Hill, and from the tops of houses which were covered with men, women, and children. The night . . . presented the whole awful spectacle [sight] of shot and shells, and rockets, shooting and bursting through the air."

—Reporter for the *Salem Gazette*, quoted in *The Rockets' Red Glare*, by Scott S. Sheads

The Americans refused to surrender Fort McHenry. The British chose to retreat instead of continuing to fight.

✔ **Reading Check: Sequencing** What did Great Britain's military forces do after destroying much of the nation's capital? moved on to Baltimore, bombarded Fort McHenry, but withdrew when the Americans did not surrender

---

★ The Battle of New Orleans

After the attack on Washington, the British launched another offensive. From their Caribbean bases, they attacked New Orleans. They hoped to capture the city and thus take control of the Mississippi River. Andrew Jackson was in command of the U.S. forces around New Orleans. British troops advanced to within seven miles of the city. Startled, Jackson ordered his forces to make a stand. Jackson's troops were a mix of regular soldiers, state militia, and pirates led by Jean Laffite. They quickly constructed a wall of dirt and logs and waited for the attack.

The **Battle of New Orleans** began on the morning of January 8, 1815. Some 5,300 British troops attacked Jackson's force of 4,500. The British began marching toward the U.S. defenses under the cover of a thick morning fog. As they drew near, the air cleared. They were exposed to heavy fire from U.S. riflemen and artillery. Caught on an open field, the British were cut down with frightening speed. A militia member recalled the scene. "The field was entirely covered with . . . bodies. In some places they were lying in piles of several, one on top of the other." By the time the battle ended, more than 2,000 British soldiers had been killed or wounded. The Americans had suffered about 70 casualties.

✔ **Reading Check: Finding the Main Idea** What occurred at the Battle of New Orleans? Andrew Jackson and his troops won a convincing victory over a larger British force.

✪ REVIEW AND ASSESS

Have students complete the **Section 4 Review** on p. 355. Then have students complete **Daily Quiz 11.4**. As **Alternative Assessment**, you may want to use the warship graphic organizer or the commemorative stamp lesson from this section.

✪ RETEACH

Have students complete **Main Idea Activity for English Language Learners and Special-Needs Students 11.4**. Then ask them to create an annotated time line covering significant events of the War of 1812. Next to each event, have students identify the date it occurred and provide a brief summary of what happened and why the incident was important.
ENGLISH LANGUAGE LEARNERS

✪ EXTEND

Give students blank outline maps of the United States. Have them create a map depicting significant battles in the War of 1812. (You may want to give them a list of battles to include.) Have students create a legend for the map, identifying which side won each battle. Ask students to label each event, list the date each battle occurred, and identify which side won the battle. Finally, display students' maps throughout the classroom.
BLOCK SCHEDULING

⭐ Ending the War

Before the battle at New Orleans, New England Federalists gathered at Hartford, Connecticut, to oppose the war. This gathering became known as the **Hartford Convention**. Some delegates to the convention wanted New England to withdraw from the United States. However, moderate members convinced the convention to send a delegation to meet with Congress to try to increase states' rights.

Before this delegation reached Washington, however, news reached North America that the war had ended. Some critics accused them of treason. The Federalists' attempt to challenge the power of the national government proved costly. Humiliated, the Federalists lost much of their political power.

The peace agreement that caught the Federalists by surprise was the **Treaty of Ghent**. It had been signed in Belgium on December 24, 1814, before the Battle of New Orleans took place. After months of frustrating negotiations, U.S. and British diplomats finally agreed to end the war. Each nation returned the territory it had conquered. However, the diplomats found no solutions to the problems of impressment or trade embargoes. Both sides agreed to address the remaining issues once there was peace. For the United States, the War of 1812 was a narrow escape from potential disaster. But Americans were proud that their young nation had stood up to the mighty British.

✔ **Reading Check: Identifying Cause and Effect** What led to the Hartford Convention, and what effect did it have on the political future of the Federalist Party? New England opposition to the war, wanted to withdraw from the Union or increase states' rights; Federalist Party declined rapidly

THE GRANGER COLLECTION, NEW YORK

Interpreting the Visual Record

Peace treaty *The signing of the Treaty of Ghent was a relief for two nations tired of war.* **How does this image contrast with the battle scenes from the War of 1812?**

attack on Washington—British defeat U.S. forces and set fire to the White House; Battle of New Orleans—Jackson leads a major U.S. victory over British troops that actually took place after a peace treaty ending the war had been signed

❸ a. fought on the side of the British, helping them capture Fort Detroit; but they suffered serious defeats at the Battle of the Thames and the Battle of Horseshoe Bend.
b. British outnumbered Americans and burned Washington, D.C., but were defeated at Fort McHenry in Baltimore.

❹ Students' diary entries will vary, but should include the threat made at the Hartford Convention, terms of the Treaty of Ghent, and significance of the Battle of New Orleans.

CHAPTER 11 REVIEW ANSWERS

The Chapter at a Glance
Students' flash cards will vary but should include the main events of the chapter and the dates they occurred.

Identifying People and Ideas
Students' sentences should indicate an understanding of the following definitions:

1. chief justice of the Supreme Court who established the principle of judicial review

2. the Supreme Court has the right to declare an act of Congress unconstitutional

Section 4 Review

go.hrw.com Homework Practice Online
keyword: SA3 HP11

❶ **Identify and explain:**
• Oliver Hazard Perry
• Battle of Lake Erie
• Battle of the Thames
• Red Eagle
• Andrew Jackson
• Battle of Horseshoe Bend
• Battle of New Orleans
• Hartford Convention
• Treaty of Ghent

❷ **Comparing and Contrasting** Copy the chart below. Use it to compare and contrast the significant details of the major military battles fought on land and sea during the War of 1812.

Battle	Details (Winner, Location, Importance)

❸ **Finding the Main Idea**
a. What role did American Indians play in the War of 1812?
b. How did the war progress in the East?

❹ **Writing and Critical Thinking**
Evaluating Imagine that you are a member of President Madison's cabinet in 1815. Write a diary entry describing the events that took place at the end of the War of 1812 and their significance.

Consider the following:
• the Hartford Convention
• the Treaty of Ghent
• the Battle of New Orleans

REPRODUCIBLE
▶ Vocabulary Activity 11

TECHNOLOGY
▶ Chapter 11 Test Generator (on the One-Stop Planner)
▶ Global Skill Builder CD–ROM
▶ HRW Go site

REINFORCEMENT, REVIEW, AND ASSESSMENT
▶ Chapter 11 Review, pp. 355–357
▶ Chapter 11 Tutorial for Students, Parents, Mentors, and Peers

▶ Chapter 11 Test (Form A or B)
▶ Alternative Assessment Handbook
▶ Chapter 11 Test for English Language Learners and Special-Needs Students

★ **REVIEW**

Have students complete the **Chapter 11 Review** on pages 356–57.

★ **ASSESS**

Use one of the chapter tests to assess students' understanding of the content. For **Alternative Assessment**, see the **Alternative Assessment Handbook**.

3. purchase of land from France that doubled the size of the United States

4. expedition ordered by Jefferson to explore the Louisiana Purchase Territory

5. practice of forcing subjects to serve in the army or navy

6. Shawnee chief who wished to unite the American Indians of the Northwest Territory, the South, and the eastern Mississippi Valley; Americans defeated his forces, which eroded his support

7. members of Congress who supported declaring war on Great Britain

8. battle in which Jackson defeated the British after the signing of the Treaty of Ghent

9. gathering of New England Federalists to discuss the War of 1812

10. treaty between U.S. & Great Britain ending the War of 1812

Understanding Main Ideas

1. the Bank of the United States

2. Marbury wanted the Court to uphold the commission that former president Adams had issued.

3. they were vital to American trade

4. Great Britain and France go to war; both countries pass laws forbidding the U.S. to trade with their enemies; the *Chesapeake* incident; the Embargo and Non-Intercourse Acts; Congress declares war on Britain.

Chapter **11** Review

The Chapter at a Glance
Examine the visual summary of the chapter below. Create a set of flash cards listing the chapter's main events and the dates on which they occurred. Use your flash cards with a classmate to review the chapter content.

The Nation at War and Peace

1801
Marbury v. *Madison* gives the Supreme Court the power of judicial review.

1803
The United States doubles its size by making the Louisiana Purchase.

1807–09
Congress passes the Embargo and Non-Intercourse Acts.

1811
William Henry Harrison defeats Tecumseh's forces at the Battle of Tippecanoe.

1812
The War of 1812 begins between Great Britain and the United States.

1814
Federalists hold the Hartford Convention to protest the War of 1812.

1814
The Treaty of Ghent ends the War of 1812.

1815
Andrew Jackson wins the Battle of New Orleans.

Identifying People and Ideas
Use the following terms or people in historically significant sentences.
1. John Marshall
2. judicial review
3. Louisiana Purchase
4. Lewis and Clark expedition
5. impressment
6. Tecumseh
7. War Hawks
8. Battle of New Orleans
9. Hartford Convention
10. Treaty of Ghent

Understanding Main Ideas
Section 1 *(Pages 334–37)*
1. What Federalist policy did President Jefferson leave in place?
2. Why did the Supreme Court review *Marbury* v. *Madison*?

Section 2 *(Pages 338–43)*
3. Why were New Orleans and the Mississippi River important to the United States?

Section 3 *(Pages 344–49)*
4. Starting with the war between Great Britain and France, list the series of events that led to the U.S. declaration of war on Britain in 1812.

Section 4 *(Pages 350–55)*
5. Was the War of 1812 a success from the American point of view? Explain your answer, considering the reasons why war was declared.

You Be the Historian— Reviewing Themes
1. **Constitutional Heritage** What was the significance of the *Marbury* v. *Madison* decision, and what issues did it resolve?
2. **Geography** Why did President Jefferson send Lewis and Clark to explore the West, and what important information did they bring back?
3. **Global Relations** What conflicts arose between the United States and American Indians along the western frontier?

Thinking Critically
1. **Evaluating** Do you think that Thomas Jefferson was right to purchase Louisiana despite his concerns that doing so was unconstitutional? Explain your answer.
2. **Supporting a Point of View** Write a speech arguing whether or not Congress should declare war on Great Britain in 1812.
3. **Drawing Inferences and Conclusions** What danger did the United States risk when it declared war on Britain in 1812?

Organize students into four groups and assign each group one of the chapter's sections. Give each group a large sheet of butcher paper and have them illustrate the major events covered in the section they were assigned. Ask them to include captions for each illustration. Have members of each group present his or her group's work to the class. **ENGLISH LANGUAGE LEARNERS** , **COOPERATIVE LEARNING**

Portfolio Extensions

1. Cooperative Learning

Have students complete this activity in small groups. Ask them to write a play about Tecumseh based on information provided in this chapter. Students should prepare and present scenes with Tecumseh in different roles. Show Tecumseh (a) meeting with General Harrison; (b) discussing the Indian confederation with the Prophet; (c) asking leaders of the Creek nation to join his confederation; and (d) meeting with the Prophet after the Battle of Tippecanoe.

2. Linking to Community

Tell students that Francis Scott Key's "Star-Spangled Banner" celebrated America's victorious defense of Fort McHenry in 1814. Then have students write a poem or a short song about a person or group in their community who has produced a creative way to celebrate important events or achievements in that community. The person or group selected can be living in the community now or in the past.

Social Studies Skills Workshop

Interpreting Maps

Study the map below. Then use the information on the map to help you answer the questions that follow.

The Creek War

1. According to the map, where did the American victory in the Creek War take place?
   a. between the Alabama and Tallapoosa Rivers
   b. in Georgia near the border with the Mississippi Territory
   c. in Florida near the border with the Mississippi Territory
   d. in the Mississippi Territory near the border with Georgia

2. Based on your knowledge of the period, why was it significant that Jackson led his forces on to New Orleans after defeating the Creek?

Analyzing Primary Sources

Read the following quote from historian David Ramsay, who commented on the Louisiana Purchase in 1804, and then answer the questions that follow.

❝History affords no example of the acquisition of such important benefits, at so moderate a price, and under such favorable circumstances. . . . [Aside from independence and the Constitution] the acquisition of Louisiana is the greatest political blessing ever conferred on these states.❞

3. Which of the following best describes Ramsay's view of the Louisiana Purchase?
   a. The purchase was very valuable to the nation but still too expensive.
   b. The purchase was one of the most impressive achievements of the United States.
   c. The price of the purchase was fair, but the United States had little to gain from the new territory.
   d. The purchase was even more important than the Constitution.

4. What do you think Ramsay means when he calls the Louisiana Purchase "the greatest political blessing ever conferred on these states"?

5. Based on your knowledge of the period, do you agree or disagree with Ramsay's viewpoint on the importance of the Louisiana Purchase? Explain your answer.

Alternative Assessment

Building Your Portfolio

Interdisciplinary Connection to the Arts
Using the library and other available sources, research the role of the USS *Constitution* ("Old Ironsides") in the War of 1812. Use this information to build a model or make a sketch of the warship. Then use your model or sketch as a visual aid for a short oral report that you present to the class. Have a classmate ask and answer questions related to your work on the model.

🖳 internet connect

Internet Activity: go.hrw.com
keyword: SA3 CF11

Choose a topic on the Expanding Nation to:
● Explore the American West with Lewis and Clark.
● Research the causes and effects of the War of 1812, and write an analysis of its impact.
● Review the outcome of the last general election and compare it to the election of 1800.

---

5. Students responses will vary.

You Be the Historian— Reviewing Themes

1. defined the powers of the Supreme Court's powers more clearly; established the principle of judicial review

2. wanted them to explore the LA Purchase Territory; information about paths to the Rockies, animal and plant life, groups of American Indians in the West

3. Indians were angered by the Treaty of Greenville; Tecumseh tried to establish a confederacy to stop American expansion

Thinking Critically

1. Students' answers will vary.

2. Students' speeches will vary.

3. if the United States had lost the war, it might also have lost its independence

Skills Workshop

1. d

2. because the Treaty of Ghent had been signed already

3. b

4. purchasing Louisiana greatly expanded the nation's territorial and political power

5. Students' answers will vary.

LET'S GET STARTED!

Ask students to identify the age of the oldest person they know, such as a grandparent or a neighbor. *(Students' responses will most likely be under 100 years old.)* Then ask students if they have ever heard the United States referred to as a young country. Point out to students that the United States is just over 220 years old, probably more than twice the age of the oldest person that students know. Then ask the class to think of the United States as a developing child. In its first years, it was like an infant—13 states born along the Atlantic coastline. Then over time, it began to have growth spurts—growing larger and more self-sufficient with each addition of territory. Tell students that they will learn more about the growth of the United States in this unit.

★ TEACH

Have students read the Connecting to Geography lesson. Choose one or more of the following activities to explore the Connecting to Geography content with students.

★ Economics

Western Migration.
The economic potential of the western territories prompted many Americans to head west during the early 1800s. Only 1,000 settlers lived in present-day Alabama in 1800. Twenty years later, 128,000 people lived there. Mississippi experienced slower but still substantial growth rates. In 1800 some 8,000 Americans lived there. In 1820 the population reached 75,000. Louisiana more than doubled its population between 1810 and 1820, growing from 77,000 to 153,000 residents during that 10-year period.

CRITICAL THINKING
How did most settlers who moved to the southern regions hope to make their fortune?

ANSWER: They turned to agricultural pursuits. Some students might note that they used slave labor to grow cotton.

SKILLS ANSWERS
1. 5.7 million
2. 1810–1820

Connecting to Geography

The Growing Republic

In 1790 the United States was a new nation. The 13 states were all located on the eastern coast of North America. But pioneers had already begun to head west beyond the Appalachian Mountains. In 1803 the United States bought Louisiana from France. This Louisiana Purchase nearly doubled the size of the country.

The United States remained mostly a nation of farmers. Much of the young country's wealth, however, was based on trade with foreign nations.

Population and Trade

In 1790 the United States had nearly 4 million people. It stretched from the Atlantic Ocean to the Mississippi River. As the nation grew, so did its trade with other countries. But international conflicts sometimes caused foreign trade to rise or fall dramatically.

Geography Skills
Interpreting Bar Graphs

1. **Human Systems** How much did the U.S. population increase between 1790 and 1820?
2. **Analyzing Information** During which ten-year periods did the U.S. population increase the most?

U.S. Population Growth, 1790–1820

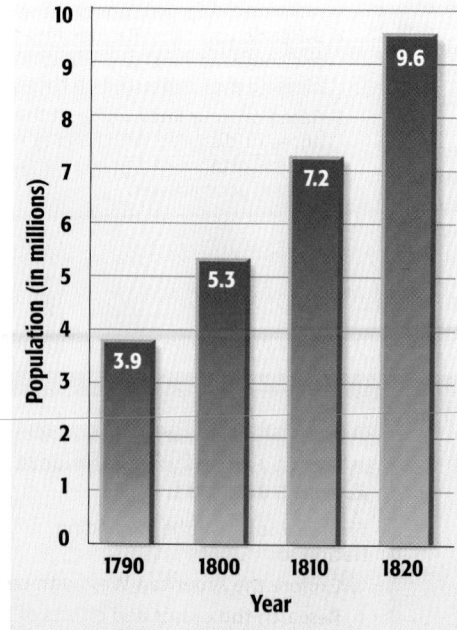

Population (in millions)

Year	Population
1790	3.9
1800	5.3
1810	7.2
1820	9.6

Source: *Historical Statistics of the United States*

History Note 1
The U.S. population more than doubled between 1790 and 1820. The number of Americans in the West grew particularly fast. In 1790 about 4 percent of the U.S. population lived west of the Appalachian Mountains. By 1820 this figure had grown significantly.

LEVEL 1: Review the information on p. 360 with students. Remind them that the United States was a country of many influences. Have students use newspapers and magazines to create a collage either 1) illustrating some of the nations that claimed territory in the United States or 2) illustrating American Indian influences that persist in today's culture. Have volunteers present their collages to the class.

ENGLISH LANGUAGE LEARNERS , COOPERATIVE LEARNING

 ALL LEVELS: Ask half of the class to imagine that they are importers of goods and the other half to imagine that they are exporters. Then assign each student a 10-year span from the graph on p. 359. Pair students with the same time period so that one student is an importer and one an exporter. Have students use the graph and the History Note on p. 359 along with what they have learned in class to explain trends in trade for their assigned time period. Ask pairs to share their information with the class.

ENGLISH LANGUAGE LEARNERS , COOPERATIVE LEARNING

 LEVEL 2: Have students use the map on p. 361 and the graph on p. 358 to create a dual-purpose time line for the period of 1790–1820. The time line will illustrate the physical growth of the United States as well as its population growth. Using five-year intervals, students should show U.S. population growth (in rounded figures) above the line and illustrate U.S. land growth (identifying the name of the territory and the current states located in its area) below the line.

Early American merchants sometimes listed their goods for sale in papers like this one. Decorated plates were one of many trade items.

History Note 2

Great Britain remained an important U.S. trading partner after the American Revolution. In 1790 more than a third of U.S. exports went to Britain. However, between 1790 and 1820 international conflicts sometimes made foreign trade difficult.

U.S. Imports and Exports, 1790–1820

○—○ Imports
○—○ Exports

Source: *Historical Statistics of the United States*

Geography **Skills**
Interpreting Line Graphs

1. Was the value of U.S. exports usually higher or lower than the value of imports from 1790 to 1820?
2. **Drawing Inferences and Conclusions** When were the values of U.S. exports and imports lowest? Why do you think trade was so low at those times?

ABBY ALDRICH ROCKEFELLER FOLK ART MUSEUM

This painting shows a scene of an ideal farm in the late 1700s.

★ Global Relations

Trade with Europe.
During the early years of the republic, the majority of U.S. exports were sent to Europe. Of the $20 million worth of goods exported in 1790, $13 million were shipped to Britain, France, Germany, and other European countries. Between 1790 and 1820, U.S. exports to non-European countries exceeded U.S.. exports to European countries only twice, in 1808 and 1814. In 1808 the United States exported $22 million worth of goods, but only $7 million went to Europe. In 1814, exports totaled only $7 million, with a mere $1 million worth of goods arriving in Europe.

CRITICAL THINKING

What types of events might lead to a drop in trade with a particular nation?

ANSWER: Students might suggest conflict with that nation or conflicts among other nations that cause unsafe shipping.

SKILLS ANSWERS
1. lower
2. 1814; Students might suggest that the United States and Great Britain were at war from 1812 through the beginning of 1815.

Upon completion, ask the class to identify any patterns or connections between the two fields of data. (*Students' time lines should reflect that the population increased with land growth.*)

 LEVEL 3: Explain to the class that as the nation grew in population, many settlers moved west to claim land. Have students read the History Note on p. 358. Then ask them to imagine what it must have been like for the people who were used to living in isolation to suddenly become surrounded by the people who were moving west. Organize the class into small groups and have each group create a skit that reflects the reactions of those already on the frontier to the western settlers. Have each group perform its skit for the class.
COOPERATIVE LEARNING

★ CLOSE

Have students look at the map on p. 361. Ask students to create a description of the United States in the 1820s for someone who has never been to the United States. Students should answer some or all of the following questions in their descriptions: What states and territories make up each geographic region of the United States? What other nations have claims to lands near parts of the United States? What bodies of water form natural boundaries for the United States? What is the distance from the northernmost point to the southernmost point of the United States? What is the distance from the easternmost point to the westernmost point of the United States? Once students have completed the assignment, have volunteers present their descriptions to the class.

★ Citizenship

The Treaty of Greenville.
Eleven American Indian nations signed the Treaty of Greenville, which gave most of the Ohio Valley to the United States. Representatives from the Delaware, Kaskaskia, Kickapoo, Miami, Ojibwa, Ottawa, Piankasha, Shawnee, and other nations met at a fort in northwestern Ohio to sign the treaty. In exchange for the lands that they gave away, the American Indians received a guarantee that the lands they retained would be off-limits to U.S. settlers. However, the government did not enforce the agreement, and settlers continued to move onto Indian lands.

CRITICAL THINKING

What options did the Ohio Valley Indians have to respond to the broken treaties?

ANSWER: They could either go to war or move west.

SKILLS ANSWERS

1. Cherokee, Chickasaw, Choctaw, Creek, Iroquois, Miami, Potawatomi, Sauk Fox, Shawnee

2. mountainous, few rivers

3. in Florida, in present-day Texas, and in the Southwest and the Far West

---

The Expanding Nation

The territory of the United States expanded greatly between 1790 and 1820. But the United States still competed with American Indians and foreign nations for land.

The United States, 1790

[Map of the United States, 1790, showing territories, rivers, mountains, and Native American tribes]

Legend:
- U.S. territory
- Spanish territory
- British territory
- Disputed territory
- Northwest Territory
- Spanish settlements and missions
- UTE Native American tribe

0   250   500 Miles
0   250   500 Kilometers
Albers Equal-Area Projection

Geography **Skills**
Interpreting Political Maps

1. What major American Indian peoples still populated U.S. territory in 1790?
2. **Physical Systems** In what ways was the physical geography of western North America different from the central and eastern parts of the continent?
3. **Summarizing** In what parts of the present-day United States were many Spanish settlements located?

History Note 3

The United States in 1790 was primarily a rural nation, with the vast majority of people living on farms. Only 24 U.S. cities had a population of more than 2,500.

History Note 4

Many American Indians in the West resisted the movement of settlers onto their lands. However, gradually most American Indian groups lost their lands to the expanding United States. By the 1790s treaties opened land to settlers throughout the Trans-Appalachian West. These areas included lands in Georgia, New York, North Carolina, and present-day Tennessee. A series of battles took place with American Indians in the Ohio Valley region. After a 1795 treaty, nearly two thirds of what is now the state of Ohio was opened for settlement.

Have students review the information in the Connecting to Geography Unit 5. Then have students complete Geography and History Quiz 5.

⭐ RETEACH

Tell students that you can often learn a lot about a time period by looking at paintings and photos from that particular time period. Have students look at the painting on p. 359. Then have them write a few sentences explaining what everyday life may have been like in early America. Encourage students to describe the chores that people appear to be doing, the plants and animals around them, and the types of housing and transportation shown. **ENGLISH LANGUAGE LEARNERS**

⭐ EXTEND

Have students interview at least 10 people in their community about their backgrounds and the places from which their families originated—family members are not permitted. Then instruct students to tally the class's results and convert the figures into percentages of the total group surveyed. Have students create a pie chart representing the diversity of people in their community. Then provide students with census figures about the ethnic makeup of the U.S. population. Have students create a pie chart representing this information. Finally, have students write a paragraph describing how their community's ethnic makeup compares to that of the United States. **BLOCK SCHEDULING**

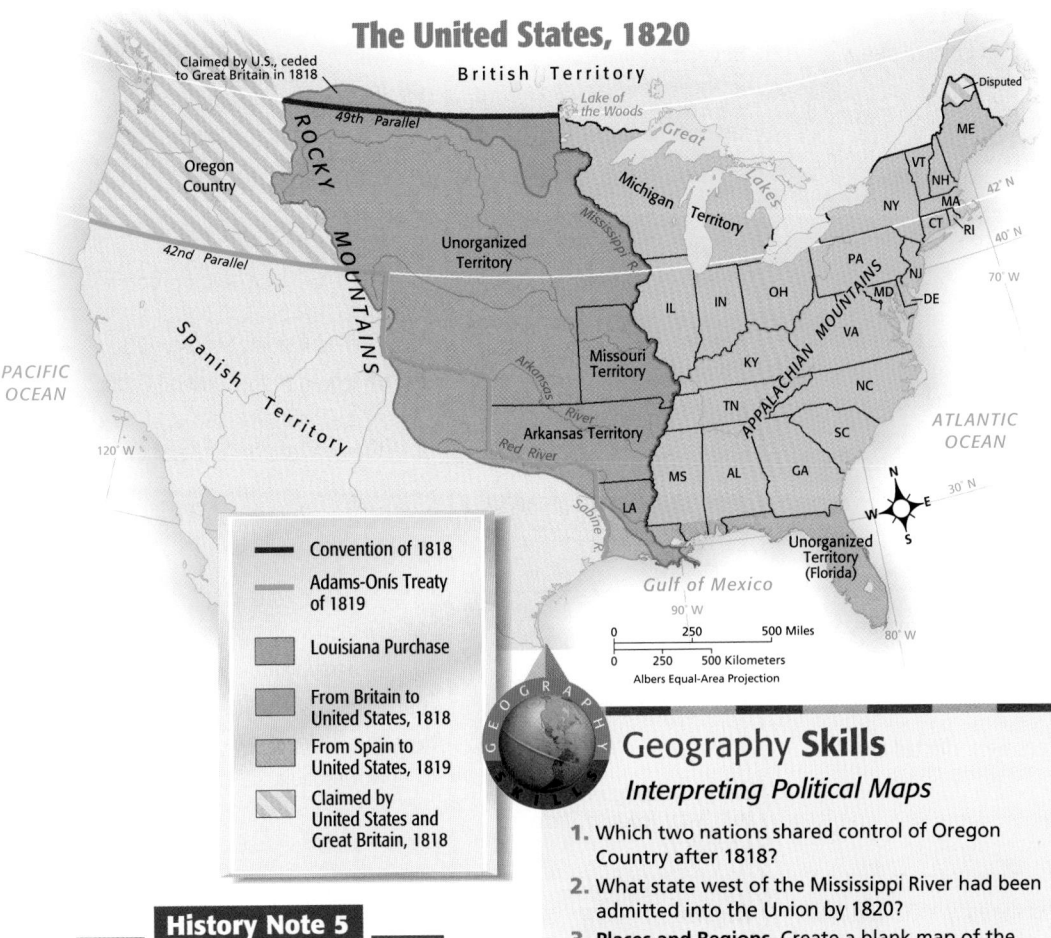

The United States, 1820

Legend:
- Convention of 1818
- Adams-Onís Treaty of 1819
- Louisiana Purchase
- From Britain to United States, 1818
- From Spain to United States, 1819
- Claimed by United States and Great Britain, 1818

Geography Skills
Interpreting Political Maps

1. Which two nations shared control of Oregon Country after 1818?
2. What state west of the Mississippi River had been admitted into the Union by 1820?
3. **Places and Regions** Create a blank map of the United States. Ask a fellow student to draw in the U.S. borders established by the Convention of 1818 and the Adams-Onís Treaty of 1819.
4. **Analyzing Information** What physical features helped form the western boundary of the Louisiana Purchase and the Adams–Onís Treaty?

Interdisciplinary Connection

▶MATH◀

Land. In 1790 the United States and its territories totaled 888,811 square miles. The Louisiana Purchase of 1803 added an additional 827,192 square miles of land. After the 1819 treaty negotiations with Spain, the United States received Florida, which as 58,560 square miles, as well as other territories that totaled 13,443 square miles.

ACTIVITY: Have students determine the size of the United States at the end of 1803 and at the end of 1819. *(1803—1,716,003 square miles; 1819—1,788,006 square miles).* Then have students determine the percentage of the 1819 total that came from the Louisiana Purchase *(46.3 percent)* and the lands acquired from Spain *(4 percent).*

SKILLS ANSWERS
1. the United States and Great Britain
2. Louisiana
3. the Rocky Mountains, the 42nd parallel, and the Red River

History Note 5

Immigration has always been an important contributor to the U.S. population. The original thirteen colonies that became the United States were mostly populated by immigrants from Great Britain. There were also sizable numbers of immigrants from Germany. After the Revolutionary War, overall immigration slowed. By 1820 more people were coming to the United States from Ireland than from Great Britain.

History Note 6

As American settlers moved westward, the abundance of land and other resources helped support large families. In fact, the average American household was significantly larger than households in Europe. An average free household in the United States had 6 members, compared to an average of 4.5 persons in British homes. A higher birthrate and rising standard of living in the United States help explain this difference in size.

Objectives	Pacing Guide	Reproducible Resources
SECTION 1: **The Rise of Nationalism** (pp. 364–67) ★ Examine how the United States settled its land disputes with Great Britain and Spain. ★ Analyze President Monroe's reasons for issuing the Monroe Doctrine, and describe its most important points.	**Regular** 2 days **Block Scheduling** 1 day *Block Scheduling Handbook with Team Teaching Strategies, Chapter 12*	**RS** Guided Reading Strategy 12.1
SECTION 2: **Expansion and Improvements** (pp. 368–73) ★ Discuss the issues that the Missouri Compromise was supposed to address. ★ Analyze how improvements in transportation affected the United States. ★ Explain why the 1824 presidential election was controversial.	**Regular** 2 days **Block Scheduling** 1 day *Block Scheduling Handbook with Team Teaching Strategies, Chapter 12*	**RS** Guided Reading Strategy 12.2 **PS** Biography Reading 12: Henry Clay **E** Hands-On History Activity: Writers of Your Region
SECTION 3: **The Age of Jackson** (pp. 374–79) ★ Examine how Jacksonian Democracy was a sign of change in American politics. ★ Explore how tariff disputes lead to the nullification crisis and how President Jackson responded to it. ★ Describe why President Jackson was against a national bank and how his resistance affected the economy.	**Regular** 2 days **Block Scheduling** 1 day *Block Scheduling Handbook with Team Teaching Strategies, Chapter 12*	**RS** Guided Reading Strategy 12.3 **PS** American History Political Cartoon 6: Jackson and the Bank **E** Creative Teaching Strategy: Continuum
SECTION 4: **Indian Removal** (pp. 380–84) ★ Explain why the federal and state governments began an American Indian removal policy. ★ Examine how American Indians such as the Cherokee resisted removal. ★ Describe how American Indians were affected by the removal from their lands.	**Regular** 2 days **Block Scheduling** 1 day *Block Scheduling Handbook with Team Teaching Strategies, Chapter 12*	**RS** Guided Reading Strategy 12.4 **SM** Geography Activity 12: The Seminole Wars **PS** Primary Source Reading 12: The Trail of Tears **RS** Graphic Organizer 12: Contributors to the New Nation
SECTION 5: **American Culture** (pp. 385–88) ★ Examine the favorite writers of the early 1800s and what they wrote about. ★ Describe the focus of the Hudson River school.	**Regular** 1.5 days **Block Scheduling** .5 day *Block Scheduling Handbook with Team Teaching Strategies, Chapter 12*	**RS** Guided Reading Strategy 12.5 **PS** Literature Reading 12: "Rip Van Winkle"

Chapter Resource Key

PS	Primary Sources	**A**	Assessment		Music
RS	Reading Support	**REV**	Review		Video
IC	Interdisciplinary Connections	**ELL**	Reinforcement and English Language Learners		Internet
E	Enrichment		Transparencies		Holt Presentation Maker Using Microsoft® PowerPoint®
SM	Skills Mastery		CD-ROM		

 One-Stop Planner CD-ROM

See the *One-Stop Planner* for a complete list of additional resources for students and teachers.

One-Stop Planner CD–ROM

It's easy to plan lessons, select resources, and print out materials for your students when you use the **One-Stop Planner CD–ROM with Test Generator.**

Technology Resources	**Reinforcement, Review, and Assessment**

 One-Stop Planner, Lesson 12.1
Homework Practice Online

REV Section 1 Review, p. 367
A Daily Quiz 12.1
ELL Main Idea Activity 12.1
ELL English Audio Summary 12.1
ELL Spanish Audio Summary 12.1

 One-Stop Planner, Lesson 12.2
 American Music Selection 9: "The Erie Canal"
 Holt Researcher: American History CD–ROM
Homework Practice Online

REV Section 2 Review, p. 373
A Daily Quiz 12.2
ELL Main Idea Activity 12.2
ELL English Audio Summary 12.2
ELL Spanish Audio Summary 12.2

 One-Stop Planner, Lesson 12.3
Homework Practice Online
HRW Go site

REV Section 3 Review, p. 379
A Daily Quiz 12.3
ELL Main Idea Activity 12.3
ELL English Audio Summary 12.3
ELL Spanish Audio Summary 12.3

 One-Stop Planner, Lesson 12.4
 Everyday Life in America Transparency 7: Portrait of Native Americans, 1833
 Linking Geography and History Transparency 12: Native American Resistance, 1830–1861
CNN. Presents America: Yesterday and Today, Beginnings to 1914 Segment: Living in America–the Choctaw
Homework Practice Online

REV Section 4 Review, p. 384
A Daily Quiz 12.4
ELL Main Idea Activity 12.4
ELL English Audio Summary 12.4
ELL Spanish Audio Summary 12.4

 One-Stop Planner, Lesson 12.5
 Art in American History Transparency 5: Monticello, and Transparency 9: Fur Traders Descending the Missouri
Homework Practice Online

REV Section 5 Review, p. 388
A Daily Quiz 12.5
ELL Main Idea Activity 12.5
ELL English Audio Summary 12.5
ELL Spanish Audio Summary 12.5

internet connect

HRW ONLINE RESOURCES
GO TO: go.hrw.com
Then type in a keyword.

TEACHER HOME PAGE
KEYWORD: SA3 Teacher

CHAPTER INTERNET ACTIVITIES
KEYWORD: SA3 CF12
• learn about the war of independence in Greece.
• research James Fenimore Cooper and the development of an American culture in art and literature.
• create a newspaper about Andrew Jackson and the politics of the 1830s.

CHAPTER ENRICHMENT LINKS
KEYWORD: SA3 CH12

ONLINE ASSESSMENT
Homework Practice
KEYWORD: SA3 HP12

Standardized Test Prep
KEYWORD: SA3 STP12

Rubrics
KEYWORD: SS Rubrics

ONLINE MAPS, CHARTS, AND GRAPHS
KEYWORD: SA3 MCG
• Male Suffrage
• Slavery Compromises

CONTENT UPDATES
KEYWORD: SS Content Updates

HOLT PRESENTATION MAKER
KEYWORD: SA3 PPT12

ONLINE READING SUPPORT
KEYWORD: SS Strategies

CURRENT EVENTS
KEYWORD: S3 Current Events

Meeting Individual Needs

Ability Levels

Level 1 Basic-level activities designed for all students encountering new material

Level 2 Intermediate-level activities designed for average students

Level 3 Challenging activities designed for honors and gifted-and-talented students

English Language Learners Activities that address the needs of students with Limited English Proficiency

Chapter Review and Assessment

IC Vocabulary Activity 12
 Global Skill Builder CD–ROM
HRW Go site
REV Chapter 12 Tutorial for Students, Parents, Mentors, and Peers
REV Chapter 12 Review, pp. 389–91
Chapter 12 Test Generator (on the One-Stop Planner)

A Chapter 12 Test (Form A or B)
A Alternative Assessment Handbook
A Chapter 12 Test for English Language Learners and Special-Needs Students

Build on What You Know

If You Were There...

Ask students to answer the following question:

What would you do to help the country?

Consider:
- the economy
- relations with foreign countries

You Be the Historian

What's Your Opinion?

To help students create their **Themes** Journal entries, provide the following examples of appropriate **agree**/**disagree** statements.

EXPLORING THE TIME LINE
GL BAL EVENTS

CHAPTER

12 A New National Identity
(1812–1840)

These five-dollar gold coins were issued by the U.S. Mint.

The Erie Canal was opened in 1825 and greatly reduced the cost of shipping goods from Buffalo to New York City.

UNITED STATES

1816 James Monroe is elected president.

1817 Work on the Erie Canal begins.

1819 Spain and the United States sign the Adams-Onís Treaty in February, giving Florida to the United States.

In March the Supreme Court establishes the constitutionality of the Second Bank of the United States in *McCulloch v. Maryland.*

1824 John Quincy Adams is elected president.

1812	1815	1818	1821	1824

1815 Napoléon returns to power in France but is defeated at the Battle of Waterloo.

1819 Simon Bolívar becomes president of Gran Colombia.

1822 Brazil declares independence from Portugal.

1824 Simon Bolívar becomes president of Peru.

WORLD

The Brazilian Empire used this flag after it declared independence from Portugal.

The Duke of Wellington led an army of allied European nations to victory over Napoléon's French forces at the Battle of Waterloo.

Build on What You Know

The United States had survived a second war with Great Britain. Although the nation was at peace, there were still unresolved disputes with foreign powers. A rising sense of nationalism and an expansion of democracy played key roles in shaping American identity as the young nation began to assert itself.

Global Relations

Agree Nations can resolve land issues through mediation.

Disagree Land is too valuable to surrender without a fight.

Citizenship

Agree In a strong democracy, all people must have the right to vote.

Disagree The military strength of a democracy makes it strong.

Constitutional Heritage

Agree The federal government should not be all-powerful.

Disagree The federal government is supreme and all states must follow its laws.

THE GRANGER COLLECTION, NEW YORK

This picture of Jackson was carried by supporters during one of his presidential campaigns.

Andrew Jackson, shown standing before a crowd of well-wishers, received a record number of popular votes in 1828.

The Whig Party. The Whig Party was formally established in 1834. This new political party was a loose coalition of groups that opposed President Andrew Jackson. The Whigs believed Jackson held too much power and was becoming a kinglike tyrant. One reason for the lack of success of the Whigs was that they never fully established a party program. In 1836 the Whigs nominated three candidates, hoping to appeal to all sections of the United States and divide the electoral vote. It was not until the presidential election of 1840, when their candidate William Henry Harrison won the election, that the Whigs gained enough political power to become a dominant force in the federal government. Unfortunately for the Whigs, Harrison died after only a month in office and his successor, John Tyler, failed to fulfill Whig expectations.

CRITICAL THINKING

Why might John Tyler have failed to meet Whig expectations?

ANSWER: Students' might suggest that even though Tyler was Harrison's vice president, he did not support Whig legislation or policies, or that his opinions were not as strong as Harrison's.

1828 Andrew Jackson is elected president.

1830 Congress passes the Indian Removal Act.

1834 Opponents of Andrew Jackson form the Whig Party.

1836 Martin Van Buren is elected president.

1838 The Trail of Tears begins, as U.S. troops remove the Cherokee from Georgia.

1827   1830   1833   1836   1839

1829 The Ottoman Empire recognizes the independence of Greece.

1832 A British reform bill doubles the number of British men who can vote.

1835 Dutch colonists in Africa, known as the Boers, begin their Great Trek into the African interior.

1839 The Opium War breaks out between Britain and China.

If you were there . . .
What would you do to help the country?

You Be the Historian

What's Your Opinion? Do you **agree** or **disagree** with the following statements? Support your point of view in your journal.

- **Global Relations** Disputes over land can be resolved without armed force.
- **Citizenship** Voting rights make a democracy stronger.
- **Constitutional Heritage** States should have the right to ignore federal laws with which they disagree.

Section 1

OBJECTIVES

★ Examine how the United States settled its land disputes with Great Britain and Spain.

★ Analyze President Monroe's reasons for issuing the Monroe Doctrine, and describe its most important points.

SECTION **1** RESOURCES

REPRODUCIBLE

▶ Guided Reading Strategy 12.1

TECHNOLOGY

▶ One-Stop Planner, Lesson 12.1

▶ Homework Practice Online

REINFORCEMENT, REVIEW, AND ASSESSMENT

▶ Section 1 Review, p. 367

▶ Daily Quiz 12.1

▶ Main Idea Activity 12.1

▶ English Audio Summary 12.1

▶ Spanish Audio Summary 12.1

LET'S GET STARTED!

Write the following phrase on the chalkboard: *Good Feelings.* As students enter the classroom, ask them how they would explain the phrase to a foreign visitor. *(Students' responses will vary but students will most likely relate their responses to their personal experiences.)* Tell students that the expression was used to describe the way U.S. citizens felt during President Monroe's term of office. Explain to students that in Section 1 they will study the reasons that Monroe's presidency is known as the Era of Good Feelings.

Section 1

The Rise of Nationalism

Read to Discover

1. How did the United States settle its land disputes with Great Britain and Spain?
2. Why did President Monroe issue the Monroe Doctrine, and what were its most important points?

WHY IT MATTERS TODAY

Border disputes often lead to more serious international conflicts. Use **CNN fyi.com** or other **current events** sources to learn about a recent border dispute between countries. Record your findings in your journal.

Identify

- James Monroe
- Rush-Bagot Agreement
- Convention of 1818
- Adams-Onís Treaty
- Simon Bolívar
- Monroe Doctrine

The Story Continues

James Monroe greatly admired the French republic. Yet he believed that the United States could become the greatest republic ever. He shared these views with his daughter Eliza while they walked through the streets of Paris. When Eliza noted that the French had better roads, Monroe answered, "That's true, our country may be likened to a new house. We lack many things, but we possess the most precious of all—liberty!"

James Monroe was close friends with former presidents Thomas Jefferson and James Madison.

★ The Era of Good Feelings

After the War of 1812, the United States enjoyed a time of peace. National pride began to grow. By 1817, journalists had begun calling this time the Era of Good Feelings. The previous year **James Monroe**, a Republican, had easily won the presidency over Federalist Rufus King. Running unopposed, Monroe won re-election in 1820. During his presidency, the United States resolved several conflicts with foreign powers.

The Treaty of Ghent had ended the war with Britain. However, the United States and British Canada still disagreed about who controlled the waterways along their borders. Both countries wanted to keep their navies and fishing rights on the Great Lakes. In the spring of 1817, the two sides compromised by reaching the **Rush-Bagot Agreement**.

★ TEACH

Have students read Section 1 and complete Guided Reading Strategy 12.1. Choose one or more of the following activities to explore the section content with students. For further suggestions on block scheduling or team teaching, see the *Block Scheduling Handbook with Team Teaching Strategies.*

LEVEL 1: Discuss President Monroe's reasons for issuing the Monroe Doctrine and its most important points with the class. Then give each student a large sheet of butcher paper, and tell them that they have been hired to place billboards at U.S. ports of entry. Explain to students that the purpose of these billboards is to convey the Monroe Doctrine's message to foreign diplomats and naval personnel in a visually appealing design. **ENGLISH LANGUAGE LEARNERS**

HOMEWORK Have students write a paragraph explaining whether the United States had a right or duty to limit European access to the Western Hemisphere.

ALL LEVELS: Copy the graphic organizer on the next page onto the chalkboard, omitting the italicized answers. Have students complete the organizer to learn how the United States settled its land disputes with Great Britain and Spain. **ENGLISH LANGUAGE LEARNERS**

Secretary of State Richard Rush negotiated this treaty. It limited naval power on the Great Lakes for both the United States and British Canada. Another treaty, known as the **Convention of 1818**, gave the United States fishing rights off parts of the Newfoundland and Labrador coasts. It also set the border between the United States and Canada at the 49th parallel. This border extended as far west as the Rocky Mountains. In addition, both countries agreed to jointly occupy part of the Pacific Northwest.

✔ **Reading Check: Finding the Main Idea** How did the United States use compromise to settle its border disputes with British Canada? It reached the Rush-Bagot Agreement and the Convention of 1818.

★ The Issue of Florida

Another dispute involved the U.S. border with Spanish Florida. Some Americans wanted to settle in the area. Others were angered by raids on U.S. towns made by Seminole Indians from Florida. The Seminole also aided runaway slaves. In 1818 Secretary of State John Quincy Adams held talks with Spanish diplomat Luis de Onís about allowing American settlers into Florida. Meanwhile, President Monroe sent troops under the command of General Andrew Jackson to secure the border.

In April 1818 Jackson's troops invaded Florida to capture Seminole raiders, thus beginning the First Seminole War. During the war, Jackson fought the Spanish as well as the Seminole. He took over most of Spain's important military posts and overthrew the governor of Florida. He commited these acts against Spain without receiving direct orders from President Monroe.

Jackson's actions upset both British and Spanish leaders. "We can hardly believe that any thing so offensive to public decorum [proper behavior] could be admitted, *even in America!*" reported one London

★★★★★★★★★★★★
That's Interesting!
★★★★★★★★★★★★

Mistaken Identity Can you imagine the president of the United States being mistaken for a clerk? It happened to James Monroe. When a European diplomat paid a visit to the White House during Monroe's presidency, he came upon a man writing at a desk. The man had no wig and wore a dirty waistcoat spotted with ink. Ragged slippers hung on his feet. The diplomat was surprised that the president would hire such a messy assistant. Imagine his shock when he discovered this man was the president himself!

Interpreting the Visual Record

The Fourth of July *By 1819, when Joseph Krimmel painted* Fourth of July Celebration in Centre Square, *the Fourth of July had become a popular holiday celebrating the birth of the young United States.* **What parts of this picture suggest that a national holiday is being celebrated?**

★ Citizenship

The Election of 1816.
In the race for the presidency, James Monroe had no difficulty gaining President Madison's support, but he did have problems winning his party's nomination. Noting that Thomas Jefferson, Madison, and Monroe were all Virginians, some Democratic-Republicans argued that the presidential candidate in 1816 should come from a different state. These people supported Secretary of War William Crawford, who was from Georgia. In a party meeting during March 1816, Monroe defeated Crawford for the party nomination by just 11 votes. Daniel Tompkins of New York easily won the vice presidential nomination.

CRITICAL THINKING

Why would some party members oppose the election of another Virginian to the presidency?

ANSWER: Students might suggest that Virginia's interests might dominate government policy if the president always came from that state.

Visual Record Answer

Students might suggest that the flags indicate a national holiday is being celebrated.

Compromise with Great Britain

Rush-Bagot Agreement Terms:

- limited naval power on the Great Lakes

Convention of 1818 Terms:

- gave the United States fishing rights off parts of Newfoundland and Labrador coasts
- established a border between the United States and Canada at the 49th parallel, as far west as the Rockies
- agreed to joint occupation of the Pacific Northwest

Compromise with Spain

Adams-Onís Treaty Terms:

- Spain gave Florida to the United States.
- The United States gave up claims to present-day Texas.
- United States took responsibility for up to $5 million of United States citizen's claims against Spain.

LEVEL 3: Have students write a newspaper article about the Monroe Doctrine. The class should write either from a U.S. perspective or a European perspective. Encourage students to include a headline and a cartoon or illustration. Finally, lead a class discussion on the various perspectives on the Monroe Doctrine.

★ CLOSE

Have each student create a chart comparing the conflicts over the northern and southern borders of the United States. Have students consider the following topics on their charts: the nation with which the conflict occurred, the causes of the disagreement, the actions taken to resolve the disputes, and the final results.

★ Citizenship

Politics and the Monroe Doctrine. The Monroe Doctrine is remembered as an important foreign policy declaration, but it also played a role in the presidential ambitions of John Quincy Adams. Adams hoped to succeed Monroe in the White House, but he knew that many Americans were suspicious of him because he desired close relations with Great Britain. When the British wanted to issue a joint declaration opposing European influence in the Americas, Adams persuaded Monroe to issue the doctrine without British involvement. Strongly nationalistic Americans approved of this decision, and Adams was not attacked as pro-British in the 1824 election.

CRITICAL THINKING

How can domestic political issues influence foreign affairs?

ANSWER: Student answers might mention that political leaders will try to reflect popular opinion in formulating policy.

ANALYZING PRIMARY SOURCES ANSWERS

1. Monroe warned that European "interposition" in Latin America would be seen as hostile to the U.S.
2. Students' answers will vary.

Analyzing Primary Sources

Drawing Inferences and Conclusions How would the reader know that Jackson is a powerful leader? by the willingness of so many soldiers to rise up at his call

journal. Most Americans, however, were in favor of Jackson. One U.S. newspaper of the time described Jackson's popularity and power.

History Makers Speak

"Among the people of the West, his popularity is unbounded [unlimited]. . . . At his call, 50,000 of the most efficient warriors on this continent would rise, armed, and ready for any enemy."

—*Niles' Weekly Register*, quoted in *A Diplomatic History of the American People*, by Thomas A. Bailey

Jackson's presence in Florida helped convince Spanish leaders to settle all border disputes with the United States in the **Adams-Onís Treaty** of 1819. Under this treaty, Spain gave East Florida to the United States and gave up its claims to West Florida. In return, the United States gave up its claims to what is now Texas. The United States also agreed to take responsibility for up to $5 million of U.S. citizens' claims against Spain.

✔ **Reading Check: Summarizing** What disagreements did the United States have with Spain over Florida, and how were these settled? border disputes; by the Adams-Onís Treaty, which gave Florida to the United States for claims to Texas and paying claims of U.S. citizens

★ The Monroe Doctrine

At the time of the Adams-Onís Treaty, Spain had other problems. The Spanish colonies of Central and South America began to challenge Spanish rule. By the early 1820s most of these Latin American countries had declared independence from Spain. Revolutionary fighter

Historical Document

THE MONROE DOCTRINE

On December 2, 1823, President James Monroe issued what became known as the Monroe Doctrine. The following is an excerpt from the doctrine, which has had a significant effect on U.S. foreign policy.

We . . . declare that we should consider any attempt on their [European powers'] part to extend their [political] system to any portion of this hemisphere as dangerous to our peace and safety.

With the existing colonies or dependencies of any European power we have not interfered and shall not interfere. But with the governments who have declared their independence and maintained it, and whose independence we have . . . acknowledged, we could not view any **interposition**[1] for the purpose of **oppressing**[2] them, or controlling in any other manner their destiny, by any European power in any other light than as the **manifestation**[3] of an unfriendly disposition toward the United States.

---

[1] **interposition:** interference [2] **oppressing:** unjustly ruling [3] **manifestation:** evidence

Analyzing Primary Sources

1. What warning did President Monroe give to the European powers in the Monroe Doctrine?
2. What do you think is most important about this document?

A replica of the Monroe Doctrine

★ REVIEW AND ASSESS

Have students complete the **Section 1 Review** on p. 367. Then have students complete **Daily Quiz 12.1**. As **Alternative Assessment**, you may want to use the compromise graphic organizer or the newspaper exercise in this section's lessons.

★ RETEACH

Have students complete **Main Idea Activity for English Language Learners and Special-Needs Students 12.1**. Then tell students that they have been asked by President Monroe to create from the Monroe Doctrine an outline that he can refer to while giving a speech. Have students work in groups to write their outlines. Then display the outlines around the classroom, and ask a volunteer from each group to present his or her group's outlines. **ENGLISH LANGUAGE LEARNERS**, **COOPERATIVE LEARNING**

★ EXTEND

Organize the class into two groups. Have one group find examples of how the United States has relied on the Monroe Doctrine, while the other group looks for examples of European opposition to this policy. Ask members of each group to present their findings to the class. **COOPERATIVE LEARNING**, **BLOCK SCHEDULING**

<u>Simon Bolívar</u>, hailed as *the Liberator,* led many of these struggles. The revolutions in Latin America reminded most American leaders of the American Revolution. As a result, they supported the struggles for independence. In 1818 the *Nashville Whig* reported a toast given at a public dinner in Tennessee.

Simon Bolívar led the revolutions against Spanish rule in what are now the nations of Bolivia, Columbia, Ecuador, and Peru.

> **❝***The patriots of South America:* palsied [paralyzed] be the arm that would wrest [take] from them the standard of liberty for which they have so nobly struggled. Six cheers!**❞**
>
> —*Nashville Whig,* quoted in *Life of Andrew Jackson* by James Parton

Yet Latin American independence worried President Monroe. He thought that European powers might try to take control of the newly independent Latin American countries. Secretary of State Adams and President Monroe decided to warn European powers not to interfere with the Americas. Delivered on December 2, 1823, this warning became known as the **Monroe Doctrine**. It stated that foreign powers should not create new colonies in North and South America. The United States would view any European interference with Latin American governments as a hostile act.

Some Europeans strongly criticized the Monroe Doctrine. The French foreign minister said that the doctrine "ought to be resisted by all the powers having commercial or territorial interests in the hemisphere." Despite such threats, few European countries challenged the Monroe Doctrine, which has played a major role in shaping U.S.–Latin American relations.

✔ **Reading Check: Analyzing Information** What did the Monroe Doctrine accomplish? It discouraged European nations from further colonizing North and South America.

Section 1 Review

go.hrw.com Homework Practice Online keyword: SA3 HP12

❶ Identify and explain:
• James Monroe
• Rush-Bagot Agreement
• Convention of 1818
• Adams-Onís Treaty
• Simon Bolívar
• Monroe Doctrine

❷ Sequencing Copy the graphic organizer below. Use it to describe how the United States responded to foreign-policy problems during Monroe's presidency. List the date of each response.

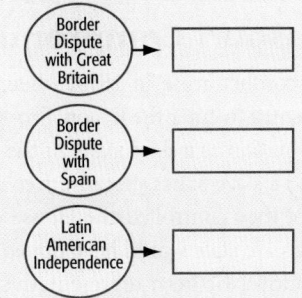

❸ Finding the Main Idea
a. How did the United States settle its conflict with Great Britain over Canada, and why was resolving the conflict important to both nations?

b. What caused a dispute between the United States and Spain during Monroe's presidency, and how was this dispute settled?

❹ Writing and Critical Thinking
Supporting a Point of View Imagine that you are a U.S. ambassador. Write a memo to the secretary of state explaining your opinion of the Monroe Doctrine.

Consider the following:
• the main points of the doctrine
• U.S. views on Latin American independence
• the potential dangers of European involvement in Latin America

A New National Identity **367**

Section 2

OBJECTIVES

★ Discuss the issues that the Missouri Compromise was supposed to address.

★ Analyze how improvements in transportation affected the United States.

★ Explain why the 1824 presidential election was controversial.

SECTION 2 RESOURCES

REPRODUCIBLE

▶ Guided Reading Strategy 12.2

▶ Biography Reading 12: Henry Clay

TECHNOLOGY

▶ One-Stop Planner, Lesson 12.2

▶ American Music Selection 9: "The Erie Canal"

▶ Holt Researcher: American History CD–ROM

▶ Homework Practice Online

REINFORCEMENT, REVIEW, AND ASSESSMENT

▶ Section 2 Review, p. 373

▶ Daily Quiz 12.2

▶ Main Idea Activity 12.2

▶ English Audio Summary 12.2

▶ Spanish Audio Summary 12.2

 **LET'S GET STARTED!**

Write the following instructions on the chalkboard: *Name cities, states, and countries you have visited.* As students enter the classroom, have them write down an answer to the instructions. Then ask students who have traveled great distances to explain how long their trips took and the type of transportation they used. *(Students' responses will vary, but students should describe a relatively short amount of time making use of airplanes, buses, cars, ships, or trains.)* Explain to students that in this Section 2 they will learn how improvements in transportation affected travel and communication in the United States during the early 1800s.

Section 2

Expansion and Improvements

Read to Discover

1. What issues was the Missouri Compromise supposed to address?
2. How did improvements in transportation affect the United States?
3. Why was the 1824 presidential election controversial?

WHY IT MATTERS TODAY

Transportation is still very important in our daily lives. Use **CNNfyi.com** or other **current events** sources to learn about transportation issues in the United States. Record your findings in your journal.

Identify

- Henry Clay
- Missouri Compromise
- American System
- Cumberland Road
- Erie Canal
- John Quincy Adams

The Story Continues

In the early 1800s, more Americans moved west. Most were looking for land and opportunity. An Ohio migrant described the scene in 1816. "The western country continues to rise in population and importance with unabated [unstoppable] rapidity." The writer mentioned the town of Mount Pleasant, Ohio. It grew from 7 families to about 90 families in just 10 years. As more Americans pushed west, debates arose over what laws would govern the newly settled lands.

Wagons were important for both settlement and trade on the western frontier.

★ The Missouri Compromise

A major regional conflict arose in 1819, when Congress considered the application of Missouri to enter the Union. Pro-slavery leaders in Missouri wanted to join the nation as a slave state. At the time, the Union included 11 free states and 11 slave states. Because free states in the North had a greater population, they controlled the House of Representatives. However, adding a new slave state would have tipped the balance in the Senate in favor of the South. Northern representatives in the House therefore passed a legislative amendment that would accept Missouri as a slave state

Have students read Section 2 and complete Guided Reading Strategy 12.2. Choose one or more of the following activities to explore the section content with students. For further suggestions on block scheduling or team teaching, see the *Block Scheduling Handbook with Team Teaching Strategies*.

LEVEL 1: Organize the class into several small groups. Assign half the groups the role of Jackson supporters and the other groups the role of Adams supporters. Have each group write a letter to the editor expressing its views on the controversy surrounding the election of 1824 and its outcome. Finally, have a volunteer from each group present his or her group's letters to the class.

ENGLISH LANGUAGE LEARNERS , COOPERATIVE LEARNING

---

with certain restrictions. Importing slaves into Missouri would become illegal. The amendment also required all children of Missouri slaves to be set free when they reached age 25. These proposed limits on slavery angered southern politicians.

Some senators, such as Rufus King of New York, opposed any expansion of slavery. "The existence of slavery impairs [harms] the industry and the power of a nation," he argued. North Carolina senator Nathaniel Macon wanted to continue adding slave states. "Why depart from the good old way, which has kept us in quiet, peace, and harmony?" he asked. Eventually, the Senate rejected the amendment. Missouri was still not a state.

To settle this dispute, Kentucky representative **Henry Clay** helped Congress reach the **Missouri Compromise**. This agreement had three main conditions.

1. Missouri would enter the Union as a slave state.
2. Maine would join the Union as a free state.
3. Slavery would be prohibited in any new territories or states formed north of 36°30' latitude—Missouri's southern border.

Another Kentucky representative, Benjamin Hardin, urged support for this compromise. He warned that regional differences over slavery threatened national unity.

Henry Clay had a long and distinguished political career and was noted for his efforts in Congress to achieve compromise between the North and the South.

History Makers Speak

❝It is north and east against the south and the west. It is a great geographical line that separates the contending [competing] parties. And those parties, when so equally divided, shake mighty empires to their center, and break up the foundations of the great deep, that sooner or later, if not settled, will rend in twain [break in two] this temple of liberty.❞

—Benjamin Hardin, quoted in *Major Problems in the History of the American South, Volume I,* edited by Paul D. Escott and David R. Goldfield

Congress passed the Missouri Compromise in 1820. Maine became a state on March 15 of that year, and Missouri was admitted to the Union on August 10, 1821.

Clay earned the nickname the Great Pacificator, or peacemaker, for his efforts on behalf of the compromise. However, there were still strong disagreements between the North and the South over the expansion of slavery into the West. This controversial issue would continue to divide the nation.

✔ **Reading Check: Identifying Cause and Effect** Why did Henry Clay propose the Missouri Compromise, and what were its key points? to prevent conflict over the admission of Missouri to the Union; see list above

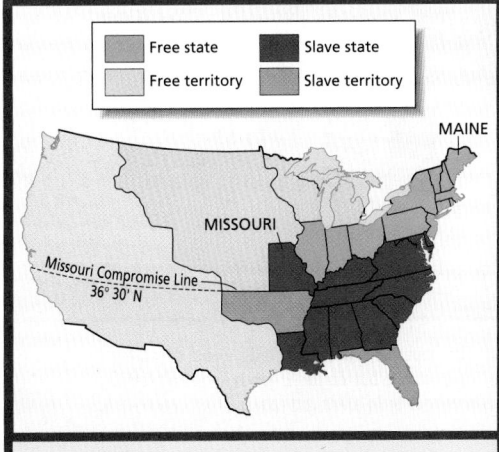

| Free state | Slave state |
| Free territory | Slave territory |

MAINE

MISSOURI

Missouri Compromise Line 36° 30' N

The Missouri Compromise

Interpreting Maps The Missouri Compromise allowed Maine to enter the Union as a free state and Missouri as a slave state.

Skills Assessment Places and Regions After the Missouri Compromise, how many slave states were there, and how many free states?

★ **Geography**

The Missouri Compromise. The votes in the House of Representatives on the provisions of the Missouri Compromise revealed a regional split. All but 5 of 100 northern representatives voted in favor of the bill to ban slavery in the Louisiana Purchase north of Missouri's southernmost boundary. A little more than half of the 76 southern representatives approved this measure. However, 87 northerners voted against a bill that permitted Missouri to include slavery in its constitution if it so desired, while all 76 southern representatives voted in favor. Only 14 northerners voted for this measure, while another 4 northerners abstained. Most northerners who voted in favor did so because they feared that further controversy might result in the end of the Union.

CRITICAL THINKING

What might the voting reveal about slavery and the Missouri Compromise?

Answer: Students might suggest that its passage depended on the small number of representatives who were willing to compromise.

MAP ANSWER

12 slave states and 12 free states

Science, Technology & Society

Roads. Americans' experiences during the War of 1812 contributed to the growing interest in a system of improved roads. Because the British blockaded the U.S. coastline, American merchants and farmers were forced to rely on overland transportation to get goods to market. They discovered that the roads were terrible. A four-horse team pulling a wagon full of goods took 75 days to make the journey from Worcester, Massachusetts, to Charleston, South Carolina. At the war's end, many Americans decided that something had to be done about the poor roads.

CRITICAL THINKING

What new developments in transportation helped solve the problem of poor roads?

ANSWER: Students' responses may vary but might include turnpikes and canals.

VISUALIZING HISTORY ANSWERS

1. He felt that a tariff would help domestic industries by keeping Americans from buying foreign goods.

2. Students' responses will vary.

Technology Resources

 American Music Selection 9: "The Erie Canal"

Research on the ROM

Free Find:
Henry Clay
After reading about Henry Clay on the **Holt Researcher CD–ROM**, create a poster in support of Clay for president. Be sure your poster shows his many accomplishments.

★ Internal Improvements

Henry Clay believed that a strong national economy would prevent regional conflicts. To strengthen the economy, he wanted a protective tariff. A tariff, Clay stated, would help domestic industries by keeping Americans from buying foreign goods. He wanted the tariff revenue to be used to improve roads and canals, or artificial waterways. These internal improvements would connect the regions of the country and make trade easier. Clay's plan became known as the **American System**.

Many people liked the idea of uniting the country through internal improvements. In 1816 a western citizen talked about these changes. "I believe the time [is] not very distant," he said, "when the wealth and resources of the western country will be brought almost to your doors." However, some members of Congress were against Clay's plan. They believed that the Constitution did not permit the federal government to spend money on internal improvements. Clay answered that the possible gains for the country justified federal action. Congress did pass a protective tariff, yet little of the money was used for internal improvements. Many state governments and private citizens continued to invest in improving the country's internal transportation systems.

✔ **Reading Check: Identifying Points of View** Why did some Americans believe the country needed internal improvements to build up the national economy? *Improved transportation would connect regions and make trade easier.*

The American System

The American System was Henry Clay's plan to strengthen the U.S. economy by protecting U.S. industries and improving national transportation.

 An American-made fur hat might cost $1.50 to buy.

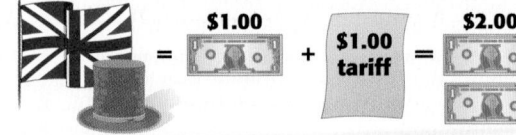 An imported British fur hat would be cheaper . . . but the tariff would raise the cost.

Clay hoped such protective tariffs would encourage Americans to buy domestic goods and also provide money to build roads and canals.

Visualizing History

1. **Economics** Why did Henry Clay want a tariff?

2. **Connecting to Today** Do you think that the American System would work in today's economy? Explain your answer.

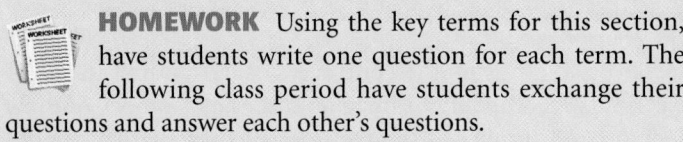 **HOMEWORK** Using the key terms for this section, have students write one question for each term. The following class period have students exchange their questions and answer each other's questions.

Note: To help students make meaningful connections between events in American history and those in their hometown, use the Chapter 12 **Hands-On History** activity, Writers of Your Region.

 LEVEL 3: Organize the class into two groups—one supporting the inclusion of Missouri as a free state and the other opposing it. Give each group time to prepare arguments supporting its position. Encourage students to consider in their arguments the regional issues that affected this national dispute. Then moderate a debate between the two sides. (*Students' arguments supporting will likely suggest that it should be allowed to become a new state. Students' arguments opposing will likely mention that inclusion of Missouri as a free state would upset the balance of power.*) Finally, discuss how the Missouri Compromise failed to settle the issue of slavery in Missouri. **COOPERATIVE LEARNING**

Interpreting the Visual Record

The National Road *The Fairview Inn was a stopping place for merchants and settlers traveling the National Road.* **How busy does the road appear to be in this image?**

★ New Roads and Canals

In the early 1800s most roads in the United States were made of dirt, making land travel difficult. British actress Frances Kemble described one New York road on which she had struggled during a visit to the United States in the 1830s.

 "The wickedest road, I do think, the cruellest, hard-heartedest road, that ever [a] wheel rumbled upon. Through bog [wet spongy ground] and marsh, and ruts [wheel tracks], wider and deeper than any . . . ruts I ever saw, with the roots of trees protruding [sticking out] across our path."

—Frances Anne (Kemble) Butler, *Journal*

The **Cumberland Road** was the first road built by the federal government. It ran from Cumberland, Maryland, to Wheeling, a town on the Ohio River in present-day West Virginia. Construction began in 1815, and by 1818 the road reached Wheeling. Then the Panic of 1819 hurt the economy, stopping further expansion. Construction on the road began again in the 1820s. In 1833 the National Road, as the extended road was called, stretched to Columbus, Ohio. It reached all the way to Illinois by 1850.

Water transportation was usually quicker, easier, and cheaper than overland travel. However, many areas of the country did not have rivers to connect them to other towns. Some Americans tried to make water transportation easier by building canals. During the early 1800s canal construction increased dramatically in the United States, particularly in the Northeast.

One of the largest projects was the **Erie Canal**, running from Albany to Buffalo, New York. Albany is located on the Hudson River, which feeds into New York Bay, and Buffalo is located on Lake Erie. Governor DeWitt Clinton of New York worked for many years to get approval for the project. Begun in 1817, it was completed in 1825. The Erie Canal

Analyzing Primary Sources

Making Generalizations and Predictions How might travel over roads such as this one affect a nation? It might discourage contact and trade among people, preventing a stronger culture and economy.

★ Economics

The Canal-Building Boom. The success of the Erie Canal sparked a canal boom throughout the United States; between 1816 and 1840 approximately 3,226 miles of canals were built. Yet canal construction was expensive. A stone turnpike cost between $5,000 and $10,000 per mile, while the average canal cost between $20,000 and $30,000 per mile. The total cost of the canals built between 1816 and 1840 is estimated to have been about $125 million. In addition, canals were expensive to repair and maintain; the high costs led to a decline in canal building.

CRITICAL THINKING

Why did canals cost so much to build?

Answer: Students might suggest that engineering difficulties, such as those faced by the builders of the Erie Canal, contributed to the high costs.

★★★★★★★★★★★★
That's Interesting!
★★★★★★★★★★★★

In order to finance road construction without spending large sums of public money, some states, particularly those in the North, permitted private companies to build turnpikes, or toll roads. New York had some 4,000 miles of turnpikes, and Pennsylvania had an estimated 2,400 miles of toll roads by 1832. By 1830 Maryland, however, had only 300 miles of turnpikes.

Denny Schillings of Homewood, Illinois, suggested the following activity:

ALL LEVELS: Have each student draw one political cartoon depicting the need for better roads in the West and another cartoon depicting the advantages of canals over other transportation methods of the period. Ask volunteers to present their cartoons to the class. Finally, lead a class discussion on how improvements in transportation affected the United States. **ENGLISH LANGUAGE LEARNERS**

★ CLOSE

Describe to students the controversy surrounding the 1824 election. Ask students to imagine that they support Andrew Jackson and think that the House of Representatives should have selected him as president rather than Adams. Have students make signs or banners protesting the House's decision to choose Adams. Then have students create signs or banners protesting Henry Clay's appointment as secretary of state. Ask them to include the historical arguments in their work. Have volunteers present their signs to the class. Finally, discuss how the election hurt Adams.

Science, Technology & Society

The Erie Canal. In 1817 New York governor DeWitt Clinton convinced the state legislature to authorize the expenditure of $7 million for the construction of the Erie Canal. Stretching from Buffalo to Albany, New York, the canal was 363 miles (584 km) long, 40 feet (12 m) wide, and 4 feet (1.2 m) deep. Along the route, the canal had to cross the mountains and rise 500 feet (150 m). To accomplish this feat, the canal engineers used 83 locks. There were no roads; only humans and horses were available for power. Rocks had to be blasted away with black powder, and aqueducts were used to cross streams. Despite these challenges, the canal opened on October 25, 1825.

ACTIVITY: Ask students to conduct research on other canals that are still used today and to prepare a list of the canals.

CONNECTING TO SCIENCE AND TECHNOLOGY ANSWER

They had to be able to raise and lower the water level because the surrounding land was hilly.

Visual Record Answer

(for p. 371)

Students might suggest that the road appears to be very busy.

CONNECTING TO
SCIENCE AND TECHNOLOGY

Building the Erie Canal

In 1817 New York began building the Erie Canal to connect Buffalo to Albany. One early difficulty was that much of the land between the two cities is hilly. Engineers solved this problem by using locks. A lock is a section of a canal with large gates at either end. Water inside the lock can be raised or lowered, allowing boats to move up and down hills. Today the Erie Canal is a tourist attraction and carries sightseers. The canal has also become part of American folklore, inspiring songs such as "Fifteen Miles on the Erie Canal." What challenges did engineers overcome in building the Erie Canal?

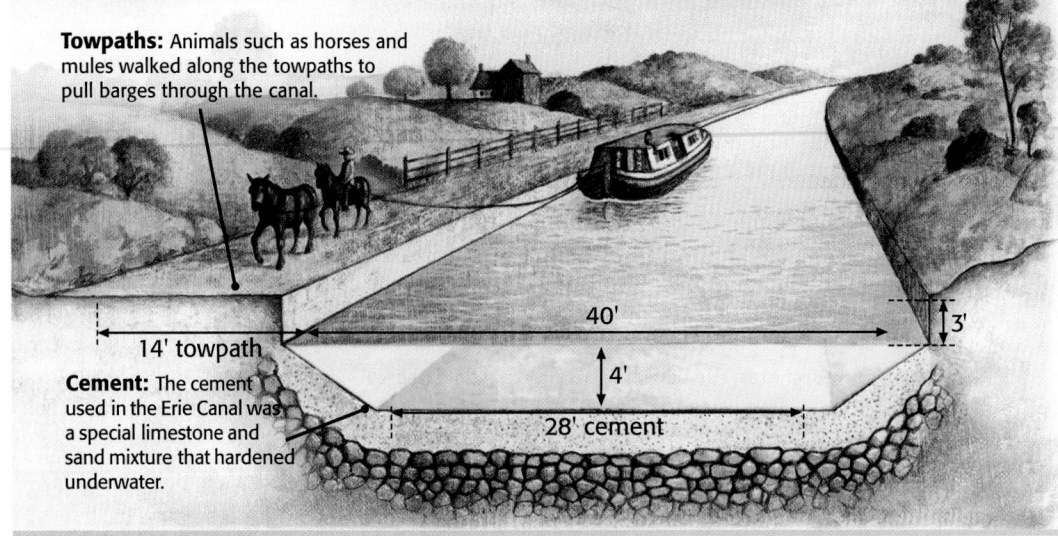

Towpaths: Animals such as horses and mules walked along the towpaths to pull barges through the canal.

Cement: The cement used in the Erie Canal was a special limestone and sand mixture that hardened underwater.

14' towpath

40'

3'

4'

28' cement

cost New York taxpayers millions of dollars, but it proved to be worth the expense. The canal allowed goods and people to move between all towns on Lake Erie and New York City. When the canal opened, a speaker at the opening ceremony called it a triumph of technology and praised its builders.

Analyzing Primary Sources

Identifying Points of View What qualities of the Erie Canal most impressed this speaker? *longest canal, lowest cost, least time to build, great benefits*

History Makers Speak

"They have built the longest canal in the world, in the least time, with the least experience, for the least money and to the greatest public benefit."

—Anonymous, quoted in *The Americans: The National Experience,* by Daniel Boorstin

The success of the Erie Canal helped start a canal-building boom across the country. South Carolina governor George McDuffie also sponsored a canal project. He hoped to make Charleston the center of southern Appalachian trade, wanting it to become "the New York of the South."

✔ **Reading Check: Summarizing** How did the creation of new roads and canals aid the economy? *They improved the ease and speed of transporting goods and people while reducing costs.*

★ REVIEW AND ASSESS

Have students complete the **Section 2 Review** on p. 373. Then have students complete **Daily Quiz 12.2.** As **Alternative Assessment,** you may want to use the improvements graphic organizer or the Teacher to Teacher activity in this section's lessons.

★ RETEACH

Have students complete **Main Idea Activity for English Language Learners and Special-Needs Students 12.2.** Then organize students into three groups. Assign each group one of the section's three objectives, and ask each group to create a 10-question quiz about its objective, writing the answers on a separate page. Have each group exchange its quiz with another group to answer. Then discuss questions with which other groups had trouble. **ENGLISH LANGUAGE LEARNERS , COOPERATIVE LEARNING**

★ EXTEND

Organize the class into groups. Have students use the library to obtain information on transportation from 1815 to 1840, and today. Give each group a large sheet of poster board and have them make drawings that compare and contrast the transportation methods used then and now. Then ask groups to annotate each picture. **COOPERATIVE LEARNING , BLOCK SCHEDULING**

★ The Election of 1824

Although Henry Clay had tried to build up a national economy, the country still faced many regional differences. The presidential election of 1824 showed these divisions. One of the two main candidates was Secretary of State **John Quincy Adams**. The other was Andrew Jackson, who had become a senator from Tennessee. Both men ran as Republicans. Jackson won the most popular votes, but he did not have enough electoral votes to win office. Under the rules set forth in the Constitution, the House of Representatives had to choose the winner. Speaker of the House Henry Clay influenced the vote by backing Adams. The House chose Adams as president. In response, Jackson's supporters claimed that Adams had made a "corrupt bargain" with Clay. These accusations only increased after Adams chose Clay to be his secretary of state.

The election controversy weakened President Adams's congressional and public support. He was already unpopular in the slaveholding South. He thus had little support when he asked for more federal money for canals, education, roads, and scientific research. Congress rejected most of these plans. However, it agreed to pay for some road and canal projects.

As president, John Quincy Adams supported higher education and tried unsuccessfully to establish a national university.

✔ **Reading Check: Finding the Main Idea** Why did John Quincy Adams have weak public and congressional support during his presidency?
He did not win the popular vote; his appointment of Henry Clay led to accusations of corruption; and his proposals for internal improvements were unpopular.

Section 2 Review

go.hrw.com Homework Practice Online
keyword: SA3 HP12

1 Identify and explain:
• Henry Clay
• Missouri Compromise
• American System
• Cumberland Road
• Erie Canal
• John Quincy Adams

2 Summarizing Copy the graphic organizer below. Use it to describe how the debate over slavery affected the growth of the North, South, and West in the 1820s.

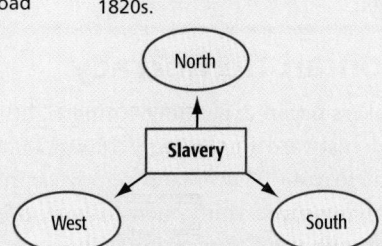

3 Finding the Main Idea
a. How did new transportation systems affect the expansion and development of the nation?

b. What caused the controversy surrounding the 1824 presidential election?

4 Writing and Critical Thinking
Supporting a Point of View Imagine that you are Henry Clay. Write a letter to a friend in Missouri explaining your reasons for proposing the Missouri Compromise.

Consider the following:
• the balance of power between slave and free states in Congress
• the prohibition of slavery in territory north of latitude 36°30'
• the compromise's effect on national unity

Section 2 Review
ANSWERS

1 Identify
• Henry Clay, p. 369
• Missouri Compromise, p. 369
• American System, p. 370
• Cumberland Road, p. 371
• Erie Canal, p. 371
• John Quincy Adams, p. 373

2 slavery debate led to: Maine admitted as pro-North free state; Missouri admitted as pro-South slave state; new rules on slavery in the West

3 a. They allowed remote areas to reach port cities and thereby enter the world marketplace.
b. Jackson won the popular vote but did not have enough electoral votes to win office. The House, led by Speaker Henry Clay, decided the election in favor of Adams. This led Jackson's supporters to make accusations of corruption.

4 Students' letters will vary but should explain the reasoning behind the Missouri Compromise.

Section 3

OBJECTIVES

⭐ Examine how Jacksonian Democracy was a sign of change in American politics.

⭐ Explore how tariff disputes led to the nullification crisis, and how President Jackson responded.

⭐ Describe why President Jackson was against a national bank and how his resistance affected the economy.

SECTION 3 RESOURCES

REPRODUCIBLE

▶ Guided Reading Strategy 12.3
▶ American History Political Cartoon 6: Jackson and the Bank

TECHNOLOGY

▶ One-Stop Planner, Lesson 12.3
▶ Homework Practice Online
▶ HRW Go site

REINFORCEMENT, REVIEW, AND ASSESSMENT

▶ Section 3 Review, p. 379
▶ Daily Quiz 12.3
▶ Main Idea Activity 12.3
▶ English Audio Summary 12.3
▶ Spanish Audio Summary 12.3

Section 3

The Age of Jackson

Read to Discover

1. How was Jacksonian Democracy a sign of change in American politics?
2. How did tariff disputes lead to the nullification crisis, and how did President Jackson respond?
3. Why was President Jackson against a national bank, and how did his opposition affect the economy?

WHY IT MATTERS TODAY

Voting is the foundation of our democracy. Use CNNfyi.com or other **current events** sources to learn about a recent local, state, or federal election. Record your findings in your journal.

Define

- nominating conventions
- spoils system
- kitchen cabinet
- states' rights
- nullification crisis

Identify

- Andrew Jackson
- Democratic Party
- John C. Calhoun
- Martin Van Buren
- Tariff of Abominations
- Daniel Webster
- *McCulloch v. Maryland*
- Whig Party
- Panic of 1837
- William Henry Harrison

This small figure of a frog was meant to encourage voters to "Croak for the Jackson Wagon."

The Story Continues

John Quincy Adams once described himself as "a man of reserved, cold . . . and forbidding [threatening] manners." Many citizens viewed Adams as part of an old, upper-class culture—wealthy people out of touch with the country's needs. Political rallies of the 1820s showed that the people wanted a more lively leader. The wild gatherings held by Andrew Jackson's supporters amazed politicians. One writer noted that Jackson's appeal proved there "must be a new order of things."

⭐ Jacksonian Democracy

Western lawmakers began expanding voting rights in the 1790s. These changes spread eastward in the early 1800s. Many more Americans gained the right to vote. Many states removed property requirements for voting, allowing more white men to vote. Some political parties began holding **nominating conventions**. These were public meetings to select the party's presidential and vice presidential candidates.

Have students read Section 3 and complete Guided Reading Strategy 12.3. Choose one or more of the following activities to explore the section content with students. For further suggestions on block scheduling or team teaching, see the *Block Scheduling Handbook with Team Teaching Strategies.*

LEVEL 1: Lead a class discussion that highlights the ways that Jacksonian Democracy represented a change in U.S. politics. Then ask students to create a song or poem that explains the significance of Jacksonian Democracy. Encourage students to highlight Jackson's humble upbringing and his attempts to limit wealthy citizens' influence over politics, or his use of the spoils system. Ask volunteers to sing or read their songs or poems to the class. **ENGLISH LANGUAGE LEARNERS**

 ALL LEVELS: Write the expression *Jacksonian Democracy* on the chalkboard. Have students work in pairs to create a crossword puzzle based on information related to the phrase using people and key terms from the section as answers. Have pairs exchange their crossword puzzles and fill in the answers. Then have students return the completed puzzles to authors for grading. Finally, lead a class discussion on how Jacksonian Democracy was a sign of change in U.S. politics. **ENGLISH LANGUAGE LEARNERS , COOPERATIVE LEARNING**

Expanded voting rights and conventions let more people become active in politics. Historians began calling this democratic expansion Jacksonian Democracy after popular politician **Andrew Jackson**.

Not everyone gained greater political power, however. In 1820 women were not allowed to vote in any state. In addition, free African Americans had no voting rights in most states. The supporters of Andrew Jackson were mostly farmers, frontier settlers, and southern slaveholders. They believed their leader would defend the rights of the common people and the slave states.

Many of these Americans believed that a "corrupt bargain" between Henry Clay and John Qunicy Adams had stolen the 1824 election from Jackson. These people got together to make sure that Jackson would become the next president. They began to call themselves Democrats and formed the **Democratic Party**. Many people who backed President Adams began calling themselves National Republicans. In the presidential election of 1828, Adams ran as a National Republican, while Jackson ran as a Democrat. Jackson chose Senator **John C. Calhoun** of South Carolina as his vice presidential running mate.

✔ **Reading Check: Finding the Main Idea** What led to the creation of the Democratic Party? increased access of common people to the political process and belief that Jackson had been robbed of election in 1824

☆ Jackson's Victory

The 1828 campaign focused a great deal on the candidates' personalities. Jackson's campaigners described him as a war hero. They said he had been born poor and rose to success through his own hard work. They contrasted this image with Adams, a Harvard-educated man whose father had been the second U.S. president. Some of Jackson's supporters also described Adams as being out of touch with everyday people. Even an ally of Adams said that he was as "cold as a lump of ice." In turn, Adams's supporters said Jackson was hot tempered, crude, and ill equipped to be president. Yet, when the election was over, Jackson and Calhoun had won with a record number of popular votes.

Jackson's supporters saw his victory as a win for the common people. One Kentucky newspaper editor described the feeling. "It was a proud day for the people. General Jackson is *their own* president." To show this, a crowd of Jackson voters celebrated his inauguration with a huge party on the White House lawn. The party caused a great deal of property damage. Some people feared that the mob at the White House was a sign of trouble. Margaret Bayard Smith recalled the inauguration party.

History Makers Speak 66What a scene did we witness! . . . a rabble, a mob, of boys, . . . women, children, scrambling, fighting, romping. . . . But it was the people's day, and the people's President, and the people would rule. 99

—Margaret Bayard Smith, quoted in *Eyewitness to America,* edited by David Colbert

---

Andrew Jackson

Andrew Jackson's nickname was Old Hickory. The name reflected his reputation for being extremely tough, like the hard wood of a hickory tree. He was born in 1767 in South Carolina. By the time he was 13 years old both his parents had died. Jackson moved to North Carolina, where he became a lawyer, and then to Tennessee. He earned respect as a military leader during the War of 1812 and later represented Tennessee in the U.S. Senate. In 1828 he won the presidency in a landslide.

Jackson believed in being a take-charge president. He vetoed more bills during his presidency than all the previous presidents combined. He also had a quick temper with people who disagreed with his views. He was popular with the common people, however. They saw him as a simple man who had gained great influence and respect through hard work. **Why was Andrew Jackson so popular?**

Analyzing Primary Sources
Drawing Inferences and Conclusions How did this scene reflect Jacksonian Democracy? It showed the involvement of the common people in politics.

★ Citizenship

Political Conventions.
In September 1831 the Anti-Masonic Party held the first national political convention for nominating candidates in Baltimore, Maryland. The convention was attended by 116 delegates from 13 states. The National Republicans, who opposed Andrew Jackson, held their convention in December in Baltimore. Despite a winter storm, 168 delegates from 18 states attended. Representatives from 23 states convened for the Democratic convention in Baltimore in May 1832.

☑ internet connect

TOPIC: Politics
GO TO: go.hrw.com
KEYWORD: SA3 CF12

Have students use the library or access the Internet through the HRW Go site to find information about one of these three parties. Then, using standard grammar, spelling, sentence structure, and punctuation, students should write a speech that might have been given at one of these conventions.

PRESIDENTIAL PROFILE ANSWER

Jackson seemed to represent the common man who worked hard and achieved greatness.

ALL LEVELS: Copy the following graphic organizer onto the chalkboard, omitting the italicized answers. Have students complete the graphic organizer to explore how tariff disputes led to the nullification crisis and how President Jackson responded.
ENGLISH LANGUAGE LEARNERS

HOMEWORK Have students create a report card grading Jackson as president. Have students grade Jackson on domestic and economic policies, and on his popularity. Ask students to provide examples from the text to support each grade.

Note: For an additional teaching idea, see the Chapter 12 Continuum activity in the **Creative Teaching Strategies** handbook.

STEPS LEADING TO THE NULLIFICATION CRISIS

Southern states asserted their right to nullify protective tariffs, which they argued hurt their economy. → *Jackson condemned nullification.* → *Jackson threatened to send federal troops to South Carolina to enforce federal laws.*

⭐ Biography

Jacksonian Democracy.
In the early 1900s historians argued that Andrew Jackson's election signaled the triumph of common people over social elites. Recently, historians have argued that Jackson's followers actually hoped to increase their *own* economic opportunities and to become more like the elites. Historians do agree that the excitement over politics in the 1820s and 1830s marked a turning point in U.S. political history.

CRITICAL THINKING

What changes to the political process may have contributed to this turning point?

ANSWER: Students may mention that nominating conventions and the elimination of property requirements meant that more people could participate in politics than ever before.

CITIZENSHIP AND YOU ANSWER
delegates are chosen in different ways; the number of delegates is larger; delegates are a more diverse group, use of Internet

Citizenship and You
Political Conventions

Before the 1830s U.S. presidential candidates were selected by members of Congress from each political party. In the election of 1832, however, the major parties began holding national conventions. There they chose their candidate for president. Each state held a convention to choose its delegates to the national meeting.

Many important changes have taken place over the years in party politics. For example, the number of delegates attending conventions has risen a great deal as the population has grown. In 1831 only 116 delegates attended the first convention. However, in 2000 the Democratic National Convention had 5,000 delegates. In addition, minorities, women, and young people have become an important influence on conventions. How have political nominating conventions changed over time?

George W. Bush at the 2000 Republican National Convention

Jackson rewarded some of his supporters with government jobs—a practice known as the **spoils system.** This term comes from the saying "to the victor belong the spoils [valued goods] of the enemy." However, Jackson changed few government positions, replacing less than one fifth of federal officeholders. Secretary of State **Martin Van Buren** was one of Jackson's strongest allies in his official cabinet. President Jackson also relied a great deal on an informal group of trusted advisers. This group was called the **kitchen cabinet** because its members sometimes met in the White House kitchen.

✔ **Reading Check: Analyzing Information** What effect did Jackson's election have on the government? He used the spoils system to some degree and formed the kitchen cabinet. In general he brought a more informal and more popular style to the presidency. [✷ 8.5F, 8.23B, 8.30B]

⭐ Conflict over Tariffs

One of the first challenges President Jackson faced was a growing regional conflict over tariffs. Northern manufacturers wanted high tariffs to protect their new industries from foreign competition, which came mostly from Great Britain. British companies could drive smaller American firms out of business by selling factory goods more cheaply than Americans could afford to make them. Protective tariffs blocked this practice.

However, the South had little industry to protect. The southern economy relied on agriculture, particularly cotton exports. Southerners imported most of their manufactured goods. High tariffs made these goods more expensive and also angered some of the South's European trading partners. Southerners thus wanted low tariffs. Westerners were divided on the tariff issue. Northern areas tended to support tariffs. For example, Kentucky wanted tariffs to protect its hemp industry, while further south, westerners tended to oppose tariffs.

In 1828, under strong pressure from northern manufacturers, Congress passed a tariff with very high rates. Angry southerners called the law the **Tariff of Abominations.** (An abomination is a hateful thing.) Some southern politicians saw the tariff as one way the federal government was abusing its power over the states.

✔ **Reading Check: Identifying Points of View** Why were the North, South, and West divided over the benefits of high tariffs? The North wanted to protect its industries; the South wanted to keep import prices low; and the West was split between the two sides. [✷ 8.5B, 8.7A, 8.13C, 8.30B]

⭐ The Nullification Crisis

Vice President John C. Calhoun, an experienced politician, helped lead opposition to the tariff. He wrote a statement in support of **states' rights.** People who favor states' rights believe that the federal government's authority is strictly limited by the Constitution. Calhoun's statement said that states had the right to nullify, or cancel, any federal law

LEVELS 2 AND 3: Organize the class into four groups and assign each group one of the following topics: *McCulloch* v. *Maryland*, the Tariff of Abominations, the nullification crisis, or the Panic of 1837. Have each group research its assigned topic and create a 10-minute presentation either explaining how the tariff disputes led to the nullification crisis and President Jackson's subsequent response or explaining the reasons that President Jackson opposed a national bank and how his resistance affected the economy. The presentation should be similar to a television documentary. You may wish to have students assume the following roles within each group: narrator, special guests, on-location reporters, and audio-visual design crew. Have each group present its documentary to the class. If possible, videotape each presentation and replay the tape for the class. **COOPERATIVE LEARNING**

---

they considered unconstitutional. The dispute between the state and federal governments became known as the **nullification crisis**. Calhoun warned that states had the right to rebel if their rights were violated. Senator **Daniel Webster** of Massachusetts disagreed. He vowed, "Liberty and Union, now and forever, one and inseparable!"

South Carolina tested the nullification theory after Congress passed a new tariff in 1832. The South Carolina state legislature passed a resolution declaring that the 1828 and 1832 tariffs were "null, void . . . [and not] binding upon this State, its officers or citizens." Calhoun resigned from the vice presidency in support of his home state. Some thought the federal government would use force to collect the tariff duties. South Carolina officials said the state would withdraw from the Union if this happened.

Jackson was strongly against nullification. "I consider, then, the power to annul [cancel] a law of the United States . . . incompatible with [contrary to] the existence of the Union," he said. Jackson said he would send U.S. troops into South Carolina to enforce federal laws. However, he did not have to take this step, because the two sides reached a compromise. Congress agreed to lower the tariffs little by little over several years. South Carolina's leaders agreed to enforce the tariff law. However, they still believed that nullification was legal.

✔ **Reading Check: Summarizing** What led to the nullification crisis, and why was it significant? Southern states asserted their power to nullify protective tariffs, which most southerners opposed. It demonstrated the nation's growing problem over the issue of states' rights.

⭐ The Second Bank of the United States

President Jackson upheld federal authority in the nullification crisis. However, he did not always support greater federal power. For example, he was against the Second Bank of the United States, which Congress had founded in 1816. Many states had also opposed the Bank and had taken action against it. For example, several states, including Maryland, passed laws that taxed branches of the national bank. James McCulloch, cashier of the Bank's branch in Maryland, refused to pay this tax. The state took him to court, and the resulting case, **McCulloch v. Maryland**, went all the way to the U.S. Supreme Court.

The Court, led by Chief Justice John Marshall, made two important rulings in the case. The Court supported the Bank's constitutionality. First, Marshall said that the elastic

Interpreting Political Cartoons

Jackson against the Bank *This political cartoon shows President Andrew Jackson, on the left, using his veto stick to fight against the Bank of the United States and its state branches.* **Why do you think the artist portrayed the Bank as a monster with many heads?**

COLLECTION OF THE NEW-YORK HISTORICAL SOCIETY

LEVEL 3: Lead a class discussion on the case of *McCulloch* v. *Maryland* and President Jackson's attempts to defeat the Second Bank of the United States. Have students work in groups to create an outline of a chapter that might have appeared in Andrew Jackson's memoirs. The outline should include Jackson's thoughts about *McCulloch* v. *Maryland* and attempts to defeat it, the significance of *McCulloch* v. *Maryland*, and how Jackson's defeat of the Bank affected the economy. **COOPERATIVE LEARNING**

★ CLOSE

Have students use information from this section to create a flowchart that links the key terms. *(Students' charts may vary but might draw an arrow from a box containing the term* states' rights *to a box containing the term* nullification crisis. *On the arrow linking the two terms, students could write that some supporters of states' rights advocated the nullification crisis.)*

Using Visual Resources

Political Art. The illustration on the following page is a lithograph that was used as political propaganda during the presidential election campaign in 1840. Its caption read, "*The Log Cabin:* presidential candidate William H. Harrison welcoming a veteran with his legendary...hospitality."

ACTIVITY: Ask students to analyze the information on the following page about the election campaign in 1840. Have students create a chart that pairs objects in the picture with their value as propaganda for Harrison.

CONNECTING TO MATH ANSWERS
1. $7,403;
2. Students' line graphs may vary but should illustrate the information presented in the chart.
3. Students' answers may vary, but students might mention that debt declined from $48,565,000 to $38,000.

Visual Record Answer

(for p. 379)
Students might suggest that it shows that he comes from a humble background.

CONNECTING TO
MATH

Just the Facts

U.S. Debt from 1800 to 1840
(in thousands of dollars)

Year	Debt
1800	82,976
1805	82,312
1810	53,173
1815	99,834
1820	91,016
1825	83,788
1830	48,565
1835	38,000
1840	3,573

Using Mathematical Skills

1. What was the difference in the debt between 1800 and 1840?

2. Create a line graph that illustrates changes in the national debt between 1800 and 1840.

3. Imagine that you are a Democratic politician in 1836. Write a speech that summarizes the change in the national debt during Jackson's presidency.

clause of the Constitution allowed Congress to establish the Bank. This ruling was a broad interpretation of the implied powers of Congress. The Court also decided that federal law was superior to state law—an idea that challenged the principle of states' rights. This ruling meant that Maryland could not tax or interfere with the Bank.

This victory was not enough for Nicholas Biddle, the Bank's director, who decided to make the Bank a presidential issue. The Bank's charter was due to expire in 1836. Rather than wait, Biddle pushed for a bill to renew the Bank's charter in 1832. Jackson campaigned strongly for the defeat of this bill. "I will kill it," he promised. Jackson vetoed legislation to renew the charter. He then issued this strongly worded statement.

History Makers Speak ❝It is to be regretted that the rich and powerful too often bend the acts of government to their selfish purposes. . . . By attempting to gratify their desires, we have in the results of our legislation arrayed [positioned] section against section, interest against interest.❞

—Andrew Jackson, quoted in *The Annals of America*

Congress could not gather the two-thirds majority needed to override Jackson's veto. Jackson also weakened the Bank's power by moving most of its funds to state banks, which his opponents called pet banks. In many cases, these state banks used the funds to offer credit to people buying land. While this practice helped promote expansion in the West, it also led to inflation.

In the summer of 1836, Jackson tried to slow this inflation. He did this by ordering Americans to use only gold or silver—instead of paper bank notes—to buy government-owned land. This policy did not help the national economy as Jackson had hoped. However, Jackson did improve the economy by lowering the national debt.

✔ **Reading Check: Contrasting** What positions did John Marshall and Andrew Jackson take on the Second Bank of the United States? Marshall ruled the national bank constitutional and above state laws. Jackson moved the Bank's funds to state banks and vetoed its renewal.

★ Van Buren's Presidency

Jackson was still very popular with voters in 1836 at the end of his second term. However, his actions had angered members of Congress, many of whom believed he had abused his presidential powers. In 1834 a group of Jackson opponents had formed the **Whig Party**. Many Whigs supported the idea of a weak president and a strong legislature. In 1836 the Whigs nominated four candidates to run for president against Martin Van Buren, the Democratic candidate and former vice president under Jackson. Despite this opposition, with strong support from Jackson, Van Buren won the election.

The people never liked Van Buren the way they had liked Jackson, however. Shortly after Van Buren took office, the country experienced a financial crisis. Called the **Panic of 1837**, this crisis led to a severe

Martin Van Buren became the new vice president when Andrew Jackson won re-election in 1832.

THE GRANGER COLLECTION, NEW YORK

economic depression. The policies of the pet banks and Jackson's plan to curb inflation had helped lead to the panic. Nevertheless, Van Buren received the blame for it. The financial crisis hurt President Van Buren's re-election campaign in 1840. The Whigs ran **William Henry Harrison**, a general from the Battle of Tippecanoe, as their candidate. He and John Tyler, his running mate, ran under the popular campaign slogan "Tippecanoe and Tyler too."

The Whigs called Van Buren a friend of the rich and claimed Harrison was the friend of the common people. Harrison had actually been born to a wealthy family. However, the Whigs' emphasis on his war record and log-cabin roots made Harrison seem like a rugged man from the frontier, similar to Jackson. More than 75 percent of the eligible voters turned out for this election. Although the popular vote was close, Harrison won the electoral college in a landslide, gaining 234 electoral votes to Van Buren's 60. The Whigs had achieved their goal of winning the presidency.

THE GRANGER COLLECTION, NEW YORK

Interpreting the Visual Record

Log cabin *This 1840 campaign illustration supposedly shows the log cabin where William Henry Harrison grew up.* **Why might showing Harrison in a setting like this have helped his popularity?**

✔ **Reading Check: Identifying Cause and Effect** How did Jackson's policies affect the economy, and what was the result for Van Buren? Jackson's actions against the national bank and his inflation policy contributed to the Panic of 1837. This hurt Van Buren's presidency.

Section 3 Review

go.hrw.com **Homework Practice Online**
keyword: SA3 HP12

1 **Define and explain:**
• nominating conventions
• spoils system
• kitchen cabinet
• states' rights
• nullification crisis

2 **Identify and explain:**
• Andrew Jackson
• Democratic Party
• John C. Calhoun
• Martin Van Buren
• Tariff of Abominations
• Daniel Webster
• *McCulloch v. Maryland*
• Whig Party
• Panic of 1837
• William Henry Harrison

3 **Summarizing** Copy the graphic organizer below. Use it to describe the main events of Jackson's presidency and the major changes in politics that took place during that time.

Jacksonian Presidency
_____
_____
_____
(Jacksonian Era)
_____
_____
Jacksonian Democracy

4 **Finding the Main Idea**
a. What caused the nullification crisis, and how did President Jackson deal with this issue?

b. Why did President Jackson veto the renewal of the Second Bank of the United States, and what effect did this have on the economy?

5 **Writing and Critical Thinking**
Analyzing Information Imagine that you are a reporter covering the effect of Jackson's election. Write a newspaper article describing the rise of Jacksonian Democracy.

Consider the following:
• expansion of voting rights and nominating conventions
• formation of the Democratic Party
• Jackson's appeal to the common people

Section 4

OBJECTIVES

⭐ Explain why the federal and state governments began an American Indian removal policy.

⭐ Examine how American Indians such as the Cherokee resisted removal.

⭐ Describe how American Indians were affected by the removal from their lands.

Section 4

Indian Removal

Read to Discover

1. Why did the federal and state governments begin an American Indian removal policy?
2. How did American Indians such as the Cherokee resist removal?
3. How were American Indians affected by the removal from their lands?

WHY IT MATTERS TODAY

Many American Indians were forced to leave their homes to live on reservations. Use **CNNfyi.com** or other **current events** sources to identify a group of people being forced to leave their homeland today. Record your findings in your journal.

Identify

• Black Hawk
• Indian Removal Act
• Indian Territory
• Bureau of Indian Affairs
• Treaty of Dancing Rabbit Creek
• Sequoya
• John Ross
• *Worcester* v. *Georgia*
• Trail of Tears
• Osceola

Black Hawk refused to leave his homeland.

The Story Continues

As American settlers moved west, American Indian leaders talked about the best way to deal with them. Keokuk, a Sauk leader from Illinois, wanted to compromise and avoid a war. Another Sauk leader named Black Hawk disagreed. He believed that U.S. officials had bribed Keokuk and other Indian leaders to gain their support. Black Hawk firmly resisted all attempts to take American Indian lands.

⭐ The Black Hawk War

In 1827 the federal government decided to end years of conflict between American Indians and U.S. settlers in Illinois. Officials ordered the removal of all Indians from the state. **Black Hawk** and his followers ignored the removal policy, rejecting the very idea of land ownership.

History Makers Speak

❝My reason teaches me that land cannot be sold. The Great Spirit gave it to his children to live upon. So long as they occupy and cultivate it they have the right to the soil. Nothing can be sold but such things as can be carried away.❞

—Black Hawk, quoted in *Atlas of the North American Indian,* by Carl Waldman

Have students read Section 4 and complete Guided Reading Strategy 12.4. Choose one or more of the following activities to explore the section content with students. For further suggestions on block scheduling or team teaching, see the *Block Scheduling Handbook with Team Teaching Strategies.*

LEVEL 1: Explain why the federal and state governments began an American Indian removal policy and then explain the circumstances surrounding the case of *Worcester v. Georgia* to the class. Then tell students about President Jackson's refusal to uphold the Court's decision. Organize the class into two groups. Have students on one side of the classroom create headlines for possible articles in the *Cherokee Phoenix,* based on events leading up to Jackson's refusal to uphold the decision. Instruct the other side of the classroom to create headlines that might have accompanied articles dealing with the same subject in other newspapers of the time. *(Students' headlines will vary, but headlines from the Cherokee Phoenix might include the victory of the Worcester v. Georgia case or the failure of Jackson to uphold the Court's decision. Headlines from other newspapers might praise Jackson for his stance on removing the Cherokee.)* Then lead a class discussion on how the Cherokee resisted removal.

ENGLISH LANGUAGE LEARNERS , COOPERATIVE LEARNING

When the Sauk returned from their winter hunt in 1830, they found that white settlers had moved into their village. But Black Hawk and his followers refused to be pushed out. Although his forces were flying a white flag, U.S. troops fired on them. Black Hawk then decided to fight. Indian groups began to raid American settlements and attack U.S. troops. However, by August 1832 the Sauk forces were running out of food and supplies. Black Hawk surrendered and gave up leadership of the Sauk. By 1850 the U.S. Army had removed the American Indians living within the old Northwest Territory.

✔ **Reading Check: Finding the Main Idea** What was the outcome of the Black Hawk War?

★ The Indian Removal Act

Indian removal was also an issue in the Southeast. American Indians had long lived in settlements stretching from Georgia to Mississippi. However, President Jackson and other political leaders wanted to open this land to settlement by American farmers. They said that Indians in the Southeast should move to lands in the West. Under pressure from Jackson, Congress passed the **Indian Removal Act** in 1830. This act authorized the removal of American Indians who lived east of the Mississippi River.

Congress then established **Indian Territory** as a new Indian homeland. This area contained most of what is now Oklahoma.

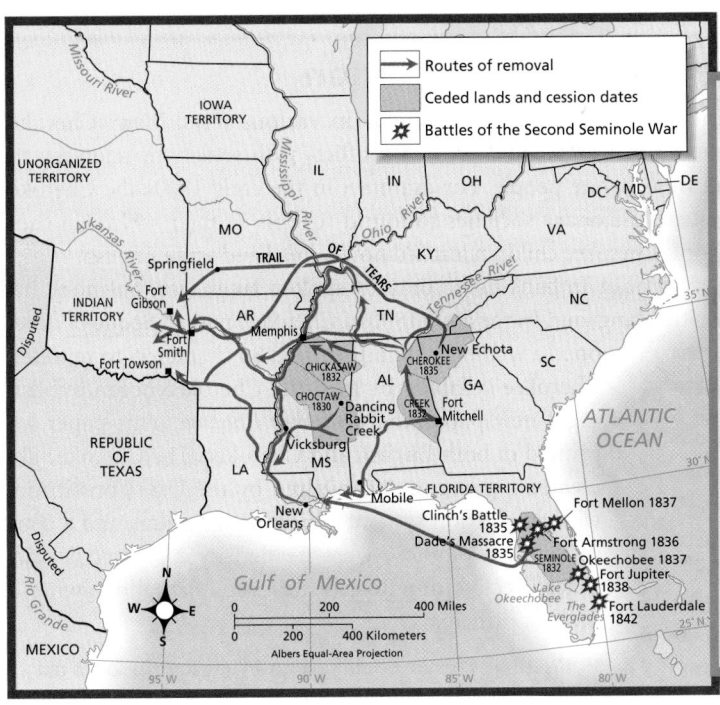

Indian Removal from the Southeast, 1830s

Interpreting Maps The Indian Removal Act of 1830 allowed the president to move American Indians in the Southeast to new lands west of the Mississippi River. American Indians were forced from their homes and marched hundreds of miles to the new Indian Territory.

Skills Assessment

1. **Locate** From what present-day state were the Cherokee removed?
2. **Analyzing Information** Which American Indian group traveled the greatest distance to Indian Territory?

Interdisciplinary Connection

▶Literature◀

Black Hawk's Autobiography. In 1833 a publisher released an account of Black Hawk's life that was purported to be an autobiography. Black Hawk supposedly dictated his tale to Antoine LeClaire, who translated it into English and passed it on to a newspaper editor, who prepared the manuscript for publication. Some scholars have refuted the autobiography, arguing that there is no proof that Black Hawk dictated its contents. However, many scholars believe that Black Hawk did tell the story that was published under his name.

ACTIVITY: Have students write a paragraph based on an interview conducted with a fellow student. Then ask students to compare the paragraph to the original oral account, discussing the ways in which the story changed when it was written down.

MAP ANSWERS
1. Georgia
2. the Seminole

Technology Resources

 CNN Presents America: Beginnings to 1914 Segment: Living in America—The Choctaw

ALL LEVELS: Copy the following graphic organizer onto the chalkboard, omitting the italicized answers. Have students complete the organizer to explain why the federal and state governments began an American Indian removal policy. **ENGLISH LANGUAGE LEARNERS**

Reasons for American Indian Removal Policy

to end disputes between American Indians and settlers

to open up American Indian land to settlers

ALL LEVELS: Lead a class discussion on the routes traveled by the various nations that were forced to move to the Indian Territory. Give students a blank outline map of the United States and ask them to create a key identifying which color represents each nation's route. Have students fill in the names of each state and significant geographic features encountered by the nations. Then have them mark, using the determined color, the routes traveled by each nation. Display maps around the classroom for other students to view. Finally, discuss with the class how the American Indians were affected by removal from their lands. **ENGLISH LANGUAGE LEARNERS**

★ Citizenship

The Indian Removal Act.

Many members of Congress opposed the passage of the Indian Removal Act. New Jersey Senator Theodore Frelinghuysen delivered a three-day-long speech opposing the act. He argued that the United States should live up to its treaties with American Indians. He also argued that removal was unnecessary because Indians were complying with U.S. policies and gradually adopting the customs of the white settlers. Frelinghuysen reminded his fellow senators about the moral implications of their decision.

CRITICAL THINKING

What moral implications do you think Frelinghuysen might have mentioned with regard to the removal of the American Indians?

ANSWER: Students' might suggest peoples' obligations to deal fairly with one another, and to live up to their word.

Visual Record Answer

It enabled the Cherokee to develop a written language.

Technology Resources

 Everyday Life in America Transparency 7: Portrait of Native Americans, 1833

Interpreting the Visual Record

A new alphabet *Sequoya poses with the Cherokee alphabet he developed in the bottom image, while above him is a page from a Cherokee primer.* **Why would the creation of an alphabet be important?**

THE GRANGER COLLECTION, NEW YORK

Some supporters of this plan argued that it would protect American Indians. John C. Calhoun believed that removal would prevent more conflicts with American settlers. "One of the greatest evils to which they are subject is that incessant [constant] pressure of our population," he noted. Congress also approved the creation of the **Bureau of Indian Affairs** to oversee federal policy toward American Indians.

The Choctaw were the first American Indians sent to Indian Territory. After the Mississippi legislature abolished the government of the Choctaw, some Choctaw leaders signed the **Treaty of Dancing Rabbit Creek**. This treaty gave more than 7.5 million acres of their land to the state. The Choctaw journeyed from Mississippi to Indian Territory during the winter of 1831–32. The trip was disastrous. Federal officials in charge of the move did not provide enough food or supplies. As a result, about one fourth of the Choctaw died of cold, disease, and starvation. News of the U.S. treatment of the Choctaw caused other American Indians to resist removal. Some Creek decided to stay on their lands, located mainly in Alabama, but state officials ordered their forced removal. In 1836, federal troops led some 14,500 captured Creek, many in chains, to Indian Territory.

The Chickasaw, mostly from Mississippi, were moved west in the winter of 1837–38. They had been promised better supplies on their trip to Indian Territory. Yet, Chickasaw lives were also lost during removal.

✔ **Reading Check: Comparing** What was the Indian Removal Act, and how did it affect the Choctaw, Creek, and Chickasaw? federal act that authorized the removal of eastern American Indians; all three groups sent on harsh journeys to Indian Territory

★ The Cherokee Nation

American Indians resisted removal in various ways. Many Cherokee believed that they could prevent conflicts with settlers by adopting the culture of white people. For example, in the early 1800s the Cherokee invited missionary societies to found schools in their towns. In these schools Cherokee children learned how to read and write English.

American Indians used complex spoken languages, but none had a written language. In the early 1800s a Cherokee named **Sequoya** developed a writing system that used 86 characters to represent Cherokee syllables. In 1828 the Cherokee began publishing a newspaper, the *Cherokee Phoenix*. This paper was printed in both English and Cherokee. The Cherokee also created a government inspired by the U.S. Constitution with an election system, a bicameral council, and a court system. All of these were headed by a principal chief. Voters elected **John Ross**, a successful plantation owner, as the first principal chief.

✔ **Reading Check: Summarizing** What contributions did Sequoya make to Cherokee culture? Sequoya developed a written Cherokee language.

Section 5

OBJECTIVES

⭐ Examine the favorite writers of the early 1800s and what they wrote about.

⭐ Describe the focus of the Hudson River school.

 **LET'S GET STARTED!**

Write the following name on the chalkboard: *Rip Van Winkle.* As students enter the classroom, ask them what they know about the story. *(Students' responses will vary, but students should point out that the character Rip Van Winkle slept for 20 years, and when he awoke, he found that the world had changed.)* Relate Washington Irving's story to the class and discuss as a class the changes that might occur 20 years from now. Then tell students that in Section 5 they will learn more about how changes in society affected writers such as Washington Irving.

Section 5

American Culture

Read to Discover

1. Who were the favorite writers of the early 1800s, and what did they write about?
2. What was the focus of the Hudson River school?

WHY IT MATTERS TODAY

Art and literature are important parts of a country's culture. Use **CNN fyi.com** and other **current events** sources to find an example of art or literature that reveals the culture of a country of your choice. Record your findings in your journal.

Identify

- Washington Irving
- James Fenimore Cooper
- Catharine Maria Sedgwick
- Hudson River school
- Thomas Cole
- George Caleb Bingham

SECTION 5 RESOURCES

REPRODUCIBLE

▶ Guided Reading Strategy 12.5
▶ Literature Reading 12: "Rip Van Winkle"

TECHNOLOGY

▶ One-Stop Planner, Lesson 12.5
▶ Art in American History Transparency 9: Fur Traders Descending the Missouri
▶ Homework Practice Online

REINFORCEMENT, REVIEW, AND ASSESSMENT

▶ Section 5 Review, p. 388
▶ Daily Quiz 12.5
▶ Main Idea Activity 12.5
▶ English Audio Summary 12.5
▶ Spanish Audio Summary 12.5

The Story Continues

In 1817 Virginia politician William Wirt published a popular biography of Revolutionary leader Patrick Henry. Wirt spent years researching his book. Yet he found that Henry was not as exciting as he had hoped. "The incidents of Mr. Henry's life are extremely monotonous [boring]," Wirt told a friend. "It is all speaking, speaking, speaking." To make his book more exciting, Wirt exaggerated certain events. Some critics accused him of rewriting history. Despite these complaints, Wirt's book helped make Patrick Henry a hero for a whole generation of Americans.

Patrick Henry was seen as a hero of the American Revolution.

⭐ American Tales

Many developments in American life led to the success of William Wirt's biography of Patrick Henry. For example, much of the public was interested in the Revolutionary era. Wirt represented a growing number of writers who wrote about the heroes of the Revolution. These writers inspired pride in the United States. Unlike Wirt, however, most of these writers used fictional characters to represent American ideals.

One of the first American writers to gain international fame was **Washington Irving**. Born in 1783, he was named after George

★ TEACH

Have students read Section 5 and complete Guided Reading Strategy 12.5. Choose one or more of the following activities to explore the section content with students. For further suggestions on block scheduling or team teaching, see the *Block Scheduling Handbook with Team Teaching Strategies.*

LEVEL 1: Show the class several famous landscape paintings. Tell students that before the 1830s, most American painters focused on portraits of individuals and that it was a group of artists known as the Hudson River school that began to focus on and paint the American landscape. Have students draw or paint the landscape around their community. Ask volunteers to present their work to the class. Discuss the similarities and differences of students' views of their surroundings. **ENGLISH LANGUAGE LEARNERS**

 ALL LEVELS: Copy the following graphic organizer onto the chalkboard, omitting the italicized answers. Have students complete the chart to discover the favorite writers of the early 1800s and what they wrote about. **ENGLISH LANGUAGE LEARNERS**

FAVORITE AMERICAN WRITERS OF THE EARLY 1800s	
Writers	**Subjects**
Washington Irving, James Fenimore Cooper, Catharine Maria Sedgwick	*American Revolution, settlement, and the landscape*

Science, Technology & Society

Improvements in Printing. Improvements in printing technology allowed publishers to increase their output and lower their costs. For example, James Fenimore Cooper's works had originally cost a dollar per volume. With improved technology, a new edition was released in the late 1830s at only 25 cents per volume.

CRITICAL THINKING

How might improvements in printing promote interest in American literature?

ANSWER: Students might suggest that publishers released more books with lower costs, which allowed more people to buy and read them.

CONNECTING TO THE ARTS ANSWER

Students might suggest that suspense is created by the look on Ichabod Crane's face.

CONNECTING TO THE ARTS

The Legend of Sleepy Hollow The literature of the early 1800s often inspired artists. In his painting *The Headless Horseman Pursuing Ichabod Crane*, artist John Quidor captures one of the most frightening scenes in Washington Irving's story "The Legend of Sleepy Hollow." Here Crane, the local schoolmaster, flees a headless rider that he believes is an evil spirit. How does the artist show the drama of this scene?

Washington. Irving's writing often dealt with American history. He often wrote humorous stories, using a style of writing called satire. Through satire, Irving warned that Americans should learn from the past and be cautious about the future. He shared this idea in one of his best-known short stories, "Rip Van Winkle." Rip Van Winkle is a man who falls asleep during the time of the American Revolution. He wakes up 20 years later to a society he does not recognize. Irving published this and another well-known tale, "The Legend of Sleepy Hollow," in an 1819–20 collection.

Irving was one of the first American writers to gain respect in Europe. In fact, European writers helped shape his humorous style. Irving believed that the United States should not give up European traditions altogether. He said, "We are a young people . . . , and we must take our examples and models in a great degree, from the existing nations of Europe."

✔ **Reading Check: Finding the Main Idea** How did Washington Irving help make American writing more respected? He wrote popular satirical stories that were admired in Europe and that continued some European traditions.

★ James Fenimore Cooper

In some of his most popular works, Irving combined European influences with American settings and characters. His work served as a bridge between European writing traditions and American writers exploring new styles. Perhaps the best known of these new writers was **James Fenimore Cooper**. Cooper was born to a wealthy New Jersey family in 1789. He never saw the American frontier, but stories about

LEVEL 3: Discuss the growth of historical fiction in the United States, and ask for examples of works by writers such as James Fenimore Cooper and Catharine Maria Sedgwick. (*Students' responses should mention* The Last of the Mohicans *or* Hope Leslie.) Have students write a short story that uses fictional characters to portray a historical event discussed in this chapter. Encourage volunteers to read their stories to the class.

HOMEWORK Have students use the library or other resources to find drawings, paintings, or photographs of American architectural styles of the post-Jacksonian, pre–Civil War period. Have students create a visual comparison between Georgian architecture and Greek and Roman architecture.

★ CLOSE

To conclude the lesson, show students a work of art from the Hudson River school and a work of art from an earlier period. Have students compare the works of art, and ask them to identify major differences. Finally, lead a class discussion on how literature and art changed in the early 1800s.

---

the West and the American Indians who lived there interested him. These topics became the focus of his best-known works.

In 1823 Cooper published *The Pioneers*. This novel was the first of five books that featured the heroic character Natty Bumppo. Together these books were called the Leatherstocking Tales. This series told of settling the western frontier. Cooper's hero, Bumppo, was a frontiersman who found truth in nature. Cooper's stories also included historical events. For example, *The Last of the Mohicans* takes place during the French and Indian War. By placing his fictional characters in the middle of a real historical event, Cooper popularized a type of writing called historical fiction.

★ Catharine Maria Sedgwick

Some critics, such as poet Russell Lowell, said that Cooper's characters were not interesting. They particularly criticized the women in his stories. Cooper's female characters seemed to have no purpose other than to be saved by the hero. Other authors of historical fiction, such as **Catharine Maria Sedgwick**, created more interesting heroines. In 1822 Sedgwick published her first novel, *A New England Tale*. This story describes the landscape and culture of New England life.

Another popular book by Sedgwick, *Hope Leslie*, was a historical novel set in Massachusetts in the 1600s. To make this 1827 novel realistic, Sedgwick did major research into the culture of the Mohawk Indians, who had lived in the area at the time. Some readers did not like Sedgwick's description of the Pilgrims. She included unpleasant parts of their lives, such as their superstitions and intolerance, in her novels. Sedgwick defended her work saying that it accurately showed both the strengths and weaknesses of early Americans in New England.

❛❛These were the vices [bad habits] of their age. . . . They had a most generous and self-devoting zeal [energy] to the cause of liberty, so far as they understood it, but they were still in the thraldom [captivity] of . . . superstition.❜❜

—Catharine Maria Sedgwick, from *Life and Letters of Catharine M. Sedgwick*, edited by Mary E. Dewey

Sedgwick hoped that Americans could learn new ideas from reading about the lives of the Pilgrims.

Sedgwick was the most successful female author of her time, writing six books. Through her work, she also challenged commonly held ideas about women. For example, in *Married or Single?* Sedgwick, who never married, rejected the idea that all women had to marry. She hoped the novel would "lessen the stigma [disgrace] placed on the term, old maid."

✔ **Reading Check: Analyzing Information** How did American writers such as Cooper and Sedgwick describe the growth of a new cultural identity in the United States? They wrote about American subjects such as the frontier, the American landscape, and the experiences of early American settlers.

Catharine Maria Sedgwick hoped that her novels would teach people about America while entertaining them.

THE GRANGER COLLECTION, NEW YORK

★ REVIEW AND ASSESS

Have students complete the **Section 5 Review** on p. 388. Then have students complete **Daily Quiz 12.5**. As **Alternative Assessment,** you may want to use the favorite writers graphic organizer or the drawing and painting activities in this section's lessons.

★ RETEACH

Have students complete **Main Idea Activity for English Language Learners and Special-Needs Students 12.5**. Then ask students to think about the following question: *How did popular writers and artists reflect changes in American culture?* Have students review material from the section and list ways that writers and artists reflected the growth and change of American culture. **ENGLISH LANGUAGE LEARNERS**

★ EXTEND

Have students choose a work by Washington Irving, James Fenimore Cooper, Catharine Maria Sedgwick, or another American historical fiction writer of the period. Tell students to read the selection they chose and prepare an oral report on it. Have students identify the actual historical event depicted in the story. Ask each student to present his or her report to the class. Finally, lead a class discussion on ways that each of the selected works reflect the basic ideas discussed in the section. **BLOCK SCHEDULING**

Section 5 Review
ANSWERS

❶ Identify
• Washington Irving, p. 385
• James Fenimore Cooper, p. 386
• Catharine Maria Sedgwick, p. 387
• Hudson River school, p. 388
• Thomas Cole, p. 388
• George Caleb Bingham, p. 388

❷ Writers—Irving, Cooper, Sedgwick; Painters—Cole, Bingham, Hudson River school; American Cultural Identity—American landscapes, the frontier, and people's relationship to their American environment

❸ a. Irving—why Americans should learn from their past and be cautious about their future; Cooper—settling the American frontier; Sedgwick—New England scenery, focused on historical accuracy, women's issues and early settlement
b. American landscapes, usually from the Hudson River valley

❹ Students' stories will vary but should describe American painters, writers, and the cultural landscape.

CONNECTING TO LITERATURE ANSWERS
(for p. 389)

1. They have lost their lands to European settlers.

2. They are going into decline and will soon disappear as a people.

3. Students might suggest that he feels that he should bring this matter to the public's attention.

Thomas Cole painted The Notch in the White Mountains in 1839.

Analyzing Primary Sources
Identifying Points of View According to Bryant, why was Cole's painting uniquely American? It portrayed the American landscape "peculiar to our country."

★ A New Style of Art

The writings of Irving and Cooper also inspired painters. These artists began to paint landscapes that showed the history of America and the beauty of the land. Earlier American painters, such as John Singleton Copley, were portrait painters. By the 1830s a group of artists called the **Hudson River school** emerged. These artists primarily painted landscapes. Their name came from the subject of many of their paintings—the Hudson River valley.

Thomas Cole was the leader of the group. He had moved to the United States from Britain in 1819 and soon recognized the unique qualities of the American landscape. As his work gained fame, he encouraged other American artists to show the beauty of nature. Observer William Bryant praised Cole's painting.

 History Makers Speak
❝[It] carried the eye over scenes of wild grandeur peculiar to our country, over our aerial mountain tops with their mighty growth of forests never touched by the axe, along the bank of streams never deformed by culture and into the depth of skies bright with the hues [colors] of our own climate.❞
—William Bryant, quoted in *Art and Life in America*, by Oliver W. Larkin

By the 1840s many American artists were combining rugged landscapes with scenes of frontier life. For example, **George Caleb Bingham** tried to show the ruggedness of the West. As the country grew, the new styles of art and literature helped form a new American national identity.

✔ **Reading Check: Finding the Main Idea** How did the style of American art change to reflect the American way of life in the early 1800s? It began to focus on the American landscape and the people who lived in it.

Section 5 Review

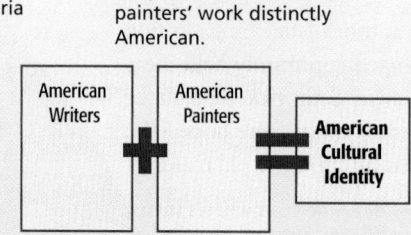
go. hrw .com **Homework Practice Online**
keyword: SA3 HP12

❶ Identify and explain:
• Washington Irving
• James Fenimore Cooper
• Catharine Maria Sedgwick
• Hudson River school
• Thomas Cole
• George Caleb Bingham

❷ Summarizing Copy the graphic organizer below. Use it to identify the shared characteristics that made early American writers' and painters' work distinctly American.

American Writers **+** American Painters **=** American Cultural Identity

❸ Finding the Main Idea
a. Who were some major early American authors, and what did they write about?
b. What subjects did Thomas Cole and the other Hudson River school artists paint?

❹ Writing and Critical Thinking
Analyzing Information Imagine that you are an art student visiting America from Europe in the 1840s. Write a story to tell your classmates that describes how American culture reflects the American way of life.
Consider the following:
• the work of popular American writers
• the work of popular American painters

CONNECTING TO *Literature*

The Last of the Mohicans

James Fenimore Cooper

James Fenimore Cooper was the first major American novelist. His novels helped create the myth of the frontier and the American frontier hero. Natty Bumppo, also called Leatherstocking and Hawkeye, is the hero of the five novels called the Leatherstocking Tales. Chingachgook, a Mohican Indian, is also an important character in the popular stories. Cooper did not have direct experience with American Indians or the frontier. He simply read books and listened to the stories his father told. Nevertheless, Cooper's novels brought the frontier to life for many readers. Cooper had a wide audience in the United States and Europe. His novels have remained popular since his death in 1851. The following excerpt is from The Last of the Mohicans, *set during the French and Indian War. In this passage Chingachgook tells Hawkeye about the Mohicans' recent history.*

"The first pale-faces who came among us spoke no English. They came in a large canoe, when my fathers had **buried the tomahawk**[1] with the redmen around them. Then, Hawkeye," he continued, betraying his deep emotion . . . : "then, Hawkeye, we were one people, we were happy. The salt lake gave us its fish, the wood its deer, and the air its birds. We took wives who bore us children; we worshipped the Great Spirit; and we kept the **Maquas**[2] beyond the sound of our songs of triumph! . . .

"The Dutch landed, and gave my people the **fire-water**;[3] they drank until the heavens and the earth seemed to meet, and they foolishly thought they had found the Great Spirit. Then they parted with their land. Foot by foot, they were driven back from the shores, until I, that am a chief and a **sagamore**,[4] have never seen the sun shine but through the trees, and have never visited the graves of my fathers. . . .

"Where are the blossoms of those summers!—fallen, one by one: so all of my family departed, each in his turn, to the land of spirits. I am on the hill-top, and most go down into the valley; and when Uncas follows in my footsteps, there will no longer be any of the blood of the sagamores, for my boy is the last of the Mohicans."

Understanding What You Read

1. **Literature and History** According to the story told by Chingachgook, what has happened to the Mohicans?

2. **Literature and History** What does Chingachgook mean by going down into the valley, and how is this significant for the Mohicans?

3. **Literature and You** Why do you think that Cooper chose to portray the decline of the Mohicans in this way?

---

[1]**buried the tomahawk:** made peace
[2]**Maquas:** their enemy
[3]**fire-water:** alcoholic beverages
[4]**sagamore:** a lesser chief of the Algonquian

REVIEW AND ASSESSMENT RESOURCES

REPRODUCIBLE
▶ Vocabulary Activity 12

TECHNOLOGY
▶ Chapter 12 Test Generator (on the One-Stop Planner)
▶ Global Skill Builder CD–ROM
▶ HRW Go site

REINFORCEMENT, REVIEW, AND ASSESSMENT
▶ Chapter 12 Review, pp. 389–91
▶ Chapter 12 Tutorial for Students, Parents, Mentors, and Peers

▶ Chapter 12 Test (Form A or B)
▶ Alternative Assessment Handbook
▶ Chapter 12 Test for English Language Learners and Special-Needs Students

★ REVIEW

Have students complete the **Chapter 12 Review** on pages 390–91.

★ ASSESS

Use one of the chapter tests to assess students' understanding of the content. For **Alternative Assessment**, see the **Alternative Assessment Handbook**.

Understanding Main Ideas

1. President Monroe was concerned that European nations would try to gain influence in the newly liberated Latin American nations, so he issued the Monroe Doctrine. It kept European countries from intervening in Latin America.

2. Missouri wanted to enter the Union as a slave state, which would upset the balance between slave and free states; it provided for the admission of Missouri as a slave state and Maine as a free state, as well as the prohibition of slavery north of latitude 36° 30'.

3. Northern manufacturers supported the tariff. Southerners imported most of their goods and thus would have to pay higher prices, opposed the tariff.

4. He believed the Bank gave wealthy Americans too much influence on the government.

5. The Sauk, the Seminole, and the Creek used armed resistance, while the Cherokee, turned to the courts for protection.

6. American Revolution, American landscape, American settlement, women's issues

You Be the Historian— Reviewing Themes

1. Canada—the Rush-Bagot Agreement and the Convention of 1818; Spain—the Adams-Onís Treaty

---

Chapter **12** Review

The Chapter at a Glance
Examine the visual summary of the chapter below. Use the chapter's main ideas to create a five-section outline that you might give to a classmate to study.

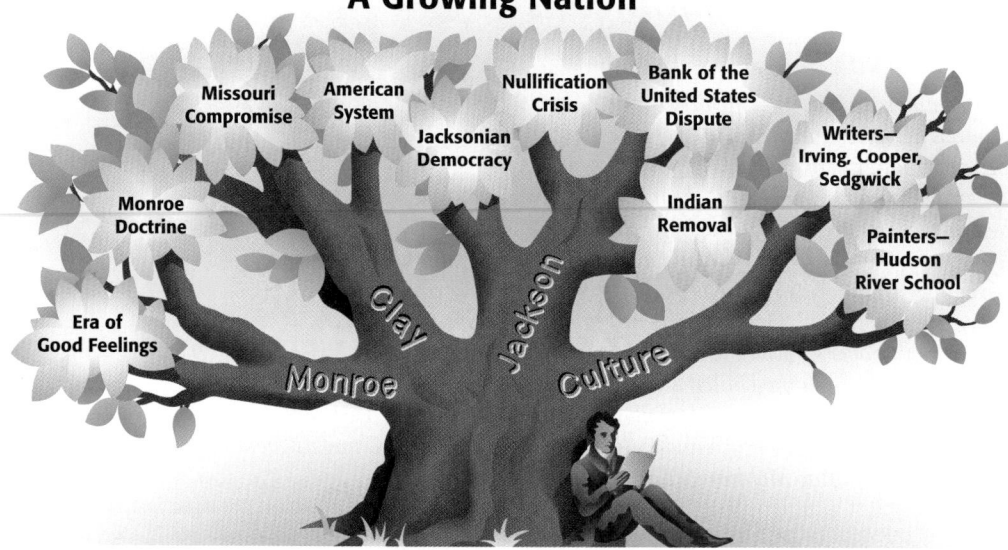

A Growing Nation

Identifying People and Ideas
Use the following terms or people in historically significant sentences.
1. Monroe Doctrine
2. Henry Clay
3. American System
4. Democratic Party
5. John C. Calhoun
6. nullification crisis
7. *McCulloch* v. *Maryland*
8. *Worcester* v. *Georgia*
9. Trail of Tears
10. Hudson River school

Understanding Main Ideas
Section 1 (*Pages 364–367*)
1. What effect did the revolutions in Latin America have on U.S. foreign policy, and what was the impact of the U.S. response?

Section 2 (*Pages 368–373*)
2. What led to the Missouri Compromise, and what did it achieve?

Section 3 (*Pages 374–379*)
3. How did the issue of protective tariffs divide northerners and southerners?
4. Why did President Jackson veto the rechartering of the Second Bank of the United States?

Section 4 (*Pages 380–384*)
5. How did American Indians resist removal to Indian Territory?

Section 5 (*Pages 385–388*)
6. What topics did early American authors write about?

You Be the Historian— Reviewing Themes
1. **Global Relations** How did the United States settle its border disputes with British Canada and Spanish Florida?
2. **Citizenship** How did U.S. political parties change between the elections of 1820 and 1828?
3. **Constitutional Heritage** What did Chief Justice John Marshall and the Supreme Court decide in *McCulloch* v. *Maryland* and *Worcester* v. *Georgia*, and how did these cases affect the power of state governments?

Thinking Critically
1. **Comparing** What was similar about the disputes that led to the Missouri Compromise and the nullification crisis?
2. **Contrasting** How did protective tariffs affect the economies of the North, the South, and the West?
3. **Analyzing Information** How did American culture develop in the 1820s?

RETEACH

Organize students into five groups and assign each group one of the chapter's sections. Give each group a large sheet of butcher paper and have students make a flowchart showing how the major events depicted in the section are related. Display the finished flowcharts around the classroom and ask volunteers from each group to explain the connections depicted on their groups' charts to the class.
**ENGLISH LANGUAGE LEARNERS ,
COOPERATIVE LEARNING**

Portfolio Extensions

1. Cooperative Learning
Have students read Washington Irving's "Rip Van Winkle" or "The Legend of Sleepy Hollow." Organize students into groups. Then have each group discuss the story and how it fulfills Irving's desire to create American myths and legends. Finally, ask groups to write a short play that summarizes the story that they have read. Each group may wish to perform the play for the class. **COOPERATIVE LEARNING**

2. Linking to Community
Ask students to determine the American Indian group that was nearest to the region where they live during the 1800s. Have students investigate the group's history during the past 200 years. Then have students create a map that visually illustrates the group's experiences up to the present.

Interpreting Political Cartoons
Study the editorial cartoon of Andrew Jackson below. Then answer the questions that follow.

BORN TO COMMAND.

OF VETO MEMORY.

HAD I BEEN CONSULTED.

THE GRANGER COLLECTION, NEW YORK

KING ANDREW THE FIRST.

1. Which of the following statements best describes the artist's attitude about Jackson?
   a. Jackson should be king.
   b. Jackson is a strong leader.
   c. Jackson has vetoed too many bills.
   d. Jackson is behaving more like a king than an elected leader.

2. Is the artist in favor of or opposed to Jackson's policies?

Analyzing Primary Sources
Read the following quote from Senator John C. Calhoun concerning tariffs and states' rights, then answer the questions that follow.

> "The truth can no longer be disguised, that the peculiar domestick institutions of the Southern States [that is, slavery], and the consequent direction which that and her soil and climate have given to her industry, has placed them in regard to taxation . . . in opposite relation to [against] the majority of the Union; against the danger of which, if there be no protective power in the reserved rights of the states, they must in the end be forced to rebel."

3. Why does Calhoun think that the South is opposed to the tariff that the other states support?
   a. The southern economy, based on agriculture and slavery, is very different from that of the North and other parts of the Union.
   b. Southern politicians believe that the tariff and other taxes like it are unconstitutional.
   c. The South fears that it might be attacked by other states in the Union.
   d. The true reasons why the South opposes the tariff are hidden.

4. Based on your knowledge of the period, do you think that President Jackson would have agreed or disagreed with Senator Calhoun's views?

2. Political parties became better organized and more important between 1820 and 1828.

3. that the Second Bank of the United States was constitutional, that the Cherokee nation was a distinct community under the jurisdiction of the federal government and the state of Georgia had no legal authority over them; said that the state governments had to follow the federal government's laws

Thinking Critically
1. They both involved disagreements between northern states and southern states.

2. Answers may vary but should be supported with examples from Jackson's presidency.

3. Americans saw their own history, environment, and experiences as very different from those of Europeans. Examples include historical fiction and landscape paintings.

Skills Workshop
1. d

2. opposed to

3. b

4. Students should say that Jackson opposed the idea of nullification on the tariff so he would probably disagree with senator Calhoun's views.

Building Your Portfolio

Interdisciplinary Connection to Geography
Select a region of the country (either the South, the Northeast, or the Midwest). Then create a brochure that might be used to attract settlers or immigrants to that region in the 1830s. Your brochure should focus on the region's culture, economy, and historical points of interest.

internet connect

**Internet Activity: go.hrw.com
keyword: SA3 CF12**

Choose an activity about the New National Identity of America to:
● Learn about other wars of independence.
● Research the development of an American culture in art and literature.
● Create a newspaper about Andrew Jackson and the politics of the 1830s.

✪ TEACH

ALL LEVELS: Explain to students that cause and effect is rarely simple and that few effects have only one cause. Have students review the material on *Marbury* v. *Madison* on textbook pages 336–337. Ask them to copy the cause-and-effect chart about the case from this page and to use the material from the text to expand it. Encourage students to reflect the fact that many causes led to the case and that the case itself had a number of other effects. Once they have expanded the chart, have students search the text for the clue words and phrases that helped them identify the relationships they showed in their charts. Ask them to finalize their cause-and-effect charts by adding the clue words and phrases on the lines to show the connections between events.

ENGLISH LANGUAGE LEARNERS

UNDERSTANDING CAUSE AND EFFECT

Have students choose a current event and search newspapers over the past month for its causes. Ask them to create a cause-and-effect chart and to use the clue words and phrases on this page to write a paragraph describing the causes that led up to the event. Encourage students to draw inferences about cause and effect by speculating on what effects the event they studied may have on future events.

SKILLS ANSWERS

1. Students' answers will vary.
2. Students' diagrams will vary, but they should include impressments, embargo attempts, American Indian unrest, and the War Hawks.

Social Studies Skills
WORKSHOP

Identifying Cause and Effect

Identifying and understanding cause-and-effect relationships is crucial to the study of history. To investigate why events happen and what else may have happened because of these events, historians often ask questions such as: What immediate activities may have triggered the event? What past activities may have led up to the event? Who was involved?

How to Identify Cause and Effect

1. **Look for clues.** Certain words and phrases are immediate clues. They reveal the existence of a cause-and-effect relationship in history. The following chart lists some examples of clue words and phrases.

Clue Words and Phrases	
Cause	**Effect**
because	as a consequence
brought about	as a result of
gave rise to	depended on
inspired	originating from
led to	outcome
produced	proceeded from
provoked	resulting in
the reason	this led to

2. **Identify the relationship.** Read carefully to identify how historical events may be connected. Writers do not always state the link between cause and effect. Therefore, you must read very carefully. You may have to draw your own conclusions about the cause or the effect of an event.

3. **Check for complex connections.** Beyond the immediate cause and effect, check for other more complex connections. For example, an event might have multiple causes or effects. Effects may also be the causes of further events.

The following diagram presents an important cause-and-effect relationship involving the *Marbury* v. *Madison* Supreme Court case. In 1801 President John Adams appointed William Marbury as a federal judge. The new secretary of state, James Madison, refused to give Marbury his commission. This led Marbury to take his case to the Supreme Court. Chief Justice John Marshall decided that the Court did not have the power to force the government to give Marbury his commission. This ruling produced the principle of judicial review, which allows the Supreme Court to decide whether an act of Congress is constitutional.

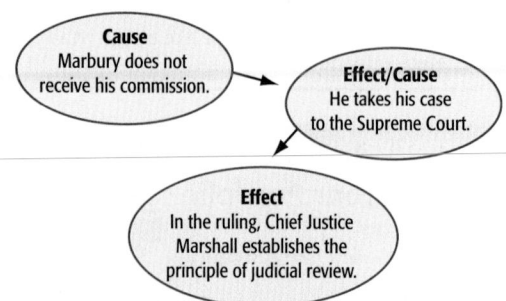

Practicing the Skills

1. Identify the clue words used in the example above.
2. Reread Chapter 11, Section 3, of your textbook, which discusses the causes of the War of 1812.

Draw a diagram like the one above, showing the relationships between the important events leading up to the War of 1812.

LEVELS 2 AND 3: Once the students have given their presentations outlined in the History in Action lesson to the class, inform them that Congress has approved their plan. Have them write a story from the viewpoint of a settler who is thinking about moving west. In their stories, students should discuss the positives and negatives influencing their decisions. Students should also say if the presentations influenced their decision in any way. Ask volunteers to read their stories to the class.

LEVEL 3: Have students imagine that they are members of an American Indian nation living west of the Mississippi River as settlers began moving west. Tell students that they have been appointed by members of their nation to approach President Jefferson about their concerns for how westward expansion will impact their way of life. Then have each student write a letter to the president outlining their concerns and explaining what effects the expansion might have on American Indians.

History in Action

UNIT 5 SIMULATION

You Solve the Problem . . .

How Do You Encourage Westward Expansion during the Early 1800s?

Complete the following activity in small cooperative groups. It is 1803. Thomas Jefferson has purchased the Louisiana Territory from France. The United States has expanded to the Mississippi River. You are a member of a congressional subcommittee that will propose a plan to Congress to encourage westward expansion. Follow these steps to solve your problem.

 **1. Gather Information.** Use your textbook and other resources to find information that might influence your plan of action for encouraging westward expansion. Be sure to use what you learned from the unit's Skills Workshop on Identifying Cause and Effect to help you find an effective solution to this problem. For example, you might consider why people choose to settle new lands and what effects their settlements may have. You may want to divide different parts of the research among group members.

2. List and Consider Options. After reviewing the information you have gathered, list and consider the options you might recommend for encouraging westward expansion. Your final solution to the problem may be easier to reach if you consider as many options as possible. Be sure to record your possible options for your presentation.

 **3. Consider Advantages and Disadvantages.** Now consider the advantages and disadvantages of taking each option. Ask yourselves questions like: "What are the main benefits of westward expansion for the nation and for individuals?" Once you have considered the advantages and disadvantages, record them as notes for your presentation.

 4. Choose, Implement, and Evaluate a Solution. After considering the advantages and disadvantages, you should plan and create a presentation. Be sure to make your proposal very clear. You will need to support your proposed plans for encouraging westward expansion by including information you gathered and by explaining why you rejected other possible options or solutions. Your presentation needs to be visually appealing so that you can get Congress to support your proposal. When you are ready, decide which group members will make each part of the presentation, and then take your solution to Congress (the rest of the class). Good luck!

History in Action
Encourage students to investigate other historical issues that have come before Congress throughout U.S. history. Then have students choose one issue or event and have them incorporate the problem-solving steps found on this page into a proposal. Ask students to present their proposal to Congress (the class) in order to persuade Congress to their point of view.

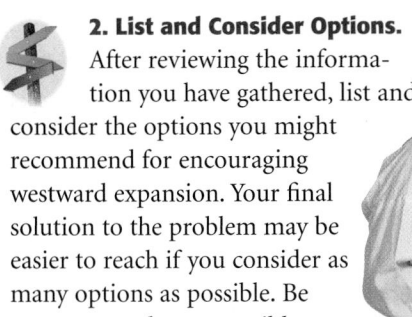

CHAPTER 13

Industrial Growth in the North

During the early 1800s the use of machinery and interchangeable parts dramatically changed the rate at which goods such as cloth could be produced. The changes in manufacturing were coupled with dramatic changes in transportation as railroads and new types of ships quickened the pace of American life. New devices such as the telegraph and the sewing machine also revolutionized daily life in the United States.

CHAPTER 14

Agricultural Changes in the South

After the Revolutionary War the price of southern cash crops declined. However, the invention of the cotton gin created a new cash crop for the South. The southern economy came to be dominated by cotton, and many southern ports developed a lively overseas trade. Cotton production depended heavily on slave labor. Under the southern slave system, Africans forced to come to America suffered terrible conditions and had to perform hard labor. In spite of this, slaves developed a deep religious sense and a rich culture.

Internet Activity

Northern Factories

internet connect

TOPIC: Northern Factories
GO TO: go.hrw.com
KEYWORD: SA3 Factory Life

Have students search the Internet through the HRW Go site for information on factory life during the early 1800s. Have students use the information that they obtain along with information from the Young People in History feature on the opposite page to write a diary entry, using standard grammar, spelling, sentence structure, and punctuation, from the perspective of a child working in a factory during the early 1800s.

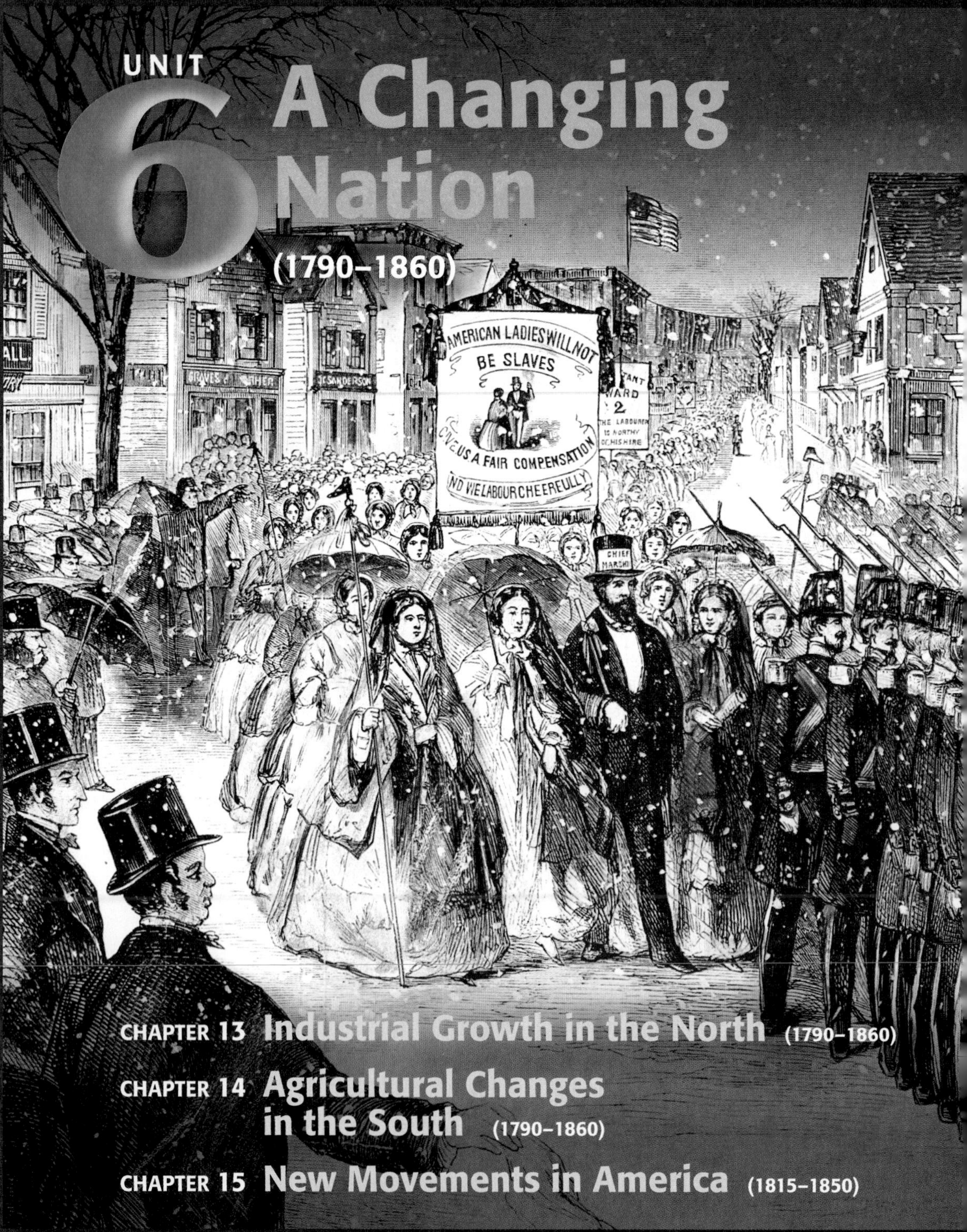

UNIT
6 A Changing Nation
(1790–1860)

Between 1790 and 1850, life and culture in the United States changed dramatically. Americans began to try to find more intense meaning in their lives through deeper religious commitment or though romantic art and transcendental thought. Waves of immigrants led to the rapid growth of cities. At the same time, a number of Americans attempted to improve social conditions.

Share the information in the chapter overviews with students. Write each of the unit's chapter titles as headings on the chalkboard. Use the first two headings to create a comparison chart of what students expect will be the differences and similarities between the North and the South based on information that they have learned about the regions thus far. Have students create a dialogue between a southerner and a northerner, reflecting their knowledge. Call on volunteers to act out their dialogues. After you have finished the unit, ask students to evaluate how closely their ideas matched the actual events of the chapters and to revise their dialogues according to what they have learned. Encourage students to consider the information about reform movements when revising their dialogues.

Young People
IN HISTORY
Young Workers

By the mid-1800s teenage girls throughout New England were working and earning money of their own. These teenagers included girls in the city and in the country. Girls in rural areas usually worked out of their homes. They wove cloth, braided hats, or stitched together shoes. Girls in the cities often did needlework or found work as housekeepers or cooks.

In Fitzwilliam, New Hampshire, many young women made hats to be sold at the local store. They were usually not paid in money, but in store credit. Martha Alexander was 18 years old when she began making hats. Over a period of nearly four years, she braided 341 hats. Her store credit allowed her to buy teacups, saucers, and plates for her upcoming marriage.

Other New England girls worked in textile mills. In Lowell, Massachusetts, about half of the young women working in the mills were between the ages of 15 and 19 when they first arrived. Despite the long hours, many girls enjoyed their work in the mills. It gave them independence and relieved the isolation of farm life. The girls used their hard-earned money in many ways. Many of them sent money home to help their families or saved it for their future. Some girls spent their money on clothes and recreation, such as plays and concerts.

Textile mills often employed young workers.

Some teenagers found that life at the mills opened up a bright, new future for them. Lucy Larcom worked in the Lowell mills while she was a teenager and wrote about her experiences.

❝And I was everyday making discoveries about life, and about myself. . . . I found that the crowd was made up of single human lives, not one of them wholly uninteresting, when separately known. . . . I defied the machinery to make me its slave. Its incessant discords [constant noise] could not drown the music of my thoughts. . . . I know that I was glad to be alive, and to be just where I was.❞

If You Were There   *What sorts of jobs would you be interested in?*

LEFT PAGE: *These workers from a shoe factory in Lynn, Massachusetts, went on strike in 1860.*

Mass-Produced Art. The engraving on the opposite page of striking women workers from a shoe factory was mass-produced. During the mid-1800s producing prints of famous subjects, portraits, and American scenery became a highly profitable business. Mass-produced prints such as this one would cost anywhere from 25 cents to $3. The price was low enough that many Americans used prints to decorate their homes. These works were first printed in black and white, and then a group of young people, each in charge of a different color, would fill in the colors. Eventually, the prints were created by using a color process that no longer required the painstaking labor of the colorists.

CRITICAL THINKING

Why might a printmaker choose to produce an image of this strike?

ANSWER: Students might suggest that a print may have mass appeal because people would be interested in seeing this major event. A printmaker might also want to use the image to spread news about the strike.

	Objectives	Pacing Guide	Reproducible Resources
SECTION 1: **The Industrial Revolution and America** (pp. 398–403)	✴ Discuss how Samuel Slater contributed to the growth of the textile industry in the Northeast. ✴ Explain how Eli Whitney's ideas benefited manufacturing. ✴ Describe how events before and during the War of 1812 aided the growth of manufacturing in the United States.	**Regular** 2 days **Block Scheduling** 1 day *Block Scheduling Handbook with Team Teaching Strategies, Chapter 13*	**RS** Guided Reading Strategy 13.1 **RS** Graphic Organizer 13: The Growth of Industry
SECTION 2: **Changes in Working Life** (pp. 404–09)	✴ Examine how the Rhode Island and Lowell systems differed. ✴ List the ways that the introduction of factories influenced the daily life of workers in the northeastern United States. ✴ Describe how Sarah G. Bagley and other reformers contributed to the early labor movement.	**Regular** 2 days **Block Scheduling** 1 day *Block Scheduling Handbook with Team Teaching Strategies, Chapter 13*	**RS** Guided Reading Strategy 13.2 **PS** Literature Reading 13: Transportation in the United States **PS** Primary Source Reading 13: The Lowell Girls **E** Hands-On History Activity: Working Conditions in a Local Industry
SECTION 3: **The Transportation Revolution** (pp. 410–14)	✴ Describe how the Transportation Revolution changed life in the United States. ✴ Discuss the effect of the Supreme Court case *Gibbons* v. *Ogden*. ✴ Analyze how the growth of the railroads benefited the nation.	**Regular** 2 days **Block Scheduling** 1 day *Block Scheduling Handbook with Team Teaching Strategies, Chapter 13*	**RS** Guided Reading Strategy 13.3 **SM** Geography Activity 13: The National Road **PS** Biography Reading 13: Robert Fulton
SECTION 4: **More Technological Advances** (pp. 415–19)	✴ Describe the ideas Samuel Morse drew upon in order to invent the telegraph. ✴ Explain how new developments benefited factory and farm work. ✴ Identify the new inventions Cyrus McCormick and Isaac Singer developed.	**Regular** 1.5 days **Block Scheduling** .5 day *Block Scheduling Handbook with Team Teaching Strategies, Chapter 13*	**RS** Guided Reading Strategy 13.4 **E** Creative Teaching Strategy: Analyzing Political Cartoons

Chapter Resource Key

PS	Primary Sources	**A**	Assessment
RS	Reading Support	**REV**	Review
IC	Interdisciplinary Connections	**ELL**	Reinforcement and English Language Learners
E	Enrichment		Transparencies
SM	Skills Mastery		CD-ROM

 Music
 Video
 Internet
 Holt Presentation Maker Using Microsoft® PowerPoint®

 One-Stop Planner CD-ROM

See the *One-Stop Planner* for a complete list of additional resources for students and teachers.

One-Stop Planner CD-ROM

It's easy to plan lessons, select resources, and print out materials for your students when you use the **One-Stop Planner CD-ROM with Test Generator.**

Technology Resources	Reinforcement, Review, and Assessment

 One-Stop Planner, Lesson 13.1
 American History Simulations CD-ROM: Choosing a Factory Site
 Homework Practice Online
 HRW Go site

REV Section 1 Review, p. 403
A Daily Quiz 13.1
ELL Main Idea Activity 13.1
ELL English Audio Summary 13.1
ELL Spanish Audio Summary 13.1

 One-Stop Planner, Lesson 13.2
 Exploring America's Past Video Segment: Factory Girls; Teacher's Guide, pp. 20–21
 Holt Researcher: American History CD-ROM
Homework Practice Online

REV Section 2 Review, p. 409
A Daily Quiz 13.2
ELL Main Idea Activity 13.2
ELL English Audio Summary 13.2
ELL Spanish Audio Summary 13.2

 One-Stop Planner, Lesson 13.3
 Linking Geography and History Transparency 10: Growth of Transportation 1840
 CNN Presents America: Yesterday and Today, Beginnings to 1914 Segment: Rebuilding the Riverboats
 Homework Practice Online
 HRW Go site

REV Section 3 Review, p. 414
A Daily Quiz 13.3
ELL Main Idea Activity 13.3
ELL English Audio Summary 13.3
ELL Spanish Audio Summary 13.3

 One-Stop Planner, Lesson 13.4
 Homework Practice Online

REV Section 4 Review, p. 418
A Daily Quiz 13.4
ELL Main Idea Activity 13.4
ELL English Audio Summary 13.4
ELL Spanish Audio Summary 13.4

internet connect

HRW ONLINE RESOURCES
GO TO: go.hrw.com
Then type in a keyword.

TEACHER HOME PAGE
KEYWORD: SA3 Teacher

CHAPTER INTERNET ACTIVITIES
KEYWORD: SA3 CF13
Choose an activity to:
• create a database and graph of the economic and social impact of the McCormick Reaper.
• learn about clipper ships.
• write a biography of Samuel Slater.

CHAPTER ENRICHMENT LINKS
KEYWORD: SA3 CH13

ONLINE ASSESSMENT
Homework Practice
KEYWORD: SA3 HP13

Standardized Test Prep
KEYWORD: SA3 STP13

Rubrics
KEYWORD: SS Rubrics

ONLINE MAPS, CHARTS, AND GRAPHS
KEYWORD: SA3 MCG
• The National Road
• The National Debt
• Transportation Methods

CONTENT UPDATES
KEYWORD: SS Content Updates

HOLT PRESENTATION MAKER
KEYWORD: SA3 PPT13

ONLINE READING SUPPORT
KEYWORD: SS Strategies

CURRENT EVENTS
KEYWORD: S3 Current Events

Meeting Individual Needs

Ability Levels

Level 1 Basic-level activities designed for all students encountering new material

Level 2 Intermediate-level activities designed for average students

Level 3 Challenging activities designed for honors and gifted-and-talented students

English Language Learners Activities that address the needs of students with Limited English Proficiency

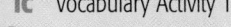

Chapter Review and Assessment

IC Vocabulary Activity 13
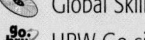 Global Skill Builder CD-ROM
HRW Go site
REV Chapter 13 Tutorial for Students, Parents, Mentors, and Peers
REV Chapter 13 Review, pp. 419–21
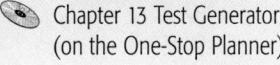 Chapter 13 Test Generator (on the One-Stop Planner)
A Chapter 13 Test (Form A or B)

A Alternative Assessment Handbook
A Chapter 13 Test for English Language Learners and Special-Needs Students

Build on What You Know

If You Were There...

Ask students to answer the following question:

What kind of invention would you try to develop?

Consider:

- the technological needs of the time period
- economic conditions and available resources

You Be the Historian

What's Your Opinion?

To help students create their **Themes** Journal entries, provide the following examples of appropriate **agree**/**disagree** statements.

EXPLORING THE TIME LINE
AMERICAN EVENTS

📶 **internet** connect

TOPIC: *Gibbons* v. *Ogden*
GO TO: go.hrw.com
KEYWORD: SA3 CF13

Have students access the Internet through the HRW Go site to research the background of *Gibbons* v. *Ogden* and its effect on both the regulation of commerce and the limitation of the powers of federal and state governments. Then have students research other landmark cases related to the commerce clause. Tell them to create a chart that contains the following information: the name of the case, the issues of the case, and how the case influenced the evolving concepts of federal and state powers.

CHAPTER

13 Industrial Growth in the North
(1790–1860)

The invention of the steel plow increased farm productivity.

Steamboats made river travel easier.

UNITED STATES

1793 Samuel Slater helps build a mill in Rhode Island for spinning cotton thread.

1807 Robert Fulton's *Clermont* becomes the first commercially successful steamboat.

1818 Eli Whitney invents the milling machine, which can make complex parts for many kinds of equipment.

1824 *Gibbons* v. *Ogden,* a case dealing with the power of the federal government to regulate commerce, reaches the Supreme Court.

1790	**1800**	**1810**	**1820**

1790 The first steam-powered mill opens in Great Britain.

1796 British doctor Edward Jenner develops an inoculation to prevent people from getting smallpox.

Dr. Edward Jenner

1814 Sweden and Norway are united in the Treaty of Kiel.

1821 Greece starts fighting for its independence from the Ottoman Empire.

WORLD

The manufacture of cloth was one of the first breakthroughs in the Industrial Revolution.

Build on What You Know

In the early 1800s Americans began to feel an increased sense of national pride, which led to new styles of art and literature. The country was also beginning to experience revolutions in industry and transportation. Factories, railroads, and steamships were built throughout the nation, particularly in the Northeast. These helped the U.S. economy grow rapidly.

Government

Agree   It is the duty of the government to regulate new kinds of technology and transportation.

Disagree   Government and business must be kept separate.

Science, Technology & Society

Agree   Technology changes the way people work.

Disagree   Technology may not affect the work of some people.

Economics

Agree   Improvements in transportation strengthen the national economy.

Disagree   Developments in transportation might threaten economic stability.

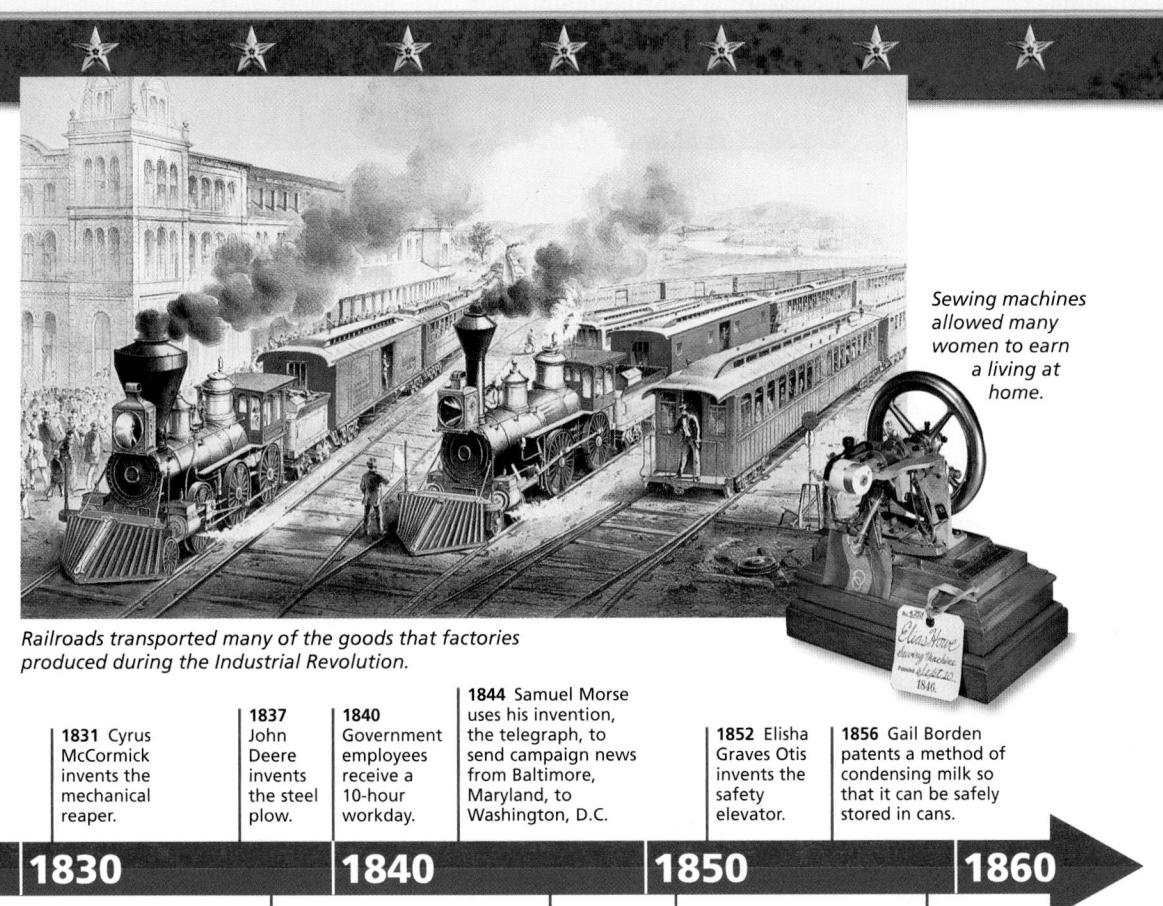

Railroads transported many of the goods that factories produced during the Industrial Revolution.

Sewing machines allowed many women to earn a living at home.

1831 Cyrus McCormick invents the mechanical reaper.

1837 John Deere invents the steel plow.

1840 Government employees receive a 10-hour workday.

1844 Samuel Morse uses his invention, the telegraph, to send campaign news from Baltimore, Maryland, to Washington, D.C.

1852 Elisha Graves Otis invents the safety elevator.

1856 Gail Borden patents a method of condensing milk so that it can be safely stored in cans.

1830   **1840**   **1850**   **1860**

1838 The *Sirius* becomes the first steamship to cross the Atlantic Ocean entirely under steam power.

1847 The British Factory Act limits the working day to 10 hours for women and children.

1851 The Great Exhibition in London displays inventions from around the world.

1859 Construction of the Suez Canal begins in Egypt.

If you were there . . .
What kind of invention would you try to develop?

You Be the Historian

Themes Journal

What's Your Opinion? Do you **agree** or **disagree** with the following statements? Support your point of view in your journal.

- **Government** Governments have the right to control new kinds of technology and transportation.
- **Science, Technology & Society** Technology changes the way people work whether they want it to or not.
- **Economics** Improved transportation leads to a stronger national economy.

The Great Exhibition of 1851. After the success of the French Industrial Exposition of 1844, talk began about having a similar exhibition in London. The British government was not interested at first, however. Though France held many exhibitions, Great Britain hosted mainly small local events. Britain's Prince Albert lobbied for a large, privately funded event. In January 1850, the Royal Commission finally agreed. Construction then began on a massive site. In 1851, Great Britain hosted its industrial-art exhibition, the largest event of its kind up to that time. The Great Exhibition of 1851 was a huge financial success. Before the doors opened, enough tickets had been sold to achieve a profit. By the time the doors closed six months later, 6 million people had visited the exhibition. The queen herself is said to have attended most every day.

ACTIVITY: Have students conduct research at the library to find and support an answer to the following question: *What other public exhibitions have met with similar success?* Have students write responses and present their findings to the class. Ask students to use standard grammar, spelling, sentence structure, and punctuation while drafting their response.

Section 1

OBJECTIVES

★ Discuss how Samuel Slater contributed to the growth of the textile industry in the Northeast.

★ Explain how Eli Whitney's ideas benefited manufacturing.

★ Describe how events before and during the War of 1812 aided the growth of manufacturing in the United States.

LET'S GET STARTED!

Write the following statement on the chalkboard: *Name an invention that would make people's lives easier.* As students enter the classroom, have them write down their ideas. *(Students' ideas might include devices to aid communications, daily life, transportation, etc.)* Have students explain why the invention would be useful and describe how it could improve people's lives. Call on volunteers to explain their ideas to the class. *(Students' ideas will vary.)* Tell students that in Section 1 they will learn how new technology in the early 1800s spurred the first stages of the Industrial Revolution in the United States.

Section 1

The Industrial Revolution and America

Read to Discover

1. How did Samuel Slater contribute to the growth of the textile industry in the Northeast?
2. How did Eli Whitney's ideas benefit manufacturing?
3. How did events before and during the War of 1812 aid the growth of manufacturing and free enterprise in the United States?

WHY IT MATTERS TODAY

Each year inventors apply for patents and copyrights for their new inventions and products. Use CNNfyi.com or other **current events** sources to learn more about some of the different items that have been invented in recent years. Record your findings in your journal.

Define

• textiles
• technology
• interchangeable parts
• mass production

Identify

• Industrial Revolution
• Richard Arkwright
• Samuel Slater
• Eli Whitney

In the 1700s, women like the ones in this picture worked to prepare wool for spinning.

The Story Continues

In 1761 the British Society of Arts issued an advertisement. It asked for "the best invention of a machine that will spin six threads of wool . . . or cotton, at one time." The society also wanted this machine to "require but one person to work and attend it." The advertisement offered a cash reward for such an invention. The reward and the possibility that such a machine would increase profits attracted many entrepeneurs. The society's advertisement reflected a growing demand for new machinery to meet industrial needs.

★ The Industrial Revolution

At the beginning of the 1700s, most people in Europe and the United States were farmers. They made by hand much of what they needed at home. Some families sold extra cloth to merchants. In towns a few skilled workers—such as blacksmiths, carpenters, and shoemakers—made manufactured goods by hand in their own shops.

★ TEACH

Have students read Section 1 and complete Guided Reading Strategy 13.1. Choose one or more of the following activities to explore the section content with students. For further suggestions on block scheduling or team teaching, see the *Block Scheduling Handbook with Team Teaching Strategies.*

 LEVEL 1: Lead a discussion on Samuel Slater's and Eli Whitney's inventions and ask students to identify each inventor's contributions to the Industrial Revolution. *(Students should mention Samuel Slater's textile mills and Eli Whitney's development of interchangeable parts and mass production.)* Have students work in pairs to develop at least four headlines that show how each invention contributed to the economy and benefited manufacturing. Have volunteers present their headlines to the class.
ENGLISH LANGUAGE LEARNERS , COOPERATIVE LEARNING

ALL LEVELS: Organize the class into pairs. Have each pair write an interview with Eli Whitney, discussing his development of interchangeable parts and the importance of the process of mass production. Instruct students to base the interviews on material from the section. Have one student act as the interviewer and the other as Eli Whitney. Ask pairs to present their interviews to the class.
ENGLISH LANGUAGE LEARNERS , COOPERATIVE LEARNING

These ways of life had stayed the same for generations. However, by the mid-1700s changes in Great Britain were creating a greater demand for manufactured goods. As agriculture and roads improved, cities and populations grew. Overseas trade also expanded, and merchants found that traditional manufacturing methods could not produce enough goods to meet everyone's needs. People explored ways to use machines to make items quickly and efficiently. These changes led to the **Industrial Revolution**, a period of rapid growth in the use of machines in manufacturing and production.

The first important breakthrough of the Industrial Revolution took place in how **textiles,** or cloth items, were made. Before the Industrial Revolution, spinning thread took much more time than making cloth. Several workers were needed to spin enough thread to supply a single weaver. In 1770 Englishman James Hargreaves patented a small inexpensive machine called the spinning jenny. This new spinning wheel was powered by hand. Using it, a worker could produce many threads at the same time. Soon the spinning jenny was being used in homes across Britain.

A year earlier, Englishman **Richard Arkwright** had brought a more dramatic change to the textile industry. He patented a large spinning machine, called the water frame, that ran on waterpower. Arkwright's machine could create dozens of cotton threads at one time. Later versions could make even more threads. The machine lowered the cost of cotton cloth and increased the speed of production. In addition, Arkwright's invention was the first machine that could make high-quality thread. The water frame was too large to fit in people's homes and needed a source of power. These needs led merchants to build large textile mills, or factories, filled with spinning machines near streams. Merchants also began hiring people to come work in their mills.

✔ **Reading Check: Sequencing** List the steps in their proper order that led to the establishment of factories in Great Britain. greater demand for manufactured goods in Britain; new textile machinery invented; factories built to house machines and workers

Daily Life

Factory Work Before the late 1700s, most people made cotton thread and cloth in their homes. Workers had much independence. In addition, they could set their own pace of work. This situation changed as factories were built. Many women and children joined the workforce. The woman shown here is using a spinning jenny to make many threads at once. In addition, many skilled weavers were forced to join unskilled factory workers and work for the same pay. Some weavers rioted and broke machines in protest. Why might operating a machine like this one require careful attention?

★ Using Visual Resources

Carding. The image on the previous page shows a woman carding fibers, or preparing them for spinning. Carding involves untangling, cleaning, and collecting the fibers into neat bunches. Early weavers used their fingers or thorns to card fibers, while people living in the 1700s, such as the woman in the illustration, used flat pieces of wood with wires embedded in them. With the development of new textile-manufacturing processes, machines frequently performed this task.

CRITICAL THINKING

Why did wool have to be carded before it could be used for weaving?

ANSWER: It came directly from sheep and was dirty and tangled.

DAILY LIFE ANSWER
to avoid injuries or accidents

THE GRANGER COLLECTION, NEW YORK

HOMEWORK Have students find articles, with pictures if possible, about industries in the United States today. If their articles contain pertinent information about the attributes of each industry, ask students to list them as follows: size (of the building and the workforce), working conditions, availability of natural resources, etc.

 ALL LEVELS: Copy the following graphic organizer onto the chalkboard, omitting the italicized answers. Have students complete the flowchart to show the innovations of Eli Whitney and Samuel Slater and the effects the inventions had on the Industrial Revolution.
ENGLISH LANGUAGE LEARNERS

Innovation	Samuel Slater →	Innovation
• *machine production of cotton thread* • *interchangeable parts* • *mass production*	Eli Whitney →	• *successful use of machinery in mills* • *easy to assemble and replace* • *goods cost less*

✪ Biography

Samuel Slater. Samuel Slater was born in Belper, England, where he lived until he immigrated to the United States in 1789. His first factory, which he, William Almy, and Smith Brown jointly owned, eventually employed more than 100 people. Just before he died in 1835, Slater owned or partially owned at least 10 textile mills and two machine shops across New England. Collectively, these operations housed 25,000 spindles and employed 1,000 men, women, and children.

Visual Record Answer

Students might suggest that it could provide work for the town's inhabitants.

Interpreting the Visual Record

Mills *The textile mill built by Samuel Slater used nearby waterfalls to turn waterwheels that powered the mill machinery.* **How do you think a textile mill might change a town like the one in the picture?**

★★★★★★★★★★★
That's Interesting!
★★★★★★★★★★★

Slater's Secrets Can you imagine building a factory from memory? Well, that's what Samuel Slater had to do when he came to America. Parliament had passed a law to prevent British mill machines or their designs from leaving Great Britain. But American businesses were offering rewards to anyone who brought the secrets of mill machinery to America. In 1789 these offers convinced mechanic Samuel Slater to memorize the designs of several mill machines. Then posing as a farmworker, Slater boarded a ship. He wasn't carrying anything illegal—all the secrets were in his mind! Once he reached the United States, Slater built the first American mill machine from memory.

✪ Slater and His Secrets

The new textile machines allowed Great Britain to produce cloth faster and cheaper than other countries could. **Samuel Slater** was a skilled British mechanic who knew how to build these machines. Slater immigrated to the United States. Soon after arriving, he sent a letter to Moses Brown, who owned a textile business in New England. Slater claimed he could improve the way American textiles were manufactured.

Brown had one of his workers test Slater's knowledge of machinery, and Slater passed the test. Businessmen Smith Brown and William Almy formed a partnership with Slater. In 1790 they built their first mill, located in Pawtucket, Rhode Island. The production of cotton thread by machine had begun. Although mill workers made the thread, families wove it into cloth at home or in small shops. Slater ran the mill and the machinery. He was very confident that the new machines would be a success.

 "If I do not make as good yarn as they do in England, I will have nothing for my services, but will throw the whole of what I have attempted over the bridge."

—Samuel Slater, quoted in *The Ingenious Yankees,* by Joseph and Francis Gies

Slater's hopes came true. The Pawtucket mill became a success. Hannah Slater, Samuel's wife, even invented a type of cotton thread used for sewing. This thread became a popular item in the United States and Europe. Americans soon began building more textile mills, most of which were located in the Northeast. In New England in particular, investors saw the potential for making large profits and thus were willing to invest money in the mills. New England also had many fast-flowing rivers to supply power. Fewer mills were built in the South, partly because investors in the region concentrated on expanding agriculture.

✔ **Reading Check: Finding the Main Idea** What problem did American textile manufacturers face, and how did Samuel Slater help them solve it?
They did not have textile machines like those in Great Britain. Slater built the first of these machines in the United States.

A Manufacturing Breakthrough

Despite these great changes, most manufacturing was still done by hand. For example, in the late 1790s the U.S. government worried about a possible war with France, it wanted more muskets to equip the army. However, skilled workers made the parts for each weapon by hand. No two parts were exactly alike, and carefully fitting all the pieces together for each musket took much time and skill. As a result, U.S. gun makers could not produce the muskets quickly enough. Factories needed better **technology**—the tools used to produce items or to do work. In 1798 inventor **Eli Whitney** tried to address some of these problems. Whitney wanted to make guns for the U.S Army. He had new ideas about how this could be done using water-powered machinery. Whitney also came up with the idea of manufacturing using **interchangeable parts**. Products with interchangeable parts are made from pieces that are exactly the same. The products are thus easier to assemble and broken parts are easier to replace.

Whitney believed that this idea was a "new principle" in manufacturing, but his goal was difficult to achieve. To make his plans work he needed to invent new tools to do the job.

History Makers Speak
❝The tools which I contemplate [plan] are similar to an engraving [picture] on a copper plate from which may be taken a great number of impressions [copies] perceptibly alike [the same].❞

—Eli Whitney, quoted in *Technology in America*, edited by Carroll W. Pursell Jr.

Analyzing Primary Sources
Identifying Points of View
What did Whitney hope his tools would let him do?
Make many exact copies of the same thing

Early artisans had to create and fit together each part of a machine by hand, a time-consuming process that required great skill.

SPOTLIGHT
on Industry

Organize the class into groups. Have each group research how technological developments in various industries have changed people's lives at home and at work. Have each group create a pamphlet for their peers that describes and illustrates the changes that took place. Encourage groups to exchange and compare one another's pamphlets.

BLOCK SCHEDULING , COOPERATIVE LEARNING

SPOTLIGHT
on Science, Technology & Society

Ask students to prepare records, in the form of journal entries, of Eli Whitney's observations as he tested interchangeable parts for muskets. As they write, encourage students to speculate on the significance of this development. Lead a class discussion on the significance of interchangeable parts.

BLOCK SCHEDULING

☆ CLOSE

Have students make a flowchart showing the effects of the Industrial Revolution and the technological innovations discussed in this section. Call on volunteers to present their flowcharts to the class.

★ Economics

Mass Production. With mass production came a new problem for factory owners— how to motivate workers to attend to their machines. Factory work was not physically hard, but it involved considerable boredom, monotony, and stress. Some British factory owners tried to create a new work discipline and encourage workers to be more attentive by attempting to control their workers' private lives as well as their work lives. Business owners therefore established company towns. In these towns factory owners built and owned all the stores and housing.

CRITICAL THINKING

How did company towns extend factory owners' control over their employees' lives?

ANSWER: Students should suggest that by controlling workers' jobs, housing, and shopping, company towns left workers with few choices regarding their lives.

8.29A, 8.29C, 8.30B

Technology Resources

American History Simulations CD–ROM: Choosing a Factory Site

LINKING PAST TO PRESENT ANSWER

Students' answers will vary, but suggested reasons may include— to make money, to learn secrets that protect national security, or to compete better in certain markets.

LINKING PAST to PRESENT ★

Keeping Industrial Secrets

For hundreds of years, countries have spied on one anothers' businesses and industries. For example, more than 1,000 years ago Persia stole precious silkworms from China. Today such spying is called industrial espionage. Usually spies hope to steal the secret of some valuable invention or idea. Automobile plans and even cookie recipes have been stolen. High-tech companies, such as makers of airplane or computer chips (see below), are also targets.

Sometimes spies are sent to learn secrets to protect national security. Other times industrial secrets simply help businesses make money. Experts believe that stolen secrets may cost American companies billions of dollars each year. What are some reasons a company or country might steal industrial secrets?

Whitney promised to build 10,000 muskets in two years. At the time, this was an incredible number. The federal government gave Whitney money to build his factory. However, designing the machines and training the workers took him longer than he expected. After two years he still had not produced a single musket. So in 1801 Whitney was called to Washington, D.C., to give a demonstration.

Whitney stood before President John Adams and Vice President Thomas Jefferson. He had brought an assortment of parts for 10 guns. He then randomly chose parts and quickly assembled them. To the amazement of his audience, Whitney repeated the process several times. Witness Elizur Goodrich recalled the event. "All Judges & Inspectors unite in a declaration that they [the muskets] are superior [better] to any [other muskets]."

Whitney proved that American inventors could keep up with and improve upon the new British technology. Other businesses did have success with **mass production**—making large numbers of goods that are exactly alike. For example, in the early 1800s Seth Thomas began mass-producing thousands of inexpensive clocks.

✔ **Reading Check: Summarizing** How did Eli Whitney influence American manufacturing? He introduced ideas of interchangeable parts and using machinery for mass production, making goods less expensive.

★ A Slow Start for Manufacturing

Manufacturing in the United States grew slowly. In 1810 Secretary of the Treasury Albert Gallatin suggested reasons why the United States had few factories.

History Makers Speak

❝[The reasons include] . . . the superior attractions of agricultural pursuits [farming], . . . the abundance of land compared with the population, the high price of labor, and the want [lack] of sufficient capital [investment].❞

—Albert Gallatin, quoted in *Who Built America*, edited by Bruce C. Levine et al.

Gallatin reasoned that few people would choose to work in a factory if they could own their own farm instead. In Great Britain, on the other hand, land was scarce and expensive. As a result, fewer people were able to buy farms. Only a few industries had found a place in the U.S. economy. These included cotton goods, flour milling, weapons, and the production of iron.

Because Britain had plenty of factory workers, British manufacturers were able to produce large amounts of goods at low cost. They could charge lower prices for the goods, which made it difficult for American manufacturers to compete. This situation discouraged Americans from investing money to build new factories and machinery.

✔ **Reading Check Finding the Main Idea** Why did Great Britain lead the United States in the growth of manufacturing in the early 1800s? Land was cheaper in the United States, which encouraged farming. Land was more expensive in Great Britain, and wages were cheaper.

★ REVIEW AND ASSESS

Have students complete the **Section 1 Review** on p. 403. Then have students complete **Daily Quiz 13.1.** As **Alternative Assessment**, you may want to use the advertisement or pamphlet exercise in this section's lessons.

★ RETEACH

Have students complete **Main Idea Activity for English Language Learners and Special-Needs Students 13.1.** Ask them to write one descriptive sentence using each key term discussed in the section. Once students have finished, have them rewrite their sentences replacing each term with a blank space. Have students exchange their sentences and fill in the blank

spaces. Then have students return the sentences to their authors for grading. **ENGLISH LANGUAGE LEARNERS ,**
COOPERATIVE LEARNING

★ EXTEND

Have students use the library to research the life of a major figure discussed in this section. Then have each student prepare an obituary detailing that person's contribution to the Industrial Revolution. Collect the obituaries and distribute copies of the collections to the class. Ask students to read the collection, and then lead a discussion on each individual.
BLOCK SCHEDULING

★ The War of 1812 and Manufacturing

Manufacturing began to change around the time of the War of 1812. Since the 1790s, wars in Europe had interfered with U.S. trade. American customers were no longer able to get all the manufactured goods they needed. During the war British ships also blockaded eastern seaports, preventing foreign ships from delivering goods. Americans began to buy the items they needed from American manufacturers. As profits grew, manufacturers spent more money expanding their factories. State banks and private investors began to lend money to manufacturers for their businesses.

At the same time, many Americans began to realize that the United States had been relying too much on foreign goods. Thomas Jefferson, who had once opposed manufacturing, began to change his mind. He, too, realized that the United States was too dependent on imports. Jefferson explained that "to be independent for the comforts of life we must fabricate [make] them ourselves. We must now place the manufacturer by the side of the agriculturalist [farmer]." If the United States could not meet its own needs, it would be weak and open to attack.

In February 1815, New Yorkers celebrated the end of the war and return of free trade. The streets were decorated and filled with representatives of ships loaded with goods. "With Peace and Commerce, American Prospers," declared one display. Eager New Yorkers prepared to lead the United States into a period of industrial growth. After the war, northern manufacturers used northern politicians to pass higher tariffs on foreign goods to protect U.S. companies.

✔ **Reading Check Analyzing Information** How did the War of 1812 aid the growth of American manufacturing and the free enterprise system?
During the war Americans could not get foreign goods. American manufacturers began to sell more of their goods and make greater profits, which encouraged them to expand their factories. Americans also realized that they were too dependent on foreign goods.

This clock was made in a factory opened by Seth Thomas in 1812.

During the war Americans could not get foreign goods. American manufacturers began to sell more of their goods and make greater profits, which encouraged

Section 1 Review

Homework Practice Online
keyword: SA3 HP13

1 **Define** and explain:
• textiles
• technology
• interchangeable parts
• mass production

2 **Identify** and explain:
• Industrial Revolution
• Richard Arkwright
• Samuel Slater
• Eli Whitney

3 **Summarizing** Copy the chart below. Use it to list the key events that led to the growth of factories and changes in daily life in the United States.

Invention	How the Invention Changed Manufacturing
Arkwright	
Slater	
Whitney	

4 **Finding the Main Idea**
a. Why were more factories built in New England than in the southern states?

b. In what ways did the War of 1812 lead to the growth of manufacturing in the United States?

5 **Writing and Critical Thinking**
Supporting a Point of View Imagine that you are an American manufacturer seeking a bank loan in order to expand your factory in 1814. Write your best argument to convince the bank to give you the money you need.

Consider the following:
• the benefits of mass production
• the need for American-made goods
• your entrepeneurship and profit potential

Section 1 Review
ANSWERS

1 **Define**
• textiles, p. 399
• technology, p. 401
• interchangeable parts, p. 401
• mass production, p. 402

2 **Identify**
• Industrial Revolution, p. 399
• Richard Arkwright, p. 399
• Samuel Slater, p. 400
• Eli Whitney, p. 401

3 Arkwright: invented a water frame spinning machine; made merchants build factories; Slater: designed the first American textile mill that used British machinery; started the growth of the American textile industry; Whitney: used machinery to make smaller goods and interchangeable parts which led to mass production; led to the cheaper manufacture of goods

4 a. more rivers and streams, which provided the water power factories needed to run their machinery; more investors to support new factories
b. before the war U.S. trade with Great Britain and France stopped; blockades during the war meant that foreign ships could not deliver goods; greater profits made by American manufacturers led to greater investment

5 Students' arguments will vary, but should include the benefits of mass production, the need for American-made goods, and new ideas regarding bank loans.

Industrial Growth in the North **403**

Section 2

OBJECTIVES

⭐ Examine how the Rhode Island and Lowell systems differed.

⭐ List the ways in which the introduction of factories influenced the daily life of workers in the northeastern United States.

⭐ Describe how Sarah G. Bagley and other reformers contributed to the early labor-union movement.

SECTION 2 RESOURCES

REPRODUCIBLE

▶ Guided Reading Strategy 13.2

▶ Literature Reading 13: Transportation in the United States

▶ Primary Source Reading 13: The Lowell Girls

TECHNOLOGY

▶ One-Stop Planner, Lesson 13.2

▶ Exploring America's Past Video Segment: Factory Girls; Teacher's Guide, pp. 20–21

▶ Holt Researcher: American History CD–ROM

▶ Homework Practice Online

REINFORCEMENT, REVIEW, AND ASSESSMENT

▶ Section 2 Review, p. 409

▶ Daily Quiz 13.2

▶ Main Idea Activity 13.2

▶ English Audio Summary 13.2

▶ Spanish Audio Summary 13.2

 **LET'S GET STARTED!**

As students enter the classroom, ask them to read Primary Source Reading 13: "The Lowell Girls." Then ask students why a labor union might be helpful or harmful, using the reading as a reference point. *(Students' responses will vary but should point out that labor unions are designed to negotiate on behalf of workers to obtain better pay and working conditions for their members.)* Tell students that in Section 2 they will learn about the problems in the early 1800s that caused workers to form unions and how American society viewed their efforts.

Section 2

Changes in Working Life

Read to Discover

1. How were the Rhode Island system and the Lowell system different?

2. In what ways did the introduction of factories influence the daily life of workers in the northeastern United States?

3. How did Sarah G. Bagley and other reformers contribute to the early labor-union movement?

WHY IT MATTERS TODAY

The U.S. government makes laws governing many working conditions. Use **CNNfyi.com** or other **current events** sources to learn about one of these laws. Record your findings in your journal.

Define

• trade unions
• strikes

Identify

• Rhode Island system
• Francis Cabot Lowell
• Lowell system
• Sarah G. Bagley

The Story Continues

Smith Wilkinson was a boy in Pawtucket, Rhode Island, when Samuel Slater built his first textile mill there. After it opened, Wilkinson got a job at the mill. "I was then in my tenth year," remembered Wilkinson, "and went to work with him [Slater], and began attending the breaker [a machine]." In the early 1800s many children worked in the textile mills. Children even younger than Wilkinson might work as many as 12 hours a day. Wilkinson spent much of his life working in mills. Eventually he ran one himself.

Textile companies used cloth labels like this one.

⭐ Factory Families

Many mill owners in the United States could not find enough people to work in their factories. At first, Samuel Slater used apprentices—young men who worked for several years to learn the trade. However, these young men often did only simple work. Their jobs included feeding cotton into the machines and cleaning the mill equipment. Apprentices like James Horton ran away from Slater's mill because "Mr. Slater . . . keep me always at one thing. I might have stayed there until this time and never knew nothing."

Have students read Section 2 and complete Guided Reading Strategy 13.2. Choose one or more of the following activities to explore the section content with students. For further suggestions on block scheduling or team teaching, see the *Block Scheduling Handbook with Team Teaching Strategies.*

LEVEL 1: Organize the class into two groups—one supporting Slater's Rhode Island system and the other encouraging the use of the Lowell system. Have each group define their labor system, and reasons to support it. Then lead a discussion comparing these two systems. **ENGLISH LANGUAGE LEARNERS**, **COOPERATIVE LEARNING**

ALL LEVELS: Copy the following graphic organizer onto the chalkboard, omitting the italicized answers. Have students complete the chart by listing the ways the daily life of each type of worker changed by working at northeastern mills. **ENGLISH LANGUAGE LEARNERS**

Types of Workers	Changes in Daily Life
• Families • Unmarried women • Craftspeople	• *worked in factories instead of on farms* • *began working in factories* • *were forced to change working conditions to compete*

Eventually Slater began to hire entire families who would move to Pawtucket and work in the mills. This practice allowed Slater to fill his labor needs at a low cost. Children as well as adults worked in the mills. On many farms children already worked to help their families. Therefore, few people complained about them working in factories instead. H. Humphrey, an author of books on raising children, told parents that children needed to be useful. Humphrey wrote, "If he [a child] will not study, put him on to a farm, or send him into the shop, or in some other way provide regular employment for him." The machines made many tasks in the mill simple enough for children to perform. Mill owners paid children very low wages. Adults usually earned as much in a day as most children did in a week.

Slater's practice of hiring families and dividing factory work into simple tasks became known as the **Rhode Island system**. Mill owners throughout the Northeast adopted Slater's methods. Owners advertised for "Men with growing families wanted." They also sent recruiters to poor communities to find new workers.

✔ **Reading Check: Summarizing** What problem did Slater have in his mills, and how did he solve it? He had a hard time keeping apprentices in his factories because of the dull work. He decided to hire entire families, including children.

Interpreting the Visual Record

New opportunities *Some people left farm life to go to work in textile factories.* **How would you describe the mix of workers shown in this picture?**

★ The Lowell System

Not all mill owners followed Samuel Slater's system. **Francis Cabot Lowell**, a businessman from New England, developed a very different approach. His ideas completely changed the textile industry in the Northeast. First, Lowell decided to build a water-powered loom based on one he had seen in Great Britain. This loom could both weave thread and spin cloth in the same mill. Lowell's other idea was to hire young unmarried women from local farms instead of entire families. These practices became known as the **Lowell system**.

Lowell received financial help from the investors of the Boston Manufacturing Company. They finished building the first textile mill to use the Lowell system in 1814. It was located in Waltham, Massachusetts. "From the first starting of the first power loom there was not . . . doubt about the success," wrote one investor. In 1822 the company built a larger mill in a town later named Lowell, Massachusetts. Visitors to Lowell were amazed by the machinery. The clean factories and the neatly kept boardinghouses for the workers also impressed them.

Visual Record Answer

Students might suggest that they appear to be of varied ages and of both sexes.

Research on the  **R◉M**

Free Find:
Francis Cabot Lowell
After reading about Francis Cabot Lowell on the **Holt Researcher CD-ROM**, create an advertisement for jobs in one of Lowell's factories. Include descriptions of the work and the benefits that are offered.

Note: To help students make meaningful connections between events in American history and those in their hometown, use the chapter 12 **Hands-On History** activity, Working Conditions in a Local Industry.

TEACHER TO TEACHER

Cynthia Gore of San Jose, California, suggested the following activity:

ALL LEVELS: Lead a discussion on the advantages and disadvantages of being a union member in the mid-1800s. Then have each student create a political cartoon depicting either an advantage or a disadvantage of being in a union. Instruct students to create captions or funny sayings to accompany their drawings.
ENGLISH LANGUAGE LEARNERS

★ Culture

Working Women. In addition to the mills, women living in the 1800s had other opportunities for work. In one study of New England's working women, a historian found that the positions open to a woman often depended on her race and ethnicity. Women who were native to New England could find clerical and sales jobs, while daughters of immigrants often found semiskilled factory work. African Americans and new immigrants were largely limited to domestic and personal service. Teachers often came from relatively prosperous farming families. Often, those who did not marry earned such low wages that they never gained economic independence.

CRITICAL THINKING

What would be the advantages of working in a factory instead of working on a farm?

ANSWER: Students might mention the opportunity to meet other women or the chance to gain economic independence.

CONNECTING TO LITERATURE ANSWERS

1. She says it assumes that the readers understand the intensity of the work involved.
2. Students' responses will vary but should mention repetitious factory work.

CONNECTING TO Literature

The *Lowell Offering*

The Lowell Offering *began publication in 1840. This monthly magazine featured editorials, poems, and stories about the lives of mill workers. In many ways the* Lowell Offering *gave an unrealistic view of mill life. The December 1845 cover, for example, showed a setting that looked more like a garden than a factory mill. The artist who created the cover apparently followed magazine policy by ignoring the harsh realities of mill life. In 1845 Harriet Farley, the editor of the* Offering, *defended the image of Lowell shown in the magazine.*

We have been accused of representing unfairly the relative advantages and disadvantages of factory life. . . . Are we guilty? . . . We have never published anything which our own experience had convinced us was unfair. But, if in our sketches, there is too much light, and too little shade, let our excuse be found in the circumstances which have brought us before the public. We have not thought it necessary to state . . . that our life was a **toilsome**[1] one—for we supposed that would be universally understood, after we had stated how many hours in a day we **tended**[2] our machines. We have not thought a constant repetition of the fact necessary, that our life was one of confinement; when it was known that we work in one spot of one room. These facts have always been so generally understood that the worth, happiness and intelligence, which really exists, have been undervalued.

---

[1]**toilsome:** difficult [2]**tended:** watched

Understanding What You Read

1. **Literature and History** Why does Harriet Farley say the *Lowell Offering* describes factory life as it does?
2. **Literature and You** What kind of description would you write of the Lowell factory if you worked there?

The young female mill workers soon became known as Lowell girls. The mills paid them between $2 and $4 each week. The workers paid $1.25 for room and board. These wages were much better than women could earn teaching or doing domestic work. Many young women from across New England came to Lowell. They wanted the chance to earn money instead of working on the family farm and earning nothing. The typical Lowell girl stayed at the mills for about four years.

Unlike other factory workers, the Lowell girls were encouraged to use their free time to take classes and form women's clubs. They even wrote their own magazine, the *Lowell Offering*. Lucy Larcom, who started working in Lowell at age 11, later praised her fellow workers.

Analyzing Primary Sources
Drawing Inferences and Conclusions How do you think Larcom's background influenced her opinion of the Lowell girls? Possible answers: because Larcom grew up among the Lowell girls or because she was one, she thought highly of them.

 History Makers Speak "I regard it as one of the privileges [advantages] of my youth that I was permitted to grow up among those active, interesting girls, whose lives . . . had principle [ideals] and purpose distinctly their own."

—Lucy Larcom, *A New England Girlhood*

LEVEL 2: Organize the class into groups. Each group should assume the role of a member of a family of factory workers in the northeastern United States during the Industrial Revolution. Roles may include: a parent or a young child who works or an older child organizing for labor reform. Have each group write a journal entry about how their lives have changed since the factories came to town.

ENGLISH LANGUAGE LEARNERS , COOPERATIVE LEARNING

LEVEL 3: Have students imagine that they work for the New England Workingmen's Association. Then ask students to write a speech for Sarah G. Bagley that is designed to raise money for the association's efforts to improve working conditions in the mills. Have students summarize the following issues in their speeches: child labor, the 10-hour workday, work contracts for shorter hours, and union organization. Call on volunteers to present their speeches to the class. Finally, have students describe how Bagley and others contributed to the early labor-union movement.

For many women, however, the disadvantages of mill work outweighed the good points. The workday was between 12 and 14 hours long, and daily life was carefully controlled. Ringing bells ordered workers to breakfast or lunch. Throughout the 1800s, mill owners steadily increased the size and speed of their machines. They forced employees to work harder and faster to keep up with the equipment. According to an 1846 newspaper, each Lowell girl usually had to look after three looms. "Doing so requires constant attention," said the article. In addition, the spinning rooms were also filled with cotton dust, which caused health problems for workers.

✔ **Reading Check: Contrasting** In what ways were the Lowell system and the Rhode Island system different? young women workers vs. entire families of workers; Lowell girls encouraged to study and form clubs

⭐ Workers Organize

Factories continued to spread in the 1800s, and craftspeople—people who made goods by hand—felt threatened. Factories produced low-priced goods quickly. To compete with factories, shop owners had to hire more workers and pay them less money. Shoemaker William Frazier complained about this situation in the mid-1840s. "We have to sit on our seats from twelve to sixteen hours per day, to earn one dollar."

The wages of factory workers also stayed the same or even went down as people competed for jobs. A wave of immigration in the 1840s brought in new people willing to work for low pay. More immigrants

Organize a mock trial before the U.S. Supreme Court for the case of *Commonwealth* v. *Hunt*. Organize the class into four groups and assign each group one of the following roles: (a) attorneys who will research and present the arguments for the workers; (b) attorneys who will research and present the arguments for the state; (c) judges, who will research the decision of the Supreme Court, including dissenting opinions; and (d) reporters, who will write newspaper articles at the end of the proceedings on the background of the case, the trial, and the significance of the Court's decision. Then conduct the proceeding with individuals from the groups playing their respective roles. At the conclusion of the proceedings, have the judges issue the Court's decision and explain their reasoning.

COOPERATIVE LEARNING , BLOCK SCHEDULING

☆ CLOSE

Have students prepare recruitment brochures seeking employees for Slater's mills. Ask students to consider the following questions: What segment of society might want to work in a mill? What incentives would appeal to possible employees? Why would a person want to work in one of Slater's mills? When students have completed their brochures, have them take turns reading one another's work. Finally, lead a discussion on conditions in the mills during this period.

COOPERATIVE LEARNING

★ Biography

Sarah G. Bagley. Historians believe that Sarah G. Bagley was born in Meredith, New Hampshire. In the fall of 1836, she was employed by the Hamilton Manufacturing Company, a cotton mill in Lowell. Initially, Bagley seemed to like factory life, writing "Pleasures of Factory Life" for the *Lowell Offering* in 1840. However, by 1844 Bagley had founded the Lowell Female Labor Reform Association. Denied the ability to print her views in the *Lowell Offering*, she gave a speech on July 4, 1844, denouncing the periodical. In February 1846, Bagley took a job as a superintendent of the newly opened Lowell telegraph office and became the first female telegraph operator.

ACTIVITY: Have students imagine Sarah G. Bagley's speech denouncing the *Lowell Offering* and stating her views on factory life. Ask students to write an excerpt from such a speech using standard grammar, spelling, sentence structure and punctuation.

Visual Record Answer

Students might note the expressions of the family members or the bare walls and furniture of the house.

Interpreting the Visual Record

The Panic of 1837 *This cartoon shows bill collectors paying a visit to a family with its starving children.* **How does this image reflect the hard times that people faced during the Panic of 1837?**

Analyzing Primary Sources

Identifying Points of View
How does the quotation reflect manufacturers' concerns that trade unions hurt free enterprise? They thought trade unions hurt the ability of companies to compete.

came to the Northeast, where the mills were located, than to the South. At the Lowell mills, pay decreased and working conditions worsened. Some Lowell girls refused to keep working. Eventually, immigrants replaced the Lowell girls. Competition also came from people who had become unemployed during the Panic of 1837. Some 50,000 workers in New York City alone had lost their jobs.

Skilled workers thus faced low wages, long hours, and the fear of losing their jobs. These concerns led many skilled workers to form groups called **trade unions.** Trade unions tried to improve pay and working conditions for their members. In time, factory workers also formed trade unions. Most employers and factory owners did not want their workers to join unions. Employers often refused to hire union workers. In 1836 a group of New York employers expressed a typical business owner's opinion.

History Makers Speak
❝We consider such associations [unions] illegal because they are harmful to trade and prevent us from competing successfully with manufacturers of similar goods in our neighboring towns and cities.❞

—New York employers group, from *Voices of America*, edited by Thomas R. Frazier

Union members wanted to get business owners to listen to them. Sometimes they staged protests called **strikes.** Workers on strike refuse to work until their employers meet their demands. Most early strikes were not very successful, however. Courts and police usually supported companies rather than striking union members. Union members wanted new laws that would protect workers. Many decided to become more politically active. One union warned its members not to vote for "proud members of the upper class who cannot subscribe to [believe in] the . . . principles [ideals] of the workers." The group asked workers to vote instead for candidates who supported working people.

✔ **Reading Check: Analyzing Information** What issues concerned workers in the mid-1800s, and how did they respond? the growth of factories, lower wages, the increase in immigration, increased competition for jobs; formed trade unions and staged strikes

☆ REVIEW AND ASSESS

Have students complete the **Section 2 Review** on p. 409. Then have students complete **Daily Quiz 13.2**. As Alternative Assessment, you may want to use the labor speech or mock trial exercises in this section's lessons.

☆ RETEACH

Have students complete **Main Idea Activity for English Language Learners and Special-Needs Students 13.2.** Organize the class into three groups and assign each group one of the Read to Discover questions. Have each group draw a picture illustrating its answer to the assigned question. Then have a volunteer from each group present his or her group's drawing to the class. **ENGLISH LANGUAGE LEARNERS** , **COOPERATIVE LEARNING**

☆ EXTEND

Have students use the library to research the similarities and differences between labor unions in the mid-1800s and today. Instruct students to list issues that labor unions were trying to resolve during each time period. Then have students write a union's labor contract on behalf of employees for each time period. Ask volunteers to present their contracts to the class. **BLOCK SCHEDULING**

⭐ Labor Reform Efforts

One of the strongest voices in the union movement belonged to mill worker **Sarah G. Bagley**, who founded the Lowell Female Labor Reform Association in 1844. The association made public the struggles of factory laborers. One of Bagley's causes was to fight for shorter working hours. In 1840 President Martin Van Buren had granted a 10-hour workday to many federal employees. Bagley wanted this rule to also apply to employees of private businesses. At the time, these men and women often worked 12 to 14 hours, typically six days a week. Huldah Stone, a reformer, attacked this practice. She wrote, "Call ye this *life*—to labor, eat, drink and die?"

Many working men and women supported the 10-hour workday campaign, despite the opposition of business owners. In 1845 Sarah Bagley was elected vice president of the New England Workingmen's Association. She was also put in charge of the 10-hour-day reform. This election made her the first woman to hold such a high-ranking position in the American labor movement.

The unions achieved some legal victories. Connecticut, Maine, New Hampshire, Ohio, Pennsylvania, and a few other states passed 10-hour-workday laws. However, companies could often avoid these new laws by making workers sign special contracts agreeing to work longer hours. For factory workers in other states, long hours remained common. Union supporters continued to fight for work reforms during the 1800s.

This union banner was created by the New York chapter of the United Brotherhood of Carpenters and Joiners.

✔ **Reading Check: Finding the Main Idea** What were the main goals of union reformers such as Sarah G. Bagley, and what did they achieve?
better working conditions and a shorter workday; got some 10-hour-workday laws passed

Section 2 Review

go.hrw.com **Homework Practice Online**
keyword: SA3 HP13

1 **Define** and explain:
• trade unions
• strikes

2 **Identify** and explain:
• Rhode Island system
• Francis Cabot Lowell
• Lowell system
• Sarah G. Bagley

3 **Categorizing** Copy the web diagram below. Use it to fill in information about how each person or group of people contributed to changes in workers' daily lives.

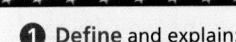

Business Leaders → Changes in Lives of Workers ← Lowell & Slater ← Bagley & Trade Unions

4 **Finding the Main Idea**
a. Imagine that you are a mill owner. Decide whether you will use the Rhode Island system or the Lowell system. Explain your choice.

b. How effective were Sarah G. Bagley and other reformers in helping industrial workers? Explain your answer.

5 **Writing and Critical Thinking**
Analyzing Information Imagine that you are a factory worker who also writes for a workers' magazine. Write a short column called "Factory Life" describing how factories have changed daily life for workers in the Northeast.

Consider the following:
• the effects of factories on farm families
• the effects of factories on craftspeople
• the disadvantages and advantages of mill work

Section 2 Review
ANSWERS

1 **Define**
• trade unions, p.408
• strikes, p. 408

2. Identify
• Rhode Island system, p. 405
• Francis Cabot Lowell, p. 405
• Lowell system, p. 405
• Sarah G. Bagley, p. 409

3 Slater: hired families to work in his factories, including children, divided work into simple tasks, introduced the Rhode Island system, which was followed in many other factories; Lowell: hired young unmarried women to work in his factories, provided women an opportunity to earn more money than they would as teachers or domestic workers, introduced waterpowered looms so mills; Bagley: founded the Lowell Female Labor Reform Association, led the reform effort to establish a 10-hour workday for factory workers; trade unions: encouraged workers to strike for better wages and conditions; business owners: offered people new ways of earning money and better wages, often made workers work under unhealthy conditions, made the work of craftspeople harder

4 a. Rhode Island system: relied on family labor; and the Lowell system: relied on the labor of young unmarried women
b. Bagley: leader in labor associations, promoted a shorter workday; other reformers: organized strikes and political activity

5 Students' articles will vary.

Section 3

OBJECTIVES

★ Describe how the Transportation Revolution changed life in the United States.

★ Discuss the effect of the Supreme Court case *Gibbons* v. *Ogden*.

★ Analyze how the growth of railroads benefited the nation.

Section 3

The Transportation Revolution

Read to Discover

1. How did the Transportation Revolution change life in the United States?
2. What was the effect of the Supreme Court case *Gibbons* v. *Ogden*?
3. How did the growth of railroads benefit the nation?

WHY IT MATTERS TODAY

Today inventors are working to improve transportation. Use CNN fyi.com or other **current events** sources to identify a new advance in or idea for transportation. Record your findings in your journal.

Identify

- Transportation Revolution
- Robert Fulton
- *Clermont*
- *Gibbons* v. *Ogden*
- Peter Cooper

The Story Continues

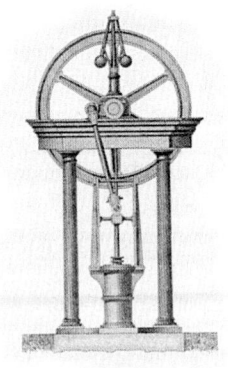

This picture shows an early design for a steam engine.

In 1806 inventor Robert Fulton returned to America from Europe. Neither the French nor the British wanted to give him money to build his steam-powered ships. Still, Fulton continued his work. In August 1807 he took his boat, which doubters called Fulton's Folly, out on the Hudson River. He traveled up the river, passing sailboats along the way. Instead of being a disaster, Fulton's Folly was a success. The steamboat was faster than sailboats and did not rely on the wind for power. Fulton's boat revolutionized water transportation.

★ New Ways to Travel

In addition to the Industrial Revolution, during the 1800s the United States experienced a **Transportation Revolution**—a period of rapid growth in the speed and convenience of travel. Americans expanded roads and built thousands of miles of canals in the Northeast. Two important new forms of transportation were also invented: the steamboat and the railroad. Both relied on steam engines to supply power.

Have students read Section 3 and complete Guided Reading Strategy 13.3. Choose one or more of the following activities to explore the section content with students. For further suggestions on block scheduling or team teaching, see the *Block Scheduling Handbook with Team Teaching Strategies.*

LEVEL 1: Lead a discussion on changes caused by and the effects of the Transportation Revolution. Have students create drawings illustrating the innovations of the Transportation Revolution. Ask students to include a label for their drawing indicating how these innovations changed life in the United States. Display the finished drawings around the room for students to view. **ENGLISH LANGUAGE LEARNERS**

 HOMEWORK Pose the following question to the class: *If the Transportation Revolution had included the needs of all Americans, how might it have been different, if at all?* Have each student use material from the section to answer the question and write a formal response in the form of an editorial.

The Transportation Revolution helped the expansion of free enterprise by opening up new markets across the country. Shipping times were greatly reduced. In 1817 shipping cargo from Cincinnati, Ohio, to New York City took almost two months. By the early 1850s that same trip took only one week. Shipping costs also fell. For example, a merchant might pay $100 to ship a load of goods by land across New York State. It would cost that merchant only $5 to ship the same goods by canal. Along with goods, people and information moved more easily and quickly.

The growth in communication, trade, and travel also encouraged the development of new towns. In 1835 one foreign visitor commented on the rapid spread of transportation networks in America.

 History Makers Speak ❝The Americans . . . have already changed the whole order of nature for their own advantage. They have joined the Hudson to the Mississippi, and made the Atlantic Ocean communicate with the Gulf of Mexico, across a continent.❞

—Alexis de Tocqueville, *Democracy in America*

✔ **Reading Check: Comparing** List the key benefits the Transportation Revolution brought to free enterprise and daily life. free enterprise: cheaper, easier, and faster shipping; daily life: improved travel and communication, new towns developed

⭐ The Steamboat

One of the first breakthroughs of the Transportation Revolution occurred with water transportation. American and European inventors had developed steam-powered boats in the late 1700s. American **Robert Fulton** tested a model steamboat design in 1803 in France.

Analyzing Primary Sources
Drawing Inferences and Conclusions How is Tocqueville suggesting that the growth of transportation has changed the United States? Students might suggest that it has connected different parts of the nation.

Interpreting the Visual Record
Steamboats *Because they made it cheaper and faster to travel upstream, steamboats were used for a variety of purposes.* **What are the steamboats in the picture being used for?**

 **Technology Resources**
CNN Presents America: Beginnings to 1914 Segment: Rebuilding the Riverboats

Visual Record Answer
They are transporting people.

ALL LEVELS: Copy the following graphic organizer onto the chalkboard, omitting the italicized answers. Have students complete the chart by listing the new forms of transportation including the railroad, discussed in this section and the way or ways in which they changed and benefited American daily life. **ENGLISH LANGUAGE LEARNERS**

Effects of Developments	**Steamships** • *eased the transport of goods* • *encouraged Midwestern settlement*
	Railroads • *increased economic development* • *linked communities* • *aided the growth of cities*
	Telegraph • *made information readily available*

Interdisciplinary Connection

▶Science◀

Engineering. Riverboat captains on U.S. rivers such as the Ohio, the Missouri, and the Mississippi claimed that Oliver Evans's engine was the best machine for these rivers. Evans designed a smaller, more powerful engine that used steam at a much higher pressure. Evans's engine made shallow rivers easier to navigate, and helped captains deal with changing currents and obstructions in the water.

CRITICAL THINKING

Why might Evans's engine be more risky for riverboat captains to use than steam engines?

ANSWER: Students might suggest that Evans's engine was a high-pressure engine, which often exploded.

CONNECTING TO SCIENCE AND TECHNOLOGY ANSWER

Steam engines allowed people to live and work in a wider variety of locations. Steam engines could also give people the freedom to choose when they did their work as well.

Technology Resources

Linking Geography and History Transparency 10: Growth of Transportation, 1840

Several years passed before Fulton could test a full-sized commercial steamboat in the United States. Fulton's ship was called the ***Clermont***. On August 9, 1807, the *Clermont* traveled up the Hudson River without any trouble. A demand for a steamboat ferry service soon arose. Within a few months Fulton and his partners had earned back all the money they had spent building the ship.

The steamboat was well suited to river travel. It could move quickly against the current and did not rely on wind power. Steamboats cut months off the time it had taken to travel from New Orleans to Pittsburgh, Pennsylvania. Before the steamboat was invented, people rarely traveled upstream by boat. However, the steamboat made such trips easier and cheaper. The price of a trip upriver fell by some 90 percent from 1815 to 1860. Westerners found it easier to send goods, such as grain and lumber, to eastern markets. Steamboats also made it easier for eastern companies to ship their goods to western buyers. Increased trade and cheaper transportation encouraged more settlers to move to the Midwest.

CONNECTING TO SCIENCE AND TECHNOLOGY

The Age of Steam

Before the Industrial Revolution began, people used natural sources of energy to do work. These sources included animals, waterpower, and wind power. Steam power provided a new source of energy. The first steam engines were built in the early 1700s in Europe. In the 1800s American Oliver Evans helped develop a smaller and more powerful steam engine. This engine was ideal for steamboats running on the Mississippi River or trains racing across the American countryside. Engineers continued to use and improve steam engines throughout the 1800s. **How do you think steam engines changed the way people lived and worked?**

LEVEL 3: Ask students to imagine that they are newspaper reporters covering the Supreme Court. Then have students write an article explaining the effects of the Supreme Court ruling in *Gibbons* v. *Ogden*. Have students include the expected favorable and unfavorable reactions to the ruling. Ask volunteers to read their paragraphs to the class.

Have students review material from the section to evaluate travel experiences on clipper ships, steamboats, and railroads. Then have each student write a review that rates each form of transportation, using a four-star system. Remind them to describe the advantages and disadvantages of each method. Call on volunteers to read excerpts from their reviews to the class.

BLOCK SCHEDULING

SPOTLIGHT
on Transportation
Ask students to imagine that they are critics during the mid-1800s who have been asked to travel the country to critique the new forms of transportation in the United States.

★ CLOSE
Draw students' attention to the end of this section and ask them to speculate in a paragraph about other inventions that may have also had an effect on transportation.

Steamboat travel was dangerous. The engines could build up too much pressure and explode. But these risks did not stop steamboats from becoming common on the Mississippi River. More than 500 of them were in use by 1840. By the 1850s steamboats were also being used to carry people and goods across the ocean.

✔ **Reading Check: Finding the Main Idea** How did steamboat travel benefit Americans? *River travel and shipping became faster and cheaper.*

★ Gibbons v. Ogden

The growth of the steamboat shipping industry led to the first Supreme Court ruling on commerce between states. Thomas Gibbons was operating his steamboats between New Jersey and Manhattan using a federal license. However, he did not have a state license to travel in New York waters. New York had already given Aaron Ogden a monopoly on the steamboat business. When Ogden sued Gibbons and won, Gibbons appealed.

The case of **Gibbons v. Ogden** reached the Supreme Court in 1824. The Court ruled that Gibbons had the right to operate in New York. Chief Justice John Marshall spoke for the Court and explained that the federal law overruled the state law. Thus Gibbons's federal license had priority over Ogden's state license.

The Marshall Court's ruling reinforced the federal government's authority over the states. In doing so he also expanded the definition of commerce to include the transportation of people. *Gibbons* v. *Ogden* was one of Marshall's most important decisions. Over time, the interpretation of commerce has even come to include the use of new communications technology. The decision also tore down a barrier to free enterprise by eliminating Ogden's state monopoly.

✔ **Reading Check: Summarizing** Explain the events surrounding *Gibbons* v. *Ogden* and how the ruling affected the power of the federal government. *See above bold-faced term and description.*

★ American Railroads

What the steamboat did for water travel, the train did for travel on land. Steam-powered trains had first been developed in Britain in the early 1800s, but they did not become popular in the United States until the 1830s. About 1830 **Peter Cooper** built the *Tom Thumb*. Although this locomotive was small, it had great power and speed. Railroad fever spread throughout the United States, particularly in the North. By 1840, railroad companies had laid about 2,800 miles of track. French economist Michel Chevalier described Americans as having "a perfect passion for railroads."

Engineers and mechanics had to overcome physical obstacles such as steep mountains, swift rivers, and tight curves. To meet these challenges,

CONNECTING TO
MATH

Just the Facts

The Railroad Boom, 1830–1860

Year	Miles of Railroad Operated
1830	23
1835	1,098
1840	2,818
1845	4,633
1850	9,021
1855	18,374
1860	30,626

Using Mathematical Skills

1. How much more track was in operation in 1840 than in 1830?

2. Create a line graph that illustrates changes in the total amount of railroad track operated from 1830 to 1860.

3. Imagine that you are a business leader in 1860. Using the figures above, prepare a speech to give to a group of investors. Explain why you think starting a new railroad company is or is not a good idea.

★ Geography

The Railroad in the Midwest. In 1850 Illinois was still a frontier state, with 8 of its 10 cities located on Lake Michigan or along the Mississippi or Illinois Rivers. Railroads brought a population explosion to formerly small Illinois towns. By 1853 Chicago had a rail route to the east coast and it boasted several routes to the Mississippi River by 1855. Between 1850 and 1855, Cairo, Illinois, grew from 300 to 1,300 inhabitants; Vandalia from 360 to 1,000; Freeport from 1,400 to 5,000; and Urbana from 500 to 1,145.

ACTIVITY: Have students imagine that they live in Cairo, Illinois. Then ask them to write a series of journal entries that reflect the changes in town life between 1850 and 1855 as a result of the railroad.

CONNECTING TO MATH ANSWERS
1. about 100 times more track in 1840

2. Students' line graphs should accurately display the chart data.

3. Students' answers may vary. Students will probably note the steady increases in the miles of railroad in operation and predict future growth and profits for the industry.

Have students complete the **Section 3 Review** on p. 414. Then have students complete **Daily Quiz 13.3**. As **Alternative Assessment**, you may want to use the exercise about being critics or the article on *Gibbons* v. *Ogden* in this section's lessons.

★ **RETEACH**

Have students complete **Main Idea Activity for English Language Learners and Special-Needs Students 13.3.** Have students write the section's headings on a sheet of paper, leaving a space between each heading. Then ask students to list the main ideas of each heading in the appropriate space.

ENGLISH LANGUAGE LEARNERS

★ **EXTEND**

Have students use the library to compile data on the growth of railroads between 1830 and 1860. Assign students one of the following topics: the number of miles of track in the United States, the freight volume shipped by rail in the United States, or the amount of federal aid provided to assist the growth of railroads. Have students create bar graphs depicting data on their assigned topics. **BLOCK SCHEDULING**

Section 3 Review
ANSWERS

❶ **Identify**
- Transportation Revolution, p. 410
- Robert Fulton, p. 411
- *Clermont*, p. 412
- *Gibbons* v. *Ogden*, p. 413
- Peter Cooper, p. 413

❷ steamboat: Robert Fulton tests the *Clermont* on the Hudson River in 1807; more than 500 steamboats are in use on Mississippi River by 1840; railroad: Peter Cooper builds the Tom Thumb about 1830; railroad companies lay about 2,800 miles of track by 1840, by 1860 railroad companies have built about 30,000 miles of railroads linking most major cities in the eastern United States.

❸ a. reinforced the federal government's authority over the states; expanded commerce to include the transportation of people and the use of new inventions
b. increased the country's economic development and linked communities together.

❹ Students' dialogues will vary but should reflect an understanding of how steamboats and railroads affected settlement patterns. Dialogues should also include the effect they had on free enterprise.

Transportation Methods of the Mid-1800s

TYPE OF TRANSPORTATION	AVERAGE SPEED	SHIPPING COSTS
Roads	2 miles per hour by wagon 6–8 miles per hour by stagecoach	$0.12 per ton per mile
Canals	1.5–5 miles per hour	$0.045 per ton per mile
Steamboats	around 20 miles per hour	$0.007 per ton per mile
Clipper Ships (Ocean Travel)	11.5–17 miles per hour (depending on weather)	$10.00 per ton for trans-Atlantic shipment
Railroads	around 20 miles per hour (including stops)	$0.06 per ton per mile

Source: George Rodger Taylor, *The Transportation Revolution, 1815 to 1860*

they built faster and more powerful steam locomotives.

Trains were the fastest form of transportation most people had ever experienced. Train wrecks were common, however, whenever engineers trying to stay on schedule traveled too fast. Englishman Charles Richard Weld was on a railroad car that flew off the tracks. To his amazement, the other passengers praised the engineer for trying to keep on schedule.

The free enterprise system helped the railroad system grow. Railroad companies knew they could earn a great deal of money transporting factory goods, freight, and people. By 1860 about 30,000 miles of railroad had been laid, and railroads linked most major cities in the eastern United States. Railroad companies became some of the most powerful businesses in the nation. As the railroad system grew, manufacturers and farmers were able to send their goods to distant markets. Thus, they could look for markets with the best prices. Competition in national markets also lowered prices for consumers.

Railroads contributed to the nation's physical growth as well. They helped cities grow because trains brought new residents as well as raw materials for industry and construction.

✔ **Reading Check: Analyzing Information** In what ways did the railroads affect the economy of the United States? Transporting goods and people between regions became easier and faster, aiding city growth.

Section 3 Review

go. hrw .com Homework Practice Online
keyword: SA3 HP13

❶ **Identify and explain:**
- Transportation Revolution
- Robert Fulton
- *Clermont*
- *Gibbons* v. *Ogden*
- Peter Cooper

❷ **Sequencing** Copy the time line below. Use it to create a flowchart listing the key events that led to the emergence of the steamboat and the railway locomotive in the United States.

The Emergence of the Steamboat and Locomotive

1790s Steam-powered boats developed	Early 1800s Steam trains	1807	1830	1840	1860

❸ **Finding the Main Idea**
a. What were the results of the Supreme Court case *Gibbons* v. *Ogden*?

b. In what ways did railroads in the United States benefit from the free enterprise system?

❹ **Writing and Critical Thinking**
Summarizing Write a dialogue between an American and a visitor from another country discussing how the Transportation Revolution has affected the nation's development.
Consider the following:
- the invention of steamboats and railroads
- the benefits for free enterprise
- the growth of cities

Section 4

OBJECTIVES

- ☆ Describe the ideas Samuel Morse drew upon in order to invent the telegraph.
- ☆ Explain how new developments benefited factory and farm work.
- ☆ Identify the new inventions Cyrus McCormick and Isaac Singer developed.

Section 4

More Technological Advances

Read to Discover

1. What ideas did Samuel Morse draw upon in order to invent the telegraph?
2. How did new developments benefit factory and farm work?
3. What new inventions did Cyrus McCormick and Isaac Singer develop?

WHY IT MATTERS TODAY

New technology continues to dramatically change the daily lives of people around the world. Use CNNfyi.com or other **current events** sources to learn about inventions for the home that have made life easier for people. Record your findings in your journal.

Define

- telegraph

Identify

- Samuel F. B. Morse
- Morse code
- John Deere
- Cyrus McCormick
- Isaac Singer

The Story Continues

On May 24, 1844, Samuel Morse sat down in the Capitol Building in Washington. He was about to conduct the first public test of his new device. His friend Annie Elsworth wrote down a message on a slip of paper. Morse read the message. He then used his invention to send Elsworth's message instantly to Baltimore, Maryland, about 40 miles away. His associate in Baltimore quickly sent the message—"What hath God wrought?"—back to Morse. This exchange had taken place in only a minute.

The telegraph marked the beginning of a new age of communications.

☆ Messages by Wire

In 1832 **Samuel F. B. Morse** invented the **telegraph**, which could send information over wires across great distances. To develop the telegraph, Morse studied electricity and magnetism. Around 1800 Italian scientist Alessandro Volta had built the first battery, which provided a steady supply of electricity. About 20 years later, André-Marie Ampère of

★ TEACH

Have students read Section 4 and complete Guided Reading Strategy 13.4. Choose one or more of the following activities to explore the section content with students. For further suggestions on block scheduling or team teaching, see the *Block Scheduling Handbook with Team Teaching Strategies.*

 ALL LEVELS: Copy the following graphic organizer onto the chalkboard, omitting the italicized answers. Have each student complete the organizer to illustrate how new developments benefited factory and farm work.

ENGLISH LANGUAGE LEARNERS , COOPERATIVE LEARNING

LEVEL 1: Have students explain the inventions of Singer, Deere, and McCormick. List their comments on the chalkboard. As a class, discuss the effects or benefits these developments had on factory or home life.

ENGLISH LANGUAGE LEARNERS

Technological Developments Benefiting Factory and Farm Work

Steam power allowed business owners to build factories in places that did not have streams or waterfalls to power the factory.

Improved machinery was introduced as a substitute for manual labor.

John Deere's steel plow eased farmers' work.

Cyrus McCormick's reaper made harvesting more efficient.

★ Linking Past to Present

Telegraphs: Hello and Goodbye. Shortly after Samuel Morse helped start the telegraph boom, he received government funding to run a transmission cable along rail lines from Baltimore to Washington. Telegraphs soon broadcast news across the United States and in Europe. Western Union routed a transcontinental line in 1861. In 1866, cables were run across the Atlantic Ocean. Cable technology of the 1870s enabled multiple use along a single line. After Edison patented the telephone in 1876, telegraph and telephone messages shared the same lines. Despite fears that the telephone would replace it, telegraph technology flourished for many years. In the 1980s, the telegraph's other services having at long last been replaced by the teletypewriter, e-mail, and the postal service, the telegraph took a bow to the telephone.

ACTIVITY. Have students conduct research to determine why the telephone outlived the telegraph, and to speculate whether the telephone will be replaced by a currently developing technology.

BIOGRAPHY ANSWER

Morse needed to earn money to support his family.

Visual Record Answer

Students might suggest the telegraph.

BIOGRAPHY

Samuel F. B. Morse
(1791–1872)

Like steamboat creator Robert Fulton, American Samuel Morse began his career as a painter rather than an inventor. In 1832 Morse was a widower struggling to raise his three children alone. He became interested in the idea of sending messages electrically. Morse hoped he could invent a device that would earn him enough money to support his family. In time, earnings from the telegraph made Morse extremely wealthy. **What motivated Samuel Morse to invent the telegraph?**

Interpreting the Visual Record

Communication revolution *Several new inventions greatly increased the speed of communication in the 1800s. What do you see in the picture that might have improved communication?*

France determined some of the rules governing the relationship between electricity and magnetism. Morse was the first person to put the work of these scientists together in a practical machine. He spent years trying to achieve his goal of creating the telegraph.

The telegraph sent pulses of electric current through a wire. The telegraph operator tapped a bar, called a telegraph key, that controlled the length of each pulse. At the other end of the wire, these pulses were changed into clicking sounds. A short click was called a dot, while a long click was called a dash. Morse's assistant, Alfred Lewis Vail, developed a system known as **Morse code**. In Morse code, different combinations of dots and dashes are used to stand for letters of the alphabet. For example, *dot dot dot, dash dash dash, dot dot dot* is the distress call SOS. Skilled telegraph operators could send and receive many words every minute.

Several years passed before Morse could connect two locations with telegraph wires. Even then, people doubted that he was actually reading messages sent from miles away. They claimed that he was making lucky guesses. Morse's break came during the 1844 Democratic National Convention in Baltimore, Maryland. A telegraph wired news of a presidential candidate's nomination to politicians in Washington. The politicians responded, "Three cheers for the telegraph!" Telegraphs were soon sending and receiving information for businesses, the government, newspapers, and private citizens.

The telegraph grew with the railroad. Telegraph companies strung telegraph lines on poles alongside railroads across the country. They established telegraph offices in many train stations. Thousands more miles of telegraph were added every year in the 1850s. The first transcontinental line was finished in 1861. By the time he died in 1872, Morse was famous across the United States.

✔ **Reading Check: Evaluating** How did scientific discoveries help make Morse's invention of the telegraph possible? Morse drew on the ideas of Alessandro Volta and André-Marie Ampère about electricity and magnetism.

⭐ New Factories

At the start of the Industrial Revolution, most factories ran on waterpower. Over time, however, factory owners began using steam power to run their machines. This shift brought major changes to the nation's industrial growth. While water-wheels remained popular in many areas, water-powered factories had to be built near fast-flowing streams or waterfalls. The use of steam engines allowed business owners to build their factories almost anywhere. Yet the Northeast was still home to most of the nation's industry. By 1860 New England alone had as many factories as the entire South.

Some companies decided to build their factories closer to cities and transportation centers. This location gave them easier access to workers, allowing them to lower the cost of labor. Being closer to cities also reduced shipping costs. As factories moved, so did the nation's population. Cities soon became the center of industrial growth. People from rural areas as well as foreign countries flocked to the cities to take factory jobs.

Americans also improved the designs of many kinds of machines. Mechanics invented tools that could cut and shape metal, stone, and wood with great precision. Englishman Joseph Whitworth wrote a report on American manufacturing in 1854. He noted how much Americans used their new inventions.

> **"**[Americans] call in the aid of machinery in almost every department [area] of industry. Wherever it can be introduced as a substitute for manual labor, it is universally [widely] and willingly resorted [turned] to.**"**
>
> —Joseph Whitworth, quoted in *From the American System to Mass Production*, by David A. Hounshell

By the 1840s this new machinery was able to produce interchangeable parts. Gunmakers at the federal Springfield Armory in Massachusetts finally achieved Eli Whitney's dream. They built weapons using interchangeable parts and mass production. Within a short period of time, the growing machine-tool industry was even making customized equipment. By 1859 the value of the products of American industry was greater than the value of crops. Inventions also spread quickly in America. For example, just 15 years after the sewing machine was invented, America had 15 times as many sewing machines as England.

✔ **Reading Check: Finding the Main Idea** How did new technology change the way goods were manufactured? Business owners had more freedom in where to locate their factories, and they were able to use interchangeable parts and mass production methods.

This pin-making machine was one of the technological advances developed during the early 1800s.

Analyzing Primary Sources
Identifying Points of View
What does Whitworth's opinion of American industry seem to be? Answers will vary, but students might suggest that Whitworth is impressed by how Americans have found ways to use machines to help them make work more efficient.

⭐ Historical Sidelight

The American Farm. Inventions such as the steel plow and mechanical reaper dramatically reduced the time and effort required to perform farm work. Farmers became able to plant and harvest far more with these machines than they were able to do by hand. Between 1820 and 1840, the percentage of people working on farms went from 71.8 to 68.6. The numbers continued to decline, falling to 58.9 in 1860, 57.1 in 1880, and 37.5 in 1900. Figures went from 27 percent to 17.4 percent from 1920 to 1940, plummeting to 6.1 percent 20 years later. By 1980 only 2.7 percent of Americans worked on farms, and that figure had bottomed out at 2.5% by 1994.

ACTIVITY. Have students graph the figures and share observations about what they see.

★ Better Farm Equipment

During the 1830s technology began transforming the farm as well as the factory. In 1837 blacksmith **John Deere** saw that his farming friends in Illinois had problems plowing the thick soil because the dirt stuck to their iron plows. Deere thought that a steel blade like one he had seen in a sawmill, might slice through the earth. His steel plow design was a success. By 1846 Deere was selling 1,000 plows per year. His business continued to prosper as more farmers moved west.

While Deere's plow made planting wheat easier, harvesting it was still time-consuming and difficult. About the same time Deere developed his plow, **Cyrus McCormick** was developing a new harvesting machine. He later recalled, "I was often advised by my father and family to abandon [my work]." Despite this advice, he went on to create the mechanical reaper, which cut down wheat quickly and efficiently.

McCormick continued to improve his design, and in the 1840s he sold his first machines. He later entered the device in international competitions, where it achieved great success. McCormick soon began mass-producing his reapers in a large factory in Chicago. His factory was one of the first to use steam-engine technology to run its saws and other machines. McCormick overcame competition from other inventors and became a millionaire. McCormick's business talents and marketing ideas contributed to his great success. His company advertised, gave demonstrations, and provided a repair and spare-parts department. The company also allowed customers to buy on credit.

The combination of Deere's plow and McCormick's reaper allowed midwestern farmers to plant and harvest huge fields of wheat. The process was both fast and cheap. In 1830 harvesting an acre of wheat took 20 hours. McCormick's farm machinery eventually reduced that time to an hour per acre. By 1860 farmers in the United States were producing more than 170 million bushels of wheat and more than 800 million bushels of corn a year.

New advertisements helped sell farm machinery, such as the McCormick reaper shown below, to farmers.

✔ **Reading Check: Analyzing Information** What marketing methods did McCormick use to help sell his farm equipment? He advertised, gave demonstrations, and provided repair and spare-parts services to gain customers.

★ Changing Life at Home

Some inventions of the Industrial Revolution simply made life easier. When Alexis de Tocqueville of France visited the United States, he identified what he called a very American quality.

History Makers Speak
❝[Americans want] to be always making life more comfortable and convenient, to avoid trouble, and to satisfy the smallest wants [desires] without effort and almost without cost.❞

Alexis de Tocqueville, *Democracy in America*

☆ **REVIEW AND ASSESS**

Have students complete the **Section 4 Review** on p. 418. Then have students complete **Daily Quiz 13.4.** As **Alternative Assessment,** you may want to use the slogan or magazine article proposal exercises in this section's lessons.

☆ **RETEACH**

Have students complete **Main Idea Activity for English Language Learners and Special-Needs Students 13.4.** Then ask students to look at the terms listed in the Define and Identify segments of the Section Review. Ask students to place the terms into the following categories: communications,

farming, or home life. Finally, for each category have students write a few sentences describing each Define and Identify term. **ENGLISH LANGUAGE LEARNERS**

☆ **EXTEND**

Have students use the library to find information about advances in plows and reapers since the mid-1800s. Have students create a series of illustrations depicting how these farm machines have changed over the years. Have students write a brief summary next to each illustration explaining its improvements over the previous model. **BLOCK SCHEDULING**

The sewing machine was one of these many conveniences. Elias Howe, a factory apprentice in Lowell, Massachusetts, first invented the sewing machine. However, <u>Isaac Singer</u> made improvements to this design. His Singer sewing machine grew increasingly popular in the 1850s. It had a clever design and was easy to use. Early advertisements claimed, "Even a child can run it." Singer worked very hard to promote his product. Like McCormick, he also allowed customers to buy goods on credit and provided service with sales. Singer's strategies worked well. Many women bought sewing machines to try to earn a living at home by making clothing for large companies. In some homes, fancy sewing machines became signs of wealth. By 1860 Singer's company was the world's largest maker of sewing machines.

Other advances improved on everyday items. In the 1830s iceboxes cooled by large blocks of fresh ice became available, allowing people to store fresh food safely. Iron cookstoves began replacing cooking fires and stone hearths. Companies also began to mass-produce old inventions cheaply. This method allowed many families to afford household items such as clocks.

More cities also built public water systems. Some wealthy families had water pumps installed inside their houses. However, very few homes had plumbing above the first floor. Hotels were often the first buildings in a city to have such advances. Other useful items were developed during this period. For example, matches were introduced in the 1830s, and the safety pin was invented in 1849. All of these inventions helped make life at home more convenient for an increasing number of Americans.

By the late 1800s many American homes had sewing machines.

✔ **Reading Check Comparing** How did the different labor-saving inventions affect daily life? Women were able to sew at home for pleasure or profit with sewing machines; iceboxes stored food safely; iron cookstoves made cooking easier; and pumps allowed families to have water inside.

Section 4 Review

keyword: SA3 HP13

❶ **Define and explain:**
• telegraph

❷ **Identify and explain:**
• Samuel F. B. Morse
• Morse code
• John Deere
• Cyrus McCormick
• Isaac Singer

❸ **Summarizing** Copy the graphic organizer below. Use it to show the significant technological developments of the 1800s and who created them. Then briefly explain each development's significance.

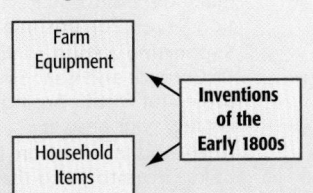

❹ **Finding the Main Idea**
a. What are the key factors that contributed to Samuel Morse's invention of the telegraph and its success?

b. How did the introduction of steam power affect manufacturing and the U.S. population?

❺ **Writing and Critical Thinking**
Identifying Cause and Effect Imagine that you are a reporter in the mid-1800s. Write an article explaining to your readers how the new inventions are improving life at home and at work.

Consider the following:
• improved production methods
• the usefulness of new household conveniences
• the marketing methods used to sell goods

REVIEW AND ASSESSMENT RESOURCES

REPRODUCIBLE
▶ Vocabulary Activity 13

TECHNOLOGY
▶ Chapter 13 Test Generator (on the One-Stop Planner)
▶ Global Skill Builder CD–ROM
▶ HRW Go site

REINFORCEMENT, REVIEW, AND ASSESSMENT
▶ Chapter 13 Review, pp. 419–21
▶ Chapter 13 Tutorial for Students, Parents, Mentors, and Peers

▶ Chapter 13 Test (Form A or B)
▶ Alternative Assessment Handbook
▶ Chapter 13 Test for English Language Learners and Special-Needs Students

★ REVIEW
Have students complete the **Chapter 13 Review** on pages 420–21.

★ ASSESS
Use one of the chapter tests to assess students' understanding of the content. For **Alternative Assessment**, see the **Alternative Assessment Handbook**.

Understanding Main Ideas

1. Samuel Slater's mill was the first in America to use a British design.

2. Samuel Slater used the Rhode Island system, which used families to provide labor. Francis Cabot Lowell used the Lowell system, which used young unmarried women to provide labor.

3. to improve working conditions, get better pay, and work fewer hours

4. Both made it easier and cheaper for people and goods to travel. This led more people to settle in the Midwest and the cities.

5. Deere developed the steel plow, and McCormick invented the mechanical reaper—both inventions made farming easier and more efficient.

6. made daily chores easier, kept food fresh longer

You Be the Historian— Reviewing Themes

1. The Court ruled that a federal steamboat operating license superseded a state-issued license. The ruling established that the federal government could regulate interstate transportation and new inventions as part of interstate commerce.

2. Factory jobs were created, many of them in cities, leading more people to move to cities. The daily work patterns of many Americans were also changed.

3. Steamboats and railroads made it easier and cheaper to ship goods, which contributed to an increase in American markets.

Chapter **13** Review

The Chapter at a Glance
Examine the visual summary of the chapter below. Make a chart listing the inventions you think were most important and explain why. Share your chart with another student. Place each invention in the appropriate category.

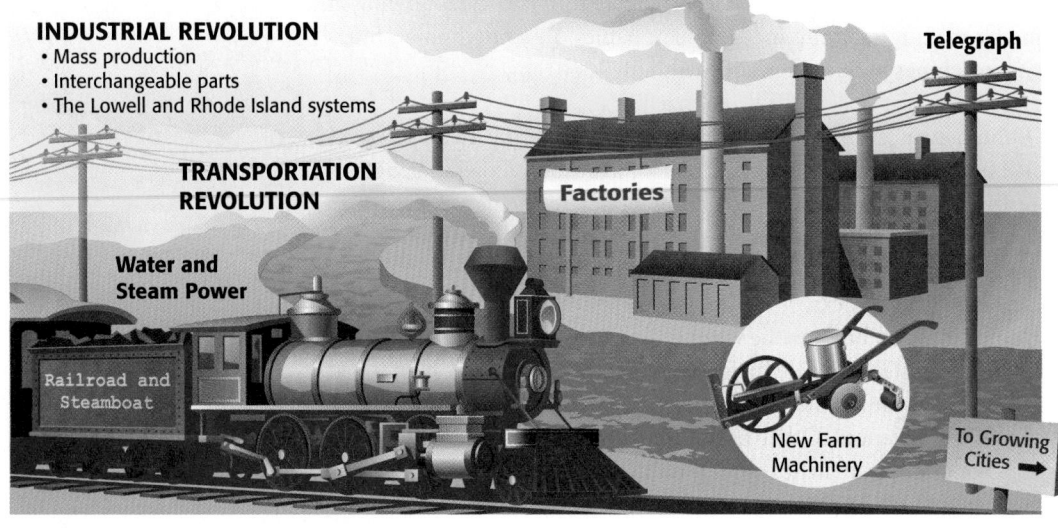

INDUSTRIAL REVOLUTION
- Mass production
- Interchangeable parts
- The Lowell and Rhode Island systems

TRANSPORTATION REVOLUTION

Water and Steam Power

Railroad and Steamboat

Factories

Telegraph

New Farm Machinery

To Growing Cities

Identifying People and Ideas
Use the following terms or people in historically significant sentences.
1. Industrial Revolution
2. interchangeable parts
3. mass production
4. Lowell system
5. Sarah G. Bagley
6. Transportation Revolution
7. Robert Fulton
8. *Gibbons* v. *Ogden*
9. telegraph
10. Cyrus McCormick

Understanding Main Ideas
Section 1 *(Pages 398–403)*
1. How did the innovations of Samuel Slater and Eli Whitney contribute to the growth of American manufacturing?

Section 2 *(Pages 404–409)*
2. What were the characteristics of the two main factory systems that developed in New England?
3. Why did workers organize trade unions?

Section 3 *(Pages 410–414)*
4. How did the steamboat and the railroad affect the growth of cities?

Section 4 *(Pages 415–419)*
5. Compare the contributions made by John Deere and Cyrus McCormick to American farming.

6. How did the different types of home appliances make daily life easier?

You Be the Historian— Reviewing Themes
1. **Government** What did the Supreme Court rule in *Gibbons* v. *Ogden*, and what was significant about the case?
2. **Science, Technology & Society** How did the growth of factories change American life?
3. **Economics** How did the Transportation Revolution benefit the U.S. economy and free enterprise?

Thinking Critically
1. **Drawing Inferences and Conclusions** How do you think the U.S. free enterprise system helped make the Industrial Revolution and Transportation Revolution possible?
2. **Supporting a Point of View** Do you think Cyrus McCormick and Isaac Singer would have been so successful without using new sales methods? Explain your answer.
3. **Analyzing Information** Explain the influence of key inventors and their inventions on the industrial growth of the United States during the 1800s.

⭐ RETEACH

Have students imagine that they were born in 1790 and that it is now 1860. Ask students to create a scrapbook that shows how much the United States has changed during their lives. Students should include drawings of the inventions that have altered their lives and describe how each affected communications, work, or home life. Encourage volunteers to share their scrapbooks with the class. **ENGLISH LANGUAGE LEARNERS**

Portfolio Extensions

1. Interdisciplinary Connection to Geography

Have students create a map of the United States. Tell them to use the information provided in the chapter to locate where industrial growth and major improvements in transportation took place. Students should label these places on the map using appropriate map symbols. Then using their map as a guide, students should create a list of areas in the United States that they think were most affected by the Industrial and Transportation Revolutions.

2. Linking to Community
Tell students that many creative men and women contributed to the technological growth of the nation. Tell students to use current events sources to find out about someone in their community who has invented or developed an item of significance. Students should present an oral report on this person and his or her invention to the class.

Social Studies Skills Workshop

Interpreting Charts

Study the chart below. Then use the information on the chart to help you answer the questions that follow.

> **Causes and Effects of the Industrial Revolution in America, 1790–1860**
>
> **Long-Term Causes**
> Industrial Revolution in Britain
> Transportation Revolution (canals, improved roads, railroads, steamboats)
> Introduction of steam power
> Growing cities
> Rise in immigration
>
> **Immediate Causes**
> Technological innovations by individuals such as Samuel Slater and Eli Whitney in early 1800s
> War of 1812
> Founding of Lowell mills, 1822
> Tariffs on foreign manufactured goods
>
> **The Industrial Revolution in America, 1790–1860**
>
> **Effects**
> Economic growth
> More manufactured goods produced at lower prices
> Factory jobs change working habits and conditions
> Women and children become wage-earners

1. Which of the following was not an immediate cause of the Industrial Revolution in America?
   a. the War of 1812
   b. the Lowell mills
   c. tariffs on foreign goods
   d. a rise in immigration

2. Based on your knowledge of the period, how do you think the long-term causes listed on the chart contributed to the Industrial Revolution in the United States?

Analyzing Primary Sources

Read the following quote by John H. B. Latrobe, a railroad developer, and then answer the questions that follow.

> ❝In the beginning, no one dreamed of steam upon the [rail]road. Horses were to do the work . . . ; relays of horses trotted the cars from place to place. . . . There was this difficulty about introducing an English [steam] engine on an American road. An English road was virtually a straight road. An American road had curves. . . . For a brief season it was believed that this feature of the early American roads would prevent the use of locomotive engines.❞

3. Which of the following statements best describes the problem with using steam engines on early American railroads?
   a. Americans wanted to use horses to pull railcars.
   b. American railroads had too many curves in them.
   c. All the steam engines were built in England.
   d. People were afraid of steam locomotives.

4. Based on your knowledge of the period, what are some ways in which Americans could have made railroads work in the American environment?

📄 internet connect

Internet Activity: go.hrw.com
keyword: SA3 CF13

Choose an activity on Industrial Growth in the North to:
- Create a database and graph of the economic and social impact of the McCormick reaper.
- Create an annotated map of the Erie Canal.
- Write a biography of Samuel Slater.

Thinking Critically

1. Students' answers will vary but should indicate that the free enterprise system encouraged people to enter the business world and take risks.

2. Students should note that both men used advertising, installment buying, repair services, and so forth to encourage people to buy their products.

3. Slater brought the new water-powered textile technology necessary to start factories. Whitney introduced the mass production and interchangeable parts later used by people such as McCormick and Singer. Steam power helped factories relocate, while the telegraph improved communication and provided information.

Skills Workshop
1. d

2. Answers will vary, but should note that: the Industrial Revolution in Britain encouraged Americans to develop industries; the Transportation Revolution helped bring goods and people together faster and more cheaply; steam power helped run factories and vehicles; and growing cities and more immigrants provided bigger centers of industry and many potential factory workers.

3. b

4. Answers will vary, but students will probably note either: changing the environment by building tunnels, bridges and so forth to make the railroads straighter, or building bigger, stronger, more maneuverable locomotives.

Objectives	Pacing Guide	Reproducible Resources
SECTION 1: **The Growth of Cotton** (pp. 424–27) ★ Explain what happened to agriculture and slavery in the South immediately after the American Revolution. ★ Analyze the effect of the cotton gin on the South and slavery. ★ Investigate the effects of the cotton boom on the South's economy.	**Regular** 2 days **Block Scheduling** 1 day *Block Scheduling Handbook with Team Teaching Strategies, Chapter 14*	**RS** Guided Reading Strategy 14.1 **SM** Geography Activity 14: A Southern Plantation
SECTION 2: **The Southern Economy** (pp. 428–32) ★ Describe how trade affected the southern economy. ★ Determine why crops other than cotton were important to the southern economy. ★ Identify the kinds of factories that were located in the South.	**Regular** 1.5 days **Block Scheduling** 1 day *Block Scheduling Handbook with Team Teaching Strategies, Chapter 14*	**RS** Guided Reading Strategy 14.2 **PS** Primary Source Reading 14: The Southern Economy **E** Creative Teaching Strategy: Open Interviewing
SECTION 3: **Southern Society** (pp. 433–37) ★ Describe what life was like for southern planters and owners of small farms. ★ Analyze what the urban South was like. ★ Examine the challenges free African Americans faced in the South.	**Regular** 2 days **Block Scheduling** 1 day *Block Scheduling Handbook with Team Teaching Strategies, Chapter 14*	**RS** Guided Reading Strategy 14.3 **PS** Biography Reading 14: Fanny Kemble **E** Hands-On History Activity: Your State's Agriculture
SECTION 4: **The Slave System** (pp. 439–43) ★ Explain what work and daily life were like for most slaves. ★ Describe how slaves used family, religion, and other aspects of their culture to help them cope with the slave system. ★ Identify ways that enslaved African Americans challenged the slave system.	**Regular** 1.5 days **Block Scheduling** .5 day *Block Scheduling Handbook with Team Teaching Strategies, Chapter 14*	**RS** Guided Reading Strategy 14.4 **PS** American History Political Cartoon 7: Slavery in America and England **PS** Literature Reading 14: Incidents in the Life of a Slave Girl **RS** Graphic Organizer 14: Living Conditions for Slaves

Chapter Resource Key

PS	Primary Sources	**A**	Assessment	Music	
RS	Reading Support	**REV**	Review	Video	
IC	Interdisciplinary Connections	**ELL**	Reinforcement and English Language Learners	Internet	
E	Enrichment		Transparencies	Holt Presentation Maker Using Microsoft® PowerPoint®	
SM	Skills Mastery		CD-ROM		

 One-Stop Planner CD-ROM

See the *One-Stop Planner* for a complete list of additional resources for students and teachers.

One-Stop Planner CD–ROM

It's easy to plan lessons, select resources, and print out materials for your students when you use the **One-Stop Planner CD–ROM with Test Generator.**

Technology Resources	Reinforcement, Review, and Assessment

 One-Stop Planner, Lesson 14.1
Homework Practice Online

REV Section 1 Review, p. 427
A Daily Quiz 14.1
ELL Main Idea Activity 14.1
ELL English Audio Summary 14.1
ELL Spanish Audio Summary 14.1

 One-Stop Planner, Lesson 14.2
 Holt Researcher: American History CD–ROM
 Homework Practice Online
 HRW Go site

REV Section 2 Review, p. 432
A Daily Quiz 14.2
ELL Main Idea Activity 14.2
ELL English Audio Summary 14.2
ELL Spanish Audio Summary 14.2

 One-Stop Planner, Lesson 14.3
 Holt Researcher: American History CD–ROM
American History Interactive Maps CD–ROM: The Cotton Plantation
 Homework Practice Online

REV Section 3 Review, p. 437
A Daily Quiz 14.3
ELL Main Idea Activity 14.3
ELL English Audio Summary 14.3
ELL Spanish Audio Summary 14.3

 One-Stop Planner, Lesson 14.4
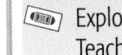 Exploring America's Past Video Segment: Slavery and the South; Teacher's Guide, pp. 22–23
 American Music Selection 11: "Wayfaring Stranger"
 CNN Presents America: Yesterday and Today, Beginnings to 1914 Segment: A Slave Memorial
 Homework Practice Online

REV Section 4 Review, p. 443
A Daily Quiz 14.4
ELL Main Idea Activity 14.4
ELL English Audio Summary 14.4
ELL Spanish Audio Summary 14.4

Meeting Individual Needs

Ability Levels

Level 1 Basic-level activities designed for all students encountering new material

Level 2 Intermediate-level activities designed for average students

Level 3 Challenging activities designed for honors and gifted-and-talented students

English Language Learners Activities that address the needs of students with Limited English Proficiency

internet connect

HRW ONLINE RESOURCES
GO TO: go.hrw.com
Then type in a keyword.

TEACHER HOME PAGE
KEYWORD: SA3 Teacher

CHAPTER INTERNET ACTIVITIES
KEYWORD: SA3 CF14
Choose an activity to:
• learn about slave revolts in Haiti and the abolition of slavery in France.
• understand sugar production and make a flow chart.
• research and report on the Tredegar Iron Works.

CHAPTER ENRICHMENT LINKS
KEYWORD: SA3 CH14

ONLINE ASSESSMENT
Homework Practice
KEYWORD: SA3 HP14

Standardized Test Prep
KEYWORD: SA3 STP14

Rubrics
KEYWORD: SS Rubrics

ONLINE MAPS, CHARTS, AND GRAPHS
KEYWORD: SA3 MCG
• Agriculture and Slavery
• Slaveholding Families, 1850
• Southern Population, 1850

CONTENT UPDATES
KEYWORD: SS Content Updates

HOLT PRESENTATION MAKER
KEYWORD: SA3 PPT14

ONLINE READING SUPPORT
KEYWORD: SS Strategies

CURRENT EVENTS
KEYWORD: S3 Current Events

Chapter Review and Assessment

IC 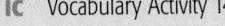 Vocabulary Activity 14
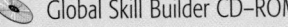 Global Skill Builder CD–ROM
 HRW Go site
REV Chapter 14 Tutorial for Students, Parents, Mentors, and Peers
REV Chapter 14 Review, pp. 444–45
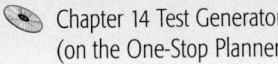 Chapter 14 Test Generator (on the One-Stop Planner)
A Chapter 14 Test (Form A or B)

A Alternative Assessment Handbook
A Chapter 14 Test for English Language Learners and Special-Needs Students

14

Build on What You Know

If You Were There...

Ask students to answer the following question:

What type of business would you start in the South?

Consider:

• the economy and climate of the South

• the type of business opportunities available

You Be the Historian

What's Your Opinion?

To help students create their **Themes** Journal entries, provide the following examples of appropriate **agree**/**disagree** statements.

CHAPTER

14 Agricultural Changes in the South

(1790–1860)

Eli Whitney's cotton gin had a simple design but made a tremendous impact on the southern economy.

In addition to being an inventor, Jean Étienne Boré served as the first mayor of New Orleans under American rule.

UNITED STATES

1793 Eli Whitney invents the cotton gin, which enables southern farmers to grow more cotton.

1795 Jean Étienne Boré invents a new sugar-processing system.

1808 A congressional ban on the importing of slaves into the United States takes effect.

1790	**1800**	**1810**	**1820**

WORLD

1794 France ends slavery in its colonies.

1806 The British cotton industry employs more than 250,000 workers.

1807 Parliament bans the slave trade in the British Empire.

1825 A revolt against the Russian czar is crushed.

After Britain banned the slave trade, British warships tried to stop slave ships on the high seas.

Build on What You Know

While industrial growth was changing the society of the North, a distinct southern culture emerged. The South's agricultural economy relied on the labor of enslaved African Americans. Southern society was led by planters and also included yeomen, poor whites, and free African Americans.

Science, Technology & Society

Agree Many technological advancements are not related to the growth of manufacturing.

Disagree Improvements in technology can be linked to the growth of manufacturing.

Economics

Agree Product specialization can lead to superior quality and knowledge of a product.

Disagree Concentrating on one product limits the ability to adapt to changes in the market.

Culture

Agree Only the predominant group in each region will express its culture.

Disagree Many cultures can exist simultaneously in the same region.

Southern cotton plantations depended upon the labor of enslaved African Americans.

Slaves produced crafts, such as this quilt below showing stories from the Bible, that reflected their cultural and spiritual beliefs.

1831 Nat Turner's Rebellion leads to fears of further slave revolts in the South.

1845 The U.S. Naval Academy opens in Annapolis, Maryland.

1848 Joseph R. Anderson becomes owner of the Tredegar Iron Works, the South's only large iron factory.

1860 The South grows two thirds of all cotton in the United States.

1830 **1840** **1850** **1860**

1835 Alexis de Tocqueville publishes *Democracy in America.*

1837 Victoria is crowned queen of Great Britain.

1854 The disease cholera spreads through London.

The United States Naval Academy. The United States Naval Academy located in Annapolis, Maryland, was founded in 1845. George Bancroft, the secretary of the navy, wanted to establish a school to improve the methods of training midshipmen. The original course was for five years, two at the academy and three at sea. The current course of four years at the academy with a summer practice cruise was instituted during a reorganization that occurred in 1850.

CRITICAL THINKING

Do you think the original course would have been better at training midshipmen?

ANSWER: Students' responses will vary, but some students might suggest that the midshipmen's training was longer and therefore more comprehensive.

If you were there . . .
What type of business would you start in the South?

You Be the Historian

Themes Journal

What's Your Opinion? Do you **agree** or **disagree** with the following statements? Support your point of view in your journal.

- **Science, Technology & Society** New technology does not always lead to the growth of manufacturing.

- **Economics** Concentrating on making one product will lead to economic success.

- **Culture** Each region of the country has only one distinct culture.

Section 1

OBJECTIVES

⭐ Explain what happened to agriculture and slavery in the South immediately after the American Revolution.

⭐ Analyze the effect of the cotton gin on the South and slavery.

⭐ Investigate the effects of the cotton boom on the South's economy.

📻 LET'S GET STARTED!

Write the following question on the chalkboard: *What inventions have changed people's lives?* As students enter the classroom, have them answer the question. *(Students' responses may include airplanes, automobiles, telephones, and trains.)* Tell students that perhaps one of the most influential inventions in early U.S. history was Eli Whitney's cotton gin. Detail its purpose to students and tell them that the cotton gin revolutionized the southern economy. Explain to the class that the growth of this industry also spread the practice of slavery throughout the South. Tell students that in Section 1 they will learn more about the cotton gin and its effects on the South.

Section 1

The Growth of Cotton

Read to Discover

1. What happened to agriculture and slavery in the South immediately after the American Revolution?
2. What effect did the cotton gin have on the South and slavery?
3. How did the cotton boom affect the South's economy?

WHY IT MATTERS TODAY

After 1800 the southern economy came to depend more and more on the production of cotton. Use **CNN fyi**.com or other **current events** sources to find a region or a country whose economy today depends on one major product. Record your findings in your journal.

Define

- cotton gin
- cotton belt

Identify

- Eli Whitney

The Story Continues

This fan was owned by a wealthy southerner.

COLONIAL WILLIAMSBURG FOUNDATION

O n an August day in 1770, slaveholder Landon Carter rode out to view his tobacco crops. He was pleased by the thick healthy plants he saw. Carter was a successful plantation owner in Virginia. He and his neighbors believed that the ability to produce good crops reflected a person's good character. "I know in this neighborhood people are very fond of speaking meanly of their neighbor's Crops," he noted. "However, when I ride out, I declare I do not see any so good [as mine]."

⭐ The South's Agricultural Economy

Successful plantation owners like Landon Carter saw farming as an art to be passed down from generation to generation. Southerners prided themselves on their ties to the land. Many believed that the future of the United States rested on agriculture. Thomas Jefferson expressed this view.

Analyzing Primary Sources

Identifying Points of View
What was Jefferson's attitude toward independent farmers?

He saw them as God's chosen people, virtuous, without corruption or immorality.

 History Makers Speak

❝Those [independent white farmers] who labor in the earth are the chosen people of God. . . . Corruption of morals in the mass of cultivators [farmers] is a phenomenon [event] of which no age nor nation has furnished an example.❞

—Thomas Jefferson, quoted in *The Annals of America*

Have students read Section 1 and complete Guided Reading Strategy 14.1. Choose one or more of the following activities to explore the section content with students. For further suggestions on block scheduling or team teaching, see the *Block Scheduling Handbook with Team Teaching Strategies*.

LEVEL 1: Explain the significance of the cotton gin to southern agriculture. Have students write an encyclopedia entry about the device. Ask students to answer the following questions in their entries: What problem was the cotton gin invented to solve? Who invented it? What year was it invented? What effect did it have on the South and slavery?

(Students' responses should include that the cotton gin solved the problem of removing cotton seeds and was invented by Eli Whitney in 1793. Students might suggest that the cotton gin gave new life to the southern agricultural economy.) Have students take turns presenting each other's entries.

ENGLISH LANGUAGE LEARNERS

HOMEWORK Ask students to imagine that they are living in the southern United States in the early 1800s. Ask them to write a letter to a friend describing how life has changed since the American Revolution. Have students comment on how slavery and the growth of the cotton industry brought about further changes.

However, southern agriculture began to decline after the American Revolution. Prices for major cash crops such as indigo, rice, and tobacco all fell. With prices falling, landowners cut production or began switching to crops that needed less labor, like wheat. With less demand for farm workers in the Upper South, the value of slaves began to drop.

Some slaveholders freed their slaves for moral or political reasons. Certain Revolutionary leaders believed that a nation founded on liberty could not support slavery. Northern states gradually began to abolish slavery completely. In the South there were some planters, such as Richard Randolph, who freed their slaves in their wills. Randolph had come to view slavery as "the most lawless and monstrous tyranny [injustice]." As more slaves gained their freedom, some leaders predicted that slavery would eventually die out.

✔ **Reading Check: Summarizing** Why did slavery decline in the Upper South at the end of the 1700s? falling prices for South's cash crops, reduced production, ideal of liberty

In 1781 the slave Mum Bett successfully sued for her freedom in a Massachusetts court.

☆ Whitney and the Cotton Gin

Some southerners saw cotton as a cash crop that would help the economy. The expanding British and American textile industries used cotton to make cloth. However, farmers had difficulty keeping up with the demand for raw cotton because it was difficult to grow and process.

Southerners had been growing small amounts of cotton since Jamestown was founded in 1607. Long-staple, or black-seed, cotton was the easiest to process. Workers could easily remove the seeds from its long fibers. But long-staple cotton only grew well in a few places in the South.

☆ Geography

Tobacco and the South.
One farming expert observed that "there is no plant in the world that requires richer land . . . than tobacco. . . . It will grow on poorer fields, but not to yield crops that are sufficiently profitable to pay the expenses of negroes." Tobacco so badly bleached the land of nutrients that after three years, the soil required 20 years of rest before it was arable again. Before farmers learned to rotate crops, they instead rotated fields, planting tobacco on fresh land until its nutrients were exhausted.

CRITICAL THINKING
How did the introduction of tobacco affect southern society?

ANSWER: Students might suggest that agriculture began to play a central role in the southern economy and culture.

CONNECTING TO SCIENCE AND TECHNOLOGY ANSWER
It simplified and streamlined the process of removing the seeds from cotton.

CONNECTING TO
SCIENCE AND TECHNOLOGY

The Cotton Gin

Early cotton gins, or engines, could not remove the seeds from the type of cotton that would grow most easily in the South. Eli Whitney's cotton gin consisted of rollers with wire teeth set inside a box. As the rollers turned they pulled the cotton from the box but left the seeds behind. Another roller brushed away the cotton lint from the wire-teeth rollers to keep them from being clogged. Many southerners made copies of Whitney's cotton gin. Soon other inventors had improved on his original design. **What was the advantage of Whitney's design?**

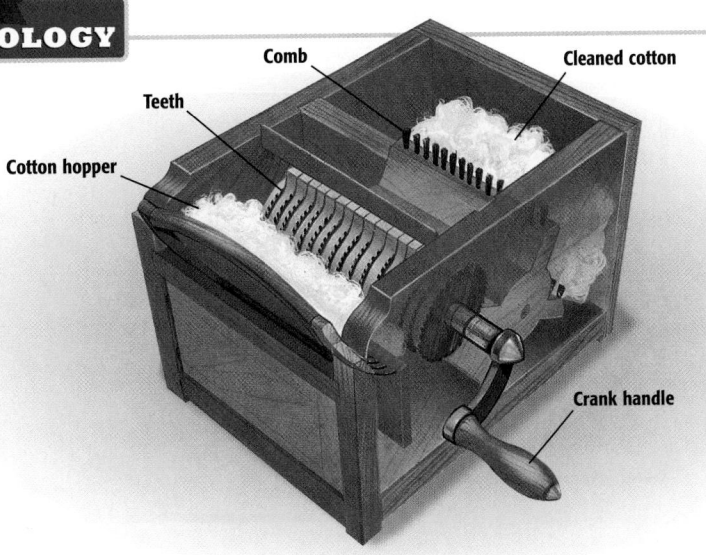

Comb

Teeth

Cleaned cotton

Cotton hopper

Crank handle

ALL LEVELS: Copy the following graphic organizer onto the chalkboard, omitting the italicized answers. Have students list the positive and negative effects of the cotton boom on the South's economy.
ENGLISH LANGUAGE LEARNERS

LEVEL 3: Ask students to develop an economic proposal that would address the problem of falling prices on indigo, rice, and tobacco. Then have students discuss what happened to agriculture and slavery in the South immediately after the American Revolution.

EFFECTS OF THE COTTON BOOM

Positive
• *helped the economy grow*
• *provided a lot of cash*

Negative
• *increased reliance on one crop*

★ CLOSE

Ask students to imagine that they are traveling in the South sometime between 1790 and 1860. Have them write a travelogue describing the following: who is working in the fields, what crops they are growing, the machinery they are using, their living quarters, and how they are being supervised.

Science, Technology & Society

The Cotton Gin.

The engraving on page 427 shows how workers ran cotton into the gin to separate the seeds from the cotton fibers. Whitney's first device of 1794 could not keep the cotton seeds separated from the lint. A chamber opened once after the lint was separated from the seed, allowing the seed to fall away from the good cotton, but some seed and lint usually clung together. Two years after Whitney invented his device, H. Ogden Holmes patented a development that allowed the separated seed to be discharged continuously, instead of just once per batch of cotton. His improvement was considerable enough to cause a controversy over which inventor should be given the most credit for the gin.

CRITICAL THINKING

Which inventor should receive credit for the gin, and why?

ANSWER: Students' answers will vary, but they should support their answer.

MAP ANSWER

Alabama, Georgia, Louisiana, Mississippi, North Carolina, South Carolina, Tennessee, Virginia

---

★★★★★★★★★★★★
That's Interesting!
★★★★★★★★★★★★

All Glory, No Gain Did you know that the inventor of the cotton gin made practically no money from his machine? It's true! After perfecting the cotton gin, Eli Whitney was given the sole right to make the machine in 1794. But others could easily make the gins, and planters did not need Whitney's help. Whitney sued planters for violating his rights, but he gained next to nothing from his legal battles. "[A]n invention can be so valuable," Whitney concluded, "as to be worthless to the inventor."

Although short-staple, or green-seed, cotton grew well across the South, removing its seeds was very hard. A worker might take an entire day to remove the seeds from just one pound of green-seed cotton. Cotton growers needed a machine that could more easily do this job.

Northerner **Eli Whitney** finally built such a machine in 1793. In 1792 Whitney had visited a Georgia plantation owned by Catherine Greene. Workers were using a machine to remove seeds from long-staple cotton. Greene asked Whitney to help improve the machine. By the following spring, Whitney had perfected a machine for removing short-staple seeds from cotton fibers.

A simple device, the **cotton gin** used a hand-cranked cylinder with wire teeth to pull cotton fibers apart from the seeds. Whitney described how his invention would improve the cotton business.

> **History Makers Speak**
> ❝One man will clean ten times as much cotton as he can in any other way before known and also clean it much better than in the usual mode [method]. This machine may be turned by water or with a horse, with the greatest ease, and one man and a horse will do more than fifty men with the old machines.❞
>
> —Eli Whitney, quoted in *Eli Whitney and the Birth of American Technology*, by Constance McLaughlin Green

Whitney's gin revolutionized the cotton industry and gave new life to southern agriculture. Planters—large-scale farmers who held more than 20 slaves—built gins that could process tons of cotton quickly. Other southerners, like William McCreight of South Carolina, established successful businesses making gins for cotton growers.

✔ **Reading Check: Finding the Main Idea** Why was the way the cotton gin worked important? *made separating seeds from cotton easier, renewed demand for slaves*

Cotton bolls

The Cotton Kingdom

Interpreting Maps The growth of the textile industry created a large demand for cotton. To meet this demand, farmers dramatically increased the area devoted to growing cotton between 1820 and 1860.

Skills Assessment Places and Regions What states were growing cotton in 1820?

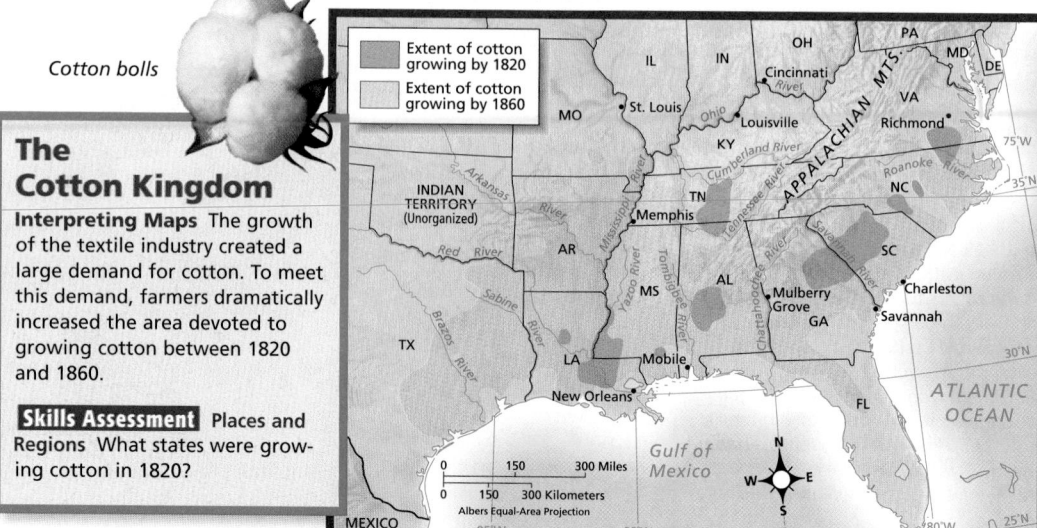

☆ REVIEW AND ASSESS

Have students complete the **Section 1 Review** on p. 427. Then have them complete **Daily Quiz 14.1**. As **Alternative Assessment**, you may want to use the cotton boom graphic organizer or the travelogue exercise in this section's lessons.

☆ RETEACH

Have students complete **Main Idea Activity for English Language Learners and Special-Needs Students 14.1**. Then have students create an annotated time line showing events in the South that changed the southern economy immediately after the American Revolution and how each event changed southern life. **ENGLISH LANGUAGE LEARNERS**,

COOPERATIVE LEARNING

☆ EXTEND

Give students blank maps of the United States. Assign each student a five-year interval from 1790 to 1860. Then have them use the library or other resources to find out what types of crops, such as cotton, rice, indigo, and tobacco, were grown in each state of the cotton belt during those years. Have students create a map key that identifies the cotton belt and provides a symbol for each crop. Then have students label the southern states that existed during that assigned five-year span and identify the quantity of each crop grown during that time. Compare maps to see changes in the quantity of each crop.

BLOCK SCHEDULING

☆ The Cotton Boom

Whitney's gin began a cotton boom. Short-staple cotton grew easily almost everywhere in the South. In theory, a farmer needed only land and labor to raise a cotton crop. By 1860 the southern states east of the Mississippi produced two thirds of all U.S. cotton. Cotton accounted for more than half of all American exports. Farmers eager to profit from the cotton boom headed west to find land. The new Cotton Kingdom included land stretching from South Carolina to Texas. This area became known as the **cotton belt**, the region that grew most of the country's cotton crop.

As the cotton belt expanded, farmers continued trying to improve the crop. In the 1830s, disease wiped out short-staple cotton in many areas. Agricultural scientists like Dr. Rush Nutt worked at breeding stronger types of cotton that were soon grown across the cotton belt.

Cotton had many advantages as a cash crop. Besides being easy to grow, it cost little to market. Unlike food staples, harvested cotton could be stored for a long time. Because cotton was lighter than other staple crops, it also cost less to transport.

Growing and harvesting cotton required many field hands. So did other southern crops, such as Louisiana sugarcane. Rather than pay wages to free workers, planters began to use more slave labor than ever before. Congress made the importation of slaves into the United States illegal in 1808. However, the growing demand for slaves led to an increase in the domestic slave trade. Many slaveholders from states like Virginia and Maryland profited by selling slaves to cotton or sugar planters from states farther south.

✔ **Reading Check: Identifying Cause and Effect** What caused the cotton boom, and how did it affect slavery and the southern economy? The cotton gin made growing cotton very profitable. The demand for slaves increased; cotton growers expanded west.

THE GRANGER COLLECTION, NEW YORK

The cotton boom led to an increased dependence on slave labor in the South.

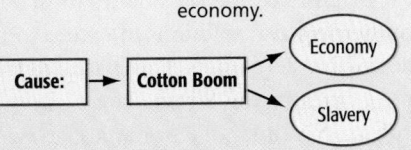

Section 1 Review

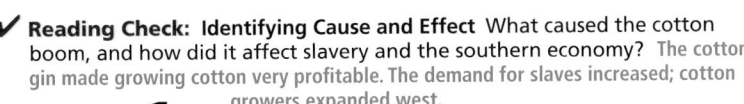

go.hrw.com **Homework Practice Online**

keyword: SA3 HP14

❶ Define and explain:
• cotton gin
• cotton belt

❷ Identify and explain:
• Eli Whitney

❸ Identifying Cause and Effect Copy the graphic organizer below. Use it to show what led to the cotton boom and what effects increased cotton production had on slavery and the southern economy.

Cause: → Cotton Boom → Economy / Slavery

❹ Finding the Main Idea
a. What happened to the Upper South's economy and to slavery in the late 1700s?

b. How did the cotton gin affect the agricultural system in the South?

❺ Writing and Critical Thinking
Analyzing Information Imagine that you are a southern planter in the cotton belt in the early 1800s. Write an advertisement for cotton seeds that explains cotton's advantages as a cash crop.

Consider the following:
• the demand for cotton
• where cotton can be grown
• cotton's storage qualities

Agricultural Changes in the South **427**

Section 2

OBJECTIVES

⭐ Describe how trade affected the southern economy.

⭐ Determine why crops other than cotton were important to the southern economy.

⭐ Identify the kinds of factories that were located in the South.

SECTION 2 RESOURCES

REPRODUCIBLE

▶ Guided Reading Strategy 14.2

▶ Primary Source Reading 14: The Southern Economy

TECHNOLOGY

▶ One-Stop Planner, Lesson 14.2

▶ Holt Researcher: American History CD–ROM

▶ Homework Practice Online

▶ HRW Go site

REINFORCEMENT, REVIEW, AND ASSESSMENT

▶ Section 2 Review, p. 432

▶ Daily Quiz 14.2

▶ Main Idea Activity 14.2

▶ English Audio Summary 14.2

▶ Spanish Audio Summary 14.2

🔊 LET'S GET STARTED!

As students enter the classroom, have students take turns reading aloud Primary Source Reading 14: The Southern Economy. Then ask students to imagine what might happen to a company that makes only one product for which there is high demand? *(Students' responses might include that the company should prosper.)* Then ask students how low product demand would affect that company. *(Students' responses may note that the company would probably suffer.)* Explain to students that although cotton was king in the pre–Civil War South, southern planters still needed to diversify their crops and businesses. Tell students that in Section 2 they will learn more about the southern economy.

Section 2

The Southern Economy

Read to Discover

1. How did trade affect the southern economy?
2. Why were crops other than cotton important to the southern economy?
3. What kinds of factories were located in the South?

WHY IT MATTERS TODAY

Southerners tried to use science to grow better crops. Use **CNNfyi.com** or other **current events** sources to find out how scientists work to improve farming today. Record your findings in your journal.

Define

• factors

• scientific agriculture

Identify

• Jean Étienne Boré

• Joseph R. Anderson

• Tredegar Iron Works

The Story Continues

In an 1858 speech before the U.S. Senate, South Carolina politician James Henry Hammond declared, "Cotton is King!" Southern senators listened closely. Like many of them, Hammond was a planter who believed that the cotton trade had turned the South into a global power. Without cotton, Hammond claimed, the world economy would fail. "No power on earth dares to make war upon it," he declared. "Who can doubt . . . that cotton is supreme?"

Cotton was typically shipped in large 400-pound bales.

⭐ The Cotton Trade

Many southerners shared James Henry Hammond's view about cotton and the cotton trade. Southerner David Christy declared, "*king cotton* is a profound [learned] statesman, and knows what measures will best sustain his throne." Great Britain became the South's most valued foreign trading partner. Southerners also sold tons of cotton to the growing textile industry in the northeastern states. This increased trade led to the growth of major port cities in the South. These cities included Charleston, South Carolina; Savannah, Georgia; and New Orleans, Louisiana.

★ TEACH

Have students read Section 2 and complete Guided Reading Strategy 14.2. Choose one or more of the following activities to explore the section content with students. For further suggestions on block scheduling or team teaching, see the *Block Scheduling Handbook with Team Teaching Strategies*.

LEVEL 1: Describe for students the growth of trade between the South and Great Britain. Give each student a blank outline map of the eastern United States and have them identify the location of each of the following port cities: Charleston, South Carolina; New Orleans, Louisiana; and Savannah, Georgia. Then ask students to speculate about why these cities developed in these locations. Finally, lead a class discussion on how trade affected the southern economy.

ENGLISH LANGUAGE LEARNERS

HOMEWORK Have students write letters to the editor expressing the importance of trade to the southern economy. Encourage students to address the need to diversify their economy with a variety of crops, and the role of factories in the South.

In these port cities, crop brokers called **factors** managed the cotton trade. Farmers sold their cotton to merchants who then made deals with factors. Merchants and factors also arranged loans to farmers who needed to buy supplies. In addition, they often advised farmers on how to invest their profits. Once farmers got their cotton to the port cities, factors arranged transport aboard trading ships.

Getting crops to the ports was a major challenge for farmers. Most southern farmers relied on the region's many rivers to ship their goods. On the Ohio and Mississippi Rivers, flatboats carried cotton and other products to port. With the invention of the steam engine, steamboats became the main method of transportation. Hundreds of steamboats soon traveled up and down the mighty Mississippi. As a result, New Orleans became a major port city.

Shipping cotton by land was very difficult in the South. The few major road projects were limited to the Southeast. Southern states were also slow to build canals. By 1850 the South had only about 14 percent of the country's total canal mileage. In addition, the South had fewer miles of railroad. Thus, the Transportation Revolution had a wider impact in the North than in the South.

✔ **Reading Check: Summarizing** How did farmers transport and sell their cotton? river transportation, particularly steamboats; sold crops with the help of factors in port cities

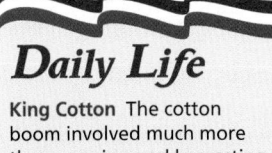

Daily Life

King Cotton The cotton boom involved much more than growing and harvesting cotton. Harvested cotton had to be ginned, pressed into bales, and then shipped to market or to warehouses. Special agents helped do everything from marketing cotton to customers to insuring crops against loss or damage. Factories were built to produce items needed by cotton farmers, such as ropes to bale cotton. As a result, cotton was part of the lives of many people beyond those who produced it. **What were some of the different tasks required to produce and sell cotton?**

★ Economics

Factors. Factors extended their networks by developing partnerships with businesspeople across the country and in Great Britain. In a single crop year, factors Heard and Simpson of Augusta, Georgia, sold cotton in Charleston, New York, Baltimore, and Liverpool, as well as Augusta. The factorage system made every cotton market in the world available to the planter, who could keep up with the price of cotton in various markets by reading newspapers. If planters were unhappy with cotton prices in one market, they could instruct their factors to send their crops elsewhere.

CRITICAL THINKING

How did planters benefit from factor networks?

ANSWER: Students might suggest that the networks made far-off markets available to southern cotton farmers.

DAILY LIFE ANSWER
Students might suggest any of the following: growing, harvesting, ginnning, pressing into bales, shipping, and marketing.

ALL LEVELS: Copy the following graphic organizer onto the chalkboard, omitting the italicized answers (shown as check marks here). Have students complete the chart by placing a check mark in the squares that correspond with the crops grown in each state.

ENGLISH LANGUAGE LEARNERS

Crops	States	VA	NC	SC	GA	AL	MS	LA	AR	TX	TN	KY	MO
cotton		✓	✓	✓	✓	✓	✓	✓	✓	✓	✓	✓	✓
corn			✓								✓		
sugar cane								✓					
wheat					✓								
hemp										✓		✓	✓
flax										✓	✓	✓	

LEVEL 2: Explain to students that factories began to spring up throughout the South during the 1800s. Then have them write journal entries from the perspective of a northerner who expects to see only cotton-related businesses. Remind students to use the text to help them detail other industries that the northerner might have seen in the South. Encourage students to refer to the cities mentioned in this section.

Note: For an additional teaching idea, see the Chapter 14 Open Interviewing activity in the **Creative Teaching Strategies** handbook.

The Cotton Trade

By the mid-1820s the South was known as the Cotton Kingdom. The region was the largest supplier of cotton in the world. During the late 1840s the South exported more than 900 million pounds of cotton per year. To supply its textile mills, Great Britain bought more than half of all cotton grown in the South. Other European countries, particularly France, also bought thousands of bales of cotton.

The success of the cotton trade made the South confident of its important position in the global economy. But cotton-growing countries such as Brazil, China, Egypt, India, and Russia were becoming significant competitors. **How did the cotton gin contribute to the increase in the South's foreign trade?**

Textile mills produced fabric sample books such as this one to show off their patterns and colors.

★ Agricultural Diversity

Some southern farmers supported **scientific agriculture**—the use of scientific methods to improve farming. One goal was to increase crop production. Scientists also wanted to protect the land used to grow cotton. Planting cotton over and over again on the same piece of land wore out the soil. Virginia farmer Edmund Ruffin wrote many articles on better ways to use fertilizers. Others told farmers to regularly change the kinds of crops that they grew on a piece of land. This practice, called crop rotation, would help keep the soil healthy. These scientific practices helped farmers protect their soil.

Some southern leaders worried that farmers relied too much on cotton. Editor James D. B. De Bow and others wanted southerners to try a variety of crops and investments. In 1847 De Bow wrote an article describing the South's problem.

66This is the great evil under which the southwest labors. She is yearly wearing out her soil in the production of one great staple, which has become ruinously [severely] low in price by reason of its great supply: she parts with this staple at prime cost, and purchases almost all her necessary appliances of comfort from abroad, not at prime cost.**99**

—James D. B. De Bow, *Commercial Review of the South and West,* March 1847

Some farmers were already growing other crops. Corn remained the most important southern food crop. By the late 1830s, the top three corn-growing states in the nation were all in the South. Tennessee, the leader, produced some 45 million bushels of corn in 1839. Kentucky and Virginia ran close behind. The South's other common food crops included rice, sweet potatoes, sugarcane, and wheat. High demand for flour in Great Britain increased the value of southern wheat. London bakers particularly liked the type of flour made from Alabama wheat.

The French introduced sugarcane to Louisiana about 1700. However, the crop never became popular until **Jean Étienne Boré** (ay-tyen bohr-AY) invented a new system for processing sugar in 1795. Using Caribbean techniques, Boré perfected a way of processing Louisiana sugarcane into granulated sugar. Louisiana became the center of the sugar industry in the United States. So important was sugar to the state's economy that many planters described Boré as the "savior of Louisiana."

Some southern farmers also produced cash crops other than cotton. Production of tobacco, the South's first major cash crop, was particularly time-consuming. Many farmers prepared their harvested tobacco for market by curing, or drying, it in small barns. In 1839 a slave discovered a way to improve the drying process. By using heat from burning

LEVEL 3: Explain to students the importance of growing a variety of crops. Have each student write a short story describing a southern community that becomes dependent on cotton production. Instruct students to depict the following: the importance of cotton to the community, a natural disaster that threatens the cotton industry, and the community's reaction to the disaster. *(Students' stories should include the introduction of new crops or industries after the cotton industry was threatened.)* Then have students exchange and read each other's stories. Finally, lead a class discussion on the importance of diversifying an economy.

COOPERATIVE LEARNING

★ CLOSE

Have students create advertisements for the products of local southern farmers that are to be sold at an upcoming farmers' market. Encourage students to choose a city or state as a location for the farmers' market. Have students refer to the section for information on crops that were produced in their chosen area.

charcoal, workers could cure tobacco more quickly. This discovery boosted tobacco farming, but tobacco still took much longer to process than most crops.

Partly as a result of the cotton boom, hemp and flax became major cash crops. Their fibers were used to make rope and sackcloth. Farmers across the cotton belt used rope produced in Kentucky, Missouri, and Tennessee to bundle cotton into bales.

✔ **Reading Check: Comparing** How did southerners use scientific agriculture and new technology to improve crop production in the South?
improved fertilizer use and crop rotation; improved sugar and tobacco processing

★ Southern Factories

Southern industries sprang up to serve the needs of farmers. The rope industry was one example. Some, such as the lumber industry, benefited from new technology. In 1803 the nation's first steam-powered sawmill was built in Donaldsonville, Louisiana. Factories were not as common in the South as they were in the Northeast, however. Many of the first factories in the South were built to process crops.

Turning sugarcane into sugar, for example, required many machines. Writer Mark Twain once described the interior of a southern sugar-processing factory. "[It was] a wilderness of tubs and tanks and vats and filters, pumps, pipes, and machinery." Some southerners, such as Hinton Rowan Helper, believed that the South needed even more industries.

> **History Makers Speak**
> ❝We should . . . keep pace with the progress of the age. We must expand our energies, and acquire habits of enterprise and industry; we should arouse ourselves from the couch of lassitude [laziness], and inure [set] our minds to thought and our bodies to action.❞
> —Hinton Rowan Helper, *The Impending Crisis of the South: How to Meet It*

Research on the R⊙M

Free Find:
Agriculture and Slavery
After reading about agriculture and slavery on the **Holt Researcher CD–ROM,** imagine that you are a farmer trying to get financial backing to produce a crop. Write a brief proposal explaining the crop you have chosen and why you think it will sell.

Analyzing Primary Sources
Identifying Points of View
What did Helper think the South's economy needed?
more enterprise and industry

⋆ REVIEW AND ASSESS

Have students complete the **Section 2 Review** on p. 432. Then have them complete **Daily Quiz 14.2**. As **Alternative Assessment**, you may want to use the crops graphic organizer or the short story exercises in this section's lessons.

⋆ RETEACH

Have students complete **Main Idea Activity for English Language Learners and Special-Needs Students 14.2**. Then have students write the section's headings and subheadings on a sheet of paper, leaving a space between each. Ask students to list the main ideas of each heading and subheading in the appropriate space. **ENGLISH LANGUAGE LEARNERS**

⋆ EXTEND

Organize the class into three groups. Assign each group one of the section's Reading Check questions. Have each group create a public service announcement that summarizes information about the assigned question. Encourage students to create visual aids to highlight important points. Have each group present its public service announcement to the class.
COOPERATIVE LEARNING , BLOCK SCHEDULING

Section 2 Review
ANSWERS

❶ Define
• factors, p. 429
• scientific agriculture, p. 430

❷ Identify
• Jean Étienne Boré, p. 430
• Joseph R. Anderson, p. 432
• Tredegar Iron Works, p. 432

❸ Diversify: dependence on agricultural production and low income during poor crop years; soil depletion, poor crop quality, falling prices, incomes; supply exceeds demand, prices and incomes fall; need to purchase manufactured goods at higher prices from outside suppliers; expand industry: modernize southern economy; less reliance on cotton

❹ a. the economy grew
b. they were built to produce staple crops such as sugar some factories also produced iron

❺ Students' letters will vary, but they should include the wealth created by cash crops like cotton, tobacco, hemp and flax. Arguments for crops other than cotton should mention that cotton depletes the soil.

Interpreting the Visual Record

Working at the mill *This textile mill in Columbus, Georgia, was one of the relatively few factories in the South during the early 1800s.* **Does this mill appear to be located in the countryside or in a city?**

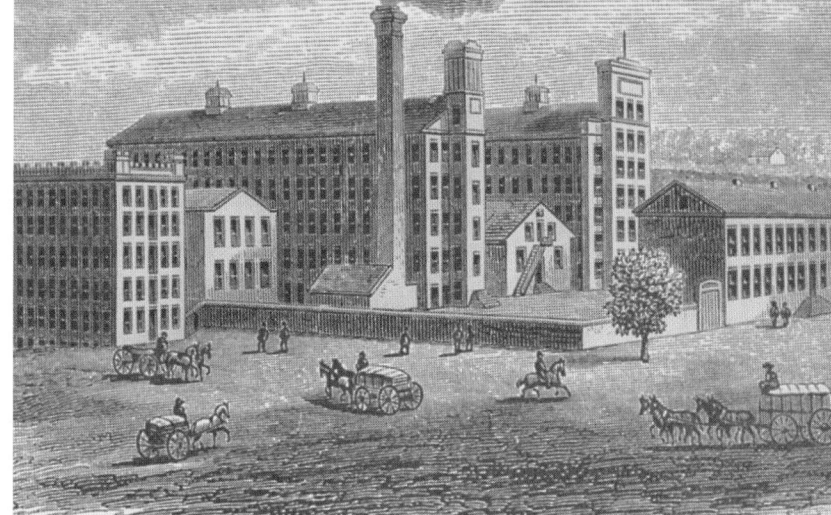

Joseph R. Anderson, a graduate of the military academy at West Point, followed Helper's advice. In 1848, he became the owner of the **Tredegar Iron Works** in Richmond. His company had the only large southern factory that made iron products. By 1860 Anderson had turned his factory into one of the most productive iron works in the nation. Tredegar produced boilers, bridge materials, cannons, locomotives, steam engines, and other products.

The South's industrial growth lagged behind that of the North. Cash crops, like tobacco and cotton, seemed to promise great wealth. As a result, most farmers and planters invested in more land and slaves in order to grow more cotton. They poured their profits into the developing plantation system, not into southern industry.

✔ **Reading Check: Summarizing** What kinds of factories were most common in the South, and why did the South build fewer factories than the North? *factories to process staple crops; because southern investors preferred agriculture*

Section 2 Review

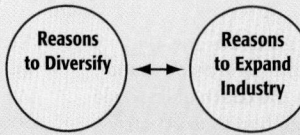
Homework Practice Online
keyword: SA3 HP14

❶ Define and explain:
• factors
• scientific agriculture

❷ Identify and explain:
• Jean Étienne Boré
• Joseph R. Anderson
• Tredegar Iron Works

❸ Summarizing Copy the graphic organizer below. Use it to show the reasons that James D. B. De Bow and others advised southerners to grow a variety of crops and why Helper and others advised southerners to expand industry.

Reasons to Diversify ↔ Reasons to Expand Industry

❹ Finding the Main Idea
a. How did international trade affect the South's economy?

b. What were typical factories in the South designed to manufacture?

❺ Writing and Critical Thinking
Supporting a Point of View Imagine that you are a southern farmer. Write a letter to your relatives explaining what crops you have decided to grow. Be sure to explain your choices.

Consider the following:
• the markets for southern crops
• the most common southern crops
• the effect of crops on the soil

Section 3

OBJECTIVES

- ⭐ Describe what life was like for southern planters and owners of small farms.
- ⭐ Analyze what the urban South was like.
- ⭐ Examine the challenges free African Americans faced in the South.

📀 LET'S GET STARTED!

Have each student write a list describing how farmers and city residents each contributed to southern culture. Have volunteers share their lists with the class. *(Students' lists will vary.)* Write students' responses on the chalkboard. Tell students that in Section 3 they will learn what life was like for planters, small farmers, slaves, and southern urban dwellers prior to the Civil War.

Section 3

Southern Society

Read to Discover

1. What was life like for southern planters and owners of small farms?
2. What was the urban South like?
3. What challenges did free African Americans face in the South?

WHY IT MATTERS TODAY

The lifestyles of rural and urban southerners varied in important ways. Use **CNNfyi.com** or other **current events** sources to learn about issues affecting the lives of city residents and rural Americans in one area of the United States today. Record your findings in your journal.

Define
- yeomen

Identify
- Mark Twain

SECTION 3 RESOURCES

REPRODUCIBLE
- ▶ Guided Reading Strategy 14.3
- ▶ Biography Reading 14: Fanny Kemble

TECHNOLOGY
- ▶ One-Stop Planner, Lesson 14.3
- ▶ Holt Researcher: American History CD–ROM
- ▶ American History Interactive Maps CD–ROM: The Cotton Plantation
- ▶ Homework Practice Online

REINFORCEMENT, REVIEW, AND ASSESSMENT
- ▶ Section 3 Review, p. 437
- ▶ Daily Quiz 14.3
- ▶ Main Idea Activity 14.3
- ▶ English Audio Summary 14.3
- ▶ Spanish Audio Summary 14.3

The Story Continues

Many writers romanticized southern life. They wrote about what they saw as its unique characteristics. In 1832 Baltimore writer John Pendleton Kennedy, one of the first novelists to write about plantations, wrote *Swallow Barn*. The story glorifies the lives of planter families. In one scene, the narrator described his ideal of southern life. It was "a thousand acres of good land, an old manor-house, . . . a hundred [slaves], a large library, a host of friends, . . . and . . . a house full of pretty, intelligent, and docile [obedient] children." A booming market in plantation novels followed the publication of Kennedy's book. In reality, however, plantation life was very different from the scenes in Kennedy's writing.

A wealthy southern family might own finely crafted furniture such as this chair.

THE GRANGER COLLECTION, NEW YORK

⭐ The Planters

Popular fiction often made it seem that all white southerners had many slaves and lived on large plantations. This was hardly the case. In the first half of the 1800s, about one third of white southern families had slaves. Fewer families had plantations. Despite their small numbers, these planters had a powerful influence over the South. Many served as

✪ TEACH

Have students read Section 3 and complete Guided Reading Strategy 14.3. Choose one or more of the following activities to explore the section content with students. For further suggestions on block scheduling or team teaching, see the *Block Scheduling Handbook with Team Teaching Strategies.*

 LEVEL 1: Lead a class discussion about what life was like for southern planters and owners of small farms. Then assign each student one of the occupations discussed in this section. Have students write a classified ad seeking individuals to fill that position. Students should describe characteristics that candidates for that position need to possess. For example, if someone is seeking yeoman farmers, qualified candidates should be willing to put in long hours at a variety of tasks for little profit.
ENGLISH LANGUAGE LEARNERS

Note: To help students make meaningful connections between events in American history and those in their own hometown, use the Chapter 14 **Hands-On History** activity, Your State's Agriculture.

★★★★★★★★★★★★
That's Interesting!
★★★★★★★★★★★★

Authorities in most states were reluctant to interfere with the head of the household's authority. This was particularly true in some southern states such as South Carolina, where the husband was legally considered the head of the household and therefore dominant in all matters. In fact, one South Carolina judge declared that women had no legal rights of their own.

Technology Resources
 American History
Interactive Maps CD–ROM:
The Cotton Plantation

The children of planters often received a privileged upbringing.

political leaders. As the wealthiest members of southern society, planters also greatly influenced the economy. Some showed off their wealth by living in beautiful mansions. Many others chose to live more simply. A visitor described wealthy planter Alexander Stephens's estate as "an old wooden house" surrounded by weeds. Some planters saved all their money to buy more land and slaves.

Male planters were primarily concerned with raising crops and supervising slave laborers. They left the running of the plantation household to their wives. The planter's wife oversaw the raising of their children and supervised the work of all slaves within the household. Slave women typically cooked, cleaned, and helped care for the planter's children. Wives also took on the important social duties of the family. For example, many southern leaders discussed political issues at the dances and dinners hosted by their wives.

Planters often arranged their children's marriages based on business interests. Lucy Breckinridge, the daughter of a wealthy Virginia planter, was married by arrangement in 1865. Three years earlier, she had described in her journal how she dreaded the very thought of marriage. "A woman's life after she is married, unless there is an immense amount of love, is nothing but suffering and hard work." How Breckinridge's life in her own arranged marriage would have turned out cannot be known. She died of typhoid fever just months after her wedding.

✔ **Reading Check: Finding the Main Idea** How did planters maintain their influence in southern society? political leadership, wealth, social prestige, arranged marriages

✪ Southern Society and Culture

Most southern white women married **yeomen**, or owners of small farms. Yeomen made up the majority of southern farmers. Typically they held few slaves or none at all. By 1860 about 80 percent of all southern farmers owned their own land. The typical yeoman farm averaged about 100 acres. Yeomen took great pride in their work. In 1849 a young Georgia man wrote that "I desire above all things to be a 'Farmer.' It is the most honest, upright, and sure way of securing all the comforts of life." In fact, most yeomen families had few material comforts. They worked long days at many tasks. "My life is one of toil," wrote yeoman Ferdinand Steel in 1839, "but blessed be God that it is as well with me as it is." Many yeomen farmers hoped one day to become planters themselves.

Some yeomen earned enough money to buy a few slaves. Yet, unlike the planters, yeomen generally worked side by side with slaves. Many planters believed they should maintain their control over slaves by treating them harshly.

Planters and yeomen alike often looked down on the poorest of white southerners. These landless people made up less than 10 percent

Corn was the most common food crop grown in the South, and many yeomen produced it.

ALL LEVELS: Copy the following graphic organizer onto the chalkboard, omitting the italicized answers. Have students complete the organizer to analyze what the urban South was like. **ENGLISH LANGUAGE LEARNERS**

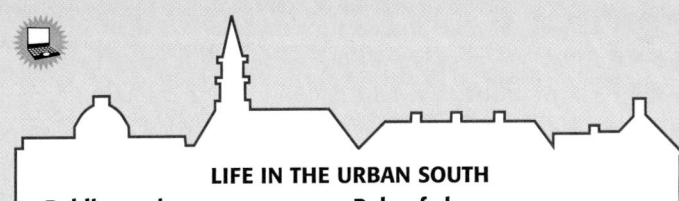

LIFE IN THE URBAN SOUTH

Public services
• *water systems*
• *well-maintained streets*
• *public education*

Role of slavery
• *manual labor*
• *domestic servants*
• *other skills*

The Southern Population, 1860

Total Population

- Nonslaveholding whites
- Slaves
- Slaveholding whites
- Free African Americans
- Other

1%
2%
16%
47%
34%

Slaveholding Households

- Fewer than 10 slaves
- 10–49 slaves
- 50–99 slaves
- 100 or more slaves

1%
2%
25%
72%

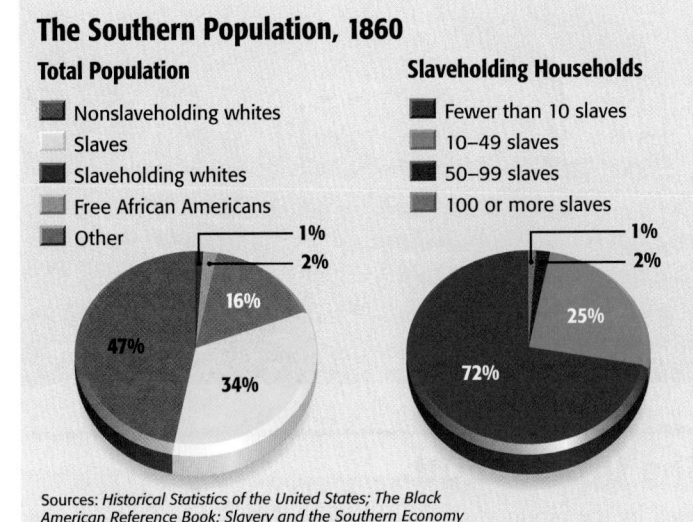

Sources: *Historical Statistics of the United States; The Black American Reference Book; Slavery and the Southern Economy*

Interpreting Graphs Despite the importance of slavery to the South's agricultural economy, most southerners held no slaves.

Skills Assessment

1. Which group made up the largest percentage of the southern population?
2. What percent of slaveholding households had 100 or more slaves?

of the white southern population. Most of them lived on lands that were not suited to growing cash crops. They survived by hunting, fishing, raising a few animals, tending small gardens, and doing odd jobs for money.

White southerners did share a common culture in many ways. For example, religion was central to southern social life. Farm families were often isolated from one another. They might see their neighbors only at church events, such as revivals or socials. Although they were not allowed to become ministers, rural women often played volunteer roles in their churches.

Other wealthy white southerners used religion to justify their position in society and the institution of slavery. They argued that God created some people, like themselves, to rule over African Americans. This belief set them against those northern Christians who believed that God opposed slavery.

Some southern writers tried to increase national awareness of southern culture. Charleston, South Carolina, attracted many writers who gathered to discuss their poems, short stories, and essays. Most southern writers, such as John Pendleton Kennedy, greatly romanticized southern culture—particularly life on plantations. Some later writers provided a more even-handed look at southern society during the mid-1800s. Among these writers was Samuel Clemens, better known by his pen name, **Mark Twain**. He based this pen name on river slang for shallow water only two fathoms deep. Several of Twain's most popular works, such as *The Adventures of Huckleberry Finn* and *The Adventures of Tom Sawyer*, are set in the South.

✔ **Reading Check: Comparing and Contrasting** How were planters, yeomen, and poor whites similar to and different from each other?
Planters were leaders, large landholders, and slaveholders. Yeomen owned land, but not all held slaves. Poor whites had neither land or slaves.

Caroline Howard Gilman began a successful career as a southern writer in the 1830s.

⭐ Culture

Southern Women.
Women's roles were greatly limited during the 1800s, particularly in the South. Southern women had little exposure to the social or political realm. Henry Hughes of Mississippi argued that "a baby is better fitting a woman than an oration. She is intended for home duties, labors and responsibilities. Her physical characteristics prove this. . . . [She has] not physical power to be anything other than home folk."

CRITICAL THINKING
Why might some women be resistant to this kind of thinking?

ANSWER: Students might suggest that it indicates women are somehow inferior and thus should not have the same rights as men.

GRAPH ANSWERS
1. nonslaveholding whites
2. 1 percent

LEVEL 3: Ask students to imagine that they are free African Americans living in the South prior to 1860. Have students use information from the section to create an oral history describing how they gained their freedom, the economic opportunities that were available to them, and the challenges that they faced in their communities. Encourage volunteers to present their histories to the class.

HOMEWORK Ask students to imagine that they are southern planters who just moved to the city. Have them write a journal entry describing how life in the city is different from the life of a small planter.

★ CLOSE

Tell students that southern cities were similar to northern cities in many ways. Have students write newspaper articles describing life in a southern city. Ask them to discuss the following topics in their articles: the services provided by city government, the image of their cities that southern business leaders wanted to portray, and the business opportunities and challenges for free African Americans. Ask volunteers to present their articles to the class. Finally, lead a discussion on southern urban life prior to the Civil War.

★ Daily Life

Free African Americans.
Free African Americans were more likely to live in southern cities than in rural areas. By 1860, free African Americans outnumbered slaves 10 to 1 in Baltimore and 5 to 1 in Washington. On the eve of the Civil War, New Orleans was home to 10,000 free African Americans. These African Americans often faced discrimination in the cities, in spite of the fact that they were free. An example of such discrimination was an 1832 Baltimore law that stated that free African Americans were subject to the same treatment and punishment as slaves.

ACTIVITY: Have students imagine that they are recently freed slaves moving to a major southern city. Ask them to write a paragraph describing their hopes and fears about what they will find when they arrive.

Visual Record Answer

Students might suggest cotton bales.

Interpreting the Visual Record

Busy port *Many of the larger southern cities, such as Charleston, South Carolina, and New Orleans, Louisiana, were also busy seaports.* **What goods can you see being prepared for shipment on the dock?**

Research on the R★M

Free Find:
South Carolina
After looking at the population figures for South Carolina on the **Holt Researcher CD–ROM,** imagine that you are a member of the Census Bureau. Create a line graph showing the changes in the population of South Carolina from 1800 to 1850.

★ The Urban South

Influenced by the products of the plantations, the urban economy was also an important part of the South. But cities had many different businesses, people, and social organizations. City residents often took on many key roles in their communities. James A. Cowardin of Richmond, Virginia, was a typical urban business leader who also edited a small newspaper and served in the state legislature.

In many ways, southern cities were like those in the North. City governments built public water systems and provided well-maintained streets. Public education was available in some places. Sometimes wealthy residents gave large sums of money to charities—from orphanages to public libraries. Southern urban leaders wanted their cities to appear as modern as possible. They hoped to impress foreign visitors who came to the South to do business.

As on plantations, slaves did much of the work in southern cities. Slaves worked as domestic servants, in mills, in shipyards, and at skilled jobs. Compared with rural white southerners, urban whites were more likely to hold slaves. Many business leaders held slaves or hired them from nearby plantations.

✔ **Reading Check: Finding the Main Idea** What were public services and slavery like in southern cities? Cities supplied water systems, streets, and in some places education; slaves did much of the manual labor, though some slaves were skilled and some worked as house servants.

★ Free African Americans

Some free African Americans also found work in southern cities. In 1860 more than half of all free African Americans were living in the South. Some were the descendants of slaves who had been freed after the American Revolution. Still others had won their freedom, often by running away.

Free African Americans who lived in southern cities worked in a variety of jobs, mostly as skilled artisans. A small number became fairly successful in their businesses. Free African Americans in rural areas

✪ REVIEW AND ASSESS

Have Students complete the **Section 3 Review** on p. 437. Then have them complete **Daily Quiz 14.3**. As **Alternative Assessment**, you may want to use the newspaper articles or the occupations exercises from this section's lessons.

✪ RETEACH

Have students complete **Main Idea Activity for English Language Learners and Special-Needs Students 14.3**. Then have them create annotated mobiles depicting society before the Civil War. Have students portray the various occupations, show the inequality among the races, and portray a southern urban community. Ask students to write an annotation on the back of each part of the mobile that explains their mobiles to the class. **ENGLISH LANGUAGE LEARNERS**

✪ EXTEND

Have students use the library or other resources to find information about the percentage of southern society that nonslaveholding whites, slaves, slaveholding whites, and free African Americans represented. Assign students a 10-year interval from 1790 to 1850 to research. Have students create a pie chart with a corresponding key to summarize the information they find. Ask students to identify significant changes, over time in the proportion of each group represented. **BLOCK SCHEDULING**

often hired out their services to plantations. A few of them were quite financially successful. Churches often served as the center of social life for free southern African Americans. In the early 1800s free and enslaved African Americans in Charleston, South Carolina, started a rare independent-church movement.

Free African Americans faced constant discrimination. White southerners feared that free African Americans would try to encourage slave rebellions. Many cities and states passed laws limiting the rights of free African Americans. Most could not vote, travel freely, or hold certain types of jobs. In some places, laws forced them to have a white person represent them in their business dealings.

An 1806 Virginia law banned former slaves from living in the state without special permission. Jemima Hunt, a free African American woman, was able to buy the freedom of Stephen, her husband. She asked the Virginia legislature to grant him permission to stay in the state.

 History Makers Speak ❝Your petitioner [Hunt] farther states that she has a numerous family of Children by the said Stephen, who are dependent upon the daily labor of herself & husband for a support, & without the assistance of her husband Stephen they must suffer.❞

—Jemima Hunt, quoted in *Enduring Voices, Volume I: To 1877*, edited by James J. Lorence

Many white southerners felt that free African Americans could not take care of themselves. "The status of slavery is the only one for which the African is adapted," wrote one white Mississippian. But free African Americans proved that they could survive outside the slave system. As a result, many white southerners viewed them as a threat to the institution of slavery.

✔ **Reading Check: Summarizing** What economic, legal, and social challenges did free African Americans face in southern society? discrimination and limited access to voting, travel, employment, and business activities

Some African Americans had to wear badges such as this one to prove that they were free.

Analyzing Primary Sources
Identifying Points of View
Why was it important for Jemima Hunt to have her husband with her? She needed him to help her support their children.

Section **3** Review

 **go.hrw.com Homework Practice Online**
keyword: SA3 HP14

❶ **Define** and explain:
• yeomen

❷ **Identify** and explain:
• Mark Twain

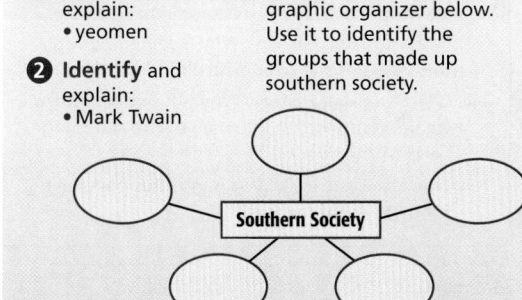
Southern Society

❸ **Categorizing** Copy the graphic organizer below. Use it to identify the groups that made up southern society.

❹ **Finding the Main Idea**
a. How were the lives of planters different from and similar to the lives of yeomen?
b. What was life like in southern cities?

❺ **Writing and Critical Thinking**
Analyzing Information Imagine that you are a novelist living in the South. Write a short story about a free African American living in the South in the early 1800s. Make sure your characters also include at least one planter, one yeoman, and one slave.
Consider the following:
• the views of most white southerners about slavery
• characteristics of life in rural and urban areas
• relations between whites and free African Americans

CONNECTING TO *Literature*

Life on the Mississippi
Mark Twain

Samuel Langhorne Clemens, better known as Mark Twain, was born in 1835 in Missouri. One of America's most humorous writers, Twain enriched his works by using local color—writing that expresses the culture and language of a particular region. In the following passage from Twain's book Life on the Mississippi, *he recalls a lesson from Mr. Bixby, a steamboat pilot who taught him to pilot a riverboat on the Mississippi River.*

Mark Twain wrote several books about life on and around the Mississippi River.

Nothing ever had the same shape when I was coming downstream as it had **borne**[1] when I went up. I mentioned these little difficulties to Mr. Bixby. . . . It was plain that I had got to learn the shape of the river in all the different ways that could be thought of—upside down, wrong end first, inside out, **fore-and-aft**,[2] and **"thort-ships"**[3]—and then know what to do on gray nights when it hadn't any shape at all. So I set about it. In the course of time I began to get the best of this knotty lesson, and my **self-complacency**[4] moved to the front once more. Mr. Bixby was all fixed, and ready to start it to the rear again. He opened on me after this fashion—

"How much water did we have in the idle crossing at Hole-in-the-Wall, trip before last?"

I considered this an outrage. I said—

"Every trip, down and up, the **leadsmen**[5] are singing through that tangled place for three quarters of an hour on a stretch. How do you reckon I can remember such a mess as that?"

"My boy, you've got to remember it. You've got to remember the exact spot and the exact **marks**[6] the boat lay in when we had the **shoalest**[7] water, in every one of the five hundred shoal places between St. Louis and New Orleans; and you mustn't get the shoal soundings and marks of one trip mixed up with the shoal soundings and marks of another, either, for they're not often twice alike. You must keep them separate."

When I came to myself again, I said—

"When I get so that I can do that, I'll be able to raise the dead, and then I won't have to pilot a steamboat to make a living. I want to retire from this business. I want a slush-bucket and a brush; I'm only fit for a **roustabout**.[8] I haven't got brains enough to be a pilot; and if I had I wouldn't have strength enough to carry them around, unless I went on crutches."

"Now drop that! When I say I'll **learn**[9] a man the river, I mean it. And you can depend on it, I'll learn him or kill him."

Understanding What You Read

1. **Literature and History** Why is remembering the shape of the river difficult?

2. **Literature and History** Why is it important for steamboat pilots to know all of the changing parts of the river?

3. **Literature and You** Why might this passage be funny to some readers?

---

[1]**borne:** held
[2]**fore-and-aft:** front and back
[3]**"thort-ships":** shore to shore
[4]**self-complacency:** lack of concern

[5]**leadsmen:** workers who measure the water's depth
[6]**marks:** measurements of water depth

[7]**shoalest:** most shallow
[8]**roustabout:** laborer on a boat
[9]**learn:** teach

Section 4

OBJECTIVES

- ★ Explain what work and daily life were like for most slaves.
- ★ Describe how slaves used family, religion, and other aspects of their culture to help them cope with the slave system.
- ★ Identify ways that enslaved African Americans challenged the slave system.

🔊 LET'S GET STARTED!

Write the following instruction and question on the chalkboard: *Read the opening paragraph of Section 4 on page 439. What does it say about the life of slaves?* As students enter the classroom have them follow the instruction and respond to the question. *(Students' responses may vary, but students should point out that slaves did not often have control over many aspects of their lives. Students should also point out that for many slaves, the only way to obtain their freedom was to run away.)* Tell students that in Section 4 they will learn more about the lives of slaves.

Section 4

The Slave System

Read to Discover

1. What were work and daily life like for most slaves?
2. How did slaves' family, religion, and other aspects of their culture help them cope with the slave system?
3. How did enslaved African Americans challenge the slave system?

WHY IT MATTERS TODAY

Spirituals were one aspect of slave culture. Use **CNNfyi.com** or other **current events** sources to find out how art, literature, or music serves as part of a group's culture today. Record your findings in your journal.

Define

- folktales
- spirituals

Identify

- Nat Turner
- Nat Turner's Rebellion

SECTION 4 RESOURCES

REPRODUCIBLE

- ▶ Guided Reading Strategy 14.4
- ▶ American History Political Cartoon 7: Slavery in America and England
- ▶ Literature Reading 14: Incidents in the Life of a Slave Girl
- ▶ Graphic Organizer 14: Living Conditions for Slaves

TECHNOLOGY

- ▶ One-Stop Planner, Lesson 14.4
- ▶ Exploring America's Past Video Segment: Slavery and the South; Teacher's Guide, pp. 22–23
- ▶ American Music Selection 11: "Wayfaring Stranger"
- ▶ CNN Presents America: Beginnings to 1914 Segment: A Slave Memorial
- ▶ Homework Practice Online

REINFORCEMENT, REVIEW, AND ASSESSMENT

- ▶ Section 4 Review, p. 443
- ▶ Daily Quiz 14.4
- ▶ Main Idea Activity 14.4
- ▶ English Audio Summary 14.4
- ▶ Spanish Audio Summary 14.4

The Story Continues

Harriet Jacobs was born into slavery in 1813. Jacobs worked for many years in a doctor's household. Determined that her children would not live as slaves, Jacobs ran away. "I had . . . a mother's love for my children," she explained. "I resolved that out of the darkness . . . a brighter dawn should rise for them." Jacobs knew that it would be hard to survive as a runaway slave, but she was hopeful. "My master had power and law on his side . . . ," Jacob noted. "I had a determined will."

This slave auction poster identifies and describes the people that the company planned to sell.

★ Slaves and Work

Although treatment of enslaved African Americans varied, most slaveholders tried to get as much work as they could out of slaves. Enslaved people living on small farms usually did a wide variety of jobs. On large plantations most slaves were assigned to specific tasks. The majority of slaves worked in the fields. Drivers, who were sometimes slaves themselves, made sure that slaves followed orders. Drivers also carried out punishments.

★ TEACH

Have students read Section 4 and complete Guided Reading Strategy 14.4. Choose one or more of the following activities to explore the section content with students. For further suggestions on block scheduling or team teaching, see the *Block Scheduling Handbook with Team Teaching Strategies.*

 LEVEL 1: Explain to students that slaves often worshiped in secret. Have them think about what an African American parent might have said to his or her children about how to deal with being a slave. Instruct students to write a few sentences offering advice from a parent to a child encouraging the child to rely on his or her community, culture, and religion to cope with the slave system. Encourage students to use material from the section as examples in their advice. Allow time for volunteers to present their advice to the class. Then lead a class discussion on the coping mechanisms that slaves used. **ENGLISH LANGUAGE LEARNERS**

HOMEWORK Assign students one of the Reading Check questions from the section. Have students write poems or songs that address that question.

Interdisciplinary Connection

▶Math◀

Slaves' Daily Lives. Some supporters of slavery attempted to justify the institution by arguing that the "wages" that slaves earned in food and shelter were roughly equivalent to the wages that factory workers earned in the North. One slave supporter wrote that "a slave consumes in meat two hundred pounds of bacon or pork, costing . . . $8; thirteen bushels of Indian corn, costing $2; this makes up his food. Now for salt and medicines add $1, and it runs thus; a year's food is $11. Their clothing . . . $7.50." These figures were probably exaggerated by slave owners to help justify their livelihood.

ACTIVITY: Based on the slavery supporters' figures, have students determine the daily rate of pay a slave earned for his "wages," given a workweek of six days *(six cents a day).*

Visual Record Answer

Students might suggest that it helps preserve the reverence of the gathering.

Interpreting the Visual Record

Funeral *Slaves often tried to practice their religious beliefs and ceremonies out of sight of slaveholders. Here a group of slaves conducts a funeral at night in the woods.* **Why do you think slaves might have wanted privacy for a ceremony like this one?**

DETAIL OF JOHN ANTROBUS, PLANTATION BURIAL, (1860) OIL ON CANVAS, THE HISTORICAL NEW ORLEANS COLLECTION

Slaveholders used shackles like this metal collar and these leg irons to punish slaves.

Most plantation owners used the gang labor system. In this system all hands worked on the same task at the same time. They usually worked from sunup to sundown. Former slave Harry McMillan had worked on a plantation in South Carolina. He recalled that the field hands usually did not even get a break to eat lunch. "You had to get your victuals [food] standing at your hoe," he remembered.

Men, women, and even children older than about 10 usually did the same work. Hardly anything, even sickness and poor weather, stopped the work. "The times I hated most was picking cotton when the frost was on the bolls [seed pods]," recalled former Louisiana slave Mary Reynolds. "My hands git sore and crack open and bleed."

Some slaves worked as butlers, cooks, or nurses in the planter's home. These slaves often had better food and clothing than field hands. But they often worked longer hours. They had to serve the planter's family 24 hours a day. House servants could also be sent to work in the fields. On larger plantations, some slaves worked at skilled jobs such as blacksmithing or carpentry. Sometimes planters let these slaves hire out their services to other people. In this way, some skilled slaves earned enough money to buy their freedom. For example, William Ellison earned his freedom by working for wages as a cotton gin maker. For years he worked late at night and on Sundays. He bought his freedom with the money he earned. Eventually, he was also able to buy the freedom of his wife and daughter.

✔ **Reading Check: Categorizing** What were some of the different types of work that slaves did on plantations? Most slaves did field work. Some worked as cooks, nurses, or butlers around the planter's home. On larger plantations, some slaves worked in skilled jobs such as blacksmithing or carpentry.

★ Life under Slavery

Generally, slaveholders tended to view slaves as property, not as people. Some slaves were bought, worked, and sold to make a profit. Slave traders even kidnapped free African Americans and then sold them into slavery. For example, Solomon Northup was kidnapped in Washington. He spent 12 years as a slave, "shut out from the sweet light of liberty." He finally proved his identity and gained his release.

working slower

CHALLENGING THE SLAVERY SYSTEM

violent revolts

running away

Most slaves received very poor clothing and shelter. They lived in small cabins with dirt floors, leaky roofs, and few furnishings. Field hands like Delia Garlic recalled that her slave clothing "was made out of the cheapest cloth that could be bought." Some slaves tried to brighten up their clothes by using old scraps of cloth to sew designs on the fabric. In this way, they individualized the clothing given to them by the planters. Likewise, many slaves did what they could to improve their food rations. Some planters allowed slaves to keep their own vegetable gardens, and chickens for eggs. If they had time, slaves might catch fish or pick berries.

Some planters offered more food or better living conditions to encourage slaves' obedience. However, many slaveholders used punishment instead. Some would punish one slave in front of others as a warning to them all. Harry McMillan recalled some of the punishments he witnessed.

 History Makers Speak "The punishments were whipping, putting you in the stocks [wooden frames to lock people in] and making you wear irons and a chain at work. Then they had a collar to put round your neck with two horns, like cows' horns, so that you could not lie down. . . . This also kept you from running away for the horns would catch in the bushes. Sometimes they dug a hole like a well with a door on top. This they called a dungeon keeping you in it two or three weeks or a month, or sometimes till you died in there."

—Harry McMillan, quoted in *Major Problems in the History of the American South, Volume I,* edited by Paul D. Escott and David R. Goldfield

To further control slaves' actions, many states had strict slave codes that limited what slaves could do. Some laws prohibited slaves from traveling far from their homes. Teaching slaves to read or write was usually illegal. Slaves thus did not have freedom of movement and the benefits of simple education.

✔ **Reading Check: Analyzing Information** How did slaveholders try to keep slaves under control? Slaveholders used incentives or more often punishment to encourage slaves to be more obedient.

Analyzing Primary Sources

Making Generalizations and Predictions What effect do you think the treatment Harry McMillan describes would have on slave workers? Answers may vary. Students may suggest that fear would cause slaves to be more obedient, or that punishments would make slaves more resentful and angry.

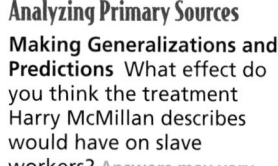

Interpreting the Visual Record

Auction *Families of enslaved African Americans were often broken up at auctions.* **Why might an auction like this one frighten an enslaved person?**

 Visual Record Answer

Students might suggest that the families of those being auctioned are being torn apart, and that to other slaves in attendance are therefore afraid the same thing will happen to them.

 **Technology Resources**

Exploring America's Past Video Segment: Slavery and the South; Teacher's Guide, pp. 22–23

Search 17511, Play to 22923 Videodisc Red Side B See *Teacher's Guide* for Spanish barcode.

441

Steve Munzel of Palo Alto, California, suggested the following activity:

 ALL LEVELS: Have students review material from this section and from Chapter 13 to compare and contrast a day in the life of a southern field slave and a Lowell girl. Allow students to convey the information in any appropriate fashion that they choose. (*Students' comparisons will vary, but some students may choose written reports, while others might perform skits or submit drawings.*) **ENGLISH LANGUAGE LEARNERS**

 LEVEL 3: Explain to students that daily life was often very difficult for slaves and who usually had little hope of gaining their freedom. Ask students to write a dialogue between two slaves, arguing for an end to slavery. Ask students to mention what working and living conditions were like for slaves.

★ CLOSE

Have each student design a quilt square, on paper or with fabric, that illustrates an aspect of the slaves' community or religion, or a method of challenging slavery. Attach the squares to create a quilt and display it in the classroom.

★ Biography

Nat Turner. Some historians have suggested that Nat Turner knew he would never completely escape his pursuers after the revolt. By remaining in the area of the rebellion, Turner would be captured and tried legally, rather than being lynched. This would ensure that he could deliver a final statement. Turner, with lawyer T.R. Gray, wrote his "Confessions" from his jail cell.

CRITICAL THINKING

Why did Nat Turner rebel?

ANSWER: Students might suggest that he believed that God had called upon him to overthrow slavery.

Technology Resources

 American Music
Selection 11:
"Wayfaring Stranger"

Technology Resources

 CNN Presents America:
Beginnings to 1914
Segment: A Slave Memorial

BIOGRAPHY ANSWER

a solar eclipse

Research on the **R⊙M**

Free Find:
Nat Turner's Confession
After reading Nat Turner's Confession on the **Holt Researcher CD-ROM**, imagine that you are a journalist from the North. Write a brief article summarizing Nat Turner's views.

BIOGRAPHY

Nat Turner

(1800–1831)

Nat Turner grew up believing he was called by God to do something important. As a child on a Virginia plantation, he gained a reputation among the other slaves for his religious beliefs and intelligence. Turner became a well-respected minister in the local slave community. In 1827 he even baptized a white overseer. When a solar eclipse took place in 1831, Turner interpreted it as a sign that the time had come to start a revolt. What event led Nat Turner to believe that he should start a slave revolt?

★ Slave Culture

Despite the harsh realities of daily life, many slaves took comfort in their community and culture. They worked hard to maintain strong ties to one another and to their heritage. The most important unit of slave communities was the family. Most slaves feared being separated from their families more than physical punishment. Josiah Henson never forgot the day that he and his family were sold at a slave auction. His mother begged the slaveholder who bought her to buy Josiah also. If he did, then she would have at least one of her children with her. The slaveholder refused, and Henson's entire family was separated. "I must have been then between five or six years old," he recalled years later. "I seem to see and hear my poor weeping mother now."

Enslaved parents made sure that children never forgot their heritage. They passed down family histories, as well as African customs and traditions. They also told **folktales**, or stories with a moral, to teach lessons about how to survive under slavery. Folktales often warned slaves not to trust slaveholders, who were often represented in the stories by powerful animals. Clever characters called tricksters were used to show slaves how to survive by outsmarting slaveholders.

Religion was also an important part of slave culture. By the early 1800s many slaves were Christians. White ministers often tried to use religion to control slaves. They preached that God wanted slaves to obey slaveholders. However, enslaved African Americans noted that the Bible suggested that all people are equal in God's eyes. They came to see themselves as God's chosen people. Much like the Hebrew slaves in ancient Egypt, slaves in the South had faith that they would someday live in freedom.

Some slaves used **spirituals**, emotional Christian songs that blended African and European music, to express their religious beliefs. For example, "The Heavenly Road" reflected slaves' belief in their equality in the eyes of God.

 Primary Sources "Come, my brother, if you never did pray,
I hope you may pray tonight;
For I really believe I'm a child of God
As I walk in the heavenly road."

—Anonymous, quoted in *Afro-American Religious History,* edited by Milton C. Sernett

Slaves blended aspects of traditional African religions with those of Christianity. For example, spirituals developed in part out of a dance called the ring shout, which was based on African ceremonial dances performed in a ring. Slaves worshipped in secret, out of sight of the slaveholder. Some historians have called slave religion the invisible institution.

✔ **Reading Check: Summarizing** What did slaves use to keep a sense of community among themselves? *families, folktales, and spirituals*

★ **REVIEW AND ASSESS**

Have students complete the **Section 4 Review** on p. 443. Then have them complete **Daily Quiz 14.4**. As **Alternative Assessment**, you may want to use the challenges to slavery graphic organizer or the Teacher to Teacher exercise from this section's lessons.

★ **RETEACH**

Have students complete **Main Idea Activity for English Language Learners and Special-Needs Students 14.4**. Ask students to create a list of five questions about material in this section to ask other students. Instruct students to take turns asking each other their questions and correcting one another's answers. Finally, discuss any topics that students are having difficulty understanding. **ENGLISH LANGUAGE LEARNERS**, **COOPERATIVE LEARNING**

★ **EXTEND**

Encourage students to skim a novel that covers slaves' resistance to planters' authority. Have each student write down descriptive words used in the book to depict the treatment of slaves and their attempts to resist authority. Then have students write their own essays using descriptive words from their lists to portray slaves' lives. **BLOCK SCHEDULING**

★ Challenging Slavery

Slaves rebelled in small ways against the slave system on a daily basis. Sometimes this meant working slower to protest long hours in the fields. Other times it meant running away for a few days. Some slaves tried to escape, but most left only for short periods, usually to see relatives. However, thousands of enslaved people did manage to escape to the North.

Although violent slave revolts were rare, white southerners lived in fear that they would occur. Denmark Vesey planned a rebellion in Charleston, South Carolina, in 1822, but he was found out and stopped before it could be carried out. Authorities executed most of those involved. The most violent slave revolt in the United States occurred in 1831. **Nat Turner**, a slave from Virginia, believed that God had called on him to end slavery. **Nat Turner's Rebellion** began on an August night in 1831. Turner led a group of slaves that set out to kill slaveholders and their families. The rebels killed about 60 white people in the area.

More than 100 slaves were killed in an attempt to put down the rebellion. Turner himself was caught within weeks and executed on November 11, 1831. After the rebellion, many states strengthened their slave codes. The codes were meant to place stricter controls on the slave population. Despite the resistance of enslaved people, slavery continued to spread.

✔ **Reading Check: Finding the Main Idea** What was Nat Turner's Rebellion, and what happened as a result? Turner and other slaves revolted against slavery but were defeated. Slave codes were strengthened to control the slave population more strictly.

THE GRANGER COLLECTION, NEW YORK

Interpreting the Visual Record

Nat Turner's Rebellion *Nat Turner believed that his revolt was justified.* "I am willing to suffer the fate that awaits me," he said. **Why do you think Turner and his fellow rebels are in the swamp?**

Visual Record Answer

Students might suggest that they are hiding.

**Section 4 Review
ANSWERS**

❶ **Define**
• folktales, p. 442
• spirituals, p. 442

❷ **Identify**
• Nat Turner, p. 443
• Nat Turner's Rebellion, p. 443

❸ Coping with slavery–building families, remembering heritage, folktales, spirituals; Challenging slavery–working slowly, running away, rebelling

❹ a. received poor food, clothing and shelter; endured long, hard days of repetitive labor
b. Students may suggest that because the rebellion failed, others chose not to try. They may point out that after the rebellion, southern states increased their control of slave populations as the system of slavery spread.

❺ Students' articles will vary but students should include information on family life, religion, and the importance of folktales and spirituals.

Section 4 Review

go.hrw.com **Homework Practice Online**
keyword: SA3 HP14

❶ **Define and explain:**
• folktales
• spirituals

❷ **Identify and explain:**
• Nat Turner
• Nat Turner's Rebellion

❸ **Evaluating** Copy the graphic organizer below. Use it to describe life under slavery.

Life as a Slave
- Coping with Slavery
- Challenging Slavery

❹ **Finding the Main Idea**
a. What was a typical working day in the life of a slave like?
b. How do you think Nat Turner's Rebellion affected the lives of southern slaves who did not take part in the revolt?

❺ **Writing and Critical Thinking**
Summarizing Imagine that you are a historian interviewing a former slave in the late 1800s. Write a half-page article on how enslaved people coped with the slave system.
Consider the following:
• slave families
• the role of religion in the lives of slaves
• the importance of folktales and spirituals

REPRODUCIBLE
▶ Vocabulary Activity 14

TECHNOLOGY
▶ Chapter 14 Test Generator (on the One-Stop Planner)
▶ Global Skill Builder CD–ROM
▶ HRW Go site

REINFORCEMENT, REVIEW, AND ASSESSMENT
▶ Chapter 14 Review, pp. 444–45
▶ Chapter 14 Tutorial for Students, Parents, Mentors, and Peers

▶ Chapter 14 Test (Form A or B)
▶ Portfolio Assessment Handbook
▶ Chapter 14 Test for English Language Learners and Special-Needs Students

★ **REVIEW**
Have students complete the **Chapter 14 Review** on pages 444–45.

★ **ASSESS**
Use one of the chapter tests to assess students' understanding of the content. For **Alternative Assessment**, see the **Alternative Assessment Handbook**.

CHAPTER **14** REVIEW ANSWERS

The Chapter at a Glance
Students' quizzes will vary but should include information on the main ideas expressed in each section.

Identifying People and Ideas
Students' sentences should indicate an understanding of the following definitions:

1. invented the cotton gin

2. removed seeds from cotton fibers

3. area from South Carolina to east Texas, where most of the country's cotton crop grew

4. crop brokers who managed the trade between planters and their customers

5. invented a new sugar-processing system

6. the only large southern factory that made iron products

7. small landowning farmers

8. stories with a moral to teach lessons about how to survive slavery

9. emotional Christian songs that blended African and European traditions

10. a slave rebellion in Virginia, led by Nat Turner

Understanding Main Ideas

1. demand from textile industry and invention of the cotton gin

2. slavery clashed with the ideal of liberty for some, and cash crops such as tobacco,

Chapter **14** Review

The Chapter at a Glance
Examine the visual summary of the chapter below. Create a five-question quiz on how the main ideas in each section are related to each other to exchange with a classmate.

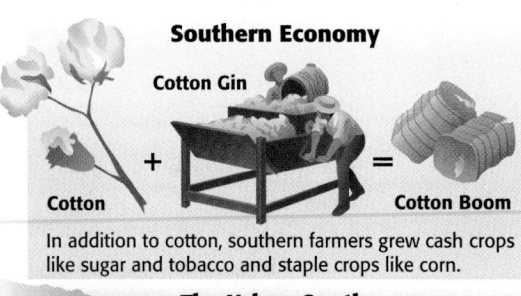

Southern Economy

Cotton + Cotton Gin = Cotton Boom

In addition to cotton, southern farmers grew cash crops like sugar and tobacco and staple crops like corn.

The Urban South

Factories   Cities

The South had fewer factories and large cities than the North. Most free African Americans lived in urban areas.

Southern Society

Planters were at the top of southern society, which also included yeoman farmers, poor whites, and enslaved and free African Americans. Planters were the largest slaveholders.

Understanding People and Ideas
Use the following terms or people in historically significant sentences.
1. Eli Whitney
2. cotton gin
3. cotton belt
4. factors
5. Jean Étienne Boré
6. Tredegar Iron Works
7. yeomen
8. folktales
9. spirituals
10. Nat Turner's Rebellion

Understanding Main Ideas
Section 1 (Pages 424–427)
1. Why did cotton production increase in the 1800s?
2. Why did slavery seem to decline after the American Revolution, and why did it increase again in the 1800s?

Section 2 (Pages 428–432)
3. What did southerners mean when they proclaimed that "Cotton is King"?
4. What kinds of factories existed in the South in the 1800s?

Section 3 (Pages 433–438)
5. How were the economic interests of planters and yeomen similar?
6. What kind of discrimination did free African Americans face in the South?

Section 4 (Pages 439–443)
7. What role did family and religion play in the lives of enslaved African Americans?

You Be the Historian— Reviewing Themes
1. **Science, Technology & Society** How did the invention of the cotton gin by Eli Whitney lead to an increased demand for slave labor in the South?
2. **Economics** How did the cotton boom affect the economy and society of the South?
3. **Culture** How did slavery influence southern African American culture in the 1800s?

Thinking Critically
1. **Analyzing Information** Why did the southern economy develop differently from that of the North in the 1800s?
2. **Comparing and Contrasting** How were the lives of free southern African Americans different from and similar to the lives of slaves? Consider political and social factors.
3. **Finding the Main Idea** What effects did the cotton gin and scientific agriculture have on life in the South?

Have students imagine that they are living in the antebellum South and have been asked to create a time capsule. Instruct them to provide information about the Reading Check questions from the chapter in their time capsules. Encourage them to include newspaper articles, letters, illustrations, maps, charts, and graphs in the time capsule.

Portfolio Extensions

1. Cooperative Learning Have students work in teams to prepare for a debate on the following topic. Resolved: the dependence on cotton was bad for the southern economy in the early 1800s. Ask students to use the library and their textbook to research reasons why dependence on one staple crop such as cotton may or may not have been good for the economy. Then have students use this information to help their team argue in support of its positions on the resolution.

2. Linking to Community Tell students that the novels of white southerners and the folktales of southern slaves show two different views of the South. Have students prepare a poster that summarizes different perspectives given by two persons in their community on a major issue, development, or trend. The persons can be people living in the community today or in the past.

Social Studies Skills Workshop

Interpreting Graphs
Study the graph below. Then use the information on the graph to help you answer the questions that follow.

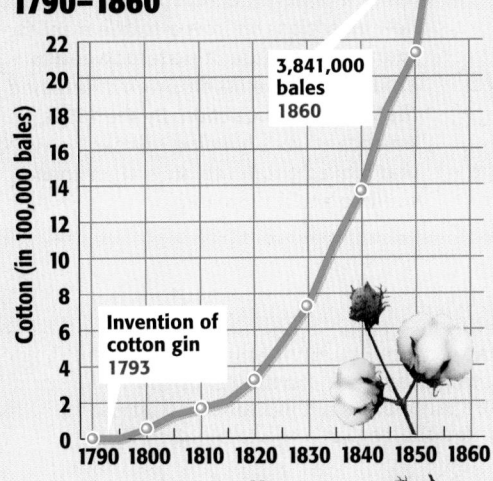

U.S. Cotton Production, 1790–1860

3,841,000 bales 1860

Invention of cotton gin 1793

Cotton (in 100,000 bales)

1790 1800 1810 1820 1830 1840 1850 1860

Year

Source: *Historical Statistics of the United States*

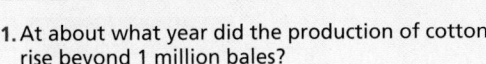

1. At about what year did the production of cotton rise beyond 1 million bales?
   a. 1840
   b. 1835
   c. 1830
   d. 1825

2. Based on the graph and your knowledge of the period, what event contributed to the increase in cotton production in the South?

Analyzing Primary Sources
Read the following quote by planter Bennet H. Barrow, and then answer the questions that follow.

❝If I employ a laborer to perform a certain quantum [amount] of work per day, and I agree to pay him a certain amount for the performance of said work when he has accomplished it, I of course have no further claim on him for his time or services [when he is done]—but how different is it with a slave. . . . If I furnish my [slave] with every necessary of life, . . . am I not entitled to an exclusive right to his time? . . . A plantation might be considered as a piece of machinery; to operate successfully, all of its parts should be uniform [the same].❞

3. Which of the following best describes Barrow's attitude toward slaves?
   a. A planter should treat slaves like parts of a machine and have control over all their time.
   b. Slavery is actually more expensive than paying people's wages.
   c. Once they have finished their work, slaves should have free time to themselves.
   d. Plantations should make use of modern machinery as well as slaves.

4. According to his own words, how would Barrow expect to treat free workers whom he paid wages?
   a. They would have to work for him whenever he wanted.
   b. He would pay them only when he was satisfied with their work.
   c. When they finished a job, their free time would be their own.
   d. He would expect to provide for all of their needs in addition to paying wages.

indigo, and rice saw a decrease in price; an agricultural boom based on cotton

3. the South's economy was built on it

4. iron and lumber.

5. both were devoted to the cotton-based, plantation-oriented, slave-labor agricultural system

6. limited rights; most could not vote, hold certain jobs, travel freely, or conduct business freely

7. helped slaves cope with their bondage

You Be the Historian— Reviewing Themes
1. sparked a cotton boom that required a large labor force, namely slaves

2. fueled the southern economy, and created a wealthy agricultural society

3. many slaves found comfort through their community and religion

Thinking Critically
1. cotton boom renewed demand for slaves, strengthened plantations system

2. free African Americans held some rights that slaves did not, but like slaves they faced discrimination in a society dominated by white southerners

3. both contributed to the growth of agriculture

Skills Workshop
1. b

2. the invention of the cotton gin

3. a

4. c

Alternative Assessment

Building Your Portfolio

Interdisciplinary Connection to Literature
Create a folktale that enslaved African American parents might have told their children. Use animals to represent the main characters. Have one of the characters play the trickster's role—to outwit a stronger creature. The folktale should try to teach a moral lesson about how to survive in slavery. Present your folktale to the class, and have students discuss the story's lesson.

☑ **internet connect**

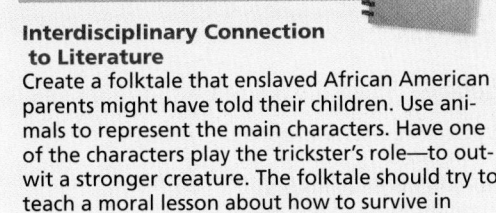

Internet Activity: go.hrw.com
keyword: SA3 CF14

Choose a topic on Agricultural Changes in the South to:
● Learn about slave revolts in Haiti and the abolition of slavery in France.
● Understand sugar production and make a flow chart.
● Research and report on the Tredegar Iron Works.

LET'S GET STARTED!

Ask students to raise their hand if they have ever lived in a house other than the one in which they currently live. Explain to them that many Americans will move several times during their lives. Then ask student why they think American move so often. *(Students' responses will vary, but students may mention job or educational opportunities.)* Point out to students that in the first half of the 1800s, this willingness of Americans to move led to the growth of major industrial areas and the outward expansion of the United States. Furthermore, to meet the needs of this mobile population, new, more efficient technology and transportation systems had to be created. Tell students that they will learn about the nation's growing economy in this unit.

★ TEACH

Have students read the Connecting to Geography lesson. Choose one or more of the following activities to explore the Connecting to Geography content with students.

★ Historical Sidelight

Transportation Systems.
Railroads and canals were not the only routes of travel in the early 1800s. In some states, private companies financed and built turnpikes, roads upon which travelers were required to pay a toll. In New England by 1840, more than $6.5 million of private funds had been spent to build turnpikes. Pennsylvania had an estimated 2,400 miles of toll roads by 1832. Private companies had financed the majority of the cost of these roads.

ACTIVITY: Have students conduct research at the library to obtain more information about turnpikes. Ask students to choose a particular turnpike and to write a report, using standard grammar, spelling, sentence structure, and punctuation, about its history, usage, and whether it still exists today.

SKILLS ANSWERS
1. North and Northeast
2. 17.7 percent

Connecting to Geography

A Growing Economy

 From 1790 to 1860, the economy of each region of the United States grew and developed in very different ways. The economies of the South and the West were based largely on farming. The economy of the North was increasingly focused on industry.

In some ways these differences worked together to help the nation grow. For example, the South provided some raw materials, such as cotton, to northern factories. The Midwest provided large supplies of food, which helped feed the growing population of northern cities.

American manufacturing grew in the late 1700s and early 1800s. This growth was made possible by the invention and development of new technologies. For example, new inventions improved textile manufacturing, and the use of waterpower was expanded. These developments increased the speed of production. By the 1830s, Americans were building railroad networks that moved goods rapidly and inexpensively to and from market.

The North

The North developed an industrial economy partly because of its geography and superior transportation system. Farmland in the North was not generally suited for large-scale agriculture. Industrial development was thus necessary for the region's economic growth.

Distribution of U.S. Manufacturing Establishments, 1860

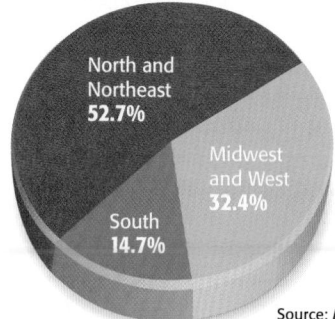

North and Northeast 52.7%

Midwest and West 32.4%

South 14.7%

Source: *Encyclopedia of American History*

History Note 1

By 1860 only about one in seven U.S. factories and other manufacturing establishments were located in the South. As industry increased in the North, so did the region's urban population. Cities, particularly those in the Northeast and Midwest, grew larger as factories provided more and more jobs. In the South, which had fewer factories, urban growth was much slower.

 ## Geography Skills

Interpreting Pie Graphs

1. What region had the largest percentage of the nation's manufacturing establishments in 1860?
2. **Comparing** How much greater was the percentage of manufacturing establishments in the Midwest and West than in the South in 1860?

LEVEL 1: Explain to students that the United States used rivers to transport the majority of its goods during the 1800s, despite the fact that many of the rivers in the East have numerous waterfalls and rapids. Have students look at the map on p. 447 and have them brainstorm ways engineers might overcome this problem. *(Students' brainstorming might include transporting over land via railroad or wagon.)* Have volunteers present their ideas to the class.

ENGLISH LANGUAGE LEARNERS

ALL LEVELS: Have students refer to the maps on p. 447 and have them create directions to give to an employee who needs to transport a large shipment of textile goods from Lewiston, Maine, to Cincinnati, Ohio. Advise students that because of the time and expense, they are to travel by wagon for as little of the journey as possible and that because of limited cargo space for personal items, they will need to stop frequently to pick up supplies. Instruct students to include the following in their directions: the mode of transportation *(railroad, canal, or wagon)* that the employee will use to travel from city to city; the distance each segment of the trip will cover; and the direction the employee will need to travel on each leg of the journey. Have volunteers report their direction to the class. (As an option, you may want to trace students' routes on an overhead projector to provide both visual and auditory presentations of each route.) **ENGLISH LANGUAGE LEARNERS**

Industry in the North, 1860

Legend:
— Railroad
— Canal
— Canalized river

Scale: 0 — 75 — 150 Miles
0 — 75 — 150 Kilometers
Albers Equal-Area Projection

Industries
- Clothing accessories
- Food products
- Iron or steel
- Machinery or equipment
- Paper
- Textiles
- Weaponry
- Diverse industries
- Clocks, watches
- Other

History Note 2

Improved transportation networks in the North encouraged industrial expansion. Businesses shipped goods on rivers, the Great Lakes, and the growing networks of canals and railroads. The benefits of expanded transportation networks on industrial growth could be clearly seen in New England in the first half of the 1800s. Connecticut, Massachusetts, and Rhode Island provide good examples of this important relationship.

Geography Skills

Interpreting Thematic Maps

1. Have a fellow student look at this map. Then ask him or her to create a bar graph comparing the number of iron, steel, and textile industries in the North.

2. **Environment and Society** How do you think the construction of so many railroads and canals helped northern industry?

3. **Analyzing Information** What geographic features made New England more suitable for early industries?

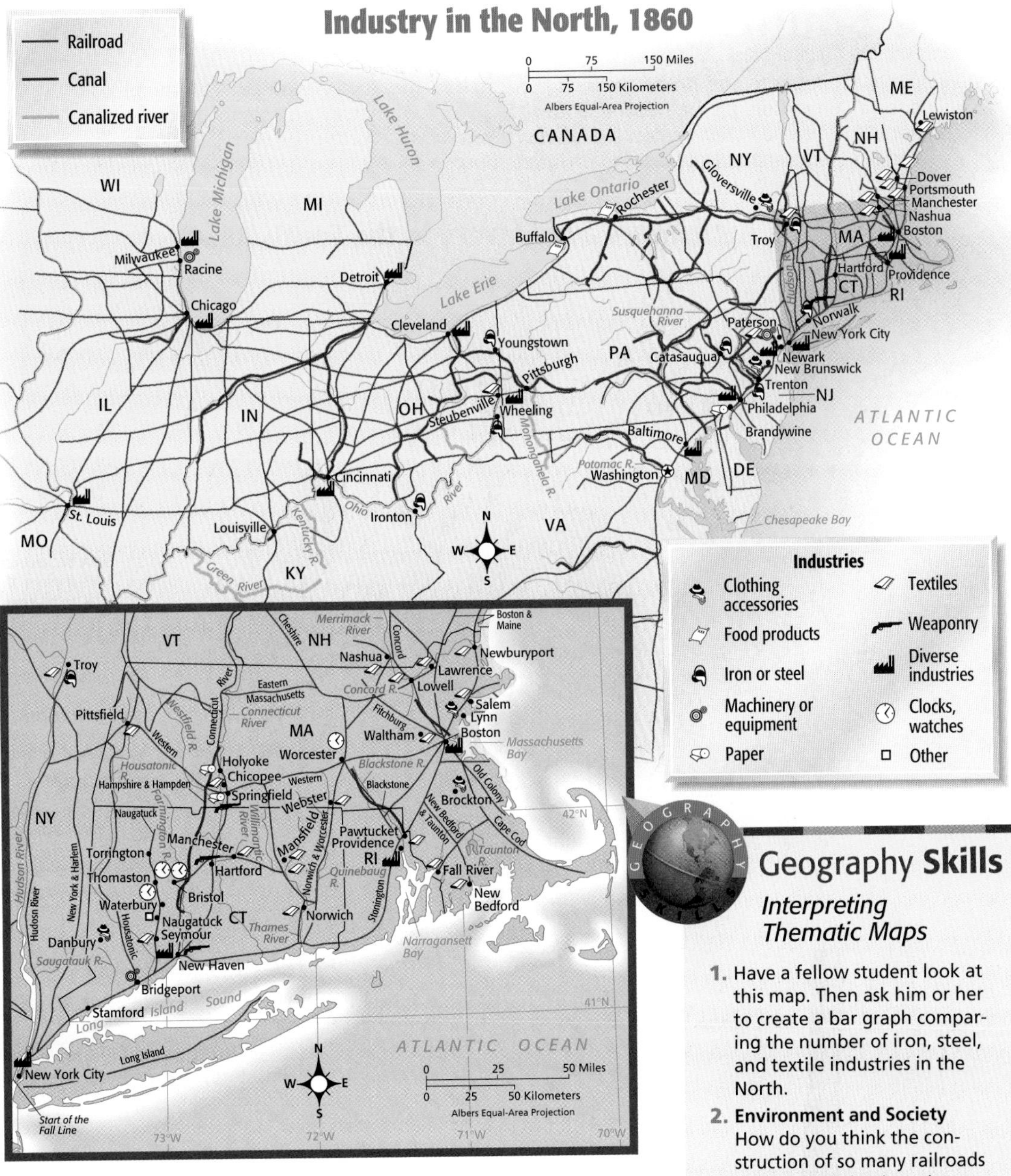

★ Economics

Free African Americans in the North. Not all Americans shared in the wealth that industrial growth brought to the North during the 1800s. Many free African Americans—some of whom were escaped slaves from the South—lived in poverty because they were unable to find decent jobs with good wages. One historian has estimated that almost 90 percent of the African Americans in New York City held low-paying jobs. As more European immigrants entered the United States, they competed with African Americans for jobs.

CRITICAL THINKING

Why might African Americans be unable to find higher paying jobs in the North?

ANSWER: Students might suggest that they competed for jobs with immigrants and faced discrimination.

SKILLS ANSWERS

1. Students' graphs will vary but should accurately reflect the information found on the map.

2. easier to transport; lower shipping costs; more jobs

3. Students might suggest improved transportation networks and access to water.

LEVEL 3: Ask students to examine the graphs and maps on pp. 446–49 and to write a short essay describing the contribution that geography made to the formation of the northern and southern economies and to the related growth of urban populations. Have students describe how geography affected transportation and the crops that could be grown. Have volunteers read their essays to the class. Finally, lead a discussion summarizing the effect that geography had on both economies.

★ CLOSE

Explain to students that maps are not only a method for illustrating information but can also be a source of specific information. Have students use information from the map Industry in the North, 1860—located on p. 447—as a reference, have students create a table showing the types of industry in each state in 1860. Then have students list the types of industry shown on the map as headings for the horizontal axis and the states shown on the map as headings for the vertical axis. Ask students to place an X in any square that connects a state to an industry it had in 1860.

★ Economics

Southern Industry.

Manufacturing did take place in the South, but not on the same scale as it did in the North. By 1860 approximately 132,000 southerners worked in factories, creating more then $200 million worth of goods. However, 84 percent of southern workers still worked on farms in 1860; that same year, only 40 percent of northerners were still involved in agriculture. In addition, southerners had a great deal of their money tied up in slave ownership, leaving them very little money to start factories.

CRITICAL THINKING

Why were fewer northerners involved in agriculture?

ANSWER: Students might suggest environmental conditions were better for farming in the South.

SKILLS ANSWERS

1. cotton, corn

2. sugarcane—Louisiana and Texas; tobacco—Kentucky, North Carolina, Tennessee, and Virginia

3. cotton

The South

While industry in the North grew, agriculture in the South boomed. The invention of the cotton gin in 1793 encouraged growth in southern cotton production. However, as that region's economy grew, so did disapproval in the North and the West of the South's use of slave labor.

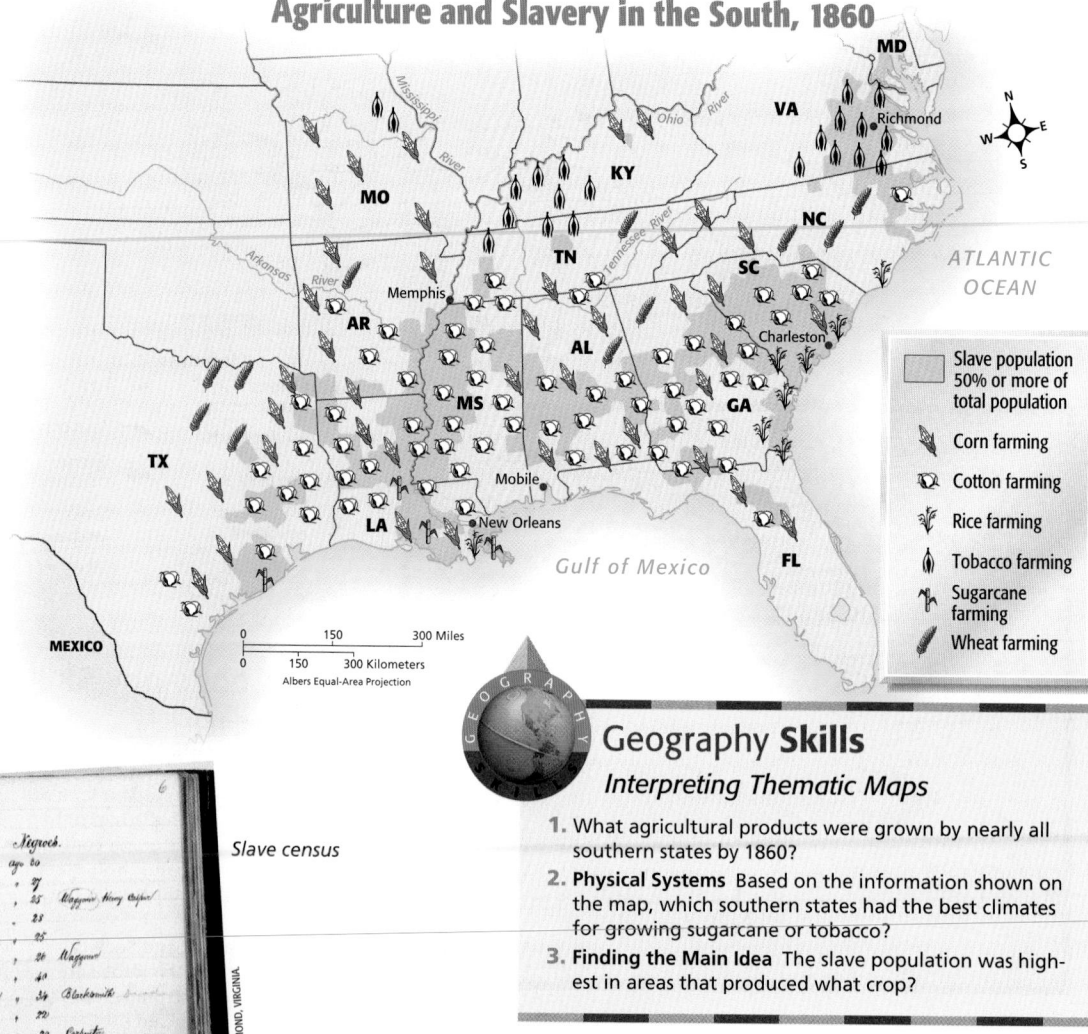

Agriculture and Slavery in the South, 1860

Legend:
- Slave population 50% or more of total population
- Corn farming
- Cotton farming
- Rice farming
- Tobacco farming
- Sugarcane farming
- Wheat farming

Slave census

THE MUSEUM OF THE CONFEDERACY, RICHMOND, VIRGINIA. PHOTOGRAPHY BY KATHERINE WETZEL

Geography Skills
Interpreting Thematic Maps

1. What agricultural products were grown by nearly all southern states by 1860?

2. **Physical Systems** Based on the information shown on the map, which southern states had the best climates for growing sugarcane or tobacco?

3. **Finding the Main Idea** The slave population was highest in areas that produced what crop?

History Note 3

American cotton production boomed in the first half of the 1800s. Cotton production was concentrated within a region called the cotton belt, which ran from South Carolina to eastern Texas. In 1860 the United States exported more than $190 million worth of cotton, most of it grown in the cotton belt.

Have students review the information in Connecting to Geography Unit 6. Then have students complete Geography and History Quiz 6.

★ **RETEACH**

Have students look at the maps in this activity. Ask them to identify the minimum number of states a person would have to visit in order to see every type of crop and industry shown on the maps. Have students provide the number of states, list the name of each state that a person would need to visit, and identify the crops and industries in each of those states.

ENGLISH LANGUAGE LEARNERS

Have students use the library or other available resources to obtain current information about the major industries in each of the states shown on the maps on p. 447. Then have students create a map depicting the dominant industries in these states. Instruct them to create a key identifying each type of industry found on the map. Finally, have students review both the maps they created and the map on p. 447 and discuss with the class how the economies of these states have changed or remained the same. **BLOCK SCHEDULING**

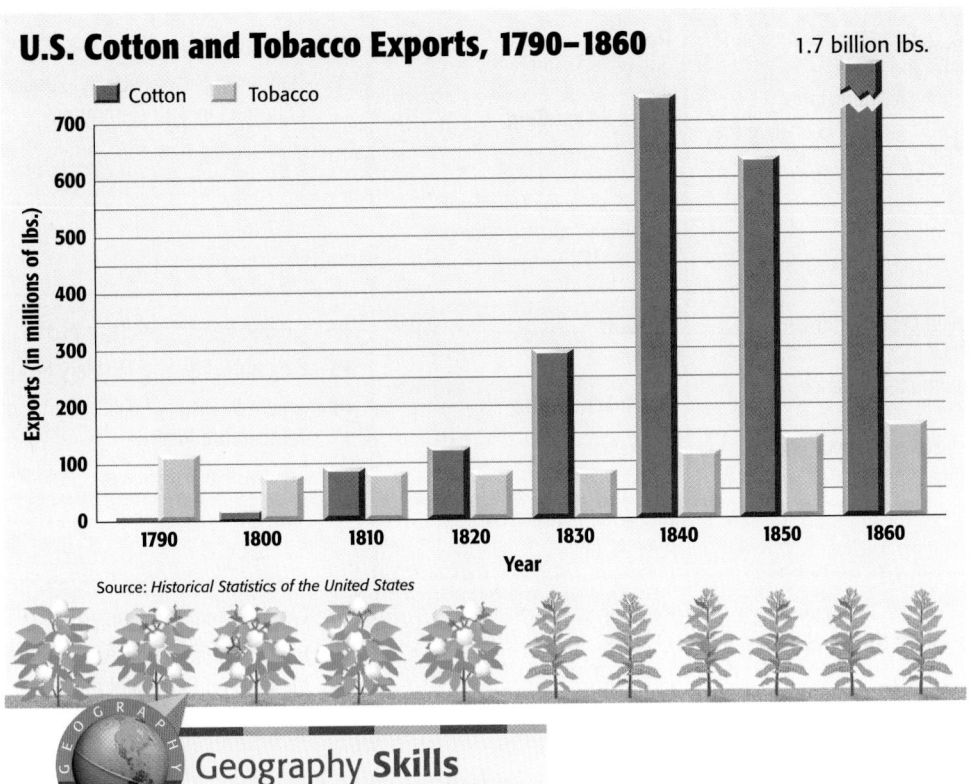

U.S. Cotton and Tobacco Exports, 1790–1860

1.7 billion lbs.

Source: *Historical Statistics of the United States*

Slaves returning from a hard day of laboring in the fields

Geography **Skills**

Interpreting Bar Graphs

1. By what year had the amount of cotton exports overtaken the amount of tobacco exports?
2. **Summarizing** Show this bar graph to a classmate. Have this person write a paragraph describing the general trends in tobacco and cotton exports from 1790 to 1860.

History Note 4

Together Alabama, Georgia, Louisiana, and Mississippi produced about two thirds of the cotton in the United States in 1860. States that produced smaller amounts of cotton often produced larger amounts of other agricultural products. For example, in 1860 Virginia produced relatively little cotton. However, it produced nearly 30 percent of the nation's tobacco. South Carolina produced nearly two thirds of the nation's rice in that year.

Changes in Cotton Gins.
Prior to the Civil War, slaves were used in almost every aspect of cotton production, including carrying the cotton after it was picked and operating the plantation's cotton gin. After the war, however, it was harder to get enough workers to complete this task, so innovators decided to create a labor-saving cotton gin. Robert Munger developed a system that moved the cotton from the field directly to the gin, where it was processed. This invention raised the cost of the average gin so that public gins began to replace the gins found on individual plantations.

CRITICAL THINKING

Why was it harder for plantation owners to find people to work the cotton gins after the Civil War?

ANSWER: Students' answers will vary, but students may mention that African Americans who were freed during the Civil War may not have wanted to return to the same work they were performing before the war.

SKILLS ANSWERS

1. 1810
2. Students' paragraphs will vary but should reflect an increase in both, with cotton overtaking tobacco.

Objectives	Pacing Guide	Reproducible Resources
SECTION 1: **America's Spiritual Awakening** (pp. 452–56) ✪ Examine how religion affected Americans during the Second Great Awakening. ✪ Describe the transcendentalists' views of American society. ✪ Identify some ideas of the romantic movement.	**Regular** 1.5 days **Block Scheduling** 1 day *Block Scheduling Handbook with Team Teaching Strategies, Chapter 15*	**RS** Guided Reading Strategy 15.1 **SM** Geography Activity 15: Utopian Communities
SECTION 2: **Immigrants and Cities** (pp. 457–61) ✪ Explain why so many Irish and German immigrants came to the United States in the 1840s and 1850s. ✪ Discuss some Americans' reactions to immigrants. ✪ Describe what caused U.S. cities to grow, and analyze the benefits and problems this growth created.	**Regular** 2 days **Block Scheduling** 1 day *Block Scheduling Handbook with Team Teaching Strategies, Chapter 15*	**RS** Guided Reading Strategy 15.2 **E** Hands-On History Activity: Public Education in Your Community
SECTION 3: **Reforming Society** (pp. 462–68) ✪ Analyze how reformers improved prisons in the early 1800s. ✪ Examine why reformers started the temperance movement. ✪ Determine how Americans' educational opportunities changed during the early and mid-1800s.	**Regular** 2 days **Block Scheduling** 1 day *Block Scheduling Handbook with Team Teaching Strategies, Chapter 15*	**RS** Guided Reading Strategy 15.3 **PS** Biography Reading 15: Mary Lyon **PS** American History Political Cartoon 5: Temperance Reform **E** Creative Teaching Strategy: Role-Playing
SECTION 4: **The Movement to End Slavery** (pp. 469–74) ✪ Explore why some Americans became abolitionists. ✪ Identify ways that abolitionists spread the movement's message. ✪ Investigate why some Americans opposed abolition.	**Regular** 1.5 days **Block Scheduling** 1 day *Block Scheduling Handbook with Team Teaching Strategies, Chapter 15*	**RS** Guided Reading Strategy 15.4 **PS** Primary Source Reading 15: "An Appeal to the Colored Citizens of the World"
SECTION 5: **Women's Rights** (pp. 475–79) ✪ Explain the effect that the abolitionist movement had on the women's rights movement. ✪ Identify some of the goals of the women's rights movement. ✪ Analyze the purpose and significance of the Seneca Falls Convention.	**Regular** 1.5 days **Block Scheduling** .5 days *Block Scheduling Handbook with Team Teaching Strategies, Chapter 15*	**RS** Guided Reading Strategy 15.5 **PS** Literature Reading 15: Encouraging Women's Rights **RS** Graphic Organizer 15: Early Reform Movements

Chapter Resource Key

PS Primary Sources	**A** Assessment	Music	
RS Reading Support	**REV** Review	Video	
IC Interdisciplinary Connections	**ELL** Reinforcement and English Language Learners	 Internet	
E Enrichment	Transparencies	 Holt Presentation Maker Using Microsoft® PowerPoint®	
SM Skills Mastery	CD-ROM		

 One-Stop Planner CD-ROM

See the *One-Stop Planner* for a complete list of additional resources for students and teachers.

One-Stop Planner CD–ROM

It's easy to plan lessons, select resources, and print out materials for your students when you use the **One-Stop Planner CD–ROM with Test Generator.**

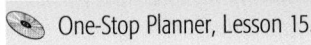

Technology Resources

- One-Stop Planner, Lesson 15.1
- Exploring America's Past Video Segment: Spirit of the Times; Teacher's Guide, pp. 24–25.
- Art in American History Transparency 11: Thunderstorm in the Rocky Mountains
- Homework Practice Online
- HRW Go site

- One-Stop Planner, Lesson 15.2
- Linking Geography and History Transparency 13: Sources of Immigration, 1831–1860
- CNN Presents America: Yesterday and Today, Beginnings to 1914 Segment: The Irish Potato Famine
- Homework Practice Online

- One-Stop Planner, Lesson 15.3
- Everyday Life in America Transparency 9: Message Art: Temperance in the Early 1800s
- Homework Practice Online
- HRW Go site

- One-Stop Planner, Lesson 15.4
- Everyday Life in America Transparency 8: Portrait of a Prosperous African American
- American Music Selection 12: "Follow the Drinking Gourd"
- Holt Researcher CD–ROM
- Homework Practice Online

- One-Stop Planner, Lesson 15.5
- American History Simulations CD–ROM: Reform: Making a Difference
- Holt Researcher CD–ROM
- Homework Practice Online

Reinforcement, Review, and Assessment

- **REV** Section 1 Review, p. 456
- **A** Daily Quiz 15.1
- **ELL** Main Idea Activity 15.1
- **ELL** English Audio Summary 15.1
- **ELL** Spanish Audio Summary 15.1

- **REV** Section 2 Review, p. 461
- **A** Daily Quiz 15.2
- **ELL** Main Idea Activity 15.2
- **ELL** English Audio Summary 15.2
- **ELL** Spanish Audio Summary 15.2

- **REV** Section 3 Review, p. 468
- **A** Daily Quiz 15.3
- **ELL** Main Idea Activity 15.3
- **ELL** English Audio Summary 15.3
- **ELL** Spanish Audio Summary 15.3

- **REV** Section 4 Review, p. 474
- **A** Daily Quiz 15.4
- **ELL** Main Idea Activity 15.4
- **ELL** English Audio Summary 15.4
- **ELL** Spanish Audio Summary 15.4

- **REV** Section 5 Review, p. 478
- **A** Daily Quiz 15.5
- **ELL** Main Idea Activity 15.5
- **ELL** English Audio Summary 15.5
- **ELL** Spanish Audio Summary 15.5

internet connect

HRW ONLINE RESOURCES
GO TO: go.hrw.com
Then type in a keyword.

TEACHER HOME PAGE
KEYWORD: SA3 Teacher

CHAPTER INTERNET ACTIVITIES
KEYWORD: SA3 CF15
Choose an activity to:
- Write a journal entry from the point of view of Henry David Thoreau.
- Research the leaders and beliefs of the Transcendentalist movement.
- Write a biography of Dorothea Dix.

CHAPTER ENRICHMENT LINKS
KEYWORD: SA3 CH15

ONLINE ASSESSMENT
Homework Practice
KEYWORD: SA3 HP15

Standardized Test Prep
KEYWORD: SA3 STP15

Rubrics
KEYWORD: SS Rubrics

ONLINE MAPS, CHARTS, AND GRAPHS
KEYWORD: SA3 MCG
- Utopian Communities
- The Underground Railroad
- Boston, 1850
- Reform and Society
- Social Reform

CONTENT UPDATES
KEYWORD: SS Content Updates

HOLT PRESENTATION MAKER
KEYWORD: SA3 PPT15

ONLINE READING SUPPORT
KEYWORD: SS Strategies

CURRENT EVENTS
KEYWORD: S3 Current Events

Meeting Individual Needs

Ability Levels

Level 1 Basic-level activities designed for all students encountering new material

Level 2 Intermediate-level activities designed for average students

Level 3 Challenging activities designed for honors and gifted-and-talented students

English Language Learners Activities that address the needs of students with Limited English Proficiency

Chapter Review and Assessment

- **IC** Vocabulary Activity 15
- Global Skill Builder CD–ROM
- HRW Go site
- **REV** Chapter 15 Tutorial for Students, Parents, Mentors, and Peers
- **REV** Chapter 15 Review, pp. 479–81
- Chapter 15 Test Generator (on the One-Stop Planner)

- **A** Chapter 15 Test (Form A or B)
- **A** Alternative Assessment Handbook
- **A** Chapter 15 Test for English Language Learners and Special-Needs Students

Build on What You Know

If You Were There...

Ask students to answer the following question:

What social issues would you choose to work on?

Consider:

• how slavery shaped the entire country

• how social ills could be improved

You Be the Historian

What's Your Opinion?

To help students create their **Themes** Journal entries, provide the following examples of appropriate **agree/disagree** statements.

EXPLORING THE TIME LINE
AMERICAN EVENTS

internet connect

TOPIC: Abolitionist Newspapers
GO TO: go.hrw.com
KEYWORD: SA3 CF15

Have students access the Internet through the HRW Go site to research the influence of abolitionist newspapers written by William Lloyd Garrison and Frederick Douglass. Then have them create a visual display for their research. Students should include primary sources and biographical information about each man. Students' displays should also illustrate how each individual represented the abolitionist point of view in his newspapers.

CHAPTER
15   New Movements in America
(1815–1850)

William Lloyd Garrison's antislavery banner announced, "I WILL BE HEARD."

Horace Mann fought for better salaries for teachers.

THE GRANGER COLLECTION, NEW YORK

UNITED STATES

1817 Thomas Gallaudet founds a school for people who are hearing impaired.	**1821** Emma Willard starts the Troy Female Seminary.	**1831** William Lloyd Garrison begins publishing the abolitionist newspaper *The Liberator*.	**1837** Horace Mann becomes the first secretary of education in Massachusetts.

1815	**1820**	**1825**	**1830**	**1835**

WORLD

1822 The American Colonization Society founds the city of Monrovia on Africa's west coast.

1829 French educator Louis Braille creates a system of writing that uses raised dots for people who are blind.

Slavery is banned in Mexico.

1834 A law abolishing slavery in the British Empire goes into effect.

Monrovia became the capital of the African nation Liberia.

THE GRANGER COLLECTION, NEW YORK

Build on What You Know

The North and South developed very different economies during the early 1800s. Rising immigration led to population growth, especially in the North. As the country faced new challenges, social reform movements emerged in response. Many people joined groups to fight alcohol abuse, end slavery, or improve education.

Culture

Agree You should strive to help those who are less fortunate.

Disagree You have no responsibility to help people who are less fortunate.

Economics

Agree Immigration brings people with a desire to succeed, thereby benefiting the economy.

Disagree A strong American economy should help Americans, not people from other countries.

Citizenship

Agree American citizens have the right to work to change laws.

Disagree The laws of the United States were carefully crafted to be fair to everyone.

Organizers of the Seneca Falls Convention based the Declaration of Sentiments in part on the Declaration of Independence.

During the mid-1800s, large numbers of German and Irish immigrants came to the United States.

1848 The first meeting for women's rights—the Seneca Falls Convention—is held in New York.

1850 Nathaniel Hawthorne publishes *The Scarlet Letter.*

1855 Boston lets African American children attend white schools.

1860 About 13 percent of the American population is foreign born.

1840	1845	1850	1855	1860

1840 The World's Anti-Slavery Convention is held in London.

1845 A potato famine in Ireland causes more Irish to move to the United States.

1860 In England Florence Nightingale founds the first school for training nurses.

In 1907 Florence Nightingale became the first woman to receive Britain's Order of Merit.

You Be the Historian

Themes Journal

What's Your Opinion? Do you **agree** or **disagree** with the following statements? Support your point of view in your journal.

- **Culture** People should try to improve the lives of the less fortunate.
- **Economics** Immigration makes a country's economy grow.
- **Citizenship** Citizens should try to change laws that they feel are unjust.

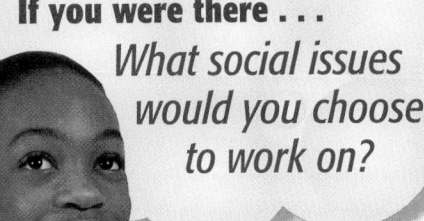

If you were there . . .
What social issues would you choose to work on?

★ Biography

Florence Nightingale. Despite her family's protests, Englishwoman Florence Nightingale went to Germany at the age of 30 to study nursing. When she returned to England, she became the superintendent of a London hospital. Nightingale was so successful at reorganizing that institution that she was appointed head of a group of nurses who were sent to care for the wounded in the Crimean War. She arrived at the front in 1854 and immediately started to improve the war hospitals. Through donations and by using her own money she supplied bedding, clothing, eating utensils, and food to the wounded soldiers. By the end of her first year in the Crimea, the mortality rate among wounded soldiers had decreased dramatically.

CRITICAL THINKING

Why do you think Florence Nightingale's family objected to her becoming a nurse?

ANSWER: Students might suggest that her family did not think women should work or be exposed to disease and disorder.

Section 1

OBJECTIVES

- ★ Examine how religion affected Americans during the Second Great Awakening.
- ★ Describe the transcendentalists' views of American society.
- ★ Identify some ideas of the romantic movement.

LET'S GET STARTED!

Write the following question on the chalkboard: *What changes in traditional belief systems, religion, and ways of treating people do you think could improve society?* As students enter the classroom, allow time for them to respond. *(Students' responses will vary.)* Tell students that in Section 1 they will learn about how ideas for improving traditional institutions sparked new social and artistic movements in the early to mid-1800s.

SECTION 1 RESOURCES

REPRODUCIBLE

- ▶ Guided Reading Strategy 15.1
- ▶ Geography Activity 15: Utopian Communities

TECHNOLOGY

- ▶ One-Stop Planner, Lesson 15.1
- ▶ Exploring America's Past Video Segment: Spirit of the Times; Teacher's Guide, pp. 24–25
- ▶ Art in American History Transparency 11: Thunderstorm in the Rocky Mountains
- ▶ Homework Practice Online
- ▶ HRW Go site

REINFORCEMENT, REVIEW, AND ASSESSMENT

- ▶ Section 1 Review, p. 456
- ▶ Daily Quiz 15.1
- ▶ Main Idea Activity 15.1
- ▶ English Audio Summary 15.1
- ▶ Spanish Audio Summary 15.1

DAILY LIFE ANSWER
(for p. 453)
Students might suggest that the attendees are praying and lifting their hands to God.

Section 1

America's Spiritual Awakening

Read to Discover

1. How did religion affect Americans during the Second Great Awakening?
2. What were the transcendentalists' views of American society?
3. What were some ideas of the romantic movement?

WHY IT MATTERS TODAY

Art is a way to learn more about a culture or a community. Use **CNNfyi.com** or other **current events** sources to learn more about an American writer who is alive today. Record your findings in your journal.

Define

- transcendentalism
- utopian communities

Identify

- Second Great Awakening
- Charles Grandison Finney
- Ralph Waldo Emerson
- Margaret Fuller
- Henry David Thoreau
- Thomas Cole
- Nathaniel Hawthorne
- Edgar Allan Poe
- Emily Dickinson
- Walt Whitman

Traveling ministers were key to the success of the Second Great Awakening.

The Story Continues

In her early teens, New Yorker Huldah Baldwin began thinking seriously about her spiritual life. When she became deathly ill, she asked relatives and friends to come to her bedside. She was concerned about the state of their souls. She pleaded with her family members as death grew near. "O live for him [God] that we may meet hereafter and enjoy a blessed eternity together." Such deep religious beliefs were increasingly common in the early 1800s in New York.

★ The Second Great Awakening

Beginning in the 1790s some Americans took part in a movement of Christian renewal called the **Second Great Awakening**. It swept through towns across upstate New York and through the frontier regions of Kentucky, Ohio, Tennessee, and South Carolina. By the 1820s and 1830s this new interest in religion had spread to New England, the Appalachians, and the South.

★ **TEACH**

Have students read Section 1 and complete Guided Reading Strategy 15.1. Choose one or more of the following activities to explore the section content with students. For further suggestions on block scheduling or team teaching, see the *Block Scheduling Handbook with Team Teaching Strategies.*

LEVELS 1 AND 2: Draw two columns on the chalkboard. Have students suggest things that people want but do not need, and write their suggestions in one column. Then have them suggest items that are essential to survival, and write those things in the second column. Lead a discussion in which students explain their choices, and compare the two lists. Organize students into small groups and have them imagine that, like transcendentalist Henry David Thoreau, they have isolated themselves from society. Have them write journal entries describing the transcendentalists' views of society. **ENGLISH LANGUAGE LEARNERS ,**
COOPERATIVE LEARNING

<u>Charles Grandison Finney</u> was one of the most important leaders of the Second Great Awakening. After experiencing a dramatic religious conversion in 1821, Finney left his career as a lawyer and began preaching. Speaking in a forceful and direct style, Finney challenged some traditional Protestant beliefs. He told congregations that each individual was responsible for his or her own salvation. He also believed that sin was avoidable. Finney held prayer meetings that would last for days. Many people converted to Christianity during these revivals. Finney told these converts to demonstrate their faith by doing good deeds.

Finney's preaching angered some traditional ministers like Lyman Beecher of Boston. Beecher wanted to prevent Finney from holding revivals in the city. "You mean to carry a streak of fire to Boston. If you attempt it, as the Lord liveth, I'll meet you . . . and fight every inch of the way." However, the First Amendment guarantee of freedom of religion prevented local or state governments from passing laws banning the new religious practices. Ministers were thus free to spread their message of faith and salvation to whomever wished to listen.

As a result of their efforts, church membership across the country grew a great deal during the Second Great Awakening. Many of these new church members were women. African Americans were among those drawn to the new religious movement. Some became Baptist, Methodist, or Presbyterian ministers. The African Methodist Episcopal Church spread across the Middle Atlantic states. Although the movement had begun in the Northeast and on the frontier, the Second Great Awakening renewed Americans' religious faith throughout the country.

✔ **Reading Check: Finding the Main Idea** How did the Second Great Awakening affect Americans? It renewed their religious faith, and led to increased church membership, particularly among African Americans and women.

In 1794 Richard Allen founded the Bethel African Methodist Episcopal Church in Philadelphia.

Daily Life

Revival Meetings Religious revivals swept the United States in the early 1800s. Some meetings drew up to 20,000 people at a time to huge outdoor camps. James Finley, who later became a Methodist preacher, described one revival as a "vast sea of human beings [that] seemed to be agitated as if by a storm." Preachers traveled from town to town, urging sinners to seek salvation. **How does this image portray the emotional qualities of a revival meeting?**

★ **Culture**

The End of the World.
This new interest in religion touched a preacher named William Miller in the 1840s. He attracted around 100,000 followers with his proclamation that the apocalypse, or the end of the world, would occur sometime between 1843 and 1844. When the apocalypse did not occur, Millerites revised their beliefs. Some of today's denominations have been influenced by Millerite doctrines.

CRITICAL THINKING
What religious purposes might Miller's "end of the world" belief have served?

ANSWER: Students might suggest that followers could be convinced to convert or change their ways since they believed the end of the world was so near.

Technology Resources

 Exploring America's Past Video Segment: Spirit of the Times; Teacher's Guide, pp. 24–25.

Search 22931, Play to 29183
Videodisc Red Side B
See *Teacher's Guide* for Spanish barcode.

THE GRANGER COLLECTION, NEW YORK

Interpreting the Visual Record

Utopian communities *Brook Farm, a utopian community in Massachusetts, attracted a number of famous writers.* **What do you see in this picture that might attract people to live there?**

Analyzing Primary Sources

Drawing Inferences and Conclusions Why did Thoreau live in a cabin in the woods? Students might say that he wanted to live a simpler life.

★ Transcendentalism and Utopian Communities

Some New England writers and thinkers found spiritual inspiration in **transcendentalism**. Transcendentalism was the belief that people could transcend, or rise above, the material things in life, such as money and personal belongings. Transcendentalists believed that people should depend on themselves instead of upon outside authority. Some important figures who believed in this philosophy were **Ralph Waldo Emerson**, **Margaret Fuller**, and **Henry David Thoreau**.

Emerson wrote an essay titled "Self-Reliance" in 1841. In this essay, he said that Americans depended too much on institutions and traditions. Emerson wanted people to follow their personal beliefs and use their own judgment. "What I must do is all that concerns me, not what the people think," he wrote. Fuller edited the transcendentalist publication *The Dial*. In 1845 she wrote a book called *Woman in the Nineteenth Century*. In it, she said that women had the right to choose their own paths in life. Some people saw her as a champion of women's rights.

Thoreau also believed in self-reliance and did not trust institutions. He expressed many of his ideas in *Walden, or Life in the Woods*, published in 1854. For two years, Thoreau lived alone in a small cabin in Massachusetts. He wrote about his experiences living near Walden Pond.

Primary Sources
"I went to the woods because I wished to live deliberately [with a purpose], to front [experience] only the essential facts of life, and see if I could learn what it had to teach, and not, when I came to die, discover that I had not lived."

—Henry David Thoreau, *Walden*

In the 1840s some transcendentalists formed a community at Brook Farm, Massachusetts. Brook Farm did not last very long, however. It was one of many experiments with **utopian communities** that took place in America. These communities tried to form a perfect society on Earth. Some Americans founded utopian communities as places to practice their religious beliefs. In 1774 Ann Lee started a community of Shakers—so named because their bodies would often shake during worship. By the 1830s this group had about 6,000 members living in various communities. The Shakers did not believe in private ownership of property and lived a very plain lifestyle. The furniture they made reflected their simple approach to life.

LEVEL 3: Lead a discussion on the Second Great Awakening, focusing on the ideas it spread and how it affected the people who responded to it. Ask students to imagine that they are Charles Grandison Finney and are touring the country preaching the ideas of the Second Great Awakening. Ask students to write a speech that Finney might have given that explains how religion could affect Americans during the Second Great Awakening.

HOMEWORK Have students create either a poem or a work of art in the romantic style. Also have the students that create a work of art write a caption to accompany their artwork, explaining how their work reflects the romantic movement. Display students' work and captions in the classroom for others to view.

☆ CLOSE

Remind students that a utopian society is designed to be a "perfect society" in which all community members divide responsibilities equally and work for the greater good of the community. Have students plan their own utopia, describing the following: the form of government they would establish, the way work would be shared among the community members, what schools would be like, and what the lifestyle would be like. Encourage students to include ideas that were used by the societies discussed in the textbook. Have volunteers present their ideas to the class.

Other utopian communities were based on social philosophies. Many groups wanted men and women to be equal. Mary Paul, a member of a group in Red Bank, New Jersey, explained this view. She said that in the community "both men and women have the *same pay* for the *same* work." Such utopian communities allowed people to pursue spiritual and cooperative lifestyles. However, only a few of these communities lasted very long. Most groups failed to get their members to work together well enough for the community to survive.

✔ **Reading Check: Identifying Points of View** How did transcendentalists believe people should live? by following their personal ideas and their own judgment, and simply, without regard to wealth or possessions

★ The American Romantics

Ideas about spirituality, the simple life, and nature also shaped painters and writers in the early 1800s. Some artists became part of the romantic movement, which began in Europe and drew upon the idea that each person brings a unique view to the world. Romantic artists such as **Thomas Cole** painted the American landscape. These images of nature and the wilderness contrasted with the large cities and the corruption that many Americans saw in Europe.

During this time the number of notable American authors grew. Many female authors, such as Ann Sophia Stephens, wrote historical fiction. These works became very popular during the mid-1800s. One of the best-known examples of romantic literature is *The Scarlet Letter*. This novel by New England writer **Nathaniel Hawthorne** describes Puritan life in the 1600s. Hawthorne's friend Herman Melville was a writer and a former sailor who wrote tales of the sea. *Moby-Dick* and *Billy Budd* are some of his more famous works.

Along with novels, American romantic authors also wrote many famous short stories and poems. **Edgar Allan Poe**, for example, is best known for his short stories and poetry. A verse from Poe's haunting poem, "The Raven," follows.

> **❝Once upon a midnight dreary,[1]
> while I pondered,[2] weak and weary,
> Over many a quaint[3] and curious
> volume of forgotten lore[4] —
> While I nodded, nearly napping,
> suddenly there came a tapping,
> As of some one gently rapping,
> rapping at my chamber door—
> ''Tis some visiter,' I muttered,
> 'tapping at my chamber door—
> Only this and nothing more.'❞**

—Edgar Allan Poe, "The Raven," from *Anthology of American Literature*, edited by George McMichael

---

[1]**dreary:** gloomy [2]**pondered:** thought [3]**quaint:** odd [4]**lore:** legends

This illustration shows a scene from Edgar Allen Poe's poem "The Raven."

Interdisciplinary Connection

▶Literature◀

A Lady Romantic. Emily Dickinson was one of the few female authors who found her literary voice within the American Romantic movement. Although some of Dickinson's poems were published before 1955, it wasn't until that time that all 1,775 were edited and compiled into a three-volume set—nearly 80 years after her death. Dickinson's unusual poetic style was slow to earn praise from critics, but it inspired a new generation of poets who liked her imagery and symbolism. The fact that she seldom left her home and that her poetry covered such a wide range of styles and emotions has made understanding her life and categorizing her poetry difficult.

CRITICAL THINKING

Why was Dickinson's poetry inspirational to poets nearly a century after her death?

ANSWER: Students might suggest that its use of imagery and symbolism appealed to a later generation.

CONNECTING TO LITERATURE ANSWER
(for p. 456)
Dickinson's poetry was her form of communication with the public.

★ REVIEW AND ASSESS

Have students complete the **Section 1 Review** on p. 456. Then have students complete **Daily Quiz 15.1.** As **Alternative Assessment**, you may want to use the romantic movement graphic organizer or the Finney speech in this section's lessons.

★ RETEACH

Have students complete **Main Idea Activity for English Language Learners and Special-Needs Students 15.1.** Then have each student write a question about the Second Great Awakening, the transcendentalists, and the romantic movement. Organize the class into two teams and conduct a game

show style review session. **ENGLISH LANGUAGE LEARNERS , COOPERATIVE LEARNING**

★ EXTEND

Lead a discussion about the American romantics, focusing on how they treated the following themes: the beauty and power of nature contrasted with corrupt European civilizations, expansion of the United States onto the frontier, American individualism, democracy, and the beauty and power of nature contrasted with Western civilizations. Have students review a work by an artist or writer discussed in this section. Tell them to identify the themes that the work addresses, rate the work using a four-star system, and describe its influence on American culture in the 1800s. **BLOCK SCHEDULING**

Section 1 Review
ANSWERS

❶ Define
- transcendentalism, p. 454
- utopian communities, p. 454

❷ Identify
- Second Great Awakening, p. 452
- Charles Grandison Finney, p. 453
- Ralph Waldo Emerson, p.454
- Margaret Fuller, p. 454
- Henry David Thoreau, p. 454
- Thomas Cole, p. 455
- Nathaniel Hawthorne, p. 455
- Edgar Allen Poe, p. 455
- Emily Dickinson, p. 456
- Walt Whitman, p. 456

❸ religion—individual responsibility for salvation, sin was avoidable; philosophy—transcendentalism, utopian communities; art—romantic movement; and literature—romantic movement

❹ a. period of widespread evangelism that spread from the northeast throughout the country; renewed religious faith, church membership increased, African Americans and women became particularly involved
b. criticized reliance on institutions and traditions and their focus on material possessions

❺ Students' poems will vary but should reflect the ideas of the romantic movement and the student's perspective.

CONNECTING TO *Literature*

"This Is My Letter to the World"

Emily Dickinson

Born in 1830, Emily Dickinson led a quiet life in Amherst, Massachusetts. Her first published collection of poetry included the following selection.

This is my letter to the World
That never wrote to Me—
The simple News that Nature told—
With tender Majesty

Her Message is committed
To Hands I cannot see—
For love of Her—Sweet—countrymen
Judge tenderly—of Me.

Understanding What You Read
Literature and History What does Dickinson mean by her "Letter to the World"?

The United States produced several other gifted American poets during this period. These writers included **Emily Dickinson**, Henry Wadsworth Longfellow, John Greenleaf Whittier, and **Walt Whitman**. Only two of Dickinson's poems were published during her lifetime, both anonymously. After her death in 1886, her family discovered hundreds of her poems, some written on loose scraps of paper. Longfellow was the best-known poet of the mid-1800s. His long story-poems, such as *Hiawatha*, the *Courtship of Miles Standish*, and *Tales of a Wayside Inn* became favorites in many American households. Whittier spoke out against slavery in works such as *Poems Written during the Progress of the Abolition Question.*

Walt Whitman praised both American individualism and democracy in his simple, unrhymed poetry. His work *Leaves of Grass*, published in 1855, is noted for its distinct style. Whitman expressed his view of America's poetic gifts in the preface to *Leaves of Grass*. "Americans of all nations at any time upon the earth have probably the fullest poetical nature," he wrote. "The United States themselves are essentially the greatest poem."

✔ **Reading Check: Analyzing Information** What was the romantic movement, and who were some of the major American artists and writers of this movement? a movement that began in Europe and that drew on individual perspective; see discussion above

go. hrw .com **Homework Practice Online**
keyword: SA3 HP15

Section 1 Review

❶ Define and explain:
- transcendentalism
- utopian communities

❷ Identify and explain:
- Second Great Awakening
- Charles Grandison Finney
- Ralph Waldo Emerson
- Margaret Fuller
- Henry David Thoreau
- Thomas Cole
- Nathaniel Hawthorne
- Edgar Allan Poe
- Emily Dickinson
- Walt Whitman

❸ Summarizing Copy the graphic organizer below. Use it to identify the new ideas that emerged from religion, philosophy, art, and literature during the early 1800s.

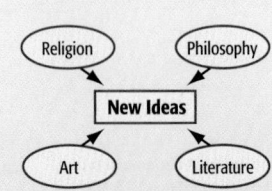

❹ Finding the Main Idea
a. What was the Second Great Awakening, and what effect did it have on religious life in America?

b. How did the transcendentalists describe American society?

❺ Writing and Critical Thinking
Analyzing Information Imagine that you are an American poet in the early 1800s. Write a poem on a subject of your choice based on the style of the romantics.

Consider the following:
- the work of other romantic poets and writers
- your personal perspective on life
- an appeal to your readers' emotions

Section 2

OBJECTIVES

★ Explain why so many Irish and German immigrants came to the United States in the 1840s and 1850s.

★ Discuss some Americans' reactions to immigrants.

★ Describe what caused U.S. cities to grow, and analyze the benefits and problems this growth created.

🎵 LET'S GET STARTED!

As students enter the classroom, distribute maps of the world. Ask students to fill in their maps with the birthplaces of some famous U.S. citizens who were born in foreign countries. *(Students' maps will vary.)* Then ask for volunteers to share their maps with the class. Tell students that in Section 2 they will learn about how the United States is made up of people from many different nations and about immigration to the United States in the mid-1800s.

Section 2

Immigrants and Cities

Read to Discover

1. Why did so many Irish and German immigrants come to the United States in the 1840s and 1850s?
2. How did some Americans react to immigrants?
3. What caused U.S. cities to grow, and what benefits and problems did this growth create?

WHY IT MATTERS TODAY

Many immigrants are still drawn to the United States today. Use CNNfyi.com or other **current events** sources to learn why people immigrate to the United States. Record your findings in your journal.

Define

- nativists
- middle class
- tenements

Identify

- Know-Nothing Party

SECTION 2 RESOURCES

REPRODUCIBLE

▶ Guided Reading Strategy 15.2

TECHNOLOGY

▶ One-Stop Planner, Lesson 15.2

▶ Linking Geography and History Transparency 13: Sources of Immigration, 1831–1860

▶ CNN Presents America: Beginnings to 1914 Segment: The Irish Potato Famine

▶ Homework Practice Online

REINFORCEMENT, REVIEW, AND ASSESSMENT

▶ Section 2 Review, p. 461
▶ Daily Quiz 15.2
▶ Main Idea Activity 15.2
▶ English Audio Summary 15.2
▶ Spanish Audio Summary 15.2

The Story Continues

Irish immigrants to the United States traveled in tightly packed sections of ships. They received little fresh air or light on their long journey. Dozens of immigrants suffered and died from fever and disease. In Herman Melville's story *Redburn*, a cabin boy describes one such journey in which fever had a terrible effect on the passengers. "By their own countrymen, they were torn from the clasp [embrace] of their wives . . . and with hurried rites [ceremonies], were dropped into the ocean." Of the millions of immigrants who left their homes in the mid-1800s, not all made it safely across the Atlantic.

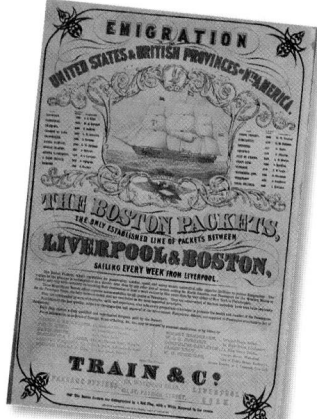

Advertisements like this one encouraged people to immigrate to the United States.

★ Waves of Immigrants

In the mid-1800s large numbers of immigrants crossed the Atlantic Ocean to begin new lives in the United States. More than 4 million immigrants settled in the United States between 1840 and 1860, most of them from Europe. More than 3 million of these immigrants were German or Irish. Many immigrants were fleeing economic or political troubles in their native countries.

Have students read Section 2 and complete Guided Reading Strategy 15.2. Choose one or more of the following activities to explore the section content with students. For further suggestions on block scheduling or team teaching, see the *Block Scheduling Handbook with Team Teaching Strategies*.

LEVEL 1: Discuss with students the reasons that many Irish and German immigrants came to the United States in the 1840s and 1850s. *(Students' responses should suggest that many Irish immigrants came to escape the potato blight, starvation, and disease, and that many German*

immigrants came to escape persecution and pursue economic opportunities.) Have students imagine that they are either Irish or German immigrants traveling to the United States. Have them prepare a series of drawings illustrating the reasons they left their homeland, their experiences on the ship, and what they hope to find in the United States. Display students' work around the classroom. **ENGLISH LANGUAGE LEARNERS**

Note: To help students make meaningful connections between events in American history and those in their own hometown, use the Chapter 14 **Hands-On History** activity, Public Education in Your Community.

★ **Daily Life**

German Aid Societies.
New immigrants faced many dangers in the United States, including scam artists and dangerous jobs. Some societies formed to help newcomers adjust to and prosper in their new country. They also helped focus on poor traveling and housing conditions for immigrants. The German Society of the City of New York was one such organization. The group worked for the passage of state and federal laws to protect immigrants, and succeeded despite heavy opposition. The German Society still exists today.

CRITICAL THINKING
What types of activities do you think the German Society might sponsor today?

ANSWER: Students might suggest activities that foster German cultural awareness or laws that help German immigration.

CONNECTING TO MATH ANSWERS
1. domestic servants
2. Students' graphs should present an accurate depiction of statistics in the chart.
3. Students' letters will vary but should mention the number of occupations in which immigrants can find work.

CONNECTING TO
MATH

Just the Facts

Some Occupations of Immigrants in New York, 1855

Occupation	Total Number of Workers	Foreign-Born Workers
Bakers	3,692	3,323
Blacksmiths	2,642	2,159
Leather workers	1,386	980
Jewelers	1,705	1,037
Carpenters	7,531	4,863
Clerks	13,929	5,921
Dressmakers/ seamstresses	9,819	6,606
Shoemakers/ tailors	19,354	18,600
Domestic servants	31,749	29,470
Merchants	6,299	1,705
Physicians	1,469	566

Using Mathematical Skills

1. Which occupation had the highest number of immigrant workers in 1855?
2. Create a bar graph that compares the total number of workers to the number of foreign-born workers.
3. Imagine that you are an immigrant. Write a letter to family members overseas, using the statistics in this chart to persuade them to immigrate to New York City.

Most immigrants from the British Isles during this period were Irish. In the mid-1840s potato blight, a disease that causes rot, left many families in Ireland with little food. Tomas Francis Meagher, an Irish leader, sadly commented, "One business survives! . . . That fortunate business . . . is the Irish coffin-maker's." More than 1 million Irish people died of starvation and disease. Even more fled to the United States. Most Irish immigrants were very poor. Many settled in towns and cities in Massachusetts, New Jersey, New York, and Pennsylvania. Those who did not live in cities commonly worked on building canals and railroads. Irish women often worked as domestic servants for wealthy families, laboring 16 hours or more a day. Irish men in the cities could usually find only unskilled work. As an 1849 Boston health committee reported, low wages forced most Irish immigrants to live in poor housing.

Nevertheless, some immigrants enjoyed a new feeling of equality. Patrick Dunny wrote home to his family about this situation.

History Makers Speak

66 People that cuts a great dash [style] at home . . . think it strange [in the United States] for the humble class of people to get as much respect as themselves. 99

—Patrick Dunny, quoted in *Who Built America?*, by Bruce Levine et al.

Many Germans also came to the United States during this time. In 1848, numbers of German people had revolted against harsh rule. Some educated Germans came to the United States to escape persecution during this time. However, most of them came for economic reasons. Working-class Germans began to leave as well. These immigrants came in search of new economic opportunity and freedom from government control. While most Irish immigrants were Catholics, German immigrant groups included Protestants, Catholics, and Jews.

Many German immigrants arrived in the United States with money in hand. Germans were more likely than the Irish to become farmers and to live in rural areas. They moved particularly to midwestern states such as Michigan, Ohio, and Wisconsin where more land was available than in the eastern United States. German immigrants—like the Irish—often had to take low-paying jobs, despite their skills. The *Chicago Daily Tribune* declared that the German immigrant population was "fitted to do the cheap . . . labor of the country."

✔ **Reading Check: Comparing and Contrasting** What factors—both similar and different—led Irish and German people to immigrate to the United States in the mid-1800s? Irish—to find jobs, escape potato blight, starvation, disease; Germans—to escape persecution, pursue economic opportunity

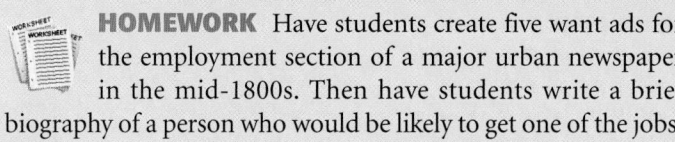

HOMEWORK Have students create five want ads for the employment section of a major urban newspaper in the mid-1800s. Then have students write a brief biography of a person who would be likely to get one of the jobs.

ALL LEVELS: Discuss with students the reasons for the growth of U.S. cities. Then copy the following graphic organizer onto the chalkboard, omitting the italicized answers. Ask students to complete the organizer by listing the problems and benefits of growing U.S. cities during the mid-1800s. **ENGLISH LANGUAGE LEARNERS**

Growth of U.S. Cities	
Problems	**Benefits**
• *overcrowding*	• *job opportunities*
• *poorly built housing*	• *growth of middle class*
• *poor sanitation*	• *entertainment and cultural life*
• *no permanent fire or police force*	
• *diseases and epidemics*	
• *lack of public services*	

⭐ The Nativist Response

Industrialization and the waves of people from Europe greatly changed the American labor force. The chance of getting farmland in the Midwest drew many immigrants to this area. Industrial jobs in the Northeast drew many immigrants who filled the need for cheap labor in many towns and cities. These new workers fueled the local economies, which led to the creation of new jobs for clerks, merchants, supervisors, and professional workers.

Yet many native-born citizens feared losing their jobs to immigrants who might work for lower wages. Many native-born Americans also felt threatened by the different cultures and religions of immigrant groups. Before Catholic immigrants arrived, most people living in the United States were Protestants. American Protestants did not always trust Catholic immigrants because of long-standing conflicts between Catholics and Protestants in Europe. Americans who held such views and who opposed immigration were called **nativists**.

In the 1840s and 1850s some of these people became politically active. One of their main goals was to try to stir up anti-immigrant feeling. An 1844 election flyer gave Americans a warning.

History Makers Speak
❝Look at the . . . thieves and vagabonds [tramps], roaming about our streets . . . monopolizing [taking] the business which properly belongs to our own native and true-born citizens.❞

—Election flyer, quoted in *Who Built America?*, by Bruce Levine et al.

In 1849, nativists founded a secret society that became a political organization known as the **Know-Nothing Party**. The party was so named because when asked questions by outsiders, its members usually answered, "I know nothing." The Know-Nothings wanted to keep Catholics and immigrants out of public office. They also wanted immigrants to have to live in the United States for at least 21 years before they could become citizens. Party politicians had some success, winning several state elections during the 1850s. They also controlled the Massachusetts legislature for a short time.

✔ **Reading Check: Analyzing Information** How did anti-Catholicism contribute to the views of nativists and the creation of the Know-Nothing Party? Many nativists did not trust Catholic immigrants. The Know-Nothing Party tried to keep Catholics and immigrants out of public office.

Analyzing Primary Sources
Identifying Bias Why might a reader think that the author of this quotation is a nativist? calling immigrants names, showing fear of immigrants' economic competition

A protest by a nativist group led to this riot in Philadelphia in 1844. Similar riots took place elsewhere in the country.

THE GRANGER COLLECTION, NEW YORK

Technology Resources
Linking Geography and History Transparency 13: Sources of Immigration, 1831–1860

Technology Resources
CNN Presents America: Beginnings to 1914 Segment: The Irish Potato Famine

⚡ CLOSE

Have students write diary entries describing a day in the life of an immigrant. Entries should explain political and social problems that immigrants faced. Encourage volunteers to read their entries to the class.

★ Geography

Life in Rural America.

Social life in rural areas differed greatly from that in the city. Visits with extended family and neighbors provided entertainment for people living in the country. The frequency of these get-togethers depended on the distance people lived from each other. Families on isolated southern plantations met only occasionally for dances, barbecues, and weddings, while men and women in small New England towns might enjoy regular evening visits with neighbors. New Hampshire resident Horace Greeley remembered his parents gathering with neighbors in the evenings to sing and tell stories. Country stores also served as gathering places for neighbors to share the latest town news.

CRITICAL THINKING

Why were patterns of social entertainment in rural areas different from those in the city?

ANSWER: Students might suggest that the availability of resources as well as the distances that people lived from each other affected social patterns.

VISUALIZING HISTORY ANSWERS

1. rural migration, immigration from Europe, transportation revolution, industrial revolution

2. Students might suggest that cities continue to grow for many of the same reasons.

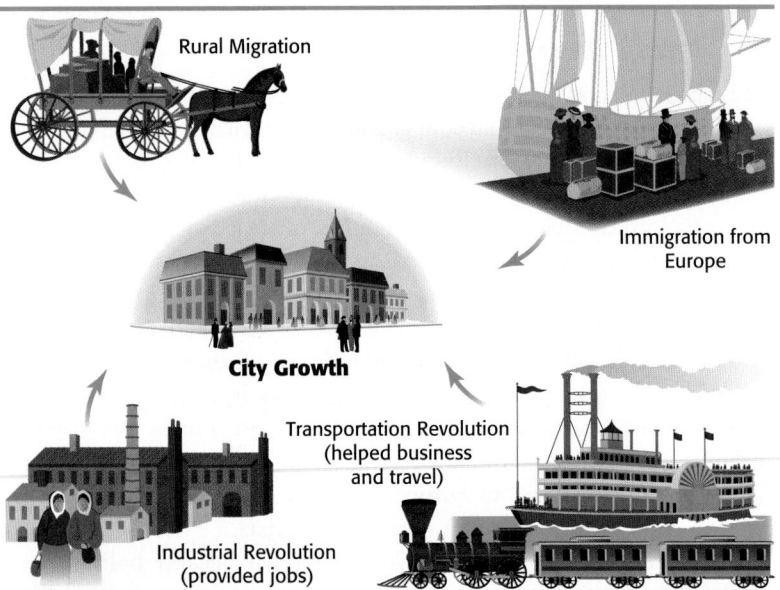

Urban Growth

American cities in the Northeast began to grow rapidly in the mid-1800s.

Visualizing History

1. **Geography** What factors contributed to the growth of American cities?

2. **Connecting to Today** How do you think these factors influence urban growth today?

Rural Migration

Immigration from Europe

City Growth

Transportation Revolution (helped business and travel)

Industrial Revolution (provided jobs)

★★★★★★★★★★★★
That's Interesting!
★★★★★★★★★★★★

Where are the police? Can you imagine a city of more than 500,000 people without a permanent police force? Well, that's just what New York City was like before 1853. Before permanent forces were created, a volunteer night watch patrolled the city. During the daytime, an officer called a constable was on duty. He was paid a fee for each crime that he and his assistants helped stop. Private citizens were also asked to catch criminals. As cities grew larger, crime often grew out of hand. Many constables took bribes to ignore crimes. So the people of New York City created a paid police force.

★ The Growth of Cities

The Industrial Revolution led to the creation of many new jobs in U.S. cities. These city jobs drew immigrants as well as migrants from rural areas. The Transportation Revolution helped connect cities and made it easier for people to move to them. As a result of these two trends, U.S. cities grew rapidly during the mid-1800s. Cities in the northeastern and Middle Atlantic states grew the most. By the mid-1800s three quarters of the country's manufacturing jobs were in these areas.

The rise of industry and the growth of cities changed American life. Those who owned their own businesses or worked in skilled jobs benefited most from the changes. The families of these merchants, manufacturers, professionals, and master craftspeople made up a growing social class. This new **middle class** was a social and economic level between the wealthy and the poor.

In the growing cities, people found entertainment and an enriched cultural life. Many enjoyed visiting places such as libraries and clubs. In the early 1800s people also attended urban theaters. Favorite pastimes, such as bowling and playing cards, also provided recreation for urban residents.

Cities during this time were compact and crowded. Many people walked to work. Wagons carried goods down streets paved with stones, making a noisy, busy scene. One person noted that the professionals in New York City always had "a hurried walk."

✔ **Reading Check: Summarizing** How did the Industrial Revolution and the Transportation Revolution affect life in American cities? new jobs, new economic opportunities, new middle class, improved cultural life, busy and noisy

⭐ Urban Problems

American cities in the early and mid-1800s faced many challenges as a result of their rapid growth. Because public and private transportation was limited, many city residents lived within a short distance of their workplaces. The crowded conditions meant that poor wage workers, members of the rising middle class, and the wealthy often lived near each other. Poor city dwellers often felt that they were treated unfairly by the rich—who in turn often accused the poor of being rude and violent. Disagreements between these social classes led to increasing conflict and sometimes even led to riots.

Other major problems in most large cities were the lack of safe housing and public services. Many people, particularly immigrants, could afford to live only in dirty, overcrowded buildings called **tenements**. Many cities did not have clean water, public health regulations, or clean ways to get rid of garbage and human waste. Diseases spread easily in these unhealthy conditions. In 1832 and 1849, for example, New York City suffered cholera epidemics that killed thousands of people.

Urban areas also became centers of criminal activity. Most cities—including New York City, Boston, and Philadelphia—had no permanent police force to fight crime. Instead, they used volunteer night watches, which offered little protection. Fire protection was often poor as well. Most cities were served by volunteer fire companies. Firefighters had to use hand pumps and buckets to put out fires. All of these conditions combined to make life difficult for many city residents.

During the 1800s poor city residents often lived in overcrowded tenement neighborhoods like this one.

✔ **Reading Check: Analyzing Information** What were some of the problems caused by urbanization? overcrowding, poor housing, disease, conflict between social classes, no permanent police or fire force, general lack of public services

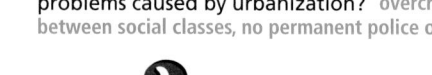

Section 2 Review

go.hrw.com Homework Practice Online

keyword: SA3 HP15

1 **Define** and explain:
• nativists
• middle class
• tenements

2 **Identify** and explain:
• Know-Nothing Party

3 **Identifying Cause and Effect** Copy the graphic organizer below. Use it to identify the causes and effects of immigration and of urban growth.

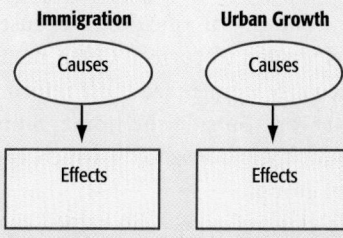

Immigration
Causes → Effects

Urban Growth
Causes → Effects

4 **Finding the Main Idea**
a. Why did many German and Irish people immigrate to the United States between 1840 and 1860?

b. Why did nativists oppose immigration in the mid-1800s?

5 **Writing and Critical Thinking**
Evaluating Imagine that you are visiting a northeastern American city in the mid-1800s. Create a postcard showing a city street scene. On the back of the card, write a short letter to a friend back home that describes the scene.

Consider the following:
• the benefits of city growth
• the problems caused by city growth
• immigration to cities

Section 3

OBJECTIVES

- ★ Analyze how reformers improved prisons in the early and mid-1800s.
- ★ Examine why reformers started the temperance movement.
- ★ Determine how Americans' educational opportunities changed during the early and mid-1800s.

Section 3

Reforming Society

Read to Discover

1. How did reformers improve prisons in the early and mid-1800s?
2. Why did reformers start the temperance movement?
3. How did Americans' educational opportunities change during the early and mid-1800s?

WHY IT MATTERS TODAY

Many Americans today take part in reform efforts. Use **CNNfyi.com** or other **current events** sources to learn about current campaigns for efforts such as education reform. Record your findings in your journal.

Define

- temperance movement
- common-school movement

Identify

- Dorothea Dix
- Lyman Beecher
- Horace Mann
- Catharine Beecher
- Emma Willard
- Mary Lyon
- Samuel Gridley Howe
- Thomas Hopkins Gallaudet

Dorothea Dix helped improve the prison system in the United States.

The Story Continues

In 1841 Dorothea Dix visited a jail in Cambridge, Massachusetts, to teach a Sunday school class. What she saw there shocked her. Mentally ill women were jailed beside common criminals in dirty cells. Dix became angry at the conditions she found there and in other Massachusetts jails. As a result, she began to work to improve the care of mentally ill people across the country. She joined many other women reformers in the early and mid-1800s.

★ Prison Reform

The teachings of the Second Great Awakening had inspired many people to try to improve society. The growth of cities had caused social problems that many Americans wanted to correct. Often members of the growing middle class, particularly women, led these reform efforts. Many of these women did not work outside the home. Some hired domestic servants to help care for their households, which gave them more time to take part in reform groups.

Dorothea Dix was a middle-class reformer who helped change the prison system in the United States. After visiting prisons throughout

Have students read Section 3 and complete Guided Reading Strategy 15.3. Choose one or more of the following activities to explore the section content with students. For further suggestions on block scheduling or team teaching, see the *Block Scheduling Handbook with Team Teaching Strategies.*

LEVELS 1 AND 2: Draw two columns on the chalkboard. Title the first column *Reform Movement,* and the second column *New Laws/Actions Taken.* First, have students list the specific reform movements discussed in the chapter. (*Students' lists should include prison reform, temperance movement, common-school movement, women's educational reform, African American educational reform, and teaching people with disabilities.*) Then have students volunteer answers to fill in the rest of the chart. (*Students' answers should include: prison reform: separate facilities created for mentally ill people, juvenile criminals sent to reform schools instead of prison, houses of correction created; temperance movement: several states banned the sale of alcohol; common-school movement: school budgets and teachers' salaries increased, the school year became longer, teacher training; women's educational reform: college-level institutions and colleges for women opened; African American educational reform: some colleges began to accept African Americans, black colleges founded; teaching people with disabilities: schools for people with disabilities were opened, school workers received training.*)

ENGLISH LANGUAGE LEARNERS

Massachusetts, Dix reported the terrible conditions. Mentally ill people were often jailed with criminals. Dix told the state legislature of her findings in this speech.

History Makers Speak

> ❝I come to present the strong claims of suffering humanity . . . the miserable, the desolate [deserted], the outcast . . . to call your attention to the present state of insane persons confined within this Commonwealth, in cages, closets, cellars, stalls, pens! Chained, naked, beaten with rods, and lashed into obedience.❞

—Dorothea Dix, from *Memorial to the Legislature of Massachusetts*

In response, the government of Massachusetts created special, separate facilities for mentally ill people. The influence of Dix's work spread across the country. Eventually more than 100 state hospitals where mentally ill people received more professional care were built.

Other reformers protested the treatment of young offenders. Children who committed crimes such as begging or stealing were treated the same as adult criminals. Boston mayor Josiah Quincy asked that these young people be given different punishments than adults. In the 1820s several state and local governments founded reform schools for children who were once housed in prisons. In these schools children lived under strict rules. While living there, they received vocational training—learning useful skills through work.

Some reformers also tried to end the overcrowding and cruel conditions in prisons. Their efforts led to the creation of houses of correction. These institutions did not use punishment alone. Instead, they tried to change prisoners' behavior through education.

✔ **Reading Check: Summarizing** How did reformers try to change prisons in the early 1800s? special facilities for mentally ill; different sentences for child offenders; improved conditions; and rehabilitation

Dorothea Dix opposed the use of cages like this one to confine mentally ill people.

Reformers wanted to help prison inmates become productive citizens. These inmates are learning to make hats.

★ Biography

Dorothea Dix. Dorothea Dix was born in 1802 to a middle-class family in rural Maine, but she grew up with other family members in Boston. Her first community activities involved education. She opened a school in 1821 and published several educational books. In 1836 poor health forced her to quit teaching and go to England for a long rest. While in England, Dix met people involved in humanitarian causes, which increased her own interest in reform efforts. She returned to Boston in 1837, where she began her reform efforts in 1841.

internet connect

TOPIC: Dorothea Dix
GO TO: go.hrw.com
KEYWORD: SA3 CF15

Have students search the Internet through the HRW Go site for more information on Dorothea Dix. Ask them to write a brief biography of her life, using standard grammar, spelling, sentence structure, and punctuation.

ALL LEVELS: Copy the following graphic organizer onto the chalkboard, omitting the italicized answers. Then have students complete the organizer with the causes and effects of the American temperance movement.

ENGLISH LANGUAGE LEARNERS

The Temperance Movement

Cause: *belief that alcohol abuse led to social problems, such as family violence, poverty, and criminal behavior*

Cause: *prevention of alcohol abuse*

Cause: *worry over the effects of alcohol*

Effects: *Maine and 12 other states passed laws making the sale of alcohol illegal*

★ Citizenship

Opposition to Prohibition.

Some people opposed prohibition, or laws that made it illegal to produce or sell alcohol. Even if they supported temperance, these opponents believed that the church, and not the state, should provide the moral leadership to control the abuse of alcohol.

CRITICAL THINKING

Why might people believe in temperance but not in prohibition?

ANSWER: Students might suggest that these people believed that the state should not make laws to control moral behavior.

Technology Resources

Everyday Life in America Transparency 9: Message Art: Temperance in the Early 1800s

Visual Record Answer

Students might suggest the picture of the "perfect" family could encourage people to give up drinking.

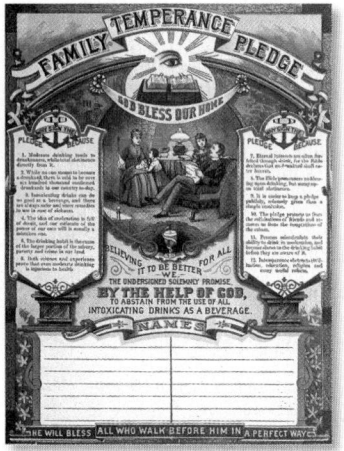

Interpreting the Visual Record

Temperance *Posters like this one urged people to stop drinking and thus help their families.* **How do the scenes in this picture encourage people to give up drinking?**

★ Campaigning against Alcohol Abuse

A number of reformers also worked to prevent alcohol abuse. Many people believed that Americans were drinking liquor at an alarming rate in the early and mid-1800s. During the 1830s the average alcohol consumption per person was seven gallons a year. Abraham Lincoln recalled that in his youth liquor was an "angel of death." Many reformers believed alcohol abuse caused social problems such as family violence, poverty, and criminal behavior.

Americans' worries about the effects of alcohol led to the growth of a **temperance movement**. This social reform effort urged people to stop drinking hard liquor and limit drinking of beer and wine to small amounts. Various groups such as the American Temperance Society and the American Temperance Union helped spread this message. Minister **Lyman Beecher** spoke widely about the evils of alcohol. He said that people who drank alcohol were "neglecting the education of their families—and corrupting their morals."

Many people across the country were in favor of the temperance movement. However, some people believed that temperance alone would not fix social problems caused by alcohol abuse. People such as Neal Dow of Maine wanted to outlaw the sale of alcohol. Dow's efforts resulted in the Maine Law of 1846, which made selling alcohol illegal in the state. Banning the sale of alcohol became a major goal of reformers. By 1855 a dozen other states had passed laws like the one in Maine.

✔ **Reading Check: Finding the Main Idea** What were the goals of the temperance movement? to get people to stop drinking hard liquor and drink beer and wine only in small amounts; to attempt to prevent social problems caused by alcohol abuse

★ Education in America

Another problem facing America in the early 1800s was poor public education. As immigration increased, reformers argued that education would help Americans become good workers and citizens. Most families in the United States believed education was important. However, they did not expect their children to receive a great deal of formal schooling. Many children worked in factories or on farms to help support their families. Parents generally wanted their children to be able to read the Bible, write, and do simple math.

The availability of education varied a great deal throughout the United States. New England had the most schoolhouses, while the South and the West had the fewest. Most schoolteachers were untrained young men. They often taught for a short time before becoming farmers or practicing another trade. Teachers usually worked in small, poorly built schoolhouses, teaching students of many ages and abilities. As reformer Horace Mann wrote, students ranged from "infants just out of their cradles" to "men . . . enrolled in the militia."

Note: For an additional teaching idea, see the Chapter 14 Open Interviewing activity in the **Creative Teaching Strategies** handbook.

 ALL LEVELS: Organize students into three groups. Assign each group one of the following topics about educational reform: the common-school movement, women's education, African American schools, or teaching people with disabilities. Have students create annotated time lines covering the years between 1800 and 1860 that include significant events of their reform movement. Students should include a title and a brief caption summarizing each event on their time lines. **ENGLISH LANGUAGE LEARNERS**, **COOPERATIVE LEARNING**

Mary reciting her Lesson.

THE GRANGER COLLECTION, NEW YORK

GALLERY OF AMERICAN ART, PHILLIPS ACADEMY

Science, Technology & Society

Publishing School Textbooks. Although classroom instruction in the United States remained limited, technological and economic developments made it possible for an increasing number of students to take advantage of education. New printing techniques made producing textbooks less costly. In addition, books became more widely distributed. These developments meant that more schools could serve more students for longer periods of time.

CRITICAL THINKING

Why might an increase in textbooks bring about improvements in education?

ANSWER: Students might suggest that fewer students would be required to share books and that more students could be taught in a classroom.

The textbooks most often used in public schools in the mid-1800s were the McGuffey's *Readers*. William Holmes McGuffey, an educator and Presbyterian minister, put together these textbooks. They were made up mostly of selections from British and American literature. McGuffey's *Readers* were used to teach students about moral and social values as well as literature and reading.

People from different backgrounds received very different educations in the United States. Rich people could send their children to private schools or hire private tutors. However, poor children could only attend public school. Girls could attend school, but parents kept them home more often than boys. The result was that fewer girls learned to read.

Interpreting the Visual Record

Early schools *Many children attended one-room schoolhouses in their local communities. Primers such as the one shown above were the most common textbooks.* **How is the school shown here similar to or different from yours?**

★ The Common-School Movement

To teach children the necessary values and skills, reformers called for better schools. People in the **common-school movement** wanted all children educated in a common place, regardless of class or background. **Horace Mann** was the leading voice for education reform in the mid-1800s. He explained the idea of the common school.

History Makers Speak ❝It is on this common platform that a general acquaintance-ship [friendship] should be formed between the children of the same neighborhood. It is here that the affinities [bonds] of a common nature should unite them together.❞

—Horace Mann, quoted in *The Age of the Common School, 1830–1865*, by Frederick M. Binder

Analyzing Primary Sources

Supporting a Point of View Do you agree with Horace Mann's idea? Why or why not? answers may vary but should reflect an understanding of the common-school philosophy

Mann became the first secretary of education for Massachusetts in 1837. The former lawyer and state legislator worked very hard—speaking, traveling, and writing—to help improve children's education. He doubled the state school budget and helped teachers earn better salaries. He also made the school year longer and founded the first school for teacher training.

Visual Record Answer

Students might suggest that their schools have more than one room and there are individual desks for students.

LEVELS 2 AND 3: Describe the conditions in prisons during the 1800s. Have students imagine that they are members of a an organization that is seeking prison reform. Then ask students to think about living conditions, who should be placed in prisons, the privileges prisoners should be allowed, and how to deal with juvenile offenders. Ask students to suggest what they might include in a bill of rights for prisoners. *(Student's responses will vary but should include humanitarian reforms to counter the inhumane conditions.)* Write students' suggestions on the chalkboard. Then ask students to compare their ideas to the actual reform efforts made in the early 1800s. *(Students' comparisons should indicate the creation of special facilities for the mentally ill, different sentences*

for child offenders, improvement of overcrowded and inhumane conditions, and rehabilitation through education.)

ENGLISH LANGUAGE LEARNERS

LEVEL 3: Have students create graphic organizers comparing how educational opportunities changed during the early 1800s for the following groups: women, African Americans, and individuals with disabilities. Tell students that their organizers should include the following information: pioneers and leaders of the movement, schools involved in the reform movement, geographical areas in which each reform movement took place, and the long-term effects of each movement. Have volunteers share their organizers with the class.

★ Citizenship

Graduates of Troy Seminary. Emma Willard believed that women's education was critical to the success of the nation because women could best train its future citizens. The graduates of Willard's Troy Seminary extended the educator's influence and philosophy from New England to the South. An example of a typical graduate of Troy Seminary was Caroline Livy, who became principal of the local female academy in Rome, Georgia. More than 5,000 girls attended Livy's school under her leadership.

CRITICAL THINKING

How did Willard's educational philosophy spread throughout the country?

ANSWER: Students should note that graduates of Willard's Seminary headed their own schools throughout the country.

ANDOVER, MA   GIFT OF MAXIM KAROLIK, COURTESY, MUSEUM OF FINE ARTS   BOSTON

Beyond grade school, classes for women were usually separated from classes for men.

Mann's ideas on education spread throughout the United States, and to Latin America and Europe as well. Mann won over many other educators by saying that "the common school, improved and energized, may become the most effective . . . of all the forces of civilization." Mann's work set the standard for education reform throughout the country.

✔ **Reading Check: Summarizing** Why did Horace Mann want to improve schools, and what did he accomplish? concerned about the quality of education; supported common-school movement, increased budget and salaries, extended school year, and founded first teacher training school

★ Women's Education

The education reform movement also created greater opportunities for women. Before the 1820s few women in the United States could attend classes beyond grade school. **Catharine Beecher**, daughter of Lyman Beecher, grew up in a family committed to social reform. She became one of the most effective reformers of women's education in the early 1800s.

Catharine Beecher believed that women were better at teaching the moral lessons that made good citizens. "Let every woman become so . . . refined in intellect that her taste and judgment will be respected," she wrote. Beecher started an all-female academy in Hartford, Connecticut. She also wrote several important essays, including *On the Education of Female Teachers.*

In 1821 the citizens of Troy, New York, called on educator **Emma Willard** to found a college-level institution for women. Willard's Troy Female Seminary was the first school of its kind in the United States. At this school women studied many different subjects, ranging from mathematics to philosophy. Between 1821 and 1872, more than 12,000 women attended the school.

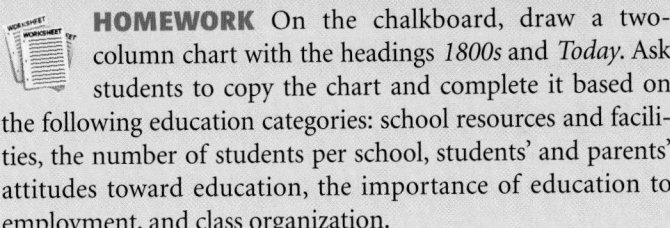

HOMEWORK On the chalkboard, draw a two-column chart with the headings *1800s* and *Today*. Ask students to copy the chart and complete it based on the following education categories: school resources and facilities, the number of students per school, students' and parents' attitudes toward education, the importance of education to employment, and class organization.

✪ CLOSE

Ask each student to write a magazine article based on the following question: *How relevant are the reform movements of the 1800s for modern society?* Ask students to identify how the individual reform movements affected either temperance, prisons, or education.

Several women's colleges opened in the 1830s. One of these colleges was Mount Holyoke Seminary in Massachusetts, founded by educator **Mary Lyon** in 1837. Lyon answered critics of her work by saying, "I am doing a great work, I cannot come down." In 1837 Oberlin College, located in Ohio, became the first co-educational college in the United States. This meant that both men and women were allowed to study there.

✪ African American Schools

Free African Americans also enjoyed some benefits of education reform. Although African Americans found more educational opportunities, they almost always went to separate schools from white students. The New York African Free School, which had opened in New York City in 1787, produced some notable scholars and leaders, such as Henry Highland Garnet.

The people of Philadelphia also supported the development of African American education. By 1800 the city had seven schools for black students. In 1820 Boston opened a separate elementary school for African American children. Also, in 1855 the city began allowing African Americans to attend white schools. However, James Thomas, a free African American in Tennessee, described the unequal education that many received in the 1830s.

 History Makers Speak ❝School was kept occasionally. It was regarded a great favor to have it allowed at any time. Each pupil or scholar paid one dollar per month. Often there was no school because there was no teacher.❞

—James Thomas, quoted in *From Slavery to Freedom,* by John Hope Franklin and Alfred A. Moss Jr.

African Americans rarely attended college because only a few institutions of higher education would accept them. In 1835 Oberlin became the first to do so. Harvard later joined Oberlin in accepting African Americans. Black colleges also began to be founded in the 1840s. For example, in 1842 the Institute for Colored Youth and in 1849 Avery College were opened in Philadelphia.

As the examples above show, free African Americans did have some opportunities to attend school in the Midwest and the North. In the South, however, fewer free African Americans were able to obtain an education. Laws in the South prevented most slaves from receiving any education, in part due to southern whites' fears of potential slave rebellions.

✔ **Reading Check: Comparing** What educational challenges did women and African Americans face in the 1800s? a lack of regular schooling, few institutions of higher education

Mount Holyoke Seminary was one of the country's best schools for women.

Analyzing Primary Sources
Making Generalizations and Predictions How might citizens solve the problem with schooling that Thomas describes? Answers may vary; students may suggest devoting tax revenues to hire permanent teachers.

⭐ Historical Sidelight

Education in the South. Free African Americans in the South had difficulty obtaining an education because many southern states made it illegal to teach them. Nevertheless, many free African Americans were able to learn basic reading and writing through church schools, private tutors, and a few private schools supported by wealthy African Americans.

CRITICAL THINKING

Why do you think it was difficult for free African Americans in the South to receive an education?

ANSWER: Students might suggest that whites feared that education would cause African Americans to demand more rights and would lead to uprisings.

★ ★ ★ ★ ★ ★ ★ ★ ★ ★

Section 3 Review ANSWERS

❶ **Define**
- temperance movement, p. 464
- common-school movement, p. 465

❷ **Identify**
- Dorothea Dix, p. 462
- Lyman Beecher, p. 464
- Horace Mann, p. 465
- Catharine Beecher, p. 466
- Emma Willard, p. 466

★ REVIEW AND ASSESS

Have students complete the **Section 3 Review** on p. 468. Then have students complete **Daily Quiz 15.3**. As **Alternative Assessment**, you may want to use students' annotated time lines or educational reform charts in this section's lessons.

★ RETEACH

Have students complete **Main Idea Activity for English Language Learners and Special-Needs Students 15.3**. Then have each student create an outline that highlights information about the various reform movements and that contains blank spaces where names or concepts would be located. Have each student exchange outlines with another student for

completion, and then return the outlines for grading. **ENGLISH LANGUAGE LEARNERS** , **COOPERATIVE LEARNING**

★ EXTEND

Have students use the library to research the life and contributions of one of the following reformers: Catharine Beecher, Dorothea Dix, Samuel Gridley Howe, Horace Mann, Josiah Quincy, or Emma Willard. Ask students to create a certificate of commendation from the president to give to the reformer they researched. Commendations should include the person's name, a description of the problem the person is associated with fighting, a summary of the person's efforts, and the signature of the president who was in office at the time. **BLOCK SCHEDULING**

- Mary Lyon, p. 467
- Samuel Gridley Howe, p. 468
- Thomas Hopkins Galluadet, p. 468

❸ Prisons and mental health: Dorothea Dix, Josiah Quincy; improved inhumane conditions, young offenders given different punishments from adults, first houses of correction and reform schools established, separate facilities created for mentally ill; Temperance: Lyman Beecher, Neal Dow; state laws banning the sale of alcohol; Education: Horace Mann, Catharine Beecher, Emma Willard, Mary Lyon, Samuel Gridley Howe, Thomas Gallaudet; common-school reform increased teacher salaries and extended the school year; women's academies and schools for African Americans opened, education of visually and hearing impaired Americans improved, Perkins Institution opened, first free American school for people with hearing impairments opened in Hartford, CT

❹ a. created special separate facilities for mentally ill; tried to get different sentences for child offenders & improvement of overcrowding and inhumane conditions; new houses of correction and reform schools that tried to change prisoners' behavior through education
b. an end to violence, poverty, and criminal behavior they blamed on alcohol, by banning or limiting its use

❺ Students' speeches will vary but should focus on educational reforms.

This typewriter produced raised dots representing the alphabet created by Louis Braille for visually impaired people.

★ Teaching People with Disabilities

Efforts to improve education also helped people with special needs. **Samuel Gridley Howe** worked to improve the education of visually impaired Americans. Howe also worked for education reform, prison reform, and care for mentally ill people. In 1831 Howe opened a school called the Perkins Institution in Massachusetts for people with visual impairments. He trained the school's workers to address the particular needs of the students. He also traveled to 17 other states to talk about teaching visually impaired people. Howe ran the Perkins Institution for 45 years. During this time he showed that people with visual impairments could lead economically and socially productive lives.

After graduating from Yale College, **Thomas Hopkins Gallaudet** worked to improve the education and lives of people who were hearing impaired. He went to Europe for two years to study ways to teach such students. In 1817, after he returned to the United States, Gallaudet founded the first free American school for people with hearing impairments in Hartford, Connecticut. He served as the school's principal until 1830. After he retired from the school, Gallaudet became a professor of philosophy of education at New York University. He called for special schools to train teachers and wrote textbooks for children and people with hearing impairments. Gallaudet University in Washington, D.C., was named in his honor. Thus, school reformers helped people in many parts of American society during the early and mid-1800s.

✔ **Reading Check: Summarizing** What kinds of schools were founded for people with disabilities? Samuel Gridley Howe founded Perkins Institution, a school for people with visual impairments; Thomas Gallaudet founded the first free American school for people with hearing impairments.

Section **3** Review

go.hrw.com Homework Practice Online
keyword: SA3 HP15

❶ **Define** and explain:
- temperance movement
- common-school movement

❷ **Identify** and explain:
- Dorothea Dix
- Lyman Beecher
- Horace Mann
- Catharine Beecher
- Emma Willard
- Mary Lyon
- Samuel Gridley Howe
- Thomas Hopkins Gallaudet

❸ **Categorizing** Copy the chart below. Use it to match reform leaders with their respective movements and the accomplishments of each movement.

Movement	Leaders	Accomplishments
Prison & Mental Health Reform		
Temperance		
Education		

❹ **Finding the Main Idea**
a. Describe the ways that reformers changed prisons and the treatment of the mentally ill.

b. What did members of the temperance movement try to achieve?

❺ **Writing and Critical Thinking**
Summarizing Imagine that you are Horace Mann visiting a foreign country. Write a speech that describes the ways in which many more Americans gained the opportunity to receive an education in the early and mid-1800s.

Consider the following:
- education for women
- education for African Americans
- educating people with disabilities

Section 4

OBJECTIVES

★ Explain why some Americans became abolitionists.

★ Identify ways that abolitionists spread the movement's message.

★ Investigate why some Americans opposed abolition.

🔊 *LET'S GET STARTED!*

Write the following statement on the chalkboard: *All students with brown eyes will take a pop quiz today, while the rest of the class will play a game.* As students enter the classroom, allow time for them to write down their feelings about the statement. *(Students' responses will vary.)* Ask students to point out how unfair this situation is. Then lead a discussion on restricting individuals' freedom based on their physical characteristics. Tell students that in Section 4 they will learn about the plight of slaves as they sought to gain freedom and the conflicts between groups that advocated slavery and groups that opposed it.

Section 4

The Movement to End Slavery

Read to Discover

1. Why did some Americans become abolitionists?
2. How did abolitionists spread the movement's message?
3. Why were some Americans against abolition?

WHY IT MATTERS TODAY

Citizens still organize to seek changes in laws. Use CNNfyi.com or other **current events** sources to learn more about a group trying to change a law. Record your findings in your journal.

Define

- abolition
- emancipation

Identify

- Robert Finley
- American Colonization Society
- David Walker
- William Lloyd Garrison
- *The Liberator*
- American Anti-Slavery Society
- Angelina and Sarah Grimké
- Frederick Douglass
- Underground Railroad
- Harriet Tubman

SECTION 4 RESOURCES

REPRODUCIBLE

▶ Guided Reading Strategy 15.4

▶ Primary Source Reading 15: "An Appeal to the Colored Citizens of the World"

TECHNOLOGY

▶ One-Stop Planner, Lesson 15.4

▶ Everyday Life in America Transparency 8: Portrait of a Prosperous African American

▶ American Music Selection 12: "Follow the Drinking Gourd"

▶ Homework Practice Online

REINFORCEMENT, REVIEW, AND ASSESSMENT

▶ Section 4 Review, p. 474

▶ Daily Quiz 15.4

▶ Main Idea Activity 15.4

▶ English Audio Summary 15.4

▶ Spanish Audio Summary 15.4

The Story Continues

During the mid-1800s John Fairfield helped enslaved African Americans escape to freedom in the North. Fairfield traveled throughout the South under different disguises. Sometimes he posed as a slaveholder. Other times he dressed as a trader, or a peddler. Once he led 28 slaves to freedom by disguising them as part of a funeral procession. Most antislavery activists did not take such risks. However, they all helped a movement that grew much stronger in the mid-1800s.

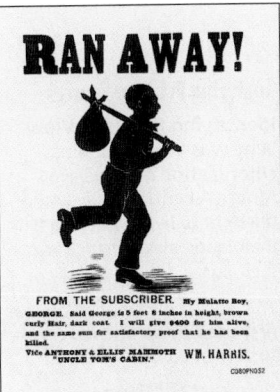

RAN AWAY!

FROM THE SUBSCRIBER. My Mulatto Boy, GEORGE. Said George is 5 feet 8 inches in height, brown curly hair, dark coat. I will give $400 for him alive, and the same sum for satisfactory proof that he has been killed.

Vide ANTHONY & ELLIS MAMMOTH "UNCLE TOM'S CABIN." WM. HARRIS.

Newspapers often published advertisements for the capture of runaway slaves.

★ Abolition

During the 1830s Americans who had been against slavery for years began to take organized action. They formed a movement to support **abolition**, or a complete end to slavery, in the United States. Some of these people wanted immediate **emancipation**. Through emancipation, all enslaved African Americans would be freed from slavery.

469

Have students read Section 4 and complete Guided Reading Strategy 15.4. Choose one or more of the following activities to explore the section content with students. For further suggestions on block scheduling or team teaching, see the *Block Scheduling Handbook with Team Teaching Strategies.*

 LEVEL 1: Have volunteers read to the class the text under the "Abolition" heading. Ask students to volunteer reasons why people became abolitionists, and write their responses on the chalkboard. *(Students' responses should include that some people wanted to abolish slavery in the United States; some wanted a complete end to slavery with full equality for African Americans; some wanted to end slavery but did not support full equality for African Americans; some opposed slavery on religious grounds; some thought slavery was morally wrong; and some wanted to send freed African Americans to new colonies in Africa.)* Then have students write a headline explaining the attraction of the abolitionist movement, and draw an illustration for an article that might appear in an abolitionist newspaper.

ENGLISH LANGUAGE LEARNERS

☆ Culture

Abolition and Religion.
For many abolitionists, religion was the primary reason for opposing slavery. These abolitionists argued that slavery went against the teachings of Christianity because Jesus preached that all people were joined in universal brotherhood. They also believed slavery contradicted the Christian principle that all people were created in the image of God. James G. Birney wrote *A Letter to the Ministers and Elders* in 1834 and Theodore Weld wrote *The Bible Against Slavery* in 1837 to make the Christian argument against slavery.

CRITICAL THINKING

Why did many abolitionists base their views on religion?

ANSWER: Students should suggest that many abolitionists' religious views taught them that slavery was morally wrong.

GLOBAL CONNECTIONS ANSWER
British warships began stopping slave ships in the Atlantic and Indian Oceans to free the slaves they found.

GLOBAL CONNECTIONS

British Abolitionists

Many American abolitionists looked to Great Britain for examples of how to fight slavery. Britain had outlawed the slave trade in 1807. In 1834 a law abolishing slavery in the British Empire went into effect. However, British antislavery work did not stop there. In 1840 the British and Foreign Anti-Slavery Society held the World's Anti-Slavery Convention in London. Convention members asked the British government to pressure other countries to end slavery as well. In the mid-1800s British warships began stopping slave ships in the Atlantic and Indian Oceans and freeing the slaves they found. **How did British abolitionists try to end slavery outside of Britain?**

Analyzing Primary Sources
Identifying Points of View
Why was Walker against colonization? He believed African Americans had earned the right to live in America with their labor; also, America was their home.

This antislavery medallion was first used by an antislavery society in London.

Abolitionists were in the minority in the United States, but they were very vocal. They came from many different backgrounds and wanted to ban slavery for different reasons. The Quakers were among the first groups to challenge slavery on religious grounds. The Quakers had begun working for abolition during colonial times. Some ministers of the Second Great Awakening also believed that slavery was morally wrong. People such as Charles Grandison Finney and Theodore Weld moved many others to take up the cause of abolition. Other abolitionists pointed to the ideals of the Declaration of Independence. They reminded people that the American Revolution supported equality.

Abolitionists disagreed about what ending slavery should mean for African Americans. Some abolitionists thought that African Americans should be treated the same as white Americans. Many others, however, opposed full social and political equality for African Americans.

Some antislavery reformers wanted to send freed African Americans to Africa to start new colonies there. They thought that this would prevent conflicts between different races in the United States. Many Americans supported this view. J. C. Galloway of North Carolina described this idea. "It is impossible for us [whites] to be happy, if . . . they [freed African Americans] are to remain among us," he wrote.

In 1817 a minister named **Robert Finley** started the **American Colonization Society**. Five years later the society founded the colony of Liberia on the west coast of Africa. About 12,000 African Americans eventually settled in Liberia. However, many who were once in favor of colonization later turned against it. Some African Americans also opposed the colonization movement. **David Walker** was one such person. In an 1829 essay, *Appeal to the Colored Citizens of the World*, Walker explained why he was against colonization.

 History Makers Speak ❝The greatest riches in all America have arisen from our blood and tears: And they [whites] will drive us from our property and homes, which we have earned with our blood.❞

—David Walker, quoted in *From Slavery to Freedom,*
by John Hope Franklin and Alfred A. Moss Jr.

✔ **Reading Check: Contrasting** How did some abolitionists' goals differ?
Some wanted full equality for African Americans, which others opposed.

☆ Spreading the Abolitionist Message

Abolitionists found many ways to further their cause. Some abolitionists went on speaking tours or wrote newspaper articles and pamphlets. Editor Horace Greeley became a strong voice in the movement through the *New York Tribune*. Others, like John Greenleaf Whittier, spread the abolitionist message through their poetry and literature. **William Lloyd Garrison** published an abolitionist newspaper. This newspaper, ***The Liberator***, first appeared in 1831. Garrison became one of the most outspoken and

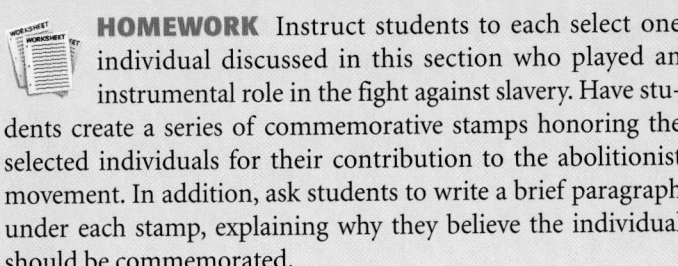

Spreading the Message	
Working to End Slavery	**Working to Keep Slavery**
• *speaking tours and lectures* • *newspapers* • *pamphlets and essays* • *poetry, plays, and slave narratives* • *abolitionist societies* • *essays* • *petitions to Congress*	• *newspaper editorials* • *political speeches* • *threats to abolitionists* • *federal laws*

controversial leaders of the movement. In 1833 Garrison helped found the **American Anti-Slavery Society**. This group wanted immediate emancipation and racial equality for African Americans. Garrison later became the group's president.

Both *The Liberator* and the Anti-Slavery Society relied on the support of free African Americans. Members of the society spread antislavery literature throughout the North and Midwest. They also sent petitions to Congress. In these petitions, they asked for an end to all federal support of slavery. Then in 1840 the American Anti-Slavery Society split. One group wanted immediate freedom for enslaved African Americans. This group also believed women should take part in the abolition movement on an equal basis with men. The other group wanted slower emancipation and a limited role for women.

Angelina and Sarah Grimké, two white southern women, became well-known antislavery activists of the 1830s. The sisters were members of a slaveholding family in South Carolina. They did not share their parents' support of slavery, however. Instead, they moved to Philadelphia and joined the abolition movement. Angelina Grimké tried to bring other white southern women to the cause. She wrote a pamphlet titled *Appeal to the Christian Women of the South* in 1836.

History Makers Speak ❝I know you do not make the laws, but . . . if you really suppose you can do nothing to overthrow slavery, you are greatly mistaken. . . . Try to persuade your husband, father, brothers and sons that slavery is a crime against God and man.❞

—Angelina Grimké, quoted in *The Grimké Sisters from South Carolina*, edited by Gerda Lerner

This essay was quite popular in the North. As a result, the Grimké sisters became the first women to speak before male and female audiences of the Anti-Slavery Society. The sisters gave lectures and formed dozens of female antislavery societies. In 1839 they wrote *American Slavery As It Is* with Angelina's husband, abolitionist leader Theodore Weld. This book was one of the most important antislavery writings of the time.

✔ **Reading Check: Finding the Main Idea** How did the members of the Anti-Slavery Society fight slavery? *through speeches, publications, and petitions to Congress*

Analyzing Primary Sources
Evaluating Sources How did Grimké believe women could help bring an end to slavery? *by persuading the men in their lives that slavery was wrong*

THE GRANGER COLLECTION, NEW YORK

William Lloyd Garrison's The Liberator *became one of the most widely read abolitionist newspapers in the North.*

LEVEL 3: Ask students to write a dialogue that might have occurred between an abolitionist and an advocate of slavery during the 1800s. Dialogues should focus on whether slavery should be allowed to continue in the United States. Have students include material from this section identifying why abolitionists fought for slaves' freedom and why advocates sought to maintain the institution of slavery.

SPOTLIGHT
on the Underground Railroad

Tell students that it was illegal to help a slave escape. Then ask them to imagine that they are town officials in the South looking to put a stop to the activities of the Underground Railroad. To do so, they think they must capture Harriet Tubman, a famous "conductor" along the escape route. Have students create a wanted poster that includes a sketch of Tubman, a description of her crimes (how she helped slaves escape), and the reward for her capture. **BLOCK SCHEDULING**

★ Global Relations

African American Abolitionists in Europe.
Many African Americans who spoke out against slavery in the United States also traveled to Europe to spread their message. Frederick Douglass, Charles Remond, and Henry Garnet—editor of the abolitionist newspaper the *National Watchman*—were just a few of the speakers who visited countries such as France, Germany, and Great Britain. These African American abolitionists made important connections between reformers in Europe and those in the United States.

ACTIVITY: Have students conduct additional research on one of the abolitionists mentioned above. Then ask them to write a speech from that person's perspective, using standard grammar, spelling, sentence structure, and punctuation. Have the students deliver their speeches to the class.

Technology Resources
 American Music Selection 12: "Follow the Drinking Gourd"

CONNECTING TO LITERATURE ANSWER
He wanted to expose the slavery system and encourage people to end it.

CONNECTING TO *Literature*

Narrative of the Life of Frederick Douglass

In 1845 Frederick Douglass published the first of three autobiographies describing his life as a slave and his abolitionist efforts once he gained his freedom. In the following excerpt he explains the purpose of his autobiography.

> Sincerely and earnestly hoping that this little book may do something toward throwing light on the American slave system, and **hastening**[1] the glad day of deliverance to the millions of my **brethren**[2] in bonds—faithfully relying on the power of truth, love, and justice, for success in my humble efforts—and solemnly pledging myself anew to the sacred cause,—I **subscribe**[3] myself, Frederick Douglass.

[1]**hastening:** quickening   [3]**subscribe:** pledge
[2]**brethren:** brothers and sisters

Understanding What You Read
Literature and History Why did Frederick Douglass write his narrative?

★ African Americans Fight against Slavery

Many former slaves were very active in the antislavery movement. **Frederick Douglass**, who escaped from slavery at age 20, became one of the most important African American leaders of the 1800s. Douglass had secretly learned to read and write as a boy. In addition, his public-speaking skills greatly impressed the members of the Anti-Slavery Society. In 1841 they asked Douglass to give regular lectures. Speaking at a Fourth of July celebration in 1852, he captured the audience's attention with his powerful voice.

 History Makers Speak
❝The blessings in which you, this day, rejoice, are not enjoyed in common. . . . This Fourth of July is *yours*, not *mine*. You may rejoice, I must mourn.❞

—Frederick Douglass, quoted in *From Slavery to Freedom*, by John Hope Franklin and Alfred A. Moss Jr.

Douglass went on many speaking tours in the United States and Europe. He also published a pro-abolition newspaper called *North Star* and wrote several autobiographies.

African Americans such as Charles Remond and Sojourner Truth also helped the abolitionist cause. Truth became famous in the antislavery movement for her dramatic and fiery speeches. In 1842 Remond asked the Massachusetts legislature to end racial discrimination in the state. "It is JUSTICE I stand here to claim, and not FAVOR for either complexion [skin color]," he declared.

Other African Americans wrote slave narratives about their experiences. In 1861 abolitionists helped publish *Incidents in the Life of a Slave Girl* by Harriet Jacobs, one of the few slave narratives written by a woman. William Wells Brown wrote an antislavery play and an antislavery novel called *Clotel*. These writers and many other African Americans contributed significantly to the abolitionist cause.

★ The Underground Railroad

By the 1830s a loosely organized group had begun helping slaves escape from the South. Free African Americans, former slaves, and a few white abolitionists worked together to create the **Underground Railroad**. This network of people arranged transportation and hiding places for

TEACHER TO TEACHER

Anastacio Asuncion of San Jose, California, suggested the following activity:

🇺🇸 **ALL LEVELS:** Have students use their textbook or the library to find information that will help them map the common routes of escaped slaves. (Accounts of actual escapes along with historical maps may be needed.) Encourage students to research the approximate distance traveled each day and to illustrate this information by using breaks in the route. Also have students calculate the approximate distance of the entire route. **ENGLISH LANGUAGE LEARNERS**

CLOSE

Assign each student one of the following individuals: Frederick Douglass, John Fairfield, Robert Finney, William Lloyd Garrison, Angelina Grimké, Sarah Grimké, Robert Purvis, Charles Remond, Sojourner Truth, or Harriet Tubman. Ask each student to write a paragraph describing the individual's contributions to the fight against slavery—without mentioning the individual's name. Have students place their finished paragraphs in a box. Then ask volunteers to pick a paragraph from the box, and read it to the class. Have other students identify the figure described in the paragraph. **COOPERATIVE LEARNING**

---

fugitives, or escaped slaves. Often wearing disguises, fugitives moved along the "railroad" at night, guided by the North Star. They stopped to rest during the day at various "stations." These stations were the homes of abolitionists known as conductors. The conductors hid the fugitives in barns, attics, and other secret locations. They would then send word to the next station farther north that they were on the way.

The most famous and daring conductor on the Underground Railroad was **Harriet Tubman**. When Tubman herself escaped in 1849, she left behind her husband, parents, sisters, and brothers. She returned to the South 19 times. Tubman successfully led her family and more than 300 other slaves to freedom. She never lost a fugitive. At one time the reward for Tubman's capture climbed to $40,000. Historians estimate that 40,000 slaves used the Underground Railroad to reach freedom between 1810 and 1850.

✔ **Reading Check: Analyzing Information** How did free African Americans and former slaves try to end slavery? through speeches, writings, and the Underground Railroad

MAP ANSWERS
1. Mississippi, Tennessee, Kentucky, Illinois, and Indiana
2. Bahamas, Canada, Cuba, and Mexico

Harriet Tubman

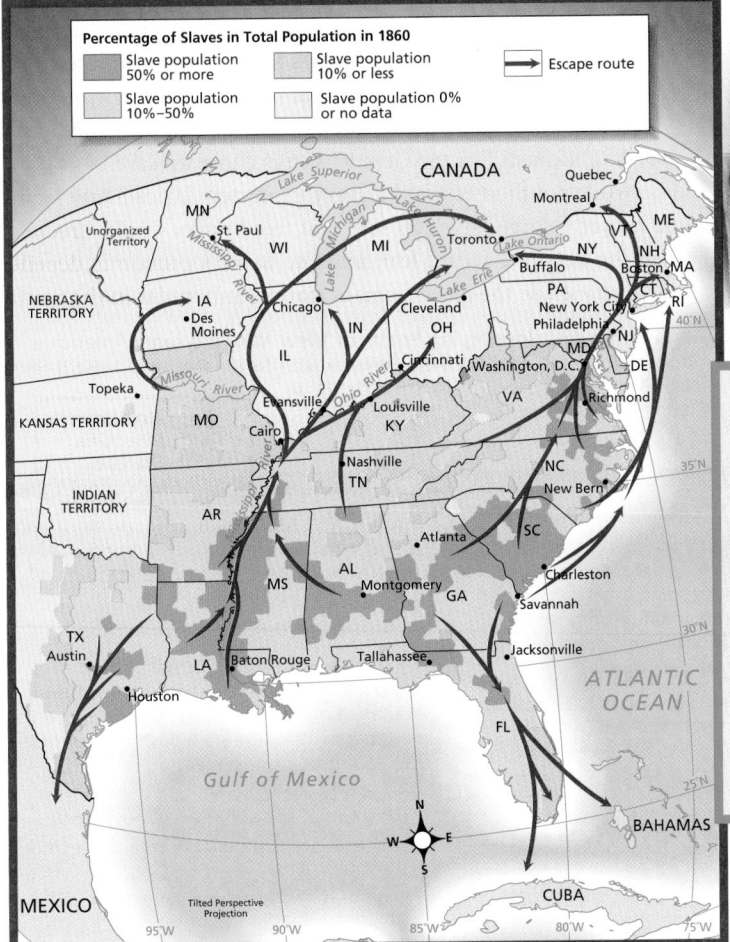

Percentage of Slaves in Total Population in 1860
- Slave population 50% or more
- Slave population 10%–50%
- Slave population 10% or less
- Slave population 0% or no data
- → Escape route

The Underground Railroad

Interpreting Maps The Underground Railroad helped thousands of slaves escape to freedom.

Skills Assessment
1. **Places and Regions** Through which states might slaves pass if they were escaping from Alabama to Ohio?
2. **Analyzing Information** To what destinations besides the northern states did slaves escape?

⭐ REVIEW AND ASSESS

Have students complete the **Section 4 Review** on p. 474. Then have students complete **Daily Quiz 15.4.** As **Alternative Assessment,** you may want to use students' dialogues or abolitionist biographies in the section's lessons.

⭐ RETEACH

Have students complete **Main Idea Activity for English Language Learners and Special-Needs Students 15.4.** Then ask them to review the Define and Identify terms, and write what they have learned about each term. When students have finished, ask volunteers to present their definitions to the class.
ENGLISH LANGUAGE LEARNERS

⭐ EXTEND

Have students use the library to obtain a copy of one pamphlet, publication, speech, or narrative mentioned in this section. Ask students to read the document and summarize key points in a short essay. Encourage students to focus on how the selection advocates the abolitionist movement. **BLOCK SCHEDULING**

Section 4 Review
ANSWERS

❶ Define
• abolition, p. 469
• emancipation, p. 469

❷ Identify
• Robert Finley, p. 470
• American Colonization Society, p. 470
• David Walker, p. 470
• William Lloyd Garrison, p. 470
• *The Liberator*, p. 470
• American Anti-Slavery Society, p. 471
• Angelina and Sarah Grimké, p. 471
• Frederick Douglass, p. 472
• Underground Railroad, p. 472
• Harriet Tubman, p. 473

❸ opposed slavery on religious grounds, or because it was politically and morally hypocritical compared with the Declaration of Independence; methods—speaking tours, newspapers, pamphlets, petitions to Congress, and writing poetry, plays, and other literature

❹ a. because of their racism, fear of losing jobs, and fear of losing the basis of the southern economy
b. tension would likely grow between abolitionists and slavery supporters, forcing Congress to discuss slavery issues when new territories became part of the Union

❺ Students' posters will vary but should focus on the goals of the abolitionists.

THE GRANGER COLLECTION, NEW YORK

Southern defenders of slavery used images like this one to argue that American slaves enjoyed a better life than British factory workers.

⭐ Opposition to Abolition

Many white northerners did not believe in equal treatment for African Americans. Newspaper editors and politicians often warned that freed slaves would move north and take jobs from white workers. Leaders of the abolitionist movement received threats. Some northerners joined violent mobs that attacked African Americans and burned antislavery literature.

The federal government also stood in the way of the abolitionist movement. Between 1836 and 1844 the U.S. House of Representatives used a Gag Rule to prevent discussion of the thousands of antislavery petitions it received. This rule effectively violated the First Amendment right of citizens to petition the government. But southern congressmen were against any debate about slavery, and many northern congressmen just wanted to avoid the issue.

Many white southerners thought slavery was a vital part of the South's economy and culture. White southerners also generally believed that outsiders had no business interfering with their way of life. After Nat Turner's Rebellion in 1831, open talk of the slavery question disappeared in the South. Abolitionists like the Grimké sisters chose to leave.

Some white southerners said slavery protected African Americans. Virginia lawyer George Fitzhugh said that freed slaves would "freeze or starve" in the North. Racism, fear, and the South's economic dependence on slavery made the idea of emancipation unpopular in the South.

✔ **Reading Check: Identifying Points of View** Why did some Americans oppose emancipation? Northern white workers feared they would lose their jobs; southerners believed slavery was central to their economy and culture.

Section 4 Review

go.
hrw
.com

Homework Practice Online
keyword: SA3 HP15

❶ Define and explain:
• abolition
• emancipation

❷ Identify and explain:
• Robert Finley
• American Colonization Society
• David Walker
• William Lloyd Garrison
• *The Liberator*
• American Anti-Slavery Society
• Angelina and Sarah Grimké
• Frederick Douglass
• Underground Railroad
• Harriet Tubman

❸ Analyzing Information
Copy the graphic organizer below. Use it to explain why some Americans joined the abolitionist movement and the methods they used to fight slavery.

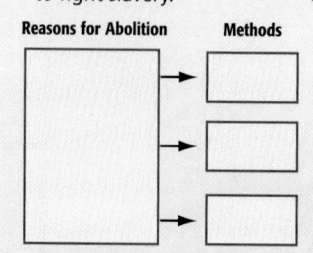

Reasons for Abolition → **Methods**

❹ Finding the Main Idea
a. For what reasons did many Americans in the North and the South oppose abolition?

b. How might the issue of slavery lead to conflict as the United States expanded?

❺ Writing and Critical Thinking
Supporting a Point of View Imagine that you are a member of one of the antislavery societies in 1840. Create a poster announcing your group's next meeting.

Consider the following:
• the goals of the abolitionist movement
• why Americans should become active in the movement
• ways or methods to persuade other Americans to join the cause

474 Chapter 15

Section 5

OBJECTIVES

- ★ Explain the effect that the abolitionist movement had on the women's rights movement.
- ★ Identify some of the goals of the women's rights movement.
- ★ Analyze the purpose and significance of the Seneca Falls Convention.

LET'S GET STARTED!

Write the following statement on the chalkboard: *List three famous women from the 1900s.* As students enter the classroom, allow time for them to respond. *(Students' lists will vary.)* Have students share their lists with the class, and then discuss how each of these women has influenced others' lives. Then tell students that some of the women they identified might not have had the opportunity to demonstrate their talents if the women's rights movement of the 1800s had never taken place. Tell students that in Section 5 they will learn about how the women's rights movement started, who played instrumental roles in it, and how the movement influenced society.

Section 5

Women's Rights

Read to Discover

1. How did the abolitionist movement affect the women's rights movement?
2. What were some goals of the women's rights movement?
3. What was the purpose of the Seneca Falls Convention, and why was it significant?

WHY IT MATTERS TODAY

The women's rights movement is still active in the United States today. Use **CNNfyi.com** or other **current events** sources to learn about the important roles women play in America today. These roles include positions in business, government, and society in general. Record your findings in your journal.

Identify

- Elizabeth Cady Stanton
- Lucretia Mott
- Seneca Falls Convention
- Declaration of Sentiments
- Lucy Stone
- Susan B. Anthony

SECTION 5 RESOURCES

REPRODUCIBLE

- ▶ Guided Reading Strategy 15.5
- ▶ Literature Reading 15: Encouraging Women's Rights
- ▶ Graphic Organizer 15: Early Reform Movements

TECHNOLOGY

- ▶ One-Stop Planner, Lesson 15.5
- ▶ American History Simulations CD–ROM: Reform: Making a Difference
- ▶ Homework Practice Online

REINFORCEMENT, REVIEW, AND ASSESSMENT

- ▶ Section 5 Review, p. 479
- ▶ Daily Quiz 15.5
- ▶ Main Idea Activity 15.5
- ▶ English Audio Summary 15.5
- ▶ Spanish Audio Summary 15.5

The Story Continues

In February 1838 Angelina Grimké nervously prepared to speak before the Massachusetts legislature. "I never was so near fainting under the tremendous pressure of feeling," she wrote her future husband. "My heart almost died within me." Grimké planned to present antislavery petitions to the 1,500 people gathered. However, she felt a great responsibility. She was the first woman to speak before a legislature in the United States. As she spoke, Grimké bravely addressed both the issue of abolition and the question of women's rights.

Angelina Grimké was one of the first women to speak on behalf of the American Anti-Slavery Society.

★ The Influence of Abolition

Many female abolitionists, such as the Grimké sisters and Sojourner Truth, later became part of the women's rights movement of the mid-1800s. These women found that they had to defend their right to speak in public, particularly when a woman addressed both men and women. For example, members of the press, the clergy, and even some male abolitionists criticized the Grimké sisters for speaking in public. These critics believed that women should not give public speeches, and

TEACH

Have students read Section 5 and complete Guided Reading Strategy 15.5. Choose one or more of the following activities to explore the section content with students. For further suggestions on block scheduling or team teaching, see the *Block Scheduling Handbook with Team Teaching Strategies.*

LEVEL 1: Have volunteers read the text under the "The Influence of Abolition" heading. After the first paragraph has been read, ask students why some people opposed women's efforts in the abolitionist movement.

(Students' responses should mention that these people criticized women for giving public speeches and believed that women should not go beyond traditional roles.) After the rest of the section has been read, ask students which women were prominent in both movements and what actions these women took in the women's rights movement. *(Students' responses should include the Grimké sisters, particularly Sarah Grimké, who published a pamphlet arguing for women's rights, and Sojourner Truth, who gave speeches about women's rights.)* Finally, ask students what effects that the abolitionist movement had on the women's rights movement. **ENGLISH LANGUAGE LEARNERS**

Female Abolitionists and Religion. Women in the early 1800s did not participate in political discussions about slavery—it would not have been respectable to do so. Once slavery became a religious concern, however, women felt it was their right and often their duty to become involved in the antislavery movement; the public viewed religion as an appropriate activity for women. Some women abolitionists, such as Lucretia Mott, were part of socially active religious groups. Others received support from religious officials in their efforts to promote women's antislavery societies.

CRITICAL THINKING

How did religion open the antislavery movement to women?

ANSWER: Students might suggest that women's participation in the religious debate about slavery was acceptable to the public, even though their participation in political discussions on the issue was not considered appropriate.

Technology Resources

 American History Simulations CD–ROM: Reform: Making a Difference

BIOGRAPHY ANSWER

She experienced equality with boys.

476

they did not want women to leave their traditional female roles. However, the Grimkés had a different view. They told their critics that women had a moral duty to lead the antislavery movement.

In 1838 Sarah Grimké published a pamphlet arguing for equal rights for women. She titled the essay "Letters on the Equality of the Sexes and the Condition of Women."

 History Makers Speak ❝I ask no favors for my sex. . . . All I ask our brethren [brothers] is, that they will take their feet from off our necks, and permit us to stand upright on that ground which God designed us to occupy.❞

—Sarah Grimké, quoted in *The Grimké Sisters from South Carolina,* edited by Gerda Lerner

Sarah Grimké also argued for equal educational opportunities. She pointed out laws that negatively affected women and called for equal pay for equal work.

Sojourner Truth was another powerful speaker for both abolition and women's rights. Writer Harriet Beecher Stowe said that she had never spoken "with anyone who had more . . . personal presence than this woman." Truth stood six feet tall and was a confident speaker. She often recalled her experiences as a slave. In 1851 she gave a speech at a women's rights convention. In her speech, she challenged the audience members not to think of women as the "weaker sex."

 History Makers Speak ❝That man over there says that women need to be helped into carriages and lifted over ditches, and to have the best place everywhere. Nobody ever helps me into carriages or over mud puddles, or gives me any best place. . . . Look at me! I have ploughed and planted and . . . no man could head [outwork] me. And ain't I a woman?❞

—Sojourner Truth, quoted in *A History of Women in America,* by Carol Hymowitz and Michaele Weissman

Truth and other supporters of the women's rights movement were determined to be heard.

✔ **Reading Check: Identifying Cause and Effect** Why did some people oppose women's efforts in the abolitionist movement, and how did this opposition affect the women's rights movement? They believed women should not go beyond traditional female roles; it strengthened the women's rights movement.

★ Women's Rights

Publications about women's rights first appeared in the United States shortly after the American Revolution. However, women's concerns did not become a national movement for many more years. This change took place when women took part in reform and abolition efforts. Other social changes also led to the rise of the movement. Women took advantage of better educational opportunities. They also learned how to organize more effectively by working together in reform groups. Some

Analyzing Primary Sources

Identifying Points of View Using your own words, explain how Sarah Grimké wants women to be treated.
the same as men are treated

 Sojourner Truth traveled throughout New England preaching the word of abolition and women's rights.

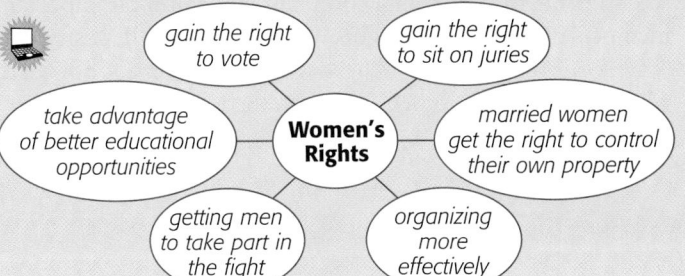
men also took part in the struggle for women's rights. Many activists were upset that women could not vote. In addition, married women in many states had little or no control over their own property.

Many people, both men and women, did not agree with some of the goals of the women's rights movement. Many women believed that they did not need any new rights. They said that women were not unequal to men, only different. Some critics believed that women should not try to work for social changes in public. In other words, they should work for change at home from within their families. "Let her not look away from her own little family circle for the means of producing moral and social reforms," wrote T. S. Arthur. His advice appeared in a popular women's magazine called *The Lady at Home*.

Some people also thought that women did not have the physical or mental strength to survive without men's protection. Such people believed that a woman needed to be under a man's authority. They also believed that her husband should control her property. Despite this strong opposition, women still pursued their goal of greater rights.

✔ **Reading Check: Summarizing** Why were some people against the goals of the women's movement? Critics believed women should influence society from the home; believed women were not unequal, just different; and believed they could not survive without men's protection.

★ The Seneca Falls Convention

In 1840 **Elizabeth Cady Stanton** attended the World's Anti-Slavery Convention in London, England, while on her honeymoon. Stanton had to watch the meeting separately from her husband, however, because women could not participate. Women in attendance had to sit in a separate gallery of the convention hall, hidden from the men's view by a curtain. In protest, William Lloyd Garrison sat with them, refusing to join a proceeding that did not allow women's equal participation.

This treatment of women abolitionists angered Stanton and her new friend, **Lucretia Mott**. Stanton later wrote that they "resolved to hold a convention as soon as we returned home." Mott and Stanton planned to "form a society to advance the rights of women." Eight years passed, however, before Stanton and Mott sent out a notice announcing the **Seneca Falls Convention**. The meeting, which began on July 19, 1848, in Seneca Falls, New York, launched an organized women's rights movement. This convention was the first public meeting about women's rights to be held in the United States.

To present their case, the convention organizers wrote a **Declaration of Sentiments** based on the language of the Declaration of Independence. The document detailed their beliefs about social injustice toward women. Some 100 people signed the Declaration of Sentiments.

Some 240 people attended the Seneca Falls Convention, including some men such as Frederick Douglass. Most of these reformers also worked in the temperance or antislavery movements. In addition,

BIOGRAPHY

Elizabeth Cady Stanton
(1815–1902)

Elizabeth Cady grew up in a wealthy family near Albany, New York. Her father, a judge, had a strong influence on her life. When Cady asked her father's opinion of her accomplishments, he replied sadly, "My daughter, you should have been a boy." Yet Cady did enjoy a happy childhood in which boys and girls played together. Cady did very well in school and attended a female seminary. In 1840 Cady married antislavery activist Henry Stanton, and they had seven children. She went on to become one of the most important leaders of the women's rights movement. She was a primary author of the Declaration of Sentiments. **What was significant about Stanton's childhood?**

SPOTLIGHT
on Women's Rights

Bring current newspapers and magazines to class, and encourage students to do the same. Ask them to create collages titled *Women's Rights* that highlight significant advances or issues in the women's rights movement. Have students explain their collages to the class. **BLOCK SCHEDULING**

★ CLOSE

Ask students to skim this section and take notes on important members of the women's rights movement. Then have students write brief biographies of these women that reflect how each woman influenced women's rights in the United States.

Section 5 Review
ANSWERS

❶ Identify
- Elizabeth Cady Stanton, p. 477
- Lucretia Mott, p. 477
- Seneca Falls Convention, p. 477
- Declaration of Sentiments, p. 477
- Lucy Stone, p. 479
- Susan B. Anthony, p. 479

❷ Abolitionist movement—female activists joined antislavery societies and spoke out against slavery; women abolitionists—Sarah and Angelina Grimké, Sojourner Truth, Elizabeth Cady Stanton, Lucy Stone, and Susan B. Anthony felt they had to defend a woman's right to speak against slavery; women's rights movement—women began to organize to fight for rights for the first time in the United States

❸ a. social equality, equal pay for equal work, improvement in women's property laws, and right to vote
b. because of the way women were treated at the World's Anti-Slavery Convention in London and to advance the rights of women; led to the Seneca Falls Declaration of Sentiments and was the first women's rights conference

---

several women who worked in nearby factories participated in the convention as well. For example, 19-year-old Charlotte Woodward signed the Declaration of Sentiments because she was tired of making gloves for low wages. Woodward earned pennies that she then had to turn over to her father.

Women had spoken out for their rights earlier. However, the Seneca Falls Convention marked the first time that women in the United States organized as a group to promote their rights.

✔ **Reading Check: Finding the Main Idea** Why was the Seneca Falls Convention important? It brought together many reformers and was the first public meeting on women's rights in the United States.

Historical Document

1848 SENECA FALLS DECLARATION OF SENTIMENTS

A woman speaking before the Seneca Falls Convention

THE GRANGER COLLECTION, NEW YORK

On July 19 and 20, 1848, people gathered in Seneca Falls, New York, to discuss women's rights. Elizabeth Cady Stanton and Lucretia Mott had organized the event. They also helped write the Declaration of Sentiments. Signed by some 100 people, this document helped shape the future of the women's rights movement.

We hold these truths to be **self-evident:**[1] that all men and women are created equal; that they are **endowed**[2] by their Creator with certain **inalienable**[3] rights; that among these are life, liberty, and the pursuit of happiness. . . .

The history of mankind is a history of repeated injuries and **usurpations**[4] on the part of man toward woman, having in direct object the establishment of an absolute **tyranny**[5] over her. To prove this, let facts be submitted to a **candid**[6] world.

He has never permitted her to exercise her inalienable right to . . . [the vote]. . . .

He has taken from her all right in property, even to the wages she earns. . . .

He has **monopolized**[7] nearly all the profitable employments, and from those she is permitted to follow, she receives but a scanty **remuneration.**[8] He closes against her all the avenues to wealth and distinction which he considers most honorable to himself. . . .

He has denied her the **facilities**[9] for obtaining a thorough education, all colleges being closed against her. . . .

He has endeavored, in every way that he could, to destroy her confidence in her own powers, to lessen her self-respect, and to make her willing to lead a dependent and **abject**[10] life. . . .

Resolved, That woman is man's equal—was intended to be so by the Creator, and the highest good of the race demands that she should be recognized as such.

---

[1]**self-evident:** obvious
[2]**endowed:** provided
[3]**inalienable:** permanent
[4]**usurpations:** seizures

[5]**tyranny:** unjust rule
[6]**candid:** fair
[7]**monopolized:** taken control of

[8]**remuneration:** payment
[9]**facilities:** means
[10]**abject:** hopeless

Analyzing Primary Sources

1. What are some of the injustices that the declaration describes?
2. How is the Declaration of Sentiments modeled after the Declaration of Independence?
3. Are the rights demanded in the declaration granted to women in the United States today? Explain your answer.

☆ REVIEW AND ASSESS

Have students complete the **Section 5 Review** on p. 479. Then have students complete **Daily Quiz 15.5**. As **Alternative Assessment**, you may want to use students' promotional pieces or women's rights letters in the section's lessons.

☆ RETEACH

Have students complete **Main Idea Activity for English Language Learners and Special-Needs Students 15.5**. Then have students create a chart with the following categories: *Education, Career Opportunities, Wages, Role in Politics,* and *Community Involvement.* Have students complete their charts to show the rights women did or did not have in these areas in the 1830s. **ENGLISH LANGUAGE LEARNERS**

☆ EXTEND

Have students use the library to research Sojourner Truth's speech, "Ain't I a Woman?" Ask students to write a literary critique of her speech, describing whether or not they feel she was an appealing speaker to women during the 1800s. **BLOCK SCHEDULING**

★ The Continuing Struggle

Although women's rights activists encountered many difficulties, they continued working together after the Seneca Falls Convention. **Lucy Stone** and Susan B. Anthony, along with Elizabeth Cady Stanton, became the most important leaders. Lucy Stone was a well-known member of the Anti-Slavery Society. She soon took on the cause of women's rights as well. During the early years of the women's rights movement, Stone became known as a gifted speaker.

Susan B. Anthony brought strong organizational skills to the women's rights movement. Anthony was largely responsible for turning the fight for women's rights into a political movement. As a single woman who supported herself, women's economic struggles were of particular importance to her. Anthony argued that women and men should receive equal pay for equal work and that women should be allowed to enter traditionally male professions such as law.

Anthony led a campaign to change laws regarding women's property rights. She wrote in her diary that no woman could be free without "a purse of her own." Anthony organized a network to cover every area of New York State. She collected more than 6,000 signatures to petition for a new property rights law. In 1860 New York finally gave married women ownership of their wages and property. Other states in the Northeast and Midwest followed with similar laws. Other major reforms, such as the right to vote, were not achieved at this time. However, more American women than ever before became actively involved in efforts to attain equal rights.

In 1979 Susan B. Anthony became the first American woman to be depicted on U.S. currency.

✔ **Reading Check: Comparing** What were some of the contributions of women's rights leaders Lucy Stone and Susan B. Anthony? Stone—powerful speaker; Anthony—turned women's movement into a political movement; worked to change women's property rights

Section 5 Review

keyword: SA3 HP15

① Identify and explain:
• Elizabeth Cady Stanton
• Lucretia Mott
• Seneca Falls Convention
• Declaration of Sentiments
• Lucy Stone
• Susan B. Anthony

② Summarizing Copy the graphic organizer below. Use it to explain how the women's rights movement grew out of the abolitionist movement.

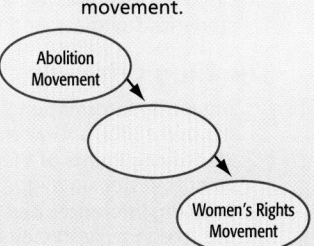

Abolition Movement

Women's Rights Movement

③ Finding the Main Idea
a. What were the main goals of the women's rights movement?

b. Why did Elizabeth Cady Stanton and Lucretia Mott organize the Seneca Falls Convention, and what did it achieve?

④ Writing and Critical Thinking
Supporting a Point of View Imagine that you are a women's rights activist in the mid-1800s. Write an editorial responding to criticism of the women's rights movement.

Consider the following:
• women speaking in public
• women's traditional roles in society
• husbands' control of their wives' property

④ Students' editorials will vary but should focus on the goals of the women's rights movement.

CHAPTER 15 REVIEW ANSWERS

The Chapter at a Glance
Students' flash cards will vary but should include information about reform movements and their accomplishments.

Identifying People and Ideas
Students' sentences should indicate an understanding of the following definitions:

1. period of Christian renewal that began in the 1790s and spread by the 1820s and 1830s

2. important transcendentalist who believed in self-reliance and did not trust institutions

3. native-born citizens who opposed immigration

4. poorly designed urban housing structures that were often dirty, overcrowded, and unsafe

5. the leading educational reformer in the mid-1800s

6. movement that sought immediate emancipation and racial equality for African Americans

7. activist and author for abolition and the women's rights movement

8. former slave who became one of the most important African American leaders of the 1800s

New Movements in America **479**

CHAPTER

15

REVIEW AND ASSESSMENT RESOURCES

REPRODUCIBLE
▶ Vocabulary Activity 15

TECHNOLOGY
▶ Chapter 15 Test Generator (on the One-Stop Planner)
▶ Global Skill Builder CD–ROM
▶ HRW Go site

REINFORCEMENT, REVIEW, AND ASSESSMENT
▶ Chapter 15 Review, pp. 479–81
▶ Chapter 15 Tutorial for Students, Parents, Mentors, and Peers

▶ Chapter 15 Test (Form A or B)
▶ Alternative Assessment Handbook
▶ Chapter 15 Test for English Language Learners and Special-Needs Students

★ REVIEW

Have students complete the **Chapter 15 Review** on pages 480–81.

★ ASSESS

Use one of the chapter tests to assess students' understanding of the content. For **Alternative Assessment**, see the **Alternative Assessment Handbook**.

9. women's rights activist who co-organized the Seneca Falls Convention

10. meeting that took place in 1848 in Seneca Falls, New York, that launched the women's rights movement

Understanding Main Ideas

1. thought people could transcend the material things in life

2. Thomas Cole, Ann Sophia Stephens, Nathaniel Hawthorne, Herman Melville, Edgar Allen Poe, Emily Dickinson, Henry Wadsworth Longfellow, John Greenleaf Whittier, Walt Whitman

3. a search for better jobs and an escape from persecution in homelands

4. prison reform, care for the mentally ill, temperance, education for children, women, African Americans, and people with disabilities

5. thought slavery was morally wrong for religious and/or political reasons; wanted social and legal equality for African Americans, while others were more interested in ending slavery or in legal rather than social equality

6. social equality, equal pay for equal work, improvement in women's property laws, and the right to vote

You Be the Historian— Reviewing Themes

1. encouraged people to try to improve themselves and society as a whole; inspired utopian communities, the temperance movement, and abolition; also increased the participation of women in reform efforts

Chapter **15** Review

The Chapter at a Glance

Examine the visual summary of the chapter below. Then create a set of flash cards listing the key leaders of each reform movement on one side of the card and one key accomplishment on the other side. Use the flash cards to review the chapter material with a classmate.

PRISON REFORM
• Better treatment for criminals, orphans, and people with mental illnesses

TEMPERANCE
• Limit alcohol consumption
• Ban the sale of alcohol

EDUCATION
• Common schools for all children
• Colleges for women
• Schools for African Americans and the disabled

ABOLITION
• End slavery in the United States
• Full social and political equality for African Americans wanted by some abolitionists

WOMEN'S RIGHTS
• Right to vote
• Equal property rights

Identifying People and Ideas

Use the following terms or people in historically significant sentences.
1. Second Great Awakening
2. Henry David Thoreau
3. nativists
4. tenements
5. Horace Mann
6. abolition
7. Angelina Grimké
8. Frederick Douglass
9. Elizabeth Cady Stanton
10. Seneca Falls Convention

Understanding Main Ideas

Section 1 *(Pages 452–456)*
1. What did the transcendentalists and members of utopian communities believe?
2. Who were some of the most important artists and authors of the romantic movement?

Section 2 *(Pages 457–461)*
3. What caused the increase in immigration to the United States during the mid-1800s?

Section 3 *(Pages 462–468)*
4. What social issues did reformers address in the early to mid-1800s?

Section 4 *(Pages 469–474)*
5. Why did people join the abolitionist movement, and what were their goals?

Section 5 *(Pages 475–479)*
6. What were the major goals of the women's rights movement?

You Be the Historian— Reviewing Themes

1. **Culture** How did the Second Great Awakening affect the reform movements of the mid-1800s?
2. **Economics** How did U.S. immigration between 1840 and 1860 affect the economy?
3. **Citizenship** Choose three of the following people and explain how they worked to end slavery: Robert Finley, David Walker, William Lloyd Garrison, Angelina and Sarah Grimké, Frederick Douglass, and Harriet Tubman.

Thinking Critically

1. **Analyzing Information** How did cities change in the mid-1800s, and what caused these changes?
2. **Identifying Points of View** Why did nativists want to restrict immigration to the United States?
3. **Drawing Inferences and Conclusions** How did the freedoms protected by the First Amendment aid the Second Great Awakening and social reform movements?

RETEACH

Organize students into five groups and assign each group one of the chapter's sections. Have each group create diagrams illustrating the highlights of the assigned section including any relevant individuals, events, or dates. Then have each group present its work to the class.

ENGLISH LANGUAGE LEARNERS ,
COOPERATIVE LEARNING

Portfolio Extensions

1. Interdisciplinary Connection to the Arts

Have students design a mural honoring one of the reformers that they read about in the chapter. Have them depict scenes from the person's life as well as his or her accomplishments. Then ask students to write a brief paragraph about the mural. In the paragraph they should explain why they selected this person from all of the prominent reformers in the 1800s.

2. Linking to Community Have students design their own ideal community using the examples described in this chapter as models. Then ask students to make a list of at least seven rules for members of their new utopian community.

Social Studies Skills Workshop

Interpreting Graphs

Study the graph below. Then use the information on the graph to help you answer the questions that follow.

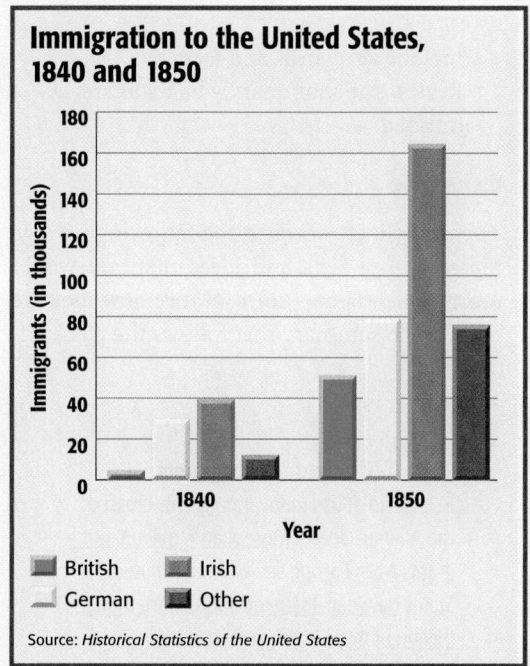

Immigration to the United States, 1840 and 1850

Immigrants (in thousands) / Year

Legend: British, Irish, German, Other

Source: *Historical Statistics of the United States*

1. Based on your knowledge of the period, what events could have led to the increase in the number of German and Irish immigrants to the United States between 1840 and 1850?

2. Which of the following statements was not true for 1850?
   a. The Irish were the largest group of immigrants to the United States.
   b. The number of German immigrants rose greatly from 1840.
   c. There were fewer immigrants from Britain than in 1840.
   d. There were nearly 80,000 immigrants from "Other" countries in 1850.

Analyzing Primary Sources

Read the following quote by abolitionist William Lloyd Garrison, then answer the questions that follow.

❝I will be as harsh as truth, and as uncompromising as justice. On this subject, I do not wish to think, to speak, or write, with moderation. . . . I am in earnest—I will not equivocate [lie]—I will not excuse—I will not retreat a single inch—AND I WILL BE HEARD.❞

3. What is the best interpretation for what Garrison means by, "I will be as harsh as truth, and as uncompromising as justice"?
   a. He will treat everyone equally.
   b. He will be truthful and fair in what he writes about slavery.
   c. He will pursue abolition no matter how long it takes or whom he offends.
   d. He will punish slaveholders for their crimes.

4. Based on your knowledge of the period, why do you think Garrison felt he needed to state his determination so forcefully?

5. Whom do you think Garrison was addressing when he made the statement above?

Alternative Assessment

Building Your Portfolio

Linking to Community
As a group, select an issue that you think is important to your community today. Plan a campaign to educate the public about this issue. Assign each group member one of the following roles—artist, speechwriter, or presenter. The artists should design a poster explaining the issue. The speechwriters should write a script for a speech about the issue. Finally, the presenters should formally deliver the speech and artwork to the class.

internet connect

Internet Activity: go.hrw.com
keyword: SA3 CF15

Access the Internet through the HRW Go site to learn about the Astor Place riot of 1849 and how the riot reflected developments in drama and urban society in the 1800s. Then imagine that radio had been invented during this time and conduct a radio broadcast with one of the actors or witnesses of the riot. Include direct references to your research in your broadcast.

---

2. helped fuel economic growth, particularly in cities

3. Finley—started the American Colonization Society; Walker—wrote and spoke against slavery; Garrison—published the *Liberator* and established the American Anti-Slavery Society; Grimkés—wrote and spoke against slavery; Douglass—wrote and spoke against slavery and published the *North Star*; Tubman—guided slaves to freedom on the Underground Railroad

Thinking Critically

1. dramatic increase in urban population and jobs; cities became crowded & unsanitary; need arose for public services; Industrial Revolution, Transportation Revolution, and immigration

2. belief that immigrants could not assimilate into American culture, fear of losing jobs to immigrants, fear of immigrants' religious background

3. Students' answers will vary.

Skills Workshop

1. many Irish immigrants came to escape, starvation, and disease; many German immigrants came to escape persecution and pursue economic opportunities

2. c

3. c

4. Students' answers will vary, but students will probably note that many people condoned the practice of slavery and that Garrison was speaking out against slavery and for justice.

5. those who condoned slavery

★ TEACH

ALL LEVELS: Have students turn back to p. 331 and reread the passage on northern factories. Ask students to identify the main ideas of the passage. Next, organize the students into groups. Have each group take notes to find details to support the main ideas and key vocabulary terms from the chapter. Then bring the groups together and share the notes to make a class list. Discuss how the students chose which details to include in their notes. Next, have the students individually create a summary of the passage with only their notes. Have volunteers read their summaries to the class. Stress the importance of specific details in notes. Finally, ask students to make a list of all the words they could not identify and to define them for their notes.

ENGLISH LANGUAGE LEARNERS , COOPERATIVE LEARNING

STUDY SKILLS

Assign each student a theme from Chapter 15. Themes might include the following: immigration, the movement to end slavery, and so on. Have students locate passages in the text that match the theme. Ask them to take notes on the passages. Once they have finished, have each student trade papers with another student. Let the second student write a summary from the first student's notes. Allow volunteers to read their summaries to the class. As a class, discuss the varying level of detail in the summaries.

SKILLS ANSWERS

1. Students' notes will vary.
2. Students' summaries will vary.

Social Studies Skills
W O R K S H O P

Study Skills

Taking notes and summarizing are key study skills. The following activities will help you develop and practice these skills.

Taking Notes

Taking notes helps you identify the main points of whatever you are studying, whether it is a book or a lecture. You should write your notes in your own words to help you understand them. Try to use the following steps when taking notes:

1. Identify the subject or main topic.
2. Identify the main ideas.
3. Note interesting and important details.
4. Identify key vocabulary terms.
5. Review your notes shortly after you write them.

Summarizing

Taking good notes can be very helpful when creating a summary—a brief statement of the important ideas in what you are studying. Summaries are a good tool to use when doing research for a report or presentation. The following strategies will help you write a summary:

- Write the summary in paragraph form, using as few words as possible without being inaccurate or too brief.

- Include key words and facts.
- Review your summary when you are finished.

Example

The underlined words in the following passage represent key facts and ideas that you would record when taking notes. Notice how they are used in the summary that follows the passage.

> **Waves of Immigrants**
> In the mid-1800s many immigrants crossed the Atlantic Ocean. <u>More than 4 million immigrants from Europe</u> settled in the United States <u>between 1840 and 1860</u>. <u>More than 3 million</u> of these immigrants arrived <u>from Ireland and Germany</u>. <u>Many immigrants were fleeing from economic or political troubles</u> in their native countries.

Summary More than 3 million Irish and German immigrants came to the United States between 1840 and 1860. Many immigrants came because of economic or political problems at home.

Practicing the Skills

1. Look at Chapter 15: Section 4, The Movement to End Slavery. Read the subsection titled The Underground Railroad. On your own paper, take notes by writing down the key words and phrases from each paragraph.

2. Now look at the notes that you have taken. Using only these notes and the strategies outlined above, write a short summary of the subsection. Show your summary to another student to see if he or she can understand the subject based on your summary.

ALL LEVELS: Explain to students that many factors influence the decision to immigrate. Organize the class into small groups. Have the groups brainstorm possible reasons for emigrating from Europe in the 1800s. (*Students' answers will vary but should include family pressures, economic opportunities, and political and religious conflicts.*) Ask groups to study and to take notes on the flyer that was created regarding the items immigrants might need in their new country. Then have each group summarize, in a one-act play, the family's reaction to the flyer detailing what they should and should not bring. If the family wishes to bring more items, have students explain what and why. Finally, ask groups to present their plays to the class.

ENGLISH LANGUAGE LEARNERS , COOPERATIVE LEARNING

History in Action

UNIT 6 SIMULATION

You Make the Decision . . .

What Should Immigrants Bring with Them to the United States?

Complete the following activity in small cooperative groups. It is the mid-1800s and America is the land of opportunity. Many people are coming to the United States from other countries to start new lives. Usually traveling in tightly packed sections of ships, immigrants are limited in what they can bring with them to America. Your community has asked you to serve on a committee to develop a flier that will identify for immigrants what items to bring with them to make the successful transition to life in the United States. Follow these steps to reach your decision.

1. Gather Information. Use your textbook and other resources to find information that might help you decide which items immigrants need to bring to America to start their new lives. Be sure to use what you learned from this unit's Skills Workshop on Summarizing and Taking Notes to help you record the information that you gather. You may want to divide different parts of the research among group members.

2. Identify Options. After reviewing the information you have gathered, consider the options for items to recommend. Your final decision may be easier to reach if you consider as many options as possible. Be sure to record your possible options for the preparation of your flier.

3. Predict Consequences. Now consider what might be the outcome if immigrants decide to bring or not to bring each of these items. Ask yourselves questions like: "Will the immigrants have enough room to bring these items on the ship?" Once you have predicted the consequences, record them as notes for the preparation of your flier.

4. Take Action to Implement Your Decision. After you have considered your options, you should plan and create your flier to present to the community board. Be sure to make your decision on which items immigrants should bring to the United States very clear. You will need to support your decisions by including information you gathered and by explaining why you rejected other options. Your flier needs to be visually appealing to the community board. When you are ready, decide which committee members will present each part of the flier, and then take your flier to the community board (the rest of the class). Good Luck!

History in Action Ask students to imagine that they are immigrants who have been in the United States for one year. Have students draft a letter to the Immigration Board outlining whether the provisions and items that were recommended in the flyer were adequate and why or why not. Encourage students to include any additional information that may be of use to the board in aiding new immigrants. Students should incorporate the decision-making steps found in the simulation on this page into their letter that summarizes their points and thoughts regarding the flyer and its usefulness.

⭐ CHAPTER 16
Expanding West

During the 1800s Americans continued to push the boundaries of their nation west. In the Southwest, residents of the Spanish colony of Mexico rebelled, forming their own republic. Some grew unhappy with the Mexican government, revolted, and created the nation of Texas. In the meantime, other settlers braved difficult trails to reach Oregon and California.

⭐ CHAPTER 17
Manifest Destiny and War

In the 1840s many Americans believed that their country was meant to expand as far west as the Pacific Ocean—a belief known as Manifest Destiny. This belief led many people to settle in territories outside the U.S. borders. Eventually, these settlers' hopes for statehood led to tensions with Britain and a war with Mexico. The Mexican War ended in a U.S. victory, which increased U.S. territory. In 1849 the discovery of gold in California increased both the number of people in that territory and the speed with which it became a state.

Internet Activity

Pioneers and Artists

internet connect

TOPIC: Artists and the West
GO TO: go.hrw.com
KEYWORD: SA3 Artists and the West

Many western expeditions included artists, who went along to record the plants and animals as well as the beauty of the landscape. Have students search the Internet through the HRW Go site for information about artists who traveled west, such as John Audubon, Albert Bierstadt, Karl Bodmer, George Catlin, and Alfred Miller. Have students collect pictures by and information about the artists. Then organize the class into groups. Have groups refer to these pictures in order to prepare a report to the president of the United States describing the recently acquired territories in the West.

UNIT 7
The Nation Expands West
(1790–1860)

CHAPTER 16 Expanding West (1790–1850)

CHAPTER 17 Manifest Destiny and War (1840–1860)

Share the information in the chapter overviews with students. Have them brainstorm a list of items that they think characterized both the Southwest and the Northwest before settlement. Then have them brainstorm a list of items that characterize Arizona, California, New Mexico, Oregon, and Texas today. Have half of the class write letters from the perspective of settlers to the new western territories in the 1800s and have the other half write letters from the perspective of someone moving to these areas now. Ask students to use their letters to describe the opportunities that people think they might find in these places. Organize students into pairs. Have pairs compare and look for similarities between their letters. Later, when you have finished the unit, refer to these letters and have students evaluate how closely their ideas about the motives of western settlers reflect the actual motivations described in this unit.

Young People

IN HISTORY

Young Pioneers

The young pioneers who set out for the West with their families in the 1840s and 1850s showed great courage. They knew that hardship and perhaps death lay ahead on the western trails. Young Martha Gay traveled to Oregon in the 1850s. She remembered, "We often saw human skulls bleached by sun and storms lying scattered around" along the trail.

Many teenagers were willing to push ahead, regardless of the conditions. Young Nancy Kelsey was one of the first group of pioneers to head for California in 1841. When the group's horses began to tire, Kelsey and the others had to leave their wagons at the Great Salt Lake. She recalled their struggles.

❝We had a difficult time to find a way down the [Sierra Nevada] mountains. . . . We were then out of provisions [supplies], having killed and eaten all our cattle. I walked barefeeted until my feet were blistered and lived on roasted acorns for two days.❞

Young pioneers travel across the western frontier in the 1800s.

Kelsey arrived in California soon afterward.

Young pioneers worked hard every day to keep their families healthy and safe. Older boys watched the livestock. Even boys as young as 12 took turns standing watch around the wagon train at night. Teenage girls took care of their younger brothers and sisters and helped with chores.

Teenagers still found ways to have fun during the trip. They played music and danced during the evenings. Fifteen-year-old Mary Margaret Hezlep stitched patch blocks for a quilt during her trip to California. The blocks tell the story of her journey. Other young pioneers brought along books like *The Life of Daniel Boone*, *Pilgrim's Progress*, and *Robinson Crusoe* to read. Some teenagers kept diaries.

If You Were There *What would you do for fun while traveling along the pioneer trails?*

LEFT PAGE: *In the mid-1800s, Emanuel Gottlieb Leutze painted this scene of the frontier, titled* Westward the Course of Empire Takes Its Way.

★ **Using Visual Resources**

Westward Expansion. Although he was raised in the United States, painter Emanuel Leutze spent much of his life in Düsseldorf, Germany. There he was an outspoken critic of the autocratic German government of the time. A woman once asked him why he painted *Westward the Course of Empire Takes Its Way.* She asked, "Did you not mean this group [shown on the opposite page] to teach a new gospel to this continent, a new truth which this part of the world is to accept?" According to the woman's memoirs, Leutze told her that she "was the first American that had understood his picture."

ACTIVITY: Have students study the picture closely to determine what each figure reveals about westward expansion. Then have them write caption bubbles for what each of the figures might be saying or thinking.

Objectives	Pacing Guide	Reproducible Resources
SECTION 1: **The Spanish West and Southwest** (pp. 488–91) ★ Examine how society was structured in Spanish California, New Mexico, and Texas. ★ Identify the events leading to the establishment of the republic of Mexico. ★ Describe how the Mexican war for independence affected California and Texas.	**Regular** 1.5 days **Block Scheduling** .5 day *Block Scheduling Handbook with Team Teaching Strategies, Chapter 16*	**RS** Guided Reading Strategy 16.1
SECTION 2: **Texas Gains Independence** (pp. 492–96) ★ Identify the reasons why many U.S. settlers in Texas rebelled against the Mexican government. ★ Analyze the most important events of the Texas Revolution. ★ Explain the result of the Texas Revolution.	**Regular** 2 days **Block Scheduling** 1 day *Block Scheduling Handbook with Team Teaching Strategies, Chapter 16*	**RS** Guided Reading Strategy 16.2 **PS** Biography Reading 16: Stephen F. Austin
SECTION 3: **The Lone Star Republic** (pp. 497–501) ★ Identify the difficulties American Indians and Tejanos faced in the republic of Texas. ★ Explain what drew new immigrants to Texas. ★ Describe the economic and foreign challenges that faced the Texas government.	**Regular** 2 days **Block Scheduling** 1 day *Block Scheduling Handbook with Team Teaching Strategies, Chapter 16*	**RS** Guided Reading Strategy 16.3 **RS** Graphic Organizer 16: The Republic of Texas **E** Hands-On History Activity: Famous Buildings in Your Community
SECTION 4: **Oregon and the Far West** (pp. 502–07) ★ Identify the reasons Americans first traveled to the Rocky Mountains and farther west. ★ Explain why Americans decided to settle in Oregon Country. ★ Describe what life was like on the Oregon Trail.	**Regular** 2 days **Block Scheduling** 1 day *Block Scheduling Handbook with Team Teaching Strategies, Chapter 16*	**RS** Guided Reading Strategy 16.4 **SM** Geography Activity 16: The Fur Traders **PS** Primary Source Reading 16: The Road to Oregon **E** Creative Teaching Strategy: Decision Tree
SECTION 5: **California and the Southwest** (pp. 508–11) ★ Identify the reasons Americans started traveling to California in the early 1800s. ★ Explain why American merchants established a new route to New Mexico. ★ Describe the types of images frontier artists painted.	**Regular** 1.5 days **Block Scheduling** 1 day *Block Scheduling Handbook with Team Teaching Strategies, Chapter 16*	**RS** Guided Reading Strategy 16.5 **PS** Literature Reading 16: On a California Ranch

Chapter Resource Key

PS	Primary Sources	**A**	Assessment
RS	Reading Support	**REV**	Review
IC	Interdisciplinary Connections	**ELL**	Reinforcement and English Language Learners
E	Enrichment		Transparencies
SM	Skills Mastery		CD-ROM

 Music

 Video

 Internet

Holt Presentation Maker Using Microsoft® PowerPoint®

One-Stop Planner CD-ROM

See the *One-Stop Planner* for a complete list of additional resources for students and teachers.

One-Stop Planner CD-ROM

It's easy to plan lessons, select resources, and print out materials for your students when you use the **One-Stop Planner CD-ROM with Test Generator.**

Technology Resources

One-Stop Planner, Lesson 16.1
Homework Practice Online

One-Stop Planner, Lesson 16.2
Exploring America's Past, Video Segment: Remember the Alamo; Teacher's Guide, pp. 26–27
CNN Presents America: Yesterday and Today, Beginnings to 1914 Segment: Excavating the Alamo
Homework Practice Online
HRW Go site

One-Stop Planner, Lesson 16.3
Homework Practice Online
HRW Go site

One-Stop Planner, Lesson 16.4
Holt Researcher: American History CD-ROM
Homework Practice Online

One-Stop Planner, Lesson 16.5
American History Interactive Maps CD-ROM: San Francisco: Mission to Metropolis
Art in American History Transparency 10: See-non-ty-a, an Iowa Medicine Man
Homework Practice Online

Reinforcement, Review, and Assessment

REV Section 16 Review, p. 491
A Daily Quiz 16.1
ELL Main Idea Activity 16.1
ELL English Audio Summary 16.1
ELL Spanish Audio Summary 16.1

REV Section 2 Review, p. 496
A Daily Quiz 16.2
ELL Main Idea Activity 16.2
ELL English Audio Summary 16.2
ELL Spanish Audio Summary 16.2

REV Section 3 Review, p. 501
A Daily Quiz 16.3
ELL Main Idea Activity 16.3
ELL English Audio Summary 16.3
ELL Spanish Audio Summary 16.3

REV Section 4 Review, p. 507
A Daily Quiz 16.4
ELL Main Idea Activity 16.4
ELL English Audio Summary 16.4
ELL Spanish Audio Summary 16.4

REV Section 5 Review, p. 510
A Daily Quiz 16.5
ELL Main Idea Activity 16.5
ELL English Audio Summary 16.5
ELL Spanish Audio Summary 16.5

internet connect

HRW ONLINE RESOURCES
GO TO: go.hrw.com
Then type in a keyword.

TEACHER HOME PAGE
KEYWORD: SA3 Teacher

CHAPTER INTERNET ACTIVITIES
KEYWORD: SA3 CF16
Choose an activity to:
• report on the Texas Revolution.
• compare and contrast the Texas Declaration of Independence with the US Declaration of Independence.
• write a biography of Juan Seguín.

CHAPTER ENRICHMENT LINKS
KEYWORD: SA3 CH16

ONLINE ASSESSMENT
Homework Practice
KEYWORD: SA3 HP16

Standardized Test Prep
KEYWORD: SA3 STP16

Rubrics
KEYWORD: SS Rubrics

ONLINE MAPS, CHARTS, AND GRAPHS
KEYWORD: SA3 MCG
• Settlements in Texas, 1850
• The Texas War of Independence
• Oregon Country
• Major Overland Routes to the West by 1860

CONTENT UPDATES
KEYWORD: SS Content Updates

HOLT PRESENTATION MAKER
KEYWORD: SA3 PPT16

ONLINE READING SUPPORT
KEYWORD: SS Strategies

CURRENT EVENTS
KEYWORD: S3 Current Events

Meeting Individual Needs

Ability Levels

Level 1 Basic-level activities designed for all students encountering new material

Level 2 Intermediate-level activities designed for average students

Level 3 Challenging activities designed for honors and gifted-and-talented students

English Language Learners Activities that address the needs of students with Limited English Proficiency

Chapter Review and Assessment

IC Vocabulary Activity 16
Global Skill Builder CD-ROM
HRW Go site
REV Chapter 16 Tutorial for Students, Parents, Mentors, and Peers
REV Chapter 16 Review, pp. 511–13
Chapter 16 Test Generator (on the One-Stop Planner)

A Chapter 16 Test (Form A or B)
A Alternative Assessment Handbook
A Chapter 16 Test for English Language Learners and Special-Needs Students

Build on What You Know

If You Were There...

Ask students to answer the following question:

Why would you settle in the West?

Consider:

- the type of work you would like to perform
- how your life will change upon moving

You Be the Historian

What's Your Opinion?

 To help students create their **Themes** Journal entries, provide the following examples of appropriate **agree**/**disagree** statements.

EXPLORING THE TIME LINE

GLOBAL EVENTS

internet connect

TOPIC: Antonio López de Santa Anna
GO TO: go.hrw.com
KEYWORD: SA3 CF16

Have students access the Internet through the HRW Go site to research Antonio López de Santa Anna. Then have them write a biography of the controversial leader of the republic of Mexico. Remind students to use standard grammar, punctuation, spelling, and sentence structure in their biographies.

CHAPTER

16 Expanding West

(1790–1850)

By the 1810s fur trappers were already crossing the Rocky Mountains in search of wild game and new trading partners.

Moses Austin played an important role in bringing U.S. settlers to Texas.

UNITED STATES

1811 John Jacob Astor founds the fur-trading post Astoria on the Columbia River.

1821 Moses Austin becomes the first American to receive a contract to bring settlers to Texas.

| 1800 | 1805 | 1810 | 1815 | 1820 |

WORLD

1810 The Mexican war for independence begins.

1821 Mexico wins its independence from Spain.

1824 Mexico creates a republican constitution.

The national flag of Mexico features an eagle at its center.

This mural celebrates the efforts of Father José María Morelos y Pavón to win independence for Mexico.

Build on What You Know

By the mid-1800s there were many different reform movements changing American society. Some Americans saw the West as a place for a fresh start and a way to avoid overcrowding in the East. These settlers' quest for land brought them into conflict with Mexican citizens and the many different American Indian groups living in the region.

Citizenship

Agree Citizens are free to separate from a government they feel is oppressive.

Disagree Citizens have an obligation to obey the government that they have chosen.

Culture

Agree New foods, languages, traditions, and religions diversify a regional culture.

Disagree Combining cultures threatens a regional identity.

Geography

Agree People seek to settle desirable land.

Disagree Dangerous lands should be left uninhabited.

ALBERT BIERSTADT, "EMIGRANTS CROSSING, THE PLAINS," 1867, OIL ON CANVAS, A.0117; NATIONAL COWBOY HALL OF FAME, OKLAHOMA CITY, OK

After the Battle of San Jacinto, Texan leader Sam Houston accepted the surrender of Mexican general Santa Anna.

Albert Bierstadt's painting Emigrants Crossing the Plains *shows settlers moving west to Oregon Country in the mid-1800s.*

1836 Mexican troops defeat the Texan forces at the Alamo in San Antonio on March 6.

On April 21 Sam Houston leads Texans to victory over Mexican troops at San Jacinto.

1827 The United States and Great Britain agree to continue joint occupation of Oregon Country.

1835 The Texas Revolution begins.

1843 A territorial government is set up in Oregon Country.

1844 Texas president Sam Houston signs a peace agreement with Mexico.

1825   1830   1835   1840   1845

1833 General Antonio López de Santa Anna becomes president of Mexico.

1837 Reformers in Canada rebel against the government.

THE GRANGER COLLECTION, NEW YORK

Santa Anna was one of Mexico's most influential military and political leaders from the 1820s to the 1840s.

You Be the Historian

Themes Journal

What's Your Opinion? Do you **agree** or **disagree** with the following statements? Support your point of view in your journal.

- **Citizenship** A group of people have the right to declare independence from their country.
- **Culture** Immigration always brings positive change to a region.
- **Geography** People seek to settle only certain types of land.

If you were there . . .
Why would you settle in the West?

Texas and statehood. Although they had been denied membership to the Union in 1837, Texans remained hopeful of becoming a state. Tired of the wait for annexation, however, Texas formally withdrew that offer of annexation in 1838 and promptly set about establishing its own foreign policy. In 1839 and 1840, under President Mirabeau Lamar, Texas signed treaties with Belgium, France, Great Britain, and the Netherlands. Throughout this time, Texas remained willing to join the Union, but was not invited to do so as abolitionists feared upsetting the balance between slaveholding and nonslaveholding states. Furthermore, President Andrew Jackson did not want trouble with Mexico. Soon, however, Jackson feared Texas's foreign allies more than he feared its enemies. (In 1843 Britain and France negotiated peace between Texas and Mexico, bringing Great Britain too close to the Union for comfort.) U.S. secretary of state Abel P. Upshur offered to reopen annexation talks with Sam Houston, who eventually agreed.

ACTIVITY: Have students prepare a time line sequencing events that led from the initial proposal of Texas's annexation to its final acceptance.

Section 1

OBJECTIVES

⭐ Examine how society was structured in Spanish California, New Mexico, and Texas.

⭐ Identify the events leading to the establishment of the republic of Mexico.

⭐ Describe how the Mexican war for independence affected California and Texas.

SECTION 1 RESOURCES

REPRODUCIBLE

▶ Guided Reading Strategy 16.1

TECHNOLOGY

▶ One-Stop Planner, Lesson 16.1

▶ Homework Practice Online

REINFORCEMENT, REVIEW, AND ASSESSMENT

▶ Section 1 Review, p. 491

▶ Daily Quiz 16.1

▶ Main Idea Activity 16.1

▶ English Audio Summary 16.1

▶ Spanish Audio Summary 16.1

LET'S GET STARTED!

Write the following statement on the chalkboard: *Speculate about mixing people of two different cultures and how this can affect the peoples' lifestyles and cultures.* As students enter the classroom, have them write down their responses. *(Students' responses may include that one culture becomes dominant, they both remain unique, or that the cultures enhance each other.)* Tell students that in Section 1 they will learn more about how the mixture of Spanish and American Indian peoples affected their respective lifestyles and how the resultant culture reflects aspects of both.

Section 1

The Spanish West and Southwest

Read to Discover

1. How was society structured in Spanish California, New Mexico, and Texas?
2. What events led to the establishment of the republic of Mexico?
3. How did the Mexican war for independence affect California and Texas?

Identify

- Californios
- Tejanos
- Father Miguel Hidalgo y Costilla
- Agustín de Iturbide

WHY IT MATTERS TODAY

Missions are just one example of the Hispanic heritage of the United States. Use **CNNfyi.com** or other **current events** sources to find out about other ways our nation is influenced by its Hispanic heritage. Record your findings in your journal.

The style of the San Miguel Chapel was common to many colonial churches in northern New Spain.

The Story Continues

Bishop Pedro Tamarón y Romeral toured northern New Spain in 1760. When visiting Santa Fe, Tamarón was particularly interested in the town's churches, which were all built from adobe. This building style, adopted from the Pueblo Indians, was just one example of how Spanish towns on the frontier combined European and American Indian ways of life.

⭐ Life in Northern New Spain

New Spain's northern frontier was made up of California, New Mexico, and Texas. New Mexico was the oldest and most important of these provinces, with its capital at Santa Fe. By the mid-1800s settlers lived in small villages scattered across New Mexico. These Spanish colonists were influenced greatly by the Pueblo Indians of the region. In turn, the Spanish changed many aspects of Pueblo life, bringing new tools and new foods, such as peaches, to the region. The Pueblo introduced the Spanish

Have students read Section 1 and complete Guided Reading Strategy 16.1. Choose one or more of the following activities to explore the section content with students. For further suggestions on block scheduling or team teaching, see the *Block Scheduling Handbook with Team Teaching Strategies.*

LEVEL 1: Write the events leading to the establishment of the republic of Mexico in random order on the chalkboard. Have students work in pairs to identify the proper sequence. Discuss each event as a class.

ENGLISH LANGUAGE LEARNERS , COOPERATIVE LEARNING

ALL LEVELS: Copy the following graphic organizer onto the chalkboard, omitting the italicized answers. Have students complete the chart by adding details about how society was structured in each region. When students have completed their graphic organizers, discuss the comparisons and contrasts with the class.

ENGLISH LANGUAGE LEARNERS

Spanish California	New Mexico	Texas
mission system, each mission one day apart from the next	*small villages scattered throughout the region*	*mission system, scattered about settlement held back by American Indian defense against it*

to southwestern foods such as beans and corn. The Spanish also began to build with adobe, as the Pueblo did.

Life in California was very different from life in New Mexico. Missions were the center of California's colonial life. Between 1769 and 1823 the Spanish built 21 missions in California along the coast from San Diego to San Francisco. Each California mission was one day's travel from the next. Spanish military forts called presidios protected the missions from attack. New Spain's leaders also hoped this military presence would keep the British and Russians out of the region.

The missions held a great deal of land, which was used for farming and ranching. American Indians who lived on mission lands and were supervised by Catholic priests performed most of this labor. The crowded living conditions in the California missions led to outbreaks of disease that killed tens of thousands of mission Indians over the years.

The missions supported themselves into the 1800s. Often they sold their goods to local communities. Colonist Guadalupe Vallejo remembered the early days of Spanish California.

History Makers Speak

❝We were the pioneers of the Pacific coast, building towns and Missions while General [George] Washington was carrying on the war of the Revolution.❞

—Guadalupe Vallejo, quoted in *Sketches of Early California*, edited by Donald DeNevi

Spanish colonists in California were known as **Californios**. They were basically cut off from the rest of New Spain because of the great distance. This isolation was one reason that only some 3,200 Spanish people lived in California by 1821.

✔ **Reading Check: Contrasting** How was life for Spanish settlers in New Mexico and California different? In New Mexico, settlers lived in small villages; in California, society centered around the missions.

Analyzing Primary Sources

Making Generalizations and Predictions How do you think Vallejo would say that the Spanish and English colonists were similar?

Answers will vary, but students might suggest that both groups were attempting to build new societies.

THE GRANGER COLLECTION, NEW YORK

Interpreting the Visual Record

Mission life *Missions such as San Diego de Alcala, shown here, controlled much of the land in early Spanish California.* **Does the setting shown in this picture appear to be agricultural or industrial? Explain your answer.**

Linking Past to Present

Changing Religious Beliefs. The Christian view of existence and afterlife often differed from American Indians' beliefs. For example, many American Indians found it hard to accept the idea that immortality was a reward for a lifetime of good deeds. They believed that rewards were given in this life, and the afterlife was simply an idealized version of the world they already knew. To overcome such disbelief or resistance, missionaries sometimes modified Christian beliefs and rituals to adapt them to those of American Indian cultures.

CRITICAL THINKING

How might missionaries modify religious rites to appeal to American Indian cultures?

ANSWER: Students might suggest that missionaries might change Christian rites to resemble those of the American Indians.

Visual Record Answer

Students might suggest that the trees and countryside would indicate an agricultural setting.

LEVELS 2 AND 3: Ask students to imagine that they are residents of either California or Texas following the Mexican war for independence. Then have them write a letter to a family member who lives elsewhere describing the effects the war has had on their region. Have students include in their letters their feelings about the war.

HOMEWORK Ask students to imagine that they are either Californios, Tejanos, mestizos, American Indians, or Anglos living in the northern provinces. Then have them create a banner describing how Mexican independence and how the decline of the mission system affected the lives of their chosen group.

★ CLOSE

Ask students to compose a poem or a song summarizing their impressions of the effect of the Mexican war for independence had on the lives of people living in the three northern provinces.

★ Using Visual Resources

Father Hidalgo. Father Miguel Hidalgo y Costilla was born into an established Mexican family. His father managed a large hacienda and sent his son to a Jesuit college and later to another religious institution. While he was serving as a priest, Hidalgo met the men who would become his co-conspirators. The revolutionaries' plan was simple—imprison the rich Spaniards, confiscate their property, and overthrow any authority that opposed their revolution. In the painting on this page, Father Hidalgo is wearing his priest's robes and holding a document enscribed with the *Grito de Dolores*.

CRITICAL THINKING
Why do you think people followed Father Hidalgo?

ANSWER: Students may point to his plan to eliminate the upper class.

Father Miguel Hidalgo y Costilla led a rebellion against Spain.

★ Early Texas

The Spanish built up to 40 missions in Texas, but the mission system in Texas was weaker than the one in California. One reason was that the Texas missions were located far apart from each other. In addition, the Spanish often fought local American Indians, such as the Comanche and the Apache. Because of this fighting, fewer Spanish settlers moved to Texas during the early 1700s.

The Spanish government responded by offering land grants to settlers. By the mid-1700s only a few thousand Spanish settlers, called **Tejanos** (tay-HAH-nohs), were living in what is now Texas. They introduced new breeds of cattle and soon created a cattle-ranching society on the huge Texas grasslands.

The Comanche and the Apache still controlled much of Texas, however, limiting Spanish expansion. Viceroy Bernardo de Gálvez commented on the situation in the late 1700s. According to Gálvez, "A bad peace with all the [Indian] tribes which ask for it would be more fruitful [helpful] than the gains of a successful war."

★ Mexico Gains Independence

In September 1810 about 80,000 poor American Indians and mestizos in Mexico joined in revolt against Spanish rule. **Father Miguel Hidalgo y Costilla**, a Mexican priest from the town of Dolores, led this rebellion. The rebels hoped that independence would improve their living conditions. Their rallying call was the Grito de Dolores, or "Cry of Dolores." The cry went, "Long live our Lady of Guadalupe, down with bad government, death to the Spaniards!"

Support for Father Hidalgo grew. As his army marched across the countryside, he began reforms, such as ending the enslavement and unfair taxation of American Indians. But Father Hidalgo could not unite all of Mexico's villages. In 1811 the Spanish defeated the rebels and killed the priest.

Father José María Morelos y Pavón continued the revolution and Hidalgo's reforms. Morelos fought bravely until his capture in 1815. Finally, in 1821 under **Agustín de Iturbide** (ee-toor-BEE-day), the rebels defeated the Spanish. Mexico had won its independence. Although he did not have great political support, Iturbide made himself Mexico's emperor. After only two and a half years the army made him step down. A new congress created the Constitution of 1824, which made Mexico a republic. The country included what is now Arizona, California, Nevada, New Mexico, Texas, and Utah. It also contained parts of Colorado, Kansas, Oklahoma, and Wyoming.

✔ **Reading Check: Sequencing** Describe in the order that they took place the events that led to the creation of the republic of Mexico. **1810–11: Revolt by Indians and mestizos against Spanish rule fails; 1815: rebel leader Father Morelos captured; 1821: Iturbide defeats the Spanish, gaining Mexican independence; 1824: Mexico becomes a republic.**

★ Changes in California and Texas

In 1833 Mexico ended the Spanish mission system in California, and officials gave the mission lands to Californios. A group of about 500 families created large ranchos, or ranches. The largest ranchos had up to 90,000 acres of land and huge herds of cattle. American Indians did much of the hard physical labor on ranches and farms. For most American Indians, life did not improve greatly with the end of the mission system.

In his novel *Two Years before the Mast,* American Richard Henry Dana Jr. wrote about his many encounters with Californio culture. In one small town, a local man served a feast to Dana and his friend.

Primary Sources ❝We took out some money and asked him how much we were to pay. He shook his head and crossed himself, saying that it was charity—that the Lord gave it to us.❞

—Richard Henry Dana Jr., *Two Years before the Mast*

After Mexico's war for independence, Texas merged with the Mexican province of Coahuila (koh-ah-WEE-lah) to form a single state called Coahuila y Texas. Fighting during the war had killed or chased away many Tejanos. By 1821 only about 2,500 of them were left, mostly on scattered ranches and in a few towns, such as San Antonio. Mexican officials worried that so few people could not protect all of Texas. The government decided to recruit more settlers to help protect the northern frontier from American Indian attacks or possible invasion by another nation.

✔ **Reading Check: Summarizing** What changes did the new Mexican government make in California and Texas? The government ended California's mission system, gave land to Californios, and encouraged settlement in Texas.

Interpreting the Visual Record

Californios *The Californios developed a reputation as skilled horse riders. They were also known for their generosity to guests.* **What characteristics of this horseman suggest his wealth?**

Visual Record Answer

Students might suggest that his style of dress suggests wealth.

Section 1 Review
ANSWERS

❶ **Identify**
• Californios, p. 489
• Tejanos, p. 490
• Father Miguel Hidalgo y Costilla, p. 490
• Agustín de Iturbide, p. 490

❷ Texas under Spain: weak mission system, Tejano population of about 9,000, cattle-ranching society, American Indian attacks on settlers, government encouraged settlement; Texas under Mexico: Tejano population of only a few thousand, fear of attack by American Indians and Great Britain; California under Spain: missions at center of society, farming and ranching done by Indians who lived at the missions, California under Mexico: government ended the mission system, Indians left the missions to work on the farms and ranches

❸ a. wanted to improve their living conditions; effect—eventually, Mexico became an independent republic
b. large effect: influenced settlement patterns and introduced new foods and ideas to the Spanish settlers; little effect because they had less power than settlers

❹ Students' journal entries will vary, but should include an awareness of settlement patterns, the role of American Indians, and the population in each region.

Section 1 Review

❶ **Identify** and explain:
• Californios
• Tejanos
• Father Miguel Hidalgo y Costilla
• Agustín de Iturbide

❷ **Comparing and Contrasting** Copy the chart below. Use it to compare and contrast the key characteristics of Texas and California before and after Mexico gained its independence.

	Spanish Rule	Mexican Rule
Texas		
California		

❸ **Finding the Main Idea**
a. Why did American Indians and mestizos join forces to revolt against their Spanish rulers, and what effect did this have on Mexico?

b. How much of an effect do you think American Indians had on Spanish settlement in California, New Mexico, and Texas?

❹ **Writing and Critical Thinking**
Summarizing Imagine that you are a trader traveling through the Spanish territories of California, New Mexico, and Texas. Write a journal entry that lists how society was structured in each of these regions.

Consider the following:
• settlement patterns
• the role of American Indians
• the population in each region

go.hrw.com Homework Practice Online
keyword: SA3 HP16

Section 2

OBJECTIVES

★ Identify the reasons why many U.S. settlers in Texas rebelled against the Mexican government.

★ Analyze the most important events of the Texas Revolution.

★ Explain the result of the Texas Revolution.

Visual Record Answer

(for p. 493)

Students might suggest that with his gun raised, he appears ready to fight.

LET'S GET STARTED!

Write the following question onto the chalkboard: *When is it right for you to fight against apparently hopeless odds for a cause that you support?* As students enter the classroom, ask them to think about what set of circumstances would make it appropriate to fight an apparently losing battle. *(Students' suggestions will vary.)* Call on volunteers to explain their answers to the class. Then briefly explain the circumstances surrounding the battle of the Alamo. Tell students that in Section 2 they will learn the reasons why Texans revolted against Mexican rule.

Section 2

Texas Gains Independence

Read to Discover

1. Why did many U.S. settlers in Texas rebel against the Mexican government?
2. What were the most important events of the Texas Revolution?
3. What was the result of the Texas Revolution?

WHY IT MATTERS TODAY

Throughout the world many groups are struggling for political independence. Use **CNNfyi.com** or other **current events** sources to find out about one of these groups. Record your findings in your journal.

Define

• *empresarios*

Identify

• Stephen F. Austin
• Antonio López de Santa Anna
• Alamo
• Battle of Goliad
• Sam Houston
• Battle of San Jacinto

The Story Continues

In 1819 James Long led a group of Mississippi traders into Spanish Texas. The group built a fort by Galveston Bay, but Long and others were arrested in 1822 by Mexican troops. His wife, Jane, pregnant with their second child, stayed at the fort with their daughter. She survived the winter but left for Louisiana after learning of her husband's death. However, she was determined to return to Texas someday.

Jane Long had to protect herself and her children from American Indian attacks at Galveston Bay.

★ American Settlers in Texas

The new Mexican republic wanted to attract more people to Texas. Mexico hired **empresarios**, or agents, to bring settlers to Texas. In exchange, these *empresarios* received land—as much as 67,000 acres for every 200 families. American Moses Austin was an early *empresario* who died before he could bring anyone to Texas. However, in 1821 his son **Stephen F. Austin** selected a colony site on the lower Colorado River. Then he began carefully choosing settlers, including Jane Long. These first 300 families became known as the Old Three Hundred.

Austin worked to keep the peace between the Mexican government and the American settlers. His devotion to Texas helped make the

★ TEACH

Have students read Section 2 and complete Guided Reading Strategy 16.2. Choose one or more of the following activities to explore the section content with students. For further suggestions on block scheduling or team teaching, see the *Block Scheduling Handbook with Team Teaching Strategies*.

LEVEL 1: Lead a class discussion about the important events of the Texas Revolution, and its results. Draw an outline map of Texas and northern Mexico on the chalkboard. Call on volunteers to label the Alamo, the battle of Goliad, and the San Jacinto. List responses near each label.

ENGLISH LANGUAGE LEARNERS

ALL LEVELS: Copy the following graphic organizer onto the chalkboard, omitting the italicized answers. Have students complete the time line to help them sequence the important events surrounding the Texas Revolution. Display the time lines around the classroom, and have students compare and contrast them.

ENGLISH LANGUAGE LEARNERS

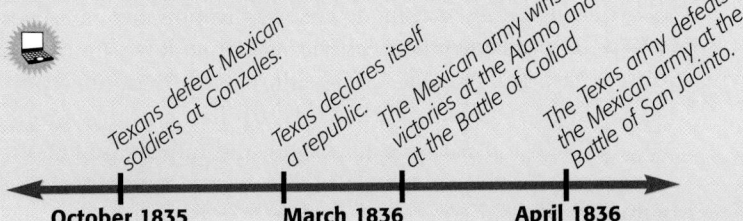

Texans defeat Mexican soldiers at Gonzales.

Texas declares itself a republic.

The Mexican army wins victories at the Alamo and at the Battle of Goliad.

The Texas army defeats the Mexican army at the Battle of San Jacinto.

October 1835 **March 1836** **April 1836**

colony a success. Other American and Mexican *empresarios*, such as John McMullen and Martín de León, brought more settlers. By 1834 more than 20,000 Americans had moved to Texas.

Most American settlers came from the southern states. In some parts of the South, the letters *GTT*—"Gone To Texas"—commonly appeared on empty houses. The promise of cheap or free land attracted most of these families. Each man could receive 640 acres, with additional land for his wife and each child. Other grants offered about 4,600 acres of free land to every married man.

✔ **Reading Check: Finding the Main Idea** Why did Americans move to Texas? They wanted the land offered by the Mexican government.

★ Trouble in Texas

By 1821 Mexico had set requirements for all foreign immigrants. They had to become Mexican citizens, obey Mexican laws, and support the Roman Catholic Church. However, most U.S. settlers were not interested in adapting to Mexican culture or becoming Mexican citizens.

By 1830 there were many more American settlers than Tejanos in Texas. These settlers often ignored Mexican laws, acting as if they were still in the United States and not on Mexican soil. Many American settlers came to Texas illegally and felt little loyalty to Mexico. Mexican officials

Interpreting the Visual Record

Rebellion *Stephen F. Austin pursued peaceful relations with the Mexican government, but was ultimately unsuccessful.* **What does Austin seem prepared to do in this painting?**

★ Historical Sidelight

European Colonists.
Mexican diplomats worried that too many U.S. citizens had settled in Texas and feared that Mexico might lose control of the territory. They consequently altered their policy regarding Texas and set about attempting to fill it with colonists of their own choosing. They considered Irish, German, and Swiss-Catholic farmers to be the best prospects to colonize Texas because their beliefs and backgrounds were different from most Americans.

CRITICAL THINKING

Why would the Mexican government have preferred European immigrants over U.S. settlers?

ANSWER: U.S. settlers might try to make Texas part of the United States

MAP ANSWERS

1. San Jacinto
2. Students might suggest that Mexican forces led by Santa Anna had to travel a great distance and cross several rivers.

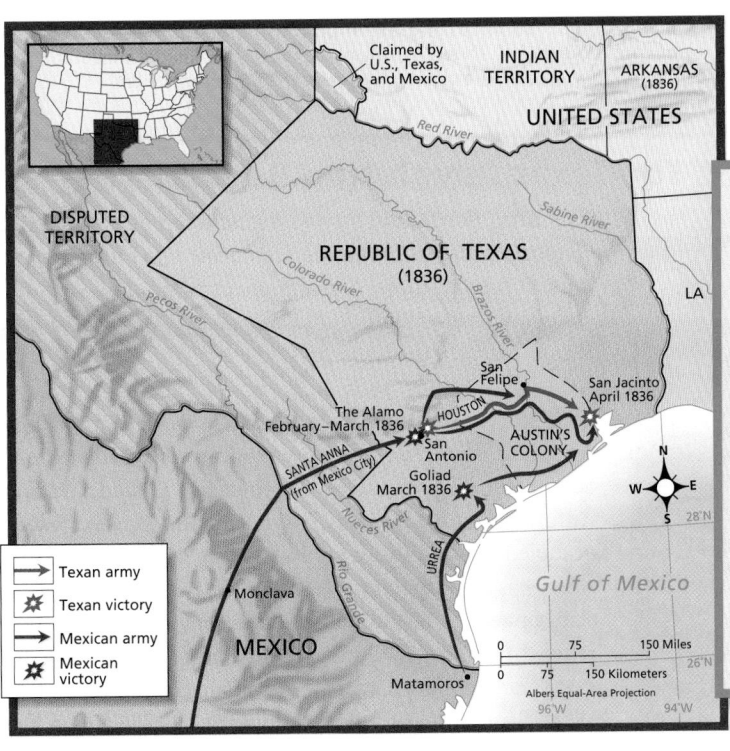

Claimed by U.S., Texas, and Mexico

INDIAN TERRITORY

ARKANSAS (1836)

UNITED STATES

Red River

DISPUTED TERRITORY

REPUBLIC OF TEXAS (1836)

LA

Sabine River

Colorado River

Pecos River

Brazos River

San Felipe

San Jacinto April 1836

The Alamo February–March 1836

HOUSTON

SANTA ANNA (from Mexico City)

San Antonio

AUSTIN'S COLONY

Goliad March 1836

Nueces River

URREA

Rio Grande

Gulf of Mexico

28°N

→ Texan army
✹ Texan victory
→ Mexican army
✹ Mexican victory

Monclava

MEXICO

Matamoros

0   75   150 Miles
0   75   150 Kilometers
Albers Equal-Area Projection

96°W   94°W   26°N

The Texas War for Independence

Interpreting Maps After defeats at Goliad and the Alamo, Texans rallied behind their leader, Sam Houston, and won a decisive victory at San Jacinto.

Skills Assessment

1. **The World in Spatial Terms** What battle took place within the boundaries of Austin's Colony?
2. **Drawing Inferences and Conclusions** In terms of geography, what advantage did the Texans have over the Mexican forces?

Technology Resources

 CNN Presents America: Beginnings to 1914 Segment: Excavating the Alamo

ALAMO COLLECTION, PHOTOGRAPH COURTESY THE DAUGHTERS OF THE REPUBLIC OF TEXAS LIBRARY, CT9723

James Pyne of Flossmoor, Illinois, suggested the following activity:

 LEVEL 2: Have students imagine that they are *empresarios* working to create a promotional pamphlet that will encourage Americans to migrate to Texas. The pamphlet should include information about the opportunities available to willing pioneers, the requirements they would have to meet in order to acquire land, and information about Mexico and its governmental regulations affecting Texas. The pamphlet should also capture the essential spirit of the migration of Americans during the 1820s and early 1830s. Encourage students to include diagrams, drawings, maps, slogans, and other items. **COOPERATIVE LEARNING**

LEVEL 3: Based on their understanding of the interactions between Tejanos, U.S. settlers, and the Mexican government, have students prepare a solution to resolve the differences between the groups. Proposals should begin with an analysis of the reasons why many U.S. settlers rebelled against the Mexican government, and should then continue with suggestions for stifling rebellion against the Mexican government, and preventing Texas from becoming independent. Have students advocate either more local government control or more control by the Mexican government.

Historical Sidelight

The Alamo. The Alamo was a small walled mission that consisted of a number of buildings. The Sacristy, a long building that was next to the church, was used by the Texan defenders as officers' quarters and a provisions storehouse. During the siege this room sheltered a number of people not involved in the fighting, including a woman and her infant. The Alamo compound also included a separate building that housed the kitchen, several cannon sites, trenches, and a makeshift hospital.

CRITICAL THINKING

How had the Texans altered the Alamo's original purpose?

ANSWER: The Alamo was changed from a Franciscan mission into a military fort.

Analyzing Primary Sources
Supporting a Point of View
How does this statement show Austin's feelings about the Mexican government?
He does not believe that the government can be negotiated with.

The outnumbered Texan defenders at the Alamo could only hope to keep the Mexican army outside the walls.

complained about this lack of respect for their government. One Mexican warned the country's minister of war and navy, "Either the [Mexican] government occupies Texas now, or it is lost forever." For their part, some Texans—Americans and Tejanos alike—argued that they were not fairly represented in Mexico's government. These Texans thought Mexico's central government was too powerful. They called for the Mexican Constitution of 1824 to be more strictly followed.

Mexico responded by enforcing its laws more strictly. For example, the Mexican government limited American immigration in 1830. Officials worked to keep settlers from bringing slaves, which concerned settlers who were slaveholders. Tariffs on goods from the United States were raised, and Mexico sent more soldiers to Texas.

While these actions angered many Texans, Stephen F. Austin tried to keep the peace. In 1833 Austin went to Mexico with a petition asking for more self-government, but he was thrown in jail. That same year General **Antonio López de Santa Anna** was elected president of Mexico. Santa Anna suspended Mexico's republican constitution in 1834. Austin was released from jail after a year and a half. Soon he called for all Texans to rebel against Mexico.

 History Makers Speak
"War is our only resource [option]. There is no other remedy [solution]. We must defend our rights, ourselves, and our country by force of arms."

—Stephen F. Austin, quoted in *Lone Star,* by T. R. Fehrenbach

✔ **Reading Check: Summarizing** What policies of the Mexican government caused Texans to rebel? The Mexican government limited immigration, kept out slaves, added more soldiers, and refused to give Texas more independence.

The Texas Revolution Begins

The Texas Revolution started in the town of Gonzales in October 1835, when the Mexican army tried to remove a cannon located there. A group of rebels stood next to the gun with a flag reading "Come and take it." In a brief battle, Texans defeated the Mexican soldiers.

In November 1835 a group of Texans formed a temporary government with the goals of defeating Santa Anna and restoring Mexico's republican constitution. Texas volunteers soon captured the towns of Goliad and San Antonio. Led by William Travis and Jim Bowie, Texans occupied the **Alamo**, an old mission in San Antonio. Santa Anna was determined to put down the rebellion and led an army of about 1,800 troops to San Antonio. Travis, however, refused to retreat. Volunteers including Juan Seguín and frontiersman Davy Crockett joined the Alamo defenders. When Santa Anna arrived on February 23, 1836, Travis had

HOMEWORK Ask students to prepare headlines with two accompanying stories announcing the results of the Texas Revolution. Each story should be written from one of the following perspectives: an American settler, a Mexican soldier, a U.S. official, or a Mexican official.

★ CLOSE

Organize the class into groups. Assign each group a major event in the Texas Revolution. Have groups prepare news dispatches summarizing their events. Dispatches should contain a headline, a report on the event and its aftermath, and speculation about its causes. Dispatches should also analyze both the implications of a Mexican victory and its probable effect on both resistance in Texas and world opinion. Call on volunteers to read their group's dispatch to the class.

COOPERATIVE LEARNING

Interpreting the Visual Record

Independence The delegates to the Convention of 1836 are shown here listening to the Texas Declaration of Independence. **How do the delegates appear to be responding to the declaration?**

only 189 troops. For 13 days the Mexican troops surrounded the Alamo. Travis sent Seguín on a daring mission through enemy lines to try to get reinforcements. Despite the terrible odds, Travis also wrote a bold letter. It was addressed "To the People of Texas and All Americans in the World."

> **History Makers Speak**
>
> **❝I shall never surrender or retreat. . . . I call on you in the name of Liberty, of patriotism, and everything dear to the American character, to come to our aid with all dispatch [speed]. . . . If this call is neglected I am determined to sustain [keep] myself as long as possible and die like a soldier who never forgets what is due his honor and that of his country. VICTORY OR DEATH.❞**
>
> —William Travis, from *Documents of Texas History*, edited by Ernest Wallace and David M. Vigness

Before dawn on March 6, 1836, the Mexican army attacked. Although the Mexicans suffered heavy losses, they soon overpowered the Texans. All the defenders of the Alamo were killed. Santa Anna spared the lives of a few people not involved in the fighting, including Susanna Dickinson. Along with others, she spread the story of the fall of the Alamo throughout Texas. The news increased support for the revolution. "Remember the Alamo!" became a rallying cry in Texas and the United States.

Following the victory at the Alamo, Mexican forces attacked the Texas troops near the town of Goliad. The Texans were greatly outnumbered. At the **Battle of Goliad** Texas commander James Fannin chose to surrender. Santa Anna ordered the execution of Fannin and almost all of his soldiers. This act outraged many Texans and shocked some of the Mexican troops. Francita Alavez, a nurse, hid several of Fannin's men. Because of her, they escaped the firing squads, and she became known as the Angel of Goliad for this act of mercy.

✔ **Reading Check: Supporting a Point of View** Do you think that the early battles of the Texas Revolution were a success or a failure for the Texans? Explain your answer. Answers may vary. Students should explain that the Texans suffered major defeats, but they may note that the Alamo and Goliad greatly increased support for the revolution.

Susanna Dickinson was one of the few survivors of the Alamo.

★ Citizenship

Declaring Independence. George Campbell Childress is considered the author of the Texas Declaration of Independence. He was born in 1804 in Tennessee and eventually became an attorney and newspaper publisher in Nashville. In 1836 Childress moved to Texas and less than a month later was elected to the Constitutional Convention. Although the convention appointed five men to write the declaration, it is thought that Childress wrote it alone. Unlike Thomas Jefferson, who worked for 17 days on the U.S. Declaration of Independence, Childress wrote the Texas declaration in one night.

🖳 internet connect

TOPIC: Texas Independence
GO TO: go.hrw.com
KEYWORD: SA3 CF16

Have students use the library or search the Internet through the HRW Go site to obtain a copy of the Texas Declaration of Independence. They should then compare it to the U.S. Declaration of Independence. Ask students the following question: *What concepts did the authors of the Texas document borrow from the U.S. declaration?*

☆ REVIEW AND ASSESS

Have Students complete the **Section 2 Review** on p. 496. Then have students complete **Daily Quiz 16.2**. As **Alternative Assessment**, you may want to use the promotional pamphlet or news dispatch exercises in this section's lessons.

☆ RETEACH

Have students complete **Main Idea Activity for English Language Learners and Special-Needs Students 16.2**. Then assign each student one of the key terms from the Define and Identify lists in the Section Opener. Have each student prepare a brief descriptive clue to the term's identity. Call on volunteers to offer their clues and ask the class to identify each correct term. Continue until all of the terms have been identified correctly. **ENGLISH LANGUAGE LEARNERS**

☆ EXTEND

Organize the class into two groups for a debate. Have one group support Travis's decision to remain at the Alamo and the other oppose it. Have students use the library to gather information in order to support their groups' arguments in a debate on the following question: *Would it have been better to abandon the Alamo, join other rebellious forces, and present a stronger, united front against General Santa Anna's advancing army?*
COOPERATIVE LEARNING , BLOCK SCHEDULING

★ ★ ★ ★ ★ ★ ★ ★ ★ ★ ★ ★

Section 2 Review
ANSWERS

❶ **Define**
• *empresarios*, p. 492

❷ **Identify**
• Stephen F. Austin, p. 492
• Antonio López de Santa Anna, p. 494
• Alamo, p. 494
• Battle of Goliad, p. 495
• Sam Houston, p. 496
• Battle of San Jacinto, p. 496

❸ October 1835: Texans defeat Mexican soldiers at Gonzalez; March 1836: Texas declares itself a republic, the Mexican army is victorious at the Alamo and Battle of Goliad; April 1836: Texans defeat Mexican army at the the Battle of San Jacinto

❹ a. American settlers wanted more self-government, the Mexican government became angry that Texans would not follow its laws, passed stricter ones, and sent troops to Texas; when the Texas Revolution ended, Texas was an independent country
b. Students should recognize similarities in greater representation in government, fighting for a cause they believed in, and the right to self-defense.

❺ Students' songs will vary, but should reflect an understanding of the causes of the Texas Revolution, the events at the Alamo and the Battle of Goliad, as well as the implications of a Mexican defeat.

Despite some criticism of his leadership, Sam Houston led the Texas army to victory over Mexico.

☆ Texas Becomes a Republic

Four days before the Battle of the Alamo, Texas delegates had met to declare independence from Mexico. Within two weeks they had written a constitution. Both the Texas Declaration of Independence and Constitution were modeled on those of the United States. However, there were some differences between the Texan and U.S. documents. For example, the Texas Constitution specifically made slavery legal. The delegates elected politician David Burnet as temporary president. They chose *empresario* Lorenzo de Zavala as vice president.

Sam Houston became the commander in chief of the new Texas army. Outnumbered and untrained, Houston's soldiers had to retreat east. The Texans finally made a stand at San Jacinto, near the present-day city of Houston. Santa Anna was confident of victory and had chosen his campsite carelessly. As a result, the Mexican army had poor defenses. On the afternoon of April 21, 1836, many of the Mexican soldiers were resting. They awoke to the sounds of Houston's forces attacking the camp and shouting "Remember the Alamo! Remember Goliad!" The **Battle of San Jacinto** had begun. Caught by surprise, Santa Anna's troops were driven back and trapped in the nearby woods. One Mexican officer later recalled the scene. "The enemy's cavalry surrounded the grove [woods], while his infantry ... [pursued] us with fierce and bloodthirsty feelings."

The defeat destroyed Santa Anna's army. Texans captured the Mexican leader and forced him to sign a treaty giving Texas its independence. Santa Anna was thrown out of power when he returned home. Although the fighting was over, many Mexican officials did not truly accept that Texas was now independent.

✔ **Reading Check: Finding the Main Idea** What was the importance of the Battle of San Jacinto? It led to the defeat of the Mexican army and Santa Anna's agreement to grant Texas independence.

Section **2** Review

★ ★

go.hrw.com **Homework Practice Online**
keyword: SA3 HP16

❶ **Define** and explain:
• *empresarios*

❷ **Identify** and explain:
• Stephen F. Austin
• Antonio López de Santa Anna
• Alamo
• Battle of Goliad
• Sam Houston
• Battle of San Jacinto

❸ **Sequencing** Copy the time line below. Use it to list the important events surrounding the Texas Revolution.

October 1835 —
March 1836 ◁—
April 1836 —

❹ **Finding the Main Idea**
a. What events led to the Texas Revolution, and what change resulted from it?

b. How might Texans have called upon the ideals of the American Revolution in their fight?

❺ **Writing and Critical Thinking**
Supporting a Point of View Imagine that you are a Texan under Sam Houston's command. You want to inspire your fellow soldiers before the Battle of San Jacinto. Write a song that will inspire the troops.

Consider the following:
• the causes of the Texas Revolution
• events at the Alamo and the Battle of Goliad
• what will happen if Mexico is defeated

Section 3

OBJECTIVES

⭐ Identify the difficulties American Indians and Tejanos faced in the Republic of Texas.

⭐ Explain what drew new immigrants to Texas.

⭐ Describe the economic and foreign challenges that faced the Texas government.

🔊 LET'S GET STARTED!

As students enter the classroom, assign each of them one of the following perspectives: an American settler, a Tejano, a Mexican, an American Indian, or a European. Then ask them to decide whether or not President Jackson should have annexed Texas in 1837. *(Students' responses will vary but should reflect the opinion of their assigned perspective.)* Have students explain their reasoning and list their replies on the chalkboard. Tell students that in Section 3 they will learn about the effects that annexation had on the many peoples of Texas.

Section 3

The Lone Star Republic

Read to Discover

1. What difficulties did American Indians and Tejanos face in the Republic of Texas?
2. What drew new immigrants to Texas?
3. What economic and foreign challenges faced the Texas government?

Define
• annex

Identify
• Republic of Texas
• Mirabeau Lamar

WHY IT MATTERS TODAY

In recent years, different regions of the world have become independent nations. Use **CNNfyi.com** or other **current events** sources to find out about the problems facing new nations' governments. Record your findings in your journal.

SECTION 3 RESOURCES

REPRODUCIBLE
▶ Guided Reading Strategy 16.3
▶ Graphic Organizer 16: The Republic of Texas

TECHNOLOGY
▶ One-Stop Planner, Lesson 16.3
▶ Homework Practice Online
▶ HRW Go site

REINFORCEMENT, REVIEW, AND ASSESSMENT
▶ Section 3 Review, p. 501
▶ Daily Quiz 16.3
▶ Main Idea Activity 16.3
▶ English Audio Summary 16.3
▶ Spanish Audio Summary 16.3

The Story Continues

In December 1836 President Andrew Jackson faced a difficult decision. Texas had declared its independence from Mexico earlier that year. Congress had asked Jackson to recognize, or formally accept, the new Texas government. However, Mexico still considered Texas a part of its territory. In a speech to Congress, Jackson described his problem. He said that the people of Texas "are bound to many of our citizens by ties of friendship and kindred [family] blood." Yet in his view it was too soon to take sides in the fight between Texas and Mexico.

This was the flag adopted by the Republic of Texas.

⭐ Texas Faces the World

The independent nation of Texas was called the **Republic of Texas**. Its capital was the new town of Houston. Voters elected Sam Houston, victor at San Jacinto and a former governor of Tennessee, as president. **Mirabeau Lamar** was chosen as vice president.

In 1837 the new government asked the United States to **annex**, or take control of, Texas. The vast majority of Texans hoped that Texas

Have students read Section 3 and complete Guided Reading Strategy 16.3. Choose one or more of the following activities to explore the section content with students. For further suggestions on block scheduling or team teaching, see the *Block Scheduling Handbook with Team Teaching Strategies.*

LEVEL 1: Organize students into pairs. Have one student from each pair write down one sentence describing the economic challenges faced by the Texas government. Have the other student write down one sentence describing its foreign challenges. Have pairs discuss their sentences.
ENGLISH LANGUAGE LEARNERS , COOPERATIVE LEARNING

 ALL LEVELS: Copy the following graphic organizer onto the chalkboard, omitting the italicized answers. Have each student complete the chart by describing the various challenges and conditions American Indians, immigrants, and Tejanos faced in the republic of Texas.
ENGLISH LANGUAGE LEARNERS

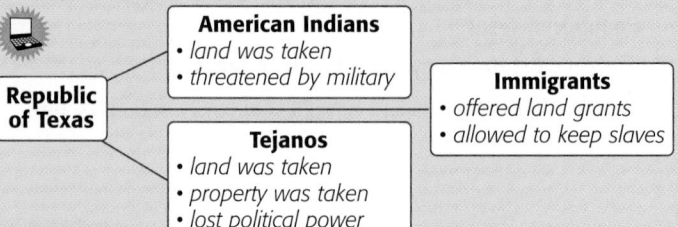

Republic of Texas

American Indians
• *land was taken*
• *threatened by military*

Immigrants
• *offered land grants*
• *allowed to keep slaves*

Tejanos
• *land was taken*
• *property was taken*
• *lost political power*

★ Biography

Juan Seguín. While he was mayor of San Antonio, Juan Seguín was greatly concerned about the effect American settlers were having on his fellow Tejanos. He believed the primary cause of hostilities between these groups was conflict over land. During the early 1840s Seguín noted that "the American straggling adventurers . . . were already beginning to work their intrigues against the native families whose only crime was, that they owned large tracts of land and desirable property." Seguín felt he had to protect these Texas families.

BIOGRAPHY

Juan Seguín
(1806–1890)

Born to an important San Antonio family in 1806, Juan Seguín became a well-known Tejano politician. Seguín led a troop of Tejano cavalry in the victory at San Jacinto.

After the war, Seguín served in the Texas Senate and later became mayor of San Antonio. In 1842 Seguín moved his family to Mexico because of rising tensions between Anglos and Tejanos. **What role did Seguín play in the winning of Texas independence?**

internet connect

TOPIC: Juan Seguín
GO TO: go.hrw.com
KEYWORD: SA3 CF16

Have students use the library or search the Internet through the HRW Go site for more information on Juan Seguín. Then ask them to add to the Biography on this page with the information they found using standard grammar, spelling, sentence structure, and punctuation.

BIOGRAPHY ANSWER
He served as a captain in the Texas cavalry and led a troop of Tejanos in the victory at San Jacinto.

would eventually become a U.S. state. Most Texas leaders, including Houston, supported this decision. In contrast, Lamar wanted to expand the republic to the west and increase its power.

Members of the U.S. Congress wanted to annex Texas, but President Andrew Jackson was concerned because Texas supported slavery. Adding Texas to the Union would upset the balance between free states and slave states. Jackson also did not want to go to war with Mexico over Texas. He recognized Texas as an independent nation, but he would not annex it. Martin Van Buren, the next U.S. president, did the same. France recognized the Texas government in 1839, and Great Britain did so the next year. However, Mexico still refused to agree that its former province had become an independent country.

✔ **Reading Check: Finding the Main Idea** Why did Texas not immediately become part of the United States? U.S. presidents feared upsetting the balance between slave and free states, and wanted to avoid war with Mexico.

★ American Indians and Tejanos

As a young man, Sam Houston had lived with the Cherokee in Tennessee. His experience led him, as president of Texas, to support a peaceful relationship with American Indians. However, Texas's Indian policy changed in 1838 when Mirabeau Lamar became president. Lamar demanded that American Indians leave their homelands and follow all Texas laws. He threatened military action if they refused.

Fighting soon broke out with American Indian groups such as the Cherokee and the Comanche. Comanche raids on Texan settlements increased. Many Texans believed that the Cherokee were plotting with Mexico to overthrow the republic. After Houston was elected to a second term as president in 1841, the fighting slowed. By then, however, Texans had forced most American Indians from their eastern lands.

Relations between Tejanos and American settlers also suffered under the new republic. Tejanos often faced unfair treatment. Tejanos lost land, political power, and property. This situation angered many Tejanos who had taken part in Texas's war for independence. Juan Seguín, a hero of the revolution and the mayor of San Antonio, described some of the problems faced by Tejanos.

Analyzing Primary Sources
Identifying Points of View How do you think Seguín feels about attacks against Tejanos? Answers will vary, but the students might note disappointment or sadness after fighting in the war of independence.

 History Makers Speak
"At every hour of the day and night, my countrymen [Tejanos] ran to me for protection against the assaults [attacks] . . . of these [American] adventurers. . . . Were not the victims my own countrymen, friends, and associates?"

—Juan Seguín, quoted in *Anglos and Mexicans in the Making of Texas, 1836–1986,* by David Montejano

Despite such treatment, many Tejanos chose to remain in Texas.

✔ **Reading Check: Summarizing** What problems did American Indians and Tejanos face in the new nation of Texas? Indians were pushed off of their lands, and Tejanos were treated unfairly and lost their land, property, and political power.

LEVELS 2 AND 3: Organize the class into six groups. Assign each group one of the following roles: African Americans, American Indians, German immigrants, Mexicans, Tejanos, or Texans originally from elsewhere in the United States. Then ask students to prepare a headline and news story describing what drew them to Texas, the government policies that affected their group, any difficulties their group faced in the new republic, the interactions among the groups, and where each group settled. Have volunteers read his or her group's articles to the class. **COOPERATIVE LEARNING**

 HOMEWORK As agents of the newly independent republic of Texas, have students prepare advertisements inviting U.S. settlers and Europeans to migrate to the republic. Have students include reasons why Texas might appeal to new settlers and describe incentives offered to encourage settlement in Texas.
ENGLISH LANGUAGE LEARNERS

Note: To help students make meaningful connections between events in American history and those in their own hometown, use the Chapter 16 **Hands-On History** activity, Famous Buildings in Your Community.

New Immigrants

In 1836 the population of Texas was approximately 52,700, including some 22,700 American Indians, African Americans, and Tejanos. To increase the republic's population, Texas leaders decided to offer land grants to American and European settlers. In the years 1840 and 1841 alone, the government gave out nearly 37 million acres. The Texas population grew by about 100,000 from 1836 to 1847. By 1845 so many immigrants were arriving daily that they had to wait for hours at ferry crossings. As more people came, settlements expanded to the north and west.

The largest group of immigrants to Texas was from the United States. They came in search of land and economic opportunities, particularly after the economic depression caused by the Panic of 1837. One Texan reported to a New Orleans newspaper about the rush of U.S. settlers to Texas. "All are land-hunting, seeking sugar, cotton, and stock farm lands."

The majority of these settlers came from southern states. Most were small farmers who did not own slaves. However, because the Constitution of 1836 made slavery legal, many slaveholders were also attracted to the Republic. As a result, the population of enslaved African Americans in Texas increased from some 5,000 in 1836 to almost 70,000 by 1845.

Life for slaves was difficult. Long days of hard labor and the threat of harsh punishments were common. The laws of the republic also made life difficult for free African Americans. In 1840 the Texas Congress passed a

THE GRANGER COLLECTION, NEW YORK

Daily Life

Austin, Texas As more settlers came to Texas, the population began to spread to the west. Leaders such as Mirabeau Lamar worried that the republic's capital, Houston, was too far from such settlements. In 1839 the Congress selected the tiny settlement of Waterloo in central Texas to be the site of the new capital. Officials renamed the town Austin in honor of Stephen F. Austin. **Looking at the picture, what challenges do you think officials faced in preparing Austin to be the republic's capital?**

LEVELS 2 AND 3: Based on the material from this section, have students prepare several entries for Sam Houston's diary. Entries should cover the problems Texas faced with the national economy as well as in its dealings with Mexico. Then call on volunteers to read their entries. Write key events or developments on the chalkboard, sequencing them in chronological order.

⭑ CLOSE

Remind students that when Texas became independent, many people wanted the United States to annex it, but instead Texas remained independent. Now that they have studied the history of Texas from 1836–44, ask students to reconsider if it would have been wise for the United States to have annexed Texas in 1836, and whether by 1844 it was more or less advisable to do so. Ask students to explain their reasoning, and compare and contrast their thinking with the ideas suggested in the *Let's Get Started!* activity in this section. Ask students to judge whether their reasoning has changed. If so, have them explain how and why it has changed. If not, have them describe what confirmed their original thinking.

⭑ Culture

Germans in Texas. The German immigrants who came to Texas were a diverse group. They included Protestants, Catholics, and Jews; abolitionists and slaveholders; farmers and townspeople. Most came seeking economic prosperity, while a few were fleeing the 1848 revolution and seeking political refuge. Few came for religious freedom.

CRITICAL THINKING

What traditions did Germans bring to Texas?

ANSWER: Students may suggest the following: music, theater, dance, language, food.

LINKING PAST TO PRESENT ANSWER

Students might suggest that Texans hold holiday celebrations, practice traditional art forms, and host arts and crafts festivals.

law that banned free African Americans from immigrating to Texas. The law stated that free African Americans living in Texas would have to leave within two years or be sold into slavery. Although this legal deadline was later postponed, by 1850 there were fewer than 400 free African Americans reported as living in Texas.

Germans made up the largest group of European immigrants to Texas. In 1843 the Congress required laws to be published in German as well as English. Germans established farming communities. They also founded towns such as New Braunfels and Fredericksburg, both in central Texas. German immigrant Gustav Dresel described the rapid growth in the 1840s.

History Makers Speak ❝There was land in abundance. . . . The lawyers . . . accepted payment in land. The innkeepers received so and so many hundreds of thousands of acres of land for board [food] and lodging from the army officers or big estate owners.❞

—Gustav Dresel, quoted in *Gustav Dresel's Houston Journal*, translated and edited by Max Freund

German customs had a strong influence on the culture of many towns in central Texas. Other European immigrants came to Texas from France, Ireland, and Poland. Czech immigrants from central Europe also settled in Texas. Each of these groups brought with it different traditions in areas such as architecture, food, and music.

✔ **Reading Check: Analyzing Information** What attracted settlers to the Republic of Texas, and what was life like for African Americans there? The government offered large land grants to settlers. Life was difficult for slaves and laws were biased against free African Americans.

⭑ Struggles of the Republic

With its small, scattered population, Texas faced many challenges as an independent country. During the years of the republic, only four Texas towns—Galveston, Houston, New Braunfels, and San Antonio—had more than 1,000 residents. Travel between the newer settlements was slow, difficult, and often dangerous.

Texas also had significant economic problems. Its economy was based largely on farming and ranching with very little industry. Although the republic was rich in resources, particularly in land, it had little cash. Taxes on imports and property failed to bring in much revenue. As a result the new nation was almost bankrupt. Texas's debt rose dramatically, while the value of its paper currency dropped sharply.

The government's lack of funds made it difficult for Texas to defend its vast territory. Due to problems with discipline among some of the soldiers, President Houston was forced to disband most of the Texas army. For defense and frontier protection, he relied instead on militia companies and the Texas Rangers. Formed in 1835, the Rangers were a frontier defense force that later acted as law officers as well. To make

LINKING
★ PAST *to* PRESENT ★

Ethnic Traditions

In Texas a wide range of cultures influence everything from food to holidays. Holiday celebrations like Diez y Seis de Septiembre are among many Texas traditions that date back to the first Tejano settlers. Diez y Seis celebrates the call for Mexican independence on September 16, 1810.

Thousands of European immigrants moved to Texas in the 1840s, bringing their customs with them. For example, a modern festival in the city of New Braunfels features traditional German music and polka dancing.

Every year the Institute of Texan Cultures in San Antonio hosts the Folklife Festival. Texans from 70 counties representing different backgrounds participate. How do Texans currently honor their ethnic traditions?

Texas children participate in a German festival.

★ REVIEW AND ASSESS

Have Students complete the **Section 3 Review** on p. 501. Then have students complete **Daily Quiz 16.3**. As **Alternative Assessment**, you may want to use the advertisement or newspaper exercises in this section's lessons.

★ RETEACH

Have students complete **Main Idea Activity for English Language Learners and Special-Needs Students 16.3**. Then organize the class into three groups, and assign each group one of the Read to Discover questions. Have each group answer its question. Then form new groups consisting of one student from each of the three original groups. Have members of the new groups discuss the answers to their respective questions.
ENGLISH LANGUAGE LEARNERS , **COOPERATIVE LEARNING**

★ EXTEND

Have students locate primary and secondary sources at the library to investigate the history of relations between Mexico and the Texas Republic in the years following the war and before the signing of the 1844 treaty. Then ask students to imagine that they are representatives of the republic of Texas in 1844. Have them write a recommendation considering the terms of the treaty and whether to pursue possible annexation to the United States. **BLOCK SCHEDULING**

Economic problems meant that paper money issued by the Republic of Texas steadily decreased in value, making it harder to buy goods and services.

matters worse, Mexico still considered Texas to be its property. President Mirabeau Lamar vowed to fight Mexico if necessary. Upon taking office he declared, "If peace can only be obtained by the sword, let the sword do its work."

In 1841 Lamar authorized a military attack on Santa Fe in the Mexican territory of New Mexico. The invasion lacked the approval of the Texas Congress and failed miserably. Mexico responded by sending its troops into Texas. The Mexican army even took control of San Antonio on two occasions. After Sam Houston returned to the presidency in 1841, he worked hard to end the fighting. Finally, Texas and Mexico signed a peace treaty in 1844.

✔ **Reading Check: Finding the Main Idea** What problems did Texas have with its economy and its dealings with Mexico? Texas had very little revenue, a large debt, and fought with little success against Mexico.

Section 3 Review

Homework Practice Online
keyword: SA3 HP16

① **Define** and explain:
  • annex

② **Identify** and explain:
  • Republic of Texas
  • Mirabeau Lamar

③ **Categorizing** Copy the graphic organizer below. Use it to explain the major problems that challenged the Republic of Texas.

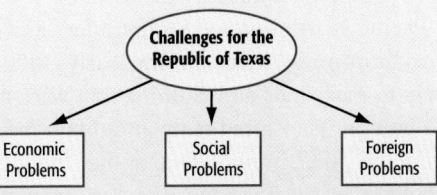

Challenges for the Republic of Texas

Economic Problems | Social Problems | Foreign Problems

④ **Finding the Main Idea**
  a. Explain the problems American Indians, Tejanos, Mexicans, and African Americans experienced in the Republic of Texas.

  b. Why do you think many Texans wanted Texas to become part of the United States?

⑤ **Writing and Critical Thinking**
  Analyzing Information Imagine that you are a Texas official. Create an advertisement to encourage immigrants to move to Texas.

  Consider the following:
  • the availability of land
  • economic opportunities
  • the reasons that settlers are wanted

Section 3 Review
ANSWERS

① **Define**
  • annex, p. 497

② **Identify**
  • Republic of Texas, p. 497
  • Mirabeau Lamar, p. 497

③ economic problems: lack of cash, rising public debt, devaluation of money, narrow economy; social problems: fighting with American Indians, problems with discrimination against Tejanos, laws against free African Americans, disputes over slavery; foreign problems: the U.S. would not annex it, hard to defend its borders, fighting with Mexico, invasion by Mexico

④ a. American Indians pushed off of their lands; Tejanos and Mexicans: treated unfairly by American settlers, and lost land, property, and political power; African Americans: enslaved, and the few free African Americans not allowed to live in Texas
  b. most Texans came from the United States

⑤ Students' advertisements will vary but should include the availability of land, economic opportunities, and the reasons why settlers were wanted.

Section 4

OBJECTIVES

⭐ Identify the reasons Americans first traveled to the Rocky Mountains and farther west.

⭐ Explain why Americans decided to settle in Oregon Country.

⭐ Describe what life was like on the Oregon Trail.

SECTION 4 RESOURCES

REPRODUCIBLE

▶ Guided Reading Strategy 16.4

▶ Geography Activity 16: The Fur Traders

▶ Primary Source Reading 16: The Road to Oregon

TECHNOLOGY

▶ One-Stop Planner, Lesson 16.4

▶ Holt Researcher: American History CD–ROM

▶ Homework Practice Online

REINFORCEMENT, REVIEW, AND ASSESSMENT

▶ Section 4 Review, p. 507

▶ Daily Quiz 16.4

▶ Main Idea Activity 16.4

▶ English Audio Summary 16.4

▶ Spanish Audio Summary 16.4

Section 4

Oregon and the Far West

Read to Discover

1. Why did Americans first travel to the Rocky Mountains and farther west?
2. Why did Americans decide to settle in Oregon Country?
3. What was life like on the Oregon Trail?

WHY IT MATTERS TODAY

In the 1800s, Oregon was known as a place that offered the opportunity for a new life to Americans and immigrants. Use **CNNfyi.com** or other **current events** sources to find out why Oregon is in the news today. Record your findings in your journal.

Define

• mountain men
• rendezvous

Identify

• John Jacob Astor
• Marcus and Narcissa Whitman
• Oregon Trail

The clothing of fur trappers was often influenced by American Indian styles.

The Story Continues

Fur trapper Manuel Lisa was one of the earliest explorers of the Rocky Mountains. Lisa once wrote to the famous explorer William Clark. "I go a great distance while some are considering whether they will start today or tomorrow." In 1807 Lisa led an expedition up the Missouri River. The explorers braved deadly river rapids and freezing weather. In the winter, he stopped at the Little Bighorn River, in present-day Montana. Lisa's accomplishment helped blaze the westward trail for future generations.

⭐ The Fur Traders

Most of the first non–American Indians who traveled to the Rocky Mountains and the Pacific Northwest were fur traders and trappers. They were known as **mountain men**. In the early 1800s eastern companies wanted furs to make hats and clothing that were popular in the United States and Europe. They hired many mountain men to bring back the furs of beavers and other animals. One of the largest businesses that bought furs from trappers was the American Fur Company, owned by **John Jacob Astor**.

★ TEACH

Have students read Section 4 and complete Guided Reading Strategy 16.4. Choose one or more of the following activities to explore the section content with students. For further suggestions on block scheduling or team teaching, see the *Block Scheduling Handbook with Team Teaching Strategies.*

LEVEL 1: Have students imagine that they are deciding whether to remain in the northeast or move west to Oregon to join other families from their area who have recently moved there. Tell students to list reasons to stay and reasons to go. Then poll the class to determine whether more students would stay or go. Call on volunteers to explain their reasoning. **ENGLISH LANGUAGE LEARNERS**

HOMEWORK Have students prepare a bulletin board sign encouraging people to migrate to Oregon Country.

Mountain men lived lonely and often dangerous lives. They trapped animals on their own, far from towns and settlements. Mountain men such as Jedediah Smith, Manuel Lisa, and Jim Bridger survived many hardships during their search for wealth and adventure. To survive on the frontier, mountain men adopted American Indian customs and clothing. In addition, mountain men often married American Indian women. The Indian wives of trappers often worked hard to contribute to their success.

Pioneer William Ashley saw that bringing furs out of the Rocky Mountains was expensive. He asked his traders to stay in the mountains and meet once a year to trade and socialize. This practice helped make the fur trade more profitable. The yearly meeting was known as the **rendezvous**. At the rendezvous, mountain men and American Indian trappers sold their furs to fur company agents. It was thus important to bring as many furs as possible. One trapper described the people at a typical rendezvous in 1837. He saw Americans, Canadian French, some Europeans, and "Indians, of nearly every tribe in the Rocky Mountains."

The rendezvous was filled with celebrating and storytelling. At the same time, the meeting was also about conducting business. Western artist Alfred Jacob Miller described how trade was begun in the rendezvous camp.

This 1841 drawing of Fort Walla Walla in Oregon Country shows fur trappers and American Indians meeting to trade. Fur coats such as the one shown were commonly worn by fur trappers.

> **History Makers Speak**
>
> ❝The Fur Company's great tent is raised; the Indians erect their picturesque [beautiful] white lodges; the accumulated [collected] furs of the hunting season are brought forth and the Company's tent is a . . . busy place.❞
>
> —Alfred Jacob Miller, quoted in *The Fur Trade of the American West,* by David J. Wishart

Analyzing Primary Sources
Summarizing According to Miller, what groups participated in the rendezvous? traders, the Fur Company, and American Indians

The stories and rugged lives of the mountain men caught the American imagination. However, the era of American fur trading in the Pacific Northwest lasted only a short time. By the 1840s the demand for beaver furs had fallen because fashions changed. Too much trapping had also greatly lowered the number of beavers. Some mountain men gave up their work and moved back east. Others began guiding farmers, miners, and ranchers to the West. In the 1840s these new settlers replaced the mountain men on the frontier.

✔ **Reading Check: Analyzing Information** What economic and environmental conditions did mountain men have to face? Their profits were based on personal effort and the demand for furs, which collapsed. They faced harsh outdoor conditions and a decreasing supply of beavers.

★ Geography

Astoria. Astoria served as the headquarters for the Pacific Fur Company. In the early 1800s it was the most distant outpost in the United States west of the Rocky Mountains. Astoria was actually populated by few U.S. citizens, however. American Indians, French Canadians, Hawaiians, Scots, and a few U.S. citizens made up Astoria's population. The frontier trading post symbolized the shared aspirations for personal wealth held by people with a wide variety of backgrounds and political allegiances.

ACTIVITY: Have students write diary entries that describe what a day in the life of a person living in Astoria or some other part of Oregon country might have been like using standard grammar, spelling, sentence structure, and punctuation.

ALL LEVELS: Copy the following graphic organizer onto the chalkboard, omitting the italicized answers. Have students complete the diagram to compare and contrast the reasons that the first settlers traveled to the Rocky Mountains and farther west with the reasons that Americans later settled the Oregon Country.

ENGLISH LANGUAGE LEARNERS

LEVEL 2: Have students write a letter from either Marcus or Narcissa Whitman to eastern friends who are missionaries. In the letters, have students explain their decision to settle in Oregon Country, how the fur trade affected their lives in the West, and their hopes and dreams for the future. Then ask students to "mail" their letters to other members of the class. Call on volunteers to explain whether the letters they received would persuade them to move to Oregon Country.

First Settlers
fur to trade

Both
*seek fortune
opportunity*

Later Settlers
*spread Christianity,
farm, mine,
or ranch*

It is not surprising that Narcissa Whitman became a missionary—by the age of 16 she had already pledged her life to missionary work. It would be 12 more years before she had her chance to fulfill that promise, however. Although Whitman had signed up with the American Board of Commissioners for Foreign Missions, she was unable to go west as they were not in the habit of sending single women out to the frontier to perform missionary work. Marcus Whitman, who had just returned from his first trip to Oregon Country, spent a weekend with Narcissa's family in 1836. The couple decided to marry and headed west that same year to perform missionary work together. Finally, Narcissa was able to live her dream.

The Long Way Home
Can you imagine traveling to Oregon via Antarctica? That's what some pioneers did in the 1800s! Not everyone wanted to spend four months walking from the East Coast to Oregon. So they went by water around the tip of South America and along the edge of Antarctica. But this trip sometimes took a year! Some pioneers tried a short-cut by crossing what is now Panama and waiting for a boat. Sometimes they waited for months. Many of the ships that picked up these pioneers were not safe and sank before reaching the West Coast.

Narcissa Whitman and another missionary's wife were the first white women known to have crossed North America.

Oregon Country

In 1811 American merchant John Jacob Astor founded Astoria as a center for the fur trade. It was located at the mouth of the Columbia River in the Pacific Northwest. This small outpost was one of the earliest American settlements in the region later called Oregon Country.

At the beginning of the 1800s, Oregon Country was occupied by American Indians. These Indian groups included the Cayuse, the Flathead, the Nez Percé, and the Shoshone. Great Britain, Russia, Spain, and the United States also claimed this region. The United States based its claim on the exploration of merchant captain Robert Gray, who had reached the mouth of the Columbia River in 1792.

In 1819 Spain and the United States signed the Adams-Onís Treaty. Spain gave up all claims to land beyond the northern border of what is now California. In 1824 Russia also signed a treaty with the United States. Russia gave up its land claims up to the southern border of what is now Alaska. These treaties left American Indians, Britain, and the United States as rivals for the Pacific Northwest.

The United States and Britain had signed a treaty in 1818 that allowed both countries to occupy Oregon Country. In 1827 they decided to extend this treaty. The agreement did not state how long this shared ownership would last, however. Both sides wanted to maintain use of the Columbia River and its surrounding land. Still, neither country was willing to start a war over the territory.

The British were interested in the Pacific Northwest primarily for the fur trade. Only a few British or Canadians settled in the area. In contrast, many Americans had begun heading to Oregon Country.

✔ **Reading Check: Summarizing** What nations claimed Oregon Country, and how were their claims resolved? Spain, Russia, Britain, and the United States all claimed Oregon. Through treaties the United States ended up sharing Oregon Country with Britain.

The Missionary Spirit

Missionaries were among the first Americans to settle in Oregon Country. The Second Great Awakening had brought a new religious spirit to the United States. Some churches decided to bring Christianity to American Indians in the Far West. Oregon Country was one such destination. In 1836, missionaries **Marcus and Narcissa Whitman** went there to convert American Indians to Christianity.

The Whitmans settled in Walla Walla, in present-day Washington State. They founded a mission called Waiilatpu. However, the Whitmans had limited success bringing Christianity to the local Cayuse Indians. Narcissa Whitman found her new life difficult and lonely. She wrote to her sister in 1846, "My health has been so poor, and my family has increased so rapidly, that it [frontier life] has been impossible."

LEVEL 3: Organize the class into groups. Have them imagine that they are a group of travelers about to head west along the Oregon Trail. Have them use the textbook to identify problems they are likely to encounter along the way. Have students group the problems according to common elements, such as supplies and weather. Then instruct each group to select one of the problems listed and then figure out a solution to it. Call on volunteers to present their solutions to the class. Have students vote on whether to accept the proposed solution. Finally, ask students to identify factors that made it difficult for enthusiastic groups to plan for their trek across the Oregon Trail. **COOPERATIVE LEARNING**

★ CLOSE

Have each student create an illustration for a history book depicting one of the main events or developments covered in this section. Students should include a caption that relates their illustration back to one of the Read to Discover questions. **ENGLISH LANGUAGE LEARNERS**

Note: For an additional teaching idea, see the Chapter 16 Decision Tree activity in the **Creative Teaching Strategies** handbook.

Despite the challenges the Whitmans faced, Marcus Whitman remained hopeful. He wrote letters encouraging more Americans to move out west. "I have no doubt our greatest work is . . . to aid the white settlement of this country," he wrote to his parents. He also made trips back east to recruit more settlers.

The Whitmans' efforts ended in tragedy. Settlers stopping at Waiilatpu brought diseases that led to an epidemic that killed many Cayuse children. In anger a group of Cayuse killed the Whitmans and at least 10 others.

✔ **Reading Check: Identifying Cause and Effect** Why did the Whitmans go to Oregon Country, and what were the effects of their efforts?
Missionaries wanted to convert American Indians and guide new settlers. Settlers brought disease, and the local Indians killed the missionaries.

★ A New Life Out West

Missionaries were not the only early American settlers in the Pacific Northwest. Thousands of people from the Midwest also moved to Oregon Country. These families looked to the West as a place where they could improve their lives. They had learned that Oregon Country offered rich farmland, great forests, rivers full of fish, and a good climate. Newspapers encouraged people to move. Many settlers also decided to go west following the economic hardships of the Panic of 1837.

A new territorial government was set up in 1843. It started a system of land grants to attract even more settlers. After 1843 each married man who settled in Oregon could claim 640 acres of land. In May 1843 the *Ohio Statesman* reported, "The Oregon fever is raging in almost every part of the Union."

Most of the new settlers moved into the Willamette Valley. The majority stayed and prospered in what is now Oregon. Others settled in what is now the state of Washington. The population growth in the region led to increased conflict with American Indians. It also caused greater tension with Great Britain over control of Oregon Country.

✔ **Reading Check: Finding the Main Idea** What attractions did Oregon Country hold for American settlers? rich land for farming, rivers full of fish, a good climate

Interpreting the Visual Record

Mission in Oregon *The Whitmans provided rest and shelter at their Waiilatpu mission for many settlers arriving in Oregon Country.* **Why might settlers want to stop at a place like Waiilatpu?**

Research on the R⊙M

Free Find:
Narcissa Whitman
After reading about Narcissa Whitman on the **Holt Researcher CD–ROM**, write a fictional journal entry describing her daily life as a missionary in the West.

★ Biography

Joe Lewis. Lewis, a Roman Catholic American Indian, joined the Cayuse in killing the Whitmans and 11 others. Lewis came to Oregon in 1847 with a group of priests and French settlers. He made his way to the Whitmans' settlement, and though poor, quickly prospered because he was able to speak English, French, and some Nez Percé. Lewis caused disturbances at the settlement, however, and was sent away by the Whitmans. Later, he returned to lead the massacre.

CRITICAL THINKING

Why might the Cayuse have followed Lewis?

ANSWER: Students may respond that they followed Lewis because he had lived in the settlement and knew it well.

Visual Record Answer

Students might suggest that it appears to be a peaceful and beautiful place to stay.

SPOTLIGHT
on the West

Before class, prepare a list of geographic features, trails, and sites of key historical events that were referred to in this section. Give students outline maps of the western United States and instruct them to locate and label each item from the list as it is identified in the section. Tell them to write brief descriptions of each item they identified on a separate sheet of paper as they read the section. **BLOCK SCHEDULING**

SPOTLIGHT
on Oregon Country

On an outline map of the western United States, similar to the one used in the previous activity, have students show the developing controversy over control of Oregon Country. Have students locate, label, and date the border established by the Adams-Onís Treaty, the border agreed on with Russia in 1824, and the joint occupation of Oregon Country agreed on by Great Britain and the United States. On a separate sheet of paper, have students provide brief descriptions of each border they identified. Finally, lead a class discussion about the controversy surrounding control of the area. **BLOCK SCHEDULING**

★ Geography

Oregon. Pioneers interested in Oregon Country were products of earlier frontiers. Most came from Illinois, Indiana, Kentucky, Ohio, and Missouri. Most were poor farmers. Oregon was an attractive new territory because it promised economic success without requiring new farming techniques. Rich, fertile land was also readily available. Settlers simply transplanted their skills to a more rewarding setting.

ACTIVITY: Ask students to list the items they would take if they were moving from Ohio to Oregon Country. Be sure that they describe the significance of each item.

MAP ANSWER
The Mormon Trail and the Oregon Trail; the South Pass

★ The Oregon Trail

Many of the settlers moving to Oregon Country and other western areas followed the **Oregon Trail**. The Oregon Trail stretched more than 2,000 miles across the northern Great Plains and the Rocky Mountains. Traveling the trail challenged the strength and determination of pioneer families. Pioneers started their journey in Independence or St. Joseph, Missouri, or Council Bluffs, Iowa. The trail followed the Platte and Sweetwater Rivers over the Plains. After it crossed the Rockies, the trail split into two paths, one to Oregon Country and the other to California.

The pioneers' journey usually began after the rainy season ended in late spring. The trip lasted about six months. A family of four needed about $600 to buy the supplies necessary for making the trip—a lot of money at a time when laborers made around $1.50 per day. Young families

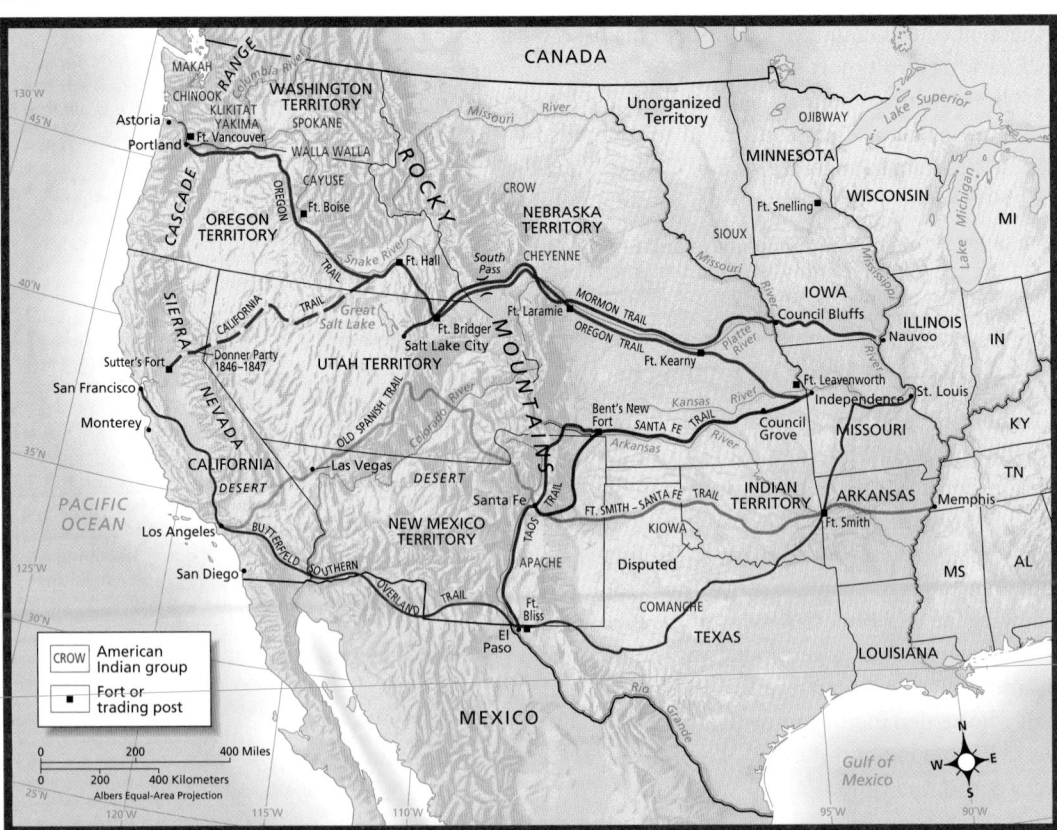

Major Overland Routes to the West

Interpreting Maps The rough terrain and a lack of constant water supply made many of the overland routes extremely difficult.

Skills Assessment The World in Spatial Terms What trails led between Fort Laramie and Fort Bridger, and what pass allowed settlers to cut through the Rocky Mountains?

☆ REVIEW AND ASSESS

Have Students complete the **Section 4 Review** on p. 507. Then have students complete **Daily Quiz 16.4**. As **Alternative Assessment,** you may want to use the Marcus or Narcissa Whitman letter or map exercises in this section's lessons.

☆ RETEACH

Have students complete **Main Idea Activity for English Language Learners and Special-Needs Students 16.4**. Then ask each student to prepare a newspaper headline summarizing a major topic that was discussed in this section. Write students' headlines on sheets of butcher paper. Call on volunteers to provide information that might be included in an article based on the headlines, and write the information on the appropriate sheet of butcher paper. Lead a review on any topics that students are having difficulty understanding.

ENGLISH LANGUAGE LEARNERS

☆ EXTEND

Have students search the library to locate excerpts from primary sources by people describing their experiences along the Oregon Trail, such as letters, diaries, and journals. Instruct students to compile a list summarizing the recurring themes, problems, attitudes, and moods that are found in the entries. Then have each student write a short story based upon the list of themes that describes the Oregon Trail experience. **BLOCK SCHEDULING**

made up most groups of settlers. They gathered in wagon trains for the trip. There could be as few as 10 wagons or as many as several dozen in a wagon train.

Shortages of food, supplies, and water were a constant problem for many wagon trains. Pioneers also faced rough weather and natural barriers, such as rivers and mountains. Travelers often got confused over the best route to take.

Pioneers often walked to save their animals' strength. They kept up a tiring pace, traveling from dawn until dusk. Settler Jesse Applegate recalled the advice he received from an experienced Oregon pioneer: "Travel, *travel*, TRAVEL. . . . Nothing is good that causes a moment's delay."

At the end of each day, much work remained to be done, such as unpacking, cooking, cleaning, and looking after children and livestock. Martha Ann Morrison recalled that when the men were busy, "the women helped pitch [set up] the tents, helped unload, and helped yokeing up [harnessing] the cattle." Children helped out their parents with the day-to-day work. One out of every five pioneers was a child.

American Indians from many different groups also helped the pioneers. Indians often acted as guides, carried messages between wagon trains, and traded food for goods. Although newspapers reported American Indian "massacres" of pioneers, few settlers died because of Indian attacks. The settlers who arrived safely in Oregon and California found generally healthy and pleasant climates. They also found fertile valleys for farming. By 1845 about 5,000 settlers occupied the Willamette Valley. Thousands more Americans chose to brave the dangers of the Oregon Trail to find new opportunities in the West.

Pioneers had to make room in their wagons to carry supplies, household goods, and sick people.

✔ **Reading Check: Supporting a Point of View** Do you think that life in the West was worth the risk for families who went there? Explain your answer. Students might say that the risk was too high and give examples of sickness, hunger, and bad weather; others might say the rewards of the trip justified the risk.

Section 4 Review

go. hrw .com Homework Practice Online
keyword: SA3 HP16

❶ Define and explain:
• mountain men
• rendezvous

❷ Identify and explain:
• John Jacob Astor
• Marcus and Narcissa Whitman
• Oregon Trail

❸ Summarizing Copy the web diagram below. Use it to explain why the following groups of people traveled to the Rocky Mountains and farther west and what challenges they faced.

```
          ┌──────────┐
          │ Pioneers │
          └──────────┘
              ▲
  ┌─────────────────┐
  │  Why Americans  │
  │   Headed West   │───────┐
  └─────────────────┘       │
      │                     ▼
      ▼               ┌─────────────┐
┌──────────┐          │ Missionaries│
│ Mountain │          └─────────────┘
│   Men    │
└──────────┘
```

❹ Finding the Main Idea
a. What factors led to the rise and decline of the fur trade?
b. How did missionaries influence future settlement in Oregon?

❺ Writing and Critical Thinking
Supporting a Point of View Imagine that you are a pioneer on your way to Oregon. Write a letter to a friend back east to tell him or her about life on the trail.

Consider the following:
• hardships and dangers
• activities and chores
• interactions with American Indians

★★★★★★★★★★★★★★
Section 4 Review
ANSWERS

❶ Define
• mountain men, p. 502
• rendezvous, p. 503

❷ Identify
• John Jacob Astor, p. 502
• Marcus and Narcissa Whitman, p. 504
• Oregon Trail, p. 506

❸ mountain men: to collect furs for eastern merchants; lived solitary, dangerous lives; missionaries: to convert American Indians to Christianity; lived difficult lives, did not have much success with conversion, faced Indian hostility; pioneers: wanted to establish farms or start their lives over, long, difficult journies

❹ a. the rise: eastern companies hired mountain men to bring back furs; the decline: fur fashions fell out of style and animals were overhunted
b. helped open the Oregon Trail, were enthusiastic about Oregon, recruited more American settlers

❺ Students' letters will vary but should include an awareness of the hardships and dangers, the activities and chores, and the interactions with American Indians.

Section 5

OBJECTIVES

- ✪ Identify the reasons Americans started traveling to California in the early 1800s.
- ✪ Explain why American merchants established a new route to New Mexico.
- ✪ Describe the types of images frontier artists painted.

SECTION 5 RESOURCES

REPRODUCIBLE

- ▶ Guided Reading Strategy 16.5
- ▶ Literature Reading 16: "On a California Ranch"

TECHNOLOGY

- ▶ One-Stop Planner, Lesson 16.5
- ▶ American History Interactive Maps CD–ROM: San Francisco: Mission to Metropolis
- ▶ Art in American History Transparency 10: See-non-ty-a, an Iowa Medicine Man
- ▶ Homework Practice Online

REINFORCEMENT, REVIEW, AND ASSESSMENT

- ▶ Section 5 Review, p. 511
- ▶ Daily Quiz 16.5
- ▶ Main Idea Activity 16.5
- ▶ English Audio Summary 16.5
- ▶ Spanish Audio Summary 16.5

Section 5

California and the Southwest

Read to Discover

1. Why did Americans start traveling to California in the early 1800s?
2. Why did American merchants establish a new route to New Mexico?
3. What types of images did frontier artists paint?

WHY IT MATTERS TODAY

Today the U.S. wilderness is a place for recreation instead of survival. Use **CNNfyi.com** or other **current events** sources to find out about nature activities around the country. Record your findings in your journal.

Identify

- Donner party
- John Sutter
- Sutter's Fort
- George Catlin

This Mexican gold coin was used as currency in California.

The Story Continues

In 1835 American Richard Henry Dana Jr. arrived in San Francisco Bay on board a merchant ship. Dana and the crew spent a few days ashore. He admired the climate, calling it "as near to being perfect as any in the world." He also praised the nearby town of Yerba Buena. It supplied traders and whaling ships with food. Dana's crew then set sail for more destinations on the California coast. As they left the bay, Dana glanced up at the hills and made a prediction. "If California ever becomes a prosperous [rich] country, this bay will be the center of its prosperity."

✪ Going to California

In the 1830s and 1840s California was still under Mexican rule. The main route to California started with the Oregon Trail. At the Snake River in present-day Idaho, the trail split. Settlers who wanted to go to California took the southern route, known as the California Trail. This route ran through a mountain range called the Sierra Nevada. American emigrants

★ TEACH

 Have students read Section 5 and complete Guided Reading Strategy 16.5. Choose one or more of the following activities to explore the section content with students. For further suggestions on block scheduling or team teaching, see the *Block Scheduling Handbook with Team Teaching Strategies*.

 LEVEL 1: Organize the class into five groups. Assign each group one of the following topics: California Trail, Donner party, Sutter's Fort, Santa Fe Trail, or frontier art. Have each group create drawings depicting a summary of why people went west and how they got there.
ENGLISH LANGUAGE LEARNERS , COOPERATIVE LEARNING

ALL LEVELS: Copy the following graphic organizer onto the chalkboard, omitting the italicized answers. Have students complete the organizer by identifying the reasons that people traveled to California in the early 1800s. When students have completed their graphic organizers, call on volunteers to share their organizers with the class.
ENGLISH LANGUAGE LEARNERS

Why they went to California
to settle, to trade with Mexican merchants, to paint

and traders on the California Trail tried to cross these mountains before the season's first snows.

The **Donner party** was a group of western travelers with bad luck and poor judgment. The party began its journey west in the spring of 1846. Trying to find a shortcut, the group left the main trail and got lost. When the Donner party reached the Sierra Nevada, they became trapped by heavy snows. Virginia Reed later wrote to her sister about the party's struggles to survive the winter.

> **History Makers Speak**
> ❝There was 15 in the cabin we was in and half of us had to lay [in] a bed all the time. . . . there was 10 starved to death. . . . It snowed and would cover the cabin all over so we could not get out for 2 or 3 days.❞
>
> —Virginia Reed, quoted in *Ordeal by Hunger: The Story of the Donner Party*, by George R. Stewart

A rescue party found the starving and freezing group in February 1847. Of the original 87 travelers, 42 had died.

Although more Americans were traveling along the California Trail, few actually settled in California. Instead, California became a meeting ground for merchants from Mexico and the United States. American merchants traded manufactured goods for gold and silver coins, cowhides, and tallow (animal fat used to make soap and candles) from Mexico.

Mexicans and American Indians made up most of California's population. Mexican officials did not want many Americans to settle in the province. However, in 1839 they did give Swiss immigrant **John Sutter** permission to start a colony. **Sutter's Fort** was located near the Sacramento River and soon became a popular rest stop for many American immigrants. These new arrivals praised Sutter's generosity and helpfulness. By the mid-1840s some Anglo-Californians were publishing guidebooks encouraging other settlers to move west.

✔ **Reading Check: Finding the Main Idea** Why were most Americans interested in California? Some wanted to settle there, but most wanted to trade for Mexican goods.

COURTESY OF THE CALIFORNIA HISTORY ROOM, CALIFORNIA STATE LIBRARY, SACRAMENTO, CALIFORNIA

The members of the Donner party found themselves trapped by high snows in the Sierra Nevada.

Interpreting the Visual Record

Sutter's Fort *Many Americans chose Sutter's Fort as their destination in California.* **What parts of this drawing help explain why the colony was called a fort?**

THE GRANGER COLLECTION, NEW YORK

LEVEL 3: Organize the class into groups and have each group create a guidebook about the Mexican province of California in the early 1840s. Guidebooks should include articles addressing the needs of settlers and traders, and the types of images painted by frontier artists. Students should include information on the following subjects: economic opportunities, attractions, trails from the East, and why the new route to the region was established. They might also provide advice about what to bring and when to travel.
COOPERATIVE LEARNING

HOMEWORK Ask students to create a frontier-style image along with a few sentences explaining what qualities make it similar to the frontier art of the 1800s.

✪ CLOSE

Have students create flowcharts that identify and sequence the ways that the Mexican territories and the United States became more closely connected. Tell students to start with Mexican officials wanting to limit the number of U.S. settlers traveling to the region and to include the influence that Sutter's Fort and trails connecting the territories had on merging Mexican and U.S. cultures.

CONNECTING TO THE ARTS ANSWER
Students might suggest that eastern audiences wanted to learn more about American Indians.

Technology Resources

Art in American History Transparency 10: See-non-ty-a, an Iowa Medicine Man

---

★ ★ ★ ★ ★ ★ ★ ★ ★ ★

Section 5 Review
ANSWERS

❶ Identify
• Donner party, p. 509
• John Sutter, p. 509
• Sutter's Fort, p. 509
• George Catlin, p. 511

❷ California Trail: used by settlers on their way to California; Santa Fe Trail: went to New Mexico; established by traders; Both: used as trade routes; challenged those who traveled on them

❸ a. American merchants earned high profits trading with Mexican merchants
b. merchants and traders wanted to travel into the region, to earn money through trade, so they started the Santa Fe Trail which settlers would later be able to use

❹ Students' reviews will vary but should include an awareness of how western artists depicted American Indian life and culture, their images of landscapes, and artists' personal interests in the West.

CONNECTING TO
THE ARTS

George Catlin Artists like George Catlin brought images of the West to the rest of the country. Catlin is best known for his paintings of American Indians. From 1830 to 1836 he traveled throughout the western Great Plains. He painted portraits and important events such as buffalo hunts and religious ceremonies. In the East, thousands of people viewed Catlin's paintings. Today his many paintings provide a valuable record of American Indian culture. **Why do you think Catlin's paintings were so popular with people in the East?**

Analyzing Primary Sources
Drawing Inferences and Conclusions What seems to be Magoffin's reaction to the wreck of the wagon? Answers will vary. Students might note that she seems calm despite the great destruction.

★ Other Southwestern Trails

Other major western trails at this time were mostly used as trade routes to the Southwest rather than as routes for settlers. Unlike the Spanish, the Mexican government agreed to allow American merchants to come to New Mexico. American traders seized this opportunity by starting the Santa Fe Trail.

The trail ran from Independence, Missouri, to Santa Fe, New Mexico. American merchants loaded their wagon trains with cloth and other manufactured goods. In Santa Fe they exchanged these products with Mexican merchants for horses, mules, and silver.

The long trip across the desert and mountains was difficult and dangerous. Yet traders took the risk because a successful journey could earn high profits. The U.S. government also offered these merchants protection by sending troops and providing money to ensure American Indian cooperation. By the mid-1800s the traders were even traveling to southern California by following the Old Spanish Trail, which began in Santa Fe.

In 1846 Susan Shelby Magoffin became one of the first white women to travel on the Santa Fe Trail. She made this dangerous journey with her husband and their load of trade goods. At one point their wagon plunged into a gully, or small valley, an event she later described.

History Makers Speak ❝To see the wreck of that carriage now with the top and sides entirely broken to pieces, [one] could never believe that people had come out of it alive.❞

—Susan Shelby Magoffin, from *Down the Santa Fe Trail and into Mexico*, edited by Stella M. Drumm

✔ **Reading Check: Summarizing** Why did American traders establish the Santa Fe Trail? to profit from trade with Mexico

★ **REVIEW AND ASSESS**

Have Students complete the **Section 5 Review** on p. 511. Then have students complete **Daily Quiz 16.5**. As **Alternative Assessment**, you may want to use the California immigration graphic organizer or frontier art exercises in this section's lessons.

★ **RETEACH**

Have students complete **Main Idea Activity for English Language Learners and Special-Needs Students 16.5**. Ask students to create an outline summarizing their impressions of the Far West and its attraction for Americans of the early and mid-1800s. **ENGLISH LANGUAGE LEARNERS**

★ **EXTEND**

Have students use the library to find information from both primary and secondary sources about life on a westward trail. Ask students to compose a song or poem that describes a day's journey on the trail and things seen along the way. Encourage volunteers to share their poems or songs with the class.

BLOCK SCHEDULING

★ Frontier Artists

Stories of the people and scenery in the West inspired some artists to travel with explorers to the frontier. <u>George Catlin</u> gave up a career as a portrait painter in Philadelphia to go west. He painted more than 500 images of American Indians, including spiritual and military leaders. In 1840 he wrote, "I have visited forty-eight tribes . . . containing in all 400,000 souls." When Catlin returned to the East, thousands of people flocked to his art shows. His paintings were the only images many would ever see of the American West. Catlin made his shows more exciting by showing Indian clothing, giving talks, and telling tales about life in the West.

Artist Alfred Jacob Miller traveled through the Rocky Mountains, painting striking images of the landscape. He also created portraits of the mountain men who hunted and trapped in remote regions. Other artists such as John Mix Stanley and Seth Eastman also painted American Indians and the western environment. Not all of these artists had great talent, and their paintings often exaggerated the things that they saw. Together, however, the works of these artists became extremely popular in the East and in Europe. Their paintings captured people's imaginations and shaped their ideas about the West.

✔ **Reading Check: Drawing Inferences and Conclusions** What did western artists depict, and why do you think their work was so popular? Students should understand that Americans were fascinated with the rugged landscape and different peoples depicted by the western artists.

Interpreting the Visual Record

Western art *Frontier artist John Mix Stanley painted* Buffalo Hunt on the South-western Plains. **What does this painting suggest about the risks and skills involved in the buffalo hunt?**

CHAPTER 16 REVIEW ANSWERS

The Chapter at a Glance
Students' sentences will vary but should include information on the importance of each term as it relates to American settlement in the West.

Identifying People and Ideas
Students' sentences should indicate an understanding of the following definitions:

1. Spanish settlers in colonial Texas

2. led Indians and mestizos in the revolution against Spanish rule in Mexico

3. *empresario* who contracted to recruit settlers to Texas, brought the Old Three Hundred to Texas, and eventually called for Texans to revolt against Mexico

4. commander in chief of the Texas army, then president of the republic of Texas

5. battle where Houston's army defeated Santa Anna's army

6. to take control of something, as in the United States's option to take control of Texas

7. hunters and merchants who traveled to the Rocky Mountains and Pacific Northwest

8. owner of the American Fur Company, one of the nation's largest at the peak of the fur trade

Section **5** Review

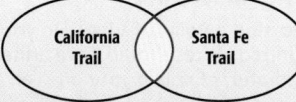
go.hrw.com **Homework Practice Online**
keyword: SA3 HP16

❶ Identify and explain:
• Donner party
• John Sutter
• Sutter's Fort
• George Catlin

❷ Comparing and Contrasting Copy the diagram below. Use it to compare and contrast the characteristics of the California Trail and the Santa Fe Trail.

California Trail / Santa Fe Trail

❸ Finding the Main Idea
a. Why did some Americans traveling west go to California or New Mexico?

b. Who established the early trails from the United States to the Southwest, and how did the trails benefit others?

❹ Writing and Critical Thinking
Analyzing Information Imagine that you are an art historian studying images of American Indian life in the American West. Write a review of a piece you might see and describe what it represents.

Consider the following:
• how western artists showed American Indian life and culture
• images of landscapes
• artists' personal interest in the West

REPRODUCIBLE

▶ Vocabulary Activity 16

TECHNOLOGY

▶ Chapter 16 Test Generator (on the One-Stop Planner)

▶ Global Skill Builder CD–ROM

▶ HRW Go site

REINFORCEMENT, REVIEW, AND ASSESSMENT

▶ Chapter 16 Review, pp. 511–13

▶ Chapter 16 Tutorial for Students, Parents, Mentors, and Peers

▶ Chapter 16 Test (Form A or B)

▶ Alternative Assessment Handbook

▶ Chapter 16 Test for English Language Learners and Special-Needs Students

★ REVIEW

Have students complete the **Chapter 16 Review** on pages 512–13.

★ ASSESS

Use one of the chapter tests to assess students' understanding of the content. For **Alternative Assessment,** see the **Alternative Assessment Handbook.**

---

9. located in California, a popular destination for American immigrants

10. painter who specialized in portraits of American Indians

Understanding Main Ideas

1. The new government ended the mission system in California and gave the mission lands to Californios. Texas's population had decreased so the new government encouraged settlement.

2. Texans defeat Mexican soldiers at Gonzales and San Antonio; the Mexican army defeats Texans at the Alamo and the Battle of Goliad; and Texas wins its independence at the Battle of San Jacinto.

3. Texas did not have much money and was faced with a growing debt military problems with Mexico. American Indians were pushed from their land, and Tejanos often lost land, property, and political power.

4. Mountain men earned money by trapping animals for fur, missionaries wanted to convert American Indians to Christianity, and families wanted to start new lives in this rich land.

5. Merchants could earn a great deal of money trading with Mexicans in these regions.

Chapter **16** Review

The Chapter at a Glance

Examine the visual summary of the chapter below. Use standard grammar, spelling, sentence structure, and punctuation to write a sentence about each label attached to an image in the visual summary. In pairs, discuss the sentences that you write.

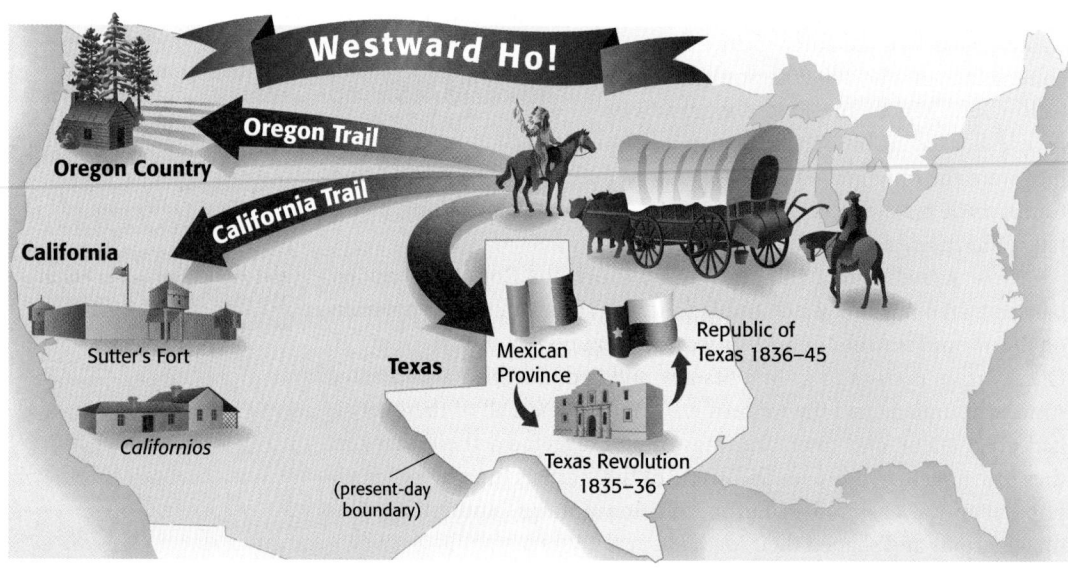

Identifying People and Ideas

Use the following terms or people in historically significant sentences.

1. Tejanos
2. Father Miguel Hidalgo y Costilla
3. Stephen F. Austin
4. Sam Houston
5. Battle of San Jacinto
6. annex
7. mountain men
8. John Jacob Astor
9. Sutter's Fort
10. George Catlin

Understanding Main Ideas

Section 1 (Pages 488–491)

1. What changes took place in California and Texas soon after Mexico won its independence?

Section 2 (Pages 492–496)

2. List in the proper sequence the important events of the Texas Revolution.

Section 3 (Pages 497–501)

3. What problems did the Republic of Texas and some of its citizens face?

Section 4 (Pages 502–507)

4. Why did different groups of Americans journey west of the Rocky Mountains to Oregon Country?

Section 5 (Pages 508–511)

5. What new economic opportunities did California and New Mexico offer?

You Be the Historian— Reviewing Themes

1. **Citizenship** Describe the series of events that led Texans to declare their independence from Mexico.

2. **Culture** How did German immigrants affect the Republic of Texas?

3. **Geography** How was the geography of the Pacific Northwest different from that of the Southwest, and why do you think people settled in each region?

Thinking Critically

1. **Supporting a Point of View** Do you think that the United States should have annexed Texas immediately? Explain your answer.

2. **Analyzing Information** How did religion play a role in the settlement of Oregon Country?

3. **Comparing** What attracted American settlers to Oregon Country and Texas?

★ **RETEACH**

Organize the class into groups. Assign each group one of the chapter's sections. Have each group summarize the main ideas from its assigned section to develop a segment of a documentary that deals with the United States expanding westward. Then have each group present its section of the documentary to the class. Lead a class discussion reviewing significant events in the westward expansion of the United States.

ENGLISH LANGUAGE LEARNERS ,

COOPERATIVE LEARNING

Portfolio Extensions

American History

1. Cooperative Learning

Organize the class into five groups. Have each group assume the role of one of the following groups of people who lived in the republic of Texas: U.S. settlers, German immigrants, free African Americans, Apache and Comanche, and Tejanos. Have each group write a short speech about the difficulties they face. The speech should conclude with suggestions for ways to make Texas a better place. Have each group present its speech to the class.

2. Linking to Community

Have students conduct research on the Americans (or European colonists) who first settled the region in which their community is located. Then have students create a diorama of their information. Students' dioramas should include who the settlers were, why they came to the region, what they found/did there, and how they influenced the region.

Social Studies Skills Workshop

Interpreting Maps

Study the map below. Then use the information on the map to help you answer the following questions.

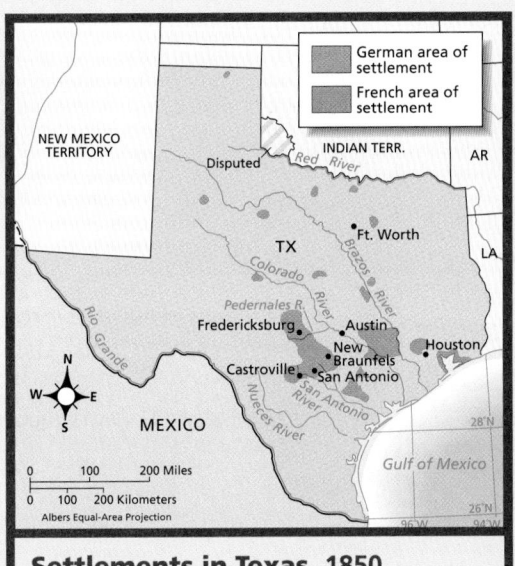

Settlements in Texas, 1850

1. What cities were located within the German area of settlement?
   a. Castroville and San Antonio
   b. Fort Worth and Castroville
   c. Fort Worth and Houston
   d. Fredericksburg and New Braunfels

2. Based on your knowledge of the period and the information shown on the map, why do you think Texans moved the capital from Houston to Austin?

Analyzing Primary Sources

Read the following quote by Mrs. W. W. Buck, a pioneer on the Oregon Trail, and then answer the questions that follow.

❝Of course, we were all anxious to hear about the country we were bound for, and our captain said Doctor White, tell us about Oregon. He jumped upon the wagon tongue and all our eyes and ears were open to catch every word. He said: 'Friends, you are traveling to the garden of Eden, a land flowing with milk and honey. And just let me tell you, the clover grows wild all over Oregon, and when you wade [walk] through it, it reaches your chin.' We believed every word, and for days, I thought that not only our men, but our poor tired oxen, stepped lighter for having met Dr. White.❞

3. Which of the following statements best describes the reaction of the pioneers to Dr. White's speech?
   a. They were not interested in hearing stories about Oregon.
   b. Some people doubted what Dr. White told them.
   c. They wanted Dr. White to lead their wagon train.
   d. They were happy and encouraged by the news.

4. Based on your knowledge of the period, how do you think Dr. White's description of Oregon compares with the actual situation that settlers in Oregon Country encountered?

You Be the Historian— Reviewing Themes

1. Texans did not agree with the laws made by the Mexican government and felt they did not have enough say in these laws.

2. They established farming communities and towns and protested slavery.

3. Pacific Northwest—more rainfall and water and thus a more lush environment; Southwest—desert conditions in many places. Inexpensive land drew settlers to both regions, and in both places people founded missions, hoping to convert American Indians to Christianity.

Thinking Critically

1. Students' answers will vary.

2. Missionaries wanting to convert American Indians to Christianity went to Oregon.

3. rich land for growing crops or raising animals

Skills Workshop

1. d

2. to keep the capital central to the growing and westward shifting population

3. d

4. Students' descriptions will vary but should reflect a knowledge of the situation in Oregon at that time.

Alternative Assessment

American History

Building Your Portfolio

Interdisciplinary Connection to the Arts

Select an artist of the American West and write a critique of one or more of that person's works. Use the library to find information about the artist. Your critique should examine the artist's point of view, use of color, and choice of subject matter. Artists may include, but are not limited to, the following: Albert Bierstadt, George Caleb Bingham, Karl Bodmer, and George Catlin.

🖥 internet connect

Internet Activity: go.hrw.com
keyword: SA3 CF16

Access the Internet through the HRW Go site to locate databases, primary and secondary sources, and interviews about the causes of the Texas Revolution. Then write a report, using these sources to support your point of view. Make sure you evaluate the accuracy of your sources and use standard grammar, punctuation, sentence structure, and spelling in your report.

Objectives	Pacing Guide	Reproducible Resources
SECTION 1: **Manifest Destiny and Expansion** (pp. 516–21)	★ Analyze how Americans' belief in manifest destiny affected western expansion. ★ Explain how the United States acquired Oregon and Texas. ★ Discuss events that led to the Mexican War.	**Regular** 2 days **Block Scheduling** 1 day *Block Scheduling Handbook with Team Teaching Strategies, Chapter 17*	**RS** Guided Reading Strategy 17.1 **PS** American History Political Cartoon 8: James Polk and Foreign Policy **E** Hands-On History Activity: Your State's Boundaries
SECTION 2: **The Mexican War** (pp. 522–26)	★ Describe Americans' reaction to the declaration of war against Mexico. ★ Examine the major events and battles of the war. ★ Explain the terms of the treaty that ended the Mexican War.	**Regular** 2 days **Block Scheduling** 1 day *Block Scheduling Handbook with Team Teaching Strategies, Chapter 17*	**RS** Guided Reading Strategy 17.2 **PS** Primary Source Reading 17: Opposition to the Mexican War
SECTION 3: **More Settlers Head West** (pp. 528–32)	★ Analyze the conflicts caused by new U.S. settlement in the Southwest. ★ Discuss the interaction between various cultures in the Southwest. ★ Explain why the Mormons moved to the West and what they achieved there.	**Regular** 1.5 days **Block Scheduling** .5 day *Block Scheduling Handbook with Team Teaching Strategies, Chapter 17*	**RS** Guided Reading Strategy 17.3 **SM** Geography Activity 17: Spanish Missions in California **PS** Biography Reading 17: Brigham Young
SECTION 4: **The Gold Rush** (pp. 533–39)	★ Discuss why many people headed west to California in 1849. ★ Describe what life was like in gold rush mining camps and towns. ★ Analyze how the gold rush changed California.	**Regular** 1.5 days **Block Scheduling** 1 day *Block Scheduling Handbook with Team Teaching Strategies, Chapter 17*	**RS** Guided Reading Strategy 17.4 **PS** Literature Reading 17: The Squatter and the Don **RS** Graphic Organizer 17: American Settlement and Expansion **E** Creative Teaching Strategy: Open-Ended Statements

Chapter Resource Key

PS	Primary Sources	**A**	Assessment		Music
RS	Reading Support	**REV**	Review		Video
IC	Interdisciplinary Connections	**ELL**	Reinforcement and English Language Learners		Internet
E	Enrichment		Transparencies		Holt Presentation Maker Using Microsoft® PowerPoint®
SM	Skills Mastery		CD–ROM		

 **One-Stop** Planner CD–ROM

See the *One-Stop Planner* for a complete list of additional resources for students and teachers.

One-Stop Planner CD-ROM

It's easy to plan lessons, select resources, and print out materials for your students when you use the **One-Stop Planner CD-ROM with Test Generator.**

Technology Resources

 One-Stop Planner, Lesson 17.1
 Holt Researcher: American History CD-ROM
Homework Practice Online
HRW Go site

 One-Stop Planner, Lesson 17.2
 CNN. Presents America: Yesterday and Today, Beginnings to 1914 Segment: Choosing Sides in the War with Mexico
Homework Practice Online

 One-Stop Planner, Lesson 17.3
Homework Practice Online

 One-Stop Planner, Lesson 17.4
Holt Researcher: American History CD-ROM
American History Simulations CD-ROM: The Gold Rush
 American Music Selection 10: "Joe Bowers"
Homework Practice Online
HRW Go site

Reinforcement, Review, and Assessment

REV Section 1 Review, p. 521
A Daily Quiz 17.1
ELL Main Idea Activity 17.1
ELL English Audio Summary 17.1
ELL Spanish Audio Summary 17.1

REV Section 2 Review, p. 526
A Daily Quiz 17.2
ELL Main Idea Activity 17.2
ELL English Audio Summary 17.2
ELL Spanish Audio Summary 17.2

REV Section 3 Review, p. 532
A Daily Quiz 17.3
ELL Main Idea Activity 17.3
ELL English Audio Summary 17.3
ELL Spanish Audio Summary 17.3

REV Section 4 Review, p. 539
A Daily Quiz 17.4
ELL Main Idea Activity 17.4
ELL English Audio Summary 17.4
ELL Spanish Audio Summary 17.4

internet connect

HRW ONLINE RESOURCES
GO TO: go.hrw.com
Then type in a keyword.

TEACHER HOME PAGE
KEYWORD: SA3 Teacher

CHAPTER INTERNET ACTIVITIES
KEYWORD: SA3 CF17
Choose an activity to:
• research the causes and effects of the Mexican War.
• conduct an interview with James K. Polk and Henry David Thoreau.
• learn about the journey west to California during the Gold Rush.

CHAPTER ENRICHMENT LINKS
KEYWORD: SA3 CH17

ONLINE ASSESSMENT
Homework Practice
KEYWORD: SA3 HP17

Standardized Test Prep
KEYWORD: SA3 STP17

Rubrics
KEYWORD: SS Rubrics

ONLINE MAPS, CHARTS, AND GRAPHS
KEYWORD: SA3 MCG
• Settlements in Texas, 1850
• Transportation Methods
• The Mormon Trail

CONTENT UPDATES
KEYWORD: SS Content Updates

HOLT PRESENTATION MAKER
KEYWORD: SA3 PPT17

ONLINE READING SUPPORT
KEYWORD: SS Strategies

CURRENT EVENTS
KEYWORD: S3 Current Events

Meeting Individual Needs

Ability Levels

Level 1 Basic-level activities designed for all students encountering new material

Level 2 Intermediate-level activities designed for average students

Level 3 Challenging activities designed for honors and gifted-and-talented students

English Language Learners Activities that address the needs of students with Limited English Proficiency

Chapter Review and Assessment

IC Vocabulary Activity 17
 Global Skill Builder CD-ROM
HRW Go site
REV Chapter 17 Tutorial for Students, Parents, Mentors, and Peers
REV Chapter 17 Review, pp. 540–41
Chapter 17 Test Generator (on the One-Stop Planner)

A Chapter 17 Test (Form A or B)
A Alternative Assessment Handbook
A Chapter 17 Test for English Language Learners and Special-Needs Students

Build on What You Know

If You Were There...

Ask students to answer the following question:

How would you react to efforts to make the country even bigger?

Consider:

- the economic and social consequences
- the methods necessary to enlarge the area

You Be the Historian

What's Your Opinion?

To help students create their **Themes** Journal entries, provide the following examples of appropriate **agree**/**disagree** statements.

EXPLORING THE TIME LINE
AMERICAN EVENTS

☑ internet connect

TOPIC: The Election of 1840
GO TO: go.hrw.com
KEYWORD: SA3 CF17

Have students access the Internet through the HRW Go site to locate and use primary and secondary sources on the election of 1840. Have them identify the points of view of the candidates and the historical context surrounding the election of William Henry Harrison as president. Then ask them to create a visual display, such as a campaign poster, that illustrates the issues, results, and political importance of the election.

CHAPTER
17 Manifest Destiny and War
(1840–1860)

John Gast's 1879 painting shows the spirit of manifest destiny leading settlers and modern technology westward across the continent.

UNITED STATES

1840 William Henry Harrison is elected president.

1845 John O'Sullivan coins the phrase *manifest destiny*. This term is used to promote westward expansion.

1846 The United States declares war on Mexico.

1848 Gold is discovered in California on January 24.

The Treaty of Guadalupe Hidalgo is signed on February 2, ending the Mexican War and granting the United States California and other western territories.

| 1840 | 1842 | 1844 | 1846 | 1848 |

WORLD

1842 China gives Great Britain control of the island of Hong Kong.

1844 The United States negotiates a trade treaty with China.

1847 Liberia, an African nation founded by former slaves from the United States, becomes an independent republic.

This Chinese punch bowl depicts trading centers at the port of Guangzhou (Canton).

China ceded Hong Kong to the British in the Treaty of Nanking.

Build on What You Know

By 1840 the United States was roughly twice its original size. Americans had been moving west ever since the country won its independence. Many Americans believed it was their country's destiny to extend to the Pacific Coast. While this idea encouraged the United States to acquire more territory, it also led to tensions with other nations.

Global Relations

Agree Conquering other countries is the best way to gain more land.

Disagree The United States gained Louisiana by purchasing it from France.

Culture

Agree Conflict occurred with American Indians when European settlers first arrived in North America.

Disagree The French and the American Indians encountered each other without conflict.

Geography

Agree Settlers are likely to use resources in the same ways that they did in their old homelands.

Disagree Settlers will adapt to their new environment by using whatever resources are most plentiful.

Newly arrived gold-seekers in San Francisco were forced to live in tent communities on Telegraph Hill as the town struggled to keep up with its rapid growth.

Wooden rockers like this one were used for mining gold.

1850 The population of San Francisco exceeds 25,000.

1853 Under the Gadsden Purchase the United States buys part of what is now Arizona and New Mexico from Mexico.

1850 **1852** **1854** **1856** **1858**

1851 A huge gold rush takes place in the colony of Victoria in Australia.

1852 The South African Republic is created.

1858 Great Britain assumes formal control of India.

The gold found in Victoria was often in the form of nuggets that were of great size and value.

If you were there . . .
How would you react to efforts to make the country even bigger?

You Be the Historian

Themes Journal

What's Your Opinion? Do you **agree** or **disagree** with the following statements? Support your point of view in your journal.

- **Global Relations** Nations only grow through conquest.
- **Culture** When different groups first meet, conflict is bound to take place.
- **Geography** Settlers moving to new areas react to the environment just as they did in their old homes.

EXPLORING THE TIME LINE
GLOBAL EVENTS

★ Global Relations

The Opium Wars. The British government gained control of Hong Kong in 1843 through the signing of the Treaty of Nanking. The Treaty of Nanking ended the fighting between the British and Chinese in what was known as the first Opium War. The first Opium War began in 1839 as hostilities developed between the Chinese and Western traders. The Chinese government seized all opium warehouses hoping to stop the trade.. The hostilities between the two countries increased when drunken British sailors killed a Chinese villager, and the British government then refused to allow the Chinese government to try the sailors. Fighting quickly broke out, but the superior British forces were soon victorious. During the second Opium War and other conflicts, Great Britain gained more control of parts of China.

CRITICAL THINKING

Why might the British have wanted more control of other parts of China?

ANSWER: Students might suggest that the British wanted to expand their empire, and increasing control over China was a way to achieve that expansion.

Section 1

OBJECTIVES

⭐ Analyze how Americans' belief in manifest destiny affected western expansion.

⭐ Explain how the United States acquired Oregon and Texas.

⭐ Discuss events that led to the Mexican War.

SECTION 1 RESOURCES

REPRODUCIBLE

▶ Guided Reading Strategy 17.1

▶ American History Political Cartoon 8: James Polk and Foreign Policy

TECHNOLOGY

▶ One-Stop Planner, Lesson 17.1

▶ Holt Researcher: American History CD–ROM

▶ Homework Practice Online

▶ HRW Go site

REINFORCEMENT, REVIEW, AND ASSESSMENT

▶ Section 1 Review, p. 521

▶ Daily Quiz 17.1

▶ Main Idea Activity 17.1

▶ English Audio Summary 17.1

▶ Spanish Audio Summary 17.1

LET'S GET STARTED!

Write the following statement and question on the chalkboard: *There is a territory near the United States with vast reserves of lumber, fertile farmland, and mineral resources. However, this territory also has its own culture and government. Should the United States annex this territory?* Allow time for students to respond. *(Students' responses will vary, but students should support their opinions.)* Explain to students that in Section 1 they will learn about how the United States faced this problem in the 1840s surrounding the ideas of manifest destiny.

Section 1

Manifest Destiny and Expansion

Read to Discover

1. How did Americans' belief in manifest destiny affect western expansion?
2. How did the United States acquire Oregon and Texas?
3. What events led to the Mexican War?

WHY IT MATTERS TODAY

The United States still has close relations with Canada and Mexico today. Use **CNNfyi.com** or other **current events** sources to learn about one policy of the United States today that affects either Canada or Mexico. Record your findings in your journal.

Define

• manifest destiny

Identify

• John O'Sullivan
• John Tyler
• Henry Clay
• James K. Polk
• Zachary Taylor

THE
UNITED STATES MAGAZINE,
AND
DEMOCRATIC REVIEW.

The Democratic Review was one of several magazines that supported western expansion.

The Story Continues

In 1843 South Carolina senator John C. Calhoun gave a speech to Congress. In it he described the great changes he had seen during his lifetime. "In the period of thirty-two years which have elapsed [passed] since I took my seat . . . [the] frontier has receded [moved] 1,000 miles to the west," he noted proudly. Then he talked about the future. "Our population is rolling toward the shores of the Pacific with an impetus [force] greater than what we realize." Calhoun believed that if the United States was patient and avoided unnecessary wars, it would become the strongest nation in the world.

⭐ The Roots of Manifest Destiny

By the 1840s many Americans shared Senator Calhoun's view. The United States, they thought, was sure to expand all the way to the Pacific Ocean. They believed that nothing could stop this growth from taking place. This expansionist view became known as **manifest destiny**. The term was first used by **John O'Sullivan**, a New York editor.

Have students read Section 1 and complete Guided Reading Strategy 17.1. Choose one or more of the following activities to explore the section content with students. For further suggestions on block scheduling or team teaching, see the *Block Scheduling Handbook with Team Teaching Strategies*.

LEVEL 1: Have each student create a *Cause and Effect* chart for the events leading to the Mexican War. For example, students might list the annexation of Texas as a cause and the border dispute with Mexico as an effect. Ask volunteers to present their charts to the class.
ENGLISH LANGUAGE LEARNERS

Interpreting the Visual Record

Heading west *In Emanuel Gottlieb Leutze's painting* Westward the Course of Empire Takes Its Way, *a scout points the way west for the eager settlers.* **Based on this image, do you think the artist has a positive view of westward expansion? Why or why not?**

Science, Technology & Society

Western Exploration.
Between 1840 and 1860 the U.S. government spent as much as one third of the national budget on scientific studies, particularly in the West. The government published the records of western explorations and studies—which covered the ecology, ethnography, geography, and geology of the West—in multivolume sets that included maps and lithographs.

CRITICAL THINKING

Why did the federal government spend so much money on western expansion?

ANSWER: Students might suggest that it wanted to understand the territory it had gained and find out more about territory that it hoped to gain.

Visual Record Answer

Students might suggest yes since the people in the painting seem excited and eager about the land that lay before them.

History Makers Speak
❝The American claim is by the right of our manifest destiny to overspread and to possess the whole of the continent which Providence [God's blessing] has given us for the development of the great experiment of liberty. We are the nation of human progress, and who will, what can, set limits to our onward march?❞

—John O'Sullivan, quoted in *"It's Your Misfortune and None of My Own,"* by Richard White

Analyzing Primary Sources
Identifying Points of View
Why did O'Sullivan think that Americans were meant to rule the continent? He thought the United States was the nation of human progress, chosen by God to spread the blessings of liberty.

The roots of manifest destiny lay in Americans' economic, political, and social experiences. Many Puritan colonists had believed North America was a promised land that God had given to them so they could set up a new society. This society would then become a religious example to the rest of the world. Puritans hoped others would follow the Protestant teachings of the Reformation.

The American Revolution added to the idea that America was special. Patriots believed that the United States would prove to the rest of the world that democracy could work in a large and growing country. Thomas Jefferson and James Madison also believed that the American people needed new lands to settle to prevent increased social tensions as city populations grew larger.

After the United States became independent, there were strong economic reasons to expand. As the eastern population grew, people sought more room. Farmers wanted more land to grow crops, and industry needed more natural resources. Businesses wanted more markets for American goods. Soon business leaders, pioneers, and politicians were looking to the West and its millions of acres of land.

John O'Sullivan first used the phrase manifest destiny *in his magazine the* Democratic Review.

✔ **Reading Check: Summarizing** What were the social, political, and economic roots of the American belief in manifest destiny? social: Puritan goal of carrying out Reformation; political: success of democracy and freedom; economic: pressure for land, resources, and markets

ALL LEVELS: Have students read the John O'Sullivan quotation about manifest destiny on page 517. Then have them create a cartoon or illustration that captures Americans' belief in manifest destiny. Finally, lead a discussion on how the idea affected western expansion.

ENGLISH LANGUAGE LEARNERS

ALL LEVELS: Copy the following graphic organizer onto the chalkboard, omitting the italicized answers. Have students complete the organizer to learn how the United States acquired Texas and Oregon.

ENGLISH LANGUAGE LEARNERS

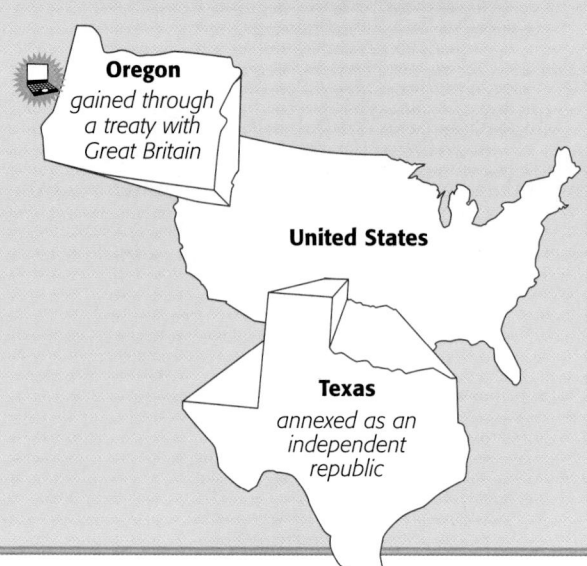

Oregon
gained through a treaty with Great Britain

United States

Texas
annexed as an independent republic

★ Geography

Migration to Texas.
Englishman William Bollaert described the reasons that Americans and Europeans should settle in Texas after he visited the region in 1842 and 1843. "These new lands of Texas merely require 'scraping' and a crop of corn or cotton comes up the first year," he wrote. Bollaert argued that Americans needed only to repeat the farming skills and techniques used in other parts of the country to be successful in Texas. European immigrants—even without work skills—could expect "a peaceful home, a plentiful table" and if not for themselves, then their children "would have rich plantations and farms."

CRITICAL THINKING

What potential difficulties may Bollaert have overlooked in his description of Texas?

ANSWER: Students might suggest conflicts over land and property with Texas Indians, cultural conflicts with Tejanos, and the hardships of starting a farm.

VISUALIZING HISTORY ANSWERS

1. Students might suggest that people of other cultures probably had differing viewpoints based on whether or not the westward expansion affected them.

2. Students' responses will vary.

★ Gone West

By the 1840s many Americans had accepted the idea of manifest destiny. They thought that the United States had been chosen by God to spread its democratic, economic, and religious values. Americans would fulfill this destiny by spreading across the continent. In the process, Americans believed they would bring liberty, improve the land, and spread the Christian gospel. At the same time, this westward movement of people would reduce social tensions in the East, such as overcrowding in the cities. Expansion would allow the growing eastern population to find new opportunities on the frontier.

Belief in manifest destiny encouraged many Americans to build settlements beyond the boundaries of the United States. They moved to places such as California, Oregon, and Texas. Settlers in Oregon were attracted by the rich farmland. One woman, for example, recalled the stories told by an Oregon pioneer, who said, "Friends, you are traveling to the garden of Eden, a land flowing with milk and honey."

There were already thousands of American Indians and Mexicans living in the West. Yet most supporters of manifest destiny ignored this fact. As Americans saw it, the West was not being fully developed by the people living there. Politicians and settlers wanted to bring farms and industry to the region. They felt that by doing this Americans would be improving the West.

✔ **Reading Check: Identifying Points of View** How did believers in manifest destiny view the West? *as underdeveloped land to which American settlers would bring many political and social benefits*

Expanding Westward

Many Americans believed that the United States had a special destiny to expand across the continent.

Visualizing History

1. **Culture** How do you think people of other cultures and nations viewed the idea of manifest destiny?

2. **Connecting to Today** What special purpose in the world do you think the United States has today?

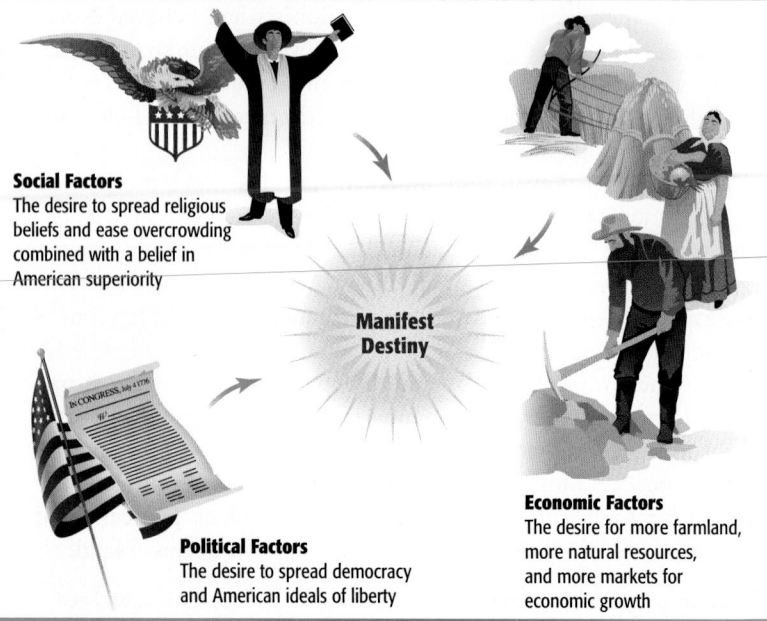

Social Factors
The desire to spread religious beliefs and ease overcrowding combined with a belief in American superiority

Manifest Destiny

Political Factors
The desire to spread democracy and American ideals of liberty

Economic Factors
The desire for more farmland, more natural resources, and more markets for economic growth

LEVEL 2: Have students write a letter to President Polk supporting or protesting the ultimatum of "Fifty-four forty or fight!" Letters should discuss the background of the controversy and the effects of territorial acquisitions such as Oregon and Texas.

LEVEL 3: Have students imagine that they are members of the House of Representatives in 1846 who are debating Polk's request for a declaration of war against Mexico. Ask students to prepare speeches outlining the background of the conflict.

Note: To help students make meaningful connections between events in American history and those in their own hometown, use the Chapter 17 **Hands-On History** activity, Your State's Boundaries.

The Election of 1844

President <u>John Tyler</u> helped make western expansion an important subject in the election of 1844. Tyler had been elected as William Henry Harrison's vice president in 1840. He became president when Harrison died in April 1841. Tyler was a pro-slavery Whig from Virginia, who wanted to extend the political power of the southern slave states. Tyler believed that the annexation of Texas would help by adding another slave state to the country.

Tyler's ideas about Texas started a national debate. Many Whigs disagreed with his expansionist beliefs. As a result, he was too unpopular within his own party to win the 1844 presidential nomination. Instead, the Whigs chose Senator <u>Henry Clay</u> of Kentucky as their candidate. When Clay began his presidential campaign, he said he was against the annexation of Texas. After being pressured by southern voters, however, he decided halfheartedly to support annexation. Many of his original backers became angry when Clay changed his mind. The Democratic Party chose former Tennessee governor <u>James K. Polk</u> as its presidential candidate. Unlike Clay, Polk strongly favored acquiring both Texas and Oregon.

The idea of manifest destiny played an important part in the campaign. There were rumors that the Republic of Texas might end slavery, and southern politicians feared the loss of a potential slave state. It was also rumored that independent Texas might become an ally of Great Britain. If this were to happen, Americans would again be facing British power, this time at the Texas border.

When the votes had been counted, Polk had defeated Clay by a very narrow margin. Clay believed his defeat was caused by "a most extraordinary combination of adverse [bad] circumstances." Polk, on the other hand, insisted that the American people had voted for his views on westward expansion.

✔ **Reading Check: Finding the Main Idea** What were the major issues in the election of 1844, and how did the major political parties view them?
American expansion into Oregon and the annexation of Texas; Whigs divided by issues, Democrats in favor

⭐ Acquiring New Territory

President Polk quickly set out to fulfill his campaign promises. He was sure that he could bring Oregon and Texas into the United States. In the 1810s and 1820s Russia and Spain had given up their claims to Oregon Country. Britain and the United States had agreed to occupy the area together. As more Americans settled there, they began to ask that Oregon become part of the United States. Polk wanted to protect these settlers' interests. Some politicians saw other opportunities. They thought that Oregon Country would offer a Pacific port for the growing United States trade with China.

THE GRANGER COLLECTION, NEW YORK

James K. Polk

James K. Polk was born into a wealthy Tennessee farming family in 1795. After graduating from college, Polk practiced law before serving in the House of Representatives. He became Speaker of the House and later served as governor of Tennessee. However, Polk was not well known nationally when nominated by the Democratic Party as its presidential candidate. He did not let this discourage him during the campaign. He promised voters that as president he would make every effort to annex Texas and acquire Oregon. As president, Polk considered himself "the hardest working man in this country." What were Polk's major goals as president?

⭐ Presidential Profiles

James K. Polk. Many historians consider James K. Polk to have been one of the most effective U.S. presidents. Polk worked toward a well-thought-out set of goals, skillfully used his cabinet to carry out his plans, maintained regular contact with congressional leaders, and though of himself as the people's representative in government.

☑ internet connect

TOPIC: James K. Polk
GO TO: go.hrw.com
KEYWORD: SA3 CF17

ACTIVITY: Have students use the library or search the Internet through the HRW Go site to find information on President Polk. Then ask them to use the information to write a brief biography of his life using standard grammar, spelling, sentence structure, and punctuation.

PRESIDENTIAL PROFILES ANSWER
to expand the United States by annexing Texas and acquiring Oregon

★ CLOSE

Have students list the chain of events that resulted from the belief in manifest destiny. Then have students write a one-paragraph definition explaining the term's implications and meaning.

★ Historical Sidelight

Great Britain and U.S. Territory. The conflict between the United States and Great Britain over control of Oregon was not the first time Britain had to fight for this area. In 1790 Spain and Great Britain almost went to war over a part of Vancouver Island. Because of Spain's military weakness, Great Britain was able to gain control of western Canada.

CRITICAL THINKING

Ask students to imagine that the United States was not able to keep Oregon as part of their territory. How would life be different for those in present-day Oregon?

ANSWER: Students' responses will vary, but students might suggest that those living in present-day Oregon would be citizens of Canada and have different rights and responsibilities.

Visual Record Answer

Students might suggest seemingly fertile land and access to water.

Research on the R●M

Free Find:
Oregon
After reading about Oregon on the **Holt Researcher CD–ROM**, create a line graph showing the increase in Oregon's population after it became a U.S. territory.

Interpreting the Visual Record

New settlements *As more pioneers came to Oregon Country, they began founding settlements such as Oregon City, built in 1829 along the Willamette River.* **What environmental features do you see in the picture that might have made this a good place for settlers to live?**

Meanwhile, Britain and the United States disagreed over where in Oregon to draw the U.S.-Canada border. War between the two countries seemed possible. American expansionists cried, "Fifty-four forty or fight!" This slogan referred to the 54°40' parallel, the line to which Americans wanted their northern territory to extend. However, neither side truly wanted a war. Congressman Robert C. Winthrop expressed this wish. "This question, from its very nature, is . . . one for negotiation, compromise, and amicable [friendly] adjustment." In 1846 Britain and the United States signed a treaty that gave the United States all Oregon land south of the 49th parallel. This treaty drew the present-day border between Canada and the United States in the Pacific Northwest. Oregon became a U.S. territory in August 1848.

Polk and his supporters also wanted to acquire Texas. By March 1845 Congress had already approved annexation and needed only the support of the Republic of Texas. Many Americans continued to move to Texas, and Texas politicians hoped that joining the United States would help solve the republic's financial and military problems. Editor John O'Sullivan spoke for the expansionists. He wrote, "It is time . . . for common sense to give in to what is inevitable." The Texas Congress approved annexation in June, and Texas became the 28th state in December 1845. This action angered the Mexican government, which considered Texas a "stolen province."

✔ **Reading Check: Summarizing** How did compromise settle the dispute over Oregon? The United States signed a treaty with Great Britain to divide Oregon Country.

THE GRANGER COLLECTION, NEW YORK

☆ REVIEW AND ASSESS

Have students complete the **Section 1 Review** on p. 521. Then have them complete **Daily Quiz 17.1**. As **Alternative Assessment**, you may want to use the manifest destiny cartoon or the Texas and Oregon organizer exercise in this section's lessons.

☆ RETEACH

Have students complete **Main Idea Activity for English Language Learners and Special-Needs Students 17.1**. Then give each student a blank outline map of the United States.

Ask students to label the territories discussed in this section, identify the dates of acquisition, and note key ideas or facts related to each territory's acquisition.
ENGLISH LANGUAGE LEARNERS

☆ EXTEND

Have students research the lives and careers of the presidential candidates in 1844—James K. Polk and Henry Clay. Have students give a 10-minute speech in support of one of the candidates. **BLOCK SCHEDULING**

★ War Breaks Out

Mexico reacted to the annexation of Texas by cutting off all diplomatic ties with the United States. Mexico also ordered American settlers to leave California and banned further American immigration there. The Mexican government continued to reject the Texas and U.S. claim that the Rio Grande marked the southern border of Texas, arguing that the real southern border lay along the Nueces River farther north.

In June 1845 Polk ordered General **Zachary Taylor** to take U.S. troops into the disputed border region. Polk said that this force was intended to protect Texas from a possible Mexican attack. Meanwhile, Polk sent diplomat John Slidell to Mexico City to negotiate the Texas boundary dispute. The president also told Slidell to offer to buy California and New Mexico from the Mexican government for $30 million. However, when Slidell arrived in Mexico City, officials there refused to speak to him, making negotiations impossible.

In March 1846 General Taylor led his troops to the Rio Grande and made camp. In April the Mexican commander insisted that General Taylor remove the U.S. forces from the region, or else "arms and arms alone must decide the question." Taylor refused to move. Mexican soldiers then crossed the river and attacked a group of 63 U.S. soldiers. They killed 11 Americans, wounded 5 others, and captured the rest.

When the news reached Polk, he quickly prepared to inform Congress. On May 11, 1846, Polk declared, "Mexico has shed American blood upon the American soil." Polk's war message had its desired effect. Two days later Congress declared war on Mexico.

✔ **Reading Check: Identifying Cause and Effect** What problem arose from the annexation of Texas, and what happened as a result? dispute about the border between the United States and Mexico; resulted in an armed clash that provoked war between the two nations

The artwork on this cigar case shows General Zachary Taylor leading his troops across the Rio Grande.

Section 1 Review

go.hrw.com
Homework Practice Online
keyword: SA3 HP17

❶ **Define and explain:**
• manifest destiny

❷ **Identify and explain:**
• John O'Sullivan
• John Tyler
• Henry Clay
• James K. Polk
• Zachary Taylor

❸ **Analyzing Information** Copy the graphic organizer below. Use it to give examples of expansion and conflict brought about by the American belief in manifest destiny.

Manifest Destiny
→ Expansion
→ Conflict

❹ **Finding the Main Idea**
a. What were the results of the treaty signed by Great Britain and the United States in 1846?

b. How did Texas become part of the United States?

❺ **Writing and Critical Thinking**
Supporting a Point of View Imagine that you are a newspaper reporter in 1846. Write a brief article explaining Congress's declaration of war on Mexico.

Consider the following:
• the idea of manifest destiny
• the annexation of Texas

Section 1 Review
ANSWERS

❶ **Define**
• manifest destiny, p. 516

❷ **Identify**
• John O'Sullivan, p. 516
• John Tyler, p. 519
• Henry Clay, p. 519
• James K. Polk, p. 519
• Zachary Taylor, p. 521

❸ Expansion—annex Texas, Oregon Treaty; Conflict—war with Mexico

❹ a. war avoided, United States given Oregon lands below the 49th parallel
b. annexed by United States; annexation approved by Texas

❺ Students' articles will vary but should address the idea of manifest destiny, list the territories gained by the United States in the 1840s, and discuss relations between Texas and Mexico before 1845.

Manifest Destiny and War **521**

Section 2

OBJECTIVES

⭐ Describe Americans' reaction to the declaration of war against Mexico.

⭐ Examine the major events and battles of the war.

⭐ Explain the terms of the treaty that ended the Mexican War.

SECTION 2 RESOURCES

REPRODUCIBLE

▶ Guided Reading Strategy 17.2

▶ Primary Source Reading 17: Opposition to the Mexican War

TECHNOLOGY

▶ One-Stop Planner, Lesson 17.2

▶ **CNN** Presents America: Beginnings to 1914 Segment: Choosing Sides in the War with Mexico

▶ Homework Practice Online

REINFORCEMENT, REVIEW, AND ASSESSMENT

▶ Section 2 Review, p. 526

▶ Daily Quiz 17.2

▶ Main Idea Activity 17.2

▶ English Audio Summary 17.2

▶ Spanish Audio Summary 17.2

🔊 *LET'S GET STARTED!*

As students enter the classroom, ask them to imagine a situation in which their best friend or a family member has made a decision with which the students disagree. Tell them to think about what their reaction might be. *(Students' responses will vary.)* Explain to students that many Americans disagreed about U.S. foreign policy when the United States went to war with Mexico during the mid-1800s. Then tell them that despite the enthusiasm for manifest destiny, the war met with heated opposition. Tell students that in Section 2 they will learn more about the Mexican War.

Section 2

The Mexican War

Read to Discover

1. How did Americans react to the declaration of war against Mexico?
2. What were the major events and battles of the war?
3. What were the terms of the treaty that ended the Mexican War?

WHY IT MATTERS TODAY

Nations and groups continue to go to war with one another. Use **CNNfyi.com** or other **current events** sources to learn about an armed conflict somewhere in the world today. Record your findings in your journal.

Identify

• Henry David Thoreau
• Stephen Kearny
• Bear Flag Revolt
• John C. Frémont
• Winfield Scott
• Treaty of Guadalupe Hidalgo
• Mexican Cession
• Gadsden Purchase

This illustration shows an American soldier during the Mexican War.

The Story Continues

The days following Polk's war message to Congress were full of angry debate. Some members of the Whig Party believed that the president had intentionally started the conflict with Mexico. Congressman Garrett Davis of Kentucky spoke bitterly. "It is our own President who began this war." The House of Representatives, however, stood firmly by the president. The House stated in its declaration of war that the conflict was started "by the act of the Republic of Mexico."

⭐ Responses to War

News of the declaration of war spread across the country. At the beginning of the war, the U.S. Army was greatly outnumbered by Mexican forces. U.S. soldiers had better weapons and equipment, however. To strengthen the army during the Mexican War, the U.S. government called for 50,000 volunteers. Some 200,000 volunteers answered the call. Many of the volunteers were young men who saw the war as a grand adventure in a foreign land. The Mexican War was the first U.S. war fought mainly on foreign soil. It was also the first time many newspapers covered a

★ TEACH

Have students read Section 2 and complete Guided Reading Strategy 17.2. Choose one or more of the following activities to explore the section content with students. For further suggestions on block scheduling or team teaching, see the *Block Scheduling Handbook with Team Teaching Strategies*.

ALL LEVELS: Copy the following graphic organizer onto the chalkboard, omitting the italicized answers. Have students complete the time line to show the major events and battles of the Mexican War. Display the time lines around the classroom for other students to view. **ENGLISH LANGUAGE LEARNERS**

LEVEL 1: Give each student a blank outline map of the southwestern United States and Mexico. Have him or her label major battles in the Mexican War and include facts that show the importance of each battle. Display maps around the room and invite students to observe the work of their classmates. **ENGLISH LANGUAGE LEARNERS**

| **May 1846** *Taylor pushes Mexican forces into Mexico.* | **August 1846** *California is controlled by American forces.* | **September 1847** *U.S. troops under Scott capture Mexico City.* |

| **June 1846** *Kearny joins the fighting in California.* | **February 1847** *Santa Anna and Taylor battle at Buena Vista.* |

U.S. conflict. Reporters used horses to send articles back East quickly. In addition, the war was one of the first to be photographed.

On the home front, many men and women supported the soldiers. They collected supplies and wrote patriotic poems and songs. One popular war song urged soldiers to "Arm and strike for liberty!" For many Americans the war led to greater national pride. Many people who supported the war argued that it would spread republican values.

Not all Americans supported the war, however. Many members of the Whig Party thought that the conflict was unjustified and unnecessary. The conflict also upset people who were against expansion or war. Transcendentalist writer and philosopher **Henry David Thoreau** went to jail for refusing to pay taxes because he believed they would support the war in Mexico.

Northern abolitionists opposed the Mexican War, fearing that the United States might gain lands in the Southwest. If so, they reasoned, southern states would try to establish slavery in these new lands. But some pro-slavery southerners worried that new territories might choose to ban slavery. This concern led southern politicians such as John C. Calhoun to question the goals of the Mexican War. Thoreau's fellow transcendentalist Ralph Waldo Emerson predicted that these disagreements over the Mexican War would further divide Americans.

This painting shows Mexican cavalry charging U.S. Army cannons in the Battle of Palo Alto.

History Makers Speak

"The United States will conquer Mexico, but it will be as the man swallows the arsenic [a poison], which brings him down in turn. Mexico will poison us."

—Ralph Waldo Emerson, quoted in *Battle Cry of Freedom*, by James M. McPherson

Analyzing Primary Sources

Drawing Inferences and Conclusions What do you think Emerson meant when he said that "Mexico will poison us"? Students might say that disagreements over the war would divide Americans.

✔ **Reading Check: Summarizing** What reasons did Americans such as Henry David Thoreau give for opposing the Mexican War? They opposed expansion, feared the growth of slavery, opposed war or thought it unnecessary.

★ American Victories

While supporters and opponents of the war argued, the fighting had already started. Even before the official declaration of war, General Zachary Taylor's soldiers fought and won battles south of the Nueces River. He defeated Mexican forces at Palo Alto and Resaca de la Palma on May 8 and 9, 1846. Taylor's victories drove the Mexican troops back into Mexico. Taylor then crossed the Rio Grande and occupied Matamoros. While Taylor waited for reinforcements, Polk ordered Brigadier General **Stephen Kearny** to attack New Mexico. Kearny took the city of Santa Fe without a fight. He claimed the entire territory of New Mexico for the United States. Then Kearny marched toward southern California in June 1846.

HOMEWORK Have students imagine that they are volunteer soldiers in the Mexican War. Ask students to write a series of journal entries discussing their decision to volunteer, their experiences in battle, and their feelings about the terms of the Treaty of Guadalupe Hidalgo. Remind students to include historical details from the section in their entries.

LEVEL 2: Organize a panel discussion in which groups of students represent the viewpoint of the following people: President Polk, Congressman Abraham Lincoln, army volunteers, Henry David Thoreau, Ralph Waldo Emerson, John C. Calhoun, a northern abolitionist, and a representative of the Mexican government. Have students prepare to discuss the following questions: What were the causes of the war? Was the United States justified in their reactions to declaring war? On what terms should the war end? Serve as a moderator for the discussion and make certain that all groups have a chance to respond.

Interdisciplinary Connection

▶Art◀

Representations of the Mexican War. The fact that Americans could receive relatively current information about the Mexican War through the telegraph affected artistic representations of the conflict. Richard Caton Woodville's painting *News From the Mexican War* shows several men gathered around a newspaper, excitedly reading about the latest events. Reporters and printmakers were able to make thousands of chromolithograph prints of the war's heroes, which were used as propaganda. Many lithographs were solely based on news reports—not on eyewitness accounts—and therefore often mistakenly represented events. For example, some showed the early battles taking place before grand mountains or in the jungle, when in reality they were fought on a coastal prairie.

CRITICAL THINKING

Why would heroic-looking scenes of the Mexican War be used as propaganda?

ANSWER: Students might suggest to encourage more people to enlist or otherwise support the war.

MAP ANSWERS
1. Doniphan
2. Students might suggest that with each victory the U.S. became more confident and assured of victory.

The Mexican War, 1846–1847
Interpreting Maps Within months of declaring war, U.S. forces had captured all the major cities and towns along the coast of California and controlled much of the territory north of Mexico City.

Skills Assessment
1. **Human Systems** Which U.S military commander led forces from Santa Fe to Chihuahua?
2. **Drawing Inferences and Conclusions** How did U.S. victories in Mexican territory help the troops go on to win the Mexican War?

California settlers raised this flag in 1846 to declare their independence from Mexico.

At the same time, a small group of American settlers near the town of Sonoma revolted against the Californios. These rebels declared that California was an independent republic. To represent this new nation, the rebels created a flag with a single star and a grizzly bear. As a result, the rebellion was called the **Bear Flag Revolt**. Army explorer **John C. Frémont** played an important part in the revolt. Frémont had been leading an expedition across the Sierra Nevada when he heard that the United States might go to war with Mexico. Frémont returned to the Sacramento Valley. Upon his arrival, he encouraged Americans to revolt and then joined them.

While the revolt was taking place, the U.S. Navy took Monterey, the capital of the Mexican province of California. Naval forces then planned another invasion of California, aided by the arrival of Kearny's army from New Mexico. The towns of San Diego, Los Angeles, and San Francisco soon fell to the Americans. In August 1846, Commodore Robert Stockton declared that California belonged to the United States. Some Californios continued to resist until early 1847, when they surrendered. General Kearny was appointed governor of California by President Polk.

✔ **Reading Check: Summarizing** How did the United States gain control of California during the Mexican War? As American settlers declared independence from Mexico, Kearny's army joined naval forces under Stockton to defeat Mexico.

Denny Schillings of Homewood, Illinois, suggested the following activity:

LEVEL 3: Have students use their textbooks and notes to review information about the Treaty of Guadalupe Hildalgo. Organize students into groups, assigning each to represent either opposition to the treaty or support for the treaty. Each group should produce a set of historical documents that includes the following items: (1) a map showing land acquisitions, (2) a summary outlining the provisions of the treaty, and (3) a position statement clarifying the group's view on the treaty. **COOPERATIVE LEARNING**

★ CLOSE

Ask students to write a one-paragraph essay that explains whether the United States was justified in declaring war against Mexico. Call on volunteers to present their paragraphs, list their replies on the chalkboard, and group them according to their similarities.

★ The War's End

In Mexico, Taylor finally got his reinforcements. His army soon drove the Mexican army deeper into Mexico. At the heavily fortified city of Monterrey, U.S. troops won a hard-fought battle. Both sides spent a few months trying to improve their positions. General Santa Anna then took over Mexico's government. He led his army north in February 1847, clashing with Taylor's forces at Buena Vista.

Santa Anna sent the outnumbered U.S. soldiers a note demanding their surrender, but General Taylor refused. After two days of hard fighting, Santa Anna's men retreated under the cover of darkness.

Taylor's success earned him popularity with his troops and back home. Soldiers called him Old Rough-and-Ready. Taylor's popularity troubled President Polk, who feared the general might run for president in 1848. Polk was also concerned that Taylor might not be able to win the war. For these reasons, Polk gave the command to General **Winfield Scott**, known as Old Fuss and Feathers.

Scott sailed down to the port of Veracruz, which was the strongest fortress in Mexico. On March 29, after an 88-hour artillery attack, Veracruz fell to Scott's army. The next part of the plan was to attack Mexico City.

Scott's men pushed some 200 miles inland to the heart of Mexico. Santa Anna tried to stop the U.S. forces at Cerro Gordo in mid-April. With a daring uphill attack on the Mexican position, U.S. soldiers won a key victory. By August 1847, U.S. troops were at the edge of Mexico City.

After a truce failed to end the war, Scott ordered a massive attack on Mexico City. Mexican soldiers and civilians fought fiercely. At a military school atop the steep and fortified hill of Chapultepec, young cadets bravely defended their position. Finally, on September 14, 1847, U.S. soldiers captured the Mexican capital.

✔ **Reading Check: Sequencing** List the major battles that brought an end to the Mexican War in their proper sequence. Buena Vista, Veracruz, Cerro Gordo, Chapultepec, fall of Mexico City

Biography

Zachary Taylor. Taylor's troops started calling him Old Rough and Ready because he dressed informally. He rarely wore a uniform or any emblem of his rank. One officer claimed, "He looks more like an old farmer going to market with eggs to sell than anything."

CRITICAL THINKING

Why might Taylor's informal style of dress make him a popular military figure?

ANSWER: Students might suggest that he seemed uninterested in self-glorification.

Visual Record Answer

Students might suggest that it appears to be a very orderly culture and that the military is a prominent part of that culture.

Interpreting the Visual Record

The end of the war *U.S. soldiers entered Mexico City in September 1847. Santa Anna fled the country soon afterward.* **What does the painting suggest about the culture of Mexico?**

☆ REVIEW AND ASSESS

Have students complete the **Section 2 Review** on p. 526. Then have them complete **Daily Quiz 17.2**. As **Alternative Assessment**, you may want to use the panel discussion or the Mexican War time line exercises in this section's lessons.

☆ RETEACH

Have students complete **Main Idea Activity for English Language Learners and Special-Needs Students 17.2**. Then have students identify the significance of the Treaty of Guadalupe Hildalgo. Ask students to briefly discuss both from the American point of view and from the Mexican point of

view, the progress of the war and whether its benefits exceeded its costs. **ENGLISH LANGUAGE LEARNERS**

☆ EXTEND

Have students use the library or other resources to find information about the Mexican War, including key military figures, battles, and diplomatic efforts. Then ask each of them to put together a written or oral report using the information they found. Encourage students to include visual aids and to present their reports to the class. **BLOCK SCHEDULING**

Section 2 Review
ANSWERS

❶ Identify
- Henry David Thoreau, p. 523
- Stephen Kearny, p. 523
- Bear Flag Revolt, p. 524
- John C. Frémont, p. 524
- Winfield Scott, p. 525
- Treaty of Guadalupe Hidalgo, p. 526
- Mexican Cession, p. 526
- Gadsden Purchase, p. 526

❷ Taylor's forces drive Mexican troops back into Mexico; Kearny takes Santa Fe; rebels declare California independent in the Bear Flag Revolt; Santa Anna's troops retreat; Scott and troops lay siege; young cadets defend a military school; Scott and his troops push inland and finally capture Mexico City

❸ a. thought the war helped fulfill America's manifest destiny; feared it would lead to the expansion of slavery
b. United States gained the Mexican Cession for $15 million paid to Mexico

❹ Students' reports will vary, but reports should include the Bear Flag Revolt as well as the actions of Kearny's and Stockton's forces.

★★★★★★★★★★★★
That's Interesting!
★★★★★★★★★★★★

An Unpopular Peace Can you imagine being fired for negotiating a peace treaty? That's what happened to Nicholas Trist. President Polk had sent Trist, a State Department official, to help end the war with Mexico. Trist had little success for months, but he finally got his chance when Scott captured Mexico City. However, Polk had ordered Trist back to Washington to receive new instructions. Not wanting to lose his chance for a treaty, the diplomat ignored his orders. He stayed in Mexico and negotiated the Treaty of Guadalupe Hidalgo. When Polk first heard about the treaty, he was so angry that he fired Trist!

The Treaty of Guadalupe Hidalgo

★ More New Territories

The war ended after Scott took Mexico City. The **Treaty of Guadalupe Hidalgo** marked the new peace. Signed in February 1848, it ceded, or turned over, much of Mexico's northern territory to the United States. Known as the **Mexican Cession**, this land included the present-day states of California, Nevada, and Utah. It also included most of Arizona and New Mexico and parts of Colorado and Wyoming. The United States also got the area claimed by Texas north of the Rio Grande. The Mexican Cession totaled more than 500,000 square miles. It increased the size of the United States by almost 25 percent. The United States agreed to pay Mexico $15 million and to assume claims of more than $3 million held by American citizens against Mexico. The treaty also addressed the status of Mexicans in the Mexican Cession.

The treaty itself caused a controversy. Some Americans wanted to take all of Mexico. Antislavery and antiwar activists, people who thought that Mexicans would not make good republican citizens, and Whigs were all against the treaty. Polk answered them by pointing out the benefits the United States would gain from the treaty. The Senate ratified the treaty in March 1848. James Gadsden, U.S. minister to Mexico, negotiated the **Gadsden Purchase** in December 1853. Under the terms of the purchase, the U.S. government paid Mexico $10 million for the southern parts of what are now Arizona and New Mexico. With this purchase, the continental boundaries of the United States were finally fixed.

✔ **Reading Check: Finding the Main Idea** How did the American victory in the Mexican War affect the United States? Although the treaty was controversial, the Mexican Cession increased the territory of the nation by about 25 percent.

Section 2 Review

go.hrw.com **Homework Practice Online**
keyword: SA3 HP17

❶ Identify and explain:
- Henry David Thoreau
- Stephen Kearny
- Bear Flag Revolt
- John C. Frémont
- Winfield Scott
- Treaty of Guadalupe Hidalgo
- Mexican Cession
- Gadsden Purchase

❷ Sequencing Copy the graphic organizer below. Use it to show the sequence of major events leading to the end of the Mexican War.

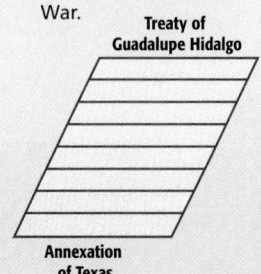

Treaty of Guadalupe Hidalgo

Annexation of Texas

❸ Finding the Main Idea
a. Why did some Americans support the Mexican War, and what reasons did other Americans give for opposing the war?

b. What did each side gain in the Treaty of Guadalupe Hidalgo?

❹ Writing and Critical Thinking
Summarizing Imagine that you are a U.S. soldier in California during the Mexican War. Write a short report to your commanders describing how the United States gained control of California.

Consider the following:
- Polk's offer to buy California
- the Bear Flag Revolt
- actions by Kearny's and Stockton's forces

SPOTLIGHT
on Henry David Thoreau

Have students read the excerpt from Henry David Thoreau's essay about civil disobedience on this page. Call on volunteers to read the excerpt aloud, then discuss Thoreau's ideas. Discuss circumstances under which Thoreau's concept of civil disobedience might be applied. Finally, ask students to write responses to Thoreau that defend, modify, or repudiate his position. **BLOCK SCHEDULING**

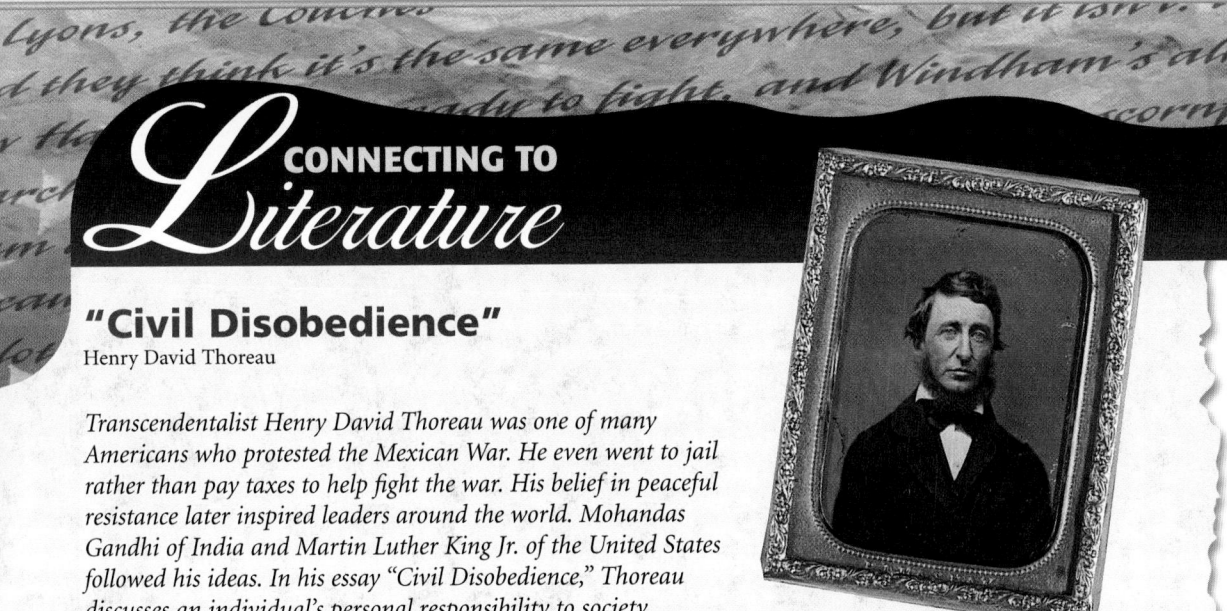

CONNECTING TO *Literature*

"Civil Disobedience"
Henry David Thoreau

Transcendentalist Henry David Thoreau was one of many Americans who protested the Mexican War. He even went to jail rather than pay taxes to help fight the war. His belief in peaceful resistance later inspired leaders around the world. Mohandas Gandhi of India and Martin Luther King Jr. of the United States followed his ideas. In his essay "Civil Disobedience," Thoreau discusses an individual's personal responsibility to society.

Henry David Thoreau argued for nonviolent opposition to the Mexican War.

I heartily accept the motto, "That government is best which governs least"; and I should like to see it acted up to more rapidly and **systematically.**[1] Carried out, it finally amounts to this, which also I believe—"That government is best which governs not at all"; and when men are prepared for it, that will be the kind of government which they will have. Government is at best but an **expedient;**[2] but most governments are usually, and all governments are sometimes, **inexpedient**[3]. . . . The government itself, which is only the **mode**[4] which the people have chosen to execute their will, is equally liable to be abused and **perverted**[5] before the people can act through it. Witness the present Mexican war, the work of . . . a few individuals using the standing government as their tool; for, in the outset, the people would not have consented to this measure. . . .

Unjust laws exist: shall we be content to obey them, or shall we **endeavor**[6] to amend them, and obey them until we have succeeded, or shall we **transgress**[7] them at once? Men generally, under such a government as this, think that they ought to wait until they have persuaded the majority to alter them [the laws]. They think that, if they should resist, the remedy would be worse than the evil. But it is the fault of the government itself that the remedy is worse than the evil. It makes it worse. Why is it not more **apt**[8] to anticipate and provide for reform? Why does it not cherish its wise minority . . . ?

If the injustice is part of the necessary friction of the machine of government, let it go, let it go: **perchance**[9] it will wear smooth—certainly the machine will wear out. If the injustice has a spring, or a pulley, or a rope, or a crank, exclusively for itself, then perhaps you may consider whether the remedy will not be worse than the evil; but if it is of such a nature that it requires you to be the agent of injustice to another, then, I say, break the law.

Understanding What You Read

1. **Literature and History** Under what conditions does Thoreau support breaking the law?
2. **Literature and You** Do you agree with Thoreau that it is acceptable to peacefully break a law that has been passed by the government? Why or why not?

---

[1]**systematically:** regularly
[2]**expedient:** means to an end
[3]**inexpedient:** unwise
[4]**mode:** method
[5]**perverted:** twisted
[6]**endeavor:** try
[7]**transgress:** break
[8]**apt:** suitable
[9]**perchance:** maybe

Biography

Henry David Thoreau. When he was 16, Thoreau entered college at Harvard, where he was judged such an "oddity in literary matters that his writings will never probably do him any justice." While at Harvard, Thoreau refused to wear the required black coat; instead he wore a green one. Thus, few of his former classmates were surprised when he ended up spending a night in jail for refusing to pay his taxes. Ralph Waldo Emerson, Thoreau's friend and mentor, visited him in jail and reportedly asked, "What are you doing in there?" Thoreau answered, "What are you doing out there?"

CRITICAL THINKING

What did Thoreau mean by his reply to Emerson?

ANSWER: Students might suggest that he implied that if Emerson shared Thoreau's principles, Emerson would also be willing to go to jail.

CONNECTING TO LITERATURE ANSWERS

1. the law forces you to do an injustice to another person
2. Students' responses will vary, but students should display an understanding of Thoreau's idea of civil disobedience.

Section 3

OBJECTIVES

★ Analyze the conflicts caused by new U.S. settlement in the Southwest.

★ Discuss the interaction between various cultures in the Southwest.

★ Explain why the Mormons moved to the West and what they achieved there.

★ LET'S GET STARTED!

As students enter the classroom, ask them to imagine what might happen if their homes were suddenly taken over by their neighbors. *(Students' responses will vary, but students might say that a feud would start with the neighbors and that they might try to get the authorities to intervene.)* List responses on the chalkboard. Explain to students that this was the situation in the Southwest after the Mexican War, when settlers, speculators, and trappers moved in and encroached upon longtime inhabitants of the area. Tell students that in Section 3 they will learn about the conflicts and opportunities that resulted from U.S. territorial acquisitions.

Section 3

More Settlers Head West

Read to Discover

1. What conflicts did new U.S. settlement cause in the Southwest?
2. How did various cultures interact in the Southwest?
3. Why did the Mormons move to the West, and what were their achievements there?

Identify

• Joseph Smith
• Mormons
• Brigham Young
• Mormon Trail

WHY IT MATTERS TODAY

California, Texas, and the Southwest continue to be areas of rapid growth today. Use **CNN fyi.com** or other **current events** sources to learn about a city or region in the West or Southwest that is experiencing growth due to immigration or migration. Record your findings in your journal.

THE SQUATTER

AND

THE DON.

A NOVEL DESCRIPTIVE OF CONTEMPORARY OCCURRENCES IN CALIFORNIA.

BY

C. LOYAL.

SAN FRANCISCO
1885

COURTESY THE BANCROFT LIBRARY

The Squatter and the Don *described the efforts of a Californio family to keep their land.*

The Story Continues

In her novel *The Squatter and the Don,* María Amparo Ruiz de Burton described the struggles of the Californios. A Californio landowner herself, Ruiz de Burton put her family's anger and despair into the words of her characters. "Is it possible that there is no law to protect us; to protect our property?" asked Doña Josefa Alamar. "The treaty said that our rights would be the same as those enjoyed by all other American citizens," Don Mariano Alamar answered her. "[But] we have had no one to speak for us."

★ Conflicts over Land

After the Mexican War, a flood of traders, trappers, settlers, and speculators moved to the Southwest. Most Mexicans, Mexican Americans, and American Indians faced legal, economic, and social discrimination. American newcomers struggled against longtime residents to control the land. They also competed to control other valuable resources, such as water and minerals.

★ **TEACH**

Have students read Section 3 and complete Guided Reading Strategy 17.3. Choose one or more of the following activities to explore the section content with students. For further suggestions on block scheduling or team teaching, see the *Block Scheduling Handbook with Team Teaching Strategies.*

LEVEL 1: Have students imagine that they are Mormons who have made the journey to Utah. Have students create diary entries describing significant events that happened along the journey. Students should also include reasons why they were moving west as well as what they planned to achieve when they arrived. Ask students to include information about Joseph Smith, Brigham Young, and the Mormon settlement in Salt Lake City. Have students present their diary entries to the class. **ENGLISH LANGUAGE LEARNERS**

Interpreting the Visual Record

New customs *This image shows a Mexican family in the 1800s making tortillas at home. What customs do you see in the image that American settlers might adopt from this family?*

★ Culture

American Indians in the Mexican War. Many California Indians fought with Captain Frémont in California. Although the army promised to pay them for their services, they often received only receipts that promised future payment. Many of the volunteers became angry, thinking that the U.S. government had deceived them. In an attempt to appease them, Frémont offered some of the American Indian volunteers old horses that had been roaming around the U.S. fort. It was not until 1858 that Congress repaid some of the receipts, and others were never repaid.

CRITICAL THINKING

Why might these American Indians begin raiding farmers and ranchers after they left the army?

ANSWER: Students might suggest that they needed food or money to support their families, since they had not been paid.

Visual Record Answer

Students might suggest various homemaking customs.

The Treaty of Guadalupe Hidalgo promised to protect the property rights of residents of the Mexican Cession. However, the U.S. government often made Mexican American landowners go to court to prove that they had titles to their land. These legal battles often bankrupted landowners. In the 1850s magazine writer John S. Hittell described the situation faced by Californios.

History Makers Speak

“It was not their fault that the Mexican land system differed from the American. . . . It was severe hardship for owners of land under grants from Mexico, that they should be required to sue the government of the United States, or lose their land.”

—John S. Hittell, from *A Documentary History of the Mexican Americans,* edited by Wayne Moquin with Charles Van Doren

Analyzing Primary Sources

Identifying Points of View Why does Hittell think that Mexican landowners were treated unfairly? Because American courts ignored Mexican land titles and forced Mexican landowners to go to court to keep their lands.

In other areas, new settlers usually ignored Mexican legal ideas such as community property or community water rights. Conflicts over the ownership of cattle and sheep were also common. Some rich Tejanos tried to protect their property by marrying into powerful Anglo families.

The steady arrival of new settlers and the policies of the U.S. government greatly affected American Indians in the Southwest. In some areas, new white settlers soon outnumbered Indians. These settlers often tried to take control of valuable water resources and grazing lands. Settlers rarely respected Indian holy places, such as mountain lakes and burial grounds. Sometimes Indian raiding parties took settlers' cattle and attacked settlements. In response, angry westerners fought the raiding parties. They also often attacked Indian tribes or villages that were not involved in the fighting, thus causing new conflicts.

✔ **Reading Check: Identifying Cause and Effect** What were the causes and results of conflict between Anglo settlers, Mexican Americans, and American Indians? Anglos claimed the right to control land and other resources held by the other groups. Mexican Americans sought protection in the American courts or by marrying into Anglo families. Indians sometimes attacked Anglo settlements and property.

HOMEWORK Have students make a graphic organizer that shows the cultural exchanges that occurred in the Southwest among the American Indian, Anglo, and Mexican cultures.

ALL LEVELS: Copy the following graphic organizer onto the chalkboard, omitting the italicized answers. Use it to help students better understand the interactions between different cultures as more settlers moved to the southwest. **ENGLISH LANGUAGE LEARNERS**

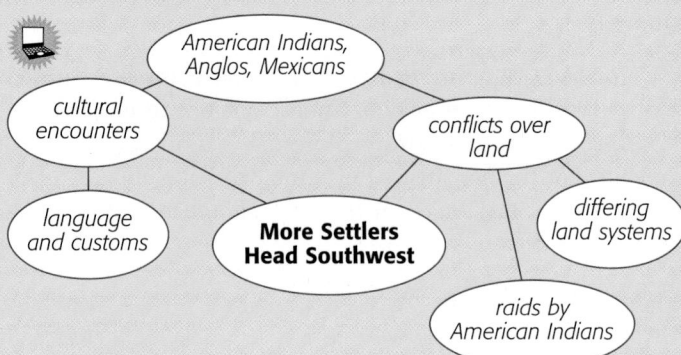

⭐ Culture

Tejano Celebrations. In 1851, Henry Kinney held a fiesta in Corpus Christi that represented the liveliness of Tejano culture. At Kinney's party, girls and women wore fancy dresses made of brightly colored fabrics, while the men put on intricately decorated sombreros and silver-trimmed pants. Tejanos also showed off beautiful silver and leatherwork in their ornamental saddles and bridles. In addition to dancing, fiestas often included games, such as the wheel of fortune and acrobatic demonstrations. Fiestas also included delicious refreshments such as *dulces* [sweet cakes], chocolates, and lemonade.

CRITICAL THINKING

How do you think Tejano fiestas differed from Anglo dances?

ANSWER: Students might suggest the way people dressed, the entertainment, the food, and the types of dances.

Visual Record Answer

Students might suggest the pretty countryside and a community environment.

LINKING PAST TO PRESENT ANSWER
(for p. 531)
Because water was scarce, Mormons passed laws to control its use. The laws made sure that water was used to benefit the community, not just individuals.

Interpreting the Visual Record

San Antonio *By 1860, San Antonio had become the largest city in Texas.* **What qualities of the city shown in this painting do you think would attract settlers?**

COURTESY OF THE WITTE MUSEUM, SAN ANTONIO, TEXAS

⭐ Cultural Encounters

Despite conflicts, American Indian, Mexican, and Anglo cultures influenced one another in the Southwest. As American settlers made homes there, they adopted some of the customs and practices of the peoples they met.

In settlements with large Mexican American populations, laws were often printed in both English and Spanish. The Spanish language was also important in trade and daily life, especially in California, New Mexico, and Texas. Place-names such as San Antonio, San Diego, and Taos show the Mexican and American Indian heritage of the Southwest. Communities throughout the Southwest regularly celebrated both Mexican and American holidays. One example was Diez y Seis de Septiembre, which celebrates the declaration of the Grito de Dolores in Mexico in 1810. This holiday became popular in Texas. In addition, there were numbers of French and German immigrants in towns of Central Texas. In these towns, people kept many of their traditional customs.

Mexican and American Indian knowledge and traditions also shaped the local economies of many American communities in the Southwest. Mexican Americans taught Anglo settlers about mining in the rugged mountains. The ranching communities of the West were first started by Mexican settlers. These communities grew as new ranchers moved in and new markets opened. In addition, Mexican Americans introduced new types of saddles, clothing, and other equipment to American ranchers. Adobe, a building material originally developed by the Anasazi, was adopted from the Pueblo by the Spanish. It was commonly used in Arizona, California, and New Mexico. In addition, new settlers adopted Mexican and American Indian foods such as beans, tamales, and tortillas.

Trade also changed the Southwest and the people living there. Even small communities were pulled into the growing market economy. For

LEVEL 3: Have students write a dialogue between the following three characters living in the new U.S. territories of the Southwest: a U.S. citizen who has just moved there, an American Indian, and a Mexican American. Have each character describe changes and conflicts brought about by settlement in the southwest and ways of adapting to the changes.

★ CLOSE

Ask students to write essays describing what they consider to be the most important issue that arose from the migration of Americans to the Southwest. Ask volunteers to read their papers, and encourage class discussion. List the issues suggested by students' essays, then group them according to similarities.

example, the Navajo made more handwoven woolen blankets to sell to Americans. The Navajo also became known as skilled silversmiths. They had learned the metalworking craft from Mexican American settlers.

Americans, in turn, brought manufactured goods and money to the Southwest. They brought new firearms and other trade goods. Settlers and traders also brought new breeds of animals from elsewhere in the United States. As a result, the economies of many Mexican American and American Indian communities in the Southwest began to change.

✔ **Reading Check: Categorizing** What cultural and economic influences did American Indians and Mexican Americans have on Anglo settlers in the Mexican Cession? cultural: use of both Spanish and English, celebration of holidays; economic: Mexican mining and ranching, adobe, trade goods, use of Indian and Mexican foods

★ The Mormons

One group of American settlers traveled to the West in search of religious freedom. In 1830 a young man named **Joseph Smith** founded the Church of Jesus Christ of Latter-Day Saints in western New York. The members of this church became known as **Mormons**. Smith told his followers that he had found and translated a set of golden tablets containing religious revelations. These writings became the Book of Mormon.

The Mormons stressed hard work and community, and their church membership grew rapidly. However, some Mormon beliefs and practices made them the target of persecution. For example, some Mormon men practiced polygamy—in which one man is married to several women at the same time.

In the early 1830s Smith and his growing number of converts left New York. They formed new communities, first in Ohio and then in Missouri. The Ohio settlement's bank went under during the Panic of 1837. Moving on to Missouri, Mormons left their settlement when they were chased away by a mob of local people. Their next settlement, at Nauvoo, Illinois, was quite successful. The city grew to some 20,000 converts. But an anti-Mormon mob murdered Smith in jail in 1844. "I can tell you it is a sorrowful time here at present," wrote Mormon Sarah Scott after Smith's death. Following Smith's murder, **Brigham Young** became the head of the Mormon Church. The Mormons decided to move west to build a new community. Young chose what is now Utah as the group's new home. At the time, Utah was still Mexican territory, outside the boundaries of the United States.

Young was a gifted leader who carefully planned the long trip west. An advance party arrived at a pass overlooking the Great Salt Lake in July 1847. Follower Erastus Snow recalled Young's words: "This is the place whereon we will plant our feet." These pioneers began preparing the area for other Mormon immigrants.

Tens of thousands of Mormons took to the **Mormon Trail**. Many pushed or pulled heavy handcarts along the rough ground. Mormons

This Navajo woman is using traditional methods to weave a woolen blanket.

LINKING
★ PAST to PRESENT ★

Water Usage in the West

When the Mormons arrived at the Great Salt Lake in Utah, they saw a barren plain. Mormon leader Brigham Young created strict rules about water use. Young allowed individuals to build dams, but they had to use the water for beneficial purposes such as farming, mining, or manufacturing. In any dispute over water use, the good of the community outweighed the interests of individuals.

In 1902 the federal government created the Bureau of Reclamation. The bureau built dams, reservoirs, and canals to bring additional water to dry western regions. Today the bureau manages all the water in 17 states west of the Mississippi River. **How has the environment shaped federal water management in the West?**

★ REVIEW AND ASSESS

Have Students complete the **Section 3 Review** on p. 532. Then have them complete **Daily Quiz 17.3**. As **Alternative Assessment**, you may want to use the dialogue activity or the Mormon diary exercise from this section's lessons.

★ RETEACH

Have students complete **Main Idea Activity for English Language Learners and Special-Needs Students 17.3**. Then ask each student to list changes that took place in the West because of U.S. settlement. Discuss students' lists in class.

ENGLISH LANGUAGE LEARNERS

★ EXTEND

Have students write an epic poem about U.S. expansion into the Southwest during the mid-1800s. Epics are usually very long, written in an elevated style, and focus on a main hero. Ask students to write their poems about the interactions between American Indians, Mexican, and U.S. settlers, and to refer to events, ideas, people, and places, discussed in this section. Ask volunteers to present their poems to the class.

BLOCK SCHEDULING

★ ★ ★ ★ ★ ★ ★ ★ ★ ★ ★

Section 3 Review
ANSWERS

❶ Identify
• Joseph Smith, p. 531
• Mormons, p. 531
• Brigham Young, p. 531
• Mormon Trail, p. 531

❷ Factors—conflicting Spanish and Anglo legal traditions, lack of respect for American Indian rights and holy places, Anglo ideas of cultural superiority; Groups Affected—Mexicans and American settlers, American Indians, Mexicans and American Indians

❸ a. ownership of land, cattle, and sheep; and use of water resources and grazing lands
b. persecuted for their religious differences; turned Utah into an inhabitable area where farmers prospered and Mormons found refuge

❹ Students' journals will vary but should accurately express the characteristics of American Indian, Anglo, and Mexican cultures, include the idea of manifest destiny, and describe conflicts between the three cultures.

Interpreting the Visual Record

The Mormon Trail *After Joseph Smith was murdered, Mormons moved west to Utah.* **What challenges does the illustration show the Mormons facing?**

fleeing persecution in the East and the Midwest were joined by converts immigrating to America from Great Britain and Scandinavia.

The Mormons selected a desert valley for their new home and established a very disciplined community. "Those that do not like our looks and customs are at liberty to go where they please," Brigham Young declared. The main Mormon settlement at Salt Lake City became a thriving community with broad roads and surrounding farms. After his arrival in 1847, Young chose the site for the Mormons' Great Temple. In December 1860 the Mormon population of Utah stood at about 40,000.

✔ **Reading Check: Finding the Main Idea** Why did Mormons move to the West? to escape religious persecution and to gain religious freedom

Section 3 Review

❶ Identify and explain:
• Joseph Smith
• Mormons
• Brigham Young
• Mormon Trail

❷ Summarizing Copy the chart below. Use it to show three factors that made interaction among new Anglo settlers, Mexican Americans, and American Indians difficult in the Mexican Cession.

Factors	Groups Affected

❸ Finding the Main Idea
a. What conflicts arose among American settlers, American Indians, and Mexican Americans as more settlers moved into the West and the Southwest?

b. What caused the Mormons to move to the West, and what did they accomplish there?

❹ Writing and Critical Thinking
Analyzing Information Imagine that you are a traveler to the Southwest in the mid-1800s. Write a journal entry describing how Mexican, American Indian, and Anglo cultures are mingling in the region.
Consider the following:
• characteristics of American Indian, Anglo, and Mexican cultures
• the idea of manifest destiny
• conflicts between the three cultures

go.hrw.com
Homework Practice Online
keyword: SA3 HP17

Section 4

OBJECTIVES

- ★ Discuss why many people headed west to California in 1849.
- ★ Describe what life was like in gold rush mining camps and towns.
- ★ Analyze how the gold rush changed California.

Section 4

The Gold Rush

Read to Discover

1. Why did many people head west to California in 1849?
2. What was life like in gold rush mining camps and towns?
3. How did the gold rush change California?

WHY IT MATTERS TODAY

Individuals, corporations, and nations still search for and use Earth's mineral wealth. Use **CNNfyi.com** or other **current events** sources to learn about discoveries of oil, precious metals, or other minerals in recent years. Record your findings in your journal.

Define

- forty-niners
- prospect

Identify

- California Gold Rush
- Biddy Mason

The Story Continues

In the early 1840s there were still relatively few Americans in California. On January 24, 1848, James W. Marshall made a discovery that suddenly changed this situation. Marshall recalled that he was working that day near Sutter's Mill in California when he glanced down. "My eye was caught with the glimpse of something shining in the bottom of the ditch. . . . I reached my hand down and picked it up; it made my heart thump, for I was certain it was gold. The piece was about half the size and of the shape of a pea."

Advertisements like this one encouraged travelers to move to California.

★ The Forty-Niners

John Sutter, the owner of Sutter's Mill, soon learned that gold had been discovered on his property. At first, according to Sutter, he could not believe it. "I thought something had touched Marshall's brain." When Sutter saw the gold, however, he "was fairly thunderstruck." Both men agreed to keep the discovery a secret. However, when they went to examine the work site the next day, they met a Spanish-speaking Indian worker holding a nugget and shouting, "Oro [gold]! Oro! Oro!" Sutter's workers soon quit to search for gold. Stories of the discovery spread across the country. President Polk added to the national excitement by

★ **TEACH**

Have students read Section 4 and complete Guided Reading Strategy 17.4. Choose one or more of the following activities to explore the section content with students. For further suggestions on block scheduling or team teaching, see the *Block Scheduling Handbook with Team Teaching Strategies*.

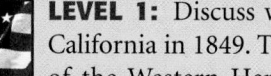

LEVEL 1: Discuss with students why people went to California in 1849. Then have students illustrate a map of the Western Hemisphere that shows the various routes that people traveled to make their way to California during the gold rush. Have students note the major obstacles along each route. Display the maps around the classroom.
ENGLISH LANGUAGE LEARNERS

American Indian Lands of Gold. Because gold was found outside the boundaries of John Sutter's land grant, he had to negotiate with the Yalesumne Indians to use it. Sutter and his partner, James Marshall, were given permission to cut timber, build a sawmill, grow crops, and open mines. In return, Sutter and Marshall agreed to build two millstones and to grind the Yalesumne's grain. Each year they gave the Yalesumne $150 worth of clothing and tools, and at the end of 20 years, the land would return to the Yalesumne.

ACTIVITY: Have students write an entry about the gold rush from John Sutter's diary using standard grammar, spelling, sentence structure, and punctuation.

MAP ANSWER
Sutter's Fort (Sacramento)

CONNECTING TO SCIENCE AND TECHNOLOGY ANSWER
(for p. 535)
caused soil erosion, clogged rivers

Technology Resources

American History Simulations CD–ROM: The Gold Rush

The California Gold Rush

Interpreting Maps California drew national attention after the discovery of gold at Sutter's Mill.

Skills Assessment Places and Regions What city is located at the junction of three trails and a supply route?

Map legend:
- Gold mining area
- Leading gold mine
- Trails to California
- Leading supply route

UTAH TERR.

Truckee R. / Lake Tahoe / Carson River / Sacramento River / American R. / San Joaquin R.

SIERRA NEVADA

Sutter's Fort (Sacramento) / Sutter's Mill / CALIFORNIA / San Francisco / Stockton

January 24, 1848: James Marshall discovers gold while building a sawmill.

By 1850, San Francisco grows to a booming port of more than 25,000 people.

PACIFIC OCEAN

0   20   40 Miles
0   20   40 Kilometers
Albers Equal-Area Projection

Mining tools

---

confirming the California gold strike in his farewell message to Congress in December 1848.

In 1849 the **California Gold Rush** caused a huge rise in California's population. That year about 80,000 gold-seekers came to California, hoping to strike it rich. These migrants were known as **forty-niners**. As one Iowa woman who left with her husband to find gold recalled, "At that time the 'gold fever' was contagious, and few, old, or young, escaped the malady [sickness]." Nearly 80 percent of the forty-niners were Americans, while the rest came from all over the world.

Most of the forty-niners braved long and often dangerous journeys to reach California. Many easterners and Europeans took one of two major sea routes. One route went down the Atlantic coast and up the Pacific coast of South America. The other combined ship and land travel across Nicaragua or the Isthmus of Panama. The trip around Cape Horn at the tip of South America took six to nine months but was fairly safe. The Central American route was much shorter, but travelers had to cross jungles. They risked catching deadly diseases such as malaria or yellow fever.

Midwestern gold-seekers usually traveled west in wagon trains along overland routes. Some of these forty-niners took a northern route from Missouri or Iowa through the South Pass of the Rocky Mountains. Others followed a southern trail that went through Santa Fe and the southwestern deserts. With luck, a wagon train could cover the roughly 2,000 miles to the gold fields in about three months. Overland travelers were commonly delayed by poor planning, bad weather, and rough ground, however. Many travelers did not bring enough water and other supplies to last through the hot Nevada deserts. Buying supplies along the way was very expensive.

Whatever their method of travel, most forty-niners arrived in San Francisco. The port town had a fine natural harbor and was located close to the newly discovered gold strikes. For these reasons, San Francisco became a convenient trade center and stopping point for travelers. As a result, San Francisco grew more rapidly than any other city in the world at the time. Its population jumped from about 800 in March 1848 to more than 25,000 by 1850.

✔ **Reading Check: Identifying Cause and Effect** Why did the forty-niners go to California, and what effect did they have on the area's population?
They went to find gold; the population grew rapidly.

⭐ Gold Fever

Few of the forty-niners had any previous gold-mining experience. Some people had quick success. Most of the forty-niners, however, found the work to be difficult and time-consuming. The forty-niners would **prospect**, or search, for gold along the banks of streams or in shallow surface mines. The early forty-niners worked an area that ran for 70 miles in northern California. Later, the forty-niners began searching for gold in the Sierra Nevada mountain range.

Early miners frequently banded together to prospect for gold. The first person to arrive at a site would "stake a claim." The miners agreed that each would keep a share of whatever gold was discovered. When one group abandoned a claim, more recent arrivals often took it over, hoping for success. Sometimes two or more groups staked rival claims in the same area. In the early gold rush days, before courts were established, this competition led to conflicts—some of them violent.

CONNECTING TO
SCIENCE AND TECHNOLOGY

Early Mining Methods

Most gold miners in California searched for gold by using water to separate gold particles from lighter rock and dirt. Common tools included pans and larger wooden devices such as cradles, rockers, and sluice boxes. To get the steady flow of water they needed, miners often built small dams and directed the water to their claims. Sometimes the miners' digging and tree cutting caused soil erosion. Piles of dirt and rock washed downstream from mining camps, clogging rivers. How did mining sometimes affect the environment?

Sluice box

Riffles, or ridges, to catch gold

Carpeting to catch gold particles

535

California Gold Rush

- *Settlers from other countries and other parts of the United States move to California.*
- *The economy booms with the discovery of gold and other businesses related to mining.*
- *The sudden increase in population allows California to become a state very quickly.*

In 1853 California's yearly gold production peaked at more than $60 million. Individual success stories inspired many miners. One lucky man got two and a half pounds of gold after only 15 minutes of work. Two African American miners found a rich gold deposit that became known as Negro Hill in honor of their discovery. But the vast majority of gold rush miners did not become rich. Forty-niner Alonzo Delano commented that the "lean, meager [thin], worn-out and woe-begone [sorrowful] miner . . . might daily be seen at almost every point in the upper mines." The good luck that made some miners wealthy never came to thousands of gold-seekers. Most of them found little but misery and debt.

✔ **Reading Check: Finding the Main Idea** How successful were most of the forty-niners? Few prospectors became rich; most failed to strike gold and wound up in debt instead.

★ Mining Camps and Towns

Mining camps sprang up wherever enough people gathered to look for gold. Mining camps often disappeared as quickly as they were built, as rich claims opened up and other claims dried out. Miners found themselves making money one day and broke the next. Under these circumstances, theft and miscommunication were common. There were rarely any local authorities to provide law and order. Some early miners tried to prevent violence and stealing, but others lived wild and often dangerous lives. William Perkins was concerned when he visited the Sonora mining camp in 1850. "It is surprising how indifferent [uncaring] people become to the sight of violence and bloodshed in this country."

Daily Life

Mining camps Some areas in California grew so fast that new arrivals had to live in tents. Most of the residents in these camps were young, unmarried men. Crime, drinking, fighting, and gambling were common problems in these temporary communities, which often had names like Hangtown or Poker Flat. The few women who migrated to California found towns like Columbia, shown below, to be very different from what they left behind. **What parts of this scene suggest that the town has grown rapidly?**

THE GRANGER COLLECTION, NEW YORK

LEVEL 2: Ask students to write a short story or diary entries about a California resident during the mid-1800s who witnessed how the gold rush changed California. Have volunteers present their stories or entries to the class.

LEVEL 3: Have students review the experiences of Chinese immigrants in California that is described in the text. Have them use the information to write a series of letters from a Chinese immigrant to his or her family in China, encouraging or discouraging them to take the journey to California. Letters should include detailed descriptions of life in mining camps and towns. Encourage students to consider what problems might affect the family's decision to come to California.

Miners in the camps came from many cultural backgrounds. Most miners were young, unmarried men. Only around five percent of gold rush immigrants were women or children. Some married women did make the journey to California with their husbands, however. These hardworking wives generally made good money by cooking meals, washing clothes, and operating boardinghouses. Catherine Haun recalled her first home in California.

History Makers Speak

"We were glad to settle down and go housekeeping in a shed that was built in a day of lumber purchased with the first fee. . . . For neighbors, we had a real live saloon. I never have received more respectful attention than I did from these neighbors."

—Catherine Haun, from *Ordinary Americans*, edited by Linda R. Monk

Haun's husband, who was a lawyer, concluded that practicing law was actually more profitable than panning for gold. He was one of many people who found that they could make a good living by supplying miners with food, clothing, equipment, or services. Miners paid high prices for basic necessities because the large amounts of gold in circulation caused severe inflation in California. A loaf of bread, for example, might cost five cents back East, but it would sell for 50 to 75 cents in San Francisco. Eggs sold for $1 apiece. Prices could rise even higher when goods had to be shipped to isolated mining camps. There was also a great demand for mining supplies such as clothes, shovels, nails, and mercury. Clipper ships, known for their speed, could not bring enough of these goods to meet the demand. People who found ways to supply needed goods or services could sell to the highest bidder.

Some settlers took full advantage of these free-enterprise conditions. **Biddy Mason** and her family arrived in California as slaves. They were brought there by a Georgia slaveholder during the gold rush years. He quickly discovered that most Californians opposed slavery. Mason and her family gained their liberty and moved to the small village of Los Angeles. By working as a nurse for $2.50 a week and doing domestic work, Mason saved enough money to buy some land. Over time, Mason's property increased in value from $250 to $200,000. She became one of the wealthiest landowners in California. Mason used one of her houses to help needy travelers. In addition, she used some of her money to support education for African American children. Mason found in California an even greater prize than gold—her freedom.

✔ **Reading Check: Summarizing** What role did free enterprise play in the economic life of the mining camps? Many settlers made their fortunes by supplying scarce goods at high prices to the miners.

CONNECTING TO MATH

Just the Facts

Gold Production, 1847–1860
(in thousands of fine troy ounces)

Year	Amount	Year	Amount
1847	43	1854	2,902
1848	484	1855	2,661
1849	1,935	1856	2,661
1850	2,419	1857	2,661
1851	2,661	1858	2,419
1852	2,902	1859	2,419
1853	3,144	1860	2,225

Using Mathematical Skills
1. How much did gold production increase between 1848 and 1849? Why do you think this happened?
2. Create a graph that shows the annual production of gold and silver for this period.
3. Imagine that you are an economic adviser to the president of the United States. Prepare a written report in which you discuss how increased gold production might affect prices, especially in California.

Perhaps 1,000 of the prospectors in California were African Americans.

Science, Technology & Society

The Daily Drudgery of Mining. Few of the thousands of prospectors who flocked to California to find their fortunes realized how difficult mining for gold would be. Most gold miners worked 50 pans during a 10-hour day. The tasks of digging the dirt to fill the pans, separating the dirt, and swirling the water to reveal the gold were physically demanding. One forty-niner said that prospecting combined "the various arts of canal-digging, ditching, laying stone walls, ploughing, and hoeing potatoes."

CRITICAL THINKING

What other factors would have made mining difficult?

ANSWER: Students might suggest that the distance from provisions, the living conditions, and the high prices for supplies added to the difficulties.

CONNECTING TO MATH ANSWERS
1. a four-fold increase; discovery of gold in California
2. Students' graphs will vary but should accurately display the annual production of gold and silver.
3. Students' reports will vary, but students might report that an increase in gold production would probably increase the supply of gold more than the demand for gold and cause prices to decline.

LEVEL 3: Have students prepare a newspaper for a mining town based on information from this section. The paper should include stories about miners that describe their successes and failures, life in the mining town, and town problems and possible solutions. Encourage students to also create advertisements for jobs, goods, and services as well as drawings that illustrate life in the town and its inhabitants.

★ CLOSE

Have students compare the effects that the gold rush had on California with the lists that they created in the *Let's Get Started!* activity about how a gold discovery might affect their town. Ask students to decide if some of the changes that occurred in California could have happened in their town. Create a large list on the chalkboard of students' suggestions about how the discovery of gold affected California.

Research on the R⊙M

Free Find:
California
After reading about California on the **Holt Researcher CD–ROM,** imagine that you work for the state tourism board. Create a short pamphlet describing California's natural resources.

★ Immigrants to California

The lure of gold attracted miners from around the world to California. Many were from countries that had had few people move to the United States in the past. Famine and economic hardships in southeastern China encouraged many Chinese men to come to America. They looked for fortunes in the American West. These immigrants were known in Chinese as *gam saan haak,* or "travelers to Gold Mountain." Most of them hoped to find great wealth and then return home to China. Between 1849 and 1853 some 24,000 young Chinese men migrated to California. "From far and near we came and were pleased," wrote merchant Lai Chun-Chuen in 1855.

Chinese immigrants soon found that many Americans did not welcome them, however. In 1852 California placed a high monthly tax on all foreign miners. Chinese miners had no choice but to pay this tax if they wished to prospect for gold in California. Chinese workers were also the targets of violent attacks in the mining camps. The legal system offered little protection. It often favored Americans over Chinese and other immigrants.

Many Chinese immigrants continued working in the gold mines, despite such treatment. Some looked for different jobs, and many opened their own businesses. A California newspaper reported that Chinese worked as "ploughmen, laundrymen, placer miners, woolen spinners and weavers, domestic servants, cigar makers, [and] shoemakers."

Prospectors also came to California from Europe, Mexico, and South America. Some 20,000 immigrants had come to California in 1849 alone. Like most American gold-seekers, these new arrivals intended to return home after they had made their fortunes. However, even when they did not become rich, many decided to stay. Some who remained in California became successful business owners. Levi Strauss, a German immigrant, earned his fortune by making tough denim work pants to sell to miners.

✔ **Reading Check: Comparing and Contrasting** How were Chinese immigrants similar to and different from other immigrants who came to California? While many made their fortunes by supplying goods or services rather than by mining for gold, the Chinese were more likely to be the objects of antiforeigner prejudice.

Interpreting the Visual Record

Immigrant workers *Chinese miners faced steep taxes, harsh working conditions, and discrimination in the gold fields.* **What parts of this image suggest harsh working conditions?**

COURTESY OF THE CALIFORNIA HISTORY ROOM, CALIFORNIA STATE LIBRARY, SACRAMENTO, CALIFORNIA. IMAGE HAS BEEN ALTERED.

★ REVIEW AND ASSESS

Have students complete the **Section 4 Review** on p. 443. Then have them complete **Daily Quiz 17.4**. As **Alternative Assessment**, you may want to use the gold rush outfitter or the newspaper exercises from this section's lessons.

★ RETEACH

Have students complete **Main Idea Activity for English Language Learners and Special-Needs Students 17.4.** Organize students into six groups and assign each group one of the main parts of this section. Have each group prepare an illustration depicting the main point of the section assigned to them. Have groups present their illustrations to the class.

ENGLISH LANGUAGE LEARNERS , COOPERATIVE LEARNING

★ EXTEND

Have students research the growth of San Francisco from 1840 to 1860. Ask students to identify changes in the city and why these changes occurred. Have students prepare oral reports based on their findings, and have them include visual aids.

BLOCK SCHEDULING

★ Growth in the West

During the Spanish and then Mexican periods of settlement, California's population had grown slowly. The arrival of the forty-niners changed this dramatically. Almost overnight, business growth, gold mining, and trade transformed California's economy. As the gold rush faded, frontier society became more stable. Great wealth became more difficult to achieve, but with luck and hard work, immigrants could build good lives for themselves in the West.

Fast population growth had negative consequences for many Californios and California Indians. One early observer of the gold rush described why.

Clipper ships provided transportation to California.

 "The Yankee regarded every man but a native American [meaning a white U.S. citizen] as an interloper [trespasser], who had no right to come to California and pick up the gold of 'free and enlightened citizens.'"

—W. Kelly, quoted in *The Other Californians,* by Robert F. Heizer and Alan F. Almquist

Californio Mariano Vallejo observed California's growing population. "The good ones were few and the wicked many," he concluded.

Without the gold rush, California would probably have continued to grow slowly. It would have become a U.S. territory and eventually a state. The California Gold Rush changed this, however. California's population explosion made it eligible for statehood only two years after being acquired by the United States. Along with the gold rush came an economic boom. This boom led to growth in agriculture and industry.

✔ **Reading Check: Finding the Main Idea** What political effect resulted from California's rapid population growth? eligible for statehood within two years of the discovery of gold

Section 4 Review

go.hrw.com Homework Practice Online
keyword: SA3 HP17

1 Define and explain:
• forty-niners
• prospect

2 Identify and explain:
• California Gold Rush
• Biddy Mason

3 Evaluating Copy the web diagram below. Use it to show how the gold rush changed California.

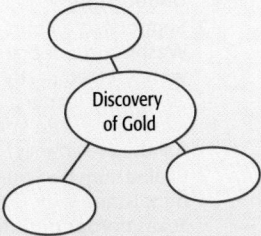
Discovery of Gold

4 Finding the Main Idea
a. What caused people to travel to California in 1849?
b. How were the mining camps an example of free enterprise?

5 Writing and Critical Thinking
Summarizing Imagine that you are a prospector looking for gold in California. Write a letter to your family back home telling them about life in the local mining town.

Consider the following:
• law and order in the town
• available goods and services
• the diversity of the population

★ Section 4 Review
ANSWERS

1 Define
• forty-niners, p. 534
• prospect, p. 535

2 Identify
• California Gold Rush, p. 534
• Biddy Mason, p. 537

3 rapid population growth, economic boom, statehood, social tensions between groups

4 a. wanted to find gold and become wealthy
b. few regulations on trade, cost of goods was completely under the control of supply and demand giving many people a chance to make money even if they did not look for gold

5 Students' letters will vary but students should include information on law and order in the town, the availability of goods and services, and the diversity of the population.

REVIEW AND ASSESSMENT RESOURCES

REPRODUCIBLE
▶ Vocabulary Activity 17

TECHNOLOGY
▶ Chapter 17 Test Generator (on the One-Stop Planner)
▶ Global Skill Builder CD–ROM
▶ HRW Go site

REINFORCEMENT REVIEW AND ASSESSMENT
▶ Chapter 17 Review, pp. 540–41
▶ Chapter 17 Tutorial for Students, Parents, Mentors, and Peers

▶ Chapter 17 Test (Form A or B)
▶ Alternative Assessment Handbook
▶ Chapter 17 Test for English Language Learners and Special-Needs Students

★ REVIEW

Have students complete the **Chapter 17 Review** on pages 540–541.

★ ASSESS

Use one of the chapter tests to assess students' understanding of the content. For **Alternative Assessment**, see the **Alternative Assessment Handbook**.

CHAPTER 17 REVIEW ANSWERS

The Chapter at a Glance
Students' fill-in-the-blank statements will vary, but should include information on the main ideas.

Identifying People and Ideas
Students' sentences should indicate an understanding of the following definitions:

1. belief that the U. S. was meant to expand across the continent to the Pacific Ocean

2. campaigned for the annexation of TX and OR; elected president in 1844

3. transcendentalist writer; protested Mexican War by not paying his taxes and was jailed

4. small group of American settlers who revolted against the Californios and formed an independent republic

5. land gained from Mexico as a result of the Treaty of Guadalupe Hidalgo

6. religious group founded by Joseph Smith in 1830; established a settlement at Salt Lake City

7. led Mormons to present-day Utah

8. sudden rise in immigration to CA in 1849 in search of gold

9. name given to those who traveled to CA in 1849 in hopes of finding gold

10. search for gold

Understanding Main Ideas
1. economic: pressure for land, resources, & markets; political: success of democracy & freedom; social: maintain social peace

---

Chapter 17 Review

The Chapter at a Glance
Examine the visual summary of the chapter below. Create five fill-in-the-blank statements that show the cause-and-effect relationship between two items in the visual summary. Give the questions to a classmate to answer.

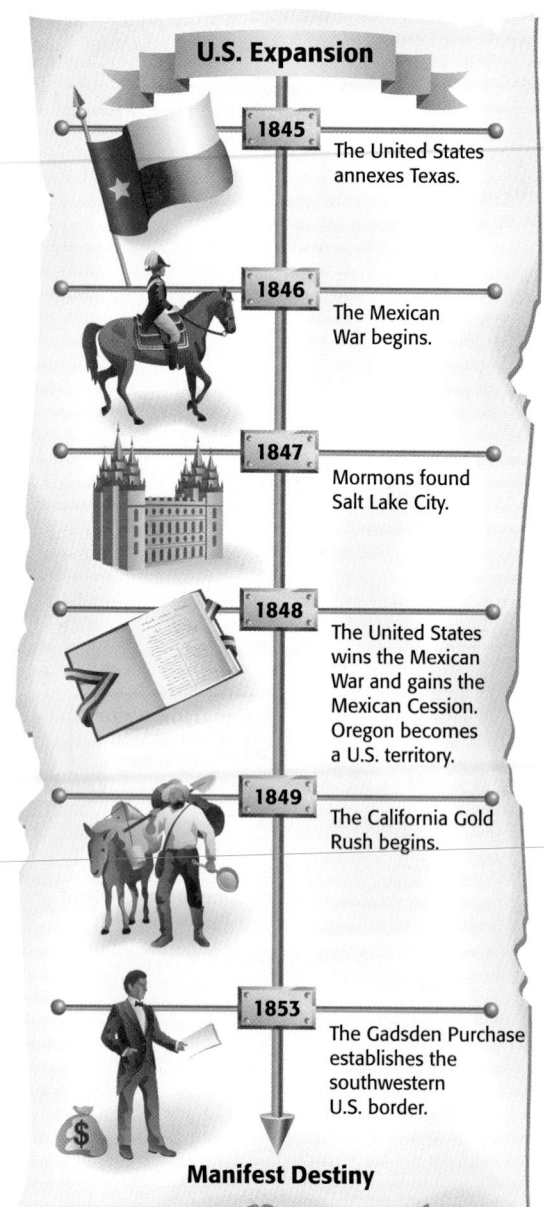

U.S. Expansion

1845 — The United States annexes Texas.

1846 — The Mexican War begins.

1847 — Mormons found Salt Lake City.

1848 — The United States wins the Mexican War and gains the Mexican Cession. Oregon becomes a U.S. territory.

1849 — The California Gold Rush begins.

1853 — The Gadsden Purchase establishes the southwestern U.S. border.

Manifest Destiny

Identifying People and Ideas
Use the following terms or people in historically significant sentences.
1. manifest destiny
2. James K. Polk
3. Henry David Thoreau
4. Bear Flag Revolt
5. Mexican Cession
6. Mormons
7. Brigham Young
8. California Gold Rush
9. forty-niners
10. prospect

Understanding Main Ideas
Section 1 *(Pages 516–21)*
1. What were the economic, political, and social origins of the idea of manifest destiny?
2. Why did the United States declare war against Mexico?

Section 2 *(Pages 522–27)*
3. What lands did the United States gain as a result of the Mexican War?

Section 3 *(Pages 528–32)*
4. Why did Mormons move west?

Section 4 *(Pages 533–39)*
5. How did the discovery of gold in California affect the region and the United States?
6. Why did Chinese immigrants come to California, and how were they treated?

You Be the Historian— Reviewing Themes
1. **Global Relations** How did Texas, Oregon, and California become parts of the United States?
2. **Culture** What conflicts arose as a result of the encounters among Mexican Americans, American Indians, and Anglos in the Mexican Cession?
3. **Geography** How did the Mormons adapt to their new environment?

Thinking Critically
1. **Analyzing Information** How did the idea of manifest destiny affect the growth of the United States?
2. **Supporting a Point of View** Several presidents—Washington, Jackson, and Taylor for example—were elected partly because of their popularity as military leaders. Do you think military experience is an important qualification for the presidency? Explain your answer.
3. **Evaluating** Do you think Mexico should have negotiated with the United States over the Texas border dispute instead of going to war? Explain your answer.

RETEACH

Have students work in groups to create time lines for the following territories: Texas, Oregon, California, and Utah. Have students include major events in the history of the assigned area. Have groups explain their time lines to the class and lead a discussion on how the events on their time line affected the West and the United States.

ENGLISH LANGUAGE LEARNERS ,
COOPERATIVE LEARNING

Portfolio Extensions

American History

1. Cooperative Learning

Organize the class into three groups. Ask each group to imagine that it is holding a Mexican American festival highlighting Mexican contributions to American culture. Then have them complete one of the following activities: select a traditional Mexican dish and prepare it for your class; make a piñata and give an oral report to your class on the history of the piñata; find a Mexican short story on the topic of your choice and read it to the class.

2. Linking to Community

Henry David Thoreau was a dissenter who chose to use nonviolent actions to express his views. Have students prepare an oral report on someone in their community who has participated in a nonviolent form of protest. The person can be someone from the community today or someone who lived there in the past.

Social Studies Skills Workshop

Interpreting Political Cartoons

Study the political cartoon on the Mexican War below. Then answer the questions that follow.

THE GRANGER COLLECTION, NEW YORK

VOLUNTEERS FOR TEXAS

1. What is the soldier nearest the front of the cartoon holding at his shoulder?
   a. a rifle
   b. a briefcase
   c. an umbrella
   d. a treaty

2. Based on your knowledge of the period and your understanding of the cartoon, what message do you think the artist is trying to convey about Mexican War volunteers and the war itself?

Analyzing Primary Sources

Read the following quote by John O'Sullivan, which discusses the annexation of Texas, and then answer the questions that follow.

> **"It is time now for opposition to the annexation of Texas to cease [end], all further agitation of the waters of bitterness and strife [fighting], . . . even though it may perhaps be required of us as a necessary condition of the freedom of our institutions, that we must live on forever in a state of unpausing struggle and excitement upon some subject of party division or other. But, in regard to Texas, enough has now been given to party. It is time for the common duty of patriotism to the country to succeed; or . . . it is at least time for common sense to acquiesce [accept] with decent grace in the inevitable and the irrevocable."**

3. Which of the following statements best summarizes what the author is saying?
   a. With freedom comes responsibility.
   b. Americans should stop disagreeing about the future of Texas and accept annexation.
   c. American political parties spend too much time disagreeing about important issues.
   d. Patriotism is more important than any other responsibility that a U.S. citizen might have.

4. What does O'Sullivan mean when he says that disagreement and party divisions are "a necessary condition of the freedom of our institutions"?
   a. People will never get along.
   b. Americans enjoy arguing.
   c. People in a democracy will disagree because they have the freedom to express their views.
   d. Political parties are essential to democracy.

5. Based on what you know about the period, whom do you think O'Sullivan was addressing?

Alternative Assessment

American History

Building Your Portfolio

Interdisciplinary Connection to Economics

Complete the following activity in small groups. Imagine that you and your partners are planning to open a general store in a California mining camp. Create a poster showing the layout of your store and labeling the different items you will sell. Create advertisements to show your products. For each item, write one or two sentences explaining why you think it will be profitable.

internet connect

Internet Activity: go.hrw.com
keyword: SA3 CF17

Choose a topic about Manifest Destiny and War to:

● Research the causes and effects of the Mexican War.

● Conduct an interview with James K. Polk and Henry David Thoreau.

● Learn about the journey westward to California during the Gold Rush.

---

2. Mexican soldiers attacked U.S. troops on land the U.S. claimed.

3. CA and most of the present-day southwest; Rio Grande river was border between Texas and Mexico

4. escape religious persecution

5. led to the CA Gold Rush, drawing forty-niners from around the world & increasing its population.

6. often the victims of antiforeigner prejudice.

You Be the Historian—Reviewing Themes

1. TX was annexed; OR was acquired as a result of a treaty with Britain; CA was gained as part of the Mexican Cession under the Treaty of Guadalupe Hidalgo.

2. conflicts over different legal traditions, land titles, water rights, livestock and other property, respect for holy places, attitude of cultural superiority

3. developed new water use laws & new systems of irrigation for farming

Thinking Critically

1. caused westward expansion

2. Students' responses will vary.

3. Answers should reflect an understanding of what the U.S. would gain by going to war with Mexico

Skills Workshop

1. c

2. Students' responses will vary.

3. b

4. Students might suggest he is addressing those opposed to annexation.

5. Students' responses will vary.

LET'S GET STARTED!

Place a current map of the United States on an overhead projector. Cover up approximately one third of the land mass shown on the western side of the map. Ask students to discuss ways that America would be different had these states not become part of the United States. (*Students' answers will vary, but students may point out that other cultures or nations may have been created in this area or point out that the nation would have a drastically lower population and a limited supply of certain foods, such as California oranges or Idaho potatoes.*) Explain to students that many of today's western states did not become part of the United States until after 1845 and that as a result of admitting the western states, the U.S. population became more diverse. Tell students that they will learn about westward expansion in this unit.

★ TEACH

Have students read the Connecting to Geography lesson. Choose one or more of the following activities to explore the Connecting to Geography content with students.

★ Linking Past to Present

Texas Population. The 2000 census revealed that 20,851,820 people lived in Texas. Approximately 52.4 percent of the population was white; about 32 percent was Hispanic, and 11.5 percent was African American. The remaining percentage of Texans came from other ethnic backgrounds. This ethnic diversity reflected the state's history. Further, the population of Texas continues to grow as the population grew by over 22 percent from 1990 to 2000.

CRITICAL THINKING

Why might Texans be increasingly living in cities?

ANSWER: Students might mention that the state's economy is no longer dependent of farming and ranching.

SKILLS ANSWERS

1. Independence (Westport), Missouri

2. Arizona, California, Nevada, New Mexico, Utah, parts of western Colorado, and Wyoming

---

Connecting to Geography

Westward Expansion

After the Louisiana Purchase of 1803, the boundaries of the United States stretched roughly from the Atlantic Ocean to the Rocky Mountains. Gradually, American pioneers moved across the Mississippi River, pushing the frontier of American farms and settlements farther west.

In 1846 Britain and the United States agreed to divide Oregon Country, using the 49th parallel as a boundary line. The land south of the 49th parallel became U.S. territory. In 1848, after a war with Mexico, the United States added California and the Southwest. The present southern boundary of the United States was set in 1853.

The Early West

The United States annexed Texas in 1845. After winning the war with Mexico, the United States added the lands of the Mexican Cession. This vast area extended west from Texas to the Pacific Ocean. Combined with Oregon Country and the Gadsden Purchase, these new lands added more than 1.2 million square miles to the United States.

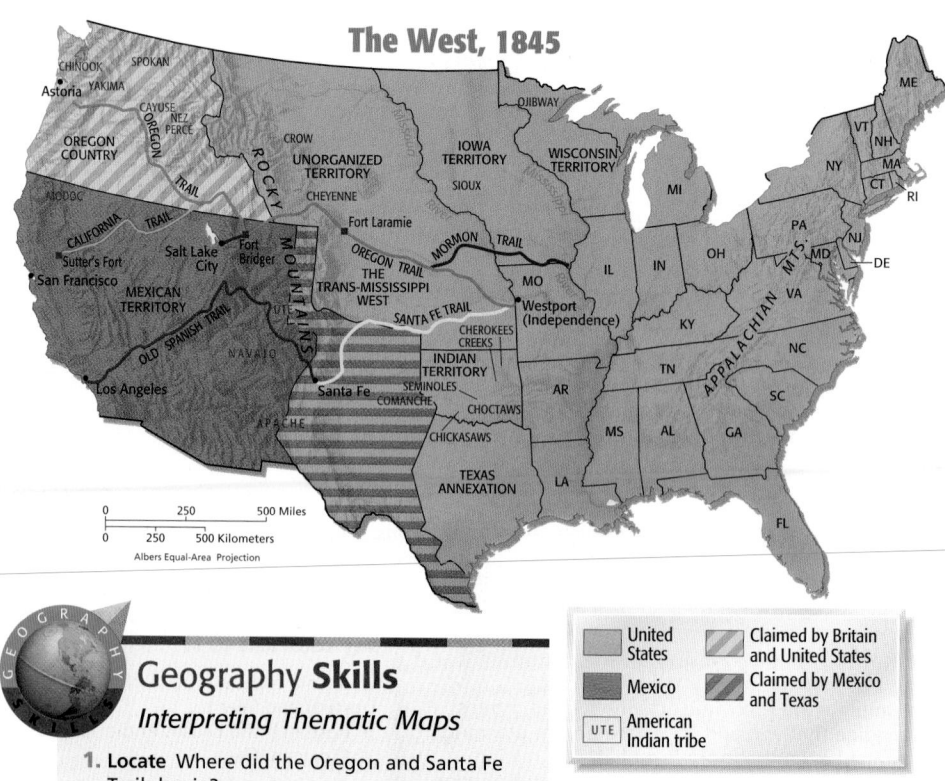

The West, 1845

Legend:
- United States
- Mexico
- UTE American Indian tribe
- Claimed by Britain and United States
- Claimed by Mexico and Texas

Geography **Skills**
Interpreting Thematic Maps

1. **Locate** Where did the Oregon and Santa Fe Trails begin?

2. **Comparing** Compare this map to the U.S. map on page 543. What current states occupy land that was Mexican territory in 1845?

LEVEL 1: Ask students to pretend that they currently live in a developing country and want to immigrate to the United States. On a sheet of paper they are to list the reasons they might have for wanting to immigrate. After students have completed their lists, organize the class into groups of three or four students. Have the students in the groups compare each other's lists in order to write a master list that they can present to the class. *(Students' lists might include economic opportunity, educational benefits, protection of rights and freedoms, and so on.)* Lead a class discussion asking students if the reasons to immigrate would be different if they were coming from a developed nation with a similar economy or similar constitutional protections.

ENGLISH LANGUAGE LEARNERS , COOPERATIVE LEARNING

 ALL LEVELS: Lead a class discussion about the regional populations in the United States today. Then have students review the map on p. 544 illustrating The West Today. Then ask students to create a pie graph depicting the percentage of regional populations in the United States today using the map as a reference.

ENGLISH LANGUAGE LEARNERS

 LEVEL 2: Have students review the facts and figures from the pie graphs on p. 545. Then have students convert the information from the visual format to a written report also incorporating the information from the History Note and the chapters within the unit. Encourage students to share their reports with the class.

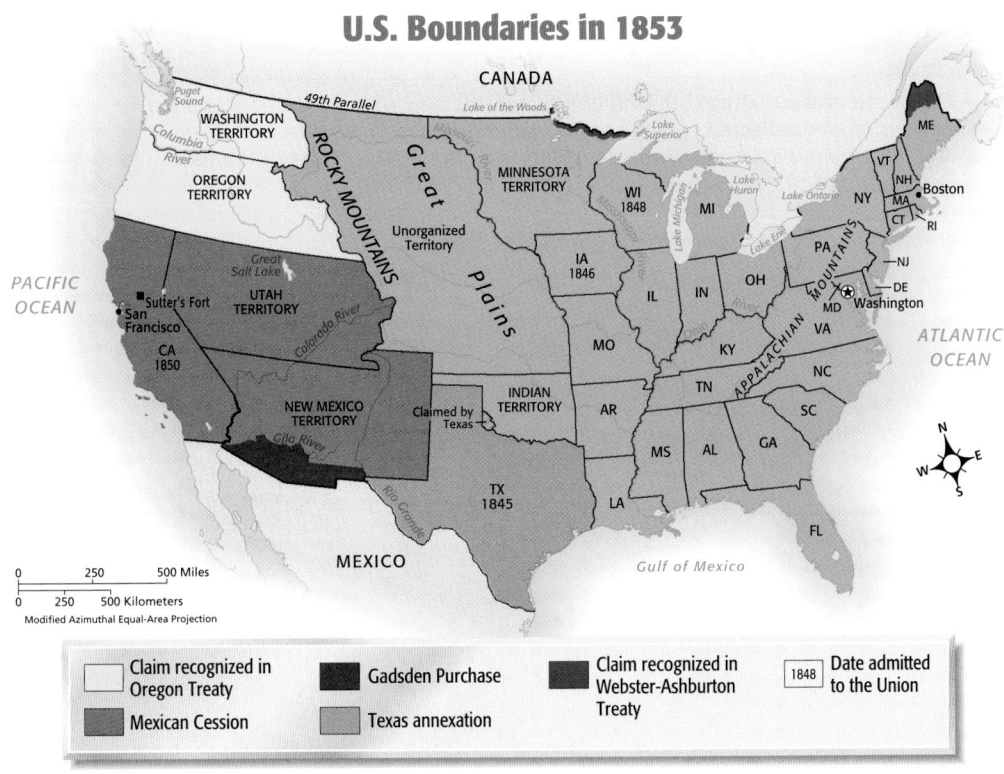

U.S. Boundaries in 1853

Legend:
- Claim recognized in Oregon Treaty
- Mexican Cession
- Gadsden Purchase
- Texas annexation
- Claim recognized in Webster-Ashburton Treaty
- 1848 Date admitted to the Union

Geography Skills
Interpreting Thematic Maps

1. What states and territories were formed in the new U.S. lands?
2. **Places and Regions** What river became the boundary between Texas and Mexico?
3. **Summarizing** Compare this map to the current map of the United States on page 544. What two current states include territory from the Gadsden Purchase? What three states were formed from Oregon Country?

Many settlers heading to the West had to cross the Rocky Mountains.

History Note 1

The territory granted to the United States in the Mexican Cession had long belonged to Spain and then Mexico. Yet the Hispanic population there was outnumbered by settlers from the United States by 1850.

★ Global Relations

The Texas Boundary.
Disputes between the United States and Mexico over the location of the Texas boundary continued for several years after the 1845 annexation. In 1848 with the Treaty of Guadalupe Hildago the two nations agreed that the middle of the deepest channel of the Rio Grande would serve as the boundary. However, the river often changed its course, and in 1884 both nations claimed to own Morteritos, an island in the middle of the river. The issue was resolved through peaceful means when Mexico agreed to recognize U.S. control over the island and the United States agreed to ratify a formal treaty to solve problems that might arise in the future if the river changed its course.

CRITICAL THINKING
For what reasons do nations need to agree upon boundary lines?

ANSWER: Students might suggest to prevent conflicts over resources, law enforcement, and other issues that might arise near an international boundary.

SKILL ANSWERS
1. Washington Territory, Oregon Territory, Utah Territory, New Mexico Territory, states of California and Texas
2. the Rio Grande
3. Arizona and New Mexico; Oregon, Idaho, and Wyoming

LEVEL 3: Have students imagine that they have been asked to help gather valuable information for the next census. The information will help officials prepare future budgets and predict future population growth. Then tell students that they will be preparing a report that illustrates the changes in immigration to the United States from 1850 to 1994. Refer students to the graphs and note on p. 545 to obtain information about the changes. Then lead a discussion in which students speculate on reasons that these shifts in immigration have occurred. *(Students' speculations might note that Mexico is close to the United States, making it easier for immigrants to travel here. They might also speculate that difficulties in the home nation or a desire to earn a better living might motivate immigrants to come to the United States.)*

☆ CLOSE

Have students look at the map on p. 542 and compare it with the modern map of the United States on p. 544. Ask students to make a list identifying the states that were eventually created from the land claimed by Great Britain, Mexico and the United States. Lead a discussion about the significant historical events (e.g., the Mexican War, the Gadsden Purchase) that had a major effect on the creation of the current boundaries of the United States. **ENGLISH LANGUAGE LEARNERS**

★ Geography

Hispanics in the United States. The 1990 census revealed that 22,354,059 Americans, or 9 percent of the population, claimed Hispanic heritage. Almost a third of Hispanic Americans—7,687,938 people—lived in California, where they made up almost 26 percent of the population. Texas had the second greatest number—4,339,905—of Hispanic Americans. Vermont had the lowest, with only 3,661 Hispanic Americans counted in the census.

CRITICAL THINKING

Why might Texas and California have more Hispanic Americans than other states?

ANSWER: Students might suggest that Hispanics would choose to live in these states because they were once part of Mexico and have retained a measure of their Hispanic population and culture.

The West Today

The southwestern United States has historical ties with Spain and Mexico. These ties are reflected in the people and culture of the region. The largest concentration of Hispanic Americans is found in the Southwest.

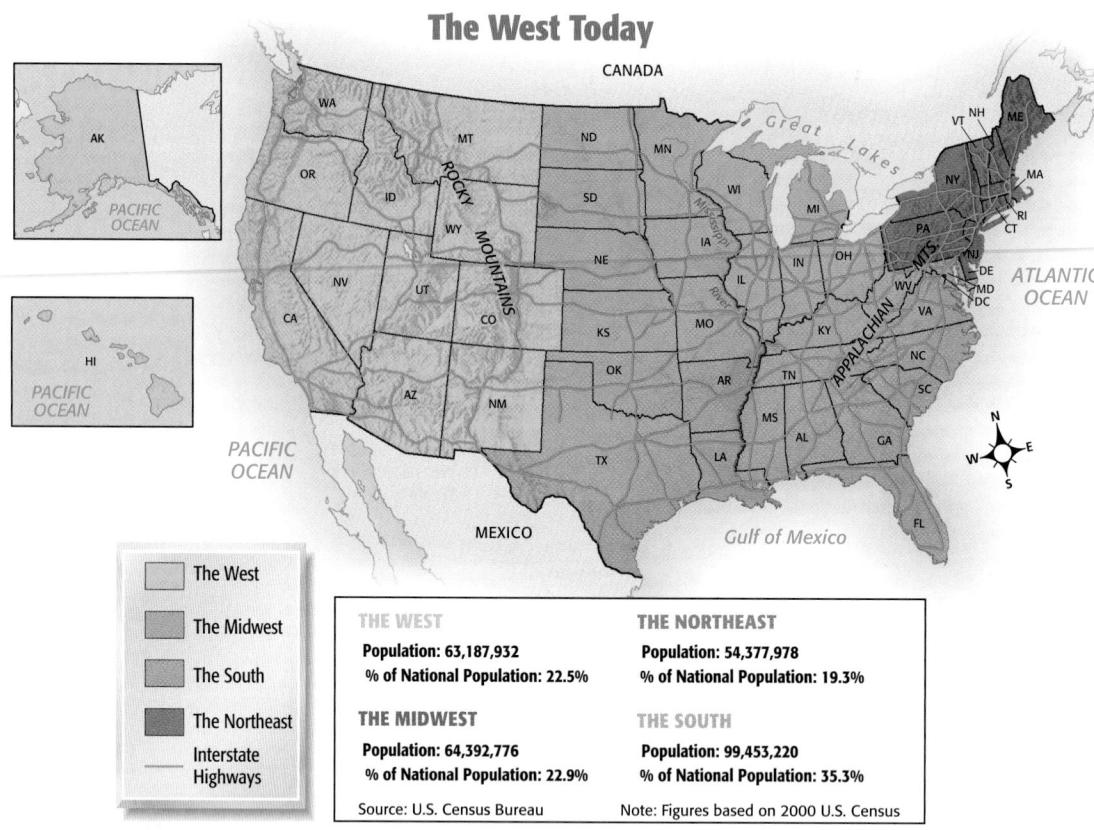

The West Today

THE WEST	THE NORTHEAST
Population: 63,187,932	Population: 54,377,978
% of National Population: 22.5%	% of National Population: 19.3%
THE MIDWEST	THE SOUTH
Population: 64,392,776	Population: 99,453,220
% of National Population: 22.9%	% of National Population: 35.3%

Legend: The West, The Midwest, The South, The Northeast, Interstate Highways

Source: U.S. Census Bureau   Note: Figures based on 2000 U.S. Census

Geography **Skills**

Interpreting Charts and Thematic Maps

1. **The World in Spatial Terms** Which region of the United States has the largest area?
2. **Human Systems** What region of the United States has the highest population?
3. **Drawing Inferences and Conclusions** What environmental conditions might have contributed to the large populations of the South and West?

History Note 2

According to the 2000 census, there were about 19.7 million Hispanic or Latino Americans living in California, Texas, Arizona, and New Mexico. This figure is more than half the total Hispanic population of the entire United States. California also has nearly 3.7 million Asian Americans and some 2.25 million African Americans, making it the most diverse state in the nation.

545

★ REVIEW AND ASSESS

Have students review the information in Connecting to Geography Unit 7. Then have students complete Geography and History Quiz 7.

★ RETEACH

Ask students to choose two of the graphs shown in this activity and re-create them in a different form. Explain to students that they should not change the title of the graph or any of the data. Instead, they should merely represent the information in a different way. Have volunteers present their work to the class.

ENGLISH LANGUAGE LEARNERS

★ EXTEND

Have students use the library and the Census Bureau to obtain information about the percentage of Hispanics that make up each of the states in the Southwest. With the information obtained from the library and/or the Census Bureau, instruct students to prepare pie graphs illustrating the percentage of Hispanic population in each of the states of the Southwest. Ask volunteers to share their pie graphs with the class.

BLOCK SCHEDULING

Sources of Immigration to the United States in 1850

Total number of immigrants in 1850: 369,980

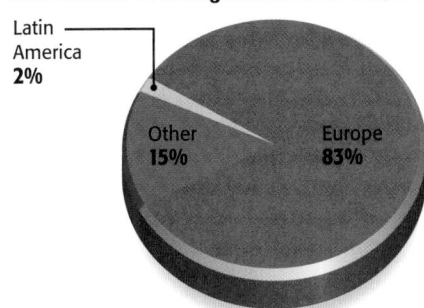

Latin America 2%

Other 15%

Europe 83%

Source: *Datapedia of the United States, 1790–2000: America Year by Year*

Geography **Skills**
Interpreting Pie Graphs

1. Create a bar graph showing the percentages of emigrants from the regions shown in 1850.
2. **Finding the Main Idea** Which part of the world provided most of the immigrants to the United States in 1850?

History Note 3

California has become a major entry point for immigrants to the United States. About one quarter of all immigrants to the United States in 1998 entered through California. In recent years, Latin America, particularly Mexico, has provided about half of all immigrants to the United States.

A Chinese American celebration

Foreign-Born U.S. Population in 2000 by Region of Origin

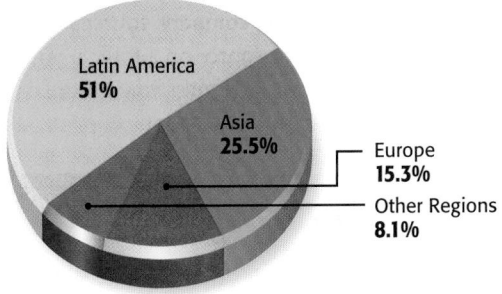

Latin America 51%

Asia 25.5%

Europe 15.3%

Other Regions 8.1%

Source: U.S. Census Bureau, *Current Population Survey,* March 2000

Geography **Skills**
Interpreting Pie Graphs

1. Which part of the world provided the highest percentage of the foreign-born population in the United States in 2000?
2. **Human Systems** Compare the pie graphs for the years 1850 and 2000. Then create a five-question quiz on the information contained in the graphs.
3. **Making Generalizations and Predictions** In what ways do you think the change in immigration from 1850 to today has changed or will change the nation? Explain your answer.

★ Linking Past to Present

Immigration to California. California remains a favored destination for immigrants from Asia. More than 37 percent of Chinese immigrants who arrived in the United States in 1991 decided to live in California, as did more than half of Filipino immigrants. Other Asian nations whose emigrants have lived in California in large numbers include Korea, Taiwan, and Vietnam.

CRITICAL THINKING

Why do many Asian immigrants choose to live in California?

ANSWER: Students might suggest that California borders the Pacific Ocean, making it an easier destination for Asian immigrants.

SKILL ANSWERS
1. Students' graphs will vary.
2. Europe

SKILLS ANSWERS
1. Latin America
2. Students' quizzes will vary.
3. Students might suggest that the immigration changes from 1850 to 2000 have led to a much more diversified nation composed of a variety of cultures, religions, and languages, yet bound by a common belief in the Constitution and its protections.

☆ TEACH

ALL LEVELS: Ask students to reread the excerpt from Thoreau's essay "Civil Disobedience" on page 527. Ask students to describe the historical background of the essay and explain Thoreau's purpose. Then ask them to use context clues in the passage to describe the audience that Thoreau seemed to be addressing. Next, ask students to identify words and phrases that show Thoreau's bias, particularly when he describes the war as being started by people who want to use the government as their "tool" or when he explains "the remedy is worse than the evil." Ask students to compare Thoreau's opinions with the textbook coverage of the war with Mexico. Organize students into groups. Have groups write one paragraph showing how they would incorporate short quotations from "Civil Disobedience" into a book on the war.

ENGLISH LANGUAGE LEARNERS

USING PRIMARY AND SECONDARY SOURCES

Have students choose both a primary and secondary source on the historical subject of their choosing. Then have them write a report, using standard grammar, spelling, sentence structure, and punctuation, comparing the two works and considering the audience and whether there was bias in either account.

SKILL ANSWERS

1. primary—firsthand historical information; secondary—descriptions or interpretations written after an event has occurred by people not directly connected to an event

2. a wider perspective

3. In explaining their choices, students should give the characteristics that make each of their choices a primary or a secondary source.

Social Studies Skills
WORKSHOP

Using Primary and Secondary Sources

There are many sources of firsthand historical information. These sources include diaries, editorials, letters, and legal documents such as wills and titles. All of these are *primary sources.* Newspaper reports are also considered primary sources. However, they are typically written after an event has taken place. The same is true for personal memoirs and autobiographies. These works are usually written late in a person's life. The editorial cartoons, paintings, and photographs that make up history's visual record are also primary sources. Primary sources are valuable historical tools that allow a close-up look at the past.

Secondary sources are descriptions or interpretations of historical events written after the events have occurred by persons who did not take part in or witness the events. Biographies, encyclopedias, history books, and other reference works are examples of secondary sources. Writers of secondary sources have the advantage of knowing the long-range consequences of events. This knowledge helps shape their viewpoints.

How to Study Primary and Secondary Sources

1. **Study the material carefully.** Consider the nature of the material. Is it verbal or visual? Is it based on firsthand information or on the accounts of others? Note the major ideas and supporting details.

2. **Consider the audience.** Ask yourself: For whom was this message originally meant? Whether a message was intended, for example, for the general public or for a specific private audience may have influenced its style or content.

3. **Check for bias.** Watch for certain words or phrases that signal a one-sided view of a person or event.

4. **When possible, compare sources.** Study more than one source on a topic if you can. Comparing sources gives you a more complete and balanced account.

Practicing the Skill

1. How are secondary sources different from primary sources?

2. What advantages do secondary sources have over primary sources?

3. Select a topic from Unit 7. Write a brief report on this topic, using one primary source and one secondary source. Explain why each source is considered a primary or a secondary source.

ALL LEVELS: Explain to students that whenever they have a big decision to make, they should look at all possible options and the consequences for each option. Remind them that choices they will make in life have consequences. Then, in order to illustrate the possible options and consequences that they have compiled in their History in Action activity, groups may either record their findings in chart form or make two hanging mobiles. One mobile should show the reasons for moving westward, and the other mobile should show the reasons against moving westward. The consequences should be attached by string or tape to the corresponding reason. Have groups present their findings to the class.

ENGLISH LANGUAGE LEARNERS , COOPERATIVE LEARNING

History in Action

UNIT 7 SIMULATION

You Make the Decision . . .

Should Your Family Move Westward to the Great Plains?

Complete the following activity in small cooperative groups. It is early 1838. Your family has lived very comfortably in the East for generations. However, following the economic hardships of the Panic of 1837, the lure of moving west for adventure, riches, and land is very tempting. Your family includes your spouse and three children, all under the age of 15. You have to decide whether your family will move westward onto the Great Plains. You have to prepare a presentation that will convince the rest of your family that your decision is best for all of them. Follow these steps to reach your decision.

1. Gather Information. Use your textbook and other resources to find information that might help you decide whether to move your family westward. Be sure to use what you learned from this unit's Skills Workshop on Using Primary and Secondary Sources to help you make an informed decision. You may want to divide different parts of the research among group members.

2. Identify Options. After reviewing the information you have gathered, identify the different reasons you might consider for moving or not moving to the West. Your final decision may be easier to reach if you consider as many options as possible. Be sure to record your possible options for your presentation.

3. Predict Consequences. Now take each option your group came up with and consider what might be the outcome of each course of action. Ask yourselves questions like: "Will my family be safe on the frontier?" Once you have predicted the consequences, record them as notes for your presentation.

4. Take Action to Implement Your Decision. After you have considered your options, you should plan and create your presentation. Be sure to make your decision on moving westward very clear. You will need to support your decision by including information you gathered and by explaining why you rejected other options. Your presentation needs to be visually appealing to gain the support of your family. When you are ready, decide which group members will make each part of the presentation, and then take your decision to your family (the rest of the class). Good luck!

History in Action Another way for students to weigh options and make decisions is by drawing a decision tree. Along the trunk vertical lines are drawn representing possible options. In the foliage area of the tree, space for three positive and three negative consequences for each option are provided. At the top of the tree the final choice is recorded. Have students draw the tree on a sheet of paper. Then assign students a topic in which they would have choices and have them fill in the decision tree. Possible topics should include something historical—such as how the prospective miners made their way to California, whether to declare war, admitting a state into the union, and so on. Ask volunteers to share their decision trees with the class.

★ CHAPTER 18

A Divided Nation

At the end of the war with Mexico, the United States gained more than 500,000 square miles of new territory, increasing the size of the nation by almost 25 percent. The addition of these new western lands revived the debate over slavery. Congress attempted to put the question to rest with a series of compromises, which only increased the polarization between the North and the South. Kansas in particular was the scene of violence between pro-slavery and Free-Soiler groups. Abraham Lincoln, a Republican who hoped to stop the spread of slavery, was elected to the presidency in 1860. This prompted South Carolina and six other southern states to secede and form the Confederate States of America.

★ CHAPTER 19

The Civil War

Soon after Lincoln's inauguration, South Carolina opened fire on Fort Sumter, beginning the Civil War. Initially, the South won several major battles, including the First Battle of Bull Run, the Seven Days' Battles, and the Second Battle of Bull Run. However, the North turned the tide of the war with victories in both the West and the East. The Union

Internet Activity

Underground Railroad

🖵 **internet** connect

TOPIC:
Underground Railroad
GO TO: go.hrw.com
KEYWORD: SA3 Underground Railroad

The Underground Railroad was a network of people, hiding places, and transportation organized to help escaped slaves. Have students search the Internet through the HRW Go site for information about this conduit to freedom. Have students gather stories and visual images to create an annotated map of the Underground Railroad. Use the map to show what the journey might have been like, the sorts of people the escapees might have met, and the stories those people might have heard.

UNIT 8 The Nation Breaks Apart

(1848–1865)

CHAPTER 18 **A Divided Nation** (1848–1860)

CHAPTER 19 **The Civil War** (1861–1865)

gained control of the Mississippi River with General Ulysses S. Grant's capture of Vicksburg. On the same day, Union forces defeated Confederate troops under General Robert E. Lee at Gettysburg, which proved to be the turning point of the war. American life changed dramatically during the war, which affected people on both sides at every social level.

Share the information in the chapter overviews with students. Have them name wars that they have heard about in the news. Have them discuss the causes of these wars and (if the conflicts have ended) what the consequences were for the combatants. Ask students to compile a list of the causes and consequences of war in general and to include as many ideas as they can. Have students work as a class to create a chart on a sheet of butcher paper, using arrows to show both the causes and the consequences of wars. Later, when you have finished the unit, have students return to this chart and create a similar one specifically for the Civil War.

Young People

IN HISTORY

Young Soldiers

During the Civil War, 15-year-old Union soldier Thomas Galway described a fierce battle.

"Now we are close to the enemy. They rise up in the sunken lane and pour deadly fire into us. Our men drop. . . . We go forward on the run, heads downward as if under a pelting rain. . . . We are kneeling in the soft grass and I notice for a long time that almost every blade of grass is moving. For some time I supposed that this is caused by the merry crickets; and it is not until I made a remark to that effect to one of our boys near me and notice him laugh, that I know it is bullets that are falling thickly around us!"

Galway was one of the thousands of youths who fought in the Civil War.

Both the North and the South tried to keep boys out of their armies. However, many teenagers lied about their ages in order to join. Elisha Stockwell's father would not let his 15-year-old son enlist. So, Elisha told his parents that he was going to a dance in town. Instead, he joined the Union army. Although young Stockwell did not return home for two years, he thought of home often. One such time was during his first battle, kneeling on the ground in the middle of exploding shells. "I thought what a foolish boy I was to run away and get into such a mess as I was in."

Other boys joined the army as drummers. The beat of the drum was an important way to communicate orders to soldiers. Therefore, drummer boys often found themselves the target of enemy fire. Johnny Clem went from drummer boy to fighting soldier during the Battle of Shiloh. After his drum was shattered, 11-year-old Clem picked up a gun and began firing. Within two years, Clem was promoted to sergeant.

Young Union soldiers relax between battles.

 **If You Were There** *How would you view the war?*

LEFT PAGE: *Members of the 54th Massachusetts Infantry attack Confederate soldiers at Fort Wagner.*

The 54th Massachusetts Regiment. The most famous African American regiment was the 54th Massachusetts Infantry, shown in the painting on the opposite page storming Fort Wagner. The 54th, which included two of Frederick Douglass's sons, distinguished itself by leading the charge on Fort Wagner. Half of the members of the 54th were wounded or killed during the charge. A northern journalist described the soldiers of the 54th: "Although we had seen many of the famous regiments of the English, French, and Austrian armies, we were never more impressed with the fury and majesty of war than when we looked upon the solid mass of the thousand [actually 600] black men, as they stood . . . waiting the order to advance."

 **CRITICAL THINKING**

What conclusions can you draw about the fighting during the Civil War based on the painting?

ANSWER: Students might suggest battles were often fought at close range and were dangerous.

	Objectives	Pacing Guide	Reproducible Resources
SECTION 1: **The Debate over Slavery** (pp. 552–57)	⊠ Explain how the outcome of the Mexican War affected the debate over slavery's expansion. ⊠ Examine the main conditions of the Compromise of 1850 and the views expressed for and against it. ⊠ Analyze why the Fugitive Slave Act was controversial in the North.	**Regular** 2 days **Block Scheduling** 1 day *Block Scheduling Handbook with Team Teaching Strategies, Chapter 18*	**RS** Guided Reading Strategy 18.1 **PS** Primary Source Reading 18: A Response to the Fugitive Slave Act **PS** Literature Reading 18: Narrative of the Life of Frederick Douglass, an American Slave **PS** Biography Reading 18: John C. Calhoun **E** Creative Teaching Strategy: Dialogue Debate
SECTION 2: **Trouble in Kansas** (pp. 559–63)	⊠ Explain how different regions of the country reacted to the Kansas-Nebraska Act. ⊠ Describe the ways people tried to settle the conflict over slavery in Kansas. ⊠ Depict the series of violent events that showed the growing division over slavery in the United States.	**Regular** 2 days **Block Scheduling** 1 day *Block Scheduling Handbook with Team Teaching Strategies, Chapter 18*	**RS** Guided Reading Strategy 18.2
SECTION 3: **Political Divisions** (pp. 564–68)	⊠ Analyze the effect of the Kansas-Nebraska Act on U.S. political parties. ⊠ Explain why Dred Scott sued for his freedom and how the Supreme Court ruled on his case. ⊠ Examine how Abraham Lincoln and Stephen Douglas differed in their views on slavery.	**Regular** 2 days **Block Scheduling** 1 day *Block Scheduling Handbook with Team Teaching Strategies, Chapter 18*	**RS** Guided Reading Strategy 18.3 **SM** Geography Activity 18: Southern Agriculture and the Slave Trade, 1860 **E** Hands-On History Activity: State and Federal Government Relations
SECTION 4: **Secession** (pp. 569–75)	⊠ Describe Americans' reactions to John Brown's raid on Harpers Ferry. ⊠ Analyze the factors that led to Lincoln's victory in the presidential election of 1860. ⊠ Examine the reasons why some southern states decided to leave the Union.	**Regular** 2 days **Block Scheduling** 1 day *Block Scheduling Handbook with Team Teaching Strategies, Chapter 18*	**RS** Guided Reading Strategy 18.4 **PS** American History Political Cartoon 10: Secession **RS** Graphic Organizer 18: Key Events in the Slavery Debate

Chapter Resource Key

PS	Primary Sources	**A**	Assessment		Music
RS	Reading Support	**REV**	Review		Videotape
IC	Interdisciplinary Connections	**ELL**	Reinforcement and English Language Learners	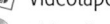	Videodisc
E	Enrichment		Transparency	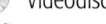	Internet
SM	Skills Mastery		CD–ROM		Holt Presentation Maker Using Microsoft® PowerPoint®

 One-Stop Planner CD–ROM

See the *One-Stop Planner* for a complete list of additional resources for students and teachers.

One-Stop Planner CD–ROM

It's easy to plan lessons, select resources, and print out materials for your students when you use the **One-Stop Planner CD-ROM with Test Generator.**

Technology Resources	**Reinforcement, Review, and Assessment**

 One-Stop Planner, Lesson 18.1

 Holt Researcher: American History CD–ROM

 Everyday Life in America Transparency 11: Slavery and Conflict

 CNN Presents America: Yesterday and Today, Beginnings to 1914 Segment: Frederick Douglass: An American Portrait

Homework Practice Online

REV Section 1 Review, p. 557
A Daily Quiz 18.1
ELL Main Idea Activity 18.1
ELL English Audio Summary 18.1
ELL Spanish Audio Summary 18.1

 One-Stop Planner, Lesson 18.2

Homework Practice Online

HRW Go site

REV Section 2 Review, p. 563
A Daily Quiz 18.2
ELL Main Idea Activity 18.2
ELL English Audio Summary 18.2
ELL Spanish Audio Summary 18.2

 One-Stop Planner, Lesson 18.3

 Exploring America's Past Video Segment: A Divided Nation; Teacher's Guide, pp. 28–29

 Holt Researcher: American History CD–ROM

Homework Practice Online

REV Section 3 Review, p. 568
A Daily Quiz 18.3
ELL Main Idea Activity 18.3
ELL English Audio Summary 18.3
ELL Spanish Audio Summary 18.3

 One-Stop Planner, Lesson 18.4

 American History Interactive Maps CD–ROM: Balancing Political Power

 American Music Selection 14: "John Brown's Body"

Homework Practice Online

REV Section 4 Review, p. 574
A Daily Quiz 18.4
ELL Main Idea Activity 18.4
ELL English Audio Summary 18.4
ELL Spanish Audio Summary 18.4

---

internet connect

go.hrw.com

HRW ONLINE RESOURCES
GO TO: go.hrw.com
Then type in a keyword.

TEACHER HOME PAGE
KEYWORD: SA3 Teacher

CHAPTER INTERNET ACTIVITIES
KEYWORD: SA3 CF18
Choose an activity to:
• understand the causes and effects of the European revolutions of 1848.
• create a newspaper on John Brown and resistance movements against slavery.
• write a biography of Franklin Pierce.

CHAPTER ENRICHMENT LINKS
KEYWORD: SA3 CH18

ONLINE ASSESSMENT
Homework Practice
KEYWORD: SA3 HP18

Standardized Test Prep
KEYWORD: SA3 STP18

Rubrics
KEYWORD: SS Rubrics

ONLINE MAPS, CHARTS, AND GRAPHS
KEYWORD: SA3 MCG
• Bleeding Kansas
• Slavery Compromises, 1820–1854

CONTENT UPDATES
KEYWORD: SS Content Updates

POWERPOINT PRESENTATIONS
KEYWORD: SA3 PPT18

ONLINE READING SUPPORT
KEYWORD: SS Strategies

CURRENT EVENTS
KEYWORD: S3 Current Events

Chapter Review and Assessment

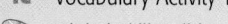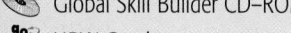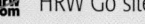

IC Vocabulary Activity 18
Global Skill Builder CD–ROM
HRW Go site
REV Chapter 18 Tutorial for Students, Parents, Mentors, and Peers
REV Chapter 18 Review, pp. 575–77
Chapter 18 Test Generator (on the One-Stop Planner)

A Chapter 18 Test (Form A or B)
A Alternative Assessment Handbook
A Chapter 18 Test for English Language Learners and Special-Needs Students

---

Meeting Individual Needs

Ability Levels

Level 1 Basic-level activities designed for all students encountering new material

Level 2 Intermediate-level activities designed for average students

Level 3 Challenging activities designed for honors and gifted-and-talented students

English Language Learners Activities that address the needs of students with Limited English Proficiency

549b

Build on What You Know

If You Were There...

Ask students to answer the following question:

How would you try to solve the country's conflicts?

Consider:

• passing new laws

• working out a compromise between northerners and southerners

You Be the Historian

What's Your Opinion?

To help students create their **Themes** Journal entries, provide the following examples of appropriate **agree**/disagree statements.

CHAPTER

18 A Divided Nation
(1848–1860)

THE GRANGER COLLECTION, NEW YORK

Harriet Beecher Stowe was the daughter of Lyman Beecher, a prominent minister and reformer.

Martin Van Buren and Charles F. Adams were the first presidential and vice presidential candidates of the Free-Soil Party.

THE GRANGER COLLECTION, NEW YORK

UNITED STATES

1848 The Free-Soil Party is formed on August 9. Zachary Taylor is elected president on November 7.	**1850** On September 9 California enters the Union as a free state. Congress passes the Fugitive Slave Act on September 18.	**1852** Harriet Beecher Stowe publishes *Uncle Tom's Cabin*.	**1853** Franklin Pierce is inaugurated as president.

1848	**1850**	**1852**	**1854**
1848 Revolutionary movements sweep across Europe.	**1850** Hundreds of thousands of peasants and workers in China join the Taiping Rebellion against the Manchu dynasty.	**1852** Louis-Napoléon declares himself Emperor Napoléon III of France.	**1853** The Crimean War begins.

WORLD

In 1848 German revolutionaries demanding a new republican government fought soldiers in the streets of Frankfurt.

Build on What You Know

After winning the Mexican War, the United States gained the Mexican Cession. Settlement of these lands renewed heated debate between northerners who opposed the expansion of slavery and southerners who supported it. Some southerners threatened to support secession if the government tried to block the westward expansion of slavery.

Geography

Agree As a country expands its borders, conflicts arise within that country.

Disagree Peaceful expansion occurs if citizens are reminded of the common good.

Citizenship

Agree The Supreme Court must uphold the Constitution, which guarantees individuals' rights.

Disagree There are some people who are not guaranteed rights under the Constitution.

Constitutional Heritage

Agree Because each state decided to join the Union, any state should be allowed to leave it.

Disagree States should not be able to leave the Union because that would weaken the country.

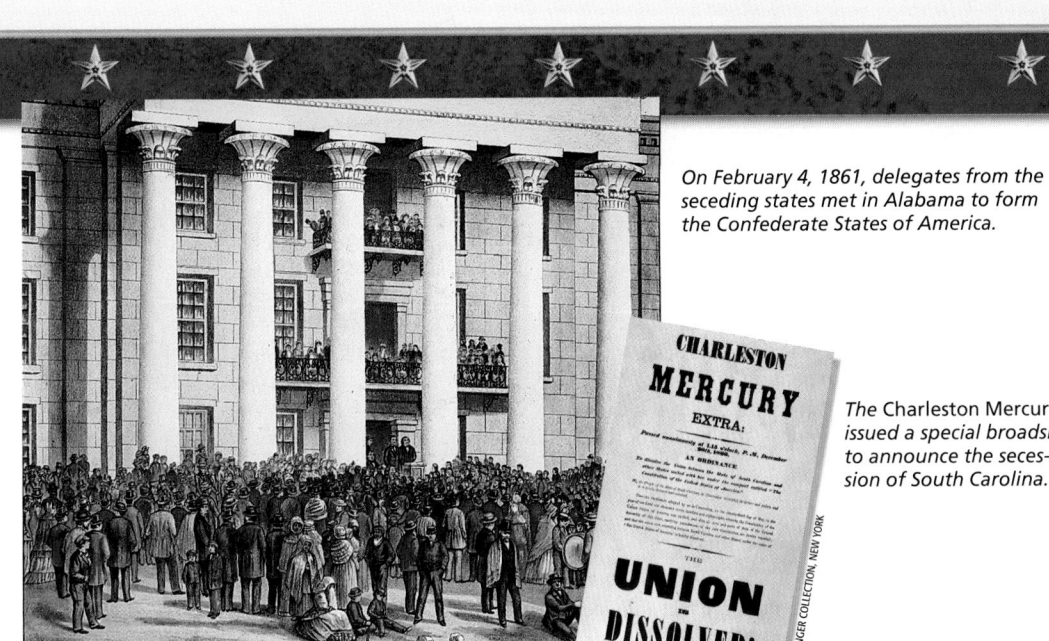

On February 4, 1861, delegates from the seceding states met in Alabama to form the Confederate States of America.

The Charleston Mercury issued a special broadside to announce the secession of South Carolina.

THE GRANGER COLLECTION, NEW YORK

1856 In the Sack of Lawrence, pro-slavery forces attack the town of Lawrence, Kansas, on May 21.

On May 24 abolitionist John Brown and his followers kill five pro-slavery settlers in the Pottawatomie Massacre.

1858 The Lincoln-Douglas debates begin in Illinois.

1859 John Brown takes control of the federal arsenal at Harpers Ferry, Virginia.

1860 Abraham Lincoln is elected president on November 6.

On December 20 South Carolina votes to secede from the United States.

1856   1858   1860   1862

1856 British and French forces defeat Russia in the Crimean War.

1857 Indian soldiers in the British army begin the Sepoy Mutiny against British control of India.

If you were there . . .

How would you try to solve the country's conflicts?

You Be the Historian

Themes Journal

What's Your Opinion? Do you **agree** or **disagree** with the following statements? Support your point of view in your journal.

- **Geography** Expansion often leads to conflict within a country.
- **Citizenship** The Supreme Court must protect all individuals' rights.
- **Constitutional Heritage** States should be able to legally leave the Union.

EXPLORING THE TIME LINE

AMERICAN EVENTS

★ Biography

Zachary Taylor. Before winning the presidency, Zachary Taylor had never held political office. His views on the extension of slavery were not well known, and he had made no public comment regarding the Wilmot Proviso. Taylor's supporters took advantage of his image as being above party politics by organizing rallies under the banners "Independent" or "No Party." However, Taylor was a southerner and a slaveholder—owning close to 200 slaves at the time of his death—which helped him to win support in the South. Interestingly, after becoming president, Taylor opposed the extension of slavery in new states.

CRITICAL THINKING

Why do you think Zachary Taylor opposed the extension of slavery?

ANSWER: Students might suggest that Taylor wanted to put an end to sectional conflict for good.

Section 1

OBJECTIVES

⭐ Explain how the outcome of the Mexican War affected the debate over slavery's expansion.

⭐ Examine the major provisions of the Compromise of 1850 and the views expressed for and against it.

⭐ Analyze why the Fugitive Slave Act was controversial in the North.

SECTION 1 RESOURCES

REPRODUCIBLE

▶ Guided Reading Strategy 18.1
▶ Primary Source Reading 18: A Response to the Fugitive Slave Act
▶ Literature Reading 18: Narrative of the Life of Frederick Douglass, an American Slave
▶ Biography Reading 18: John C. Calhoun

TECHNOLOGY

▶ One-Stop Planner, Lesson 18.1
▶ Holt Researcher: American History CD–ROM
▶ Everyday Life in America Transparency 11: Slavery and Conflict
▶ CNN Presents America: Beginnings to 1914 Segment: Frederick Douglass: An American Portrait
▶ Homework Practice Online

REINFORCEMENT, REVIEW, AND ASSESSMENT

▶ Section 1 Review, p. 557
▶ Daily Quiz 18.1
▶ Main Idea Activity 18.1
▶ English Audio Summary 18.1
▶ Spanish Audio Summary 18.1

LET'S GET STARTED!

Write the following question on the chalkboard: *What are some important compromises that politicians might be called on to make?* As students enter the classroom, allow time for them to respond. *(Students' responses might include health care issues, criminal sentencing, or border disputes.)* Use students' examples to explain the differences between economic, political, and moral issues. Lead a discussion about how an initial short-term political compromise might make a long-term moral solution even more difficult. Tell students that in Section 1, they will learn about how the Compromise of 1850 dealt with economic, political, and moral issues.

Section 1

The Debate over Slavery

Read to Discover

1. How did the outcome of the Mexican War affect the debate over the expansion of slavery?
2. What were the main conditions of the Compromise of 1850, and what reasons were given for supporting or opposing it?
3. Why was the Fugitive Slave Act controversial in the North?

WHY IT MATTERS TODAY

Congressional compromises are still an important part of the U.S. government. Use CNN**fyi**.com or other **current events** sources to learn about a recent issue that has led to compromise legislation in Congress. Record your findings in your journal.

Define

- sectionalism
- popular sovereignty

Identify

- Wilmot Proviso
- Free-Soil Party
- Henry Clay
- Daniel Webster
- Compromise of 1850
- Fugitive Slave Act
- Anthony Burns
- *Uncle Tom's Cabin*
- Harriet Beecher Stowe

The Story Continues

O n August 8, 1846, the members of the U.S. House of Representatives slowly returned from dinner. They resumed their talk of the ongoing war with Mexico. It was one of the hottest nights of the summer. Ice water and fans were in heavy demand. As the representatives began to talk about the possible outcomes of the war, a congressman from Pennsylvania asked to speak. David Wilmot held the floor for 10 minutes—and changed the course of history.

This illustration shows the U.S. Capitol as it looked in the 1800s.

⭐ The Expansion of Slavery

Victory in the Mexican War in 1848 added more than 500,000 square miles to the United States and renewed the bitter debate over the expansion of slavery. The Missouri Compromise of 1820 had let Missouri enter the Union as a slave state. The Compromise divided the rest of the Louisiana Purchase into free and slave territory. Slavery was not allowed north of latitude 36°30'. President James K. Polk and others now wanted to run the 36°30' line to the Pacific coast, dividing the Mexican Cession into free and slave territory.

Have students read Section 1 and complete Guided Reading Strategy 18.1. Choose one or more of the following activities to explore the section content with students. For further suggestions on block scheduling or team teaching, see the *Block Scheduling Handbook with Team Teaching Strategies.*

LEVEL 1: Ask students to volunteer the terms of the Fugitive Slave Act, and write their answers on the chalkboard. (*Students should include: federal crime to help runaway slaves, runaways could be arrested in areas where slavery was illegal; slaveholders and their agents could use documents and white witnesses to prove ownership to U.S. commissioners; fugitives could*

not testify in their own defense; and so on.) Then go over each point on the list, discussing who would most likely benefit and why. Ask students which specific points of the Fugitive Slave Act they think northerners would most oppose. (*Students' responses might suggest that northerners would object to the lack of trial by jury and the apparent bribe given to commissioners to send suspected fugitives back to the South.*)

ENGLISH LANGUAGE LEARNERS

HOMEWORK Ask students to create political cartoons supporting or opposing the Fugitive Slave Act. Have students include a caption that addresses an issue involved in the controversy. Post the cartoons around the classroom.

Some northerners wanted to prohibit slavery in all parts of the Mexican Cession. During the war, Representative David Wilmot had proposed a plan known as the **Wilmot Proviso**. It stated that "neither slavery nor involuntary servitude shall ever exist in any part of [the] territory." The House of Representatives, which had a northern majority, passed the proviso, but it died in the Senate, where the South had more power. Although the Wilmot Proviso never became law, the debate over the plan showed the growing **sectionalism** of the country. Sectionalism happens when people favor the interests of one region over the interests of the country as a whole.

Senator Lewis Cass of Michigan hoped to solve the conflict over slavery in new territories. He pushed for **popular sovereignty**, which would allow voters in a territory to decide whether they wanted to ban or allow slavery. They would make their choice by electing antislavery or pro-slavery representatives to their territorial legislatures. Based on the will of the majority, these legislatures then would pass laws either to ban or to allow slavery.

The debate over slavery in the Mexican Cession dominated the presidential campaign of 1848. However, neither the Democrats nor the Whigs took a clear position on slavery in the West. For this reason, thousands of antislavery northerners formed a new political party. In August 1848 in Buffalo, New York, they formed the **Free-Soil Party**. The Free-Soilers supported the Wilmot Proviso. They chose former president Martin Van Buren of New York as their candidate. The new party won 10 percent of the popular vote. This helped Whig candidate Zachary Taylor, a Mexican War hero, win a narrow victory over Democratic opponent Lewis Cass.

The California Gold Rush caused a population boom that allowed California to skip the territorial stage and apply directly for admission into the Union. This raised the issue of whether California would join as a free state or a slave state. Most Californians did not want slavery and hoped to enter the Union as a free state. However, doing so would upset the balance between free and slave states.

To many southerners such a step was unacceptable. "We are about permanently to destroy the balance of power between the sections," warned Senator Jefferson Davis of Mississippi. He and many other southerners declared that they would oppose the admission of California to the Union as a free state.

✔ **Reading Check: Contrasting** How were the Wilmot Proviso and the principle of popular sovereignty different? The Wilmot Proviso would have banned slavery completely in the new territories while popular sovereignty would have allowed each territory to decide the issue.

CONGRESSIONAL SCALES, A TRUE BALANCE.

Interpreting Political Cartoons

Balancing act *The controversy over the Wilmot Proviso forced President Zachary Taylor to try to balance antislavery and pro-slavery interests.* **How does the cartoonist show Taylor's efforts to preserve peace?**

"General Taylor Never Surrenders" is the motto of this 1848 Zachary Taylor campaign button.

GENERAL TAYLOR NEVER SURRENDERS

★ **Biography**

David Wilmot. When David Wilmot introduced his proviso to Congress in 1846, he gained national attention. However, the proviso interrupted his political career. During his 1850 run for re-election to the House, many Democrats refused to support Wilmot but favored James Buchanan instead. He later became a Republican. Lincoln offered him a position in his cabinet, but Wilmot was elected to the Senate and chose to serve in Congress instead.

CRITICAL THINKING

Why would some Democrats be angry with Wilmot?

ANSWER: His proviso created divisions within the party over the status of slavery.

POLITICAL CARTOONS ANSWER

Students might suggest that he's trying to balance both sides.

★ The Compromise of 1850

<u>Henry Clay</u> had helped settle the Missouri crisis of 1819–20 and the nullification crisis of 1832–33. This senator from Kentucky, nicknamed "The Great Compromiser," now stepped forward with another plan. Clay's proposal had five main parts.

1. He urged Congress to let California enter the Union as a free state.

2. He called for the rest of the Mexican Cession to be organized as a federal territory. In this territory—already called New Mexico—popular sovereignty would decide the status of slavery.

3. He addressed a border dispute between Texas and New Mexico. He called on Texas to give up its claim to all land east of the upper Rio Grande. In exchange, the federal government would pay Texas's old debts. These debts remained from its days as an independent republic.

4. He called for an end to the slave trade—but not slavery—in the country's capital.

5. He called for a new, more effective fugitive slave law.

Almost immediately, Clay's plan came under fire. Senator William Seward of New York spoke for antislavery northerners. He demanded the admission of California "directly, without conditions, without qualifications, and without compromise." Senator John C. Calhoun of South Carolina spoke for many in the South. Near death, Calhoun was so weak that another senator had to read his speech. Calhoun argued that letting California enter as a free state would destroy the balance

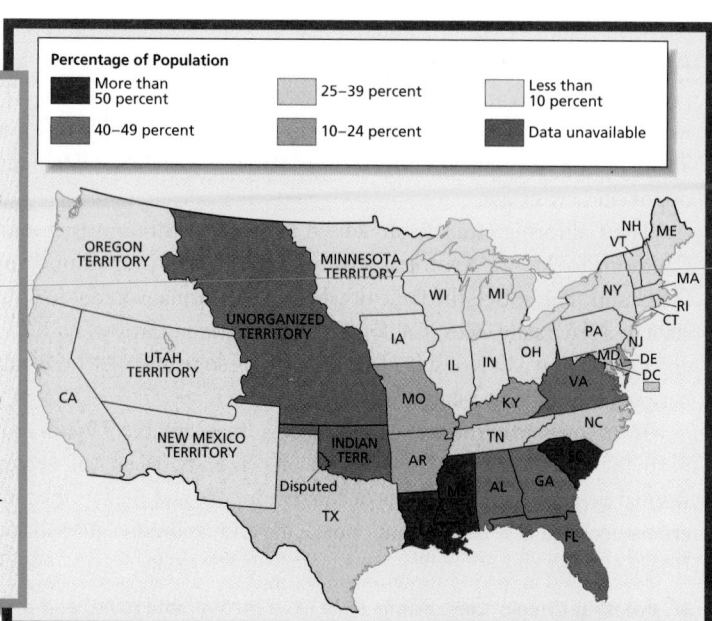

African American Population in 1850

Interpreting Maps African Americans made up 15 percent of the total U.S. population in 1850. However, in slave states African Americans accounted for a much higher percentage.

Skills Assessment

1. **Human Systems** In what states did African Americans make up more than 50 percent of the population?
2. **Analyzing Information** What was the trend in African American population heading from the South to the North and the West?

Percentage of Population

- More than 50 percent
- 40–49 percent
- 25–39 percent
- 10–24 percent
- Less than 10 percent
- Data unavailable

LEVEL 3: Organize the class into five groups. Then ask students to hold mock congressional hearings about the main conditions of the Compromise of 1850. Assign each group the role of a congressional investigative committee assigned to one of the following key issues of the compromise: letting California enter as a free state; making New Mexico a federal territory practicing popular sovereignty; having Texas give up some land claims in exchange for the federal government's paying off its old debts; ending the slave trade; or implementing a new fugitive slave law. Each committee should use material from the section to prepare a report citing the advantages and disadvantages of its issue. They should also recommend for or against its adoption and support their recommendation. After hearing each committee's report, have the class vote on the compromise. Conclude with a discussion on the various trade-offs that were a part of the Compromise of 1850. **COOPERATIVE LEARNING**

THE GRANGER COLLECTION, NEW YORK

between the two sections of the country. The slave states could not "remain in the Union consistently with their honor and their safety," he said. Calhoun asked that they be allowed "to separate and part in peace."

Others, such as Senator **Daniel Webster** of Massachusetts, were in favor of Clay's plan. Although Webster himself was opposed to the expansion of slavery, he argued that preserving the Union was more important than any regional differences.

 History Makers Speak **"**I wish to speak today, not as a Massachusetts man, nor as a Northern man, but as an American. . . . I speak today for the preservation of the Union. Hear me for my cause.**"**

—Daniel Webster, quoted in *Battle Cry of Freedom*, by James M. McPherson

Webster criticized northern abolitionists and scolded southerners who spoke of breaking away from the Union. He also argued that fighting over slavery in the West was unnecessary. Because of the soil and climate in this region, he claimed, the kinds of crops for which slave labor was used would not grow.

The **Compromise of 1850** became law in September of that year. It accomplished most of what Clay had wanted. California entered the Union as a free state. The rest of the Mexican Cession was divided into two territories. In these territories—Utah and New Mexico—the status of slavery would be decided by popular sovereignty. Texas agreed to give up its land claims in New Mexico. In exchange, the federal government gave Texas the financial help it needed. Finally, the compromise outlawed the slave trade in the nation's capital and produced a new fugitive slave law that replaced the previous law of 1793.

✔ **Reading Check: Summarizing** How did the Compromise of 1850 attempt to resolve conflicts over the expansion of slavery? See list on p. 554 and paragraph above.

Analyzing Primary Sources

Drawing Inferences and Conclusions How did Senator Webster avoid sectionalism in his speech? He stressed the importance of speaking as an American, and not as a man from a particular region or state.

 **Research on the R⬤M**

Free Find:
John C. Calhoun
After reading about John C. Calhoun on the **Holt Researcher CD-ROM**, create a political profile of him. Be sure to give details of Calhoun's life and explain his positions on important political issues of the era.

Technology Resources
Everyday Life in America Transparency 11: Slavery and Conflict

Visual Record Answer

Students might suggest that he is the central figure in the image.

Have students prepare flyers either supporting or opposing the Compromise of 1850. Flyers should explains students' positions and predict what will happen if Congress enacts the compromise. Have volunteers present their letters to the class.

SPOTLIGHT
on the Slavery Issue

Have students make a list of the political leaders discussed in Section 1 who were important to the slavery issue. *(Students' lists should include John C. Calhoun, Lewis Cass, Henry Clay, Daniel Webster, and David Wilmot.)* Then have students make a chart illustrating the political leaders' positions.

(Students' charts should include the following information: Wilmot: opposed slavery, proposed the Wilmot Proviso; Cass: wanted to compromise, proposed popular sovereignty; Clay: wanted to compromise, proposed the Compromise of 1850; Calhoun: supported slavery, told Congress that the slave states could not remain in the Union if California joined as a free state; Webster: wanted to compromise, supported the Compromise of 1850) Incorporate the students' charts into one master chart on a large sheet of butcher paper. **BLOCK SCHEDULING**

Interdisciplinary Connection

►Literature◄

Slave Narratives. Frederick Douglass's autobiography is only one of a number of slave narratives. One historian has estimated that more than 6,000 such narratives exist. The earliest known narrative, the story of Adam, the "servant of John Saffin, Esquire," was published in 1703. Douglass's work is probably the best known. Four different versions were published, the first (and today the rarest) in 1845. A revised edition released in 1892 was the last.

ACTIVITY: Have students obtain a copy of Douglass's autobiography and read aloud a passage relating to the treatment he received when he was a slave. Have students write a summary of the conditions Douglass faced, using standard grammar, spelling, sentence structure, and punctuation.

Technology Resources

 CNN Presents America: Beginnings to 1914 Segment: Frederick Douglass: An American Portrait

BIOGRAPHY ANSWER

Students might suggest that his autobiography gave so much detail that he was in danger of being arrested as a fugitive slave.

BIOGRAPHY

Frederick Douglass
(1817–1895)

Frederick Douglass was born to an enslaved family in Maryland. At age 20, he escaped to freedom in the North. There he began speaking and writing for the abolition movement. In 1845 he published the *Narrative of the Life of Frederick Douglass*. The detail in this autobiography forced him to leave the country to avoid being arrested as a fugitive slave. He returned in 1847 and bought his freedom. He started an antislavery newspaper, which he named *North Star*. In the first issue, Douglass called on other former slaves to join his crusade for freedom. Why did Douglass have to leave the country?

Analyzing Primary Sources

Identifying Points of View
How did Delany react to the new fugitive slave law? He threatened to resist it with lethal force.

★ The Fugitive Slave Act

One part of the Compromise of 1850 kept slavery very much on the minds of Americans. The **Fugitive Slave Act** made it a federal crime to help runaway slaves. The act even let officials arrest runaways in areas where slavery was illegal. Under the new law, slaveholders and their agents could take suspected fugitive slaves before U.S. commissioners. They would then try to prove ownership through documents or through the testimony of white witnesses. In contrast, the accused fugitives could not testify in their own defense. Commissioners who rejected a slaveholder's claim received $5 for their services. Those who returned a suspected fugitive to the slaveholder in the South received $10. Anyone who hid or otherwise helped a runaway slave faced six months in jail and a $1,000 fine.

In the 10 years after Congress passed this law, 343 fugitive slave cases came under the commissioners' review in the North. The accused fugitive was declared free in only 11 of these cases. Such numbers worried many African Americans living in the North—free individuals as well as former slaves. Thousands of African Americans went to Canada to escape potential prosecution under the Fugitive Slave Act.

The Fugitive Slave Act upset many northerners. They did not agree with the lack of a trial by jury. These northerners also disliked the higher fee given to commissioners who returned fugitives. This apparent bribe encouraged commissioners to send a suspected fugitive slave back to the South. As expected, abolitionists led the protests against the new law. One abolitionist said it was every citizen's duty to make sure that the new law was "resisted, disobeyed at all hazards." Martin R. Delany, a doctor and a leading African American abolitionist, spoke publicly to the mayor of Pittsburgh, Pennsylvania.

 History Makers Speak

❝If any man approaches that house in search of a slave—I care not who he may be . . . if he crosses the threshold of my door, and I do not lay him a lifeless corpse at my feet, I hope the grave may refuse my body a resting place, and righteous Heaven my spirit a home.❞

—Martin R. Delany, quoted in *The Negro Caravan,* edited by Sterling A. Brown, Arthur P. Davis, and Ulysses Lee

In general, northerners who resisted the Fugitive Slave Act did so without using violence. However, blood was spilled on several occasions. In 1854, for example, the case of **Anthony Burns** caught the nation's attention. Burns, a fugitive slave from Virginia, was arrested and jailed in Boston. A group of abolitionists in the city tried to rescue Burns by force. A deputy marshal was killed in the attempt, but Burns was eventually returned to slavery in Virginia.

✔ **Reading Check: Finding the Main Idea** How did many northerners respond to the Fugitive Slave Act? They were offended. They objected to the lack of trial by jury and the apparent bribe given to commissioners to send suspected fugitives back to the South.

☆ **REVIEW AND ASSESS**

Have students complete the **Section 1 Review** on p. 557. Then have students complete **Daily Quiz 18.1**. As **Alternative Assessment**, you may want to use the political cartoons or letters to Congress in this section's lessons.

☆ **RETEACH**

Have students complete **Main Idea Activity for English Language Learners and Special-Needs Students 18.1**. Ask students to use the terms listed in the Define and Identify sections in five different sentences that explain how the issue of slavery increased tensions among Americans between 1846 and 1852. When students are finished, pair them and have them read each

other's sentences. Then have each student write five study questions to go along with the sentences.

ENGLISH LANGUAGE LEARNERS, **COOPERATIVE LEARNING**

☆ **EXTEND**

Have students use the library to obtain information about the Nashville Convention of 1850, which drew attention to the possibility of southern secession. Then ask students to imagine that they are delegates to that convention. Have students write diary entries explaining their reactions to the results of the convention, commenting on the opinions expressed by other delegates, and describing whether the convention was a success or failure. **BLOCK SCHEDULING**

THE GRANGER COLLECTION, NEW YORK

THE GRANGER COLLECTION, NEW YORK

Abolitionists protested the arrest of suspected fugitive slaves, such as the capture shown above.

★ Antislavery Literature

Abolitionists in the North used the stories of fugitive slaves such as Anthony Burns to help their cause. They also made use of slave narratives, which became popular around 1840. Among the best known were the narratives of Frederick Douglass and Sojourner Truth. Truth's narrative differed from most other slave narratives in two ways. First, its central character was a woman. Second, Truth had been a slave not in the South but in New York.

No other literary work, however, had the influence of _Uncle Tom's Cabin_. This powerful antislavery novel was written by **Harriet Beecher Stowe**. Stowe was born into a religious family in Connecticut and moved to Ohio at the age of 21. There she met with fugitive slaves and learned about the cruelty of slavery. The passage of the Fugitive Slave Act of 1850 greatly angered Stowe, so she decided to write a book that would show northerners what slavery was really like.

Uncle Tom's Cabin was published in 1852. The main character is a kindly old slave named Tom, who is separated from his wife and sold. Tom becomes the slave of a cruel cotton planter in Louisiana. The novel sparked outrage in the South and gained praise in the North. Within 10 years, more than 2 million copies of _Uncle Tom's Cabin_ were sold in the United States. The book's popularity caused one northerner to remark that Stowe had created "two millions of abolitionists."

✔ **Reading Check: Analyzing Information** How did literature help the antislavery movement? Stories of fugitive slaves, slave narratives, and novels such as _Uncle Tom's Cabin_ made people aware of the cruelty of slavery and convinced some people to become abolitionists.

Section 1 Review

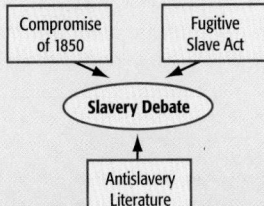

**go. Homework
hrw Practice
.com Online**
keyword: SA3 HP18

1 **Define** and explain:
• sectionalism
• popular sovereignty

2 **Identify** and explain:
• Wilmot Proviso
• Free-Soil Party
• Henry Clay
• Daniel Webster
• Compromise of 1850
• Fugitive Slave Act
• Anthony Burns
• _Uncle Tom's Cabin_
• Harriet Beecher Stowe

3 **Contrasting** Copy the diagram below. Use it to explain how the Compromise of 1850, Fugitive Slave Act, and antislavery literature related to the debate over the expansion of slavery.

```
[Compromise   [Fugitive
of 1850]      Slave Act]
        ↘    ↙
     (Slavery Debate)
           ↑
      [Antislavery
       Literature]
```

4 **Finding the Main Idea**
a. How did U.S. territory change after the Mexican War ended, and how did this change renew the debate over slavery?
b. What did the Compromise of 1850 propose? Why did Senator Daniel Webster support it, and why did Senator John C. Calhoun oppose it?

5 **Writing and Critical Thinking**
Supporting a Point of View Imagine that you are a northerner who is opposed to the Fugitive Slave Act. Create a handbill that you would pass out at a town meeting to persuade members of your community to protest the law.
Consider the following:
• lack of trial by jury
• "bribes" given to commissioners
• examples of abolitionist protests

**Section 1 Review
ANSWERS**

1 **Define**
• sectionalism, p. 553
• popular sovereignty, p. 553

2 **Identify**
• Wilmot Proviso, p. 553
• Free-Soil Party, p. 553
• Henry Clay, p. 554
• Daniel Webster, p. 555
• Compromise of 1850, p. 555
• Fugitive Slave Act, p. 556
• Anthony Burns, p. 556
• _Uncle Tom's Cabin_, p. 557
• Harriet Beecher Stowe, p. 557

3 Compromise of 1850—sparked debate between leaders; Fugitive Slave Act—result of Compromise of 1850, angered abolitionists; Antislavery Literature—educated and persuaded people

4 a. territory increased by 500,000 square miles; northerners and southerners could not agree on status of slavery in new territories
b. 1) admit CA as free state; 2) organize rest of Mexican Cession as a federal territory where popular sovereignty would decide slavery question; 3) TX would give up claim to land east of Rio Grande and federal government would assume TX's debt; 4) end to slave trade in nation's capital; 5) more effective fugitive slave law; Webster—believed it would preserve the Union; Calhoun—argued that admission of California would destroy the balance between slave and free states

5 Students' handbills will vary.

SPOTLIGHT
on *Uncle Tom's Cabin*

Have students prepare a book jacket for *Uncle Tom's Cabin*. Ask them to include a picture or drawing accompanied by the title on the front cover; a brief summary of the book's contents on the jacket's end flaps; the title, author, and publisher on the spine; and comments about the book's influence on the back cover. **BLOCK SCHEDULING**

SPOTLIGHT
on Slavery

Have students find examples of slave narratives, abolitionist newspapers, or books such as *Uncle Tom's Cabin*. Then ask students to perform dramatic readings of key excerpts that illuminate the major ideas of their selection. Encourage students to find works that highlight information discussed in this section. **BLOCK SCHEDULING**

Interdisciplinary Connection

▶Literature◀

Reactions to *Uncle Tom's Cabin*. Harriet Beecher Stowe sent advance copies of her novel to several important Europeans, including Prince Albert of England and author Charles Dickens. English readers loved the book. Forty different publishers released editions, most of them unauthorized, selling approximately 1.5 million copies. Interest in Stowe's work prompted songwriters to write music about the evils of slavery. People in London lined up to attend a play based on the novel, prompting one newspaper to describe the trend as "Tom-mania."

CRITICAL THINKING

Why did *Uncle Tom's Cabin* capture the interest of the British people?

ANSWER: Students might suggest that the British were concerned about the institution of slavery, which no longer existed in their country.

CONNECTING TO LITERATURE ANSWERS

1. the United States

2. to oppose slavery because of its cruelty and injustice

CONNECTING TO *Literature*

Uncle Tom's Cabin
Harriet Beecher Stowe

Like Mark Twain, Harriet Beecher Stowe was a local-color writer, concentrating on describing regional culture and language. Stowe wrote mostly about New England. However, she is best remembered for Uncle Tom's Cabin, *a powerful novel about slavery. In the following passage, Simon Legree is a northerner who has moved south and become a cruel slaveholder. He has ordered Sambo, a slave driver, to whip Tom. Legree wants to learn what Tom knows about the disappearance of two slaves. Tom, a slave, is one of the main characters of the novel. He has maintained his religious faith despite the brutality he has witnessed and experienced. The scene shows the consequences of slavery—both to the suffering slave and to the soul of the slaveholder. The criticism of slavery in the first and last paragraphs is the author's voice.*

Uncle Tom's Cabin helped convince many Americans of the moral wrongs of slavery.

Scenes of blood and cruelty are shocking to our ear and heart. What man has nerve to do, man has not nerve to hear. What brother-man and brother-Christian must suffer, cannot be told us, even in our secret chamber, it so **harrows up**[1] the soul! And yet, oh my country; these things are done under the shadow of thy laws! O, Christ! thy church sees them, almost in silence! . . . "He's most **gone**,[2] **Mas'r**,[3]" said Sambo, touched, in spite of himself, by the patience of his victim.

"Pay away, till he give up! Give it to him!—give it to him!" shouted Legree. "I'll take every drop of blood he has, unless he confesses!"

Tom opened his eyes, and looked upon his master. "Ye poor miserable crittur!" he said, "there ain't no more ye can do! I forgive ye, with all my soul!" and he fainted entirely away.

"I b'lieve, my soul, he's done for, finally," said Legree, stepping forward, to look at him. "Yes, he is! Well, his mouth's shut up, at last,—that's one comfort!"

Yes, Legree; but who shall shut up that voice in thy soul? that soul, **past repentance**,[4] past prayer, past hope, in whom the fire that never shall be quenched is already burning!

Understanding What You Read

1. **Literature and History** In the opening paragraph, whom does Stowe criticize for allowing slavery to occur?

2. **Literature and You** What do you think Stowe is asking of the reader?

[1]**harrows up:** frightens or shocks
[2]**gone:** dead
[3]**Mas'r:** master

[4]**past repentance:** beyond the ability to turn away from sin; past regret

Section 2

OBJECTIVES

⭐ Explain how different regions of the country reacted to the Kansas-Nebraska Act.

⭐ Describe the ways people tried to settle the conflict over slavery in Kansas.

⭐ Depict the series of violent events that showed growing division over slavery in the United States.

Section 2

Trouble in Kansas

Read to Discover

1. How did different regions of the country react to the Kansas-Nebraska Act?
2. In what ways did people try to settle the conflict over slavery in Kansas?
3. What series of violent events showed growing division over slavery in the United States?

WHY IT MATTERS TODAY

In the 1850s events in Kansas affected the entire nation. Use **CNNfyi.com** or other **current events** sources to learn about events in one part of the country that have affected the entire country. Record your findings in your journal.

Identify

- Franklin Pierce
- Stephen Douglas
- Kansas-Nebraska Act
- Pottawatomie Massacre
- Charles Sumner
- Preston Brooks

The Story Continues

Franklin and Jane Pierce spent the morning taking a peaceful carriage ride just outside Boston, Massachusetts. On their way back to their hotel in the city, they saw a horseman racing toward them. When the rider reached the Pierces' carriage, he shouted the news. The Democratic convention in Baltimore, Maryland, had nominated Franklin Pierce for the presidency. The Pierces were stunned.

The Democratic Party nominated Franklin Pierce for president in 1852.

⭐ The Election of 1852

As the Democratic convention opened in 1852, there were four leading candidates for the presidential nomination. It soon became clear, however, that no one could win a majority of votes. After nearly 50 ballots, the frustrated delegates chose **Franklin Pierce**. Pierce was a little-known politician from New Hampshire. However, he and his party promised to honor the Compromise of 1850 and enforce the Fugitive Slave Act. Thus, many southerners saw Pierce "as reliable as Calhoun himself" on the slavery question.

The Whigs also held their convention in Baltimore in 1852. The divided party hoped to repeat earlier successes by nominating a well-

Have students read Section 2 and complete Guided Reading Strategy 18.2. Choose one or more of the following activities to explore the section content with students. For further suggestions on block scheduling or team teaching, see the *Block Scheduling Handbook with Team Teaching Strategies*.

LEVEL 1: On the chalkboard make a chart with the first column labeled *The South* and the second column labeled *The North*. Ask students to fill in the chart with examples of how each of these regions reacted to the Kansas-Nebraska Act. Write students' answers on the chalkboard. (*Students' answers should include: the South—strongly supported*

the act, wanted it to become a slave territory; North—felt outrage, believed it was part of a plan to turn free territory into slave territory, attended protest meetings, sent anti-Nebraska petitions to Congress.) Then organize the class into groups. Have each group write a petition to encourage Congress to stop the Kansas-Nebraska Act from becoming law.
ENGLISH LANGUAGE LEARNERS , COOPERATIVE LEARNING

ALL LEVELS: Copy the graphic organizer on the following page onto the chalkboard, omitting the italicized answers. Have students complete the chart with the series of violent events that show the growing division over slavery in the United States. **ENGLISH LANGUAGE LEARNERS**

★ Biography

Franklin Pierce. Franklin Pierce's commitment to his family greatly influenced his career. In 1842 he retired from the U.S. Senate because his wife wanted to return to their home in New Hampshire. In 1846 President James K. Polk offered to make Pierce U.S. attorney general, but Pierce refused, again because of family obligations. Although Pierce turned down several political appointments, he announced in 1852 that he would not reject the presidential nomination, which prompted the Democrats to nominate him when they could not agree on any other candidate.

☑ **internet** connect

TOPIC: Franklin Pierce
GO TO: go.hrw.com
KEYWORD: SA3 CF18

Have students use the library or access the Internet through the HRW Go site to obtain information on Franklin Pierce. Ask students to create a resumé that chronicles his career.

MAP ANSWER
The United States created Kansas Territory, Nebraska Territory and Washington Territory were created.

known soldier for the presidency. They passed over Millard Fillmore, who had become president after Zachary Taylor's death. Instead, the Whigs chose Winfield Scott, a hero from the Mexican War. Although Scott was born in Virginia, many southerners did not trust him because he had not completely supported the Compromise of 1850.

The Democrats won the election by a large margin. Pierce won 27 of the 31 states. Even Scott's home state of Virginia voted for Pierce. Whig Representative Lewis Campbell of Ohio feared the worst after this painful defeat. "We are slayed," he cried. "The party is dead—dead—dead!"

✔ **Reading Check: Identifying Cause and Effect** Who won the 1852 presidential election, and how did the election affect the Whig Party?
Democrat Franklin Pierce; some Whigs feared their party would die

★ The Kansas-Nebraska Act

Since entering Congress in the mid-1840s, **Stephen Douglas** had supported building a railroad to the Pacific. Douglas wanted a line running from Chicago, in his home state of Illinois. To build this railroad, however, the rest of the Louisiana Purchase had to be made into a federal territory. The Missouri Compromise banned slavery in this region, meaning that the land would eventually become free states.

Southerners in Congress did not support Douglas's plan. They wanted a line running from New Orleans across Texas. It would run through the already organized territory of New Mexico and into southern California. However, Douglas was determined to have the railroad start in Chicago. Thus, he asked a few key southern senators to support

Compromise of 1850	Kansas-Nebraska Act, 1854
OREGON TERR.	WASHINGTON TERR.
MINNESOTA TERR.	OREGON TERR.
UNORGANIZED TERR.	NEBRASKA TERR.
UTAH TERR.	MINNESOTA TERR.
CALIFORNIA	UTAH TERR.
Missouri Compromise line (36°30'N)	KANSAS TERR.
NEW MEXICO TERR.	NEW MEXICO TERR.
INDIAN TERR.	INDIAN TERR.
Disputed	Disputed

■ Free state　□ Free territory　■ Slave state　□ Slave territory　■ Popular sovereignty

Slave and Free Territory in 1850 and 1854
Interpreting Maps The Compromise of 1850 and the Kansas-Nebraska Act of 1854 gave new states and territories the right to vote on whether to allow slavery.

Skills Assessment Places and Regions How did the status and boundaries of the western territories change between 1850 and 1854?

Pro-slavery settlers and free-soilers arm themselves.

A pro-slavery posse sets fire to some buildings and destroys the printing presses in Lawrence, Kansas.

Abolitionist John Brown leads the Pottawatomie Massacre, killing five pro-slavery men.

After Massachusetts representative Charles Sumner criticizes pro-slavery Kansans, Preston Brooks, a representative from South Carolina, canes him.

LEVEL 3: Ask students to imagine that they are members of Congress after the Civil War has ended. Then organize a mock congressional hearing to discover how the division over slavery led to violent events in the United States prior to the Civil War. Remind students that they should determine what, if anything, could have been done to avoid the violence. Have each group present its decision to the class.
COOPERATIVE LEARNING

Comparing the Compromises

As disagreements over the expansion of slavery divided the nation, congressional leaders tried to find a compromise that would end sectional disagreements.

Missouri Compromise

No slavery in new states north of 36° 30' line

Missouri joins the Union as a slave state

Maine joins the Union as a free state

Henry Clay

Compromise of 1850

California joins the Union as a free state

New Mexico and Utah Territories to use popular sovereignty to decide status of slavery

Stronger fugitive slave law passed

Slave trade ended in Washington, D.C.

Border dispute between New Mexico and Texas is resolved

Henry Clay

Daniel Webster

John C. Calhoun

Kansas-Nebraska Act

Kansas and Nebraska Territories are created

No more 36° 30' boundary for slave states

Kansas and Nebraska Territories will use popular sovereignty

Stephen Douglas

Visualizing History

1. **Government** What are the main similarities and differences among the three compromises?

2. **Connecting to Today** Do you think compromise is still an important political tool today? Why or why not?

his plan. They said they would give up their plans for a southern railroad route. In return, they wanted the new territory west of Missouri opened up to slavery.

In January 1854 Douglas introduced what became the **Kansas-Nebraska Act**. This plan would divide the rest of the Louisiana Purchase into two territories—Kansas and Nebraska. In each territory, popular sovereignty would decide the question of slavery. Douglas's plan would remove the Missouri Compromise's restriction on slavery north of the 36°30' line.

Antislavery northerners were outraged. Some called the proposal a "gross violation of a sacred pledge." They thought it was part of a southern plot to turn free territory into a "dreary region . . . inhabited by masters and slaves." All across the North, citizens attended protest meetings and sent anti-Nebraska petitions to Congress. However, the measure carried strong southern support. Douglas and President Pierce also tried to get their fellow Democrats to vote for it. The measure passed the Senate in March and the House two months later. The president signed the act into law on May 30, 1854. Lost in the controversy was Douglas's proposed railroad to the Pacific. Congress would not approve the construction of such a railroad until 1862.

Advertisements like this 1855 poster encouraged settlers to buy land in Kansas.

✔ **Reading Check: Finding the Main Idea** Why were antislavery northerners angry about the Kansas-Nebraska Act? It eliminated the Missouri Compromise's restriction on slavery north of 36°30'.

LEVEL 3: Organize students into small groups. Have groups create a newspaper reporting events associated with "Bleeding Kansas" and the ways people tried to settle the controversy over the extension of slavery in Kansas. The paper should include stories on the Kansas-Nebraska Act and the issue of slavery in the territories. It should also include interviews with key figures, editorial comment on the emergence of two competing territorial governments, and political cartoons describing the controversy. **COOPERATIVE LEARNING**, **BLOCK SCHEDULING**

HOMEWORK Tell students to imagine that they are living in Kansas during the "Bleeding Kansas" period. Then ask students to create five journal entries, each focusing on a different event that took place in Kansas.

★ CLOSE

Organize students into groups and ask them to consider the following questions: *How might the Kansas-Nebraska Act have been changed to prevent the violence of "Bleeding Kansas"? What steps should have been taken to settle the Kansas issue peacefully?* Ask each group to prepare a plan and explain it to the class. Ask the class to speculate on why political figures of the 1850s did not use such a plan. **COOPERATIVE LEARNING**

Antislavery activist Henry Ward Beecher helped raise money to send weapons to abolitionist settlers in Kansas.

THE GRANGER COLLECTION, NEW YORK

★ "Bleeding Kansas"

Both northern and southern politicians saw that a contest had begun. As a result, antislavery and pro-slavery groups rushed to get people to Kansas. Senator William Seward of New York spoke on the issue.

> **History Makers Speak** ❝Gentlemen of the Slave States, since there is no escaping your challenge, I accept it in behalf of the cause of freedom. We will engage in competition for . . . Kansas, and God give victory to the side which is stronger in numbers as it is in right.❞
>
> —William Henry Seward, quoted in *The Impending Crisis, 1848–1861,* by David M. Potter

Elections for the Kansas territorial legislature were held in March 1855. To ensure a pro-slavery victory, thousands of men crossed the border from Missouri, voted in Kansas, and then returned home. As a result, the territorial legislature, located at Lecompton, had a huge pro-slavery majority. The new legislature passed a series of strict pro-slavery laws. One law made it a crime to question anyone's right to hold slaves. Another law stated that anyone caught helping a fugitive slave could be punished by death. In protest, antislavery Kansans formed their own legislature 25 miles away in Topeka.

By early 1856 Kansas had two governments and an angry population divided into two armed camps. Many of the pro-slavery settlers had brought guns with them to the new territory. Meanwhile antislavery settlers had asked for shipments of weapons from their friends in the East. With both sides heavily armed, violence soon broke out. In May 1856 a pro-slavery grand jury charged the leaders of the antislavery government with treason. A posse of more than 700 men rode to Lawrence, where they destroyed buildings and printing presses.

Abolitionist John Brown decided that it was his duty to punish pro-slavery forces for the so-called Sack of Lawrence. He said it was time to

Interpreting the Visual Record

The Sack of Lawrence *A pro-slavery force came to the town of Lawrence seeking to arrest antislavery leaders. When they could not find these people, they attacked the rest of the town, killing one man. **How does this image portray the violence of the pro-slavery settlers?***

THE GRANGER COLLECTION, NEW YORK

★ REVIEW AND ASSESS

Have students complete the **Section 2 Review** on p. 563. Then have students complete **Daily Quiz 18.2.** As **Alternative Assessment,** you may want to use the student's Kansas-Nebraska Act petitions or the violence in Kansas graphic organizers.

★ RETEACH

Have students complete **Main Idea Activity for English Language Learners and Special-Needs Students 18.2.** Then ask them to create charts with the following headings on the horizontal axis: *the Kansas-Nebraska Act, the beating of Charles Sumner,* and *the settlement of Kansas;* and *North* and *South* as

headings on the vertical axis. Have students complete the organizer by filling in the general opinions of people from both regions regarding each issue. **ENGLISH LANGUAGE LEARNERS**

★ EXTEND

Have students use the library to research the conflict between the territorial governments established at Lecompton and Topeka. Then have students use their findings to write a recommendation to the president stating which of the two models the U.S. government should recognize. **BLOCK SCHEDULING**

"strike terror in the hearts of the pro-slavery people." Brown was a New Englander who moved to Kansas in 1855 with some of his sons. On the night of May 24, 1856, he led a group of seven men along Pottawatomie Creek in eastern Kansas. They killed five pro-slavery men in what became known as the **Pottawatomie Massacre**. Kansas collapsed into a state of civil war. About 200 people were killed in the months that followed. The events in "Bleeding Kansas" became front-page stories in many of the country's newspapers.

Conflict also swept Congress, where Senator **Charles Sumner** of Massachusetts gave a speech called "The Crime Against Kansas." In it, he criticized pro-slavery efforts in Kansas and insulted Senator Andrew Pickens Butler of South Carolina. Representative **Preston Brooks**, a relative of Butler, was greatly upset. On May 22, 1856, Brooks approached Sumner in the Senate chamber and beat him unconscious with a walking cane. A newspaper editor in Virginia praised Brooks's actions.

THE GRANGER COLLECTION, NEW YORK

Preston Brooks was fined $300 by a federal court for his attack on Charles Sumner, who was unable to return to the Senate until after a three-year absence.

History Makers Speak
❝We consider the act good in conception [thought], better in execution. . . . These vulgar [rude] abolitionists in the Senate . . . must be lashed into submission [surrender]. Sumner, in particular, ought to have nine-and-thirty [lashes] early every morning.❞

—*Richmond Enquirer,* June 2, 1856

Analyzing Primary Sources

Identifying Bias How can you tell that the speaker supports the spread of slavery? by the fact that he approved of Brooks's actions

Dozens of southerners sent Brooks new canes. In the North Sumner's beating outraged many people, who called the attacker Bully Brooks.

✔ **Reading Check: Comparing and Contrasting** How did northerners and southerners react to events involving Kansas? See discussion above.

Section 2 Review

go.hrw.com **Homework Practice Online**
keyword: SA3 HP18

❶ **Identify** and explain:
• Franklin Pierce
• Stephen Douglas
• Kansas-Nebraska Act
• Pottawatomie Massacre
• Charles Sumner
• Preston Brooks

```
Kansas-
Nebraska Act
```

❷ **Sequencing** Copy the graphic organizer below. Use it to describe the Kansas-Nebraska Act and the conflicts that followed in the order that they occurred.

❸ **Finding the Main Idea**
a. What did northerners and southerners think of the Kansas-Nebraska Act?

b. How did antislavery forces hope to prevent slavery in Kansas, and how did pro-slavery groups influence the Kansas territorial elections in 1855?

❹ **Writing and Critical Thinking**
Summarizing Imagine that you are a historian writing about the beating of Charles Sumner by Preston Brooks. Write a half-page essay describing the events leading up to the beating and the public's reactions.

Consider the following:
• reasons for the attack
• northern reactions to the beating
• southern reactions to the beating

Section 3

OBJECTIVES

- ⭐ Analyze the effect of the Kansas-Nebraska Act on U.S. political parties.
- ⭐ Explain why Dred Scott sued for his freedom and how the Supreme Court ruled on his case.
- ⭐ Examine how Abraham Lincoln and Stephen Douglas differed in their views on slavery.

📻 LET'S GET STARTED!

Write the following question on the chalkboard: *How would the U.S. political system change if the two major political parties divided into three or four groups competing for power?* As students enter the classroom, allow time for them to respond. *(Students' responses might include that there would be less consensus on political issues or that there would be a greater variety of ideas in the political system.)* Tell students that in Section 3, they will learn how the issue of slavery divided the two major political parties so deeply that by the presidential election of 1860 there were actually four candidates running for president on major party tickets.

Section 3

Political Divisions

Read to Discover

1. How did the Kansas-Nebraska Act affect U.S. political parties?
2. Why did Dred Scott sue for his freedom, and how did the Supreme Court rule on his case?
3. How did Abraham Lincoln and Stephen Douglas differ in their views on slavery?

WHY IT MATTERS TODAY

Supreme Court decisions have a major impact on life in the United States. Use **CNNfyi.com** or other **current events** sources to learn about how a recent Supreme Court decision will affect the whole country. Record your findings in your journal.

Identify

- Republican Party
- James Buchanan
- John C. Frémont
- Dred Scott
- Roger B. Taney
- *Dred Scott* decision
- Abraham Lincoln
- Lincoln-Douglas debates
- Freeport Doctrine

The Story Continues

On July 5, 1854, hundreds of people met at the town of Jackson, Michigan, to form a new political party. "We will . . . be known as Republicans," they declared in their platform. They promised to uphold the principles of republican government. They also said they would fight the spread of slavery "until the contest be terminated."

This crowd has gathered to hear a speaker at the first Republican National Convention.

THE GRANGER COLLECTION, NEW YORK

⭐ New Divisions

Political unrest led Whigs, some Democrats, Free-Soilers, and abolitionists to join and form the **Republican Party** in 1854. These different groups united to oppose the spread of slavery in the West. The Kansas-Nebraska Act of 1854 had once again raised this issue and divided the Democratic and Whig Parties. Under pressure from Senator Stephen Douglas and President Franklin Pierce, nearly 60 northern Democrats had voted for the Kansas-Nebraska bill. They suffered politically for their support, however. In the next congressional elections, only seven of the northern Democrats who voted for the bill kept their seats in the House of Representatives.

564

★ **TEACH**

Have students read Section 3 and complete Guided Reading Strategy 18.3. Choose one or more of the following activities to explore the section content with students. For further suggestions on block scheduling or team teaching, see the *Block Scheduling Handbook with Team Teaching Strategies.*

LEVEL 1: Have students volunteer Abraham Lincoln's beliefs about slavery, the status of African Americans, and racial equality. Write students' answers on the chalkboard. *(Students' responses should include that Lincoln believed that slavery was wrong, slavery should not expand farther West, African Americans were entitled to all the natural rights listed in the Declaration of Independence, and African Americans were not necessarily the social or political equals of whites.)* Then ask students about Stephen Douglas's reactions to Lincoln's beliefs during their series of debates. *(Students' responses should explain that Douglas claimed that Lincoln said that African Americans were equal to whites, and that he also accused Lincoln and the Republicans of wanting to make every state a free state, which would lead to warfare.)* **ENGLISH LANGUAGE LEARNERS**

The Kansas-Nebraska Act was even more damaging to the Whigs. Every northern Whig voted against Douglas's bill. Most southern Whigs, however, voted for it.

The presidential election of 1856 showed just how divided the country was becoming. Some longtime Whigs and Democrats joined the Know-Nothing Party, which quickly fell apart over the slavery issue. Northern delegates left the convention hall when southerners refused to support the repeal of the Kansas-Nebraska Act. Many northerners later supported the Republican Party. Those Know-Nothings who remained behind chose former president Millard Fillmore as their presidential candidate.

The Democrats knew that they could not nominate anyone closely associated with the Kansas-Nebraska Act, which ruled out President Pierce and Senator Douglas. They chose **James Buchanan** of Pennsylvania instead. Buchanan had served roughly 20 years in Congress and as Polk's secretary of state for 4 years. Most importantly, he had not been involved in the Kansas-Nebraska controversy.

At their first presidential nominating convention, the Republicans chose **John C. Frémont** as their candidate. Frémont had little political experience, but his opposition to the spread of slavery appealed to Republicans. Although the Republicans also favored issues such as protective tariffs, they generally were seen as a "single-issue party." Their antislavery platform meant the Republicans had almost no supporters outside of the free states.

Some white southerners even said that they would not accept a Republican victory in the election. A politician from Georgia made a prediction: "The election of Frémont would be the end of the Union." On election day, Buchanan won 14 of the 15 slave states and 5 of the free states, the rest of which went to Frémont. Fillmore, meanwhile, won only one state—Maryland. Buchanan won the election.

✔ **Reading Check: Summarizing** How did the Kansas-Nebraska Act affect political parties in the 1856 election? Republicans opposed the Act. It hurt northern Democratic supporters and split the Whig and Know-Nothing Parties.

★★★★★★★★★★★★
That's Interesting!
★★★★★★★★★★★★

Watching Every Dime Would you remember to correct the error if you underpaid a bill by three cents? It was everyday policy for James Buchanan to follow such precision in his accounting. Throughout his life, he kept books in which he carefully recorded every penny that he earned or spent. While serving as ambassador to Great Britain, Buchanan recorded such daily details as how much he spent on pins and suspender buttons. One time during his presidency he realized he had underpaid by three cents for some food. Even though the merchant ignored the error, the president made sure the owner received his three pennies.

★ **Citizenship**

The Republicans.
Meetings to organize a new political party began in early 1854. Historians believe that the first such meeting took place in the Congregational Church of Ripon, Wisconsin, on February 28 of that year. On March 20, the day after Congress passed the Kansas-Nebraska Act, the townspeople again met at the church. The Whig and Free-Soil parties in Ripon agreed to disband. A committee consisting of three Whigs, one Free-Soiler, and one Democrat convened to begin the business of forming a new party and organizing the first Republican Party meeting, which was held in Jackson, Michigan, that summer.

ACTIVITY: Have students use the library to find information about the Republican Party. Ask students to create a time line describing the formation of the party and significant events in its history.

James Buchanan's inaugural parade stretched far down the streets of Washington, D.C.

THE GRANGER COLLECTION, NEW YORK

A Divided Nation **565**

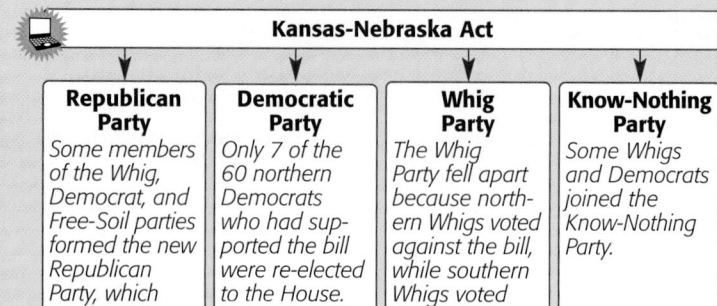

Kansas-Nebraska Act

Republican Party	Democratic Party	Whig Party	Know-Nothing Party
Some members of the Whig, Democrat, and Free-Soil parties formed the new Republican Party, which opposed the spread of slavery.	*Only 7 of the 60 northern Democrats who had supported the bill were re-elected to the House.*	*The Whig Party fell apart because northern Whigs voted against the bill, while southern Whigs voted for it.*	*Some Whigs and Democrats joined the Know-Nothing Party.*

Dred Scott argued that living on free soil had made him a free man.

Analyzing Primary Sources

Identifying Points of View What concerned Lincoln about the *Dred Scott* decision? that the Supreme Court might make slavery legal in free states

⭐ The *Dred Scott* Decision

Just two days after Buchanan became president, the Supreme Court issued a ruling that threw the country back into crisis. This case involved **Dred Scott**, the slave of an army surgeon from St. Louis, Missouri. In the 1830s Scott had gone with the surgeon on tours of duty in Illinois and the northern part of the Louisiana Purchase. In 1846 Scott sued for his freedom after returning to Missouri. He argued that he had become free when he lived in free territory.

The case reached the U.S. Supreme Court in 1856. The justices—a majority of whom were from the South—had three key issues before them. First, the Court had to rule on whether Scott was a citizen of the United States. This ruling would determine if he was able to sue in federal court. Second, the Court had to decide if the time he had spent living on free soil made him free. Third, the Court had to decide whether the ban on slavery in parts of the Louisiana Purchase was constitutional. This last ruling would affect the Missouri Compromise.

The Chief Justice of the Supreme Court was **Roger B. Taney** (TAW-nee). Taney came from a slaveholding family in Maryland. He wrote the majority opinion in the ***Dred Scott* decision** in March 1857. Taney said the nation's founders believed that African Americans "had no rights which a white man was bound to respect." He therefore concluded that African Americans were not citizens under the U.S. Constitution. Thus, Dred Scott did not have the right to file suit in federal court.

Taney then said that living on free soil had not made Scott free. Thus, "his *status*, as free or slave, depended on the laws of Missouri." Finally, Taney said that the Missouri Compromise restriction on slavery north of 36°30' was unconstitutional. He used the Fifth Amendment as support. It said no one could "be deprived of life, liberty, or property without due process of law." Slaves were considered property, so Congress could not ban someone from taking slaves into a federal territory.

Most white southerners cheered the decision. It "covers every question regarding slavery and settles it in favor of the South," reported a Georgia newspaper. The ruling stunned many northerners. Republicans were particularly upset by the Court's ruling on the Missouri Compromise. Indeed, some northerners feared that the spread of slavery would not stop with the federal territories. Illinois lawyer **Abraham Lincoln** warned about the Court's future rulings.

History Makers Speak

"We shall *lie down* pleasantly dreaming that the people of *Missouri* are on the verge of [close to] making their state *free*; and we shall *awake* to the *reality*, instead, that the *Supreme* Court has made *Illinois* a *slave* state."

—Abraham Lincoln, from *The Collected Works of Abraham Lincoln*, edited by Roy P. Basler

✔ **Reading Check: Summarizing** What were the three key issues in the Supreme Court's ruling on the *Dred Scott* case? See the discussion in the third and fourth paragraphs above.

LEVEL 3: Have students imagine that they are newspaper reporters covering the *Dred Scott* case. Then have students write an interview they might have conducted with Scott in which they discuss why he sued for his freedom, the Supreme Court's decision, and Scott's reaction to it. Have volunteers share their interviews with the class.

HOMEWORK Have students imagine that they are abolitionists who have just read about the *Dred Scott* decision. Have them write letters to Chief Justice Taney explaining their objections to the decision.

☆ CLOSE

Ask students to make three vertical columns on a blank piece of paper with the following headings: *Democratic*, *Republican*, and *Whig*. Under each heading, have students briefly identify key members of each party, their views on slavery, and how the slavery issue affected the political fortunes of each party.

☆ The Lincoln-Douglas Debates

At the time of the *Dred Scott* decision, few people outside of Illinois knew Abraham Lincoln. A native of Kentucky, he had moved to the Midwest in 1816. Lincoln became involved in politics, serving four terms in the Illinois legislature and one term in Congress. A longtime Whig, he joined the Republican Party in 1856. He supported the party's efforts to halt the spread of slavery.

In 1858 Illinois Republicans nominated Lincoln for a U.S. Senate seat. His opponent was Democrat Stephen Douglas, who had represented Illinois in the Senate since 1847. Douglas was well known for the Kansas-Nebraska Act, so Lincoln tried to take advantage of his opponent's fame. He challenged Douglas to a series of debates throughout the state.

Thousands of people attended the **Lincoln-Douglas debates**. In each of the seven debates, Lincoln stressed that the central issue in the campaign involved slavery and its future in the West. Lincoln said that the Democrats wanted to spread slavery across the continent. As a Republican, Lincoln believed that slavery was wrong. Lincoln added that "one of the methods of treating it as a wrong is to make provision [ensure] that *it shall grow no larger*." Lincoln also said that African Americans were "entitled to all the natural rights" listed in the Declaration of Independence. He specifically named "the right to life, liberty, and the pursuit of happiness."

Some voters asked Lincoln about his views on racial equality. He replied that African Americans were not necessarily the political or social equals of whites. However, "in the right to eat the bread . . . which his own hand earns, he [an African American] *is my equal and the equal of Judge Douglas*." Douglas insisted that Lincoln "thinks that the Negro is his brother. . . . Those of you who believe that the Negro is your equal . . . of course will vote for Mr. Lincoln." Douglas hoped that these statements would shock many voters and cost Lincoln votes.

Research on the ROM

Free Find:
Stephen Douglas
After reading about Stephen Douglas on the **Holt Researcher CD–ROM**, imagine that you are hosting one of the Lincoln-Douglas debates. Write a speech that introduces Stephen Douglas to the crowd of spectators.

Interpreting the Visual Record

Political debate *The Lincoln-Douglas debates established the reputation of Abraham Lincoln as a gifted public speaker. In this painting of the fourth debate in the series, Lincoln is standing to speak and Stephen Douglas is seated to Lincoln's right.* **What is the mood of the politicians and audience members shown in this painting?**

☆ **REVIEW AND ASSESS**

Have students complete the **Section 3 Review** on p. 568. Then have students complete **Daily Quiz 18.3**. As **Alternative Assessment**, you may want to use the student's political party graphic organizer or Scott interviews in the section's lessons.

☆ **RETEACH**

Have students complete **Main Idea Activity for English Language Learners and Special-Needs Students 18.3**. Then ask students to make a list of the important people they have read about in this section. Have students explain how each person advanced or delayed the political dispute over slavery during this period. **ENGLISH LANGUAGE LEARNERS**

☆ **EXTEND**

Have students use the library to find additional information on the Lincoln-Douglas debates. Ask students to use their research to write a brief skit focusing on Americans' reactions the debates. Students should focus on each candidate's opinions about slavery, popular sovereignty, and state control versus federal control of slavery in the territories, and who supported each candidate. **BLOCK SCHEDULING**

Section 3 Review
ANSWERS

❶ Identify
• Republican Party, p. 564
• James Buchanan, p. 565

• John C. Frémont, p. 565

• Dred Scott, p. 566
• Roger B. Taney, p. 566
• *Dred Scott* decision, p. 566
• Abraham Lincoln, p. 566
• Lincoln-Douglas debates, p. 567
Freeport Doctrine, p. 568 8.31A

❷ Election of 1856—destroyed the Whig and Know-Nothing parties also fell apart because of internal conflicts over slavery; *Dred Scott* decision—southerners very happy and many northerners stunned; Lincoln-Douglas Debates—Lincoln warned against the extension of slavery and dangers of a divided country; Douglas believed people living in a territory should decide whether or not they wanted to allow slavery and that the country could exist half slave and half free

❸ a. it led some to form the Republican Party, hurt northern Democrats who voted for the bill, split Whigs into northern and southern groups who refused to work with each other, thereby killing the party

b. claimed that living on free soil for three years made him free; Court ruled that he was still a slave because African Americans were not citizens and therefore had no legal right to sue in federal court

❹ Students' letters will vary but should express the differing views on slavery.

Supporters of Stephen Douglas made this wooden campaign doll.

Douglas also criticized Lincoln for saying that the country could not remain "half slave and half free." He said that the Republicans wanted to make every state a free state. If this happened, he warned, it would only lead to "a dissolution [destruction] of the Union" and "warfare between the North and the South."

The second debate was held in the northern Illinois town of Freeport. At this meeting, Lincoln pointed out the difference between the Democrats' belief in popular sovereignty and the terms of the *Dred Scott* decision. He asked Douglas to explain how Congress could allow the citizens of a federal territory to ban slavery if Congress itself could not ban it. Douglas's response became known as the **Freeport Doctrine**. "It matters not" what the Supreme Court decides about slavery, responded Douglas.

 66The people have the lawful means [way] to introduce it or exclude it [shut it out] as they please, for the reason that slavery cannot exist a day or an hour anywhere, unless it is supported by local police regulations.**99**

—Stephen Douglas, quoted in *Stephen A. Douglas*, by Robert W. Johannsen

The Freeport Doctrine would put control of the slavery question back in the hands of American citizens. The doctrine helped Douglas win the Senate seat. However, Lincoln had made a strong showing in the debates. As a result, he became one of the important leaders of the new Republican Party.

✔ **Reading Check: Contrasting** How did Douglas oppose Lincoln's views on slavery and African Americans? Douglas tried to shock voters by saying Lincoln thought African Americans were his equals and accused Lincoln of trying to split the Union.

keyword: SA3 HP18

Section 3 Review

❶ Identify and explain:
• Republican Party
• James Buchanan
• John C. Frémont
• Dred Scott
• Roger B. Taney
• *Dred Scott* decision
• Abraham Lincoln
• Lincoln-Douglas debates
• Freeport Doctrine

❷ Analyzing Information Copy the chart below. Use it to identify examples of deepening political divisions caused by the slavery issue.

Event	Results
Election of 1856	
Dred Scott decision	
Lincoln-Douglas debates	

❸ Finding the Main Idea
a. How did different political parties respond to the Kansas-Nebraska Act?

b. What did Dred Scott claim made him free, and how did the Supreme Court rule in his case?

❹ Writing and Critical Thinking
Summarizing Imagine that you are an Illinois resident who attended the Lincoln-Douglas debates. Write a letter to a friend in another state explaining the candidates' views on the spread of slavery.

Consider the following:
• Lincoln's views on slavery and racial equality
• Douglas's response to Lincoln
• the Freeport Doctrine

Section 4

OBJECTIVES

⭐ Describe Americans' reactions to John Brown's raid on Harpers Ferry.

⭐ Analyze the factors that led to Lincoln's victory in the presidential election of 1860.

⭐ Examine the reasons why some southern states decided to leave the Union.

Section 4

Secession

Read to Discover

1. How did Americans react to John Brown's raid on Harpers Ferry?
2. What factors led to Lincoln's victory in the presidential election of 1860?
3. Why did some southern states decide to leave the Union?

WHY IT MATTERS TODAY

There is still diversity among the different regions of the United States. Use CNNfyi.com or other **current events** sources to identify issues or features that show these differences. Record your findings in your journal.

Define

• secession

Identify

• John Brown's raid
• John C. Breckinridge
• Constitutional Union Party
• John Bell
• John J. Crittenden
• Confederate States of America
• Jefferson Davis

The Story Continues

After the Pottawatomie Massacre, John Brown was a hunted man. He left Kansas and eventually returned to New England. There Brown was frustrated that most abolitionists wanted to end slavery without using violence. "Talk! talk! talk!" he said with disgust after attending a meeting of the New England Anti-Slavery Society. "That will never free the slaves. What is needed is action—action."

John Brown believed that violence was the only way to end slavery.

⭐ The Raid on Harpers Ferry

In 1858 John Brown worked to start a slave uprising. He wanted to attack the federal arsenal, or military storehouse, in Virginia and seize the weapons stored there. He then planned to arm the slaves in the surrounding area. Brown was prepared to take hostages or kill any white southerners who stood in the way. He urged his fellow abolitionists to give him enough money to recruit, train, and supply a small army. However, after nearly two years of preparation, Brown's band had about 20 men, including three of his sons and himself.

On the night of October 16, 1859, **John Brown's raid** began. Brown and his men entered Harpers Ferry, Virginia. The town lay next to the Potomac River, about 55 miles northwest of Washington, D.C. Brown

★ TEACH

Have students read Section 4 and complete Guided Reading Strategy 18.4. Choose one or more of the following activities to explore the section content with students. For further suggestions on block scheduling or team teaching, see the *Block Scheduling Handbook with Team Teaching Strategies.*

LEVEL 1: Ask students to imagine that they are southerners and that Lincoln has just been elected to the presidency. Ask students to think about why they do not want Lincoln to be president and what they are afraid will happen as a result of his election. Then have students create posters to share their views. Use students' posters to begin a class discussion on why most southern states decided to leave the Union. **ENGLISH LANGUAGE LEARNERS**

★ Biography

John Brown. John Brown was born in 1800 in the city of Torrington, Connecticut. Twice married, he had a total of 20 children. Brown tried his hand at several businesses, including hide tanning and sheepherding, but never succeeded. While he lived in Pennsylvania during the 1820s, his barn served as a way station for escaped slaves on the Underground Railroad. Brown moved his family many times before finally arriving in Kansas in 1855. After his experiences in Kansas, his friends noted that Brown had become obsessed with the fight against slavery.

CRITICAL THINKING

What does Brown's willingness to use his property as a way station for escaped slaves on the Underground Railroad reveal?

ANSWER: Students might suggest that Brown had a strong interest in abolition well before the events in Kansas.

Technology Resources

American Music Selection 14: "John Brown's Body"

GLOBAL CONNECTIONS ANSWER

Students might suggest that the extreme emotion displayed by each side may have convinced Hugo that the two sides would never agree on whether slavery should be allowed.

GLOBAL CONNECTIONS

Reactions to John Brown's Raid

News of the raid on Harpers Ferry raised strong emotions across the Atlantic, particularly in Great Britain. British politician William Edward Forster expressed his views. "Whatever John Brown may have done toward freeing the slaves . . . he has exposed the utter [complete] weakness of the slave system." Other Europeans also praised Brown and the abolitionist cause.

In early 1860 the French writer Victor Hugo made a prediction. He thought that Brown's execution would lead to the breakup of the United States. "Between the North and the South stands the gallows of Brown," Hugo wrote. "Union is no longer possible: such a crime cannot be shared." **Why might Victor Hugo have said that Brown's raid would lead to the breakup of the Union?**

John Brown, shown here kissing an African American child, was led to his execution on December 2, 1859.

THE METROPOLITAN MUSEUM OF ART

first took over the federal arsenal. Then he sent several of his men into the countryside to get slaves to come to Harpers Ferry.

Brown hoped enslaved African Americans would join him. None did. They most likely knew they would be severely punished if they were caught taking part in an uprising. Instead, white southerners from Harpers Ferry and the surrounding area armed themselves and attacked Brown. Eight of his men and three local men were killed in the exchange of gunfire. Brown and some of his followers retreated to the safety of a firehouse.

Federal troops arrived in Harpers Ferry on the night of October 17. The following morning Colonel Robert E. Lee ordered a squad of marines to storm the firehouse. In a matter of seconds, the marines killed two more of Brown's men. They captured the rest—including Brown.

★ Judging John Brown

Brown was quickly charged and convicted of treason, murder, and conspiracy to stir up slave rebellion. Some of the men who took part in the raid received death sentences. On the way to his execution, John Copeland—a fugitive slave—defended his actions. "If I am dying for freedom, I could not die for a better cause—I had rather die than be a slave!" On November 2, convinced that he also would be sentenced to death by the state of Virginia. Brown delivered a memorable speech.

History Makers Speak
❝It is unjust that I should suffer such a penalty. . . . I believe that to have interfered . . . in behalf of His [God's] despised [hated] poor, is no wrong, but right. Now, if it is deemed [thought] necessary that I should forfeit [give up] my life for the furtherance of the ends of justice, and mingle [mix] my blood . . . with the blood of millions in this slave country whose rights are disregarded by wicked, cruel, and unjust enactments, I say, let it be done.❞
—John Brown, quoted in *John Brown, 1800–1859,* by Oswald Garrison Villard

As expected, the judge ordered Brown to be hanged. The sentence was carried out a month later, on December 2, 1859.

Many people in the North mourned the death of John Brown. Novelist Louisa May Alcott referred to him as "Saint John the Just." Not everyone who opposed slavery supported Brown's actions, however. Abraham Lincoln said Brown "agreed with us in thinking slavery wrong." He continued, "That cannot excuse violence, bloodshed, and treason." Most southern whites—including slaveholders and non-slaveholders—felt threatened. White southerners worried that a "John Brown the Second" might attack another southern target. One South Carolina newspaper wrote about these fears. "We are convinced the safety of the South lies only outside the present Union." Another journal from the same state was more blunt: "The sooner we get out of the Union, the better."

✔ **Reading Check: Summarizing** How did northerners differ in their reactions to John Brown's raid and execution? Many northerners supported Brown's actions and mourned his death, while some northerners such as Lincoln believed Brown's use of violence was wrong.

ALL LEVELS Copy the following graphic organizer onto the chalkboard, omitting the italicized answers. Ask students to complete the chart with events and attitudes that became important factors in Lincoln's election to the presidency in 1860. **ENGLISH LANGUAGE LEARNERS**

Factors in Support of Lincoln in 1860	Factors against Support of Lincoln in 1860
• *Democratic Party split in two.* • *Constitutional Union Party formed and elected a presidential candidate.* • *Breckinridge and Bell split the electoral votes of the slave states.*	• *Seward was the leading Republican candidate.* • *Lincoln did not win the nomination until the third ballot.*

Population Distribution in 1860

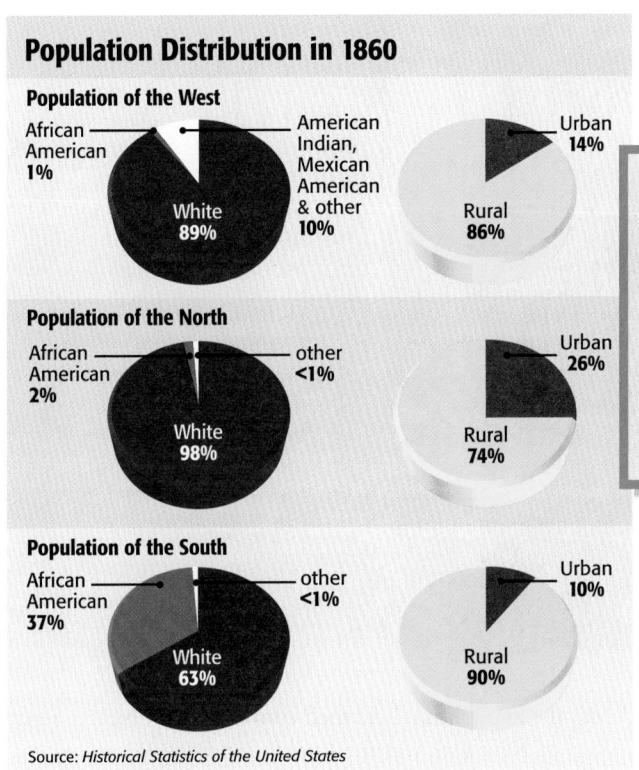

Population of the West

African American 1%
White 89%
American Indian, Mexican American & other 10%

Urban 14%
Rural 86%

Population of the North

African American 2%
White 98%
other <1%

Urban 26%
Rural 74%

Population of the South

African American 37%
White 63%
other <1%

Urban 10%
Rural 90%

Source: *Historical Statistics of the United States*

Interpreting Graphs The vast majority of people in each region lived in rural areas.

Skills Assessment

1. **Human Systems** Which region had the highest percentage of urban residents?
2. **Comparing** Which regions of the country were predominantly white and rural?

★ The Election of 1860

In this mood of distrust, Americans prepared for another presidential election. The Democrats were the first party to meet to nominate a presidential candidate in 1860. They met in Charleston, South Carolina, in late April. Yet the northern and southern members of the party could not agree on a candidate. When they could not agree, the party split in two. The Democrats met again six weeks later in Baltimore. Northern Democrats chose Senator Stephen Douglas. Southern Democrats backed the current vice president, **John C. Breckinridge** of Kentucky. Breckinridge strongly supported slavery in the territories. He did not believe, however, that a Republican victory in the election would give states the right to break up the Union.

Meanwhile, in early May some northerners and southerners—many of them former Whigs—decided to form a new political party. Called the **Constitutional Union Party**, its platform was simple. It recognized "no political principles other than the Constitution of the country, the Union of the states, and the enforcement of the laws." Members of this new party also met in Baltimore, Maryland. They selected **John Bell** of Tennessee as their presidential candidate. Bell was a slaveholder, but he had been against the Kansas-Nebraska Act in 1854.

★ Citizenship

Constitutional Union Party. The Constitutional Union Party claimed that because platforms "have had the effect to mislead and deceive the people, and at the same time to widen the political divisions of the country," it would release only a brief platform. In fact, party members hoped to unify the country by rising above the slavery dispute. This strategy was popular in the Upper South. Party candidate John Bell won the states of Kentucky, Tennessee, and Virginia. However, after the outbreak of the Civil War the party disintegrated.

ACTIVITY: Have students research the Constitutional Union Party and write a sample platform for the party.

Technology Resources

American History Interactive Maps CD–ROM: Balancing Political Power

GRAPH ANSWERS
1. the north
2. all of the regions

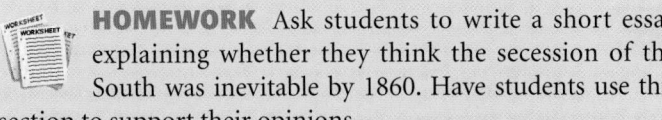

HOMEWORK Ask students to write a short essay explaining whether they think the secession of the South was inevitable by 1860. Have students use this section to support their opinions.

TEACHER TO TEACHER

Pat Tobbe of Louisville, Kentucky, suggested the following activity:

LEVEL 2: Have students create a time line describing events between 1848 and 1860 that contributed to the growing division in the nation. Ask them to use one color to represent events that angered, disturbed, or caused controversy among abolitionists and northerners and another color to represent events that angered slavery proponents and southerners.

★ Economics

The Tariff Issue. Slavery was not the only issue that divided northerners and southerners in the presidential election of 1860. Northerners and southerners also held vastly different views on economic issues. Northerners favored a national bank, internal improvements, a federally funded transcontinental railroad, and free-labor and free-market systems. Southerners opposed these measures, believing that they would disrupt their plantation economic system and lifestyle. Republicans also favored a high protective tariff for manufacturers. This appealed to northern industrialists. Indeed, the Morrill Tariff of 1861 raised the prices of foreign goods, while allowing American manufacturers to raise their prices as well.

ACTIVITY: Use newspapers or other current events sources to discover what tariffs the federal government supports today.

DAILY LIFE ANSWER
Students might suggest that they hoped to eventually gain the right to vote.

THE GRANGER COLLECTION, NEW YORK

Daily Life

Political parties Crowds gathered at the 1860 Republican National Convention, the second time the Republicans had fielded a presidential candidate. The 1850s had seen the rise and fall of several political parties as Americans struggled to address the slavery issue. The Free-Soil, Know-Nothing, and Whig Parties had all collapsed or been greatly weakened during this period. Shortly before the Republican convention met, yet another political party—the Constitutional Union Party—had formed. Voters thus faced many choices but seemingly few solutions to the divisions that plagued the nation. Why do you think women would have attended the Republican convention although they did not yet have the right to vote?

In mid-May the Republicans held their convention in Chicago. Senator William Seward of New York was the leading candidate. However, many Republicans worried that his strong antislavery views made him a poor choice. Thus, Abraham Lincoln won the nomination on the third ballot. Lincoln was a moderate who was against the spread of slavery. He said, however, that he would not try to abolish slavery where it already existed.

The four-man election contest was really a pair of two-man contests. Lincoln challenged Douglas for the North's electoral votes. Bell and Breckinridge competed for those of the South. Douglas, Bell, and Breckinridge each knew he might not win the election. However, they hoped to win enough votes to prevent Lincoln from winning in the electoral college. Such an outcome would send the election to the House of Representatives.

In this they failed. Lincoln won the race. Although he gained less than 40 percent of the overall popular vote, he won 180 of the 183 electoral votes in the free states. Breckinridge and Bell split the electoral votes of slave states, with the exception of Missouri. Douglas had the second-highest number of overall popular votes. However, he won only one state—Missouri—outright. He finished with just 12 electoral votes. The election results angered many southerners. Lincoln did not carry a single southern state, yet he would be the next president. This election was a strong reminder of how the South was losing its political power on the national level.

✔ **Reading Check: Finding the Main Idea** How did Lincoln and the Republican Party win the presidential election of 1860? Lincoln won nearly all the electoral votes in the free states, while Breckinridge and Bell split the electoral votes in the slave states, giving Lincoln a majority.

LEVEL 3: Explain to students that Americans had various reactions to John Brown's raid on Harpers Ferry, based on their moral interpretations of the events and of slavery in general. Assign students different regions of the country and have them write emotional speeches that might have been given in their region regarding Harpers Ferry. Ask volunteers to read their speeches to the class. After each speech is finished, have students from a different region of the country challenge the speaker.

 **SPOTLIGHT**
on the Election of 1860
Have students create a mock up of the front pages of four newspapers describing the results of the election of 1860. The newspapers should be from four different regions or states, and each should support a different candidate.
BLOCK SCHEDULING

Breaking with the Union

Many southern whites believed that once in power, Lincoln would move to abolish slavery in the South. They feared this action would destroy the South's economy and society. Lincoln insisted he would not change slavery in the southern states. He had said, however, that slavery had to end at some point in the future. That was enough to greatly concern many southerners. A man in Mississippi urged white southerners to act quickly to protect their interests. "Let us rally . . . before the enemy can make good his promise to overwhelm us."

Just four days after Lincoln's election, South Carolina's legislature called for a special convention. There delegates met to consider the question of **secession**, the act of formally withdrawing from the Union. The convention opened in Charleston on December 17, 1860. After three days of speeches, all of the delegates voted to secede. They wanted to dissolve "the union now subsisting [existing] between South Carolina and other States."

The Constitution does not directly address the issue of secession. Therefore, southerners who wanted to secede believed that there was no constitutional barrier to a state leaving the Union. They pointed out that each of the original states had voluntarily joined the Union. Each of these states had held a special state convention to ratify the Constitution. Surely, southerners reasoned, states could also leave the Union by the same process.

This banner supports Republican candidates Abraham Lincoln and Hannibal Hamlin.

MAP ANSWERS
1. New York, Lincoln
2. Douglas

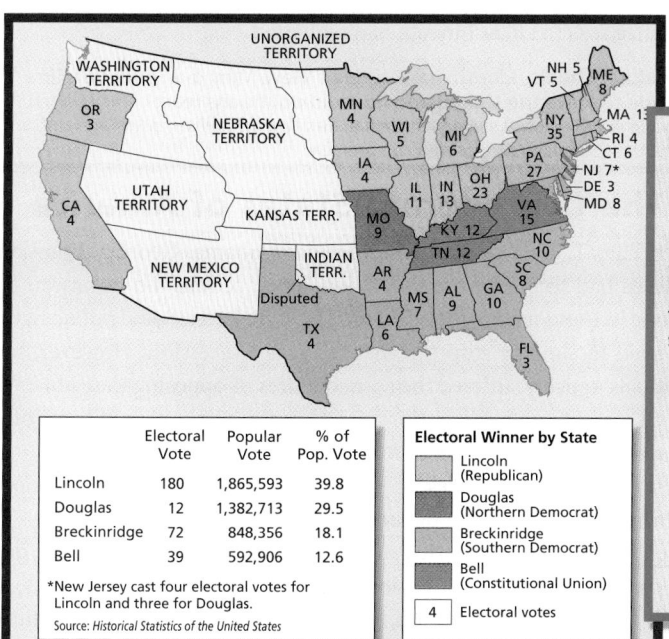

The Election of 1860

Interpreting Maps The division between North and South was clearly reflected in the election of 1860. Lincoln's victory increased tensions between the regions, and secession soon followed.

Skills Assessment

1. **Places and Regions** Which state had the most electoral votes, and which candidate won this state?
2. **Analyzing Information** Which candidates finished second to Lincoln in the electoral and popular votes?

	Electoral Vote	Popular Vote	% of Pop. Vote
Lincoln	180	1,865,593	39.8
Douglas	12	1,382,713	29.5
Breckinridge	72	848,356	18.1
Bell	39	592,906	12.6

*New Jersey cast four electoral votes for Lincoln and three for Douglas.
Source: Historical Statistics of the United States

Electoral Winner by State
- Lincoln (Republican)
- Douglas (Northern Democrat)
- Breckinridge (Southern Democrat)
- Bell (Constitutional Union)
- 4 Electoral votes

Assign each student a border or a Confederate state. Then have them use the library to find information on the secession movement in that assigned state. Ask students to determine the issues at stake and to find out how the decision regarding secession was made. Then organize a meeting of leaders from the assigned states. In that meeting, have students act as representatives of the states they researched and explain the states' reasons for remaining in the Union or seceding.

BLOCK SCHEDULING

⚝ CLOSE

Ask students to speculate on what would have happened had President-elect Lincoln urged acceptance of the Crittenden Compromise. Ask students to predict how such an agreement would have affected secession of the southern states and the slavery issue in general. Have students write scripts for short films or plays based on the above situation.

CONNECTING TO MATH ANSWERS

1. 39
2. Students' graphs should correctly illustrate the statistics.
3. Students' speeches will vary.

★ ★ ★ ★ ★ ★ ★ ★ ★

Section 4 Review ANSWERS

❶ **Define**
• secession, p. 573

❷ **Identify**
• John Brown's raid, p. 569
• John C. Breckinridge, p. 571
• Constitutional Union Party, p. 571
• John Bell, p. 571
• John J. Crittenden, p. 574
• Confederate States of America, p. 574
• Jefferson Davis, p. 574

❸ fear of another event like John Brown's raid; Lincoln's election as president and fears that he would abolish slavery

❹ a. many in the North mourned the death of John Brown and revered him, Southern whites felt threatened
b. other candidates split the electoral votes in the South, assuring Lincoln a victory when he won almost all the northern states' electoral votes

❺ Students' speeches will vary but should discuss southern secession.

CONNECTING TO
MATH

Just the Facts

Slave and Free States in Congress

Number of Representatives

Year	Slave states	Free states
1820	90	113
1830	99	125
1840	88	114
1850	89	118
1860	84	123

Source: *Historical Statistics of the United States*

Using Mathematical Skills

1. What was the largest gap between representatives of free and slave states?

2. Create a line graph that illustrates the statistics in the chart above. Label the *x*-axis "Number of Representatives," and label the *y*-axis "Year."

3. Imagine that you are a southern politician in 1860. Write a speech describing the trend that has taken place in the House between 1820 and 1860 and what it means to southern politics.

Critics of secession flatly rejected this idea. President Buchanan said that the Union was not "a mere voluntary association of States, to be dissolved at pleasure by any one of the contracting parties." President-elect Abraham Lincoln agreed. He said, "No State, upon its own mere motion, can lawfully get out of the Union." Lincoln added, 'They can only do so against [the] law, and by revolution."

While South Carolina representatives were meeting, Congress reviewed a plan to preserve the Union. Senator **John J. Crittenden** of Kentucky proposed a series of constitutional amendments to satisfy the South. One would extend the line created by the Missouri Compromise to the Pacific coast. It would allow slavery in all territories "now held, or hereafter acquired" south of this line. Another would use federal money to pay slaveholders who could not recover their fugitive slaves in the North. Crittenden hoped his plan would address the chief fears of slaveholders. He also hoped that the country would avoid secession and a civil war.

President-elect Lincoln did not agree with this plan. To express his views, he sent many letters to Republicans in the Senate. In these letters he asked Congress to vote against Crittenden's plan. "Entertain [consider] no proposition for a compromise in regard to the extension of slavery," Lincoln wrote. "The tug has to come and better now than later." A Senate committee voted on the Crittenden Compromise. Every Republican on the committee rejected it, as Lincoln had requested.

✔ **Reading Check: Identifying Points of View** Why did South Carolina decide to leave the Union, and how did politicians react? They feared that Lincoln would abolish slavery. Buchanan and Lincoln said secession was unconstitutional; Crittenden proposed a compromise.

★ The Confederate States of America

By February 1, 1861, Mississippi, Florida, Alabama, Georgia, Louisiana, and Texas had seceded from the Union. Their actions did not mean that everyone in these states supported secession, however. Some public figures even tried to slow or stop the march toward secession. However, such individuals quickly suffered the consequences of opposing the public will. In Texas, for example, Governor Sam Houston was removed from office for standing in the way of secession.

On February 4, delegates from six of the seven seceding states met in the town of Montgomery, Alabama. They established a new nation—the **Confederate States of America**, also known as the Confederacy. The delegates passed their new constitution on February 8. The document closely resembled the U.S. Constitution in many ways. However, the constitution of the Confederacy guaranteed that its citizens could hold slaves.

their groups' answers to the entire class.

★ REVIEW AND ASSESS

Have students complete the **Section 4 Review** on p. 575. Then have students complete **Daily Quiz 18.4.** As **Alternative Assessment,** you may want to use the time lines or Lincoln election graphic organizer from this section's lessons.

★ RETEACH

Have students complete **Main Idea Activity for English Language Learners and Special-Needs Students 18.4.** Then organize students into small groups. Ask groups to re-read the objectives at the beginning of this section. Have each group discuss the objectives in round-robin style, with one student in each group recording the answers. Then have recorders read their groups' answers to the entire class.

ENGLISH LANGUAGE LEARNERS , COOPERATIVE LEARNING

★ EXTEND

Assign each student a border or a Confederate state. Have them use the library to research the secession movement in that state. Ask students to determine the issues at stake within the assigned state and to find out how the decision regarding secession was made. Then organize a meeting of the provisional government of the Confederate States of America. In the meeting, have students act as representatives of the states they researched and explain the states' reasons for leaving the Union.

BLOCK SCHEDULING

<u>Jefferson Davis</u> of Mississippi was elected president of the Confederate States of America. Alexander H. Stephens of Georgia became vice president. Davis was a graduate of West Point and a veteran of the Mexican War. He had been secretary of war under President Pierce and had served in the Senate until Mississippi left the Union. Davis had opposed secession as late as 1860, although he believed that states had the right to secede. But his loyalty to the South outweighed his hopes for peace. With his military background, Davis hoped to be appointed general in command of Mississippi's troops. He did not seek the presidency of the Confederacy. He greeted the news of his election with silence. Davis's wife, Varina, wrote about his reaction.

❝He looked so grieved that I feared some evil had befallen [happened to] our family. After a few minutes' painful silence he told me [what the telegram contained], as a man might speak of a sentence of death.❞

—Varina Davis, *Jefferson Davis: A Memoir*

Davis was a highly intelligent and hardworking politician. He also was very loyal to his friends. However, he tended to involve himself in details that would have been better left to his staff. Furthermore, his devotion to his friends often clouded his judgment. These personal qualities would increase the difficulty of the challenges he would face as president of the Confederacy.

As an officer during the Mexican War, Jefferson Davis had led U.S. forces to victory in the Battle of Buena Vista.

THE GRANGER COLLECTION, NEW YORK

✔ **Reading Check: Summarizing** What did the seceding states do in 1860 and 1861 after leaving the Union? formed the Confederate States of America, wrote a new constitution closely modeled on the U.S. Constitution, elected Jefferson Davis president

---

Section 4 Review

Homework Practice Online
keyword: SA3 HP18

1 **Define** and explain:
• secession

2 **Identify** and explain:
• John Brown's raid
• John C. Breckinridge
• Constitutional Union Party
• John Bell
• John J. Crittenden
• Confederate States of America
• Jefferson Davis

3 **Summarizing** Copy the graphic organizer below. Use it to identify the causes of the secession of southern states in 1860 and 1861.

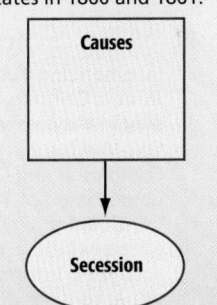

4 **Finding the Main Idea**
a. Describe the northern and southern reactions to John Brown's raid on Harpers Ferry.

b. How did the four-way race for president help Lincoln win the election of 1860?

5 **Writing and Critical Thinking**
Supporting a Point of View Imagine that you are a foreign ambassador witnessing the conflicts over slavery in the United States. Write a speech for your home country that responds to South Carolina's secession from the Union.

Consider the following:
• reasons for secession
• whether or not the Constitution mentions secession
• your support for or opposition to South Carolina's secession

---

REPRODUCIBLE

▶ Vocabulary Activity 18

TECHNOLOGY

▶ Chapter 18 Test Generator
(on the One-Stop Planner)

▶ Global Skill Builder
CD–ROM

▶ HRW Go site

**REINFORCEMENT,
REVIEW, AND
ASSESSMENT**

▶ Chapter 18 Review,
pp. 575–77

▶ Chapter 18 Tutorial
for Students, Parents,
Mentors, and Peers

▶ Chapter 18 Test
(Form A or B)

▶ Alternative Assessment
Handbook

▶ Chapter 18 Test for English
Language Learners and
Special-Needs Students

★ **REVIEW**

Have students complete the
Chapter 18 Review on pages
576–77.

★ **ASSESS**

Use one of the chapter tests to
assess students' understanding
of the content. For **Alternative
Assessment,** see the **Alternative
Assessment Handbook.**

**Understanding
Main Ideas**

1. 1) admit California as a slave
state; 2) organize rest of Mexican
Cession as a federal territory in
which popular sovereignty would
decide the slavery question;
3) Texas would give up claim
to land east of the Rio Grande
and the federal government would
assume Texas's debt; 4) end to
slave trade in the nation's capital; 5) more effective fugitive
slave law

2. free—were threatened with
being sent South without a fair
trial, many moved to Canada
to escape the law;
enslaved—made successful
escapes more difficult

3. Both pro-slavery and antislavery forces formed their own governments, while some from both
sides turned to violence.

4. created to represent antislavery groups and was primarily an
antislavery power

5. Lincoln—Republican,
Douglas—northern Democrats,
Breckinridge—southern
Democrats, Bell—Constitutional
Union Party

6. election of Lincoln, fear of
growing northern political influence, and fear that slavery would
be restricted or abolished

**You Be the Historian—
Reviewing Themes**

1. Americans had to determine
the status of slavery in the new
region

Chapter **18** Review

The Chapter at a Glance

Examine the visual summary of the chapter below. Make notes about each topic
listed in the image. Then use the notes to create a simple board game to be played
with a partner. Each player must explain the topics he or she lands on to continue
proceeding along the "pathway to secession."

The Balance
Is Broken

Secession

Northern Complaints

Southern Complaints

• Fugitive Slave Act
• Kansas-Nebraska Act
• "Bleeding Kansas"
• Dred Scott decision
• Westward expansion
of slavery

• Uncle Tom's Cabin
• "Bleeding Kansas"
• John Brown's raid
• Lincoln's election
• Growing power of
the North

The United States   of America

Compromise
of 1850

Identifying People and Ideas

Use the following terms or people in historically
significant sentences.

1. sectionalism
2. Free-Soil Party
3. Daniel Webster
4. Stephen Douglas
5. Republican Party
6. Dred Scott
7. John Brown's raid
8. secession
9. Confederate States of
America
10. Jefferson Davis

Understanding Main Ideas

Section 1 *(Pages 552–558)*

1. What were the parts of the Compromise of 1850?
2. How did the Fugitive Slave Act affect free and
enslaved African Americans?

Section 2 *(Pages 559–563)*

3. How did pro-slavery and antislavery forces
oppose each other in Kansas?

Section 3 *(Pages 564–568)*

4. Why was the Republican Party created, and what
goals did it promote?

Section 4 *(Pages 569–575)*

5. How did each of the four presidential candidates
in 1860 view the slavery issue?

6. What led many of the southern states to leave
the Union?

You Be the Historian—
Reviewing Themes

1. **Geography** Why did the Mexican Cession renew
tensions about slavery between northern and
southern states?
2. **Citizenship** How did the *Dred Scott* decision
affect African Americans, and what was the
response to the decision?
3. **Constitutional Heritage** What legal argument did
South Carolina's officials use to justify secession?

Thinking Critically

1. **Summarizing** What roles did the politicians
John C. Calhoun, Henry Clay, and Daniel Webster
play in the compromise efforts prior to the
Civil War?
2. **Comparing and Contrasting** How were the
Compromise of 1850 and the Missouri
Compromise similar, and how were they
different?
3. **Analyzing Information** How did both congressional conflicts and efforts to compromise
contribute to greater divisions within the
United States?

★ RETEACH

Have students create a list of what they consider to be the five most important events leading to the South's secession and the five most important people involved with these events. Have volunteers share their lists with the class.

ENGLISH LANGUAGE LEARNERS

Portfolio Extensions

American History

1. Cooperative Learning

Organize students into groups. Ask them to imagine that they are publishers in the 1850s. Tell them that they have been hired to promote one of the works of abolitionist literature popular in the northern United States. Then ask each group to create a poster to advertise one of these works. Possibilities include *Narrative of the Life of Frederick Douglass*, the *Narrative of Sojourner Truth*, or *Uncle Tom's Cabin*. Remind groups that their poster should clearly state what the work is about. It should explain why people would want to buy and read the book.

2. Linking to Community
Tell students that many northerners and southerners held strong beliefs about the expansion of slavery. Activists in their community also hold strong beliefs and work hard to promote them. Ask students to choose a community leader in their town or region to interview about an issue such as education or public services. Ask volunteers to present their interviews to the class.

Social Studies Skills Workshop

Interpreting Maps

Study the map below. Then use the information on the map to help you answer the following questions.

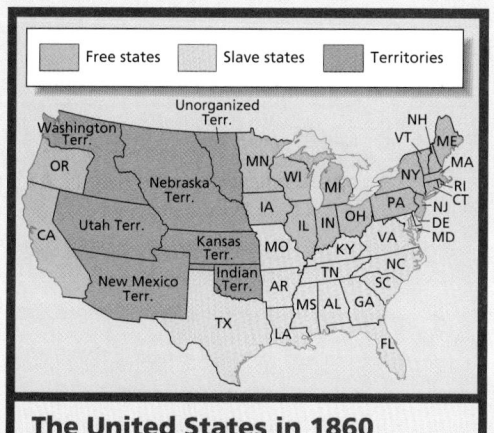

The United States in 1860

1. How many slave states and free states were there in 1860?
   a. 13 slave states, 20 free states
   b. 15 slave states, 16 free states
   c. 14 slaves states, 18 free states
   d. 15 slave states, 18 free states

2. What would the total number of senators have been for the slave states and for the free states in 1860?
   a. 30 and 36
   b. 28 and 36
   c. 30 and 34
   d. 30 and 32

3. Based on the map and your knowledge of the period, where do you think southern politicians hoped to add additional slave states to the Union?

Analzying Primary Sources

Read the following quote by a reader of Harriet Beecher Stowe's *Uncle Tom's Cabin* and answer the questions that follow.

❝My Dear Mrs. Stowe,—I sat up last night until long after one o'clock, reading and finishing "Uncle Tom's Cabin." I *could not* leave it any more than I could have left a dying child. . . . I thought I was a thoroughgoing abolitionist before, but your book has awakened so strong a feeling of indignation and of compassion that I seem never to have had *any* feeling on this subject till now. But what can we do? Alas! Alas! what *can* we do?❞

4. Which of the following statements best describes the letter writer's feelings about *Uncle Tom's Cabin*?
   a. The criticism of slavery offended her greatly and made her angry.
   b. The book made her want to do even more to try to abolish slavery.
   c. The book changed her mind about slavery, which had not bothered her before.
   d. The book does not matter because nobody can do anything about slavery.

5. Based on your knowledge of the period, why would such reactions to *Uncle Tom's Cabin* have been important to the relationship between the North and the South?

2. It argued that African Americans were not citizens. Abolitionists were outraged, and some thought that the decision would allow slavery to spread.

3. The states had voluntarily joined the Union, so they could voluntarily leave it.

Thinking Critically

1. Students' responses will vary but should include information from the textbook.

2. Similar—both tried to resolve conflicts over the expansion of slavery in western territories. Different—the Missouri Compromise outlawed slavery in some territories and permitted it in others, while the Compromise of 1850 did not automatically outlaw slavery in any territory.

3. Students' responses will vary, but each disagreement, such as the Wilmot Proviso or the Brooks beating, divided extremists on both sides. Each compromise upset northern republicans and abolitionists, who felt the South was bullying the North.

Skills Workshop

1. d

2. a

3. the West in general and the Kansas Territory in particular

4. b

5. Students should note that the book stirred greater support for abolition in the North and angered many southerners.

Alternative Assessment

American History

Building Your Portfolio

Cooperative Learning
As a group, prepare a chart showing the political parties that were formed from 1848 to 1860. The chart should include information on the year the party was formed (and ended, if applicable), the party's platform, presidential candidates, and region of strongest support. Add appropriate images to your chart and write a paragraph to explain the importance of third parties in political elections.

⬛ internet connect

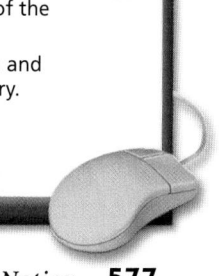

Internet Activity: go.hrw.com
keyword: SA3 CF18

Choose a topic on the Divided Nation to:
- Understand the causes and effects of the European revolutions of 1848.
- Create a newspaper on John Brown and resistance movements against slavery.
- Research Supreme Court decisions regarding slavery.

19 The Civil War

CHAPTER RESOURCE MANAGER

Objectives	Pacing Guide	Reproducible Resources
SECTION 1: **The War Begins** (pp. 580–84) ★ Describe what led to the bombardment of Fort Sumter and explain why this event was important. ★ Identify which side of the conflict Arkansas and the Upper South joined and explain why. ★ Explain why both the North and the South wanted to claim the border states. ★ Analyze the strategies each side followed at the beginning of the war.	**Regular** 2 days **Block Scheduling** 1 day *Block Scheduling Handbook with Team Teaching Strategies, Chapter 19*	**RS** Guided Reading Strategy 19.1 **PS** American History Political Cartoon 10: Secession
SECTION 2: **The War in the East** (pp. 585–89) ★ Identify the battles that the Confederates won in Virginia, and analyze why they were important. ★ Explain what stopped the northward advance of the Confederate army. ★ Examine the significance of the *Monitor* and the *Virginia*.	**Regular** 2 days **Block Scheduling** 1 day *Block Scheduling Handbook with Team Teaching Strategies, Chapter 19*	**RS** Guided Reading Strategy 19.2 **PS** American History Political Cartoon 11: Changing Union Leadership **PS** Literature Reading 19: Miss Ravenel's Conversion from Secession to Loyalty
SECTION 3: **The War in the West** (pp. 590–93) ★ Examine General Ulysses S. Grant's strategy for the Union army in the West. ★ Explain why the fall of Vicksburg, Mississippi, was important. ★ Describe the fighting that took place in the Far West.	**Regular** 2 days **Block Scheduling** 1 day *Block Scheduling Handbook with Team Teaching Strategies, Chapter 19*	**RS** Guided Reading Strategy 19.3 **PS** Primary Source Reading 19: A Confederate Girl's Diary **SM** Geography Activity 19: The Siege of Vicksburg
SECTION 4: **Life during the War** (pp. 594–99) ★ Determine how different groups in the North reacted to Abraham Lincoln's Emancipation Proclamation. ★ Identify the ways that African Americans and women contributed to the war effort. ★ Explain how northerners and southerners responded to the new draft laws.	**Regular** 2 days **Block Scheduling** 1 day *Block Scheduling Handbook with Team Teaching Strategies, Chapter 19*	**RS** Guided Reading Strategy 19.4 **PS** American History Political Cartoon 12: Copperheads **PS** Biography Reading 19: Clara Barton **E** Hands-On History Activity: A Song for Your Community, Region, or State
SECTION 5: **The Tide of the War Turns** (pp. 600–05) ★ Examine why the Battle of Gettysburg was important. ★ Identify the campaigns that were launched in Virginia and the Lower South. ★ Explain how and when the war finally ended.	**Regular** 2 days **Block Scheduling** 1 day *Block Scheduling Handbook with Team Teaching Strategies, Chapter 19*	**RS** Guided Reading Strategy 19.5 **RS** Graphic Organizer 19: Civil War Battles **E** Creative Teaching Strategy: Predicting Consequences

Chapter Resource Key

PS	Primary Sources	**A**	Assessment	Music	
RS	Reading Support	**REV**	Review	Video	
IC	Interdisciplinary Connections	**ELL**	Reinforcement and English Language Learners	 Internet	
E	Enrichment		Transparencies	 Holt Presentation Maker Using Microsoft® PowerPoint®	
SM	Skills Mastery		CD–ROM		

 One-Stop Planner CD-ROM

See the *One-Stop Planner* for a complete list of additional resources for students and teachers.

One-Stop Planner CD–ROM

It's easy to plan lessons, select resources, and print out materials for your students when you use the *One-Stop Planner CD–ROM with Test Generator.*

Technology Resources	Reinforcement, Review, and Assessment

Technology Resources

- One-Stop Planner, Lesson 19.1
- American History Simulations CD–ROM: Global Politics and the Civil War
- Homework Practice Online

Reinforcement, Review, and Assessment

- REV Section 1 Review, p. 584
- A Daily Quiz 19.1
- ELL Main Idea Activity 19.1
- ELL English Audio Summary 19.1
- ELL Spanish Audio Summary 19.1

- One-Stop Planner, Lesson 19.2
- American Music Selection 13: "All Quiet Along the Potomac"
- Everyday Life in America Transparency 12: Photograph of Civil War Casualties
- Homework Practice Online

- REV Section 2 Review, p. 589
- A Daily Quiz 19.2
- ELL Main Idea Activity 19.2
- ELL English Audio Summary 19.2
- ELL Spanish Audio Summary 19.2

- One-Stop Planner, Lesson 19.3
- Linking Geography and History Transparency 14: The War in the East and the West, 1861–1863
- Homework Practice Online

- REV Section 3 Review, p. 593
- A Daily Quiz 19.3
- ELL Main Idea Activity 19.3
- ELL English Audio Summary 19.3
- ELL Spanish Audio Summary 19.3

- One-Stop Planner, Lesson 19.4
- Exploring America's Past Video Segment: A Country Torn Apart; Teacher's Guide, pp. 30–32
- Holt Researcher: American History CD–ROM
- CNN. Presents America: Yesterday and Today, Beginnings to 1914 Segment: Clara Barton and the Legacy of War
- Homework Practice Online
- HRW Go site

- REV Section 4 Review, p. 599
- A Daily Quiz 19.4
- ELL Main Idea Activity 19.4
- ELL English Audio Summary 19.4
- ELL Spanish Audio Summary 19.4

- One-Stop Planner, Lesson 19.5
- Art in American History Transparency 13: Near Andersonville
- Holt Researcher: American History CD–ROM
- Homework Practice Online
- HRW Go site

- REV Section 5 Review, p. 605
- A Daily Quiz 19.5
- ELL Main Idea Activity 19.5
- ELL English Audio Summary 19.5
- ELL Spanish Audio Summary 19.5

internet connect

HRW ONLINE RESOURCES
GO TO: go.hrw.com
Then type in a keyword.

TEACHER HOME PAGE
KEYWORD: SA3 Teacher

CHAPTER INTERNET ACTIVITIES
KEYWORD: SA3 CF19
Choose an activity to:
- view photographs and write a poem describing the life of a soldier in the war.
- research Civil War authors.
- create a 3D model of the battlefield at Gettysburg.

CHAPTER ENRICHMENT LINKS
KEYWORD: SA3 CH19

ONLINE ASSESSMENT
Homework Practice
KEYWORD: SA3 HP19

Standardized Test Prep
KEYWORD: SA3 STP19

Rubrics
KEYWORD: SS Rubrics

ONLINE MAPS, CHARTS, AND GRAPHS
KEYWORD: SA3 MCG
- Battle of Gettysberg
- Southern Railroads
- Union and Confederacy
- Soldiers' Occupations

CONTENT UPDATES
KEYWORD: SS Content Updates

HOLT PRESENTATION MAKER
KEYWORD: SA3 PPT19

ONLINE READING SUPPORT
KEYWORD: SS Strategies

CURRENT EVENTS
KEYWORD: S3 Current Events

Meeting Individual Needs

Ability Levels

Level 1 Basic-level activities designed for all students encountering new material

Level 2 Intermediate-level activities designed for average students

Level 3 Challenging activities designed for honors and gifted-and-talented students

English Language Learners Activities that address the needs of students with Limited English Proficiency

Chapter Review and Assessment

- IC Vocabulary Activity 19
- Global Skill Builder CD–ROM
- HRW Go site
- REV Chapter 19 Tutorial for Students, Parents, Mentors, and Peers
- REV Chapter 19 Review, pp. 607–09
- Chapter 19 Test Generator (on the One-Stop Planner)

- A Chapter 19 Test (Form A or B)
- A Alternative Assessment Handbook
- A Chapter 19 Test for English Language Learners and Special-Needs Students

CHAPTER

19

Section 1   *The War Begins*

Section 2   *The War in the East*

Section 3   *The War in the West*

Section 4   *Life during the War*

Section 5   *The Tide of the War Returns*

Build on What You Know

If You Were There...

Ask students to answer the following question:

Would you support or oppose secession?

Consider:

- whether or not human freedom is worth going to war over

- whether or not your business would benefit

You Be the Historian

What's Your Opinion?

To help students create their **Themes** Journal entries, provide the following examples of appropriate **agree**/disagree statements.

EXPLORING THE TIME LINE

GLOBAL EVENTS

CHAPTER

19

The Civil War
(1861–1865)

The fierce fighting at the First Battle of Bull Run surprised many Americans who had expected the war to be over swiftly.

THE GRANGER COLLECTION, NEW YORK

UNITED STATES

| **1861** Confederate guns open fire on Fort Sumter in South Carolina on April 12. | **1861** Confederate forces win the first battle of the Civil War on July 21 at Bull Run Creek in Virginia. | **1862** The *Monitor* fights the *Virginia* on March 9. | **1862** On December 13 General Robert E. Lee wins a major victory at Fredericksburg, Virginia. | **1863** The Emancipation Proclamation goes into effect on January 1. |

1861   1862   1863

1861 On March 17 nationalist leader Giuseppe Garibaldi declares Victor Emmanuel II king of Italy.

1862 Jean-Henri Dunant of Switzerland proposes the creation of the International Red Cross.

WORLD

Together, Giuseppe Garibaldi and Victor Emmanuel II helped unify Italy.

This medal was used by the International Red Cross.

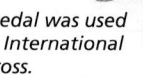

Build on What You Know

In the 1850s the North and the South were strongly divided over the issue of slavery. The election of Republican Abraham Lincoln as president in 1860 led 11 southern states to leave the Union. When the North refused to accept this secession, the opposing views of each side soon led to a terrible civil war between North and South.

Science, Technology & Society

Agree Technological advances improve one's chances in a war.

Disagree Technology is only one factor in gaining an advantage in war.

Economics

Agree Supporting a war drains a nation's resources.

Disagree War provides a market for many resources.

Citizenship

Agree Soldiers and civilians have a duty to support their country in war.

Disagree People who disagree with a war's cause should not support it.

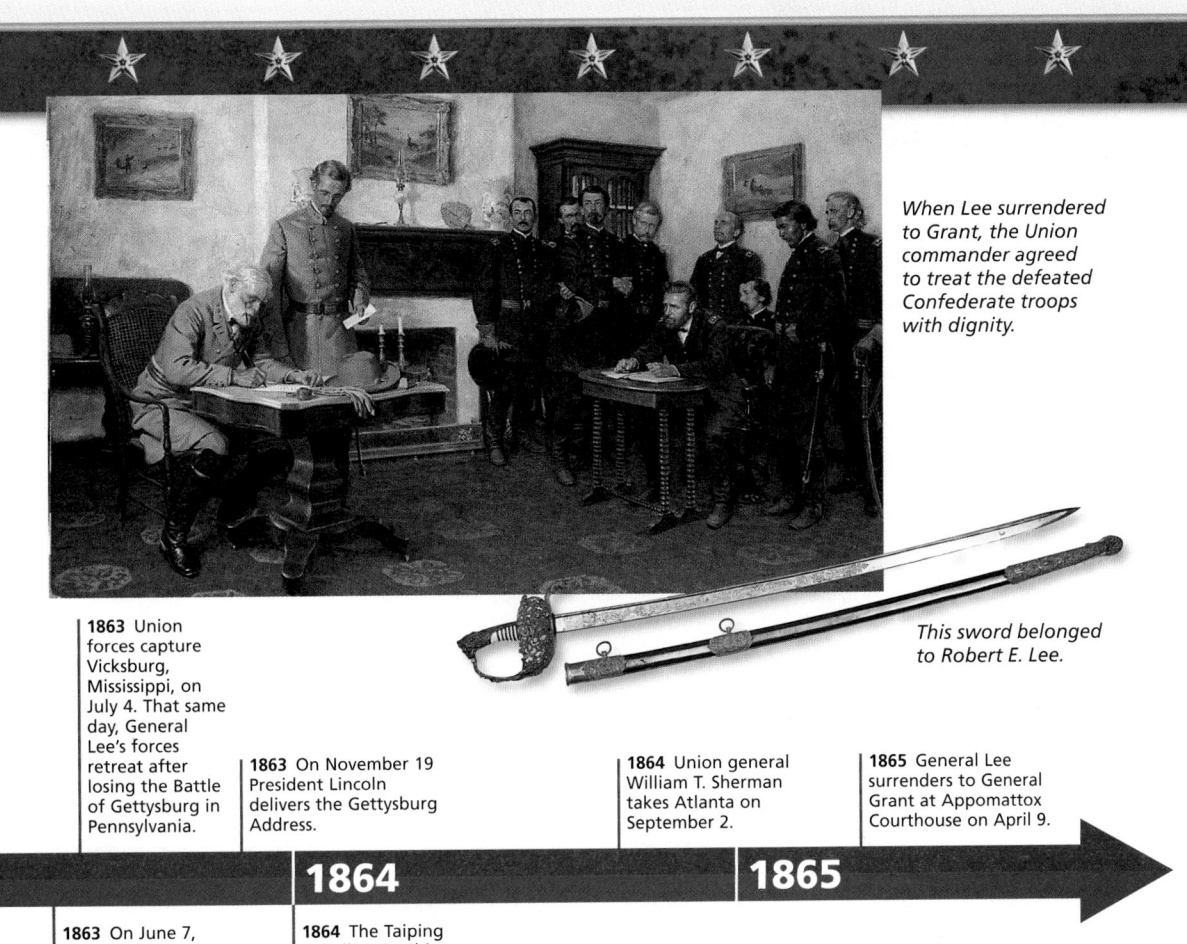

When Lee surrendered to Grant, the Union commander agreed to treat the defeated Confederate troops with dignity.

This sword belonged to Robert E. Lee.

1863 Union forces capture Vicksburg, Mississippi, on July 4. That same day, General Lee's forces retreat after losing the Battle of Gettysburg in Pennsylvania.

1863 On November 19 President Lincoln delivers the Gettysburg Address.

1864 Union general William T. Sherman takes Atlanta on September 2.

1865 General Lee surrenders to General Grant at Appomattox Courthouse on April 9.

1864

1865

1863 On June 7, French forces capture Mexico City.

1864 The Taiping Rebellion in China ends after the capture of Nanjing in July.

If you were there . . .
Would you support or oppose secession?

You Be the Historian

What's Your Opinion? Do you **agree** or **disagree** with the following statements? Support your point of view in your journal.

- **Science, Technology & Society** New technology always makes wars easier to win.
- **Economics** Wars are bad for a nation's economy.
- **Citizenship** All citizens have a duty to support their government during a war.

★ Historical Sidelight

Gettysburg. After the Confederate victories in Chancellorsville and Fredericksburg, General Robert E. Lee set his sights on Union territory. Seeking recognition from abroad and hoping to further dampen his opponent's spirits, Lee brought the Army of Northern Virginia up the Shenandoah Valley heading north. General Richard Ewell, a fellow Confederate officer, was ordered to bring his troops in for backup. That move turned out to be more hindrance than help, however. As Ewell and his men made their way up the Potomac, they cut Lee off from his cavalry chief, Jeb Stuart. For three days Lee received no reports on Union troop movements from Stuart and this may have cost him the battle. The Union forces won, successfully turning back a Confederate invasion of the North.

CRITICAL THINKING

Why would Gettysburg have been an important victory for the Confederates?

ANSWER: Students' responses may include that they would win foreign recognition, access to Union land and would dampen spirits in the North.

Section 1

OBJECTIVES

- ⭐ Describe what led to the bombardment of Fort Sumter and explain why this event was important.
- ⭐ Identify which side of the conflict Arkansas and the Upper South joined and explain why.
- ⭐ Explain why both the North and the South wanted to claim the border states.
- ⭐ Analyze the strategies each side followed at the beginning of the war.

🔊 LET'S GET STARTED!

Write the following question on the chalkboard: *What grievances did some southerners have with the federal government prior to the Civil War?* As students enter the classroom, have them write down their responses. (*Students' responses might include that some southerners thought the federal government was ignoring their rights and this eventually led to the Civil War.*) Tell students that in Section 1 they will learn how the resulting struggle between the North and the South as well as the importance of the border states to both sides as the war began.

Section 1

The War Begins

Read to Discover

1. What led to the bombardment of Fort Sumter, and why was this event important?
2. Which side of the conflict did Arkansas and the Upper South join, and why?
3. Why did both the North and the South want to claim the border states?
4. What strategies did each side follow at the beginning of the war?

Define
- border states
- cotton diplomacy

Identify
- Fort Sumter
- Abraham Lincoln
- Elizabeth Blackwell
- Winfield Scott

WHY IT MATTERS TODAY

Many countries around the world are currently experiencing civil wars. Use **CNN fyi.com** or other **current events** sources to find out about some of these places. Record your findings in your journal.

The Spirit of '61 was used as a symbol of Union pride on recruiting posters.

The Story Continues

When Abraham Lincoln took office, seven states had already left the Union. He wanted to keep more southern states from seceding. Lincoln gave his inaugural address on March 4, 1861. He pledged that he would not try to end slavery in the South. He also promised the South that the federal "government will not assail [attack] you. You can have no conflict without being yourselves the aggressors." At the same time, however, Lincoln spoke of his intention to preserve the Union.

⭐ Lincoln Faces a Crisis

The South did not respond to these calls for unity. Confederate officials were already taking over many federal mints, arms storehouses, and forts. One important federal post was **Fort Sumter**, located near Charleston, South Carolina. The fort controlled the entrance to Charleston Harbor. By early March 1861 the federal troops at Fort Sumter were running low on supplies. Instead of ordering the troops to surrender, President **Abraham Lincoln** decided to resupply them.

★ TEACH

Have students read Section 1 and complete Guided Reading Strategy 19.1. Choose one or more of the following activities to explore the section content with students. For further suggestions on block scheduling or team teaching, see *the Block Scheduling Handbook with Team Teaching Strategies.*

 ALL LEVELS: Copy the following graphic organizer onto the chalkboard, omitting the italicized answers. Have students complete the chart to identify the events that led to the bombardment of Fort Sumter. Then have students draw a circle around the entry that explains why this event was important. **ENGLISH LANGUAGE LEARNERS**

 LEVEL 1: Ask students to write a newspaper headline and two subheads announcing the bombardment of Fort Sumter. Then have each student write an editorial outline on what led to the bombardment of Fort Sumter, and explaining why this event was important.
ENGLISH LANGUAGE LEARNERS

Events at Fort Sumter →
- *Lincoln became president.*
- *The South took over federal forts.*
- *Federal troops refused to surrender.*
- *Confederate guns opened fire.*
- *The Civil War began.*

LINCOLN'S FIRST INAUGURAL ADDRESS

In the following excerpt from Abraham Lincoln's first inaugural address, he discusses the disagreements that led to the nation's greatest crisis.

I hold that, in contemplation of universal law, and of the Constitution, the Union of these States is perpetual.[1] . . .

It follows from these views that no State, upon its own mere motion,[2] can lawfully get out of the Union, —that resolves[3] and ordinances[4] to that effect are legally void; and that acts of violence, within any State or States, against the authority of the United States, are insurrectionary[5] or revolutionary, according to circumstances.

I therefore consider that, in view of the Constitution and the laws, the Union is unbroken. . . . I trust this will not be regarded as a menace, but only as the declared purpose of the Union that it *will* constitutionally defend, and maintain itself. In doing this there needs to be no bloodshed or violence; and there shall be none, unless it be forced upon the national authority. . . .

One section of our country believes that slavery is *right*, and ought to be extended, while the other believes it is *wrong*, and ought not to be extended. This is the only substantial[6] dispute. . . .

My countrymen, one and all, think calmly and *well*, upon this whole subject. . . . In *your* hands, my dissatisfied fellow countrymen, and not in *mine*, is the momentous issue of civil war.

Analyzing Primary Sources
1. According to Lincoln, what do the Constitution of the United States and the laws of the government say about the Union?
2. What does Lincoln say is the main dispute between the states?

[1]**perpetual:** everlasting
[2]**motion:** action
[3]**resolves:** resolutions
[4]**ordinances:** laws
[5]**insurrectionary:** rebellious
[6]**substantial:** important

Before the supply ships arrived, however, South Carolina demanded that the Union troops leave the fort. The fort's commander, Major Robert Anderson, refused to do so. He told the southerners, "Gentlemen, I will await your fire."

Before sunrise on April 12, 1861, Confederate guns opened fire on Fort Sumter. The Civil War had begun. A witness wrote that the first shots brought "every man, woman, and child in the city of Charleston from their beds." The fort withstood 34 hours of Confederate bombardment. Then Anderson had no choice but to surrender.

The attack on Fort Sumter outraged the North. Lincoln declared that the South was in rebellion and asked the state governors to provide 75,000 militiamen to help put down the revolt. Mary Boykin Chesnut, whose husband became a Confederate general, wrote about the events in her diary.

History Makers Speak "I did not know that one could live in such days of excitement. . . . Everybody tells you half of something, and then rushes off . . . to hear the last news."

—Mary Boykin Chesnut, *Mary Chesnut's Civil War,* edited by C. Vann Woodward

✔ **Reading Check: Drawing Inferences and Conclusions** How do you think states' rights issues contributed to the attack on Fort Sumter? Students might say that South Carolina believed it had the right to take over Fort Sumter from the federal government, which disagreed.

April 12, 1861
The Confederacy attacks Fort Sumter, starting the Civil War.

Analyzing Primary Sources
Drawing Inferences and Conclusions How do Chesnut and the people around her regard the start of the Civil War? with anticipation and excitement

---

★ Presidential Profiles

Lincoln's Arrival in Washington. Before his inauguration, Lincoln went on a speaking tour of five northern states. His last scheduled stop was Baltimore, a pro-slavery city. Many Republican leaders feared for Lincoln's safety and urged him not to speak in Baltimore but to head straight to Washington. The trip to Baltimore was canceled. Lincoln arrived in Washington at 6 A.M., while a train thought to be carrying him arrived in Baltimore that afternoon to an angry crowd chanting cheers in support of the South.

CRITICAL THINKING
What might have happened if Lincoln had gone on to Baltimore?

ANSWER: Students may conclude that the angry crowd could have rioted and tried to hurt Lincoln.

ANALYZING PRIMARY SOURCES ANSWERS
1. He says that the Union will last forever, that the Union is legally impossible to destroy, and that no state has the authority to leave the Union by itself.
2. One section of the country favors slavery, while the other opposes it.

Cynthia Gore of San Jose, California, suggested the following activity:

ALL LEVELS: Explain to students that in the Civil War both sides needed to recruit soldiers. Assign students either the North or South and have them make recruitment posters for their side. Also have students use information from the text and class discussion to design a brochure outlining the need for volunteers and stating the cause for which the side was fighting. **ENGLISH LANGUAGE LEARNERS**

LEVEL 3: Have students write a memoir, similar to one Abraham Lincoln or Jefferson Davis might have written, about the importance of the border states (including Arkansas and the Upper South). Ask students to identify which side of the conflict Arkansas and the Upper South joined, and explain why. Also, have students explain why both the North and the South wanted to claim the border states. Finally, discuss the reasons that northerners and southerners might have had different views on the participation of these states.

★ Using Visual Resources

Enlisting Soldiers.

Although recruitment posters such as the one on this page were used in the North to convince men to enlist, at the beginning of the war neither side needed to advertise for recruits. After Fort Sumter, men rushed to enlist. However, if all these men had entered the Union army, the government would not have been able to equip, pay, or transport them.

CRITICAL THINKING

Why might it have been easy to convince some people to join the war effort after Fort Sumter?

ANSWER: Students might suggest that people felt strong support for their side's cause.

MAP ANSWERS

1. Confederacy—Alabama, Arkansas, Florida, Georgia, Louisiana, Mississippi, North Carolina, South Carolina, Tennessee, Texas, and Virginia; Union—California, Connecticut, Delaware, Illinois, Indiana, Iowa, Kansas, Kentucky, Maine, Maryland, Massachusetts, Michigan, Minnesota, Missouri, New Hampshire, New Jersey, New York, Ohio, Oregon, Pennsylvania, Rhode Island, Vermont, West Virginia, and Wisconsin.

2. If Maryland joined the Confederacy, the Capital would be surrounded by Confederate states.

The Union and Confederacy in 1861

Interpreting Maps After the 1860 election many slave states left the Union to form the Confederacy.

Skills Assessment

1. **Places and Regions** What states made up the Confederacy, and what states made up the Union?
2. **Analyzing Information** How was the state of Maryland strategically important to the Union in relationship to Washington, D.C.?

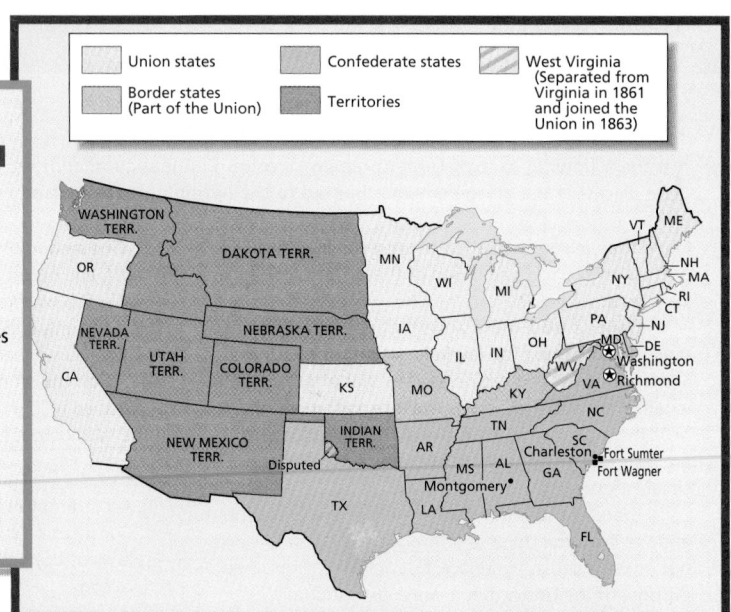

The Union printed recruitment posters such as this one to encourage volunteers for the war effort.

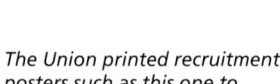
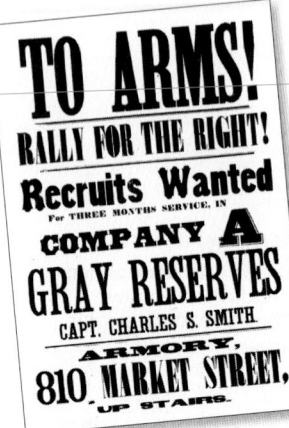

★ Choosing Sides

Democratic senator Stephen Douglas supported Lincoln's call for troops. He declared, "Every man must be for the United States or against it." The free northern states were solidly in the Union. Meanwhile, slave states that had not joined the Confederacy had to choose sides. The states of the Upper South—North Carolina, Tennessee, and Virginia—all joined the Confederacy soon after Lincoln's request for troops. So did Arkansas. "The South must go with the South," wrote a North Carolinian. The Upper South provided the Confederacy with soldiers and industrial resources. Richmond, Virginia, became the Confederacy's capital.

Four slave states—Delaware, Kentucky, Maryland, and Missouri—bordered the North. The position of these **border states** made them important to both the North and the South. Kentucky and Missouri controlled key stretches of the Ohio and Mississippi Rivers. The federal capital of Washington, D.C., was located within Maryland.

Slaveholders in Delaware supported secession, but they were few in number. In Kentucky, Missouri, and Maryland, however, people were deeply divided. Troops from Kentucky and Missouri served with each side in the war. There were riots against Union soldiers in Maryland. However, these three states eventually voted against secession. Lincoln sent federal troops into Maryland and into western Virginia, whose population was mostly loyal to the Union. People in the region set up their own state government. The new state of West Virginia joined the Union in 1863.

✔ **Reading Check: Comparing and Contrasting** Identify the similarities and differences between the Upper South and the border states. All were slave states, and many had strategic value. Border states stayed in the Union, and the Upper South joined the Confederacy.

★ The Volunteer Spirit

Neither side was prepared for war. Therefore, both sides depended on volunteers. At the start of the war, the Union army had only 16,000 troops. Thousands of volunteers quickly joined the army. One Union recruit from the Midwest explained why he signed up.

> **History Makers Speak**
> ❝[It is] a duty I owe to my country and to my children to do what I can to preserve this government as I shudder to think what is ahead for them if this government should be overthrown.❞
>
> —Union soldier, quoted in *Battle at Bull Run,* by William C. Davis

Virginian Thomas Webber also defended his way of life. He wanted to fight "against the invading foe [enemy] who now pollute the sacred soil of my beloved native state." Many southern volunteers shared his view. Early in the war, Union soldiers asked one southerner why he was fighting. He replied, "I'm fighting because you're down here."

In the border states, members of the same family often joined opposing sides in the war. The president's Kentucky-born wife, Mary Todd Lincoln, had four brothers who fought for the Confederacy. Disagreements over the war deeply divided many friends and families.

Civilians on both sides also helped the war effort. They raised money, provided aid for soldiers and their families, and ran emergency hospitals. Dr. **Elizabeth Blackwell**, the first woman to earn a medical license, helped convince President Lincoln to form the U.S. Sanitary Commission in June 1861. The Sanitary, as it was known, had tens of thousands of volunteers. They sent bandages, medicines, and food to Union army camps and hospitals. Staff and volunteers also worked to keep the Union troops healthy.

✔ **Reading Check: Analyzing Information** How did civilians help the war effort in both the North and the South? They raised money, helped soldiers and their families, and ran hospitals.

★ The North versus the South

At the beginning of the war, the North had several key advantages over the South. The much larger population of the North provided more soldiers. The North had most of the nation's factories and more shipyards. It also had a better network of railways, which allowed for more efficient transportation. Finally, the Union was able to raise more money to spend on the war.

The Confederacy also had advantages. The South's military tradition provided it with many skilled officers. In addition, the South needed only to defend itself until the North grew tired of the war. In contrast, the North had to defeat southern forces and occupy large areas of enemy territory.

Both the Union and the Confederacy based their military strategies on their strengths. Union general **Winfield Scott** developed the Union's

THE GRANGER COLLECTION, NEW YORK

Abraham Lincoln

Abraham Lincoln was born on February 12, 1809, in Kentucky. He entered politics in 1834, serving four terms in the state legislature of Illinois and one in the U.S. House of Representatives. He helped spread the message of the new Republican Party in the 1850s and was elected president in 1860. Lincoln was a strong leader during the Civil War. With the Emancipation Proclamation, he began the process of freeing the slaves.

Today Lincoln is one of four presidents whose image is carved into the monument at Mount Rushmore, South Dakota. President's Day, a federal holiday, is held on the third Monday of every February near his birthday. **What were some of Lincoln's major accomplishments as a political leader?**

Many Confederate soldiers came from rural areas to fight for the South.

THE MUSEUM OF THE CONFEDERACY, RICHMOND, VIRGINIA
PHOTOGRAPHY BY KATHERINE WETZEL

Have students complete the **Section 1 Review** on p. 584. Then have students complete **Daily Quiz 19.1**. As **Alternative Assessment**, you may want to use the strategy proposal or the stamp exercise in this section's lessons.

★ RETEACH

Have students complete **Main Idea Activity for English Language Learners and Special-Needs Students 19.1**. Then have students draw a scale-shaped organizer and label one side *North* and the other *South*. Have students complete the graphic organizer by weighing the advantages that each side had at the beginning of the war. **ENGLISH LANGUAGE LEARNERS**

★ EXTEND

Organize the class into four groups. Assign one border state to each group *(Delaware, Kentucky, Missouri, or Maryland)*. Have groups use the library to research what life was like in their states just before the outbreak of the Civil War. Then have each group analyze its research to determine why its state chose to support or oppose the Union. Have each group present its findings in a brief, illustrated report. Ask for volunteers to share their group's report with the class. **COOPERATIVE LEARNING**, **BLOCK SCHEDULING**

POLITICAL CARTOON ANSWER
Students might say the blockade was intended to squeeze the South.

★ ★ ★ ★ ★ ★ ★ ★ ★ ★

Section 1 Review ANSWERS

❶ Define
• border states, p. 582
• cotton diplomacy, p. 584

❷ Identify
• Fort Sumter, p.580
• Abraham Lincoln, p. 580
• Elizabeth Blackwell, p. 583
• Winfield Scott, p. 583

❸ slave states that joined: Delaware, Kentucky, Maryland, Missouri; North Carolina, Tennessee, Virginia, Arkansas; Advantages: large population, many factories and shipyards, good network of railways; skilled officers, needed only to defend itself; Disadvantages: had to defeat and occupy large areas of enemy territory; had fewer people, factories, and shipyards, less money, weaker transportation system; Strategies: destroy the South's economy through a naval blockade of seaports, divide the Confederacy and cut its communications by controlling the Mississippi River; defend itself and wear down the Union's will to fight, take Washington.

❹ a. held a strategic position at the port of Charleston; began Civil War
b. decided to join the Confederacy and secede from the Union; felt greater loyalty to the South

❺ Students' plans will vary.

SCOTT'S GREAT SNAKE.

Interpreting Political Cartoons

Scott's Great Snake *This cartoon shows Union general Winfield Scott's plan to block-ade the Confederacy as a giant snake wrapped around the southern coastline.* **Why do you think the artist chose to represent the blockade plan as a snake squeezing the Confederacy?**

basic two-part strategy. He wanted to destroy the South's economy through a naval blockade of southern seaports. Scott also wanted to gain control of the Mississippi River to divide the Confederacy and cut its communications. Scott believed that this strategy would defeat the Confederacy "with less bloodshed than by any other plan." However, it would take time to succeed. Many northern leaders also called for a direct attack on Richmond, the Confederate capital.

The Confederacy's early strategy was to defend its territory and to wear down the Union's will to fight. Its offensive plan focused on taking Washington, D.C. Confederate president Jefferson Davis played a major role in the war. A demanding leader, Davis became so involved in war planning that he went through six secretaries of war in four years.

Davis and other Confederate leaders also tried to win foreign allies through **cotton diplomacy**. Cotton diplomacy was based on the southern belief that the British government would support them because cotton was important to Great Britain's textile industry. The British, however, had a large supply of cotton stockpiled when the war began. They were also able to get cotton from India and Egypt.

The strategies of the North and the South led to a war that was fought on land and at sea. As leaders made their plans, soldiers on both sides prepared to fight.

✔ **Reading Check: Supporting a Point of View** Which side do you think was best prepared for victory? Explain your answer. Answers will vary.

Section 1 Review

go. **Homework**
hrw **Practice**
.com **Online**
keyword: SA3 HP19

★ ★

❶ Define and explain:
• border states
• cotton diplomacy

❷ Identify and explain:
• Fort Sumter
• Abraham Lincoln
• Elizabeth Blackwell
• Winfield Scott

❸ Summarizing
Copy the chart below. Use it to identify key characteristics of the North and the South at the start of the Civil War.

	The North	The South
Slave states that joined		
Advantages		
Disadvantages		
Strategies		

❹ Finding the Main Idea
a. Why did the Confederates attack Fort Sumter, and what happened as a result?

b. What did Arkansas, North Carolina, Tennessee, and Virginia decide about the Confederacy, and why did they make this decision?

❺ Writing and Critical Thinking
Analyzing Information Imagine that you are an adviser to President Lincoln. Write a plan that describes how the Union can keep the border states from seceding.

Consider the following:
• possible military actions
• the loyalty of the states' citizens

Section 2

OBJECTIVES

- ⭐ Identify the battles that the Confederates won in Virginia and analyze why they were important.
- ⭐ Explain what stopped the northward advance of the Confederate army.
- ⭐ Examine the significance of the *Monitor* and the *Virginia*.

 **LET'S GET STARTED!**

As students enter the classroom, organize them into rows and have one row of students stand to one side of the room and the remaining rows stand on the other side. Explain that each row represents an army troop. Then ask the students, *Who would win a battle if one side had more troops than the other side?* Allow students time to answer. (*Students' responses may include that the side with the most troops would probably win.*) Next ask students what could alter that outcome. (*Students' responses may include the following: better leadership, better weapons, or the advantage of knowing the terrain where the battle is fought.*) Tell students that in Section 2 they will learn about the significant early battles of the war.

Section 2

The War in the East

Read to Discover

1. What battles did the Confederates win in Virginia, and why were they important?
2. What stopped the northward advance of the Confederate army?
3. What was the significance of the *Monitor* and the *Virginia*?

WHY IT MATTERS TODAY

During the Civil War, powerful new types of warships were developed. Use **CNNfyi.com** or other **current events** sources to find out about the types of ships used by the U.S. Navy today. Record your findings in your journal.

Define
- ironclad

Identify
- Thomas "Stonewall" Jackson
- First Battle of Bull Run
- George B. McClellan
- Robert E. Lee
- Seven Days' Battles
- Second Battle of Bull Run
- Battle of Antietam

The Story Continues

After the fall of Fort Sumter, northerners demanded bold action. The Confederate Congress was supposed to meet in Richmond on July 20, 1861. Union troops gathered in Washington during the early summer. A northern newspaper headline urged, "Forward to Richmond! Forward to Richmond! The Rebel Congress Must Not Be Allowed to Meet There." President Lincoln decided to listen to public opinion. He ordered an attack on the Confederate capital.

This drum was used by the Union army.

⭐ Two Armies Meet

The first major clash of Union and Confederate armies took place in July 1861. President Lincoln had General Irvin McDowell lead about 35,000 troops from Washington toward Richmond. The soldiers were barely trained. McDowell complained that they "stopped every moment to pick blackberries or get water; they would not keep in the ranks."

The two armies met about 30 miles outside of Washington, near Manassas Junction, Virginia. Some 35,000 Confederates were lined along Bull Run Creek. At first the Union troops drove the left side of the

☆ **TEACH**

Have students read Section 2 and Complete Guided Reading Strategy 19.2. Choose one or more of the following activities to explore the section content with students. For further suggestions on block scheduling or team teaching, see the *Block Scheduling Handbook with Team Teaching Strategies.*

 LEVEL 1: Ask students to use information from the text and class discussion to draw illustrations of the *Virginia* and the *Monitor.* Have students write captions next to their illustrations, describing the significance of these ships. *(Students' captions should indicate that the* Virginia *was an iron-plated Confederate steamship which sank two of the Union's wooden warships. The* Monitor *was a Union ironclad that, after several hours of fighting, forced the* Virginia *to withdraw).*
ENGLISH LANGUAGE LEARNERS

 ALL LEVELS: Copy the graphic organizer on the following page onto the chalkboard, omitting the italicized answers. Have students complete the chart by listing the battles the Confederates won in Virginia and analyzing their importance, as well as the key Union victory.
ENGLISH LANGUAGE LEARNERS

★ **Economics**

Richmond. By the time the First Battle of Bull Run was fought, the population of Richmond had grown to 38,000. The city was built along the James River and had strong trading ties with the rest of the commercial world. The result of these ties was prosperity for its citizens. Richmond's factories produced flour, iron, meal, and tobacco. Before the Civil War, Richmond ranked thirteenth in the country and first in the South for the value of its manufactured goods.

CRITICAL THINKING

What factors may have contributed to Richmond's economic success?

ANSWER: Students might suggest that Richmond had access to a river that led to the Atlantic Ocean, and it was close to northern markets and to southern materials.

 Technology Resources
American Music
Selection 13: "All Quiet Along the Potomac"

MAP ANSWERS
1. Antietam, Union victory
2. Fair Oaks and Seven Days

Analyzing Primary Sources
Drawing Inferences and Conclusions Based on Coffin's observation, what do you think the soldiers had expected war to be like?
Answers will vary, but students might suggest less violent and more civilized.

Civil War photographs such as this one showed civilians the horrors of the battlefield.

The War in the East, 1861–1862
Interpreting Maps One Union objective was to capture the Confederate capital of Richmond.

Skills Assessment
1. **Human Systems** What battle took place in Maryland, and what was the outcome?
2. **Summarizing** What two battles took place within 25 miles of each other?

Confederate line back. However, a unit led by General **Thomas "Stonewall" Jackson** held firmly in place. Jackson's example inspired the other Confederate troops. "There is Jackson standing like a stone wall!" one southern officer cried out. "Rally behind the Virginians!" General "Stonewall" Jackson ordered his troops against the northern line. They charged forward, letting out the terrifying rebel yell.

Northern journalist Charles Coffin saw the battle. He described the confusion and shock of the fighting.

 History Makers Speak ❝There is smoke, dust, wild talking, shouting; hissings, howlings, explosions. It is a new, strange, unanticipated [surprising] experience to the soldiers of both armies, far different from what they thought it would be.❞

—Charles Coffin, quoted in *Voices of the Civil War,* by Richard Wheeler

Fresh southern troops soon arrived, driving the Union army back. Soon the northerners were retreating to Washington. The Confederates might have captured the Union capital if they had not been so tired and disorganized. In the **First Battle of Bull Run**, the Confederacy broke the Union's hopes of winning the war quickly and easily.

✔ **Reading Check: Analyzing Information** Why did the Confederates win the First Battle of Bull Run? They received reinforcements, rallied around General Jackson, and charged forward aggressively.

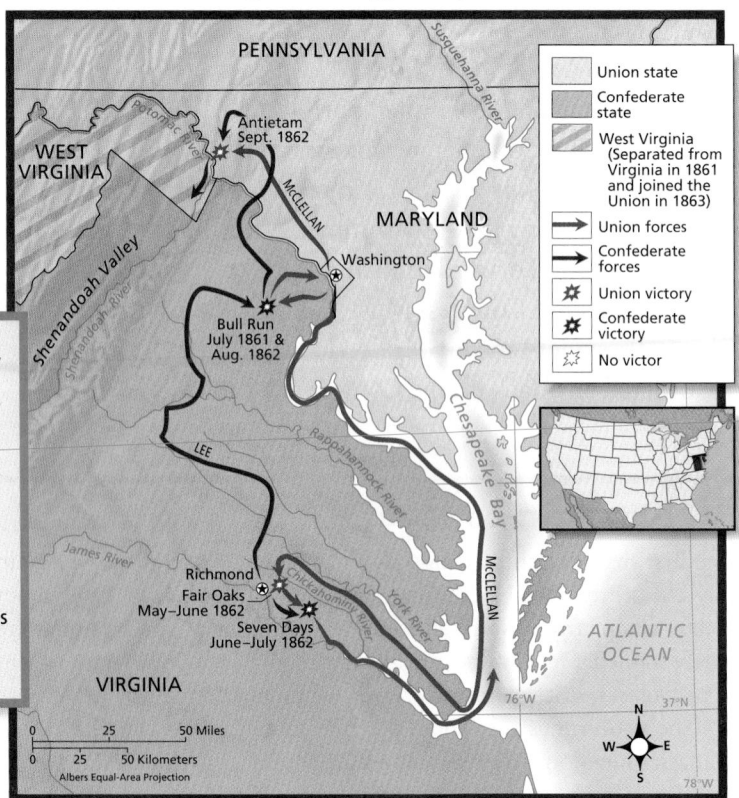

ALL LEVELS: Organize the class into eight groups. Assign each group one of the three key Confederate battles discussed in this section *(First Battle of Bull Run, Second Battle of Bull Run, Seven Days' Battles)* or the Union victory that stopped the advance of the Confederate army *(Battle of Antietam)*. Have each group use the textbook to write a newspaper headline that describes the events and an outline for an article that analyzes the significance of the assigned battle. *(Students' articles will vary but should include an awareness that the First Battle of Bull Run, Seven Days' Battles, and Second Battle of Bull Run were all Confederate victories that forced Union troops to withdraw from Virginia; Battle of Antietam was a Union victory that stopped the Confederates' northward advance.)* For each battle, have one group write from the perspective of a northern newspaper and the other group from that of a southern newspaper. Ask volunteers to share their group's article with the class.

COOPERATIVE LEARNING

★ More Battles in Virginia

Lincoln still wanted to capture Richmond. He sent his new commander, General **George B. McClellan**, back into Virginia. By early April 1862 McClellan and a huge force were camped near Yorktown, Virginia, southeast of Richmond. McClellan did not attack, however, because he thought his troops were outnumbered. This gave the Confederates time to strengthen Richmond's defenses. In early May, McClellan finally took Yorktown. The Union army forced the southern troops to retreat. At the end of the month, the two armies fought again near Richmond.

President Jefferson Davis put General **Robert E. Lee** in charge of the Confederate army in Virginia in June 1862. Lee was one of the most talented officers on either side. A graduate of the U.S. Military Academy at West Point, he had served in the Mexican War. Later, Lee was an engineer for the Army Corps of Engineers. He had also led the federal troops that captured John Brown at Harpers Ferry. Lincoln had even asked Lee in 1861 to command the Union forces. Although Lee was against slavery and secession, he was loyal to the South. As he told a northern friend, "I cannot raise my hand against my birthplace, my home, my children." When Virginia left the Union, Lee resigned from the U.S. Army and returned home.

During the summer of 1862, General Lee strengthened his positions. Then he began attacking, hoping to push McClellan's army away from Richmond. After scouting Union positions, Lee attacked on June 26, 1862. During the next week, the two armies fought five separate times. This fighting became known as the **Seven Days' Battles**. Confederate general D. H. Hill described one failed attack. "It was not war—it was murder." The Confederates suffered more than 20,000 casualties, and the Union suffered nearly 16,000. However, Lee forced McClellan to retreat from the area around Richmond.

Next, Lincoln ordered General John Pope to advance directly on Richmond from Washington. Pope told his soldiers, "Let us look before us and not behind. Success and glory are in the advance." To stop the Union forces, Lee sent Jackson's troops around Pope's right side. Then Lee's main force fell upon the Union's left side. This battle became known as the **Second Battle of Bull Run**. Caught off guard, Pope's army fell apart. By the end of August 1862, Lee had pushed most of the Union forces out of Virginia. He then decided to take the war into the North.

General Robert E. Lee was widely respected in both the North and the South for his leadership and daring strategies.

✔ **Reading Check: Summarizing** How did Lee's forces drive the Union army from Virginia? attacked in the Seven Days' Battles; defended themselves in the Second Battle of Bull Run

The Civil War **587**

LEVEL 3: Have students write victory songs for the Confederate forces. Songs should identify the battles the Confederates won in Virginia and include details about why they were important.

HOMEWORK Have students write one *I am . . .* poem about the *Monitor* and one about the *Virginia*. Students should use their poems to describe the significance of their vessels.

★ CLOSE

Organize the class into four groups. Assign each group one of the battles discussed in this section. Then have each group create a commercial for an upcoming documentary on their assigned battle. The commercials should be designed to create interest in the show by highlighting significant information about the group's particular battle.

ENGLISH LANGUAGE LEARNERS , COOPERATIVE LEARNING

★ Economics

Blockade Runners. The blockade-running business was quite profitable for those willing to risk being targets of northern ships. For example, salt, which sold for $6.50 a ton in the Bahamas, went for $1,700 in the South; while coffee, which sold for $249 in the Bahamas, brought $5,500. A successful blockade captain could earn $5,000 on one run, while a captain in the merchant service would only earn about $150 for equivalent work.

CRITICAL THINKING

Do you think many southern captains would be interested in becoming blockade runners?

ANSWER: Students might suggest that some captains would be willing to risk their lives to make the extra profit.

CONNECTING TO SCIENCE AND TECHNOLOGY ANSWER

Students should suggest that his cameras could only take pictures of still objects.

Technology Resources

Everyday Life in America Transparency 12: Photograph of Civil War Casualties

---

★ The Battle of Antietam

Confederate leaders hoped a victory on northern soil might break the Union's spirit and convince European powers to aid the South. On September 4, 1862, some 40,000 Confederate soldiers entered Maryland. Union soldiers, however, found a copy of Lee's battle plan, which General McClellan used to plan a counterattack. On September 17, 1862, the armies met along Antietam Creek in Maryland. The **Battle of Antietam** lasted for hours. By the end of the day, the Union had suffered more than 12,000 casualties, and the Confederates more than 13,000. Antietam was the bloodiest single-day battle of the war, but the Union won a key victory.

Antietam cost Lee many of his troops and stopped his northward advance. However, McClellan allowed Lee to retreat to Virginia. Two months later, tired of McClellan's delays, Lincoln took the command in the East away from him.

✔ **Reading Check: Finding the Main Idea** How did the Battle of Antietam help the Union? first Union victory; stopped Lee's advance

CONNECTING TO
SCIENCE AND TECHNOLOGY

Photography and the Civil War

In 1862 Mathew Brady shocked the people of New York with his photographs from the Battle of Antietam. Brady and other photographers followed the Union army to record events with their cameras. The early cameras were bulky and hard to set up quickly. They could only be used to take pictures of still objects. As a result, the photographs of the Civil War were mostly portraits of soldiers and scenes of camp life. Brady's pictures of battlefields were taken only after the fighting had stopped. Why did Brady not show images of battle?

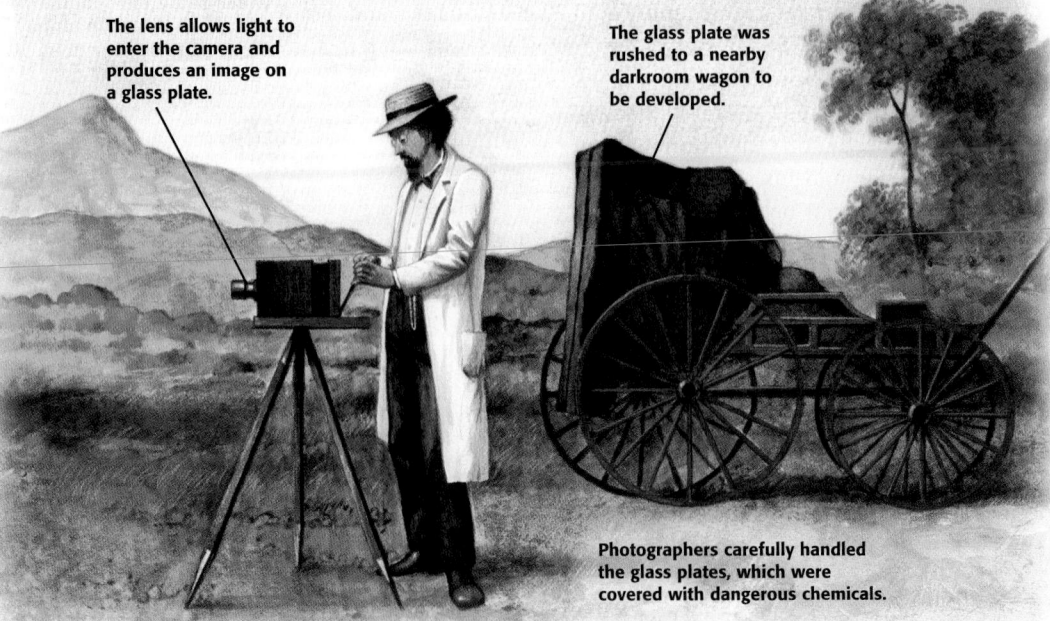

The lens allows light to enter the camera and produces an image on a glass plate.

The glass plate was rushed to a nearby darkroom wagon to be developed.

Photographers carefully handled the glass plates, which were covered with dangerous chemicals.

★ The War at Sea

While the two armies fought for control of the land, the Union controlled the sea. The North had most of the U.S. Navy's small fleet and enough industry to build more ships. The Union navy blockaded the South, cutting off southern trade and hurting the economy. The blockade was hard to maintain because the Union navy had to patrol thousands of miles of coastline from Virginia to Texas. The South used small, fast ships called blockade runners to outrun the larger Union warships and reach trading ports. These ships, however, could not make up for the South's loss of trade.

The Confederacy turned to a new type of warship, the **ironclad**, which was heavily armored with iron. The Confederates had turned a captured Union ship into an ironclad, renamed the *Virginia*. One Union sailor described it as "a huge half-submerged crocodile." In early March 1862 the ironclad sailed north into Hampton Roads, Virginia. Union ships guarded access to this important waterway. Before nightfall, the *Virginia* easily sank two of the Union's wooden warships while suffering only minor damage.

However, the Union navy had already built its own ironclad. The *Monitor* had unusual new features such as a revolving gun turret. Although small, the *Monitor* carried powerful guns and had thick plating. When the *Virginia* returned to Hampton Roads on March 9, 1862, the *Monitor* was waiting. After several hours of fighting neither ship was seriously damaged, but the *Monitor* forced the *Virginia* to withdraw. This success saved the Union fleet and kept the blockade going.

✔ **Reading Check: Identifying Cause and Effect** Why did the Confederates send the *Virginia* to sea in 1862, and what was the result? to damage the Union navy and weaken the North's blockade of southern seaports; had success at first but was finally driven off by the Union *Monitor*.

Interpreting the Visual Record

Ironclads *The duel of the* Virginia *and the* Monitor *was the first naval battle between ironclad ships.* **What features of these ships do you think made them more effective in combat?**

Section 2 Review
ANSWERS

❶ **Define**
• ironclad, p. 589

❷ **Identify**
• Thomas "Stonewall" Jackson, p. 586
• First Battle of Bull Run, p. 586
• George B. McClellan, p. 587
• Robert E. Lee, p. 587
• Seven Days' Battles, p. 587
• Second Battle of Bull Run, p. 587
• Battle of Antietam, p. 588

❸ First Battle of Bull Run, Seven Days' Battles, Second Battle of Bull Run—VA, Confederate victories that forced Union forces to withdraw; Hampton Roads—VA, battle between the *Virginia* and the *Monitor*, Union victory ensuring continued blockade; Battle of Antietam—MD, Union victory that stopped the Confederates' northward advance

❹ a. Students' responses will vary.
b. battle introduced a major change in naval warfare; if the *Virginia* had won, it would have helped the South break the Union blockade

❺ Students' interviews will vary, but should reflect an understanding of why Lee fought for the South, his training and experience, and the South's strategy.

Section 2 Review

Homework Practice Online
keyword: SA3 HP19

❶ **Define** and explain:
• ironclad

❷ **Identify** and explain:
• Thomas "Stonewall" Jackson
• First Battle of Bull Run
• George B. McClellan
• Robert E. Lee
• Seven Days' Battles
• Second Battle of Bull Run
• Battle of Antietam

❸ **Summarizing** Copy the graphic organizer below. Use it to identify the battles of the Civil War that took place in 1861 and 1862, which side won each, and their significance.

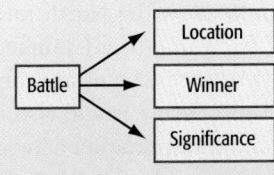

Battle → Location
Battle → Winner
Battle → Significance

❹ **Finding the Main Idea**
a. Of the Confederate victories in Virginia, which do you think was the most important? Explain your answer.

b. Why was the victory of the *Monitor* over the *Virginia* in 1862 important?

❺ **Writing and Critical Thinking**
Identifying Points of View Imagine that you are a war correspondent. Write an imaginary interview with Robert E. Lee.

Consider the following:
• why Lee is fighting for the South
• Lee's training and experience
• the South's strategy

Section 3

OBJECTIVES

- ★ Examine General Ulysses S. Grant's strategy for the Union army in the West.
- ★ Explain why the fall of Vicksburg, Mississippi, was important.
- ★ Describe the fighting that took place in the Far West.

SECTION 3 RESOURCES

REPRODUCIBLE

- ▶ Guided Reading Strategy 19.3
- ▶ Primary Source Reading 19: A Confederate Girl's Diary
- ▶ Geography Activity 19: The Siege of Vicksburg

TECHNOLOGY

- ▶ One-Stop Planner, Lesson 19.3
- ▶ Linking Geography and History Transparency 14: The War in the East and the West, 1861–1863
- ▶ Homework Practice Online

REINFORCEMENT, REVIEW, AND ASSESSMENT

- ▶ Section 3 Review, p. 593
- ▶ Daily Quiz 19.3
- ▶ Main Idea Activity 19.3
- ▶ English Audio Summary 19.3
- ▶ Spanish Audio Summary 19.3

Section 3

The War in the West

Read to Discover

1. What was General Ulysses S. Grant's strategy for the Union army in the West?
2. Why was the fall of Vicksburg, Mississippi, important?
3. What fighting took place in the Far West?

WHY IT MATTERS TODAY

The brave actions of the soldiers and civilians who participated in the Civil War are remembered today. Use **CNNfyi.com** or other **current events** sources to find out about different ways that soldiers are honored. Record your findings in your journal.

Identify

- Ulysses S. Grant
- Battle of Shiloh
- David Farragut
- John C. Pemberton
- Siege of Vicksburg
- Battle of Pea Ridge

Heavy mortars like this one were used to lob artillery shells onto forts.

The Story Continues

In February 1862 General Ulysses S. Grant led Union forces into Tennessee. Grant hoped to capture two important forts—Fort Henry and Fort Donelson. With help from Union gunboats, Grant took Fort Henry on February 6. He then attacked Fort Donelson six days later. The Confederate commander of Fort Donelson asked to discuss surrender terms. Grant replied, "No terms except an unconditional and immediate surrender can be accepted." The Confederate officer had no choice. Grant got his surrender and the fort.

★ Western Strategy

Union strategy in the West focused on controlling the Mississippi River. This strategy would allow the North to cut the eastern states of the Confederacy off from important sources of food production in the western states of Arkansas, Louisiana, and Texas. From bases on the Mississippi, the Union army would also be able to attack the South's communication and transportation network.

Ulysses S. Grant was the most important figure in the war in the West. A graduate of West Point, Grant had served in the Mexican War.

TEACH

Have students read Section 3 and Complete Guided Reading Strategy 19.3. Choose one or more of the following activities to explore the section content with students. For further suggestions on block scheduling or team teaching, see the *Block Scheduling Handbook with Team Teaching Strategies.*

LEVEL 1: Ask students to describe the events and implications of the battles covered in this section, in particular students should examine General Ulysses S. Grant's strategy for the Union army in the West. *(Students' descriptions should include an awareness that Grant wanted to gain control of the Mississippi in order to cut off the Confederacy*

from sources of food production and to enable attacks on the South's communication and transportation networks.)
ENGLISH LANGUAGE LEARNERS

 HOMEWORK Have students design a newsmagazine's table of contents listing the major battles of the western war with a brief description of the implications of each battle. **ENGLISH LANGUAGE LEARNERS**

 ALL LEVELS: Copy the graphic organizer on the following page onto the chalkboard, omitting the italicized answers. Have students complete the chart to identify the strategies and implications of each battle listed, including why the fall of Vicksburg, Mississippi, was important.
ENGLISH LANGUAGE LEARNERS

He later resigned from the army. When the Civil War broke out, Grant quickly volunteered to serve with the Union army. By September 1861, Lincoln had made him a general. Grant's strength in battle set him apart. *"I can't spare this man,"* Lincoln said of Grant. *"He fights."*

By late February 1862, Union forces had captured Nashville. They controlled Kentucky and much of Tennessee. By the spring the Union controlled key stretches of the Tennessee and Cumberland Rivers, as well as some important southern railroads. General Grant advanced south along the Tennessee River toward Mississippi. Following orders, he halted just north of the border. There, near a creek and a church named Shiloh, he waited for additional Union troops.

On April 6, 1862, the Confederates began the **Battle of Shiloh**. Catching Grant by surprise, they pushed his army back. Grant ordered his troops to hold their ground, whatever the cost. During the night, more Union soldiers arrived. On April 7, Grant began a counterattack. By evening's end, the Confederates were in retreat, and the Union had won greater control of the Mississippi River valley. The Battle of Shiloh was one of the first major battles of the war. Teenage Union soldier John Cockerill looked out in shock at the dead soldiers on the battlefield. "The blue and gray were mingled [mixed] together . . . as though they had bled to death while trying to aid each other," he wrote.

✔ **Reading Check: Analyzing Information** What role did the Battle of Shiloh play in Grant's western strategy? *It gave Union forces greater control of the Mississippi River valley.*

⭐ Fighting for the Mississippi River

General Grant and other Union commanders wanted to capture key southern positions along the Mississippi River. The Union navy would first try to take the port of New Orleans, the largest city in the South. The Union could then send forces up the Mississippi to join Grant's army advancing from the north. However, two forts guarded the approach to New Orleans from the Gulf of Mexico.

The capture of New Orleans fell to Flag Officer **David Farragut**. He was a daring Union naval leader from Tennessee who had refused to serve in the Confederacy. Unable to destroy the forts guarding New Orleans, Farragut decided to sail boldly past them. Before dawn on April 24, 1862, Farragut ordered his warships to advance through a hail of Confederate fire. His ships arrived in New Orleans the next day, and the city surrendered on April 29. Farragut then sailed farther up the Mississippi River. Next he took Baton Rouge, Louisiana, and Natchez, Mississippi. After that, only the strong defenses at Vicksburg, Mississippi, stood in his way.

The southern defenders of Vicksburg had an important advantage—the city's high bluffs overlooking the river. These bluffs allowed the Confederates under General **John C. Pemberton** to cover the area with heavy guns. Previous attempts to take Vicksburg by land and sea had failed.

Ulysses S. Grant was working as a businessman when the Civil War broke out.

★★★★★★★★★★★★
That's Interesting!
★★★★★★★★★★★★

Civil War historian Shelby Foote points out a number of characteristics that made Ulysses S. Grant a great general. Not the least of these was his ability to concentrate. Foote describes Grant working at his desk and needing to get something from across the room: He did not get out of his crouched position. He simply crossed the room, picked up the item while he was still bent over, and returned to his desk without ever losing his train of thought.

 Technology Resources

Linking Geography and History Transparency 14: The War in the East and the West, 1861–1863

★★★★★★★★★★★★
That's Interesting!
★★★★★★★★★★★★

Cave Homes Would you believe that during the Siege of Vicksburg people lived in underground caves? It's true! To protect themselves from the Union cannons, many people moved into caves dug into the hillsides. Caves for a single family usually had one or two rooms. Some large caves could hold as many as 200 people. People furnished their caves with carpets, rocking chairs, and mirrors. They also built shelves into the walls to hold books, candles, flowers, and water jugs.

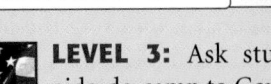

Strategies		Implications
• Union holds its ground, despite surprise attack.	**Battle of Shiloh**	• gave Union greater control of the Mississippi River valley.
• Union attacked southern forces at Jackson, obliterating Vicksburg's reinforcements.	**Seige of Vicksburg**	• gave the Union total control of the Mississippi River, cutting off the western states (AK, LA, TX)
• Fought to protect Union forts in the Midwest.	**Battle of Pea Ridge**	• gave the Union control over Missouri

LEVEL 3: Ask students to imagine they are the aide-de-camp to General Grant. As part of this responsibility, each student should write a report for the War Department in Washington, about either the Battle of Shiloh or the Siege of Vicksburg. Ask students to describe the fighting that took place in the Far West and examine General Grant's strategy for the Union army in the West. Have students conclude with personal commentary on the importance of the victory, and a list of recommendations for future actions. Have volunteers present their work to the class.

★ CLOSE

Organize the class into groups. Have each group write journal entries that a northern soldier might have written, about battles and strategy to gain control of the Mississippi.
COOPERATIVE LEARNING

★ Geography

The Caves of Vicksburg.

Vicksburg was built on the side of a hill that was easy to dig yet also firm enough for solid excavation. During the Siege of Vicksburg, the city's residents burrowed a system of more than 500 caves into the side of the hill. Women and children took shelter in these caves when Union soldiers launched their artillery attacks. The people of Vicksburg brought furniture, rugs, and cookstoves into the caves, which they staffed with their slaves.

CRITICAL THINKING

Why did some Union troops call Vicksburg "prairie dog village?"

ANSWER: Students might suggest that it was because residents of Vicksburg essentially moved their households underground, like prairie dogs.

MAP ANSWERS

1. Tennessee
2. Chickamauga

The War in the West, 1862–1863

Interpreting Maps After the Union victories at Murfreesboro and Chattanooga, the Union was in position to divide the Upper and Lower South.

Skills Assessment

1. **Human Systems** In which western state did the most battles take place?
2. **Analyzing Information** What Confederate victory took place in the West?

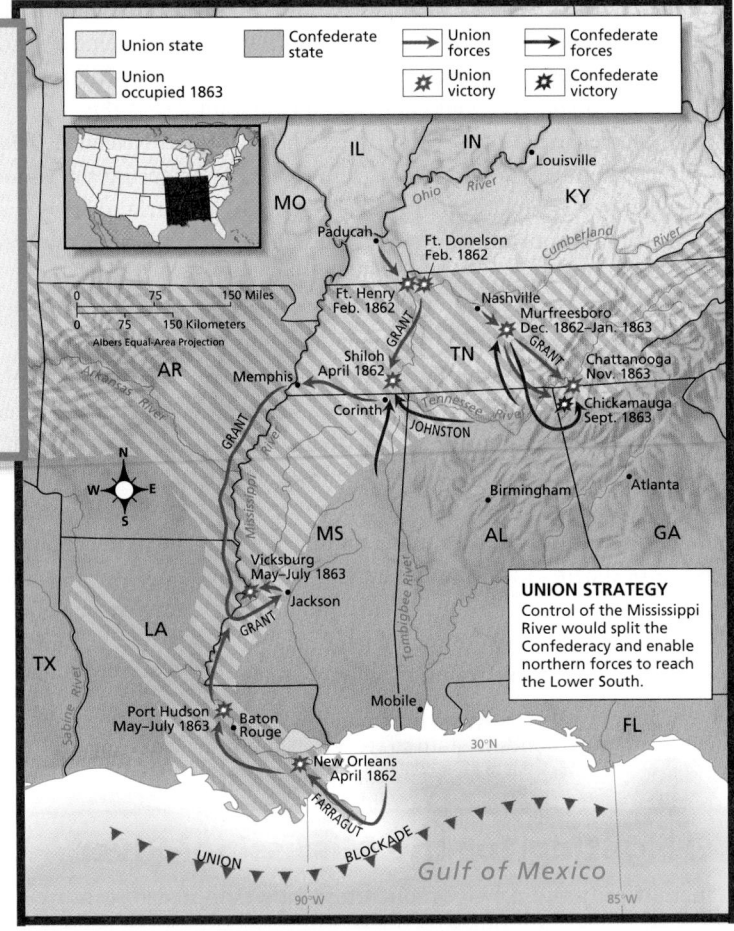

UNION STRATEGY
Control of the Mississippi River would split the Confederacy and enable northern forces to reach the Lower South.

July 4, 1863
General Grant's troops capture Vicksburg.

Analyzing Primary Sources

Supporting a Point of View What reason do the soldiers give Pemberton for thinking that surrender is necessary?
The army is out of food, and the troops are ready to rebel unless they are fed or they surrender.

In the spring of 1863 General Grant blocked southern forces from aiding Vicksburg. He then surrounded the city with his troops. The **Siege of Vicksburg** lasted about six weeks. As supplies ran out, the residents and soldiers inside the city survived by eating horses, dogs, and rats. "We are utterly [completely] cut off from the world, surrounded by a circle of fire," wrote one woman. "People do nothing but eat what they can get, sleep when they can and dodge the shells." In late June a group of Confederate soldiers sent General Pemberton a warning letter.

 History Makers Speak **"The army is now ripe for mutiny [rebellion], unless it can be fed. If you can't feed us, you'd better surrender us, horrible as the idea is."**

—Confederate soldiers at Vicksburg, quoted in *The Civil War*, by Geoffrey C. Ward

There was no real hope of relief. Pemberton surrendered Vicksburg on July 4, 1863, giving the Union control of the Mississippi River.

✔ **Reading Check: Summarizing** What events led to the Union gaining control of the Mississippi River in 1863? Union forces captured New Orleans, followed by other cities on the river, and finally captured Vicksburg.

★ The Far West

Fighting also took place in Arkansas and Missouri, along the Texas coast, and in New Mexico. Little or no fighting occurred in California, which was strongly pro-Union. In August 1861, Confederate forces from Texas marched into New Mexico. Union forces advancing from Colorado defeated the Confederates at Glorieta Pass, near Santa Fe, New Mexico. The Union victory ended Confederate hopes of controlling the Southwest.

The Confederates also tried to take Missouri. Union forces turned the Confederates back in their attempt to seize the federal arsenal at St. Louis in the summer of 1861. In March 1862, Union forces and pro-Confederate Missourians met at the **Battle of Pea Ridge** in northwestern Arkansas. Some American Indians, mainly Cherokee, fought on the side of the Confederates. They hoped that Confederate leaders would give the Indian nations greater independence than the Union had. In addition, slavery was legal in Indian Territory, and some American Indians who were slaveholders supported the Confederacy. Despite being outnumbered, the Union forces won the Battle of Pea Ridge. This victory gave the Union the upper hand in Missouri, but its hold was far from complete. Pro-Confederate units remained active in the region throughout the war. They attacked Union forts and raided towns in Missouri and Kansas forcing Union commanders to keep valuable troops stationed in the area.

Much of the fighting in the West involved the struggle for control of the Mississippi River. Neither side had many troops to spare for the fighting in the Far West.

✔ **Reading Check: Summarizing** What was the significance of the Battle of Pea Ridge, and what fighting took place afterward? It gave the Union limited control over Missouri. Confederates continued to attack Union forts and raid towns in the region.

Section 3 Review

Homework Practice Online
keyword: SA3 HP19

❶ **Identify** and explain:
  • Ulysses S. Grant
  • Battle of Shiloh
  • David Farragut
  • John C. Pemberton
  • Siege of Vicksburg
  • Battle of Pea Ridge

❷ **Identifying Cause and Effect** Copy the graphic organizer below. Use it to identify causes and effects of the listed battles.

Cause		Battles		Effect
	→	Battle of Shiloh	→	
	→	Capture of New Orleans	→	
	→	Siege of Vicksburg	→	
	→	Battle of Pea Ridge	→	

❸ **Finding the Main Idea**
  a. How did General Grant plan to win the war in the West?
  b. Describe the battles that Confederate and Union forces fought in the Far West.

❹ **Writing and Critical Thinking**
  Evaluating Imagine that you are a soldier fighting with the Confederacy at Vicksburg. Write a poem describing the siege and what you think the effect of the battle will be.
  Consider the following:
  • the hardships faced by the people in the city
  • why the results of the battle are important

Section 4

OBJECTIVES

★ Determine how different groups in the North reacted to Abraham Lincoln's Emancipation Proclamation.

★ Identify the ways that African Americans and women contributed to the war effort.

★ Explain how northerners and southerners responded to the new draft laws.

SECTION 4 RESOURCES

REPRODUCIBLE

▶ Guided Reading Strategy 19.4
▶ American History Political Cartoon 12: Copperheads
▶ Biography Reading 19: Clara Barton

TECHNOLOGY

▶ One-Stop Planner, Lesson 19.4
▶ Exploring America's Past Video Segment: A Country Torn Apart; Teacher's Guide, pp. 30–32
▶ Holt Researcher: American History CD–ROM
▶ CNN Presents America: Beginnings to 1914 Segment: Clara Barton and the Legacy of War
▶ Homework Practice Online
▶ HRW Go site

REINFORCEMENT, REVIEW, AND ASSESSMENT

▶ Section 4 Review, p. 599
▶ Daily Quiz 19.4
▶ Main Idea Activity 19.4
▶ English Audio Summary 19.4
▶ Spanish Audio Summary 19.4

Section 4

Life during the War

Read to Discover

1. How did different groups in the North react to Abraham Lincoln's Emancipation Proclamation?
2. How did African Americans and women contribute to the war effort?
3. How did northerners and southerners respond to the new draft laws?

WHY IT MATTERS TODAY

During the Civil War, President Lincoln faced opposition from many Democrats in Congress. Use **CNNfyi.com** or other **current events** sources to find out about a current conflict between the president and members of the opposing party in Congress. Record your findings in your journal.

Define

• contrabands
• *habeas corpus*

Identify

• Emancipation Proclamation
• 54th Massachusetts Infantry
• Copperheads
• Clara Barton

Secretary of State William H. Seward was a key member of Lincoln's cabinet.

The Story Continues

In July 1862 President Lincoln met privately with members of his cabinet, including William H. Seward, to discuss freeing the slaves in the South—a topic of great concern to him. Lincoln felt that slavery strengthened and supported the South. "We must free the slaves or be ourselves subdued [defeated]," he explained. Lincoln's cabinet members told him to wait for a better time to put his plan into action.

★ Freeing the Slaves

President Lincoln supported freeing slaves if it would help the North win the war. Many people in the North wanted to end slavery for other reasons. Some wished to punish southern slaveholders for their role in causing the war. Others argued that continuing slavery would lead to future conflict between the North and the South.

Lincoln faced two problems concerning emancipation, or the freeing of the slaves. First, he feared that northern prejudice against African Americans might weaken support for the war if emancipation became a Union goal. He was also afraid that some northerners would

Have students read Section 4 and Complete Guided Reading Strategy 19.4. Choose one or more of the following activities to explore the section content with students. For further suggestions on block scheduling or team teaching, see the *Block Scheduling Handbook with Team Teaching Strategies.*

LEVEL 1: As a class, summarize the major points of the Emancipation Proclamation. Then lead a discussion on the importance of the document. Ask students to identify how different groups in the North reacted to Abraham Lincoln's Emancipation Proclamation. (*Students'*

responses should reflect the knowledge that African Americans celebrated; some people, like the Copperheads, thought it went beyond the war's purpose of restoring the Union; and abolitionists thought that it did not go far enough.) Encourage students to speculate why each group may have felt the way it did.

ENGLISH LANGUAGE LEARNERS

 HOMEWORK Have students write a letter, reacting to the Emancipation Proclamation to the editor of a local newspaper. Remind students that they can use arguments presented in this section to support their points of view.

Emancipation in 1863

Interpreting Maps The Emancipation Proclamation freed slaves in states that were in rebellion against the Union. The Proclamation did not, however, free slaves in Union states or in areas occupied by Union troops.

Skills Assessment

1. **Places and Regions** In which states were slaves granted freedom by the Emancipation Proclamation?

2. **Summarizing** What was the location of most of the states where slaveholding remained legal?

Map legend:
- Union state
- Border state
- Confederate state
- Territory
- Area of legal slaveholding
- Area in which slavery was abolished by the Emancipation Proclamation

consider slaves to be property that southerners had the right to keep. In addition, the Constitution did not give the president the power to end slavery in the United States.

Lincoln decided to issue a military order freeing slaves only in areas controlled by the Confederacy. Lincoln felt that his authority to end slavery did not apply to the loyal, slaveholding border states. He also did not want to anger citizens in these states.

President Lincoln waited for a northern victory in the East before announcing his plans. The Battle of Antietam was the victory he needed. On September 22, 1862, Lincoln called for all slaves in Confederate-controlled areas to be freed. This **Emancipation Proclamation** went into effect on January 1, 1863. News of the order encouraged southern slaves to escape when they heard that Union troops were nearby. This loss of slave labor hurt the southern economy and the Confederate war effort. Many African Americans and northerners praised the Emancipation Proclamation. Abolitionist Frederick Douglass called January 1, 1863, "the great day which is to determine the destiny [fate] not only of the American Republic, but that of the American Continent." There was also popular support for the Proclamation in Great Britain and France.

Many northern Democrats, however, opposed the Emancipation Proclamation. They wanted only to restore the Union, not to end slavery. A few abolitionists, on the other hand, argued that Lincoln had not gone far enough. William Lloyd Garrison complained that the president had left "slavery, as a system . . . , still to exist in all the so-called loyal Slave States."

✔ **Reading Check: Contrasting** In what different ways did people in the North view the Emancipation Proclamation? Some supported it, some thought it went too far, and others thought it did not go far enough because slavery was still legal.

GLOBAL CONNECTIONS

Reactions to Emancipation

Abraham Lincoln's Emancipation Proclamation drew the attention of many people in Europe. Some workers from Manchester, England, wrote to the president. "We joyfully honor you . . . [for] your belief in the words of your great founders: 'All men are created free and equal.'" A British noble praised the Union's high moral purpose in the Civil War. Giuseppe Garibaldi, an Italian leader, hailed Lincoln as "the heir of the aspirations [dreams] of . . . [abolitionist] John Brown." **How did some Europeans react to the Emancipation Proclamation?**

★ Culture

African American Soldiers. Thousands of African Americans tried to enlist in the Union army, but they were turned down. President Lincoln was concerned that the border states might rebel if African Americans were allowed to serve. As early as 1861 several Union commanders used fugitive slaves as laborers, seamen, and servants. African Americans could not officially serve in the Union army until July 1862.

CRITICAL THINKING

Why do you think Lincoln changed his position on allowing African Americans to enlist?

ANSWER: Students might suggest that Lincoln realized that African American soldiers could help the Union.

MAP ANSWERS

1. Alabama, Arkansas, Florida, Georgia, Louisiana, Mississippi, North Carolina, South Carolina, Texas, and Virginia

2. the border between North and South

GLOBAL CONNECTIONS ANSWER

They were pleased that it was passed and believed it upheld the basic principles upon which the United States was founded.

★ Citizenship

Daily Life

African American soldiers Frederick Douglass encouraged African Americans to fight in the Union army, calling it their "golden opportunity." Many men responded to the call. Despite making up only 2 percent of the North's population, African Americans made up nearly 10 percent of the Union army by the end of the war. Although they faced discrimination, many soldiers celebrated the opportunity to fight for freedom. **What reasons do you think African Americans would have had for joining the Union army cause despite facing discrimination?**

Analyzing Primary Sources

Identifying Points of View According to Douglass, what will serving as soldiers accomplish for African Americans?

Their service to their country will prove that they have earned the right to be U.S. citizens.

★ African Americans and the War

The question of whether to permit African Americans to serve in the military also troubled many northern leaders. The Union navy had already been accepting African American volunteers. Since the war began, abolitionists had called for the Union army to recruit African Americans as well. Frederick Douglass stated that military service would help African Americans earn equal rights.

 History Makers Speak
❝Once let the black man get upon his person the brass letters, U.S.; . . . and a musket on his shoulder and bullets in his pocket, and there is no power on earth which can deny that he has earned the right to citizenship.❞

—Frederick Douglass, quoted in *Battle Cry of Freedom*, by James McPherson

Northern leaders also saw a practical reason to enlist African Americans—the Union needed soldiers. Congress allowed the army to sign up African American volunteers as laborers in July 1862. The War Department also gave **contrabands**, or escaped slaves, the right to join the Union army in South Carolina. Free African Americans in Louisiana and Kansas also formed units in the Union army.

By the spring of 1863, African American units were fighting in the field with the Union army. They took part in a Union attack on Port Hudson, Louisiana, in May 1863. The **54th Massachusetts Infantry** consisted mostly of free African Americans. In July 1863 this regiment played a key role in the attack on South Carolina's Fort Wagner. Lewis Douglass, Frederick Douglass's son, fought in the battle. "My regiment [unit] has established its reputation as a fighting regiment—not a man flinched," he proudly wrote later. The 54th became the most famous African American unit of the war.

About 180,000 African Americans served with the Union army during the war. Despite discrimination, African American soldiers fought bravely. For most of the war, African Americans received less pay than white soldiers. They were usually led by white officers. They also faced greater danger from Confederate troops, who often killed African American prisoners of war or sold them into slavery. In 1864 President Lincoln suggested rewarding African American soldiers in Louisiana by giving them the right to vote. He also wrote a letter praising the contributions of African Americans to the military effort.

History Makers Speak ❝Abandon all the posts now possessed by black men, surrender all these advantages to the enemy, and we would be compelled [forced] to abandon the war in three weeks.❞

—Abraham Lincoln, quoted in *Battle Cry of Freedom*, by James McPherson

✔ **Reading Check: Finding the Main Idea** Why did African Americans serve in the Union army despite the problems they faced? hope of gaining U.S. citizenship; to end or push back slavery; pride in military service

⭐ Problems in the North

The issue of ending slavery added to the problems already brewing in the North. Northerners were growing upset by the length of the war and the increasing number of casualties. A group of northern Democrats led by Clement L. Vallandigham of Ohio began to speak out against the war. War supporters compared these Democrats to a poisonous type of snake, calling them **Copperheads**. Many Copperheads were midwesterners who sympathized with the South, objected to abolition, and wanted the war to end. Vallandigham asked what the war had gained and then said, "Let the dead at Fredericksburg and Vicksburg answer."

Lincoln believed the Copperheads threatened the war effort. To stop them, he suspended the right of *habeas corpus*—the constitutional

Analyzing Primary Sources
Identifying Points of View
How does Lincoln view African American soldiers? He thinks they are necessary to a successful war effort.

THE GRANGER COLLECTION, NEW YORK

Interpreting Political Cartoons
The Copperheads *In this cartoon, northern Democrats who called for peace are shown as deadly copperhead snakes threatening the Union.* **Why do you think the artist chose to depict these politicians in this way?**

LEVEL 3: Organize the class into three groups. Have one of the groups represent African Americans, another represent Copperheads, and the third represent the abolitionists. Then ask students to write the script for a panel discussion in which representatives of all sides are asked questions dealing with their differences in opinion to determine how different groups in the North reacted to Abraham Lincoln's Emancipation Proclamation. Ask groups to write a few sentences outlining their side's position and to formulate questions to ask panelists that will reveal the major differences in opinion between Copperheads and Republicans. *(Students' questions may include: How do you see your life changing as a result of the Proclamation? What, do you feel, are the strong points of the Proclamation?)* Finally, have students perform the panel discussions. **COOPERATIVE LEARNING**

★ CLOSE

Ask students to create two lists: one listing northern criticisms of the war and the other listing southern criticisms. Have students write each government's response next to each criticism. Finally, lead a discussion on the difficulties both governments had in maintaining support for their war effort.

Interdisciplinary Connection

▶Literature◀

Walt Whitman. When the brother of poet Walt Whitman was injured in the Battle of Fredericksburg, Whitman traveled to Virginia to find him. After this exposure to army hospitals, Whitman volunteered as a nursing aide in Washington. His Civil War experience inspired his collection of poetry, *Drum Taps*.

▣ internet connect

TOPIC: Civil War Authors
GO TO: go.hrw.com
KEYWORD: SA3 CF19

ACTIVITY: Have students use the library or search the Internet through the HRW Go site to find information on authors who wrote about their Civil War experiences. Have students identify the words authors used to express their experiences.

Technology Resources

CNN Presents America: Beginnings to 1914
Segment: Clara Barton and the Legacy of War

Research on the ROM

Free Find:
Mary Boykin Chesnut
After reading about Mary Boykin Chesnut on the **Holt Researcher CD–ROM**, imagine that you are writing an entry in her journal. Describe the situation faced by the Confederacy during a particular period of the Civil War.

Southerner Mary Boykin Chesnut kept an extensive journal describing her experiences during the Civil War.

protection against unlawful imprisonment. By ignoring this protection, Union officials could put their enemies in jail without either evidence or trial. Lincoln's actions greatly angered Democrats.

More debate arose in March 1863 when Congress passed a law allowing men to be drafted into military service. Critics noted that dishonesty in the draft was common. Wealthy people could legally buy their way out of military service. The Copperheads complained that it was unfair to force unwilling white men to fight for the freedom of southern slaves.

Other critics shared this belief. In July 1863, riots targeting African Americans and draft officials broke out in New York City. Many of the rioters were poor immigrants afraid of losing their jobs to freed African Americans. Rioters damaged a great deal of property and killed more than 100 people before Union troops could stop the violence.

✔ **Reading Check: Identifying Cause and Effect** Why were people unhappy with Lincoln's war policies, and how did Lincoln attempt to deal with them? The war was long and bloody. Lincoln signed a draft law and ignored the right of *habeas corpus* to silence Democratic opposition.

★ Southern Struggles

The South also faced many challenges. The North's naval blockade took a heavy toll on southerners. Soldiers did not have enough supplies. "Every day we grow weaker. . . . Already they [Confederate soldiers] begin to cry out for more ammunition, and already the blockade is beginning to shut it all out," wrote Mary Boykin Chesnut. The value of Confederate money fell as southern exports dropped. The price of food, clothing, and medicine shot up as supplies ran low. Basic items such as bread cost more than most people could afford.

The severe shortages caused unrest in the South. In the spring of 1863, food riots took place in several southern cities, including Richmond. Southern officials ordered local newspapers not to mention these riots. Confederate president Jefferson Davis feared that the news would embarrass the South and encourage the North to keep fighting.

The government of the Confederacy faced problems because its officials disagreed on many issues. There was also controversy among southerners over their new draft law, approved by Davis in 1862 despite much criticism. One problem was that the southern draft did not apply to men who held many slaves. This rule angered poor southerners, who generally held few, if any, slaves. Confederate private Sam Watkins wrote that the draft law "raised the howl of 'rich man's war, poor man's fight.'" The draft was very unpopular in rural areas such as western North Carolina. Hatred of the draft and some pro-Union feeling in this region led to protests. Some southerners even took up arms against Confederate officials.

✔ **Reading Check: Comparing** What problems did both northerners and southerners have with the new draft laws, and how did they show their feelings? Both opposed the draft; protests and riots took place in both the North and South.

Have students complete the **Section 4 Review** on p. 599. Then have students complete **Daily Quiz 19.4.** As **Alternative Assessment,** you may want to use the monologue or the political cartoon exercises in this section's lessons.

★ RETEACH

Have students complete **Main Idea Activity for English Language Learners and Special-Needs Students 19.4.** Then ask students to create a storyboard depicting women's and African Americans' contributions to the Civil War. Have students create illustrations along with captions explaining the

items they depict. Ask volunteers to share their storyboards with the class. **ENGLISH LANGUAGE LEARNERS**

★ EXTEND

Have students use the library to search for information on women's contributions to the Civil War. Have each student write a biographical sketch on one woman's contributions or write an essay describing women's overall contributions to the war effort. Encourage students to share their research with the class. **BLOCK SCHEDULING**

★ Life on the Home Front

In both the North and the South, the war effort involved people at all levels of society. People too young or too old for military service worked in factories, on farms, and in other areas. Southern women also ran farms and plantations after their husbands and sons went to war.

Women played an important role in providing medical care for soldiers. Dorothea Dix headed more than 3,000 women who served as paid nurses in the Union army. <u>Clara Barton</u> worked as a volunteer, organizing the collection of medicine and supplies for delivery to Union troops on the battlefield. Barton often remained at field hospitals to comfort the wounded. Her work formed the basis for what would become the American Red Cross. Women in the South also cared for sick and wounded soldiers. For example, Sally Louisa Tompkins established a hospital in Richmond.

The efforts of these women volunteers were very important. Soldiers faced great dangers in daily life as well as in battles. For every day of fighting, soldiers spent weeks living in uncomfortable and unhealthy camps. They faced bad weather, disease, and unsafe food. About twice as many Civil War soldiers died of disease than died in combat.

Military prisoners also suffered greatly during the Civil War. The worst conditions were at Andersonville, in southwestern Georgia. Thousands of Union soldiers were held there with no shelter and little food. Following her visit to the prison, southerner Eliza Andrews was told that "at one time the prisoners died at the rate of a hundred and fifty a day."

✔ **Reading Check: Analyzing Information** How did southern and northern women affect the war efforts? They worked on farms and in factories, and they provided medical care on battlefields and in field hospitals.

Interpreting the Visual Record

Camp life *Civil War soldiers on both sides often brought their families to camp with them.* **What do you think some of the advantages and disadvantages of soldiers having their families with them might be?**

Visual Record Answer
Students' responses will vary.

Section 4 Review
ANSWERS

❶ **Define**
- contrabands, p. 596
- *habeas corpus,* p. 597

❷ **Identify**
- Emancipation Proclamation, p. 595
- 54th Massachusetts Infantry, p. 596
- Copperheads, p. 597
- Clara Barton, p. 599

❸ Women: worked as nurses for the Union, worked on farms and in factories, volunteered medical care; African Americans: served in the Union army; Draft Protesters: rioted in the North, took up arms in the South, spoke against the war and draft laws

❹ a. African Americans: supported it but felt they also needed the right to vote; abolitionists: pleased but thought that the entire system of slavery should be abolished; Copperheads: thought the Emancipation Proclamation went too far and that the Union should not fight for the freedom of enslaved African Americans
b. ignored *habeas corpus* and passed a draft law

❺ Students' articles should display an understanding of responses to the draft laws, and the contributions of African Americans and women.

Section 4 Review

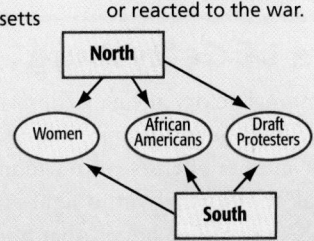

go.
hrw
.com **Homework Practice Online**
keyword: SA3 HP19

❶ **Define** and explain:
- contrabands
- *habeas corpus*

❷ **Identify** and explain:
- Emancipation Proclamation
- 54th Massachusetts Infantry
- Copperheads
- Clara Barton

❸ **Categorizing** Copy the graphic organizer below. Use it to list the ways that people in different parts of society contributed to or reacted to the war.

> **North**
> Women — African Americans — Draft Protesters
> **South**

❹ **Finding the Main Idea**
a. Describe how each of the following groups reacted to the Emancipation Proclamation: African Americans, abolitionists, and Copperheads.

b. What actions did Lincoln take that angered Democrats in the North?

❺ **Writing and Critical Thinking**
Summarizing Imagine that you are a foreign journalist reporting on the war in the North and the South. Write a half-page newspaper article about life on the home front.

Consider the following:
- responses to new draft laws
- the contributions of African Americans
- the contributions of women

Section 5

OBJECTIVES

⭐ Examine why the Battle of Gettysburg was important.

⭐ Identify the campaigns that were launched in Virginia and the Lower South.

⭐ Explain how and when the war finally ended.

SECTION 5 RESOURCES

REPRODUCIBLE
▶ Guided Reading Strategy 19.5
▶ Graphic Organizer 19: Civil War Battles

TECHNOLOGY
▶ One-Stop Planner, Lesson 19.5
▶ Holt Researcher: American History CD–ROM
▶ Art in American History Transparency 13: Near Andersonville
▶ Homework Practice Online
▶ HRW Go site

REINFORCEMENT, REVIEW, AND ASSESSMENT
▶ Section 5 Review, p. 605
▶ Daily Quiz 19.5
▶ Main Idea Activity 19.5
▶ English Audio Summary 19.5
▶ Spanish Audio Summary 19.5

Section 5

The Tide of the War Turns

Read to Discover
1. Why was the Battle of Gettysburg important?
2. What campaigns were launched in Virginia and the Lower South?
3. How and when did the war finally end?

WHY IT MATTERS TODAY

Many people participate in reenactments of Civil War battles or visit national parks located on Civil War battle sites. Use **CNNfyi.com** or other **current events** sources to find out about either a historical reenactment taking place today or a historical national park. Record your findings in your journal.

Define
• total war

Identify
• Battle of Gettysburg
• George G. Meade
• George Pickett
• Pickett's Charge
• Gettysburg Address
• Wilderness Campaign
• William Tecumseh Sherman
• Appomattox Courthouse

General Stonewall Jackson was shot during the Battle of Chancellorsville.

The Story Continues

In May 1863 General Lee's troops defeated a larger Union force near the town of Chancellorsville, Virginia. The fighting was heavy. While riding at the front lines, Lee's trusted general Stonewall Jackson was accidentally shot by his own troops. Doctors cut off Jackson's left arm in an effort to save his life. Still, his condition grew worse. When Lee found out that Jackson was hurt, he told an aide, "Tell him to . . . come back to me as soon as he can. He has lost his left arm, but I have lost my right." Jackson died just a few days after the battle ended.

⭐ The Battle of Gettysburg

In addition to the stunning victory at Chancellorsville, the Confederates also triumphed at Fredericksburg, Virginia. These successes encouraged General Lee to launch another offensive into Union territory. As before, his goals were to break the North's will to fight and to capture much-needed supplies for his army. Lee hoped that another victory would turn the tide of war in the Confederacy's favor.

In mid-June 1863 Lee cut across northern Maryland into southern Pennsylvania. Lee's forces gathered near a small town called Gettysburg. Lee was unaware that Union soldiers were just northwest of the town. When a Confederate raiding party went to Gettysburg for supplies, the troops came under fire. This event triggered the **Battle of Gettysburg**. Some 75,000 Confederate soldiers faced about 90,000 Union troops.

The battle began on July 1, 1863. The Confederates pushed the Union line back to Cemetery Ridge, just south of the town. The Confederate forces occupied nearby Seminary Ridge. On July 2 Lee ordered an attack on the left side of the Union line. The bold charge of Union colonel Joshua Chamberlain's troops at Little Round Top, however, helped turn back the Confederates. Then General **George G. Meade** placed more soldiers on the Union line.

Lee planned to rush the center of the Union line. This task fell to three divisions of Confederate soldiers. General **George Pickett** commanded the largest unit. In the late afternoon, about 14,000 men took part in **Pickett's Charge** up Cemetery Ridge. The attack was a disaster. Confederate lieutenant G. W. Finley was part of the charge. "Men were falling all around us, and cannon and muskets were raining death upon us," he wrote. Fewer than half of Pickett's troops reached the top of the ridge. All those who reached the Union wall were captured or killed. Only about 6,500 men returned to the Confederate rear. Lee ordered Pickett to organize his division for a possible counterattack. "General Lee, I *have* no division now," Pickett replied. "The battle was now over," wrote Union lieutenant Jesse Young, "but nobody knew it."

✔ **Reading Check: Identifying Cause and Effect** What led to the Battle of Gettysburg, and what was its outcome? Lee decided to launch an offensive into Union territory; the Union troops defeated the Confederates.

July 1–3, 1863: *The Battle of Gettysburg takes place, ending in Union victory.*

May–June 1864: *The Wilderness Campaign weakens Lee's forces in Virginia.*

Sept. 2, 1864: *Atlanta falls to Sherman's forces.*

Dec. 10, 1864: *Sherman's army invades Savannah.*

April 2, 1865: *Grant surrounds Lee's army in Richmond.*

April 9, 1865: *Lee surrenders to Grant.*

LEVEL 3: Organize the class into an even number of groups. Have each group write a special newspaper section covering the surrender at Appomattox and the possible long-term consequences of the Civil War. Assign the northern point of view to half of the groups and the southern view to the other half. Each student should contribute something to his or her group's project: an article, a political cartoon, or an editorial. **COOPERATIVE LEARNING**

Note: For an additional teaching idea, see the Chapter 19 Predicting Consequences activity in the **Creative Teaching Strategies** handbook.

Science, Technology & Society

Early Photography. No pictures captured Lincoln's image as he delivered the Gettysburg Address. The speech lasted only about two minutes—much shorter than the average speech of the era—and the photographer was still setting up his camera when Lincoln sat down. One historian has pointed out that Lincoln spoke so briefly that the photographer probably did not even have time to get his camera's shutter open.

internet connect

TOPIC: Early Photography
GO TO: go.hrw.com
KEYWORD: SA3 CF19

ACTIVITY: Have students use the library or search the Internet through the HRW Go site to find more information about photography during the mid- to late 1800s. Lead the class in a discussion about the development of photographic technology.

July 4, 1863

Union troops win the Battle of Gettysburg.

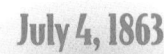

★ A Turning Point

Rain slowed Meade's troops, allowing Lee to retreat from Gettysburg on July 4 and return to Virginia. Nonetheless, Gettysburg was a turning point in the war. Lee's troops would never again launch an attack onto northern soil. The Union victory at Gettysburg took place on the same day as General Grant's capture of Vicksburg in Mississippi. These critical victories made northerners believe that the Confederacy could be defeated. The Union triumph at Gettysburg, however, had come at a high price. Union casualties numbered more than 23,000. The Confederacy suffered more than 28,000 casualties.

President Lincoln expressed the Union's new sense of confidence and commitment. He delivered the **Gettysburg Address** on November 19, 1863. This short, moving speech is one of the most famous in American history. Lincoln spoke of the importance of liberty, equality, and democratic ideals. He reminded listeners that the war was being fought to protect these cherished principles. Lincoln dedicated himself and the rest of the North to winning the war and preserving the Union. He knew that a difficult road still lay ahead.

✔ **Reading Check: Drawing Inferences and Conclusions** Why do you think Lincoln talked about liberty, equality, democratic ideals, and unity in the Gettysburg Address? to remind Americans of why the war was being fought; to make Americans more willing to keep fighting the difficult war

This painting shows Robert E. Lee with some of his generals at his side in 1863.

HOMEWORK Ask students to review Section 5. Then have them write down the various subheadings. Ask students to write one or two sentences under each subheading that convey its main idea.
ENGLISH LANGUAGE LEARNERS

 LEVEL 3: Ask students to write an informative essay about the Battle of Gettysburg as well as the campaigns that were launched in Virginia and the Lower South. In their essays, students should explain the importance of each event. Ask volunteers to read their essays to the class.

SPOTLIGHT
on the Gettysburg Address
Ask students to imagine that they are reporters at the dedication of the Gettysburg Cemetery. Have them write a summary of President Lincoln's speech and describe how it was received. Refer students to the copy of the address in the Historical Documents section of the chapter and encourage them to quote and comment on segments of the address. Ask volunteers to read their summaries to the class.
BLOCK SCHEDULING

Interpreting the Visual Record

Battles *During the Civil War, soldiers on each side were often ordered to charge well-defended positions, leading to very high casualties.* **Whose perspective is the artist trying to portray? Explain your answer.**

⭐ Grant's Drive to Richmond

Lincoln was impressed with General Grant's successes at Vicksburg and in the West. He brought Grant to the East and gave him command of the Union army. In early 1864 Grant forced Lee to fight a series of battles in Virginia that stretched Confederate soldiers and supplies to their limits.

From May through June, the opposing armies fought a series of battles in northern and central Virginia. Union troops launched the **Wilderness Campaign** with about 100,000 men against 70,000 Confederates. The first battle took place in early May about 50 miles northwest of Richmond. Grant then ordered General Meade southeast to Spotsylvania. There the fighting raged for 10 days. Over the next month, Union soldiers pressed the Confederate troops back to just north of Richmond. The Battle of Cold Harbor took place from June 1 to June 3, only 10 miles northeast of Richmond. It was Grant's worst defeat of the campaign. During one brief assault some 7,000 Union troops were killed or wounded. The battle ended Grant's plans to advance on the Confederate capital.

Union forces suffered incredible losses in the Wilderness Campaign, with twice as many casualties as their Confederate opponents. Even so, Grant continued his aggressive strategy. He knew he would be getting additional soldiers, but that Lee was running low on troops. Grant slowly but surely pressed forward. He told another officer, "I propose to fight it out along this line if it takes all summer."

After Cold Harbor, Grant moved south of Richmond. He had hoped to take the key railroad junction at Petersburg, Virginia. Lee's army, however, formed a solid defense. Grant called off his attack and prepared to lay siege to Petersburg. Grant was winning the war, but he had not captured Richmond. This failure was discouraging for Lincoln.

✔ **Reading Check: Analyzing Information** Why was Grant's 1864 campaign in Virginia successful despite the huge casualties? The campaign also took a huge toll on Lee's army, which could not get more reinforcements, and the Union army got closer to Richmond.

★★★★★★★★★★★
That's Interesting!
★★★★★★★★★★★

A Desperate Plan Did you know that near the end of the war the Confederacy considered having slaves serve in its army? It's true! As the South lost thousands of soldiers, some leaders suggested that slaves should serve in the army. They would then be freed after the war was over. Lee was in favor of this plan. Another general, however, was upset at the thought of drafting African Americans. He wrote, "If slaves will make good soldiers, our whole theory of slavery is wrong." In early 1865 the Confederate president Jefferson Davis had signed a "Negro Soldier Law." The war ended, however, before this law had much effect on Confederate forces.

⭐ Daily Life

Desertion in the Civil War. The Confederate army had higher rates of desertion than the Union army. By the end of 1864, nearly half of all Confederate soldiers had left the ranks. Some men went home to their families, others joined guerrilla groups that preyed both on soldiers and civilians, and still others hid in the mountains or forests. Some deserters even joined the Union army.

CRITICAL THINKING

Why do you think the Confederate army had more deserters than the Union army?

ANSWER: Students might suggest that soldiers deserted because the Confederacy lost more battles than the Union did or because the draft was less popular in the South than in the North.

Technology Resources
 Art in American History Transparency 13: Near Andersonville

Visual Record Answer

Students might suggest that the artist is trying to portray the Union's perspective because of the presence of U.S. flags.

SPOTLIGHT
on Civil War Battles

Have students search the library to find information on the battles covered in this section. Ask students to develop the design for a Web site that shows how the war progressed after Gettysburg. The main page should provide a general overview of the push that led to Union victory, with links to other battles and events leading up to and including Lee's surrender at Appomattox. The linked pages should provide information about specific battles and key events. Encourage students to explain their sites to the class. **BLOCK SCHEDULING**

⊠ CLOSE

Explain to students that the chances for Lincoln's re-election seemed to increase as the North began to gain an advantage over the South. Have students develop campaign posters that could have been used to support Lincoln. Encourage students to include events discussed in this section such as the Battle of Gettysburg, Sherman's march, and so on, as reasons to offer support for Lincoln. **ENGLISH LANGUAGE LEARNERS**

★★★★★★★★★★★
That's Interesting!
★★★★★★★★★★★

Do you think it would be safe for a president to take a walk alone at night during times as volatile as the Civil War? That is exactly what President Lincoln did. Every night President Lincoln would walk to the War Department to hear news about the Civil War. There he received telegraph reports updating him on the Union's progress in the war. It is unlikely that Lincoln's advisers worried about his safety on his trips alone at night. The War Department was stationed in a building just across the White House lawn.

Visual Record Answer

Students might suggest that the cannons might indicate a total-war strategy.

Interpreting the Visual Record

Total war *General William Tecumseh Sherman, shown above, led his Union troops on a destructive March to the Sea.* **What evidence of Sherman's total-war strategy can you identify in the scene shown above?**

★ Sherman Strikes the South

Lincoln needed a victory to help him win re-election in 1864. The bold campaign of General **William Tecumseh Sherman** provided this key victory. Sherman carried out the Union plan to destroy southern railroads and industries. In the spring of 1864, Sherman marched south from Tennessee with 100,000 troops. His goal was to take Atlanta, Georgia. From May through August, Sherman's army moved steadily through the Appalachian Mountains toward Atlanta. Several times, Sherman avoided defenses set up by Confederate general Joseph Johnston.

In July Sherman was within sight of Atlanta. His troops drove back Confederate forces trying to protect the city. The Confederate troops retreated as Sherman held Atlanta under siege. Atlanta fell to Sherman on September 2, 1864. Much of the city was destroyed by artillery and fire. Sherman ordered the residents who still remained to leave. The loss of Atlanta cost the South an important railroad link and center of industry. The victory also showed northerners that progress was being made in defeating the South. This success helped convince Union voters to re-elect Lincoln in a landslide.

Shortly after the election, General Sherman began his next attack. His goal was the port city of Savannah, Georgia. In mid-November 1864 Sherman left Atlanta with a force of about 60,000 men. He said he would "make Georgia howl!"

On his March to the Sea, Sherman waged **total war**—destroying both civilian and military resources. Sherman felt that total war would ruin the South's economy and its ability to fight. He ordered his troops to destroy railways, bridges, crops, livestock, and other resources. They burned plantations and freed slaves. Sherman's army reached Savannah on December 10, 1864. They left behind them a wide path of destruction more than 250 miles long. Sherman believed his tactics would hasten the end of the war.

✔ **Reading Check: Sequencing** List the key events in Sherman's march through the South in 1864 in their proper sequence. See paragraphs above for dates and events.

☆ **REVIEW AND ASSESS**

Have students complete the **Section 5 Review** on p. 605. Then have students complete **Daily Quiz 19.5**. As **Alternative Assessment**, you may want to use the newspaper article or the Web site exercises in this section's lessons.

☆ **RETEACH**

Have students complete **Main Idea Activity for English Language Learners and Special-Needs Students 19.5.** Organize the class into three groups and assign to each group one of the Read to Discover questions from this section. Have each group develop an answer to present to the class. Then ask each group to decide on the best format to use when presenting its answer to the class, such as an oral presentation or a play. Finally, have each group make its presentation. **ENGLISH LANGUAGE LEARNERS , COOPERATIVE LEARNING**

☆ **EXTEND**

Assign each student a battle mentioned in this section. Have them use the library to find information on historical museums or reenactments that deal with the battle. Then have students use this information to create a bulletin-board display about his or her assigned battle. **BLOCK SCHEDULING**

☆ The South Surrenders

In early April Sherman closed in on the last Confederate defenders in North Carolina. Grant finally broke through the Confederate defenses at Petersburg. On April 2 Lee was forced to retreat from Richmond. As Union troops poured into the Confederate capital, the final days of the war began.

By the second week of April 1865, Grant had surrounded Lee's army and demanded its surrender. Lee hoped to join the remaining Confederates in North Carolina, but Grant cut off his escape just west of Richmond. Trapped in the small town of **Appomattox Courthouse**, Lee concluded that the situation was hopeless.

The Union and Confederate leaders met on Palm Sunday, April 9, 1865. There Lee signed the surrender documents, ending the long bloody war. Grant later wrote that he found the scene at Appomattox Courthouse more tragic than joyful.

 History Makers Speak 66I felt . . . sad and depressed at the downfall of a foe [enemy] who had fought so long and valiantly [bravely], and had suffered so much for a cause, though that cause was, I believe, one of the worst for which a people ever fought.99

—Ulysses S. Grant, *Personal Memoirs*

The Civil War had deep and lasting effects. Almost 620,000 Americans lost their lives in the four years of fighting. It was the most costly conflict in American history. Bitterness over the war would linger in both the North and the South for many years as the nation tried to heal its wounds and rebuild.

✔ **Reading Check: Finding the Main Idea** Why did Lee surrender? Grant's army had surrounded him, and he was unable to reach the remaining Confederates in North Carolina.

General Robert E. Lee signs the surrender documents. "There is nothing left for me to do but go and see General Grant," Lee had said. "I would rather die a thousand deaths."

April 9, 1865

General Lee surrenders to General Grant at Appomattox Courthouse.

Section 5 Review

 **go. hrw .com Homework Practice Online**
keyword: SA3 HP19

1 **Define** and explain:
• total war

2 **Identify** and explain:
• Battle of Gettysburg
• George G. Meade
• George Pickett
• Pickett's Charge
• Gettysburg Address
• Wilderness Campaign
• William Tecumseh Sherman
• Appomattox Courthouse

3 **Sequencing** Copy the graphic organizer below. Use it to fill in and explain the events that led to the end of the Civil War.

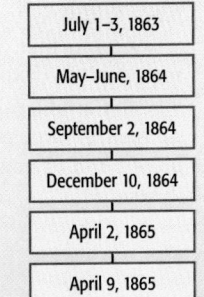

| July 1–3, 1863 |
| May–June, 1864 |
| September 2, 1864 |
| December 10, 1864 |
| April 2, 1865 |
| April 9, 1865 |

4 **Finding the Main Idea**
a. How might the war have been different if Confederate forces had won the Battle of Gettysburg in 1863?

b. How did the Union win the war in the East and in the South?

5 **Writing and Critical Thinking**
Evaluating Imagine that you are either a northern or southern soldier present at Appomattox Courthouse. Write an account of General Lee's surrender.

Consider the following:
• the campaign against Richmond
• the relations between northerners and southerners

★★★★★★★★★★★★★★★★★★
Section 5 Review ANSWERS

1 **Define**
• total war, p. 604

2 **Identify**
• Battle of Gettysburg, p. 601
• George G. Meade, p. 601
• George Pickett, p. 601
• Pickett's Charge, p. 601
• Gettysburg Address, p. 602
• Wilderness Campaign, p. 603
• William Tecumseh Sherman, p. 604
• Appomattox Courthouse, p. 605

3 July 1–3, 1863: Battle of Gettysburg ended in Union victory; May–June 1864: Wilderness Campaign weakens Lee's forces in Virginia; September 2, 1864: Atlanta falls to Sherman's forces; December 10, 1864: Sherman's army invades Savannah; April 2, 1865: Grant surrounds Lee's army in Richmond; April 9, 1865: Lee surrenders to Grant

4 a. Students' answers will vary.
b. Grant attacked Lee's forces in VA to stretch Confederate soldiers and supplies and to advance on Richmond. Sherman led an army through the Lower South to destroy southern railroads and industries.

5 Students' accounts will vary but should include the campaign against Richmond, the terms of the surrender, and the relations between northerners and southerners.

The Civil War **605**

605

ANALYZING PRIMARY SOURCES ANSWERS

1. the authority he holds as the commander of the U.S. military

2. Students' answers will vary, but students might suggest that Lincoln was wary of northern racism and wanted to target slaves in the Confederates states, which were at war with the Union.

ANALYZING PRIMARY SOURCES ANSWERS

1. to keep the Union together

2. He thinks they are very important—worth dying for and worth continuing the war to preserve.

1863

THE EMANCIPATION PROCLAMATION

When the Union army won the Battle of Antietam, President Lincoln felt that the timing was right for a bold move. In late September 1862 he issued a preliminary Emancipation Proclamation. On January 1, 1863, the following official Proclamation went into effect.

A poster celebrating the Emancipation Proclamation

A Proclamation by the President of the United States of America

Whereas on the twenty-second day of September, A.D. 1862, a proclamation was issued by the President of the United States, containing, among other things, the following, **to wit:**[1]

"That on the first day of January, A.D. 1863, all persons held as slaves within any state or designated part of a state, the people whereof shall then be in rebellion against the United States, shall be then, **thenceforward,**[2] and forever free; and the executive government of the United States, including the military and naval authority thereof, will recognize and maintain the freedom of such persons and will do no act or acts to **repress**[3] such persons or any of them, in any efforts they may make for their actual freedom.

"That the Executive will on the 1st day of January aforesaid, by proclamation, **designate**[4] the states and parts of states, if any, in which the people thereof, . . . shall then be in rebellion against the United States; and the fact that any state or the people thereof shall on that day be in good faith represented in the Congress of the United States by members chosen thereto at elections wherein a majority of the qualified voters of such states shall have participated shall, in the absence of strong **countervailing**[5] testimony, be **deemed conclusive**[6] evidence that such state and

the people thereof are not then in rebellion against the United States."

Now, therefore, I, Abraham Lincoln, President of the United States, by virtue of the power in me **vested**[7] as Commander-in-Chief of the Army and Navy of the United States in time of actual armed rebellion against the authority and government of the United States, and as a fit and necessary war measure for suppressing said rebellion, do, on this first day of January, A.D. 1863, and in **accordance**[8] with my purpose so to do, publicly proclaimed for the full period of one hundred days from the first day above mentioned, order and designate as the states and parts of states wherein the people thereof, . . . are in this day in rebellion against the United States. . . .

And I hereby **enjoin upon**[9] the people so declared to be free to **abstain**[10] from all violence, unless in necessary self-defense; and I recommend to them that, in all cases when allowed, they labor faithfully for reasonable wages.

And I further declare and make known that such persons of suitable condition will be received into the armed service of the United States to **garrison**[11] forts, positions, stations, and other places, and to man vessels of all sorts in said service.

And upon this act, sincerely believed to be an act of justice, warranted by the Constitution upon military necessity, I **invoke**[12] the considerate judgment of mankind and the gracious favor of Almighty God.

Analyzing Primary Sources

1. What authority did Lincoln claim allowed him to issue the Emancipation Proclamation?

2. Why do you think Lincoln did not free all slaves?

---

[1] **to wit:** namely
[2] **thenceforward:** afterward
[3] **repress:** keep down
[4] **designate:** name

[5] **countervailing:** opposing
[6] **deemed conclusive:** considered certain
[7] **vested:** given
[8] **accordance:** agreement

[9] **enjoin upon:** order
[10] **abstain:** hold back
[11] **garrison:** defend
[12] **invoke:** call upon

1863

ABRAHAM LINCOLN'S GETTYSBURG ADDRESS

On November 19, 1863, Abraham Lincoln addressed a crowd gathered to dedicate a cemetery at the Gettysburg battlefield. His short speech reminded Americans of the ideals on which the Republic was founded.

Lincoln gives the Gettysburg Address.

Four score and seven years ago our fathers brought forth on this continent, a new nation, **conceived**[1] in Liberty, and dedicated to the **proposition**[2] that all men are created equal.

Now we are engaged in a great civil war, testing whether that nation, or any nation so conceived and so dedicated, can long endure. We are met on a great battlefield of that war. We have come to dedicate a portion of that field, as a final resting place for those who here gave their lives that that nation might live. It is altogether fitting and proper that we should do this.

But, in a larger sense, we can not dedicate—we can not **consecrate**[3]—we can not **hallow**[4]—this ground. The brave men, living and dead, who struggled here, have consecrated it, far above our poor power to add or **detract**.[5] The world will little note nor long remember what we say here, but it can never forget what they did here. It is for us

the living, rather, to be dedicated here to the unfinished work which they who fought here have thus far so nobly advanced. It is rather for us to be here dedicated to the great task remaining before us—that from these honored dead we take increased devotion to that cause for which they gave the last full measure of devotion—that we here highly **resolve**[6] that these dead shall not have died in vain—that this nation, under God, shall have a new birth of freedom—and that government of the people, by the people, for the people shall not perish from the earth.

Analyzing Primary Sources

1. For what cause does Lincoln say the soldiers at Gettysburg died?

2. How does Lincoln value liberty, equality, and democracy?

---

[1] **conceived:** created
[2] **proposition:** idea

[3] **consecrate:** set apart
[4] **hallow:** make holy

[5] **detract:** take away from
[6] **resolve:** decide

The Chapter at a Glance
Students' time lines will vary but should accurately display the key events of the Civil War.

Identifying People and Ideas
1. important federal post that controlled entrance to the Charleston Harbor

2. Delaware, Kentucky, Maryland, and Missouri; position made them key to both the North and the South

3. Confederate victory that dashed Union hopes of an easy win

4. leader of the Confederate army in Virginia

5. most important Union general in the West

6. Union army's six-week long blockade that led the city to surrender

7. an order ending slavery

8. constitutional protection against unlawful imprisonment

9. important Union victory that gave the North more control of the Mississippi River valley

10. town where Union troops cornered Confederate ones, forcing a surrender and ending the war

REVIEW AND ASSESSMENT RESOURCES

REPRODUCIBLE

▶ Vocabulary Activity 19

TECHNOLOGY

▶ Chapter 19 Test Generator (on the One-Stop Planner)
▶ Global Skill Builder CD–ROM
▶ HRW Go site

REINFORCEMENT, REVIEW, AND ASSESSMENT

▶ Chapter 19 Review, pp. 607–09
▶ Chapter 19 Tutorial for Students, Parents, Mentors, and Peers

▶ Chapter 19 Test (Form A or B)
▶ Alternative Assessment Handbook
▶ Chapter 19 Test for English Language Learners and Special-Needs Students

✪ REVIEW

Have students complete the **Chapter 19 Review** on pages 608–09.

✪ ASSESS

Use one of the chapter tests to assess students' understanding of the content. For **Alternative Assessment**, see the **Alternative Assessment Handbook**.

Understanding Main Ideas

1. North: advantages—large population, many factories and shipyards, network of railways, more money; disadvantages—had to defeat & occupy large areas of enemy territory; South: advantages—skilled officers, needed only to defend itself; disadvantages—fewer people, factories, and shipyards, less money, weaker transportation system

2. showed the war would not be won easily and quickly

3. sent ships to outrun and avoid the blockade, tried to destroy the Union navy with their ironclad

4. gave the Union complete control of the river

5. bravely served in the Union army

6. VA: attacked Lee's forces repeatedly in an effort to capture Richmond; Lower South: sent Sherman to capture southern cities.

7. Grant's forces trapped Lee near Richmond, and Lee surrendered to the Union on April 9, 1865.

You Be the Historian—Reviewing Themes

1. They were heavily armored and changed the way that naval warfare would be fought.

2. War severely harmed the South's economy.

Chapter 19 Review

The Chapter at a Glance

Examine the visual summary of the chapter below. Work with a classmate to create a time line that shows the key events of the war.

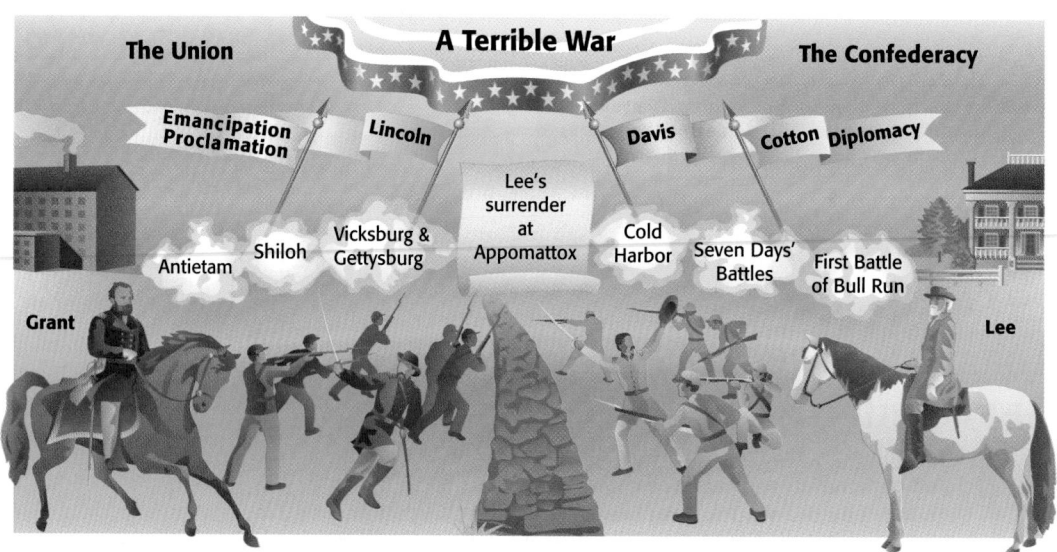

Identifying People and Ideas

Use the following terms or people in historically significant sentences.

1. Fort Sumter
2. border states
3. First Battle of Bull Run
4. Robert E. Lee
5. Ulysses S. Grant
6. Siege of Vicksburg
7. Emancipation Proclamation
8. *habeas corpus*
9. Battle of Gettysburg
10. Appomattox Courthouse

Understanding Main Ideas

Section 1 *(Pages 580–584)*

1. What advantages and disadvantages did the North and the South each have at the beginning of the Civil War?

Section 2 *(Pages 585–589)*

2. How did the First Battle of Bull Run in 1861 change many northerners' ideas about the war?
3. How did the South attempt to avoid the naval blockade?

Section 3 *(Pages 590–593)*

4. How did the Siege of Vicksburg help the Union gain control of the Mississippi River?

Section 4 *(Pages 594–599)*

5. How did African Americans help the war effort?

Section 5 *(Pages 600–605)*

6. What campaigns did Grant plan in Virginia and the Lower South?
7. How did the war end in 1865?

You Be the Historian— Reviewing Themes

1. **Science, Technology & Society** How did ironclads reflect the changes that new technology brought to the war?
2. **Economics** What effect did the war have on the South's economy?
3. **Citizenship** How did northerners and southerners oppose the war, and how did the Union and Confederate governments respond?

Thinking Critically

1. **Supporting a Point of View** Which key 1863 battle—Vicksburg or Gettysburg—do you think was the most important turning point in the war? Explain your answer.
2. **Comparing and Contrasting** In what ways were the beliefs of, and challenges faced by, Presidents Lincoln and Davis similar and different?
3. **Summarizing** What ideas about equality, government, liberty, and union did Lincoln present in his first inaugural address and the Gettysburg Address?

Organize students into five groups and assign one of the chapter's sections to each group. Have students create flowcharts on poster board or butcher paper, illustrating the development of the main topics discussed in the section. Ask groups to include all the key terms from their section and to connect these terms to the appropriate main topic.

ENGLISH LANGUAGE LEARNERS ,

COOPERATIVE LEARNING

Portfolio Extensions

American History

1. Interdisciplinary Connection to Literature

Tell students that many writers wrote about their impressions of the war. Then have them find one of these works, such as *Hospital Sketches* by Louisa May Alcott. Ask students to read the book that they have chosen and then report on it to the class.

2. Linking to Community Have students use their local library or other resources to obtain information on how individuals in their community took part in the Civil War or other important conflicts. Ask volunteers to discuss their findings with the class.

Social Studies Skills Workshop

Interpreting Graphs

Study the graph below. Then use the information on the graph to help you answer the following questions.

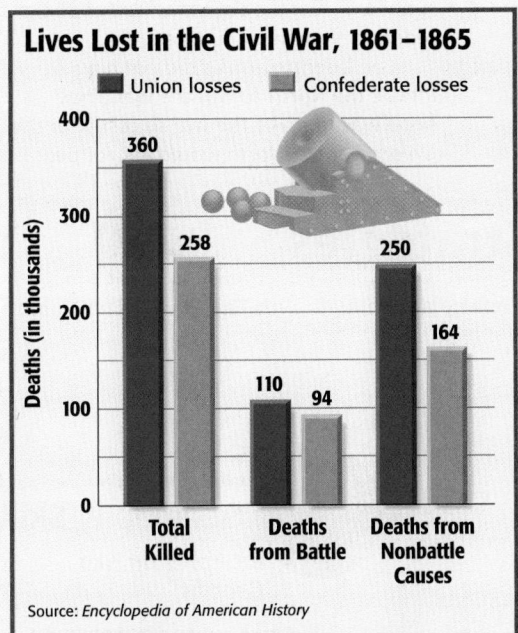

Lives Lost in the Civil War, 1861–1865

■ Union losses   ■ Confederate losses

Deaths (in thousands)

- Total Killed: 360 / 258
- Deaths from Battle: 110 / 94
- Deaths from Nonbattle Causes: 250 / 164

Source: Encyclopedia of American History

1. About how many soldiers in total were killed during the war?
   a. 418,000
   b. 618,000
   c. 102,000
   d. more than 1 million

2. About what percentage of the total deaths from battle were Union soldiers?
   a. about 66 percent
   b. about 30 percent
   c. about 54 percent
   d. 50 percent

3. Based on your knowledge of the period, why do you think the number of deaths from nonbattle causes was higher than the number of deaths caused by battles?

Analyzing Primary Sources

Read the following excerpt about the Fugitive Slave Act from Abraham Lincoln's first inaugural address, then answer the questions that follow.

❝Again, in any law upon this subject, ought not all the safeguards of liberty known in civilized and humane jurisprudence to be introduced, so that a free man be not, in any case, surrendered as a slave? And might it not be well, at the same time, to provide by a law for the enforcement of that clause in the Constitution which guarranties that 'The citizens of each State shall be entitled to all previleges and immunities of citizens in the several States?'❞

4. Which of the following statements best describes Lincoln's view of liberty?
   a. No matter what their race, no free person should ever be treated like a slave.
   b. Different laws on freedom should apply to people in different states.
   c. Slavery is wrong and should be abolished.
   d. The current Fugitive Slave Act is fair.

5. How do you think Lincoln views the government's role in preserving the equality of all citizens?

3. North and South—people opposed draft laws because they were not applied equally to rich men and poor men; antidraft riots took place in the North, and food riots took place in the South. Responses—North had antiwar Democrats whom Lincoln suppressed by suspending *habeas corpus*; Jefferson Davis blocked news of riots in the South.

Thinking Critically

1. Students' answers will vary.

2. Both men appointed aggressive military leaders and both had to deal with popular dissent at home. Lincoln suspended *habeas corpus*, and Davis censored news of food riots. Davis supported secession and slavery, while Lincoln supported neither, in principle.

3. Students should refer to the Gettysburg Address on p. 607 for their answers.

Skills Workshop

1. b

2. c

3. Students might suggest the lack of advanced medical care, the lack of supplies for many soldiers during the war, and the dangers of disease in army camps.

4. a

5. Students' answers will vary, but students should note that Lincoln is proposing a law ensuring that all citizens will have the same rights in every state, so that all will have equal treatment and rights.

Alternative Assessment

Building Your Portfolio

American History

Cooperative Learning

Organize the class into small groups. Each group will write part of a chapter for a textbook on the consequences of the Civil War. Choose one of the following topics: the roles of women during the war, the lives of soldiers, or the war's effect on former slaves and free African Americans. Each group should conduct research and then write its section. Be sure to create images, maps, or charts as needed to place in your group's section.

☑ internet connect

Internet Activity: go.hrw.com

keyword: SA3 CF19

Choose a topic about the Civil War to:

- View photographs and write a poem describing the life of a soldier in the war.
- Research Civil War authors.
- Create a 3D model of the battlefield at Gettysburg and then pose and answer questions with a partner about the events of the battle.

go. hrw .com

LET'S GET STARTED!

As students enter the classroom, ask them to name as many states as they can that made up the Union and then the Confederacy. *(Students' responses will vary but should include: Georgia, Maryland, New Jersey, Pennsylvania, Virginia, and so on.)* Have students list any information they know about the population, economy, or geography of each side. Then lead a discussion about ways that a region's geographic location and climate influence its economy. Explain to students that the major focus leading up to the Civil War was the issue of slavery. Once the war began, each side began to focus on how it could best use its resources to win the war. Tell students that they will study maps and graphs that illustrate the advantages and disadvantages each side had as well as the locations of the war's major battles that are described in this unit.

★ TEACH

Have students read the Connecting to Geography lesson. Choose one or more of the following activities to explore the Connecting to Geography content with students.

★ Global Relations

King Cotton. In 1860 the South grew two thirds of the world's cotton supply. Britain was particularly dependent on southern cotton. Approximately one quarter of the British people were involved in textile production, and three fourths of the cotton that Britain used in its textile mills was imported from the United States. Because the British economy would suffer without cotton, southerners assumed that the British would support the Confederacy during the war. However, the British had a large stockpile of cotton in 1860 and therefore did not have the need to come to the South's aid.

CRITICAL THINKING

How might the war have been different if Britain had not had a stockpile of cotton?

ANSWER: Students may suggest that he South might have received aid from Europe and could have had a better chance of winning the war.

SKILLS ANSWERS
1. the South
2. the Midwest

Connecting to Geography

Theaters of War

Geography played an important role in the development of military strategies during the Civil War. The Confederacy occupied a large stretch of land from the Atlantic Ocean to west Texas. To achieve military victory, Union leaders had to capture key parts of this large region. Union leaders planned to gain control of key river routes, railroads, and seaports. The Union wanted to stop the movement of Confederate troops and supplies across the South, as well as Confederate trade with Europe.

Confederate armies did not have to invade the North to win the war. Their hope was to make the war so costly for the Union that the North would ask for peace.

Resources and Strategies

The North entered the war with many advantages over the South. The North had more people, industry, and money.

Farm Values by Region, 1860 and 1870

Value (in billions of dollars)

Northeast   Midwest   South   West   Total U.S.

■ 1860
■ 1870

Source: *Historical Statistics of the United States*

Geography **Skills**

Interpreting Bar Graphs

1. Which region's farms had the highest total value in 1860? in 1870?
2. **Analyzing Information** Where did farms have the greatest growth in value from 1860 to 1870?

Cotton plants

LEVEL 1: Organize students into three groups. Ask students to brainstorm and compile a list of strengths and weaknesses of the North and South. *(Groups' lists will vary, but they should support their reasonings.)*
ENGLISH LANGUAGE LEARNERS , COOPERATIVE LEARNING

 **ALL LEVELS:** Ask students to refer to the bar graph on p. 611. Tell students that information from charts and graphs can be useful in highlighting differences between two topics. Explain that in this bar graph, some relevant statistics are shown that illustrate the North's advantages over the South before the Civil War. Have students use the information in the graph to write a few sentences summarizing their views on what the North's strengths were as it prepared for the Civil War. Ask

volunteers to present their summaries to the class.
ENGLISH LANGUAGE LEARNERS

 LEVEL 3: In one of the most important campaigns of the war, General Sherman led forces from Tennessee through Georgia and upward through the Carolinas. This was part of the Union's attempt to separate the Confederate capital at Richmond, Virginia, from the rest of the Confederacy. Ask students to refer to the map on p. 613 and trace the route that Sherman's troops followed in their final campaign to win the war for the North. Have students use the string method introduced in the Unit 2 Connecting to Geography lesson wrap in order to calculate the distance traveled by Sherman and his army as they journeyed from Chattanooga, Tennessee, to

Comparing the North and the South, 1860

■ North ■ South

Category	North	South
Total population	61%	39%
Railroad tracks	72%	28%
Factories	86%	14%
Total farm value	72%	28%
Cotton production	0.1%	99.9%
Horses	72%	28%
Donkeys and mules	29%	71%

Percent: 0 10 20 30 40 50 60 70 80 90 100

Source: *The Civil War Day by Day: An Almanac, 1861–1865*

Geography Skills

Interpreting Bar Graphs

1. What percentage of the nation's population lived in the North at the beginning of the war?
2. **Human Systems** What resources did the Union have more of than the Confederacy? What resources did the Confederacy have more of than the Union?
3. **Making Generalizations and Predictions** How do you think the resource advantages enjoyed by the Union affected the outcome of the Civil War?

History Note 2

The Union also had a great advantage in communications. The North controlled far more miles of telegraph line than the South. The telegraph made Union supply and reinforcement easier because field commanders could communicate quickly with officials in Washington. The South's expansion and repair of telegraph lines was hurt by a shortage of equipment and operators.

History Note 1

One of the North's major advantages was its greater population, which allowed Union generals to put more soldiers in the field. In late 1862, an estimated 300,000 Confederate soldiers faced nearly 700,000 Union soldiers. By the end of the war, the Union had about 1 million troops. Confederate soldiers probably numbered fewer than 160,000.

A telegraph key

SKILL ANSWERS

1. 61 percent
2. railroad tracks, factories, total farm value, horses, and more people; cotton, donkeys, and mules
3. Students might suggest that the advantages of population, railroad tracks, factories, and total farm value gave the Union a distinct advantage over the Confederacy.

Durham, North Carolina. Then have students determine an approximate distance that Sherman and his troops traveled between each battle. *(Students' answers should reveal the following: Chattanooga to Atlanta, 110 miles; Atlanta to Savannah, 215 miles; Savannah to Columbia, 130 miles; Columbia to Bentonville, 200 miles; Bentonville to Durham, 60 miles.)* Then have students write newspaper articles describing the direction and distance that Sherman's troops traveled. Then lead a discussion about the importance of this campaign in bringing victory to the Union army.

★ CLOSE

Remind students that pie graphs can frequently be used to illustrate the same information as bar graphs. Refer students to the bar graph on p. 611 that compares the resources of the North and South before the start of the Civil War. Then have students transfer the data from the bar graph to pie graphs. You may want to provide students with sheets of butcher paper or posterboard to allow room for several pie graphs.

Interdisciplinary Connection

▶Geography◀

Vicksburg. In 1861, before he became commander of the Union armies, Ulysses S. Grant envisioned the Union's wartime strategy. He believed that the city of Vicksburg would be on the future invasion route. Other Union officials also believed that Vicksburg would play an important role in Union strategy. Early in the war, President Lincoln told a visitor, "Let us get Vicksburg and all that country is ours. The war can never be brought to a close until that key is in our pocket."

ACTIVITY: Have students locate Vicksburg on a map. Then have them discuss the reason that Vicksburg was crucial to the Union strategy.

SKILLS ANSWERS

1. the eastern theater

2. the large number of miles of coastline

3. the Mississippi River; the river would split the western theater from the far western theater; control of the river allowed Union forces easier access to inland Confederate targets and took away the South's most important seaport, New Orleans

4. Students might suggest that a lack of access in terms of both soldiers and supplies would contribute to the lack of concentrated effort and that it was sparsely populated.

Theaters of War

Legend:
- Eastern theater
- Western theater
- Far Western theater
- → Union war strategy
- ▲ Union naval blockade
- ✪ Capital city

Geography Skills

Interpreting Thematic Maps

1. In what theater were the capitals of the Union and the Confederacy located?

2. What geographic feature of the Confederacy made the Union blockade difficult?

3. **The Uses of Geography** What river was a key to the Union strategy in the western theater? Why would controlling this river have been important?

4. **Drawing Inferences and Conclusions** Based on the map, why do you think the Union and the Confederacy concentrated little effort on the Far Western theater?

Union gunboat

History Note 3

Both the Union and the Confederacy concentrated their efforts in the eastern and western theaters of war. Battles took place on a smaller scale in the less-populated far western theater. For example, in 1862 a Confederate force of about 3,000 troops invaded the New Mexico Territory. They were eventually turned back. Part of the Union strategy when the war began was to split the Confederacy. Union commanders planned to cut off Arkansas, Louisiana, and Texas by taking control of the Mississippi River.

Have students review the information in Connecting to Geography Unit 8. Then have students complete Geography and History Quiz 8.

☆ RETEACH

Tell students to skim the notes, maps, graphs, and charts from this lesson. Ask them to make a bulleted list of the disadvantages the South faced in the Civil War, along with the advantages of the North. Then have students make a chart showing each of the battles in the war, along with the winner. Finally, lead a class discussion on the outcome of the war and its effects on the South and its economy. **ENGLISH LANGUAGE LEARNERS**

☆ EXTEND

Assign students one of the following battles: Chancellorsville, Fredericksburg, Gettysburg, or Vicksburg. Have students use the library to obtain information about their assigned battle. Then ask each student to create a bar graph that illustrates the following results of their battle: the number of soldiers sent to fight for each side and the number of soldiers who died for each side. Ask students to write who won the battle below their graphs. Have students display their work and to explain what it depicts to the class. Lead a class discussion about the importance of each battle and the total number of lives lost in these four battles.

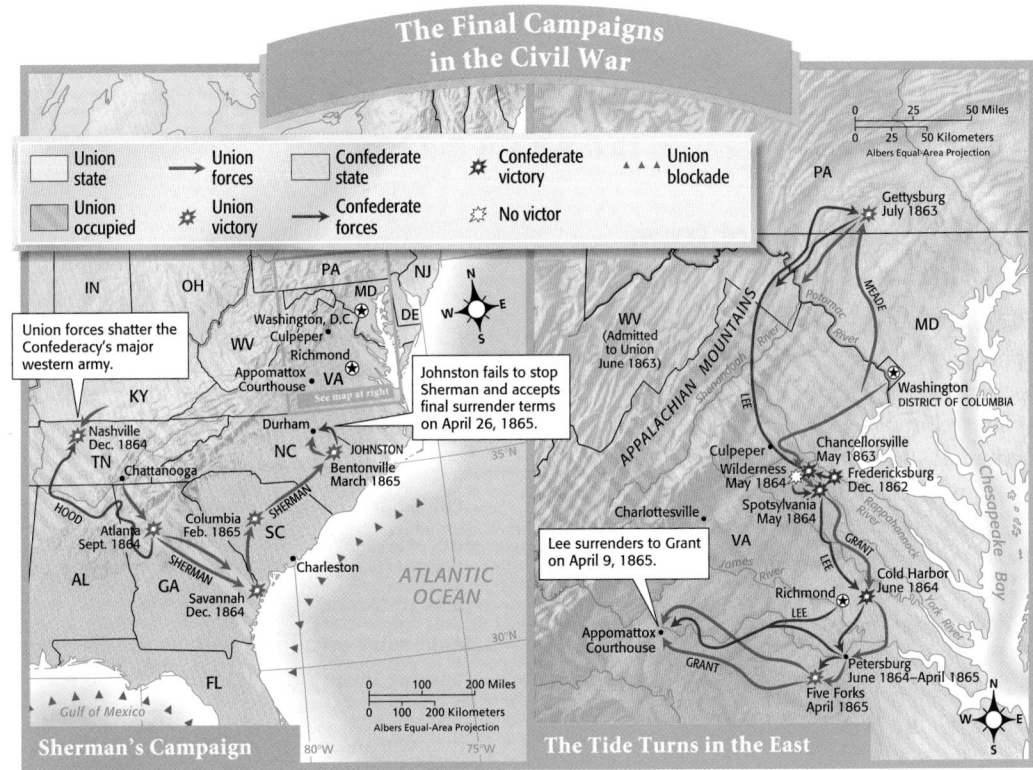

The Final Campaigns in the Civil War

| Union state | → Union forces | Confederate state | ☼ Confederate victory | ▲▲▲ Union blockade |
| Union occupied | ☼ Union victory | → Confederate forces | ☆ No victor | |

Union forces shatter the Confederacy's major western army.

Johnston fails to stop Sherman and accepts final surrender terms on April 26, 1865.

Lee surrenders to Grant on April 9, 1865.

Sherman's Campaign

The Tide Turns in the East

Geography Skills
Interpreting Thematic Maps

1. Where did Sherman's army go after taking Savannah?
2. **Locate** Identify and list in the order that they occurred the battles fought during Sherman's campaign.
3. **Drawing Inferences and Conclusions** Why did so many eastern battles occur between the James and Potomac Rivers?

History Note 4

Most of the major battles near the end of the war took place in Virginia or the Lower South. Union commanders hoped to cut off Virginia from the Lower South. To do so, General William T. Sherman led an army from Tennessee through Georgia to the Atlantic coast. Union leaders then planned to defeat Robert E. Lee's army and capture the Confederate capital of Richmond, Virginia.

THE GRANGER COLLECTION, NEW YORK

Richmond, Virginia, after the war

The March to the Sea.
After taking Atlanta, General William T. Sherman marched approximately 62,000 soldiers to the city of Savannah. He split his troops into two columns that marched up to 50 miles apart from each other. The troops covered an average of 15 miles per day. The soldiers were ordered to live off the land, taking food and other goods from the southern farms along the way. Runaway slaves and Confederate deserters followed along. Sherman's troops did not burn houses, but they destroyed everything related to slavery or the southern war effort.

CRITICAL THINKING

Why did Sherman order his troops to live off the land?

ANSWER: Students might suggest that living off the land hurt the Confederate war effort by denying supplies to Confederate troops and allowed the Union troops to travel without carrying supplies.

SKILL ANSWERS

1. to Columbia
2. Chattanooga, Atlanta, Savannah, Columbia, Bentonville, Durham
3. Students might suggest that the two capitals were located in this region.

✪ TEACH

ALL LEVELS: Have students search the unit for quotations that are statements of fact and statements of opinion. Discuss why it might be important for a history book to include both. Explain the context cues that students should look for when searching for statements of fact and statements of opinion. Then have students imagine opinions that the following sources might have published about South Carolina's firing upon Fort Sumter: a newspaper in Ohio, a newspaper in South Carolina, and Frederick Douglass's newspaper, the North Star. Have students write one or two sentences that might express the opinions of each of these newspapers. After students have written their opinions, have them write a paragraph that might be appropriate for a history textbook. The paragraph should include all three imagined opinions as well as cues to help the reader understand the difference between fact and opinion. **ENGLISH LANGUAGE LEARNERS**

DISTINGUISHING FACT FROM OPINION

Have students bring in newspaper editorials or letters to the editor from their local newspaper. Ask students to make a chart separating the verifiable statements in the letters or editorials from the statements that cannot be verified. Then have them create a third column to show how words or phrases in the documents helped them distinguish fact from opinion.

SKILLS ANSWERS

1. opinion; *we consider, vulgar abolitionists*

2. Students might suggest that he thinks that they are wrong and ought to be forced to agree with slaveholders. His approval of extreme violence and his choice of the word *vulgar* to describe abolitionists shows his bias.

Social Studies Skills
WORKSHOP

Distinguishing Fact from Opinion and Identifying Bias

Historical sources may contain both facts and opinions. Sources such as diaries, letters, and speeches usually express personal views. The ability to distinguish facts from opinions is very important. It allows you to judge the accuracy of an argument or a historical account.

When reading historical sources, try to identify a writer's bias—prejudices or strong feelings. Many famous historical people had strong opinions that appear in their writings and speeches. Remember that just because a person is famous does not mean that you must agree with his or her opinions.

How to Distinguish Fact from Opinion

1. **Identify the facts.** Ask yourself: Can the statement be proven? Determine whether the idea can be checked for accuracy in a source such as an almanac or encyclopedia. If so, the statement probably concerns a matter of fact. If not, it probably contains an opinion.

2. **Identify the opinions.** Look for clues that indicate a statement of opinion. These clues include phrases such as "I think" and "I believe," comparative words like *greatest* and *more important,* and value-filled words like *extremely* and *ridiculous.* All of these words imply a judgment and, thus, an opinion.

How to Identify Bias

1. **Evaluate the information presented.** What are the sources of information? How reliable are they? Why might a historical figure have supported one view over another? Be sure to distinguish between provable facts and someone's opinions.

2. **Make your own judgment.** Remember that many of the historical documents you read are created by people who have their own opinions and points of view. It is up to you to read each document critically and to draw your own conclusions.

Practicing the Skills

Read the excerpt below, in which a southern newspaper editor defends Representative Preston Brooks's beating of Senator Charles Sumner. Then answer the questions that follow.

❝We consider the act good in conception [thought], better in execution. . . . These vulgar abolitionists . . . must be lashed into submission. Sumner, in particular, ought to have nine-and-thirty [lashes] early every morning.❞

1. Is this excerpt an example of a fact or an opinion? Which words let you know?

2. What bias, if any, does the author express? If you found bias, how did you identify it?

LEVEL 2: Explain to students that political campaign ads contain both fact and opinion, as well as examples of propaganda. Sometimes ads concern an issue, rather than a particular political candidate. Organize students into groups. Ask groups to produce an ad that would try to convince the people of their state to support one side or the other in the Civil War—the Union or the Confederacy. Students will then present their ads to the class. Ads can be in the form of a video-taped presentation, a multimedia presentation, or a theatrical presentation.

LEVEL 3: Distribute newspaper editorials to students in the class. Ask each student to write a report explaining whether the editorial is based mostly in fact, in opinion, or a combination of both. Have students support their position with examples from the editorial.

History in Action

UNIT 8 SIMULATION

You Make the Decision . . .

Should Your Border State Support the Union or the Confederacy?

Complete the following activity in small cooperative groups. It is April 12, 1861. The Confederates have opened fire on Fort Sumter. You live in one of the four border states in which slavery is legal—Delaware, Kentucky, Maryland, or Missouri. The people in your state have strong feelings for both sides in the conflict. Your state legislature has asked a special committee to make a recommendation about which side your state should support—the Union or the Confederacy. Follow these steps to reach your decision.

1. Gather Information. Use your textbook and other resources to find information that might help you decide whether to support the North or the South in this conflict. Be sure to use what you learned from this unit's Skills Workshop on Distinguishing Fact from Opinion and Identifying Bias to help you make an informed decision. You may want to divide different parts of the research among group members.

2. Identify Options. After reviewing the information you have gathered, identify the options you might consider for which side to support in the Civil War. Your final solution to the problem may be easier to reach if you consider as many options as possible. Be sure to record your possible options for your presentation.

3. Predict Consequences. Now take each option your group came up with and consider what might be the outcome if you followed each course of action. Ask yourselves questions like: "Is it possible for our state to remain neutral during this conflict?" Once you have predicted the consequences, record them as notes for your presentation.

4. Take Action to Implement Your Decision. After you have considered your options, you should plan and create your presentation. Be sure to make your decision on whether to support the North or the South very clear. You will need to support your committee's recommendation by including information you gathered and by explaining why you rejected other options. Your presentation needs to be visually appealing to gain the support of the state legislature. When you are ready, decide which group members will make each part of the presentation, and then take your decision to the state legislature (the rest of the class). Good luck!

History in Action Ask students if they have ever tried to convince someone to see a movie or to go to a particular restaurant. Tell them that in trying to persuade someone they are using propaganda. Assign students a historical event or issue that can be viewed from both sides of the issue. Then have them conduct research at the library to obtain more information about it. After students have finished their research, have them implement the decision-making steps to formulate a viewpoint about the issue. Then have students use propaganda in a written statement to convince others of their viewpoint.

★ CHAPTER 20

Reconstruction

At the end of the Civil War, the United States faced two major challenges—to reunite the country and to define the rights of African Americans. After Lincoln's assassination, these Reconstruction policy decisions fell to the new president, Andrew Johnson. The Fourteenth Amendment was intended to give freed slaves protection and to bring much needed reforms to the South. The Fifteenth Amendment gave African American men the vote. Support for Reconstruction faded in the mid-1870s. In the Compromise of 1877, Rutherford Hayes became president and removed the last federal troops from the South. The Democrats regained control of southern state governments. Segregation, poll taxes, and Jim Crow laws eroded African American civil rights. In 1896, the U.S. Supreme Court supported "separate-but-equal" facilities in *Plessy* v. *Ferguson*. Sharecropping became a feature of southern agriculture, while the New South movement hoped to add an industrial base to strengthen the southern economy.

Internet Activity

The Assassination of President Lincoln

internet connect

TOPIC: John Wilkes Booth
GO TO: go.hrw.com
KEYWORD: SA3 John Wilkes Booth

Shortly after the beginning of his second term in office, President Lincoln went to see the play Our American Cousin. During the play John Wilkes Booth shot Lincoln. The president died the next morning. Have students search the Internet through the HRW Go site to find information about John Wilkes Booth and the circumstances surrounding the assassination of the president. Instruct students to use the information they find to create a mock FBI file about this event. The file should include at least five pieces of "evidence," such as photographs. The file should also contain a memo that analyzes and interprets the evidence presented.

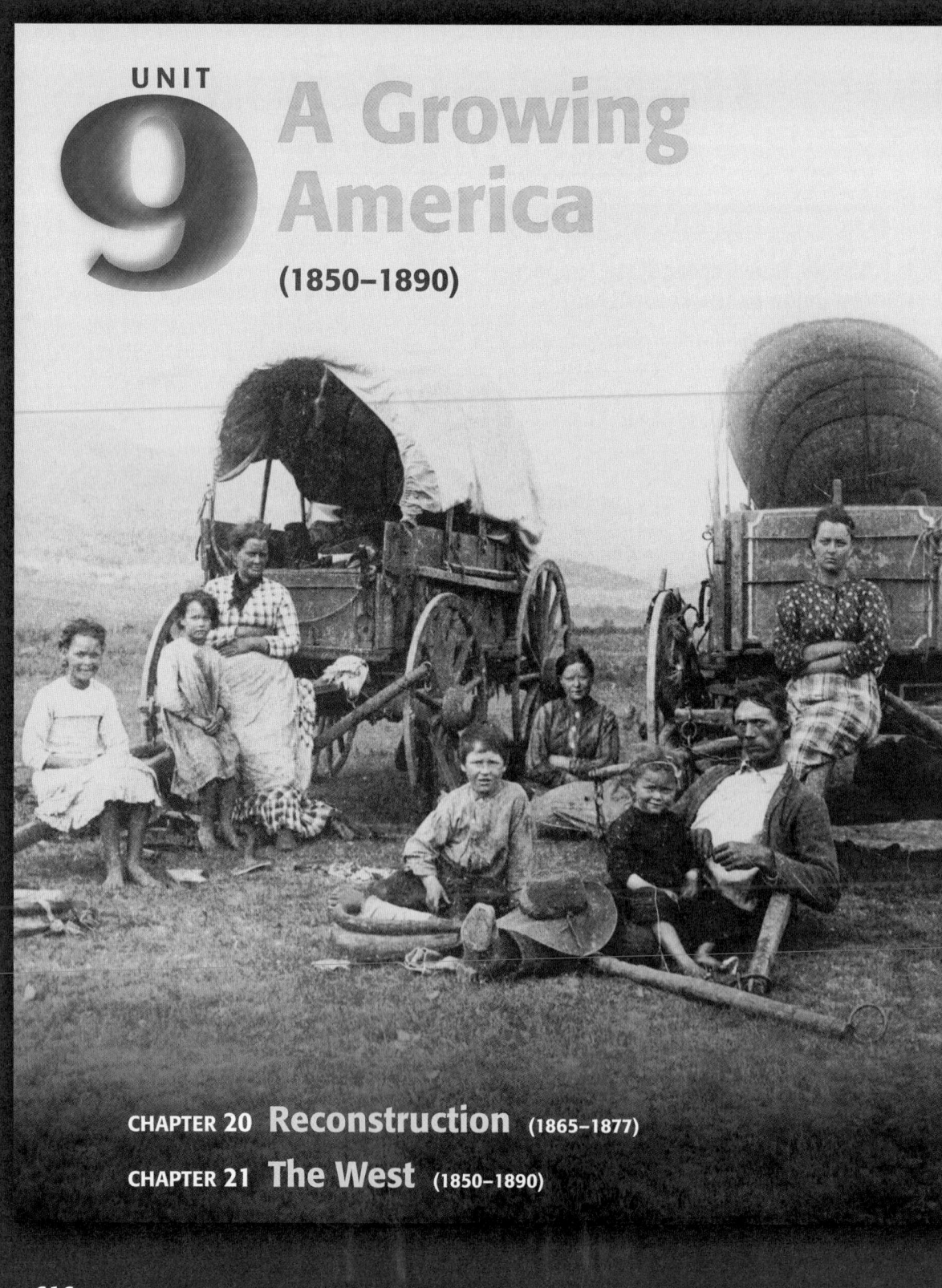

UNIT 9 A Growing America

(1850–1890)

CHAPTER 21

The West

Increasing numbers of settlers moved west in the mid-1800s. The discovery of gold drew many miners west. Conflicts soon broke out between the new settlers and American Indians. To try to control this conflict, the U.S. government forced many American Indians onto reservations. The wars between the American Indians and the U.S. Army came to an end in 1890 at the Massacre at Wounded Knee. Meanwhile, the economy of the West was greatly changed by mining, the building of the transcontinental railroad, and the rise of the Cattle Kingdom in the 1870s. The federal government's offer of free land encouraged farmers to settle in the Great Plains, and this region became known as the breadbasket of the world.

Share the information in the chapter overviews with students. Have students skim each chapter for as many place names as they can find and then make a list of them on the chalkboard. Using a large sheet of butcher paper, have the class create a map showing each place on the list. Instruct students to write in their notebooks one question about each place. As they go through the unit, have students answer the questions.

Young People

IN HISTORY

Young Cowhands

Cowhands herded Texas longhorn cattle northward across the Great Plains to be sold in Kansas railroad towns. A cattle drive of this distance required working long hours in all kinds of weather. Sometimes cowhands would run into problems with cattle thieves known as rustlers. The greatest danger, however, was a stampede.

Many cowhands began working cattle when they were children. A rancher paid young Cliff Newland 50 cents a day to haul supplies to cattle drivers 75 miles away. From this job, Newland turned to wrangling—the work of herding and caring for livestock. To help him learn to stay in the saddle while training horses, Newland's father tied him onto the seat. By age 13, Newland had already been on three cattle drives and had a job training young horses.

Not all the young cowhands were boys. At age 13, Agnes Morley and her younger brother traveled across 130 miles of harsh New Mexico landscape to sell some cattle.

Many cowhands left home to work the cattle drives while they were still children. E. C. Abbott, also known as "Teddy Blue," went on his first cattle drive when he was 11 years old. He recalled his trip up the Western Trail in 1879.

Many young cowhands like this female broncobuster gained recognition for their unique skills.

66 **That trip up the trail in '79 was my second, but in a way it was the first that counted, because I was only a button [youngster] the other time. I wasn't nineteen years old when I come up the trail with the Olive herd, but don't let that fool you. I was a man in my own estimation and a man in fact.** 99

Teddy Blue recalled a story he had once heard about a schoolteacher. She wanted a Texas cowhand to tell her about life on the trail. She asked, "Oh, Mister So-and-So, didn't the boys used to have a lot of fun riding their ponies?" He replied, "Madam, there wasn't any boys or ponies. They was all horses and men."

If You Were There *Would the life of a cowhand be appealing to you?*

LEFT PAGE: *In many western families, like this one, all family members had to work hard.*

Western Photography. Settlers moving west began traveling early each morning so they could unhitch the wagons during the heat of the day to water the animals, eat a noonday meal, and rest. Since photographers were also moving west, this time was often ideal for posing before the camera, as the group of pioneers in the photograph on the opposite page did. Photographers in the West faced special hardships because of the weight of their equipment. The camera itself was quite heavy, but the chemicals and the glass plates required for developing were even heavier. Photographers also had to take along their own darkrooms, which were too heavy to carry and had to be dragged. After carting all this equipment across rough terrain, photographers could return without a single negative. The glass plates could break if a horse stumbled or fell, and the chemical mixtures needed to fix the images were easily upset.

ACTIVITY: Ask students to write a letter back home from the perspective of one of the people in the photograph. Have volunteers share their letters with the class.

Objectives	Pacing Guide	Reproducible Resources
SECTION 1: **Rebuilding the South** (pp. 620–25) ⭐ Analyze the effect that the end of the Civil War had on African Americans in the South. ⭐ Contrast the views of Abraham Lincoln, Congress, and Andrew Johnson on Reconstruction.	**Regular** 2 days **Block Scheduling** 1 day *Block Scheduling Handbook with Team Teaching Strategies, Chapter 20*	**RS** Guided Reading Strategy 20.1 **E** Hands-On History Activity: Social Services in Your Community
SECTION 2: **The Fight over Reconstruction** (pp. 626–32) ⭐ Explain how Black Codes restricted African Americans' freedoms. ⭐ Analyze the reasons that Radical Republicans tried to impeach President Johnson. ⭐ Describe Republicans' efforts to protect the civil rights of African Americans.	**Regular** 2 days **Block Scheduling** 1 day *Block Scheduling Handbook with Team Teaching Strategies, Chapter 20*	**RS** Guided Reading Strategy 20.2 **PS** American History Political Cartoon 13: Radical Reconstruction
SECTION 3: **Reconstruction in the South** (pp. 633–38) ⭐ Describe the reforms Reconstruction governments carried out. ⭐ Analyze the factors that led to the end of Reconstruction. ⭐ Examine how southern laws and governments changed after Reconstruction ended.	**Regular** 2 days **Block Scheduling** 1 day *Block Scheduling Handbook with Team Teaching Strategies, Chapter 20*	**RS** Guided Reading Strategy 20.3 **PS** Primary Source Reading 20: *Plessy* v. *Ferguson* **PS** Literature Reading 20: Jim Crow Cars **RS** Graphic Organizer 20: Congress and Reconstruction **E** Creative Teaching Strategy: Music, Poetry, and Law
SECTION 4: **The New South** (pp. 639–43) ⭐ Describe how southern agriculture changed after the Civil War. ⭐ Explain why some business leaders hoped to create a "New South." ⭐ Discuss some popular forms of southern culture during and after Reconstruction.	**Regular** 1.5 days **Block Scheduling** 1 day *Block Scheduling Handbook with Team Teaching Strategies, Chapter 20*	**RS** Guided Reading Strategy 20.4 **PS** Biography Reading 20: George Washington Carver **SM** Geography Activity 20: Tenant Farming and Sharecropping

Chapter Resource Key

PS Primary Sources
RS Reading Support
IC Interdisciplinary Connections
E Enrichment
SM Skills Mastery

A Assessment
REV Review
ELL Reinforcement and English Language Learners
🖉 Transparencies
💿 CD–ROM

 Music
 Video
 Internet
 Holt Presentation Maker Using Microsoft® PowerPoint®

 ✨ **One-Stop** Planner CD–ROM

See the *One-Stop Planner* for a complete list of additional resources for students and teachers.

One-Stop Planner CD-ROM

It's easy to plan lessons, select resources, and print out materials for your students when you use the **One-Stop Planner CD-ROM with Test Generator.**

Technology Resources

 One-Stop Planner, Lesson 20.1

 CNN Presents America: Yesterday and Today, Beginnings to 1914 Segment: The Life of Lincoln

 Exploring America's Past Video Segment: A Play of Fate; Teacher's Guide, pp. 33–35

 Homework Practice Online

 One-Stop Planner, Lesson 20.2

 Holt Researcher: American History CD–ROM

 Homework Practice Online

 HRW Go site

 One-Stop Planner, Lesson 20.3

 Holt Researcher: American History CD–ROM

Homework Practice Online

 One-Stop Planner, Lesson 20.4

 Everyday Life in America Transparency 13: Life During Reconstruction

 American Music Selection 15: "When Johnny Comes Marching Home"

 Homework Practice Online

Reinforcement, Review, and Assessment

REV   Section 1 Review, p. 625
A   Daily Quiz 20.1
ELL   Main Idea Activity 20.1
ELL   English Audio Summary 20.1
ELL   Spanish Audio Summary 20.1

REV   Section 2 Review, p. 632
A   Daily Quiz 20.2
ELL   Main Idea Activity 20.2
ELL   English Audio Summary 20.2
ELL   Spanish Audio Summary 20.2

REV   Section 3 Review, p. 638
A   Daily Quiz 20.3
ELL   Main Idea Activity 20.3
ELL   English Audio Summary 20.3
ELL   Spanish Audio Summary 20.3

REV   Section 4 Review, p. 642
A   Daily Quiz 20.4
ELL   Main Idea Activity 20.4
ELL   English Audio Summary 20.4
ELL   Spanish Audio Summary 20.4

internet connect

HRW ONLINE RESOURCES

GO TO: go.hrw.com
Then type in a keyword.

TEACHER HOME PAGE
SA3 Teacher

CHAPTER INTERNET ACTIVITIES
KEYWORD: SA3 CF20
Choose an activity to:
• use primary and secondary sources to learn about differing views of Reconstruction.
• create a newspaper on Radical Reconstruction and the removal of Edwin M. Stanton as Secretary of War.
• research historically black colleges founded during Reconstruction.

CHAPTER ENRICHMENT LINKS
KEYWORD: SA3 CH20

ONLINE ASSESSMENT
**Homework Practice
KEYWORD: SA3 HP20**

**Standardized Test Prep
KEYWORD: SA3 STP20**

**Rubrics
KEYWORD: SS Rubrics**

ONLINE MAPS, CHARTS, AND GRAPHS
KEYWORD: SA3 MCG
• African American Colleges
• Reconstruction Amendments

CONTENT UPDATES
KEYWORD: SS Content Updates

HOLT PRESENTATION MAKER
KEYWORD: SA3 PPT20

ONLINE READING SUPPORT
KEYWORD: SS Strategies

CURRENT EVENTS
KEYWORD: S3 Current Events

Meeting Individual Needs

Ability Levels

Level 1 Basic-level activities designed for all students encountering new material

Level 2 Intermediate-level activities designed for average students

Level 3 Challenging activities designed for honors and gifted-and-talented students

English Language Learners Activities that address the needs of students with Limited English Proficiency

Chapter Review and Assessment

IC   Vocabulary Activity 20
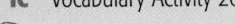 Global Skill Builder CD–ROM
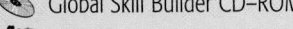 HRW Go site
REV   Chapter 20 Tutorial for Students, Parents, Mentors, and Peers
REV   Chapter 20 Review, pp. 643–45
 Chapter 20 Test Generator (on the One-Stop Planner)

A   Chapter 20 Test (Form A or B)
A   Alternative Assessment Handbook
A   Chapter 20 Test for English Language Learners and Special-Needs Students

Section 1   Rebuilding the South

Section 2   The Fight over Reconstruction

Section 3   Reconstruction in the South

Section 4   The New South

Build on What You Know

If You Were There...

Ask students to answer the following question:

How would you try to reunite the nation?

Consider:

• the tensions that might still exist between northerners and southerners

• the economic problems that existed after the war

You Be the Historian

What's Your Opinion?

To help students create their **Themes** Journal entries, provide the following examples of appropriate **agree**/**disagree** statements.

EXPLORING THE TIME LINE

GLOBAL EVENTS

☐ internet connect

TOPIC: Suez Canal and Transportation
GO TO: go.hrw.com
KEYWORD: SA3 CF20

Have students access the Internet through the HRW Go site to research the construction of the Suez Canal and the role of canals for transportation in the nineteenth century. Then ask students to create an annotated diagram or model in which they illustrate their research. Have them include a short quiz and an answer key. Tell students to quiz their friends about the research displayed in their model or diagram.

CHAPTER

20 Reconstruction
(1865–1877)

The race riots in New Orleans led to the deaths of 34 African Americans.

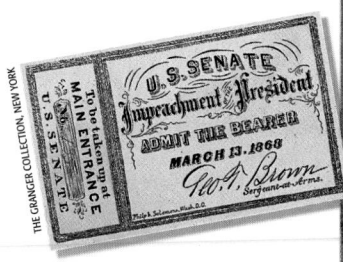

This ticket allowed a spectator to observe President Andrew Johnson's impeachment trial.

THE GRANGER COLLECTION, NEW YORK

UNITED STATES

1865 The Thirteenth Amendment is ratified, abolishing slavery.

1866 Race riots break out in New Orleans.

1867 Congress passes the first federal Reconstruction Act.

1868 President Andrew Johnson is impeached on February 24.

On July 28 the Fourteenth Amendment is ratified by the states, granting African Americans citizenship.

On November 3 Union general Ulysses S. Grant is elected president.

1870 On February 25, Hiram Revels becomes the first African American in the U.S. Senate.

The Fifteenth Amendment is ratified on March 30, giving African Americans the right to vote.

| 1865 | 1866 | 1867 | 1868 | 1869 | 1870 | 1871 |

WORLD

1868 The Meiji dynasty returns to power in Japan.

1869 The Suez Canal opens, linking the Mediterranean and Red Seas.

1870 France and the German state of Prussia go to war against each other.

1871 France loses the Franco-Prussian War.

This image shows the opening-day procession of ships through the Suez Canal.

Build on What You Know

The Civil War left two major issues unresolved. First, the federal government had to decide the conditions by which the defeated southern states could rejoin the Union. Second, it had to define the rights of African Americans freed by the Emancipation Proclamation. As southerners tried to rebuild their lives, the nation attempted to heal its wounds.

Constitutional Heritage

Agree   As our society changes, so should our Constitution.

Disagree   The Constitution is thorough and should remain intact forever.

Government

Agree   A civil war would not have occurred if the established government had been a strong one.

Disagree   A civil war does not indicate a poor existing government.

Culture

Agree   Cultural expression, such as art and literature, often reflects changing political ideas.

Disagree   Political changes do not affect the culture or the expression of culture in a society.

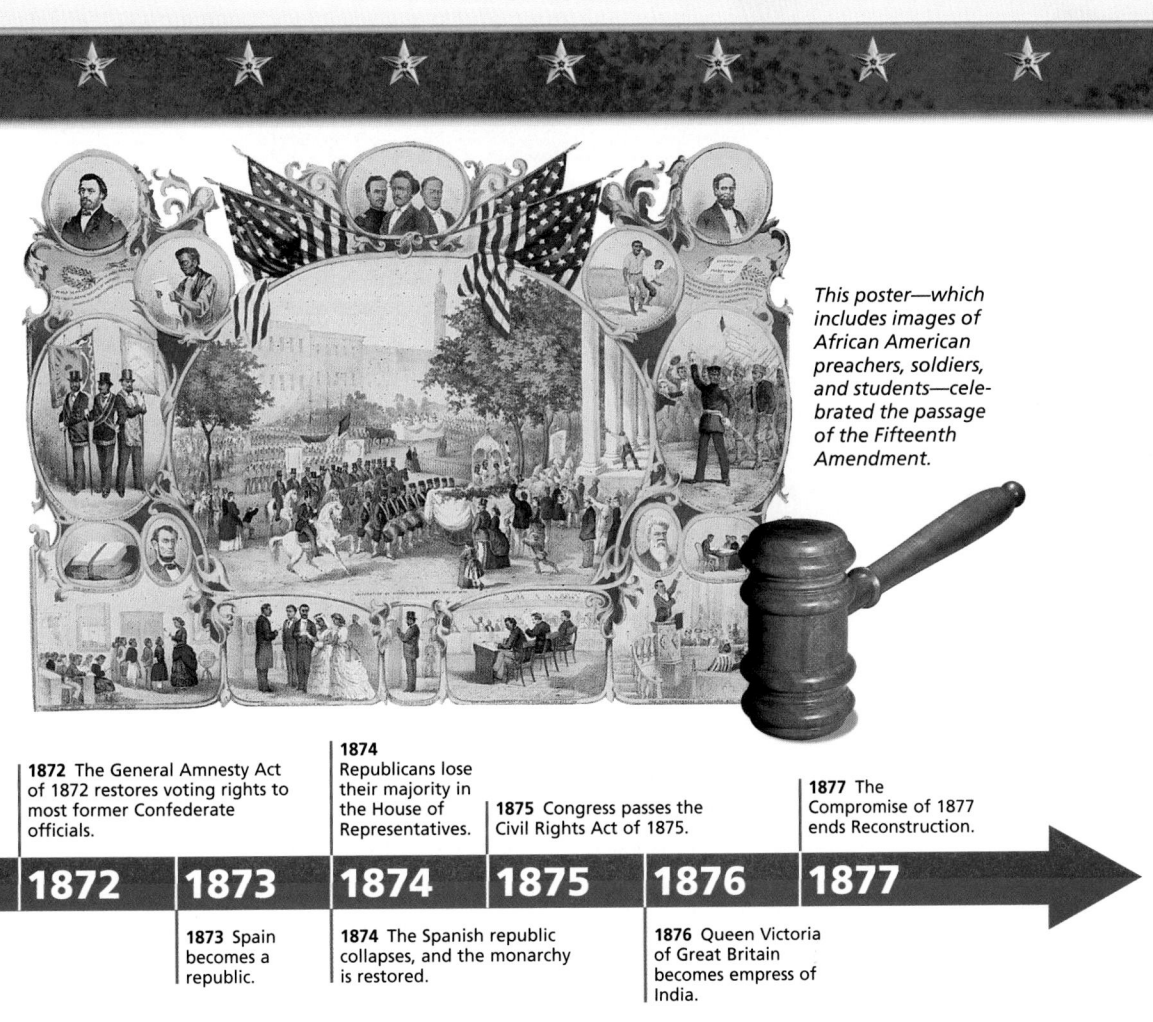

This poster—which includes images of African American preachers, soldiers, and students—celebrated the passage of the Fifteenth Amendment.

1872 The General Amnesty Act of 1872 restores voting rights to most former Confederate officials.

1874 Republicans lose their majority in the House of Representatives.

1875 Congress passes the Civil Rights Act of 1875.

1877 The Compromise of 1877 ends Reconstruction.

| 1872 | 1873 | 1874 | 1875 | 1876 | 1877 |

1873 Spain becomes a republic.

1874 The Spanish republic collapses, and the monarchy is restored.

1876 Queen Victoria of Great Britain becomes empress of India.

EXPLORING THE TIME LINE

AMERICAN EVENTS

★ Biography

Hiram Revels. Hiram Revels was the first African American to become a U.S. senator. He began his political career as a state senator in Mississippi in 1869 and was elected to the U.S. Senate the following year. He was elected to the U.S. Senate to fill the position vacated by Jefferson Davis, the former Confederate president. After leaving the Senate, Revels became president of Alcorn College in Mississippi. Although he was dismissed from that position in 1874, he returned to Alcorn in 1876 and remained as president until his retirement.

ACTIVITY: Have students imagine that they are going to interview Hiram Revels. Ask students to develop a series of questions, using standard grammar, spelling, and punctuation, that students would like to ask Revels about his life and political career.

If you were there . . .
How would you try to reunite the nation?

You Be the Historian

What's Your Opinion? Do you **agree** or **disagree** with the following statements? Support your point of view in your journal.

- **Constitutional Heritage** Amending the Constitution is necessary to keep up with changes in government and society.
- **Government** New governments are necessary to rebuild a nation after a civil war.
- **Culture** Political changes bring about new forms of cultural expression.

Section 1

OBJECTIVES

- ★ Analyze the effect that the end of the Civil War had on African Americans in the South.
- ★ Contrast the views of Abraham Lincoln, Congress, and Andrew Johnson on Reconstruction.

SECTION 1 RESOURCES

REPRODUCIBLE

▶ Guided Reading Strategy 20.1

TECHNOLOGY

▶ One-Stop Planner, Lesson 20.1
▶ CNN. Presents America: Beginnings to 1914 Segment: The Life of Lincoln
▶ Exploring America's Past Video Segment: A Play of Fate; Teacher's Guide, pp. 33–35
▶ Homework Practice Online

REINFORCEMENT, REVIEW, AND ASSESSMENT

▶ Section 1 Review, p. 625
▶ Daily Quiz 20.1
▶ Main Idea Activity 20.1
▶ English Audio Summary 20.1
▶ Spanish Audio Summary 20.1

LET'S GET STARTED!

As students enter the classroom, have them create lists of all the steps that are necessary to make a peanut butter and jelly sandwich. *(Students' lists will vary but should include obtaining bread, peanut butter, and jelly, spreading the ingredients on the bread, and putting the bread together to form a sandwich.)* Once the lists are finished, have volunteers write their steps on the chalkboard. Point out the differences that exist between the lists. Tell students that in Section 1 they will learn about the different plans that people created for Reconstruction.

Section 1

Rebuilding the South

Read to Discover

1. What effect did the end of the Civil War have on African Americans in the South?
2. How did President Lincoln, Congress, and President Johnson differ in their views on Reconstruction?

WHY IT MATTERS TODAY

Nations today continue to rebuild after wars or natural disasters. Use CNNfyi.com or other **current events** sources to find a modern country or region that is rebuilding after a destructive event or period. Record your findings in your journal.

Define

- amnesty

Identify

- Reconstruction
- Ten Percent Plan
- Wade-Davis Bill
- Thirteenth Amendment
- Freedmen's Bureau
- John Wilkes Booth
- Andrew Johnson

The Story Continues

When the Civil War ended, much of the South lay in ruins. Union troops had destroyed many major southern cities and railroads, wrecking trade and commerce. In the countryside, farms had suffered a similar fate. Harvests of corn, cotton, rice, and other important crops were well below normal prewar levels. In South Carolina, Mary Boykin Chesnut wrote in her diary about another problem faced by southerners in many communities—isolation. "We are shut in here. . . . All RR's [railroads] destroyed—bridges gone. We are cut off from the world."

Much of Richmond, Virginia, burned in the last days of the war.

★ Planning Reconstruction

After the South's surrender, tired southern soldiers returned home to find that the world they had left behind was gone. Because of high food prices and widespread crop failures, many southerners faced starvation. The Confederate money most southerners held was now worthless. Banks failed and merchants went bankrupt because people could not repay their debts. Former Confederate general Braxton Bragg found that "*all, all* was lost, except my debts."

★ TEACH

Have students read Section 1 and complete Guided Reading Strategy 20.1. Choose one or more of the following activities to explore the section content with students. For further suggestions on block scheduling or team teaching, see the *Block Scheduling Handbook with Team Teaching Strategies*.

LEVEL 1: Have students create two lists: one listing conditions faced by African Americans in the South before the Civil War, the other listing conditions faced by African Americans in the South after the Civil War. *(Students' lists will vary but should reflect an understanding of how the Civil War changed African Americans' daily lives.)* Finally, lead a class discussion on how the end of the Civil War affected African Americans in the South.

ENGLISH LANGUAGE LEARNERS

Note: To help students make meaningful connections between events in American history and those in their own hometown, use the Chapter 20 **Hands-On History** activity, Social Services in Your Community.

The U.S. government faced the question of how to deal with the defeated southern states. **Reconstruction** was the process of reuniting the nation and rebuilding the southern states without slavery. It lasted from 1865 to 1877.

President Lincoln wanted to reunite the nation as quickly and painlessly as possible. He had proposed a plan for readmitting the southern states even before the war ended. Lincoln wanted to offer southerners **amnesty**, or an official pardon, for all illegal acts supporting the rebellion. To receive amnesty, southerners had to swear an oath of loyalty to the United States and accept a ban on slavery. Once 10 percent of voters in a state made these pledges, they could form a new government. The state then could be readmitted to the Union. Louisiana quickly elected a new state legislature under this **Ten Percent Plan**. Other southern states that had been occupied by Union troops followed Louisiana back into the Union.

Some politicians pointed out that Congress had the power to admit new states. They argued that Congress, not the president, should control the southern states' return to the Union. Also, many Republican members of Congress simply disagreed with Lincoln's Ten Percent Plan. Two Republicans—Senator Benjamin Wade and Representative Henry Davis—had an alternative to Lincoln's plan. Under the **Wade-Davis Bill**, a state had to meet two conditions before it could rejoin the Union.

★ Geography

African Americans in Southern Cities.

Emancipation changed the face of southern cities. Before the war, not many African Americans lived in southern cities. The few who did often lived in the same neighborhoods as whites. After the war, the African American population doubled in the 10 largest southern cities. Newly freed slaves moved from the country to the city, looking for better jobs and safer living conditions. They settled on the edges of cities and in neighborhoods that were segregated from white residents.

CRITICAL THINKING

What other aspects of city life do you think attracted African Americans after the war?

ANSWER: Students might mention that newly freed people might have more freedom to build their own lives in a city. For example, they might have more opportunities to attend churches, join organizations, and take part in a wide variety of cultural events.

ANALYZING PRIMARY SOURCES ANSWERS

1. Slavery was tearing the Union apart, and the government had the right to stop its territorial enlargement.

2. Students' responses will vary.

3. He is asking the nation to heal wounds, to care for those hurt by the war, and to unite again in peace.

Historical Document

1865

LINCOLN'S SECOND INAUGURAL ADDRESS

On March 4, 1865, President Lincoln laid out his approach to Reconstruction in his second inaugural address. As this excerpt shows, Lincoln hoped to peacefully reunite the nation and its people.

"On the occasion corresponding to this four years ago, all thoughts were anxiously directed to an **impending**[1] civil war. . . . One eighth of the whole population were colored slaves, not **distributed**[2] generally over the Union, but localized in the southern part of it. These slaves **constituted**[3] a peculiar and powerful interest. All knew that this interest was somehow the cause of the war. To strengthen, **perpetuate**,[4] and extend this interest was the object for which the **insurgents**[5] would **rend**[6] the Union even by war, while the Government claimed no right to do more than to restrict the territorial enlargement of it. . . . With **malice**[7] toward none; with charity for all; with firmness in the right, as God gives us to see the right, let us strive on to finish the work we are in, to bind up the nation's wounds, to care for him who shall have borne the battle, and for his widow, and his orphan—to do all which may achieve and cherish a just, and a lasting peace."

[1]**impending:** coming
[2]**distributed:** spread
[3]**constituted:** formed
[4]**perpetuate:** continue
[5]**insurgents:** rebels
[6]**rend:** tear apart
[7]**malice:** hatred

Analyzing Primary Sources

1. What does Lincoln believe the spread of slavery was doing to the Union, and how does he believe the government had to respond?
2. How do you think Lincoln views the issue of freeing the slaves?
3. How does Lincoln's speech promote union and equal treatment?

ALL LEVELS: Copy the following graphic organizer onto the chalkboard, omitting the italicized answers. Have students complete the organizer to list some of the different views of Abraham Lincoln, Congress, and Andrew Johnson on Reconstruction. **ENGLISH LANGUAGE LEARNERS**

Reconstruction Views

Lincoln's Views
—*Any southern state with at least 10 percent of its voters making a loyalty pledge could establish a new state government and be readmitted to the union.*

Johnson's Views
—*similar to Lincoln's Ten Percent Plan*
—*Wealthy southerners and former Confederate officials would need a presidential pardon to qualify for amnesty.*

Congress's Views
—*Under the Wade-Davis bill, a state had to meet two conditions before it could join the Union:*
1. It had to ban slavery.
2. A majority of the adult males had to take the loyalty oath.

★ Citizenship

Pocket Veto. The U.S. Congress approved the Wade-Davis Bill just before it adjourned. The end of the congressional session made it possible for President Lincoln to use a "pocket" veto to kill the measure. In effect, the president put the bill in his pocket and refused to sign it. If a president does not sign a bill within 10 days while Congress is in session, a bill automatically becomes a law without the president's signature. However, if Congress is adjourned, a bill dies if the president does not sign it. A pocket veto cannot be overturned by congressional vote.

ACTIVITY: Ask students to imagine that they are members of Congress in 1864. Have them work in committees to write a plan that they think Lincoln would have accepted for readmitting the states. Encourage students to consider what rules they would set to ensure that ex-Confederates would support the Union and end slavery. Remind students to use standard grammar, spelling, sentence structure, and punctuation in their plans.

Technology Resources

 CNN. Presents America: Beginnings to 1914 Segment: The Life of Lincoln

First, it had to ban slavery. Second, a majority of adult males in the state had to take the loyalty oath. However, only southerners who swore that they had never supported the Confederacy could vote or hold office. Because of this rule, the Wade-Davis Bill made it much harder for southern states to rejoin the Union than did Lincoln's plan. President Lincoln refused to sign this bill into law. He thought that few southern states would agree to meet its requirements.

✔ **Reading Check: Contrasting** How did Lincoln's Ten Percent Plan and the Wade-Davis Bill treat southerners differently? See the definitions of the plans given above.

★ The Thirteenth Amendment

One issue Republicans agreed on was abolishing slavery. The Emancipation Proclamation had freed slaves only in the Confederate states that had not been occupied by Union forces. Slavery continued in the border states. In addition, many people feared that the federal courts might someday declare the Emancipation Proclamation unconstitutional.

On January 31, 1865, at Lincoln's urging, Congress proposed the **Thirteenth Amendment** to the Constitution. It made slavery illegal throughout the United States. The amendment was ratified and took effect on December 18, 1865. When abolitionist William Lloyd Garrison heard the news, he declared that his work was now finished. He called for

Many African American families bought family records like this one after the war.

Aid for Freedpeople

Interpreting Maps In order to help African Americans, the Freedmen's Bureau and several private aid societies distributed food and clothing, set up hospitals, and operated schools.

Skills Assessment

1. **Places and Regions** According to the map, which states had major private aid projects?
2. **Drawing Inferences and Conclusions** Why do you think that most private aid societies had their headquarters in northern states?

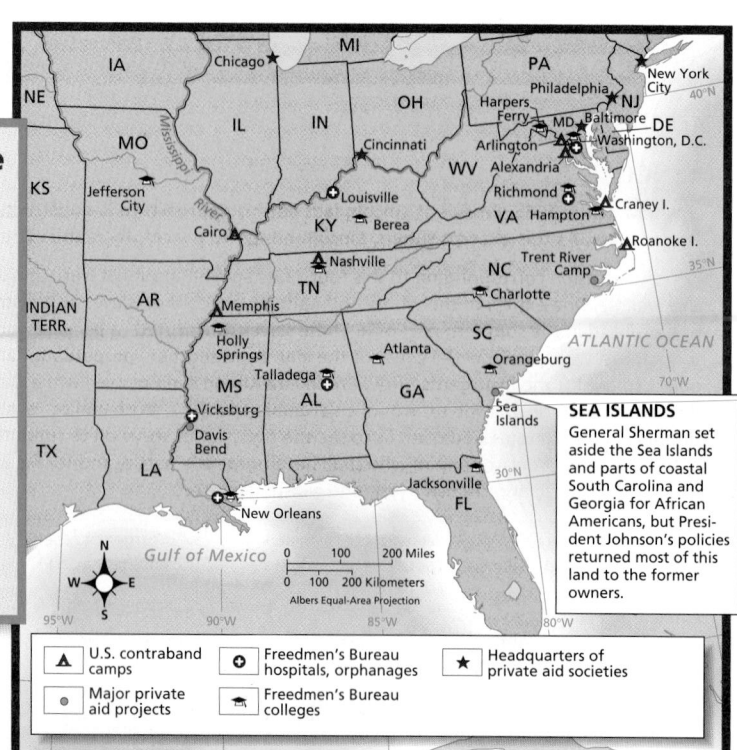

SEA ISLANDS
General Sherman set aside the Sea Islands and parts of coastal South Carolina and Georgia for African Americans, but President Johnson's policies returned most of this land to the former owners.

Legend:
- ▲ U.S. contraband camps
- ● Major private aid projects
- ✚ Freedmen's Bureau hospitals, orphanages
- Freedmen's Bureau colleges
- ★ Headquarters of private aid societies

George Wood of Portland, Texas, suggested the following activity:

 ALL LEVELS: Have students create a chart that compares and contrasts the different Reconstruction plans suggested by Lincoln, Republicans in Congress, and Johnson. Charts should include categories that describe (a) how the plan will bring the South back into the Union, (b) what consequences southern states will face as a result of withdrawing from the Union, and (c) how the plan will help freedpeople.

Once students have finished, review the chart or questions with the class. **ENGLISH LANGUAGE LEARNERS**

 LEVEL 3: Assign each student the role of a Confederate soldier, a freedperson, or an agent of the Freedmen's Bureau. Have students assume their roles and ask them to write to the newspaper editor stating which Reconstruction plan they favor and why they support it. After students have written their letters, organize the class into small groups. Using their letters as guides, each group should then create a graphic organizer identifying the strengths and weaknesses of each plan. Finally, lead a class discussion on the different views Abraham Lincoln, Congress, and Andrew Johnson had on Reconstruction. **COOPERATIVE LEARNING**

Interpreting the Visual Record

New schools *This school for freedpeople was established in Vicksburg, Mississippi.* **What does this image reveal about the ages of students in these early schools?**

the American Anti-Slavery Society to break up. Not all abolitionists agreed, however. Frederick Douglass insisted that "slavery is not abolished until the black man has the ballot [vote]."

Freedom did bring many changes to the lives of former slaves. Many couples held ceremonies to legalize marriages that had not been recognized under slavery. Many people searched for relatives who had been sold away from their families years earlier.

Some former slaves began to test their new freedom of movement. A South Carolina woman explained this need. "I must go, if I stay here I'll never know I'm free." Freedom to travel was just the first step on a long road toward equal rights and a new way of life. Adults took new last names. They insisted on being called Mr. or Mrs., rather than by their first name or by nicknames.

Across the South, freedpeople also demanded the same economic and political rights as white citizens. Henry Adams, a former slave, argued that "if I cannot do like a white man I am not free." Many former slaves wanted their own land to farm. Near the end of the Civil War, General William Tecumseh Sherman issued an order setting aside coastal lands in South Carolina, Georgia, and Florida for former slaves. However, the federal government soon returned these lands to the original owners. Many former slaves remained unsure about their future. They did not know where they would live, what kind of work they would do, and what rights they had.

✔ **Reading Check: Summarizing** What did the Thirteenth Amendment achieve, and how did this change the lives of enslaved African Americans? It abolished slavery. African Americans gained freedom but found it necessary to struggle for equal rights.

HOMEWORK Have students write a one-page summary of the three Reconstruction plans discussed in the section. Ask students to also include how each plan affected African Americans in the South.

⭐ CLOSE

Organize the class so that every student has a partner. You might want to pair students who are having difficulty with the material with peer tutors. Have one student in each pair state everything he or she knows about one of the following topics: the conditions affecting former Confederate soldiers and freedpeople at the end of the war; or the elements of the three Reconstruction plans described in this section. The second student should take notes on what the first student says. When finished, the person taking notes should add information that might have been overlooked by his or her partner. Then students should switch tasks with their partner and repeat the process until both topics have been covered.

COOPERATIVE LEARNING

LINKING PAST *to* PRESENT

Historically Black Colleges and Universities

After the Civil War, colleges for African Americans were established in the South. These schools, now known as historically black colleges and universities, offered traditional education, training, and teaching degrees. At one time, laws in many states prohibited African Americans from attending white schools. Today, however, many students choose historically black colleges and universities for their emphasis on African American identity and history. According to United Negro College Fund president William H. Gray III, students receive valuable support from the faculty, administration, and fellow students. **What do historically black colleges and universities provide their students?**

African American students studying art

⭐ The Freedmen's Bureau

In 1865 Congress established the <u>Freedmen's Bureau</u>. Its purpose was to provide relief for all poor people—black and white—in the South. Under Oliver O. Howard, the Bureau distributed food to the poor and supervised labor contracts between freedpeople and their employers. The Bureau also assisted African American war veterans.

In addition, the Freedmen's Bureau helped promote education in the South. Laws against educating slaves had kept most of them from learning to read or write. The Bureau and other groups established schools and provided books and teachers. Some former slaves also organized their own education efforts. African Americans opened schools in abandoned buildings. Some white southerners, however, burned down schools and attacked teachers and students. But by 1869, more than 3,000 schools had been established. More than 150,000 students attended these schools. The Freedmen's Bureau helped establish several colleges for African Americans, including Howard University in Washington, D.C., and Fisk University in Nashville, Tennessee. Students quickly filled the new classrooms, and working adults attended classes in the evening.

✔ **Reading Check: Analyzing Information** How did the Freedmen's Bureau help to provide educational reform in the South? It supported public education for former slaves by providing books and teachers and by founding schools and colleges.

⭐ A New President

On the evening of April 14, 1865, President Lincoln and his wife attended a performance of *Our American Cousin* at Ford's Theatre in Washington. During the play, <u>John Wilkes Booth</u> sneaked into the president's theater box and shot him. Booth was a southerner who opposed Lincoln's policies. Lincoln was rushed to a boardinghouse across the street, where he died at about 7:30 the next morning. Across the North people were stunned and saddened by the news of Lincoln's death. His body was sent home to Springfield, Illinois, for burial. Vice President <u>Andrew Johnson</u> was sworn into office that morning. Reconstruction was now his responsibility.

Republicans liked President Johnson because he seemed to favor a tougher approach to Reconstruction than Lincoln had. Johnson's plan for bringing southern states back into the Union was similar to Lincoln's plan. Johnson gave amnesty to all southerners who took an oath of loyalty and who agreed to support the abolition of slavery. However, wealthy southerners and former Confederate officials would need a presidential pardon to qualify for amnesty. In the end, this restriction was not as harsh as it might seem. Johnson shocked Republicans by eventually pardoning more than 7,000 people.

✔ **Reading Check: Finding the Main Idea** How did Lincoln's assassination affect the nation? It caused widespread grief and switched responsibility for Reconstruction to Andrew Johnson.

☆ REVIEW AND ASSESS

Have students complete the **Section 1 Review** on p. 625. Then have them complete **Daily Quiz 20.1**. As **Alternative Assessment**, you may want to use the Reconstruction plans graphic organizer or the Reconstruction Plans chart from the Teacher to Teacher activity in this section's lessons.

☆ RETEACH

Have students complete **Main Idea Activity for English Language Learners and Special-Needs Students 20.1**. Then ask students to imagine that they work for the Freedmen's Bureau and are in charge of obtaining contributions to help

run the organization. Have students create flyers explaining the Bureau's goals and asking for contributions to help run programs. **ENGLISH LANGUAGE LEARNERS**

☆ EXTEND

Remind students of the loss that was felt by many soldiers who returned home after the war to find their homes destroyed or their families gone. Have students write a poem or song that depicts these feelings. Encourage students who play a musical instrument to put their lyrics to music. Have students share their work with the rest of the class. **BLOCK SCHEDULING**

☆ President Johnson's Reconstruction Plan

Johnson's plan for Reconstruction established a system for setting up new southern state governments. First, he appointed a temporary governor for each state. Then southerners who had taken the loyalty oath elected delegates to a convention that would revise their state's constitution. Next, voters elected new state officials and representatives to the U.S. Congress. Each new state government was required to declare that secession was illegal. It also had to refuse to pay Confederate debts. No state could rejoin the Union until it had met these requirements. Governments already set up under Lincoln's Ten Percent Plan—in Arkansas, Louisiana, Tennessee, and Virginia—were allowed to remain in place.

By the end of 1865 all the southern states except Texas had created new governments. Johnson approved them all and declared that the United States was restored. Newly elected representatives soon came to Washington, D.C., from each reconstructed southern state. But Congress refused to allow them to take their seats in the House and Senate.

Republicans complained that many of the new southern representatives had been military officers and political leaders of the Confederacy. For example, Alexander H. Stephens, the newly elected U.S. senator from Georgia, had been the vice president of the Confederacy. Many Republicans did not believe that people like Stephens were truly loyal to the United States. Congress therefore refused to readmit the reconstructed southern states into the Union. Clearly, the nation was still divided over who should control Reconstruction and what direction it should take.

✔ **Reading Check: Summarizing** What steps did Johnson require southern states to take in order to be readmitted into the Union? *loyalty oath; support for abolition; revised state constitution; election of new state officials, representatives, and senators*

Lincoln's funeral procession was witnessed by thousands of mourners.

Section 1 Review

go.hrw.com **Homework Practice Online**
keyword: SA3 HP20

1 Define and explain:
amnesty

2 Identify and explain:
- Reconstruction
- Ten Percent Plan
- Wade-Davis Bill
- Thirteenth Amendment
- Freedmen's Bureau
- John Wilkes Booth
- Andrew Johnson

3 Comparing and Contrasting Copy the graphic organizer below. Use it to describe the three plans for Reconstruction that were developed over time.

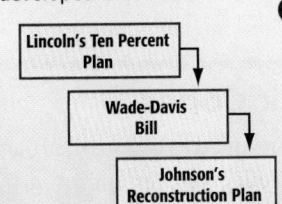

4 Finding the Main Idea
a. How did life in the South begin to change for African Americans after the Civil War?

b. What effect did Lincoln's assassination have on Reconstruction?

5 Writing and Critical Thinking
Summarizing Imagine that you are a southern newspaper editor in 1865. Write a brief editorial that describes the condition of the South after the Civil War.

Consider the following:
- the economic condition of the South
- the political situation of the ex-Confederate states
- the effect of the Thirteenth Amendment

Section 1 Review
ANSWERS

1 Define
- amnesty, p. 621

2 Identify
- Reconstruction, p. 621
- Ten Percent Plan, p. 621
- Wade-Davis Bill, p. 621
- Thirteenth Amendment, p. 622
- Freedmen's Bureau, p. 624
- John Wilkes Booth, p 624
- Andrew Johnson, p. 624

3 Ten Percent Plan: offered southern states amnesty if 10% of voters took a loyalty oath and swore to support a ban on slavery; Wade-Davis Bill: required southern states to ban slavery, only southerners who swore that they had never supported the Confederacy could vote or hold office; Johnson's Plan: gave amnesty to all southerners who took a loyalty oath and agreed to support the abolition of slavery, returned all property to pardoned southerners

4 a. they began to test the limits of their new freedom by legalizing marriages, taking new last names, insisting on being called Mr. or Mrs., and trying to obtain their own farmland

b. Students might suggest that if Lincoln had lived, his Ten Percent Plan would have treated southerners less harshly.

5 Students' editorials will vary.

Section 2
OBJECTIVES

⊠ Explain how Black Codes restricted African Americans' freedoms.

⊠ Analyze the reasons that Radical Republicans tried to impeach President Johnson.

⊠ Describe Republicans' efforts to protect the civil rights of African Americans.

🔊 LET'S GET STARTED!

As students enter the classroom, ask them to identify reasons to remove a president from office. (*Students' responses should indicate that a president can be removed for conviction of treason, bribery, or other high crimes and misdemeanors.*) List their replies on the chalkboard. Read Article II, Sections 1 and 4 of the Constitution to the class. These deal with the presidential oath of office and the reasons that a president may be impeached. Ask students to compare their reasons with those listed in the Constitution. Then tell students that in Section 2 they will learn more about the attempted impeachment of President Andrew Johnson.

Section 2

The Fight over Reconstruction

Read to Discover

1. How did Black Codes restrict African Americans' freedoms?
2. Why did Radical Republicans try to impeach President Johnson?
3. How did Republicans try to protect the civil rights of African Americans?

WHY IT MATTERS TODAY

In the 1860s the Radical Republicans used their control of Congress to pass major laws. Use **CNNfyi.com** or other **current events** sources to identify which political party controls each house of Congress today and one piece of legislation that party is trying to pass. Record your findings in your journal.

Identify

• Black Codes
• Radical Republicans
• Thaddeus Stevens
• Civil Rights Act of 1866
• Fourteenth Amendment
• Reconstruction Acts
• Fifteenth Amendment

A federal soldier protects an African American man from violence.

The Story Continues

To test his newfound freedom, in 1865 Henry Adams left the plantation where he had been a slave. A group of white men stopped Adams on the road, demanding to know who owned him. When Adams replied that he was a free man, the strangers beat him. Such violent attacks were not unusual in the South in the years following the Civil War. Many white southerners opposed and feared African Americans' freedom. This resentment also affected local authorities and state governments.

★ The Black Codes

In 1866 Congress continued to debate the rules for restoring the Union. Meanwhile, new state legislatures approved by President Johnson had already begun passing laws to deny African Americans' civil rights. "This is a white man's government, and intended for white men only,"

★ TEACH

Have students read Section 2 and complete Guided Reading Strategy 20.2. Choose one or more of the following activities to explore the section content with students. For further suggestions on block scheduling or team teaching, see the *Block Scheduling Handbook with Team Teaching Strategies.*

LEVEL 1: Pair students and have them write brief paragraphs outlining the goals of the Fourteenth Amendment, the Fifteenth Amendment, the Civil Rights Act of 1866, and the Reconstruction Acts. Then ask each student to mention what all of these acts have in common. *(Students' responses will vary, but students should mention that all of the acts were ways Republicans tried to protect African Americans' civil rights.)* **ENGLISH LANGUAGE LEARNERS , COOPERATIVE LEARNING**

declared Governor Benjamin F. Perry of South Carolina. Soon every southern state passed **Black Codes**—laws that greatly limited the freedom of African Americans.

Black Codes required African Americans to sign work contracts. This arrangement created working conditions similar to those experienced under slavery. In most southern states, any African American who could not prove he or she had a job could be arrested. Their punishment might be one year of forced labor without pay. African Americans were also prevented from owning guns. In addition, African Americans were not allowed to rent property in cities.

The Black Codes alarmed African Americans. As one Civil War veteran asked, "If you call this Freedom, what do you call Slavery?" African Americans organized to oppose the codes. One group sent a petition to officials in South Carolina.

History Makers Speak
❝We simply ask . . . that the same laws which govern *white men* shall govern *black men*; that we have the right of trial by a jury of our peers; that schools be established for the education of *colored children* as well as white . . . that, in short, we be dealt with as others are—in equity [equality] and justice.❞

—Petition by an African American convention, quoted in *There Is a River: The Black Struggle for Freedom in America,* by Vincent Harding

Such calls for equality had little effect on the new state governments, however.

✔ **Reading Check: Finding the Main Idea** How were southern African Americans treated after the Civil War, and why did they receive this treatment? White southerners feared the freedom of African Americans and passed Black Codes to keep them in conditions similar to slavery.

★ The Radical Republicans

The Black Codes angered many Republicans who felt the South was returning to its old ways. Most Republicans were moderates who wanted the South to have loyal state governments. They also believed that African Americans should have rights as citizens. Most moderates hoped that the national government would not have to force the South to follow federal laws.

Radical Republicans wanted the southern states to change much more than they already had before they could return to the Union. Like the moderates, they thought the Black Codes were cruel and unjust. Radicals, however, wanted the federal government to be much more involved in Reconstruction. They feared that too many southern leaders

THE GRANGER COLLECTION, NEW YORK

Under the Black Codes, white southerners could arrest unemployed African Americans and auction their labor to the highest bidder.

Analyzing Primary Sources
Identifying Points of View What rights did these African Americans want? They wanted the same rights as whites.

Thaddeus Stevens was one of the most vocal Radical Republicans in Congress.

Andrew Johnson

Andrew Johnson had a long political career before becoming president. Born to a poor family in North Carolina, Johnson became a tailor's apprentice. Unhappy with this arrangement, the young Johnson ran away to Tennessee and started his own tailoring business. Eventually, he became a prosperous landowner and entered politics. However, he never forgot his humble beginnings and often criticized wealthy southern planters. Johnson served as governor of Tennessee and later as a U.S. senator from that state. When Tennessee seceded, Johnson remained loyal to the Union. The Republicans selected Johnson as Lincoln's running mate in the presidential campaign of 1864. They hoped that he would appeal to voters in the border states. He had been vice president for less than six weeks when Lincoln was assassinated. What parts of Andrew Johnson's experience prepared him for the presidency?

were still loyal to the former Confederacy. **Thaddeus Stevens** of Pennsylvania and Charles Sumner of Massachusetts were the leaders of the Radical Republicans.

A harsh critic of President Johnson, Stevens was known for his honesty and sharp tongue. He wanted economic and political justice for both African Americans and poor white southerners.

 History Makers Speak ❝Have not loyal blacks quite as good a right to choose rulers and make laws as rebel whites? Every man, no matter what his race or color . . . has an equal right to justice, honesty, and fair play with every other man; and the law should secure him those rights.❞

—Thaddeus Stevens, quoted in *Sources of the American Republic*

Sumner had been a strong opponent of slavery before the Civil War. He continued to argue for African Americans' civil rights, which included the right to vote and the right to fair treatment under the law. Both Stevens and Sumner felt that President Johnson's Reconstruction plan was a failure. Although the Radicals did not control Congress, they gained support among moderates when President Johnson ignored criticism of the Black Codes. "The same national authority that destroyed slavery must see that this other pretension [racial inequality] is not permitted to survive," said Sumner.

✔ **Reading Check: Comparing and Contrasting** How were Radical Republicans and moderate Republicans similar and different? Similar: both supported rights for African Americans; Different: Radicals wanted federal involvement to protect these rights

Johnson versus Congress

In early 1866 Congress proposed a bill to give the Freedmen's Bureau more powers. The law would allow the Freedmen's Bureau to use military courts to try people accused of violating African Americans' rights. The bill's supporters hoped that these courts would be fairer than local courts in the South. To the surprise of many members of Congress, Johnson vetoed the bill. He insisted that Congress could not pass any new laws until the southern states were represented in Congress. Johnson also argued that the Freedmen's Bureau was unconstitutional. He believed that African Americans did not need any special assistance.

Republicans responded with the **Civil Rights Act of 1866**. This act provided African Americans with the same legal rights as white Americans. President Johnson once again used his veto power. He argued that the law would give too much power to the federal government. He also rejected the principle of equal rights for African Americans. The president insisted that they did not understand "the nature and character of our institutions." Congress, however, overrode Johnson's veto.

✔ **Reading Check: Identifying Points of View** What Congressional laws did Johnson veto, and why? He vetoed laws that expanded powers of Freedman's Bureau and the Civil Rights Act of 1866. He did not agree that the federal government could pass laws affecting southern states that were not represented. In addition, he did not support equal rights for African Americans.

LEVEL 2: Tell students that they are going to serve as members of a congressional committee that is investigating the effects of how the Black Codes restricted the freedoms of African Americans. Ask students to develop testimonials to present to Congress (the class) describing how the Civil Rights Act of 1866, the Fourteenth Amendment, and the Fifteenth Amendment will bring an end to the restrictions imposed by the Black Codes. *(Students' testimonials should indicate that the Civil Rights Act of 1866 provided African Americans with the same legal rights as white Americans; the Fourteenth Amendment guaranteed citizenship and equal protection under the law to all people born or naturalized within the U.S.; the Fifteenth Amendment gave African American men throughout the United States the right to vote.)* Encourage students to use logical reasoning to support their opinions.

☆ The Fourteenth Amendment

Republicans feared the Civil Rights Act might be overturned. To protect civil rights laws from hostile presidents, courts, or future legislators, Republicans proposed a constitutional amendment in the summer of 1866. The **Fourteenth Amendment** included the following provisions.

1. It defined all people born or naturalized within the United States, except American Indians, as U.S. citizens.
2. It guaranteed to citizens the equal protection of the laws.
3. It said that states could not "deprive any person of life, liberty, or property, without due process of law."
4. It banned many former Confederate officials from holding state or federal offices.
5. It made state laws subject to review by federal courts.
6. It gave Congress the power to pass any laws needed to enforce any part of the amendment.

President Johnson and most Democrats opposed the Fourteenth Amendment. As a result, civil rights for African Americans became a key issue in the 1866 congressional elections. Republican candidates asked Americans to support civil rights by voting for the Republican Party. Johnson traveled around the country defending his Reconstruction plan, but his tour was of little help to Democratic Party candidates.

Two major riots in the South also hurt Johnson's campaign. On May 1, 1866, a dispute in Memphis, Tennessee, took place between local police and black Union soldiers. The dispute turned into a three-day wave of violence against African Americans. By the time the riots ended, 46 African Americans were dead. About three months later, another riot took place in New Orleans when African Americans attempted to hold a peaceful political demonstration. This time 34 African Americans and three white Republicans were killed. Federal troops had to restore order.

✔ **Reading Check: Summarizing** What issue did the Fourteenth Amendment address, and how did it affect the congressional elections of 1866?
It addressed civil rights and made civil rights for African Americans a major issue in the elections.

Research on the R·OM

Free Find:
Civil Rights Act of 1866
After reading about the Civil Rights Act of 1866 on the **Holt Researcher CD–ROM**, create an illustrated diagram that shows what rights former slaves had before and after Congress passed the act.

☆ Citizenship

The Firing of Stanton.
President Lincoln appointed Edwin Stanton secretary of war shortly after the Civil War began. Stanton's able leadership contributed to the Union victory. Although he continued as secretary of war under Johnson, Stanton did not agree with Johnson's Reconstruction policies. The secretary called for more severe punishment of the southern states. He also supported the Republicans' act that created the Freedmen's Bureau and the Civil Rights Act of 1866. Shortly before Johnson fired Stanton, the secretary of war was helping congressional Republicans draft the new Reconstruction laws. It was Stanton's support of Johnson's Republican opponents that caused Johnson to fire Stanton.

☑ **internet** connect

TOPIC: Stanton
GO TO: go.hrw.com
KEYWORD: SA3 CF20

ACTIVITY: Have students use the library or search the Internet through the HRW Go site to find information about Edwin Stanton. Have students draw up a letter that Stanton might have written in defense of himself and his beliefs. Have students use standard grammar, spelling, sentence structure, and punctuation in their letters.

THE GRANGER COLLECTION, NEW YORK

Interpreting the Visual Record

Johnson's tour *President Andrew Johnson often got into arguments with audience members during his speaking tour in 1866. When someone cried out, "Hang Jeff Davis!" Johnson replied angrily, "Why not hang Thad Stevens?"* **What does this image tell you about how Johnson traveled on his tour?**

LEVEL 3: Have students imagine that they are northern journalists who have been assigned to expose unfair southern laws. Have each student write an article on one of these laws. Combine these articles into a newspaper that is designed to promote justice for African Americans and explain how the Black Codes restricted African Americans' freedoms.

 HOMEWORK Have students create a flowchart that illustrates the relationships between the key terms for this section. Ask them to add drawings to enhance their charts.

Going to the Polls. "The Great Epoch in the history of our race has at last arrived," wrote African American Robert Fitzgerald about the election of 1868. He was talking about southern African Americans exercising their right to vote. African American voters took part in election parades and attended Republican meetings during the campaign. In many parts of the South, however, African Americans faced intimidation and violence when taking part in political events. In some towns, whites closed down polls on election day or blocked African Americans from voting. In Louisiana, government officials refused to protect African American voters from violent acts by whites and even advised African Americans to stay away from the polls.

CRITICAL THINKING

How do you think violence against African American voters affected the election of 1868?

ANSWER: Students might suggest that violence most likely resulted in fewer votes for Grant and other Republican candidates, since many African Americans were kept from voting.

Visual Record Answer

(for p. 629)

Students should suggest that he traveled by train.

★ Congress Takes Charge

The 1866 elections gave the Republican Party a commanding two-thirds majority in both the House and the Senate. This majority gave the Republicans the power to override any presidential veto. In addition, the Republicans became united as the moderates joined with the Radicals. Together they called for a new form of Reconstruction.

In March 1867 Congress passed the first of several **Reconstruction Acts**. These laws divided the South into five districts, with a U.S. military commander in control of each district. The military would remain in the South until the southern states rejoined the Union. To be readmitted, a state had to write a new state constitution supporting the Fourteenth Amendment. Finally, the state had to give African American men the right to vote.

President Johnson disagreed strongly with the Reconstruction Acts. He argued that African Americans did not deserve the same treatment as white people. The Reconstruction Acts, he said, used "powers not granted to the federal government or any one of its branches." Republicans knew

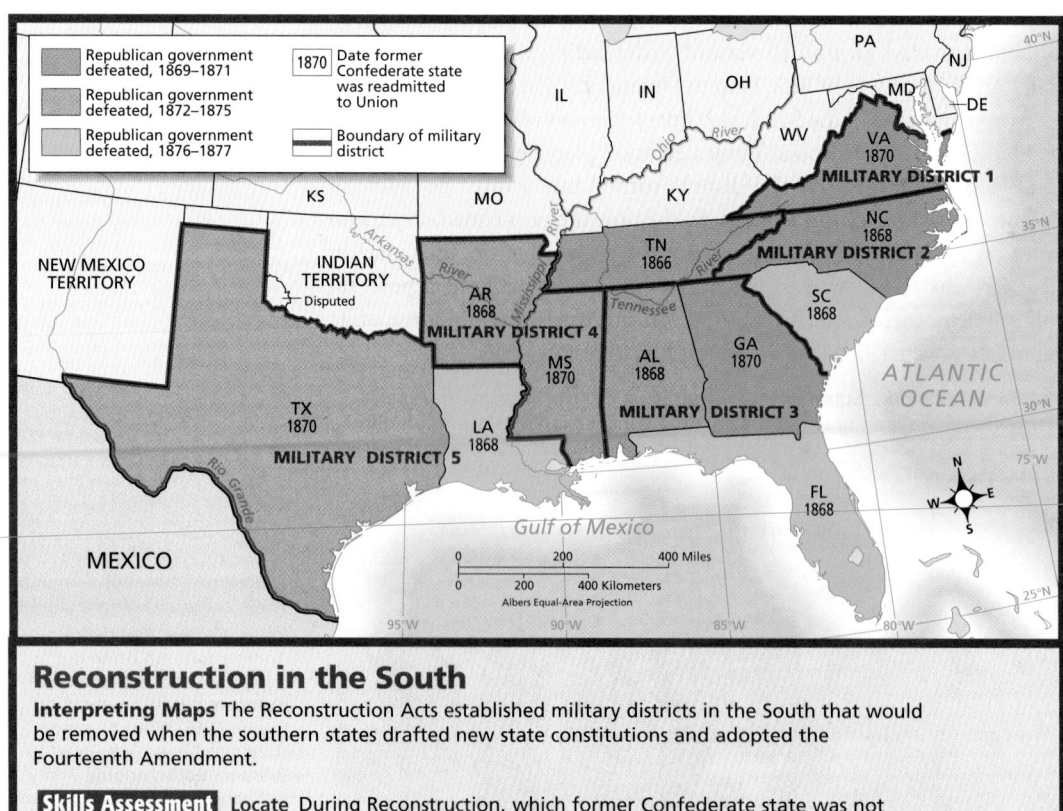

Reconstruction in the South

Interpreting Maps The Reconstruction Acts established military districts in the South that would be removed when the southern states drafted new state constitutions and adopted the Fourteenth Amendment.

Skills Assessment Locate During Reconstruction, which former Confederate state was not part of a military district?

LEVEL 3: As a class, conduct a mock impeachment trial for President Andrew Johnson. Organize the class into four groups. Have one group act as impeachment managers for the House of Representatives who are presenting the case against the president. Have the second group prepare a defense of the president. Have the third group act as the Senate, which is preparing questions to ask representatives of both sides and voting at the end of the trial whether or not to convict. Have the fourth group act as reporters who are observing the trial and preparing a news story describing the events. After the trial, discuss with students what happened during each aspect of the case. **COOPERATIVE LEARNING**

★ CLOSE

Ask students to write a journal entry describing whether they think the rights of freedpeople were adequately protected by the passage of the Fourteenth and Fifteenth Amendments. Encourage students to consider the events in this section when exploring their opinions.

that Johnson did not support their Reconstruction policies, so they passed a law to limit his power. This law prevented the president from removing cabinet officials without the U.S. Senate's approval. Johnson quickly broke the law by firing Edwin Stanton, the secretary of war.

The House of Representatives responded by voting to impeach the president. Impeachment is the process used by a legislative body to bring charges of wrongdoing against a public official. This was the first time in U.S. history that a president had been impeached. The next step, under Article I of the Constitution, was a trial in the Senate. If a two-thirds majority of the senators found Johnson guilty, he would be removed from office.

Although Johnson was unpopular with Republicans, some of them believed he was being judged unfairly. Others did not trust the president *pro tempore* of the Senate, Benjamin Wade, who would become president if Johnson were removed from office. By a single vote, Senate Republicans failed to convict Johnson. Even so, the trial broke his power.

THE GRANGER COLLECTION, NEW YORK

President Andrew Johnson's impeachment trial in the Senate attracted many onlookers.

✔ **Reading Check: Analyzing Information** What was the purpose of the Reconstruction Acts, and how did they affect the South? to protect African American rights; divided South into five military districts, required new state constitutions and ratification of Fourteenth Amendment, gave African Americans the vote

★ The Election of 1868

The Democratic Party did not nominate Johnson for another term in 1868. Instead, the Democrats chose former New York governor Horatio Seymour as their presidential candidate. The Republicans selected Ulysses S. Grant. As a war hero, Grant appealed to many northern voters. He had no political experience but supported the congressional Reconstruction plan. He ran under the slogan "Let Us Have Peace."

Shortly after Grant was nominated, Congress readmitted seven southern states—Alabama, Arkansas, Florida, Georgia, Louisiana, North Carolina, and South Carolina. (Tennessee already had been readmitted in 1866.) Under the terms of readmission, these seven states approved the Fourteenth Amendment. They also agreed to let African American men have the vote. However, white southerners used violence to keep African Americans away from the polls during the presidential election.

Despite such tactics, hundreds of thousands of African Americans voted for Grant and the "party of Lincoln." The *New Orleans Tribune* reported that many former slaves "see clearly enough that the Republican party [is] their political life boat." African American votes helped Grant win a narrow victory.

✔ **Reading Check: Analyzing Information** What voters did Grant appeal to in the presidential election of 1868? northern voters and newly enfranchised African Americans

★★★★★★★★★★★★
That's Interesting!
★★★★★★★★★★★★

Ulysses S. Grant was born Hiram Ulysses Grant. After being accepted to the U.S. Military Academy at West Point, Grant decided to change his name to Ulysses Hiram. However, Grant was commissioned under the name Ulysses S. Grant. Because Grant claimed the middle initial stood for nothing, many of his colleagues began to call him U.S. Grant or Uncle Sam Grant.

MAP ANSWER
(for p. 630)
Tennessee

Visual Record Answer
(for p. 632)
Students might say former slaves, new businessman, or soldiers.

★★★★★★★★★★★★
That's Interesting!
★★★★★★★★★★★★

A Good Show Can you imagine a trial becoming a social event? That's just what happened when Andrew Johnson was impeached. People had to have tickets to attend the trial, and only 1,000 were printed. William H. Crook, President Johnson's bodyguard, described the scene. "Everyone who by any possible means could get a ticket . . . [showed] it early that morning at the Capitol. The floor and galleries were crowded." Washingtonians attended in their finest clothes and hoped for a good show. However, they were soon disappointed. Few were interested in the long speeches, and President Johnson did not even appear at his trial.

★ REVIEW AND ASSESS

Have students complete the **Section 2 Review** on p. 632. Then have them complete **Daily Quiz 20.2**. As **Alternative Assessment**, you may want to use the northern journalist activity or the reasons for impeachment organizer in this section's lessons.

★ RETEACH

Have students complete **Main Idea Activity for English Language Learners and Special-Needs Students 20.2**. Then ask students to make a bulleted list of this sections key terms and definitions. Assist students with terms that they are having difficulty understanding. **ENGLISH LANGUAGE LEARNERS**

★ EXTEND

Explain to students that the effect of the Fifteenth Amendment was realized shortly after ratification. Tell students that the 1870 presidential election was one of the first tests of the amendment's effect. Have students conduct research to examine the 1870 election. Tell them to write a report to Congress that describes the amendment's effect on the 1870 election. Have students describe attempts that were made to keep African Americans from voting. Then ask them to analyze African Americans' influence on the outcome of the election.
BLOCK SCHEDULING

Section 2 Review
ANSWERS

❶ **Identify**
- Black Codes, p. 627
- Radical Republicans, p. 627
- Thaddeus Stevens, p. 628
- Civil Rights Act of 1866, p. 628
- Fourteenth Amendment, p. 629
- Reconstruction Acts, p. 630
- Fifteenth Amendment, p. 632

❷ 1866: Civil Rights Act which would have given African Americans the same legal status as whites and the Fourteenth Amendment defining citizenship, guaranteeing the equal protection of the laws, and preventing states from infringing on people's civil rights proposed; 1867: Reconstruction Acts providing for the military occupation of the South until former confederate states wrote new constitutions supporting the Fourteenth Amendment and granted African American men the right to vote; and 1870: the Fifteenth Amendment granting the right to vote to African American men

❸ a. forced African Americans to sign work contracts, punished those who did not have jobs, kept African Americans from owning guns, and kept African Americans from renting property in cities
b. vetoed laws affecting the Confederate states; ignored criticism of the Black Codes; worked against the re-election of Republicans in 1866; violated a federal law; and, in general, opposed Congress's plans for Reconstruction

❹ Students' slogans will vary.

Interpreting the Visual Record

Gaining the vote *This illustration shows African Americans voting after the passage of the Fifteenth Amendment.* **What types of individuals are shown in the voting line?**

★ The Fifteenth Amendment

Congressional Republicans wanted to protect their Reconstruction plan from any major changes. They believed that most African American voters would support Republican policies. In addition, some Radical Republicans argued that it was not fair that many northern states had laws that prevented African Americans from voting. After all, every southern state was now required to grant suffrage to African American men under the Republican plan.

These were some of the reasons why Congress proposed the **Fifteenth Amendment** in 1869. The amendment gave African American men throughout the United States the right to vote. Abolitionist William Lloyd Garrison praised "this wonderful, quiet, sudden transformation of four millions of human beings from . . . the auction block to the ballot-box." The amendment went into effect in 1870, and it was one of the last important Reconstruction measures passed at the federal level.

The Fifteenth Amendment did not please every reformer, however. Writer and editor Henry Adams commented that the Fifteenth Amendment was "more remarkable for what it does not than for what it does contain." For example, the act did not guarantee African Americans the right to hold public office. It also did not extend the right to vote to all Americans. This particularly upset women's rights activists, many of whom believed it was unfair to grant African American men the vote while still denying suffrage to all American women. Many women's rights activists opposed the amendment for this reason.

✔ **Reading Check: Finding the Main Idea** What did the Fifteenth Amendment achieve? It gave African American men the right to vote throughout the country.

Section 2 Review

★ ★ ★ ★ ★ ★ ★ ★ ★ ★ ★ ★ ★ ★ ★ ★ ★ ★ ★ ★

go. Homework
hrw Practice
.com Online
keyword: SA3 HP20

❶ **Identify** and explain:
- Black Codes
- Radical Republicans
- Thaddeus Stevens
- Civil Rights Act of 1866
- Fourteenth Amendment
- Reconstruction Acts
- Fifteenth Amendment

❷ **Sequencing** Copy the time line below. Use it to list, in order, the reform legislation Congress proposed or passed as part of Reconstruction. Include the significance of each law or amendment.

Congressional Reconstruction

1866　1867　　　　　　1870

❸ **Finding the Main Idea**
a. In what ways did the Black Codes restrict the freedom of African Americans?

b. Why did Radical Republicans want to remove President Johnson from office?

❹ **Writing and Critical Thinking**
Identifying Points of View Imagine that you are a member of the Republican Party. Write a slogan that might have been used by the Republican Party to appeal to voters in either the 1866 congressional elections or the 1868 presidential election.

Consider the following:
- how the party tried to protect the rights of African Americans
- new amendments and congressional laws
- differences between moderate and Radical Republicans

Section 3

OBJECTIVES

- ⭐ Describe the reforms Reconstruction governments carried out.
- ⭐ Analyze the factors that led to the end of Reconstruction.
- ⭐ Examine how southern laws and governments changed after Reconstruction ended.

Section 3

Reconstruction in the South

Read to Discover

1. What reforms did Reconstruction governments carry out?
2. What factors led to the end of Reconstruction?
3. How did southern laws and governments change after Reconstruction ended?

WHY IT MATTERS TODAY

During Reconstruction, there were many Republican governments in the South. As Reconstruction ended, Democrats gained power. Use **CNNfyi.com** or other **current events** sources to learn which political party is leading a southern state today. Record your findings in your journal.

Define

- carpetbaggers
- scalawags
- poll tax
- segregation

Identify

- Hiram Revels
- Blanche K. Bruce
- Ku Klux Klan
- General Amnesty Act of 1872
- Panic of 1873
- Civil Rights Act of 1875
- Compromise of 1877
- Redeemers
- Jim Crow laws
- *Plessy* v. *Ferguson*

The Story Continues

Governments elected with the support of African American voters took control of most southern states. Planter Henry William Ravenel expressed concerns about the future in his daily journal. "The experiment [Reconstruction] is now to be tried. . . . It produces a financial, political, and social revolution [in] the South." Ravenel worried about how the actions of the new governments would affect southern society.

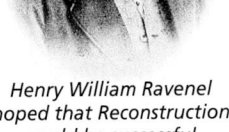

Henry William Ravenel hoped that Reconstruction would be successful.

⭐ Reconstruction Governments

The Republican Party controlled most southern governments, partly because the Fourteenth Amendment banned many former Confederates, who were Democrats, from holding office. Most of the Republican officeholders were unpopular with the majority of white southerners.

Some northern-born Republicans had moved south after the war. Many white southerners called these Republicans **carpetbaggers**. Supposedly the northerners carried all their possessions in bags made from

Have students read Section 3 and complete Guided Reading Strategy 20.3. Choose one or more of the following activities to explore the section content with students. For further suggestions on block scheduling or team teaching, see the *Block Scheduling Handbook with Team Teaching Strategies.*

LEVEL 1: Organize students into small groups. Have each group develop a list of factors that led to the end of Reconstruction. *(Students' lists will vary but should include violence, the Panic of 1873, or the election of 1876.)* Then have each group choose one factor from its list and analyze in detail how that factor contributed to the end of Reconstruction. Ask a volunteer from each group to present his or her group's findings. **ENGLISH LANGUAGE LEARNERS** , **COOPERATIVE LEARNING**

☆ Historical Sidelight

Carpetbaggers. Contrary to their reputations, most so-called carpetbaggers were well-educated professionals, such as lawyers, journalists, and business leaders. Many of these northerners were members of the Union army who decided to remain in the South after the war. Those who won political office during Reconstruction generally supported equal rights for African Americans. Some were even asked to run for office by freedpeople. In economic matters, however, these northerners were more moderate. They hoped to build railroads and modernize the southern economy, but few supported land grants for freedpeople.

CRITICAL THINKING

How do you think these northerners wanted to change the southern economy?

ANSWER: Students might suggest that they probably wanted to reform the southern economy so that it would be more like that of the North.

Visual Record Answer

Students might suggest because they were the first African American members of Congress.

This is an example of the type of carpetbag from which the nickname carpetbaggers developed.

Interpreting the Visual Record

Representatives *The first African American members of Congress included, from left to right, Hiram Revels, Benjamin Turner, Robert DeLarge, Josiah Walls, Jefferson Long, Joseph Rainey, and Robert Elliott.* **What was significant about the election of these politicians?**

THE GRANGER COLLECTION, NEW YORK

---

carpeting. Many southerners resented these northerners, believing that they had moved south to profit from Reconstruction. Some of the newcomers wanted to help former slaves. Others hoped to make money while rebuilding the southern economy.

Southern Democrats cared even less for white southern Republicans. They referred to them as **scalawags**, or "mean fellows." Democrats believed that these southerners had betrayed the South by voting for the Republican Party. Many southern Republicans were small farmers who had supported the Union during the war. Others, like Mississippi governor James Alcorn, were former members of the Whig Party. They preferred to become Republicans rather than join the Democrats.

African Americans were the largest group of southern Republican voters. During Reconstruction, more than 600 African Americans were elected as representatives to state legislatures. Of these politicians, 16 were elected to Congress. Other African Americans held important state offices such as lieutenant governor, treasurer, and secretary of state. Many more held local offices in counties throughout the southern states. Apart from their regular duties, African American politicians helped enforce laws that white officials ignored. In Georgia, for example, Justice of the Peace Tunis Campbell protected African Americans from attack by angry whites. One African American called Campbell "the champion of their rights and the bearer of their burden."

African American politicians came from many different backgrounds. **Hiram Revels** was born free in North Carolina and went to college in Illinois. He became a Methodist minister and served as a chaplain in the Union army. In 1870 Revels became the first African American in the U.S. Senate. He took over the seat previously held by Jefferson Davis in Mississippi. Unlike Revels, **Blanche K. Bruce** grew up in slavery in Virginia. He became an important Republican in Mississippi and served one term as a U.S. senator.

Reconstruction governments provided money for many new programs and organizations. They helped to establish some of the first state-funded public school systems in the South. They also built new hospitals, prisons, and orphanages and passed laws prohibiting discrimination against African Americans. Southern states under Republican control spent large amounts of money. They aided the construction or repair of railroads, bridges, and public buildings. These improvements were intended to help the southern economy recover from the war. To get the money for these projects, the Reconstruction governments raised taxes and issued bonds.

✔ **Reading Check: Summarizing** What reforms did Reconstruction state governments carry out? They funded schools and other public institutions, prohibited racial discrimination, and built or repaired railroads, bridges, and public buildings.

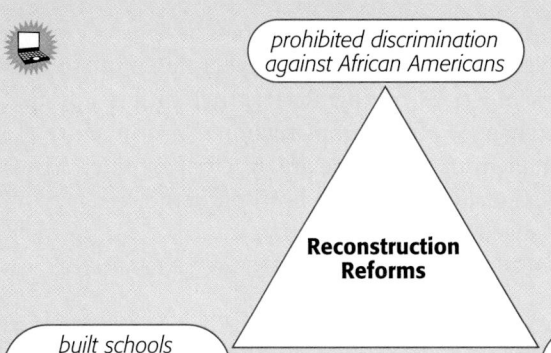

★ Opposition to Reconstruction

Despite these efforts to rebuild the South, most white southerners opposed Reconstruction. Democrats claimed that the Reconstruction governments were corrupt and illegal. They also disliked having federal soldiers stationed in their states. Many white southerners disapproved of African American officeholders.

In 1866 a group of white southerners in Tennessee created the **Ku Klux Klan**. This secret society opposed civil rights, particularly suffrage, for African Americans. Klan members wore robes and disguises to hide their identities. The Klan used violence and terror against African Americans, white Republican voters, and public officials. The Klan's membership grew rapidly as it spread throughout the South. In response, Congress passed laws that made it a federal crime to interfere with elections or to deny citizens equal protection under the law. Within a few years the Klan was no longer an organized threat, but violence against African Americans and Republicans continued throughout the 1870s.

✔ **Reading Check: Finding the Main Idea** What was the purpose of the Ku Klux Klan? to oppose civil rights for African Americans

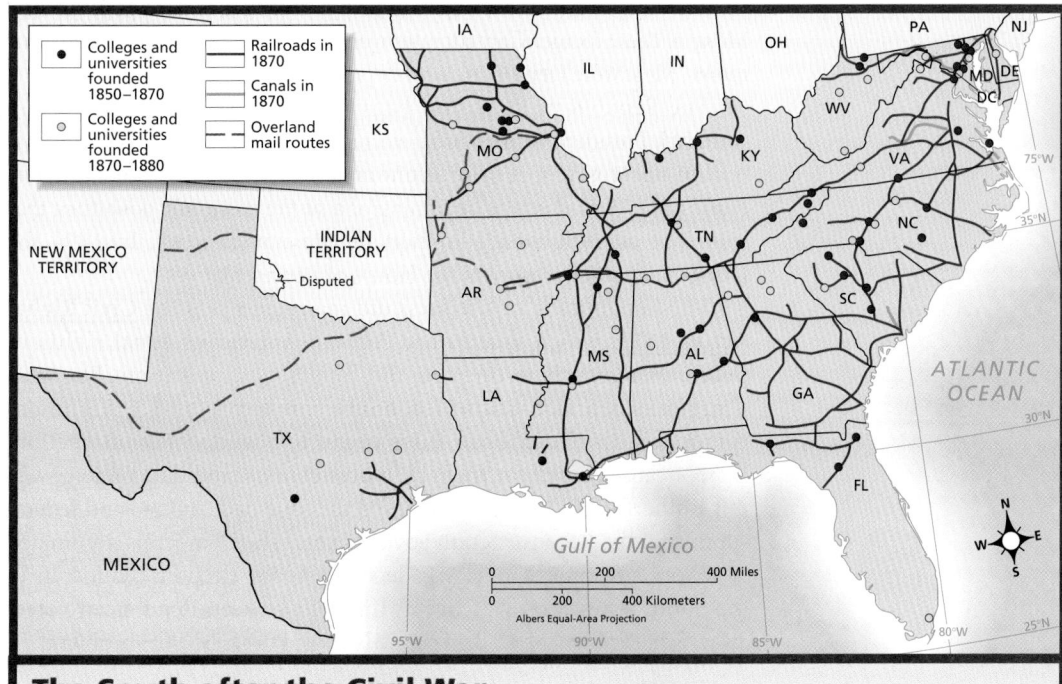

The South after the Civil War
Interpreting Maps After the Civil War many Reconstruction programs contributed to the rapid growth in transportation and education in the South.

Skills Assessment Places and Regions How many colleges and universities were founded in Alabama from 1850 to 1870?

ALL LEVELS: Pair students. Then have pairs create a graphic organizer that displays what the southern government was like during Reconstruction, and how that government changed after Reconstruction. Then organize the pairs into small groups. Have the groups compare their organizers. Finally, lead a discussion on how southern laws and governments changed after Reconstruction.

ENGLISH LANGUAGE LEARNERS , COOPERATIVE LEARNING

LEVEL 3: Have students use their textbooks or class notes to determine the main factors that led to the end of Reconstruction. Then ask students to decide which factor they believe was the most important. *(Students' responses should include: Democrats claim that the Reconstructionist governments were unjust and illegal; white southerners disapproval of African American officeholders; the financial Panic of 1873, which hurt the Republican Party; Republicans losing control of the House of Representatives to the Democrats in 1874; and the Compromise of 1877.)* Have students prepare for a class debate to support the factor they chose. Finally, lead the debate to determine which factor played the most important role in leading to the end of Reconstruction.

Interdisciplinary Connection

▶Math◀

The Popular Vote. The votes in the presidential election of 1876 broke down along regional lines. Hayes won the majority of nonsouthern states, while Tilden dominated the South.

ACTIVITY: Copy the following chart onto the chalkboard and have students use it to determine what percentage of the ex-Confederate states Tilden won by popular vote *(73 percent)* and what percentage Hayes won *(27 percent). (If students are having trouble, you might want to review the steps for determining percentages—divide the total number of ex-Confederate states and move the decimal point two places to the right.)*

Popular Vote, Election of 1876		
State	Rutherford Hayes	Samuel Tilden
AL	68,708	102,989
AR	38,649	58,086
FL	23,849	22,927
GA	50,533	130,157
LA	75,315	70,508
MS	52,603	112,173
NC	108,484	125,427
SC	91,786	90,897
TN	89,566	133,177
TX	45,013	106,372
VA	95,518	140,770

Interpreting the Visual Record

Disputed votes *A special Election Commission heard testimony on disputed returns from the presidential election of 1876.* **Why do you think so many people gathered to watch these proceedings?**

★ The End of Reconstruction

The violence of the Ku Klux Klan was not the only challenge to Reconstruction. The **General Amnesty Act of 1872** allowed former Confederates, except those who had held high ranks, to hold public office. Many of these former Confederates were soon elected to southern governments. Most were Democrats who opposed Reconstruction.

The Republican Party also began losing its power in the North. Although President Grant was re-elected in 1872, scandals in his administration upset voters. A poor economy also hurt the Republicans. The **Panic of 1873** marked the beginning of a severe economic downturn that soon put an estimated 2 million people out of work. In 1874 the Democrats gained control of the House of Representatives.

The Republicans in Congress did manage to pass the **Civil Rights Act of 1875**, which guaranteed African Americans equal rights in public places such as theaters and public transportation. But with Americans worried about economic problems and government corruption, the Republican Party began to abandon Reconstruction. Republicans selected for their 1876 presidential candidate Ohio governor Rutherford B. Hayes. He believed the time had come to end federal support of the Reconstruction governments. The Democrats nominated New York governor Samuel J. Tilden. During the election, Democrats in the South again used violence at the polls to keep Republican voters away. Senator Blanche K. Bruce of Mississippi described the problem.

Analyzing Primary Sources
Summarizing How did Democrats act to ensure that Republicans were defeated at the polls? Voting was corrupted, and the threat of violence prevented some from voting at all.

History Makers Speak
❝In many parts of the State corrupt and violent influences were brought to bear [used] . . . changing the number of votes cast; . . . threats and violence were practiced directly upon the masses of voters . . . to deter [prevent] them from [voting].❞

—Blanche K. Bruce, quoted in *Crossing the Danger Water*, edited by Deirdre Mullane

LEVEL 3: Have students imagine that they are a journalist who has been observing the changes in the southern government after the Civil War. Have each student write an article that discusses the reforms implemented by Reconstruction governments, as well as how southern laws and governments changed after Reconstruction ended. Ask volunteers to present their articles to the class.

★ CLOSE

Arrange a panel of students to discuss who was responsible for Reconstruction's failure to reform southern society. Have students take turns participating in the discussion and offering their opinions. Then tell students that no single group can take the blame for Reconstruction's failure. Explain to students that there were many factors that contributed to Reconstruction's failure.

Note: For an additional teaching idea, see the Chapter 20 Music, Poetry, and Law activity in the **Creative Teaching Strategies** handbook.

The election between Hayes and Tilden was very close. Tilden appeared to have won. Republicans, however, challenged the electoral votes in Oregon and three southern states. A special Election Commission of 10 members of Congress and five Supreme Court justices settled the issue. The commission narrowly decided to give all the disputed votes to Hayes, who thus won the election by one electoral vote. In the **Compromise of 1877**, the Democrats agreed to accept Hayes's victory. In return, they wanted all remaining federal troops removed from the South. They also asked for funding for internal improvements in the South and the appointment of a southern Democrat to the president's cabinet. Shortly after he took office in 1877, President Hayes removed the last of the federal troops from the South.

✔ **Reading Check: Sequencing** What issues led up to the Compromise of 1877, and how did it affect Reconstruction? economic crisis, weakening congressional support for Reconstruction, and disputed electoral votes given to Hayes; federal troops were removed from the South

★ Jim Crow and *Plessy* v. *Ferguson*

Gradually, Democrats regained control of state governments in the South. These Democrats were called **Redeemers**. They came from a variety of backgrounds. Texas governor Richard Coke, like many other Redeemers, was a former officer in the Confederate army. Some Redeemers came from business backgrounds. In general, Redeemers wanted to reduce the size of state government and limit the rights of African Americans. They lowered state budgets and got rid of social programs. The Redeemers cut property taxes and reduced public funding for schools.

Redeemers set up the **poll tax** in an effort to deny the vote to African Americans. The poll tax was a special tax people had to pay before they could vote. Some states also targeted African American voters by requiring them to pass a literacy test. A so-called grandfather clause written into law affected men whose fathers or grandfathers could vote before 1867. In those cases, a voter did not have to pay a poll tax or pass a literacy test. As a result, almost every white man could escape the voting restrictions, while few black men could.

Redeemer governments also introduced legal **segregation**, the forced separation of whites and African Americans in public places. **Jim Crow laws**—laws that required segregation—were common in southern states in the 1880s. African Americans had to stay in different hotels than whites. They had to sit in separate theater sections and ride in separate railcars. One white southerner described the segregated areas that African Americans were forced to use as "the most uncomfortable, uncleanest, and unsafest place[s]."

African Americans challenged Jim Crow laws in court. In 1883, however, the U.S. Supreme Court ruled that the Civil Rights Act of 1875 was unconstitutional. The Court also ruled that the Fourteenth

Interpreting Political Cartoons

Compromise of 1877 *Some saw the Compromise of 1877 as the only way to avoid violence in the South after the disputed election results.* **Why do you think the artist chose to show a hand grasping at a pistol?**

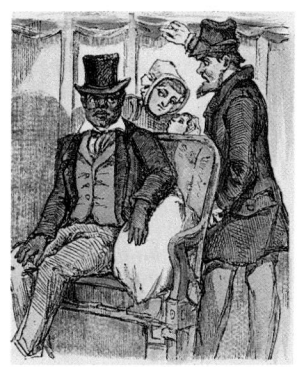
This African American man is being ordered to leave a whites-only railroad car.

★ Daily Life

Violence. After the Civil War, freedpeople faced daily the threat of violence, including beating, assault, and even murder. Many southerners refused to accept that African Americans had the freedom to control their own lives and exercise their rights. White southerners attacked and sometimes killed African American men, women, and children.

CRITICAL THINKING

How could the threat of violence have affected freedpeople?

ANSWER: Students might suggest that freedpeople might have tried to avoid whites because they feared becoming targets of violence.

POLITICAL CARTOON ANSWER

Students might suggest it symbolizes the South reaching for violent means.

Visual Record Answer

(for p. 636)
Students might suggest that people were invested and interested in the outcome of the election.

★ REVIEW AND ASSESS

Have students complete the **Section 3 Review** on p. 638. Then have them complete **Daily Quiz 20.3.** As **Alternative Assessment,** you may want to use the end of Reconstruction group activity, or the Reconstruction reforms article activity in this section's lessons.

★ RETEACH

Have students complete **Main Idea Activity for English Language Learners and Special-Needs Students 20.3.** Explain to students that the government wants them to evaluate Reconstruction's success. Have students review material from this section to determine their opinion on the subject. Students should write short summaries of their findings. **ENGLISH LANGUAGE LEARNERS**

★ EXTEND

Ask students to read aloud the Supreme Court's decision in the case of *Plessy* v. *Ferguson.* Have students research the arguments presented in the case. Then ask students to imagine that they are John Marshall Harlan, the only Supreme Court justice who disagreed with the Court's decision. Have students write a dissenting opinion that argues against the Court's decision. Have students point out the constitutional grounds on which their opinions are based and to describe the negative effects that they think will result from the decision. **BLOCK SCHEDULING**

★★★★★★★★★★★★★★★★★

Section 3 Review
ANSWERS

1 Define
• carpetbaggers, p. 633
• scalawags, p. 634
• poll tax, p. 637
• segregation, p. 637

2 Identify
• Hiram Revels, p. 634
• Blanche K. Bruce, p. 634
• Ku Klux Klan, p. 635
• General Amnesty Act of 1872, p. 636
• Panic of 1873, p. 636
• Civil Rights Act of 1875, p. 636
• Compromise of 1877, p. 637
• Redeemers, p. 637
• Jim Crow laws, p. 637
• *Plessy* v. *Ferguson,* p. 638

3 violence; the Panic of 1873; the election of 1876

4 a. building of schools and other public institutions, past laws that prohibited discrimination against African Americans, and built or repaired railroads, bridges, and public buildings.
b. reduced the size and cost of government, cut taxes, reduced funding for schools, worked to reduce African American voting, and introduced Jim Crow laws

5 Students' letters will vary, but should express how the ruling is related to the Fourteenth Amendment, Redeemer governments in the South, and Jim Crow laws.

Research on the R⊙M

Free Find:
Plessy v. *Ferguson*
After reading about *Plessy* v. *Ferguson* on the **Holt Researcher CD–ROM,** imagine that you are a newspaper reporter working at the time of the Supreme Court decision. Write a newspaper article about the case and the Court's decision.

Analyzing Primary Sources
Identifying Points of View
What does it mean to say that the Constitution is "color-blind"? The Constitution does not permit different treatment for people of different races.

Amendment applied only to the actions of state governments. This ruling allowed private individuals and businesses to practice segregation.

In 1896 the U.S. Supreme Court returned to the issue of segregation in the case **Plessy v. Ferguson.** Homer Plessy, an African American, had purchased a ticket on a Louisiana train. When he refused to leave the whites-only section of the train car, he was arrested. Louisiana's Jim Crow laws did not allow African Americans to ride in cars with whites. Plessy's lawyers argued that the law violated his right to equal treatment under the Fourteenth Amendment.

The Court ruled that segregation was allowed if "separate-but-equal" facilities were provided for African Americans. Among the justices, only John Marshall Harlan disagreed with the Court's decision. He explained his disagreement in a dissenting opinion.

> **History Makers Speak** ❝In the eye of the law, there is in this country no superior, dominant [controlling], ruling class of citizens.... Our Constitution is color-blind, and neither knows nor tolerates classes among citizens. In respect of civil rights, all citizens are equal before the law.❞
>
> —John Marshall Harlan, quoted in *American Issues*

Despite Harlan's view, segregation became widespread across the country. African Americans were forced to use separate public schools, libraries, and parks. When they existed, these facilities were usually of poorer quality than those created for whites. In practice, these so-called separate-but-equal facilities were separate and unequal.

✔ **Reading Check: Making Generalizations and Predictions** Why might the *Plessy* v. *Ferguson* decision make it hard to establish racial equality? *By upholding the Jim Crow laws, the decision made segregation constitutional.*

Section 3 Review

go. hrw .com **Homework Practice Online**
keyword: SA3 HP20

★★★★★★★★★★★★★★★★★★★★★★★★★★★★★

1 Define and explain:
• carpetbaggers
• scalawags
• poll tax
• segregation

2 Identify and explain:
• Hiram Revels
• Blanche K. Bruce
• Ku Klux Klan
• General Amnesty Act of 1872
• Panic of 1873
• Civil Rights Act of 1875
• Compromise of 1877
• Redeemers
• Jim Crow laws
• *Plessy* v. *Ferguson*

3 Evaluating Copy the graphic organizer below. Use it to identify the factors leading to the end of Reconstruction.

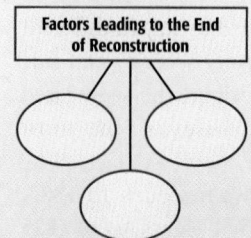
Factors Leading to the End of Reconstruction

4 Finding the Main Idea
a. What reforms took place under the Reconstruction state governments?

b. Describe laws passed by the new southern state governments after Reconstruction ended.

5 Writing and Critical Thinking
Supporting a Point of View Imagine that you are a Republican who opposes the *Plessy* v. *Ferguson* ruling. Write a letter to a friend in the North that expresses your views on the ruling.

Consider the following:
• the Fourteenth Amendment
• the actions of Redeemer governments in the South
• Jim Crow laws

Section 4

OBJECTIVES

⭐ Describe how southern agriculture changed after the Civil War.

⭐ Analyze why some business leaders hoped to create a "New South."

⭐ Discuss some popular forms of southern culture during and after Reconstruction.

🔊 **LET'S GET STARTED!**

As students enter the classroom ask them to identify the resources they would need in order to be a successful farmer. (*Students' responses will vary but might include land, a barn, seeds, farm machinery, and a source of water.*) List their answers on the chalkboard. Tell students that during and after Reconstruction, poor African Americans and whites often lacked land and the money to buy it. Explain to students that because of this lack of resources poor farmers often turned to new ways of earning a living. Tell students that in Section 4 they will learn about changes in the culture of the South following the Civil War and during and after Reconstruction.

Section 4

The New South

Read to Discover

1. How did southern agriculture change after the Civil War?
2. Why did some business leaders hope to create a "New South"?
3. What were some popular forms of southern culture during and after Reconstruction?

WHY IT MATTERS TODAY

Many large corporations today try to diversify, or produce a variety of goods and services, rather than relying on one product. Use **CNNfyi.com** or other **current events** sources to find a modern company that makes many different products. Record your findings in your journal.

Define

• sharecropping

Identify

• Henry W. Grady
• Mary Noailles Murfree
• Joel Chandler Harris
• Charles W. Chesnutt

The Story Continues

After farming for years, Charley White and his wife, Lucille, had saved enough money to buy their own farm in Texas. White later reflected on the purchase. "The house wasn't much more than a shack." But that it belonged to them made all the difference. "It just set us on fire. We didn't seem to get half as tired, or if we did we didn't notice it." Lucille White told her husband that "even the rocks look pretty." For many African American farmers, however, owning their own farms remained just a dream.

Sharecroppers and other poor farmers often planted gardens to help provide food for their families.

⭐ Sharecropping

Few African Americans in the South could afford to buy or even rent farms. Moving west also was costly. Many African Americans, therefore, remained on plantations. Others tried to make a living in the cities.

African Americans who stayed on plantations often became part of a system known as **sharecropping**, or sharing the crop. Landowners provided the land, tools, and supplies, while sharecroppers provided the labor. At harvest time the sharecropper often had to give most of the

☆ TEACH

Have students read Section 4 and complete Guided Reading Strategy 20.4. Choose one or more of the following activities to explore the section content with students. For further suggestions on block scheduling or team teaching, see the *Block Scheduling Handbook with Team Teaching Strategies*.

LEVEL 1: Lead a class discussion on the various forms of southern entertainment or culture discussed in this section. Then have students create folk ballads that are similar to those created during that era. Have students include references to southern culture during and after the Reconstruction era in their work. **ENGLISH LANGUAGE LEARNERS**

 HOMEWORK Have students use the library to research popular forms of southern culture during and after Reconstruction, as well as for present-day southern society. Then have students compare the popular forms of culture for the two eras in an essay noting the similarities and differences.

☆ Daily Life

The General Store.

General stores grew in importance after the Civil War because of the need for farm credit. The general stores that dotted the South served many functions: grocery store, department store, and hardware store. General stores also served as banks, pharmacies, and meeting places. Both African American and white customers traveled over bad roads to buy clothing, food, medicines, and other staple goods that they could not grow or make themselves. Store owners extended credit—at interest rates as high as 40 percent—for these purchases as well as for seed and equipment to plant crops. Local farmers gathered to hold meetings of fraternal societies at general stores. Community members also gathered at the store to hear local gossip and political news.

CRITICAL THINKING

Why was the general store such an important institution in the South?

ANSWER: Students might suggest that it provided services that were critical to everyday life.

VISUALIZING HISTORY ANSWERS

1. They face unfair merchants or landowners, or poor harvests.
2. Students' answers will vary, but they might suggest the government as a resource.

The Sharecropping Cycle

The sharecropping system trapped many black and white farmers in a cycle of poverty.

Visualizing History

1. **Economics** What economic disadvantages did sharecroppers face?
2. **Connecting to Today** What policies or programs might help poor farmers today?

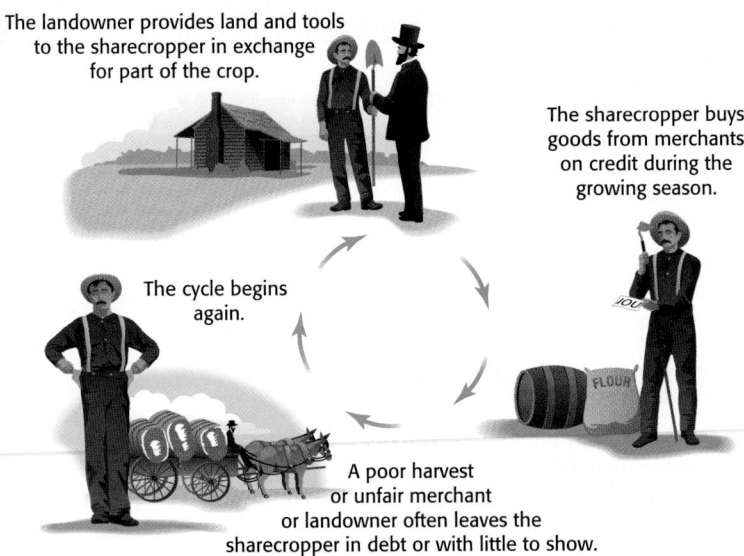

The landowner provides land and tools to the sharecropper in exchange for part of the crop.

The sharecropper buys goods from merchants on credit during the growing season.

The cycle begins again.

A poor harvest or unfair merchant or landowner often leaves the sharecropper in debt or with little to show.

Analyzing Primary Sources

Identifying Points of View According to Douglass, how did merchants keep sharecroppers in debt? by charging the highest prices for the poorest goods

crop to the owner. Whatever remained belonged to the sharecropper. Many sharecroppers hoped to save enough money from selling their share of the crops to one day be able to buy a farm. Unfortunately, only a few ever achieved this dream.

Most sharecroppers instead lived in a cycle of debt. When they needed food, clothing, or supplies, most families had to buy goods on credit because they had little cash. When sharecroppers sold their crops, they hoped to pay off these debts. However, bad weather, poor harvests, or low crop prices often made this impossible. Merchants sometimes cheated sharecroppers by charging them for items they did not buy. Some landowners also cheated sharecroppers by taking more than their fair share of the crops. Abolitionist Frederick Douglass complained about this poor treatment of sharecroppers.

 History Makers Speak "The merchant puts him [the sharecropper] off with his poorest commodities [goods] at highest prices, and can say to him take these or nothing. . . . By this means the laborer is brought into debt, and hence is kept always in the power of the landowner."

—Frederick Douglass, quoted in *Enduring Voices*

As a result of such practices, most sharecroppers found themselves ever deeper in debt. They owed more at the end of the harvest than they had when they planted their crops.

Most sharecroppers grew cotton, one of the South's most important cash crops. When too many farmers planted cotton, however, the supply became too great. As a result, the price per bale dropped. One man wrote his father about a drop in the price of cotton. "It nearly ruined us. . . . But getting ready to plant cotton again."

The New South

Why business leaders hoped to develop a "New South" economy	How business leaders hoped to develop a "New South" economy
• *to take advantage of southern resources* • *to diversify and modernize the southern economy*	• *build textile mills* • *draw labor away from farms and into factories*

Many farmers understood the drawbacks of planting cotton. However, they felt too much pressure from banks or landlords to change their ways. "Cotton raising has grown to be a necessity more than a choice," a farmer in Alabama said. A southern farmer explained why so many sharecroppers depended on cotton.

History Makers Speak "Cotton is the thing to get credit on in this country. . . . You can always sell cotton. You leave home with a wagon load of cotton and you will go home that night with money in your pocket; you load up your wagon with wheat or corn . . . and I doubt some days whether you could sell it."

—Anonymous farmer, quoted in *The Promise of the New South*, by Edward L. Ayers

✔ **Reading Check: Finding the Main Idea** How did the sharecropping system limit the economic freedom of southern farmers? Cotton supply often exceeded demand; low prices and unfair landowners kept sharecroppers in debt.

⭐ Southern Industry

The southern economy suffered through cycles of good and bad years as cotton prices went up and down. Some business leaders hoped industry would strengthen the southern economy. They wanted to create a "New South." **Henry W. Grady**, an Atlanta newspaper editor, was a leader of the New South movement. Grady and his supporters wanted to take advantage of the South's resources. With its cotton production and cheap and abundant labor, the South could build textile mills and other factories.

The most successful industrial development in the South involved textile production. Businesspeople built textile mills in many small towns to produce cotton fabric. Hundreds of people from rural areas came to work in the mills. However, few cotton mills hired African Americans.

Work in the cotton mills appealed to farm families who had trouble making ends meet. As one mill worker explained, "It was a necessity to move and get a job, rather than depend on the farm." Recruiters sent out by the mills promised good wages and steady work. Entire families often worked in the same mill. Mills employed large numbers of women and children. Many children started working at about the age of 12. Women did most of the spinning and were valued workers. However, few women had the opportunity to advance within the company.

Mill work was often unpleasant. One unhappy worker described it as "the same thing over and over again. . . . The more you do, the more they want done." Workers often labored 12 hours a day, six days a week. Cotton dust and lint filled the air. This unhealthy air caused asthma and an illness known as brown-lung disease. Fast-moving machinery caused injuries and even some deaths. Despite the long hours and dangerous working conditions, wages were low. But mill work did offer an alternative to farming.

✔ **Reading Check: Comparing and Contrasting** How was work in the cotton mills similar to and different from sharecropping? Both occupations kept poor people poor, but while sharecroppers depended on the uncertainty of the cotton market and were victims of merchants and landlords, mill workers had the benefit of certain, if low, wages.

CONNECTING TO MATH

Just the Facts

Cotton Production and Price

Year	Bales produced	Price per pound
1876	4,474,000	9.71¢
1877	4,773,000	8.53¢
1878	5,074,000	8.16¢
1879	5,756,000	10.28¢
1880	6,606,000	9.83¢
1881	5,456,000	10.66¢
1882	6,949,000	9.12¢
1883	5,713,000	9.13¢
1884	5,682,000	9.19¢
1885	6,576,000	8.39¢

Using Mathematical Skills

1. In how many of the years shown on the chart did the price of cotton go up?

2. Use these figures to create two line graphs, one showing cotton production from 1876 to 1885 and the other showing cotton prices during the same period.

3. What happened to cotton production each time the price rose to over 10 cents a pound? Why do you think this was the case?

A young African American girl working in the cotton fields
THE GRANGER COLLECTION, NEW YORK

⭐ Economics

Railroads. From 1877 to 1900 the South built railroad lines at a faster rate than the nation as a whole. In 1860 the South had only about 10,000 miles of railroads. By 1900 some 60,000 miles of railroads—one third of the country's lines—connected southern towns and cities to the rest of the nation. Railroad building had an immediate effect on the southern economy. Farmers profited by cutting railroad ties from their land and selling them to the railroad companies. Farm families also made money by selling chickens, eggs, meat, and other farm products to the railroad workers.

CRITICAL THINKING
How do you think the railroads helped the southern economy in the long term?

ANSWER: Students might suggest that railroads would help the southern economy by shipping more crops and other goods to more areas.

CONNECTING TO MATH ANSWERS
1. four
2. Students' line graphs should include data from the chart.
3. The first time it rose; the second time it dropped. Students might suggest that higher prices led to increased production.

LEVEL 3: Ask students to write a short story that describes the experiences of a poor southern farmer trying to improve his or her life after the Civil War. The story should describe how southern agriculture changed after the Civil War and include references to the labor system, economic changes, and agricultural changes that are depicted in this section. Ask volunteers to read their stories to the class and invite other students to comment on them.

★ CLOSE

Ask students to list the ways that life in the New South differed from life in the Old South. Then organize the class into small groups and have members share their lists with one another and create a chart comparing and contrasting the two lifestyles.
COOPERATIVE LEARNING

CONNECTING TO THE ARTS ANSWER
They brought African American music to a wider audience and helped raise money for Fisk University.

Technology Resources
 Everyday Life in America Transparency 13: Life during Reconstruction

Technology Resources
 American Music Selection 15: "When Johnny Comes Marching Home"

★ ★ ★ ★ ★ ★ ★ ★ ★ ★ ★

Section 4 Review
ANSWERS

❶ **Define**
• sharecropping, p. 639
❷ **Identify**
• Henry W. Grady, p. 641
• Mary Noailles Murfree, p. 642
• Joel Chandler Harris, p. 642

• Charles W. Chesnutt, p. 642

❸ textile mills and factory wage laborers; sharecropping and economic dependence on cotton

---

CONNECTING TO
THE ARTS

The Fisk Jubilee Singers
During Reconstruction, students from Fisk University in Nashville, Tennessee, formed the Fisk Jubilee Singers. They traveled widely, touring the North in 1871 and 1872. They later performed in Europe. As they brought African American music, such as spirituals, to a wider audience, they made Fisk University famous. They also raised enough money to help the university build its first permanent building. Other African American colleges, such as Hampton Institute in Virginia, formed similar singing groups. As a result, the popularity of spirituals increased. **What is notable about the Fisk Jubilee Singers?**

★ Southern Literature

The New South movement sought to modernize the South. Many southerners looked to the arts to keep their longstanding traditions alive, however. Southern literature gained national popularity in the late 1800s. Part of the reason for this was that many southern stories involved people and places in the South that seemed exciting and even exotic to northerners.

Mark Twain wrote many stories about the South, including *The Adventures of Tom Sawyer*. He was considered to be the most famous writer about the South at the end of Reconstruction. **Mary Noailles Murfree** wrote popular short stories and novels about the mountain people of eastern Tennessee. George Washington Cable wrote novels about the African American community in New Orleans. Cable used his writing to protest racial prejudice in the South. **Joel Chandler Harris** wrote short stories about fictional plantation life. His main character was a slave named Uncle Remus, who taught lessons by reciting folktales. Harris based his work on stories he was first told by enslaved African Americans.

Many white southern writers set their stories in a pre–Civil War South full of beautiful plantations and happy slaves. **Charles W. Chesnutt**, an African American, did not share this romantic image. Born in Ohio but raised in North Carolina, his plantation stories showed the greed and cruelty of slaveholders. Many of his short stories are collected in a book called *The Conjure Woman*.

✔ **Reading Check: Analyzing Information** What were the most common topics of southern literature in the late 1800s? *country folk, protests of racial prejudice, plantation life, and slavery*

JUBILEE SINGERS, COURTESY OF FISK UNIVERSITY

Have students complete the **Section 4 Review** on p. 643. Then have them complete **Daily Quiz 20.4**. As **Alternative Assessment**, you may want to use the poor southern farmer short story or the "New South" organizer in this section's lessons.

★ RETEACH

Have students complete **Main Idea Activity for English Language Learners and Special-Needs Students 20.4**. Then ask students to make a list of important ideas, people, and places, found in this section. Have students create another list that contains explanations of each term. Then have each student exchange his or her lists with another student to match the terms to the definitions. **ENGLISH LANGUAGE LEARNERS , COOPERATIVE LEARNING**

★ EXTEND

Have students use the library to obtain information about southern mill workers and working conditions in the mills. Have students write a campaign speech for a southern reformer who is seeking to improve the conditions in the mills. Encourage students to be as descriptive as possible when explaining the working conditions and to offer suggestions for changes in the mills. **BLOCK SCHEDULING**

★ Southern Music

Southern music also grew in popularity after the Civil War. Some of the musical instruments popular in the South were the fiddle, the banjo, and the guitar. Fiddle players provided the music for square dancing, a favorite pastime.

One of the most important types of songs in the South was the spiritual. Spirituals were based on Christian hymns and African music sung in the days of slavery. The lead singer often called out a verse that the rest of the singers would repeat. Sometimes the lead singer might change the words slightly to reflect current events. The lyrics usually described the sorrows of slavery and the hope for freedom. One of the best-known spirituals was "Swing Low, Sweet Chariot." It expressed a longing for the promised land, where African Americans would be free from slavery.

Dancing parties were a common pastime in many parts of the South.

Primary Sources

"Swing low, sweet chariot,
Comin' for to carry me home,
Swing low, sweet chariot,
Comin' for to carry me home,
I look'd over Jordan, an' what did I see,
Comin' for to carry me home,
A band of angels comin' after me,
Comin' for to carry me home,
If you get-a there befo' I do,
Tell all my friends I'm comin' too."

—From *Crossing the Danger Water*, edited by Deirdre Mullane

Analyzing Primary Sources

Drawing Inferences and Conclusions What does "home" represent in "Swing Low, Sweet Chariot"? Students might suggest the promised land of freedom or heaven.

✔ **Reading Check: Making Generalizations and Predictions** How might the universal themes of spirituals have helped them become popular in the late 1800s? Answers will vary. Students might suggest that the music expressed themes such as the desire of people to be free, the importance of religion in guiding the way, and the joy of anticipating heaven.

Section 4 Review

go.hrw.com **Homework Practice Online**
keyword: SA3 HP20

1 **Define** and explain:
• sharecropping

2 **Identify** and explain:
• Henry W. Grady
• Mary Noailles Murfree
• Joel Chandler Harris
• Charles W. Chesnutt

3 **Summarizing** Copy the graphic organizer below. Use it to show the main characteristics of the southern economy after the Civil War.

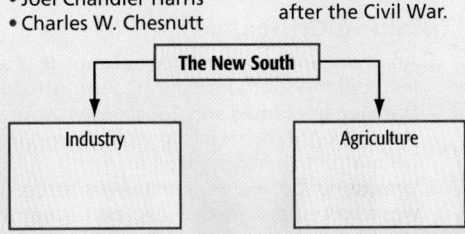
The New South
Industry
Agriculture

4 **Finding the Main Idea**
a. How did the sharecropping system work, and what were its drawbacks for southern farmers?

b. Why did some business leaders want to develop southern industry?

5 **Writing and Critical Thinking**
Evaluating Imagine that you are a northern newspaper reporter in the South after the Civil War. Write a story that explains to northern readers how southern literature and music express the views of African Americans about life in the South.
Consider the following:
• the writings of African American southerners
• the importance of spirituals
• the lyrics to "Swing Low, Sweet Chariot"

---

4 a. Former slaves and poor whites relied on landowners for supplies, tools, and land, and in return received a share of the crop they grew. Drawbacks included dependence on landowners and merchants; the uncertainty of crop prices; and low income or no income at all for the sharecropper.
b. to take advantage of southern resources such as cotton and cheap labor to diversify and modernize the southern economy

5 Students' stories will vary.

CHAPTER 20 REVIEW ANSWERS

The Chapter at a Glance
Students' quizzes will vary.

Identifying People and Ideas
Students' sentences should indicate an understanding of the following definitions:

1. made slavery illegal

2. provided relief for poor people in the South

3. Lincoln's vice president; became president in 1865

4. laws that limited the freedom of African Americans

5. guaranteed citizenship and equal protection to all people born or naturalized in the United States except American Indians

6. gave African American men the right to vote

7. the first African American U.S. senator

REVIEW AND ASSESSMENT RESOURCES

REPRODUCIBLE
▶ Vocabulary Activity 20

TECHNOLOGY
▶ Chapter 20 Test Generator (on the One-Stop Planner)
▶ Global Skill Builder CD–ROM
▶ HRW Go site

REINFORCEMENT, REVIEW, AND ASSESSMENT
▶ Chapter 20 Review, pp. 643–645
▶ Chapter 20 Tutorial for Students, Parents, Mentors, and Peers

▶ Chapter 20 Test (Form A or B)
▶ Alternative Assessment Handbook
▶ Chapter 20 Test for English Language Learners and Special-Needs Students

★ REVIEW
Have students complete the **Chapter 20 Review** on pages 644–45.

★ ASSESS
Use one of the chapter tests to assess students' understanding of the content. For **Alternative Assessment**, see the **Alternative Assessment Handbook**.

---

8. compromise in which southern Democrats accepted Hayes as president if troops were removed form the South

9. Supreme Court decision that held segregated facilities legal as long as they were of equal quality

10. agricultural system in which people farmed land owned by someone else

Understanding Main Ideas
1. difference was in the oath Confederates had to take to be pardoned

2. Fourteenth and Fifteenth Amendments, Civil Rights Act of 1866, and the Reconstruction Acts

3. vetoed laws affecting the South; did not try to stop Black Codes; worked against the re-election of Republicans; violated a federal law

4. by building public institutions, prohibiting discrimination against African Americans, and building or repairing bridges, buildings and railroads

5. violence, the Panic of 1873, the election of 1876

6. Writers depicted Southern slavery as cruel, and spirituals expressed a longing for freedom.

You Be the Historian— Reviewing Themes
1. 13th—abolished slavery, 14th—made African Americans citizens, and 15th—gave them the right to vote.

Chapter 20 Review

The Chapter at a Glance
Examine the visual summary of the chapter below. Use it to write a five-question quiz for a classmate.

Reuniting the Nation

The Thirteenth, Fourteenth, and Fifteenth Amendments are ratified, ending slavery, granting equal protection to all citizens, and giving African Americans the vote. Other civil rights laws are also passed.

The Reconstruction Acts divide the South into military districts and install new governments. The changes lead to conflict between African Americans and white southerners and Republicans and Democrats.

The Compromise of 1877 ends Reconstruction. Legal segregation is upheld in the South by Jim Crow laws and by the Supreme Court ruling in *Plessy v. Ferguson.*

Identifying People and Ideas
Use the following terms or people in historically significant sentences.
1. Thirteenth Amendment
2. Freedmen's Bureau
3. Andrew Johnson
4. Black Codes
5. Fourteenth Amendment
6. Fifteenth Amendment
7. Hiram Revels
8. Compromise of 1877
9. *Plessy* v. *Ferguson*
10. sharecropping

Understanding Main Ideas
Section 1 *(Pages 620–625)*
1. How did the Reconstruction plans of Lincoln, the Radical Republicans, and Johnson differ?

Section 2 *(Pages 626–632)*
2. List the major parts of Congress's plan for Reconstruction.
3. Why did the Radical Republicans impeach President Johnson?

Section 3 *(Pages 633–638)*
4. How did Reconstruction state governments try to change and help rebuild the South?
5. What events helped bring about the end of Reconstruction?

Section 4 *(Pages 639–643)*
6. How did African American literature and music contrast with the romantic image of the South painted by many white southern writers?

You Be the Historian— Reviewing Themes
1. **Constitutional Heritage** How did the Thirteenth, Fourteenth, and Fifteenth Amendments protect the rights of African Americans?
2. **Government** How did Reconstruction affect governments in the South?
3. **Culture** What contributions did African Americans make to southern society, government, and culture after the Civil War?

Thinking Critically
1. **Analyzing Information** What economic problems did the South face during Reconstruction?
2. **Drawing Inferences and Conclusions** How do you think Abraham Lincoln would have viewed Reconstruction had he lived to see it?
3. **Evaluating** Do you think that Reconstruction was a success or a failure? Explain your answer, considering the perspectives of all groups involved.

Organize students into four groups and assign each group one of the chapter's sections. Give each group a sheet of butcher paper, markers, and other materials and ask students to develop a collage depicting the main points of their section. Then have each group develop an oral presentation that explains its collage.

**ENGLISH LANGUAGE LEARNERS ,
COOPERATIVE LEARNING**

Portfolio Extensions

1. Cooperative Learning

Have students complete the following activity in small groups. Ask students to imagine that members of their team are agents of the Freedmen's Bureau traveling throughout the South during Reconstruction. Students should conduct research to find out the conditions in which former slaves lived, their relations with former slaveholders and other white southerners, and the way in which they were treated by southern governments organized under President Johnson in 1865. Instruct students to prepare and give an oral report to a congressional committee that is studying conditions in the South.

2. Linking to Community

Tell students that southern Redeemers wanted to reduce the size of government and cut taxes. Have students prepare a poster about a person or group in their community who accomplished similar goals. Ask students the following question: what were the consequences of those goals?

Social Studies Skills Workshop

Interpreting Political Cartoons

Study the political cartoon of Reconstruction below. Then answer the questions that follow.

THE GRANGER COLLECTION, NEW YORK

THE "STRONG" GOVERNMENT 1869—1877.

1. Which of the following best describes the message that the artist is trying to present?
   a. Poor people in the South are forced to work on behalf of the rich.
   b. The South is being unfairly punished by the harsh military rule of the federal government.
   c. Military forces have taken control of President Grant and the federal government.
   d. The South is helping carry the burdens of the rest of the nation.

2. Based on your knowledge of the period and the imagery in this cartoon, do you think the artist would have been pleased by the Compromise of 1877? Explain your answer.

3. Based on your knowledge of the period, what do you think the carpetbag in the cartoon is supposed to represent?
   a. the military power of the federal government
   b. the corrupt politics of Grant's administration
   c. northern Republicans who have moved south to take part in Reconstruction
   d. the desire of southerners to move away from the Reconstruction South

Analyzing Primary Sources

Read the following excerpt from a southern African American newspaper in 1866, then answer the questions that follow.

❝The future looks dark, and we predict, that we are entering upon the greatest political contest that has ever agitated the people of the country—a contest, in which, we of the South must be for the most part spectators [observers]; not indifferent [unconcerned] spectators, for it is about us that the political battle is fought. The issue is fairly joined [begun].❞

4. Which of the following statements best describes the viewpoint of the author?
   a. Reconstruction will unite the country peacefully and smoothly.
   b. Reconstruction will divide the nation, and the South can do little to control it.
   c. Few people in the South care one way or the other about Reconstruction.
   d. Southerners will play a major role in determining Reconstruction policies.

5. Based on your knowledge of the period, do you think these predictions were accurate? Explain your answer.

Alternative Assessment

Building Your Portfolio

Interdisciplinary Connection to the Arts

Write a poem or song describing how an African American who was set free at the end of the Civil War might have felt. If you create a poem, find an image to illustrate it. If you write a song, select a musical style in which you want it to be performed.

📶 internet connect

Internet Activity: go.hrw.com
keyword: SA3 CF20

Access the Internet through the HRW Go site to locate and use primary and secondary sources to acquire information on the differing points of view of Reconstruction. Then assume the point of view of someone living during the time and create a newspaper that reflects the historical context of Reconstruction and the frame of reference which influenced its participants.

---

2. Southerners had to take loyalty oaths before they could form new state governments and rejoin the Union; some states had governors appointed by the president; Congress passed Reconstruction Acts dividing the South into five military districts, and requiring all southern states to create new constitutions supporting the 14th Amendment and giving African American men voting rights; Republicans gained political power; and African Americans held government jobs.

3. They wrote about southern society, popularized spirituals, and began to vote and run for office.

Thinking Critically

1. sharecropping, the building of factories, the growth of a wage-laboring class, and the continued dependence on cotton

2. Students' responses will vary.

3. Students might point out that the Union was restored and slavery abolished, but Redeemer governments and economics placed African Americans in conditions similar to slavery.

Skills Workshop

1. b

2. Students' responses will vary, but students should support their answer.

3. c

4. b

5. Students' answers will vary, but some might agree that Reconstruction divided people and that the South did not have much say in the process.

	Objectives	Pacing Guide	Reproducible Resources
SECTION 1: **The Wars for the West** (pp. 648–54)	★ Identify the animals the Plains Indians used, and explain why they were important. ★ Explain the causes and results of the conflicts between American Indians and American settlers in the West. ★ Describe how the reservation system and the Dawes Act affected the American Indians.	**Regular** 2 days **Block Scheduling** 1 day *Block Scheduling Handbook with Team Teaching Strategies, Chapter 21*	**RS** Guided Reading Strategy 21.1 **PS** Biography Reading 21: Sarah Winnemucca **RS** Graphic Organizer 21: Settling the West
SECTION 2: **Miners and Railroads** (pp. 655–59)	★ Describe some of the challenges of mining in the West. ★ Examine the obstacles that the builders of the transcontinental railroad faced. ★ Evaluate how the transcontinental railroad affected the settlement and development of the West.	**Regular** 2 days **Block Scheduling** 1 day *Block Scheduling Handbook with Team Teaching Strategies, Chapter 21*	**RS** Guided Reading Strategy 21.2 **E** Hands-On History Activity: Your Region's Transportation Systems
SECTION 3: **The Cattle Kingdom** (pp. 660–65)	★ Identify the factors that led to the cattle boom. ★ Describe what life was like for cowboys. ★ Analyze the causes of the Cattle Kingdom's decline.	**Regular** 2 days **Block Scheduling** 1 day *Block Scheduling Handbook with Team Teaching Strategies, Chapter 21*	**RS** Guided Reading Strategy 21.3 **PS** Primary Source Reading 21: Cowhands and Cattle Drives **E** Creative Teaching Strategy: Structured Discussion
SECTION 4: **Farming the Great Plains** (pp. 666–71)	★ Identify the groups that settled the Great Plains and examine their reasons for moving there. ★ Discuss how the environment of the Great Plains affected settlers' farming methods. ★ Describe what life was like on the Great Plains for settlers and explain how they adapted to the conditions.	**Regular** 1.5 days **Block Scheduling** .5 day *Block Scheduling Handbook with Team Teaching Strategies, Chapter 21*	**RS** Guided Reading Strategy 21.4 **SM** Geography Activity 21: Oklahoma Land Rush **PS** Literature Reading 21: The Life of an Ordinary Woman

Chapter Resource Key

PS	Primary Sources	**A**	Assessment	Music
RS	Reading Support	**REV**	Review	Video
IC	Interdisciplinary Connections	**ELL**	Reinforcement and English Language Learners	Internet
E	Enrichment		Transparencies	 Holt Presentation Maker Using Microsoft® PowerPoint®
SM	Skills Mastery		CD–ROM	

 One-Stop Planner CD–ROM

See the *One-Stop Planner* for a complete list of additional resources for students and teachers.

One-Stop Planner CD–ROM

It's easy to plan lessons, select resources, and print out materials for your students when you use the ***One-Stop Planner CD–ROM with Test Generator.***

Technology Resources	Reinforcement, Review, and Assessment

 One-Stop Planner, Lesson 21.1

 Linking Geography and History Transparency 12: Native American Resistance, 1830–1861 and Transparency 12A: Native American Resistance, 1830–1890

 Exploring America's Past Video Segment: The Last Generation; Teacher's Guide, pp. 36–37

Art in American History Transparency 15: Navajo Eye Dazzler Blanket

 Homework Practice Online

 HRW Go site

- **REV** Section 1 Review, p. 654
- **A** Daily Quiz 21.1
- **ELL** Main Idea Activity 21.1
- **ELL** English Audio Summary 21.1
- **ELL** Spanish Audio Summary 21.1

 One-Stop Planner, Lesson 21.2

Everyday Life in America Transparency 14: Currier and Ives View of the West, 1868

American History Simulations CD–ROM: The Gold Rush

CNN Presents America: Yesterday and Today, Beginnings to 1914 Segment: Railroad Ties

Linking Geography and History Transparency 10 A: Growth of Transportation, 1840–1890

 Homework Practice Online

- **REV** Section 2 Review, p. 659
- **A** Daily Quiz 21.2
- **ELL** Main Idea Activity 21.2
- **ELL** English Audio Summary 21.2
- **ELL** Spanish Audio Summary 21.2

 One-Stop Planner, Lesson 21.3

 American Music Selection 16: "O Bury Me Not"

 Homework Practice Online

- **REV** Section 3 Review, p. 665
- **A** Daily Quiz 21.3
- **ELL** Main Idea Activity 21.3
- **ELL** English Audio Summary 21.3
- **ELL** Spanish Audio Summary 21.3

 One-Stop Planner, Lesson 21.4

 Everyday Life in America Transparency 16: Farming Technology, Late 1800s

 Holt Researcher: American History CD–ROM

 Homework Practice Online

- **REV** Section 4 Review, p. 670
- **A** Daily Quiz 21.4
- **ELL** Main Idea Activity 21.4
- **ELL** English Audio Summary 21.4
- **ELL** Spanish Audio Summary 21.4

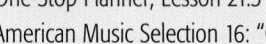

internet connect

HRW ONLINE RESOURCES
GO TO: go.hrw.com
Then type in a keyword.

TEACHER HOME PAGE
KEYWORD: SA3 Teacher

CHAPTER INTERNET ACTIVITIES
KEYWORD: SA3 CF21
Choose an activity to:
- learn the facts and mythology surrounding the Pony Express.
- research Geronimo and other American Indian leaders and write a biography of their actions during the Indian wars of the Plains and Southwest.
- analyze the myths and realities of the West and the ways in which it shaped the United States.

CHAPTER ENRICHMENT LINKS
KEYWORD: SA3 CH21

ONLINE ASSESSMENT
Homework Practice
KEYWORD: SA3 HP21

Standardized Test Prep
KEYWORD: SA3 STP21

Rubrics
KEYWORD: SS Rubrics

ONLINE MAPS, CHARTS, AND GRAPHS
KEYWORD: SA3 MCG
- Mining Centers
- U.S. Government and the West
- Oklahoma Land Rush

CONTENT UPDATES
KEYWORD: SS Content Updates

HOLT PRESENTATION MAKER
KEYWORD: SA3 PPT21

ONLINE READING SUPPORT
KEYWORD: SS Strategies

CURRENT EVENTS
KEYWORD: S3 Current Events

Meeting Individual Needs

Ability Levels

Level 1 Basic-level activities designed for all students encountering new material

Level 2 Intermediate-level activities designed for average students

Level 3 Challenging activities designed for honors and gifted-and-talented students

English Language Learners Activities that address the needs of students with Limited English Proficiency

Chapter Review and Assessment

- **IC** Vocabulary Activity 21
- Global Skill Builder CD–ROM
- HRW Go site
- **REV** Chapter 21 Tutorial for Students, Parents, Mentors, and Peers
- **REV** Chapter 21 Review, pp. 671–73
- Chapter 21 Test Generator (on the One-Stop Planner)
- **A** Chapter 21 Test (Form A or B)

- **A** Alternative Assessment Handbook
- **A** Chapter 21 Test for English Language Learners and Special-Needs Students

Build on What You Know

If You Were There...

Ask students to answer the following question:

What kind of work would you do in the West, and why?

Consider:

- the types of opportunities available
- the working conditions in each industry

You Be the Historian

What's Your Opinion?

To help students create their **Themes** Journal entries, provide the following examples of appropriate **agree**/disagree statements.

EXPLORING THE TIME LINE

AMERICAN EVENTS

🖵 internet connect

TOPIC: Pasteurization
GO TO: go.hrw.com
KEYWORD: SA3 CF21

Have students access the Internet through the HRW Go site to research pasteurization and other scientific discoveries of Louis Pasteur. Have students write a report that discusses Pasteur's scientific achievements, the difficulties he faced, and the impact of his discoveries on daily life. Remind students to use standard grammar, spelling, punctuation, and sentence structure in their reports.

CHAPTER

21 The West
(1850–1890)

Fort Laramie was a fur-trading post built in 1834.

This stamp shows a rider with the Pony Express.

UNITED STATES

1851 The Treaty of Fort Laramie is signed.	**1860** The Pony Express begins delivering mail between the East and West.	**1862** Congress passes the Homestead Act.	**1869** The first transcontinental railroad is completed.	**1874** Gold is discovered in the Black Hills of the Dakota Territory.
1850	**1855**	**1860**	**1865**	**1870**

WORLD

1855 Paris holds a world's fair.

1864 French scientist Louis Pasteur invents the process of pasteurization.

People flocked to the 1855 World's Fair in Paris, shown below.

Cans like this one were used to store meat.

Build on What You Know

After the Civil War, the U.S. population grew rapidly. Settlements spread throughout the West. A flood of miners, ranchers, and farmers transformed the western landscape and adapted to their new environment. Often, however, these new settlers came into conflict with American Indians already living in the region.

Economics

Agree The government must fund business development so people in underdeveloped regions can prosper.

Disagree Businesses and people in underdeveloped areas are responsible for creating their own prosperity.

Culture

Agree One group always imposes its cultural beliefs and customs upon another.

Disagree Different groups live peacefully by sharing resources and learning about each other's cultural beliefs and customs.

Geography

Agree People form communities to survive and prosper within difficult environmental conditions.

Disagree The difficulty of facing harsh environmental conditions is not worth the possibility of failure.

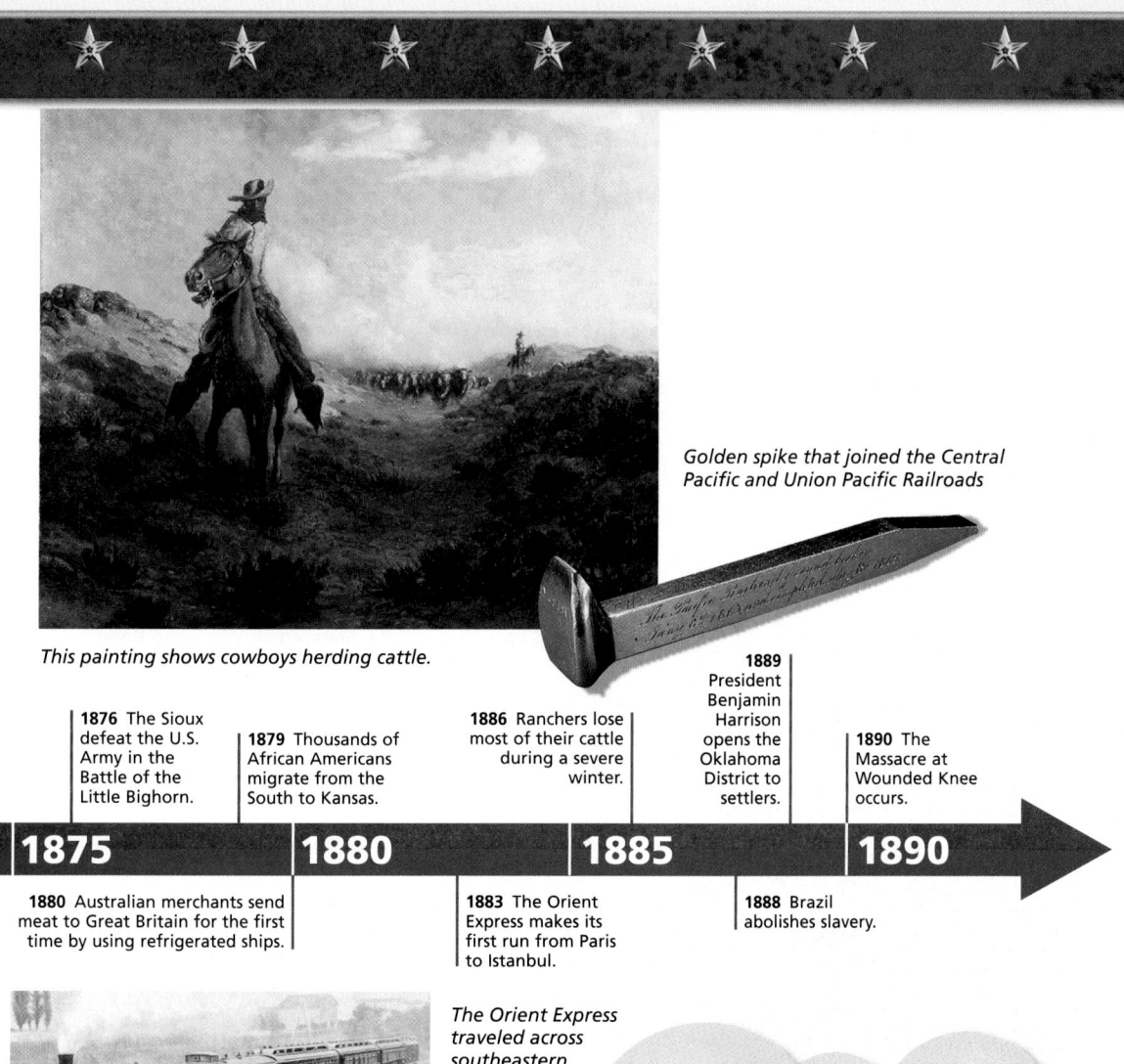

This painting shows cowboys herding cattle.

Golden spike that joined the Central Pacific and Union Pacific Railroads

1876 The Sioux defeat the U.S. Army in the Battle of the Little Bighorn.

1879 Thousands of African Americans migrate from the South to Kansas.

1886 Ranchers lose most of their cattle during a severe winter.

1889 President Benjamin Harrison opens the Oklahoma District to settlers.

1890 The Massacre at Wounded Knee occurs.

1875   **1880**   **1885**   **1890**

1880 Australian merchants send meat to Great Britain for the first time by using refrigerated ships.

1883 The Orient Express makes its first run from Paris to Istanbul.

1888 Brazil abolishes slavery.

The Orient Express traveled across southeastern Europe.

You Be the Historian

What's Your Opinion? Do you **agree** or **disagree** with the following statements? Support your point of view in your journal.

- **Economics** The federal government should promote economic development in underdeveloped regions.
- **Culture** Cultural conflict will result when two different groups come into contact.
- **Geography** People will endure harsh environmental conditions in order to have new opportunities.

If you were there . . . *What kind of work would you do in the West, and why?*

The Orient Express.
On October 4, 1883, the Orient Express, the first European transcontinental railroad, took about 40 passengers on its initial trip. The line ran from Paris to Constantinople (which is present-day Istanbul). Since no railcar had ever been built with such luxury in mind, Georges Nackelmeyer's line became a favorite among Europe's social elite and royalty. It is possible that Nackelmeyer got his inspiration from American Pullman cars. Shortly after he returned from a trip to the United States, his Compagnie des Wagons-Lits began production on the luxury line in 1876. The Orient Express ran continually from 1883 to 1977 (with two service suspensions for World Wars I and II), when it closed following a long period of declining passenger volume. The Orient Express line was reopened in 1982 by an American named James Sherwood. It still runs today, though along several shortened lines.

CRITICAL THINKING

Why do you think the Orient Express eventually declined in popularity?

ANSWER: Students might suggest that automobiles and airplanes became more convenient and faster ways to travel.

Section 1

OBJECTIVES

⭐ Identify the animals the Plains Indians used, and explain why they were important.

⭐ Explain the causes and results of the conflicts between American Indians and American settlers in the West.

⭐ Describe how the reservation system and the Dawes Act affected the American Indians.

🔊 LET'S GET STARTED!

As students enter the classroom, ask them if anyone in the class has ever had to move to another city or state because of a parent's job. Encourage students who have moved to discuss how they felt about moving. (*Students' feelings may include the following: nervous, excited, eager, scared.*) Ask students to identify how their lives have changed as a result of the move. (*Students' responses may include the following: they found new friends, they have a better house, or they miss their old friends.*) Tell students that in Section 1 they will learn how the U.S. government forced the Plains Indians to leave their lands and how the Indian's lives changed as a result.

SECTION 1 RESOURCES

REPRODUCIBLE

▶ Guided Reading Strategy 21.1
▶ Biography Reading 21: Sarah Winnemucca
▶ Graphic Organizer 21: Settling the West

TECHNOLOGY

▶ One-Stop Planner, Lesson 21.1
▶ Linking Geography and History Transparency 12: Native American Resistance, 1830–1861 and Transparency 12A: Native American Resistance, 1830–1890
▶ Exploring America's Past Video Segment: The Last Generation; Teacher's Guide, pp. 36–37
▶ Art in American History Transparency 15: Navajo Eye Dazzler Blanket
▶ Homework Practice Online
▶ HRW Go site

REINFORCEMENT, REVIEW, AND ASSESSMENT

▶ Section 1 Review, p. 654
▶ Daily Quiz 21.1
▶ Main Idea Activity 21.1
▶ English Audio Summary 21.1
▶ Spanish Audio Summary 21.1

Section 1

The Wars for the West

Read to Discover

1. What animals did the Plains Indians use, and why were they important?
2. What caused conflicts between American Indians and American settlers in the West, and what were the results of these conflicts?
3. How did the reservation system and the Dawes Act affect American Indians?

WHY IT MATTERS TODAY

Many American Indians continue to live on reservations. Use **CNNfyi.com** or other **current events** sources to find out about American Indians living on reservations today. Record your findings in your journal.

Define

• reservations

Identify

• Treaty of Fort Laramie
• Crazy Horse
• Treaty of Medicine Lodge
• George Armstrong Custer
• Sitting Bull
• Battle of the Little Bighorn
• Ghost Dance
• Massacre at Wounded Knee
• Geronimo
• Sarah Winnemucca
• Dawes General Allotment Act

THE GRANGER COLLECTION, NEW YORK

The Cheyenne used shields like this one in battle.

The Story Continues

Like many Sioux before him, Standing Bear was eager for his first buffalo hunt. "Watch the buffalo closely. . . . They are very quick and powerful," warned his father. When he got close to the buffalo herd, Standing Bear recalled, "I realized how small I was." He brought down a buffalo and rode proudly back to camp to give his mother the animal's skin. Buffalo hunts were important to American Indians' ways of life on the Great Plains.

⭐ The Plains Indians

The Great Plains lie roughly between the 98th meridian and the Rocky Mountains. They stretch north into Canada and south into Texas. Despite their sometimes harsh conditions, the region was home to the Plains Indians. Groups such as the Apache and the Comanche lived in Texas and what is now Oklahoma. The Cheyenne and the Arapaho lived in different parts of the central Plains. The Pawnee lived in Nebraska. To the north were the Sioux, who spread from Minnesota to Montana.

Have students read Section 1 and complete Guided Reading Strategy 21.1. Choose one or more of the following activities to explore the section content with students. For further suggestions on block scheduling or team teaching, see the *Block Scheduling Handbook with Team Teaching Strategies.*

LEVEL 1: Have students write two journal entries from the point of view of a Plains Indian. Have one entry explain what life was like before the Dawes Act and the reservation system and another entry describe how the Dawes Act and reservation system affected the American Indians. *(Students' entries should include an awareness that before this act, Plains Indians freely migrated and hunted before the Dawes act but lost land, hunting rights, and cultural traditions after it.)* **ENGLISH LANGUAGE LEARNERS**

For survival, Plains Indians depended on two animals—the horse and the buffalo. The Spanish brought horses to America in the 1500s. Plains Indians learned to ride horses and used them to follow the buffalo herds. They used the buffalo for food, shelter, and tools. The Plains Indians prospered and by 1850 some 75,000 American Indians were living on the Plains.

Miners and settlers began crossing the Great Plains in the mid-1800s. To protect these travelers, U.S. officials sent agents to negotiate treaties with the Plains Indians. The first major agreement was the **Treaty of Fort Laramie**, signed with northern Plains nations in Wyoming in 1851. Two years later, several southern Plains nations signed a treaty at Fort Atkinson in Nebraska. These treaties accepted Indian claims to much of the Great Plains. They also allowed Americans to build forts and roads and to travel across Indian homelands. The U.S. government promised to pay for any damages to Indian lands.

✔ **Reading Check: Analyzing Information** What compromise did the United States and American Indians reach to allow miners and settlers to cross Indian lands? Treaties accepted Indian land claims. The United States could build on Indian lands but had to pay for damages.

Sioux moccasins

That's Interesting!

Just how did the Comanche get their name? The Spanish were the first to use the term *Comanche*, but according to anthropologist Marvin K. Opler, the term actually came from the Ute word *Komantcia*, which means "anyone who wants to fight me all the time." To the Spanish, *Komantcia* sounded like *Comanche*.

Technology Resources

Linking Geography and History Transparency 12: Native American Resistance, 1830–1861 and Transparency 12A: Native American Resistance, 1830–1890

MAP ANSWER

Oklahoma

Indian Reservations and Battles to 1890

Interpreting Maps As more and more settlers moved to the West, American Indians were forced to accept treaties that placed them on reservations.

Skills Assessment Human Systems Which present-day state contained the most reservation lands?

Conflicts arose because settlers and miners wanted to use American Indian lands. As a result, the U.S. government created the reservation system and enacted the Dawes Act.

Reservation system	Dawes Act
Reservations prevented Indians from hunting buffalo and deprived Indians of many cultural traditions.	*The Dawes Act split up reservations, resulted in the loss of more land than all wars combined, did not provide citizenship, and failed to improve Indians' lives.*

Several African American cavalry regiments served in the western U.S. Army. American Indians nicknamed these African American troops, who were known for their courage and discipline, "buffalo soldiers."

THE GRANGER COLLECTION, NEW YORK

⭐ War on the Plains

The treaties did not keep the peace for long. Gold was discovered in what is now Colorado in 1858. The news brought thousands of miners to the West, where they soon clashed with the Cheyenne and the Arapaho. In 1861 the U.S. government negotiated a new treaty with these Indians. The treaty created **reservations**, areas of federal land set aside for American Indians. The government expected Indians to stay on the reservations, which made hunting buffalo almost impossible.

Many American Indians refused to live on reservations. Some continued to fight, while others shared the view of Cheyenne chief Black Kettle. "It is not my intention or wish to fight the whites," he declared. He did not get his wish. In November 1864, U.S. Army troops attacked Black Kettle's camp on Sand Creek in southeastern Colorado. The soldiers killed about 200 men, women, and children. Black Kettle was among the Cheyenne who escaped the Sand Creek Massacre.

Pioneers and miners continued to cross the Great Plains. Many miners used the Bozeman Trail, which ran from Wyoming to Montana. To protect the miners, the U.S. Army built forts along the trail, which ran through Sioux hunting grounds. Sioux chief Red Cloud responded to the army's actions with war. In late 1866 a chief named **Crazy Horse** and a group of Sioux ambushed 81 cavalry troops, killing them all.

William Tecumseh Sherman, the famous Civil War general, was in charge of the western armies. He threatened the "extermination [of the Sioux] men, women, and children." The army had little success in this effort, however, and asked Red Cloud to negotiate. Red Cloud responded, "When we see the soldiers moving away and the forts abandoned, then I will come down and talk." In 1868 the U.S. Army closed the Bozeman Trail and abandoned the forts along it. Many Sioux then moved to the Black Hills Reservation in Dakota Territory.

Meanwhile, the U.S. government was also asking southern Plains Indians to move off their lands. In the 1867 **Treaty of Medicine Lodge**, most of these peoples agreed to live on reservations. However, many of them did not want to give up their hunting grounds. Fighting soon broke out between the Comanche and the Texans. The U.S. Army and the Texas Rangers were unable to defeat the Comanche forces in battle. So U.S. forces cut off the Comanche's access to food. The Comanche could not survive under these conditions. In 1875 Quanah Parker, the last of the Comanche war leaders, surrendered.

✔ **Reading Check: Summarizing** What was the federal policy toward Plains Indians in the 1860s and 1870s? to sign treaties placing Indians on reservations and fight those Indians who resisted

★ The U.S. War with the Sioux

As fighting on the southern Plains ended, new trouble was starting to the north. In 1874 Lieutenant Colonel **George Armstrong Custer**'s soldiers found gold in the Black Hills of the Dakota Territory. The U.S. government responded by insisting that the Sioux sell their reservation land in the Black Hills. **Sitting Bull**, a Sioux leader, protested these new demands.

 History Makers Speak

❝What treaty that the whites have kept has the red man broken? Not one. What treaty that the white man ever made with us have they kept? Not one.❞

—Sitting Bull, quoted in *Touch the Earth*, by T. C. McLuhan

Other Sioux leaders listened to Sitting Bull and refused to give up the Black Hills. Fighting soon broke out between the U.S. Army and the Sioux.

Custer, a Civil War veteran, was in command of the U.S. Army 7th Cavalry. On June 25, 1876, his scouts found a Sioux camp along the Little Bighorn River in Montana. Leading 264 of his soldiers, Custer raced ahead without waiting for any backup forces. The Battle of the Little Bighorn followed. Sioux forces, led by Crazy Horse and Sitting Bull, surrounded Custer and his troops. Sitting Bull's cousin Pte-San-Waste-Win described the fighting. "The soldiers fired many shots, but the Sioux shot straight and the soldiers fell dead. When we came to the hill . . . Long Hair [Custer] lay dead among the rest." Newspapers called the battle "Custer's Last Stand."

The **Battle of the Little Bighorn** was the worst defeat the U.S. Army had suffered in the West. It was also the Sioux's last major victory. In late 1877 Crazy Horse was killed in prison after surrendering to the U.S. Army.

Analyzing Primary Sources
Identifying Points of View
Why did Sitting Bull not trust the U.S. government? He believed the government never kept its treaties.

Interpreting the Visual Record

The Battle of the Little Bighorn *The 7th Cavalry suffered a devastating defeat at the hands of Sioux forces at the Battle of the Little Bighorn.* **What advantages does the illustration show each side having?**

THE GRANGER COLLECTION, NEW YORK

LEVEL 3: Organize the class into small groups and have them use their textbooks to review one of the following conflicts between American Indians and American settlers in the West: the Battle of the Little Bighorn, the Long Walk, or the Massacre at Wounded Knee. Each group should then create a one-act play depicting the incident. Each group should select a narrator to explain the events of the conflict and describe the significance of these events. Have groups include the causes and results of the conflict between American Indians and American settlers in the West.

COOPERATIVE LEARNING

LEVEL 3: Have students create a grid that compares and contrasts the treatment of the American Indian nations discussed in this section. On the vertical axis, have students list the Indian nations. On the horizontal axis, have students identify possible interactions each nation had with the U.S. government, particularly those in relation to the reservation system and the Dawes Act. *(Students' entries may include such interactions as signing a treaty, moving to a reservation, and going to war.)* Then have students place a check mark in each box that corresponds to the Indian nation mentioned and the interactions that occurred. Once students have finished, discuss students' observations as well as the effects that the reservation system and the Dawes Act had on each of the American Indian nations.

★ Biography

Chief Joseph. Chief Joseph is said to have been a brave and peace-loving man who recommended complying with the U.S. government's policies. His followers, however, did not wish to do so. After he was taken prisoner, he was sent to Oklahoma. He was later sent to Colville Reservation in Washington State, where he died in 1904.

CRITICAL THINKING

What do you think the government should have done in response to Chief Joseph's request? Why?

ANSWER: Students might suggest that Joseph and his people should have been allowed to return to their homeland.

Technology Resources
Art in American History Transparency 15: Navajo Eye Dazzler Blanket

---

CONNECTING TO LITERATURE ANSWER

He says he is tired, heartsick, and sad about seeing his people die.

BIOGRAPHY ANSWER

(for p. 653)

Students may reason that he was admired for his intelligence, resourcefulness, and because he could be relied upon in times of danger.

CONNECTING TO *Literature*

"I Will Fight No More Forever"

Chief Joseph

Chief Joseph led the Nez Percé from 1871 to 1877. He gave the following speech to the U.S. Army officers who took him prisoner on October 5, 1877. Chief Joseph died in 1904.

Tell General Howard I know his heart. What he told me before, I have in my heart. I am tired of fighting. Our chiefs are killed. . . . The old men are all dead. It is the young men who say yes and no. **He who led on the young men**[1] is dead. It is cold and we have no blankets. The little children are freezing to death. My people, some of them, have run away to the hills, and have no blankets, no food; no one knows where they are—perhaps freezing to death. I want to have time to look for my children and see how many I can find. Maybe I shall find them among the dead. Hear me, my chiefs. I am tired; my heart is sick and sad. From where the sun now stands I will fight no more forever.

[1] **He who led on the young men:** Joseph's brother, Alokut

Understanding What You Read

Literature and History Why has Chief Joseph chosen to "fight no more forever"?

Ghost Dance shirt

Sitting Bull fled to Canada with a few of his followers. With two of their most important leaders gone, the northern Plains Indians soon surrendered.

In 1881 Sitting Bull and his Sioux followers returned from Canada. They had run out of food during the hard winter. "I wish it to be remembered," Sitting Bull said, "that I was the last man of my tribe to surrender my rifle." He joined most of the Sioux on Standing Rock Reservation in Dakota Territory.

Wovoka, a Paiute Indian, began a religious movement known as the **Ghost Dance**. He predicted the arrival of a paradise for American Indians. Indians who performed the dance believed that it would lead to a new life free from suffering. In this paradise, the buffalo herds would return, and the settlers would disappear. When the Ghost Dance spread across the Plains, U.S. officials feared it would lead to a Sioux uprising. While following orders to arrest Sitting Bull, reservation police killed the Sioux leader in 1890. In response, many Sioux left the reservations. Later that year, the U.S. Army found a camp of Sioux near Wounded Knee Creek in South Dakota. When the two groups faced one another, a shot rang out. The U.S. troops began firing and killed about 150 Indians. Known as the **Massacre at Wounded Knee**, this attack was the last major event of more than 25 years of war on the Great Plains.

✔ **Reading Check: Sequencing** List the conflicts between the Great Plains Indians and U.S. forces in the order that they occurred.
Sand Creek Massacre, attack on cavalry troops, conflict over Treaty of Medicine Lodge, surrender of Comanche, Battle of the Little Bighorn, death of Crazy Horse, Massacre at Wounded Knee

★ Indians in the Southwest and Far West

Far from the Great Plains, other American Indians resisted being moved to reservations. The Navajo lived in what became Arizona and New Mexico. In 1863 when the U.S. government ordered them to settle on a reservation, the Navajo refused. In response, Kit Carson, a former scout, led U.S. troops in raids on the Navajo's fields, homes, and livestock.

LEVEL 3: Organize the class into an even number of small groups. Pair each group with another group. Then have one group in each pair represent U.S. settlers' interests and have the other group represent American Indians' interests in the West. Pairs should solve the problems between the U.S. settlers and the Plains Indians by formulating a compromise that satisfies both groups. Ask each pair of groups to present its solution and to explain how the causes of the conflicts influenced them to reach the terms of their compromise. **COOPERATIVE LEARNING**

★ CLOSE

Ask students to make a chart about the Plains Indians that has the following four columns: *Life before Conflict, Causes of Conflict, Conflict Resolution,* and *Life after Resolution.* Under each topic, have students write a one or two-sentence summary of the Plains Indians' situation. Discuss the changes in the Plains Indians' lives with the class.
ENGLISH LANGUAGE LEARNERS

When the Navajo ran out of food and shelter, they started surrendering to the U.S. Army. In 1864 the army led Navajo captives on the Long Walk. This 300-mile march took the Navajo across the desert to a reservation at Bosque Redondo, New Mexico. Along the way, hundreds of Navajo died. At Bosque Redondo the Navajo suffered harsh conditions. In 1868 they negotiated for a new reservation located in Arizona and New Mexico.

The U.S. government had promised to let the peaceful Nez Percé keep their homelands in northeastern Oregon. Within a few years, however, settlers asked the government to remove them. The government ordered the Nez Percé to a reservation in what is now Idaho. Nez Percé leader Chief Joseph reluctantly agreed to move. Before leaving, a few angry Nez Percé killed some local settlers. Fearing that U.S. forces would fight back, the Nez Percé fled. The U.S. Army chased this band of about 700 Indians across what are now Idaho, Wyoming, and Montana. Although outnumbered, the band defeated or avoided the army for weeks before trying to escape to Canada. Less than 40 miles from the border, U.S. troops overtook and surrounded the Nez Percé. Chief Joseph surrendered on October 5, 1877. The U.S. government sent the Nez Percé to a reservation in what is now Oklahoma.

By the 1880s most American Indians had stopped fighting. The Apache of the Southwest, however, continued to battle the U.S. Army. The Apache were raiders, known for their ability to survive in the desert. In the 1870s the U.S. Army gathered some Apache on a reservation in San Carlos, Arizona. One Apache called the reservation "nothing but cactus, rattlesnakes, heat, rocks, and insects."

A Chiricahua Apache named **Geronimo** and his small band of raiders left the reservation and avoided capture until 1884. The following year Geronimo escaped again. When the U.S. Army caught him, he broke free once more on the way to the reservation. "I feared treachery [dishonesty]," he said. This time the army sent 5,000 soldiers and 500 Apache scouts to capture Geronimo and 24 of his followers. Finally, in September 1886, he surrendered, ending the Apache armed resistance. The U.S. government sent Geronimo and many Chiricahua Apache to Florida as prisoners of war.

✔ **Reading Check: Identifying Cause and Effect** What led to some of the conflicts that took place between American settlers and American Indians in the 1800s, and what were the results of these conflicts? reservation policies; Navajo and Nez Percé forced onto reservations; Chiricahua Apache sent to Florida

★ Policy and Protest

By the 1870s many American Indian peoples were living on reservations. Indian leaders spoke out against the reservation system. They complained that government agents stole food and money meant for Indians. In addition, reservation land was usually not useful for farming or buffalo hunting. As a result, many Indians were starving.

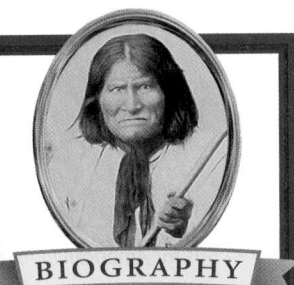

BIOGRAPHY

Geronimo
(1829–1909)

Many Apache found it difficult to get along with Geronimo. He had grown bitter after Mexican soldiers killed his mother, wife, and children. Despite this bitterness, other Apache admired Geronimo for his intelligence and his ability to handle difficult situations.

Geronimo led his own band of troops. He was captured several times, but usually managed to escape. Geronimo finally surrendered to U.S. troops in 1886. His courage and determination to remain free made Geronimo a legend. **Why was Geronimo admired by other Apache?**

★ Biography

Geronimo. Geronimo, whose Apache name, Goyathlay, means "one who yawns," is one of the few Indian leaders during the wars for the West to have died from natural causes. After his final surrender, Geronimo was sentenced to perform hard labor in a Florida work camp. In 1894, he was sent to Fort Sill, Oklahoma, where he died on February 17, 1909. According to those who worked with him in Oklahoma, Geronimo never lost his fighting spirit and volatile disposition. When General George Crook visited a schoolhouse on the Oklahoma reservation in 1890, he found Geronimo bearing a stick and threatening any children who misbehaved.

◪ internet connect

TOPIC: Geronimo
GO TO: go.hrw.com
KEYWORD: SA3 CF21

ACTIVITY: Have students use the library or search the Internet through the HRW Go site to find information on Geronimo. Then ask them to use standard grammar, spelling, sentence structure, and punctuation to write a diary entry that Geronimo might have written during his lifetime.

THE GRANGER COLLECTION, NEW YORK

Sarah Winnemucca went to Washington, D.C., to ask for reforms for American Indians.

In the late 1870s a Paiute Indian named **Sarah Winnemucca** became one of the first American Indians to call for reforms. She gave lectures on the problems of the reservation system and eventually pleaded her case in Washington, D.C. After listening to her, "many people were moved to tears," according to one spectator. Writer Helen Hunt Jackson also pushed for reform. In 1881 she published *A Century of Dishonor*. This book criticized the federal government's treatment of Indians. Jackson wrote that "it makes little difference where one opens the record of the history of the Indians; every page and every year has its dark stain." The popularity of her writings helped spread the reform message.

Many reformers believed that American Indians would be better off if they adopted the ways of white people. The **Dawes General Allotment Act**, passed by Congress in 1887, reflected this view. It tried to lessen the traditional influences on Indian society by making land ownership private rather than shared. Reservation lands were to be divided into 160-acre plots for families and 80 acres for single adults. The act also promised U.S. citizenship to American Indians.

After breaking up reservation land, the government sold the acreage that remained. As a result, Indians lost much of the land that they occupied before the Dawes Act. Reformers had hoped the Dawes Act would help American Indians. Instead, it resulted in the loss of about two thirds of their land. As enforced, the Dawes Act also did not lead to citizenship for many American Indians. Overall, the new policy failed to improve Indians' lives.

✔ **Reading Check: Drawing Inferences and Conclusions** How did reformers who fought for American Indian rights influence Indians' lives? Many reformers supported the Dawes Act which gave Indians private ownership of land and promised them U.S. citizenship. The act led to the loss of more Indian land and failed to improve Indians' lives.

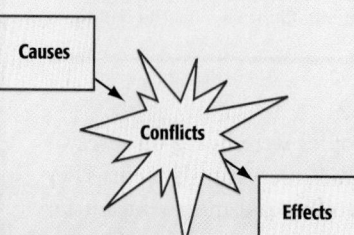

go. Homework
hrw Practice
.com Online
keyword: SA3 HP21

Section 1 Review

❶ Define and explain:
• reservations

❷ Identify and explain:
• Treaty of Fort Laramie
• Crazy Horse
• Treaty of Medicine Lodge
• George Armstrong Custer
• Sitting Bull
• Battle of the Little Bighorn
• Ghost Dance
• Massacre at Wounded Knee
• Geronimo
• Sarah Winnemucca
• Dawes General Allotment Act

❸ Identifying Cause and Effect Copy the graphic organizer below. Use it to list the causes and effects of conflicts between the United States and American Indians in the West.

Causes

Conflicts

Effects

❹ Finding the Main Idea
a. Why were the horse and the buffalo important to the lives of Plains Indians?

b. Why do you think the Ghost Dance was important to American Indians on the Great Plains?

❺ Writing and Critical Thinking
Comparing and Contrasting Imagine that you are an American Indian who has been affected by the Dawes Act. Write a letter to a member of Congress describing how your life has changed.

Consider the following:
• life on reservations
• the positive and negative aspects of land ownership
• the value of citizenship

Section 2

OBJECTIVES

- ★ Describe some of the challenges of mining in the West.
- ★ Examine the obstacles that the builders of the transcontinental railroad faced.
- ★ Evaluate how the transcontinental railroad affected the settlement and development of the West.

🔊 *LET'S GET STARTED!*

As students enter the classroom, ask them what problems could arise for people working in a mine or laying a railroad line. (*Students' responses might mention dangerous conditions such as mines emitting poisonous gases or collapsing, or poor working conditions such as long hours, hard work, or low pay.*) Then tell students that in Section 2 they will learn about these problems, how they were overcome, and why railroads and mining became major contributors to quick settlement in the West.

Section 2

Miners and Railroads

Read to Discover

1. What were some of the challenges of mining in the West?
2. What obstacles did the builders of the transcontinental railroad face?
3. How did the transcontinental railroad affect the settlement and development of the West?

WHY IT MATTERS TODAY

Railroads are still an important means of transportation in the United States. Use **CNNfyi.com** or other **current events** sources to learn about the role of railroads in the U.S. transportation system today. Record your findings in your journal.

Define

- bonanza
- boomtowns
- transcontinental railroad

Identify

- Comstock Lode
- Pony Express
- Pacific Railway Acts
- Leland Stanford

SECTION 2 RESOURCES

REPRODUCIBLE

▶ Guided Reading Strategy 21.2

TECHNOLOGY

▶ One-Stop Planner, Lesson 21.2
▶ Everyday Life in America Transparency 14: Currier and Ives View of the West, 1868
▶ American History Simulations CD–ROM: The Gold Rush
▶ CNN Presents America: Beginnings to 1914 Segment: Railroad Ties
▶ Linking Geography and History Transparency 10 A: Growth of Transportation, 1840–1890
▶ Homework Practice Online

REINFORCEMENT, REVIEW, AND ASSESSMENT

▶ Section 2 Review, p. 659
▶ Daily Quiz 21.2
▶ Main Idea Activity 21.2
▶ English Audio Summary 21.2
▶ Spanish Audio Summary 21.2

The Story Continues

In 1858 gold was discovered in Colorado. After traveling west to see the new mine, *New York Tribune* editor Horace Greeley announced that the "discovery is . . . the richest and greatest [gold mine] in America." Thousands of prospectors raced west to the mining region around Pikes Peak. Many labeled their wagons "Pikes Peak or Bust." Most of them soon learned that Greeley had been fooled about the richness of the strike. The early prospectors had started the rush by filling part of the mine with extra gold.

The dream of finding pieces of gold ore like this one drew miners to the West.

★ The Mining Booms

The following year miners found gold and silver in western Nevada. The strike became known as the **Comstock Lode**, named after miner Henry Comstock. This time the wealth was real. The Comstock Lode was a **bonanza**— a large deposit of precious ore. Over the next 20 years, the Comstock Lode produced over $500 million worth of gold and silver. It took expensive equipment to remove the silver and gold trapped within the quartz rock. Large companies bought up claims from miners who

Have students read Section 2 and complete Guided Reading Strategy 21.2. Choose one or more of the following activities to explore the section content with students. For further suggestions on block scheduling or team teaching, see the *Block Scheduling Handbook with Team Teaching Strategies*.

Note: To help students make meaningful connections between events in American history and those in their own hometown, use the Chapter 21 **Hands-On History** activity, Your Region's Transportation Systems.

LEVEL 1: As a class, list the geographic characteristics of your state or region. Discuss the problems or advantages these characteristics might present to people when building a railroad or digging mines. Finally, have students compare the obstacles/advantages in their area to those faced when building the transcontinental railroad or mining in the West in the late 1800s. *(Students' responses should indicate an understanding that miners faced unbearable heat, poor air, floods and cave-ins, fire, unsafe equipment; and that rail workers faced harsh terrain, hostile Indians, rough weather, and a lack of food and supplies.)* Conclude with a class discussion about how mining and railroads affected settlement in the west.
ENGLISH LANGUAGE LEARNERS

★ **Economics**

Mining Unions. In 1864 the Miners' Protective Association (MPA), in response to the harsh working conditions associated with mining the Comstock Lode, organized the first miner's strike. The demands of the MPA—increased wages, improved working conditions, and shorter hours—spread throughout the mining industry. In 1893 the labor movement expanded to the city of Butte, Montana. There, the Western Federation of Miners (WFM) organized other labor groups in the hope of preventing the U.S. military from intervening in labor disputes. By 1903 the WFM had more than 50,000 members.

CRITICAL THINKING

What purpose do unions serve?

ANSWER: Unions provide a central agency that promotes the well-being of a specific group of workers.

Technology Resources

Everyday Life in America Transparency 14: Currier and Ives View of the West, 1868

Visual Record Answer

Students might suggest poorly lit shafts and low oxygen levels.

THE GRANGER COLLECTION, NEW YORK

Interpreting the Visual Record

Prospectors *This image shows prospectors at the entrance of a mineshaft.* **What challenges do you think these miners faced?**

Analyzing Primary Sources

Supporting a Point of View Judging from Twain's description, would you have chosen to live in a boomtown? Why or why not? Answers may vary, but students should note the excitement or the risk of living in a boomtown.

could not afford such equipment. As a result, mining became a big business in the West, dominated by corporations.

As companies dug bigger and deeper mines, the work became more dangerous. Miners had to use unsafe equipment such as wall-less elevator platforms. Many of the poorly lit tunnels had so little oxygen that candles would not burn. Dust from drilling also caused serious lung problems. Unexpected explosions killed or injured many miners. When there were cave-ins or floods from underground springs, miners were sometimes killed or trapped below ground. The threat of fire in the mines was also a great concern. In deeper tunnels, temperatures sometimes rose above 130° F. With all these hazards, mining was probably the most dangerous job in the country. In the West, worries about safety and pay led miners to form several labor unions in the 1860s.

Some miners came from the eastern United States. Others emigrated from Europe, Central and South America, Australia, and Asia. Some Mexican immigrants and Mexican Americans were skilled in assaying, or testing, the contents of valuable ore. Despite their skill, they were often denied the better-paying mining jobs. Chinese immigrants faced similar job discrimination.

✔ **Reading Check: Summarizing** How did mining affect the western economy, and what were its risks? Mining became a big business in the West, drawing corporations and immigrant workers from around the world. It was a dangerous occupation—see specific risks above.

★ **Mining Towns**

Mining booms also produced **boomtowns**. These towns were communities that sprang up when a mine opened. They often disappeared just as quickly when the mine closed down. Most boomtowns had general stores, saloons, and boardinghouses. However, they were also dangerous places that lacked basic law and order. In his autobiographical work *Roughing It*, Mark Twain described Virginia City during its boom years.

History Makers Speak

❝[It] had grown to be the 'livest' town . . . that America had ever produced. The sidewalks swarmed with people. . . . The streets themselves were just as crowded. . . . Money-getting schemes . . . were . . . in every brain.❞

—Mark Twain, *Roughing It*

There were few women or families in most boomtowns. In 1860, for example, there were more than 75 men to each woman in Virginia City. Most women who lived in mining towns faced lives of hard work and

ALL LEVELS: Copy the following graphic organizer onto the chalkboard, omitting the italicized answers. Have students complete the organizer to show the challenges encountered by miners and rail workers in the West.
ENGLISH LANGUAGE LEARNERS

Miners
• *unbearable heat*
• *poor air that often lacked oxygen*
• *floods and cave-ins*
• *fire*
• *unsafe equipment*

Rail workers
• *harsh terrain*
• *American Indian attacks*
• *rough weather*
• *lack of food and supplies*

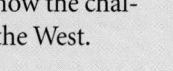
LEVEL 2: Organize the class into two groups. Assign one group to review the difficulties associated with mining in the West, and have the other group review the obstacles faced by the builders of the transcontinental railroad. Students may use their textbooks as a reference. Then ask each group to prepare a short television news documentary that describes these difficulties. Each group should present their documentaries to the class. **COOPERATIVE LEARNING**

---

few friends. "I was never so lonely and homesick in all my life," wrote one young woman. Women contributed to the local economy by washing, cooking, making clothes, and chopping wood. They also raised families, taught in schools, and wrote for local newspapers. Their work helped turn some mining camps into successful permanent towns.

✔ **Reading Check: Finding the Main Idea** Why were boomtowns created, and what was life like there? built around gold and silver mines; exciting, crowded, risky, few families or women

⭐ Linking East and West

As more Americans began moving west, the need to send goods and information between the East and West increased. In 1860 the **Pony Express** was formed to meet this need. This company used a system of messengers on horseback to carry mail between relay stations on a route about 2,000 miles long. Telegraph lines, which sent messages faster, soon put the Pony Express out of business, however.

Americans thought of other ways to improve communication and travel across the United States. Some Americans wanted to build a **transcontinental railroad** to connect the East to the West. As a result, the federal government passed the **Pacific Railway Acts** of 1862 and 1864. These acts gave railroad companies loans and large land grants, which could be sold to pay for construction costs. Congress had granted tens of millions of acres of public land to railroad companies. In exchange, the government asked the railroads to carry U.S. mail and troops at lower rates. The railway acts inspired many companies to begin laying tracks.

✔ **Reading Check: Analyzing Information** What innovations helped link the East and the West? the Pony Express, the transcontinental railroad, and the telegraph

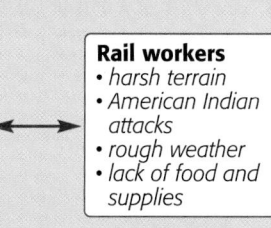
Railroad building in the West involved overcoming many physical obstacles and dangers. Here Chinese workers celebrate the completion of a tunnel in the Sierra Nevada.

HOMEWORK Have students create a chart comparing and contrasting the challenges faced by miners and rail workers.

LEVEL 3: Have students create an advertising campaign for a railroad company seeking to increase public awareness of the company's influence on the settlement and development of the West. Campaigns should include the speed of travel, the improvements in communications, and the growth of western businesses. Have students design posters with at least two paragraphs of advertising copy and illustrations that promote the railroad.

★ CLOSE

List the Great Plains states on the chalkboard. Have students brainstorm facts about each state. *(Students' facts may include main cities, products produced, and main attractions.)* Finally, discuss with students whether they believe mining, railroads, or both were responsible for the current development of the Great Plains states.

Interpreting the Visual Record
Celebration *The Central Pacific and Union Pacific connected their tracks at Promontory in Utah Territory.* **Why would the completion of the transcontinental railroad have been a cause for celebration?**

This advertisement for the Union Pacific Railroad praised the speed and comfort of railroad travel to the West.

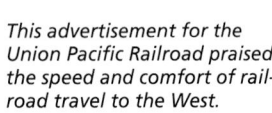

★ The Great Race

Two companies, the Central Pacific and the Union Pacific, led the race to complete the transcontinental railroad. In February 1863 the Central Pacific began building east from Sacramento, California. At the end of the year, the Union Pacific started building west from Omaha, Nebraska.

The Union Pacific hired thousands of railroad workers, including Irish immigrants and Civil War veterans. The Central Pacific hired many Chinese immigrants. The railroad's part-owner **Leland Stanford** praised these Chinese workers, but he paid them less than white laborers. Chinese crews were also given the most dangerous tasks and longer hours. However, Chinese workers could earn much more money working for the Central Pacific than in China.

Railroad companies faced many geographic challenges. The Central Pacific workers struggled to cross the Sierra Nevada range in California. Large amounts of explosives were used to blast a way through the mountains. In the winter of 1866, snowdrifts more than 60 feet high trapped and killed many workers. Meanwhile, the Union Pacific's workers faced harsh weather on the Great Plains.

For both lines, providing food and supplies for their workers was vital. To feed their workers, the railroad companies often relied on local resources. Professional hunters such as William "Buffalo Bill" Cody shot thousands of buffalo to feed workers for the Union Pacific.

Congress required the two railroads to connect at Promontory, Utah. On May 10, 1869, workers and reporters watched the two lines finally meet. In a dramatic ceremony, a golden spike was used to connect the railroad tie joining the two tracks. The transcontinental railroad had united the East and the West.

✔ **Reading Check: Summarizing** What difficulties did the builders of the transcontinental railroad face? Workers faced discrimination, harsh terrain, rough weather, and difficulty getting food and supplies.

★ REVIEW AND ASSESS

Have students complete the **Section 2 Review** on p. 659. Then have students complete **Daily Quiz 21.2**. As **Alternative Assessment**, you may want to use the news documentary or interview in this section's lessons.

★ RETEACH

Have students complete **Main Idea Activity for English Language Learners and Special-Needs Students 21.2**. Then ask them to imagine that they work in the mines or for one of the railroad companies. Have them make a list that both describes their work conditions and also displays an awareness

of the contributions they are making to the development of the West. Ask for volunteers to share their lists with the class.

ENGLISH LANGUAGE LEARNERS

★ EXTEND

Organize the class into two groups. Ask one group to research specific mining pioneers of the West and the other group to research well-known figures in the railroad industry. Have each student write a brief biographical sketch on one of these people. Then have the groups use these sketches to create a trade magazine for the industry they researched.

COOPERATIVE LEARNING , BLOCK SCHEDULING

★ The Effects of the Railroads

The transcontinental railroad increased both economic and population growth in the West. Railroad companies provided better transportation for people and goods. They also sold land to settlers, encouraging people to move west. In addition, railroads saved time. The Union Pacific advertised that a trip from Omaha, Nebraska, to San Francisco, California, would take four days. By wagon the trip took about a month.

In addition, the new railroads helped businesses. Western timber and mining companies shipped wood and metals east by railroad. In exchange, eastern factories shipped manufactured goods to the West.

Railroad companies encouraged investors to put their money into the railroad business, which they did—sometimes unwisely. Railroad speculation and the collapse of railroad owner Jay Cooke's banking firm helped start the Panic of 1873. A depression soon followed. By the 1880s many of the smaller western railroads were deep in debt. Despite such setbacks, Americans remained interested in railroad investments. In 1865 only about 35,000 miles of railroad track existed, but by 1890 about 199,000 miles were in operation. Railroads had become the biggest industry in the United States.

✔ **Reading Check: Finding the Main Idea** How did the railroad affect the settlement and development of the West? It increased economic growth and the population by transporting people and goods, shortening travel times, encouraging settlement by selling land, and helping businesses.

Population of Omaha

102,555

1,833

1860 **1900**

Sources: Bureau of the Census; U.S. Department of Commerce

Interpreting Graphs In 1863 the Union Pacific Railroad laid its tracks through the city of Omaha, Nebraska, causing the population to soar.

Skills Assessment Analyzing Information How much did Omaha's population increase between 1860 and 1900?

Technology Resources

Linking Geography and History Transparency 10A: Growth of Transportation, 1840–1890

★ ★ ★ ★ ★ ★ ★ ★ ★ ★ ★

Section 2 Review ANSWERS

❶ **Define**
• bonanza, p. 655
• boomtowns, p. 656
• transcontinental railroad, p. 657

❷ **Identify**
• Comstock Lode, p. 655
• Pony Express, p. 657
• Pacific Railway Acts, p. 657
• Leland Stanford, p. 658

❸ Mining—became a big business employing many people, encouraged other people and businesses to settle in boomtowns; Railroads—improved communication and transportation for people and goods, encouraged settlement by selling land, and made business easier

❹ a. the eastern United States, Europe, Central and South America, Asia, Mexicans and Mexico; heat unbearable, lack of oxygen, floods and cave-ins, fire, and unsafe equipment

b. discrimination against immigrant workers, harsh terrain, conflict with American Indians, rough weather, and a lack of food and supplies

❺ Students' songs will vary but should reflect an understanding of the challenges of building railroads, how the railroads changed western life, and in particular how railroads improved communication between family members.

Section 2 Review

★ ★

Homework Practice Online
keyword: SA3 HP21

❶ **Define** and explain:
• bonanza
• boomtowns
• transcontinental railroad

❷ **Identify** and explain:
• Comstock Lode
• Pony Express
• Pacific Railway Acts
• Leland Stanford

❸ **Comparing** Copy the graphic organizer below. Use it to compare how mining and railroads led to the settlement and development of the West.

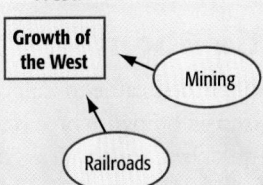

❹ **Finding the Main Idea**
a. Where did miners come from, and why was their job one of the most dangerous in the West?

b. What were some of the difficulties faced in building a transcontinental railroad?

❺ **Writing and Critical Thinking**
Summarizing Imagine that you are a railroad worker. Write a short song that might have been sung in your community after the connection of the Union Pacific and the Central Pacific Railroads.
Consider the following:
• the challenges of building the railroad
• how the railroad will change life in the West
• improved communication between family members

659

Section 3

OBJECTIVES

★ Identify the factors that led to the cattle boom.

★ Describe what life was like for cowboys.

★ Analyze the causes of the Cattle Kingdom's decline.

SECTION 3 RESOURCES

REPRODUCIBLE

▶ Guided Reading Strategy 21.3

▶ Primary Source Reading 21: Cowhands and Cattle Drives

TECHNOLOGY

▶ One-Stop Planner, Lesson 21.3

▶ American Music Selection 16: "O Bury Me Not"

▶ Homework Practice Online

REINFORCEMENT, REVIEW, AND ASSESSMENT

▶ Section 3 Review, p. 665

▶ Daily Quiz 21.3

▶ Main Idea Activity 21.3

▶ English Audio Summary 21.3

▶ Spanish Audio Summary 21.3

🔊 LET'S GET STARTED!

Write the following statement on the chalkboard: *Based on your impressions from watching television and movies, describe what a cowboy's life was like.* As students enter the classroom, allow time for them to respond. *(Students' responses may include the following: solitary, lonely, busy, exciting, adventurous, and fun.)* Explain to students that while some of what they see in the media is an accurate portrayal of cowboys, much of it is glorified. Tell the class that in Section 3 they will learn about the lives of cowboys and ranchers and their contributions to the growth of the West.

Section 3

The Cattle Kingdom

Read to Discover

1. What led to the cattle boom?
2. What was life like for cowboys?
3. What caused the decline of the Cattle Kingdom?

WHY IT MATTERS TODAY

Cattle ranching continues to be important to the economy of many western states. Use **CNN fyi.com** or other **current events** sources to learn about cattle ranching today. Record your findings in your journal.

Define

- Texas longhorn
- open range
- range rights
- vaqueros
- roundup
- cattle drive
- range wars

Identify

- Joseph McCoy
- Cattle Kingdom
- Elizabeth Collins
- Nat Love
- Chisholm Trail

The Story Continues

The Texas longhorn was well suited to living on the Plains.

In the mid-1800s Texas ranchers began gathering huge herds of wild cattle. One rancher described how ranchers let their herds roam. "Cattle are permitted to range . . . over a large surface of country, thirty, forty, and even fifty miles in extent [size]." Keeping track of these roaming cattle required great skill. The ranch hands who did this work faced many hardships. However, one rancher believed that ranch hands liked their work. "The young men that follow this 'Cow-Boy' life . . . generally become attached to it," he wrote. These cowboys and ranchers helped start the cattle-ranching industry in the West.

★ The Cattle Boom

Spanish settlers brought their cattle to California and Texas in the 1700s. These cattle later mixed with English breeds to create the **Texas longhorn**. This breed spread quickly throughout western Texas. Longhorn cattle were lean and tough, with horns up to five feet across. Many butchers said the longhorn had too little meat. They called it "8 pounds of hamburger

Have students read Section 3 and complete Guided Reading Strategy 21.3. Choose one or more of the following activities to explore the section content with students. For further suggestions on block scheduling or team teaching, see the *Block Scheduling Handbook with Team Teaching Strategies.*

LEVEL 1: Have students create a job description for a cowboy. They should include an overall description of the job's responsibilities as well as a description of what life was like for a cowboy. *(Students' descriptions should mention that cowboys had lives of hard work and low pay, with many dangers. Cattle towns had hotels, saloons, and restaurants to serve the needs of cowboys who were paid in town at the end of a drive.)* Once students have completed their descriptions, lead a class discussion about cowboy life during the 1870s.
ENGLISH LANGUAGE LEARNERS

on 800 pounds of bone and horn." Nonetheless, settlers preferred to raise longhorns. Because the animals needed very little water and could survive harsh weather, they were more suitable for the environment.

Following the Civil War, the demand for beef increased in the East. The expanding economy and growing population created the higher demand. A steer worth $3 to $6 in Texas could be sold for $38 in Kansas. In New York it could be sold for $80. Nobody drove the longhorns to eastern markets, however. In addition to the problem of distance, people feared the western cattle would infect eastern farm animals with a disease called Texas fever.

In 1867 businessman **Joseph McCoy** had an idea. He decided "to establish a market whereat the southern . . . [rancher] and the northern buyer would meet." McCoy built pens for cattle in the small town of Abilene, Kansas. The Kansas Pacific Railroad line went through Abilene. As a result, cattle could be shipped by rail from there. Soon many Texas ranchers were making the trip north to sell their herds of cattle.

Around the same time, cattle ranching began to expand onto the Great Plains. The tough longhorns did well on the Plains. Ranchers began taking their cattle north to Colorado, Wyoming, Nebraska, and Montana. They built many ranches in the region stretching from Texas north to Canada. Eventually, this area became known as the **Cattle Kingdom**. Throughout the area, ranchers grazed their huge herds on public land called the **open range**. This land had once been occupied by Plains Indians and buffalo herds.

✔ **Reading Check: Finding the Main Idea** What factors led to the cattle boom? Economic and population expansion created a greater demand for beef; cattle pens were built near the rail lines so ranchers could ship cattle to the East; ranching expanded onto the Great Plains.

★ The Ranches

One person who saw the profits to be made in ranching was **Elizabeth Collins**. She and her husband had had trouble mining gold, so they decided "to discontinue the business of mining and engage in that of cattle raising." She moved to the Teton Valley in Montana and started ranching. She was so successful that she earned the name Cattle Queen of Montana.

Collins was just one of many ranchers who became wealthy during the cattle boom. Charles Goodnight started the first ranch in the Texas Panhandle. It was more than 250 miles from any town or railroad.

Daily Life

Cattle Towns Long cattle drives ended at a town located along a railroad. In these towns, brokers bought cattle to ship east on railroad cars. Early cattle towns consisted of little more than a general store, a hotel or boardinghouse, a railroad depot, and a stockyard. Towns that drew enough business grew larger. They bustled with activity from spring to fall when the long drives took place. Prosperous cattle towns attracted businesspeople, doctors, lawyers, and their families. Once families arrived, the cattle towns built schools, hired teachers, and established police forces to maintain order. **How did the railroad contribute to the growth of western towns and businesses?**

Elizabeth Collins became a successful cattle rancher in Montana.

★ Historical Sidelight

The Rancher and Native Animals. The introduction and subsequent breeding of cattle in the West had a detrimental effect on animals native to the region. In a campaign to kill all animals that might prey on their livestock, ranchers poisoned the animal carcasses that predators would later eat. Huge numbers of bears, mountain lions, coyotes, ground squirrels, and prairie dogs were killed. In some cases, these animals were eliminated from the region entirely. To protect the grazing lands for their livestock, ranchers also killed any native animals that might eat the grass intended for the cattle or sheep. In Colorado, one ranching family killed 1,080 antelope that had been grazing on the grasslands that the family had claimed for its cattle.

CRITICAL THINKING
What was the ranchers' incentive to kill native species?

ANSWER: The ranchers were motivated by the economic need to protect their livestock investment.

DAILY LIFE ANSWER
Students should suggest that the railroad brought people West.

HOMEWORK Have students write a letter applying for the job of a cowboy. Students should include previous experience and skills that will help them in the job as well as reasons why they want the position.

ALL LEVELS: Copy the following graphic organizer onto the chalkboard, omitting the italicized answers. Have students complete the organizer to depict the reasons for the rise and fall of the Cattle Kingdom.
ENGLISH LANGUAGE LEARNERS

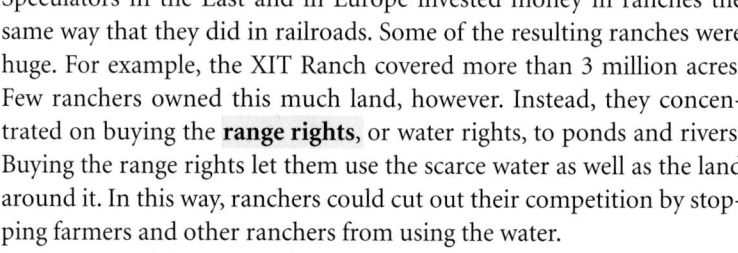

Cattle Kingdom

Rise
- *Economic and population growth increased the demand for beef.*
- *McCoy's cattle pens near rail lines eased cattle shipment to the East.*
- *Ranching expanded on the Great Plains.*

Fall
- *Beef prices were low.*
- *Competition for grazing lands increased.*
- *Harsh weather made raising cattle difficult.*

Speculators in the East and in Europe invested money in ranches the same way that they did in railroads. Some of the resulting ranches were huge. For example, the XIT Ranch covered more than 3 million acres. Few ranchers owned this much land, however. Instead, they concentrated on buying the **range rights**, or water rights, to ponds and rivers. Buying the range rights let them use the scarce water as well as the land around it. In this way, ranchers could cut out their competition by stopping farmers and other ranchers from using the water.

Because of the remote locations of many ranches, some ranchers served as the local authorities. Joseph McCoy described the view of a cattle rancher. He saw himself as "an independent sovereign [ruler] . . . capable of conducting his affairs in his own way." Mary Jaques, who lived on a Texas ranch for two years, noted ranchers' many different skills.

History Makers Speak

❝The ideal ranchman must be butcher, baker, carpenter, . . . blacksmith, plain cook, milker. . . . It is a fact that each of these trades will have to be practiced to some extent sooner or later.❞

—Mary Jaques, *Texan Ranch Life: With Three Months through Mexico in a "Prairie Schooner"*

✔ **Reading Check: Analyzing Information** How did ranchers influence western life? by acquiring huge amounts of land, gaining range rights to scarce water supplies, and acting as local authorities

---

Analyzing Primary Sources

Drawing Inferences and Conclusions Why do you think it was necessary for ranchers to have so many skills? Students might say it was necessary because ranches were usually far from other people who had these skills.

★ **The Cowboys**

The workers who took care of ranchers' cattle were known as cowhands or cowboys. Cowboys borrowed many of their techniques from Mexican **vaqueros** (vah-KER-ohs), ranch hands who cared for cattle and horses. From the vaqueros came the western saddle, the lariat—a rope used for lassoing cattle—and the leather chaps cowboys wore over their pants for protection against the thorny brush. The cowboys borrowed the vaqueros' broad felt hat. However, they changed it into the familiar high-peaked cowboy hat. Cowboys also adopted the bandanna, a cloth that covered the face to protect it from dust. Sometimes it served as a handkerchief or bandage as well. Many cowboys were Mexican Americans or African Americans, like **Nat Love**, who wrote an autobiography about his life as a cowboy. Although most cowhands were men, some women worked alongside cowboys.

Gathering the cattle together was known as a **roundup**. During spring roundups, cowboys branded young calves and horses with a ranch's unique mark to prevent thieves from selling stolen horses and cattle.

Cowboys faced the danger of cattle thieves, bad weather, and unpredictable livestock. Although they worked hard, wages were low, and few were able to make enough money to start their own ranches. Despite these factors, many cowboys like Nat Love enjoyed their days on the range.

Nat Love

Cowboys borrowed many types of clothes, equipment, and cattle-driving methods from the vaqueros.

ALL LEVELS: Lead a class discussion on the causes of the rise and ultimate decline of the Cattle Kingdom. *(Students' responses should include that economic growth, population expansion, McCoy's shipping, and ranching led to the rise, and that low prices, competition for grazing lands and harsh weather led to its decline.)* Then organize the class into several small groups. Have each group create a comic book that highlights the major events and changes that took place in the cattle industry during the mid-1800s. Comic books should depict these significant details: the breeding of Texas longhorn cattle, the building of holding pens and processing plants for cattle along railroad lines, the use of the open range and the buying of range rights, the growth of cattle towns, range wars, and the end of the open range. **ENGLISH LANGUAGE LEARNERS**, **COOPERATIVE LEARNING**

LEVEL 2: Ask students to write an encyclopedia entry explaining what led to the cattle boom. *(Students' entries should include an increased demand for beef.)*

★ Cattle Drives and Cattle Towns

One of the cowboy's most important and dangerous duties was the **cattle drive**. On these long journeys, cowboys herded cattle to the market or to the northern Plains for grazing. These trips usually lasted several months and covered hundreds of miles. The **Chisholm Trail** was one of the earliest and most popular routes for cattle drives. It was blazed, or marked, by Texas cowboy Jesse Chisholm in the late 1860s. This trail ran from San Antonio, Texas, to the cattle town of Abilene, Kansas. Charles Goodnight blazed a trail leading from Texas to New Mexico Territory, which became known as the Goodnight-Loving Trail. One of the most heavily used routes, the Western Trail, headed north from San Antonio to Dodge City, Kansas.

Cowboys herded their cattle through harsh country. They lived for months with "no tents or shelter of any sort other than [their] blankets," as cowboy James H. Cook recalled. The cattle could be difficult to handle, and they might stampede during storms. Then cowboys would have to track down the strays and round them up again. At night, cowboys had to stand watch over the cattle herds. Most cowboys were happy to reach the end of a cattle drive.

A large cattle town such as Dodge City or Abilene usually lay at the end of the trail. Small businesses sprang up as more cowboys passed through these towns. Some of these businesses were owned or operated by women. For example, Malinda Jenkins became a successful businesswoman who ran several boardinghouses.

Boardinghouses, hotels, saloons, and restaurants depended on tired cowboys spending money when they were in town. Cowboys spent their pay on food, hot baths, and comfortable beds after weeks on the trail. At times, rowdy cowboys could make life in cattle towns rough and violent. There were rarely shoot-outs in the streets, but disorderly behavior was common. Law officials such as Wyatt Earp became famous for keeping the peace in cattle towns.

✔ **Reading Check: Analyzing Information** How did the railroad affect the location and development of cattle trails and cattle towns? The railroad turned some western towns into cattle towns where cowboys drove in cattle to be shipped to the East; businesses such as hotels, saloons, and restaurants developed in these towns to serve the needs of cowboys.

★ Daily Life

The Chuck Wagon. Trail crews were often led by an older cowboy who could no longer withstand the long, harsh days on horseback. Serving as cook, doctor, dentist, and entertainer, he rode on the chuck wagon. This vehicle was a sturdy wagon with iron axles and wide tires. Carrying the entire crew's food, bedrolls, firewood, tools, and personal possessions, the cook would ride ahead of the crew to set up the next night's camp, start a fire, and prepare coffee and meals.

ACTIVITY: Have students draw pictures of what they think the inside of a chuck wagon might have looked like. Then have students label each item and explain its purpose.

Technology Resources

 American Music Selection 16: "O Bury Me Not"

Visual Record Answer

Students might suggest that it brought a rush of people and activity to the town.

LEVEL 3: Tell students that they will take part in a mock trial in which a rancher is suing a farmer. The farmer's new fence has made it impossible for the rancher's cattle to access water from a nearby river. Roles include the defense, the plaintiff, attorneys, the judge, and the jury. Students should use information from the text to create arguments for both the farmer and the rancher. *(Students' arguments may include that the person who pays for land that has a water source has a right to use it as they see fit, or another argument may be that water must be shared since it is a natural resource.)* After all the testimony has been heard, have the jury decide whether the rancher has a legitimate claim.
COOPERATIVE LEARNING

✪ CLOSE

Have students create a crossword puzzle using the key terms from this section. Then organize the class into pairs and have them exchange puzzles. After completing each other's puzzles, have pairs check each other's work. **COOPERATIVE LEARNING**

Note: For an additional teaching idea, see the Chapter 21 Structured Discussion activity in the **Creative Teaching Strategies** handbook.

★ Economics

Cowboys to Cattle Ranchers.
During the early days of the cattle industry, the economic rewards of the cattle drive often extended to the cowboys as well as to the ranch owners. In many instances, a cowboy was paid with a portion of the cattle he had helped brand. Cowboys could also take and raise motherless calves, or mavericks, whose ownership could not be determined. As the price of cattle rose and available land became scarce large cattle corporations eventually put an end to these practices.

CRITICAL THINKING

How would ranchers benefit from allowing cowboys to own their own cattle?

ANSWER: Students might suggest that cowboys could learn the importance of ownership and heighten their sense of responsibility. Ranchers would also avoid having to raise so much cash at one time.

MAP ANSWER
the Rocky Mountains

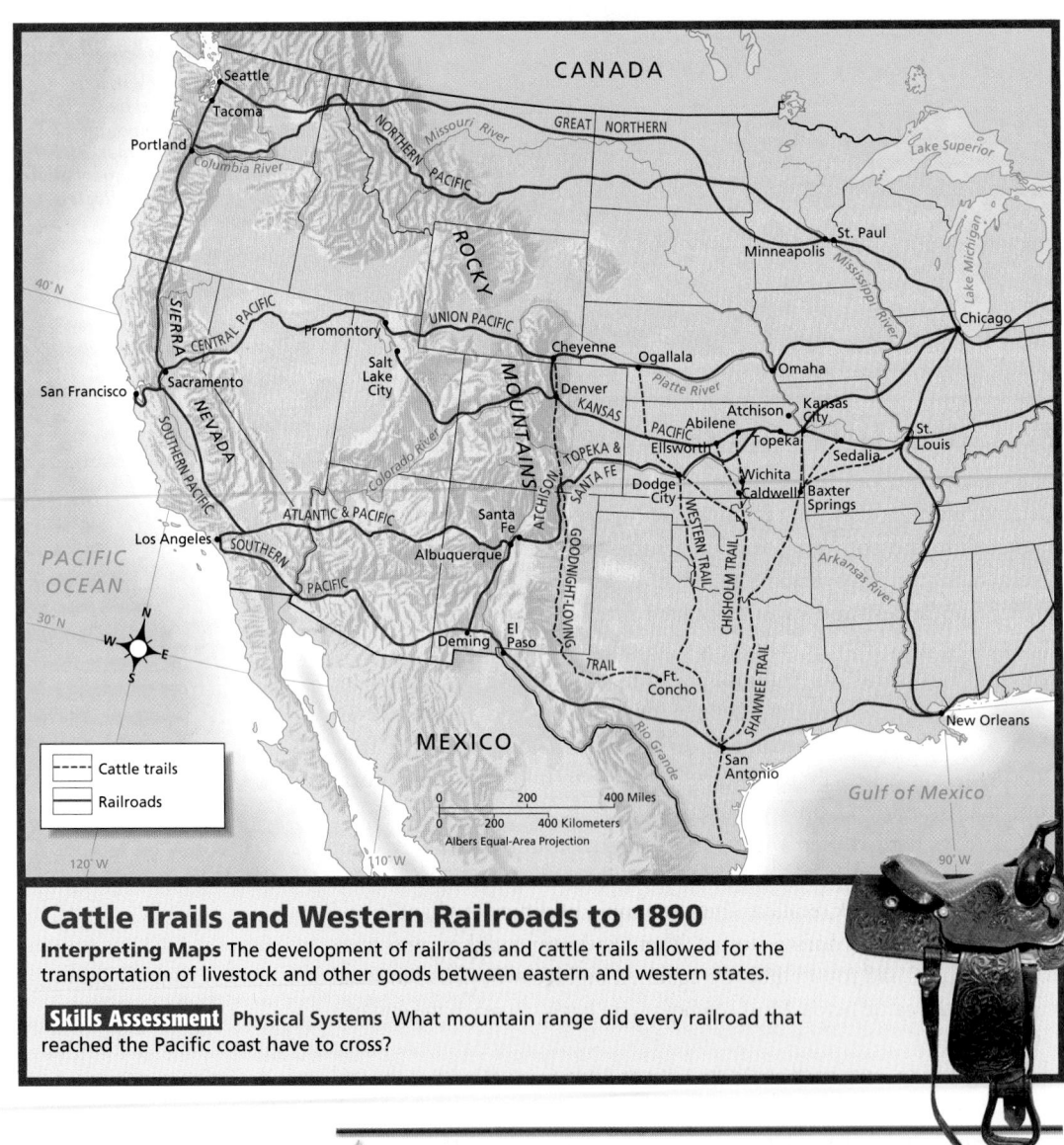

Cattle Trails and Western Railroads to 1890

Interpreting Maps The development of railroads and cattle trails allowed for the transportation of livestock and other goods between eastern and western states.

Skills Assessment Physical Systems What mountain range did every railroad that reached the Pacific coast have to cross?

★ The End of the Open Range

In the early 1880s the introduction of the refrigerator railroad car made it possible to carry meat from packing plants to eastern cities. As the national demand for beef grew, cities such as Chicago, Illinois, became famous for their meatpacking plants.

While the cattle business boomed, ranchers faced more competition for use of the open range. Farmers began to buy range land on the Great Plains where cattle had once grazed. Smaller ranchers also began competing with the large ranchers for land. Then in 1874 Joseph Glidden patented barbed wire, which allowed westerners to fence off large areas of land at a low cost.

☆ REVIEW AND ASSESS

Have students complete the **Section 3 Review** on p. 665. Then have students complete **Daily Quiz 21.3**. As **Alternative Assessment**, you may want to use the job description or comic book exercise in this section's lessons.

☆ RETEACH

Have students complete **Main Idea Activity for English Language Learners and Special-Needs Students 21.3**. Then pair students. Ask the pairs to write each key word from this section on a small piece of paper and to place them inside a hat or box. Partners should take turns choosing a slip of paper and making an accurate statement about the word written on it.

ENGLISH LANGUAGE LEARNERS , COOPERATIVE LEARNING

☆ EXTEND

Remind students that the growth of the cattle industry in the 1870s was connected to the growth of the railroad industry. Have students use the library to obtain information about the towns or regions that were significant to the cattle industry. Have students create a map identifying these towns or regions. Students should also include a map key that identifies whether each area was known for cattle ranching, its holding pens, its meat processing, or its consumer market. Then have students label key railroad routes and the cities. **BLOCK SCHEDULING**

As barbed wire came into wider use, large ranchers moved quickly to fence in the open range and valuable water sources, keeping out farmers and smaller ranchers. Some farmers and small ranchers cut the fences and moved onto the land or stole cattle in response. This competition led to **range wars** between large ranchers, small ranchers, and farmers. Large ranchers often won these battles, but few could let their cattle roam free on public land.

Cattle ranchers also fought with sheep owners. As the number of sheep grew even greater in the 1880s, so did the competition for grasslands. Sheep chewed the grass down so far that there was nothing left for the cattle. Despite threats and violence against them, sheep ranchers still usually did well in the West.

By the 1880s some 7.5 million cattle roamed the Great Plains. With the U.S. economy in a depression, cattle prices dropped in 1885. To improve prices, ranchers began to bring eastern cattle to the western range. These cattle produced more beef than the Texas longhorns but were not well adapted to the conditions on the Plains.

In 1885 and 1886 disaster struck the Cattle Kingdom. The huge cattle herds on the Plains had eaten much of the prairie grass that ranchers depended on for feed. Unusually severe winters in both years made the ranching situation even worse. Thousands of cattle died, and most ranches lost at least 30 percent of their herds. Many ranchers were ruined financially. Cattle towns were also hit hard. While cattle ranching continued, it became more costly. Ranchers were forced to buy winter feed for their cattle and to reduce the size of their herds. Low prices, harsh weather, and greater competition for grazing land brought an end to the reign of the Cattle Kingdom.

✔ **Reading Check: Finding the Main Idea** Why did the Cattle Kingdom come to an end? *Low prices, competition for grazing lands, and harsh weather led to the end of the Cattle Kingdom.*

THE GRANGER COLLECTION, NEW YORK

Before Joseph Glidden invented barbed wire, westerners had not built fences because traditional fencing materials, such as stone and lumber, were scarce in the Great Plains.

Section 3 Review

Homework Practice Online
keyword: SA3 HP21

① **Define** and explain:
• Texas longhorn
• open range
• range rights
• vaqueros
• roundup
• cattle drive
• range wars

② **Identify** and explain:
• Joseph McCoy
• Cattle Kingdom
• Elizabeth Collins
• Nat Love
• Chisholm Trail

③ **Analyzing Information** Copy the graphic organizer below. Use it to describe the factors that caused the boom and then the bust of the Cattle Kingdom.

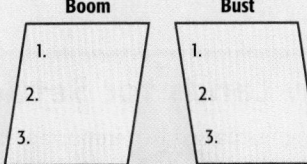

Boom	Bust
1.	1.
2.	2.
3.	3.

④ **Finding the Main Idea**
a. What was cowboy life like?

b. In what ways did the cattle boom show the benefits of free enterprise in the West?

⑤ **Writing and Critical Thinking**
Summarizing Imagine that you are a cowboy during the late 1800s. Write a diary entry explaining what your daily life is like.

Consider the following:
• salary
• work on ranches and cattle drives
• freedom on the open range

★ ★ ★ ★ ★ ★ ★ ★ ★
Section 3 Review
ANSWERS

❶ Define
• Texas longhorn, p. 660
• open range, p. 661
• range rights, p. 662
• vaqueros, p. 662
• roundup, p. 662
• cattle drive, p. 663
• range wars, p. 665

❷ Identify
• Joseph McCoy, p. 661
• Cattle Kingdom, p. 661
• Elizabeth Collins, p. 661
• Nat Love, p. 662
• Chisholm Trail, p. 663

❸ Boom—1. economic and population expansion created greater demand for beef, 2. McCoy created a new western marketplace by building cattle pens near the rail lines so cattle could be shipped to the East, 3. ranching expanded on to the Great Plains. Bust—1. low prices, 2. competition for grazing lands, 3. harsh weather

❹ a. hard work and low pay, with many dangers such as cattle thieves, the cattle themselves, and bad weather
b. created new western markets, brought money to local towns and to individual ranchers, and provided jobs in the East and West

❺ Students' diary entries will vary but should reflect an awareness of a cowboy's daily life, including salary, work on ranches and cattle drives, and freedom on the open range.

Section 4

OBJECTIVES

⭐ Identify the groups that settled the Great Plains, and examine their reasons for moving there.

⭐ Discuss how the environment of the Great Plains affected settlers' farming methods.

⭐ Describe what life was like on the Great Plains for settlers, and explain how they adapted to the conditions.

SECTION 4 RESOURCES

REPRODUCIBLE

▶ Guided Reading Strategy 21.4

▶ Geography Activity 21: Oklahoma Land Rush

▶ Literature Reading 21: The Life of an Ordinary Woman

TECHNOLOGY

▶ One-Stop Planner, Lesson 21.4

▶ Everyday Life in America Transparency 16: Farming Technology, Late 1800s

▶ Holt Researcher: American History CD–ROM

▶ Homework Practice Online

REINFORCEMENT, REVIEW, AND ASSESSMENT

▶ Section 4 Review, p. 670

▶ Daily Quiz 21.4

▶ Main Idea Activity 21.4

▶ English Audio Summary 21.4

▶ Spanish Audio Summary 21.4

🔊 **LET'S GET STARTED!**

Write the following scenario on the chalkboard: *The U.S. government is giving away 160-acre plots of land to any U.S. citizen willing to pay a small fee and move to where the land is located. Would you go, and why?* As students enter the classroom, give them time to write down their response. *(Students' responses indicating 'yes' may reason that it's free, it could be a nice change of life, it's an excellent opportunity. Students responses indicating 'no' may reason that it's risky, the land could be inferior, or they don't want to leave their friends and family.)* Explain to students that the government followed this policy in the 1860s, and many people faced that choice. Tell students that in Section 4 they will learn about who went to the Great Plains, why they went, and what they faced when they arrived.

Section 4

Farming the Great Plains

Read to Discover

1. What groups settled the Great Plains, and what were their reasons for moving there?
2. How did the environment of the Great Plains affect settlers' farming methods?
3. What was life on the Great Plains like for settlers, and how did they adapt to the conditions?

WHY IT MATTERS TODAY

Farming is still central to the economy of the Great Plains states, as well as much of the world. Use **CNNfyi.com** or other **current events** sources to learn about new farming methods being developed today. Record your findings in your journal.

Define

- sodbusters
- dry farming

Identify

- Homestead Act
- Morrill Act
- Exodusters
- Cyrus McCormick

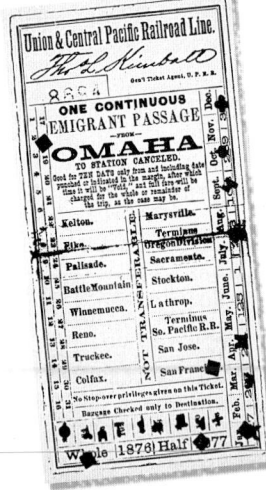

A pioneer's rail ticket

The Story Continues

In 1879 Scottish writer Robert Louis Stevenson took the transcontinental railroad across the United States. Most of the other passengers were settlers moving to the West. When a passenger began to play the song "Home Sweet Home," all conversation stopped. "The faces began to lengthen," noted Stevenson. Then "an elderly, hard-looking man . . . [asked] the performer [to] stop. 'I've heard about enough of that,' he [said]. 'Give us something about the good country we're going to.'" The passengers agreed, and the performer began to play music for dancing. Despite being homesick, most settlers hoped to build a better life in the West.

⭐ New Lands for Settlement

In 1862 Congress passed two important land-grant acts that helped open the West to settlers. The **Homestead Act** gave government-owned land to small farmers. Any adult who was a U.S. citizen or planned to become one could receive 160 acres of land. In exchange, homesteaders paid a small

TEACH

Have students read Section 4 and complete Guided Reading Strategy 21.4. Choose one or more of the following activities to explore the section content with students. For further suggestions on block scheduling or team teaching, see the *Block Scheduling Handbook with Team Teaching Strategies*.

 LEVEL 1: Lead a class discussion on what life on the Great Plains was like for farmers and settlers in the 1860s. *(Students' responses may include that people on the Great Plains faced extreme temperatures, tough sod, and loneliness.)* On the chalkboard, list the ways these conditions affected farming methods and the ways settlers adapted to them. **ENGLISH LANGUAGE LEARNERS**

ALL LEVELS: Copy the following graphic organizer onto the chalkboard, omitting the italicized answers. Have students complete the chart to identify the groups that settled the Great Plains and list the reasons why those groups moved there. **ENGLISH LANGUAGE LEARNERS**

Group	Reason
• *Exodusters* • *Norwegian, Swedish, Danish, German, and Czech immigrants*	• *equal rights* • *more economic opportunity* • *land grants*

registration fee. They also promised to live on the land for five years. The **Morrill Act** granted more than 17 million acres of federal land to the states. The act required each state to sell this land and use the money to build colleges, such as Texas A&M, to teach agriculture and engineering.

The federal government also offered land in what is now Oklahoma. Some of this land had belonged to Creek and Seminole Indians. In April 1889, officials opened these lands to homesteaders. Within a month of the government's announcement, more than 50,000 people rushed to Oklahoma to stake their claims. In all, the settlers claimed more than 11 million acres of former Indian land in the Oklahoma land rush.

✔ **Reading Check: Contrasting** List the different land acts that the federal government passed, and explain how they were different. See key terms above for specific information.

Interpreting the Visual Record

Westward expansion *The thousands of settlers who moved west formed many new communities.* **How does this picture show settlers modifying their physical environment?**

★ Settling the Plains

People from all over the country chose to move west. Settlers who had already moved to the Great Plains often chose to move again after a few years. All of these settlers hoped to find success on the Plains, often by starting their own farms. Many farming families moved from areas where farmland was becoming too scarce or expensive, such as New England. Others were the descendants of earlier pioneers to the Midwest. To encourage the presence of families and settlements in the West, the Homestead Act granted land to unmarried women.

The promise of land also drew a large group of Southern African Americans west. These settlers became known as **Exodusters** because of their exodus, or mass departure, from the South. Many Exodusters were sharecroppers such as John Solomon Lewis. He explained his reasons for moving his family.

 History Makers Speak

❝I one day said to the man I rented [land] from: 'It's no use, I works hard and raises big crops and you sells it and keeps the money, and brings me more and more in debt, so I will go somewhere else.'❞

—John Solomon Lewis, quoted in *Exodusters: Black Migration to Kansas after Reconstruction*, by Nell Irvin Painter

Soon black communities such as Nicodemus, Kansas, developed. They drew many African Americans west by land advertisements. Exodusters wanted more economic opportunity as well as equal rights that they were being denied in the South after Reconstruction.

Research on the ROM

Free Find:
Homestead Act
After reading about the Homestead Act on the **Holt Researcher CD-ROM**, create a newspaper ad that advertises the land available through this act.

★ Culture

Agricultural Growth.

Between 1860 and 1920 the number of farms in the United States increased by approximately 4.4 million. In 1800 there were some 450,000 farms. By 1850 the number of farms had climbed to almost 1.5 million, and by 1910 the number of farms had reached 6.4 million. As settlers moved West, the number of farms grew rapidly.

CRITICAL THINKING

Why do you think so many people became farmers in the western United States?

ANSWER: Students' responses may include that immigrants poured into the western states to join their families who had already settled and established farms there. They also searched for new economic opportunities outside of crowded eastern cities.

Many African American families, such as the Shores family shown here, moved to the Great Plains.

★★★★★★★★★★★★
That's Interesting!
★★★★★★★★★★★★

Attack of the Grasshoppers
Can you imagine the fields of the Great Plains covered in grasshoppers four inches deep? Well, that's exactly what happened in the summer of 1874. The grasshoppers appeared without warning. Within a few minutes, swarms had blocked out the Sun. These bugs liked to eat plants the best, but they didn't stop there. They ate curtains, old boots, and even straw hats. One settler said that he saw grasshoppers eating the wool off of a live sheep! One couple managed to save enough wheat for seed by swinging a clothesline in the air when the grasshoppers attacked. Other people were not so lucky.

Western homesteads also were attractive to immigrants. Like Americans, they could get land grants under the Homestead Act if they planned to become citizens and promised to stay on the land for five years. Norwegian, Swedish, Danish, German, and Czech immigrants looking for economic opportunity formed many small communities on the Great Plains. Usually, a relative made the journey to America first. Then this person wrote letters home telling other family members to come. In addition, a number of Mennonites, members of a Protestant religious group, moved to the Great Plains from Russia. They were among the first to begin large-scale farming in the region.

✔ **Reading Check: Summarizing** Who moved to the Great Plains, and why did they choose to move there? farmers from the East and Midwest, single women, African American Exodusters, Norwegians, Swedes, Danes, Germans, Czechs, Mennonites; for economic opportunity and equal rights

★ Farming on the Plains

The inexpensive land of the Great Plains drew settlers. Yet the Plains had many unique challenges. Plains settlers found a mostly flat landscape covered with grass. Settlers also encountered extreme seasons. In the winter, temperatures on the northern Plains could fall to −40° F. Hot summer temperatures in the southern Plains could reach 110° F. The climate of the Plains was much drier than in the East. Settlers also faced the threat of blizzards and tornadoes. All of these factors meant that farmers could not raise the same crops that they had grown in the East.

Farmers survived the challenges of the Great Plains by developing new farming equipment and methods. The root-filled sod, or dirt, of the Plains was so tough that it actually broke the plows of many farmers. Manufacturer John Deere's deep steel plow broke through the tough sod and enabled farmers to plant crops. This hard work of breaking up the sod earned farmers on the Plains the nickname **sodbusters**.

In the 1890s farmers on the western Plains began to learn a new method called **dry farming**. This method shifted the focus from water-dependent crops such as corn to hardier crops like a type of red wheat introduced by Mennonite farmers to the Plains. In addition, farmers left part of their fields unplanted each year to preserve water in the soil. Even on the eastern Plains, which got more rain, farmers found that the soil needed special care. These dry-farming methods helped farmers make it through drought years.

By the 1880s mechanical farming was becoming increasingly common. **Cyrus McCormick** made his fortune designing, building, and

LEVEL 3: Discuss with the class reasons why settlers were willing to move to the Great Plains. Then ask students to imagine they are railroad executives from the 1860s offering free land or houses to settlers. Ask them to write two newspaper advertisements, one designed to attract eastern farmers and one to attract new immigrants. The advertisements should emphasize the benefits of moving to the Great Plains.

HOMEWORK Have students create a short dialogue between two family members. One is convinced by the advertisement created in the previous lesson to move to the Plains. The other was not convinced. Remind students to include reasons to move to the Plains as well as the perspective of a family member who is not convinced by the advertisement and does not want to move.

SPOTLIGHT
on the Great Plains

Organize the class into small groups. Have students use the library to find accounts of everyday life on the Great Plains. Ask each group to create a skit based on the accounts they have read. Have each group assign specific roles to each member. Roles include a rancher, a cowboy, a farmer, and a pioneer woman. Then remind the groups to include a narrator who will discuss the general conditions encountered on the Plains. Have each group present its skit to the class.

COOPERATIVE LEARNING , BLOCK SCHEDULING

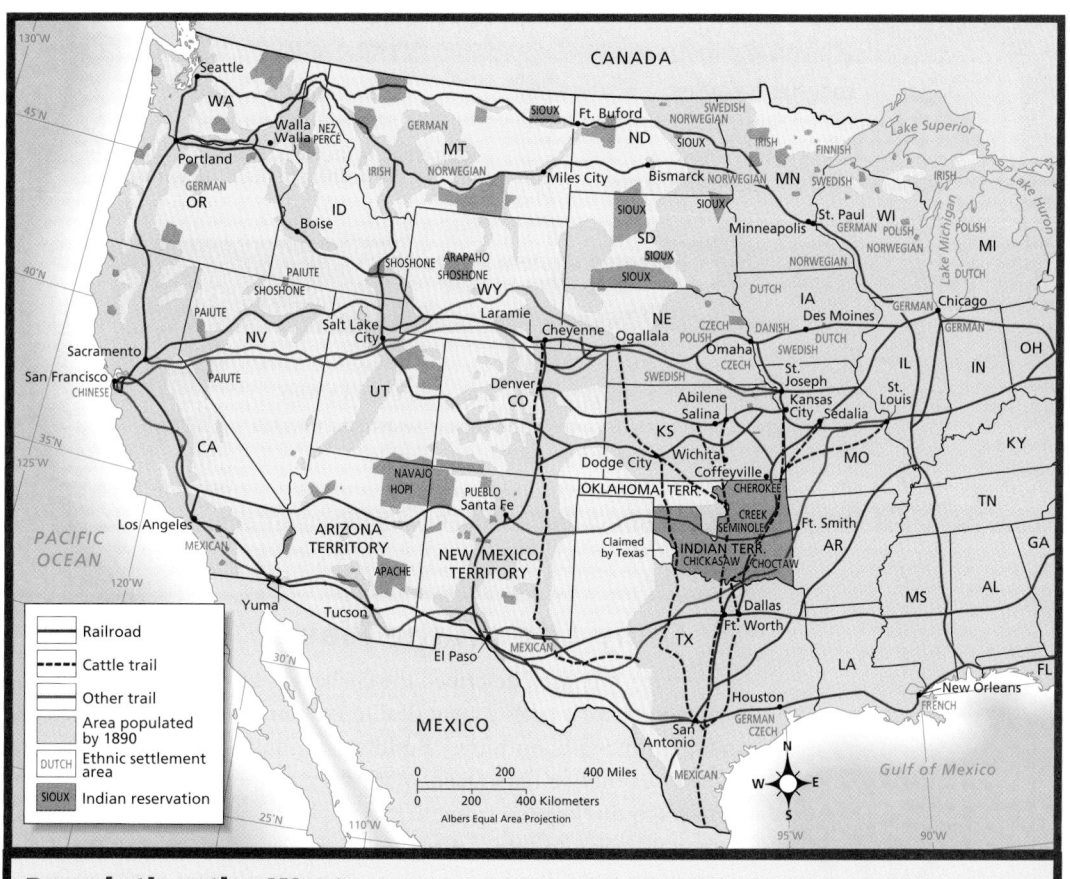

Populating the West

Interpreting Maps By 1890, settlements stretched across the western United States, which was experiencing rapid population growth.

Skills Assessment Human Systems What man-made features typically correspond with the populated areas on the map?

selling farm equipment. Horse-drawn machines such as McCormick reapers collected wheat stalks. Threshing machines separated the grain from the husk. By using machinery, farmers could harvest large fields more quickly and with fewer workers. Wealthy farmers could afford the land and machinery needed to create huge farms that employed hundreds of workers. Once they harvested their crops, farmers shipped the grain east by train. Some of it was then shipped to customers overseas. As farming technology improved, the Great Plains became known as the breadbasket of the world because of the grain that the region's farms produced.

A poster intending to persuade people to move west

✔ **Reading Check: Identifying Cause and Effect** What was the environment of the Great Plains like, and how did farmers change the region into a breadbasket? It had extreme temperatures, blizzards, tornadoes, tough soil, and droughts. They planted different crops, used new machinery, and tried scientific techniques such as dry farming.

⭐ **Daily Life**

Blizzards on the Plains.
Winter weather was said to be particularly harrowing on the Great Plains. Settlers were often struck by blizzards more severe than those in other parts of the country. A driving wind carried fine ice particles through the air with such force that no person or animal could stand to be exposed to the wind for very long. When these storms hit, settlers placed ropes along the perimeters of their houses to serve as guides to keep them from getting lost and freezing to death in the blinding snow and extreme cold.

CRITICAL THINKING
What technological advancements make Great Plains' winters more bearable today?

ANSWER: Students might suggest heating, electric streetlights, improved communications, and equipment for clearing roads.

MAP ANSWER
railroads, trails, and cattle trails

Technology Resources
 Everyday Life in America Transparency 16: Farming Technology, Late 1800s

The West **669**

SPOTLIGHT
on the Homestead Act

Have students use the library to obtain information about the influence of the Homestead Act on the settlement of the Great Plains. Ask students to focus on information about mass movements to the area, such as the migration of the Exodusters or the Mennonites. Then ask students to write a paper studying each group's reasons for moving to the Great Plains and describing how each group influenced Great Plains culture. Encourage students to share their ideas with the rest of the class. **COOPERATIVE LEARNING , BLOCK SCHEDULING**

★ CLOSE

Ask students to imagine that they live on a small farm in Virginia and want to move west. Have students write a letter to a family member or friend explaining why they want to move to the Great Plains and what they expect life will be like there.

★ ★ ★ ★ ★ ★ ★ ★ ★ ★ ★ ★

Section 4 Review
ANSWERS

❶ **Define**
- sodbusters, p. 668
- dry farming, p. 668

❷ **Identify**
- Homestead Act, p. 666
- Morrill Act, p. 667
- Exodusters, p. 667
- Cyrus McCormick, p. 668

❸ Settlers—farmers from the East and Midwest, single women, African American Exodusters, Norwegians, Swedes, Danes, Germans, Czechs, and Mennonites; Motivation—land grants, economic opportunity, and equal rights for Exodusters

❹ a. harsh weather, unfamiliar terrain, and new crops made farming difficult; farmers used new techniques such as dry farming and new equipment, including plows, reapers, and threshing machines
b. families had to work long hours, and life on the Great Plains was often lonely; families adapted by forming communities that founded churches and schools

❺ Students' advertisements will vary but should reflect an understanding of the availability of land and economic opportunity in the late 1800s, the technological advances in farming at the time, and the growth of churches and schools.

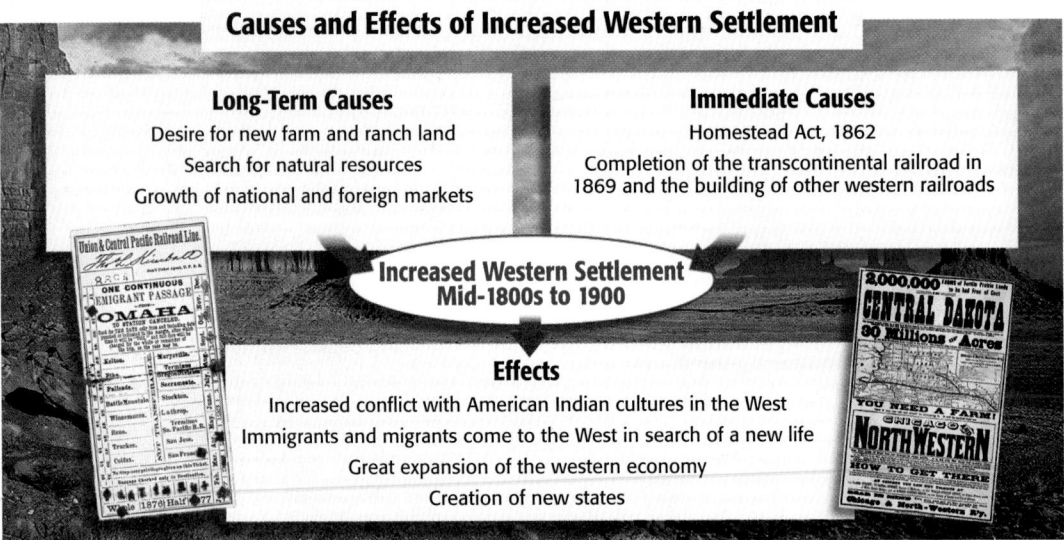

Causes and Effects of Increased Western Settlement

Long-Term Causes	Immediate Causes
Desire for new farm and ranch land	Homestead Act, 1862
Search for natural resources	Completion of the transcontinental railroad in 1869 and the building of other western railroads
Growth of national and foreign markets	

Increased Western Settlement Mid-1800s to 1900

Effects
Increased conflict with American Indian cultures in the West
Immigrants and migrants come to the West in search of a new life
Great expansion of the western economy
Creation of new states

★ Daily Life on the Plains

Settler Gro Svendsen described the challenges of Plains life. "When one begins to farm, it takes a great deal to get started—especially when one must begin with nothing." Building a house was one of the first challenges that settlers faced. With very little wood available, many families built houses from bricks of sod cut out of the ground. Although cheap to build, these sod homes were often very small and uncomfortable. Pioneer May Avery explained a few of the common problems. "The roof leaked something awful [and inside] we killed a snake or two . . . and several centipedes." For all their faults, however, the small homes did provide necessary shelter.

Once a home was built, daily chores kept pioneer families busy. For example, settlers had to make and mend their own clothes. They had no washing machines, so washing clothes was a big chore that filled the entire day. Pioneers usually made their wash soap from lye, a liquid made from wood ashes and animal fat. One pioneer woman listed 11 washday chores. She started with "build fire in back yard to heat kettle of rain water." The list ended with "brew cup of tea, set and rest and rock a spell and count blessings." Women prepared meals and often grew vegetables. They also raised chickens or made butter to earn money for the family.

Farming families raised livestock and worked hard in the fields, plowing and planting. Pioneers often had to build most of their farm buildings and repair their machinery. Children helped with many tasks around the farms. Farm families were often large, and everyone had chores.

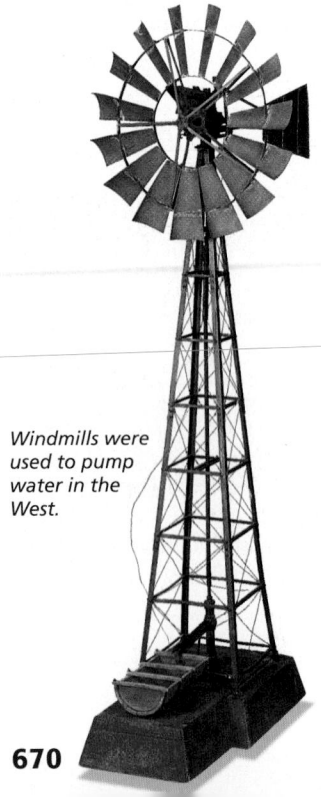

Windmills were used to pump water in the West.

✔ **Reading Check: Categorizing** What different types of work did Great Plains farmers do? They made sod bricks, clothes, and soap; they raised vegetables and livestock; and they built most buildings and repaired machinery.

★ Communities on the Great Plains

Communities were an important part of life on the Plains. Many early settlers found life on their remote farms to be extremely difficult. Esther Clark explained her mother's life as a pioneer. "It took [courage] to live twenty-four hours at a time, month in and out, on the lonely and lovely prairie." Farmers formed communities so that they could assist one another in times of need.

One of the first things that many pioneer communities did was establish a local church and a school. Churches offered a place for pioneer families to meet. Even small communities made efforts to get schools started. Many towns raised money by putting on plays or dinners. In many cases, townspeople even helped build the schools and ran them themselves. One woman recalled proudly, "They [the school board] and the pupils and I built that school house with our own hands."

Pioneer schools were usually small one-room buildings. A stove in the middle of the room provided heat, while the sunlight gave reading light. In these schools, children of all ages learned together in one class. Few children had schoolbooks. Many children went to school only part of the year because they had to help with farm work. Most teachers in these pioneer schools were young women who made little money. Frontier families worked very hard to provide communities for themselves and for their children. Through these efforts, more people found the West an appealing place to live and raise a family.

This group of pioneer students posed with their teacher in October 1893.

✔ **Reading Check: Summarizing** What roles did communities play in life on the Great Plains? They provided settlers with help and companionship. They also provided schools and churches for settlers to attend.

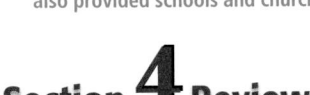

Section 4 Review

go.hrw.com Homework Practice Online
keyword: SA3 HP21

1 Define and explain:
- sodbusters
- dry farming

2 Identify and explain:
- Homestead Act
- Morrill Act
- Exodusters
- Cyrus McCormick

3 Categorizing Copy the graphic organizer below. Use it to identify the groups that settled on the Great Plains and what made them choose to move there.

Groups

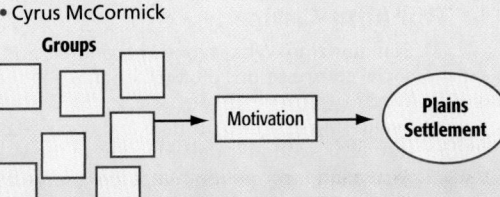

4 Finding the Main Idea
a. How did the environment of the Plains affect farming methods, and how did settlers cope with these conditions?

b. What was life on the Great Plains like, and how did pioneers adapt to this life?

5 Writing and Critical Thinking
Supporting a Point of View Imagine that you are a pioneer on the Plains in the late 1800s. Write a newspaper advertisement encouraging other people to settle the region.

Consider the following:
- availability of land and economic opportunity
- technological and scientific advances that have made Plains farming easier
- growth of churches and schools

CHAPTER

21

REVIEW AND ASSESSMENT RESOURCES

REPRODUCIBLE
▶ Vocabulary Activity 21

TECHNOLOGY
▶ Chapter 21 Test Generator (on the One-Stop Planner)
▶ Global Skill Builder CD–ROM
▶ HRW Go site

REINFORCEMENT, REVIEW, AND ASSESSMENT
▶ Chapter 21 Review, pp. 671–73
▶ Chapter 21 Tutorial for Students, Parents, Mentors, and Peers

▶ Chapter 21 Test (Form A or B)
▶ Alternative Assessment Handbook
▶ Chapter 21 Test for English Language Learners and Special-Needs Students

★ REVIEW
Have students complete the **Chapter 21 Review** on pages 672–73.

★ ASSESS
Use one of the chapter tests to assess students' understanding of the content. For **Alternative Assessment**, see the **Alternative Assessment Handbook**.

Understanding Main Ideas

1. U.S. interest in mining resources on American Indian lands, U.S. settlers crossing and settling on Indian lands; treaties, violent conflicts, forced removal of Indians to reservations

2. helped pass the Dawes General Allotment Act

3. Frequent cave-ins, toxic air, extreme heat, and unsafe equipment

4. increased growth in the West, improved communication, and depleted buffalo herds

5. resulted from free enterprise—the linking of markets by the railroads and the success of breeding longhorn cattle

6. to find economic opportunity and to take advantage of land grants

7. planted crops that grew better in the drier, more extreme weather, left some land unplanted each year, and developed new equipment that was strong enough to break up the tough sod

You Be the Historian–Reviewing Themes

1. extension of the railroad, rise of the cattle kingdom, expanded farming on the Great Plains, discovery of mine deposits, and distribution of land grants

2. caused conflict and resulted in American Indians being forced onto reservations where they could no longer hunt buffalo, or practice their cultural traditions.

3. droughts, tornadoes, and snowstorms destroyed crops, and breaking through tough sod required new plowing techniques.

Chapter 21 Review

The Chapter at a Glance
Examine the visual summary of the chapter below. Use it to create a chart listing five major events discussed in this chapter. Then give your list to a classmate and ask him or her to write the results or descriptions of these events.

The American West

As settlers moved to the West, they came into conflict with American Indians. As the last armed Indian resistance was being defeated, the U.S. government moved many tribes to reservations.

The completion of the transcontinental railroad in 1869 opened the West to more settlement. Gold and silver strikes also drew people hoping to get rich.

The railroads helped make the rise of the Cattle Kingdom possible. Cowboys drove huge herds of cattle from ranches to railway stations to be shipped to the East.

Farmers settled the Great Plains in large numbers. They overcame many hardships to make the Plains the breadbasket of America.

Identifying People and Ideas
Use the following terms or people in historically significant sentences.
1. reservations
2. George Armstrong Custer
3. Sitting Bull
4. Comstock Lode
5. Pacific Railway Acts
6. Joseph McCoy
7. Elizabeth Collins
8. Chisholm Trail
9. Homestead Act
10. Exodusters

Understanding Main Ideas
Section 1 *(Pages 648–654)*
1. What caused some of the conflicts between the United States and American Indians, and what were the results of these conflicts?
2. How did reformers change the U.S. government's Indian policy in the late 1800s?

Section 2 *(Pages 655–659)*
3. What factors made mining in the West such a dangerous job?
4. What effect did the transcontinental railroad have on western settlement?

Section 3 *(Pages 660–665)*
5. Why was there a cattle boom in the 1870s?

Section 4 *(Pages 666–671)*
6. Why did many immigrants move to the West?
7. How did settlers use new scientific methods and technology to farm on the Great Plains?

You Be the Historian— Reviewing Themes
1. **Economics** What factors led to the expansion of the economy in the West in the late 1800s?
2. **Culture** How did U.S. settlement of the West affect American Indians?
3. **Geography** In what ways did the environment of the Great Plains affect the crops that farmers planted and the farming methods they used?

Thinking Critically
1. **Summarizing** What types of economic and social contributions did women make in the West?
2. **Evaluating** List two positive and two negative results of economic development in the West.
3. **Analyzing Information** What were some of the different ways in which immigrant groups interacted with and changed the environment of the West?

★ RETEACH

Organize students into four groups and assign one of the chapter's sections to each group. Have students review their assigned section and highlight its main points in a presentation for the class. Clarify any misconceptions that students have regarding their assigned material.

**ENGLISH LANGUAGE LEARNERS ,
COOPERATIVE LEARNING**

Portfolio Extensions

American History

1. Cooperative Learning

Organize the class into groups. Ask group members to imagine that they are a family that has decided to move west in 1870. The families must make sure that they are prepared for the challenges that lie ahead. Together, the family must decide 10 things that they will take with them. Have each group brainstorm as many items as they can think of that would be helpful. Then vote on each item as a class to determine the final 10.

2. Interdisciplinary Connection to Literature/Geography/Art

Have students imagine that they are newspaper reporters from the East who have been assigned to cover the Battle of the Little Bighorn. Tell students that in order to help their readers understand more about the event, they should either write a biographical sketch of two key figures in the battle, prepare a relief map of the battle site, or create an illustration of the battle.

Social Studies Skills Workshop

Interpreting Graphs

Study the graph below. Then use the information on the graph to help you answer the questions that follow.

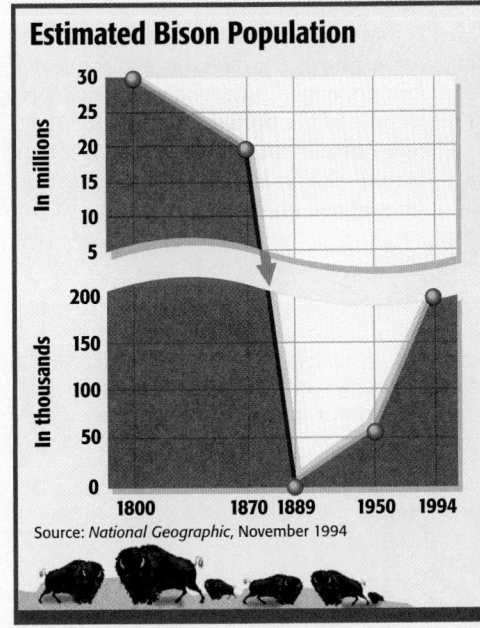

Estimated Bison Population

In millions: 30, 25, 20, 15, 10, 5
In thousands: 200, 150, 100, 50, 0

1800   1870 1889   1950 1994

Source: *National Geographic*, November 1994

1. How many buffalo (bison) were there in the United States in 1800?
   a. 30
   b. 50 million
   c. 75 million
   d. 30 million

2. How many buffalo were there in the United States in 1889?

3. Based on your knowledge of the period and of current events, what factors do you think might have accounted for the increase in the buffalo population since 1889?

Analyzing Primary Sources

Read the following quotation about cattle drives from an American cowboy song, then answer the questions.

❝It's whooping and yelling and driving the dogies;
    Oh how I wish you would go on;
It's whooping and punching and go on little dogies,
    For you know Wyoming will be your new home.

Some boys go up the trail for pleasure
    But that's where you get it most awfully wrong;
For you haven't any idea of the trouble they give us
    While we go driving them along.❞

4. Which of the following statements best describes the author's point of view?
   a. A cowboy's life is easy.
   b. Some people mistakenly believe that a cowboy's life is easy.
   c. More people should become cowboys.
   d. Cowboys do not get enough respect.

5. Based on the material that you have read about cattle drives, what problems on the trail might have led to the creation of this song? Give specific examples.

6. What do you think the lines, "It's whooping and yelling and driving the dogies" tells about cattle drives?

Thinking Critically

1. played key economic roles in cattle towns; pioneer women did much of the labor on farms essential to forging community bonds in every area of the West

2. positive—economic prosperity for thousands, establishment of colleges, development of the frontier; negative—destruction of animal species, mistreatment of American Indians and some immigrant groups

3. Chinese railroad workers—helped transform the West by building the Central Pacific Railroad; Mexican immigrants—played key parts in the mining industry; Mennonite settlers—brought new strains of wheat to the Great Plains; immigrants—helped turn the Great Plains into the nation's breadbasket.

Skills Workshop

1. d

2. less than 1,000

3. Students' answers will vary but might include an increased appreciation for wildlife or the growth of cattle ranching and domesticated food supplies.

4. b

5. Students' answers might include unpredictable livestock, cattle thieves, and bad weather.

6. Students' answers will vary but might include references to the sounds of the cattle drive.

Alternative Assessment

American History

Building Your Portfolio

Linking to Community
Mining, ranching, and farming continue to be important to the U.S. economy. Identify a person from your community who works in one of these fields. Then make a list of questions to use while interviewing this person. Conduct an interview to find out what his or her job is like today. When you finish the interview, share your results with the class.

🖃 internet connect

**Internet Activity: go.hrw.com
keyword: SA3 CF21**

Choose a topic on the West to:

● Learn the facts and mythology surrounding the Pony Express.

● Research Geronimo and other American Indian leaders and write biographies of their lives.

● Analyze the myths and realities of the West and the ways in which it shaped the United States.

LET'S GET STARTED!

As students enter the classroom, ask them to list reasons why people may move to another city or region of the country. *(Students' responses will vary but may include climate, family, or job opportunities.)* Ask students why many Americans moved to the West during the late 1800s. *(Students' answers will vary, but students may mention how the Homestead Act made westward movement more appealing or that farmers and ranchers were attracted by the availability of land.)* Explain to students that land availability and affordability were major attractions to many settlers seeking to escape population growth in the East. Mention that another factor influencing many people's decision to move westward was the possibility of mining gold and silver. Tell students that in these activities they will study maps and graphs that describe westward expansion as people sought economic opportunities in mining, ranching, and farming in this unit.

★ TEACH

Have students read the Connecting to Geography lesson. Choose one or more of the following activities to explore the Connecting to Geography content with students.

★ Citizenship

Mining. The Comstock Lode was a major mining site in north-western Nevada. In the late 1850s miners realized that the mine held silver ore. Because the ore was located deep under the ground, miners used square set timbering to brace tunnel walls as they dug deep into the rock. After 1863 many miners believed that the Comstock Lode had run dry, but new discoveries at depths of up to 3,000 feet below the surface yielded another $105 million of precious metals during the 1870s and early 1880s. Between 1860 and 1880 the Comstock Lode produced an estimated $300 million in gold and silver.

CRITICAL THINKING

Why did large companies do most of the mining at the Comstock Lode?

ANSWER: Mining at deep levels required the organization and financial backing of a large company.

SKILLS ANSWERS

1. gold and silver mines
2. Nome, Fairbanks, and Juneau in Alaska; Sacramento, California; Boise and Coeur d'Alene in Idaho; Helena, Montana; Boulder, Denver, and Cripple Creek in Colorado; Deadwood, South Dakota
3. mountainous terrain; in the Rocky Mountains, the Sierra Nevada Range, the Cascade Mountains, and the Alaska Range

Connecting to Geography

The Economy of the West

In the last half of the 1800s, great numbers of settlers followed the trails of earlier pioneers to the West. People moved west for new economic opportunities in farming, mining, and ranching.

Prospectors and miners came to California during the gold rush of 1849. Many of these settlers continued pursuing the dream of striking it rich. Cattle drives brought the ranching industry from Texas to the northern Great Plains. Growing numbers of farmers also came to the Plains to plant fields of wheat and corn.

Railroads helped bring many of these settlers west. The railroads also connected farmers, miners, and ranchers to markets in the rest of the United States. By 1890 so many people had settled in the West that the U.S. Census Bureau reported that the frontier had officially closed.

Western Mining

A mining boom in the late 1800s brought thousands of prospectors to the West. Successful strikes in western mining contributed to a huge increase in the amount of gold and silver produced in the United States.

The Mining Boom

Gold mining region | Silver mining region | Major lode

Geography Skills
Interpreting Thematic Maps

1. What types of mines surrounded Deadwood and Carson City?
2. **Environment and Society** What U.S. cities developed near gold-mining regions in the West?
3. **Comparing** In what type of terrain did most of the gold and silver strikes take place?

Mining tools

LEVEL 1: Organize students into small groups. Tell them to imagine that they are the owners of a major company. Because of company growth, they must find a location for a new plant. Ask the groups to compile a list of criteria that they consider important in the selection of a new site. *(Students' responses might include the following: the price of the building or land, ease of access, proximity to major highways, and so on.)* Compare the responses of each group and tell students that those deciding whether to move west had to consider all of their options about a new life in a new place.

ENGLISH LANGUAGE LEARNERS , COOPERATIVE LEARNING

ALL LEVELS: Remind students that westward expansion continued well into the 1900s. Ask students to create a sign that the real estate companies or land developers may have placed along railroad routes in the late 1800s to attract settlers to the West. Have students use information from the maps, notes, and graphs on pages 674–77 to determine the resources and opportunities that would have attracted the most settlers to the West. Encourage students to design their signs to attract a diverse population of miners, ranchers, and farmers. Provide students with a sheet of butcher paper and any additional art supplies they will need. Allow time for students to present their signs to the class. Have students vote on which sign they think would attract the most people to settle in the West. **ENGLISH LANGUAGE LEARNERS**

History Note 1

Individual prospectors found many of the richest gold and silver deposits in the West. Some prospectors became wealthy from their discoveries. However, the majority of the gold and silver produced was mined by corporations. Most of the profits from western mining were made by investors. They provided the money for heavy steam-powered machinery and equipment used in the mines.

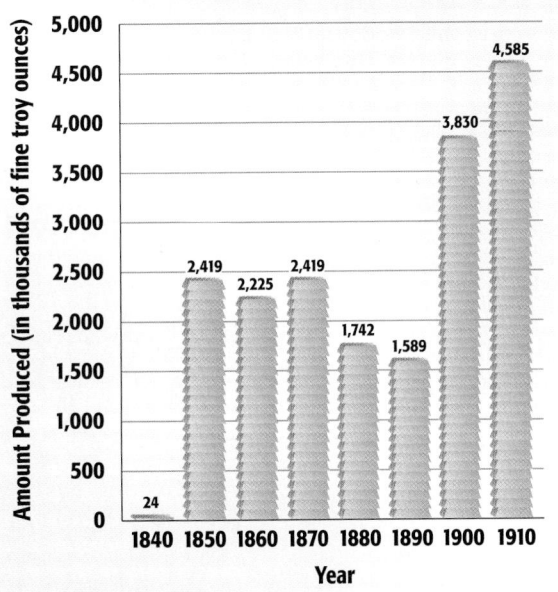

U.S. Gold Production, 1840–1910

Source: *Historical Statistics of the United States*

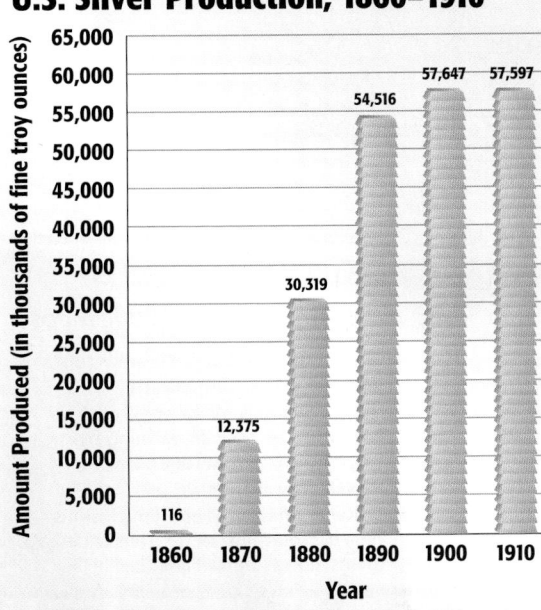

U.S. Silver Production, 1860–1910

Source: *Historical Statistics of the United States*

Geography Skills
Interpreting Bar Graphs

1. In what year shown on the graph was gold production the highest in the United States? Silver production?
2. Combine the information on these two bar graphs for the year 1860 into a pie graph comparing the amount of gold and silver produced that year.
3. **Drawing Inferences and Conclusions** What discovery would account for the dramatic increase in U.S. gold production between 1840 and 1850?

History Note 2

Gold and silver have been made into coins since around 700 B.C. These precious metals continue to be used as currency and to create jewelry and art. In addition, gold and silver are used in electronics and manufacturing. Most gold and silver mined in the United States today still comes from western states.

Science, Technology & Society

Hydraulic Mining. One mining technique used in the late 1800s involved aiming high-pressure water cannons at hills to rip away the soil in order to get at the precious metals within. The soil washed into rivers and streams, filling many of them with rocks and gravel. In the spring the clogged waterways flooded the fields of neighboring farms, often ruining the crops. The farmers protested, and the state of California began to regulate hydraulic mining in the 1890s.

CRITICAL THINKING

How might government regulation of hydraulic mining affect miner's work?

ANSWER: Students might suggest that it probably made mining much more difficult, in some cases impossible.

SKILLS ANSWERS

1. 1910, 1900
2. Students' pie graphs will vary.
3. the Comstock Lode

The Changing West

In the 1860s the U.S. government passed laws to encourage western settlement. The Homestead Act sold government-owned western lands at very low cost. The Pacific Railway Acts encouraged railroad construction. The acts gave railroad companies land for every mile of track they laid. By 1900 a network of railroad lines crossed the mountains and farmlands of the West.

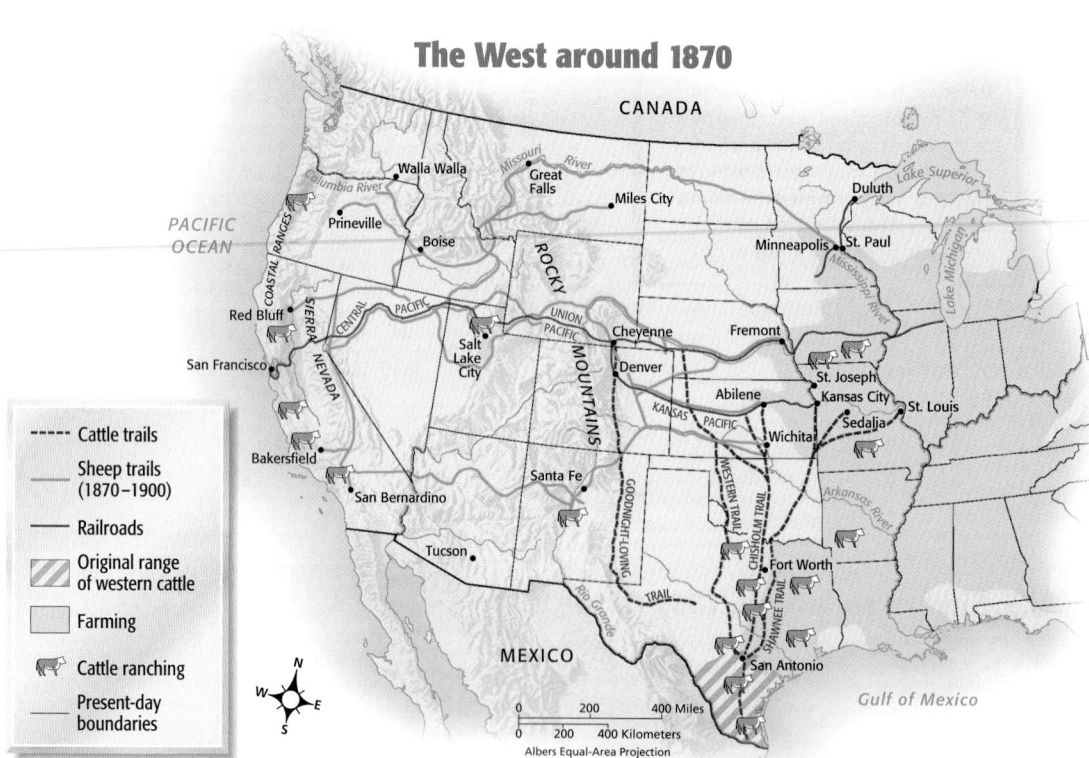

The West around 1870

History Note 3

Many of our images of the West are of cowboys and cattle drives. However, sheepherders also moved millions of sheep along a network of western trails. These experienced sheepherders were often immigrants from places like France, Mexico, and Spain. They helped move large western herds that sometimes numbered more than 10,000 sheep. One of the first great sheep drives in the West provided food for miners during the California Gold Rush.

Geography **Skills**
Interpreting Thematic Maps

1. What directions did cattle trails run? What about sheep trails?
2. **Human Systems** What areas of the West were focused on farming by around 1870? What regions were focused on ranching?
3. **Drawing Inferences and Conclusions** Why do you think cattle trails ended at towns along railroad lines?

Have students review the information in Connecting to Geography Unit 9. Then have students complete Geography and History Quiz 9.

★ RETEACH

Have students imagine that they are traveling to each of the western states discussed in this activity. Then have them create postcards from one of the states to send back home. Each postcard should identify the state the student is visiting and should include a brief description of the resources found there.

ENGLISH LANGUAGE LEARNERS

★ EXTEND

Remind students that westward expansion has significantly increased the West's population, although that growth has been unevenly dispersed throughout the western states. Have students use the library to find information about the population growth of each western state. Ask each student to create a chart that lists each western state, its current population, and its average number of people per square mile. Then ask each student to create another chart illustrating the same information from 100 years ago. Have students compare information from both charts. Lead a discussion about similarities and differences between the charts. **BLOCK SCHEDULING**

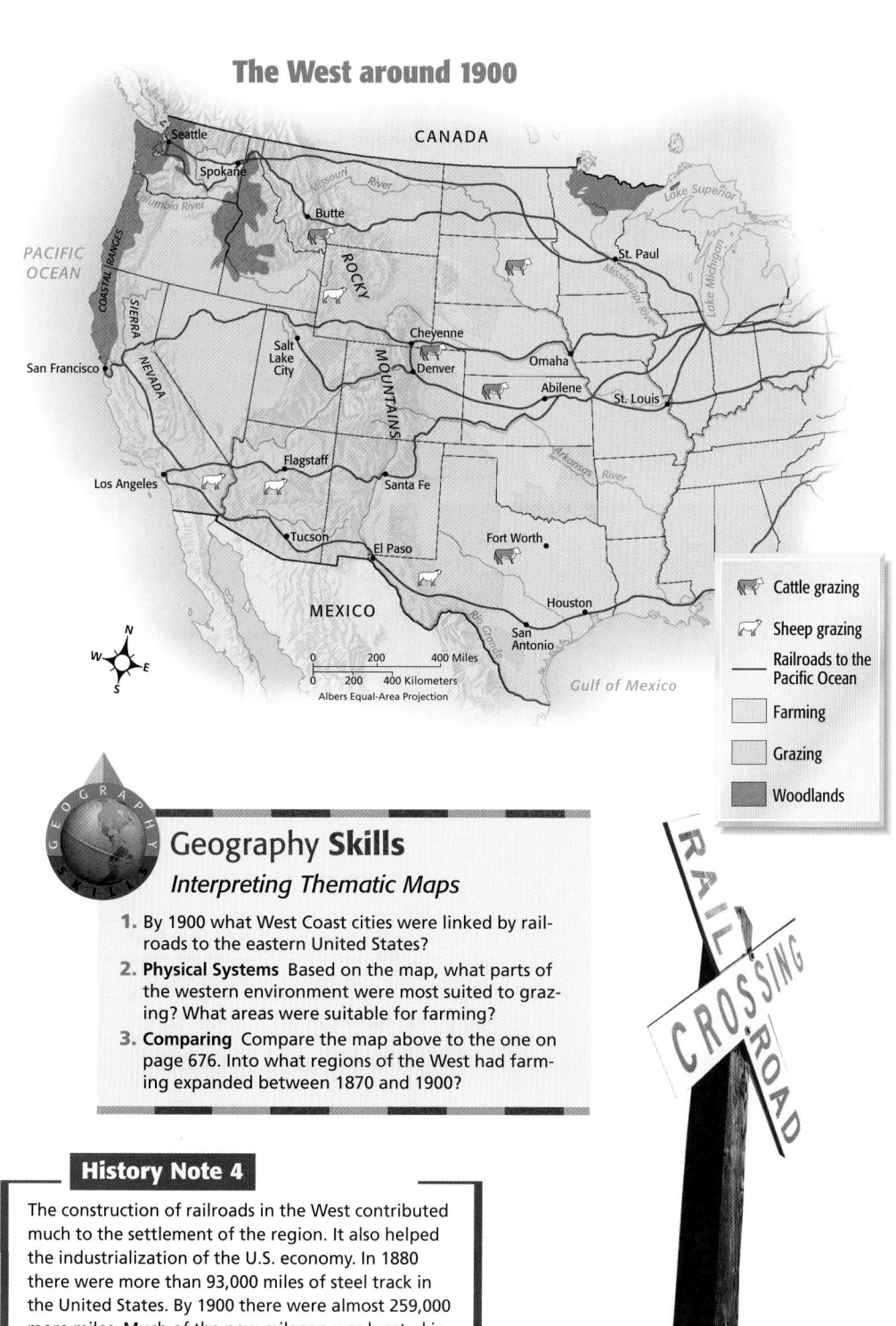

The West around 1900

Geography Skills
Interpreting Thematic Maps

1. By 1900 what West Coast cities were linked by railroads to the eastern United States?
2. **Physical Systems** Based on the map, what parts of the western environment were most suited to grazing? What areas were suitable for farming?
3. **Comparing** Compare the map above to the one on page 676. Into what regions of the West had farming expanded between 1870 and 1900?

History Note 4

The construction of railroads in the West contributed much to the settlement of the region. It also helped the industrialization of the U.S. economy. In 1880 there were more than 93,000 miles of steel track in the United States. By 1900 there were almost 259,000 more miles. Much of the new mileage was located in the rapidly growing West.

★ Economics

Building Railroads.
Because building railroads was expensive, Congress and many states passed measures to help businesses construct railroads in the West. Railroad companies received and used 188 million acres of free land in the form of grants from the federal and state governments. One company, the Northern Pacific, received nearly 40 million acres of land. In addition, Congress loaned the railroads from $16,000 to $48,000 per mile of track.

CRITICAL THINKING
Why did Congress give land to the railroads?

ANSWER: Students might suggest to encourage the rapid development of a useful, high-speed transportation network.

SKILLS ANSWERS
1. Los Angeles, San Francisco, Seattle
2. most of the area along and to the west of the Rocky Mountains as well as West Texas and the Upper Plains; 400 miles on either side of the Mississippi River, as well as river valleys in California, Washington, and Montana. Also include a small area between Denver and Cheyenne.
3. Farming had expanded to around the Rocky Mountains, the northern states, and along the West Coast.

★ TEACH

ALL LEVELS: Explain to students that the Internet offers a wealth of information and sometimes misinformation on many topics. Have students review the Social Studies Skills Workshop activity and use that information to build a mock Web page that explains how to use the Internet. Remind students to include links and other important features on their page. **ENGLISH LANGUAGE LEARNERS**

 ALL LEVELS: Organize the class into four groups. Have each group prepare a database comprised of information about each member of the group. For example, one group's database might be comprised of the number of cars the family owns, the color of the family cars, the number of pets in each family, the types of pets, and so on. Have volunteers present their group's databases to the class. **ENGLISH LANGUAGE LEARNERS , COOPERATIVE LEARNING**

USING THE INTERNET AND CREATING A DATABASE

Have students use the library or other resources to research the history of the population in their state. Then have students compile this information and create a database that could be incorporated into a Web site.

SKILLS ANSWERS

Students' databases will vary.

Social Studies Skills
WORKSHOP

Using the Internet and Creating a Database

There is a wealth of information on the Internet. However, it takes a careful approach to find accurate and useful information.

Using the Internet. There are many Web sites that concentrate on specific topics. Government sites such as the Library of Congress and the U.S. Census Bureau provide economic, historical, and political information. Other sites such as CNNfyi.com allow you to access up-to-the-minute news and information. If you are not sure which Web site might have the data you want, directories and search engines can help you search the Internet. Many Internet browsers include lists of such search tools. Whatever tool you use, reading its search tips files can help you search more efficiently.

Once you have found a Web site, you should determine whether the information it contains is reliable. Ask yourself the following questions:

- Is a well-respected organization sponsoring the site?

- Does the text contain any obvious mistakes?

- Has the Web site been updated recently, and are most of the page links active?

- Does the information appear biased?

Creating a Database. Much of the information available on the Internet is presented in database form. A database is a collection of information that is organized so that you can find the facts you need efficiently. You can also use the Internet to gather facts for creating your own database on a research topic.

Whatever information sources you use, you should follow some guidelines when creating a database.

- Give your database a clear title and use headings to identify the types of data it includes, such as dates, locations, or quantities. It is often useful to identify the source of your information as well.

- Make sure the information included under each heading follows a consistent format. For example, if your heading is STATES, it should not include data for a city.

Example

Most Populous States, 2000*		
State	**Population**	**Rank**
California	33,930,798	1
Florida	16,028,890	3
New York	19,004,973	4
Texas	20,903,994	2
*Based on Census 2000 figures		

Practicing the Skills

Search the Internet to find information on the U.S. economy. This could include information on employment, inflation, new jobs, or U.S. trade with foreign countries. Use this information to create a database that clearly displays the facts and figures about the economy that you have found.

LEVEL 2: Organize the class into groups. Ask groups to imagine that they are members of an abolition movement that has been given the task of implementing the recommendation plan devised in the problem-solving activity. Tell groups that they should create a tip sheet of action steps and answers to frequently asked questions to help those assigned the task of helping former slaves adjust to their freedom. Have volunteers present his or her group's tip sheets to the class.

 LEVEL 3: Ask students to imagine that they are a former slave adjusting to their new freedoms. Then have students write a series of diary entries explaining the problems he or she has encountered and the decisions that they have made in order to solve those problems.

History in Action

UNIT 9 SIMULATION

You Solve the Problem . . .

How Will You Help to Prepare Former Slaves for Freedom?

Complete the following activity in small cooperative groups. It is July 1865. You are on the Board of Directors of the Freedmen's Bureau. This agency was created by Congress to assist freed slaves and displaced white southerners after the Civil War. A subcommittee has been formed to plan how to prepare recently freed slaves for life after slavery. Your subcommittee will be presenting a recommendation to the rest of the Board of Directors. Follow these steps to solve your problem.

 **1. Gather Information.** Use your textbook and other resources to find information that might influence your plan of action for preparing the former slaves for freedom. Be sure to use what you learned from this unit's Skills Workshop on Using the Internet and Creating a Database to help you find an effective solution to the problem. You may want to divide different parts of the research among group members.

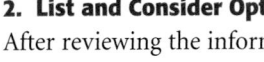 **2. List and Consider Options.** After reviewing the information you have gathered, list and consider the options you might recommend for successfully preparing former slaves for freedom. Your final solution to this problem may be easier to reach if you consider as many options as possible. Be sure to record your possible options for your presentation.

 3. Consider Advantages and Disadvantages. Now consider the advantages and disadvantages of taking each option. Ask yourselves questions like: "How can the former slaves make a living for themselves and their families?" Once you have considered the advantages and disadvantages, record them as notes for your presentation.

4. Choose, Implement, and Evaluate a Solution. After considering the advantages and disadvantages, you should plan and create a presentation. Be sure to make your proposal very clear. You will need to support your proposed methods of preparing slaves for freedom by including information you gathered and by explaining why you rejected other options. Your presentation needs to be visually appealing to the Board of Directors. When you are ready, decide which group members will make each part of the presentation, and then take your solution to the Board of Directors of the Freedmen's Bureau (the rest of the class). Good luck!

History in Action Tell students that they are pioneers in the 1800s. They are faced with the following problem-solving dilemma: After they move to the West, they must decide between becoming a sheepherder or a cattle rancher. Then have students create a pro v. con chart comparing the two lifestyles and then tell them to write a paragraph supporting the decision they ultimately make. Remind students that they should incorporate the problem-solving steps into their decision making process.

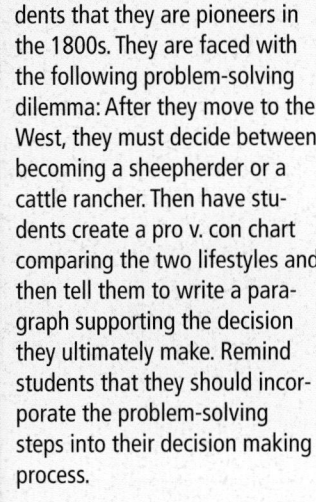

	Objectives	Pacing Guide	Reproducible Resources
SECTION 1: **Industrialization and the Progressive Era** (pp. 682–87)	★ Describe the changes in industry and business that took place in the late 1800s. ★ Explain the effects of industrialization on factory workers and farmers. ★ Analyze how progressives addressed the nation's social and political problems.	**Regular** 1 day **Block Scheduling** .5 day *Block Scheduling Handbook with Team Teaching Strategies, Chapter 22*	**RS** Guided Reading Strategy E.1 **PS** American History Political Cartoons 15: Urban Life; and 17: The Power of Trusts
SECTION 2: **World War I and Postwar America** (pp. 688–94)	★ Examine how U.S. foreign policy changed in the late 1800s and early 1900s. ★ Describe the technological and cultural changes that shaped life in the United States after World War I. ★ Analyze how President Franklin D. Roosevelt tried to solve the economic problems brought on by the Great Depression.	**Regular** 1.5 days **Block Scheduling** .5 day *Block Scheduling Handbook with Team Teaching Strategies, Chapter 22*	**RS** Guided Reading Strategy E.2 **PS** American History Political Cartoons 22: The Red Scare; and 24: FDR and the New Deal **E** Hands-On History Activity: A Snapshot of Your Community
SECTION 3: **World War II and the Cold War** (pp. 695–701)	★ Explain how the United States contributed to an Allied victory in World War II. ★ Identify how the Cold War influenced U.S. foreign policy. ★ Analyze what American society was like in the 1950s.	**Regular** 1.5 days **Block Scheduling** 1 day *Block Scheduling Handbook with Team Teaching Strategies, Chapter 22*	**RS** Guided Reading Strategy E.3 **PS** American History Political Cartoon 26: Brinkmanship **PS** Primary Source Reading Epilogue: The Path to the Atomic Bomb
SECTION 4: **Searching for Solutions** (pp. 702–06)	★ Describe the foreign-policy issues faced by Presidents Kennedy and Johnson while they were in office. ★ Define the achievements of the 1960s civil rights movement. ★ Identify the domestic challenges that the United States faced in the early 1970s.	**Regular** 1 day **Block Scheduling** .5 day *Block Scheduling Handbook with Team Teaching Strategies, Chapter 22*	**RS** Guided Reading Strategy E.4 **PS** American History Political Cartoons 28: The Vietnam War; and 29: Watergate **PS** Literature Reading Epilogue: The Autobiography of Malcolm X **E** Creative Teaching Strategy: Unfinished Story Alternatives
SECTION 5: **The Modern Era** (pp. 707–11)	★ Explain how the Cold War progressed in the 1980s. ★ Examine the legislative successes and failures of the Clinton administration. ★ Analyze how the United States took part in world affairs in the 1990s.	**Regular** 1 day **Block Scheduling** .5 day *Block Scheduling Handbook with Team Teaching Strategies, Chapter 22*	**RS** Guided Reading Strategy E.5 **PS** Biography Reading Epilogue: Madeleine Albright **SM** Geography Activity Epilogue: Nuclear Weapons in the 1990s **RS** Graphic Organizer Epilogue: A Century of War
SECTION 6: **September 11, 2001: A Day That Changed the World** (pp. 712–17)	★ Describe how the United States was attacked on September 11, 2001 and how Americans responded. ★ Explain how the events of September 11 affected the economy. ★ Evaluate the immediate steps American leaders took to find those responsible and to bring them to justice.		

Chapter Resource Key

PS	Primary Sources	**A**	Assessment	Music	
RS	Reading Support	**REV**	Review	Video	
IC	Interdisciplinary Connections	**ELL**	Reinforcement and English Language Learners	Internet	
E	Enrichment		Transparencies	Holt Presentation Maker Using Microsoft® PowerPoint®	
SM	Skills Mastery		CD-ROM		

 One-Stop Planner CD-ROM

See the *One-Stop Planner* for a complete list of additional resources for students and teachers

One-Stop Planner CD-ROM

It's easy to plan lessons, select resources, and print out materials for your students when you use the *One-Stop Planner CD-ROM with Test Generator.*

Technology Resources

 One-Stop Planner, Lesson E.1
 Everyday Life in America Transparency 18: Progressives and Children, Early 1900s
Exploring America's Past Video Segment: A New Beginning; Teacher's Guide, pp. 40–41
Holt Researcher: American History CD–ROM
Homework Practice Online
HRW Go site

 One-Stop Planner, Lesson E.2
 Linking Geography and History Transparency 15: The American Empire and Transparency 16: World War 1: The Western Front
 American Music Selection 21: "Talkin' Dust Bowl"
 Homework Practice Online
HRW Go site

 One-Stop Planner, Lesson E.3
 Linking Geography and History Transparency 20: Cold War Defenses
American History Interactive Maps CD–ROM: Living in the Cold War
Homework Practice Online

 One-Stop Planner, Lesson E.4
 Exploring America's Past Civics and Citizenship Skills Video Segment: The Citizen in Foreign Policy; Teacher's Guide, pp. 72–75
 Holt Researcher: American History CD–ROM
 Everyday Life in America Transparency 30: Protest during the Vietnam War
Homework Practice Online

 One-Stop Planner, Lesson E.5
 Exploring America's Past Video Segment: Modern America; Teacher's Guide, pp. 45–46
  CNN Presents America: Yesterday and Today, Beginnings to 1914 Segment: Eyes of the Presidency
 Homework Practice Online
HRW Go site

  CNN Presents : Yesterday and Today, September 11, 2001: A Turning Point in History

Reinforcement, Review, and Assessment
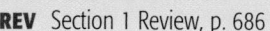

REV Section 1 Review, p. 686
A Daily Quiz E.1
ELL Main Idea Activity E.1
ELL English Audio Summary E.1
ELL Spanish Audio Summary E.1

REV Section 2 Review, p. 694
A Daily Quiz E.2
ELL Main Idea Activity E.2
ELL English Audio Summary E.2
ELL Spanish Audio Summary E.2

REV Section 3 Review, p. 701
A Daily Quiz E.3
ELL Main Idea Activity E.3
ELL English Audio Summary E.3
ELL Spanish Audio Summary E.3

REV Section 4 Review, p. 706
A Daily Quiz E.4
ELL Main Idea Activity E.4
ELL English Audio Summary E.4
ELL Spanish Audio Summary E.4

REV Section 5 Review, p. 710
A Daily Quiz E.5
ELL Main Idea Activity E.5
ELL English Audio Summary E.5
ELL Spanish Audio Summary E.5

REV Section 6 Review, p. 716

internet connect

HRW ONLINE RESOURCES
GO TO: go.hrw.com
Then type in a keyword.

TEACHER HOME PAGE
KEYWORD: SA3 Teacher

CHAPTER INTERNET ACTIVITIES
KEYWORD: SA3 Epilogue
Choose an activity to:
- create a model of the impact of technology on daily life
- analyze the Treaty of Versailles' role in creating future conflicts.
- learn about the changing role of women in the 1920s.
- write a biography on Ronald Reagan

CHAPTER ENRICHMENT LINKS
KEYWORD: SA3 CHEP

ONLINE ASSESSMENT
Homework Practice
KEYWORD: SA3 HPEP

Standardized Test Prep
KEYWORD: SA3 STPEP

Rubrics
KEYWORD: SS Rubrics

ONLINE MAPS, CHARTS, AND GRAPHS
KEYWORD: SA3 MCG
- Trench Warfare
- Weapons of World War I
- Attack on Pearl Harbor
- World War II Alliances
- Homes with Television Sets

CONTENT UPDATES
KEYWORD: SS Content Updates

HOLT PRESENTATION MAKER
KEYWORD: SA3 PPTEP

ONLINE READING SUPPORT
KEYWORD: SS Strategies

CURRENT EVENTS
KEYWORD: S3 Current Events

Meeting Individual Needs

Ability Levels

Level 1 Basic-level activities designed for all students encountering new material

Level 2 Intermediate-level activities designed for average students

Level 3 Challenging activities designed for honors and gifted-and-talented students

English Language Learners Activities that address the needs of students with Limited English Proficiency

Chapter Review and Assessment
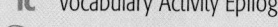

IC Vocabulary Activity Epilogue
 Global Skill Builder CD–ROM
HRW Go site
REV Epilogue Tutorial for Students, Parents, Mentors, and Peers
REV Epilogue Review, pp. 717–19
Epilogue Test Generator (on the One-Stop Planner)

A Epilogue Test (Form A or B)
A Alternative Assessment Handbook
A Epilogue Test for English Language Learners and Special-Needs Students

Section 1 Industrialization and the Progressive Era

Section 2 World War I and Postwar America

Section 3 World War II and the Cold War

Section 4 Searching for Solutions

Section 5 The Modern Era

Build on What You Know

If You Were There...

Ask students to answer the following question:

How would you react to the changes sweeping the nation?

Consider:

- the economic changes the nation is facing

- the cultural and social changes the nation is facing

You Be the Historian

What's Your Opinion?

To help students create their **Themes** Journal entries, provide the following examples of appropriate **agree/disagree** statements.

EXPLORING THE TIME LINE

GLOBAL EVENTS

internet connect

TOPIC: The Tet Offensive
GO TO: go.HRW.com
KEYWORD: SA3 CFEpilogue

Access the Internet through the HRW Go site to research the circumstances surrounding the Tet Offensive during the Vietnam War. Then create a pamphlet in which you explain how the Tet Offensive eroded American confidence in winning the war and how it reflected the different strategies of the United States and North Vietnam. Include information on political and military figures from each side.

 **Modern America**
(1877–Present)

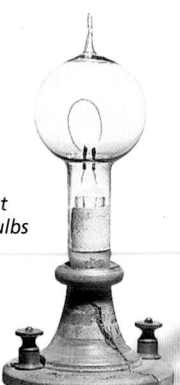

One of the first electric lightbulbs

A suffrage parade in 1912 in New York City

THE GRANGER COLLECTION, NEW YORK

UNITED STATES

1882 Thomas Alva Edison begins supplying electricity to buildings in New York City.

1920 The Nineteenth Amendment gives women the right to vote.

1929 The New York stock market crashes.

1941 A Japanese attack on the naval base at Pearl Harbor, Hawaii, on December 7 draws the United States into World War II.

| 1880 | 1900 | 1920 | 1940 |

WORLD

1898 Theodore Roosevelt leads a U.S. cavalry charge against Spanish forces in Cuba.

1917 The first U.S. troops arrive in Europe to fight in World War I.

1944 The Allies begin the D-Day invasion of France during World War II.

During World War I, millions of soldiers fought and died in trenches like this one.

Build on What You Know

After passing through the difficult years of the Civil War and Reconstruction, the United States changed in ways unimaginable to most Americans. New industrial growth transformed society and brought many new challenges. The nation also became a world power. Americans have helped shape many of the most important events of modern times.

Global Relations

Agree   Nations in conflict can resolve issues through warfare.

Disagree   Compromises and treaties have resolved many issues between nations in conflict.

Citizenship

Agree   A government should allow citizens to disagree with it.

Disagree   Citizens should support their government.

Economics

Agree   Global economic development is a responsibility of all nations.

Disagree   A nation should focus on promoting its own economic development without relying on other countries.

President George W. Bush greets the fire fighters while touring the rubble of the World Trade Center after the September 11 attack.

Neil Armstrong was the first man to walk on the Moon.

1947 President Harry S Truman declares that the United States will help any country fighting against communism.

1969 American astronaut Neil Armstrong becomes the first person to walk on the Moon.

2000 George W. Bush is elected president.

2001 On September 11, terrorists attack the World Trade Center and the Pentagon.

1960   1980   2000

1949 The United States, Great Britain, and 10 other countries form the North Atlantic Treaty Organization (NATO).

1968 The North Vietnamese launch the Tet Offensive but are driven back by U.S. troops.

1989 Germans tear down the Berlin Wall.

1991 The Soviet Union breaks apart.

1999 NATO forces begin air strikes against Yugoslavia in response to continued violence against ethnic Albanians living in the Yugoslav province of Kosovo.

People celebrating the fall of the Berlin Wall

If you were there . . .
How would you react to the changes sweeping the nation?

You Be the Historian

Themes Journal

What's Your Opinion? Do you **agree** or **disagree** with the following statements? Support your point of view in your journal.

- **Global Relations** An international conflict cannot be resolved without a war.
- **Citizenship** Citizens have a right to disagree with their government.
- **Economics** It is the responsibility of all countries to work with other countries to promote economic development.

★ Biography

Thomas Alva Edison.

One of the most noteworthy innovations of the modern age is the introduction of electricity as a power source. In 1882 Thomas Edison began supplying New York City with such power. For most people, this accomplishment alone would have been a life's work, but for Edison, it was just one of many great achievements. Edison's career, however, did not begin as an inventor. At the age of 12, Edison quit school and began working for the railroads. A few years late, Edison became an apprentice telegrapher. Initially, Edison had no problems as a telegrapher, in spite of a severe hearing loss. However, when telegraphs became equipped with a sounding key, Edison was at a disadvantage. He wanted to make telegraphic equipment that he could use even with his hearing disability. This desire sparked Edison's career as an inventor. By 1869 Edison had quit the telegraph business to embark on a life of inventing.

ACTIVITY: Have students use the library or other resources to discover other inventions attributed to Thomas Edison. Have students use standard grammar, spelling, sentence structure, and punctuation to write an encyclopedia entry of achievements based on their research.

Section 1

OBJECTIVES

- ★ Describe the changes in industry and business that took place in the late 1800s.
- ★ Explain the effects of industrialization on factory workers and farmers.
- ★ Analyze how progressives addressed the nation's social and political problems.

🔊 LET'S GET STARTED!

As students enter the classroom, ask them to identify problems that have arisen from the explosive growth of the Internet. List their replies on the chalkboard. *(Students' responses will vary but might include problems with Internet fraud or copyright infringement issues.)* Then ask students to explain which problems, if any, should be addressed by the U.S. government. Have students consider whether a governmental solution might create other unexpected problems. Allow ample time for students to explain their reasoning. Conclude by telling students that in Section 1 they will learn how the Second Industrial Revolution of the late 1800s created unanticipated, complex problems in American life and that people increasingly demanded that the government act to solve these problems.

Section 1

Industrialization and the Progressive Era

Read to Discover

1. What changes in industry and business took place in the late 1800s?
2. What effects did industrialization have on factory workers and farmers?
3. How did progressives address the nation's social and political problems?

WHY IT MATTERS TODAY

In the late 1800s business leaders drove the Second Industrial Revolution forward. Today computer technology has introduced a new generation of business leaders. Use CNNfyi.com or other **current events** sources to find out about some of these new business leaders. Record your findings in your journal.

Define

- progressives

Identify

- Second Industrial Revolution
- Bessemer process
- Sherman Antitrust Act
- Homestead strike
- Pullman strike
- Populist Party
- Seventeenth Amendment
- Eighteenth Amendment
- Nineteenth Amendment
- W. E. B. Du Bois
- Theodore Roosevelt
- Woodrow Wilson

The Story Continues

The Corliss steam engine was the most popular exhibit at the 1876 Centennial Exposition. It weighed 700 tons and towered 40 feet high. Millions of people came to view what author William Dean Howells called "an athlete of steel and iron." For many, the Corliss engine stood for the progress that modern machines made possible.

The Corliss engine ran all the equipment in the exposition's Machinery Hall.

★ The Second Industrial Revolution

During the late 1800s technological advances contributed to the **Second Industrial Revolution**. This revolution represented a period of enormous growth in U.S. manufacturing. As a result, the United States became the world's industrial leader by the mid-1890s.

Improved understanding of sciences such as chemistry and physics helped provide technological breakthroughs and improve daily life. New energy sources such as kerosene, gasoline, and electricity helped

★ **TEACH**

Have students read Section 1 and complete Guided Reading Strategies E.1. Choose one or more of the following activities to explore the section content with students. For further suggestions on block scheduling or team teaching, see the *Block Scheduling Handbook with Team Teaching Strategies*.

LEVEL 1: Have each student prepare a graphic organizer with two columns, one labeled *Social Reforms* and the other *Political Reforms*. Under each heading, have students list the following subheadings: *Achieved* and *Failed to Achieve*. Create a sample outline of the organizer on the chalkboard. Have students copy the chart and complete the organizer by entering progressives' attempts to address political and social problems. *(Students' organizers will vary but might include improvements in labor conditions, improvements in health conditions, or some of the many reform laws passed.)* When students have completed their organizers, call on volunteers to complete the organizer on the chalkboard.

ENGLISH LANGUAGE LEARNERS

---

power American industries and homes. Inventors put these power sources to work in exciting ways. The first practical motorcars ran on gasoline, and in 1903, inventors Orville and Wilbur Wright used a gasoline engine to power the world's first airplane flight. Electricity became a source of light and sound in the 1870s. Thomas Alva Edison invented an electric lightbulb in 1879 and helped build power stations to supply electricity to consumers. In 1876 Alexander Graham Bell developed the telephone to transmit the human voice over great distances. By 1900 there were almost 1.5 million telephones in America, linking many major cities.

Industry also benefited from improvements in steel production. The **Bessemer process**, developed by British inventor Henry Bessemer in the 1850s, produced steel faster and more cheaply than ever before. The increase in steel production helped feed the rapid growth of American railroads.

One of the most powerful men in the steel industry was Scottish immigrant Andrew Carnegie. Carnegie built a business empire using vertical integration—a business method in which a company controls all the steps in its manufacturing process. Carnegie owned all of the businesses needed to make steel: coal fields, iron mines, and steel mills. He was able to produce steel at much lower costs than his competitors—and in huge quantities. By 1900 Carnegie's plants produced more steel than all the mills in Great Britain put together. John D. Rockefeller was another influential business leader. Rockefeller's Standard Oil Company practiced horizontal integration—buying up all of the competing businesses in an industry. By 1880 he controlled some 90 percent of the U.S. oil-refining business.

Daily Life

Railroads Advances such as improved air brakes and Pullman sleeping cars made railroad travel safer and more comfortable. One group of businessmen heading west called their Pullman car "a beautiful . . . moving hotel." In addition, railroad owners like Cornelius Vanderbilt formed large companies, which made travel faster and more efficient. Railroads thus helped drive the economy while connecting the nation. The image here shows the Illinois Central Railroad connecting rural people to the rest of the world. What do the various images in the picture represent?

Science, Technology & Society

The Bessemer Process.

Two men—American William Kelly and Englishman Henry Bessemer—simultaneously developed ideas for improving steel manufacturing. Kelly and Bessemer both discovered that forcing air into molten iron would generate intense heat. This heat would burn the impurities out of the iron and create a high-quality steel. Bessemer actually built the machine that made possible the process bearing his name. The Bessemer process was first used in the United States in November 1864. The event occurred at a factory in Wyandotte, Michigan, which used the process in a furnace that weighed more than 2 tons.

📡 **internet** connect

TOPIC: Technology
GO TO: go.hrw.com
KEYWORD: SA3 CFEpilogue

ACTIVITY: Have students use the library or search the Internet through the HRW Go site to find information on ways technology has changed people's lives. Ask students to use standard grammar, spelling, and punctuation to write several paragraphs explaining whether technology has had positive or negative effects overall.

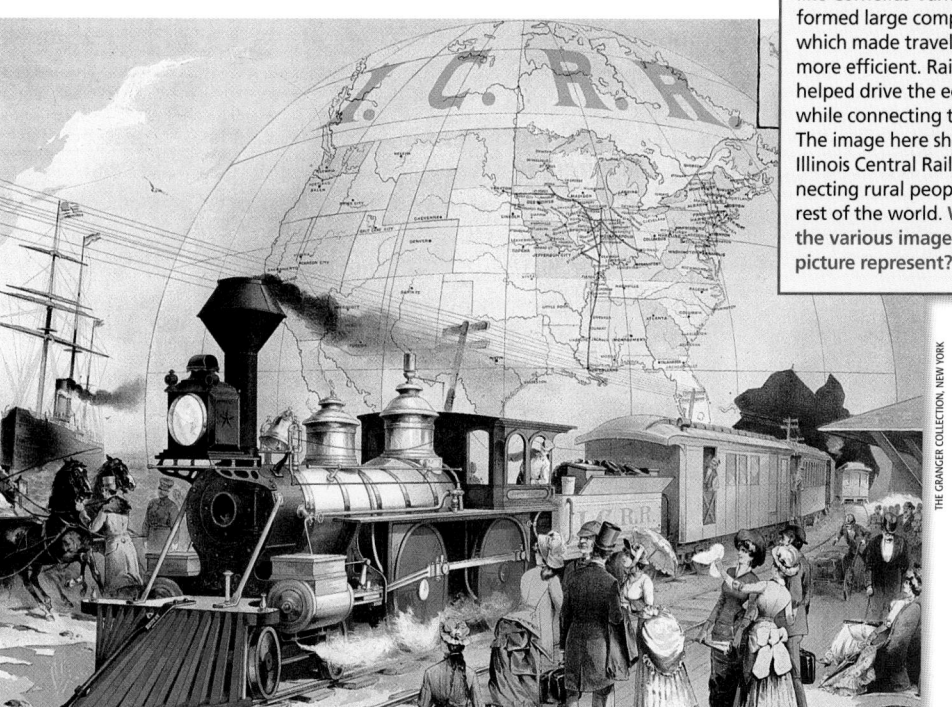

THE GRANGER COLLECTION, NEW YORK

ALL LEVELS: Copy the following graphic organizer onto the chalkboard, omitting the italicized answers. Have students complete the organizer to show the effects that industrialization had on factory workers and farmers.

ENGLISH LANGUAGE LEARNERS

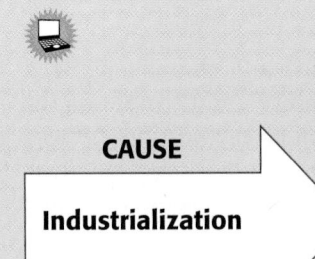

EFFECTS

CAUSE

Industrialization

Factory Workers
• *Factory workers took away jobs from skilled workers.*
• *Union members, seeking better pay and safer working conditions, went on strike.*

Farmers
• *Farmers formed organizations to seek equal economic benefits.*

Interpreting Political Cartoons

Trusts This magazine cover portrays large trusts showing off their economic power. **Why do you think the artist chose to depict trusts in this way?**

During the Second Industrial Revolution the U.S. government generally avoided interfering with business. The hope was that free enterprise would promote competition and improve economic growth. However, Rockefeller's methods drew criticism because he held a monopoly and formed a trust. A trust is a group of companies that share a board of directors. Some people felt that monopolies and trusts used unfair methods to get rid of competition and charge consumers higher prices. In 1890 Congress passed the **Sherman Antitrust Act**, which made monopolies and trusts that restricted free trade illegal. Because the law did not clearly define what a monopoly was, it was difficult for the government to make companies obey the law.

✔ **Reading Check: Summarizing** What technological and business innovations took place during the Second Industrial Revolution? new power sources; invention of airplane, Bessemer process, lightbulb, and telephone; horizontal and vertical integration

★ Industry and Agriculture

During the Second Industrial Revolution, factory owners hired fewer skilled workers. Instead, they used more machines that were run by unskilled workers. Millions of immigrants from southern and eastern Europe filled many of these new jobs. Labor unions opposed immigration because they feared that native-born workers would lose jobs.

Labor unions like the Knights of Labor and the American Federation of Labor (AFL) sometimes supported strikes in an effort to gain better pay and safer conditions for workers. The labor movement soon faced serious setbacks, however. In May 1886, workers were protesting in Chicago's Haymarket Square when a bomb went off, killing and wounding police officers. Without much evidence, the courts found eight protesters guilty of throwing the bomb. One of the eight was a union member. As a result, many people blamed labor unions for the violence at what became known as the Haymarket Riot.

Nonetheless, unions continued to strike. The **Homestead strike** began in June 1892 at a Carnegie steel mill in Homestead, Pennsylvania. Company leaders refused to let striking union members enter the mill. Workers responded by taking over the town. The strike ended after the state governor called out the militia to keep order.

In 1894 the government got involved in another labor fight. Railroad car manufacturer George Pullman had cut pay and fired some workers, so his employees went on strike. During the **Pullman strike** members of railroad unions refused to work on trains carrying Pullman cars. Their actions shut down most rail lines in the Midwest. The federal government ordered the workers to end their strike. The U.S. attorney general stated that the workers were blocking interstate trade, which violated the Sherman Antitrust Act. In this case, the government used the act to limit labor unions instead of big business. The government continued to take the side of big business for many years.

LEVEL 3: Have students write an article describing the responses of either business leaders, laborers, or farmers to changes in industry and business that took place in the late 1800s. Have students focus on business mergers, the forming of unions, farm cooperatives, and political organizations. When students have completed their articles, call on volunteers to present their articles to the class. Then point out to students that in all three cases, people formed groups to accomplish what none of them as individuals could achieve.

TEACHER TO TEACHER

Mary Beth Breshars of Fort Leonard Wood, Missouri, suggested the following activity:

LEVEL 3: Assign each student one invention or industry discussed in this section and have students use the text to research the topic's significance and describe the changes in industry and business that took place in the late 1800s. Then have students create drawings representing their assigned topics. Have students take turns presenting their drawings to the class.

From 1860 to 1900, the U.S. population more than doubled, reaching 76 million by 1900. In part to feed this growing population, the number of American farms tripled. Many farmers borrowed money to buy land and new machinery. However, more farms and larger crops led to overproduction, which led in turn to lower crop prices.

Farmers responded by forming associations as industrial workers had done. One of these groups, the National Grange, was founded in 1867. The purpose of the Grange was to allow farmers to buy and sell goods more effectively as a group. Unfortunately for farmers, most of these cooperatives failed. Farmers also formed a national political organization, the Farmers' Alliance. In 1892 the Alliance joined with labor and reform organizations to form the **Populist Party**. The Populist Party wanted government regulation of railroads. It also wanted the government to coin more silver money. Populists hoped this would put more money in circulation and help raise the prices of farm goods. Following the economic collapse known as the Panic of 1893, the Populists' calls for reform began gaining wider support. However, after its defeat in the 1896 presidential election, the Populist Party soon fell apart.

✔ **Reading Check: Comparing** How were industrial workers and farmers similar? They were similar because both formed organizations to try to improve their economic situations.

THE GRANGER COLLECTION, NEW YORK

The Grange hoped to improve the lives of small-scale farmers.

★ The Progressive Movement

Cities grew as rural residents and immigrants moved to them to find work. By 1900 about 40 percent of Americans lived in cities. Journalist Jacob Riis described the crowded living conditions of poor people in cities.

History Makers Speak
❝Nine lived in two rooms, one about ten feet square that served as parlor, bedroom, and eating room, the other a small hall room made into a kitchen.❞

—Jacob Riis, *How the Other Half Lives*

Progressives tried to address the problems caused by overcrowding in many U.S. cities.

★ CLOSE

Have each student select one individual discussed in this section who exemplifies the major changes that occurred in the nation and then write a brief summary of how the individual exemplifies the era. Once students have finished writing, call on volunteers to read their paragraphs and discuss the reasons for their selections. Finally, have students vote to determine which of the chosen individuals best exemplifies the era.

Suffrage supporters like this woman demanded action from political leaders.

Section 1 Review
ANSWERS

❶ Define
- progressives, p. 686

❷ Identify
- Second Industrial Revolution, p. 682
- Bessemer process, p. 683
- Sherman Antitrust Act, p. 684
- Homestead strike, p. 684
- Pullman strike, p. 684
- Populist Party, p. 685
- Seventeenth Amendment, p. 686
- Eighteenth Amendment, p. 686
- Nineteenth Amendment, p. 686
- W. E. B. Du Bois, p. 686
- Theodore Roosevelt, p. 687
- Woodrow Wilson, p. 687

❸ inventor—Thomas Alva Edison, Alexander Graham Bell, Bessemer; Work—electric lightbulb, the telephone, developed the Bessemer process; Importance—used by many people and industries, used for easier communication, made it faster and cheaper to produce steel; Businessperson—Andrew Carnegie, John D. Rockefeller; Work—used vertical integration in his steel business, used horizontal integration in his oil business; Importance—led to faster, more efficient rail travel, produced huge quantities of steel more cheaply than competitors, controlled some 90 percent of the U.S. oil-refining business; Social reformer—Jane Addams, Florence Kelley,

Research on the R⊙M

Free Find:
W. E. B. Du Bois
After reading about W. E. B. Du Bois on the **Holt Researcher CD–ROM**, write five interview questions that you might ask him. Then write the responses you think Du Bois might have given.

A group of reformers known as **progressives** tried to fix city problems. Many of these people were well-educated, middle-class professionals. College-educated women, who had few career choices in the late 1800s, often played an important part in the progressive movement as well.

Progressives helped citizens gain more political power. For example, they promoted the direct primary. This process let voters, not party leaders, choose candidates. In 1913 the **Seventeenth Amendment** was passed, which required the election of U.S. senators by a direct popular vote, rather than by state legislatures. In some states, citizens won the ability to propose new laws by signing petitions. Some states allowed citizens to vote on the removal of public leaders or on laws proposed by state or local governments.

Progressives also addressed social issues. They founded settlement houses—urban neighborhood centers that offered education and social activities. One example was Chicago's Hull House, begun by Jane Addams in 1889. Progressives also founded many new kindergartens and high schools. In addition, they worked to improve public health.

Reformer Florence Kelley was the head of the National Consumers' League. She led the progressive fight against child labor. The league also worked to set minimum wage laws and an eight-hour workday. Many states passed labor reform laws for women and children as a result of these efforts. New safety rules were also introduced after several tragic accidents. One of the worst accidents was the 1911 Triangle Shirtwaist Company fire in New York City, which killed some 140 workers, mostly women.

Some progressives worked for the temperance movement to outlaw or limit the drinking of alcohol. They believed that this would lower crime and poverty. The Woman's Christian Temperance Union (WCTU) helped pass the **Eighteenth Amendment** in 1919. This amendment made it illegal to produce or sell alcoholic beverages in the United States.

Women also fought for their political rights. In 1890 Elizabeth Cady Stanton and Susan B. Anthony founded the National American Woman Suffrage Association (NAWSA). In 1920 the work of the NAWSA and other women's rights groups finally led to the **Nineteenth Amendment**. This amendment gave women in the United States the right to vote.

White progressives often ignored issues such as racial discrimination. African Americans began to push for their own reforms. Journalist Ida B. Wells wrote articles exposing the lynching of African American men in the South. Booker T. Washington urged African Americans to start their own businesses and schools to improve their economic situation. Scholar **W. E. B. Du Bois** fought for equality for African Americans. Du Bois helped form the National Association for the Advancement of Colored People (NAACP) to stop racial inequality. Established in 1909, the group used the courts to attack discrimination.

✔ **Reading Check: Categorizing** List the reforms of the progressive movement, and under each reform list a group that supported it. political issues, NAWSA; social and labor issues, National Consumers' League; alcohol issues, WCTU; and racial issues, NAACP

★ The Progressive Presidents

Several presidents promoted progressive causes. President William McKinley won re-election in 1900. After his assassination in 1901, Vice President **Theodore Roosevelt** succeeded him as president. Roosevelt had strong progressive views. He proposed a policy called the Square Deal, promising to balance the interests of business, labor, and consumers for the public good. He won the presidential election of 1904, and in 1906 he signed into law the Pure Food and Drug Act. This act stopped the manufacture, sale, or transportation of mislabeled or impure food and drugs. Roosevelt also led a conservation movement to protect natural resources. He founded many national parks during his presidency.

Roosevelt helped his former cabinet member William Howard Taft win the presidency in 1908. Roosevelt did not like Taft's cautious reform policies, however, so he formed the Progressive Party. Roosevelt and his Progressive Party challenged Taft in the 1912 presidential election. Both candidates lost to **Woodrow Wilson**, a progressive Democrat. President Wilson and Congress worked together to pass strong reform laws. The Federal Reserve Act provided a federal banking system to help control the economy. The Clayton Antitrust Act of 1914 strengthened federal laws against monopolies. Wilson also favored child labor reform and lower tariffs. Wilson gained popular support because of his reforms, and won re-election in 1916.

Roosevelt's Progressive Party got the nickname the Bull Moose Party after Roosevelt told a group of supporters that he felt "as strong as a bull moose."

✔ **Reading Check: Finding the Main Idea** What key reforms were passed during the administrations of Presidents Roosevelt and Wilson? See text above for reforms.

Section 1 Review

 go. hrw .com **Homework Practice Online**

keyword: SA3 HPE

① **Define and explain:**
• progressives

② **Identify and explain:**
• Second Industrial Revolution
• Bessemer process
• Sherman Antitrust Act
• Homestead strike
• Pullman strike
• Populist Party
• Seventeenth Amendment
• Eighteenth Amendment
• Nineteenth Amendment
• W. E. B. Du Bois
• Theodore Roosevelt
• Woodrow Wilson

③ **Supporting a Point of View** Copy the chart below. Use it to list five people who were important during the Second Industrial Revolution and the Progressive Era. Then use it to explain why you believe each person listed was important.

Person	Work	Importance
Inventor		
Businessperson		
Social reformer		
Civil rights reformer		
Progressive president		

④ **Finding the Main Idea**
a. How did American industry and business change as a result of the Second Industrial Revolution?

b. How did the lives of industrial workers and farmers change as a result of the Second Industrial Revolution?

⑤ **Writing and Critical Thinking**
Summarizing Imagine that you are a journalist writing about progressive reforms. Write a newspaper article that tells about the key leaders and reforms of the Progressive Era.

Consider the following:
• political reforms
• urban and industrial conditions and reforms
• issues of equality

Section 2

OBJECTIVES

⭐ Examine how U.S. foreign policy changed in the late 1800s and early 1900s.

⭐ Describe the technological and cultural changes that shaped life in the United States after World War I.

⭐ Analyze how President Franklin D. Roosevelt tried to solve the economic problems brought on by the Great Depression.

LET'S GET STARTED!

Write the following statement on the chalkboard: *Identify elements of "the Roaring Twenties" and describe what the expression means.* As students enter the classroom, have them answer the statement. *(Students' responses will vary but might include flappers, prohibition, and the Great Depression.)* On the chalkboard, list each item under one of the following headings: *Prosperity* or *Depression.* Finally, tell students that in Section 2 they will learn about the United States during World War I, the prosperous 1920s, and the economic hard times of the depression.

SECTION 2 RESOURCES

REPRODUCIBLE

▶ Guided Reading Strategy E.2

▶ American History Political Cartoon 22: The Red Scare; and 24: FDR and the New Deal

TECHNOLOGY

▶ One-Stop Planner, Lesson E.2

▶ Linking Geography and History Transparency 15: The American Empire and Transparency 16: World War 1: The Western Front

▶ American Music Selection 21: "Talkin' Dust Bowl"

▶ Homework Practice Online

▶ HRW Go site

REINFORCEMENT, REVIEW, AND ASSESSMENT

▶ Section 2 Review, p. 694

▶ Daily Quiz E.2

▶ Main Idea Activity E.2

▶ English Audio Summary E.2

▶ Spanish Audio Summary E.2

Section 2

World War I and Postwar America

Read to Discover

1. How did U.S. foreign policy change in the late 1800s and early 1900s?
2. What technological and cultural changes shaped life in the United States after World War I?
3. How did President Franklin D. Roosevelt try to solve the economic problems brought on by the Great Depression?

WHY IT MATTERS TODAY

The United States still plays an important role in settling international conflicts. Use CNN**fyi**.com or other **current events** sources to find out about some of these conflicts and where they take place. Record your findings in your journal.

Define

- imperialism
- isolationism
- nationalism
- prohibition

Identify

- Panama Canal
- Treaty of Versailles
- Red Scare
- Jazz Age
- Harlem Renaissance
- Great Depression
- Franklin D. Roosevelt
- New Deal
- Social Security Act

THE GRANGER COLLECTION, NEW YORK

An American eagle spreads its wings over Latin America and the Pacific Ocean in this political cartoon.

The Story Continues

In 1898 Albert J. Beveridge of Indiana was running for the Senate. During his campaign Beveridge argued for greater American influence on the rest of the world. He stated, "If England can govern foreign lands, so can America." In the past, the United States had expanded only across the North American continent. However, more and more Americans began to look overseas for new lands.

⭐ The United States and the World

By the late 1800s many European countries practiced **imperialism**—a policy by which a nation creates an empire by conquering other countries or colonizing new lands. By 1914, European countries controlled much of Africa and Southeast Asia. They gained new sources of raw materials and new markets for selling goods. Many Europeans also viewed their colonies as a reason for national pride.

☆ **TEACH**

Have students read Section 2 and complete Guided Reading Strategies E.2. Choose one or more of the following activities to explore the section content with students. For further suggestions on block scheduling or team teaching, see the *Block Scheduling Handbook with Team Teaching Strategies.*

LEVEL 1: Supply each student with an outline map of the world and a list of key places dealing with changing U.S. foreign policy. Have each student prepare an annotated map that accurately locates each place on the list and that briefly explains its relevance to changing U.S. foreign policy. *(Students' maps should reflect the U.S. involvement in the Spanish-American War and World War I, the building of the Panama Canal, and U.S. involvement in Mexico.)* After students have finished their maps, display their work around the classroom. Finally, lead a discussion on how U.S. foreign policy changed in the late 1800's, and the signs indicating this change.
ENGLISH LANGUAGE LEARNERS

In the past, the United States had practiced **isolationism**—avoiding involvement in the affairs of other nations. However, many Americans began to think that expansion was needed to keep the nation's economy strong. In 1867 the United States bought Alaska from Russia, adding some 600,000 square miles to the country. Then in 1898 the United States took possession of Hawaii. The United States also traded with Japan and China.

In addition, the United States increased its involvement in Latin America. In 1895 Cuba revolted against Spanish rule. The Cubans' struggle gained the sympathy of Americans, while U.S. journalists accused the Spanish of terrible atrocities. When the U.S. battleship *Maine* exploded in the Cuban port of Havana in February 1898, many Americans blamed Spain. In mid-April the United States and Spain went to war. In addition to invading Cuba, U.S. forces swiftly overwhelmed Spanish defenders in the Philippine Islands and Puerto Rico. The fighting was over in just four months. The peace treaty placed Cuba, the Philippines, and Puerto Rico under U.S. control. Cuba became independent, while the other areas became U.S. territories.

At the urging of President Theodore Roosevelt, in 1903 the United States signed a treaty to build the **Panama Canal** across the Isthmus of Panama. The canal was finished in 1914, connecting the Atlantic and Pacific Oceans. Roosevelt further increased U.S. involvement in Latin America when he issued the Roosevelt Corollary to the Monroe Doctrine in 1904. He said that the United States would serve as "an international police power" to protect its interests in Latin America.

President Woodrow Wilson faced a foreign-policy crisis when Mexican revolutionaries overthrew that nation's dictator in 1911. American business interests and political stability in the area both were threatened. Despite several confrontations, the two countries avoided war. But the continuing political problems in Mexico encouraged nearly 240,000 Mexicans to come to the United States between 1910 and 1920.

✔ **Reading Check: Summarizing** How did U.S. foreign policy change in the late 1800s and early 1900s? The United States stopped following a policy of isolationism and became more involved in foreign affairs.

★ Geography

Nicaragua. Many members of Congress favored a canal that would cut through Nicaragua. Philippe Bunau-Varilla , an engineer for the French company initially contracted to build the canal, wanted a route through Panama. A volcano then erupted in the Caribbean, destroying a city and killing nearly 30,000 people. Following this disastrous event, Bunau-Varilla sent each U.S. senator a postage stamp picturing one of Nicaragua's many active volcanoes—one of which was located within 100 miles of the canal site that many senators favored. Congress soon came to the decision that Panama was the better location for the canal.

CRITICAL THINKING

Why would a stamp of a volcano in Nicaragua affect senators' opinions about that region as a canal site?

ANSWER: Students might mention that the stamp called attention to the potential danger that Nicaragua's volcanoes posed to a canal built in that area.

Interpreting the Visual Record

The Spanish-American War *The Rough Riders and the 9th and 10th Cavalries fight to capture an important position in Santiago, Cuba.* **How does this image show the deadliness of the fighting?**

Technology Resources

Linking Geography and History Transparency 15: The American Empire

Visual Record Answer

Students might suggest it shows close combat as well as the dead lying among the chaos.

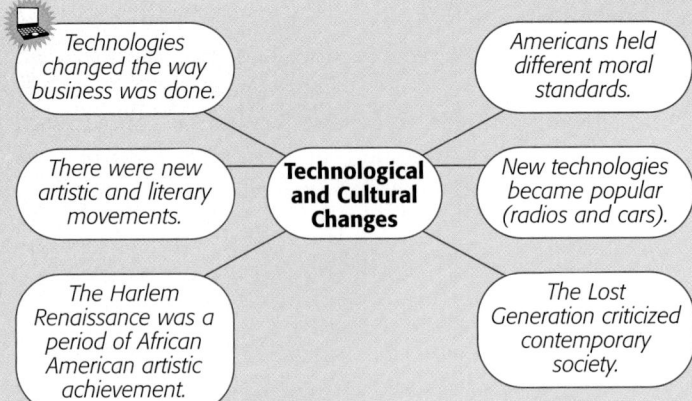

Technologies changed the way business was done.

Americans held different moral standards.

There were new artistic and literary movements.

Technological and Cultural Changes

New technologies became popular (radios and cars).

The Harlem Renaissance was a period of African American artistic achievement.

The Lost Generation criticized contemporary society.

★ Culture

African American Officers.
Many African Americans faced discrimination as they attempted to establish military careers during World War I. Although African Americans made up 13 percent of the army's enlisted personnel, they were only 1 percent of the officer corps. African Americans with college degrees hoped to receive commissions. However, the army refused to integrate the officer candidate schools. A separate school was eventually established, and some 1,100 African Americans received commissions. However, most were prevented from rising above the rank of captain, regardless of their performance.

CRITICAL THINKING

How might racial discrimination have hurt the effectiveness of the armed forces?

ANSWER: Students may suggest that racial discrimination might have created divisions within the army.

MAP ANSWERS
Marne, Somme, Verdun, Ieper

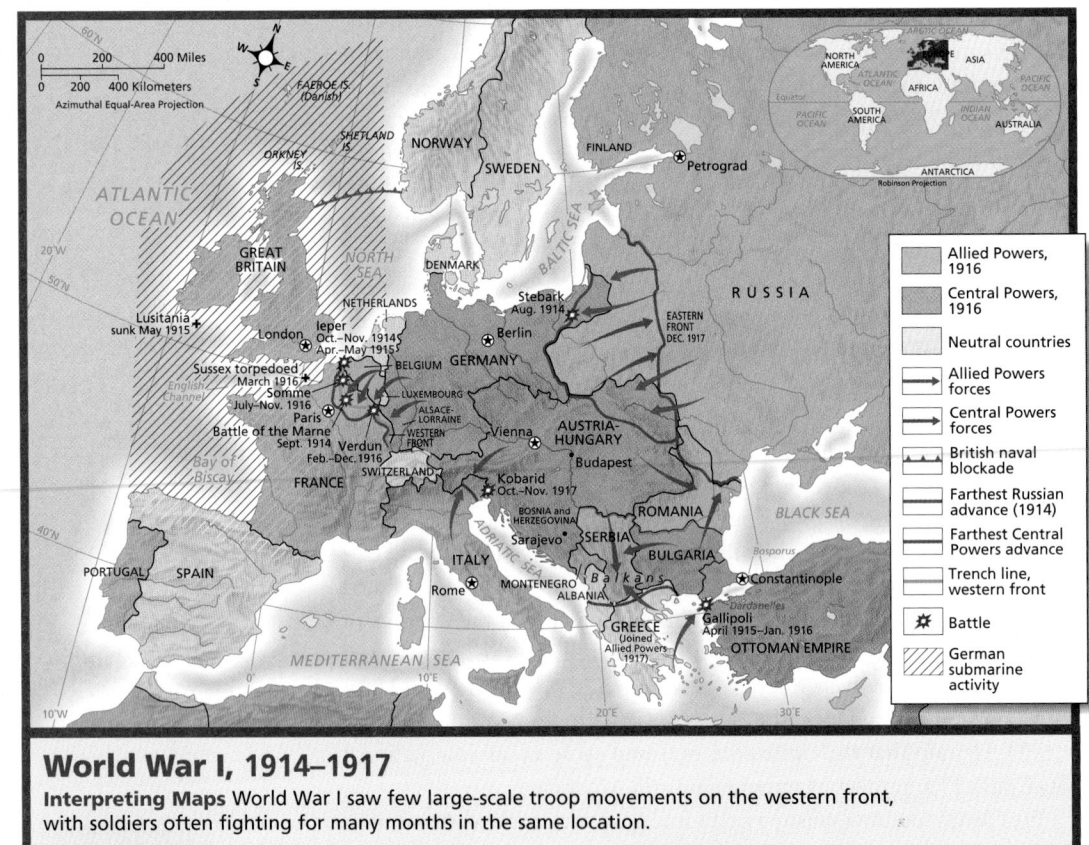

World War I, 1914–1917

Interpreting Maps World War I saw few large-scale troop movements on the western front, with soldiers often fighting for many months in the same location.

Skills Assessment Places and Regions What battles took place along the western front trench lines?

The French awarded the Croix de Guerre to Allied soldiers for bravery.

★ World War I

In the early 1900s **nationalism**—a feeling that one's nation or culture is superior to others—increased, and national tensions rose in Europe. In 1914 an assassin from Serbia killed Archduke Franz Ferdinand of Austria-Hungary and his wife. Austria-Hungary then declared war on Serbia. Within a few days a system of alliances had drawn most of the other major European nations into war. Austria-Hungary, Germany, Bulgaria, and the Ottoman Empire formed the Central Powers. They were opposed by the Allied Powers, which included France, Britain, Italy, and Russia.

World War I was unlike any other war that had ever been fought. Machine guns, poison gas, and tanks all were used for the first time. The opposing armies dug hundreds of miles of trenches, or ditches, for protection. The result was that neither side could overcome the other's defenses.

President Wilson wanted to help end the war peacefully, but neither side would negotiate. Then Germany attacked American merchant ships

LEVEL 2: Assign each student one of the following topics: causes of the Great Depression or how Franklin Roosevelt addressed the economic problems caused by the depression. Have each student use material from the section to write a detailed outline of the assigned topic. When students are finished, assign each a partner who has written on the other topic. Then ask each pair to discuss how the actions taken by Roosevelt addressed each of the causes of the Great Depression and the problems it created. *(Students' discussions should reflect New Deal programs and policies.)* Finally, call on volunteers to share their discussion with the class. **COOPERATIVE LEARNING**

LEVEL 3: Lead a class discussion on how U.S. foreign policy changed and what the signs of this change were. Have students read material from the section on the debate between imperialism and isolationism. Then have students weigh the pros and cons of each policy and write essays explaining which policy they would have supported during the early 1900s. When students have finished, call on volunteers to read their essays to the class.

---

with its submarines. On April 2, 1917, Wilson announced that "the world must be made safe for democracy." Four days later, Congress declared war on Germany.

To raise troops, Congress passed the Selective Service Act. This law required men between the ages of 18 and 45 to sign up for the draft. To raise money for the war, Congress increased taxes and sold war bonds. More than 4.5 million Americans served in the armed forces during World War I. Some 1 million women entered the labor force as soldiers headed for the war. Many Mexican Americans and African Americans also moved north to work in wartime industries. U.S. forces began arriving in France in June 1917. Their appearance turned the tide against Germany, which surrendered on November 11, 1918.

More than 8 million soldiers died in the war. Many of Europe's farms and factories were destroyed. President Wilson had a plan, called the Fourteen Points, to avoid future wars. One of these points called for the establishment of a League of Nations, an international organization dedicated to preventing future conflicts. The **Treaty of Versailles** that ended World War I included the creation of the League. The treaty also required Germany to pay billions of dollars for the costs and damages of war. The U.S. Congress, however, refused to join the League and rejected the treaty.

✔ **Reading Check: Sequencing** List the dates and details of the major events of World War I in the order that they took place. See text above for specific dates and events.

Leaders from Italy, Great Britain, France, and the United States met to draft the Treaty of Versailles, which ended World War I and created the League of Nations.

★ The Postwar Economy

After World War I, American society changed drastically. Soldiers returned home, and soon there were too many workers for too few jobs. As workers saw their incomes drop, many went on strike. Some Americans thought these strikes were evidence that Communists were trying to take over the country. Communists had successfully revolted in Russia in 1917. This led to a wave of anticommunist fear called the **Red Scare**. Although the Red Scare eventually died down, a distrust of foreigners remained.

In the 1920s the economy began to improve under Republican presidents Warren G. Harding and Calvin Coolidge. Both men were strong supporters of business. Automobile manufacturer Henry Ford helped the country's economy. He produced affordable cars by using the moving assembly line to make his factories more efficient. The automobile industry became the biggest business in the country.

The popularity of the car changed the landscape of the United States. More people moved to the suburbs and drove to their jobs in the cities.

Global Relations

Treaty of Versailles.
President Woodrow Wilson hoped that the Treaty of Versailles would heal the wounds of war and guarantee world peace. However, many Germans resented a number of the final treaty's provisions. Under the treaty, Germany lost its colonies, while the Allies were permitted to keep theirs. The treaty also contained provisions intended to humiliate the Germans. For example, one article forced the German government to take responsibility for starting the war.

📶 **internet** connect

TOPIC: The Treaty of Versailles
GO TO: go.hrw.com
KEYWORD: SA3 CFEpilogue

ACTIVITY: Have students use the library or search the Internet through the HRW Go site to find information on the Treaty of Versailles. Ask students to create a chart identifying elements of the treaty that might have contributed to future conflicts and what those conflicts might have been.

By 1927 some 15 million Ford Model Ts had been produced.

LEVEL 3: Organize the class into groups and assign each group one of the following individuals or groups: the American Liberty League, Father Charles E. Coughlin, Herbert Hoover, Huey Long, or Franklin D. Roosevelt. Have each group research the individual's or group's proposal for ending the depression. When the groups are finished, hold a round-table discussion in which groups present their assigned person's or group's plan to solve the economic problems brought on by the Great Depression. **COOPERATIVE LEARNING**

SPOTLIGHT
on the Progressive Era

Have each student select one individual discussed in this section. Then have students conduct research to obtain information on their chosen person. Ask students to write an encyclopedia entry about how that individual represents the era covered in this section. When students have finished, call on volunteers to read their paragraphs aloud and discuss the reason for their selections. Finally, have students vote to determine which of the chosen individuals best illustrates the period discussed in this section. **BLOCK SCHEDULING**

During the 1920s, young women known as flappers challenged traditional modes of dress and behavior.

Many businesses moved to the outskirts of towns, where real estate was cheaper. The automobile industry also changed the way business was done in America and abroad. Other industries copied its manufacturing and advertising methods. More products were marketed using magazines and radio advertising to encourage people to buy goods based on style.

✔ **Reading Check: Analyzing Information** How did manufacturing and marketing change in the 1920s? The assembly line made mass production cheaper. New media encouraged consumer spending.

⭐ Changes in Society

The 1920s was also a time of clashing ideals. In 1919 Congress passed the Eighteenth Amendment, calling for **prohibition.** This law banned the manufacture, sale, and distribution of alcoholic beverages. Many Americans ignored the law, and organized crime grew as gangsters supplied illegal liquor. Problems such as these led to the Twenty-first Amendment, which ended prohibition in 1933.

For many Americans, however, the 1920s was a time of fun. People enjoyed the economic boom and more free time. They listened to music and sports on the radio, and movies gained in popularity. By 1927 there were some 17,000 movie theaters in the United States. That year the first talkie—a movie with sound—appeared. Musicians and writers also made important cultural contributions. The 1920s is often known as the **Jazz Age** because of the popularity of jazz music, with its roots in the African American culture. As African Americans moved to northern cities, they brought jazz to white audiences. Harlem, a neighborhood in New York City, became the center of African American cultural life.

This period of African American artistic achievement was called the **Harlem Renaissance.** Writer and artist Elton Fax described Harlem's appeal to African Americans.

Performers such as blues singer Bessie Smith (right) and jazz musician Louis Armstrong (left) were part of the Harlem Renaissance.

History Makers Speak ❝Harlem epitomized [symbolized] a kind of freedom that we did not know: 'Once I get to Harlem, I won't need to worry about anything. Nobody's gonna bother me in Harlem.'❞

—Elton Fax, quoted in *You Must Remember This,* by Jeff Kisseloff

Poets such as Langston Hughes and Countee Cullen showed the pride that many African Americans felt for their cultural heritage.

Another group, known as the Lost Generation, included writers such as Ernest Hemingway and F. Scott Fitzgerald who criticized the shallow nature of modern American society. Overall, however, the period often referred to as the Roaring Twenties displayed Americans' positive feelings about the future.

✔ **Reading Check: Summarizing** What were the major cultural changes of the 1920s? prohibition, jazz music, Harlem Renaissance, new styles in literature, movies

★ The Great Depression

The rapid growth of the stock market fueled the economic success of the 1920s. Stock prices rose to an all-time high in September 1929. Then prices began to go down. In October 1929, nervous investors rushed to sell their stocks. Their panic caused a crash in stock values. By mid-November losses totaled about $30 billion. The stock market collapse also led to a major banking crisis. Banks began to fail, causing people across the country to lose their savings.

In the months after the crash, manufacturers cut back production and fired thousands of workers. By 1933 unemployment had risen to about 25 percent. Everywhere, people were hurt by the serious economic downturn known as the **Great Depression**. Although it began with the stock market crash, the depression touched all parts of American life. The Great Depression also affected countries throughout the world.

In the United States some people were forced to live on the streets. Unemployed people in cities formed long lines each day at soup kitchens to get free food. African Americans, Mexican Americans, and women were among the hardest hit. They were often the last employees to be hired and the first to be fired.

A lack of rain in the southern Great Plains made the situation worse for farmers in the early 1930s. Winds blew away the dry topsoil in huge clouds of dust. The area became known as the Dust Bowl. Unable to grow crops, many farmers headed west, hoping to find a better life in California. However, most only found jobs as migrant workers.

To help Americans, President Herbert Hoover cut taxes and bought farmers' extra crops. He hired people for public construction projects. However, Hoover did not believe that the government should provide direct aid. He would not give Americans food, money, or shelter. Most suffering Americans saw Hoover's actions as a sign that he did not care about their difficulties.

✔ **Reading Check: Identifying Cause and Effect** What started the Great Depression in the United States, and what effects did it have on Americans? The stock market crash started the Great Depression. Many Americans lost their jobs and their savings. Some lived on the street and did not get enough to eat.

★ The New Deal

Democrat **Franklin D. Roosevelt** won the 1932 presidential election. At his inauguration he spoke of his hopes for the future.

History Makers Speak ❝This is . . . the time to speak the truth . . . frankly [honestly] and boldly. . . . This great nation will . . . revive [recover], and will prosper [succeed]. . . . The only thing we have to fear is fear itself.❞

—Franklin D. Roosevelt, quoted in *The Annals of America*

Franklin D. Roosevelt
(1882–1945)

Franklin D. Roosevelt was born into a wealthy family in 1882. Roosevelt served in the New York legislature and as assistant secretary of the navy. In 1920 he was the Democratic vice presidential candidate. Although he was popular and intelligent, Roosevelt was not considered to be a strong leader.

Roosevelt's life changed dramatically when he suffered an attack of polio. The disease left him paralyzed in both legs. He learned to move again with the help of leg braces. He then re-entered politics, enjoying great success. Roosevelt's private battle with polio made him more compassionate and helped give him the strength to lead the nation during great crises. What event changed Roosevelt's life?

Analyzing Primary Sources
Identifying Points of View According to Roosevelt, what was most likely to keep the United States from economic recovery? fear caused by the depression

★ REVIEW AND ASSESS

Have students complete the **Section 2 Review** on p. 694. Then have them complete **Daily Quiz E.2**. As **Alternative Assessment**, you may want to use the changes after World War I organizer or the foreign policy map activities in this section's lessons.

★ RETEACH

Have students complete **Main Idea Activity for English Language Learners and Special-Needs Students E.2**. Then ask each student to write three facts pertaining to each of the section's Reading Check questions. Have students choose partners

and combine their information to create an answer to each question. **ENGLISH LANGUAGE LEARNERS , COOPERATIVE LEARNING**

★ EXTEND

Have each student use the library and other resources to find information on one piece of legislation or organization that was created as part of the New Deal. Ask students to research the history and effects of the legislation or organization. Also ask them to create annotated time lines describing important events in the history of the legislation or organization. Finally, call on volunteers to share information from their time lines with the class. **BLOCK SCHEDULING**

This magazine cover shows a happy Franklin D. Roosevelt riding to his inauguration next to the glum Herbert Hoover.

Roosevelt's plan for improving the economy was called the **New Deal**. During the first three months of his administration in 1933, Congress passed many New Deal proposals. One of Roosevelt's first acts was to close unsound banks. Congress also established the Federal Deposit Insurance Corporation (FDIC), which insured a person's bank deposits up to $5,000. In addition, Congress later passed laws to help business and industry, such as the National Industrial Recovery Act.

Roosevelt gave direct aid to poor Americans through the Federal Emergency Relief Administration (FERA). At the same time, Roosevelt started federal job programs. Congress created a relief agency known as the Works Progress Administration (WPA). Between 1935 and 1943 the WPA put millions of Americans to work building public buildings, teaching classes, and creating art. Returning to work helped restore many people's pride. New Deal legislation also brought some relief to farmers through crop subsidies.

Roosevelt appointed a number of African Americans to his administration. These leaders, as well as First Lady Eleanor Roosevelt, fought for more civil rights. In 1934 Congress passed the Indian Reorganization Act, restoring tribal rule and some tribal lands to American Indians.

The Great Depression had other positive outcomes as well. Some New Deal laws helped workers form unions. In 1935 Roosevelt signed perhaps the most far-reaching legislation of his presidency—the **Social Security Act**. The act gave pensions to retired workers. It also gave unemployment insurance to workers who lost their jobs. The New Deal programs helped to improve the lives of many Americans. However, the national economy stayed in a slump until 1940.

✔ **Reading Check: Contrasting** Contrast President Roosevelt's attempts to help poor Americans with President Hoover's. President Hoover did not believe in direct aid. Roosevelt provided direct aid through the FERA and large grants through the WPA.

Section 2 Review

go. hrw .com Homework Practice Online
keyword: SA3 HPE

❶ **Define** and explain:
• imperialism
• isolationism
• nationalism
• prohibition

❷ **Identify** and explain:
• Panama Canal
• Treaty of Versailles
• Red Scare
• Jazz Age
• Harlem Renaissance
• Great Depression
• Franklin D. Roosevelt
• New Deal
• Social Security Act

❸ **Sequencing** Copy the time line below. Use it to list the dates and a brief description of what you consider to be the five most important events that the United States was involved in between 1860 and 1940.

Key U.S. Events

1860   1900   1940

❹ **Finding the Main Idea**
a. How did U.S. foreign policy change in the late 1800s and early 1900s, and what are some examples of this change?

b. Describe the economic, social, and cultural changes that took place in the United States after World War I.

❺ **Writing and Critical Thinking**
Supporting a Point of View Imagine that you work for the administration of Franklin D. Roosevelt. Write an advertisement in support of the New Deal programs.

Consider the following:
• work programs
• the Social Security Act
• Roosevelt's leadership qualities

Section 3

OBJECTIVES

- ⭐ Explain how the United States contributed to an Allied victory in World War II.
- ⭐ Identify how the Cold War influenced U.S. foreign policy.
- ⭐ Analyze what American society was like in the 1950s.

🔊 LET'S GET STARTED!

As students enter the classroom, read excerpts from *Hiroshima* by John Hersey to the class. Then ask students to identify events that could justify the use of the atomic bomb and discuss its long-term consequences with the class. *(Students' responses will vary.)* Explain to students that in Section 3, they will learn about U.S. involvement in World War II; how the war affected the lives of Americans at home and in the armed services; how the war changed the U.S. role and position in world affairs; how in the aftermath of the war the Soviet Union, one-time ally of the United States, became its most feared enemy; and how the American fear of communism led not only to political repression but to a renewed struggle for civil rights as well.

Section 3

World War II and the Cold War

Read to Discover

1. How did the United States contribute to an Allied victory in World War II?
2. How did the Cold War influence U.S. foreign policy?
3. What was American society like in the 1950s?

WHY IT MATTERS TODAY

The United Nations continues to take an active role in worldwide peace efforts. Use **CNN fyi.com** or other **current events** sources to find an example of the UN's recent involvement in a peace effort. Record your findings in your journal.

Define

- fascism

Identify

- Nazis
- D-Day
- Holocaust
- Yalta Conference
- United Nations
- Cold War
- Truman Doctrine
- Marshall Plan
- North Atlantic Treaty Organization
- Dwight D. Eisenhower
- *Brown v. Board of Education*
- Montgomery Bus Boycott
- Martin Luther King Jr.

SECTION 3 RESOURCES

REPRODUCIBLE

- ▶ Guided Reading Strategy E.3
- ▶ American History Political Cartoon 26: Brinkmanship
- ▶ Primary Source Reading Epilogue: The Path to the Atomic Bomb

TECHNOLOGY

- ▶ One-Stop Planner, Lesson E.3
- ▶ Linking Geography and History Transparency 20: Cold War Defenses
- ▶ American History Interactive Maps CD–ROM: Living in the Cold War
- ▶ Homework Practice Online

REINFORCEMENT, REVIEW, AND ASSESSMENT

- ▶ Section 3 Review, p. 701
- ▶ Daily Quiz E.3
- ▶ Main Idea Activity E.3
- ▶ English Audio Summary E.3
- ▶ Spanish Audio Summary E.3

The Story Continues

On August 31, 1939, German troops disguised as Polish soldiers staged an attack on a radio station in their own country. The town of Gleiwitz (gly-vits) was located on the Polish border, and the German government wanted an excuse to invade Poland. Within hours, German forces were invading Poland, leading to a war that would soon spread throughout the world.

A German tank

⭐ World War II Begins

World War II was partly caused by the terms of the Treaty of Versailles, which upset some countries. For example, Italians wanted more territory. Italy's dictator, Benito Mussolini, pledged to make his country a world power through **fascism.** Fascism is a form of government that places more value on nation and race than on the individual.

🕙 Have students read Section 3 and complete Guided Reading Strategies E.3. Choose one or more of the following activities to explore the section content with students. For further suggestions on block scheduling or team teaching, see the *Block Scheduling Handbook with Team Teaching Strategies.*

🇺🇸 **LEVEL 1:** Lead a class discussion on the events of World War II and the early Cold War. Work with students to create a class time line of the main events of World War II and the early Cold-War. Have students annotate the time line to indicate how the United States contributed to an Allied victory in World War II, and how the Cold War influenced U.S. foreign policy. (*Students' annotations will vary but should include the bombing campaign against Germany, the Allied role in the Pacific against Japan, the Truman Doctrine, the Marshall Plan, the Korean War, and the Berlin Airlift.*) Encourage volunteers to add images to the time line while others add annotations. **ENGLISH LANGUAGE LEARNERS , COOPERATIVE LEARNING**

⭐ Geography

Advancements in Mapping.
In 1940, before the United States entered World War II, the U.S. Army Air Corps determined that less than 10 percent of the world was mapped well enough for them to make even the most basic pilot charts. Thus, the air force developed a program of aerial photography and reconnaissance mapping. This program relied on a new photographic process called the trimetrogon method. As a result of these efforts, huge areas that had previously gone unmapped were charted during the war years. Information from the World Aeronautical Charts, which were the result of the mapping program, are still used by countries all over the world.

CRITICAL THINKING

How could the information in the World Aeronautical Charts be useful to people after the war?

ANSWER: Students might suggest that airlines could use the information.

★★★★★★★★★★★
That's Interesting!
★★★★★★★★★★★

Hours before the landing on the Normandy beaches, U.S. and British parachutists began to drop into the French countryside—behind the German frontlines. One scholar has called this dangerous mission "a lethal lottery."

The Japanese surprise attack on Pearl Harbor was a major blow to the U.S. Pacific Fleet.

THE GRANGER COLLECTION, NEW YORK

Americans used government-issued books of ration stamps to buy scarce goods during the war.

The treaty also made Germany pay billions of dollars to the countries it had attacked. Then the Great Depression increased Germany's economic difficulties. A new leader, Adolf Hitler, appealed to many Germans. His National Socialist Party, the **Nazis**, blamed Jews, intellectuals, and Communists for Germany's problems. Hitler took over Austria and part of Czechoslovakia. At first, European leaders gave in to Hitler to avoid war with Germany. Then on September 1, 1939, Germany invaded Poland, thus starting World War II. German forces quickly overran much of Europe.

In 1940 Germany, Italy, and Japan—known as the Axis Powers—joined together. Japan had invaded China in the 1930s and hoped to gain more power in Asia. The Soviet Union joined the Allied Powers—Britain and France. The United States lent military equipment to the British but stayed out of the war. On December 7, 1941, Japanese planes launched a surprise attack on the U.S. naval base at Pearl Harbor, Hawaii. On December 8, the United States declared war on Japan. Germany and Italy then declared war on the United States.

✔ **Reading Check: Summarizing** What actions led to the outbreak of World War II? See text above for details.

⭐ Americans and the War

Americans quickly prepared for the war effort. They bought billions of dollars in war bonds. Many people, including women and African Americans, went to work in factories producing war materials. Unemployment dropped to an all-time low in 1944. Millions of men and about 300,000 women signed up for military service. About 1 million African Americans served in segregated units. Some 33,000 Japanese Americans also volunteered. They served even though the government sent more than 110,000 Japanese Americans to internment camps.

These U.S. troops were soon fighting in Europe. In 1942 and 1943 the Allies won important victories in North Africa, Italy, and the Soviet Union. On June 6, 1944, the Allies launched **D-Day**, the invasion of Nazi-occupied France. By July 2 about 1 million Allied troops had landed on the beaches of Normandy in northern France. The Allies battled their way toward Germany, which surrendered on May 7, 1945.

Fighting in the Pacific continued. Japanese forces had taken control of much of Southeast Asia and the Pacific. Allied forces pushed back the Japanese and began closing in for a final attack on Japan. President Harry Truman, who took office after Roosevelt's death in April 1945, approved using the newly developed atomic bomb on Japan. On August 6, 1945, a U.S. plane dropped an atomic bomb on Hiroshima, destroying the city.

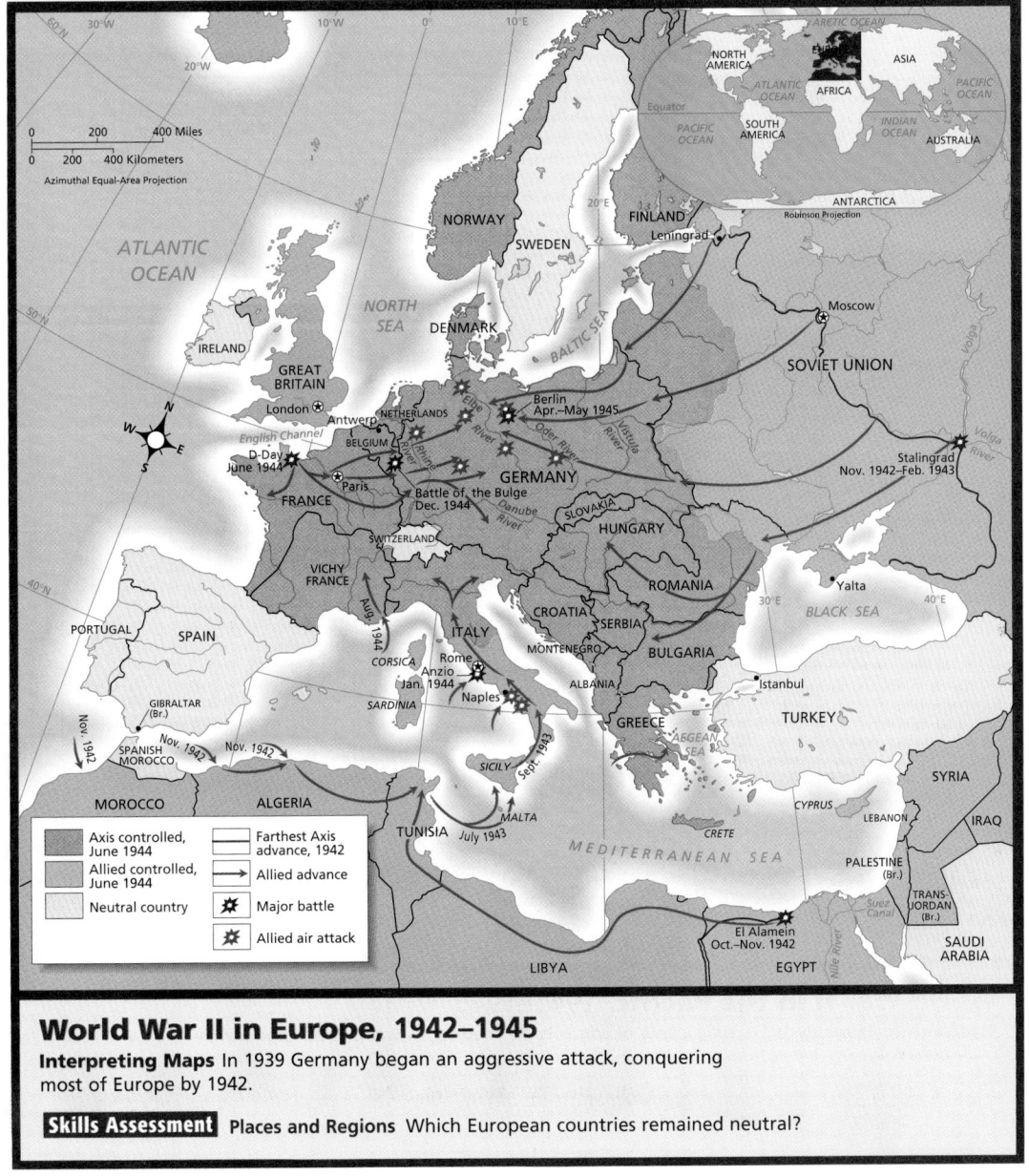

World War II in Europe, 1942–1945

Interpreting Maps In 1939 Germany began an aggressive attack, conquering most of Europe by 1942.

Skills Assessment Places and Regions Which European countries remained neutral?

ALL LEVELS: Copy the following graphic organizer onto the chalkboard, omitting the italicized answers. Have students complete the organizer to learn what American society was like in the 1950s.

ENGLISH LANGUAGE LEARNERS

K	W	L
What I Know	**What I Want to Know**	**What I Learned**
Students' responses will vary but might include the introduction of television, the beginning of the civil rights movement, and the influence of rock 'n' roll music.	*Students' responses will vary but might include how the economy changed, how leisure time changed, and how the Cold War affected Americans' lives.*	• Cold War fears influenced many aspects of American life. • The economy prospered. • Many people moved to the suburbs. • Teenagers started to listen to rock 'n' roll music. • The civil rights movement won recognition of rights for African Americans. • The nation's birthrate rose dramatically. • Many Americans moved to the Sunbelt. • Social critics warned about growing materialism of American culture.

Interdisciplinary Connection

▶**Literature**◀

The Diary of Anne Frank.
In July 1942 at the age of 14, Anne Frank, a Jewish girl living in Nazi-occupied Amsterdam, went into hiding with her family. For more than two years, the Franks hid in the back of a warehouse. To help them survive, non-Jewish friends smuggled food to the Franks. However, in August 1944 an informer told the Nazi secret police about the hideout. The Franks were captured and sent to concentration camps, where every family member died except Anne's father. After the war, friends gave him the diary she had kept while in hiding. Published as a book, *The Diary of Anne Frank* is still one of the most widely read and moving accounts of life during the Holocaust.

ACTIVITY: Encourage students to read *The Diary of Anne Frank*. Then ask students to write a book report on it using standard grammar, spelling, sentence structure, and punctuation.

MAP ANSWER
Guam, Iwo Jima, Okinawa, the Philippine Islands, and Tinian

Three days later the United States dropped a second atomic bomb on the city of Nagasaki. Japan surrendered on September 2, 1945.

World War II resulted in a tremendous loss of lives and property. Some 50 million civilians and soldiers had died, including about 400,000 Americans. It was also discovered that during the war the Nazis had murdered some 9 million people, including about 6 million Jews, in concentration camps. This tragic ordeal became known as the **Holocaust**.

✔ **Reading Check: Summarizing** How did Americans contribute to the war effort at home and abroad? See text above for specific information.

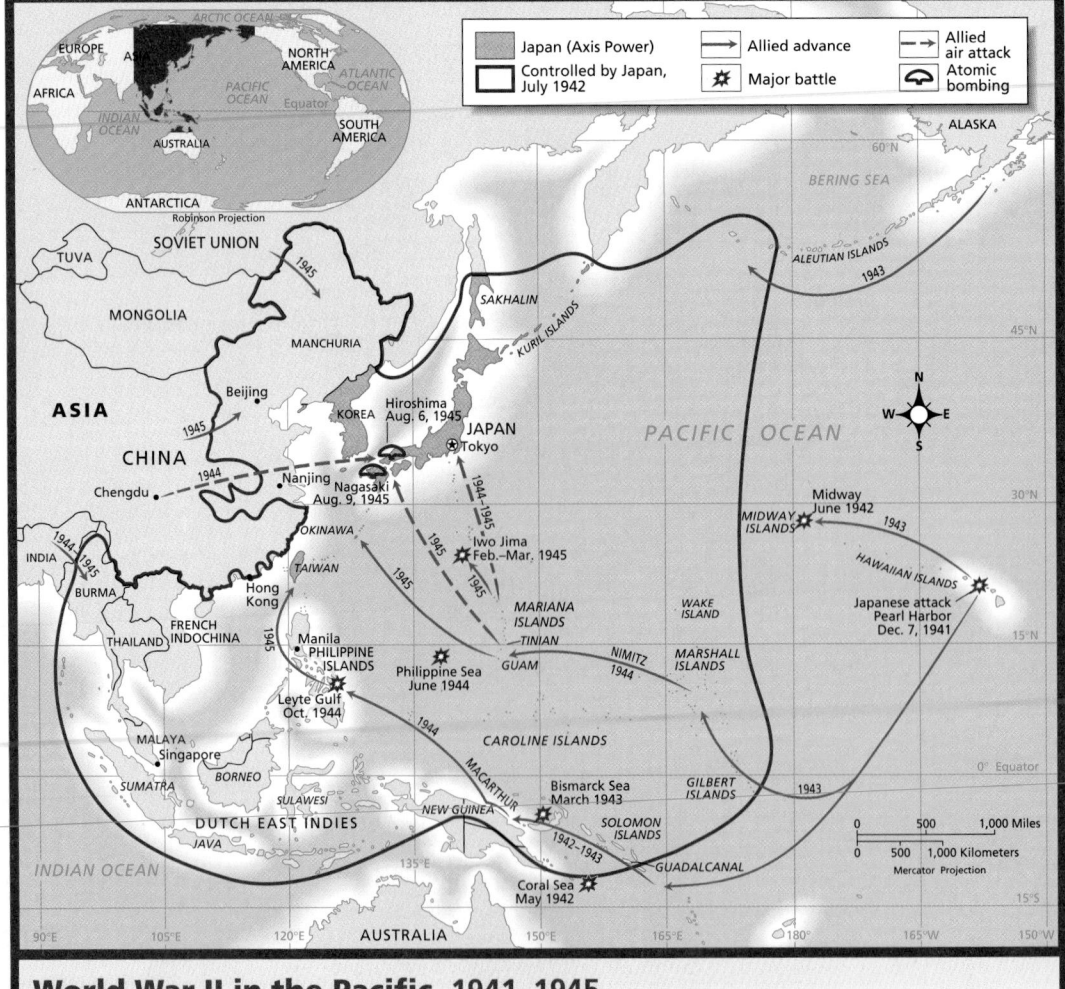

World War II in the Pacific, 1941–1945

Interpreting Maps By 1942 Japan's area of control stretched far into the Pacific and across much of eastern Asia.

Skills Assessment Places and Regions What islands did the Allies attack next after taking the Marshall Islands?

LEVEL 2: Explain to students that during World War II, many people relied on newsreel footage to provide them with information about the war. Then organize the class into several small groups and assign each group a significant event dealing with how the United States contributed to an Allied victory in World War II. Have each group create a newsreel presentation on the assigned event. To create the newsreel, students should write a script dealing with the assigned event and create drawings or photocopy pictures that highlight information from the script. Then have students tape the drawings or photocopies together and attach each end of the strip to sticks to create a scroll. Finally, have a member from each group read the script as one or more other members scroll through the visual presentation of the newsreel.

COOPERATIVE LEARNING

 LEVEL 3: Ask students to imagine that they have been assigned to write a segment of an encyclopedia entry on the early years of the Cold War. Have students reference this section while writing their segment. Students might also use charts, graphs, or images to highlight information in their entries. Ask students to include in their entry a discussion on how the Cold War influenced U.S. foreign policy. When students have finished, call on volunteers to share their work with the class.

★ The Cold War

The **Yalta Conference** was held in February 1945. President Roosevelt met with British prime minister Winston Churchill and Soviet leader Joseph Stalin. Together, they planned how to end the war. They also agreed to form the **United Nations** (UN), an organization that would settle disagreements between countries. After Germany's surrender, the Allies divided Germany. The Soviet-controlled portion became known as East Germany, while West Germany became an independent democracy. The Allies also held war crimes trials for the Nazi leaders who took part in the Holocaust and for Japanese war criminals for their crimes.

Shortly after World War II, the United States and the Soviet Union became involved in the **Cold War**, a struggle between the two nations for global power. Europe divided into the democratic West and the communist East. Winston Churchill declared that "an iron curtain has descended across the [European] Continent." In 1947 President Truman announced the **Truman Doctrine**. This policy stated that the United States would help any country fighting against communism. That same year the United States also began the **Marshall Plan**, offering some $12.5 billion to aid Europe's economic recovery. U.S. leaders hoped that countries with strong economies would not turn to communism. The Soviet Union and its allies in Eastern Europe refused American aid.

In 1948 the Soviets blockaded West Berlin, which was located within Soviet-controlled East Germany. They hoped that Western leaders would give up the city. Instead, the United States and Britain began the Berlin Airlift, flying tons of food and supplies to West Berlin. The Soviets ended their blockade in May 1949. That same year, the United States, Britain, and 10 other countries joined to form the **North Atlantic Treaty Organization** (NATO). NATO members promised to defend each other from enemy attack. The Soviet Union and other Eastern European nations later formed their own military alliance called the Warsaw Pact.

In 1949 Communists took over China. The United States worried that communism would spread throughout Asia. North and South Korea, formed after World War II, went to war in 1950. The United Nations and United States supported anticommunist South Korea, while China sent troops to aid communist North Korea. The final cease-fire in 1953 left Korea divided into two countries.

At home, the Cold War led to anticommunist feelings among Americans. The

Allied leaders, including Clement Attlee, Harry S Truman, and Joseph Stalin (seated left to right), planned the division of Germany at the Potsdam Conference in July 1945.

★ Constitutional Heritage

HUAC. Critics of the House Un-American Activities Committee (HUAC) maintained that its investigations weakened American's constitutional rights to freedom of speech, association, and due process. The 1957 Supreme Court decision in *Watkins* v. *United States* placed limitations on the congressional investigations. The Court ruled that Congress did not have the authority to expose individuals' private affairs unless performing a valid legislative function. The Court stated that in the HUAC investigations, Congress had overstepped its legislative bounds. As a result of the Court's decision, almost all of the contempt convictions that HUAC had handed out were overturned in the early to mid-1960s.

CRITICAL THINKING

What does the Court's ruling in *Watkins* v. *United States* say about the importance of constitutional guarantees?

ANSWER: Students might indicate that the Court's decision shows that the threat of communism was insufficient reason to violate the constitutional rights of U.S. citizens.

Technology Resources

Linking Geography and History Transparency 20: Cold War Defenses

Have students work in groups to prepare museum exhibits illustrating the history of your community in connection with one of the following topics: World War II, the Cold War, social trends of the 1950s, or the Civil Rights Movement. Ask students to formulate questions which they intend to answer through their exhibits. Also ask students to devise criteria by which they will locate and select artifacts, prepare text, and decide how best to display them. If possible, arrange a field trip to a local museum to familiarize students with the elements of museum exhibits. **BLOCK SCHEDULING**

✪ CLOSE

Have each student create a study guide based on this section. Ask students to leave a blank space where each term or name in the Identify portion of the Section Review should be located. Then have students exchange guides, fill in the appropriate term or name in each blank, and return the guides to their authors for grading.

★ Daily Life

The Automobile. During the 1950s automobile companies began to emphasize styling details that made the cars look sleeker and flashier. One designer, Harley Earl, set the tone for most of the cars of the era. Earl began his career in Hollywood, where he made custom cars for movie stars. In Detroit he designed cars to look like jet planes—sleek, with long finlike attachments in the rear. He covered the cars with large shiny chrome details. Flashy fins and chrome added little to cars' performance. Nonetheless, many Americans bought larger, fancier cars during the 1950s, perhaps as a symbol of their increasing prosperity.

ACTIVITY: Have students research other popular products of the 1950s and, using standard grammar, spelling, sentence structure, and punctuation, write an essay describing how they reflected 1950s culture.

Technology Resources
American History
Interactive Maps CD–ROM:
Living in the Cold War

Visual Record Answer

Students might suggest that it describes a sinister plot by Communists.

Interpreting the Visual Record

Another Red Scare *During the 1950s, many films and magazines warned that Communists at home and abroad were plotting against the United States.* **How does this poster describe the Communist threat?**

House Un-American Activities Committee (HUAC), created in 1938, began new investigations into Americans suspected of communist activities. In 1950 Wisconsin senator Joseph McCarthy shocked the nation by declaring that he had a list of hundreds of Communists who worked in the U.S. government. His accusations led to public hearings, but on television it became clear that McCarthy had little proof. However, he had already ruined the lives of many innocent people.

The Cold War shaped Americans' choice of a leader. They wanted a strong, confident president and elected **Dwight D. Eisenhower** in 1952. Eisenhower had led the Allied invasion of Europe in World War II.

By the early 1950s both American and Soviet scientists had developed powerful hydrogen bombs. The Eisenhower administration viewed nuclear arms and technology as crucial to ending the spread of communism. Eisenhower, therefore, based his foreign policy on brinkmanship. This was the willingness to go to the brink, or edge, of war to oppose communism.

The United States and the Soviet Union also competed in a space race. The Soviets sent *Sputnik*, the first artificial satellite, into space in October 1957. Americans were shocked to find themselves falling behind the Soviets. In January 1958 the United States launched its first satellite. Later that year, Congress established the National Aeronautics and Space Administration (NASA) to advance U.S. space exploration.

Cold War defense spending led to more jobs, and the postwar years became a time of prosperity for many Americans. Incomes grew and unemployment stayed low. The United States also experienced a baby boom as the country's birthrate rose dramatically. Many middle-class Americans moved out of the cities to suburban neighborhoods. Life in the suburbs centered around families, with parks, schools, and public services. Some critics claimed that suburban life urged everyone to behave the same way with little individuality.

Television became increasingly popular and greatly shaped 1950s American culture. Television advertisements that urged people to buy the latest products affected viewers' spending habits. Young Americans also began listening to rock 'n' roll music, which drew heavily on African American rhythm and blues. Many adults said that this music was too wild and led to antisocial behavior.

✔ **Reading Check: Summarizing** What changes took place in the United States during the 1950s? **The United States followed a foreign policy based on the threat of nuclear war. The 1950s were very prosperous. There were new job opportunities. Many people moved to the suburbs.**

★ The Civil Rights Movement Begins

Some people felt that society in the 1950s held them back. Although President Truman desegregated the armed forces in 1948, many African Americans thought that he had moved too slowly. The NAACP focused on ending segregation in public education. In 1954 the Supreme Court

☆ REVIEW AND ASSESS

Have students complete the **Section 3 Review** on p. 701. Then have them complete **Daily Quiz E.3.** As **Alternative Assessment**, you may want to use the American society organizer or the encyclopedia entry activities in this section's lessons.

☆ RETEACH

Have students complete **Main Idea Activity for English Language Learners and Special-Needs Students E.3.** Then assign one term or name from the Identify portion of the Section Review to each member of the class. Have each student go to the chalkboard and write one clue about the term. If none of the class members can identify the correct term or name

from the clue, have the student write a second clue, and so on. Continue until all of the terms have been reviewed.

ENGLISH LANGUAGE LEARNERS

☆ EXTEND

Have students use the library or other resources to conduct research on major U.S. victories in World War II. Have students develop a time line that displays the progression of the war in Europe and in the Pacific Ocean. Ask students to add annotations and illustrations to enhance their work.

BLOCK SCHEDULING

ruled in **Brown v. Board of Education** that segregated public schools were unconstitutional. This decision overturned the 1896 *Plessy* v. *Ferguson* ruling that supported "separate-but-equal" institutions. Still, by 1957 only four southern states had integrated their schools. In the fall of 1957, a group of African American students tried to attend the all-white Central High School in Little Rock, Arkansas. The governor of Arkansas ordered National Guard troops to keep the students from entering the school. Eventually, President Eisenhower sent federal troops to force the governor to follow the Supreme Court's ruling.

African Americans also fought to desegregate public transportation. In 1955 Rosa Parks of Montgomery, Alabama, refused to give up her bus seat to a white passenger. She was arrested and later explained her actions.

History Makers Speak ❝Having to take a certain section [on a bus] because of your race was humiliating, but having to stand up because a particular driver wanted to keep a white person from having to stand was, to my mind, most inhumane.❞

—Rosa Parks, quoted in *Voices of Freedom*, by Henry Hampton and Steve Fayer with Sarah Flynn

Elizabeth Eckford tries to enter Little Rock's Central High School.

Nearly all African Americans in the city joined in the **Montgomery Bus Boycott**, refusing to use the city's bus system. The boycott went on for more than a year. In November 1956 the Supreme Court ruled that Montgomery's segregated bus system was illegal. The boycott encouraged other civil rights protests and also introduced the country to a young African American leader, **Martin Luther King Jr.**

✔ **Reading Check: Finding the Main Idea** How did African Americans work to gain civil rights in the 1950s? The NAACP challenged school segregation in the courts. African Americans waged a boycott against segregation in public transportation.

Section **3** Review

go. hrw .com Homework Practice Online
keyword: SA3 HPE

❶ **Define** and explain:
• fascism

❷ **Identify** and explain:
• Nazis
• D-Day
• Holocaust
• Yalta Conference
• United Nations
• Cold War
• Truman Doctrine
• Marshall Plan
• North Atlantic Treaty Organization
• Dwight D. Eisenhower
• *Brown* v. *Board of Education*
• Montgomery Bus Boycott
• Martin Luther King Jr.

❸ **Analyzing Information**
Copy the graphic organizer below. Use it to describe three key events of World War II and three key events of the Cold War.

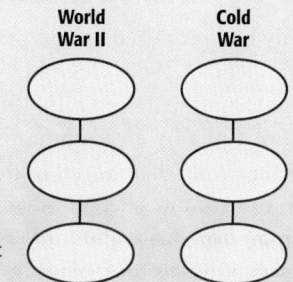
World War II / Cold War

❹ **Finding the Main Idea**
a. In what ways did the United States contribute to victory over the Axis Powers?
b. How did the Cold War affect U.S. foreign policy?

❺ **Writing and Critical Thinking**
Summarizing Imagine that you are writing a book about life in the 1950s. Design a book cover that illustrates the major events of the 1950s. The back of the book cover should include a written summary of what happened during this time period.

Consider the following:
• the Cold War
• television and rock 'n' roll
• the beginning of the civil rights movement

Section 3 Review
ANSWERS

❶ **Define**
• fascism, p. 695

❷ **Identify**
• Nazis, p. 696
• D-Day, p. 696
• Holocaust, p. 698
• Yalta Conference, p. 699
• United Nations, p. 699
• Cold War, p. 699
• Truman Doctrine, p. 699
• Marshall Plan, p. 699
• North Atlantic Treaty Organization, p. 699
• Dwight D. Eisenhower, p. 700
• *Brown* v. *Board of Education*, p. 701
• Montgomery Bus Boycott, p. 701
• Martin Luther King Jr., p. 701

❸ Students' graphic organizers will vary.

❹ a. U.S. troops fought in Europe and North Africa, took part in the bombing campaign against Germany that led to Germany's surrender, recaptured territory in Southeast Asia and the Pacific from Japan, bombed Japan, leading to its surrender
b. The United States initiated the Truman Doctrine and the Marshall Plan to fight communism abroad, fought in the Korean War, and built up its nuclear weapons and threatened to launch an attack.

❺ Students' book covers will vary but should include illustrations of major events as well as a written summary of the time period.

Section 4

OBJECTIVES

★ Describe the foreign-policy issues faced by Presidents Kennedy and Johnson while they were in office.

★ Define the achievements of the 1960s civil rights movement.

★ Identify the domestic challenges that the United States faced in the early 1970s.

LET'S GET STARTED!

As students enter the classroom read excerpts from John F. Kennedy's inaugural address. Have students write a one-paragraph reply to the president's call for Americans to serve their country. Ask students to identify whether they agree with the president's call for service and to explain their reasoning. (*Students' replies will vary based on their perspectives but the replies should explain in detail why they choose to serve or why they choose to not serve.*) Tell students that in Section 4 they will learn about attempts to solve pressing problems at home and abroad in the decade following Kennedy's inauguration. In addition, tell them they will learn how Americans grew increasingly frustrated at their government's inability to resolve both domestic and international conflicts.

Section 4

Searching for Solutions

Read to Discover

1. What foreign-policy issues did Presidents Kennedy and Johnson face while they were in office?
2. What were the achievements of the 1960s civil rights movement?
3. What domestic challenges did the United States face in the 1970s?

WHY IT MATTERS TODAY

The cost of fuel is still an important issue for Americans today. Use **CNNfyi.com** or other **current events** sources to find out about how Americans are trying to conserve energy today. Record your findings in your journal.

Define

• energy crisis

Identify

• John F. Kennedy
• Cuban missile crisis
• Lyndon Johnson
• Great Society
• Freedom Rides
• Civil Rights Act of 1964
• Voting Rights Act of 1965
• National Organization for Women
• Tet Offensive
• Richard Nixon
• Watergate
• Jimmy Carter

The Story Continues

During President John F. Kennedy's inaugural address, he urged Americans to work for a better country. "The energy, the faith, the devotion which we bring to this endeavor [effort] will light our country," the president said. "And so, my fellow Americans—ask not what your country can do for you—ask what you can do for your country."

Campaign buttons like this one urged Americans to vote for Kennedy.

★ Kennedy and Johnson

__John F. Kennedy__ had promised to "get the country moving again" if he was elected president in 1960. Once he took office, however, he faced several major international crises. In 1961, U.S. officials supported a failed invasion of Cuba by anticommunist allies. U.S.-Soviet relations worsened later that year when Soviet leader Nikita Khrushchev ordered the Berlin Wall to be built. The Wall divided East and West Berlin and kept East Germans from fleeing to the West.

The most serious crisis took place in October 1962, when U.S. spy planes discovered Soviet missiles in Cuba, only 90 miles from Florida.

Have students read Section 4 and complete Guided Reading Strategies E.4. Choose one or more of the following activities to explore the section content with students. For further suggestions on block scheduling or team teaching, see the *Block Scheduling Handbook with Team Teaching Strategies*.

LEVEL 1: Discuss foreign policy issues that faced Presidents John F. Kennedy and Lyndon B. Johnson while they were in office. (*Students' responses should include problems with Cuba, East Germany, and the Soviet Union as well as a deeper involvement in Vietnam.*) Have each student choose one of these affairs and create two political cartoons dealing with it. One cartoon should identify the issue, while the other should identify the president's reaction to it. When students have finished their cartoons, call on volunteers to present their work to the class. **ENGLISH LANGUAGE LEARNERS**

Interpreting the Visual Record

A new president *Lyndon Johnson was sworn in as president on* Air Force One *just hours after Kennedy's assassination.* **How was Johnson's swearing in different from the way most presidents take office?**

President Kennedy demanded that the Soviets remove these weapons. For the next week, the world nervously waited for the result of the **Cuban missile crisis**. Finally, the Soviets agreed to remove the missiles.

On November 22, 1963, President Kennedy was assassinated in Dallas, Texas. Within hours Vice President **Lyndon Johnson** became the new president. President Johnson assured the country that he would carry on Kennedy's work. Elected president in 1964, Johnson created a series of programs that he called the **Great Society**.

History Makers Speak

66The Great Society rests on abundance [plenty] and liberty for all. It demands an end to poverty and racial injustice [unfairness]. . . .The Great Society is a place where every child can find knowledge to enrich [improve] his mind and to enlarge his talents.99

—Lyndon Johnson, quoted in *The Annals of America*

Great Society programs provided more people with health insurance and gave federal money to schools. As a result of the Great Society programs and economic growth, fewer Americans lived in poverty.

Other challenges still remained. For example, the country went through a great deal of social conflict in the late 1960s. Young people began to disagree with many of the views and ideals of the older generation. Some young people rejected society entirely. They "dropped out" and formed a counterculture.

✔ **Reading Check: Summarizing** What challenges did Presidents Kennedy and Johnson face, and how did they deal with them? See text above for specific information.

★ The Civil Rights Movement

One of the most important movements in the 1960s was the continuing fight for civil rights. African Americans demanded equal treatment in public places. Beginning in 1960, African American students led sit-ins at segregated restaurants, refusing to leave until they were served. In 1961, civil rights activists participated in **Freedom Rides**, taking buses through several southern states to protest segregated bus stations.

Analyzing Primary Sources

Making Generalizations and Predictions How do you think Johnson might try to turn the United States into his image of the Great Society? Answers will vary, but students might suggest making sure that all Americans share in its economic wealth, that all Americans are educated, or that Americans' civil rights are protected.

Kennedy and the Freedom Rides. President John F. Kennedy was not pleased with the timing of the Freedom Rides. He was scheduled to meet with Nikita Khrushchev the next month. Kennedy worried that the Soviet leader might raise the issue of racial strife in the United States and point to the Freedom Rides as proof that American democracy did not work. Kennedy did not want to see the United States embarrassed in front of the rest of the world. He nonetheless approved protection for the Freedom Riders when they insisted on continuing.

ACTIVITY: Have students use the library or other resources to find information on the Freedom Rides. Then have students use standard grammar, spelling, and punctuation to write an editorial supporting the riders' cause and their form of protest.

Visual Record Answer

Students might suggest that it took place on an airplane after a horrific assassination.

Technology Resources

Everyday Life in America Transparency 30: Protest During the Vietnam War

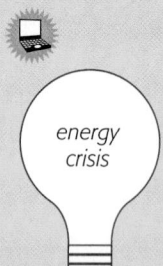
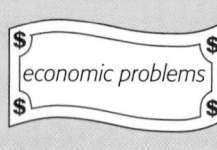

Interdisciplinary Connection

►Literature◄

The Autobiography of Malcolm X. During the last years of his life, Malcolm X worked with writer Alex Haley on an autobiography. Haley was working as a freelance journalist when he was first asked to interview Malcolm X. The assignment eventually led to Haley's work on Malcolm X's autobiography. Writing the book was a painstaking process. Malcolm X did not like being tape-recorded, so Haley had to type while Malcolm X spoke. The effort was worth it. The book, which was published in October 1965, was a huge success and gained international acclaim.

ACTIVITY: Have students read passages of *The Autobiography of Malcolm X.* Then have students explain how his beliefs differed from those of Martin Luther King Jr.

Pictured at the top are Martin Luther King Jr., his wife, Coretta, and their children. César Chávez used boycotts to draw attention to the suffering of migrant workers.

Despite violent attacks by angry white mobs, the Freedom Riders kept coming. Transportation companies and other businesses eventually ended their segregation policies.

In 1963 President Kennedy presented a new civil rights bill. Civil rights leaders planned the March on Washington to show their support. More than 200,000 men, women, and children—black and white—gathered in Washington, D.C. Martin Luther King Jr. then described his hopes for racial harmony in his "I Have a Dream" speech.

> **History Makers Speak** **❝I have a dream that my four little children will one day live in a nation where they will not be judged by the color of their skin but by the content of their character.❞**
>
> —Martin Luther King Jr., "I Have a Dream," quoted in *The Annals of America*

Congress later passed the **Civil Rights Act of 1964**. This act made it illegal for most employers to discriminate on the basis of national origin, race, religion, or sex.

In the South, threats and unfair laws kept many African Americans from voting. As a part of the Freedom Summer project of 1964, hundreds of college students went to Mississippi. They worked with African Americans there to protect their right to vote. A major voting rights campaign was then begun in Selma, Alabama. Soon afterward, President Johnson signed the **Voting Rights Act of 1965**. The act ensured every eligible U.S. citizen's right to vote. By the end of the year, nearly 250,000 new African American voters had registered.

Some African Americans did not agree with peaceful protests. Black leaders such as Malcolm X supported the use of force, when necessary, to gain civil rights. African Americans still faced economic inequality and discrimination. These issues, along with acts of police mistreatment, led to riots in cities around the country. Severe rioting followed the assassination of Martin Luther King Jr. in April 1968.

Other groups of Americans were inspired by the civil rights movement to fight for change. The Chicano movement worked to end discrimination and increase cultural pride among Mexican Americans. César Chávez led the fight to win more rights for migrant workers. The American Indian Movement (AIM) staged protests to increase awareness of American Indian issues.

Women's rights activists formed the **National Organization for Women** in 1966. In 1972 Congress passed the Equal Rights Amendment to guarantee women equal protection under the law. However, it was not ratified by a majority of states, and so did not become law. Nevertheless, women did become more involved in politics. Women also began entering professions that had been traditionally male-dominated in greater numbers.

✔ **Reading Check: Supporting a Point of View** What were civil rights activists of the 1960s trying to achieve, and how successful were they? Answers will vary but should note methods of protest, organization, and politics described above.

HOMEWORK Ask students to create charts based on this section. Students should label the columns with the names of the presidents discussed in the section and the rows *Foreign* and *Domestic*. Then have students complete the charts by filling in significant foreign and domestic affairs that occurred under each president.

Note: For an additional teaching idea, see the Chapter 22 Unfinished Story Alternatives activity in the **Creative Teaching Strategies** handbook.

★ CLOSE

Provide each student with two strips of paper cut to resemble bumper stickers. Have each student select two of the presidencies discussed in this section and create a bumper sticker for each that captures the essential theme, effect, or historical importance of it. Once students have finished creating their bumper stickers, call on volunteers to explain them to the class.

★ The Vietnam War

In 1954 the Southeast Asian nation of Vietnam won its freedom from French rule. It was divided into two countries. North Vietnam was led by Communists, and the South Vietnamese government was soon fighting against pro-communist rebels called the Vietcong.

The U.S. government did not want Communists to control South Vietnam. U.S. leaders believed that if another Asian country fell to communism, others would soon follow. Beginning with military advisers, the United States became increasingly involved in the conflict.

By 1968 more than 500,000 U.S. soldiers were serving in Vietnam. The fighting was difficult. The Vietcong and North Vietnamese troops hid in the thick jungle, launching hit-and-run attacks. Yet U.S. officials told the American public that victory was near. In late January 1968 the enemy launched a major attack on South Vietnam called the **Tet Offensive**. U.S. and South Vietnamese troops drove back the attack. However, the Tet Offensive showed that the North Vietnamese were determined to keep fighting.

The war became more and more unpopular in the United States. Students on college campuses across the country protested, and many Americans blamed Johnson and the Democrats for the war. Johnson chose not to run for re-election in 1968. Voters elected former vice president **Richard Nixon**, a Republican, who promised to bring about "peace with honor." After reaching a cease-fire agreement in January 1973, Nixon withdrew all U.S. forces. Communists took over South Vietnam in 1975. The war took the lives of more than a million Vietnamese soldiers and some 58,000 American soldiers.

✔ **Reading Check: Contrasting** How did Presidents Johnson and Nixon handle the war in Vietnam differently?
See text above for specific information.

A button calling for an end to U.S. involvement in Vietnam

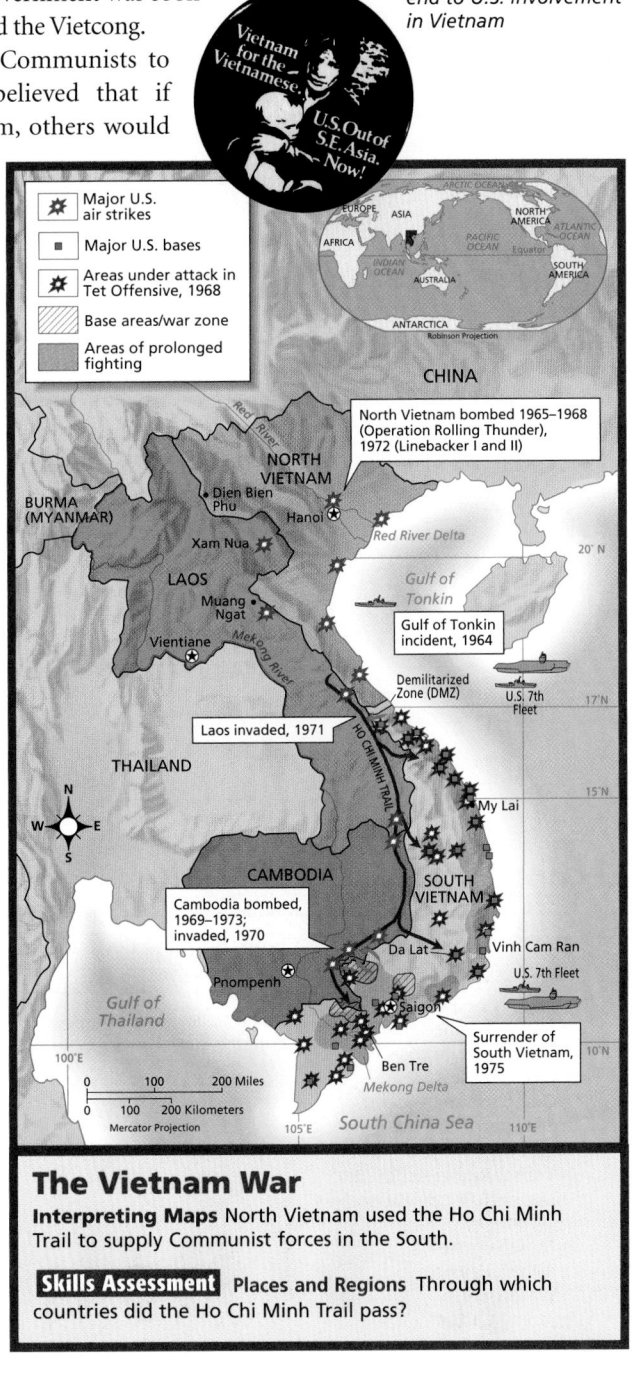

The Vietnam War

Interpreting Maps North Vietnam used the Ho Chi Minh Trail to supply Communist forces in the South.

Skills Assessment Places and Regions Through which countries did the Ho Chi Minh Trail pass?

This cartoon dollar criticizes Nixon's efforts to improve the slow economy.

★ The 1970s

In the 1970s the U.S. economy suffered from slow growth, high unemployment, and rising inflation. It got worse when the Organization of Petroleum Exporting Countries (OPEC) raised oil prices. This increase led to an **energy crisis**, with high fuel prices and low supplies of fuel.

In foreign affairs President Nixon followed a policy of détente, trying to lower military and diplomatic tensions with the Soviets. U.S. and Soviet leaders signed a treaty to limit the numbers of their nuclear missiles. In 1972 Nixon also became the first president to visit China.

A scandal called <u>Watergate</u> soon rocked Nixon's administration, however. In June 1972, five men were caught breaking into the Democratic National Committee headquarters in Washington, D.C. When Congress investigated, evidence of Nixon's involvement emerged. Nixon denied the accusations, but tape-recorded conversations showed that he had tried to cover up White House connections to the break-in. To avoid possible impeachment, Nixon resigned on August 8, 1974. Vice President Gerald Ford took office and pardoned Nixon, upsetting many Americans. Ford pursued détente and tried unsuccessfully to improve the economy.

In 1976, voters chose Democrat <u>Jimmy Carter</u> as president, hoping for change. The country's energy crisis and economic problems dragged on, however. President Carter's greatest success and his worst failure came in the Middle East. He worked out the Camp David Accords, leading to a peace treaty in 1979 between longtime enemies Israel and Egypt. But in November 1979, Iranian students took more than 50 Americans hostage in Tehran, Iran's capital.

✔ **Reading Check: Comparing and Contrasting** How were the events of the Nixon and Carter administrations similar and different? Both faced domestic economic problems and had foreign-policy successes. Nixon had Watergate and Carter had the hostage crisis.

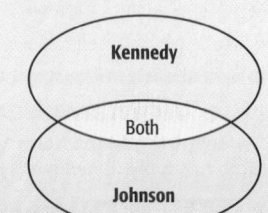

go. hrw .com **Homework Practice Online**
keyword: SA3 HPE

Section 4 Review

❶ Define and explain:
• energy crisis

❷ Identify and explain:
• John F. Kennedy
• Cuban missile crisis
• Lyndon Johnson
• Great Society
• Freedom Rides
• Civil Rights Act of 1964
• Voting Rights Act of 1965
• National Organization for Women
• Tet Offensive
• Richard Nixon
• Watergate
• Jimmy Carter

❸ Comparing and Contrasting Copy the diagram below. Use it to compare and contrast U.S. foreign policy under Presidents Kennedy and Johnson.

Kennedy

Both

Johnson

❹ Finding the Main Idea
a. What strategies did African Americans use to gain civil rights in the 1960s, and what success did they have?

b. What problems did Presidents Nixon, Ford, and Carter face?

❺ Writing and Critical Thinking
Summarizing Imagine that you are a teenager living in the 1960s. Write a letter that describes your life to a teenager from another country.

Consider the following:
• the Vietnam War
• the civil rights movement

Section 5

OBJECTIVES

⭐ Explain how the Cold War progressed in the 1980s.

⭐ Examine the legislative successes and failures of the Clinton administration.

⭐ Analyze how the United States took part in world affairs in the 1990s.

 **LET'S GET STARTED!**

Show students a map of the Soviet Union before its breakup in 1991 and a map of the East European countries that emerged after its collapse, as well as pictures of the Berlin Wall coming down. As students enter the classroom, ask them to speculate on the role that the United States played in causing these events. (*Students' responses will vary, but students might suggest that the United States was determined to succeed in establishing democracy in the former Soviet Union and in ending the Cold War.*) Finally, tell students that in Section 5 they will learn about the recent history of the United States.

Section 5

The Modern Era

Read to Discover

1. How did the Cold War progress in the 1980s?
2. What were the legislative successes and failures of the Clinton administration?
3. How did the United States take part in world affairs in the 1990s?

WHY IT MATTERS TODAY

Part of the federal government's job is to spend taxpayers' money wisely. Use **CNNfyi.com** or other **current events** sources to find out about the federal budget and issues involving the budget today. Record your findings in your journal.

Define

• supply-side economics
• Internet

Identify

• Ronald Reagan
• Iran-Contra affair
• George Bush
• War on Drugs
• Operation Desert Storm
• Bill Clinton
• Contract with America
• North American Free Trade Agreement
• Al Gore
• George W. Bush

The Story Continues

Inauguration Day 1981 was like no other in American history. President Jimmy Carter was working frantically to get Iran to free the American hostages. Before he could do so, Ronald Reagan was sworn in as president. Just moments later, the news came that the hostages indeed had been freed after being held for 444 days. Americans cheered this announcement by their new leader.

This 1980s bumper sticker urged Americans to help the economy by buying products made in the United States.

⭐ The Republican Years

Elected in 1980, President **Ronald Reagan** was a conservative Republican who supported the idea of limited government. Reagan believed in **supply-side economics**, which states that lowering taxes will help business grow. He therefore cut taxes and spending on social programs. By 1984 the economy was thriving. Yuppies, or young urban professionals, did particularly well. On the other hand, critics doubted that the economic boom was helping the poor. However, Reagan's policies and optimism made him very popular. He was easily re-elected in 1984.

Reagan's foreign policy was strongly anticommunist. He believed that the Cold War was a moral fight of "good versus evil, right against wrong."

★ Presidential Profiles

Ronald Reagan. The son of a shoe salesman, Ronald Reagan worked as a lifeguard during his teens. In 1932 Reagan took a job as a radio sportscaster. A few years later, while in California to cover baseball spring training, he took a movie screen test. Reagan's Hollywood career had begun. He went on to appear in 55 movies. During World War II he made training films for the U.S. Army Air Corps. A long-time Democrat, Reagan switched to the Republican Party when he voted for Eisenhower in the 1952 presidential election. From 1954 to 1962 he served as a host of a television show sponsored by General Electric. As a GE company spokesman, he often visited factories to talk to workers about the benefits of capitalism.

Ronald and Nancy Reagan

Under Reagan, the U.S. government spent hundreds of billions of dollars on military weapons. One of his proposals was the Strategic Defense Initiative, a space-based missile defense system. The plan was nicknamed Star Wars by the press. The defense budget increased greatly from 1981 to 1985. This spending added to the federal deficit, the amount of money the U.S. government borrows each year. The Reagan administration also helped anticommunist groups in other nations. Some top White House officials even provided aid illegally to anticommunist forces in Nicaragua, known as Contras. The **Iran-Contra affair** was the biggest scandal of the Reagan years.

U.S.-Soviet relations began to improve as the Soviet Union allowed greater political and economic openness. In 1987 Reagan met with Soviet leader Mikhail Gorbachev (gawr-buh-CHAWF) to sign the Intermediate-Range Nuclear Forces Treaty. This agreement reduced the nuclear weapons of both countries.

★ George Bush's Presidency

Ronald Reagan's vice president, **George Bush**, won the presidency in 1988. He promised to continue Reagan's policies. President Bush also supported the program known as the **War on Drugs**, a large-scale effort to keep illegal drugs out of the United States. In addition, Bush tried to improve public education.

Important changes took place throughout the world during Bush's presidency. Countries in Eastern Europe broke free from Soviet influence. The Berlin Wall was torn down in 1989, and a year later East and West Germany reunited. By the end of 1990, the Cold War had finally ended. In 1991 the Soviet Union broke up.

However, in the summer of 1990 Iraq invaded the small, oil-rich country of Kuwait. An international coalition led by the United States responded by launching **Operation Desert Storm**, an invasion to force Iraq to withdraw from Kuwait, in January 1991. U.S. Army general Colin Powell was confident of victory.

Analyzing Primary Sources

Identifying Points of View
What issues concerned General Powell at the start of Operation Desert Storm?
how long the attack would last and how many American troops would be killed

 History Makers Speak ❝I had no doubt we would be successful. We had the troops, the weapons, and the plan. What I did not know was how long it would take, and how many of our troops would not be coming home.❞

—Colin Powell, *My American Journey*

Coalition forces began a fierce, six-week bombing campaign. The ground assault that followed drove the Iraqi army from Kuwait. Some 150 U.S. soldiers, and an estimated 100,000 Iraqis had died. Victory in the Persian Gulf War boosted President Bush's popularity at home.

✔ **Reading Check: Sequencing** List important foreign-policy events from the 1980s and 1990s in the order that they occurred. Iran-Contra affair, arms-control agreements, Operation Desert Storm

ALL LEVELS: Copy the following graphic organizer onto the chalkboard, omitting the italicized answers. Have students complete the organizer to learn about U.S. involvement in world affairs in the 1990s.

ENGLISH LANGUAGE LEARNERS

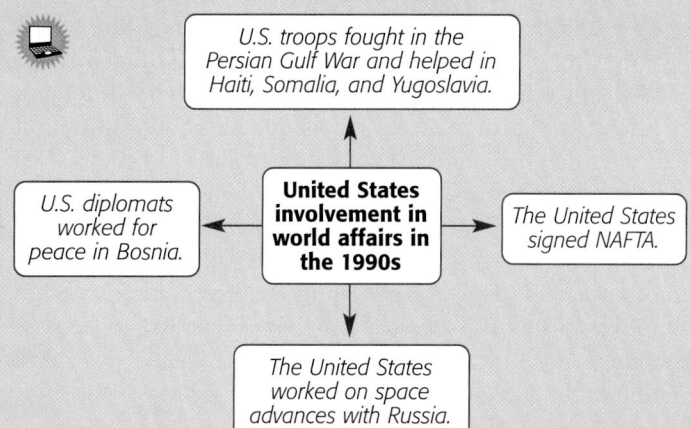

U.S. troops fought in the Persian Gulf War and helped in Haiti, Somalia, and Yugoslavia.

U.S. diplomats worked for peace in Bosnia.

United States involvement in world affairs in the 1990s

The United States signed NAFTA.

The United States worked on space advances with Russia.

⭐ The Clinton Administration

By 1992 an economic downturn had many Americans worried. In the presidential election, Bush ran against Arkansas governor **Bill Clinton**, a Democrat, and Texas billionaire Ross Perot, an independent candidate. Clinton and Perot each promised to fix the economy, while many voters felt that Bush was ignoring this issue. Clinton won the election.

President Clinton's goals included health care and welfare reform. In 1994, voters elected a Republican-controlled Congress for the first time in 42 years. Many of these Republicans had signed the **Contract with America**. A pledge to balance the budget was one of the key points of this plan. Despite opposition between Congress and the president, the two sides cooperated enough to achieve welfare reform and a balanced-budget agreement.

Clinton was re-elected in 1996 over Republican Bob Dole and Ross Perot, who ran on the Reform Party ticket. By the end of Clinton's second term, the United States had gone through the longest economic boom in its history. The stock market also experienced major gains.

Despite the strong economy and a budget surplus, questions about Clinton's personal and official conduct arose. A special prosecutor's report charged that, among other actions, Clinton had lied under oath before a grand jury. Voting largely along party lines, the House of Representatives impeached Clinton and put him on trial. The Senate, however, found Clinton not guilty of the charges, and he remained in office.

As the world's only superpower, the United States took a broader role in world affairs during Clinton's administration. U.S. troops aided many countries around the world, including Somalia and Haiti. The United States also worked for peace in the Balkans, taking part in a NATO mission in Kosovo, Yugoslavia. The end of the Cold War also led to greater U.S.-Russian cooperation. The two countries made plans to build a new space station.

Trade between countries increased in the 1990s. In 1994 the **North American Free Trade Agreement** (NAFTA) with Canada and Mexico went into effect. NAFTA allows goods, people, and services to move freely among the three countries. Many other nations expanded existing trade agreements. In January 1995 the World Trade Organization (WTO) was formed to settle economic disputes between trading partners.

Improved computer and communications technology fueled the rapid growth of the global **Internet**. This vast computer network connected businesses, governments, schools, and individuals around the world, allowing the exchange of information. More people began to use their computers to do research, share ideas, shop, and even work from home.

✔ **Reading Check: Analyzing Information** How did the end of the Cold War change U.S. foreign involvement in the 1990s? Without a major enemy, the United States became involved in more peacekeeping missions, aid missions, and friendlier relations with Russia.

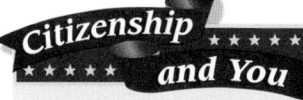

LEVEL 3: Have each student prepare a State of the Union address for President Clinton's final year in office. The address should focus on each of the following areas: legislative successes and failures of the administration and ways that the United States took part in world affairs during the administration. *(Students' speeches will vary but might include a welfare reform act, the Telecommunications Act, an Internet tax act, the U.S. involvement in Somalia, Haiti, Yugoslavia, and Bosnia.)* Have volunteers present their speeches to the class. After the speeches have been presented, invite class members to comment on the accuracy, effectiveness, and insight of the speech.

HOMEWORK Have students design a graphic organizer of the U.S. government during the late 1980s and the 1990s. Remind students to include information about the end of the Cold War, President Clinton's administration, and the U.S. involvement in foreign affairs.

⭐ CLOSE

Organize the class into small groups, assigning each group one of the presidents discussed in this section. Have each group create a segment of a television documentary covering significant events of its assigned presidency. When groups are ready, have them present their work to the class.

COOPERATIVE LEARNING

⭐ Government

Demystifying the Electoral College. It remains a puzzle to a number of Americans how one presidential candidate can win the popular election, but lose the electoral vote to an opposing candidate, and thus the presidency. Such was the case in the 2000 election when Al Gore won the popular vote but lost the election to George W. Bush, winner of the electoral vote. It was left to newscasters and political experts to remind Americans about those lessons in the voting process they had learned in school. Essentially, a state's electors are equal to its total number of senators and representatives. Thus, each state has two more votes than its proportionate population. When the popular vote cast is as close as it was in the *Bush* v. *Gore* election, it can become the number of states won that decides the outcome of the election. Put another way, the electoral college penalizes the candidate that appeals to a limited region of the country, just as it did in the 2000 election.

ACTIVITY: Have students conduct research to obtain information about other close presidential elections throughout history. Then ask them to create a chart that identifies the candidates, the parties, and the eventual outcome.

Technology Resources

CNN. Presents America: Beginnings to 1914 Segment: Eyes of the Presidency

---

A college eduation remains an important goal for many Americans. Here a student celebrates her graduation.

★★★★★★★★★★★★
That's Interesting!
★★★★★★★★★★★★

And the Winner Is... Can you imagine being told you were president... and then finding out you weren't? On November 7, 2000, all major television networks first predicted the state of Florida's 25 electoral votes would go to Al Gore. Many people believed the vice president was well on his way to victory. By about 2:00 A.M. EST, however, most networks changed their position and announced that George W. Bush had won Florida! As a result, Gore called Governor Bush to concede the election. As results from Florida continued to come in, the networks declared that Florida was now too close to call. Gore called Bush again—this time to take back his concession. It would be another five weeks before George W. Bush was declared the winner.

⭐ America in the 1990s and Beyond

Despite the economic boom, challenges still faced the country. Terrorist attacks posed threats to U.S. security. In 1993, Arab terrorists bombed the World Trade Center in New York City. Then in 1995 a federal office building in Oklahoma City, Oklahoma, was bombed. The explosion killed 168 people and hurt hundreds of others. In response to such violence, the Clinton administration passed an antiterrorism bill in 1996.

Civil rights and race relations were still important issues for many Americans in the 1990s. Both President Clinton and Attorney General Janet Reno spoke of the need for new, broader federal laws to address racially motivated crimes.

Social services caused other national concerns. The competitive job market made it increasingly important for applicants to have a college degree. At the same time, the cost of a college education grew significantly. Many Americans also worried that by the time they retired, government programs such as Social Security would be bankrupt. Many Americans therefore invested their own money for retirement.

In 2000 the Democrats nominated Vice President **Al Gore** as their presidential candidate. Gore chose Senator Joe Lieberman of Connecticut to be his running mate. Lieberman became the first Orthodox Jew to run on a major-party ticket in the United States. Gore and Lieberman ran on a promise to keep paying down the national debt. They also wanted to use the government surplus for domestic programs such as education and health care.

Republicans nominated **George W. Bush**, the son of former president George Bush and governor of Texas, as their candidate for president. Bush chose former defense secretary Dick Cheney as his running mate. Bush ran on the promise to use most of the government surplus for tax cuts. He also said that he could bring people from both parties together to work for meaningful change.

The presidential election of 2000 was unlike any political contest Americans had ever seen. The vote was so close that several states could

---

★ **REVIEW AND ASSESS**

Have students complete the **Section 5 Review** on p. 711. Then have them complete **Daily Quiz E.5**. As **Alternative Assessment**, you may want to use the State of the Union address or the Cold War time line activities from this section's lessons.

★ **RETEACH**

Have students complete **Main Idea Activity for English Language Learners and Special-Needs Students E.5**. Then assign one Reading Check question to each of four groups. Have each group prepare a poster or collage that illuminates its

answer to the question. As each group displays its work, have members of other groups attempt to identify and explain the various elements in the posters or collages.
ENGLISH LANGUAGE LEARNERS , COOPERATIVE LEARNING

★ **EXTEND**

Have students use information from the library and other resources to prepare position papers supporting or criticizing either supply-side economics or NAFTA. When students are finished writing, have volunteers present their papers to the class. **BLOCK SCHEDULING**

not declare a winner. Florida's 25 electoral votes became the key to the White House. The results of Florida's first tally were so close that recounts were called for. Court challenges over manual recounts, ballot designs, and absentee ballots kept the country in suspense for five weeks. Eventually, the issue went all the way to the Supreme Court. The Court ruled that the hand recounts that had taken place in several Florida counties were not valid. Florida's electoral votes were awarded to Bush.

Bush was sworn in on January 20, 2001. In his inauguration speech, he called for Americans to help one another.

History Makers Speak

❝I ask you to seek a common good beyond your comfort. . . . I ask you to be citizens—citizens, not subjects; responsible citizens, building communities of service and a nation of character.❞

—George W. Bush, Inaugural Address

President Bush took steps to unite Americans by choosing a diverse cabinet, including General Colin Powell, who became the first African American to serve as secretary of state. The newly seated Congress was almost equally divided between Republicans and Democrats. The Senate was split 50-50, with Vice President Cheney holding the tie-breaking vote there. In the House of Representatives, the Republicans kept a small lead. This close division showed the need for Republicans and Democrats to work together for the good of all Americans.

✔ **Reading Check: Summarizing** What national and international issues did Americans face in the 1990s and beyond? terrorism, civil rights, and a changing job market; disputed election results

George W. Bush (at top) and Al Gore (at bottom) ran an extremely close presidential contest. Bush became the first president in more than 100 years to win the electoral vote but not the popular vote.

Section 5 Review

go. hrw .com **Homework Practice Online**
keyword: SA3 HPE

1 Define and explain:
• supply-side economics
• Internet

2 Identify and explain:
• Ronald Reagan
• Iran-Contra affair
• George Bush
• War on Drugs
• Operation Desert Storm
• Bill Clinton
• Contract with America
• North American Free Trade Agreement
• Al Gore
• George W. Bush

3 Main Idea **Sequencing** Copy the graphic organizer below. Use it to describe the progress of the Cold War in the 1980s.

End of the Cold War

5.
4.
3.
2.
1.

4 Finding the Main Idea
a. On what laws did Democrats and Republicans agree or disagree?

b. In what different ways did the United States take part in world affairs in the 1990s?

5 Writing and Critical Thinking
Supporting a Point of View Imagine that you are a foreign-policy adviser for the president of the United States. Based on the events that took place in the 1990s, write a statement telling the president how to prepare for the future.

Consider the following:
• important domestic issues
• global trade
• national security

★ ★ ★ ★ ★ ★ ★ ★ ★ ★

Section 5 Review ANSWERS

1 Define
• supply-side economics, p. 707
• Internet, p. 709

2 Identify
• Ronald Reagan, p. 707
• Iran-Contra affair, p. 708
• George Bush, p. 708
• War on Drugs, p. 708
• Operation Desert Storm, p. 708
• Bill Clinton, p. 709
• Contract with America, p. 709
• North American Free Trade Agreement, p. 709
• Al Gore, p. 710
• George W. Bush, p. 710

3 Students' answers will vary but should include five steps leading to the end of the Cold War.

4 a. health care, tax cuts divided the two parties; they passed welfare reform, antiterrorism act, and balancing the budget
b. military action: Bosnia, Iraq and Kuwait, Somalia, Haiti, Yugoslavia; diplomacy: Bosnia; economic treaties: space exploration: plans for a new space station, astronauts worked aboard Mir

5 Students' statements will vary but should include considerations of domestic issues, global trade, and national security.

Section 6

OBJECTIVES

- ⭐ Describe how the United States was attacked on September 11, 2001 and how Americans responded.
- ⭐ Explain how the events of September 11 affected the economy.
- ⭐ Evaluate the immediate steps American leaders took to find those responsible and to bring them to justice.

SECTION 6 RESOURCES

TECHNOLOGY

▶ CNN. Presents: September 11, 2001: A Turning Point in History

REINFORCEMENT, REVIEW, AND ASSESSMENT

▶ Section 6 Review, p. 735

Technology Resources

 CNN. Presents: September 11, 2001: A Turning Point in History

GLOBAL CONNECTIONS ANSWER

(for p. 713)

Students might suggest that the show of compassion and solidarity provided comfort to grieving Americans.

🔊 LET'S GET STARTED!

Ask students to remember where they were when they first heard of the terrorist attacks of September 11, 2001 and to describe their reaction to the event. *(Students' responses will vary but may include shock, fear, horror, and so on.)* Tell students that in Section 6 they will learn about the attack, its economic and social consequences, and the immediate response of the United States.

Section 6

September 11, 2001: A Day That Changed the World

Read to Discover

1. How was the United States attacked on September 11, 2001, and how did Americans respond?
2. How did the events of September 11 affect the economy?
3. What immediate steps did U.S. leaders take to find those responsible and bring them to justice?

WHY IT MATTERS TODAY

The terrorist attacks of September 11, 2001, continue to affect American life and U.S. foreign policy. Use **CNNfyi.com** or other **current events** sources to learn about the latest issues and events stemming from this national tragedy.

Identify

- World Trade Center
- Pentagon
- Rudolph Giuliani
- George W. Bush
- Tom Ridge
- Donald Rumsfeld
- Colin Powell

As seen from New York Harbor, smoke, ash, and debris obscure downtown Manhattan after the terrorist attacks.

The Story Continues

On Tuesday morning, September 11, 2001, it was business as usual in the downtown financial district of New York City. In the World Trade Center complex, an estimated 10,000 employees were starting their workday. Most of them were within the Twin Towers that dominated the Manhattan skyline. On Fifth Avenue a group of pedestrians noticed a large airplane pass overhead. "We all thought it would be unusual for a plane to be flying so low over the city," recalled one man. Moments later they witnessed a terrible disaster unfold.

⭐ The Attack

At 8:48 A.M., an American Airlines passenger jet crashed into the north tower of the **World Trade Center**. The impact was devastating, as though a bomb had struck the 110-story building. Stunned men and women began evacuating the building as emergency crews rushed to the scene. Then at 9:03 A.M. a second plane slammed into the south tower and exploded.

★ TEACH

Have students read Section 6 and complete Guided Reading Strategy 6. Choose one or more of the following activities to explore the section content with students. For further suggestions on block scheduling or team teaching, see the *Block Scheduling Handbook with Team Teaching Strategies.*

LEVEL 1: Organize the class into small groups. To help students understand how the United States was attacked on September 11, 2001, ask students to create a time line of the events of that day. *(8:48 A.M.—north tower struck; 9:03 A.M.—south tower struck; 9:40 A.M.—Pentagon struck; 9:59 A.M.—south tower collapses; 10:10 A.M.—United Airlines Flight 93 crashes; 10:30 A.M.—north tower collapses.)* Then ask students to include a section on how Americans responded to the attacks in the following days. *(Students' responses should include the following: rescue workers from across the nation came to New York to aid in the rescue effort, Congress approved a relief package, and ordinary Americans donated blood and money.)* **ENGLISH LANGUAGE LEARNERS , COOPERATIVE LEARNING**

HOMEWORK Have students create a memorial that would honor those lost in the attacks of September 11, and those who contributed to the rescue efforts. Students may choose the format in which to create their memorial.

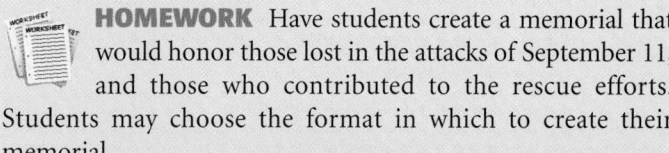

Many Americans saw the second crash broadcast live on television and realized that this was not a tragic accident but a deliberate attack. It was also soon clear that New York was not the terrorists' only target. At approximately 9:40 A.M. a third plane hit the west side of the **Pentagon**. Located just outside Washington, D.C., the Pentagon is the headquarters of the U.S. military. The impact of the crash caused massive damage and started fires deep within the huge five-sided building.

At the World Trade Center complex, hundreds of rescue workers struggled to aid victims and firefighters tried to control the raging fires. Then, further disaster struck. Just before 10:00 A.M. the south tower suddenly collapsed, followed half an hour later by the fall of the north tower. The collapse of the massive buildings killed or trapped thousands of people still inside or near the towers, including hundreds of firefighters, police officers, and other rescuers.

A fourth plane was also hijacked and still in the air over southern Pennsylvania. Passengers aboard the plane made cell phone calls indicating that they learned of the other attacks and decided to stop the terrorists on board from hitting their next target. Flight 93 crashed southeast of Pittsburgh at 10:10, between the times the World Trade Center's Twin Towers collapsed.

In downtown New York City, clouds of smoke, dust, and ash drifted through the streets. Meanwhile, emergency teams battling fires in the Pentagon were unable to search for survivors. All 265 passengers and crew aboard the four hijacked flights had been killed. Americans everywhere were shocked, wondering what was to come next.

✔ **Reading Check: Sequencing** In what order did the events on the morning of September 11, 2001, take place? A hijacked plane crashed into the north tower of the World Trade Center, and another hit the south tower. A third plane hit the Pentagon. The towers collapsed. A fourth plane crashed in Pennsylvania.

★ The Nation Responds

Government officials raced to increase rescue efforts and placed the U.S. military on full alert. The Federal Aviation Administration temporarily grounded air traffic nationwide and closed airports. Key government centers, such as the White House and the Capitol, were evacuated.

Firefighters and other rescue workers from across the nation came to New York. There they joined state and city emergency personnel searching the rubble for survivors. Their efforts were blocked by the intense heat from underground fires. New York hospitals mobilized hundreds of doctors but found, tragically, that there were relatively few survivors to treat. New York mayor **Rudolph Giuliani** said of the final death toll, "It will be more than we can bear." More than 5,500 people were killed by the attack on the World Trade Center. This number included more than 300 firefighters and many other rescue workers who were on the scene. At the Pentagon, 189 military and civilian personnel, including those on the hijacked plane, were killed.

Firefighters raise an American flag over the rubble of the World Trade Center towers.

GLOBAL CONNECTIONS

The World Reaches Out

The tragic events of September 11, 2001, drew sympathy and support from around the world. Citizens of more than 40 countries were among the missing. The European Union declared September 14 a day of mourning. British prime minister Tony Blair called the terrorist acts "an attack on the free and democratic world everywhere." The French newspaper *Le Monde* ran a headline saying, "WE ARE ALL AMERICANS." Russian and Chinese leaders gave their condolences. Even traditional opponents of the United States, such as Cuba and Iran, expressed their sympathy and regret. U.S. leaders gave thanks for these gestures and worked to form an active coalition against terrorism. **Why might global support be important to the United States?**

Science, Technology & Society

The World Trade Center. Each a little over 1,360 feet high and consisting of 110 floors, the twin towers of the World Trade Center were designed to withstand significant structural damage. Completed in the early 1970s, 200,000 tons of steel and 425,000 cubic yards of concrete went into the construction of the towers. On September 11, 2001 the buildings collapsed from the heat of the burning jet fuel which apparently softened or melted the load-bearing steel columns, resulting in the collapse of both towers.

Historical Sidelight

The Pentagon. Headquarters of the U.S. Department of Defense, the Pentagon is one of the world's largest office buildings. Although it is only five stories high, the building itself covers 29 acres. Shaped in the form of a pentagon, each of the five wedges contains more than 1 million square feet and typically houses around 5,000 employees. A Boeing 757 crashed into the left side of the first wedge where the Army military officers were located.

ACTIVITY: Have students research the history of the Pentagon and its resulting design. Then have them research other buildings of a distinctive design and make a diorama of their chosen building.

BIOGRAPHY

Rudolph Giuliani
(1944–)

As mayor of New York City, Rudy Giuliani played a key role during the early weeks of the crisis. Coordinating relief efforts, consoling victims, and calling for resolve and renewed confidence, he served as an important symbol of strength to the city and the nation as a whole. A national poll conducted following the attacks found a 95 percent approval rating for how the mayor performed his duties. Why do you think Giuliani's popularity increased after the attacks?

Analyzing Primary Sources
Drawing Inferences and Conclusions What do you think James Earl Jones means when he says what Americans share is greater than what divides them?
Students might say that a desire for freedom and democracy unites people of different backgrounds.

Congress swiftly approved a $40 billion relief package to fund emergency assistance and national security measures. The government also passed legislation that provided financial support to the families of victims. Democrats and Republicans displayed an unusual degree of cooperation in pushing through these measures.

Political leaders also tried to rally Americans' spirit on the day of the attack. Mayor Giuliani assured fellow New Yorkers, "We're going to rebuild and rebuild stronger." President **George W. Bush**, who had been in Florida visiting an elementary school, was moved to a safer location. From there, he gave a brief speech to the nation and told Americans that "we [the United States] will do whatever is necessary to protect America and Americans." Republican and Democratic members of Congress issued a joint declaration to the country from the Capitol steps. They said that the United States would not be intimidated by terrorism. The members then sang a chorus of "God Bless America."

Perhaps the greatest show of unity came from the American people themselves. Many were inspired to displays of charity and patriotism. Within two days Wal-Mart, the nation's largest retail chain, had sold its entire stock of half a million American flags. Charitable groups across the country moved swiftly to raise funds for relief efforts. Thousands of people went to Red Cross centers to donate blood.

People also came together in public to heal their wounds and show their strength. When professional sports leagues resumed their schedules, stadiums were filled with patriotic tributes and fans waving flags. Actor James Earl Jones drew cheers as he opened a mass prayer service held in New York City's Yankee Stadium.

 History Makers Speak
"Our spirit is unbroken. In fact, it is stronger than ever. Today we reaffirm our faith in the essential dignity of every individual. What we share as Americans and as human beings is far greater than what divides us."

—James Earl Jones, prayer service, September 23, 2001

Religious leaders representing many faiths led prayers for the victims and called for unity as a nation. The Boys and Girls Choir of Harlem sang a stirring version of "We Shall Overcome."

✔ **Reading Check: Summarizing** In what ways did Americans first respond to the terrorist attacks? Hospitals and rescuers took action. Congress approved a relief package. Americans displayed American flags and donated blood and money to help victims and their loved ones.

⭐ The Investigation

Immediately after the attacks, the largest criminal investigation in U.S. history began. Within 48 hours the Federal Bureau of Investigation (FBI) placed more than 4,000 special agents on the case. The FBI soon released the names of 19 suspected hijackers from several nations in the Middle East. Investigators gathered evidence suggesting that each group of hijackers included trained pilots. Some of these men had been living and training in the United States for months. Even more crucial was the identity of those who had planned these acts of terror.

A prime suspect surfaced almost immediately—Osama bin Laden. This wealthy Saudi Arabian exile was already wanted for his suspected role in earlier terrorist attacks against U.S. forces overseas. A supporter of an extreme form of Islamic fundamentalism, bin Laden had publicly called for attacks on the United States. He claimed that the United States had corrupted and oppressed Muslims. Bin Laden's global terrorism network is known as al Qaeda, or "the Base." U.S. officials believe that it is one of the few terrorist groups with the resources and organizational structure to have carried out the attacks.

Experts also agreed that the attacks of September 11 likely involved the cooperation of more than one terrorist group. Investigators from a broad range of federal agencies began a global manhunt with assistance from other nations. Investigators sifted through debris at the crash sites to find physical evidence. They also attempted to track airline, telephone, credit card, and other financial records to trace terrorists' movements. The Bush administration pledged to release conclusive evidence about the attacks as soon as it was possible to do so.

✔ **Reading Check: Analyzing Information** What early conclusions did investigators draw about who carried out the attacks, and how did they investigate them? Investigators determined that the suspected hijackers were from Middle Eastern nations and that some were trained pilots. Investigators searched through debris at the crash sites and checked telephone and financial records.

The Economic Impact

The terrorist strikes on the World Trade Center also had a high cost in economic terms. The costs related to the immediate physical damage were estimated at $25 billion. In addition, the New York Stock Exchange (NYSE) had to shut down operations for four days, the longest period of time since it closed at the beginning of World War I in 1914. When the NYSE reopened, it had one of the worst weeks in its history.

One area of particular concern was the airline industry. Major airlines were forced to shut down operations for days and faced greatly

---

Historical Document

PRESIDENT BUSH'S ADDRESS TO THE NATION

On September 20, 2001, President George W. Bush addressed the joint houses of Congress and the American people. The following is an excerpt from his speech.

Tonight we are a country awakened to danger and called to defend freedom. Our grief has turned to anger, and anger to resolution. . . .

Every nation, in every region, now has a decision to make. Either you are with us, or you are with the terrorists. From this day forward, any nation that continues to harbor or support terrorism will be regarded by the United States as a hostile regime. . . .

Great harm has been done to us. We have suffered great loss. And in our grief and anger we have found our mission and our moment. Freedom and fear are at war. The advance of human freedom . . . now depends on us. . . . We will not tire, . . . and we will not fail.

Analyzing Primary Sources

1. What did President Bush call on other nations to do?

2. How did the president say the United States would react to terrorist acts?

⭐ Culture

The Taliban. The Taliban movement began in the schools of Afghanistan and western Pakistan where a strict version of Islam was taught. In fact, Taliban means "the students" in Persian. In 1995, a civil war occurred and Mullah Muhammad Omar formed a militia composed of his students. This militia became known as the Taliban and it took control in 1996 and subsequently imposed its interpretation of Islam on its citizens. The Taliban is especially strict on women. It demands that they cover their faces, do not attend school or go to work, and are forbidden to talk to a man not related to them. It has been reported that non-followers are brutally tortured, beaten and even executed.

ACTIVITY: Have students research the government, society, and economy of Afghanistan today and submit the information in the form of a CIA special report using standard grammar, spelling, sentence structure, and punctuation.

ANALYZING PRIMARY SOURCE ANSWERS

1. He asks them to make a decision about whether to join them in the cause to eradicate terrorism.

2. He says that the United States will act with resolution.

Interpreting the Visual Record

The stock market *Concerns about a potential war and poor economic indicators caused prices on the NASDAQ stock exchange to fall dramatically after the market reopened following the terrorist attacks. European and Asian stock markets also suffered heavy losses.* **How does this photograph reflect that decline?**

increased security expenses. In addition, many people were reluctant to fly. Major airlines took heavy financial losses and laid off thousands of workers. Tourism declined severely around the nation, and companies relying on supplies shipped by air continued to have shortages. The president and Congress rushed to pass a $15 billion bail-out package to help keep the nation's airlines operating.

One of the most difficult economic problems for the government to address was falling consumer confidence. Many Americans had been concerned about the economy before the terrorist attacks. The events of September 11 raised feelings of uncertainty and made many Americans believe the country was headed for a recession. Government officials responded by emphasizing that the long-term health of the economy was strong, even if difficult times lay ahead.

✔ **Reading Check: Finding the Main Idea** What immediate effects did the terrorist attacks have on the U.S. economy? The stock market dropped and airlines took heavy financial losses. Tourism declined, and companies relying on supplies shipped by air faced shortages.

★ A Call to Action

In a national address on September 20, President George W. Bush called the attacks on the World Trade Center and the Pentagon "an act of war." He promised that the United States would bring those responsible to justice and wage war on terrorism itself. President Bush emphasized that the efforts of the United States would be aimed not only against terrorist organizations but also against national governments that supported and protected terrorists.

In his speech the president singled out one government—the ruling Taliban of Afghanistan—as a key sponsor of terror. The Taliban emerged in the mid-1990s as a splinter group of fundamentalist Muslims. Many members had fought against the Soviets during their occupation of Afghanistan. The Taliban's leaders had developed ties to Osama bin Laden, whom they later sheltered. Bush demanded that the Taliban turn Osama bin Laden over to the U.S. government.

The campaign against terrorism involved defensive and offensive measures. President Bush appointed Pennsylvania governor **Tom Ridge** to head the Office of Homeland Security, a new cabinet-level position. This office was created to coordinate the domestic national security efforts of various government agencies. Key goals included improving airport security and protecting vital systems such as transportation and power networks from attack. Political leaders such as U.S. Attorney General John Ashcroft also called for expanded law-enforcement powers to combat terrorism. This led to debate over how best to protect Americans' civil liberties while increasing domestic security.

Administration officials, including Secretary of Defense **Donald Rumsfeld**, agreed that locating and striking at terrorists outside the United States would be a lengthy and difficult task.

★ REVIEW AND ASSESS

Have students complete the **Section 6 Review** on p. 717. As **Alternative Assessment** you may want to use the quilt of heroes or journal entry exercise in this section's lessons.

★ RETEACH

Create a packet of notecards that can be sequenced describing the events of September 11, 2001 and the days that followed. Organize students into small groups and give each group a packet of cards to correctly sequence.

ENGLISH LANGUAGE LEARNERS , COOPERATIVE LEARNING

★ EXTEND

Lead a class discussion summarizing this section, and then write the following question on the board: *How have the terrorist attacks changed the United States?* Then have each student write an essay detailing how the terrorist attacks changed the United States. Encourage students to include in their essay how the attacks have affected and changed them as well.

BLOCK SCHEDULING

The Bush administration sought to fight terrorism using economic, diplomatic, and military means. The president froze the assets of individuals, groups, and companies with suspected terrorist ties. Secretary of State **Colin Powell** led U.S. efforts to build an international coalition against terrorism and to isolate the Taliban regime.

The United States also began mobilizing military forces. Aircraft carrier groups and ground troops were assembled in preparation for possible attacks on terrorist targets. On October 7, the United States and Great Britain began air strikes against Afghanistan. The strikes targeted al Qaeda and Taliban training camps, air-defense systems, and airfields, as well as Kabul, the country's capital. President Bush explained that the Taliban regime had been warned to meet American demands to surrender Osama bin Laden.

Meanwhile, as the military action continued, Americans and the military remained on alert for other possible terrorist actions. Several letters containing dried anthrax spores were sent to locations in Florida, New York City, and Washington, D.C., including Senator Tom Daschle's office. Some who handled these letters, including postal workers, became infected and died. Anthrax is a potentially deadly disease caused by spore-form bacterium. It was used in World War I as a means of biological warfare.

As U.S. leaders responded to the attacks, it was evident that a new era in global relations had begun. The events of September 11 had exposed both the vulnerability and the strength of the United States. Americans faced the uncertain future with hope and determination.

This mother and her daughter joined many Americans who attended an interfaith memorial service for the victims of the September 11 attacks.

internet connect

GO TO: go.hrw.com
KEYWORD: SS Attack
FOR: Web sites about the events of September 11, 2001, and the aftermath

✔ **Reading Check: Summarizing** What early steps did U.S. leaders take to respond to the terrorist attacks on the United States? Airport security increased. The U.S. government froze the assets of those with suspected terrorist ties and built a coalition to fight terrorism. On October 7, the United States began military action against Afghanistan.

Section 6 Review

Homework Practice Online
keyword: SF3 HPE

❶ Identify and explain:
• World Trade Center
• Pentagon
• Rudolph Giuliani
• George W. Bush
• Tom Ridge
• Donald Rumsfeld
• Colin Powell

❷ Analyzing Information
Copy the graphic organizer below. Use it to explain some of the ways in which the government responded to protect Americans and bring terrorists to justice.

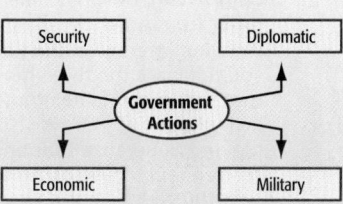

❸ Finding the Main Idea
a. Whom did investigators suspect of carrying out the terrorist attacks of September 11, 2001, and how did they pursue the investigation?
b. How did the attacks affect the economy?

❹ Writing and Critical Thinking
Evaluating Imagine that you are first learning of the attacks on September 11, 2001, and want to help however you can. Write a paragraph describing possible actions you could take to assist those in need.

Consider the following:
• the efforts of relief agencies to help victims
• the need for national unity
• the importance of tolerance

CHAPTER 22 REVIEW ANSWERS

The Chapter at a Glance
Students' lists will vary but should include important changes that took places in the late 1800s and early 1900s.

Identifying People and Ideas
Students' sentences should indicate an understanding of the following definitions:

1. period of explosive growth in U.S. manufacturing

2. a new method to make affordable steel developed in the 1850s

3. foreign policy of the United States where the nation did not get involved in the affairs of other nations

4. U.S. president who introduced the New Deal

5. a form of government that places more value on nation than individual

6. nonviolent civil rights leader who led the Montgomery Bus Boycott

7. women's rights advocacy group founded in 1966

8. scandal in which President Nixon's cover up of the break-in of Democratic National Headquarters led to his resignation in the face of impeachment

9. economic concept introduced by Ronald Reagan

10. conservative Republican president first elected in 1980

REVIEW AND ASSESSMENT RESOURCES

REPRODUCIBLE

▶ Vocabulary Activity
Epilogue

TECHNOLOGY

▶ Epilogue Test Generator
(on the One-Stop Planner)

▶ Global Skill Builder
CD–ROM

▶ HRW Go site

REINFORCEMENT, REVIEW, AND ASSESSMENT

▶ Epilogue Review,
pp. 717–19

▶ Epilogue Tutorial for
Students, Parents,
Mentors, and Peers

▶ Epilogue Test
(Form A or B)

▶ Alternative Assessment
Handbook

▶ Epilogue Test for English
Language Learners and
Special-Needs Students

★ REVIEW

Have students complete the **Epilogue Review** on pages 718–19.

★ ASSESS

Use one of the chapter tests to assess students' understanding of the content. For **Alternative Assessment**, see the **Alternative Assessment Handbook.**

Understanding Main Ideas

1. The United States became the world's industrial leader. New business practices were introduced.

2. It increasingly became involved in world affairs, particularly in Latin America.

3. Products of new technologies emerged, such as cars and radios. These technologies contributed to the booming American economy. They also introduced new ways of doing business and manufacturing. Musicians and writers contributed to cultural changes. African Americans introduced jazz music to white American culture. The Lost Generation of writers criticized modern society.

4. The United States dropped two atomic bombs on Japan, causing the country to surrender.

5. Many people were anticommunist. The government followed a military strategy that threatened nuclear attack.

6. desegregation laws, antidiscrimination laws, voting rights laws

7. by donating their time and money to help victims, donating blood, and so on

You Be the Historian— Reviewing Themes

1. World War I: German submarines attacking unarmed merchant ships; World War II: Japanese bombing the U.S. naval base at Pearl Harbor, Hawaii

---

EPILOGUE Review

The Chapter at a Glance

Examine the visual summary of the chapter below. Use it to brainstorm what you think are the most important changes that took place in the 1900s. Compare your list with a classmate's list, and then discuss how your lists are similar and different.

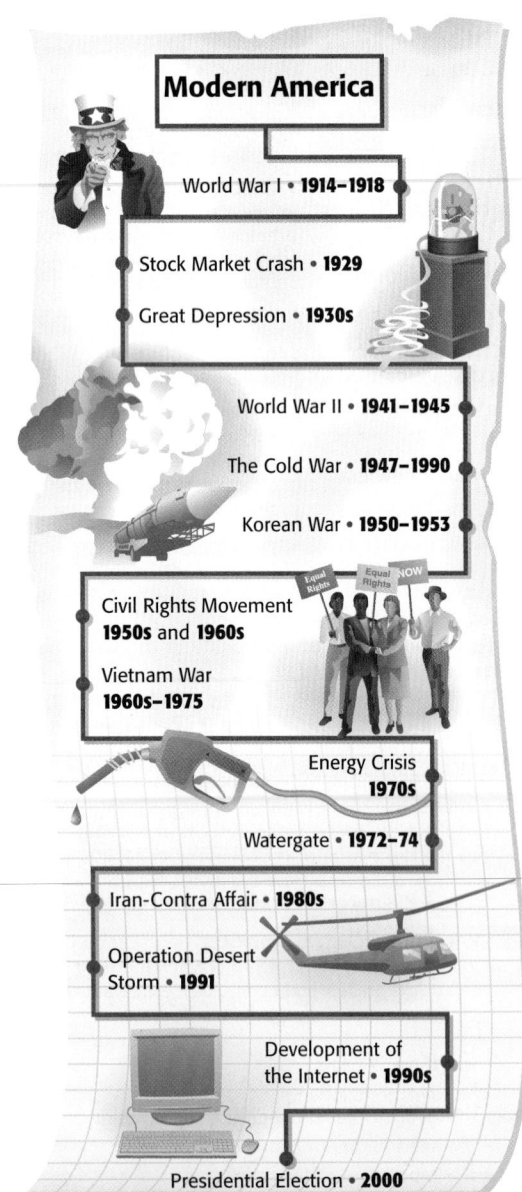

Modern America

World War I • **1914–1918**

Stock Market Crash • **1929**

Great Depression • **1930s**

World War II • **1941–1945**

The Cold War • **1947–1990**

Korean War • **1950–1953**

Civil Rights Movement **1950s** and **1960s**

Vietnam War **1960s–1975**

Energy Crisis **1970s**

Watergate • **1972–74**

Iran-Contra Affair • **1980s**

Operation Desert Storm • **1991**

Development of the Internet • **1990s**

Presidential Election • **2000**

Identifying People and Ideas

Use the following terms or people in historically significant sentences.

1. Woodrow Wilson
2. Harlem Renaissance
3. Great Depression
4. Holocaust
5. Marshall Plan
6. Martin Luther King Jr.
7. John F. Kennedy
8. energy crisis
9. supply-side economics
10. Bill Clinton

Understanding Main Ideas

Section 1 *(Pages 768–773)*
1. How did life in the United States change after World War I?

Section 2 *(Pages 774–780)*
2. How did President Roosevelt's administration help Americans get through the depression?

Section 3 *(Pages 781–786)*
3. How did the Cold War influence U.S. foreign and domestic policy?

Section 4 *(Pages 787–793)*
4. How did African Americans gain greater civil rights in the 1960s, and what were these rights?
5. What domestic and international concerns faced the United States in the 1970s?

Section 5 *(Pages 794–799)*
6. How was the United States involved with other countries in the 1980s and 1990s?

Section 6 *(Pages 800–805)*
7. How did Americans try to help after the terrorist attacks of September 11, 2001?

You Be the Historian— Reviewing Themes

1. **Global Relations** Why did the United States enter the fighting in World Wars I and II?
2. **Citizenship** What strategies did civil rights workers use in the 1950s and 1960s?
3. **Economics** How did some nations strengthen their global economic ties in the 1990s?

Thinking Critically

1. **Contrasting** How did American life in the 1930s differ from American life in the 1920s?
2. **Drawing Inferences and Conclusions** What do you think are the three most important reasons that the United States chose to take military action in the 1990s?
3. **Making Generalizations and Predictions** Based on trends you have observed in your study of the past 100 years, what do you think the next 100 years will be like?

Organize students into groups and assign each group one of the chapter's sections. Have each group create a chapter of a children's book that illustrates the most important events in the group's assigned section. Ask students to write simple text to accompany each illustration.

ENGLISH LANGUAGE LEARNERS ,
COOPERATIVE LEARNING

Portfolio Extension

American History

1. Cooperative Learning

Organize the class into groups of four or five. Assign each group one of the decades between the 1880s and the 1990s. Tell each group to imagine that they have been hired to create a time capsule of that decade to show to future Americans. Students should create a poster of the items to include in the capsule. Items should give people some idea of the major events. The items should also show how

people lived at the time. Students might want to include items that represent art, entertainment, or literature. When students have finished, have them share their work with the class.

2. Interdisciplinary Connection to the Arts
Have students choose one of the events discussed in this chapter, such as the Freedom Rides or the McCarthy hearings. Then ask students to illustrate the chosen event. Students' illustrations should be self-explanatory.

Social Studies Skills Workshop

Interpreting Political Cartoons
Study the cartoon below. Then use the cartoon to help you answer the questions that follow.

"You've got to admit we're getting Watergate behind us."

THE PARDON
COVER-UP
TRIAL
"TRANSITIONAL EXPENSES"
NIXON TAPES
SUIT

1. What is the cartoon's message?
   a. Watergate continued to trouble President Ford and the nation even after Nixon resigned.
   b. Nixon abused his powers as president.
   c. Ford was not prepared for the new responsibilities that he assumed as president.
   d. Nixon was a stronger leader than Ford.
2. What is President Ford doing and why?

Analyzing Primary Sources
Read the following quotation by Justice Sandra Day O'Connor, the first woman ever to serve on the U.S. Supreme Court, then answer the questions.

❝Judges are supposed to be objective; they're supposed to study and look at the law and apply the law to the particular case in an objective way, not from any particular point of view. So does being a woman make a difference in what answer is given? I tend to think that probably at the end of the day, a wise old woman and a wise old man are going to reach the same answer.❞

3. What point of view does Justice O'Connor express about the qualifications of women to be judges?
   a. Men make better judgments than women.
   b. Women make better judgments than men.
   c. Men and women make the same judgments.
   d. Men and women come to different conclusions.
4. What information does Justice O'Connor use to help support her conclusion?
   a. Judges are supposed to apply the law in an objective way.
   b. Justice O'Connor is well educated.
   c. Judges have many different points of view.
   d. It is important that both men and women serve on the Supreme Court.
5. Do you agree or disagree with Justice O'Connor's statement? Explain your answer.

---

2. They staged boycotts, campaigns, demonstrations, marches, protests, and sit-ins, and they used the courts.

3. They formed trade agreements and organizations.

Thinking Critically
1. Students' charts will vary.

2. For the most part in the 1920s, the American economy was experiencing a boom. People were generally optimistic. In the 1930s, however, the country was in the Great Depression.

3. Students' answers will vary, but some might mention continued efforts at bipartisanship, continuing economic prosperity, and continued struggle over issues like the environment.

Skills Workshop
1. b

2. He has added a great number of guns.

3. He has a critical attitude toward Reagan's Strategic Defense Initiative.

4. c

5. Students' answers will vary, but students may suggest that she is responding to questions as to whether a woman should be a Supreme Court justice.

6. Students' responses will vary.

Alternative Assessment

American History

Building Your Portfolio

Linking to Community
Go to a local public library or historical society, and study old copies of your local community's newspaper to learn how its residents experienced World War I. Answer the following questions in a brief written report. Who enlisted? Who was drafted? Did anyone protest U.S. involvement? What role did women and African Americans play? How did the community support troops overseas? Present your written report to the class.

📝 **internet** connect

Internet Activity: go.hrw.com
keyword: SF3 CFEP

Choose an activity on Modern America to:
● Research changes in submarine technology and the impact of submarine warfare.
● Write a biography of Louis Armstrong.
● Create an example of Berlin Wall art that portrays the breakup of the Soviet Union.

go.
hrw
.com

American pocket watch

Early American flag

Cotton, an important southern product

The Granger Collection, New York

One of the first American locomotives, c. 1830

James Madison's quill pen

Native American totem pole

HOLT

CALL TO FREEDOM

Beginnings to 1877

The Statue of Liberty

REFERENCE

Colonial pottery
Colonial Williamsburg Foundation

**Advertisement
for the Pony
Express**

Collection of the American
Numismatic Society

**U.S. coins celebrating Thomas
Jefferson's inauguration**

Presidents of the United States

The Official Portraits

1 GEORGE WASHINGTON
Born: 1732   Died: 1799
Years in Office: 1789–97
Political Party: None
Home State: Virginia
Vice President: John Adams

2 JOHN ADAMS
Born: 1735   Died: 1826
Years in Office: 1797–1801
Political Party: Federalist
Home State: Massachusetts
Vice President: Thomas Jefferson

3 THOMAS JEFFERSON
Born: 1743   Died: 1826
Years in Office: 1801–09
Political Party: Republican*
Home State: Virginia
Vice Presidents: Aaron Burr,
George Clinton

4 JAMES MADISON
Born: 1751   Died: 1836
Years in Office: 1809–17
Political Party: Republican
Home State: Virginia
Vice Presidents: George Clinton,
Elbridge Gerry

5 JAMES MONROE
Born: 1758   Died: 1831
Years in Office: 1817–25
Political Party: Republican
Home State: Virginia
Vice President: Daniel D. Tompkins

6 JOHN QUINCY ADAMS
Born: 1767   Died: 1848
Years in Office: 1825–29
Political Party: Republican
Home State: Massachusetts
Vice President: John C. Calhoun

7 ANDREW JACKSON
Born: 1767   Died: 1845
Years in Office: 1829–37
Political Party: Democratic
Home State: Tennessee
Vice Presidents: John C. Calhoun,
Martin Van Buren

* The Republican Party of the third through sixth presidents is not the party of Abraham Lincoln, which was founded in 1854.

8 MARTIN VAN BUREN
Born: 1782   Died: 1862
Years in Office: 1837–41
Political Party: Democratic
Home State: New York
Vice President: Richard M. Johnson

9 WILLIAM HENRY HARRISON
Born: 1773   Died: 1841
Years in Office: 1841
Political Party: Whig
Home State: Ohio
Vice President: John Tyler

10 JOHN TYLER
Born: 1790   Died: 1862
Years in Office: 1841–45
Political Party: Whig
Home State: Virginia
Vice President: None

11 JAMES K. POLK
Born: 1795   Died: 1849
Years in Office: 1845–49
Political Party: Democratic
Home State: Tennessee
Vice President: George M. Dallas

12 ZACHARY TAYLOR
Born: 1784   Died: 1850
Years in Office: 1849–50
Political Party: Whig
Home State: Louisiana
Vice President: Millard Fillmore

13 MILLARD FILLMORE
Born: 1800   Died: 1874
Years in Office: 1850–53
Political Party: Whig
Home State: New York
Vice President: None

14 FRANKLIN PIERCE
Born: 1804   Died: 1869
Years in Office: 1853–57
Political Party: Democratic
Home State: New Hampshire
Vice President: William R. King

15 JAMES BUCHANAN
Born: 1791   Died: 1868
Years in Office: 1857–61
Political Party: Democratic
Home State: Pennsylvania
Vice President: John C. Breckinridge

16 ABRAHAM LINCOLN
Born: 1809   Died: 1865
Years in Office: 1861–65
Political Party: Republican
Home State: Illinois
Vice Presidents: Hannibal Hamlin,
Andrew Johnson

PRESIDENTS OF THE UNITED STATES

17 ANDREW JOHNSON
Born: 1808   **Died:** 1875
Years in Office: 1865–69
Political Party: Republican
Home State: Tennessee
Vice President: None

18 ULYSSES S. GRANT
Born: 1822   **Died:** 1885
Years in Office: 1869–77
Political Party: Republican
Home State: Illinois
Vice Presidents: Schuyler Colfax,
  Henry Wilson

19 RUTHERFORD B. HAYES
Born: 1822   **Died:** 1893
Years in Office: 1877–81
Political Party: Republican
Home State: Ohio
Vice President: William A. Wheeler

20 JAMES A. GARFIELD
Born: 1831   **Died:** 1881
Years in Office: 1881
Political Party: Republican
Home State: Ohio
Vice President: Chester A. Arthur

21 CHESTER A. ARTHUR
Born: 1829   **Died:** 1886
Years in Office: 1881–85
Political Party: Republican
Home State: New York
Vice President: None

22 GROVER CLEVELAND
Born: 1837   **Died:** 1908
Years in Office: 1885–89
Political Party: Democratic
Home State: New York
Vice President: Thomas A. Hendricks

23 BENJAMIN HARRISON
Born: 1833   **Died:** 1901
Years in Office: 1889–93
Political Party: Republican
Home State: Indiana
Vice President: Levi P. Morton

24 GROVER CLEVELAND
Born: 1837   **Died:** 1908
Years in Office: 1893–97
Political Party: Democratic
Home State: New York
Vice President: Adlai E. Stevenson

25 WILLIAM MCKINLEY
Born: 1843   **Died:** 1901
Years in Office: 1897–1901
Political Party: Republican
Home State: Ohio
Vice Presidents: Garret A. Hobart,
  Theodore Roosevelt

26 THEODORE ROOSEVELT
Born: 1858   Died: 1919
Years in Office: 1901–09
Political Party: Republican
Home State: New York
Vice President: Charles W. Fairbanks

27 WILLIAM HOWARD TAFT
Born: 1857   Died: 1930
Years in Office: 1909–13
Political Party: Republican
Home State: Ohio
Vice President: James S. Sherman

28 WOODROW WILSON
Born: 1856   Died: 1924
Years in Office: 1913–21
Political Party: Democratic
Home State: New Jersey
Vice President: Thomas R. Marshall

29 WARREN G. HARDING
Born: 1865   Died: 1923
Years in Office: 1921–23
Political Party: Republican
Home State: Ohio
Vice President: Calvin Coolidge

30 CALVIN COOLIDGE
Born: 1872   Died: 1933
Years in Office: 1923–29
Political Party: Republican
Home State: Massachusetts
Vice President: Charles G. Dawes

31 HERBERT HOOVER
Born: 1874   Died: 1964
Years in Office: 1929–33
Political Party: Republican
Home State: California
Vice President: Charles Curtis

32 FRANKLIN D. ROOSEVELT
Born: 1882   Died: 1945
Years in Office: 1933–45
Political Party: Democratic
Home State: New York
Vice Presidents: John Nance Garner,
  Henry Wallace, Harry S Truman

33 HARRY S TRUMAN
Born: 1884   Died: 1972
Years in Office: 1945–53
Political Party: Democratic
Home State: Missouri
Vice President: Alben W. Barkley

34 DWIGHT D. EISENHOWER
Born: 1890   Died: 1969
Years in Office: 1953–61
Political Party: Republican
Home State: Kansas
Vice President: Richard M. Nixon

PRESIDENTS OF THE UNITED STATES

35 JOHN F. KENNEDY
Born: 1917   Died: 1963
Years in Office: 1961–63
Political Party: Democratic
Home State: Massachusetts
Vice President: Lyndon B. Johnson

36 LYNDON B. JOHNSON
Born: 1908   Died: 1973
Years in Office: 1963–69
Political Party: Democratic
Home State: Texas
Vice President: Hubert H. Humphrey

37 RICHARD M. NIXON
Born: 1913   Died: 1994
Years in Office: 1969–74
Political Party: Republican
Home State: California
Vice Presidents: Spiro T. Agnew,
Gerald R. Ford

38 GERALD R. FORD
Born: 1913
Years in Office: 1974–77
Political Party: Republican
Home State: Michigan
Vice President: Nelson A. Rockefeller

39 JIMMY CARTER
Born: 1924
Years in Office: 1977–81
Political Party: Democratic
Home State: Georgia
Vice President: Walter F. Mondale

40 RONALD REAGAN
Born: 1911
Years in Office: 1981–89
Political Party: Republican
Home State: California
Vice President: George Bush

41 GEORGE BUSH
Born: 1924
Years in Office: 1989–93
Political Party: Republican
Home State: Texas
Vice President: J. Danforth Quayle

42 BILL CLINTON
Born: 1946
Years in Office: 1993–2001
Political Party: Democratic
Home State: Arkansas
Vice President: Albert Gore Jr.

43 GEORGE W. BUSH
Born: 1946
Years in Office: 2001–
Political Party: Republican
Home State: Texas
Vice President: Richard B. Cheney

Facts About the States

STATE	YEAR OF STATEHOOD	2000 POPULATION	REPS. IN CONGRESS	AREA (SQ. MI.)	POPULATION DENSITY (SQ. MI.)	CAPITAL
Alabama	1819	4,461,130	7	51,705	86.3	Montgomery
Alaska	1959	628,933	1	591,004	1.1	Juneau
Arizona	1912	5,140,683	8	114,000	45.1	Phoenix
Arkansas	1836	2,679,733	4	53,187	50.4	Little Rock
California	1850	33,930,798	53	158,706	213.8	Sacramento
Colorado	1876	4,311,882	7	104,247	41.4	Denver
Connecticut	1788	3,409,535	5	5,018	679.5	Hartford
Delaware	1787	785,068	1	2,057	381.7	Dover
District of Columbia	—	572,059	—	69	8,290.7	—
Florida	1845	16,028,890	25	58,664	273.2	Tallahassee
Georgia	1788	8,206,975	13	58,910	139.3	Atlanta
Hawaii	1959	1,216,642	2	6,471	188.0	Honolulu
Idaho	1890	1,297,274	2	83,557	15.5	Boise
Illinois	1818	12,439,042	19	56,400	220.6	Springfield
Indiana	1816	6,090,782	9	36,291	167.8	Indianapolis
Iowa	1846	2,931,923	5	56,275	52.1	Des Moines
Kansas	1861	2,693,824	4	82,277	32.7	Topeka
Kentucky	1792	4,049,431	6	40,395	100.2	Frankfort
Louisiana	1812	4,480,271	7	48,523	92.3	Baton Rouge
Maine	1820	1,277,731	2	33,265	38.4	Augusta
Maryland	1788	5,307,886	8	10,460	507.4	Annapolis
Massachusetts	1788	6,355,568	10	8,284	767.2	Boston
Michigan	1837	9,955,829	15	58,527	170.1	Lansing
Minnesota	1858	4,925,670	8	84,068	58.6	St. Paul
Mississippi	1817	2,852,927	4	47,689	59.8	Jackson
Missouri	1821	5,606,260	9	69,697	80.4	Jefferson City
Montana	1889	905,316	1	147,046	6.2	Helena
Nebraska	1867	1,715,369	3	77,355	22.2	Lincoln
Nevada	1864	2,002,032	3	110,561	18.1	Carson City
New Hampshire	1788	1,238,415	2	9,279	133.5	Concord
New Jersey	1787	8,424,354	13	7,787	1,081.8	Trenton
New Mexico	1912	1,823,821	3	121,593	15.0	Santa Fe
New York	1788	19,004,973	29	49,576	383.4	Albany
North Carolina	1789	8,067,673	13	52,669	153.2	Raleigh
North Dakota	1889	643,756	1	70,655	9.1	Bismarck
Ohio	1803	11,374,540	18	41,222	275.9	Columbus
Oklahoma	1907	3,458,819	5	69,956	49.4	Oklahoma City
Oregon	1859	3,428,543	5	97,073	35.3	Salem
Pennsylvania	1787	12,300,670	19	45,333	271.3	Harrisburg
Rhode Island	1790	1,049,662	2	1,212	866.1	Providence
South Carolina	1788	4,025,061	6	31,113	129.4	Columbia
South Dakota	1889	756,874	1	77,116	9.8	Pierre
Tennessee	1796	5,700,037	9	42,144	135.3	Nashville
Texas	1845	20,903,994	32	266,807	78.3	Austin
Utah	1896	2,236,714	3	84,899	26.3	Salt Lake City
Vermont	1791	609,890	1	9,609	63.5	Montpelier
Virginia	1788	7,100,702	11	40,767	174.2	Richmond
Washington	1889	5,908,684	9	68,192	86.6	Olympia
West Virginia	1863	1,813,077	3	24,181	75.0	Charleston
Wisconsin	1848	5,371,210	8	56,154	95.7	Madison
Wyoming	1890	495,304	1	97,914	5.1	Cheyenne

The American Flag

The American flag is a symbol of the nation. It is recognized instantly, whether as a big banner waving in the wind or a tiny emblem worn on a lapel. The flag is so important that it is a major theme of the national anthem, "The Star-Spangled Banner." One of the most popular names for the flag is the Stars and Stripes. It is also known as Old Glory.

THE MEANING OF THE FLAG

The American flag has 13 stripes—7 red and 6 white. In the upper-left corner of the flag is the union—50 white five-pointed stars against a blue background.

The 13 stripes stand for the original 13 American states, and the 50 stars represent the states of the nation today. According to the U.S. Department of State, the colors of the flag also are symbolic:

Red stands for courage.

White symbolizes purity.

Blue is the color of vigilance, perseverance, and justice.

DISPLAYING THE FLAG

It is customary not to display the American flag in bad weather. It is also customary for the flag to be displayed outdoors only from sunrise to sunset, except on certain occasions. In a few special places, however, the flag is always flown day and night. When flown at night, the flag should be illuminated.

Near a speaker's platform, the flag should occupy the place of honor at the speaker's right. When carried in a parade with other flags, the American flag should be on the marching right or in front at the center. When flying with the flags of the 50 states, the national flag must be at the center and the highest point. In a group of national flags, all should be of equal size and all should be flown from staffs, or flagpoles, of equal height.

The flag should never touch the ground or the floor. It should not be marked with any insignia, pictures, or words. Nor should it be used in any disrespectful way—as an advertising decoration, for instance. The flag should never be dipped to honor any person or thing.

SALUTING THE FLAG

The United States, like other countries, has a flag code, or rules for displaying and honoring the flag. For example, all those present should stand at attention facing the flag and salute it when it is being raised or lowered or when it is carried past them in a parade or procession. A man wearing a hat should take it off and hold it with his right hand over his heart. All women and hatless men should stand with their right hands over their hearts to show respect. The flag should also receive these honors during the playing of the national anthem and the reciting of the Pledge of Allegiance.

THE PLEDGE OF ALLEGIANCE

The Pledge of Allegiance was written in 1892 by Massachusetts magazine (*Youth's Companion*) editor Francis Bellamy. (Congress added the words "under God" in 1954.)

I pledge allegiance to the flag of the United States of America and to the republic for which it stands, one nation under God, indivisible, with liberty and justice for all.

Civilians should say the Pledge of Allegiance with their right hands over their hearts. People in the armed forces give the military salute. By saying the Pledge of Allegiance, we promise loyalty ("pledge allegiance") to the United States and its ideals.

"THE STAR-SPANGLED BANNER"

"The Star-Spangled Banner" is the national anthem of the United States. It was written by Francis Scott Key during the War of 1812. While being held aboard a British ship on September 13, 1814, Key watched the bombardment of the U.S. Fort McHenry at Baltimore. The attack lasted 25 hours. The smoke was so thick that Key could not tell who had won. When the air cleared, Key saw the American flag that was still flying over the fort. "The Star-Spangled Banner" is sung to music written by British composer John Stafford Smith. In 1931 Congress designated "The Star-Spangled Banner" as the national anthem.

I

Oh, say, can you see, by the dawn's early light,
What so proudly we hailed at the twilight's last gleaming,
Whose broad stripes and bright stars through the perilous fight,
O'er the ramparts we watched were so gallantly streaming?
And the rockets' red glare, the bombs bursting in air,
Gave proof through the night that our flag was still there.
Oh, say, does that star-spangled banner yet wave
O'er the land of the free, and the home of the brave?

II

On the shore, dimly seen through the mists of the deep,
Where the foe's haughty host in dread silence reposes,
What is that which the breeze, o'er the towering steep,
As it fitfully blows, half conceals, half discloses?
Now it catches the gleam of the morning's first beam,
In full glory reflected, now shines on the stream.
'Tis the star-spangled banner; oh, long may it wave
O'er the land of the free, and the home of the brave!

III

And where is that band who so vauntingly swore
That the havoc of war and the battle's confusion
A home and a country should leave us no more?
Their blood has washed out their foul footsteps' pollution.
No refuge could save the hireling and slave
From the terror of flight, or the gloom of the grave:
And the star-spangled banner in triumph doth wave
O'er the land of the free, and the home of the brave!

IV

Oh! thus be it ever when freemen shall stand
Between their loved homes and the war's desolation!
Blest with victory and peace, may the heaven-rescued land
Praise the Power that hath made and preserved us a nation!
Then conquer we must, for our cause it is just,
And this be our motto: "In God is our trust!"
And the star-spangled banner in triumph shall wave,
O'er the land of the free, and the home of the brave!

Sheet Music to the national anthem

"AMERICA, THE BEAUTIFUL"

One of the most beloved songs celebrating our nation is "America, the Beautiful." Katharine Lee Bates first wrote the lyrics to the song in 1893 after visiting Colorado. The version of the song we know today is set to music by Samuel A. Ward. The first and last stanzas of "America, the Beautiful" are shown below.

O beautiful for spacious skies,
For amber waves of grain,
For purple mountain majesties
Above the fruited plain!
America! America!
God shed his grace on thee
And crown thy good with brotherhood
From sea to shining sea!

• •

O beautiful for patriot dream
That sees beyond the years
Thine alabaster cities gleam
Undimmed by human tears!
America! America!
God shed his grace on thee
And crown thy good with brotherhood
From sea to shining sea!

Important Supreme Court Cases

MARBURY v. MADISON, 1 CRANCH (5 U.S.) 137 (1803)

Significance: This ruling established the Supreme Court's power of judicial review, by which the Court decides whether laws passed by Congress are constitutional. This decision greatly increased the prestige of the Court and gave the judiciary branch a powerful check against the legislative and executive branches.

Background: William Marbury and several others were commissioned as judges by Federalist president John Adams during his last days in office. This act angered the new Democratic-Republican president, Thomas Jefferson. Jefferson ordered his secretary of state, James Madison, not to deliver the commissions. Marbury took advantage of a section in the Judiciary Act of 1789 that allowed him to take his case directly to the Supreme Court. He sued Madison, demanding the commission and the judgeship.

Decision: This case was decided on February 24, 1803, by a vote of 5 to 0. Chief Justice John Marshall spoke for the Court, which decided against Marbury. The court ruled that although Marbury's commission had been unfairly withheld, he could not lawfully take his case to the Supreme Court without first trying it in a lower court. Marshall said that the section of the Judiciary Act that Marbury had used was actually unconstitutional, and that the Constitution must take priority over laws passed by Congress.

MCCULLOCH v. MARYLAND, 4 WHEAT. (17 U.S.) 316 (1819)

Significance: This ruling established that Congress had the constitutional power to charter a national bank. The case also established the principle of national supremacy, which states that the Constitution and other laws of the federal government take priority over state laws. In addition, the ruling reinforced the loose construction interpretation of the Constitution favored by many Federalists.

Background: In 1816 the federal government set up the Second Bank of the United States to stabilize the economy following the War of 1812. Many states were opposed to the competition provided by the new national bank. Some of these states passed heavy taxes on the Bank. The national bank refused to pay the taxes. This led the state of Maryland to sue James McCulloch, the cashier of the Baltimore, Maryland, branch of the national bank.

Decision: This case was decided on March 6, 1819, by a vote of 7 to 0. Chief Justice John Marshall spoke for the unanimous Court, which ruled that the national bank was constitutional because it helped the federal government carry out other powers granted to it by the Constitution. The Court declared that any attempt by the states to interfere with the duties of the federal government could not be permitted.

GIBBONS v. OGDEN, 9 WHEAT. (22 U.S.) 1 (1824)

Significance: This ruling was the first case to deal with the clause of the Constitution that allows Congress to regulate interstate and foreign commerce. This case was important because it reinforced both the authority of the federal government over the states and the division of powers between the federal government and the state governments.

Background: Steamboat operators who wanted to travel on New York waters had to obtain a state license. Thomas Gibbons had a federal license to travel along the coast, but not a state license for New York. He wanted the freedom to compete with state-licensed Aaron Ogden for steam travel between New Jersey and the New York island of Manhattan.

Decision: This case was decided on March 2, 1824, by a vote of 6 to 0. Chief Justice John Marshall spoke for the Court, which ruled in favor of Gibbons. The Court stated that the congressional statute (Gibbons's federal license) took priority over the state statute (Ogden's state-monopoly license). The ruling also defined commerce as more than simply the exchange of goods, broadening it to include the transportation of people and the use of new inventions (such as the steamboat).

WORCESTER v. GEORGIA, 6 PET. (31 U.S.) 515 (1832)

Significance: This ruling made Georgia's removal of the Cherokee illegal. However, Georgia, with President Andrew Jackson's support, defied the Court's decision. By not enforcing the Court's ruling, Jackson violated his constitutional oath as president. As a result, the Cherokee and other American Indian tribes continued to be forced off of lands protected by treaties.

Background: The state of Georgia wanted to remove Cherokee Indians from lands they held by treaty. Samuel Worcester, a missionary who worked with the Cherokee Nation, was arrested for failing to take an oath of allegiance to the state and to obey a Georgia militia order to leave the Cherokee's lands. Worcester sued, charging that Georgia had no legal authority on Cherokee lands.

Decision: This case was decided on March 3, 1832, by a vote of 5 to 1 in favor of Worcester. Chief Justice John Marshall spoke for the Supreme Court, which ruled that the Cherokee were an independent political community. The Court decided that only the federal government, not the state of Georgia, had authority over legal matters involving the Cherokee people.

SCOTT v. SANDFORD, 19 HOW. (60 U.S.) 393 (1857)

Significance: This ruling denied enslaved African Americans U.S. citizenship and the right to sue in federal court. The decision also invalidated the Missouri Compromise, which had prevented slavery in territories north of the 36° 30' line of latitude. The ruling increased the controversy over the expansion of slavery in new states and territories.

Background: John Emerson, an army doctor, took his slave Dred Scott with him to live in Illinois and then Wisconsin Territory, both of which had banned slavery. In 1842 the two moved to Missouri, a slave state. Four years later, Scott sued for his freedom according to a Missouri legal principle of "once free, always free." The principle meant that a slave was entitled to freedom if he or she had once lived in a free state or territory.

Decision: This case was decided March 6–7, 1857, by a vote of 7 to 2. Chief Justice Roger B. Taney spoke for the Court, which ruled that slaves did not have the right to sue in federal courts because they were considered property, not citizens. In addition, the Court ruled that Congress did not have the power to abolish slavery in territories because that power was not strictly defined in the Constitution. Furthermore, the Court overturned the once-free, always-free principle.

PLESSY v. FERGUSON, 163 U.S. 537 (1896)

Significance: This case upheld the constitutionality of racial segregation by ruling that separate facilities for different races were legal as long as those facilities were equal to one another. This case provided a legal justification for racial segregation for nearly 60 years until it was overturned by *Brown* v. *Board of Education* in 1954.

Background: An 1890 Louisiana law required that all railway companies in the state use "separate-but-equal" railcars for white and

African American passengers. A group of citizens in New Orleans banded together to challenge the law and chose Homer Plessy to test the law in 1892. Plessy took a seat in a whites-only coach, and when he refused to move, he was arrested. Plessy eventually sought review by the U.S. Supreme Court, claiming that the Louisiana law violated his Fourteenth Amendment right to equal protection.

Decision: This case was decided on May 18, 1896, by a vote of 7 to 1. Justice Henry Billings Brown spoke for the Court, which upheld the constitutionality of the Louisiana law that segregated railcars. Justice John M. Harlan dissented, arguing that the Constitution should not be interpreted in ways that recognize class or racial distinctions.

LOCHNER v. NEW YORK, 198 U.S. 45 (1905)

Significance: This decision established the Supreme Court's role in overseeing state regulations. For more than 30 years *Lochner* was often used as a precedent in striking down state laws such as minimum-wage laws, child labor laws, and regulations placed on the banking and transportation industries.

Background: In 1895 the state of New York passed a labor law limiting bakers to working no more than 10 hours per day or 60 hours per week. The purpose of the law was to protect the health of bakers, who worked in hot and damp conditions and breathed in large quantities of flour dust. In 1902 Joseph Lochner, the owner of a small bakery in New York, claimed that the state law violated his Fourteenth Amendment rights by unfairly depriving him of the liberty to make contracts with employees. This case went to the U.S. Supreme Court.

Decision: This case was decided on April 17, 1905, by a vote of 5 to 4 in favor of Lochner. The Supreme Court judged that the Fourteenth Amendment protected the right to sell and buy labor, and that any state law restricting that right was unconstitutional. The Court rejected the argument that the limited workday and workweek were necessary to protect the health of bakery workers.

MULLER v. OREGON, 208 U.S. 412 (1908)

Significance: A landmark for cases involving social reform, this decision established the Court's recognition of social and economic conditions (in this case, women's health) as a factor in making laws.

Background: In 1903 Oregon passed a law limiting workdays to 10 hours for female workers in laundries and factories. In 1905 Curt Muller's Grand Laundry was found guilty of breaking this law. Muller appealed, claiming that the state law violated his freedom of contract (the Supreme Court had upheld a similar claim that year in *Lochner* v. *New York*). When this case came to the Court, the National Consumers' League hired lawyer Louis D. Brandeis to present Oregon's argument. Brandeis argued that the Court had already defended the state's police power to protect its citizens' health, safety, and welfare.

Decision: This case was decided on February 24, 1908, by a vote of 9 to 0 upholding the Oregon law. The Court agreed that women's well-being was in the state's public interest and that the 10-hour law was a valid way to protect their well-being.

BROWN v. BOARD OF EDUCATION, 347 U.S. 483 (1954)

Significance: This ruling reversed the Supreme Court's earlier position on segregation set by *Plessy* v. *Ferguson* (1896). The decision also inspired Congress and the federal courts to help carry out further civil rights reforms for African Americans.

Background: Beginning in the 1930s, the National Association for the Advancement of Colored People (NAACP) began using the courts to challenge racial segregation in public education. In 1952 the NAACP took a number of school segregation cases to the Supreme Court. These included the Brown family's suit against the school board of Topeka, Kansas, over its "separate-but-equal" policy.

Decision: This case was decided on May 17, 1954, by a vote of 9 to 0. Chief Justice Earl Warren spoke for the unanimous Court, which ruled that segregation in public education created inequality. The Court held that racial segregation in public schools was by nature unequal, even if the school facilities were equal. The Court noted that such segregation created feelings of inferiority that could not be undone. Therefore, enforced separation of the races in public education is unconstitutional.

GIDEON v. WAINWRIGHT, 372 U.S. 335 (1963)

Significance: This ruling was one of several key Supreme Court decisions establishing free legal help for those who cannot otherwise afford representation in court.

Background: Clarence Earl Gideon was accused of robbery in Florida. Gideon could not afford a lawyer for his trial, and the judge refused to supply him with one for free. Gideon tried to defend himself and was found guilty. He eventually appealed to the U.S. Supreme Court, claiming that the lower court's denial of a court-appointed lawyer violated his Sixth and Fourteenth Amendment rights.

Decision: This case was decided on March 18, 1963, by a vote of 9 to 0 in favor of Gideon. The Court agreed that the Sixth Amendment (which protects a citizen's right to have a lawyer for his or her defense) applied to the states because it fell under the due process clause of the Fourteenth Amendment. Thus, the states are required to provide legal aid to those defendants in criminal cases who cannot afford to pay for legal representation.

MIRANDA v. ARIZONA, 384 U.S. 436 (1966)

Significance: This decision ruled that an accused person's Fifth Amendment rights begin at the time of arrest. The ruling caused controversy because it made questioning suspects and collecting evidence more difficult for law enforcement officers.

Background: In 1963 Ernesto Miranda was arrested in Arizona for a kidnapping. Miranda signed a confession and was later found guilty of the crime. The arresting police officers, however, admitted that they had not told Miranda of his right to talk with an attorney before his confession. Miranda appealed his conviction on the grounds that by not informing him of his legal rights the police had violated his Fifth Amendment right against self-incrimination.

Decision: This case was decided on June 13, 1966, by a vote of 5 to 4. Chief Justice Earl Warren spoke for the Court, which ruled in Miranda's favor. The Court decided that an accused person must be given four warnings after being taken into police custody: (1) the suspect has the right to remain silent, (2) anything the suspect says can and will be used against him or her, (3) the suspect has the right to consult with an attorney and to have an attorney present during questioning, and (4) if the suspect cannot afford a lawyer, one will be provided before questioning begins.

REED v. REED, 404 U.S. 71 (1971)

Significance: This ruling was the first in a century of Fourteenth Amendment decisions to say that gender discrimination violated the equal protection clause. This case was later used to strike down other statutes that discriminated against women.

Background: Cecil and Sally Reed were separated. When their son died without a will, the law gave preference to Cecil to be appointed the administrator of the son's estate. Sally sued Cecil for the right to administer the estate, challenging the gender preference in the law.

Decision: This case was decided on November 22, 1971, by a vote of 7 to 0. Chief Justice Warren Burger spoke for the unanimous Supreme Court. Although the Court had upheld laws based on gender preference in the past, in this case it reversed its position. The Court declared that gender discrimination violated the equal protection clause of the Fourteenth Amendment and therefore could not be the basis for a law.

Gazetteer

Africa Second-largest continent. Lies in both the Northern and the Southern Hemispheres. **A10**

Alabama (AL) State in the southern United States. Admitted as a state in 1819. Capital: Montgomery. (33°N 87°W) **A1**

Alaska (AK) U.S. state in northwestern North America. Purchased from Russia in 1867. Organized as a territory in 1912. Admitted as a state in 1959. Capital: Juneau. (64°N 150°W) **A1**

Albany Capital of New York State. (42°N 74°W) **A1**

Andes Mountain range that extends along almost the entire western coast of South America. **68**

Antarctica Continent that surrounds the South Pole. **A4**

Antietam Creek Creek in northern Maryland. Site of an important Union army victory during the Civil War. **586**

Appalachian Mountains Mountain system in eastern North America that extends from Canada to central Alabama. **161**

Appomattox Courthouse Town in central Virginia where Robert E. Lee surrendered to Ulysses S. Grant, ending the Civil War. **613**

Arctic Ocean Ocean north of the Arctic Circle. **A4**

Arizona (AZ) State in the southwestern United States. Organized as a territory in 1863. Admitted as a state in 1912. Capital: Phoenix. (34°N 113°W). **A1**

Arkansas (AR) State in the south-central United States. Admitted as a state in 1836. Capital: Little Rock. (35°N 93°W) **A1**

Asia Largest continent. Occupies the same landmass as Europe. **A9**

Atlanta Capital of Georgia. (33°N 84°W) **A1**

Atlantic Ocean Body of water separating North and South America from Europe and Africa. **A4**

Austin Capital of Texas. (30°N 98°W) **A1**

Australia Island, continent, and country located between the Indian and the Pacific Oceans. Capital: Canberra. (25°S 1 35°E) **A11**

Bahamas Country in the Atlantic Ocean consisting of hundreds of islands. Captal: Nassau. **A6**

Baltimore Maryland city northeast of Washington, D.C., on the Chesapeake Bay. (39°N 76°W) **351**

Boston Capital of Massachusetts. (42°N 71°W) **187**

Brazil Republic in eastern South America. Capital: Brasília. (9°S 53°W) **A7**

Bunker Hill Hill in Boston, Massachusetts. Site of an early Revolutionary War battle. **187**

California (CA) State in the western United States. Admitted as a state in 1850. Capital: Sacramento. (38°N 121°W) **A1**

Canada Country in northern North America. Capital: Ottawa. (50°N 100°W) **A6**

Cape of Good Hope Southern tip of Africa. **36**

Caribbean Sea Arm of the Atlantic Ocean between North and South America. **A4**

Central America The southern portion of North America, beginning south of Mexico. **A6**

Charleston Port city in southeastern South Carolina. Originally called Charles Town. (33°N 80°W) **A1**

Chesapeake Bay Inlet of the Atlantic Ocean in Virginia and Maryland. **95**

Chicago City in northeastern Illinois on Lake Michigan. Major port and large U.S. city. (42°N 88°W) **A1**

China Country in East Asia with the world's largest population. Capital: Beijing. (Official name: People's Republic of China) **A9**

Colorado (CO) State in the west-central United States. Admitted as a state in 1876. Capital: Denver. (39°N 107°W) **A1**

Concord One of two northeastern Massachusetts towns (along with Lexington) where the first fighting of the Revolutionary War took place in 1775. (42°N 71°W) **187**

Connecticut (CT) State in the northeastern United States. One of the original thirteen colonies. Admitted as a state in 1788. Capital: Hartford. (41°N 73°W) **A1**

Cuba Country in the Caribbean about 90 miles south of Florida. Capital: Havana. (22°N 79°W) **A6**

Delaware (DE) State in the eastern United States. One of the original thirteen colonies. Capital: Dover. (38°N 75°W) **A1**

District of Columbia Federal district between Maryland and Virginia where the capital of the United States is located. (39°N 77°W) **A1**

El Paso City in western Texas. (32°N 106°W) **A1**

England Country of the United Kingdom that makes up most of the southern part of the island of Great Britain. Capital: London. (51°N 1°W) **A8**

Europe Continent occupying the same landmass as Asia. **A8**

Florida (FL) State in the southeastern United States. Organized as a territory in 1822. Admitted as a state in 1845. Capital: Tallahassee. (30°N 84°W) **A1**

Fort Detroit Political and trading center of the Great Lakes region located along the Detroit River. Site of what is now Detroit, Michigan. **205**

Fort McHenry U.S. fort that guarded Baltimore, Maryland, in the War of 1812. **351**

Fort Necessity Site where the French defeated British colonists in 1754, in what was the first battle of the French and Indian War. **161**

Fort Sumter Fort on Charleston Harbor, South Carolina. Attack by Confederate forces here began the Civil War. **582**

Fort Ticonderoga Fort in northern New York captured by Patriots during the American Revolution. **205**

France Country in western Europe. Capital: Paris. (46°N 1°E) **A8**

Georgia (GA) State in the southeastern United States. Admitted as a state in 1788. One of the original thirteen colonies. Capital: Atlanta. (32°N 84°W) **A1**

Germany Country in central Europe. Capital: Berlin. (51°N 8°E) **A8**

Gettysburg Town in southern Pennsylvania. (40°N 77°W) **613**

Grand Canyon Enormous gorge in northwest Arizona. **A2**

Great Basin Region including Nevada and parts of California, Idaho, Oregon, Utah, and Wyoming that was home to some American Indian nations. **11**

Great Lakes Chain of lakes located in central North America that extends across the U.S.-Canada border. Includes Lake Superior, Lake Michigan, Lake Huron, Lake Erie, and Lake Ontario. **86**

Great Plains Region of central North America that lies between the Mississippi River and the Rocky Mountains, stretching north into Canada and south into Texas. **A2**

Great Salt Lake Salty lake in northern Utah. **506**

Gulf of Mexico Gulf on the southeastern coast of North America, bordered by the United States, Mexico, and Cuba. **A6**

Hawaii (HI) U.S. state in the central Pacific Ocean that

is made up of the Hawaiian Islands. Organized as a territory in 1900. Admitted as a state in 1959. Capital: Honolulu. (20°N 157°W) **A1**

Hispaniola Island that includes the countries of Haiti and the Dominican Republic. **41**

Houston City in southeastern Texas. (30°N 95°W) **A1**

Hudson Bay Inland sea in east-central Canada. Explored by Henry Hudson in 1610. **86**

Hudson River River flowing from northeastern to southern New York. **86**

Idaho (ID) State in the northwestern United States. Admitted as a state in 1890. Capital: Boise. (44°N 115°W) **A1**

Illinois (IL) State in the north-central United States. Admitted as a state in 1818. Capital: Springfield. (40°N 90°W) **A1**

India Large republic in southern Asia. Capital: New Delhi. (28°N 77°E) **A9**

Indiana (IN) State in the north-central United States. Admitted as a state in 1816 Capital: Indianapolis. (40°N 86°W) **A1**

Indiana Territory Former territory created from the division of the Northwest Territory in 1800. Iincluded Illinois, Indiana, Wisconsin, much of Michigan, and part of Minnesota. **340**

Indian Ocean Body of water east of Africa, south of Asia, west of Australia, and north of Antarctica. **A4**

Indian Territory Former territory in the south-central United States. Set aside in 1820 as a home for forcibly displaced American Indians. **381**

Iowa (IA) State in the north-central United States. Admitted as a state in 1846. Capital: Des Moines. (42°N 94°W) **A1**

Ireland Island in the British Isles. Divided into Northern Ireland (Capital: Belfast), which is part of Great Britain, and the independent Republic of Ireland (Capital: Dublin). (54°N 8°W) **A8**

Israel Country in Southwest Asia on the eastern Mediterranean coast. Capital: Jerusalem. (32°N 34°E) **A9**

Isthmus of Panama Thin landmass that links North America to South America and separates the Atlantic and Pacific Oceans. Forms the Republic of Panama. **A6**

Italy Country in southern Europe. Capital: Rome. (44°N 11 °E) **A8**

James River River in Virginia that flows into Chesapeake Bay. **95**

Jamestown First successful English colony in America. Established in eastern Virginia in 1607. **95**

Japan Country in the western Pacific Ocean. Made up of a chain of islands. Capital: Tokyo. (37°N 134°E) **A9**

Jerusalem Capital of Israel. **A9**

Kansas (KS) State in the central United States. Organized as a territory in 1854. Admitted as a state in 1861. Capital: Topeka. (38°N 99°W) **A1**

Kentucky (KY) State in the east-central United States. Admitted as a state in 1792. Capital: Frankfort. (37°N 87°W) **A1**

Lake Erie One of the Great Lakes, located in the United States and Canada. Site of battle in War of 1812. **351**

Lexington One of two northeastern Massachusetts towns (along with Concord) where the first fighting of the American Revolution took place in 1775. (42°N 71°W) **187**

Liberia Country on the west coast of Africa, founded in 1822 as a colony for freed American slaves. (6°N 10°W) **A10**

Los Angeles Large city in southern California. (34°N 118°W) **A1**

Louisiana (LA) State in the southeastern United States carved out of the Louisiana Territory. Admitted as a state in 1812. Capital: Baton Rouge. (31°N 92°W) **A1**

Louisiana Territory Organized in 1805, extended from the Mississippi River to the Rocky Mountains and from the Gulf of Mexico to Canada, except for the Orleans Territory. **340**

Lowell Massachusetts city on the Merrimack River, northwest of Boston. (42°N 71°W) **447**

Maine (ME) State in the northeastern United States. Admitted as a state in 1820. Capital: Augusta. (45°N 70°W) **A1**

Maryland (MD) State in the east-central United States. One of the original thirteen colonies. Admitted as a state in 1788. Capital: Annapolis. (39°N 76°W) **A1**

Massachusetts (MA) State in the northeastern United States. One of the original thirteen colonies. Admitted as a state in 1788. Capital: Boston. (42°N 72°W) **A1**

Mediterranean Sea Large sea bordered by southern Europe, Southwest Asia, and northern Africa. **A8**

Mexico Country in southern North America. Capital: Mexico City. (23°N 104°W) **A6**

Michigan (MI) State in the north-central United States. Admitted as a state in 1837. Capital: Lansing. (46°N 87°W) **A1**

Minnesota (MN) State in the north-central United States. Admitted as a state in 1858. Capital: St. Paul. (46°N 90°W) **A1**

Mississippi (MS) State in the southeastern United States. Admitted as a state in 1817. Capital: Jackson. (32°N 90°W) **A1**

Mississippi River River that flows from Minnesota south to the Gulf of Mexico. **A3**

Missouri (MO) State in the central United States. Admitted as a state in 1821. Capital: Jefferson City. (38°N 93°W) **A1**

Missouri River River that flows from southern Montana and joins the Mississippi River north of St. Louis, Missouri. **A3**

Montana (MT) State in the northwestern United States. Admitted as a state in 1889. Capital: Helena. (47 N 112 W) **A1**

Montgomery Capital of Alabama. (32 N 86 W) **A1**

Montreal City in southeastern Canada founded by the French in 1642. (46°N 74°W) **86**

Nebraska (NE) State in the central United States. Admitted as a state in 1867. Capital: Lincoln. (41°N 101°W) **A1**

Netherlands Country in northwestern Europe. Capital: Amsterdam. (52°N 5°E) **A8**

Nevada (NV) State in the western United States. Organized as a territory in 1861. Admitted as a state in 1864. Capital: Carson City. (39°N 117°W) **A1**

New Amsterdam Dutch settlement on the island of Manhattan. Founded in 1620s. **89**

New England Northeastern section of the United States. Made up of Connecticut, Maine, Massachusetts, New Hampshire, Rhode Island, and Vermont. **106**

Newfoundland Island off the eastern coast of Canada. **86**

New France Former French territory in North America that included eastern Canada and the Mississippi Valley. **86**

New Hampshire (NH) State in the northeastern United States. One of the original thirteen colonies. Admitted as a state in 1788. Capital: Concord. (44°N 71°W) **A1**

New Jersey (NJ) State in the northeastern United States. One of the original thirteen colonies. Admitted as a state in 1787. Capital: Trenton. (40°N 75°W) **A1**

New Mexico (NM) State in the southwestern United States. Organized as a territory that included Arizona and part of Colorado in 1850. Admitted as a state in 1912. Capital: Santa Fe. (34°N 107°W) **A1**

New Netherland Dutch colony in North America that included parts of what are now Connecticut, Delaware, New Jersey, and New York. **89**

New Orleans Port city in southeastern Louisiana. (30°N 90°W) **A1**

New Spain Vast area of North America controlled by Spain. It extended from Mexico to California and Florida and included some Caribbean islands and also the Philippines. **75**

New Sweden Swedish colony in North America that was located along the Delaware River. **89**

New York (NY) State in the northeastern United States. One of the original thirteen colonies. Admitted as a state in 1788. Capital: Albany. (42°N 78°W) **A1**

New York City Largest city in the United States. (41°N 74°W) **A1**

North America Continent in the northern Western Hemisphere. **A6**

North Carolina (NC) State in the southeastern United States. One of the original thirteen colonies. Admitted as a state in 1789. Capital: Raleigh. (35°N 81°W) **A1**

North Dakota (ND) State in the north-central United States. Organized as part of the Dakota Territory in 1861. Admitted as a state in 1889. Capital: Bismarck. (47°N 102°W) **A1**

Northwest Territory Region of the north-central United States that extended from the Ohio and Mississippi Rivers to the Great Lakes. Later divided into what are now Illinois, Indiana, Michigan, Ohio, Wisconsin, and part of Minnesota. **225**

Nova Scotia Province of eastern Canada. **161**

Ohio (OH) State in the north-central United States. Originally part of the Northwest Territory. Admitted as a state in 1803. Capital: Columbus. (40°N 83°W) **A1**

Ohio River River that flows through Pennsylvania, Ohio, Indiana, and Illinois and empties into the Mississippi. **A3**

Oklahoma (OK) State in the south-central United States. Organized as a territory in 1890. Admitted as a state in 1907. Capital: Oklahoma City. (36°N 98°W) **A1**

Oklahoma City Capital of Oklahoma. (35°N 98°W) **A1**

Omaha City in Nebraska. (41°N 96°W) **669**

Oregon (OR) State in the northwestern United States. Admitted as a state in 1859. Capital: Salem. (43°N 1 22°W) **A1**

Oregon Country Region in northwestern North America that extended from the Pacific coast to the Rocky Mountains and from the northern border of California to Alaska. **542**

Pacific Ocean Body of water extending from the Arctic Circle to Antarctica and from western North and South America to Australia, the Malay Archipelago, and East Asia. **A4**

Panama Country in southern Central America that occupies the Isthmus of Panama. Location of the Panama Canal. Capital: Panama City. (8°N 81°W) **A6**

Pennsylvania (PA) State in the eastern United States. One of the original thirteen colonies. Admitted as a state in 1787. Capital: Harrisburg. (41°N 78°W) **A1**

Peru Country in western South America. Capital: Lima. (10°S 75°W) **A7**

Philadelphia City in southeastern Pennsylvania. Capital of the United States from 1790 to 1800. (40°N 75°W) **A1**

Philippines Country in the western Pacific Ocean. Made up of an archipelago of about 7,100 islands lying approximately 500 miles off the southeast coast of Asia. Capital: Manila. (14°N 125°E) **A9**

Pikes Peak Mountain in east-central Colorado that was part of an important mining region in the mid- to late 1800s. **340**

Pittsburgh City in southwestern Pennsylvania. (40°N 80°W) **A1**

Plymouth Site in Massachusetts where the Pilgrims first landed in North America in 1620. (42°N 71°W) **106**

Portugal Country in southwestern Europe on the western Iberian Peninsula. (38°N 8°W) **A8**

Potomac River River that flows through West Virginia, Virginia, and Maryland and empties into Chesapeake Bay. **A3**

Princeton Town in west-central New Jersey. (40°N 75°W) **205**

Providence Capital of Rhode Island. (42°N 71°W) **106**

Puerto Rico Island east of Cuba and southeast of Florida. A U.S. territory acquired in the Spanish-American War. Capital: San Juan. (18°N 67°W) **A6**

Red River River that flows from eastern New Mexico through Texas, Arkansas, and Louisiana, where it empties into the Mississippi River. **340**

Rhode Island (RI) State in the northeastern United States. One of the original thirteen colonies. Admitted as a state in 1790. Capital: Providence. (41°N 71°W) **A1**

Richmond Capital of Virginia. Capital of the Confederate States of America during the Civil War. (37°N 7°W) **586**

Rio Grande Spanish for Great River. Forms the border between Texas and Mexico. **340**

Roanoke Island Island off the coast of North Carolina. Site of early English attempt at settlement. **86**

Rocky Mountains Mountain range in western North America that extends from Alaska south to Mexico. **A2**

Russia Vast country that extends from eastern Europe through northwestern Asia. Capital: Moscow. (61°N 60°E) **A9**

Sacramento Capital of California. (38°N 121°W) **534**

Sahara Vast desert in northern Africa. **26**

St. Augustine City in northeastern Florida on the Atlantic coast. **75**

St. Lawrence River River in southeastern Canada. **86**

Salt Lake City Capital of Utah. (41°N 1 12°W) **A1**

San Antonio City in southern Texas. Site of the Mexican victory over Texas forces at the Alamo during the Texas Revolution. (29°N 99°W) **493**

San Diego City in southern California. Located on San Diego Bay, an inlet of the Pacific Ocean near the Mexican border. (33°N 1 17°W) **A1**

San Francisco City in western California on a peninsula between the Pacific Ocean and San Francisco Bay. (38°N 122°W) **534**

Santa Fe Capital of New Mexico. (35°N 106°W) **75**

Saratoga Site in eastern New York of a key battle of the Revolutionary War. **205**

Savannah Port city in southeastern Georgia. Founded by James Oglethorpe in 1733. (32°N 81°W) **117**

Scandinavia Region of northern Europe that includes Denmark, Norway, and Sweden. **A8**

Sierra Nevada Mountain range in eastern California. **A2**

South America Continent in the southern Western Hemisphere. **A7**

South Carolina (SC) State in the southeastern United States. One of the original thirteen colonies. Admitted as a state in 1788. Capital: Columbia. (34°N 81°W) **A1**

South Dakota (SD) State in the north-central United States. Organized as part of the Dakota Territory in 1861. Admitted as a state in 1889. Capital: Pierre. (44°N 102°W) **A1**

Spain Country in southwestern Europe that occupies the greater part of the Iberian Peninsula and includes the Balearic and Canary Islands. Capital: Madrid. (40°N 4°W) **A8**

Strait of Magellan Strait at the southern tip of South America that connects the southern Atlantic Ocean with the southern Pacific Ocean. **47**

Switzerland Country in central Europe. Capital: Bern. (47°N 7°E) **A8**

Tennessee (TN) State in the southeast-central United States. Admitted as a state in 1796. Capital: Nashville. (36°N 88°W) **A1**

Tenochtitlán Aztec island-city that was located on the site of what is now Mexico City. **68**

Texas (TX) State in the south-central United States. Independent republic from 1836 to 1845. Admitted as a state in 1845. Capital: Austin. (31°N 101°W) **A1**

Trenton Capital of New Jersey. (40°N 75°W) **205**

United States of America Country in central North America. Capital: Washington, D.C. (38°N 11O°W) **A1**

Utah (UT) State in the western United States. Admitted as a state in 1896. Capital: Salt Lake City. (39°N 112°W) **A1**

Valley Forge Site in southeastern Pennsylvania where General George Washington and his troops spent the harsh winter of 1777–78 during the Revolutionary War. **205**

Vermont (VT) State in the northeastern United States. Admitted as a state in 1791. Capital: Montpelier. (44°N 73°W) **A1**

Vicksburg City in western Mississippi on the bluffs above the Mississippi River. (42°N 85°W) **592**

Virginia (VA) State in the eastern United States. One of the original thirteen colonies. Admitted as a state in 1788. Capital: Richmond. (37°N 78°W) **A1**

Washington (WA) State in the northwestern United States. Bounded by British Columbia, Canada, to the north and by the Pacific Ocean to the west. Admitted as a state in 1889. Capital: Olympia. (47°N 121°W) **A1**

Washington, D.C. Capital of the United States. Located on the Potomac River between Virginia and Maryland. (39°N 77°W) **A1**

West Virginia (WV) State in the east-central United States. Part of Virginia until the area refused to join the Confederacy in 1861. Admitted as a state in 1863. Capital: Charleston. (39°N 81°W) **A1**

Wisconsin (WI) State in the north-central United States. Became part of the Northwest Territory in 1787. Admitted as a state in 1848. Capital: Madison. (44°N 91 °W) **A1**

Wyoming (WY) State in the western United States. Admitted as a state in 1890. Capital: Cheyenne. (43°N 108°W) **A1**

Yorktown Town in southeastern Virginia. Site of the last battle of the Revolutionary War. (37°N 76°W **205**

Glossary

This Glossary contains terms you need to understand as you study American history. After each key term there is a brief definition or explanation of the meaning of the term as it is used in *Call to Freedom*. The page number refers to the page on which the term is introduced in the textbook.

Phonetic Respelling and Pronunciation Guide

Many of the key terms in this textbook have been respelled to help you pronounce them. The letter combinations used in the respelling throughout the narrative are explained in the following phonetic respelling and pronunciation guide. The guide is adapted from *Webster's Tenth New College Dictionary,* *Merriam-Webster's New Geographical Dictionary,* and *Merriam-Webster's New Biographical Dictionary.*

MARK	AS IN	RESPELLING	EXAMPLE
a	alphabet	a	*AL-fuh-bet
ā	Asia	ay	AY-zhuh
ä	cart, top	ah	KAHRT, TAHP
e	let, ten	e	LET, TEN
ē	even, leaf	ee	EE-vuhn, LEEF
i	it, tip, British	i	IT, TIP, BRIT-ish
ī	site, buy, Ohio	y	SYT, BY, oh-HY-oh
	iris	eye	EYE-ris
k	card	k	KAHRD
ō	over, rainbow	oh	OH-vuhr, RAYN-boh
u̇	book, wood	ooh	BOOHK, WOOHD
ȯ	all, orchid	aw	AWL, AWR-kid
ȯi	foil, coin	oy	FOYL, KOYN
au̇	out	ow	OWT
ə	cup, butter	uh	KUHP, BUHT-uhr
ü	rule, food	oo	ROOL, FOOD
yü	few	yoo	FYOO
zh	vision	zh	VIZH-uhn

*A syllable printed in small capital letters receives heavier emphasis than the other syllable(s) in a word.

abolition An end to slavery. **469**

Adams-Onís Treaty (1819) Agreement in which Spain gave up all of Florida to the United States. **366**

Alamo Spanish mission in San Antonio, Texas, that was the site of a famous battle of the Texas Revolution in 1836; the Mexican army's victory resulted in the deaths of all the Texans defending the building. **494**

Albany Plan of Union (1754) Plan written by Benjamin Franklin and other colonial delegates that called for the colonies to unite under a common governing body. **160**

Alien and Sedition Acts (1798) Laws passed by a Federalist-dominated Congress aimed at protecting the government from treasonous ideas, actions, and people; used against members of the Democratic-Republican party. **322**

amendments Official changes, corrections, or additions to a law or constitution. **246**

American Anti-Slavery Society Group founded in 1833 by William Lloyd Garrison and others to work for immediate abolition and racial equality for African Americans. **471**

American Colonization Society Society organized in 1817 that established the colony of Liberia in West Africa as a home for free African Americans. **470**

American System Henry Clay's plan for raising tariffs to pay for internal improvements such as better roads and canals. **370**

amnesty An official pardon issued by the government for an illegal act. **621**

annex To take control of land and incorporate into a country, state, etc. **497**

Antifederalists People who opposed ratification of the Constitution. **242**

Appomattox Courthouse Virginia town where General Robert E. Lee was forced to surrender, thus ending the Civil War. **605**

apportionment The use of population to determine how many legislative representatives an area will have. **258**

apprentices People who learn skilled trades from a master craftsperson. **133**

archaeology Scientific study of the unwritten past. **5**

Articles of Confederation (1777) Document that created the first central government for the United States; was replaced by the Constitution in 1789. **225**

artifacts Remains of objects that have been made by humans. **5**

astrolabe A tool once used by navigators to determine a ship's position at sea by charting the position of the stars. **35**

backcountry Frontier region in Virginia and the Carolinas between coastal settlements and the Appalachian Mountains. **163**

Bacon's Rebellion (1676) Attack led by Nathaniel Bacon against American Indians and the colonial government in Virginia. **97**

balance of trade Relationship between what goods a country purchases from other countries and what goods it sells to other countries. **126**

Bank of the United States National bank chartered by Congress in 1791 to provide security for the U.S. economy. **309**

Battle of Antietam (1862) Union victory in the Civil War that marked the bloodiest single-day battle in U.S. military history. **588**

Battle of Brandywine Creek (1777) Revolutionary War battle in which British forces overwhelmed the Patriots in Pennsylvania. **204**

Battle of Bunker Hill (1775) Revolutionary War battle in Boston that demonstrated that the colonists could fight well against the British army. **188**

Battle of Fallen Timbers (1794) Battle between U.S. troops and an American Indian confederation resisting white settlement in the Northwest Territory; led to Treaty of Greenville. **316**

Battle of Gettysburg (1863) Union Civil War victory that turned the tide against the Confederates at Gettysburg, Pennsylvania; resulted in the loss of more than 50,000 soldiers. **601**

Battle of Goliad (1836) Mexican victory during the Texas Revolution in which Mexican leader Antonio López de Santa Anna ordered the execution of Texas soldiers after their surrender. **495**

Battle of Horseshoe Bend (1814) U.S. victory in the War of 1812 in which Andrew Jackson's troops forced Creek Indians to give up much of their land in the South. **353**

Battle of Lake Erie (1813) U.S. victory in the War of 1812, led by Oliver Hazard Perry; broke Britain's control of Lake Erie. **352**

Battle of New Orleans (1815) Greatest U.S. victory in the War of 1812; actually took place two weeks after a peace treaty had been signed ending the war. **354**

Battle of Pea Ridge (1862) Civil War battle in which Confederate forces from Missouri, joined by some American Indians, were defeated in Northwestern Arkansas. **593**

Battle of Princeton (1777) Revolutionary War battle in which the Patriots drove back British forces in New Jersey. **203**

Battle of San Jacinto (1836) Final battle of the Texas Revolution; resulted in the defeat of the Mexican army and independence for Texas. **496**

Battle of Saratoga (1777) Revolutionary War battle in New York that resulted in a major defeat of British troops; marked the Patriots' greatest victory up to that point in the war. **204**

Battle of Shiloh (1862) Civil War battle in Tennessee in which the Union army gained greater control over the Mississippi River valley. **591**

Battle of the Little Bighorn (1876) "Custer's Last Stand"; battle between U.S. soldiers, led by George Armstrong Custer, and Sioux warriors, led by Crazy Horse and Sitting Bull, that resulted in the worst defeat for the U.S. Army in the West. **651**

Battle of the Thames (1813) U.S. victory in the War of 1812, led by William Henry Harrison, that ended the Indian-British alliance in the Great Lakes. **352**

Battle of Tippecanoe (1811) U.S. victory over an Indian confederation that wanted to stop white settlement in the Northwest Territory; increased tensions between Great Britain and the United States. **347**

Battle of Trenton (1776) Revolutionary War battle in New Jersey in which Patriot forces captured more than 900 Hessian troops. **203**

Battle of Vincennes (1779) Revolutionary War battle in the West in which Patriots retook Vincennes, a mostly French town along the Wabash River, from the British. **210**

Battle of Yorktown (1781) Last major battle of the Revolutionary War; site of British general Charles Cornwallis's surrender to the Patriots in Virginia. **212**

Bear Flag Revolt (1846) Revolt against Mexico by American settlers in California who declared the territory an independent republic. **524**

Bessemer process A method of faster, cheaper steel production developed in the 1850s. **683**

bicameral legislature A lawmaking body made up of two houses. **121**

Bill of Rights First 10 amendments to the Constitution; ratified in 1791. **247**

Black Codes Laws passed in the southern states during Reconstruction that greatly limited the freedom and rights of African Americans. **627**

Black Death An epidemic that spread through Europe from 1348 to about 1350 that killed as many as 30 million people. **32**

bonanza A large deposit of precious ore. **655**

bonds Certificates that represent money the government has borrowed from private citizens. **305**

boomtowns Western communities that grew quickly because of the mining boom and often disappeared when the boom ended. **656**

borderlands Region of Spanish America where few Europeans lived; included northern Mexico, Florida, and parts of present-day Arizona, California, New Mexico, and Texas. **75**

border states Delaware, Kentucky, Maryland, and Missouri; slave states that lay between the North and the South and did not join the Confederacy during the Civil War. **582**

Boston Massacre (1770) Incident in which British soldiers fired into a crowd of angry colonists, killing five people. **172**

Boston Tea Party (1773) Protest against the Tea Act in which a group of colonists boarded British tea ships and dumped some 340 chests of tea into Boston Harbor. **174**

boycott To refuse to buy certain goods; method often used in protest movements. **169**

Brown* v. *Board of Education (1954) Supreme Court ruling that declared that segregated public schools were illegal; overturned the separate-but-equal doctrine established in 1896 case *Plessy* v. *Ferguson*. **701**

Bureau of Indian Affairs Government agency created in the 1800s to oversee federal policy toward American Indians. **382**

cabinet Group made up of the heads of the executive departments that advises the U.S. president. **260**

California Gold Rush Migration of thousands of people to California in 1849 after gold was discovered there. **534**

Californios Spanish colonists in California. **489**

capital Money or property that is used to earn more money. **33**

caravel A fast, maneuverable ship originally designed by the Portuguese. **36**

carpetbaggers Name given to northerners who moved to the South during Reconstruction. **633**

cash crops Agricultural products grown primarily to be sold for profits, not for personal use. **131**

casualties People who are killed, wounded, captured, or missing in a war. **161**

cattle drive Long journeys on which cowboys herded cattle to northern markets or grazing lands. **663**

Cattle Kingdom Area of the Great Plains, stretching from Texas to Canada, on which many ranchers raised cattle in the late 1800s. **661**

charter Official document that gives a person the right to establish a colony. **87**

checks and balances A system established by the Constitution that prevents any branch of government from becoming too powerful. **241**

Chisholm Trail Trail from San Antonio, Texas, to Abilene, Kansas, established by Jesse Chisholm in 1867 for cattle drives. **663**

circumnavigate To sail completely around. **49**

Civil Rights Act of 1866 Law that gave African Americans legal rights equal to those of white Americans. **628**

Civil Rights Act of 1875 Law guaranteeing African Americans equal rights in public places such as theaters and public transportation. **636**

Civil Rights Act of 1964 Law banning segregation in public places and prohibiting employers, unions, and universities from discriminating on the basis of color, national origin, religion, and sex. **704**

Clermont First full-sized U.S. commercial steamboat; developed by Robert Fulton and tested in 1807. **412**

Cold War Power struggle between the United States and the Soviet Union that lasted from 1945 to 1991. **699**

Columbian Exchange Transfer of plants, animals, and diseases between the Americas and Europe, Asia, and Africa. **51**

Commercial Revolution Period of economic development that began in Europe in the 1200s and greatly expanded trade. **33**

Committees of Correspondence Committees created in Massachusetts in the 1760s to help towns and colonies share information about resisting the new British laws. **169**

common-school movement Social reform efforts begun in the mid-1800s that promoted the idea of having all children educated in a common place regardless of social class or background. **465**

Common Sense (1776) Pamphlet written by Thomas Paine that criticized monarchies and convinced many American colonists of the need to break away from Britain. **190**

Compromise of 1850 Henry Clay's proposed agreement that allowed California to enter the Union as a free state and divided the rest of the Mexican Cession into two territories where slavery would be decided by popular sovereignty; also settled land claims between Texas and New Mexico, abolished the slave trade in Washington, and produced a new Fugitive Slave Act. **555**

Compromise of 1877 Agreement to settle the disputed presidential election of 1876; Democrats agreed to accept Republican Rutherford B. Hayes as president in return for the removal of federal troops from the South. **637**

Comstock Lode Nevada gold and silver deposit discovered by Henry Comstock in 1859. **655**

concurrent powers Powers that are shared by the federal and state governments. **257**

Confederate States of America Nation formed by the southern states on February 4, 1861; also known as the Confederacy. **574**

conquistadores Spanish soldiers and explorers who led military expeditions in the Americas and captured land for Spain. **66**

constitution A set of basic principles that determines the powers and duties of a government. **224**

Constitutional Convention (1787) Meeting in Philadelphia at which delegates from the states wrote the Constitution. **237**

Constitutional Union Party Political party formed in 1860 by a group of northerners and southerners who supported the Union, its laws, and the Constitution. **571**

Continental Army Army created by the Second Continental Congress in 1775 to defend the American colonies from Britain. **186**

contrabands Escaped or captured slaves taken in by the Union army during the Civil War. **596**

Contract with America Ten-point Republican reform plan created in the mid-1990s. **709**

Convention of 1818 Agreement between the United States and Great Britain that settled fishing rights and established new North American borders. **365**

convert To change beliefs. **42**

Copperheads Northern Democrats who opposed abolition and sympathized with the South during the Civil War. **597**

cotton belt Region stretching from Georgia to east Texas where most U.S. cotton was produced during the mid-1800s. **427**

cotton diplomacy Confederate efforts to use the importance of southern cotton to Britain's textile industry to persuade the British to support the Confederacy in the Civil War. **584**

cotton gin Device invented by Eli Whitney in 1793 to separate cotton plants' fibers from the seeds; revolutionized the cotton industry. **426**

Council of the Indies Group of royal officials established in 1524 that oversaw the government and enforced laws in Spanish America. **72**

covenant Sacred agreement. **104**

creditors People who lend money. **233**

Crusades (1096–1221) Series of wars launched by European Christians to gain possession of the Holy Land. **25**

Cuban missile crisis (1962) Military crisis that almost led to nuclear war until the Soviet Union agreed to remove its nuclear missiles from Cuba; in return the United States promised not to invade the island and to remove some U.S. missiles from Europe. **703**

culture Common values and traditions of a society, such as language, government, and family relationships. **6**

Cumberland Road First federal road project, construction of which began in 1815; ran from Cumberland, Maryland, to present-day Wheeling, West Virginia. **371**

D-Day June 6, 1944; Allied invasion of Nazi-occupied France during World War II. **696**

Daughters of Liberty Women's groups that used boycotts and other measures to support the colonies' resistance to the British. **171**

Dawes General Allotment Act (1887) Legislation passed by Congress that split up Indian reservation lands among individual Indians and promised them citizenship. **654**

debtors People who owe money. **233**

Declaration of Independence (1776) Statement of the Second Continental Congress that defined the colonists' rights, outlined their complaints against Great Britain, and declared the colonies' independence. **191**

Declaration of Sentiments (1848) Statement written and signed by women's rights supporters at the Seneca Falls Convention; detailed their complaints about social injustice against women. **477**

delegated powers Powers that are specifically granted to the federal government by the Constitution. **256**

Democratic Party Political party formed by supporters of Andrew Jackson after the presidential election of 1824. **375**

Democratic-Republican Party Political party founded in the 1790s that sought to preserve the power of the state governments and promote agriculture. **320**

deport To send an immigrant back to his or her country of origin. **291**

depression A steep drop in economic activity combined with rising unemployment. **233**

dissenters People who disagree with official religious or political opinions. **103**

domestication Process of breeding plants and animals for use by humans. **6**

Dominion of New England Union of northeastern American colonies created by King James II in 1686; lasted until 1689. **123**

Donner party Group of western travelers who were stranded in the Sierra Nevada during the winter of 1846-47; only 40 of the party's 87 members survived. **509**

double jeopardy Illegal act of trying a person twice for the same crime. **289**

draft A system of required service in the armed forces. **293**

Dred Scott **decision** (1857) U.S. Supreme Court ruling that declared African Americans were not U.S. citizens, that the Missouri Compromise's restriction on slavery was unconstitutional, and that Congress did not have the right to ban slavery in any federal territory. **566**

dry farming Method of farming used by Plains farmers in the 1890s that allowed them to grow certain crops with less water. **668**

due process Fair application of the law. **289**

duties Taxes on imported goods. **127**

Eighteenth Amendment (1919) Constitutional amendment that outlawed the production, sale, and transportation of alcoholic beverages in the United States; repealed in 1933. **686**

elastic clause Article I, Section 8, of the Constitution that has been interpreted as giving Congress authority to stretch its delegated powers to address issues not otherwise specified in the document; also known as the "necessary and proper clause." **257**

El Camino Real "The King's Road"; built by Spanish settlers to link communities in New Spain. **76**

electoral college Group selected from each of the states to cast votes in presidential elections. The number of each state's electors is equal to the number of its representatives and senators in Congress. The electors are expected to vote for the candidate chosen by popular vote in their states. **301**

emancipation Freedom from slavery. **469**

Emancipation Proclamation (1862) Order issued by President Abraham Lincoln freeing the slaves in areas rebelling against the Union; took effect January 1, 1863. **595**

embargo Banning of trade with a country. **345**

Embargo Act (1807) Law that prohibited American merchants from trading with other countries. **345**

eminent domain The government's power to take personal property to further the public good. **287**

empresarios Agents who were contracted by the Mexican republic to bring settlers to Texas in the early 1800s. **492**

encomienda **system** System in Spanish America that gave settlers the right to tax local Indians or to demand their labor in exchange for protecting them and teaching them skills. **74**

energy crisis Situation in the 1970s marked by high fuel prices and fuel shortages. **706**

Enlightenment Age of Reason; movement that began in Europe in the 1700s as people began examining the natural world, society, and government. **141**

English Bill of Rights (1689) Shifted political power from the British monarchy to Parliament. **125**

environments Climates and landscapes that surround living things. **6**

Erie Canal Canal that ran from Albany to Buffalo, New York; completed in 1825. **371**

executive branch Division of the federal government that includes the president and the administrative departments; enforces the nation's laws. **240**

executive order Nonlegislative directive issued by the U.S. president in certain circumstances; an executive order has the force of congressional law. **259**

Exodusters A large group of southern African Americans who settled western lands in the late 1800s. **667**

exports Items that a country sells to other countries. **126**

factors Crop brokers who managed the trade between southern planters and their customers. **429**

fascism System of military dictatorship that glorifies the nation. **695**

federalism System of government in which power is distributed between a central authority and individual states. **240**

Federalist Papers Series of essays that defended the Constitution and tried to reassure Americans that the states would not be overpowered by the proposed national government. **244**

Federalist Party Political party created in the 1790s that wanted to strengthen the federal government and promote industry and trade. **320**

Federalists People who supported ratification of the Constitution. **243**

feudalism System of government that arose during the Middle Ages in which people gave their loyalty to a lord in exchange for land or protection. **19**

Fifteenth Amendment (1870) Constitutional amendment that gave African American men the right to vote. **632**

54th Massachusetts Infantry African American Civil War regiment that played a key role in the attack on Fort Wagner in South Carolina. **596**

First Battle of Bull Run (1861) First major battle of the Civil War, resulting in a Confederate victory; showed that the Civil War would not be won easily. **586**

First Continental Congress (1774) Meeting of colonial delegates in Philadelphia to decide how to respond to increased taxes and abuses of authority by the British government; delegates petitioned King George III, listing the freedoms they believed colonists should enjoy. **184**

folktales Oral stories that often provide a moral lesson. **442**

Fort Sumter Federal outpost in Charleston, South Carolina, that was attacked by the Confederates in April 1861, sparking the Civil War. **580**

forty-niners Gold-seekers who moved to California during the gold rush. **534**

Fourteenth Amendment (1866) Constitutional amendment that, among other provisions, gave full rights of citizenship to all people born or naturalized in the United States, except for American Indians. **629**

Freedmen's Bureau Agency established by Congress in 1865 to help poor people throughout the South. **624**

Freedom Rides (1961) Bus trips through various southern states that civil rights workers used to challenge illegal bus segregation. **703**

free enterprise Economic system in which there is competition between businesses with little government control. **127**

Freeport Doctrine (1858) Argument made by Stephen Douglas during the Lincoln-Douglas debates that popular sovereignty would determine whether a state or territory could permit slavery. **568**

Free-Soil Party Political party formed in 1848 by antislavery northerners who left the Whig and Democratic Parties because neither addressed the slavery issue. **553**

French Revolution French rebellion begun in 1789 in which the French people overthrew the monarchy and made their country a republic. **310**

Fugitive Slave Act (1850) Law that made it a crime to help runaway slaves; allowed for the arrest of escaped slaves in areas where slavery was illegal and required their return to slaveholders. **556**

Fundamental Orders of Connecticut (1639) A written set of principles that made Connecticut's colonial government more democratic. **105**

Gadsden Purchase (1853) U.S. purchase of land from Mexico that included the southern parts of present-day Arizona and New Mexico. **526**

General Amnesty Act of 1872 Law that repealed Section III of the Fourteenth Amendment, which forbade former Confederates from holding public office. **634**

Gettysburg Address (1863) Speech given by Abraham Lincoln in which he praised the bravery of Union soldiers and renewed his commitment to winning the Civil War. **602**

Ghost Dance A religious movement among Plains Indians in the 1880s. **652**

Gibbons v. *Ogden* (1824) Supreme Court ruling that federal law has priority over equivalent state law; expanded definition of interstate commerce. **413**

Glorious Revolution (1688) A revolt in England against Catholic king James II that led to his overthrow and put Protestants Mary and William of Orange on the throne. **124**

glyphs Symbols or images, particularly when cut into a surface or carved in relief. **6**

Great Awakening A Christian movement that became widespread in the American colonies in the 1730s and 1740s. **137**

Great Compromise (1787) Agreement worked out at the Constitutional Convention establishing that a state's population would determine representation in the lower house of the legislature, while each state would have equal representation in the upper house of the legislature. **238**

Great Depression Serious, global economic decline that began with the crash of the U.S. stock market in 1929. **693**

Great Migration Mass migration of thousands of English people to the Americas that took place between 1630 and 1640. **104**

Great Society Series of programs introduced by President Lyndon B. Johnson to end poverty and racism. **703**

guerrilla warfare Type of fighting in which soldiers use swift hit-and-run attacks against the enemy, usually behind the battle lines. **211**

habeas corpus Constitutional protection against unlawful imprisonment. **597**

Harlem Renaissance A period of African American artistic achievement beginning in the 1920s; named after the Harlem neighborhood in New York City. **692**

Hartford Convention (1815) Meeting of Federalists at Hartford, Connecticut, to protest the War of 1812. **355**

headright System set up by the London Company that gave 50 acres of land to colonists who paid their own way to Virginia. **95**

Holocaust The Nazi's systematic killing of about 6 million European Jews and 3 million other people during World War II. **698**

Homestead Act (1862) Law passed by Congress to encourage settlement in the West by giving government-owned land to small farmers. **666**

Homestead strike (1892) Strike at Andrew Carnegie's Homestead Steel factory in Pennsylvania that erupted in violence between strikers and private detectives. **684**

House of Burgesses Colonial Virginia's elected assembly. **122**

Hudson River school Group of American artists in the mid-1800s whose pictures focused on the American landscape. **388**

hunter-gatherers People who hunt animals and gather wild plants to provide for their needs. **5**

igloos Houses that were built out of blocks of ice or other materials by the Inuit and Aleut peoples in what are now Canada and Alaska. **12**

immigrants People who move to another country after leaving their homeland. **99**

impeach To vote to bring charges against. **259**

imperialism Practice of extending a nation's power by gaining territories for a colonial empire. **688**

imports Items that a country purchases from other countries. **126**

impressment British practice of forcing people, including U.S. citizens, to serve in the British army or navy; led to increasing tensions between Great Britain and the United States in the early 1800s. **345**

indentured servants Colonists who received free passage to North America in exchange for working without pay for a certain number of years. **96**

Indian Removal Act (1830) Congressional act that authorized the removal of American Indians who lived east of the Mississippi River. **381**

Indian Territory Area covering most of present-day Oklahoma to which most American Indians in the Southeast were forced to move in the 1830s. **381**

indict To formally accuse. **287**

Industrial Revolution Period of rapid growth in the use of machines in manufacturing and production that began in the mid-1700s. **399**

inflation Increased prices for goods and services combined with the reduced value of money. **82, 232**

interchangeable parts Process developed by Eli Whitney in the 1790s that called for making each vital part of a machine exactly the same. **401**

Internet A vast global computer network that connects businesses, governments, schools, and individuals. **709**

interstate commerce Trade that is conducted between states. **232**

Intolerable Acts (1774) A set of laws, also called the Coercive Acts, passed by Parliament to punish the colonists for the Boston Tea Party and to tighten government control of the colonies. **175**

Iran-Contra affair Scandal in which officials of President Ronald Reagan's administration illegally funded Nicaraguan rebels, or contras, by secretly selling weapons to Iran. **708**

ironclads Warships heavily armored with iron. **589**

Iroquois League A political confederation of five northeastern American Indian nations—the Seneca, Oneida, Mohawk, Cayuga, and Onondaga—that made decisions concerning war and peace. **16**

Islam A faith that arose in the Middle East in the A.D. 600s under the guidance of Muhammad; its holy book is the Qur'an. **23**

isolationism National policy of avoiding involvement in other countries' affairs. **689**

Jay's Treaty (1794) Agreement negotiated by John Jay to work out problems between Britain and the United States over the western frontier trade in the Caribbean, British seizure of U.S. ships, and debts owed to British merchants. **313**

Jazz Age A popular term for the 1920s; so called because many people in that decade listened to jazz music. **692**

Jim Crow laws Laws that enforced segregation in the southern states. **637**

John Brown's raid (1859) Incident in which abolitionist John Brown and 21 other men captured a federal arsenal in Harpers Ferry, Virginia, in hopes of starting a slave rebellion. **569**

joint-stock companies Businesses formed by a group of people who jointly make an investment and share in the profits and losses. **33**

judicial branch Division of the federal government that is made up of the national courts; interprets laws, punishes criminals, and settles disputes between states. **240**

judicial review The Supreme Court's power to declare acts of Congress unconstitutional. **337**

Judiciary Act of 1789 Legislation passed by Congress that created the federal court system. **303**

Kansas-Nebraska Act (1854) Law that allowed voters in the Kansas and Nebraska territories to choose whether to allow slavery. **561**

kayaks One-person canoes almost completely enclosed by animal skins. **12**

Kentucky and Virginia Resolutions (1798–1799) Republican documents that argued the Alien and Sedition Acts were unconstitutional. **322**

kitchen cabinet President Andrew Jackson's group of informal advisers; so called because they sometimes met in the White House kitchen. **376**

kivas Circular ceremonial rooms used for religious activities by Native American peoples of the American Southwest. **14**

Know-Nothing Party Political organization founded in 1849 by nativists who supported measures making it difficult for foreigners to become citizens and to hold office. **459**

Ku Klux Klan Secret society created by white southerners in 1866 that used terror and violence to keep African Americans from obtaining their civil rights. **635**

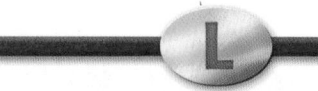

Land Ordinance of 1785 Legislation passed by Congress authorizing surveys and the division of public lands in the western region of the country. **226**

legislative branch Division of the government that proposes bills and passes them into laws. **240**

Lewis and Clark expedition Expedition led by Meriwether Lewis and William Clark that began in 1804 to explore the lands bought from France by the United States in the Louisiana Purchase. **342**

libel A false statement, usually published, that damages a person's reputation. **122**

Liberator, The Antislavery newspaper first published by William Lloyd Garrison in 1831. **470**

limited government A political principle which holds that government should be bound by laws that limit its power. **224**

Lincoln-Douglas debates Series of seven debates between Republican Abraham Lincoln and Democrat Stephen Douglas during the 1858 U.S. Senate campaign in Illinois. **567**

Line of Demarcation Boundary established by Pope Alexander VI in 1493 about 300 miles west and south of the Azores; gave unclaimed land west of the line to Spain, and east of the line to Portugal. **42**

longhouses Rectangular dwellings built by the Iroquois that were shared by several families. **16**

loose construction Way of interpreting the Constitution that allows the federal government to take actions that the Constitution does not specifically forbid it from taking. **308**

Lord Dunmore's Proclamation (1775) Statement issued by Virginia's royal governor promising freedom to any slave who fought for the British in the American Revolution. **199**

Louisiana Purchase (1803) Purchase of French land between the Mississippi River and the Rocky Mountains that nearly doubled the size of the United States. **340**

Lowell system The use of water powered textile mills that employed young unmarried women in the 1800s. **405**

Loyalists Colonists who sided with Britain in the American Revolution. **192**

Magna Carta (1215) Great Charter; agreed to by King John of England, it gave nobles and other individuals greater rights and made it clear that the nobility and monarchs must obey the law. **22**

maize Corn, the most important crop grown by Native Americans in North America and Mesoamerica. **6**

manifest destiny Belief shared by many Americans in the mid-1800s that the United States was meant to expand across the continent to the Pacific Ocean. **516**

manors Large estates held by monarchs and nobles in the Middle Ages. **19**

Marbury v. *Madison* (1803) U.S. Supreme Court case that established the principle of judicial review. **336**

Marshall Plan (1948) U.S. plan to give money to European countries to help them rebuild their economies after World War II. **699**

Massacre at Wounded Knee (1890) U.S. Army's killing of approximately 150 Sioux at Wounded Knee Creek in South Dakota; ended U.S-Indian wars on the Plains. **652**

mass production Efficient production of large numbers of identical goods. **402**

Mayflower Compact (1620) Document written by the Pilgrims that established general guidelines for self government. **99**

McCulloch v. *Maryland* (1819) U.S. Supreme Court case that declared the Second Bank of the United States was constitutional and that because it was a federal institution Maryland could not interfere with the bank's operations. **377**

mercantilism Practice of creating and maintaining wealth by carefully controlling trade. **126**

mercenaries Hired foreign soldiers. **199**

Mexican Cession (1848) Land that Mexico gave to the United States after the Mexican War through the Treaty of Guadalupe Hidalgo; included in what is now California, Nevada, and Utah; most of Arizona and New Mexico; and parts of Colorado, Texas, and Wyoming. **526**

Middle Ages Period of European history that lasted from about 500 A.D. to 1500. **19**

middle class Social and economic level between the wealthy and the poor. **460**

Middle Passage Voyage that brought enslaved Africans across the Atlantic Ocean to North America and the West Indies. **129**

migration Movement of people from one region to another. **5**

militia An army made up of civilians serving temporarily as soldiers. **158**

minutemen American colonial militia members who were supposed to be ready to fight at a minute's notice. **185**

missions Settlements established by priests in Spanish America to convert local Indians to Catholicism. **73**

Missouri Compromise (1820) Agreement proposed by Henry Clay that allowed Missouri to enter the Union as a slave state and Maine to enter as a free state; also outlawed slavery in any territories or states north of the 36°30′ line. **369**

monopoly Sole economic control of a business or product. **35**

Monroe Doctrine (1823) President James Monroe's statement forbidding further colonization in the Americas and declaring that the United States would view any attempt by a foreign country to colonize as a hostile act. **367**

Montgomery bus boycott (1955–56) African American boycott of the city buses in Montgomery, Alabama, that led to the changing of discriminatory bus rules. **701**

Mormon Trail Route by which Mormons traveled west to Utah. **531**

Mormons Members of the Church of Jesus Christ of Latter-Day Saints. **531**

Morrill Act (1862) Federal law passed by Congress that gave land to western states to encourage them to build colleges. **667**

Morse code System developed by Samuel Morse's assistant that represented each letter of the alphabet by a certain combination of dots and dashes; used with the telegraph. **416**

mountain men Men who trapped animals for fur in the Rocky Mountains and other western regions of the United States. **502**

national debt Total amount of money owed by a country to its lenders. **305**

nationalism Feeling that a specific nation, language, or culture is superior to others. **690**

National Organization for Women (NOW) Women's rights group formed in 1966. **704**

nativists U.S. citizens who opposed immigration because they were suspicious of immigrants and feared losing jobs to them. **459**

Nat Turner's Rebellion (1831) Rebellion in which Nat Turner led a group of slaves in Virginia in an unsuccessful attempt to overthrow and kill planter families. **443**

naturalized citizen A person born in another country who has been granted citizenship. **291**

Navigation Acts (1650–96) A series of English laws that required the American colonies to trade primarily with England; set duties on some goods. **127**

Nazis National Socialist Party; political group led by Adolf Hitler that rose to power in Germany in the 1930s. **696**

Neutrality Proclamation (1793) Statement made by President George Washington that the United States would not side with any of the nations at war in Europe following the French Revolution. **312**

New Deal Franklin D. Roosevelt's plan for helping the U.S. economy during the Great Depression. **694**

New Jersey Plan Proposal to create a unicameral government with representation by state rather than by population; rejected at the Constitutional Convention. **238**

Nineteenth Amendment (1920) Constitutional amendment that gave women the vote. **686**

nominating conventions Meetings where a political party selects its presidential and vice presidential candidates; first held in the 1820s. **374**

Non-Intercourse Act (1809) Law that replaced the Embargo Act and restored trade with all nations except Britain and France. **346**

North American Free Trade Agreement (NAFTA) Trade agreement among the United States, Canada, and Mexico reached in the early 1990s. **709**

North Atlantic Treaty Organization (NATO) Alliance formed in 1949 by the United States, Britain, and 10 other countries to help defend each other in case of attack. **699**

Northwest Ordinance of 1787 Legislation passed by Congress to establish a political structure for the lands in the Northwest Territory and create a system for the admission of new states. **226**

Northwest Passage A nonexistent path through North America that early explorers searched for, which would allow ships to sail from the Atlantic to the Pacific Ocean. **52**

Northwest Territory Lands including present-day Illinois, Indiana, Michigan, Ohio, Wisconsin, and part of Minnesota; organized by the Northwest Ordinance of 1787. **226**

nullification crisis A dispute between South Carolina and the federal government in the late 1820s over the state's right to nullify, or cancel, an unpopular tariff. **377**

Olive Branch Petition (1775) Peace request sent by the Second Continental Congress to Britain's King George III, who rejected it. **186**

open range Public land used by ranchers who were part of the Cattle Kingdom. **661**

Operation Desert Storm (1991) Invasion led by the United States to force Iraqi troops to withdraw from Kuwait. **708**

Oregon Trail A 2,000-mile trail stretching through the Great Plains from western Missouri to Oregon Country. **506**

Pacific Railway Acts (1862, 1864) Two laws passed by the federal government that gave loans and land grants to railroad companies to encourage them to build a transcontinental railroad. **657**

Paleo-Indians The first Americans who crossed from Asia into North America sometime between 10,000 and 3,800 B.C. **5**

Panama Canal Artificial waterway across the Isthmus of Panama; completed by the United States in 1914. **689**

Panic of 1837 A financial crisis in the United States that led to an economic depression. **378**

Panic of 1873 A financial crisis in the United States that led to an economic depression and weakened the Republican Party. **636**

pardon Freedom from punishment. **259**

Parliament The British national legislature. **121**

Patriots American colonists who fought for independence from Great Britain during the Revolutionary War. **192**

petition A formal request. **285**

Pickett's Charge (1863) Failed Confederate attack, led by General George Pickett, at the Battle of Gettysburg. **601**

Pilgrims Members of a Puritan Separatist sect that left England in the early 1600s to settle in the Americas. **99**

Pinckney's Treaty (1795) Agreement between the United States and Spain that changed Florida's border and made it easier for American ships to use the port of New Orleans. **314**

pioneers People who first settle an area. **163**

plantations Large farms that usually specialize in growing one kind of crop. **74**

planters Wealthy farmers with large plantations. **97**

Plessy v. *Ferguson* (1896) U.S. Supreme Court case that established the separate-but-equal doctrine for public facilities. **638**

political action committees (PACs) Organizations that collect money to distribute to candidates who support the same issues as the contributors. **294**

political parties Groups of people who organize to help elect government officials and influence government policies. **319**

poll tax A special tax that a person had to pay in order to vote. **637**

Pontiac's Rebellion (1763) Unsuccessful effort by Ottawa chief Pontiac and his allies to drive out British settlers on the frontier. **165**

Pony Express A system of messengers that carried mail between relay stations on a route from St. Joseph, Missouri, to San Francisco, California, in 1860 and 1861. **657**

popular sovereignty The idea that political authority belongs to the people; also a principle that would allow voters in a particular territory to decide whether to ban or permit slavery. **240, 553**

Populist Party Political party formed in 1891 that supported free coinage of silver, work reforms, immigration restrictions, and government ownership of railroads and the telegraph and telephone systems. **685**

potlatches Ceremonial events held by Indian peoples of the American Northwest at which hosts gave away most of their goods to gain respect. **12**

Pottawatomie Massacre (1856) Incident in which abolitionist John Brown and seven other men murdered pro-slavery Kansans. **563**

Powhatan Confederacy Powerful alliance of Algonquian Indians under the leadership of Wahunsonacock. **94**

precedent An action or decision that later serves as an example. **302**

presidios Spanish military bases located in the Americas. **73**

privateers Private ships authorized by a nation to attack its enemies. **312**

Privy Council Group of royal advisers who set policies for Britain's American colonies. **120**

Proclamation of 1763 British proclamation banning colonial settlement west of the Appalachian Mountains. **166**

progressives Group of reformers who worked to improve social and political problems in the late 1800s. **686**

prohibition The banning of the manufacture, distribution, and sale of alcoholic beverages. **692**

propaganda Stories and images designed to support a particular point of view. **172**

proprietors Owners. **110**

prospect To search for gold. **535**

protective tariff A tax on imported goods that raises the price of imports so people will buy domestic goods. **307**

Protestant Reformation Religious movement begun by Martin Luther and others in 1517 to reform the Catholic Church. **78**

Protestants Reformers who protested certain practices of the Catholic Church. **78**

pueblos Spanish towns in the Americas. **73**

Pullman strike (1894) Railroad strike that stopped traffic on many railroad lines until federal courts ordered the workers to return to their jobs. **684**

Puritans Protestants who wanted to reform the Church of England. **98**

Quakers Society of Friends; Protestant sect founded in 1640s in England whose members believed that salvation was available to all people. **113**

Radical Republicans Republican members of Congress who felt that southern states needed to make great social changes before they could be readmitted to the Union. **627**

range rights Rights to water on the Plains that smaller ranchers bought from larger ranchers. **662**

range wars Competition among large ranchers, small ranchers, and farmers on the Plains for the use of the open range. **665**

ratification Formal approval. **226**

Reconquista Centuries-long struggle to drive the Moors from Spain; ended in 1492 with the surrender of the kingdom of Granada. **39**

Reconstruction (1865–77) Period following the Civil War during which the U.S. government worked to reunite the nation and to rebuild the southern states. **621**

Reconstruction Acts (1867–68) Laws that put the southern states under U.S. military control and required them to draft new constitutions upholding the Fourteenth Amendment. **630**

Redcoats British soldiers who fought against the colonists in the American Revolution; so called because of their bright red uniforms. **186**

Redeemers Group of southerners who helped return the Democrats to political power in the South during Reconstruction and tried to limit the civil rights of African Americans. **637**

Red Scare A wave of anticommunist fear that swept the United States after World War I. **691**

Renaissance Rebirth of interest in the arts and learning in Europe that began in Italy in the mid-1300s and lasted until the 1600s. **34**

rendezvous Annual event held by mountain men to trade furs and socialize. **503**

repeal To abolish. **170**

representative democracy A government that is composed of representatives of the people. **256**

Republic of Texas Independent nation of Texas, which lasted from 1836 until 1848, when Texas was annexed to the United States. **497**

republicanism Support for a system of representative government known as a republic. **224**

Republican Party Political party formed in the 1850s to stop the spread of slavery in the West. **564**

reservations Federal lands set aside for American Indians. **650**

reserved powers Powers retained by the state governments or by citizens. **257**

revivals Public church gatherings at which ministers preach to a large number of people. **136**

Rhode Island System System developed by Samuel Slater in the mid-1800s, in which families were hired as textile workers. **405**

right of deposit Right to transfer goods at a destination without having to pay fees for the cargo. **313**

roundup Act of driving cattle together and collecting them into a herd. **662**

Rush-Bagot Agreement (1817) Agreement that limited naval power on the Great Lakes to the United States and British Canada. **364**

scalawags Name given to white southerners who supported Reconstruction for private gain; roughly defined as mean fellows. **634**

scientific agriculture Use of scientific techniques to improve crop production. **430**

scientific method Observation of and experimentation with natural events in order to form theories that could predict other events or behaviors. **141**

Scientific Revolution Period of great learning that began in the 1600s as European scientists, mathematicians, and astronomers looked for explanations about how the universe worked. **140**

sea dogs English sailors encouraged by Queen Elizabeth I to raid Spanish treasure ships in the late 1500s. **80**

search warrant A judge's order authorizing the search of a person's home or property to look for evidence of a crime. **286**

secession Act of formally withdrawing from an organization, such as a country. **573**

Second Battle of Bull Run (1862) Civil War battle in which the Confederate army forced most of the Union army out of Virginia. **587**

Second Continental Congress (1775) Meeting of colonial delegates in Philadelphia to decide how to react to fighting at Lexington and Concord. **186**

Second Great Awakening A period of religious evangelism that began in the 1790s and became widespread in the United States by the 1830s. **452**

Second Industrial Revolution A period of explosive growth in manufacturing and industry in the late 1800s. **682**

sect A religious group. **98**

sectionalism A devotion to the interests of one geographic region rather than those of the country as a whole. **553**

segregation Forced separation of people of different races in public places. **637**

Seneca Falls Convention (1848) First national women's rights convention, at which the Declaration of Sentiments was written. **477**

separation of powers The division of governmental power into distinct areas with different branches of government exercising different powers; prevents one branch from becoming too powerful. **257**

Separatists Radical group of Puritans who wanted to cut all ties with the Church of England. **98**

Seven Days' Battles (1862) Series of Civil War battles in which Confederate army successes forced the Union army to retreat from near Richmond, Virginia, the Confederate capital. **587**

Seventeenth Amendment (1913) Constitutional amendment allowing American voters to directly elect U.S. senators. **686**

sharecropping System used on southern farms after the Civil War in which farmers worked land owned by someone else in return for a small portion of the crops. **639**

Shays's Rebellion (1786-87) Uprising of Massachusetts farmers, led by Daniel Shays, to protest high taxes, heavy debt, and farm fore-closures. **234**

Sherman Antitrust Act (1890) Law that made it illegal to create monopolies or trusts that restrained free trade. **684**

siege Military blockade of a city or fort. **187**

Siege of Vicksburg (1863) Union army's six-week blockade of Vicksburg that led the city to surrender during the Civil War. **592**

Silk Road Overland trade route that linked China with other Asian markets as far west as the Black Sea. **25**

slave codes Laws passed in the colonies to control slaves. **132**

Social Security Act (1935) Law that provides retirement pensions and unemployment insurance to American workers. **694**

societies Groups of people who live together and share a culture. **6**

sodbusters Name given to both the Plains farmers and the plows they used to break up the region's tough sod. **668**

Sons of Liberty Secret societies formed in the mid-1700s by colonists to protest new taxes and to frighten tax collectors. **169**

Spanish Armada Large Spanish fleet defeated by England in 1588. **80**

speculators Investors who buy items at low prices in hopes that their value will rise. **305**

spirituals Emotional Christian songs sung by slaves in the South that mixed African and European elements and usually expressed slaves' religious beliefs. **442**

spoils system Politicians' practice of giving government jobs to their supporters. **376**

Stamp Act (1765) Law passed by Parliament that raised tax money by requiring colonists to pay for an official stamp whenever they bought paper items such as newspapers, licenses, and legal documents. **169**

staple crops Crops that are continuously in demand. **134**

states' rights Belief that the power of the federal government regarding the states is strictly limited. **379**

strait Narrow, winding sea passage. **48**

strict construction Way of interpreting the Constitution that allows the federal government to take only those actions the Constitution specifically says it can take. **308**

strikes Refusals of workers to perform their jobs until employers meet their demands. **408**

suffrage Voting rights. **224**

Sugar Act (1764) Law passed by the British Parliament setting taxes on molasses and sugar imported by the colonies. **167**

supply-side economics Economic theory that lowering taxes would boost the economy. **707**

Sutter's Fort Northern California colony founded by Swiss immigrant John Sutter in 1839 that became a popular destination for American immigrants. **509**

Tariff of Abominations (1828) Nickname given to a new tariff by southerners who opposed it. **376**

tariffs Taxes on imports or exports. **232**

Tea Act (1773) Law passed by Parliament allowing the British East India Company to sell its low-cost tea directly to the colonies, undermining colonial tea merchants; led to the Boston Tea Party. **173**

technology Tools used to produce goods or to do work. **401**

Tejanos Spanish settlers who lived in what is now southern Texas. **490**

telegraph Machine invented by Samuel Morse in 1837 that uses pulses of electric current to send messages across long distances through wires. **415**

temperance movement A social reform effort begun in the mid-1800s to encourage people to drink less alcohol. **464**

Ten Percent Plan President Abraham Lincoln's plan for Reconstruction; once 10 percent of voters in a for-mer Confederate state took a U.S. loyalty oath, they could form a new state government and be read-mitted to the Union. **621**

tenements Poorly built, overcrowded housing where many immigrants lived. **461**

Tet Offensive (1968) Attack by North Vietnamese and Vietcong troops against South Vietnam during the Vietnam War; demonstrated that the North Vietnamese were determined to keep fighting. **705**

Texas longhorn Hearty breed of cattle raised by ranch-ers throughout western Texas. **660**

textiles Cloth. **399**

Thirteenth Amendment (1865) Constitutional amendment that outlawed slavery. **622**

Three-Fifths Compromise (1787) Agreement worked out at the Constitutional Convention stating that three fifths of the slaves in each state should be counted as part of the state's population for determining representation in the lower house of Congress. **239**

Toleration Act of 1649 Maryland law that made restricting the religious rights of Christians a crime;

one of the first laws protecting religious tolerance to be passed in the English colonies. **110**

total war Type of war in which an army destroys its opponent's ability to fight by targeting civilian and economic as well as military resources. **604**

totems Images of ancestors or animal spirits; often carved onto tall poles by Native American peoples of the Pacific Northwest. **12**

town meeting Political meeting at which people make decisions on local issues; used primarily in New England. **122**

Townshend Acts (1767) Laws passed by Parliament placing duties on certain items imported by the colonists. **171**

trade unions Workers' organizations that try to improve pay and working conditions. **408**

Trail of Tears (1838–39) An 800-mile forced march made by the Cherokee from their homeland in Georgia to Indian Territory; resulted in the deaths of thousands of Cherokee. **383**

transcendentalism Idea that people could rise above the material things in life; philosophy shared by some New England writers in the mid-1800s. **454**

transcontinental railroad Railroad that crossed the continental United States; construction began in 1863 and was completed in 1869. **657**

Transportation Revolution Rapid growth in the speed and convenience of transportation; in the United States this began in the early 1800s. **410**

Treaty of Dancing Rabbit Creek (1830) Agreement in which the Choctaw gave up more than 10 million acres of land in Mississippi and accepted removal to Indian Territory. **382**

Treaty of Fort Laramie (1851) The first major treaty between the U.S. government and Plains Indians; allowed U.S. citizens to travel across Indian homelands. **649**

Treaty of Ghent (1814) Treaty signed by the United States and Britain ending the War of 1812. **355**

Treaty of Greenville (1795) Agreement between American Indian confederation leaders and the U.S. government that gave the United States Indian lands in the southeastern part of the Northwest Territory and guaranteed that U.S. citizens could safely travel through the region. **316**

Treaty of Guadalupe Hidalgo (1848) Treaty that ended the Mexican War and gave the United States much of Mexico's northern territory. **526**

Treaty of Medicine Lodge (1867) Agreement between the U.S. government and southern Plains Indians in which the Indians agreed to move onto reservations. **650**

Treaty of Paris (1763) Peace agreement that ended the French and Indian War. **162**

Treaty of Paris of 1783 Peace agreement that officially ended the Revolutionary War and established British recognition of the United States. **213**

Treaty of Tordesillas (1494) Treaty signed by Spain and Portugal in which both countries agreed to move the Line of Demarcation 800 miles farther west. **42**

Treaty of Versailles (1919) Treaty ending World War I; required Germany to pay billions of dollars in war costs and accept full responsibility for the war; it also established the League of Nations. **691**

Tredegar Iron Works Large iron factory that operated in Richmond, Virginia, in the early to mid-1800s. **432**

triangular trade Trading networks in which goods and slaves moved among England, the American colonies, the West Indies and West Africa. **128**

Truman Doctrine (1947) President Harry S Truman's policy that the United States would help any country struggling against communism in order to keep it from spreading. **699**

Twelfth Amendment (1804) Constitutional amendment that created a separate ballot for president and vice president. **324**

unalienable rights Basic human rights such as life, liberty, and the pursuit of happiness. **191**

Uncle Tom's Cabin (1852) Antislavery novel written by Harriet Beecher Stowe that showed northerners the violent reality of slavery and drew many people to the abolitionists' cause. **557**

Underground Railroad Network of people who helped thousands of slaves escape to the North by providing transportation and hiding places. **472**

United Nations (UN) International organization formed in 1945 for settling problems between nations. **699**

utopian community Place where people worked to establish a perfect society; such communities were popular in the United States during the late 1700s and early to mid-1800s. **454**

vaqueros Mexican cowboys in the West who tended cattle and horses. **662**

veto To cancel. **259**

viceroy A royal governor in Spanish America. **39**

Virginia Plan (1787) Plan for government proposed at the Constitutional Convention in which the national government would have three branches—executive, judicial, and legislative; representation in the legislature would be determined by state population. **237**

Virginia Statute for Religious Freedom (1786) Legislation that gave people in Virginia freedom of worship and freedom to speak their opinions about religion. **224**

Voting Rights Act of 1965 Law that ensured every eligible U.S. citizen's right to vote. **704**

Wade-Davis Bill Reconstruction plan that imposed two conditions for a former Confederate state to rejoin the United States; it had to outlaw slavery, and majority of adult males had to take a loyalty oath; those who had supported the Confederacy could not vote or hold office. **621**

War Hawks Members of Congress who wanted to declare war against Britain in the early 1800s. **348**

War on Drugs President George Bush's continuation of the government effort to stop illegal drugs from entering the United States. **708**

Watergate Scandal in which President Richard Nixon authorized a break-in of the Democratic National Committee headquarters; led to Nixon's resignation in 1974. **706**

Whig Party Political party formed by opponents of Andrew Jackson in 1834 who supported a strong legislature. **378**

Whiskey Rebellion (1794) Protests by small farmers in Pennsylvania against new taxes on whiskey and other alcohol. **316**

wigwams Small circular huts in which some north-eastern Native American peoples lived. **16**

Wilderness Campaign (May–June 1864) A series of battles between Union and Confederate forces in northern and central Virginia that stretched Confederate resources to their limit. **603**

Wilmot Proviso (1846) Proposal to outlaw slavery in the territory added to the United States by the Mexican Cession; passed in the House of Representatives but was defeated in the Senate. **553**

Worcester* v. *Georgia (1832) Supreme Court ruling that the Cherokee Nation was a distinct territory over which only the federal government had authority; ignored by both President Andrew Jackson and the state of Georgia. **383**

writs of assistance Special search warrants that allowed tax collectors to search for smuggled goods. **171**

XYZ affair (1797) Incident in which French agents attempted to get a bribe and loans from U.S. diplomats in exchange for an agreement that French privateers would no longer attack American ships; it led to an undeclared naval war between the two countries. **321**

Yalta Conference (1945) Meeting of U.S. president Franklin D. Roosevelt, British prime minister Winston Churchill, and Soviet leader Joseph Stalin to plan the future after World War II. **699**

yeomen Small landowning farmers. **434**

Glossary/Glosario

This Glossary contains terms you need to understand as you study American history. After each key term there is a brief definition or explanation of the meaning of the term as it is used in *Call to Freedom*. The page number refers to the page on which the term is introduced in the textbook.

abolition/abolición Poner fin a la esclavitud. **469**

Adams-Onís Treaty/Tratado Adams-Onís (1819) Acuerdo en el que España cede el territorio de Florida a Estados Unidos. **366**

Alamo/Álamo Misión española en San Antonio, Texas. Sitio de una famosa batalla durante la Revolución texana de 1836. La victoria del ejército mexicano dio como resultado la muerte de todos los texanos defensores del edificio. **494**

Albany Plan of Union/Plan de Unión Albany (1754) Plan redactado por Benjamin Franklin y otros delegados para pedir a las colonias que se unieran bajo un gobierno común. **160**

Alien and Sedition Acts/Leyes de no intervención extranjera (1798) Leyes aprobadas por un congreso mayoritariamente federal con la finalidad de proteger al gobierno de la influencia de ideas, acciones y personas; fueron usadas en contra de miembros del Partido Demócrata Republicano. **322**

amendments/enmiendas Cambios, correcciones o agregados hechos de manera oficial a una ley o constitución. **246**

American Anti-Slavery Society/Sociedad Estadounidense contra la Esclavitud Grupo fundado en 1833 por William Lloyd Garrison y otras personas para la abolición inmediata de la esclavitud y la igualdad racial de los afroestadounidenses. **471**

American Colonization Society/Sociedad Estadounidense de Colonización Sociedad organizada en 1817 para establecer en África Occidental una colonia llamada Liberia como hogar para los afroestadounidenses libres. **470**

American System/Sistema estadounidense Plan de alza de impuestos creado por Henry Clay para realizar mejoras internas como la reparación de caminos y canales. **370**

amnesty/amnistía Perdón oficial otorgado por el gobierno ante un acto ilegal. **621**

annex/anexar Tomar control de un territorio para incorporarlo a un estado, país, etc. **497**

Antifederalists/antifederalistas Personas que se oponían a la ratificación de la Constitución. **242**

Appomattox Courthouse/Appomattox Courthouse Poblado de Virginia donde el general Robert E. Lee fue obligado a rendirse, dando fin a la Guerra Civil. **605**

apportionment/adjudicamiento Uso de la población para determinar cuántos representantes legislativos debe tener un área determinada. **258**

apprentices/aprendices Personas que aprenden un oficio de un experto en la materia. **133**

archaeology/arqueología Estudio científico del pasado no escrito. **5**

Articles of Confederation/Artículos de la Confederación (1777) Documento que creó el primer gobierno central en Estados Unidos; fue reemplazado por la Constitución en 1789. **225**

artifacts/artefactos Restos de objetos hechos por el hombre. **5**

astrolabe/astrolabio Instrumento usado por los navegantes en algún tiempo para determinar la posición de una embarcación con base en la posición de las estrellas.

backcountry/*backcountry* Región fronteriza de Virginia y las Carolinas, localizada entre la costa y los montes Apalaches. **163**

Bacon's Rebellion/Rebelión de Bacon (1676) Ataque encabezado por Nathaniel Bacon contra los indígenas estadounidenses y el gobierno colonial en Virginia. **97**

balance of trade/balanza de intercambio Relación entre los bienes que un país adquiere de otros países y los que les vende. **126**

Bank of the United States/Banco de Estados Unidos Banco nacional rentado por el Congreso en 1791 para ofrecer seguridad a la economía de Estados Unidos. **309**

Battle of Antietam/Batalla de Antietam (1862) Victoria del Ejército de la Unión en la batalla de un solo día más sangrienta en la historia de Estados Unidos. **588**

Battle of Brandywine Creek/Batalla de Brandywine Creek (1777) Batalla de la Revolución en la que las fuerzas británicas arrasaron con los patriotas en Pennsylvania. **204**

Battle of Bunker Hill/Batalla de Bunker Hill (1775) Batalla de la Revolución que tuvo lugar en Boston y que demostró que los colonos podían luchar contra el ejército británico. **188**

Battle of Fallen Timbers/Batalla de Fallen Timbers (1794) Batalla entre las tropas estadounidenses y una confederación india estadounidense que se resistía al establecimiento de personas de raza blanca en el noroeste de Estados Unidos; esta batalla condujo al Tratado de Greenville. **316**

Battle of Gettysburg/Batalla de Gettysburg (1863) Victoria del Ejército de la Unión que revirtió las condiciones de lucha en contra de los confederados en Gettysburg, Pennsylvania. En esta batalla perdieron la vida más de 50,000 soldados. **601**

Battle of Goliad/Batalla de Goliad (1836) Victoria del ejército mexicano durante la Guerra de Texas en la que el general Antonio López de Santa Anna ordenó la ejecución de soldados texanos después de su rendición. **495**

Battle of Horseshoe Bend/Batalla de Horseshoe Bend (1814) Victoria del ejército estadounidense durante la Guerra de 1812 en la que las tropas de Andrew Jackson obligaron a los indios creek a ceder gran parte de su territorio en el sur del país. **353**

Battle of Lake Erie/Batalla del Lago Erie (1813) Victoria en la que, comandado por Oliver Hazard Perry, el ejército estadounidense puso fin al control británico del Lago Erie. **352**

Battle of New Orleans/Batalla de Nueva Orleáns (1815) Aunque ésta fue la mayor victoria del ejército estadounidense en la Guerra de 1812, tuvo lugar dos semanas después de la firma de un tratado de paz en el que se declaraba la terminación de la guerra. **354**

Battle of Pea Ridge/Batalla de Pea Ridge (1862) Batalla de la Guerra Civil en la que el ejército confederado establecido en Missouri y al que se habían unido algunos indígenas estadounidenses, fue derrotado en el noroeste de Arkansas. **593**

Battle of Princeton/Batalla de Princeton (1777) Batalla de la Revolución en la que los patriotas hicieron retroceder a las fuerzas británicas en Nueva Jersey. **203**

Battle of San Jacinto/Batalla de San Jacinto (1836) Batalla final de la Guerra de Texas en la que fue derrotado el ejército mexicano y Texas obtuvo su independencia. **496**

Battle of Saratoga/Batalla de Saratoga (1777) Batalla de la Revolución que tuvo lugar en Nueva York y en la que las fuerzas británicas sufrieron una de sus mayores derrotas y los patriotas su mayor victoria hasta ese momento. **204**

Battle of Shiloh/Batalla de Shiloh (1862) Batalla de la Guerra Civil realizada en Tennessee en la que el Ejército de la Unión adquirió mayor control sobre el Valle del Mississippi. **591**

Battle of the Little Bighorn/Batalla de Little Bighorn (1876) Última batalla del general Custer. Esta batalla entre las tropas de George Armstrong Custer y los guerreros sioux al mando de los jefes Caballo Loco y Toro Sentado produjo la mayor derrota del ejército estadounidense en el oeste. **651**

Battle of the Thames/Batalla del Támesis (1813) Victoria del ejército estadounidense al mando de William Henry Harrison que puso fin a la alianza de indios y británicos durante la Guerra de 1812. **352**

Battle of Tippecanoe/Batalla de Tippecanoe (1811) Victoria del ejército estadounidense sobre la confederación india que intentaba evitar el establecimiento de poblaciones de blancos en el noroeste. Esta batalla aumentó las hostilidades entre Gran Bretaña y Estados Unidos. **347**

Battle of Trenton/Batalla de Trenton (1776) Batalla de la Revolución que tuvo lugar en Nueva Jersey y en la que las fuerzas de los patriotas capturaron a más de 900 soldados hesianos. **203**

Battle of Vincennes/Batalla de Vincennes (1779) Batalla de la Revolución librada en el oeste, en la que los patriotas retomaron de manos de los británicos el poblado de Vincennes, de población mayoritariamente francesa y localizado en la ribera del río Wabash. **210**

Battle of Yorktown/Batalla de Yorktown (1871) La mayor batalla de la Revolución. Sitio de rendición del general británico Charles Cornwallis ante las tropas de los patriotas establecidas en Virginia. **212**

Bear Flag Revolt/Revuelta de Bear Flag (1846) Revuelta iniciada por colonos estadounidenses en contra del gobierno de México para declarar al territorio de California como una república independiente. **524**

Bessemer process/Proceso de Bessemer Proceso más económico de producción de acero, desarrollado en la década de 1850. **683**

bicameral legislature/legislatura de cámara dual Cuerpo de legisladores compuesto por las dos Cámaras. **121**

Bill of Rights/Declaración de Derechos Primeras 10 enmiendas hechas a la Constitución. Fue ratificada en 1791. **247**

Black Codes/códigos negros Decretos aprobados en los estados sureños en la época de la Reconstrucción con la finalidad de limitar al máximo la libertad y los derechos de los afroestadounidenses. **627**

Black Death/muerte negra Epidemia que se extendió por toda Europa de 1348 a 1350 y causó la muerte a 30 millones de personas. **32**

bonanza/bonanza Gran yacimiento de mineral precioso. **655**

bonds/bonos Certificados que representan el dinero de los ciudadanos tomado en préstamo por el gobierno. **305**

boomtowns/pueblos en explosión Comunidades del oeste que se desarrollaron con gran rapidez debido a la fiebre del oro, pero que desaparecieron cuando los yacimientos se agotaron. **656**

borderlands/territorio fronterizo Región dominada por España que abarcaba el norte de México, Florida y partes de los actuales estados de Arizona, Nuevo México y Texas donde vivían algunos europeos. **75**

border states/estados fronterizos Delaware, Kentucky, Maryland y Missouri. Estados ubicados entre el norte y el sur en los que se practicaba la esclavitud y que no se adhirieron a la Confederación durante la Guerra Civil. **582**

Boston Massacre/matanza de Boston (1770) Incidente en el que los soldados británicos abrieron fuego entre una multitud de colonizadores, ocasionando la muerte a cinco personas. **172**

Boston Tea Party/Motín del Té (1773) Protesta en contra de la Ley del Té en la que un grupo de colonos abordó los barcos británicos que transportaban té y echaron al mar alrededor de 340 cofres con este producto. **174**

boycott/boicot Rechazo a la compra de bienes específicos. Método usado con frecuencia como protesta contra determinados movimientos. **169**

Brown v. Board of Education/Consejo de Educación Brown (1954) Decreto de la Suprema Corte que declaraba ilegales a las escuelas públicas en las que se practicaba la segregación racial. Puso fin a la doctrina Plessy-Ferguson de separatismo, establecida en 1896. **701**

Bureau of Indian Affairs/Oficina de Asuntos Indígenas Agencia creada por el gobierno en el siglo XIX con la finalidad de hacer llegar las políticas federales a territorios habitados por tribus indígenas. **382**

cabinet/gabinete Grupo conformado por los jefes de los departamentos ejecutivos para brindar asesoría al presidente de Estados Unidos. **260**

California Gold Rush/fiebre del oro en California Migración masiva de personas a California en 1849, luego del descubrimiento de yacimientos de oro en la zona. **534**

Californios/californianos Colonos españoles que habitaron en California. **489**

capital/capital Dinero o propiedades usadas para obtener más dinero. **33**

caravel/carabela Barco rápido y fácil de maniobrar diseñado por los portugueses. **36**

carpetbaggers/aventureros Nombre dado a los norteños que emigraron al sur durante la Reconstrucción. **633**

cash crops/cultivo para la venta Nombre dado a los productos cosechados con la finalidad de obtener ganancias económicas y no para consumo personal. **131**

casualties/bajas Personas asesinadas, heridas, capturadas o extraviadas durante una guerra. **161**

cattle drive/travesía de ganado Viajes largos en los que un grupo de vaqueros arreaba ganado para llevarlo a los mercados del norte o a mejores pastizales. **663**

Cattle Kingdom/Cattle Kingdom Área de las Grandes Planicies que se extiende de Texas a Canadá en la que muchos rancheros se establecieron como productores de ganado a finales del siglo XIX. **661**

charter/carta Documento legal que da a una persona el derecho de establecer una colonia. **87**

checks and balances/revisión y balance Sistema establecido por la Constitución para evitar que cualquier rama del gobierno adquiera demasiado poder en relación con las demás. **241**

Chisholm Trail/Camino de Chisholm Camino creado por Jesse Chisholm en 1867 de San Antonio, Texas, hasta Abilene, Kansas, para realizar travesías de ganado. **663**

circumnavigate/circunnavegar Hacer una navegación completa alrededor de algo. **49**

Civil Rights Act of 1866/Ley de Derechos Civiles de 1866 Ley que daba a los afroestadounidenses derechos legales similares a los que tenían los ciudadanos de raza blanca. **628**

Civil Rights Act of 1875/Ley de Derechos Civiles de 1875 Ley que garantizaba a los afroestadounidenses igualdad de derechos en lugares públicos como teatros y medios públicos de transporte. **636**

Civil Rights Act of 1964/Ley de Derechos Civiles de 1964 Ley que prohibía la segregación racial en lugares públicos y el rechazo de patrones, sindicatos y universidades a cualquier persona por su color, nacionalidad, religión o sexo. **704**

Clermont/Clermont Primer barco comercial de vapor de grandes dimensiones, diseñado por Robert Fulton y probado en 1807. **412**

Cold War/guerra fría Periodo de lucha de poderes entre Estados Unidos y la Unión Soviética que se extendió de 1945 a 1991. **699**

Columbian Exchange/intercambio colombino Intercambio de plantas, animales y enfermedades entre Estados Unidos y Europa, Asia y África. **51**

Commercial Revolution/Revolución Comercial Periodo de auge económico iniciado en Europa en el siglo XIII con una gran expansión comercial. **33**

Committees of Correspondence/comités de correspondencia Comités creados por la Cámara de Representantes de Massachusetts en la década de 1760 para que poblados y colonias compartieran información que los ayudara a enfrentar las leyes británicas vigentes. **169**

common-school movement/Movimiento de Escuelas Comunes Reforma social iniciada a mediados del siglo XIX para fomentar la idea de que todos los niños recibieran educación en un mismo lugar sin importar su origen o clase social. **465**

Common Sense/Common Sense (1776) Folleto escrito por Thomas Paine en el que criticaba a las monarquías con la finalidad de convencer a los colonos estadounidenses de la necesidad de independizarse de Gran Bretaña. **190**

Compromise of 1850/Compromiso de 1850 Acuerdo redactado por Henry Clay en que se permitía a California ingresar a la Unión como estado libre, se proponía la división del resto del territorio cedido por México en dos partes donde el tema de la esclavitud sería reglamentado por soberanía popular, se aclaraban los reclamos de tierras entre Texas y Nuevo México, se abolía el intercambio de esclavos con Washington y se fortalecía la Ley de Esclavos Fugitivos. **555**

Compromise of 1877/Compromiso de 1877 Acuerdo en el que se definió la situación de las elecciones presidenciales de 1876. Los demócratas aceptaron al republicano Rutherford B. Hayes como presidente a cambio del retiro de las tropas federales del sur. **637**

Comstock Lode/veta de Comstock Yacimiento de oro y plata descubierto en Nevada por Henry Comstock en 1859. **655**

concurrent powers/poderes concurrentes Poderes compartidos por el gobierno federal y los gobiernos estatales. **257**

Confederate States of America/Estados Confederados de América Nación formada por los estados del sur el 4 de febrero de 1861, también conocida como Confederación. **574**

conquistadores/conquistadores Soldados y exploradores españoles que encabezaron las expediciones militares en Estados Unidos y reclamaron territorios en nombre de España. **66**

Constitution/Constitución Conjunto de principios básicos que determina los poderes y las obligaciones de un gobierno. **224**

Constitutional Convention/Convención Constitucional de Filadelfia (1787) Encuentro realizado en Filadelfia en el que delegados de los estados redactaron la Constitución. **237**

Constitutional Union Party/Partido Unido de la Constitución Partido político formado en 1860 por habitantes del norte y del sur en apoyo de la Unión, sus leyes y la Constitución. **571**

Continental Army/Ejército Continental Ejército creado por el Segundo Congreso Continental en 1775 para defender las colonias estadounidenses del dominio británico. **186**

contrabands/contrabando Esclavos que escapaban o eran capturados por el Ejército de la Unión durante la Guerra Civil. **596**

Contract with America/Contrato con Estados Unidos Reforma republicana de diez puntos creada a mediados de la década de 1990. **709**

Convention of 1818/Convención de 1818 Acuerdo entre Estados Unidos y Gran Bretaña para definir los derechos de pesca y establecer las nuevas fronteras al norte. **365**

convert/convertir Cambio de creencias religiosas. **42**

Copperheads/copperheads Demócratas del norte que se oponían a la abolición de la esclavitud y simpatizaban con las creencias sureñas durante la Guerra Civil. **597**

cotton belt/región algodonera Región que se extendía de Georgia al este de Texas en la que se producía la mayor parte del algodón cosechado en Estados Unidos a mediados del siglo XIX. **427**

cotton diplomacy/Diplomacia del algodón Esfuerzos de la Confederación por aprovechar la influencia de la industria textil británica del sur para convencer a Gran Bretaña de apoyar su causa durante la Guerra Civil. **584**

cotton gin/despepitadora de algodón Dispositivo inventado por Eli Whitney en 1793 para separar las fibras de algodón de las semillas. Este invento revolucionó la industria del algodón. **426**

Council of the Indies/Consejo de Indias Grupo de funcionarios de la realeza establecido en 1524 para vigilar las acciones del gobierno y la aplicación de las leyes españolas en América. **72**

covenant/pacto Acuerdo sagrado. **104**

creditors/acreedores Personas que prestan dinero. **233**

Crusades/Cruzadas (1096-1221) Serie de guerras emprendidas por los cristianos europeos para tomar posesión de las Tierras Santas. **25**

Cuban missile crisis /crisis de los misiles de Cuba (1962) Crisis militar que estuvo a punto de ocasionar una guerra nuclear. Finalmente, la Unión Soviética aceptó retirar sus misiles nucleares de Cuba a cambio de que Estados Unidos prometiera no invadir la isla y retirara algunos de sus misiles de Europa. **703**

culture/cultura Valores y tradiciones comunes de una sociedad, como el lenguaje, forma de gobierno y relaciones familiares. **6**

Cumberland Road/Camino Cumberland Primer proyecto federal de construcción de carreteras, iniciado en 1815 para crear caminos entre Cumberland, Maryland y el poblado en el que actualmente lleva el nombre de Wheeling, West Virginia. **371**

D-Day/Día D 6 de junio de 1944. Invasión del Ejército Aliado a la ocupación Nazi en territorio francés durante la Segunda Guerra Mundial. **696**

Daughters of Liberty/Hijas de la Libertad Grupos de mujeres que realizaron boicots y adoptaron otras medidas para apoyar la resistencia de las colonias al dominio británico. **171**

Dawes General Allotment Act/Ley de la dote general de Dawes (1887) Ley aprobada por el Congreso para dividir las reservaciones de terreno indígenas en partes individuales con la promesa de otorgarles la ciudadanía estadounidense. **654**

debtors/deudores Personas que deben dinero. **233**

Declaration of Independence/Declaración de Independencia (1776) Declaración redactada por el Segundo Congreso Continental para definir los derechos de los colonos, expresar sus quejas contra Gran Bretaña y declarar la independencia de las colonias. **191**

Declaration of Sentiments/Declaración de Sentimientos (1848) Declaración redactada y firmada por varias personas en apoyo de los derechos de las mujeres durante la Convención de Seneca Falls en la que se describía con detalle su punto de vista sobre las injusticias sociales en su contra. **477**

delegated powers/poderes delegados Poderes otorgados de manera específica por la Constitución al gobierno federal. **256**

Democratic Party/Partido Demócrata Asociación política formada por partidarios de Andrew Jackson después de las elecciones presidenciales de 1824. **375**

Democratic-Republican Party/Partido Demócrata-Republicano Asociación política formada en la década de 1790 con la finalidad de preservar el poder de los gobiernos estatales y promover la agricultura. **320**

deport/deportar Enviar a un inmigrante de regreso a su país de origen. **291**

depression/depresión Descenso considerable en la actividad económica, combinado con un alza del desempleo. **233**

dissenters/opositores Personas que están en contra de las opiniones oficiales, sean religiosas o políticas. **103**

domestication/domesticación Proceso de reproducción de plantas y animales para consumo humano. **6**

Dominion of New England/Dominio de Nueva Inglaterra Unión de algunas colonias del noreste, organizada por el Rey James II en 1686, que duró hasta 1689. **123**

Donner party/Partida Donner Grupo de viajeros del oeste extraviados en la Sierra Nevada durante el invierno de 1846-1847. Sólo 40 de los 98 viajeros sobrevivieron. **509**

double jeopardy/doble riesgo Imposibilidad legal de juzgar a una persona dos veces por el mismo crimen. **289**

draft/reclutamiento Sistema de aceptación de personal de las fuerzas armadas. **293**

Dred Scott **decision/Decisión** *Dred Scott* (1857) Decreto aprobado por la Suprema Corte en el que se declaraba que los afroestadounidenses no podían ser ciudadanos de Estados Unidos, que la restricción de la esclavitud presentada en el Compromiso de Missouri era anticonstitucional y que el Congreso no tenía derecho de abolir la esclavitud en ninguna parte del territorio federal. **566**

dry farming/cultivo de sequía Método de cultivo que usaban los agricultores de las Planicies en la década de 1890 para cosechar determinados productos con menos agua. **665**

due process/proceso debido Aplicación justa de la ley. **289**

duties/aranceles Impuestos pagados por la importación de bienes.

Eighteenth Amendment/Decimoctava enmienda (1919) Enmienda constitucional que prohibía la producción, venta y transporte de bebidas alcohólicas en Estados Unidos. Esta enmienda fue rechazada en 1933. **686**

elastic clause/cláusula elástica Artículo I, Sección 8 de la Constitución en la que se otorga al Congreso autoridad para ampliar sus poderes delegados en asuntos no especificados en la Carta Magna. **257**

El Camino Real/El camino real o "Camino del rey", construido por los colonizadores españoles para comunicar las comunidades de la Nueva España. **76**

electoral college/Colegio electoral Grupo elegido en cada estado para reunir votos en las elecciones presidenciales. El número de electores inscritos en cada estado debe ser proporcional al número de representantes y senadores en el Congreso. En cada estado, los electores deben votar por el candidato elegido por su partido. **301**

emancipation/emancipación Liberación de la esclavitud. **469**

Emancipation Proclamation/Proclamación de Emancipación (1862) decreto emitido por el presidente Abraham Lincoln para liberar a los esclavos en las áreas adheridas a la lucha contra la Unión. Tomó efecto el primero de enero de 1863. **595**

embargo/embargo Prohibición de los tratados de comercio con un país. **345**

Embargo Act/Ley de Embargo (1807) Ley que prohibía a los comerciantes estadounidenses realizar intercambios con otros países. **345**

eminent domain/expropiación Poder otorgado al gobierno para tomar propiedades particulares con la finalidad de aumentar su patrimonio. **287**

empresarios/empresarios Personas contratadas por la República mexicana para establecer poblaciones en Texas a principios del siglo XIX. **492**

encomienda **system/Sistema de** *encomienda* Sistema adoptado en Hispanoamérica para que los colonos tuvieran derecho de cobrar impuestos a los indígenas o exigirles trabajo a cambio de protección o la enseñanza de oficios específicos. **74**

energy crisis/crisis energética Situación creada a principios de la década de 1970 por el alza de los precios de los combustibles y la escasez de los mismos. **706**

Enlightenment/Ilustración Era de la razón. Movimiento iniciado en Europa en el siglo XVIII cuando las personas empezaron a adquirir más conocimientos sobre la naturaleza, la sociedad y el gobierno. **141**

English Bill of Rights/Cesión Inglesa de Derechos (1689) Cambio del poder político de la monarquía británica al parlamento inglés. **125**

environments/medio ambiente Clima y paisaje donde habitan seres vivos. **6**

Erie Canal/canal de Erie Canal que corre de Albany a Búfalo, en el estado de Nueva York. Su construcción se completó en 1825. **371**

executive branch/Poder Ejecutivo División del gobierno federal que incluye al presidente y los departamentos administrativos. Su labor es vigilar la aplicación de las leyes de la nación. **240**

executive order/acción ejecutiva Orden no legislativa emitida por el presidente en circunstancias específicas. Una acción ejecutiva tiene la validez de las leyes del Congreso. **259**

Exodusters/Éxodo Migración de afroestadounidenses del sur al oeste a finales del siglo XIX. **667**

exports/exportaciones Productos que un país vende a otros países. **126**

factors/comisionados Intermediarios que administraron el intercambio entre las plantaciones del sur y sus clientes. **429**

fascism/fascismo Sistema de dictadura militar que glorifica a la nación. **695**

federalism/federalismo Sistema de gobierno en el que el poder es distribuido entre una autoridad centralizada y varios estados. **240**

Federalist Papers/Federalist papers Conjunto de documentos que defienden y explican la Constitución con la finalidad de que los ciudadanos sepan que las leyes federales no deben sobreponerse a las de los estados. **244**

Federalist Party/Partido Federalista Asociación política creada en la década de 1790 siguiendo las ideas de Alexander Hamilton con la finalidad de fortalecer al gobierno federal y fomentar la industria y el intercambio comercial. **320**

Federalists/federales Personas que apoyaban la ratificación de la Constitución. **243**

feudalism/feudalismo Sistema de gobierno creado en la Edad Media en que los habitantes ofrecían lealtad absoluta a un señor feudal a cambio de protección. **19**

Fifteenth Amendment/Decimoquinta enmienda (1870) Enmienda constitucional que otorgaba a los afroestadounidenses el derecho al voto. **632**

54th Massachusetts Infantry/54ᵃᵛᵒ Batallón de Infantería de Massachusetts Regimiento de la Guerra Civil formado por soldados afroestadounidenses que tuvo un papel determinante en el ataque al Fuerte Wagner en Carolina del Sur. **596**

First Battle of Bull Run/Primera Batalla de Bull Run (1861) Primera batalla importante de la Guerra Civil. El ejército confederado obtuvo la victoria. En esta batalla se demostró que ninguno de los bandos ganaría la guerra con facilidad. **586**

First Continental Congress/Primer Congreso Continental (1774) Encuentro de delegados de las colonias en Filadelfia para decidir cómo responderían al cierre del Puerto de Boston, al alza de impuestos y a los abusos de las autoridades británicas. Los delegados hicieron una serie de peticiones al rey George III, incluyendo los derechos que consideraban justos para los colonos. **184**

folktales/cuentos populares Narraciones orales que con frecuencia ofrecen una moraleja. **442**

Fort Sumter/Fuerte Sumter Base federal de Charleston, Carolina del Sur, cuyo ataque por los federales en abril de 1861 dio origen a la Guerra Civil. **580**

forty-niners/gambusinos Buscadores de oro que emigraron a California durante la fiebre del oro. **534**

Fourteenth Amendment/Decimocuarta enmienda (1866) Enmienda constitucional que otorgaba derechos completos de ciudadanía a todas las personas nacidas en Estados Unidos o naturalizadas estadounidenses, con excepción de los indígenas. **629**

Freedmen's Bureau/Departamento de Asistencia Social Departamento creado por el Congreso en 1865 para ayudar a los pobres del sur del país. **624**

Freedom Rides/Viajes de la libertad (1961) Viajes en autobús de Washington, D.C., a varios estados del sur con los que los partidarios de los derechos civiles desafiaban la segregación ilegal en los autobuses. **703**

free enterprise/libre empresa Sistema económico en el que varios negocios compiten con poca intervención del gobierno. **127**

Freeport Doctrine/Doctrina de la libertad (1858) Declaración hecha por Stephen Douglas durante los debates Lincoln-Douglas en la que fomenta el uso de la soberanía popular para aprobar o rechazar la esclavitud. **568**

Free-Soil Party/Partido de la libertad de suelo Asociación política formada en 1848 por habitantes de los estados del norte que apoyaban la abolición de la esclavitud y que habían abandonado al Partido de Whig y al Partido Demócrata porque ninguno de los dos apoyaba esta causa. **553**

French Revolution/Revolución francesa Rebelión francesa iniciada en 1789 en que la población francesa se rebeló ante la monarquía y tomó el país para convertirlo en una república. **310**

Fugitive Slave Act/Ley de Esclavos Fugitivos (1850) Ley que calificaba como un crimen ayudar a un esclavo a escapar de su amo, además de permitir la captura de esclavos fugitivos incluso en zonas donde la esclavitud era ilegal para devolverlos a sus dueños. **556**

Fundamental Orders of Connecticut/Decretos Fundamentales de Connecticut (1639) Primeros principios del recién creado gobierno de Estados Unidos presentados por escrito. **108**

G

Gadsden Purchase/Compra de Gadsen (1853) Compra por parte del gobierno de Estados Unidos de territorio mexicano que incluía la región ocupada actualmente por Arizona y Nuevo México. **526**

General Amnesty Act of 1872/Ley General de Amnistía de 1872 Ley que rechazaba la Sección III de la Decimocuarta enmienda en la que se prohibía a los confederados ejercer cualquier cargo público. **634**

Gettysburg Address/Discurso de Gettysburg (1863) Discurso presentado por Abraham Lincoln en el que alababa la valentía de las tropas de la Unión y renovaba su compromiso de triunfo en la Guerra Civil. **602**

Ghost Dance/Danza de los Espíritus Movimiento religioso de los indígenas estadounidenses que se extendió en la región de las Planicies en la década de 1880. **652**

Gibbons v. Ogden/Gibbons Ogden (1824) Decreto de la Suprema Corte que establece que la ley federal tiene prioridad sobre las leyes estatales equivalentes; definición ampliada del comercio interestatal. **413**

Glorious Revolution/Revolución gloriosa (1688) Revuelta ocurrida en Inglaterra contra el rey católico James II que condujo a su destitución y al levantamiento de los protestantes Mary y William de Orange como nuevos monarcas. **124**

glyphs/glifos Símbolos o imágenes, especialmente aquellos tallados en una superficie o grabados en relieve. **6**

Great Awakening/Gran Despertar Movimiento cristiano que se extendió a todas las colonias estadounidenses en las décadas de 1730 y 1740. **137**

Great Compromise/El Gran Compromiso (1787) Acuerdo redactado durante la Convención Constitucional de Filadelfia en el que se establece que la población de un estado debe determinar su representación en la cámara baja y que cada estado debe tener igual representación en la cámara alta. **238**

Great Depression/La Gran Depresión Seria disminución de la actividad económica mundial producida por la caída del mercado de valores estadounidense en 1929. **693**

Great Migration/La Gran Migración Migración masiva de habitantes de Inglaterra a tierras americanas de 1630 a 1640. **104**

Great Society/La Gran Sociedad Serie de programas sociales presentados por el presidente Lyndon B. Johnson para terminar con la pobreza y el racismo. **703**

guerrilla warfare/guerrilla Tipo de guerra en la que los soldados realizan ataques y escapes rápidos contra el enemigo, por lo general detrás de la trinchera. **211**

H

habeas corpus/Habeas corpus Protección constitucional contra los arrestos ilegales. **597**

Harlem Renaissance/Renacimiento de Harlem Periodo de realización artística que inició en la década de 1920; lleva el nombre del vecindario de Harlem de la ciudad de Nueva York. **692**

Hartford Convention/Convención de Hartford (1815) Encuentro de federales en Hartford, Connecticut, para protestar por la Guerra de 1812. **355**

headright/concesión Sistema creado por la London Company en el que se otorgaban 50 acres de tierra a los colonos que pagaran el viaje para establecerse en Virginia. **95**

Holocaust/Holocausto Matanza sistemática con que los nazis eliminaron a casi 6 millones de judíos y 3 millones de personas de otras religiones durante la Segunda Guerra Mundial. **698**

Homestead Act/Ley Homestead (1862) Ley aprobada por el Congreso para fomentar la colonización del oeste mediante el otorgamiento de tierras a los agricultores. **666**

Homestead strike/Ataque de Homestead (1892) Ataque a la fábrica de acero de Andrew Carnegie en Homestead, Pennsylvania, que originó brotes de violencia entre atacantes y detectives privados. **684**

House of Burgesses/Casa de los burgueses Asamblea electa en Virginia durante la época de la Colonia. **122**

Hudson River school/Escuela del Río Hudson Grupo de artistas creado a mediados del siglo XIX cuya obra muestra diversos paisajes del territorio estadounidense. **388**

hunter-gatherers/cazadores personales Personas que cazaban animales y recolectaban plantas para satisfacer sus necesidades. **5**

I

igloos/iglúes Casas construidas con bloques de hielo por los habitantes de las tribus inuit y aleut en el territorio que actualmente ocupan Alaska y Canadá. **12**

immigrants/inmigrantes Personas que abandonan su país para establecerse en un país diferente. **99**

impeach/inculpar Votar para hacer cargos en contra. **259**

imperialism/imperialismo Práctica en la que una nación extiende su poder mediante la adquisición de territorios para un imperio colonial. **688**

imports/importaciones Productos que un país compra a otras naciones. **126**

impressment/Leva Práctica británica que obligaba a los colonos, incluidos los ciudadanos estadounidenses, a servir en las fuerzas armadas británicas, lo cual aumentó las fricciones entre Gran Bretaña y Estados Unidos a principios del siglo XIX. **345**

indentured servants/sirvientes por contrato Colonos que recibían pasajes gratuitos a América del Norte a cambio de trabajo sin salario por varios años. **96**

Indian Removal Act/Ley de Expulsión de Indígenas (1830) Ley redactada por el Congreso que autorizaba la remoción de indígenas que habitaban al este del río Mississippi. **381**

Indian Territory/Territorio indígena Área que abarcaba la mayor parte del actual estado de Oklahoma en la que muchas tribus indígenas del sureste fueron obligadas a establecerse durante la década de 1830. **381**

indict/procesar Acusar formalmente. **287**

Industrial Revolution/Revolución industrial Periodo de rápido desarrollo debido al uso de maquinaria en la fabricación de productos iniciado a mediados del siglo XVIII. **399**

inflation/inflación Alza de los precios de los bienes y servicios en combinación con la disminución del valor del dinero. **82, 232**

interchangeable parts/partes intercambiables Proceso desarrollado por Eli Whitney en la década de 1790 para que las partes fundamentales de todas las máquinas similares fueran exactamente iguales.

Internet/Internet Extensa red internacional por computadora que conecta negocios, gobiernos, escuelas y personas. **709**

interstate commerce/comercio interestatal Intercambio comercial entre estados. **237**

Intolerable Acts /Ley de Asuntos Intolerables (1774) Serie de decretos aprobados por el parlamento para castigar a los colonos que participaron en el Motín del Té y mantener su control sobre las colonias. **175**

Iran-Contra affair/Los contras en Irán Escándalo en el que funcionarios de la administración de Ronald Reagan patrocinaron ilegalmente a los rebeldes o contras de Nicaragua con fondos obtenidos mediante la venta secreta de armas a Irán. **708**

ironclads/acorazados buques de guerra fuertemente armados con elementos de hierro. **589**

Iroquois League/Liga de iroqueses Confederación política formada por cinco naciones indígenas del noreste de Estados Unidos (Seneca, Oneida, Mohawk, Cayuga y Onondaga) para tomar decisiones relacionadas con asuntos de guerra y de paz. **16**

isolationism/aislamiento Política en que una nación evita involucrarse en los asuntos de otras naciones. **689**

Jay's Treaty/Tratado de Jay (1794) Acuerdo negociado por John Jay para resolver los problemas entre Gran Bretaña y Estados Unidos en relación con los tratados del oeste, la incautación de barcos

estadounidenses por las autoridades británicas y las deudas con los comerciantes británicos. **313**

Jazz Age/época del jazz Término popular para designar la década de 1920. Llamada así por la gran popularidad de la música de jazz entre la población. **692**

Jim Crow laws/Leyes de Jim Craw Leyes que fomentaban la segregación en los estados del sur. **637**

John Brown's raid/Ataque de John Brown (1859) Incidente en el que el abolicionista John Brown y 21 hombres más se apropiaron de un arsenal federal en Harpers Ferry, Virginia, con la esperanza de iniciar una rebelión de esclavos. **569**

joint-stock companies/compañías de acciones combinadas Negocios formados por grupos de personas que realizan inversiones, compartiendo las ganancias y las pérdidas. **33**

judicial branch/Poder Judicial División del gobierno federal conformada por las cortes de justicia para interpretar las leyes, castigar los actos criminales y resolver disputas entre estados. **240**

judicial review/revisión judicial Poder de la Suprema Corte para declarar anticonstitucionales las acciones del Congreso. **337**

Judiciary Act of 1789/Ley judicial de 1789 Decreto aprobado por el Congreso para crear el sistema federal de aplicación de justicia. **303**

Kansas-Nebraska Act/Ley de Kansas-Nebraska (1854) Ley que permitía a los votantes de los territorios de Kansas y Nebraska decidir la aprobación o abolición de la esclavitud. **561**

kayaks/kayaks Canoas casi completamente cerradas, con capacidad para una persona, fabricadas con pieles de animales. **12**

Kentucky and Virginia Resolutions/Resoluciones de Kentucky y Virginia (1798-1799) Documentos republicanos que argumentaban el carácter anti-constitucional de las Leyes de no intervención. **322**

kitchen cabinet/gabinete de cocina Grupo informal de consejeros del presidente Andrew Jackson. Fue llamado así porque en ocasiones se reunían en la cocina de la Casa Blanca. **376**

kivas/kivas Cámaras ceremoniales circulares usadas en las actividades religiosas de los indígenas estadounidenses del suroeste. **14**

Know-Nothing Party/Partido de No Conocimiento Organización política fundada en 1849 con la finalidad de dificultar a los inmigrantes de otros países la adquisición de la ciudadanía estadounidense y su nombramiento en cargos públicos. **459**

Ku Klux Klan/Ku Klux Klan Sociedad secreta creada en 1866 por habitantes de raza blanca del sur que usaba el terror y la violencia para evitar que los afroestadounidenses obtuvieran derechos civiles. **635**

Land Ordinance of 1785/Ordenanza de territorios de 1785 Decreto aprobado por el Congreso en el que se autorizaba el uso de encuestas y la división de territorios públicos del oeste del país. **226**

legislative branch /Poder Legislativo División del gobierno federal que propone iniciativas legales y las somete a aprobación para convertirlas en leyes. **240**

Lewis and Clark expedition/expedición de Lewis y Clark Expedición encabezada por Meriwether Lewis y William Clark que partió en 1804 con la finalidad de explorar el territorio comprado por Estados Unidos a Francia en la región de Luisiana. **342**

libel/libelo Declaración falsa, generalmente impresa, que daña la reputación de una persona. **122**

Liberator, The/Liberator, The Periódico abolicionista publicado por William Lloyd Garrison a partir de 1831. **470**

limited government/gobierno limitado Principio político que establece que el gobierno debe estar confinado por leyes que limiten su poder. **224**

Lincoln-Douglas debates/debates Lincoln–Douglas Serie de siete debates entre el republicano Abraham Lincoln y el demócrata Stephen Douglas durante la campaña de 1858 para el senado por Illinois. **567**

Line of Demarcation/Línea de demarcación Límite establecido por el papa Alejandro VI en 1493 a aproximadamente 300 millas de las Islas Azores. Según el documento, los territorios no reclamados al oeste del límite pertenecían a España y los del oeste a Portugal. **42**

longhouses/grandes viviendas comunes Edificaciones rectangulares construidas en Irak, en las que habitan varias familias. **16**

loose construction/construcción suelta Interpretación de la Constitución que permite al gobierno federal tomar acciones que la misma carta magna no prohíbe de manera específica. **308**

Lord Dunmore's Proclamation/Proclamación de Lord Dunmore (1775) Declaración emitida por el gobernador real de Virginia con la promesa de otorgar su libertad a los esclavos que participaran en la lucha contra el ejército británico durante la Revolución de Independencia. **199**

Louisiana Purchase/Compra de Luisiana (1803) Adquisición del territorio localizado entre el río Mississippi y las montañas Rocosas, perteneciente al gobierno francés, que duplicó el tamaño del territorio de Estados Unidos. **340**

Lowell system/sistema Lowell Aprovechamiento de los molinos de agua en la industria textil, medida que dio empleo a muchas mujeres jóvenes solteras en el siglo diecinueve. **405**

Loyalists/leales Colonos que siempre apoyaron la causa británica durante la Revolución de Independencia. **192**

Magna Carta /Carta Magna (1215) Carta real. Acuerdo firmado por el Rey John de Inglaterra en el que se otorgaba mayores derechos a los individuos, estableciendo que incluso la nobleza y el rey debían obedecer la ley. **22**

maize/maíz El cultivo más importante de los indígenas estadounidenses en América del Norte y América Central. **6**

manifest destiny/destino manifiesto Creencia de muchos ciudadanos estadounidenses a mediados del siglo XIX que hablaba sobre la expansión de Estados Unidos hacia el Océano Pacífico. **516**

manors/feudos Estados de mayor tamaño gobernados por reyes y nobles en la Edad Media. **19**

Marbury v. Madison/Marbury versus Madison (1803) Caso de la Suprema Corte que dio origen a las revisiones judiciales. **336**

Marshall Plan/Plan Marshall (1948) Plan estadounidense que ofrecía a los países europeos ayuda económica para reconstruir su economía después de la Segunda Guerra Mundial. **699**

Massacre at Wounded Knee/Matanza de Wounded Knee (1890) Matanza de aproximadamente 150 indios Sioux en Wounded Knee, Dakota del Sur, por parte del ejército de Estados Unidos. Este episodio dio por terminados los enfrentamientos con los indios en las Planicies. **652**

mass production/producción en masa Producción eficiente de grandes cantidades de productos idénticos. **402**

Mayflower Compact/Síntesis del Mayflower (1620) Documento redactado por los colonizadores británicos que establecía los principios para gobernarse a sí mismos. **99**

McCulloch v. Maryland/McCulloch versus Maryland (1819) Caso de la Suprema Corte que declaraba que el Segundo Banco de la Nación era una empresa constitucional y que al ser una institución federal Maryland no podía intervenir en sus operaciones. **377**

mercantilism/mercantilismo Creación y conservación de riquezas mediante un control minucioso de intercambios comerciales. **126**

mercenaries/mercenarios Soldados extranjeros contratados por un salario. **201**

Mexican Cession/Cesión mexicana (1848) Tierras que México cedió a Estados Unidos mediante el Tratado de Guadalupe Hidalgo, después de la guerra entre ambos. La cesión incluía la actual California, Nevada y Utah y la mayor parte de Arizona y Nuevo México, así como parte de Colorado, Texas y Wyoming. **526**

Middle Ages/Edad Media Periodo de la historia europea entre los años 500 y 1500 d. C. **19**

middle class/clase media Estrato social y económico ubicado entre la clase rica y la clase pobre. **460**

Treaty Organization, NATO) Alianza formada en 1949 por Estados Unidos, Inglaterra y 10 países más para defenderse entre sí en caso de sufrir algún ataque. **699**

Northwest Ordinance of 1787/Ordenanza del Noroeste de 1877 Decreto aprobado por el Congreso para establecer una estructura política en el territorio del noroeste y crear un sistema de admisión de nuevos estados. **226**

Northwest Passage /Pasaje del Noroeste Camino inexistente buscado por muchos exploradores a lo largo de América del Norte para cruzar en barco del Océano Atlántico al Océano Pacífico. **52**

Northwest Territory/Territorio del Noroeste Organización del territorio que incluía los actuales estados de Illinois, Indiana, Michigan, Ohio, Wisconsin y parte de Minnesota. Creado por la Ordenanza del Noroeste en 1787. **229**

nullification crisis/crisis de anulación Disputa entre Carolina del Sur y el gobierno federal, a finales de la década de 1820, por el derecho del estado para anular o cancelar un arancel impopular. **377**

Olive Branch Petition/Petición de la rama de olivo (1775) Paz solicitada por el Segundo Congreso Continental al Rey George III de Gran Bretaña, quien decidió rechazarla. **186**

open range/campo abierto Tierras públicas aprovechadas por los rancheros que formaban parte del Cattle Kingdom. **661**

Operation Desert Storm/Operación Tormenta del Desierto (1991) Invasión de Estados Unidos al territorio iraquí con la finalidad de obligar a las tropas iraquíes a retirarse de Kuwait. **708**

Oregon Trail/Camino de Oregón Ruta de 2,000 millas que cruzaba las Grandes Planicies desde Missouri occidental hasta la región de Oregón. **506**

Pacific Railway Acts/Leyes del Ferrocarril del Pacífico (1862, 1864) Par de decretos aprobados por el gobierno federal con la finalidad de otorgar préstamos a las compañías ferroviarias para fomentar la construcción de líneas transcontinentales de ferrocarril. **657**

Paleo-Indians/paleoindígenas Los primeros habitantes de América que llegaron de Asia cruzando el Estrecho de Bering entre el 10,000 y el 3,800 a. C. **5**

Panama Canal/Canal de Panamá Canal de cruce localizado en el istmo de Panamá. Su construcción fue patrocinada por Estados Unidos y se completó en 1914. **689**

Panic of 1837/Pánico de 1837 Crisis financiera de Estados Unidos que provocó una importante depresión económica. **378**

Panic of 1873/Pánico de 1873 Crisis financiera de Estados Unidos que provocó una importante depresión económica y debilitó al Partido Republicano. **636**

pardon/perdón Liberación de un castigo. **259**

Parliament/parlamento Legislatura británica. **121**

Patriots/Patriotas Colonos estadounidenses que lucharon para independizarse de Gran Bretaña durante la Revolución. **192**

petition/petición Solicitud formal. **285**

Pickett's Charge/Ataque de Pickett (1863) Ataque fallido del ejército confederado, al mando del general George Pickett, durante la Batalla de Gettysburg. **601**

Pilgrims/peregrinos Miembros de una secta separatista puritana que emigró de Inglaterra a principios del siglo XVII para establecerse en América. **99**

Pinckney's Treaty/Tratado de Pinckney (1795) Acuerdo entre Estados Unidos y España que modificó los límites de Florida y facilitó a los barcos estadounidenses el uso del puerto de Nueva Orleáns. **314**

pioneers/pioneros Primeras personas que llegan a poblar una región. **163**

plantations/plantaciones Grandes granjas que por lo general se especializan en un cultivo específico. **74**

planters/hacendados Agricultores acaudalados dueños de grandes plantaciones. **97**

Plessy v. Ferguson/Plesy versus Ferguson (1896) Caso en el que la Suprema Corte estableció la doctrina iguales-pero-separados en los lugares públicos. **638**

political action committees/comités de acciones políticas (political action commitees, PACs) Organizaciones que recolectan dinero para distribuirlo entre los candidatos que apoyan los mismos asuntos que los contribuyentes. **294**

political parties/partidos políticos Organizaciones que ayudan a elegir funcionarios para el gobierno e influyen en las políticas gubernamentales. **319**

poll tax/impuesto de boleta Impuesto que las personas pagaban en el pasado para tener derecho al voto. **637**

Pontiac's Rebellion/Rebelión de Pontiac (1763) Ataque frustrado del jefe de la tribu ottawa, Pontiac, y sus aliados, contra los fuertes británicos de la frontera, en un intento por lograr que los colonizadores europeos abandonaran el país. **165**

Pony Express/Pony Express Sistema de mensajeros que transportaba el correo entre estaciones de relevo de St. Joseph, Missouri, a San Francisco, California, de 1860 a 1861. **657**

popular sovereignty/soberanía popular Idea de que la autoridad política pertenecía al pueblo. Principio que en una época permitió a los votantes de una región aceptar o rechazar la esclavitud. **240, 553**

Populist Party/Partido Populista Asociación política formada en 1891 para apoyar la libre producción de monedas de plata, reformas laborales y restricciones migratorias, además de asignar al gobierno la

representative democracy/democracia representativa
Gobierno compuesto por representantes del pueblo.
256

Republic of Texas/República de Texas Nación
independiente de Texas que duró de 1836 a 1848,
cuando la región se adhirió a los Estados Unidos. 497

republicanism/republicanismo Apoyo a un sistema
de gobierno representativo. 224

Republican Party/Partido Republicano Asociación
política creada en la década de 1850 para detener
la expansión de la esclavitud en el oeste. 564

reservations/reservaciones Territorios federales
exclusivos para los indígenas estadounidenses. 650

reserved powers/poderes reservados Poderes
otorgados al gobierno o a ciertos ciudadanos. 257

revivals/restauraciones Reuniones públicas eclesiásti-
cas en las que los ministros daban sermones ante
grandes cantidades de personas. 136

Rhode Island System/Sistema de Rhode Island
Sistema desarrollado por Samuel Slater a mediados
del siglo XIX con la finalidad de contratar a familias
completas para laborar en la industria textil. 405

right of deposit/derecho de depósito Derecho de
transferir bienes a otro destino sin pagar cuotas
alguna. 313

roundup/rodear Arreo del ganado formando un
círculo para formar una sola manada. 662

Rush-Bagot Agreement/Acuerdo de Rush-Bargo
(1817) Acuerdo que limitaba el poder naval en los
Grandes Lagos a embarcaciones de Estados Unidos
y Canadá. 364

scalawags/*scalawags* Nombre dado a los sureños de
raza blanca que apoyaban la Reconstrucción en
busca de ganancias económicas. Significa "pícaro",
"bribón". 634

scientific agriculture/agricultura científica Uso de
técnicas científicas para mejorar la producción
agrícola. 430

scientific method/método científico Observación y
experimentación con sucesos naturales que per-
miten elaborar teorías con el propósito de predecir
otros sucesos o comportamientos. 141

Scientific Revolution/Revolución científica Periodo
de gran aprendizaje iniciado en el siglo XVII, en el
que científicos, matemáticos y astrónomos europeos
trataron de obtener explicaciones acerca de los mis-
terios del universo. 140

sea dogs/Sabuesos de mar Marineros ingleses
patrocinados por la Reina Elizabeth I para robar los
tesoros de los navíos españoles a finales del siglo
XVI. 80

search warrant/orden de cateo Orden de un juez
que permite buscar en el hogar y posesiones de
una persona posibles evidencias de un crimen. 286

secession/secesión Retiro formal de una organización
(un país, por ejemplo). 573

**Second Battle of Bull Run/Segunda Batalla de Bull
Run** (1862) Batalla de la Guerra Civil en la que el
Ejército Confederado obligó a gran parte de las
tropas de la Unión a abandonar el territorio de
Virginia. 587

**Second Continental Congress/Segundo Congreso
Continental** (1775) Reunión de delegados de la
colonia realizada en Filadelfia para tomar decisiones
acerca de la lucha en Lexington y Concord. 186

Second Great Awakening/Segundo gran despertar
Periodo de evangelización religiosa iniciado en la
década de 1790 que se extendió por Estados
Unidos en la década de 1830. 452

**Second Industrial Revolution/Segunda Revolución
Industrial** Periodo de gran crecimiento en la
manufactura y en la industria, iniciado a fines del
siglo XIX. 682

sect/secta Grupo religioso. 98

sectionalism/regionalismo Dedicación a los intereses
de una región geográfica y no a los de un país. 553

segregation/segregación Separación obligada de personas de diferentes razas en lugares públicos. 637

**Seneca Falls Convention/Convención de Seneca
Falls** (1848) Primera convención nacional a favor
de los derechos de la mujer en la cual se redactó la
Declaración de Sentimientos. 447

separation of powers/separación de poderes
División de los poderes del gobierno en varias
ramas con el propósito de evitar que cualquiera de
ellas adopte poderes en exceso. 257

Separatists/separatistas Grupo radical de puritanos
que tenía como propósito eliminar cualquier
relación con la Iglesia Británica. 98

Seven Days' Battles/Batallas de los Siete Días (1862)
Serie de batallas de la Guerra Civil en las que el
Ejército Confederado obliga a las tropas de la Unión a
retirarse de Richmond, Virginia, la capital confederada.
587

Seventeenth Amendment/Decimoséptima enmienda
(1913) Enmienda constitucional que permite a los
votantes estadounidenses elegir directamente a sus
senadores. 686

sharecropping/cultivo compartido Sistema usado en
los campos agrícolas después de la Guerra Civil en el
que los agricultores trabajaban las tierras de alguien
más a cambio de una pequeña porción de la
cosecha. 639

Shays's Rebellion/Rebelión de Shay (1786-87)
Levantamiento de los agricultores de Massachusetts,
encabezados por Daniel Shay, para protestar por los
altos impuestos, el aumento de sus deudas y el
cierre de las granjas. 234

Sherman Antitrust Act/Ley Sherman contra los
monopolios (1890) Ley que prohibía la creación
de monopolios o firmas que restringieran el libre
comercio. 684

siege/sitio Bloqueo militar de una ciudad o fuerte. 187

Siege of Vicksburg/Sitio de Vicksburg (1863) Bloqueo de seis semanas realizado por el ejército de la Unión en Vicksburg para forzar la rendición de esa ciudad durante la Guerra Civil. **592**

Silk Road/ruta de la seda Ruta de intercambio comercial que comunicaba a China con otros mercados asiáticos hasta el Mar Negro. **25**

slave codes/códigos de esclavos Leyes aprobadas por las colonias para el control de los esclavos. **132**

Social Security Act/Ley de Seguridad Social (1935) Ley que ofrecía pensiones y seguro de desempleo a los trabajadores estadounidenses jubilados. **694**

societies/sociedades Grupos de personas que viven juntas y comparten la misma cultura. **6**

sodbusters/cortadores de césped Nombre dado a los agricultores de las Planicies y a las herramientas usadas para cortar los altos pastos de la región. **668**

Sons of Liberty/Hijos de la libertad Sociedades secretas formadas a mediados del siglo XVIII por los colonos para protestar por la creación de nuevos impuestos y para atemorizar a los recaudadores. **169**

Spanish Armada/Armada española Enorme ejército que fue derrotado por las tropas de Inglaterra en 1588. **80**

speculators/especuladores Inversionistas que compran artículos a precios bajos con la esperanza de que aumente su valor. **305**

spirituals/espirituales Canciones religiosas cantadas con gran emotividad por los esclavos del sur que combinaban elementos de origen africano y europeo para expresar sus creencias religiosas. **442**

spoils system/sistema de mimos Práctica política de ofrecer empleos a los partidarios de una causa. **376**

Stamp Act/Ley del Timbre (1765) Ley aprobada por el Parlamento en la que se obligaba a los colonos a pagar un impuesto de estampilla cada vez que compraran artículos de papel, como periódicos, licencias y documentos legales. **169**

staple crops/cultivos básicos Productos de demanda constante. **134**

states' rights/derechos estatales Creencia de que queda estrictamente limitado el poder del gobierno federal en lo que a los estados se refiere. **379**

strait/estrecho Paso angosto y serpenteante en el mar. **48**

strict construction/construcción estricta Interpretación de la Constitución que sólo permite al gobierno federal realizar las acciones expresadas de manera específica en ella. **308**

strike/huelga Negativa de un grupo de empleados a laborar hasta que sus empleadores satisfagan sus demandas. **408**

suffrage/sufragio Derecho al voto. **224**

Sugar Act/Ley del Azúcar (1764) Ley aprobada por el Parlamento británico que establece el pago de impuestos sobre la remolacha y el azúcar importada por las colonias. **167**

supply-side economics/economía lateral Teoría económica que sugiere la disminución de los impuestos para mejorar la economía. **704**

Sutter's Fort/Fuerte Sutter Colonia del norte de California fundada por el inmigrante suizo John Sutter en 1839, que se convirtió en un popular destino para los inmigrantes. **509**

Tariff of Abominations/Tarifa de abominaciones (1828) Sobrenombre dado a cada nueva tarifa de impuestos rechazada por los habitantes del sur. **376**

tariffs/aranceles Impuestos pagados por los bienes importados o exportados. **233**

Tea Act/Ley del Té (1773) Ley aprobada por el Parlamento británico que permitía a la Compañía British East India vender té a bajo costo a las colonias sin intermediarios, afectando a los comerciantes locales de té. Esta decisión dio origen al Motín del Té de Boston. **173**

technology/tecnología Herramientas usadas para producir bienes o realizar un trabajo. **401**

Tejanos/texanos Colonizadores españoles que habitaban en la región que actualmente es el norte de Texas. **490**

telegraph/telégrafo Máquina inventada por Samuel Morse en 1837 para enviar mensajes a grandes distancias mediante impulsos eléctricos transmitidos por cables. **415**

temperance movement/movimiento de abstinencia Reforma social iniciada a mediados del siglo diecinueve para fomentar la disminución en el consumo de bebidas alcohólicas. **464**

Ten Percent Plan/Plan de diez por ciento Plan de reconstrucción del presidente Abraham Lincoln. Si 10 por ciento de los votantes de un estado que había sido parte de la Confederación tomaba un voto de lealtad a la nación, tenían derecho a formar un nuevo gobierno y ser admitidos en la Unión. **621**

tenements/barracas Casas mal construidas donde vivían en hacinamiento una gran cantidad de inmigrantes. **461**

Tet Offensive/Ofensiva de Tet (1968) Ataque de las tropas de Vietnam del Norte y del Vietcong contra Vietnam del Sur que demostró el interés de éstas por permanecer en la lucha. **705**

Texas longhorn/cuernos largos Raza de ganado vacuno de gran tamaño criada por los ganaderos del oeste de Texas. **660**

textiles/textiles Ropa. **399**

Thirteenth Amendment/Decimotercera enmienda (1865) Enmienda constitucional que abolió la esclavitud. **622**

Three-Fifths Compromise/Compromiso de las tres quintas partes (1787) Acuerdo realizado durante la Convención Constitucional en el que se estableció que tres quintas partes de los esclavos de cada estado serían contados como parte de la población para determinar la representación de ese estado en el Congreso. **239**

Toleration Act of 1649/Ley de tolerancia de 1649 Ley de Maryland que calificaba como crimen la restricción de los derechos religiosos de los cristianos; fue una de las primeras leyes en proteger la libertad de credo religioso que se aprobó en las colonias inglesas. **110**

total war/guerra total Tipo de guerra en la que un ejército destruye la capacidad de lucha de su oponente mediante ataques a la población civil, la economía y los recursos militares. **604**

totems/tótems Imágenes de antepasados o animales talladas en troncos de árboles cortados por los indígenas del noroeste de la costa del Pacífico. **12**

town meeting/reunión del pueblo Reunión política en la que los habitantes de una población toman decisiones sobre temas locales. Las primeras reuniones de este tipo se realizaron en Nueva Inglaterra. **122**

Townshend Acts/Leyes Townshend (1767) Leyes aprobadas por el Parlamento para asignar aranceles a algunos de los artículos que importaban los colonos. **171**

trade unions/Sindicatos de intercambio comercial Organizaciones formadas por los trabajadores para mejorar su salario y sus condiciones laborales. **408**

Trail of Tears/Ruta de las lágrimas (1838-1839) Marcha de 800 millas que realizó de manera obligada la tribu cheroqui de su territorio natal en Georgia al nuevo territorio, en la que perdieron la vida miles de estos indígenas. **383**

transcendentalism/trascendentalismo Creencia de que las personas podían elevarse sobre los objetos materiales en vida. Movimiento popular entre los escritores y pensadores de Nueva Inglaterra a mediados del siglo XIX. **454**

transcontinental railroad/ferrocarril transcontinental Línea de ferrocarril que cruzaba Estados Unidos de un extremo a otro. Su construcción inició en 1863. **657**

Transportation Revolution/Revolución del transporte Rápido crecimiento de la velocidad y comodidad ofrecida por los medios de transporte que en Estados Unidos inició a principios del siglo XIX. **410**

Treaty of Dancing Rabbit Creek/Tratado de Dancing Rabbit Creek (1830) Acuerdo en el que la tribu choctaw cedió más de 10 millones de acres de su territorio a Mississippi y aceptó reubicarse en el nuevo territorio indígena. **382**

Treaty of Fort Laramie/Tratado del Fuerte Laramie (1851) Acuerdo entre el gobierno de Estados Unidos y los indígenas de las Planicies del norte que permitía la creación de poblaciones de blancos con la promesa de proteger el territorio indígena. **644**

Treaty of Ghent/Tratado de Ghent (1814) Acuerdo firmado por Estados Unidos y Gran Bretaña para dar fin a la Guerra de 1812. **355**

Treaty of Greenville/Tratado de Greenville (1795) Acuerdo entre la Confederación Indígena Estadounidense y el gobierno de Estados Unidos que otorgó a la nación la parte sudeste del territorio indígena ubicado al noroeste del país y garantizó la seguridad a los ciudadanos estadounidenses que viajaran por esas tierras. **316**

Treaty of Guadalupe Hidalgo/Tratado de Guadalupe-Hidalgo (1848) Acuerdo que daba por terminada la guerra contra México y daba posesión a Estados Unidos de gran parte del norte del territorio mexicano. **526**

Treaty of Medicine Lodge/Tratado de Medicine Lodge (1867) Acuerdo del gobierno de Estados Unidos y los indígenas de las Planicies en el que éstas aceptaban reubicarse a las nuevas reservaciones. **650**

Treaty of Paris/Tratado de París (1763) Acuerdo de paz que dio por terminada la guerra de los franceses contra los indígenas estadounidenses. **162**

Treaty of Paris of 1783/Tratado de París de 1783 Acuerdo de paz que oficialmente daba por terminada la Guerra Revolucionaria y en el que Gran Bretaña reconocía la soberanía de Estados Unidos. **213**

Treaty of Tordesillas/Tratado de Tordesillas (1494) Acuerdo firmado por España y Portugal en el que ambos países se comprometían a desplazar la Línea de demarcación 800 millas al oeste de su posición original en relación con las Islas Azores. **42**

Treaty of Versailles/Tratado de Versalles (1919) Acuerdo que daba por terminada la Primera Guerra Mundial. En él se obligaba a Alemania a pagar varios miles de millones de dólares por costos de guerra y a aceptar responsabilidad total por las pérdidas. Este tratado también dio origen a la Liga de las Naciones. **691**

Tredegar Iron Works/Tradegar Iron Works Gran fábrica de acero que operaba a mediados del siglo XIX en Richmond, Virginia. **432**

triangular trade/acuerdo triangular Redes de intercambio de esclavos entre Inglaterra, las colonias estadounidenses y África Occidental. **128**

Truman Doctrine/Doctrina Truman (1947) Política del presidente Harry S. Truman en la que Estados Unidos ofrecía ayuda a cualquier país que decidiera combatir el comunismo y evitar su expansión. **699**

Twelfth Amendment/Vigésima enmienda (1804) Enmienda constitucional que decretó la creación de casillas separadas para la elección de presidente y vicepresidente. **324**

unalienable rights/derechos inalienables Derechos básicos de la humanidad, como el derecho a la vida, a la libertad y a la búsqueda de la felicidad. **191**

Uncle Tom's Cabin/La cabaña del tío Tom (1852) Novela abolicionista escrita por Harriet Beecher Stowe que mostró a los habitantes del norte del país la cruda realidad de la esclavitud e hizo que muchos de ellos se adhirieran a la causa del abolicionismo. **557**

Underground Railroad/Tren clandestino Red de personas que ayudó a miles de esclavos a escapar al norte ofreciéndoles transporte y lugares para ocultarse. **472**

United Nations/Organización de las Naciones Unidas (ONU) Organización internacional establecida en 1945 con el propósito de resolver conflictos entre las naciones. **699**

utopian community/comunidad utópica Lugar en el que un grupo de personas trabaja para establecer una comunidad perfecta, como las que se popularizaron en Estados Unidos a finales del siglo XVIII y de principios a mediados del XIX. **454**

vaqueros/vaqueros Arrieros mexicanos que vivían en el oeste y se ganaban la vida arreando ganado y caballos. **662**

veto/veto Cancelación. **259**

viceroy/virrey Gobernador real de Hispanoamérica. **39**

Virginia Plan/Plan de Virginia (1787) Plan del gobierno propuesto en la Convención Constitucional para dividir al gobierno en tres ramas: El poder Ejecutivo, el Poder Legislativo y el Poder Judicial. También establecía que la representación de cada estado en la legislatura debía ser determinada por la población de ese estado. **237**

Virginia Statute for Religious Freedom/Estatutos de Virginia para la Libertad Religiosa (1786) Ley que otorgaba a los habitantes de Virginia la libertad de elegir y practicar cualquier religión, además de expresar sus opiniones religiosas. **224**

Voting Rights Act of 1965/Ley de Derecho al Voto de 1965 Ley que otorgó a todo ciudadano elegible de Estados Unidos el derecho al voto. **704**

Wade-Davis Bill/Plan Wade-Davis Plan de reconstrucción que imponía dos condiciones a los estados que habían pertenecido a la Confederación para adherirse a los Estados Unidos: abolir la esclavitud y pedir a los hombres adultos un juramento de lealtad a la nación. Sin embargo, quienes apoyaban a la Confederación no tenían derecho al voto ni podían aceptar cargos públicos. **621**

War Hawks/Halcones de guerra Integrantes del Congreso que tenían la intención de declarar la guerra a Gran Bretaña a principios del siglo XIX. **348**

War on Drugs/Guerra contra las drogas Plan del presidente George Bush que continuó el esfuerzo del gobierno por detener el tráfico ilegal de drogas en Estados Unidos. **708**

Watergate/*Watergate* Escándalo en el que el presidente Richard Nixon autorizó la desintegración del cuartel general del Comité Nacional Demócrata y lo obligó a renunciar a su cargo en 1974. **706**

Whig Party/Partido Whig Asociación política formada por oponentes de Andrew Jackson en 1834 para demandar una legislatura más fuerte. **378**

Whiskey Rebellion/Rebelión del Whisky (1794) Protesta de pequeños agricultores de Pennsylvania contra los nuevos impuestos cobrados a la producción de whisky y otras bebidas alcohólicas. **316**

wigwams/*wigwams* Pequeñas habitaciones circulares en las que vivían los indígenas estadounidenses del noreste del país. **16**

Wilderness Campaign/Campaña en despoblado (mayo-junio de 1864) Serie de batallas entre la Unión y los Confederados al norte y al centro de Virginia que estuvo a punto de agotar los recursos del Ejército Confederado. **603**

Wilmot Proviso/Propuesta Wilmot (1846) Propuesta de abolición de la esclavitud en el territorio adherido a los Estados Unidos por la cesión mexicana. Fue aprobada por la Cámara de representantes, pero rechazado por el Senado. **553**

Worcester v. Georgia/Worcester* versus *Georgia (1832) Caso en que la Suprema Corte declaró a la nación cheroqui como un territorio distinto sobre el que sólo el gobierno federal tenía autoridad. Fue ignorado por el presidente Andrew Jackson y por el estado de Georgia. **383**

writs of assistance/mandato de asistencia Garantías que permitían a los recaudadores de impuestos buscar bienes ocultos por los contribuyentes. **171**

XYZ affair/asunto XYZ (1797) Incidente en el que funcionarios franceses intentaron obtener sobornos y préstamos de diplomáticos estadounidenses a cambio de que sus barcos no atacaran más a los navíos de Estados Unidos, con lo cual se originó una batalla naval no declarada entre ambos países. **321**

Yalta Conference/Conferencia de Yalta (1945) Reunión entre el presidente Frankiln D. Roosevelt, el primer ministro de Gran Bretaña Winston Churchill y el líder soviético José Stalin para planear el futuro al término de la Segunda Guerra Mundial. **699**

yeomen/pequeños terratenientes Pequeños agricultores. **434**

Index

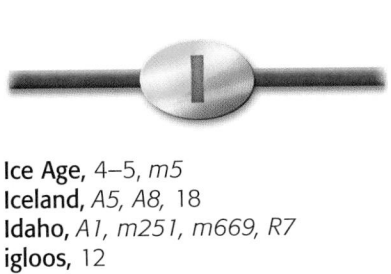

Acknowledgments

For permission to reprint copyrighted material, grateful acknowledgment is made to the following sources:

Four Winds Press, a division of Simon & Schuster, Inc: From *My Brother Sam Is Dead* by James Lincoln Collier and Christopher Collier. Copyright © 1974 by James Lincoln Collier and Christopher Collier.

Harvard University Press, Cambridge, Mass.: "World, in Hounding Me" by Sor Juana Inés de la Cruz from *A Sor Juana Anthology,* translated by A. S. Trueblood. Copyright © 1988 by the President and Fellows of Harvard College.

Harvard University Press and the Trustees of Amherst College: From "This Is My Letter to the World" from *The Poems of Emily Dickinson,* edited by Thomas H. Johnson. Copyright © 1951, 1955, 1979, 1983 by the President and Fellows of Harvard College. Published by the Belknap Press of Harvard University Press, Cambridge, Mass.

Sources Cited:

Quote by an Aztec messenger and from an Aztec poem from *The Broken Spears: The Aztec Account of the Conquest of Mexico,* Expanded and Updated Edition, edited by Miguel León-Portilla. Published by Beacon Press, Boston, 1992.

Quote by Bernal Díaz from *Cortés and the Downfall of the Aztec Empire* by Jon Manchip White. Published by Carroll & Graff Publishers, Inc., New York, 1971.

From "Across the Plains in a Prairie Schooner" by Catherine Haun from *Ordinary Americans,* edited by Linda R. Monk. Published by Close Up Publishing, 1994.

Quote by 'Abd al-Latif from *The Rise of Colleges: Institutions of Learning in Islam and the West,* translated by G. Makdisi. Published by Edinburgh University Press, 1981.

Quote by Bartolomé de Las Casas from *The Conquest of America: The Question of the Other* by Tzvetan Todorov, translated by Richard Howard. Published by HarperCollins Publishers, New York, 1984.

From "A Comparison between Ancient and Modern Ingenuity" by Alessandro Tassoni from *Philosophy, Technology and the Arts in the Early Modern Era* by Paolo Rossi, translated by Salvator Attanasio. Published by HarperCollins Publishers, New York, 1970.

From "Recantation of the Women of Andover, 1692" from *The History of the Colony and Province of Massachusetts Bay* by Thomas Hutchinson, edited by Lawrence Shaw Mayo. Published by Harvard University Press, Cambridge, 1936.

Quote by Agnolo di Tura from *The Black Death: A Turning Point in History?* edited by William Bowsky. Published by Holt, Rinehart and Winston.

From *My People the Sioux* by Luther Standing Bear. Published by Houghton Mifflin Company, New York, 1928.

Quote by Shawnee chief Tecumseh from *Indian Wars* by Robert M. Utley and Wilcomb E. Washburn. Published by Houghton Mifflin Company, Boston, 1977.

Quote by Joseph Brant and Little Turtle from *The Ohio Frontier: Crucible of the Old Northwest, 1720–1830* by R. Douglas Hurt. Published by Indiana University Press, Bloomington, 1996.

Quote by Karlsevni from *Voyages to Vinland: The First American Saga,* translated and interpreted by Einar Haugen. Published by Alfred A. Knopf, Inc., New York, 1942.

From "Newsletters Find Haven Online" by Sreenath Sreenivasan from *The New York Times,* July 7, 1997. Published by The New York Times Company, New York, 1997.

Quotes by Ibn Battuta from *A Short History of Africa* by Roland Oliver and J. D. Fage. Published by Penguin Books Ltd., 1962, 1966.

From *A Short Account of the Destruction of the Indies* by Bartolomé de Las Casas, translated by Nigel Griffin. Published by Penguin Books Ltd., London, 1992.

From *The Book of the Courtier* by Baldassare Castiglione, translated by George Bull. Published by Penguin Classics, London, 1967.

Quote by Alvise da Cadamosto and Bartholomeu Dias from *The Discoverers* by Daniel J. Boorstin. Published by Random House, Inc., New York, 1983.

Quote by Esther Clark from *Pioneer Women: Voices from the Kansas Frontier* by Joanna L. Stratton. Published by Simon & Schuster, Inc., New York, 1981.

From "The Narrative of the Expedition of Hernando de Soto" by the Gentleman of Elvas, edited by Theodore H. Lewis, from *Spanish Explorers in the Southern United States, 1528–1543.* Published by the Texas State Historical Association, Austin, 1990.

From *Ancient North America: The Archaeology of a Continent* by Brian M. Fagan. Published by Thames and Hudson Inc., New York, 1991, 1995.

Quote by the Gentleman of Elvas from *The De Soto Chronicles: The Expedition of Hernando de Soto to North America, 1539–1543,* Vol. 1, translated by James Alexander Robertson, edited by Lawrence A. Clayton et al. Published by University of Alabama Press, Tuscaloosa, 1993.

Quote by a Victorio follower from *In the Days of Victorio: Recollections of a Warm Springs Apache* by Eve Ball. Published by University of Arizona Press, Tucson, 1970.

From *Castaways: The Narrative of Alvar Núñez Cabeza de Vaca,* edited by Enrique Pupo-Walker, translated by Frances M. López-Morillas. Published by University of California Press, Berkeley, 1993.

Quote by Chester Copeland and from interview with Paul and Pauline Griffith from *Like a Family: The Making of a Southern Cotton Mill World* by Jacquelyn Dowd Hall et al. Published by University of North Carolina Press, Chapel Hill, 1987.

Quote by Josia Reams from *Class and Tennessee's Confederate Generation* by Fred Arthur Bailey. Published by University of North Carolina Press, Chapel Hill, 1987.

From interview with Madge Alford from *Indian-Pioneer Papers,* University of Oklahoma, Norman.

From an Aztec poem from *Aztec Thought and Culture: A Study of the Ancient Nahuatl Mind* by Miguel León-Portilla, translated by Jack Emory Davis. Published by University of Oklahoma Press, Norman, 1963.

From "Life and Activities in Houston" from *Gustav Dresel's Houston Journal: Adventures in North America and Texas, 1837–1841,* translated and edited by Max Freund. Published by University of Texas Press, Austin, 1954.

Quote by Hernán Cortés from *Hernán Cortés: Letters from Mexico,* translated and edited by Anthony Pagden. Published by Yale University Press, New Haven, 1986.

Photography Credits:

Abbreviated as follows: (t) top, (b) bottom, (l) left, (r) right, (c) center.

Cover and Title Page: Hitchcock House Antiques, Inc., Woodbury, CT;

Table of Contents and Front Matter: Page iv, Jerry Jacka/Courtesy Dennis Lyon Collection; v (tr), The Granger Collection, New York; (b), Musee des Beaux-Arts, Orleans, France/Bridgeman Art Library, London/New York; vi (tr, bl), North Wind Picture Archives; (bc), Courtesy the Bostonian Society, The Old State House; vii, The Granger Collection, New York; viii,(bl, t), The Granger Collection, New York; (bc), ©Laurie Platt Winfrey Inc./Woodfin Camp & Associates, Inc.; ix (bc), PRC Archive; (br), Christie's Images/SuperStock; x (tl), Carl Socolon/The Landis Valley Museum; (br), Library of Congress/PRC Archive; xi (bl), Nancy Gewitz/ Antique Textile Resources; (tr), Bettmann/CORBIS; (cr), The Granger Collection, New York; xii (bc), NASA; (br), Sally Andersen-Bruce, Museum of American Political Life; xiii (t), Independence National Historical Park Collection; (b), Culver Pictures; xiv, National Archives; xv, Library of Congress; xvi, Jeffrey Brown/Liaison Agency; xvii (tl), Paul Conklin; (tc), Independence National Historical Park Collection; xix, The Granger Collection, New York; xx (cl) Image Copyright © 2003 PhotoDisc, Inc./HRW Photo; (b), Sam Dudgeon/HRW Photo; xxi, Sam Dudgeon/HRW Photo; xxii, The Granger Collection, New York; xxv (br), HRW Photo; xxvi, from THE CIVIL WAR:FORWARD TO RICHMOND, Photograph by Al Freni, ©1983 Time-Life Books, Inc. Courtesy, Troiani Collection; xxviii, Courtesy CNNfyi.com; xxix (tl), Annie Griffiths Belt/CORBIS; (br), Ruth Fremson/AP/Wide World Photos; xxx (bl), ©Image Ideas, Inc.; (tl), Derek P. Redfearn/The Image Bank; (r), The Granger Collection, New York; xxxi (tr), COMEX/DRASSM/Xavier Desmier/Rapho Agency/Liaison Agency; (br), HRW Photo; xxxii (l), Bob Daemmrich/Stock Boston; (tr), The Granger Collection, New York; (br), Ken Cobb/Library of Congress; xxxiii, Laurence Parent; S0 (bl, cl), Annie Griffits Belt/CORBIS; (tl), Courtesy the Bostonian Society, The Old State House; (b), The Granger Collection, New York; S1 (bl), The Granger Collection, New York; (cr), Library of Congress; (br), National Archives (NARA) negative 30.60.E.082; S2 (l), National Geographic Image Collection; (cr), Library of Congress; S2(br), HRW Photo, S3 (tl), The Granger Collection, New York; S3 (b), S4, S5, S6, S8 (c), HRW Photos; S8 (br), Peter Newark's Western Americana; S9, S12, S14, S17 HRW Photo.

Unit One: Page 0 The Granger Collection, New York; 1 (r), Tate Gallery, London/Art Resource, NY. **Chapter One:** Page 2 (tl), Sam Dudgeon/HRW Photo; 2 (tr), Werner Forman Archive, British Museum, London/Art Resource, NY; 2 (bl), Roger Ressmeyer/CORBIS; 2 (bc), Adrian Neal/Stone; 3 (tr), Michael Holford; 3 (tl), ©Robert Frerck/Woodfin Camp & Associates; 4 George Lepp/Stone; 6 Dean Conger/CORBIS; 7 (t), Bodleian Library, Oxford, image MS Arch. Sheldon A.1 folio 37R; 7 (b), Alain Keler/Art Resource, NY; 8 Laurence Parent; 9 Superstock; 10 Jerry Jacka/Courtesy Dennis Lyon Collection; 12 (t), National Museum of Natural History, Smithsonian Institution, Washington, D.C./Peter Harholdt/ SuperStock; 12 (tc), Peter Newark's American Pictures; 13 Lawrence Migdale/Photo Researchers, Inc.; 14 (tr), Werner Forman/Art Resource, NY; 14 (tl), Ray Manley/SuperStock; 15 National Museum of American Art, Washington DC/Art Resource, NY; 16 Library of Congress; 17 Viking ship: The Gokstad Ship, Science Museum, London, UK/Bridgeman Art Library, London/New York; 18 "Vikings attacking a Greenland Eskimo camp," Nationalmuseet, Copenhagen, Denmark/Bridgeman Art Library, London/New York; 19 (br), Greenwich suit of armor, C. 1550, Christie's Images/Bridgeman Art Library, London, UK/New York; 19 (bl), Musee Conde, Chantilly/Giraudon; 20 Michael Holford; 21 (t), Portrait of William the Conqueror (1027-87)/Philip Mould, Historical Portraits Ltd, London, UK/Bridgeman Art Library, London/New York; 21 (b), Nik Wheeler/CORBIS; 22 The British Library; 23 museum/AKG Photo, London; 24 Ancient Art & Architecture Collection Ltd.; 25 E.T. Archive; 27 CORBIS. **Chapter Two:** Page 30 (cl), "Gambling Patoli and the god, Xochipilli," from Codex Maghabecciano, Aztec manuscript, Private Collection/Bridgeman Art Library, London/New York; 30 (b), Saint Bride Printing Library; 30 (tr), Stock Montage/SuperStock; 31 (t), Henry E. Huntington Library & Art Gallery/ SuperStock; 32 (cl), Ancient Art & Architecture Collection; 33 (t), Ancient Art & Architecture Collection; 33 (b), British Library/Art Archive; 34 (cl), Ancient Art & Architecture Collection Ltd.; 34 (b), Scala/Art Resource, NY; 35 The Granger Collection, New York; 37 Boltin Picture Library; 38 (cl), The Metropolitan Museum of Art, Gift of J.Pierpont Morgan, 1900. (00.18.2) Photograph copyright 1979 The Metropolitan Museum of Art.; 39 (t), Superstock; 40 Robert Frerck/Odyssey/Chicago; 42 (l), Bettmann/ CORBIS; 42 (t), The Granger Collection, New York; 43 The Granger Collection, New York; 44 (cl), Victoria & Albert Museum, London/Art Resource, NY; 45 Bettman/CORBIS; 46 AKG Photo; 47 museum/AKG Photo, London; 48 (t), The Granger Collection, New York; 49 Michael Holford; 50 (cl), AKG Photo; 51 (cr), Grant Heilman Photography; 52 (t), C.Chesek/ J.Becket/Negatives/Transparencies #4051, Courtesy Department of Library Services, American Museum of Natural History; 53 North Wind Picture Archives; 55 (t), Paul Dupuy Museum, Toulouse, France/Lauros-Giraudon, Paris/SuperStock; 55 (b), Image Copyright © 2003 PhotoDisc, Inc./HRW Photoc.; 55 The Granger Collection, New York; 56 (tl), National Maritime Museum/E.T. Archive; 56 (cr), Image Copyright © 2003 PhotoDisc, Inc./HRW Photoc.; 57 Richard Weiss/Peter Arnold, Inc.; 58 Image Copyright © 2003 PhotoDisc, Inc./HRW Photoc.; 59 ©Scott Camazine/Photo Researchers, Inc.; 61 Sam Dudgeon/HRW Photo.

Unit Two: Page 62 The Granger Collection, New York; 63 (c), "Sioux ball player Ah-No-Je-Nange," "He who stands on both sides," 19th century litho, Private Collection/Bridgeman Art Library, London/New York. **Chapter Three:** Page 64 (tl), Stock Montage/SuperStock; 64 (tr), Archivo General de Indias, Sevilla/SuperStock; 64 (bl), Mireille Vautier/Picture Quest; 65 (tl), The Granger Collection, New York; 65 (cr), James Stevenson/National Maritime Museum; 66 Bettmann/CORBIS; 67 (b), "The Taking of Tenochtitlan by Cortes," 1521, British Embassy, Mexico City/Bridgeman Art Library, London/New York; 67 (r), Piti Palace, Florence/E.T. Archive; 69 Bettmann/CORBIS; 70 Private Collection/Bridgeman Art Library, London/New York; 71 The Granger Collection, New York; 72 Scala/Art Resource, NY; 73 Bob Daemmrich Photo, Inc.; 74 AKG Photo, London; 75 Mark Nohl/New Mexico Magazine; 76 Art Resource, NY; 77 North Wind Picture Archives; 78 Scala/Art Resource, NY; 79 The Granger Collection, New York; 80 Bettmann/CORBIS; 81 The Granger Collection, New York; 82 (coin), Michael Holford; 82(cup), Boltin Picture Library; 84 American Museum of Natural History/Photo by Lynton Gardiner; 85 Bettmann/CORBIS; 85 The Granger Collection, New York; 87 The Granger Collection, New York. **Chapter Four:** Page 90 (tr), The Granger Collection, New York; 90 (tc), The Granger Collection, New York; 90 (bl), American Bible Society; 91 (t), Penn's Treaty with the Indians (1771-72) by Benjamin West, oil on canvas, Courtesy of the Museum of American Art of the Pennsylvania Academy of the Fine Arts Philadelphia. Gift of Mrs. Sarah Harrison (The Joseph Harrison, Jr. Collection).; 91 (tr), Layne Kennedy/CORBIS; 92 The Granger Collection, New York; 93 Colonial Williamsburg Foundation; 95 Detail from the National Portrait Gallery, Smithsonian Institution, Washington, DC/Art Resource, NY; 96 (cl), Archive Photos; 96 (bl), Colonial Williamsburg Foundation; 97 North Wind Picture Archives; 98 Detail, "Portrait of King James I and VI of Scotland," by John Whitehead Walton, (1831-85), (after Paul van Somer), The Crown Estate/Institute of Directors, London, UK/Bridgeman Art Library, London/New York; 99 Detail, Courtesy of the Pilgrim Society, Plymouth, Massachusetts; 100 The Granger Collection, New York; 101 Private Collection/ Bridgeman Art Library, London/New York; 102 The Granger Collection, New York; 103 The Granger Collection, New York; 104 North Wind Picture Archives; 107 The Granger Collection, New York; 108 CORBIS; 109 Courtesy St. Ignatius Church; 110 Enoch Pratt Free Library; 111 The Granger Collection, New York; 112 The Granger Collection, New York; 113 The Granger Collection, New York; 114 Stock Montage, Inc.; 115 The Granger Collection, New York.

Chapter Five: Page 118 (tr), Peter Newark's American Pictures; 118 (bl), Fitzwilliam Museum, University of Cambridge, UK/Bridgeman Art Library, London/New York; 118 Library of Congress; 119 (tl), Stock Montage, Inc.; 119 (tr), Science & Society Picture Library; 120 David Muench/CORBIS; 121 State Capitol, Commonwealth of Virginia, Courtesy Library of Virginia, image altered.; 122 ©Daniel MacDonald/Stock Boston; 123 The Granger Collection, New York; 124 The Granger Collection, New York; 125 The Granger Collection, New York; 126 Royal Albert Memorial Museum, Exeter, Devon, UK/Bridgeman Art Library, London/New York; 128 Courtesy of the John Carter Brown Library at Brown University; 130 Hulton Deutsch Collection Ltd./Stone; 131 Maryland Commission on Artistic Property of the Maryland State Archives. MSA SC 1545-1106; 132 (tl), The Granger Collection, New York; 132 (t), Bettmann/CORBIS; 133 The Granger Collection, New York; 134 Rare Book Department, The Free Library Of Philadelphia; 135 Maryland Historical Society, Baltimore; 136 Ken Lax, Courtesy of American Bible Society; 137 George Whitefield Preaching, by Collett/National Portrait Library, London/Bridgeman Art Library, London/New York; 138 The Granger Collection, New York; 139 Culver Pictures; 140 Scala/Art Resource, NY; 141 Culver Pictures; 142 (t), The Granger Collection, New York; 142 (b), The Granger Collection, New York; 143 Musee des Beaux-Arts, Orleans, France/Bridgeman Art Library, London/New York; 144 Detail from The Pierpont Morgan Library/Art Resource, NY; 145 Private Collection/Bridgeman Art Library, London/New York; 148 (t), Image Copyright © 2003 PhotoDisc, Inc./HRW Photoc.; 148 (c), Image Copyright © 2003 PhotoDisc, Inc./HRW Photo.; 149 (tr), Jas. Townsend & Son, Inc.; 151 (b), "The Slave Market," by Amadeo Preziosi, (1816-82), Victoria & Albert Museum/Bridgeman Art Library, London, UK/New York; 151 (t), Image Copyright © 2003 PhotoDisc, Inc./HRW Photo.; 153 Sam Dudgeon/HRW Photo.
Unit Three: 154 "Patrick Henry Before the Virginia House of Burgesses" (1851) by Peter F. Rothermel. Red HIll, The Patrick Henry National Memorial, Brookneal, Virginia.; 155 (c), Bettmann/CORBIS. **Chapter Six:** Page 156 (tl), Bettman/CORBIS; 156 (tr), The Granger Collection, New York; 156 (bl), CORBIS; 157 (tl), North Wind Picture Archives; 157 (tr), Courtesy the Bostonian Society, The Old State House; 158 Archive Photos; 159 North Wind Picture Archives; 160 The American Revolution: A Picture Sourcebook, Dover Publications, Inc.; 161 Medal commemorating the British capture of Quebec, 1759, Priviate Collection/Bridgeman Art Library, London/New York; 163 The Granger Collection, New York; 164 (t), Courtesy of the Hunt Institute for Botanical Documentation, Carnegie Mellon University, Pittsburgh, PA; 164 (b), Chief Pontiac, attributed to John Mix Stanley, Detroit Historical Society; 165 The Granger Collection, New York; 166 The Granger Collection, New York; 167 Archive Photos; 168 (b), Deposited by the City of Boston, Courtesy, Museum of Fine Arts, Boston; 169 (br), Colonial Williamsburg Foundation; 170 Courtesy of the John Carter Brown Library at Brown University; 171 Jas. Townsend & Son, Inc.; 172 CORBIS; 173 Peter Newark's American Pictures; 175 Bequest of Winslow Warren, Courtesy Museum of Fine Arts, Boston MA. Reproduced with Permission. © 2000 Museum of Fine Arts, Boston. All Rights Reserved; 176 Colonial Williamsburg Foundation; 178 (t), [neg. 1920.166] ©Collection of The New-York Historical Society; 178 (c), HRW Photo Research Library; 179 Archive Photos; 180 Image Copyright © 2003 PhotoDisc, Inc./HRW Photo.; 181 Bettmann/CORBIS. **Chapter Seven:** Page 182 (tl), Peter Newark's American Pictures; 182 (tr), Independence National Historical Park Collection; 182 (bl), North Wind Picture Archives; 182 (c), Larry Stevens/Nawrocki Stock Photo; 183 (tl), SuperStock; 183 (tr), Colonial Williamsburg Foundation; 183 Sam Dudgeon/HRW Photo; 184 The Granger Collection, New York; 185 (t), Gift of Joseph W. Revere, William B. Revere, and Edward H.R. Revere, Courtesy, Museum of Fine Arts, Boston; 185 (b), The Granger Collection, New York; 186 CORBIS; 187 Photograph courtesy of the Concord Museum, Concord, Massachusetts and the Lexington Historical Society, Inc., Lexington, Massachusetts. Photograph by David Bohl; 188 The Granger Collection, New York; 189 Victoria Smith/HRW Photo, Courtesy, Scholastic Inc.; 190 (cl), The Granger Collection, New York; 190 (bl), Library of Congress/HRW; 191 Archive Photos; 192 Peter Newark's American Pictures; 193 Culver Pictures; 194 Larry Lee/CORBIS; 198 Mount Vernon Ladies' Association; 199 (tr), Christie's Images; 199 (b), Benninghoff Collection of the American Revolution; 200 The Granger Collection, New York; 201 (l), Collection of The New-York Historical Society; 201 (r), Collection of The New-York Historical Society; 202 Anne S.K. Brown Military Collection, Brown University Library; 203 Art Resource, NY; 204 The Granger Collection, New York; 206 (tl), Erich Lessing/Art Resource, NY; 206 (cl), The Historic New Orleans Collection, Museum/Research Center, color added; 207 The Granger Collection, New York; 208 (tr), Peter Newark's American Pictures; 208 (tl), The Granger Collection, New York; 209 Courtesy of The Library of Virginia; 210 (b), The Granger Collection, New York; 210 (tl), William James Warren/CORBIS; 212 "The Battle of Yorktown" from Janice Meredith by Paul Leicester, Ford, Dodd, Mead & Co., 1899./Delaware Art Museum, Howard Pyle Collection; 213 CORBIS.
Unit Four: 218 Library of Congress; 219 (c), The Granger Collection, New York. **Chapter Eight:** Page 220 (tr), SuperStock; 220 (c), Johns Hopkins University, Larry Stevens/Nawrocki Stock Photo Inc.; 220 (bl), Prado, Madrid/Bridgeman Art Library, London/New York; 221 (t), Virginia Museum of Fine Arts, Richmond, VA. Detail of Wahsignton as Statesman at the Constitutional Convention by Junius Brutus Stearns. Gift of Edgar William and Bernice Chrysler Garbisch. Photo: Ron Jennings. ©2000 Virginia Museum of Fine Arts; 221 (l), Joseph Sohm/Chromosohm Inc./CORBIS; 222 (cl), Independence National Historical Park Collection; 223 (t), Art Archive, London/SuperStock; 223 (cr), Stock Montage, Inc.; 224 The Granger Collection, New York; 225 (b), Rare Books and Manuscripts Division, The New York Public Library, Astor, Lenox and Tilden Foundations; 226 Ted Spiegel; 227 North Wind Picture Archives; 228 (t), CORBIS; 228 (b), British Library/The Art Archive; 230 (cl), Jas. Townsend & Son, Inc.; 231 (t), Courtesy, Winterthur Museum; 232 (b), Eileen Tweedy/The Art Archive; 233 (c), The Granger Collection, New York; 233 (t), Courtesy of the Massachusetts Historical Society; 234 (t), The Granger Collection, New York; 234 (l), North Wind Picture Archives; 235 (t), Stock Montage, Inc.; 236 (cl), The Granger Collection, New York; 237 (b), The Granger Collection, New York; 237 (t), Joseph Sohm/Stock, Boston; 238 (b), Nebraska State Historical Society; 238 (t), Courtesy Winterthur Museum; 239 (t), The Library Company of Philadelphia; 241 (t), National Archives (NARA); 242 (cl), Library of Congress; 243 PRC Archive; 244 (t), The Granger Collection, New York; 246 The Granger Collection, New York; 247 The Granger Collection, New York; 250 (t), Image Copyright © 2003 PhotoDisc, Inc./HRW Photo.; 250 (c), Image Copyright © 2003 PhotoDisc, Inc./HRW Photo.; 251 H. Abernathy/H. Armstrong Roberts; 252 (t), Image Copyright © 2003 PhotoDisc, Inc./HRW Photoc.; 252 Reuters NewMedia Inc./CORBIS; 253 (all), Lance Schriner/HRW Photo. **Chapter Nine:** Page 254 (tr, tl), The Granger Collection, New York; 254 (bl), ©Hulton Getty/Liaison Agency; 254 (br), Wally McNamee/CORBIS-Sygma; 254 Sam Dudgeon/HRW Photo; 255 (tr), Bob Daemmrich/Stock Boston; 255 (tl), Lisa Quinones/Black Star; 255 (bl), Woodfin Camp & Associates; 256 Bernard Boutrit/Woodfin Camp & Associates; 257 (br), Paul S. Conklin; 257 (t), PICTOR; 258 Stock Montage, Inc.; 259 (b), Abby Aldrich Rockefeller Folk Art Museum; 259 The Granger Collection, New York; 260 Collection, the Supreme Court of the United States, courtesy The Supreme Court Historical Society; 261 Paul Conklin; 262 The Granger Collection, New York; 263 H. Armstrong Roberts; 264 Independence National Historical Park Collection; 284 Independence National Historical Park Collection; 285 The Granger Collection, New York; 286 Jeffrey Brown/Liaison Agency; 287 Bob Daemmrich Photo, Inc.; 289 Louie Psihoyos/Woodfin Camp & Associates, Inc.; 290 Sandra Baker/Liaison Agency; 291 Paul Sakuma/AP Photo/Wide World Photos; 292 Spencer Grant/PhotoEdit; 293 Jeff Greenberg /PhotoEdit; 294 (tl), Joe Marquette/AP/Wide World Photos; 294 (bl), Richard B. Levine; 295 Bob Daemmrich/Stock, Boston. **Chapter Ten:** Page 298 (tl), The Granger Collection, New York; 298 (b), Gianni Dagli Orti/CORBIS; 298 (tr), Bettmann/CORBIS; 299 (tl), Daniel Huntington 1816-1906, "The Republican Court" 1861, Oil on Canvas, 167.6 x 277.0 (66 x 109), The Brooklyn Museum 39.536.1, Gift of the Crescent-Hamilton Athletic Club; 299 (tr), The Art Archive/Yale University New Haven/Album/Joseph Martin; 300 (cl), Courtesy of the John Carter Brown Library at Brown University; 301 (t), The Granger Collection, New York; 302 Bettmann/CORBIS; 303 (t), The Granger Collection, New York; 304 (cl), National Portrait Gallery, Smithsonian Institution, Washington, DC, Gift of Henry Cabot Lodge/Art Resource, NY; 305 (c), Museum of American Financial History; 306 (tl), The Granger Collection, New York; 306 (tr), R. Foulds / Washington Stock Photo; 307 Library of Congress; 308 (t), ©Laurie Platt Winfrey Inc./Woodfin Camp & Associates; 309 (tr), Larry Stevens/Nawrocki Stock Photo; 309 (tl), The Granger Collection, New York; 310 (cl), Mansell Collection/TimePix; 311 (cr), Giraudon/Art Resource, NY; 311 (t), Giraudon/Art Resource, NY; 312 Michael Nicholson/CORBIS; 313 The Granger Collection, New York; 314 (t), The Historic New Orleans Collection; 315 (c), New York State Historical Association, Cooperstown, New York; 316 The Metropolitan Museum of Art, Gift of Edgar William and Bernice Chrysler Garbisch, 1963. (63.201.2); 317 HRW Photo Research Library; 318 (t), ©Laurie Platt Winfrey Inc./Woodfin Camp & Associates; 319 (cr), The Granger Collection, New York; 320 (b), Sally Anderson-Bruce/The Museum of American Political Life, University of Hartford, West Hartford,CT; 320 (t), McAlphin Collection, Miriam and Ira D. Wallach Division of Art, Prints and Photographs, The New York Public Library, Astor, Lenox and Tilden Foundations; 322, 324, 325, 327 (t), The Granger Collection, New York.
Unit Five: 330 Christie's Images; 331 (c), Courtesy Oregon State Archives, Mural located in Oregon State Capitol by Frank H. Schwartz c. 1938. **Chapter Eleven:** Page 332 (tl), North Wind Picture Archives; 332 (bl), Giraudon/Art Resource; 332 (tr), The Granger Collection, New York; 333 (tl), Peter Newark's American Pictures; 333 (tr), CORBIS; 334 (c), Collection of the American Numismatic Society; 334 (c), Collection of the American Numismatic Society; 335 View of the West Front of Monticello and Garden (1825) by Jane Braddick Peticolas (1791-1852) watercolor on paper, courtesy of the Thomas Jefferson Memorial Foundation, Inc., Photographer: Edward Owen.; 336 (b), Stock Montage, Inc.; 336 (tl), National Archives negative 68-2488-2 G1945-22; 337 North Wind Picture Archives; 338 North Wind Picture Library; 339 The Granger Collection, New York; 340 Fred J. Maroon; 341 Charles M. Russel, Lewis and Clark Expedition, oil on canvas, 1918, 0137.2267, From the Collection of Gilcrease Museum, Tulsa; 342 North Wind Picture Archives; 343 The Granger Collection, New York; 344 Courtesy of The Mariners' Museum, Newport News, VA; 345 North Wind Picture Archives; 346 ©The Field Museum, Neg #A93851.1c, Chicago.; 347 (t), The Granger Collection, New York; 347 (br), National Portrait Gallery, Smithsonian Institution; gift of Mrs. Herbert Lee Pratt, Jr; 348 National Portrait Gallery, Smithsonian Institution/Art Resource, NY; 349 HRW Photo Research Library; 350 Courtesy of The Mariners' Museum, Newport News, VA; 351 (t), North Wind Picture Archives; 351 Mickey Osterreicher/Black Star; 352 The Granger Collection, New York; 353 (br), ©Laurie Platt Winfrey Inc./Woodfin Camp & Associates, Inc.; 353 (bl), 354, 355 The Granger Collection, New York; 359 (tr, tl), Christie's Images; 359(ad), HRW Photo Research Library; 360 (t), Image Copyright © 2003 PhotoDisc, Inc./HRW Photo. **Chapter Twelve:** Page 362 (tr), (Detail) Collection of the New-York Historical Society, neg #34684; 362 (br), North Wind Picture Archives; 362 (tl), Larry Stevens/Nawrocki Stock Photo; 362 (tl), Larry Stevens/Nawrocki Stock Photo; 362 (bl), Victoria & Albert Museum, London/Art Resource, NY; 363 (t), HRW Photo Research Library; 363 (tl), The Granger Collection, New York; 363 (tr), The Museum of American Political Life, University of Hartford, West Hartford,CT; 363 Sam Dudgeon/HRW Photo; 364 National Portrait Gallery, Smithsonian Institution, Washington, DC/Art Resource, NY; 365 Historical Society of Pennsylvania, Fourth of July Celebration in Center Square by John Lewis Krimmel (Bc 882 K897); 366 National Archives (NARA); 367 ©Laurie Platt Winfrey Inc./Woodfin Camp & Associates, Inc.; 368 © Shelburne Museum, Shelburne, Vermont, detail of the painting "Conestoga Wagon" by Thomas Birch; 369 The Granger Collection, New York; 371 Maryland Historical Society, Baltimore, Maryland; 373 ©Laurie Platt Winfrey Inc./Woodfin Camp & Associates, Inc.; 374 Woodfin Camp & Associates; 375 National Portrait Gallery, Smithsonian Institution, Gift of the Swedish Colonial Society through Mrs. William Hacker/Art Resource, NY; 376 Karen Blier/AFP/CORBIS; 377 [neg. #42459] ©Collection of The New-York Historical Society; 378 The Granger Collection, New York; 379 The Granger Collection, New York; 380 Bettmann/CORBIS; 381 Peabody Museum-Harvard University/Photograph by Hillel Burger; 382 (b), The Granger Collection, New York; 382 (cl), Robert D. Rubic/Rare Books and Manuscripts Division, the New York Public Library, Astor, Lenox and Tilden Foundations; 383 WOOLAROC MUSEUM, BARTLESVILLE, OKLAHOMA; 384 North Wind Picture Archives; 385 Patrick Henry, (1736-99), pictured on a decorative pendant, Carnegie Institute, Pittsburgh, PA, USA/Bridgeman Art Library, London/New York; 386 Detail of The Headless Horseman Pursuing Ichabod Crane, by John Quidor, 1858,Smithsonian American Art Museum, Washington DC/Art Resource, NY; 387 The Granger Collection, New York; 388 The Granger Collection, New York; 389 Courtesy Barnes & Noble Publishing; 391 The Granger Collection, New York. **Unit Six:** 394, 395 (c), The Granger Collection, New York.
Chapter Thirteen: Page 396 (tl), Culver Pictures; 396 (tr), SuperStock; 396 (b, c), The Granger Collection, New York; 397 (tl), Library of Congress, Washington DC/SuperStock; 397 (tr), National Museum of American History, Smithsonian Institution, Washington, D.C.; 398, 399 The Granger Collection, New York; 400 Bettmann/CORBIS; 401 Bettmann/CORBIS; 402 FPG International; 403 Columned clock by Seth Thomas (1785-1859), c. 1855/Strike One, London, UK/Bridgeman Art Library, London/New York; 404 American Textile History Museum; 405, 406 The Granger Collection, New York; 407 Bettmann/CORBIS; 408 Library of Congress; 409 Bettmann/CORBIS; 410 Archive Photos; 411 Scala/Art Resource, NY; 414 Peter Newark's American Pictures; 415 Science & Society Picture Library; 416 (t), The Granger Collection, New York; 416 (b), Bettmann/CORBIS; 417 Smithsonian Institution, Washington, DC; 418 (c), Bettmann/CORBIS; 418 (b), National Museum of American History 1999/Smithsonian Institution; 419 Bettmann/CORBIS. **Chapter Fourteen:** Page 422 (tr), Louisiana State Museum; 422 (tl), Kim Neilsen/Smithsonian Institution, Washington, DC/PRC Archive; 422 (bl), North Wind Picture Archives; 423 (tr), Smithsonian Institution neg. #75-2984; 423 (tl), Christie's Images/SuperStock; 424 (c), Colonial Williamsburg Foundation; 425 (t), ; 426 (bl), Richard Hamilton Smith/CORBIS; 427 The Granger Collection, New York; 428 PRC Archive; 429 Library of Congress/ PRC Archive; 430 Courtesy, The Winterthur Library: Joseph Downs Collection of Manuscripts and Printed Ephemera; 431 North Wind Picture Archives; 432 New York Public Library; 433 (c), 434 (t), The Granger Collection, New York; 434 (b), 435 (b), Culver Pictures, Inc.; 436 Private Collection/Bridgeman Art Library, London/SuperStock; 437 Courtesy of the Charleston Museum, Charleston, South Carolina; 438 (t), CORBIS/[photographer]; 439 Stock Montage, Inc.; 440 (t), Detail of John Antrobus, Plantation Burial, (1860) oil on canvas, The Historic New Orleans Collection; 440 (bc), Chicago Historical Society, X.1354; 440 (b), Louisiana State Museum; 441 Private Collection, Photograph Courtesy of Kennedy Galleries, NY; 442 North Wind Picture Archives; 443 The Granger Collection, New York; 446 (t, c), Image Copyright © 2003 PhotoDisc, Inc./HRW Photo; 448 (b), The Museum of the Confederacy, Richmond, Virginia, Photography by Katherine Wetzel; 448 (t), Culver Pictures; 449 (b), Stock Montage, Inc. **Chapter Fifteen:** page 450 (b), The Granger Collection, New York; 450 (tl), Courtesy of the Massachusetts Historical Society; 450 (tr), The Granger Collection, New York; 451 (tr),; 451 (tl), Peter Newark's American Pictures; 451 (cl), National Army Museum, Chelsea, UK; 452 (c), Bettmann/CORBIS; 453 (b), The Granger Collection, New York; 453 (t), George Goodwin/United Methodist Church; 454 Courtesy of Massachusetts Historical Society; 455 Bettmann/CORBIS; 456 Brown Brothers; 457 (c), Courtesy of the Bostonian Society/Old State House, photo by Mark Sexton; 459 The Granger Collection, New York; 461 North Wind Picture Archives; 462 (c), The Granger Collection, New York; 463 (b), Culver Pictures; 463 (t), National Library of Medicine/PRC Archive; 464 Archive Photos; 465 (tr), The Granger Collection, New York; 465 (tl), Winslow Homer, Country School, 1873 oil on canvas, 1928.56, gift of anonymous donor, Addison Gallery of American Art, Phillips Academy, Andover, MA; 466 Anonymous, Girls Evening School, American. Pencil and watercolor, 13 1/2 x 18 1/8 in. Gift of Maxim Karolik for the M. & M. Karolik Collection of American Drawings and Watercolors, 1800-1875. Courtesy, Museum of Fine Arts, Boston.; 467 (t), The Granger

ACKNOWLEDGMENTS

Collection, New York; 467 (c), The Mount Holyoke College Archives and Special Collections; 468 ©Roger-Viollet; 469 Courtesy of the Illinois State Historical Library; 470 Photographs and Prints Division, Schomburg Center for Research in Black Culture, The New York Public Library, Astor, Lenox and Tilden Foundations; 471 The Granger Collection, New York; 472 Victoria Smith/HRW Photo; 473 (cr), North Wind Picture Archives; 474, 475 The Granger Collection, New York; 476 Archive Photos; 477 Bettmann/CORBIS; 478 The Granger Collection, New York; 479 HRW Photo; 483 Sam Dudgeon/HRW Photo.

Unit Seven: 484 Emanuel Gottlieb Leutze, Westward the Course of Empire Takes Its Way, ca. 1861, oil on canvas, 0126.1615, From the Collection of Gilcrease Museum, Tulsa; 485 (c), Bettmann/CORBIS. **Chapter Sixteen:** Page 486 (bl), The Art Archive/National History Museum Mexico City/Dagli Orti; 486 (tl), Missouri Historical Society, St. Louis; 486 (tr), Joslyn Art Museum, Omaha, Nebraska; 486 (c), United Nations; 487 (tl), Albert Bierstadt, "Emigrants Crossing the Plains," 1867, Oil on Canvas, A.011.1T: National Cowboy Hall of Fame, Oklahoma City, OK.; 487 (cl), The Granger Collection, New York; 487 (tr), Texas State Library and Archives Commission; 488 Bettmann/CORBIS; 489 The Granger Collection, New York; 490 Bettmann/CORBIS; 491 (t), Peter Newark's Western Americana; 492 From the Collections of the Fort Bend County Museum Association, Richmond, Texas.; 493 (br), Daughters of the Republic of Texas Library; 493 (t), ©Laurie Platt Winfrey Inc./Woodfin Camp & Associates, Inc.; 494 Bettmann/CORBIS; 495 (br), ©Laurie Platt Winfrey Inc./Woodfin Camp & Associates, Inc.; 495 (t), Reading of the Texas Declaration of Independence by Charles and Fanny Normann, Collection of the Joe Fultz estate, Navasota, Texas./Courtesy of the Star of the Republic Museum; 496 The San Jacinto Museum of History, Houston.; 497 The Granger Collection, New York; 498 Texas State Library and Archives Commission; 499 The Granger Collection, New York; 500 Bob Daemmrich Photography; 501 (tr), No. 75-576, The UT Institute of Texan Cultures at San Antonio; 501 (tl), Texas State Library and Archives Commission; 501 (tc), Texas State Library and Archives Commission; 502 Harcourt Brace Photo; 503 (cr), Colorado Historical Society; 503 (tr), Joseph Drayton, Indians and Trappers at Fort Walla Walla, Oregon Territory, 1841, Oregon Historical Society, Negative number OrHi 959; 504 Culver Pictures; 507 (tr), Carl Socolon/The Landis Valley Museum; 508 Collection of the American Numismatic Society; 509 (b), The Granger Collection, New York; 509 (t), Courtesy of the California History Room, California State Library, Sacramento, California. ; 510 (t), Stock Montage, Inc.; 511 (t), National Museum of American Art, Washington DC/Art Resource, NY. **Chapter Seventeen:** Page 514 (t), Library of Congress/PRC Archive; 514 (b), Mary Evans Photo Library, England; 514 (c), The Metropolitan Museum of Art, The Helena Woolworth McCaan Collection, Winfield Foundation Gift, 1958. (58.52); 515 (t), Wells Fargo Bank; 515 (cr), Courtesy of the Oakland Museum of California; 515 (c), Larry Stevens/ Nawrocki Stock Photo; 516 Courtesy Cornell University Library, Ithaca, New York; 517 (t), National Museum of American Art, Washington DC/Art Resource, NY; 517 (b), Library of Congress; 519 (t), The Granger Collection, New York; 520 The Granger Collection, New York; 521 Collection of David J. and Janice L. Frent/PRC Archive; 522 Culver Pictures, Inc.; 523 (t), Stock Montage, Inc.; 524 Society of California Pioneers; 525 Texas State Library and Archives Commission; 526 (c), National Archives; 527 National Portrait Gallery, Smithsonian Institution, Washington, DC/Art Resource, NY; 528 Courtesy The Bancroft Library, University of California, Berkeley, F855.1 B974s; 529 North Wind Picture Archives; 530 Courtesy of the Witte Museum, San Antonio, Texas; 531 CORBIS-Bettmann; 532 (tl), Bettmann/CORBIS; 532 (tr), "Handcart Pioneers" by C.C.A. Christensen, © by Intellectual Reserve, Inc. Courtesy of Museum of Church History and Art, Used by Permission.; 533 Courtesy of The Bostonian Society, Old State House; 534 Colorado Historical Society; 536 The Granger Collection, New York; 537 Courtesy of the California History Room, California State Library, Sacramento, California; 538 Courtesy of the California History Room, California State Library, Sacramento, California; 539 Peter Newark's American Pictures; 541 The Granger Collection, New York; 542 (t), Image Club Graphics ©1997 Adobe Systems; 542 (cr), Courtesy "Texas Highways" Magazine; 543 (b), Christie's Images; 544 (tr), Image Copyright © 2003 PhotoDisc, Inc./HRW Photoc.; 545 (c), Vickie Silbert/PhotoEdit; 547 Llewellyn/Pictor Uniphoto; 547 Sam Dudgeon/HRW Photo.

Unit Eight: 548 The Granger Collection, New York; 549 (t), Library of Congress. **Chapter Eighteen:** Page 550 (tl, tr), The Granger Collection, New York; 550 (bl), AKG London; 551 (tr), The Granger Collection, New York; 552 Bettmann/CORBIS; 553 (b), Steven Laschever/Museum of American Political Life, University of Hartford, West Hartford, CT; 553 (t), Library of Congress; 555 The Granger Collection, New York; 556 Nantional Archives (NARA); 557 (c), The Granger Collection, New York; 557 (t), The Granger Collection, New York; 558 Nancy Gewitz/Antique Textile Resources; 559 Collection of Janice L. and David J. Frent/PRC Archive; 561 Kansas State Historical Society; 562 (t, b), 563 (t), 564, 565, 566 The Granger Collection, New York; 567 Illinois Secretary of State; 568 National Portrait Gallery, Smithsonian Institution, Art Resource, NY; 569 Library of Congress; 570 The Metropolitan Museum of Art, Gift of Mr. and Mrs. Carl Stoeckel, 1897. (97.5) @1982 by The Metropolitan Museum of Art; 572 The Granger Collection, New York; 573 Library of Congress; 575 The Granger Collection, New York. **Chapter Nineteen:** Page 578 (tl), The Granger Collection, New York; 578 (bl), The Art Archive/Palazzo Pubblico Siena/Dagli Orti; 578 (c), Ken Cobb²/ Library of Congress; 579 (tl), National Geographic Image Collection; 579 (tr), Museum of the Confederacy, Richmond, VA. Photo by Katherine Wetzel; 580 Library of Congress; 582 Bettmann/CORBIS; 583 (br), The Museum of the Confederacy, Richmond, Virginia, Photography by Katherine Wetzel; 583 (t), The Granger Collection, New York; 584 Library of Congress; 585 from THE CIVIL WAR:FORWARD TO RICHMOND, Photograph by Al Freni, ©1983 Time-Life Books, Inc. Courtesy, Troiani Collection; 586 Bettmann/CORBIS; 587 Virginia Historic Society; 589 Bettmann/CORBIS; 590 U.S. War Dept. General Staff photo/National Archives (NARA) negative 165SB75/LCB81841055; 591 Bettmann/CORBIS; 593 Woodfin Camp & Associates; 594 North Wind Picture Archives; 596 The Historical Society of Pennsylvania; 597 The Granger Collection, New York; 598 National Portrait Gallery, Smithsonian Institution, Washington DC/Art Resource, NY; 599 Bettmann/CORBIS; 600 Anne S. Brown Military Collection, Brown University; 601 State Museum of Pennsylvania; 602 Virginia Historical Society; 603 Collection of the Mercer Museum of The Bucks County Historical Society; 604 (tl), Lloyd Ostendorf Collection; 604 (t), National Archives (NARA), negative 615.00A.004 ; 604 (t), Atlanta History Center; 605 Tom Lovell/National Geographic Image Collection (detail); 606 Library of Congress; 607 North Wind Picture Archives; 610 (bl), SuperStock; 610 (t), Image Copyright © 2003 PhotoDisc, Inc./HRW Photo.; 611 Stock Montage, Inc.; 612 Library of Congress, Manuscripts Division; 613 The Granger Collection, New York; 614 © 1995 Jeffery Titcomb/Liaison International; 615 Sam Dudgeon/HRW Photo.

Unit Nine: 616 Denver Public Library Western History Collection; 617 (c), Buffalo Bill Historical Center, Cody, Wyoming. **Chapter Twenty:** Page 618 (tl), The Granger Collection, New York; 618 (tr), Louisiana Division, Howard Tilton Memorial Library, New Orleans, LA 70118; 618 (bl), The Granger Collection, New York; 619 (tl), Library of Congress; 619 (tr), H. Armstrong Roberts; 620 The Valentine Museum; 622 Library of Congress; 623 North Wind Picture Archives; 624 © William Taufic/The Stock Market; 625 Peter Newark's Pictures; 626 Stock Montage, Inc.; 627 (t), The Granger Collection, New York; 627 (b), Bettmann/CORBIS; 628 SuperStock; 629, 631 The Granger Collection, New York; 632 North Wind Picture Archives; 633 Courtesy of South Caroliniana Library, University of South Carolina, Columbia.; 634 (b), The Granger Collection, New York; 634 (t), Private Collection/PRC Archive; 636 U.S. Senate Collection; 637 (b), The Granger Collection, New York; 637 Bettmann/CORBIS; 639 The Metropolitan Museum of Art , Morris K. Jesup Fund, 1940. (40.40). Photograph © 1985 The Metropolitan Museum of Art.; 641 The Granger Collection, New York; 642 Jubilee Singers, Courtesy of Fisk University Library, Special Collections; 643 North Wind Picture Archives; 645 The Granger Collection, New York. **Chapter Twenty-One:** Page 646 (tl), Alfred Jacob Miller, Fort Laramie. Beinecke Rare Book and Manuscript Library, Yale University;

646 (tr), Courtesy Wells Fargo Bank; 646 (bl), AKG Photo, London; 646 (c), Michael Freeman/CORBIS; 647 (tr), Iris & B. Gerald Cantor Center for Visual Arts at Stanford University; 1998.115/Gift of David Hewes; 647 (bl), Mary Evans Photo Library, England; 647 (tl), Christie's Images; 648 The Granger Collection, New York; 649 Werner Forman Archive, Pohrt Collection, Plains Indian Museum, BBHC, Cody Wyoming, USA/Art Resource, NY; 650, 651 The Granger Collection, New York; 652 The Field Museum, #A111822-2c; 653 Bettmann/CORBIS; 654 The Granger Collection, New York; 655 E.R. Degginger/Color-Pic, Inc.; 656 The Granger Collection, New York; 657 Peter Newark's Western Americana; 658 (b), Peter Newark's Western Americana; 658 (tl), Union Pacific Historical Collection; 659 Union Pacific Historical Collection; 660 ©Laurence Parent; 661 Peter Newark's Western Americana; 661 (b), Montana Historical Society, Helena; 662 (bl), Peter Newark's Western Americana; 662 (cl), Solomon D. Butcher Collection, Library of Congress; 664 ©2003 PhotoDisc; 665 The Granger Collection, New York; 666, 667 Peter Newark's Western Americana; 668 Nebraska State Historical Society; 669 ©Collection of the New-York Historical Society, negative #41800; 670 (t-bkgd) ©PI/Photo © David Hardwood/Panoramic Images, Chicago 1998; 670 (tl), Peter Newark's Western Americana; 670 (tr), The Granger Collection, New York; 670 Batavia Depot Museum, Batavia, Illinois/Courtesy, Chicago Historical Society; 671 Library of Congress; 674 (b), Colorado Historical Society; 674 (t, cr), Image Copyright © 2003 PhotoDisc, Inc./HRW Photo.; 676 National Archives (NARA) negative 30.20.E.079; 677 Image Copyright © 2003 PhotoDisc, Inc./HRW Photo.; 679 Sam Dudgeon/HRW Photo.

Epilogue: Page 680 (tl), Science Museum, London, UK/Bridgeman Art Library, London/New York; 680 (tr), The Granger Collection, New York; 680 (bl), Culver Pictures, Inc.; 681 (tr), Peter Turnley/CORBIS; 681 (bl), Robert Maass/CORBIS; 681 (tl), NASA; 682 Archive Photos; 683 The Granger Collection, New York; 684 Culver Pictures; 685 (tr), The Granger Collection, New York; 685 (b), Library of Congress #LCUSZC4-4637 DLC Detroit Publishing Co. Photo Collection; 686 Library of Congress; 687 Bettmann/CORBIS; 688 The Granger Collection, New York; 689 Library of Congress; 691 (t), The Granger Collection, New York; 691 AP/Wide World Photos; 692 (br), Archive Photos; 692 (t), John Held Jr., LIFE Magazine, © TIME Inc./Courtesy of the general libraries, The University of Texas at Austin/HRW photo by Victoria Smith; 692 (bl), Archive Photos; 693 Bettmann/CORBIS; 694 Franklin D. Roosevelt Library; 695 CORBIS; 696 (tl), HRW Photo by Sam Dudgeon, stamps courtesy Kristen Darby; 696 (tr), The Granger Collection, New York; 699 UPI/CORBIS/Bettman; 700 Archive Photos; 701 UPI/CORBIS-Bettmann Newsphotos; 702 Sally Andersen-Bruce, Museum of American Political Life; 703 AP/Wide World Photos; 704 (tl), Brown Brothers; 704 (cl), Archive Photos; 705 Sara Matthews/Swarthmore College Peace Collection; 706 Archive Photos; 707 Michael J. Okoniewski/Liaison Agency; 708 Lester Sloan/Woodfin Camp & Associates; 709 Victoria Smith/HRW Photo; 710 Ben Margot/AP/Wide World Photos; 711 (tr), Doug Mills/AP/Wide World Photos; 148149 (bc), "British Ships of War Landing Their Troops," 1768, Private Collection/Bridgeman Art Library, London/New York.

Back Matter: Page R1-R2 (bkgd), Maps Division, The New York Public Library, Astor, Lenox and Tilden Foundations; R1 (r), Sandra Baker/Liaison Agency; (cl), Colonial Williamsburg Foundation; (bcr, bcl), Collection of the American Numismatic Society; (bl), Peter Newark's Western Americana; (tl), Image Copyright © 2003 PhotoDisc, Inc./HRW Photo; R2 (tl), Image Copyright © 2003 PhotoDisc, Inc./HRW Photo; (tc), Sam Dudgeon/HRW Photo, courtesy Fred Hay; (cr), The Granger Collection, New York; (b), Independence National Historical Park Collection; (l), F. Stuart Westmorland/Allstock/Picture Quest; (r), Image Copyright © 2003 PhotoDisc, Inc./HRW Photo. Page R2-R5 (all), R6 (all except bc, br), White House Collection, copyright White House Historical Association; R6 (bc, br), The White House; R8-R11 (border), Jay Mallin Photos

Illustrator Credits

Abbreviated as follows: (t) top, (b) bottom, (l) left, (r) right, (c) center. All art, unless otherwise noted, created by Holt, Rinehart, and Winston. Text maps, feature maps, Atlas created by MapQuest.com Inc. All visual summaries, unless otherwise noted, created by Kenneth Batelman.

Table of Contents and Front Matter: Page xxiii (br), Argosy.
Unit One: Chapter One: Page 5 (b), Nenad Jakesevic.
Unit Two: Page 149 (tl), Dave Merrill/Steven Edsey & Sons; 152 (cr), Greathead Studios, Inc. **Chapter Three:** Page 82 (tl), Dave Merrill/Steven Edsey & Sons. **Chapter Five:** Page 127 (b), Argosy; 147 (tl), Greathead Studios Inc.
Unit Three: Page 178 (tl), Steven Stankiewicz. **Chapter Six:** Page 168 (t), Karen Minot; 174 (t), Leslie Kell; 177 (tl), Charles Apple. **Chapter Seven:** Page 215 (tl), Karen Minot.
Unit Four: Page 252 (t), Karen Minot; 253 (t), Charles Apple. **Chapter Eight:** Page 245 (b), Leslie Kell. **Chapter Nine:** Page 283 (b), Karen Minot; 288 (t), Karen Minot; 292 (b), Argosy. **Chapter Ten:** Page 305 (tr), Saul Rosenbaum/Deborah Wolfe Ltd.; 325 (b), Nenad Jakesevic.
Unit Five: Page 359 (tr), Dave Merrill/Steven Edsey & Sons. **Chapter Twelve:** Page 370 (b), Argosy; 372 (t), Nenad Jakesevic.
Unit Six: Page 449 (t), Karen Minot. **Chapter Thirteen:** Page 412 (b), Nenad Jakesevic; 414 (t), Leslie Kell. **Chapter Fourteen:** Page 425 (br), Craig Attebery/Jeff Lavaty Artist Agent; 435 (t), Charles Apple. **Chapter Fifteen:** Page 460 (t), Argosy; 481 (tl), Dave Merrill/Steven Edsey & Sons.
Unit Seven: Page 545 (tl), Charles Apple. **Chapter Seventeen:** Page 518 (b), Argosy; 535 (t), Nenad Jakesevic.
Unit Eight: Chapter Eighteen: Page 561 (t), Argosy; 571 (t), Saul Rosenbaum/Deborah Wolfe Ltd. **Chapter Nineteen:** Page 588 (b), Nenad Jakesevic; 609 (tl), Charles Apple.
Unit Nine: Chapter Twenty: Page 640 (t), Argosy. **Chapter Twenty-one:** Page 659 (tr), Saul Rosenbaum/Deborah Wolfe Ltd.; 670 (t), Charles Apple; 673 (tl), Charles Apple.